OXFORD HISTORY OF
THE CHRISTIAN CHURCH

Edited by
Henry and Owen Chadwick

The Church in Ancient Society

From Galilee to Gregory the Great

HENRY CHADWICK

OXFORD
UNIVERSITY PRESS

OXFORD
UNIVERSITY PRESS

Great Clarendon Street, Oxford OX2 6DP

Oxford University Press is a department of the University of Oxford.
It furthers the University's objective of excellence in research, scholarship,
and education by publishing worldwide in

Oxford New York

Auckland Bangkok Buenos Aires Cape Town Chennai
Dar es Salaam Delhi Hong Kong Istanbul Karachi Kolkata
Kuala Lumpur Madrid Melbourne Mexico City Mumbai Nairobi
São Paulo Shanghai Singapore Taipei Tokyo Toronto

Oxford is a registered trade mark of Oxford University Press
in the UK and in certain other countries

Published in the United States
by Oxford University Press Inc., New York

British Library Cataloguing in Publication Data

Data available

Chadwick, Henry, 1920–
The church in ancient society : from Galilee to Gregory the Great / Henry Chadwick.
p. cm.—(Oxford history of the Christian Church)
Includes bibliographical references.
ISBN 0–19–924695–5
1. Church history—Primitive and early church, ca. 30–600. I. Title. II. Series.
BR160 . C45 2001 270.1—dc21 2001046166

Library of Congress Cataloging in Publication Data

Data applied for

ISBN 0–19–924695–5
ISBN 0–19–926577–1 (pbk)

3 5 7 9 10 8 6 4 2

Typeset in Bembo
by Jayvee, Trivandrum, India
Printed in Great Britain
on acid-free paper by
Biddles Ltd., Guildford and King's Lynn

For Owen and Nicholas
Grandsons

PREFATORY NOTE

Special thanks are due to support from officers of Oxford University Press, especially Hilary O'Shea, Jenny Wagstaffe, Lucy Qureshi, and Dr Leofranc Holford-Strevens and to many patient librarians in both Oxford and Cambridge.

H.C.

CONTENTS

ABBREVIATIONS

ACO	*Acta Conciliorum Oecumenicorum* (1914 ff. in progress)
CCSL	Corpus Christianorum series latina
CIL	*Corpus Inscriptionum Latinarum*
CLA	*Codices Latini Antiquiores*
CSEL	Corpus Scriptorum Ecclesiasticorum Latinorum (Vienna Academy)
CTh	Codex Theodosianus
EOMIA	*Ecclesiae Occidentalis Monumenta Iuris Antiquissima*, ed. C. H. Turner
ILCV	*Inscriptiones Latinae Christianae Veteres*, ed. C. Diehl (4 vols.)
ILS	*Inscriptiones Latinae selectae*, ed. H. Dessau
JbAC	*Jahrbuch für Antike und Christentum*
JTS	*Journal of Theological Studies* (Oxford)
MGH	*Monumenta Germaniae Historica*
PWK	Pauly–Wissowa–Kroll: Real-Encyclopädie der classischen Altertums- wissenschaft
PG	Migne, Patrologia Graeca
PL	Migne, Patrologia Latina
PLRE	*Prosopography of the Later Roman Empire*
PO	Patrologia Orientalis
RAC	*Reallexikon für Antike und Christentum*
SB	Sitzungsberichte
SC	Sources Chrétiennes
TU	Texte und Untersuchungen (Berlin Academy)
ZNW	*Zeitschrift für die neutestamentliche Wissenschaft*

INTRODUCTION

During the first six hundred years of the Christian Church's existence many changes occurred. Of these the most dramatic and remarkable was the shift from being a persecuted sect which, in order to fulfil its destiny as a universal faith not tied to a particular race, had to sever the umbilical cord to Judaism, and so to capture society and the Roman empire. From embodying a counter-culture to being seen as a mainly (not invariably) conservative social force was an extraordinary step. The number of martyrs did not need to be very large for their 'witness' to be public and 'newsworthy'. Remarkably soon the Church had recruits in high society, and as early as the middle of the second century was dreaming of a day when the emperor himself would be converted. The Christians changed the dominant form of religion in the Roman empire and thereby imprinted the most important difference between ancient and medieval society.

Not that the Christians had a wholly different culture from that of 'antiquity'. They came out of a society which to educated Greeks and Romans could be labelled 'barbarian'. Defenders of Christianity devoted pages to arguing for the superiority of barbarian ethics and religious ideas. By the late third and fourth centuries the Christians were supporters of the good order and law of the Roman empire. In his commentary on Paul's epistle to the Romans Origen could say that the task of magistrates was to restrain overt and public delinquencies, whereas sins (which could be highly anti-social) had to be corrected by bishops with ecclesiastical discipline. The latter, of course, were successful only with church members acknowledging the right of the community's representative leaders to admonish and speak in the Lord's name.

Initially belonging to the ancient world, Christianity remains the faith of a high proportion of this planet's population. Its characteristic teachings and ideals still speak universally to mind and conscience in individuals, and still bond together communities across chasms of differences in education and race. To study the ancient Church is to watch the Christian society forming structures and social attitudes that have remained lasting and in the main stream permanent. The aspiration to be universal is rooted in monotheism. There is always a tendency for religions to become tribal; that is, each tribe looks to its own protecting god with whom sacrifices maintain friendly relations, and cults are mainly local. The universalizing of faith became a powerful attraction for the ideology of the Roman empire, which also claimed to be world ruler. This bequeathed the now old assumption that Christianity is the religion of Europe—old and outmoded in a twenty-first century when the core of Christian membership is in other continents. From Constantine onwards we shall see emperors wanting all their subjects to share their faith and not finding it easy to tolerate those who openly rejected it. Paganism was far from being moribund when the Christian mission went out in the world. It reconquered the centre of power with the emperor Julian but for less than two years. Julian's paganism was unsuccessful in its aspirations to be tolerant.

Like the other monotheistic religions Judaism and Islam, Christian history is beset by controversy about the interpretation of tradition, especially as enshrined in sacred texts of venerable antiquity. Between church and synagogue the hermeneutic question became central. But interpretative principles were also a matter of debate within the Christian society. Monotheism affirms that the one God alone can make himself known and that he is beyond human searching (e.g. Job 11: 7; Isa. 40: 28). The idea of revelation is integral to the whole. The problems may lie in the interpretation of the word of God, especially if that word is mediated through a diversity of texts written from differing standpoints.

Both Jews and Christians were negative towards polytheism, and regarded belief in numerous gods as a hallmark of the Gentile or 'pagan' religion round them. Greek philosophers had long been moving towards belief in only one god. In Xenophon (*Memorabilia* 1. 4, 4. 3) Socrates argued for the most high deity being a conclusion from the coherence and order of the cosmos. Cicero records the Cynic Antisthenes saying that human beings have numerous gods but nature has only one (*De natura deorum* 1. 32). An orator of the second century AD, Maximus of Tyre (11. 5), observed that despite vast disagreements over religion, all agree that there is one god, Father of everything and supreme over lesser gods. Apollonius of Tyana, sage and magician of the late first century, said that one can approach the supreme being only through mind, not material words (Eusebius, *Praep. Evang.* 4. 13). Tracts produced in Egypt during the early centuries of the empire ascribed to Thrice-Greatest Hermes a clear monotheism which, at some points, betrays influence from the book of Genesis.[1]

In general terms, the Christians were negative to pagan cult but not to philosophy or to literature unless it was pornographic, in which case many pagans were repelled too. (The poet Archilochus had a bad name for errors of taste.) Their strength in society lay in their welfare for the very poor, of whom not

[1] C. H. Dodd, *The Bible and the Greeks* (London, 1935).

a few were destitute. Food shortages were common in antiquity. Bishops of major cities found themselves performing a necessary function in gathering and distributing food (like Joseph in Egypt). During persecution, which tended especially to target people with reasonable resources and land, the poorest members of a congregation might suffer because the church chest was not being supplied with the means to buy food to distribute.

Ancient society was awash with magic and astrology, and this affected some people in all classes of society. Ancient medicine was always hazardous, but more so when physicians normally consulted astrologers and almanacs before prescribing. The quest for restoration of health dominated many lives. Some were converted to Christianity in the hope that baptism might bring a cure; if and when it failed to do so, the family might relapse to pagan cults. Amulets were widespread and could be Christianized in the form of a tiny gospel-book.

In short there was much continuity with what had gone before, but always some discontinuity.

I

THE FIRST FOLLOWERS OF JESUS

Jesus of Nazareth, a charismatic prophet from Galilee, gathered to himself a community of disciples to help in a reform of the Jewish religious tradition, which looked back to the Hebrew prophets and their expectation of divine intervention. The religious authorities of the time were not pleased by the reform element in his teaching, much concerned for the poor and social outcasts, critical of double standards among some Pharisees known for their punctilious observance of the finer points of the Law in separation from 'the people of the land'. He spoke of the need to repent and of the coming kingdom of God, which alarmed the ruling class. The Roman prefect or procurator could be stirred to think him a possible source of civil disorder. Under the prefect's authority he was crucified. But his disciples became rapidly convinced that his mission transcended death. He was a living Lord present to them in their prayers and fellowship. As they broke bread, their hearts burned within them. His tomb, surprisingly provided by a wealthy member of the Council or Sanhedrin, was found empty. Visions of the risen Master reinforced conviction that he had entrusted them with a permanent mission and by his Spirit was with them to carry it out.

He had asked them to love one another. There were initial bonds: all were Jews sharing a common set of scriptures and a sense of belonging to God's elect with an ethic of mutual aid and purity in conscious contrast with surrounding Gentile society. They shared the passionate hope that not only through past prophets but even in the present God was intervening for the vindication and salvation of his people. So their Lord was God's anointed or Messiah, in Greek 'Christos'. The Christians, as Gentile outsiders came to call them at Antioch, or Nazarenes as Jews entitled them, found themselves surrounded by a society unfriendly both from the side of conservative observant Judaism and then later from Gentiles whose gods they scorned as observant Jews did.

The various cults of polytheism were not mutually exclusive. A Gentile could offer incense to both Apollo and Isis and indeed to the emperor without raising an eyebrow. So people were baffled by a religion which was addressed to all nations and tribes and, nevertheless, was marked by a specificity and exclusive particularity that set believers apart from others.

Aversion towards them manifested by 'outsiders' was a factor in encouraging close bonding. In this respect they already had the experience of a degree of ostracism by virtue of being Jews in the Roman Empire, who were not socially integrated and were often not much liked.[1] But some of the most severe problems for Christians were internal. They did not always find it easy to love one another, as Jesus commanded them.

Because from a very early stage of development they understood their faith to carry universal significance for all, whatever their ethnic origin, they could not be content to remain as they began, an energetic group within a Judaism which already had several distinct religious associations—Sadducees, Pharisees, Essenes, or even groups encouraging the maximum of assimilation to the surrounding customs of Gentile society, highly cultivated individuals like Philo of Alexandria or Josephus who made their own the literature and philosophy of Hellenistic society but at the same time wanted to remain loyal and practising Jews.

There was a problem of a special kind in relation to such groups of orthodox Jews, namely that 'Nazarenes' (Acts 24: 5) were distinctive in their faith that Jesus of Nazareth was God's Anointed, the fulfilment of prophecy that the Messiah would come and establish the Kingdom of God on earth. Messianic belief carried with it revolutionary implications for society. Believers in Jesus had a fervent expectation of the possibility of change. When at Thessalonica the mission of Paul encountered opposition from conservatives in the synagogue, the accusation against the apostle was that by proclaiming Jesus to be Messiah 'these men have turned the world upside down' (Acts 17: 6). There had been other claimants to messiahship recorded by Josephus, Pharisee and historian, and their activities had been disturbingly seditious. Jews who wanted a quiet life whether in the study of the law of Moses or in commerce could not be enthusiastic about excited movements, especially if they were thought to involve hostile action against Roman authorities in Judaea or Galilee or against members of the Herod family put in as puppet governors. In the year 66 the Zealot faction finally began war against the Romans, and at first was successful. But Vespasian and then Titus mobilized larger forces against them, and the Jewish cause suffered catastrophic damage ending in the sack of Jerusalem in the year 70.[2] The reverberations of this disaster can be discerned at points in the gospels. Josephus, who deplored the revolt, lamented the city's ruin in language often close to that used by Jesus foreseeing the probable outcome.

The followers of Jesus dissociated themselves from the Zealot struggle. They were not the only Jews to do so. In retrospect the Nazarenes interpreted

---

[1] Observant Jews did not wish to be assimilated in the pagan society around them, and the degree of contempt towards them can be judged from the historian Tacitus' portrait in his *Histories* (below, p. 24).

[2] See Martin Goodman, *The Ruling Class of Judaea: The Origins of the Jewish Revolt* (Cambridge, 1987).

the fall of Jerusalem as divine wrath for the crucifixion of the Messiah. Pharisees interpreted the disaster as divine punishment for too much lax observance of the Mosaic law and the traditions. Among the lax observers were those Nazarenes who concluded from the call to take the gospel of Jesus to the Gentile world that this universal faith did not require of Gentile believers that they be circumcised, keep the sabbath and Jewish feasts, and observe the food laws. In hostile eyes Jewish abstinence from pork was odd, circumcision repulsive, sabbath observance an excuse for idleness. Gentiles, however, could also be impressed by the ethical quality of Jewish lives and the coherence of their families. Their monotheism had strong appeal, and their ancient sacred books commanded respect. In reply to the anti-Semitic Apion Josephus proudly reports that in every town, both Greek and barbarian, there were people who shared the custom of not working on the seventh day, kept Jewish fasts and even their food laws (2. 282). People respected Jewish rejection of abortion and sodomy (199, 202). Many inscriptions in Asia Minor record non-Jewish monotheists, worshippers of 'the most high god'.[3]

Messiah

By the title 'Messiah' Jews, especially Zealots, often (not necessarily always) expected a military, nationalist leader who was to 'restore sovereignty to Israel' and to establish a theocracy. The Messiah was to be 'the Son of David'. Among the first Christian generation several voices took the Son of David title to refer to Jesus, and this usage was familar to the apostle Paul (Rom. 1: 3) as well as being taken for granted in the genealogies in Matthew 1 and Luke 3 or Luke's infancy narrative attached to Bethlehem as 'the city of David'. At Jesus' entry to Jerusalem 'Hosanna to the Son of David' caused excitement alarming to authority. Yet Mark 12: 35–7 preserves an anecdote about Jesus which reads like a disowning of this title. Jesus was called the 'Nazarene' (Mark 14: 67), and Nazareth was not a town where Jews expected something good to come from (John 1: 46; 7: 52). Messiah was not a title of great precision.

The name 'Jesus', the Greek form of Joshua, 'Saviour', was common and in itself carried no necessarily messianic significance, though Matt. 1: 21 shows that it was capable of being so understood.

Jesus and the Pharisees

The first disciples of Jesus were not socially influential and would be classified as 'people of the land'. Jesus drew only a few individuals from the Sadducee

---

[3] See Stephen Mitchell in P. Athanassiadi (ed.), *Pagan Monotheism* (Oxford, 1999), 81–148.

ruling class in Jewish society, a conservative group known for not accepting belief in resurrection to describe the life to come. The impassioned serious-ness of his teaching impressed some Pharisees, believers in resurrection but primarily marked out by their dedication to precise strictness in observance of the Jewish law, and also some 'scribes' professionally concerned with the correct exegesis of the Law's prescriptions. That relations between Jesus and the Pharisees were or could be close and friendly may be deduced from Luke 13: 31, where Pharisees warn Jesus of hostile intent in Herod Antipas. Several other sentences in Luke imply good relations with Pharisees. Mark 12: 28–34 records scribes who positively welcomed what Jesus said about the Law. The majority of Jesus' first followers are described as Galilean fishermen and tax-collectors who collaborated with the government and were unloved by most Jews. On the opposite side, one was a former Zealot (ultra-nationalist) named Simon.

In Jesus' teaching there was a defiant bias towards the poor and despised, to harlots and men with haunted consciences, all called to repentance and faith. The Anointed of God had brought forgiveness of sins and healing to the brokenhearted. This was inherent in the process of realizing the kingdom of God. Something greater than Jonah's preaching, greater even than King Solomon, was now here (Matt. 12: 41–2). Rabbinic sages used to say that where ten were together engaged in the study of the Torah, the glory of God was with them (Mishnah, Aboth 3. 6). For believers in Jesus, where two or three were gathered in his name, he was present in their midst (Matt. 18: 20).

Son of Man

A problematic self-designation in the sayings of Jesus is the title 'Son of man'. The phrase was evidently being used with overtones of meaning that the dis-ciples were expected to grasp. On the one hand it could stress the reality and spontaneity of his humanity. On the other hand in the apocalyptic vision of Daniel 7, 'the son of man', a human figure contrasted with animal figures earlier in the vision, represents the people of God being vindicated despite all their oppression and suffering, and ascends to be seated at God's right hand and to share in the office of Judge. The phrase therefore expressed faith that present suffering would be the path to future glory. There are rabbinic and other Jewish texts in which Daniel's 'Son of man' is taken to refer to Messiah.[4]

---

[4] See W. Horbury, *JTS*, NS 36 (1985), 34–55. Concerning the variety of roles attributed to Messiah in Jewish texts see J. Klausner, *The Messianic Idea in Israel* (London, 1956).

Reform Judaism or a Gentile Mission?

One stream of the traditions about Jesus preserved in the written gospels, which became for the community standard sources for his life and teaching, records that he interpreted his mission as being limited to the Jewish people, the elect race, and hardly envisaged any extension to the Gentile world. Yet Old Testament prophets, especially Isaiah (e.g. 42: 6), had positively interpreted the Babylonian captivity to be a providential instrument to bring the light of God's holy law to enlighten the Gentile world. More than one ancient Hebrew writer had warned against the assumption that Yahweh's choice of Israel implied indifference to other races. So it would be natural for some of the missionaries sent out by Jesus (and therefore called the 'sent', 'apostles') to understand the message as needing to be carried beyond Israel to the Samaritans and beyond them to the Gentile peoples. Had this not seemed natural, there would have been no necessity for sayings such as Matt. 10: 5–6 expressly directing that those now sent out should (initially?) confine their labours to 'the lost sheep of the house of Israel'. The choice of twelve disciples, called to judge the tribes of Israel (Matt. 19: 28), presupposed a mission for the renewal of true religion within Judaism.

The two contrasting standpoints reflect a disagreement within the earliest Christian community. The congregations or house-churches for whom Matthew wrote his gospel clearly consisted mainly of Jews but with Gentile adherents. Among the Christian Jews some felt unable to support the mission to the Gentiles unless the converts submitted to the laws of the Torah in the manner of synagogue-proselytes, accepted circumcision, and observed sabbaths, feasts, and food laws. They were against the more liberal position associated with a one-time zealot in opposing the followers of the Nazarene, Saul or Paul of Tarsus, one of a number of Pharisees who adhered to the community but who was convinced that the Mosaic law could not be imposed upon Gentile converts if the Church of Jesus was to become universal. He even supplied the community with a rationale for a breach with the observant synagogue by developing a radical doctrine of 'justification by faith'; that is to say, the way of salvation is not through ethical achievement in observing the law and the traditions, constituting a right or merit before the Lord, but through faith in the mercy and love of God manifested in the sacrifice of Jesus' crucifixion, then vindicated by God raising him from the dead. Notwithstanding the divisive social consequences of this certainly profound way of putting things, Paul insisted that his missionary strategy included being 'as a Jew to Jews' as well as Gentile to the Gentiles (1 Cor. 9: 20). Five times he had preferred to accept severe synagogue discipline rather than be excluded (2 Cor. 11: 24). The structure of his thinking about God and salvation was often strikingly similar to that found in rabbinic texts.

In religious faith those with whom it is usually hardest to achieve rapport are those whose position is nearest. One would suppose that Matthew's Jewish Christians could have had friendly relations with Pharisees, with whom they shared much. Matthew 23 shows that relations were tense. This may reflect the situation after the Roman sack of Jerusalem and destruction of the Temple when the Pharisees emerged as the leading group within the synagogues of observant Judaism and regarded the Christian believers as rivals for the soul of the elect nation. The Christian Jews found themselves severely harassed by observant fellow-countrymen, and offence caused by the Gentile mission was considerable (1 Thess. 2: 14–16).[5] The supreme issue was whether or not it was true that Messiah had come. That he had was an axiom for the followers of Jesus, whether Jew or Gentile. That this lay in the future was axiomatic for most adherents of the synagogue. Yet there long remained Christians who worshipped with the synagogue on Saturday and with the Church on Sunday and ignored admonitions that they should make a choice. The practice distressed Ignatius of Antioch in Syria, and was still being debated late in the fourth century. In Paul's Gentile congregations it was a leading issue (Gal. 4: 10; Col. 2: 16). Towards the end of the first century the rabbis adopted a formula of exclusion to keep Christian Jews out of observant synagogues. To believe Jesus to be Messiah was already to be deemed an outsider, even if one's blood was wholly Hebrew. We have the paradox that strict rabbis wanted to expel Christian Jews (John 16: 2), and Gentile Christian bishops wanted to expel believers too sympathetic to the Synagogue; both were finding this task difficult.

In Matthew's gospel there is a surprising absence of reference to circumcision. Jesus is the new Moses whose sermon on the mount does not so much replace the commandments from Sinai as become superimposed. The prominence given by Matthew to the leading role assigned to Peter may readily suggest a tradition in which Paul was almost marginalized (cf. 1 Cor. 1: 12). In both Matthew and Paul there is no denial that Israel remains an elect people. Paul (Romans 9–11) interprets the Gentile mission as fulfilling Isaiah's prophecies and as a parenthetic moment in the divine plan for human history designed to provoke the Jewish people into realizing the truth of Jesus's message and authentic messiahship as he increasingly wins converts in the wider world. Antithetical as both writers appear in the spectrum of primitive Christianity, they were unanimous that without the traditions of Judaism Jesus cannot be correctly understood.

The admission of Gentiles

The disagreement whether Gentile converts should be required to observe the Torah of Moses was not for ever settled by the conference between Paul

---

[5] Observant Jews were stern to those who undermined the Law (Philo, *De spec. leg.* 2. 253).

and the 'pillar apostles', Peter, James, and John, described in Galatians 2 from a Pauline standpoint and with a later retrospect in Acts 15. Central was the question whether or not Jewish and Gentile believers could constitute a single Church and, if they could, on what terms. The account in Acts 15 describes the apostolic conference as reaching a generous conclusion, that Gentile converts were not required to keep the observances of strict Judaism, but must keep clear of idolatry, unchastity, and major breaches of the food laws (which would make common meals with Jewish believers difficult). Paul's first letter to the Corinthian church shows that these were indeed prominent issues for him and for them; but while in practice his instructions to the Corinthians come to much the same thing as the Apostolic Decree of the Jerusalem conference, there is no reference to the authority of that decision, and the reasons given for abstaining from eating meat offered in sacrifice to idols or for chastity could have astonished and alarmed Jewish believers at Jerusalem under the aegis of James, 'the Lord's brother'.

Jerusalem's centrality

Nevertheless, Paul would have lost much for his missionary congregations of Gentiles if he had not come into line with the requirements of the Jerusalem church and their leaders. Had his work failed to gain their recognition ('the right hand of fellowship'), he would have 'run in vain'. That saying implied that Paul, no less than Matthew, understood the Jewish believers at Jerusalem to be a necessary touchstone of communion in the one Church of Jesus, and that for him as much as for anyone else in the community Jews and Gentiles were alike constituent members in a single society. A similar assumption continues in later writings of the New Testament, most obviously in the Acts and in Romans 9–11 and in the epistle to the Ephesians, at least in part post-Pauline. In the apostle's lifetime it had concrete expression in the collection for the saints, money contributed by the Gentile congregations to sustain the poor believers of Jerusalem, perhaps because an experiment in communism failed.

The first-century aspiration to keep Jewish and uncircumcised Gentile believers within one single community was difficult to maintain. The epistle to the Ephesians already presupposes that the problems were severe. In the middle years of the second century Justin Martyr (*Dialogue* 46–8) knew of Jewish Christian communities who believed Jesus to be Messiah and observed the prescriptions of the Torah, perhaps also the traditions of the elders, and did not expect Gentile Christians to be circumcised or to observe the sabbath and food laws. He also knew of other Jewish groups whose only point of difference from the synagogue was belief in Jesus the Messiah. Justin was sad that Jewish and Gentile believers had ceased to be able to worship

together, and that the numerous Gentile Christians were in many cases failing to grant full recognition to their Jewish brethren.

John Baptist

Second-century evidence shows that a sect long survived attached to John
the Baptist as leader. John's following at the time of Jesus was very considerable, when his washing in Jordan offered purification to a people who evidently felt stained by the Herods. But it seems evident that a large proportion
of the disciples of Jesus were recruited from those who, like Jesus himself, had
received baptism in Jordan from John. Like Jesus, John was executed. The
gospels are probably correct in representing him as disowning the title of
Messiah and his death as a result of Herodias' anger. A second-century sect
called Mandeans claimed to continue the sect.

2

THE JEWISH MATRIX

Essenes, Therapeutae, Qumran

A community of ascetic Jews in Egypt is described by Philo of Alexandria in his work 'On the contemplative life'. He called them Therapeutae, worshippers of God devoted to the healing of the soul. Their name and life-style links them in part to a group called Essenes, the Hebrew etymology of whose title also indicates a concern for healing. To later Christian writers the Therapeutae seemed to anticipate monasticism: they avoided cities, had communal meals on a restricted diet, practised celibacy and mastery of the passions, and were devout observers of the Mosaic precepts. They interpreted the scriptures allegorically, faced sunrise for prayers, and found peace in silence.

In the time of Jesus ten miles south of Jericho near the Dead Sea at Qumran there lived a similar community of Jews consciously distinct and independent of other Jewish groups such as Pharisees and Sadducees. Their priests called themselves Sons of Zadok; perhaps (it is far from certain) they may be at least akin to, perhaps identified with, the group of Essenes described by Philo, Josephus, and the elder Pliny, who died in the eruption of Vesuvius, AD 79. The origin of this group is unclear. Possibly they had reacted to Greek ideals of piety infiltrating Palestine after Alexander the Great, especially in the time of Antiochus Epiphanes in the second century BC with his conscious programme of Hellenization.

Close by the community at Qumran in caves in the hillside texts almost certainly belonging to this community were found during the decade from 1947 onwards. The collection was scattered among eleven caves, and contained all biblical texts except Esther which had disputed status (Genesis Rabbah 36. 8), copies of the Psalms and Isaiah being particularly prominent. Included were copies of Ben Sira (Ecclesiasticus), Tobit, and the Epistle of Jeremiah. Also included were works ascribed to ancient heroes, including the book(s) of Enoch, one of these being the Book of Giants with a strongly dualistic myth of cosmic conflict. That is to say that the literature of the community had a text akin to later gnosticism on the margins of the Church. The community possessed a Rule, expositions of some of the

Hebrew prophets, and a work about war between the forces of light and those of darkness. Among the texts in the collection some show a critical stance not to the Temple at Jerusalem but to the priests responsible for its worship. One text implies a cool opinion of exegetes providing smooth glosses on the Mosaic Torah reducing its demands. The majority of the documents are non-biblical Jewish literature, but fragments of almost all the books in the Hebrew Bible have been found. Not all the texts are in Hebrew or Aramaic; some are in Greek. The finds have recovered the Hebrew original texts of some hitherto known only in Greek translation such as The Testaments of the Twelve Patriarchs. While some of the texts were evidently written within and by the community, some of the texts may have been brought to Qumran after being written elsewhere, in some cases up to two or even three hundred years before the community's life ended with the Zealot war with Rome from AD 66 onwards.

The Qumran society venerated a 'teacher of righteousness' who had taught his followers an esoteric manner of interpreting the scriptures and had suffered harassment from a wicked priest ruling over Israel. He was a founding figure for the community, but cannot be identified. Among them some refused to bear arms, but the majority took an active part in the revolt of 66 and suffered accordingly. Their communal life had resemblances to that of the disciples of Jesus. They were punctilious about correct observance of the sabbath and daily ritual washings, and that would obviously have been a difference from at least some of the disciples. Laws about ceremonial purity were intensely important to them. They had their own distinctive calendar of festivals differing from that of the Jewish authorities at Jerusalem, and preferred a solar year of 364 days to orthodox Judaism's lunar calendar of 354 days adding a month every third year or so. They forbade divorce and remarriage, disliked oaths, practised sharing of resources in a way probably close to that described in Acts 4: 32 ff. Characteristically they interpreted ancient prophecies to refer specifically to their own community.

Keen readers of apocalyptic texts, they nursed fervent messianic hopes for the coming of the Prophet promised to Moses in Deut. 18: 18 (cf. John 1: 21) and looked for the coming of two Messiahs—a priestly Messiah of Aaron and a political Messiah of Moses. The Messiah would be of the seed of David, and was prefigured in the star of Num. 24: 17. No text suggests that the 'teacher of righteousness' would become Messiah. The contrast between a Messiah of Aaron and a political Messiah of Moses who would be a Davidic leader may suggest that at least some devout Jews were conscious of tension between a military and a religious saviour, and that perhaps Jesus of Nazareth was not the only figure of his time to think there could be a Messiah whose 'nationalism' would not involve military combat.

It would be instructive for early Christian beginnings if the Qumran texts produced a clear and certain instance of a suffering Messiah; claims for such a text have not carried conviction for the learned. What is evident is that some Old Testament texts taken by early Christian writers to refer to the Messiah were also interpreted at Qumran in a messianic sense. It is also certain that the Qumran community understood itself to be living in the final age of this world and that they expected persecution. Not unnaturally the Dead Sea scrolls cast more light on contemporary Judaism than on primitive Christianity. But there are a few striking parallels to New Testament themes which raise the question whether possibly some of Jesus' followers had at one time in their lives had contact with the Qumran ascetics. Josephus' autobiography tells us that for a time he tried out the Essene way of life (*Life* 10–11). Had John the Baptist done something of the kind? Son of God (not Son of Man) is a title in Qumran texts. In one document a speculative exegesis of Melchizedek (Genesis 14) makes him a heavenly figure, which is close to the epistle to the Hebrews. A text from cave 4 offers a list of Beatitudes, showing that Matt. 5: 1 ff. was cast in a form familiar at that time.

The parallels between the New Testament texts and Dead Sea Scrolls are valuable to the historian. The closer the Qumran texts stand to the language and thought of early Christian texts, the more evident it becomes that the traditions in the canonical gospels, perhaps also some in the Gospel of Thomas transmitted in Coptic, provide a broadly reliable portrait of first-century Christianity and are not anachronistic inventions. Anachronisms and other misfits are the primary indication that a text does not belong to the alleged time and place. Similarly a high proportion of matter in the synoptic gospels is illuminated by parallels in rabbinic documents, which, although written down substantially later in time, belong to a closed society much attached to the tradition of the elders. Rabbis were saying the kind of thing preserved in the Mishnah, Midrash, and Talmud long before those collections were compiled. Parallels with sayings of Jesus can sometimes be striking. It also speaks for the value of the traditions in the synoptic gospels that although Galatians 2 and Acts 15 attest impassioned controversy about the terms of admission for Gentile believers, the gospels do not contain sayings given to Jesus which look designed to settle the question e.g. of circumcision, which is what one would expect if someone had wanted to create an authoritative decision.

The Dead Sea texts include papyrus texts in Greek. Some of these belong to the second century AD. Two small fragmentary pieces from Qumran cave 7 have been claimed to provide texts of Mark 6: 52–3 and 1 Tim. 3: 16–4: 3. The surviving damaged letters are not incompatible with this hypothesis, but may also be capable of other reconstructions. The probability of this conjecture interlocks with other hypotheses about the likely date when such Christian documents came to circulate.

Gospel traditions

For the transmission of traditions about Jesus the gospels, especially
Mark, Luke, and Matthew, are of basic importance. Their concerns were not
those of a detached historian, but were reflections of the believing communities which the evangelists represented. That does not mean that they
did not have a biographical interest. The story of Jesus, his sayings and
doings, above all his passion and resurrection, lay at the heart of what they
wanted to say. The authors of the gospels we know only from the reflection
of their face seen in their selection and discernible themes. The term 'gospel'
was the message, and only by derivation came to be applied to books,
probably as a result of the liturgical practice of reading passages from these
books at the early Christian eucharist where the people of God wanted to
hear the words of the Lord. The community by the Dead Sea did not
possess any collections of sayings from a particular teacher analogous with
the gospels. By contrast virtually every section of the story of Jesus in
the gospels presupposes his supreme authority for the community and
indeed for the human race. 'He spoke with authority, not as one of the
scribes.' 'Even the winds and the waves obey him.' The healings, apparently
almost marginal to the central point, serve to reinforce the authority
theme, which then becomes explicit in the rising crescendo of confrontation with the conservative religious authorities and expositors of the Law
in Mark 12.

In what decade the four canonical gospels were written can only be a
matter of conjecture. The impetus to gather material would naturally have
come as the twelve apostles began to die or otherwise disappear from the
scene, but also as Gentile converts wanted to know what Jesus had said
and done. The sixties and seventies of the first century AD provide one
possible context for the gospels of Mark, Matthew, and Luke. Although
John's gospel has material with affinities to that of the first three, it is so rich
in symbolist writing that one can formulate a rule that if anything can mean
more than one thing it does; this presupposes mature reflection and a date
probably in the eighties or nineties. Recognition of John's authority by
churches in the second century came more slowly than that of Matthew,
Mark, and Luke.

The terminology of the group by the Dead Sea has parallels with New
Testament language, and there are other analogies. They had officers in their
community, not only presbyters but an 'overseer' who was the society's
'shepherd' for teaching and administration. In Greek this overseer's title
would have been *epískopos*, bishop. In language and in the searching of
prophecy for messianic hopes, the Dead Sea group offer striking analogies to
the primitive Christians, but also notable differences.

Mark's messianic secret

In Mark's gospel the theme of Jesus' authority is intimately connected with an emphasis on the mystery of his status as Messiah, with an insistently repeated thesis that discernment of this truth was at the time, and is now at the time of Mark's writing, a supernatural gift not granted to all. Jewish traditions said that the identity of Messiah would be a secret that not all could penetrate, indeed that Messiah himself would not know. In Mark this notion is extended to answer the question how the elect people of God, to whom had been entrusted the oracles of God in ancient prophecy, could by a substantial majority fail to recognize their expected saviour when he came. (The fear of a loss of national identity in a universal communion is not a question raised, but Jesus in Mark 7 appears as a sharp critic of ceremonial customs and of exegeses of the Torah conflicting with natural morality.) Mark even allowed the paradoxical notion that the reason why Jesus taught through parables was an intention to enfold divine truths in obscurity; it was not the divine will that those outside the believing community should understand. Some did not have ears to hear.

At an early date observant Jews were contending that the crucifixion of Jesus could only be a sign of divine cursing in accord with Deut. 21: 23 'a hanged man is accursed by God', significantly cited by Paul in Gal. 3: 13. (A Qumran text applies this Deuteronomy verse to Crucifixion.) Paul had to warn the Corinthians (1 Cor. 12: 3) that no one could be speaking under the inspiration of the Holy Spirit if he was declaring Jesus to be anathema. He was much aware that to Jews the cross was a stumbling-block (1 Cor. 1: 23), not one of the miraculous signs by which they understood a Messiah to be accompanied. They had not seen lions lying down with lambs as the prophets suggested.

Sabbath

Although in Mark Jesus comes with an unrecognized messianic authority, he offers no challenge to the keeping of the Law of Moses. Disagreements with scribal exegetes are not whether the sabbath has to be observed but concern the manner of observance and whether this obligation overrides other duties of a more general humanity. In the age of the Second Temple leading authorities in Judaea asked for the utmost strictness in sabbath observance, a degree of strictness which later rabbinic authorities would relax in the light of circumstance and natural humanity. Jesus anticipated the view that impracticality and inhumanity can result from excessively legalistic interpretation of the Decalogue's precept. This is expressed in the memorable principle: 'The sabbath was made for man, not man for the sabbath' (Mark 2: 27), words which presuppose that the divine gift of the sabbath is not to be scorned. The large following for this Galilean teacher aroused envy (Mark 15: 10). To some scribes he appeared as an unwelcome alternative authority.

'The people of the land'

Substantial evidence in the Babylonian Talmud shows that in both Judaea and Galilee ordinary Jews, described by the very devout or by the religious authorities as 'the people of the land', did not feel bound to adhere with absolute strictness to rules about tithes and about ceremonial purity in the manner of the Pharisees and scribal interpreters of the Law. One defined oneself as belonging to the people of the land by failures to observe ritual purity before eating, to recite the Shemaʿ of Deut. 6: 4 morning and evening, to put fringes and phylacteries on garments, and to be punctilious about instructing sons in the Torah. Pharisees characteristically wished to be sure of being unpolluted, and therefore avoided contact with the people of the land, whether by trade or by accepting their hospitality. Better to cross the road than to have to salute a person not scrupulous about purity rules or tithing.

In the age of the Second Temple the number of prohibitions was increased to a burdensome extent. Any contact with leprosy or with a dead body involved serious defilement (as some Gentiles would also have thought, notably the Pythagoreans). In Jesus' parable of the Good Samaritan the priest and the Levite were consistent in judging the purity rules to override wider obligations of humanity and compassion (Luke 10: 31 f.). Express witness to the social divisiveness of this code appears in the Letter of Aristeas (106). Naturally not all people of the land were equally careless about the rules; nor were all Pharisees or rabbis equally negative about social contacts with them.

Josephus once claimed that Jews are unanimous (*c. Apion.* 2. 179). A Pharisee might hope so. In actuality rabbis were not unanimous. The school of Shammai was stricter about defilement than that of Hillel, which was more liberal. Among those who found their society shunned there was natural resentment. The Sages could hardly avoid being aware of the dislike with which they could be regarded by people who were passionately loyal Jews, ready to lay down their lives during the revolts of 66–70, 112–115, and 132–5. People of the land did not feel obliged to wear phylacteries broad or narrow or fringes long or short. It could be a burden to tithe produce to support temple clergy at Jerusalem and to give alms for the city poor. Mostly engaged in farming and trade, their daily round did not make it easy to observe ceremonial washings before food as Pharisees did.

There was rapport between the practice of less strict Jews and the criticisms of Jesus against some of the dangers of Pharisaic precisionism. The points on which criticisms by Jesus are recorded correspond more or less exactly to matters mentioned in the Talmud. People of the land could well share Jesus' judgement that to place ritual purity above a general humanity and compassion was a form of hypocrisy.

Judaism after the fall of Jerusalem

After the fall of Jerusalem in 70 the Pharisees became prominent in the reconstruction of Jewish society, and the form in which Jesus' criticisms have come to be expressed in Matthew 23 evidently represents the sense of rivalry between Pharisees and Christian Jews about the need for precise observances of the Law. With the Temple destroyed the prescribed sacrifices could not be offered unless 'sacrifice' was redefined to include prayer and Bible study. There was a sad general conviction that true prophecies had come to an end (*bSot.* 48b and elsewhere). There might still be false prophets. The Christian notion that a second Moses could come to replace the original Torah was abhorrent to the conservative rabbis (Deut. Rabbah 8. 6). So Temple cultus was now to be succeeded by disciplined study of the Torah and of the oral tradition, which was hardly less respected as given on Sinai. The *Sayings of Rabbi Nathan* (4. 9b) declare that 'the study of the Torah is dearer to God than burnt offerings'. Good works make as good an atonement as sacrifices. Justin in the second century reports that for at least some Jews the destruction of the Temple and the impossibility of sacrifices after Hadrian's paganization of Jerusalem were accepted as a providential liberation for a religion of the spirit based on the study of the Torah and the traditions with synagogue prayers (*Dial.* 117. 2). In principle such Jews shared the judgement stated by Jesus (Mark 14: 58) that if the Temple were to be destroyed, satisfactory alternative arrangements could be made within a mere three days, a saying which, in combination with the cleansing of the Temple traders, provoked deep anger among the Temple authorities, becoming an occasion for trial and handing over to Pilate. Nevertheless, in a Judaism without sacrifices or pilgrimages to the holy city it would become difficult for a less strictly observant synagogue to be distinct from a Christian group, or to exclude secret believers in Jesus the Messiah (John 9: 22). The feeling of polarity is evident in Paul's letter to the Christian Jews in Rome asking for their prayers that in his imminent visit to Jerusalem he may be delivered from 'unbelievers' (15: 31) who, at any rate temporarily, have become 'God's enemies' (11: 28). The report in Suetonius of Jews in Rome rioting 'at the instigation of Chrestus' implies that anger was running high.

The crucifixion of Jesus

In the tradition represented in St John's gospel the tension between Church and Synagogue has become a contrast between light and darkness, between those obeying the word of God and those now so hostile to this word that their father can only be the Devil (John 8: 44). In other words, the problematic unbelief of conservative Jews refusing to recognize the divine presence in the Messiah is explained by holding that they have been spiritually blinded, unable to see the light of the world. John's gospel was aware that in the eyes of these conservative observant Jews Jesus was accused of being sent by a devil and of making the claims of a madman (John 10: 19). The high priest Caiaphas judged that it was in the political interest of Israel that Jesus should be eliminated, since Roman prefects did not like messianic leaders, and it was better that one man should die than that there should be a general assault on the people (John 11: 50, 18: 14). Caiaphas' actions are presented as more political than religious in their motivation. The execution of Jesus by the Roman soldiers is seen as the result of an accidental misjudgement by a small coterie of religious and national leaders who influenced Pontius Pilate. As in Matthew, John's gospel lays a weight of responsibility on the Jewish authorities. For Josephus, Pilate made the decision but on accusations brought by Jewish leaders.

Crucifixion was a peculiarly cruel form of execution in that the torture preceding death was prolonged as long as possible, and the Romans used it especially for slaves committing murder or dangerous rebels. To Jesus' disciples it was a shattering blow, but only for a short time. It was not the end. He continued to live in a new and divine mode, anticipating the resurrection which many Jews, particularly Pharisees, believed to be the final destiny of God's elect. The disciples studied the ancient prophecies, notably Isaiah, where the servant of God suffers and is humiliated in the process of bringing salvation to Israel, or Daniel's vision of the son of man placed at God's right hand to judge the world. His dereliction on the cross and other humiliating circumstances could be found foreshadowed in Psalm 22. So the disciples concluded that Jesus was indeed the saviour not in spite of the crucifixion but because of it. The passion was a sacrifice for the sins of the world, and Jesus was the passover lamb. They continued a memorial offering of consecrated bread and wine representing the sacrifice of 'Christ our passover'. Their theology was exegesis of the Old Testament (Luke 24: 25–7).

Accordingly, Jesus who proclaimed the gospel of the kingdom is himself the gospel. The redemption is that in and by him God has visited his people, and by his life and self-sacrifice he embodied the love of God. 'The Son of man came to give his life a ransom for many' (Mark 10: 45). So in John's gospel the cross of Golgotha is no defeat but a supreme symbol of triumphant victory over the forces of evil. In the Pauline letters the theme of the cross as a sign of triumph over evil is also prominent (Col. 2: 15; cf. Eph. 1: 21–2). In the prose-poem of the Apocalypse of John 'the Lamb' is a title of conquest over diabolical adversaries. This Lamb was slain from the foundation of the world, but has become the vindicator of persecuted martyrs.

3

JEWS AND CHRISTIANS SURVIVE
ROME'S CRUSHING OF REVOLTS

Hadrian founds Aelia

Just as the eminent Rabbi Johanan ben Zakkai escaped from the Roman siege of Jerusalem in a coffin to establish his school at Yavneh near Jaffa, so also the Christian Jewish community got out of Jerusalem and is reported by Eusebius of Caesarea to have moved across the Jordan to Pella. There is no good reason to doubt the veracity of these reports. Jewish anger against Roman imperial authority continued, with a second ferocious rebellion in Egypt and Cyrene in 112–115 and then a major revolt in Hadrian's reign, 132–5, led by Bar Cocheba 'son of a star' (in rabbinic texts called Ben Koziba, 'son of a lie', no doubt because the outcome was catastrophic). Bar Cocheba was strong for observing the prescriptions of the Torah and the traditions. Christian Jews, therefore, who had a Messiah already, felt unable to participate and are reported by Justin and Jerome to have suffered accordingly. The initially successful revolt seems to have been sparked off by Hadrian's wish to legislate against circumcision and also to rebuild the ruined city of Jerusalem, mainly inhabited by a camp of Roman soldiers. Some of Bar Cocheba's coins celebrate 'the liberation of Jerusalem' and evidence, admittedly uncertain, suggests that plans to rebuild the Temple were initiated. The early Christian letter of 'Barnabas' shows that this aspiration had not died. Hadrian's builders replanned the old city, incidentally confirming the bringing of the hill of Golgotha inside the new town wall (a fact implicit in a Good Friday sermon 'On the Pascha' by Melito bishop of Sardis about thirty years later). On this site, already venerated by Christians, Hadrian erected a shrine to Aphrodite.

Hadrian called the new city after his own family name, Aelia Capitolina, which remained its official name until crusading times. It was to be strictly pagan in its cults. No Jew was to enter the city. The main temple dedicated to Jupiter Capitolinus was put on the site of the old Jewish temple with an equestrian statue of the emperor where the Holy of Holies had been.

The survival of the Jewish people and their old religion was thereafter dependent on the rabbis and on the tenacious conservatism of an unassimilated and unassimilable Judaism. This tight society was unsympathetic to Hellenized Judaism. The Greek translation of the Hebrew scriptures called the Septuagint, made at Alexandria in the third and second centuries BC, came to be distrusted. The writings of Philo and Josephus were copied by Christian scribes. Prayers of Greek synagogue liturgy survive when they became incorporated in Christian collections.

Josephus on Jesus

Two texts in the *Antiquities* of Josephus refer to Christianity: one (*AJ* 20.9.1. 200) speaks of James 'brother of Jesus entitled Christ'. The other, earlier paragraph (*AJ* 18.3.3. 63–4) raises many problems. On the one hand it describes Jesus in terms unlikely to be used by a Christian, namely that Jesus was a wise man who achieved surprising feats and whose teaching was well received by those who are pleased by the truth; on accusations brought by leading Jews Pilate condemned him to crucifixion, but those attached to him did not cease to exist and the Christian tribe has not disappeared even today. On the other hand there are phrases unlikely to be used except by a Christian interpolator, namely 'He was the Messiah . . . On the third day he appeared restored to life as foretold by the prophets.' The probability is that these words replaced something originally more neutral,[1] perhaps descriptive of popular disturbance in Jerusalem (a suggestion supported by the context in which the passage occurs), and that Josephus used words deploring the events.

Liberal Synagogues and the Church

As the Christian mission in the Gentile world gathered momentum, the synagogues of the Jewish Dispersion often provided the springboard, partly because Greek synagogues possessed the Septuagint translation of the Hebrew scriptures, partly because Gentile 'God-fearers' gathered round the community for worship, though rarely becoming proselytes. In synagogues of the Dispersion the prophet Malachi's contrast between the rejected sacrifices of Jerusalem and those of the Dispersion being accepted (1.10–110) could be applied to the situation after AD 70 (Justin, *Dialogue* 117). Christians took the prophecy to justify the Gentile mission. Probably there were instances where a local church originated in the conversion *en bloc* of a

---

[1] An Arabic version, to which S. Pines drew attention (Israel Academy, Jerusalem 1971), found in Agapius of Mabbog (tenth century) [PO 7.471], is neutral as the Greek is not, and may well preserve what Josephus wrote.

synagogue with some liberal inclination. At Rome, where there were at least nine or ten synagogues, that is likely to have been the case. Converted Jews brought with them their Septuagint Bible but also traditions of exegesis. At Qumran Bible students sought to discern fulfilment of prophecy in their own situation. Debate about the meaning of scripture when set in a situation of controversy demanded precision about the identity of books held to be sacred and authoritative.

The Old Testament canon

Josephus near the end of the first century AD provides the earliest evidence for a known canon of the Old Testament in 22 books (which he does not specify). The number 22 probably originated in a wish to have a list of books corresponding to the number of letters in the Hebrew alphabet. Since the book of Daniel was the latest book to find a place in the Hebrew canon, it is a reasonable hypothesis that the synagogue canon found its familiar shape during the second century BC. Contemporary with Josephus Rabbis in debate at Yavneh (where after AD 70 learned rabbis assembled, in effect replacing the Sanhedrin) had doubts about the Song of Solomon and the book Qoheleth (Ecclesiastes), so that the question was not then regarded as finally closed. However, disputations with Christians would have provided a stimulus for definition, notably because Greek-speaking believers, whether Jew or Gentile, were using the Septuagint as their Old Testament and this version, held (e.g. by Philo and many others) to have been inspired, included books not in the Hebrew canon. On this overplus of the Gentile Christian Old Testament over against the Rabbis' canon, see below, p. 30.

Mishnah and Talmud

The destruction of the Temple at Jerusalem reinforced the rabbis' attachment to the books of the Bible, especially the Torah or 'Teaching' (i.e. the Pentateuch) and to the oral tradition which came to be called 'Mishnah', a collection of authoritative judgements on the interpretation of the biblical laws which itself became a canon needing commentary, the 'Talmud'. The Talmud was needed because the judgements recorded in the Mishnah were not unanimous, but in time the Talmud itself became a normative exegesis and a primary subject of rabbinic studies. The fact that so many disagreements were recorded added to the zeal with which the studies were pursued. There were to be ultra-conservative rabbis who did not concede authority to Mishnah or Talmud, and adhered exclusively to the Hebrew Bible as divinely given. In addition there were those who sought mystical experiences, of

which the apostle Paul's ecstatic elevation to the third heaven to hear ineffable words (2 Cor. 12: 1–4) is the oldest instance. In time some among the
latter could become fascinated by the occult and the Kabbalah with number
mysticism and other ways of treating the Bible as a divine cryptogram.
Through the writings of Philo elements of this passed into the Christian
stream.

The possession of sacred written records of the divine Law naturally
imparted to Jewish society a powerful sense of being set apart with distinct
social customs and a desire not to be submerged or assimilated in the ethnic
'scrambled eggs' of the Graeco-Roman world. This distinctiveness was
enforced by circumcision, abstinence from pork, not working on Saturdays,
and other such customs which were the object of not very friendly comment
in Gentile society. When the historian Tacitus came to write something
about the Jewish war of 66–70, he prefaced his story with a bitingly malicious
caricature of a race which was notorious for not acknowledging the gods of
the empire.

Spiritualizing Temple and ritual

The synagogues of the Jewish Dispersion circumcised and baptized proselytes on their admission to full membership of the community. Such total
converts were rare. The Christians of the Gentile mission easily adopted a
spiritualizing understanding of Temple, ritual, circumcision, sabbath. The
theme that circumcision should be of the heart was already in Deut. 30: 6 and
Jer. 4: 4, 9: 25 f. In Paul's first letter to Corinth, the temple of God is either the
believer's body (6: 19) or the believing community (3: 16). In the epistle to
the Hebrews (6: 10) the sacrifice to embrace and supersede all sacrifices is the
self-offering of Jesus whereby as eternal high priest after the order of
Melchizedek (superior to the Levitical line) he has entered the holy of
holies in heaven. God's house, as in Paul, is the community of the Church
(3: 6). The destiny of the wandering people of God is a sabbath rest analogous
to God's rest on the seventh day of creation week.

Baptism and Eucharist

By dropping circumcision and keeping proselyte baptism the Gentile missionary churches formed their universal rite of initiation, fortified by the
awareness that Jesus himself had been baptized in Jordan by John Baptist.
Although Jesus himself had not given baptism, the apostles had done so
(John 4: 2—a sentence which may be a retort to argument on the subject),
and he had surely wished his disciples to continue the rite (Matt. 28: 19). The
Passover memorial of deliverances from bondage in Egypt, a solemn meal

with bread and wine, had been faithfully observed by Jesus and the twelve disciples on the night before the crucifixion. The memorial offering of bread and wine was continued in 'thanksgiving' (*eucharistia*) for the gift of redemption by his self-offering, his body and blood, so that the bread and wine set apart by the church by a blessing or rite of consecration was not to be received as a common meal such as one could have at home (1 Cor. 11: 22). It was a proclamation or setting forth of the Lord's death, to be continued to the end of time. Those who came to share in this act of communion were not, in Paul's exhortation, to be unworthy of receiving this bread and cup by failing to discern the sacredness of a rite not intended to satisfy hunger. 'The cup of blessing which we bless, is it not a participation in Christ's blood? The bread which we break, is it not a participation in the body of Christ?' (1 Cor. 10: 16). Already in Justin a century later *eucharistia* is an established name of the rite.

It is one thing to explain and describe how a social movement began; it is quite another to account for its survival. Believers understood the Lord to have commanded them to continue the commemoration of his self-sacrifice. Other Messianic movements of the age, reported by Josephus and by Acts 5: 33–9, did not survive. The community's continued observance of the eucharist was a factor in ensuring the Church's lasting life. For the apostle Paul it was 'the tradition' which he had received and passed on.

Easter

The depth of Christian continuity with the Church's Jewish roots is exemplified by the annual celebration of the Lord's resurrection at the time of the Jewish Passover. 'Christ our passover is sacrificed for us', wrote St Paul to the Corinthians. The Christian Jews continued to celebrate the Passover but with additional meaning in that the redemption or Exodus from the bondage of Egypt was now a salvation brought by Messiah who was also the new Moses, giver of a new law, founder of a new covenant as prophesied by Jeremiah. Passover always fell at the full moon in the month Nisan. Gradually the Christians split between those who continued to celebrate the passion and resurrection at the same time as the synagogue's Passover, on the fourteenth day of the month, and those who wanted to celebrate it on the first day of the week, when they normally met for worship (1 Cor. 16: 1). Therefore they wanted to celebrate the Christian feast on the Sunday following the first full moon after the spring equinox. That was to become the eventual norm. There could still, however, be disagreement in calculating the spring equinox. In the third century an eminent mathematician of Alexandria, Anatolius, who became bishop of Laodicea in Syria (Latakia), worked out a nineteen-year cycle for Easter. He regarded it as axiomatic that as the Jewish

Passover fell after the spring equinox, the Christian Easter must also (Eusebius *HE* 7. 32. 14ff.).[2]

Likewise the Jewish festival of Pentecost was continued in the Church but now with the commemoration of the gift of the Holy Spirit to the apostles. The Christians were keeping the main structure of the Synagogue calendar, but giving the great feasts an entirely Christian significance.

[2] By the early fourth century Alexandria had a modified form of the cycle. In time Constantinople had its own version, in the sixth century harmonized with Alexandria. The bishops of Old Rome, conscious of authority, tried to settle disagreements case by case, but as late as the fifth century found the Alexandrian cycle awkward, in contrast with Milan, which (if a letter of Ambrose about the celebration of Easter 387 is authentic) accepted it by 360.

4

THE HEBREW SCRIPTURES
IN THE CHURCH

The Septuagint

To meet the religious needs of Greek-speaking Jews of the Dispersion no longer comfortably familiar with Hebrew, a Greek version of the Pentateuch or five books of Moses was made at Alexandria in the third century BC during the reign of Ptolemy Philadelphus (284–246). Ptolemy ruled not only over Egypt but also over Judaea and had numerous Jews in his army; Egypt had a substantial Jewish population. It was claimed with probability that Ptolemy granted his patronage to the project of translation. The Greek Pentateuch became diffused beyond Alexandria among the synagogues of the Mediterranean world. In time the prophets and other writings of synagogue usage were added to the translation. The Pentateuch retained pride of place.

Probably late in the second century BC a propagandist on behalf of Judaism composed a fictitious panegyric on the origins of the Greek Pentateuch entitled the *Letter of Aristeas*. This claimed sacrosanct status for the version, produced in seventy-two days by seventy-two translators, so that it was superior to rival versions and in no need of correction or improvement. That just such a corrected text was made is certain from a Greek manuscript of the Twelve 'minor' Prophets found among the Dead Sea Scrolls, and from the use of the same form of text in Justin. Probably Aristeas had in view not only correctors of the Septuagint but also ultra-conservatives who thought no sacred text translatable without dangerous loss. Some said the Septuagint was a sin like the worship of the golden calf.

Alexandrian Jews liked to assert their presence in the city and the supremacy of monotheism against polytheism, though the Septuagint was careful to warn against scorning the religions of others (Exod. 22: 27; Deut. 7: 25). The Jews of Alexandria had an annual festival to celebrate the achievement of translation. Philo regarded the translators as divinely inspired, and this estimate became transmitted to many early Christian writers. This was the Christian Bible for both Greeks and Latins, the Bible of the apostles.[1] It would need a Hebraist like Jerome to observe that some cit-ations in Matthew's gospel presupposed the Hebrew, not the Septuagint text. Augustine regarded both Hebrew and Septuagint version as equally inspired and valid. As the prophets and the writings had become added to the Septuagint version of the Pentateuch, the title 'the Law' became a loose designation for the entire corpus of sacred Jewish books (John 10. 43; Rom. 3. 29; 1 Cor. 14. 21).

For the synagogues, naturally enough, as for Philo the Pentateuch was supreme; the prophets and the writings did not enjoy the same degree of sanctity. For the Christians, however, the prophets were supreme, and the laws of the Pentateuch were interpreted as prophecy, the Levitical directions about sacrifice and the story of Abraham and Isaac in Genesis 22 prefiguring the sacrifice of Jesus the Messiah.

Debate between observant Jews and Jewish Christians produced disagree-ment about the precise books that could be cited as authoritative. Greek-speaking Christians read the story of Susanna and thought it showed up syna-gogue elders in an unhappy light (below, p. 130). Since the text contained a Greek pun not reproducible in Hebrew, the story was unlikely to have a Hebrew original. But there it was in the Septuagint collection. The wisdom of Ben Sira became so popular among the Christians that in the West it acquired the title 'Ecclesiasticus', and a famous saying of Jesus in Matt. 11: 28 directly quotes Sir. 51: 27.[2] More problematic was the presence of a quotation from the book of Enoch in the epistle of Jude, some thinking that this guar-anteed Enoch's place in the Christian canon, while others disagreed because the book was not included in the Septuagint.

To a thoughtful Gentile it was bound to seem strange to claim that the Hebrew Bible, in a language not understood even by all Jews, could be God's universal word for all, which ought to be in a widely understood tongue such as Greek.

Belief in the inspired and authoritative quality of the Septuagint version made it possible to cite God's word in translation without a nagging anxiety that in some places the Hebrew original could be of higher authority and might mean something different. So Christian Jews could find in the Greek version of Isa. 7: 14 a prophecy of the virginal conception of Jesus (Matt. 1: 23), thereby answering objection that the Hebrew spoke not of a virgin but of a young woman. In the fifties of the second century Justin from Nablus was meeting critical questions about the reliability of the Septuagint in this pas-sage, and had to argue that Isaiah described the birth as a wonderful 'sign', which could hardly be affirmed of a young woman. He complained that

---

[1] Greek was widely understood in first-century Palestine.
[2] With Matt. 6: 12 compare Sir. 28: 2.

representatives of the Synagogue challenged the Septuagint only where they disliked Christian appeals to prophecies. Nevertheless he himself used a corrected Septuagint text for the Twelve minor Prophets.

Aquila

Disputations between Church and Synagogue moved Origen in the third century to a vast undertaking, his Hexapla, juxtaposing the Hebrew in transliteration, the Septuagint, and three or more other versions, among which special value was attached to that by Aquila. Aquila was a Gentile who, after a time as a Christian, was converted to orthodox Judaism and about 140 produced a translation of the Old Testament characterized by extreme literalness. His version was especially valued by Christian exegetes ignorant of Hebrew, since he enabled readers to see more or less exactly what the Hebrew original said without the trouble of learning the language. If his version was intended to undermine the argument from fulfilled prophecy, he was unsuccessful. Justin records that Gentile proselytes adhering to the Synagogue were much more hostile to Christians than were native Jews (*Dial.* 122. 2).

Argument about prophecy

The Christian move into the Gentile world was bound to modify the character of the appeal to ancient Hebrew prophecy. To declare Jesus to be 'Messiah', that is God's Anointed, was technical Jewish language which among Gentiles was hardly comprehensible. The title in Greek was 'Christos', meaning a person anointed with oil. A Gentile convert, unless a synagogue proselyte, had no background to make that a numinous concept. It suggested an athlete. Therefore 'Christ' rapidly became more a proper name than a title. Luke tells us that the community of the Way was first given the nickname 'Christians' in the city of Antioch, no doubt by the pagan population. Antioch was also the city from which we first meet the noun *Christianismós* (Ignatius, *Rom.* 3. 3). 'Christian' was at first no self-designation, and believers, whether Jew or Gentile, did not for some time know that that was what they were. By antithesis the Christians' name for the religion of orthodox Jews was 'Judaism' (Gal. 1: 13 f.).

Although for Jews the term 'Messiah' had various meanings (dependent on the kind of deliverance, whether religious or secular, being expected), there was widespread hope and searching of the prophets. Once the language was used in a Gentile milieu, the argument from prophecy became a demonstration that the events of Jesus' life and passion had been predicted centuries earlier. Justin noted the circularity of the argument: that miraculous events occurred was proved by the prophecies, and the inspiration of the prophets was proved by the events which they foretold. Critics questioned whether the prophecies were as clear as the argument needed. There could be more than one exegesis. Pagan critics soon began to accuse Christians of having adjusted the ancient prophecies to make them fit better, but this contention fell before the reply that the prophecies were transmitted by orthodox Jews unlikely to make changes for the convenience of the Church.

Belief that Jesus was Messiah lay at the foundation of the veneration of him as a divine figure. Justin's *Dialogue with Trypho* attests disagreement bearing on this point. Trypho met Justin's argument that texts in the Old Testament, such as the plural 'Let us make man . . .' in Genesis 1, presupposed address by the Father to the pre-existent divine Son. Trypho contended that such language was all right for Gentiles but not for strict Jewish monotheists (*Dial.* 64. 1). Trypho was also baffled by the proposition that Christ was born of a virgin. Justin concedes that messiahship is more fundamental than pre-existence or virgin birth (48. 2), and knows of Christian Jews who acknowledge Jesus to be Messiah without affirming his virgin birth (48: 4), a position which Trypho himself allows to be tenable (49: 1).

The canon

Disputations between Church and Synagogue prompted discussion concerning the identity of the books accepted as authoritative. Within the Church there long continued differences of usage about the precise content of the Old Testament. There was agreement that the scriptures included Judith, Tobit, Sirach (Ecclesiasticus), and Wisdom of Solomon, disagreement about the books of Maccabees, Baruch, the epistle of Jeremiah. As late as Justin in the mid-second century 'the scriptures' are the Old Testament. He knows Christian writings but has no fixed canon, no New Testament that might be copied in a single codex. Irenaeus a generation later is much more conscious of the need to establish which Christian books have authority, and his 'canon' (or rule) is close to that familiar to modern readers. There long remained local and regional differences.

The assumption that in the Old Testament the Hebrew retained primacy obscured a point, namely that the Septuagint was based on good Hebrew manuscripts of the third century BC, and could attest a form of text superior to that available in a manuscript roll at a nearby synagogue. A similar misunderstanding led critics in the sixteenth century to put a higher value on late Byzantine manuscripts than on Jerome's Latin version made in the fourth century and gradually becoming in the West the generally accepted version or *Vulgata*. Jerome insisted on the primacy of the Hebrew over the Greek translations. He was not concerned about the inspiration of either text, but rather on the historical witness to the apostolic tradition and its acceptance by the Church. On the books not in the synagogue canon, his formula made history: these books should continue to be read in the lectionary for guidance on ethical matters but could not safely be cited in a dispute to establish doctrine. The formula said less than might appear since there were virtually no points of dogma on which appeal would be made to these books. Jerome classified the overplus of the Septuagint over the Hebrew under the disparaging and misleading title 'Apocrypha'.

5

INTERPRETING SCRIPTURE:
PHILO AND PAUL

Letter and spirit, allegory in Philo

More complex and controversial than the canon was the question of the right principle for interpretation of scripture. Very early the Christians claimed that the redemptive work of God in Jesus the Christ was the key for a correct understanding of the law and the prophets. In controversy they could say that if leading observant Jewish authorities were rejecting their exegesis, that was of a piece with the non-recognition of Messiah and his divine authority. The stone which the builders rejected had become the chief cornerstone of God's building, and that was his Church.

It was no new step to affirm that an ancient sacred text did not necessarily mean just what its literal or external meaning seemed to say. The rabbis themselves liked meticulous literal exegesis but in the case of the Song of Songs felt bound to grant that it ought to be interpreted allegorically of God's love for Israel. At Alexandria the observant Jew Philo, insistent that understanding the symbolic meaning of the text in no way dispensed one from a literal observance of the letter, freely employed allegory on a vast scale to discover Platonic philosophy and Stoic ethics, sometimes even radical Scepticism, hidden in the less evident texts of the Pentateuch.

In classical Greece there had long been a tradition of discovering in Homer (especially in passages where the gods did not behave well) profound truths of natural philosophy and science. It had the merit of making the poet edifying for the young. Methods that Stoics applied to Homer, Philo could apply to Moses. In a code which Philo could decipher, Genesis contained a cosmogony exactly like that of Plato's dialogue the *Timaeus*.

The goal and purpose of Philo's allegorizing of the Mosaic Law derived impetus from his desire to reduce to nearly zero the particularism of Jewish tradition. By allegory the Law could be shown to be universal, indeed cosmic in its scope. The claim is explicit in his *Life of Moses* (2. 19). To obey it was for him the mark of being a citizen of the cosmos (*De opificio mundi* 1). Therefore there could be no conflict between Moses and the best moral philosophers of classical Greece. Philo was confident that Plato derived his best ideas from the study of a copy of the Pentateuch itself. These were not new themes with Philo. Jewish allegorists before him disturbed him by their opinion that for anyone who had penetrated to the symbolic sense of Moses' precepts, the precepts themselves were no longer obligatory. Philo preferred to say that, although the Levitical commands concerned the body and the world of sense, nevertheless the body serves the soul and through obedience to the physical precepts of the Law one discerns more clearly the higher truths of which they are symbols (*De migratione Abrahae* 89–93). Body and soul correspond to the literal and spiritual senses of scripture.

Philo, being a monotheist, was conscious of the polytheistic society around him at Alexandria. He answered pagan criticism that Judaism had customs which walled it off from the rest of society by the affirmation that the Jewish people were priests for the rest of the world. While pagan priests served essentially local cults and represented no more than their own people, the Jewish high priest offered for all the human race and for the natural order as well, not merely for the peace of Israel (*De spec. leg.* 1. 17). Philo interpreted monotheism to presuppose a transcendent Creator whose will is pure goodness and whose creating is an ungrudging overflow of benevolent giving, in which the divine giver remains undiminished like a spring of water or sun emitting light or a torch lighting other torches. Between this supreme first cause and this lower material world there are intermediate powers, entities whose diversity is held together by the immanent power of the divine reason or Logos. The Logos is 'the idea of ideas', first-begotten Son of the Father and even 'second God', mediator between the supreme Father and the created order. He is life, light, shepherd, manna, way, high priest, and advocate (*parákletos*). The supreme Father being too transcendent to have direct contact with this lower world, the Logos appeared in the theophanies e.g. at the burning bush to Moses. By the indwelling of the inspiring Logos, Moses was virtually elevated to a divine status.

It is sometimes thought that no monotheistic Jew could imaginably have attributed to a human being divine qualities. Philo's *Life of Moses* has to qualify any such judgement. There Moses is prophet, priest, and king. The text of Exod. 7. 1 'I make you as a God to Pharaoh' is interpreted to mean that Moses is God's viceroy mediating between God and man. The language is comparable to that which Philo uses of the Logos as a bridge between the uncreated and created order. The mapping of a frontier between divine and human in Philo is often a foggy area. His debt to Platonism inclined him to treat Mind as that by virtue of which the Logos is inherently divine (cf. *De opificio Mundi* 69).

To the contemplative soul (Philo held) God may also appear to be triad, his goodness and his power existing beside his essential being. At the heart of religion is faith, of which Abraham is the biblical symbol. The soul toils in the ascent towards divine perfection, but suddenly realizes that it has to cease from all striving and acknowledge that every virtue is achieved exclusively by God's gift. Abraham is here the model, for at the summit of human knowing, he utterly despaired of himself, and thereby opened his soul to an exact knowledge of the God who is. Without grace none can know God. 'The mind draws near to the one by whom it has been drawn.' 'The vision of God is both a seeing and a being seen.'

Philo's mystical language about the individual soul's ascent to God does not exclude the sharing of God's gifts with others; for that is the 'becoming like God' of which Plato wrote in his *Theaetetus*.

True circumcision is that of the heart (*De spec. leg.* 1. 305). Yet the Temple at Jerusalem will surely endure as long as the cosmos itself.

If several phrases in Philo's allegories anticipate language in the letters of Paul, who like Philo had roots in the Greek synagogue, there are also ideas in Philo that are more dualistic and anticipate gnostic notions. Adam and Eve first acquired bodies after their fall and their bodies are referred to as their 'coats of skins.' The soul dwells in the body as if in a tomb and carries it about as a corpse. The soul has fallen into matter, and God is redeeming it from this disaster. Unlike the gnostic sects Philo was not haunted by the problem of evil, and offered virtually no mythology about fallen angelic powers. He anticipated Origen in suggesting that souls fell as a result of satiety with the wonders of the celestial world, and suffered decline in varying degrees, some not falling so far as to be imprisoned in bodies. A few passages explain the evil in the world by the speculation that some parts of the work of creation were delegated to angels who were incompetent. The idea is reminiscent of Paul in the epistle to the Galatians (3. 19–20) where the inferior status of the Torah is deduced from the role which, by Jewish tradition, angels had played in giving it to Moses. But Philo did not like the idea that the seven planets were prisons for fallen powers. Seven was a holy number for a Jew, with the sabbath and the seven-branched candlestick or Menorah.

New Testament allegory

Philo may have influenced the author of the epistle to the Hebrews, where the sacrificial worship of the Old Testament is allegorically interpreted of the one perfect sacrifice of Jesus. His influence on the Johannine circle was no doubt more indirect. Although the apostle Paul shared some themes with Philo, the differences are more striking than the similarities. Nevertheless, the presupposition that behind the literal sense of scripture there lay a spiritual meaning allowed the apostle to see the Christian meaning as the divinely intended sense. To fail to allow it seemed to Paul the consequence of prejudice or indeed a spiritual blindness (2 Cor. 3: 15; compare Luke 24: 25).

Passages in the Hebrew prophets arraigning the people of Israel for failing to discern God's will gave controversialists the opening to assert that such failures were a lasting characteristic of a stiffnecked race. Particularly unconciliatory language is found in a speech by the deacon Stephen reported in Acts 7. Here the Jews who have failed to recognize Jesus to be Messiah are but one further instance in a long catalogue of national apostasy. Stephen voiced a negative opinion about the Temple also expressed by some Jews of the Dispersion. The opposition to him significantly came from Greek-speaking Jews of Cyrene, Alexandria, Cilicia, and Ephesus, for whom the orthodoxy of synagogues of the Dispersion was evidently fundamental. Stephen's speech forms part of a book ending with an emphatic thesis that the main body of Jews are not merely failing now to recognize the Messiah, but are never going to do so in the future (Acts 28: 23–8).

Paul's programme

That was not the unanimous judgement of the first Christian generation. The apostle Paul wrote to the Roman Christians (a community which he had not founded) that the Gentile mission was a divine parenthesis in the long providential order of history, intended to rouse the Jews to recover their sense of having a universal destiny for serving all humanity in that far-off event to which the creation moves, when 'all Israel will be saved'. Later in the immediate post-Pauline generation the Epistle to the Ephesians enunciated a programmatic vision of a universal Church in which Jewish and Gentile believers, even if with differing disciplines of practice, would be enabled to worship the one God in one unbroken fellowship.

Nevertheless, the principal figure to provide a theoretical or theological justification for the separating of the Church from its Jewish matrix was the apostle of the Gentiles, Paul. And the surviving evidence shows that he was in broad terms, if not in detail, supported by Peter. The misgivings were associated with James the Lord's brother, for whom the break with the worship of Temple and synagogue was a serious mistake. In that judgement he was certainly not in a minority of one. For centuries to come there were to be Christians, often of Gentile descent, who participated in the feasts and life of the local synagogues. The Martyrdom of Pionius 13 shows that at Smyrna in the mid-third century Christian refugees were offered hospitality by orthodox Jews, admittedly to the displeasure of the more zealous Church members. John Chrysostom at Antioch late in the fourth century was appalled to discover that a proportion of his congregation had been worshipping at the synagogue on the previous day.

All things to all men

Paul had no desire to cause offence to observant Jews (above p. 9). He was willing to compromise by consenting to the circumcision of his Gentile helper Titus (Gal. 2: 3), as he also did in the case of Timothy (Acts 16: 3). Luke reports that on James's suggestion Paul purified himself and met the expenses of four Jewish Christians in the Temple, with the motive of reassuring his many Jewish critics that he did not propose the abolition of the Mosaic Law (Acts 21: 20–7). A riot was provoked, but Paul at least showed that, with observant Jews, he wished to conform. To the Corinthians he explained that his principle was to be as a Jew to the Jews that he might win them over; to those under the Law as if under the Law, though not actually under the Law; and to those not under the Law, that is the Gentiles, as one not under law (1 Cor. 9: 19–22). The statement could have been used by enemies to prove his lack of integrity, and that this charge was being brought against him from both sides is clear from the epistles. Gal. 5: 11 shows that someone was accusing him of inconsistency in 'still preaching circumcision' (a deduction perhaps from the cases of Timothy and Titus, but possibly this complaint came from radically anti-Jewish or rather anti-Judaistic controversialists, who thought Paul was failing to teach the total discontinuity of the gospel with the Old Testament). Some of the vehemence of the epistle to the Galatians can be understood in the light of the charge that he changed his message in accordance with the prejudices of his hearers, and was merely concerned to please them rather than to be true to Christ (Gal. 1: 10). At Corinth Paul was confronted by critics who maliciously complained of his changes of mind, even about so minor a matter as his travel plans, and who unkindly grumbled that a characteristic of the apostle was to say Yes when he meant No and vice versa (2 Cor. 1: 13–24).

Paul's difficulty lay in the tension between the Jewish Christians of Jerusalem, not unsuccessful in presenting the case for Jesus' messiahship to their fellow-Jews, and the advocates of admitting Gentiles to Church membership without obligations to keep the Torah, an advocacy which inevitably undermined the work in Jerusalem. It was not easy to run with both sides, as he felt it his duty before God to try to do.

If it was going to be necessary to emancipate the Church from the Synagogue, at least Paul was determined to maintain a close link between his dispersed Gentile churches and the mother community at Jerusalem under the presidency of James, the size of which, according to Acts 21: 20, numbered 'many thousands'.

Synagogues of the Dispersion used to collect money to send each year to Jerusalem for the support of the Temple and its priests and for their distributions to the poor of the city (cf. Tobit 1: 6–7). It was not an obligation but a charitable act. The Mishnah (*Hallah*) records conflicting opinions on the subject of the acceptance of gifts from the Dispersion especially cases where they were not accepted, but provides clear evidence that they were frequent.

In Caesar's time the proconsul of Asia had to command the city of Miletus to allow the Jews to follow their customs in tithing their produce (Josephus, *AJ* 14. 10. 21. 244–6). Philo of Alexandria was censorious of Jews who failed in this regard (*De spec. leg.* 1. 153–5).[1] After the fall of Jerusalem in 70, all Jews, not only those still in Judaea, had to pay the equivalent of their Temple tax to the Roman fisc.

On the analogy of these contributions Paul agreed with the leaders of the Church at Jerusalem that he would arrange for contributions to be raised among the Gentile churches, for transmission to the Jerusalem Church for the maintenance of 'the poor' (Gal. 2. 10). The Christian community in Jerusalem was in a competitive situation in relation to observant Jews who did not acknowledge the messiahship of Jesus. Contributions from synagogues in the Dispersion would be under the control of the Temple priests, unlikely to be generous with their alms for those who had affiliated with James and the Church. Generous gifts from Gentile Christians would enable the Jerusalem leaders to keep the support of the proportion of the city poor who looked to them for help. Paul's collection for the saints was a serious matter, not an optional extra. The survival of the Church in Jerusalem was bound up with the success of the operation. Even when relations with the church at Corinth had become strained (apparent in the syntax of 2 Corinthians 8–9), he had to persist in calling for financial aid. Moreover, he did not feel confident that the church of Jerusalem would accept the money at his hands (Rom. 15: 31), a fact which betrays the degree of distrust expected.

The mission to the Gentile world met with rapid success and precipitated urgent questions. The apostle Paul never concerned himself with issues prominent in the gospels about tithe, ceremonial impurity, fringes, and phylacteries. He had to form the mind and ethic of Gentile communities for which specifically Jewish customs were remote. In any event his problem lay deeper than questions about the right interpretation of the Levitical laws. Convinced that the coming of Messiah inaugurated a new age which made the Law of Moses a stage in the education of the human race but not God's final word for all races, by what authority, he needed to say, were his converts going to order their lives? To conservative Jewish Christians he sounded dangerously like an antinomian anarchist and in one passage where he denied this to be a true account of his work, he spoke of Christ as now the source of law

[1] On gifts from dispersion synagogues to Jerusalem see Aharon Oppenheimer, *The 'Am Ha-Aretz* (Leiden, 1977), 49–51.

for himself and believers (1 Cor. 9: 21). 'The law of the Spirit of life liberated from the law of sin and death' (Rom. 8: 2). The oral tradition of Jesus' sayings had provided him with some principles, but those which Paul quotes are few—concerned with remarriage after divorce and the right of missionaries to be financially supported by their converts. His Gentile churches will have had far less access to oral traditions about Jesus than he.

At Corinth some converts took the gospel preached by Paul to teach a freedom which granted complete liberation from social conventions in regard to sex. They were asserting that in this new age of the Spirit anything goes—'all things are lawful.' In reply the apostle gladly conceded that in the new society of the Church the coming of Christ had ended the dispensation of the Law; but sexual licence was inexpedient and injured the reputation of Christians in pagan society (which at Corinth was notorious for being a hotbed of licentiousness). Despite the apostle's opposition, there long continued to be underground groups in the Church which made bold to claim the authority of Jesus himself for antinomian attitudes to sexual convention.

Paul's problem lay in the fact that while his recommended practice was no departure from the norms of good Jewish morality, his theory put an axe to the notion that the will of God for his people in the messianic age could be formulated in a legal code at all.

His Gentile converts in Galatia or at Thessalonica, Philippi, and Corinth, were not circumcised and were warned not to listen to 'Judaizers' telling them that even now they were obliged (or at least would be wise) to keep Moses' rules. At Jerusalem alarmed Jewish Christians, who looked to James the Lord's brother to be their spokesman, were asking the crucial question whether there were any rules by which Gentile converts thought themselves bound.

The conference or council at Jerusalem described in Acts 15 formulated a modest statement of guidelines, the so-called Apostolic Decree—a document with echoes elsewhere in the New Testament (Rev. 2: 20, and 24). The Decree declared that Gentile Christians should not eat meat previously offered in pagan sacrifice and then sold in the market, nor meat where the animal had been slaughtered by strangulation so as to retain the blood. Men must also have no extramarital intercourse, e.g. with their slave-girls.

In Paul's letters, especially in 1 Corinthians, the actuality and relevance of these prohibitions on fornication and on the eating of meat sacrificed to idols are writ large. The ethic of the gospel depended not on rules externally imposed but on a judgement of the informed conscience. But its hallmark was a dissent from the heathen life of ordinary Gentile society. Christians were called to live as citizens of heaven (Phil. 3: 20).

The Pauline ethical theory was intimately bound up with his understanding of 'justification by faith', a doctrine with immediate relevance to the practical question whether the Church was now to be emancipated from that Law which the apostle himself confessed to be holy, just, and good.

The apostle could contrast, to the disadvantage of the Law of Moses, the writtenness of the law with the inward life of the Spirit (Rom. 7: 6). In the third century Origen knew of Christians who took this principle to necessitate the view that what mattered was charismatic experience, not written scriptures or dominical sacraments, which both belonged to the external and material world.

The Gentile mission

The apostle Paul moved to the radical position first stated in an impassioned letter to his churches in Galatia in Asia Minor, and then more moderately affirmed in his careful letter to Rome. Both Jew and Gentile alike have fallen short. All are equally sinners and guilty before God. Whether they have the full Torah or no more than the natural guidance of conscience and natural law, they stand under the same condemnation. Indeed the Jew, having been granted greater light, has greater responsibility. But by faith in Jesus the Christ and his reconciling, atoning death, both Gentile and Jewish believers are to be granted equal access to God's forgiveness and inner renewal. Therefore to assert that after this manifestation of the mercy and universal love of God it is still necessary for faith to be supplemented by the Law and especially by circumcision (as expressive of Jewish particularism over against the Gentile society) is to derogate from the sovereignty of God's act in redemption. The one God affirmed by Hebrew monotheism is not God of the Jews only. Monotheism is incompatible with tribal particularism except insofar as that is a stage towards something universal. So those who are true descendants of Abraham are they who share his faith, not necessarily his circumcision or his ethnicity. Religion, not race, is that which defines a person before God.

The Pauline programme for the Gentile mission implied an ultimate if not immediate breach between Church and Synagogue. At the same time the mission was constructed round the Gentile cities of the empire. With a speed which can only seem astounding, the early Church moved outside its original birthplace in Jerusalem and Galilee, and the apostle of the Gentiles, as he knew himself to be, was able to forge a universal society with representation in the imperial cities. No doubt there were also a few congregations in rural districts but in ancient society it was usual for peasants to follow in religion the landowner for whom they laboured. A group of rural labourers would become Christian if their landlord was converted.

The hostility in the synagogue towards the Church, which produced a riot in Rome in the reign of Claudius about AD 50 recorded by Suetonius, was not allayed by the Gentile mission (1 Thess. 2: 14–16). Anger from the Church's side is apparent in John's Gospel where the Jews' incomprehension of Jesus is attributed to Satan: 'You cannot bear to hear my word, you are of your father the devil' (8: 43–4). The charge becomes mutual (8: 48–52). Church–Synagogue relations at Ephesus were bad.

Nevertheless Paul understood himself called to be apostle to the Gentile world, of which the capital city was Rome. If Jerusalem was a focus for the tradition of Jewish Christians, might not Rome be the focus for Gentile believers? The apostle's letter to the Roman Christians presupposes that the Church there had its roots in the conversion of a liberal synagogue, which nevertheless needed reassurance that the Pauline gospel did not mean a break with the Old Testament prophets. Gentile Christianity is presented as a parenthetic protestant movement to recall a universal catholic Judaism to its true vocation in recognizing Jesus the Messiah. Finally 'all Israel will be saved'. Not for nothing were they entrusted with the oracles of God.

While, since the apostolic council (Acts 15), Jewish Christians had in principle granted generous recognition to Gentile believers, Gentile Christians increasingly failed to return the compliment. Justin Martyr regretted this awkward fact. Once the Gentile believers regarded themselves as more authentic than their Jewish brothers and sisters, it would be no great step to regarding the capital of the Gentile world as the hub of the entire Christian world, not merely of the western half. This tendency would be taken further once the Christians of Rome and their bishops became Latin-speaking during the third century, having been Greek-speaking previously. So to Pope Leo I in the mid-fifth century Peter and Paul were the founders of a Christian city, replacing those unsatisfactory characters Romulus and Remus.

Paul and Rome

In the letter to the Roman church (15. 22) Paul announces his further travel plan, asking the church to speed him on his way to further missionary work in Spain if he is able to reach Rome as he hopes. His aspiration is therefore to take the gospel from the eastern end of the Mediterranean to the furthest West. There is also a reassurance to the Roman community that his stay with them will therefore only be brief. The latent implication is that they may feel a touch of alarm at the arrival of so controversial a figure, but he will minimize embarrassment.

The surviving letters of Paul reveal nothing of the way in which he eventually reached Rome. But the last chapters of Acts show that he was taken to Rome under arrest effected at Jerusalem and that before the governor at Caesarea he appealed to the emperor, in consequence of which the governor had no option but to send him under guard, an action which happily eliminated a difficulty for the governor. The journey turned out to be hazardous. A succession of divinely inspired situations made it possible for Paul to circumvent all obstacles finally to arrive at the capital, conducted there by Christians from Puteoli (Pozzuoli by Naples), and that in the great city he was allowed to preach the gospel initially without restriction. In Acts 27 a major Mediterranean storm and shipwreck on the shores of Malta are vividly described, underlining the author's judgement that nothing could have been less probable than the apostle's arrival in Rome. When land had nearly been reached, only the centurion's authority stopped the soldiers from killing their prisoners. When amazingly they all got safely to land, there was a snake to bite Paul. He survived. For the author of Acts the preaching of the apostle of the Gentiles in the capital of the Gentile world was a providential fact.

Christ in creation

The calling to be apostle to the Gentiles led Paul to recast the primitive apocalyptic hope of many early Christians, which he himself initially shared (as 1 Thessalonians shows). He reinterpreted the Christ who is the coming end and ultimate judge of the world to be the wisdom of God in the creation. He was thereby preparing the way for the incorporation of the Logos theology of the Hellenistic synagogue, exemplified in the writings of Philo. The doctrine of the last things was modified so that in 1 Corinthians 12 Christ and the Church are identified: the Church is his body, and therefore the last times are already being realized in the life of the community of the Spirit. This realized eschatology extends a line already present in the gospels, where Jesus is the strong man who has bound Satan.

Debate about Paul

The reception of Paul by the Church in the century after his time was cautious and hesitant. Jewish Christian communities could think with pride of his missionary achievements, but felt qualms about his more radical positions. Marcion in the 140s was to take some of Paul's arguments to an extreme conclusion and declared the Old Testament to be the unrelenting law of justice, contrasted with the loving Father first declared to the world in Jesus Christ. The orthodox 'centre' rejected Marcion and refused to jettison the Hebrew Bible used in the Septuagint version. After all, Paul had helped them to see how it should be given an exclusively Christian meaning: the Church had now expropriated it. Moreover, the affirmation that the Creator and Father to whom Jesus taught believers to pray is one God became critical in the conflict with gnostic dualism.

But Paul's low estimate of the very principle of law as an ethical code was to require modification if it was not to be dangerous. The early Gentile churches were beset by too much antinomianism to be comfortable with a subjectivism which left moral judgement entirely to the individual conscience. The suggestion that one could safely eat meat offered to idols as long as no one's conscience was offended thereby (1 Corinthians 8) seemed to churches of the second and third century very startling.

A distinction was therefore made, that Jesus Christ had abrogated the universal validity of the ceremonial law; what remained fully valid for all believers, Jewish or Gentile, was the Decalogue, with the single exception of the sabbath, which was classified with those particularist Jewish observances not now binding on Gentile believers. Paul himself had done something to prepare the ground for this distinction by pointing out, with evident force, that the Ten Commandments were simply expressions of love to God and one's neighbour. Moreover, as if in a kind of anticipatory reply to the direct criticism of his doctrine of justification by faith in the epistle 'to the twelve tribes of the Dispersion' composed in the name of James, Paul himself declared to the Corinthians that without love faith is valueless before God.

The Pauline letters, gathered into a corpus by an unknown disciple and admirer, remained a source of trouble. Gnostics could find many sentences in them to support their dualism and predestinarianism. One Christian writer early in the second century, invoking the mantle of St Peter for his pronouncements and warnings and certainly familiar with St Matthew's gospel, admonished his readers to beware of those who were twisting Paul's writings in the interest of dangerous causes. He had to concede that the letters contained many things hard to understand, but he was firm for Paul's authority (2 Pet. 3: 16). In the third century Origen would take Paul's ironic sentence in 2 Cor. 11: 6 'although I may be uneducated in words, yet I am not so in knowledge', and see in this an explanation of infelicitous language exploited by heretics. There was a problem when the texts to which deviationists particularly appealed were those held up as normative for the community.

The letters of Ignatius of Antioch early in the second century do not cite texts to settle disputes, though he evidently knew some of the apostolic epistles and may have taken them as a model for his own.

6

APOSTLES AND EVANGELISTS

The gospels

Only a minority in ancient society were capable of reading. The Church had to appoint Readers, to whom the congregation listened. Books other than the Hebrew Bible or its Septuagint version played a negligible part in the initial propagation of the faith that Jesus is the Christ. Probably after the fall of Jerusalem, which was a profound shock to the Church as well as appalling for the Synagogue, perhaps at about the time when letters of Paul were being collected to provide a point of reference, hitherto oral traditions transmitting the teaching and actions of Jesus were being put in writing and gathered. 'Gospel' meant first the message. In consequence of Mark's bold originality the word was to become the theme-title of a new genre of book, with a narrative charged with impassioned feeling reaching a climax in a long account of the Passion and ending in an extraordinary and numinous story of the empty tomb without any account of the appearances of the risen Lord. Luke's preface explains that he has drawn on first-hand witnesses, and imposed on the material an order not found in several predecessors who have composed narratives about Jesus. Luke's 'order' is no doubt more theological than merely chronological. His infancy narrative is there to show above all how, from birth, Jesus fulfilled God's ancient promises to his people. For Matthew Jesus was a new Moses who gives a new Torah for his community of disciples. And that community is the embodiment of 'the kingdom of God', a society already distinct from the Synagogue and entitled 'the Church'.

As memory began to become hazy, even though oral proclamation of the gospel would long remain preferable to books, these evangelists provided a kind of permanence in times that were mountingly precarious. They thought of themselves as more than mere reporters. Not only were they providing a support to the remembered tradition, but they were interpreting that for the needs of their own generation.

In St John's gospel the needs of the time had made the theological interpretation of the significance of Jesus so overwhelmingly primary that the historical narrative was there for its symbolic value. This method did not prevent this gospel drawing on the stock of authentic narrative material in the oral tradition, then to be moulded to a higher purpose.

Already when the fourth gospel was composed, gnostic ideas were current to the effect that a divine incarnation must be incompatible with a fully real and spontaneously human Jesus. The fourth gospel is startlingly emphatic about the human frailties of the Lord. The gospels of Mark, Matthew, and Luke were also Christological statements, never mere chronicles, and by implication their record of what the man of Nazareth said and did answered those anxious to deny both that Jesus was the Messiah of Old Testament expectation, and that he could have come 'in the flesh' (see 1 John 2. 22, 5. 1, and 4. 2).

St John's gospel ended with the observation (21. 25) that what could be recorded in books was no more than a small part of the record about Jesus. In the oral tradition there long continued to be many sayings of Jesus (technically called *agrapha*) which were not included in the gospels which the Church accepted for reading in the lectionary for worship. The dry sands of Egypt have preserved a 'Gospel of Thomas' in a Coptic version; a number of the sayings of Jesus in this Gospel occur in Greek in quotations made by ancient Christian writers, some of them in gnostic texts. The 'Gospel of Thomas' is remarkable for having no narrative framework, only a sayings-collection. The form and wording of some sayings in this collection have led to the suggestion that its tradition may well include versions of what Jesus said quite as likely to be authentic as material in the canonical gospels. In the nature of things, however, this cannot be other than speculation. Several of the sayings have passed through a gnostic milieu. Not all are of gnostic origin.

Luke–Acts

The author of the third gospel continued the story of the Church after the appearances of the risen Lord had ceased. He narrated the spreading of the gospel from Jerusalem first to Samaria, then on to Athens the citadel of Greek philosophy, and finally to Rome, capital of the Roman Empire. He saw symbolic significance in these four centres. The story divided into two main sections. In the first the Jerusalem community dominates, under the joint leadership of Peter and James the Lord's brother; it looks as if there was a harmonious agreement reached between the apostles commissioned by Jesus and the holy family, but while James remained in Jerusalem, Peter the apostle moved about from place to place. In the second half of the book the main figure is Paul the missionary who, in face of the most serious opposition, was enabled to carry the gospel to Rome itself and to preach there 'without anyone hindering him'.

The portrait of the Jerusalem community in the early chapters of the Acts is in some respects idealized, but in detail it can often be supported from information in the letters of Paul. For instance, Paul recalls that when he went to Jerusalem soon after his conversion, the Church there was led by Peter and by James the Lord's brother (Gal. 1: 16–19). Paul supports Acts in the portrayal of the Jerusalem community as the authoritative leader. Later that was where he had to go to submit to the principal apostles the terms of the gospel he was preaching among the Gentiles; and had the 'pillar' apostles not given him the right hand of fellowship, then his labours would have been in vain.

The portrait of James the Lord's brother in Acts is that of a Torah-observing Jew convinced that Jesus is Messiah and broadly sympathizing with those believing Pharisees who thought Gentile converts obliged to keep the Mosaic law, including circumcision. That portrait is in line with the epistle to the Galatians (2: 11–12). The second-century Christian writer Hegesippus relates that James was held in high respect by Jews in Jerusalem for his holiness and austerity of life, marked by daily intercessions for Israel at prayers in the Temple, but so influential in his advocacy of the recognition of Jesus as Messiah that a riot was provoked in which he was stoned to death. His authoritative position in the Church is confirmed by Paul's catalogue of the Lord's resurrection appearances (1 Cor. 15: 6) where an appearance to James is integral to the tradition.

In the second half of Acts the story has moved out of Judaea into the wider world of the eastern half of the Roman Empire. Again in detail, Acts turns out to be astonishingly accurate, e.g. taking trouble to give the correct titles to city officials, and perhaps the historian of the Roman Empire has no other source which gives so vivid a picture of life in the provinces at this period.

The value of Acts is therefore not to be disparaged. The author had a thesis to present. He saw the hand of providence in the extension of the Church from its cradle in Jerusalem to the great world of Rome.

A surprising point in the account of Paul is that the text of Acts betrays no knowledge of any letters written by the apostle. That suggests that the author did not write later than the eighties of the first century. He could have been writing in the late sixties. The Pauline Corpus had not come his way. Anti-Pauline feelings current in the Church at Jerusalem were no doubt an oblique target in the work. Among Jewish Christian communities such feelings continue to be attested well into the second century.

The second chapter of the Acts recounts the founding of the Church on the day of Pentecost with the astonished realization that this outpouring of the Holy Spirit on the apostles is destined to reach all peoples. A long catalogue is given of different provinces of the empire (possibly based on some astrological list), all of whose representatives hear in their own tongues the wonderful works of God (Acts 2: 8–11). Apparently Luke transmuted the eschatological expectation of the return of the glorified risen Lord into a hope of the extension of God's kingdom to the entire inhabited world. 'Jesus preached the kingdom of God, and what arrived was the Church'

(Loisy's famous dictum succinctly expressed Luke's intention). For the achievement of this high purpose the apostolic capture of the empire's capital in Italy would be seen as a crucial preparation.

By a series of events in which human volition played no part the apostle to the Gentile world ended in the Gentile capital. Jewish Christians looked to Jerusalem and to the holy family of which 'James the Lord's brother' was the leading figure. Paul's Gentile converts could look to their metropolis in Italy.

Missionaries other than Paul

Acts 28 records that Paul was welcomed at the port of Puteoli by Christian believers, so that evidently missionaries had already come to Italy. The community at Rome was not one founded by Paul himself, and his letters (in particular 2 Cor. 10: 14–16 and Rom. 15: 18–20) betray much sensitivity about the candidly admitted fact that, while God had called him to be apostle of the Gentiles, several Gentile churches had been founded by the labours of other unnamed missionaries. He hoped to pass on to Spain and to preach there. A generation later the Roman community understood that intention to have been fulfilled. But it was also known that he had returned to Rome, and there during the persecution of Nero (AD 64) was executed; his grave was on the road to Ostia.

From 1 Cor. 1: 12–13 it is certain that already in the fifties of the first century the Gentile mission was beset by factions. At Corinth some looked to Peter for authority, others to Paul, and a third party to the obscure figure of Apollos—described in Acts (18: 24) as being a learned Alexandrian Jew 'mighty in the scriptures' who taught accurately about Jesus; yet he had been baptized only with the baptism of John the Baptist. This last surprising phrase strongly suggests that there continued in being a society of the Baptist's disciples which, like the Gentile mission of the followers of Jesus, had now extended its activities into the world of the Jewish Dispersion and was not yet persuaded that Jesus was the Messiah of prophecy. Apollos was soon convinced of the messiahship of Jesus and evidently played an important part as a Christian teacher in Corinth.

To look to a founding apostle for the source of authoritative decisions was not easy or quick when apostles were not static or resident. Paul exercised authority more effectively by letter than by personal visits, since his physical presence was less formidable than his pen (2 Cor. 10: 10) . His conviction that his calling to be an apostle put him on the same level of authority as the Twelve (whose special position he unhesitatingly acknowledged: 1 Cor. 15: 5) was far from being universally conceded. Peter had the first place in the list of those to whom the risen Lord appeared (1 Cor. 15: 5), and in the oral tradition there circulated the story of Peter's confession at Caesarea Philippi with the first recognition of the Messiah, and of his leading role among the inner circle of disciples. Paul's emphatic insistence in his first letter to Corinth, that Jesus Christ alone is the one foundation of the Church, on which others, such as Peter, Apollos, and Paul himself, built only superstructures (1 Cor. 3: 11), naturally suggests that he was opposing alternative opinions about foundation figures, but allowing diversity otherwise.

Paul's long letter to the Roman community reflects the care with which he felt he had to write to win their confidence. The Church there was certainly familiar with the scriptures of the Old Testament (Rom. 7: 1). It is evident that they wished to hear from Paul a positive statement that God's purpose included the salvation of the Jews and that the Old Testament indeed contained 'the oracles of God'. At Rome there could well be a group of Christian Jews for whom Peter ranked higher than Paul in their estimation of apostolic authority. Be that as it may, the community at Rome retained the memory of Peter coming to Rome and suffering martyrdom there, and that Paul too had similarly suffered, perhaps in the gruesome persecution of the Roman Christians under the emperor Nero. The martyrdom of Peter was known to the editors of St John's gospel (21: 18).

In the year 165 the Roman community erected memorials to Peter and Paul, to Peter in a necropolis on the Vatican hill evidently where (perhaps rightly) he was believed to be buried, to Paul at the site of his grave on the road to Ostia. There about 200 a Roman author named Gaius could rejoice in their monuments of triumph.

The church in Jerusalem

Successive Jewish revolts against Roman power in 66–70, 112–15, and 132–5 profoundly affected the 'Nazarenes' of Jerusalem. But after Roman authority had excluded Jews from entering Hadrian's city of Aelia Capitolina, the Gentile Christian congregation retained a potent awareness of inheriting the most sacred traditions where the gospel had been acted out. In the third century they were claiming to possess the very throne on which St James had sat to preach. Their little meeting place was located in an undamaged part of the old city on the site, they believed, of the upper room where the Spirit had been poured out on the apostles at Pentecost.

The traditions of the Jerusalem Christians were regarded elsewhere as authoritative. About 160–70 Bishop Melito of Sardis, who presided over a small community juxtaposed with a large and opulent synagogue, found himself in some degree of controversy with the rabbis,[1] and visited the

---

[1] Melito's church, with other communities in Asia Minor, observed the paschal celebration of Christ's Passion on the date of the Jewish passover on the fourteenth day of the first month after the spring equinox, not necessarily on the Lord's day, Sunday. That this did not presuppose specially

church at Jerusalem to discover the limits of the Old Testament canon. During the baptismal controversy of the year 256 between Carthage and Rome, Firmilian bishop of Cappadocian Caesarea criticized the Romans' assumption that their traditional liturgical practices were of apostolic origin by remarking that the customs of Jerusalem were different. Origen had particular interest in identifying the sacred site of the gospels, already visited by pilgrims, such as the cave of the Nativity at Bethlehem. It was taken for granted that here was 'the mother of all churches'.

Shrines of the apostles

There was not always unanimity about the precise site of apostolic tombs. At Ephesus the Church treasured the memory of St John, the son of Zebedee, who died there in advanced old age. In the third century there were two alternative tombs in the city, perhaps at one time belonging to rival house-churches each claiming to have the authentic grave with the bones of the apostle. At Rome also not everyone seems to have been convinced that the official locations for the two apostolic 'founder-apostles' were correct, and a community with a rival site for both apostles buried together had celebrations on the south side of the city at the third milestone on the Appian Way. There funerary meals were consumed to honour the apostles, and devout pilgrims inscribed graffiti with their invocations, e.g. 'Paul and Peter, pray for Victor.' This shrine flourished in the middle of the third century, and may have started life in consequence of a vision giving guidance about the site to be venerated. Pilgrims who met on the Appian Way celebrated both Peter and Paul on 29 June. In the fourth century the bishops of Rome were able to reconcile the divergent traditions with a procession on 29 June which began at Constantine's church of St Peter on the Vatican hill, went on to the church of St Paul erected on the road to Ostia, and finally (at the end of what was an exhausting day) to the shrine for both apostles on the Appian Way. Harmonizing legend related that the Appian Way was the original burial place, and that in time of persecution the relics had been transferred to the separate sites which now had them (below, p. 323).

In time the visit to the Appian Way was dropped, and the site became associated with the martyr St Sebastian. In the fifth century the visit to St Paul's was deferred to 30 June, and frequented more by pilgrim visitors to Rome than by citizens of the city. The twenty-ninth of June was a date associated with the legend of Romulus, and probably the celebration implied belief that the apostles, 'founders' (as Irenaeus boldly said) of the Roman Church, were

friendly relations to the local synagogue is evident from a sermon on the Pasch by Melito preserved among the Chester Beatty and Bodmer papyri, which includes an impassioned denunciation of the people who killed the Messiah. The sermon's high rhetoric brought translations or adaptations in Latin and Coptic. See the edition by S. G. Hall.

guardians of the city. There appeared a minor disagreement whether both apostles were martyred on the same day or on the same date a year apart. For the liturgical calendar that was a matter of indifference.

A vacuum in authority

Despite the lack of information after the ending of Luke's apostolic history, something can be deduced from the later writings that came to be included in the New Testament. The generation after the deaths of Peter and Paul felt a bewildering absence of authority, and to be listened to it became necessary to write to the Gentile churches in Paul's name. At Colossae in the Lycus valley in Asia Minor the Church was being taught a theosophy which worshipped cosmic powers and required rigorous asceticism together with observance of some Jewish ceremonies. A letter was needed to explain the supremacy of Christ over all hostile cosmic forces, and to make it clear that the mortifications required of Christian believers were abstinence from sexual licence, anger, malice, smutty talk, lyings, and not merely physical abstinences and neglect to care for the body.

Already in Paul's lifetime his churches began to have resident officers. Philippi had bishops and deacons, whose duties are unspecified but from the content of Paul's letter asking for financial support appear to be responsibility for the church chest and distribution to the needy. After the apostle's death reliable pastors to guide the communities were an urgent necessity. Pastoral letters in Paul's name to his assistant Timothy and Titus provided for the installation of virtuous and respectable pastors. Late in the second century Clement of Alexandria records dispute about their authenticity (*Strom.* 2. 52. 6). Over-ambitious and prominent women were told in these letters not to aspire to pastoral office, as some were evidently doing. God's purpose for them was fulfilled in having a family (1 Tim. 1: 15); they ensured the survival of the community. The letters show concern about the good opinion of Christians among pagan neighbours. Established pastors already existed at the time of writing, since hospitality duties had led some of them to overindulgence in alcohol. The author or editor wrote as if Paul was creating a pastorate, but the letters presuppose that a ministry was already in place and was in need of correction. 1 Tim. 6: 11–21 has the tone of an ordination charge.

More serious were deviations from the tradition in both doctrine and ethics. Some deviationist teachers were propagating the opinion that all true Christians have a duty to be ascetic, vegetarian, and abstaining from marriage (1 Tim. 4: 1–4). It is, however, conceded that the Christian is called to live an austere and frugal life like a soldier in the army[2] with no wife or comforts

---

[2] Before the third century Roman soldiers were not allowed to marry.

(2 Tim. 2: 3–4), and that second marriages display a carnal spirit. Gossipy young widows too lively in their search for a second husband are disapproved (1 Tim. 5: 11–13). Rich members of the Church are warned what snares and temptations wealth brings (1 Tim. 6: 9, 17). But among low-income members there are some who neglect to provide for their families and expect the church chest to do it all (1 Tim. 5: 8; Cf. 2 Thess. 3: 10–11; Didache 12: 4–5).

Many dissensions in the Church are merely about words and are futile (1 Tim. 6: 4; 2 Tim. 2: 14, 23; Titus 3: 9). But there are also doctrines invading the communities which are indeed diabolical (1 Tim. 4: 1). There are teachers propagating a pretentious 'knowledge' or *gnosis*. The propositions of these teachers are more hinted at than specified in detail. They include the belief that resurrection is not a future experience but 'past already', probably meaning that it should be interpreted as an exalted mystical experience in this life (an opinion found in some second-century gnostic texts). The emphasis on Jesus as the one mediator between God and man may be taken to imply that the gnostic teachers knew about other intermediaries who might need to be specially propitiated by hesitant and uncertain souls. The heretics are described as creeping into houses to lead astray foolish women apparently ready to believe almost anything. Evidently it was not their method to confront the assembly as a whole with their doctrines.

For the Pastoral Epistles the foundation of all true doctrine lies first in the ancient scriptures of the Old Testament, all of which are to be accepted in the Church as inspired; that is, they are not to be valued selectively and subjectively according to the private judgement of the reader. Secondly, one must also keep undeviating adherence to authentic apostolic tradition both in the content of teaching (1 Tim. 1: 18, 6: 3; 2 Tim. 1: 13) and in the due succession of pastors appointed by the solemn laying on of hands (1 Tim. 4: 14; 2 Tim. 1: 5).

An important and surprising text in 2 Tim. 1: 15 carries the information that churches in the province of Asia (not specified by name) had come to turn away from the tradition of Paul and his doctrine. The reference may be to the flood of gnostic ideas, against which the letter to Colossae and the encyclical to the Ephesian Church constructed a bulwark. Ephesus was the location of one of the apostle's principal missionary foundations. The Apocalypse of John (2: 2) and the letters of Ignatius of Antioch record the coming of false teachers to Ephesus, but suggest that resistance had been reasonably successful.

The text in 2 Tim. 1: 15 might, however, be a witness to high tension in the province of Asia between the old believers prizing the Pauline tradition and the more recently imposed Johannine tradition. The Apocalypse of John the seer of Patmos, whose visions saw a heavenly Jerusalem with gates bearing the names of the twelve apostles of the Lamb, begins with the letters to the seven churches of Asia. At Ephesus there was a fierce struggle against 'false apostles'.

An immoralist group called Nicolaitans had been successfully rejected. At Pergamum, where the Christians lived under the shadow of the great altar of Zeus, there were contentious moral issues. There were not only Nicolaitans but also teachers declaring that the eating of meat which had been offered in sacrifice to idols was morally a matter of indifference. Their teaching was a fair representation of what the apostle Paul had told the Corinthians in 1 Corinthians 8, and the Apocalypse may therefore represent polemic against the Pauline view. The same teachers at Pergamum held a similarly indifferentist view of fornication. It is not easy to know whether this is a reference to the same view of sacrificed meat—since fornication is a common Old Testament term for idolatrous worship—or if the Pergamum moralists were content to tolerate the everyday customs whereby young men of student age (like Augustine in fourth-century Carthage) took temporary concubines until ready to marry and produce a family, or whereby converts owning domestic slaves saw no reason why they should not behave as pagan owners did and sleep with girls who were in law their private property (below, pp. 215, 357).

The indifference of 'fornication' and of eating sacrificed meat was also taught at Thyatira by a woman, called Jezebel by John the seer, who taught with a claim to prophetic inspiration. In the judgement of John the seer her doctrines were 'the deep things of Satan', no doubt because she believed them to be 'the deep things of God' of which the apostle Paul wrote to the Corinthians (1 Cor. 2: 10). Or was her doctrine that for the most advanced believers it was valuable experience to plumb the very depths of evil, so that divine mercy would visibly abound and the limitless reaches of divine forgiveness would be demonstrated?

At Laodicea a lukewarm complacent spirit had resulted from economic prosperity, probably from the adherence of well-to-do converts able to give generous support to the Church chest and so to provide good love-feasts for the poor members. Prosperity had eroded their spiritual zeal.

A cross-section of society

Writing to the Corinthians, Paul encountered converts who possessed sufficient education and enough of this world's goods to feel less than completely comfortable in a society which included 'not many wise, not many powerful people, not many of noble birth' (1 Cor. 1: 26).[3] He told them they must learn to appreciate the divine humility of the Crucifixion—the crucified Messiah so different from what the Jews expected and alien to clever Greeks whose principal love was for a well-turned argument expressed in effective

---

[3] I have not felt able to follow J. J. Meggitt's view in his learned *Paul, Poverty and Survival* (Edinburgh, 1998) that 'not many' means 'none'.

rhetoric. The passage presupposes that the Corinthian converts included at least some who were persons of substance and education. Pagan critics like Celsus in the second century displayed an aristocratic scorn of the Church as the refuge of slaves, women, and the ignorant. Origen would reply to this sneer that in his observation the make-up of the Christian community corresponded to that of a cross-section of society at large; the Church had the same proportion of poor people that the empire as a whole had. The presence of the poor and deprived in the Church was in part a consequence of the welfare services provided from the offerings made to the church chest by converts who had the resources to contribute.

The early generations of converts did not define themselves in terms of social class, and there are in any event objections of principle to the application of social theories derived from modern historical situations to ancient society on the assumption that the facts have to conform to the modern theories. It is always a prior question whether the facts can be so ascertained as to invite that kind of theory to explain them. The Christians are not easily explicable as the product of existing and discernible tensions in the framework of contemporary society. Their ethical commitment led them to create an alternative society which, to the surprise of contemporary observers, was capable of including people of diverse classes, different educational attainments, various ethnic origins, and both sexes. In consequence preachers and teachers are found operating at two levels in their language, which the simple took literally and the educated understood more symbolically.

Christians as a third race

Once the Gentile mission had separated the infant churches from the Jewish synagogues, Gentile society was puzzled and angered. Religious toleration was justified by ancient tribal custom. The second-century critic Celsus did not admire Jewish religious customs, but they were at least venerable tradition. Sceptical philosophers had long deployed argument and mockery against the myths of the gods and their temples, but atheists were few and normally reticent. Christian disbelief in the old gods, hissing disapproval as they passed a temple, aroused anger and brought persecution. Persecution, however, brought publicity and increased converts. To officials it was baffling that the Christians were not a single tribe in one locality, and had no peculiar customs or language. 'To people whose true citizenship is in heaven, everywhere they dwell is a foreign land' (*Epistle to Diognetus* 5). Neither Jews nor pagans, they were 'a third race'.

7

WOMEN AMONG JESUS' FOLLOWERS[1]

The Gospels record that among the disciples of Jesus women were a constant element, though none of the twelve apostles was female. The same presence of women appears in the Acts and in the personal greetings appended to Pauline letters. Rom. 16: 1 mentions with Andronicus a woman named Junias, 'distinguished among the apostles'. Women could be inspired prophets with charismatic gifts, like the daughters of Philip (Acts 21: 9). At Corinth they spoke with tongues as much as any (1 Cor. 11: 4). The injunction that 'women should keep silence in the assembly' (1 Cor. 14: 34) suggests that some Corinthian women had become a noisy presence which needed checking. A sharper suppression seemed necessary to the author of 1 Tim. 2: 11–14, for whom the role of women was to be quiet, to stay at home, and not to teach church members with official authority.

Widows as a class were vulnerable in ancient society, and special charitable action was needed to protect them, 1 Tim. 5: 3–16 shows that some widows were too merry for social comfort, while others were the heart and soul of the praying community. Ignatius (*Sm.* 13. 1) has a surprising greeting to 'the virgins who are called widows'. So there were groups of ascetic widows who included unmarried ladies in their society.

Tertullian regarded an excessively prominent and public role for women as a characteristic of heretical communities, where they were found to teach, exorcize, promise healings, and 'perhaps even give baptism' (*Praescr. haer.* 41. 5). In the romance of Paul and Thecla, Thecla baptizes herself, which for Tertullian was an additional ground for disparaging the story. His shift towards Montanist sympathies no doubt altered this perspective.

Admission to the order of widows was the kind of act for which the local bishop would be invited to bless and perhaps to lay on hands. Hippolytus' *Apostolic Tradition* (10) insists that this was an appointment but not an ordination to liturgical functions. In Syria feminine society was withdrawn. From Syria come the first certain prescriptions for an order of deaconesses

---

[1] Scholarly treatments are Anne Jensen, *Gottes selbstbewußte Töchter* (Freiburg i. B., 1992) = *God's Self-Confident Daughters* (Kampen, 1996), and Ute E. Eisen, *Amtsträgerinnen im frühen Christentum* (Göttingen, 1996).

appointed to assist the bishop, especially at catechism and baptism. They were also important in visiting sick women in the congregation. At first they bore the simple title 'deacon'; the feminine 'deaconess' (*diakónissa*) is a later form. During the third century there were churches where the women deacons evidently had had some part to play in the liturgy, since in 325 the Council of Nicaea had to rule that they are to be ranked with the laity. The need for such a canon implies that some churches held the opposite view.

In ancient society women who wrote books were rare, and in the Christian community almost all the surviving records were written by men. The most influential women in the life of the ancient Church were to be the ascetics, especially if they were heads of their communities, and also high-born ladies with financial resources. The latter largely contributed to the church chest and therefore to the welfare for the poor and indigent. Among the poor, widows were a fairly high proportion. At the time of the great per-secution of Diocletian the state authorities visited the church at Cirta in north Africa and demanded to investigate their property. The church library had already been removed for safety, but the officials were able to remove eight chalices, two being of gold, six of silver, numerous torches, and candles. There was a refectory with casks and vessels. In addition there was a large col-lection of shoes and clothing, eighty-two dresses for women and thirty-eight cloaks, all of which were evidently provided by the well-to-do members of the congregation to keep the poor warm during the cold north African winters.

The pagan Platonist Porphyry once sneered at the powerful role played by rich women in the choice of bishops. There could be occasions when a bishop was chosen and consecrated against the wishes of a wealthy lady. This happened at Carthage in 306 with a resulting schism led by a lady named Lucilla. She had once been insulted (as she felt) by the bishop when he was archdeacon; she waved the bone of her favourite martyr during the com-memoration of the saints at the eucharist in rebuke to the Church for failing to recognize either its authenticity or the sanctity of the martyr. The arch-deacon thought this brawling in church and rebuked her; she went off in a huff (*irata discessit*). Schism resulted (Optatus 1. 15).

In ancient society women did not play a public role with high visibility. At the eastern end of the Mediterranean upper class women wore a veil, ances-tor of the yashmak, when appearing in public. In Augustine's time in north Africa we have the earliest evidence for the custom observed in the Arab world today, by which a husband walks in front as protector, the wife a few yards behind with children and baggage. Augustine recommended that Christian couples should walk side by side (*De bono coniugali* 1).

The most widely practised form of population control in antiquity was the exposure of infants. Women, especially groups of ascetic women, played a notable role in gathering up foundlings. It has to be admitted that no evidence survives of the subsequent fortunes of the children they rescued, which in some cases may well have been wretched.

Married women often had serious problems with their husbands, and would then confide in their bishop to beg advice. Difficulty could arise if the women came in such distress that the bishop or presbyter comforting her became the object of an emotional attachment. A childless woman might turn to a holy man to ask his intercessions that God would grant her a child. When her prayers were answered, malicious whispers could suggest that the saint had contributed more than his prayers.

8

'BARNABAS', JEWISH CHRISTIANITY, TROUBLE AT CORINTH

Luke ended the Acts by delivering Paul to Rome, but then a curtain descends. A long time passed before another well-informed Christian realized that there was an important story to tell, and that a connected narrative of the Church's development would contribute to self-understanding. Nevertheless, sources exist from which deductions can be made about principal features of Church life and the problems besetting the early communities.

'Barnabas'

Debate between Church and Synagogue long continued. A letter in the name of Barnabas, one-time missionary colleague of Paul, set out to deter believers from thinking the Mosaic law obligatory for believers in Jesus, or that observant Jews and Christians shared a common covenant. At the same time the author of the letter was aware of the risks of antinomianism. The letter ended by adapting a Jewish catechism, *The Two Ways*, a copy of which was known at Qumran in Cave 4 (4Q473).[1] 'Barnabas' warns against sodomy, abortion, malicious gossip, avarice, loquacity, going to pray with unconfessed sin on the conscience.

'Barnabas' takes to extreme lengths the thesis that Christians have an exclusive proprietary right to the Old Testament. The observant Jews of the Synagogue, he contends, are singularly unintelligent to suppose that Moses could have intended his laws literally. A command not to eat pigmeat means a warning to avoid human beings resembling pigs in behaviour. The circumcision intended by the Law is that of the heart; and the fact that it is also practised among Arabs, Syrians, and Egyptians proves that there is no divine command uniquely for all the people of God in the physical ceremony. Abraham, to whom the rite was first prescribed, was really looking forward to Jesus, for he had 318 servants and the Greek for 318 is TIH, shorthand for the cross of Jesus (IH being already a scribal abbreviation for IHCOYC). Entry to the true promised land of milk and honey is by baptism. The

[1] Discoveries in the Judaean Desert, xxii (Oxford, 1996), 292.

atoning death of Jesus is foreshadowed in the Levitical scapegoat, in Moses' outstretched arms bringing victory, and in the graven serpent. The true sabbath is the final rest in heaven, the seventh age that follows the six thousand years of this world; for a day with the Lord is a thousand years (15). Here 'Barnabas' recycles matter from the book of Jubilees and Jewish millenarianism.

'Barnabas' knew of Jews in the Synagogue who, probably from meditating on Daniel 9, were dreaming of an early rebuilding of the Temple at Jerusalem with support from the Romans themselves (16: 4), as in fact would be proposed under the emperor Julian in 363. Evidently the letter of 'Barnabas' was written well before the revolt of Bar Cocheba, and probably before the revolt of 112. Barnabas' letter was in the lectionary at Alexandria during the second and third centuries, and was treated as canonical.

Jewish Christians

A wholly different estimate of the Old Testament continued among the Jewish believers. For them the catastrophic failures of Zealot rebellion against Rome were no less disastrous than for other Jews. They too were excluded from Hadrian's city of Aelia Capitolina, and communities of Christian Jews became scattered in the towns of Syria. Only a diminishing handful of Gentile Christians took interest in their fate. In Gentile Christian eyes they were an oddity: they believed in Jesus the Christ but saw no reason to abandon those historic Mosaic customs which imparted distinctiveness to Jewish people. Their self-designation, almost certainly taken over from that of the original church of Jerusalem in the time of James and attested in Paul's letters (above, p. 37), was 'the Poor' (*Ebionim*). Others called them 'Nazarenes', a term that had at one time been in general use to describe all Christians and in Arabic remained so.

Important information about these Christians comes from Justin Martyr in the middle of the second century. Justin was much concerned with the dialogue between Church and Synagogue; having been born of Gentile parents at Nablus (Neapolis) in Samaria, he had a background to encourage interest in Jewish Christians. Between the Jewish and the Gentile believers of his time, he was unaware of doctrinal differences; but he knew that Christian Jews were distinctive in their practices, keeping circumcision, sabbath, dietary rules, and Jewish festivals as Gentiles did not.

With candid regret Justin recorded that among Gentile churches the Christian Jews were widely regarded as sectarian on the ground of their practices, not their beliefs, and therefore were to be rejected as self-excluded from the universal Church. Justin thought this Gentile judgement mistaken and deficient in charity (*Dialogue* 47–8). Presumably, however, there were at least some vocal members of these Jewish communities who thought that non-observance of the Mosaic Law marked an inferior, second-class species of Christian, and thereby challenged the entire notion of one universal covenant of salvation as taught by the apostle Paul. The Christian Jews were credited, in part correctly, with holding sharply critical attitudes to Paul. They wanted to claim the authority of Peter for a doctrine of the Church more tolerant towards diversity of national customs.

A century earlier the Christian Jews had been called to sit in judgement on the new Gentile converts and to decide on what terms these distant adherents could be admitted to be citizens in the commonwealth of God. A hundred years later they found themselves facing a future in which they would become a marginalized minority, under anathema at the synagogue of their fellow Jews, and by the Gentile Christians no longer seen to be linear descendants of the destroyed Jerusalem community but regarded as bizarre deviationists, half compromising with the Synagogue and making themselves sectarian by being behind the times.

Origen reports that the 'Ebionites' or Jewish Christians were united in their rejection of canonical status for Paul and his letters, but were divided on the question of the virginal conception of Jesus, which some of them denied while others affirmed. The group which accepted the virginal conception did not, according to Eusebius of Caesarea, go on to affirm the pre-existence of the divine Son. However, Jerome, whose wanderings in Syria had brought him into direct contact with Jewish Christian communities, was in no hesitation or doubt that they were orthodox in all doctrinal respects, and did not deny the virginal conception. The agreement between Justin and Jerome weighs more in the scales than the diverse opinions of the anti-heretical writers dependent on Irenaeus. Jerome and Justin disagreed with each other on one issue: their observance of the Mosaic law led Jerome to deny that they were authentic Christians, but Justin thought that they were indeed true believers.

'The Preaching of Peter'

Echoes of Jewish-Christian opinions can be heard in an early second-century piece entitled 'The Preaching of Peter', an imaginative work incorporating some speculative theology, and attacking Pauline ideas about the Mosaic Law by attributing them to the heretic Simon Magus (Acts 8: 18–24). In particular it must be a gross error to see the destruction of the Temple as God's sign that the Mosaic Law should no longer be kept. On the other hand, the Synagogue was at fault in allowing the worship of angels and in such veneration for the moon as to allow all festivals to be determined by a lunar calendar. That the religion of the 'Greeks' ('Hellenes' in Christian usage was already becoming the term for 'pagans') must be rejected is evident; they worship merely stocks and stones. The error of the adherents of Judaism is to suppose that the Synagogue has a monopoly of the knowledge of God. The author also needed to include polemic against followers of John the Baptist, and proposed to see providence as creating things and people in pairs, with the better regularly succeeding the inferior, as Abel to Cain, or Jesus to John the Baptist. (This notion of pairs was to be attractive to the semi-gnostic school of Valentinus.)

Trouble at Corinth

While adventurous speculations were capturing the imagination of eastern Christians, the West was facing an awkward problem of order. The earliest churches were not identifiable public buildings, but private houses owned by wealthy Christians who could accommodate a congregation. A substantial city would include more than one house-church, and there was always the possibility of centrifugal forces making different congregations travel along different paths unless they could be held together by loyalty to one presiding presbyter-bishop.

During the later years of the first century (a precise date is hard to determine but perhaps three decades after Paul's martyrdom), the Christians at Corinth by a majority decision ejected the presbyter-bishops in post and installed pastors perhaps endowed with more exciting charismatic gifts. The ejected pastors, however, retained a small following and sought to bolster their weak position by inviting the support of other churches nearby, including above all the much larger community at Rome not more than two weeks' travel distant. Unhappily the contentious split became widely known in the city, and pagans found the whole affair a rich laughing matter. For other churches in the province of Achaea it was no joke. Corinth was a major port through which many passed on their way to Asia Minor or the Black Sea if they were to avoid the long often stormy sail round the Peloponnese. Visiting Christians found themselves seriously embarrassed, perhaps even subjected to rough handling with the danger of provoking suppression by the civic authorities, if they accepted hospitality from what was deemed to be the wrong faction or if they attended a Sunday eucharist celebrated by the wrong lot of pastors. In consequence the past reputation of the Corinthian church for generous hospitality to travelling Christians was severely impaired.

The community at Rome took time to react to the Corinthian cry for help. They were being subjected to unpleasant attentions from the Roman government with 'sudden and repeated disasters and misfortunes'. They had a strong consciousness of being a martyr Church since the day when, perhaps under Nero, their women had been dressed up as daughters of Danaus to be prizes for winners in an athletic contest or as Dirke who suffered a horrible death by being attached to a bull. Nero liked tragicomic mythological panto-mimes. But Roman custom particularly enjoyed dressing up prisoners in finery as preface to hellish humiliations and death. Of this the best-known instance is the soldiers' mockery of Jesus, dressing him in a purple robe with a crown of thorns imitating the radiate crown of divine rulers.[2] Plutarch describes how criminals were dressed in purple and gold wearing crowns and forced to dance, then being suddenly stripped, flogged, and incinerated.[3] Tertullian records how criminals condemned to fight beasts in the amphi-theatre were often garbed as mythological figures, then castrated like Attis or burnt alive on a pyre like Hercules.[4] There was no sparing of women unless pregnant. A woman tied to a bull might suffer the smearing of her genitals with the secretions of a cow in season; Martial had seen a woman cast in the role of Pasiphae mated with a bull.[5] It is hard to imagine a Roman mob being much entertained by women appearing as Danaus' daughters who in myth murdered their bridegrooms and were condemned to endless pouring of water into bottomless buckets, but no doubt the Romans readily devised other more spectacularly brutal horrors for them to perform as prelude to their killing.

Because of these distractions the Roman church apologized for being late in sending a letter of regret and exhortation, written in high rhetorical style and persuasive remonstrance. They did not apologize for intervening. The delay enabled them to be sure of their facts. The central theme of the Roman letter is the need for proper order in the Church of God. In the wonders of creation God has established order, in the heavenly bodies, in the limits kept by the ocean, in the singular providence (of which Virgil wrote) that winds only blow one at a time—what chaos would result if they were all to blow simultaneously! Even in the smallest things the harmony and design of nature is visible, and all this demonstrates the transcendent will of the Creator on which everything is dependent and to which it is obedient.

To this transcendent God the Corinthians must one day answer for their actions. Dissension in his Church is offensive, and those who cause it must plead with tears that their Judge will be propitious. The end will certainly come, and no one should suppose that because the end is delayed, it is never going to happen. There is no justification for doubt about the resurrection at the last day, for Christ has risen, the first-fruits of those who have fallen

[2] H. St. J. Hart in *JTS*, NS 3 (1952), 66–75.

[3] *De sera numinis vindicta* 9. 554 B. Cf. Ammianus Marcellinus 28.4.8, on 'nobles in silk robes as if led to execution.'

[4] *Apol.* 15. 2–5.

[5] *Liber spectaculorum* 5. 2, written to honour the emperor Titus in AD 80 for the celebration of the recently completed Colosseum. Martial implies that this particular form of ferocity was unusual, and it is obviously conceivable that his epigram refers to the same occasion as the first epistle of Clement. Discussion by K. M. Coleman in *Journal of Roman Studies*, 80 (1990), 66–7.

asleep. Moreover, it is analogous to the sequence in the natural order where night follows day, crops follow sowing the seed, and, in the animal order, that unique bird the phoenix dies so that its offspring may be engendered from its rotting corpse.

There is also the motive of self-respect. The Corinthians need to know themselves and their high calling as God's elect, not presuming on the grace given at their baptism but strenuously seeking what is right. In zeal and unity they should imitate the vast angelic chorus who, although numbering ten thousand times ten thousand, nevertheless chant in absolute unison: 'Holy, holy, holy is the Lord God Sabaoth, the whole creation is full of his glory.'

There are more earthly analogies. In the Roman army everything is ordered with military precision, each officer in his rank and the common soldiers obeying orders. An officerless army would be as useless as an officer-corps with no troops to command. In the human body, the head and feet are mutually necessary. (Both analogies implicitly stress obedience.) The need for humility comes from the recognition of human frailty and mortality, familiar to old Job.

At this point the argument of the letter suddenly becomes less general and more specific. In the Mosaic law precise directions are given for rites and ceremonies. There is a clear hierarchy of high priest, priest, and Levite, and the duty of laity is precisely laid down. Moreover, the place of sacrifices is given; they must be at Jerusalem, not anywhere and everywhere, and even at Jerusalem only on the Temple mount. Only authorized priests may offer, and their duties require some training and expert knowledge. The ancient penalty for breaking the rules was death. How much more careful must we Christians be!

The argument, with its echo of the epistle to the Hebrews (12: 25), does not presuppose that the Old Testament legislates for the Church (though that view was encountered by Ignatius of Antioch at Philadelphia), but rather that it provides a divinely given typological correspondence. The point is the precise care with which the ministry of the people of God needs to be handled.

The title of 'bishop' had sadly become a matter of dispute—perhaps not merely at Corinth (1 Clement 44: 1). Possibly there was already a degree of tension whether a minister with the title of 'bishop' had wider powers and responsibilities than those entitled 'presbyter'. Tactfully there is no suggestion of 'high priest'. Old Testament precedent is not taken beyond the requirement of discipline.

The worship of the Church requires decency and respect for order, and the ministers are in their pastoral office because they have received an apostolic commission. God sent Christ who sent the apostles who appointed their first converts, after testing, to be bishops and deacons of believers, thereby fulfilling the prophecy adapted from Isa. 60: 17, 'I will appoint their bishops in

righteousness and their deacons in faith.' Furthermore, the apostles had fore-
sight of the situation which has now arisen, just as Moses had in Numbers 17
when the budding of Aaron's rod vindicated the priestly tribe and disorder
was quelled. Foreseeing trouble, the apostles provided for a proper succession
of ministers; that is, they not only provided the first bishops and deacons but
directed that, when those first appointed died, 'other tested men should succeed to their service *(leitourgia)*'. The hammer-blow of the conclusion follows: 'Ministers appointed by the apostles or subsequently by others of due
standing with the consent of the entire congregation, who have faultlessly
ministered to Christ's flock in humility of mind, in peace, and with all
modesty, and who have long been well spoken of by all—these men we
consider wrongly ejected from their ministerial service.' They 'blamelessly
offered the gifts'.[6]

At Corinth near the end of the first century the controversy turns, therefore, on the permanent tenure of pastors standing at one remove from the
apostles. Ministers appointed by apostles enjoyed tenure. But was it not an
'innovation' if the same status was granted to those whom these ministers
appointed? They had not had apostles to pray and lay hands on them in
blessing, and an essential part in their ordination had been the assent of the
people.

Luke is the earliest writer to imply some assimilation of episcopal oversight
to the office of apostle (Acts 1: 20). But evidently there could be a question
whether a bishop or presbyter-bishop in the post-apostolic generation
enjoyed the degree of dominical commission that the Twelve had received.
The Corinthians evidently supposed that if their ministers were appointed by
the assent of the people, the congregation was empowered to remove them
from office and to replace them by others. In the judgement of their sister
church at Rome that was an error. The people gave assent, but the commission to minister was received from those who had themselves received such a
commission—that being derived from the commission transmitted in the
community continuous with the apostles. The Roman letter does not
identify by name or office the 'men of due standing' to whom the ejected
ministers owed their pastoral commission, but the likelihood is that they were
leading ministers from neighbouring cities whose presence assured the
community of their membership in the universal body and therefore of the
universality of recognition enjoyed by their ministers.

The Roman letter does not first assert or first establish succession at
Corinth. Continuity of ministry is taken for granted as common ground in
the debate. It is simply assumed that while apostolic authority was unique to

---

[6] 1 Clement 44. Two possible corruptions in the transmitted text occur, but the general sense or
intention of the passage is not affected.

those commissioned by Jesus, the apostles in turn realized that the world was not ending and the community would need pastors after they were gone. These pastors would do for the Church in their time much, if not all, of what the apostles had done for the first generation of believers. The assumption of continuity was natural. The ancient world thought of authority in office, e.g. in that of head of a philosophical school, as assured by due succession.

This function of ministers has to be in the one Church where unity is of its very being and those who cause splits have forsaken something at the heart of the apostolic tradition. Therefore the Roman Church asks the newly installed clergy at Corinth humbly to stand down; they can move to another city, for 'any place would be happy to receive them'. Of selfless withdrawal there were examples in Moses, Judith, and Esther, in Roman Christians who lately sold themselves into slavery to raise the money to ransom fellow-believers, and in kings who accepted voluntary exile for the good of their people, or some willing to die to avert pestilence.

It emerges, however, that the sedition at Corinth has been led by the new ministers. They are urged to be penitents for whom the entire Church will intercede as they meekly kneel before the presbyters they wrongly supplanted. It is better to be in lay status within the Church's communion than to be a presbyter and excommunicate. (It is presupposed that if an ordained minister has so sinned as to become a formal penitent, he can be restored only to lay status, not to his pastoral office).

The peroration of the Roman letter moves to an impressive conclusion by invoking the authority of God, the Lord Jesus Christ, and the Holy Spirit for the advice given to the Corinthians, and then imparts an intense solemnity to the whole document by a form of liturgical prayer. The prayer intercedes for the sick and needy and for 'our prisoners', prayers for peace and concord in both the Church and the world, and emphatically asks for wisdom to be given to the empire's rulers, much as a synagogue of the Jewish Dispersion would pray.

The letter assumes throughout that the Corinthian community is responsible for making the decision which in Roman eyes is necessary. The Corinthians are not receiving commands. But the Roman Christians will be delighted if they 'submit obediently to the letter written by us in the Holy Spirit'. A recurrent refrain is that the Romans are doing no more than remind the Corinthians of what they already know, of truths they have for the moment forgotten. The Romans' earnest prayer is that the Corinthians will 'submit not to us but to God's will'. But they will put their souls in danger if they are disobedient 'to the words spoken by Christ through us'.

The letter to Corinth was composed in the name of the Roman Church, not of a named author. But second-century evidence names the author Clement. The early episcopal lists of bishops of Rome name Clement as third or sometimes fourth bishop at about the end of the first century. There is no good reason to question this attribution of the letter. He was evidently in a leading position among the senior clergy of Rome; but there is no evidence that at this date there was one presbyter-bishop exercising monarchical authority in the city. Probably there were several 'house-churches' each with its presbyter in charge, and among these perhaps Clement had a position of seniority. In the Roman document the *Shepherd* of Hermas, Clement is mentioned as the person responsible for correspondence with other churches.

Clement, therefore, did not write with an awareness that he possessed a primacy by virtue of his office as presiding bishop and successor in jurisdiction to Peter and Paul. The letter was an admonition from one community to another in the universal Church, fulfilling a duty arising from the universality in which sister churches share.

Clement wrote the letter in good Greek with occasional reminiscences of Sophocles and Euripides. His panegyric on the heroism of the apostle Paul has echoes of the language used by Stoics about the courage of Heracles, enduring vast labours, exile, and death to earn immortal glory and to bring beneficent teaching as far as the pillars of Heracles (Straits of Gibraltar) at the boundary of the west. His exhortations to the intruded presbyters to accept voluntary withdrawal are similarly rich with ethical clichés found also in Seneca and Epictetus. In short, the author of the letter was well educated as well as being familiar with the Old Testament, and his writing presupposes that at Corinth also the recipients of the letter would appreciate the kind of arguments he uses.

Of Christian writings, Clement knew not only the epistle to the Hebrews but most of the Pauline corpus, probably Acts, 1 Peter, and James, and some of the traditions about Jesus which passed into the synoptic gospels. He shows no sign of knowing any of the Johannine writings. But sayings of Jesus rank on a par with citations from the Old Testament (13: 2). The writings of apostles have not yet achieved that exalted status. His biblical quotations are often from memory and inexact, but otherwise he quotes a recension of the Septuagint adjusted to be closer to the Hebrew. He was sure that the ancient scriptures were about Jesus. Rahab's scarlet thread (Josh. 2: 18) is a type of the redeeming blood of Christ as well as a reminder of the duty of hospitality. The significance of the death of Christ is shown by a full quotation of the 53rd chapter of the prophet Isaiah.

The Corinthians followed Roman advice; they used to read Clement's letter in their lectionary, and since the letter was a statement of universal principles not peculiar to the Corinthian situation, many other churches also read it liturgically. They were grateful that the Roman community gave a strong lead.

9

IGNATIUS OF ANTIOCH

Ignatius' letters and date[1]

Eusebius of Caesarea, a careful if not inerrant historian, reports that during Trajan's reign (98–117), indeed according to his *Chronicle* precisely in the year 107, the Church of the great city of Antioch-on-the-Orontes in Syria suffered persecution and lost its bishop Ignatius. Letters under Ignatius' name survive in three editions, a middle recension of seven letters, an expanded edition with six additional letters stressing the primacy of the see of Antioch, and an abbreviated edition of three letters extant in a Syriac version. Most of the letters insist on the authority of bishops. Fourth-century squabbles between bishops competing for power made the documents popular in that age, as Eusebius expressly remarked (*HE* 3. 36. 2). The texts would have been especially congenial to a bishop of Antioch in the 370s and 380s, at a time when he had to assert his position in competition with three rivals in a divided city. The recension known to Eusebius had seven letters in which Ignatius, under arrest, communicated with churches in Asia Minor at Philadelphia, Smyrna, Tralles, Magnesia, and Ephesus. In addition the Roman church was addressed without mention of a bishop, and also Polycarp bishop of Smyrna. This collection of seven letters was known to Irenaeus and Origen and is therefore earlier than 160–70. It is a disputed question whether they are as early as Eusebius says. A collection of Ignatius' letters was known to Polycarp, his own letter to the Philippians being a covering letter for the set. That suggests that the letters should be assigned, if not necessarily to the first decade of the second century, at least not later than the third or fourth decade. Accordingly the question of dating turns on whether enough is known of the development of the second-century Church for a confident judgement to be possible that the seven letters are somehow anachronistic in the first or second decade, but entirely possible ten or twenty years later.

Dispute on this last question cannot readily be settled. At least it is safe to say that not enough is known about the Church early in the second century

---

[1] Besides Lightfoot a good commentary on Ignatius is by W. R. Schoedel (Philadelphia, 1985).

to allow even a probability that Eusebius' dating is out of the question. Although Paul and Peter rank as authoritative figures in the letters, they contain no quotation from any document destined to form part of the New Testament. The late decades of the second century see the institution of a single bishop presiding over each local congregation as a general and accepted arrangement. If Ignatius is credited with responsibility for the 'monarchical' episcopate, the later the date ascribed to his letters, the less believable becomes this crediting. The polemic in the letters against those who expressed their faith in the divine nature of Christ by affirming that he did not really assume human flesh in the incarnation, and that his body was an optical illusion experienced by persons of immature faith, is in no way anachronistic in the first years of the second century. There is also no force in the contention that the wealth of Roman Christians presupposed in Ignatius' letter to Rome is more plausible later rather than earlier. The *Shepherd* of Hermas provides express testimony for the existence of influence and social standing among rich believers in the capital. Nothing in the letters manifests serious affinity with Justin or other apologists concerned to meet philosophical criticism. In short, if there is hesitation about assigning the martyrdom to the time of Trajan, a date later than Hadrian is unlikely to a degree.

For many centuries the text of Ignatian letters copied by medieval scribes was the longer version expanded late in the fourth century with an enhanced stress on the necessity of the bishop to impart validity to ecclesial action. The first printing of a Greek text of this long recension was in 1557. A Latin text appeared as early as 1498. But Ignatius on bishops was bound to irritate those left of centre in the Reformation. For John Calvin nothing seemed 'more disgusting than the fairy tales published under the name of Ignatius' (*Institutio*, i. 13. 29). Matters began to change in the mid-seventeenth century. In 1644 the deeply erudite Irish archbishop Ussher published at Oxford (from a manuscript in the library of Gonville and Caius College, Cambridge, cod. 395, and another owned by Bishop Richard Montague but lost with the destruction of his papers) a Latin version made by Robert Grosseteste, enabling him to identify the original corpus of seven letters known to Eusebius. Two years later Isaac Vossius printed from a Medici manuscript at Florence (Laur. pl. lvii, cod. 7, s. xi) the Greek text of six of the original letters. This codex originally contained the letter to the Romans, but that had been lost. Soon, in 1669, however, the Maurist Thierry Ruinart, assistant to Mabillon in Paris, was able to publish the letter to the Romans from a Colbert manuscript (Paris. gr. 1451, s. x), so that the original form of text was complete in Greek. That the original corpus of letters had been rediscovered was evident to Ussher. He accompanied his edition with annotation of wide erudition. He knew of the existence of the Medici manuscript, but had been unable to obtain a copy.

A fifth-century papyrus fragment at Berlin has preserved an uninterpolated text of part of Ignatius' letter to Smyrna.

In 1666 the Calvinist Jean Daillé (1594–1670) published a book attacking the authenticity not only of Dionysius the Areopagite (the spuriousness of which, argued by Lorenzo Valla in the fifteenth century, was slow to become universally accepted) but also all letters of Ignatius. Daillé on Ignatius provoked major refutation from John Pearson. Since the massive studies of Zahn and especially J. B. Lightfoot (2nd edn. 1889), the weight of opinion has been to favour the genuineness of the seven-letter recension, and while there have been learned arguments from scholars reluctant to believe in an early-second-century date, the case for accepting Zahn's and Lightfoot's main thesis has commanded a majority among scholars.

The content of the letters concerns matters more important than bishops. They are written in a highly personal and idiosyncratic style, with poetic images, unusual vocabulary, and a pervading passionate fervour. Ignatius was writing in haste under difficult circumstances, and his language did not always convey precisely what he wanted to say. The language used would be surprising at any decade of the second century. The confrontation with imminent martyrdom profoundly affected him, and the impression can be given that a proper willingness to die in union with Christ has passed into a neurotic will to die.

Voluntary provocative martyrs were easily engendered by promises of celestial joy. In the 190s Clement of Alexandria deeply disapproved of aggressive voluntary martyrs. Their attitude seemed to the emperor Marcus Aurelius, a Stoic defender of suicide, 'theatricality' in poor taste. Cyprian of Carthage under persecution in 250–8 also united idealized language about the martyr's crown with express disapproval of voluntary self-destruction.

If there were evidence of the date by which a threefold ministry of bishops, presbyters, and deacons became normal in Syria and Asia Minor, one could reason from that to Ignatius' date. But Ignatius gives the primary evidence and the argument is circular. Let it simply be observed that in Ignatius' theology there is nothing anachronistic in the early decades of the second century.

Johannine themes appear,[2] but of the canonical gospels his nearest affinity is with Matthew or oral traditions close to Matthew. There is no express quotation. Ignatius' religion had its norms in a community tradition; books were secondary, and the 'gospel' was not yet a book.

---

[2] The Gospel of John was ascribed to John the son of Zebedee in Irenaeus (*AH* 2. 22. 5, 3. 1. 4), Clement of Alexandria (Eus. *HE* 6. 14. 7), and an Armenian fragment of Papias. Probability favours the opinion that this was so from the time editors (responsible for ch. 21 at least) released it for circulation. The Gospel was integral to Tatian's *Diatessaron*. Heracleon wrote the first commentary.

Martyrdom

In Ignatius' letters we have the first light on the Church at Antioch since the disagreement between Peter and Paul about table-fellowship between Jew and Gentile (Gal. 2: 11 ff.)—in which it is unlikely that the apostle of the Gentiles emerged victorious. Nevertheless Paul's Gentile mission had its springboard there. Ignatius came of a Gentile background. He may even have owed his election as bishop to a desire on the part of a group of Christians in the city to widen the gulf between the house-churches and the city synagogues, especially because, as Ignatius' letters make clear, there were at Antioch Christian believers of Gentile birth who saw no good reason to think separation from the synagogue community right or necessary and observed their festivals. There could hardly be a more suitable time to remember the passion of Christ than Passover.

If the disagreements led to some public disorder, the attention of the Roman authorities would be drawn; Ignatius was arrested. Action on his part may have precipitated that, for he was fervent in his conviction that to die for the name of Christ was to be assured of bliss. The apostle Paul had so held (Phil. 1: 23).

With other Syrian Christians sent on ahead of him, he was to be transported to Rome (which suggests that these prisoners had Roman citizenship), there to provide entertainment for the populace and satisfaction for justice by being thrown to hungry beasts in the amphitheatre. His escort was a detachment of ten soldiers—a number which could imply that they had other prisoners as well. He found them unfriendly; they bound him in chains, which probably means that they expected a substantial bribe (cf. Acts 24: 26) or that they had heard stories of Christians miraculously liberated and hoped to forestall angelic or magical escape. However, on reaching Philadelphia in the province of Asia they allowed the bishop an astonishing freedom to meet the local church (cf. Acts 27: 3). It seems safe to assume that some rich Philadelphian Christian had greased their palms. A large bribe obtained the release from prison of a Montanist Christian named Themiso in the 170s; Tertullian judged bribery destructive of a martyr's integrity. The martyrdom of Pionios of Smyrna in the third century mentions bribes as 'the usuals'.[3] Unbribed guards were hostile.

On Ignatius' route there were stops at towns in Asia Minor with substantial Christian communities, notably at Philadelphia, Smyrna, Troas, and then in Europe at Cavalla (Neapolis). At Smyrna access was granted to bishops and other visitors from nearby churches. It was expected that those incarcerated in Roman prisons would be fed by family and friends. To prisoners

---

[3] Eus. *HE* 5. 18. 5; Tertullian, *De fuga* 5, 12; *Mart. Pionii* 11. 4–5; Libanius, *Orat.* 33. 30.

confessing their faith reverence was intense. Along the route Christians were alerted to Ignatius' coming, and in his mind the journey became a triumphal progress, no doubt to the amazement of his guards.

The ancient Church held the integrity of martyrs and confessors in the highest admiration and reverence. At the cities along Ignatius' route the Christian communities were able to receive him with extreme manifestations of pride and joy. Ignatius told Polycarp of Smyrna that his letter of greeting was 'kissing my chains'. The devout actually present to Ignatius in the flesh did their kissing literally. Tertullian (*Ad uxorem* 2. 4) records that this was usual.

At Antioch Ignatius had faced sharp challenges to his authority, especially to his endeavours to unite the Christians scattered through his large city by centralizing control of baptisms and eucharistic celebrations. This policy seems to have been unwelcome at some of the house-churches in the city, where it is likely enough that some believers broke bread without the presence of a presbyter to preside, preferring the excitements of itinerant charismatics. Ignatius found the resulting fissiparousness of his Church dangerous, laying it wide open to damaging infiltration by heretics and dissidents. At Smyrna he found a heretical group which stayed away from common prayer and eucharist, but had independent eucharists presided over by someone in a position of dignity, perhaps a presbyter or (more probably) a layman of substance (*Sm.* 6. 1).

More than one of his letters reports that at Antioch 'peace' had been restored. Perhaps persecution was past and gone. But one cannot exclude the possibility that the peace in question was a restored harmony among contending factions in his church at Antioch. Insofar as his own centralizing policy was in some quarters unpopular, this restoration of harmony may have been a consequence of his own enforced removal from the scene. But he could hardly have expressed satisfaction unless his own policies at Antioch had prevailed against the opposition, at least among the members of the community who acknowledged his authority. It cannot be assumed that Ignatius commanded the assent of the majority of Christians at Antioch. If internal dissension provoked a breach of public order, that would have given occasion for civil authority to demand the identity of the community's recognized leader. Ignatius uses language suggesting he had voluntarily come forward (*Sm.* 4. 2, cf. *Rom.* 4. 1): 'Why have I delivered myself to death . . .?' If so, was he a volunteer martyr of the type disapproved in the Martyrdom of Polycarp and later in Clement of Alexandria and Cyprian of Carthage (*ep.* 81. 1)?

Language strikingly akin to that of Ignatius occurs in the Stoic Epictetus on 'the will to die' (4. 1. 90). In reference to the 'Galilaeans' Epictetus thought this will to die a form of madness. But their fearlessness before tyrants seemed admirable (4. 7. 6). Socrates did more good by death than by any word or act in his life (4. 1. 169), a model of detachment.

A striking theme in all the letters is Ignatius' sense of triumph at the prospect of martyrdom, which is to be both an ecstatic experience of union with the crucified Lord in his passion and at the same time a glorious witnessing to God in a theatrical death at Rome before up to 50,000 pagan spectators in the lately completed Colosseum.[4] By death he will be 'imitating the suffering of my God' (*Rom.* 6. 3). From a few phrases it seems that his arrest and imminent martyrdom were not regarded so enthusiastically by critics in the church at Antioch. But for him the experience of being crunched to death between the teeth of a wild animal in the cause of God and his Church was the path to a beatific admission to paradise. Thereby he would 'attain to God'.

The letter to Rome manifested anxiety that influential Roman Christians might intercede on his behalf and thereby be able to deprive him and his Church at Antioch of the crown of martyrdom. And, he adds, how humiliating it would be (which is to say, how disastrous in histrionic terms as public statement) if, as had already occurred in a few cases to Christians condemned to the amphitheatre, the wild beasts were to take no interest in him at all.[5] Ignatius virtually stage-managed the course of his journey from Antioch to Rome and may have suspected that some in the Roman community preferred a quiet life and low profile. The Christian community in the capital certainly included citizens of considerable substance, since the *Shepherd* of Hermas, written by a Roman Christian close to Ignatius' time, contains numerous admonitions for wealthy believers, and repeatedly records the respect accorded to them in pagan society. About the last thing such Christians wanted would be the adverse publicity given to their community by the very public condemnation of some Syrian fellow-believers, including the principal officer of the Church in the great city of Antioch.

Heresies

In some of the churches near Smyrna Ignatius encountered heresies which, though he does not say so, he may already have met at Antioch. At Smyrna and its vicinity he met a group absenting themselves from their bishop's eucharist and denying that the flesh of Christ was real. At Philadelphia there was a confrontation with a group who were in controversy with their bishop

---

[4] Dedicated by Titus in June 80, 'Colosseum' was its medieval name.

[5] In the north African account of the martyrdom of Perpetua and Felicitas in 202, their male companion Saturus was tied to a boar which left him untouched but savaged the man who did the tying. Saturus was then tied to a scaffold to be attacked by a bear, but the bear stayed in its cage uninterested. A leopard then mauled him, but left him to be finished off with a sword. The story as told reflects the widespread ancient conviction, expressed for example in Horace's famous Ode 'Integer Vitae' (1. 22) and in anecdotes about Desert Fathers left uninjured by hyenas or lions (e.g. Moschus *Pratum* 107, 163, 167, 181), that wild beasts would not touch those of innocent and holy life.

because they held that for Christians supreme authority lay in the Old Testament scriptures which determined the nature of the gospel. Whether they also wanted to keep sabbaths and other Judaic practices is unclear. At Magnesia on the Maeander reports said that some were ignoring their young bishop. There was also fear that they might keep Judaic customs such as the sabbath.

The Decalogue itself required sabbath observance, and it was difficult to know by what authority the Churches were neglecting it and meeting for worship on Sundays in memorial of the Lord's resurrection. For Sunday worship there was community tradition, but no precept in the Old Testament nor in the apostolic writings. It seems possible that the 'Judaizers' felt bound to celebrate the weekly eucharist on Saturdays, and thereby divided the community. Their separate eucharist may also have been the consequence of concern to keep Jewish dietary rules. However, Ignatius' text clearly implies that the demand for the observance of the Mosaic law was coming from Gentile believers, and, since they were circumcised (*Philad.* 6), they may well have had a background before conversion and baptism in which they were synagogue proselytes subsequently attracted to Christianity and were then disturbed to find that Mosaic precepts were not being kept. At the synagogue they had submitted to circumcision; it might have been tough to be told on arrival at the church that this social sacrifice had been superfluous.

The fact that the Church defied Marcion's criticisms and insisted on keeping the Hebrew scriptures in its lectionary in the Septuagint version was bound to make permanent the presence of Christians whose faith was determined by the Old Testament. In one of his sermons on Leviticus (5. 8) Origen complains of believers who produce in the church today what they have learnt at the synagogue yesterday.

Biblical interpretation

Ignatius was content to acknowledge that as a stage in God's purpose for the world, Judaism had its valued place. But he felt certain that the Old Testament patriarchs and prophets had not actually observed the sabbath literally; already they had kept Sunday as a holy day for worship, foreseeing the day of the resurrection of Christ (*Magn.* 9. 1). The grand difference is that Christianity is universal, whereas Judaism is particular to one people (*Magn.* 10).

At Philadelphia, where Ignatius enjoyed an astonishing hour of liberty to meet with the local church, there was internal dissension about the correct interpretation of the Bible, especially about the relative authority of the Gospel proclaimed in Jesus and the Old Testament scriptures. If one side in the dispute was claiming that the Old Testament provided the criterion by

which the authenticity of the gospel message could be evaluated, the opposite point of view was upheld by the bishop of Philadelphia, who evidently
thought that the criterion for assessing the various scriptures of the Old
Testament now lay in 'the gospel'. On meeting the church Ignatius was
granted a sudden onset of charismatic inspiration and cried out in a loud
voice 'Do nothing without the bishop.' Immediately the former group took
offence, supposing that privately he had received some prior briefing about
the terms of the debate, and therefore could not be regarded as an impartial
arbiter. He was declaring agreement with the bishop without even having
heard the arguments of the opposing party, for whom it was no matter of
principle that on an issue such as this their bishop must be regarded as entitled to submission. The opposition was in effect asking by what right their
bishop and now Ignatius were entitled to set aside the inspired scriptures of
the old covenant.[6]

Closely reasoned discussion about hermeneutic principles not being his
forte, Ignatius denied possessing any previous knowledge of the local controversy. In saying what he did about the Spirit and the bishop, he was speaking under immediate inspiration of the Holy Spirit, and 'the Spirit knows
whence it comes and whither it goes', language with an echo of St John's
gospel (3: 8) or at least of Johannine tradition. When Ignatius himself
declared that his own appeal was to 'scripture' (and it is not clear whether by
that he meant the Old Testament or a written gospel such as that of Matthew
or the epistle of Clement of Rome to Corinth), he was at once accused of
begging the entire question. In any event, Ignatius had no New Testament
canon to invoke; his reliance was on the charismatic power of the ministry
representing God to his people. Of one thing he felt certain, namely that the
Spirit of God can never be found among those who separate from the common worship under the aegis of the bishop with his loyal presbyters and
deacons.

Docetism

From three of the letters it is evident that the centrifugal groups wanting to
assert their independence of the bishop were open to heretical infiltration. At
Ephesus, Tralles, and Smyrna the opinion was being propagated that real
humanity, actual flesh, could not possibly have been united to God in Jesus
Christ. Granted that God could have created a convincing optical illusion
that he had assumed human flesh in Christ, the heretics urged that the

---

[6] The Apocalypse of John of Patmos (2: 9, 3: 9) speaks of some at Philadelphia and Smyrna who,
although not Jews, claimed to be Jews and are set aside as a 'synagogue of Satan'. Probably these
were Gentile proselytes whose relationship to the Church was fiercely acrimonious.

conviction thus produced was no more than accommodation to human weakness. The flesh was in reality no reality, merely appearance. In short, the heretics held the doctrine commonly labelled 'docetism' (from *dókesis*, appearance).

Ignatius' reaction was vehement against a doctrine which in his eyes simply destroyed his hope of salvation. In strident terms he affirmed the utter physical reality of Christ's human birth and death, and loved to express his faith in a powerful series of paradoxes:

> There is one physician, fleshly and spiritual, born yet not born, God in man, true life in death, both of Mary and of God, first capable of suffering then incapable, Jesus Christ our Lord   (*Eph.* 7. 2).

> Be deaf when anyone speaks to you apart from Jesus Christ, who was of the family of David, son of Mary, who was truly born, both ate and drank, was truly persecuted under Pontius Pilate, was truly crucified and died in the sight of those in heaven and on earth and under the earth; who was also truly raised from the dead when his Father raised him. The Father will similarly raise in Christ Jesus us who believe in him, without whom we have no true life   (*Trall.* 9).

Against the docetists of Smyrna, whose names he could not bring himself to mention (*Sm.* 5. 3), Ignatius had forceful complaints. They were, he thought, 'beasts in human shape' (*Sm.* 4. 1; cf. *Eph.* 7. 1). Profound consequences followed from their denial that Christ had assumed human flesh. First, there was the fact that in their exalted otherworldly spirituality they were indifferent to the Church's social welfare for the physical sustaining of widows, orphans, prisoners, those just released from prison needing readjustment in the community, the hungry and thirsty.

Secondly, their denial of Christ's true humanity and of the actuality of his dying robbed martyrdom of its value.[7] For the meaning of martyrdom was a mystical union with the Lord in his dreadful crucifixion. The heretics were therefore depriving Ignatius of his crown. They flattered him, speaking of his noble courage. But their doctrine of Christ evacuated martyrdom of all meaning and value. Ignatius' faith took away his dread of the amphitheatre. 'Near the sword is near to God. With the beasts is to be with God' (*Sm.* 4. 2)— a saying which recalls words in the Coptic Gospel of Thomas (82): 'He who is near me is near the fire.'

A third factor making the docetists dangerous was their implicit denial of the reality of the gift of the eucharist, the body and blood of Christ being in their view unreal.

---

[7] Ignatius does not use the vocabulary of 'martyr', 'witness', which was not yet Christian usage as it would become for Justin. See G. W. Bowersock, *Martyrdom and Rome* (Cambridge, 1995). Origen (*Comm. on John* 2. 34 (28)) says 'Martyr is properly Witness, but the brotherhood keeps the title for those who have died in testimony to unbelievers.'

The heretics were therefore offering a counterfeit gospel, a manifestation of the subtlety of Satan. The seven letters have numerous references to the cosmic power of evil with diabolical snares and traps. And the urgency of the struggle against evil was given additional force by the imminence of the end. If believers asked why the end was delayed, the reasonable answer was not difficult: In his patience God was now allowing extra time for repentance (*Eph.* 11. 1; *Sm.* 9. 1). But in the meantime all believers are to be joined in conflict with 'the ruler of this world', also called the Devil or Satan.

The heretics are as malodorous as the Devil himself (*Eph.* 17. 1), and they will share Satan's destiny which is hell-fire (*Eph.* 16. 1). It was a widespread ancient belief that malevolent spirits could be detected by the stench (e.g. Augustine, *City of God* 10. 19; *Conf.* 6. 13. 23).

Among some docetist heretics, their doctrine found its springboard in the belief that flesh and blood could not imaginably be supposed to be admitted to the kingdom of God, as Paul himself conceded (1 Cor. 15: 50), and therefore that the Redeemer did not assume parts of human nature not destined to be saved. Ignatius did not formulate the reply of later orthodox writers from Irenaeus onwards that the affirmation of the resurrection of the body, in the baptismal confession of many churches, was a coherent consequence of the faith that what the Lord had assumed was what he intended to save.

Judaizers

It has been a normal pattern in church history for heretics to wish to remain recognized within the Church, anxious to persuade other believers that their position is authentic or at least a legitimate option. Schismatics on the other hand are not usually heretics, or at least seldom begin that way; but they are often parting with the parent body on some moral issue and are therefore bound by their initial consciousness of protest.

It is at first sight striking that Ignatius describes the Judaizers as organizing a division (*merismós*), whereas the docetists are a school of thought (*haíresis*) anxious to claim a legitimate place within the community and not inclined to have a distinct organization. Docetists held a point of view which Ignatius thought to be gravely wrong and in need of explicit confrontation. Some among them may have been slow to agree with him in his wish to centralize under his control the administration of the sacraments, but it does not appear that they were disposed to present the bishop with a direct challenge to his authority. The report that they 'flattered' him points rather to the opposite conclusion. They were more likely to be in the business of recruiting him to share their theological position and therefore had little wish to vex him. Defiance of his authority was not on their agenda, and many among this group may have been among his supporters when he was elected.

By contrast the Judaizing party had a separatist programme. Their observance of the sabbath with local synagogues at Antioch appeared to Ignatius a divisive act in which the whole community did not feel able to participate. On the Day of Atonement they were not likely to want to be present at an Agape or other cheerful celebration.

Probably the docetists represented a point of view that evoked sympathy in Ignatius himself, and therefore had to be disavowed with particular vehemence. In strong terms he therefore affirmed the reality of the birth and crucifixion of the Redeemer.

The star of Bethlehem

'The god of this world' had been utterly outwitted by the incognito of the Redeemer, apparently so weak and powerless in his virginal conception, birth and crucifixion 'three mysteries that cry aloud'. None of these events was understood by Satan until the new star of the Nativity of the Lord blazed forth to initiate the overthrow of all astrology and magic and to cause amazement in the other heavenly bodies (*Eph.* 19).[8] Related ideas about the failure of evil powers to realize what was happening at the crucifixion appear in the apostle Paul (1 Cor. 2: 9), in the *Ascension of Isaiah*, and in a number of early Christian texts. Among followers of Valentinus, for example, the disruption in heaven caused by the new star at the descent of the Redeemer became a favoured theme (Clement, *Exc. ex Theodoto* 74).[9] For Ignatius the birth and death of Jesus simply destroyed the power of all occult forces in the cosmos.

Astrology had been a subject to which earlier in life he seems to have given some attention (*Trall.* 5); he still felt able to take pride in his expertise on this intricate subject, though now he was a Christian, he counted it but dung.

To unbelievers the crucifying of Jesus was a scandal that blocked their way towards faith (*Eph.* 18. 1). That was because they failed to realize how his humility overthrew the prince of this world (*Trall.* 4. 1).

Unity and eucharist

A characteristic of some teachers, active in communities addressed in Ignatius' letters, was to think of salvation as liberation of the divine soul from its incarceration in the body. Ignatius thought this incompatible with the

---

[8] Like many ancient writers, Ignatius could assume that the sun, moon, and stars have souls or resident angelic powers.

[9] In his *Jewish War* (6. 289) Josephus records that a new star suspended over Jerusalem presaged the destruction of the Temple.

incarnation and so with the truth of the body and blood of the Lord in the eucharist, the very 'medicine of immortality' (*Eph.* 20. 2). 'Immortality' was the name of a well-known ancient drug in the pharmacy of medical practitioners. The phrase occurs in other writers of the period, e.g. Seneca (*Prov.* 3. 2) spoke of the hemlock drunk by Socrates as the 'medicine of immortality'. The concrete realism of Ignatius' eucharistic belief is clear from his language, but the gift is 'faith and love' (*Trall.* 8. 1). Above all, the eucharist is the bond which expresses and creates unity in the Church. Therefore one must not absent oneself from 'the bread of God' in the eucharist celebrated by the bishop, presbyters, and deacons.

The devil's masterpiece being the sowing of division and strife among believers, the united prayer of a community where there is concord destroys Satan's power. So the bishop, with the clergy who are at one with him, is sent by God to the Church to preserve unity. There is one temple, one altar (*Magn.* 7. 1).

Disunity is the consequence when the bishop is ignored, when baptism is given without his knowledge, when the eucharist is celebrated in separation from him. Without the bishop, or at least the bishop's knowledge, a eucharist lacks validity (*Magn.* 4; *Sm.* 8). Ignatius' pained language here points to the conclusion that there were groups consciously asserting their independence. He also mentions some who nominally acknowledged the bishop's title and authority, but in practice took no notice whatever of him and his clergy (*Magn.* 4). 'To do anything in the Church without the knowledge of the bishop is to do the Devil's work' (*Sm.* 9).

For Ignatius experience had shown that agreement among believers was not achieved simply by shared propositions about beliefs; it also required a common recognition of episcopal authority.

Ignatius uses sacrificial language for the eucharist but, for the minister, he never uses the term *hiereús*, priest. On the other hand such language was not far distant. As early as the Didache, the congregation was exhorted to support its prophets 'for they are your high priests', and the eucharist is there declared to realize fulfilment of Malachi's prophecy (1: 11) of sacrifices being offered to God by all nations from east to west.

Ignatius does not use the term 'laity', though had he known the first epistle of Clement he might have found the term conveniently provided with precedent. The priesthood of the whole Church 'as one person' would be stressed by Justin in the *Dialogue with Trypho* (116. 3): they are the 'high-priestly race' offering pure sacrifices as prophesied by Malachi. 'And God accepts sacrifices from no one other than his priests.'

By 200 it was explicit, in the *Apostolic Tradition* of Hippolytus and certainly representing the usage of the Roman community, that the bishop is the high priest, presiding over the sacrifice of the Church.

Bishops

Ignatius is the earliest writer to use the phrase 'the catholic Church,' in a context where he is saying that what the bishop is to a local congregation, Christ is to 'the whole' (*Sm.* 8. 2). The term 'catholic' does not yet carry the sense of 'orthodox' or 'universal' in geographical extension. The point is intrinsic indivisibility.

Ignatius is not the earliest writer to use the three titles for ministers, bishop, presbyter, deacon. The Pastoral Epistles to Timothy and Titus (of uncertain date, perhaps fairly close to Ignatius' time at Antioch) have the titles; but there is an uncertainty about the relation of bishop and presbyter. On the one hand, the two titles seem to be applicable to the same people; in other words, there are two principal ministerial orders or functions, presbyter-bishops and their deacon-assistants (as in Phil. 1: 1). On the other hand, in the Pastoral Epistles presbyters appear in the plural, the bishop in the singular. So perhaps there were churches where 'bishop' was becoming the title for one of the senior presbyters with a wider responsibility to be 'overseer' or general 'superintendent'.

In Ignatius' letters there is not the least doubt about the situation. He assumes throughout that in Syria and Asia Minor there is but one bishop in a given city, whose position in relation to his fellow-presbyters is in some degree pre-eminent, because he is in an exceptional degree the representative of the entire local Christian community (*Trall.* 1). Sources of information about the development of the churches in Syria and Asia Minor in the last quarter of the first century are so few as to make it impossible to say that Ignatius was recording a new or even a recent shift. It could have been the structure accepted there for a generation past, but the independent spirit which created problems for Ignatius was no doubt fed by a memory of how in some places things had at one time been done. The seven letters make it obvious that Ignatius never imagined himself to be creating a new ordering of ministry in the churches he was writing to. And at no city was he aware of the existence of more than one person exercising episcopal oversight, though this bishop was not isolated from his presbyters and deacons.

The qualities which Ignatius required in a bishop included firmness, patience, and gentleness (*Philad.* 1. 2). If a bishop were to be silent (presumably in contexts when his people expected utterance, perhaps of charismatic words), that silence was to be specially respected, for it has its counterpart in the divine Monarch whom he represents to his people (*Eph.* 5. 3; 15; *Philad.* 1. 1). In God silence is part of his majesty (*Magn.* 8. 2). The bishop, however, is not a lonely figure. Always he has with him presbyters and deacons. The presbyters represent the college of apostles. The deacons embody filial obedience serving the mysteries of Christ in which they are not mere ministers distributing food and drink (an instructive reference to the social role of clergy) but servants of the Church of God (*Trall.* 2. 3). In their obedience they represent the obedience of Jesus Christ, and should be respected by all (*Trall.* 3. 1). They assist the bishop in charitable disbursements.

The authority of an Ignatian bishop does not depend, however, on his personal qualities so much as on his office, and to submit to his authority is to submit not to him but to the Father of Jesus Christ the bishop of all (*Magn.* 3. 1). Those with him are assured of union with Christ and the Father (*Eph.* 5. 1). So all bishops throughout the world are in the mind of Christ (*Eph.* 3. 2). Ignatius here betrays a kind of awareness that an individual isolated bishop is no sufficient guarantee of authenticity, and that a bishop can perform his function only by sharing in the universal communion.

The letters speak with such a *fortissimo* about the importance of episcopal oversight in securing the coherence of the Church that the mistaken impression might be received of a man consumed with self-assertion. In fact he was concerned not for himself (except to the extent that he longed to be allowed the heavenly crown of the martyrs), but for the unity which the monarchical bishop existed to maintain. 'I do not give you orders,' he told the church at Ephesus, 'I speak to you as a fellow learner.' Similarly to the Christians at Tralles, 'I do not give you orders like an apostle.' Rome's dignity in the possession of commands received from Peter and Paul made it especially necessary to give that church no kind of instruction or command. In regard to himself, a lengthy catalogue of abusive and derogatory self-designations could be compiled from the seven letters.

Synagogues had a body of elders, but also had one officer with the title 'ruler of the synagogue', *archisynágogos*. It would not have seemed strange if the Gentile missionary churches quickly developed a ministerial structure in which one of the presbyters had some special degree of authority. At Jerusalem in the earliest Christian generation James the Lord's brother exercised powers of leadership. But the probability is that different regions varied in the pace at which they established a single president exercising permanent functions and superior oversight in relation to teaching, preaching, and the dispensing of the sacraments. By the second half of the second century this arrangement had become universal, but in the time of Clement of Rome and of Ignatius there are likely to have been local variations. The link explicit in Ignatius between the centralizing of authority in the bishop and the conflict with heresy offers an obvious context. But the Churches of, say, AD 100 were not all monochrome or standardized in their catechism. In some cities it may well have been the case that the 'monarchical' bishop was leader of a particular group which was not the majority in the local community. (This was the experience of Augustine of Hippo when he first became bishop there in 395–6.)

The formation of the firm ministerial structure was regarded by Ignatius as necessary for the coherence and survival of the Churches if they were to constitute a true fellowship with mutual support and exchange of gifts. Without bishops corresponding with one another by frequent letters of encouragement, visiting each other's congregations, especially when they came together for the installation of a new bishop, thereby sealing the assurance that the new bishop was a member of a much wider body which gave him and his people an indispensable validity, the very survival of Christianity would have been uncertain and precarious.

Influential Roman Christians

Nevertheless, what seemed self-evident to the 'bishop of Syria', as he called himself, may not have been so clear further west. In his letter to the Roman Church Ignatius names no bishop, not even a senior presbyter or body of presbyters. In striking contrast to Ignatius' other letters, his letter to Rome is the only one of the seven documents which fails to admonish the clergy and people to hold their bishop in greater honour and awe, or indeed to suggest respects in which their faith and way of life might possibly be capable of correction and improvement. He may have felt such exhortation superfluous. No letter is so full of flattery and praise for the distinction of the community being addressed: This is the Church which 'presides over love in the region of the Romans', is wholly devoted to the faithful keeping of the Lord's commandments, is determined not to betray the grace granted to them, and knows how to deal with the least taint of corruption, 'filtering out all alien colours' from the wine. To a church which once received commands from the apostles Peter and Paul, anything resembling an order or moral uplift from a humble bishop from Syria would be an impertinence. His one petition to this august body, so generous in giving instruction to other churches, is that they should please not use their potent influence to intercede with the effect of depriving him of his martyrdom. Ignatius is not particularly addressing Roman clergy.

His fear that some distinguished Roman Christians might well provide the *douceurs* needed to secure his release from the beasts in the amphitheatre was not utterly unreal, and is illuminated by a law in the *Digest* (48. 19. 31) directing that prisoners condemned to the beasts are not to be released as a special favour to anyone—a provision which shows it had been happening.

Ignatius' plea would make no sense, however, unless there was some penetration by Christianity into the circle of senators or their wives with access to the emperor and his close advisors. There is no ground for thinking that could not have occurred by AD 107 or 117.

So Ignatius' concern is that influential lay people will act with highminded motives with consequences that would take away his crown. The Roman

presbyters or their bishops and deacons do not enter into consideration, not
even as intercessors with the Lord on behalf of the courageous prisoner. From
the silence about Roman clergy the conclusion has sometimes been drawn
that at Rome before the middle of the second century there was no cleric
with the title and office of bishop, and no one who under some other title
exercised centralizing powers comparable to those which Ignatius was asserting for himself and his colleagues in Asia Minor. The conclusion would not
be safe on the basis of Ignatius' letter. His letter to Rome is not the only one
of the seven not to name the bishop of the community being addressed.
Writing to Smyrna, he exhorts the people to obey their bishop, but never
mentions his identity—Polycarp. Polycarp received an entirely separate personal letter. A safer ground for the judgement that Rome had not yet
acquired a concentration of authority in one man may be found in the language of the *Shepherd* of Hermas, a certainly Roman document, the material in which could well be assigned to the earliest years of the second century.
One of several papyrus fragments containing parts of the *Shepherd* which are
assigned to the second century by experts in ancient handwriting, is
confidently ascribed to the first half of the century, perhaps early in this
period.[10]

   In the *Shepherd* the clergy in authority at Rome are collectively the presbyters (Vision II 2. 6; III 9. 7–8); they 'preside over the Church'. The title
'bishops' is also used, significantly in the plural (Vision III 5. 1; Similitude
IX 27. 2). Rome being a large city, there would have been different house-
churches in different parts of the town, each with its own presbyter. But there
is strong consciousness in Hermas that at Rome he knows of only one
Church (admittedly at one point seen as a visionary lady resembling the
Sibyl). That consciousness sooner or later would encourage the development
of a single bishop with some oversight in relation to the other presbyters. It
would also be stimulated by the struggle to define orthodoxy against gnostic
heresy and Marcion, and by the controversy directly attested in Hermas
between laxist teachers too indulgent (in Hermas' opinion) to those sinning
after baptism and rigorists denying any possibility of restoration after the
once-for-all remission of baptism (cf. Heb. 6: 4). Hermas himself adopted a
via media between the contending factions, proclaiming a special revelation
that penitence was possible but only immediately, not in the long term or for
the rest of life; and the opportunity would soon pass. Consistency in the

---

[10] An ancient list of authoritative books of the New Testament age is preserved in a seventh- or
eighth-century manuscript found by L. A. Muratori (1740) in the Ambrosian library, Milan. The
list's date is disputed. It is certain that the anonymous author was opposing the widespread second-
century view that Hermas was inspired prophecy, claiming that Hermas' brother was Bishop Pius
of Rome (*c.* 140–*c.* 154) and therefore more recent than other books in his list. The list's hostility to
Montanists shows that its date is unlikely to be before 200–20.

terms of reconciliation of penitence was difficult to achieve unless there was both a consensus and a single organ of authority to see that it was implemented.

Harassment by the government could not have encouraged in Ignatius an optimistic estimate of the empire and its rulers. While he could have echoed Clement of Rome's prayer that the rulers might be granted wisdom and mercy (both rare qualities), he would probably not have felt high hopes of realization. 'The greatness of Christianity is not plausible rhetoric but to be hated by the world' (*Rom.* 3. 3). But he was anxious that the hatred be not greater than was necessary. The source from which the Church grew was the conversion of pagans now hostile. The Ephesians should behave to pagan neighbours in a brotherly manner (*Eph.* 10. 3). Polycarp of Smyrna was not to encourage slaves to suppose that the Church could rightly expend resources on the costly operation of their emancipation (*Pol.* 4. 3); for emancipation entailed a tax of 5 per cent of the slave's value (Epictetus 2. 1. 26). Such action would be regarded by non-Christian slaveowners as socially disruptive, drawing unwelcome attention to the Church as potentially undermining good order in society.

Ignatius' letters give a few indications of the social role that a bishop was expected to fulfil. For protection he was to exhort his people to trust in the protective shield of their baptism. He ought to care for the weak such as widows and slaves.

General use of the common chest needed to be subject to the bishop's authorization. Ignatius had no objection to the manumitting of slaves by individual owners, and such acts were morally meritorious. An extant deed of manumission for a female slave by her Egyptian owner, dated in the year AD 355 (P. Kellis 48, ed. K. A. Worp, Oxford, 1995) records that the owner, a former magistrate, has set her free 'because of his exceptional Christianity'. Synagogues used their common chest for emancipations.[11]

Couples marrying were to make sure of the bishop's approval. Believers dedicating themselves to celibacy should confide in the bishop but not publicise it generally among the community, lest it appear ostentatious (Polycarp 4–5).

It was good that at Tralles even the pagans held the bishop in respect (*Trall.* 3. 2). Trallian Christians should avoid actions that could give offence and even 'cause the heathen to blaspheme' (*Trall.* 8. 2). This text from Isa. 52: 5 was soon to be invoked by Christians so over-anxious not to upset pagan neighbours that they actively participated in pagan festivals, the Saturnalia

---

[11] P. Oxy. IX 1205, dated AD 291. Among studies of ancient slavery see Keith Bradley, *Slavery and Society at Rome* (Cambridge, 1994), and Peter Garnsey, *Ideas of Slavery from Aristotle to Augustine* (Cambridge, 1996).

and New Year (Tertullian attacked them, *Idol.* 14). For centuries to come bishops deplored the inebriation of the feast on 1 January. Ignatius' warning to the Trallians show that, though he himself used language about longing for martyrdom that to modern readers conveys an impression of zeal indistinguishable from irrational fanaticism, he was against suicide martyrs who used insulting gestures towards pagan temples and cult-statues.

Celibacy

A powerful stream of moral opinion within the earliest churches was sympathetic to the widely held ancient view that the physical sexuality of married love was a barrier to the higher spiritual life. While the Old Testament tradition was obviously positive about the good of marriage there were also texts, such as Exod. 19: 15 or 1 Sam. 21: 5, where abstinence is a requirement for access to the holy. Matthew's Gospel (19: 12) preserves a tradition that Jesus spoke without criticism of those who 'made themselves eunuchs for the sake of the kingdom of heaven'. The apostle Paul confronted a group at Corinth who judged conjugal relations incompatible with the life of the Spirit; he met their contention by arguing that while virginity is better, nevertheless marriage is no sin, and married couples had an obligation to meet each other's sexual need; by mutual consent they could for a time abstain to give themselves to prayer; but failure to achieve abstinence would be excusable (1 Cor. 7: 1–6). To the apostle's later readers it became a moot question whether such language was easily compatible with his judgement that marriage and conjugal relations are no sin. Some couples dedicated to the higher life lived together but abstained from sexual contact, thereby demonstrating the spirit's conquest of the flesh.

An anonymous sermon from the early decades of the second century preserved among the writings ascribed to Clement of Rome exhorts a congregation to keep their lives quite separate from the secular world of adultery, avarice, and deceit, to preserve the 'seal' of baptism undefiled, and to practise almsgiving, fasting, and prayer. Christian men should mix with women believers without being aware of their sexuality, and vice versa. The high calling is to sexual abstinence (*enkráteia*). The preacher was opposed to gnostic denial of the resurrection of the body, but welcomed the notion that the true Church is a wholly spiritual body which existed from the beginning of things and became manifest in the incarnate Christ, who is to be held to be God and the judge of living and dead.

How generally the superiority of the celibate ideal was accepted appears again in the Apocalypse of John of Patmos (14: 4), whose vision of 144,000 saints following the Lamb of God included the point that all were 'undefiled with women'.

On the margins of the Church, where gnostic influences could be potent, it easily became a matter of principle that authentic aspirers to the spiritual life would reject marriage, and this proposition became controversial (Col. 2: 22–3). Vehement opposition to it appears in 1 Tim. 4: 3.

Pliny

Ignatius' letters are rather surprisingly silent about Christians who simply lapsed and reverted to a pagan way of life and perhaps worship. In Bithynia (Asia Minor) in Ignatius' time the governor Pliny attempted, not without success, to stem an exodus from pagan temples and festivals caused by the success of a Christian mission in his province. He knew, though aware of no legal enactment, that by precedent Christians were to be arrested and after trial executed for their profession. Those who were Roman citizens he sent to Rome. But there was a problem for him in an apparently substantial number who admitted to have been Christians in the past but who had lapsed. He therefore wrote to the emperor Trajan suggesting that the lapsed could be released, and won the emperor's assent to this policy.

Pliny was not the only provincial governor to ask his emperor for guidance on procedure in dealing with Christians. The lawyer Ulpian is recorded by Lactantius (*Inst.* 5. 11. 19) to have compiled relevant rulings, all of which were emperors' replies to governors' queries.

Pliny's investigations elicited an important fact about Christians. They were very unwilling to offer sacrifice even in the apparently innocuous form of burning a little incense. That was to become the standard test of allegiance to the gods of the empire.

The upshot of the correspondence between Pliny and Trajan was that Christians were to be persecuted not for what they had done but for what they now were, with the proviso that they would be acquitted if they could show themselves no longer to be adherents by offering sacrifice in honour of the emperor and/or the gods of Rome.

IO

DIDACHE[1]

'Honour the pastor who teaches you the word of God as if he were the Lord himself.' 'Give high priority to the unity of the Church and to reconciling those groups which are inclined to schism.' These sentiments are found not only in Ignatius of Antioch but in a contemporary milieu presupposed by an even more unusual early Christian document, the *Didaché* or 'Teaching of the Twelve Apostles'. The full Greek text of this document was first recovered at Istanbul in 1873 and printed ten years later. The manuscript is now at the Greek patriarchate in Jerusalem. Its interpretation, date and region of origin are not simple to determine; Syria is a probable milieu, the city of Antioch not impossible.

The compiler of the Didache wished to write in the name of the apostles for the Church of his own day. With the conviction that the Church of the apostolic age embodied a purity of belief and practice that was coming under threat in his own time, the Didachist put together older pieces probably originating a generation before. The compiler's central concerns were for the proper morality of Christian behaviour, for due apostolic order in prayer, baptism, and eucharist, and for respect towards the resident local ministry now mainly being exercised by bishops and deacons but still finding rivalry in itinerant charismatics. The Didachist was much aware that among the wandering prophets and teachers there were numerous frauds battening on gullible congregations to raise funds to feather their own nests.

Morality is put in the first and most urgent place. The Didache incorporates a version of the originally Jewish catechism 'The Two Ways', lightly christianized (more so than the version in the epistle of Barnabas). Abstention from meat that had been offered in pagan sacrifice is an unqualified requirement in all circumstances—an edict which differs from the Pauline position stated in 1 Corinthians 8, of which the author may have been ignorant. Aphorisms from the Sermon on the Mount are joined with exhortations to avoid pride, lust, divination, magic, astrology, lying, theft,

[1] On Didache see J. P. Audet (1958) and K. Niederwimmer, 2nd edn. (Göttingen, 1993), Eng. tr. Minneapolis 1992 of first edn. Possibly the Didachist led a faction opposed by Ignatius: C. N. Jefford in *Studia Patristica* 36 (Leuven, 2001), 262–9.

avarice, meanness in alms, abortion, sodomy, and all malice. 'If the whole yoke of the Lord is too much, bear as much of it as possible.' The Didachist was anxious that his people should have no compromise with idolatry.

The compiler of the Didache shows no knowledge of any letters by the apostle Paul or of any characteristic theme of the apostle's understanding of the work of God in and through Christ. His community was one of converted Jews, determined to keep the Mosaic law with the minimum of compromise, but convinced that Jesus was the Anointed of God. A tradition of the sayings of Jesus closely akin, but not wholly identical, with some of the material in St Matthew's Gospel was known to him; he and his community had access to one of the sources that was drawn upon by Matthew. Of St Mark's Gospel he shows no knowledge.

His community was suffering harassment since he speaks of 'those who endure in the faith' and, in a cryptic phrase, declares that such believers 'will be saved by the Curse itself'—a phrase which may presuppose defiance of the thesis that, by Deut. 21. 23, a crucified person lies under a curse (above p. 17). Both Paul (Gal. 3: 13) and Justin (*Dial.* 111. 2) sought to combat the thesis. The community for which the Didache was composed was certainly in a state of tension with the Synagogue, a fact which shows that the split between Church and Synagogue cannot be attributed entirely to the actions and theology of the apostle Paul and his Gentile mission, with which the Didache seems to have no contact.

The Didachist used an archaic liturgical manual. He prescribes the correct procedure for baptism. The candidate first fasts for one or two days. An absolute requirement is that baptism is to be given in the name of Father, Son, and Holy Spirit, that is 'into the name of the Lord', and must use water. It is indifferent whether the water is cold or warm or whether it is applied by immersing the candidate or by pouring the water on his or her head. (A similar freedom would be later affirmed by Tertullian, *On Baptism* 4. 3 and in the *Apostolic Tradition* of Hippolytus, *Apost. trad.* 21.) As at the synagogue Christians should keep a fast for two days a week, but not on the synagogue's days, Monday and Thursday. The correct fast days are Wednesday and Friday. The Lord's Prayer is to be said three times a day. The Didache gives the form of text in Matthew's Gospel with the doxology at the end.

At the eucharistic thanksgiving only the baptized may receive the consecrated cup and bread. The blessing of the cup surprisingly precedes that of the broken bread (as in one form of text in Luke's account of the Last Supper). Specimen forms of prayer are given for blessing the two elements, closely akin to Jewish liturgical prayers.

The assembly is to meet weekly on the Lord's Day and, after confession of sins and the reconciliation of any quarrelling members, the Thanksgiving is celebrated. This, the Church must realize, is the worldwide sacrifice prophesied by Malachi (1: 7); i.e. the assembly must not suppose that their worship of God is a local and domestic affair without essential links to a universal offering. Moreover, the assembly particularly prays that 'as the broken bread was scattered upon the mountains but was brought together and made one, so may your Church be gathered together from the ends of the earth into your kingdom.' The Church is to pray that the entire body may be kept from evil, be perfected in love, and be gathered in holiness 'from the four winds' (Matt. 24: 31).

The Coptic version of the Didache preserves an ancient prayer which the Jerusalem manuscript and dependent church orders lost, namely a thanksgiving for incense being burned at the communal meal.

The language presupposes that the prayer which the Church is offering is expressing a unity not only with other congregations of living believers elsewhere in the empire, but with all Christians living and departed.

To provide pastors to preside at these functions, the congregation is told to appoint bishops and deacons, and is pointedly told not to look down on them as if they must be inferior to the itinerant prophets and teachers whose role seemed more charismatic and exciting, but whose specific calling was to travel about from church to church, not to provide a continuous and permanent pastorate. The author of the Didache was clearly conscious that in the first age of the Church the Christians had not immediately developed a lasting structure for their pastors. The epistle to the Hebrews thought it necessary to tell the recipients of the letter that Christians ought to be obedient to the authority of those appointed to preside over the community and added that the pastors had a solemn responsibility and would have to give account before God (13: 17). Resident pastors to whose appointment the congregation had assented needed to be respected if the coherence of the community was to be maintained. The author of the Didache was clearly aware of communities where a state nearer to the kind of anarchy described by Paul as prevailing at Corinth was normal, and where charismatic excitement was valued more than the week-by-week ministry of word and sacrament.

These Churches needed to be warned by the author of the Didache to be on their guard against fraudsters and confidence-men among the itinerant teachers and charismatic prophets who travelled from church to church living on the alms and food of the host community. Some of them were in the business of purveying heresy. Visiting prophets might simply be in search of free board and lodging. One could be sure that an itinerant charismatic prophet must be a fraud if he asked leave to stay more than two days or if, having ordered a meal when in a state of possession by the Spirit, he proceeded to consume it himself. Likewise a travelling 'apostle' who made a request for financial support could be known thereby to be a fraud. As in Paul (1 Corinthians 9), this was controversial.

However, the testing of spirits, once commended by Paul (1 Thess. 5: 21), might be a matter of delicacy. So the Didache exempts from human scrutiny a prophet who 'acts out a cosmic mystery of the Church, and then does not teach others to do what he has done.' The sentence is obscure in its reference, but might be explained from the language used in the Didache's eucharistic blessings about the Church being gathered from the four winds or from the ends of the earth, since that presupposes a conception of the Church which transcends the empirical gathering of little assemblies on earth. The Church in the Didache is an entity on a cosmic scale, and it might well require an inspired teacher to find words to give that proper expression.

The last section of the Didache contains an apocalyptic warning of an imminent antichrist figure, followed by the second coming of the Lord on the clouds.

The Didachist allows for the possibility that a true prophet may come and settle more or less permanently with a congregation. A true prophet is entitled to the support of the people, receiving the first-fruit of the vintage and the corn and even of the beasts. Such true prophets 'are your high priests' (13: 3). The prophets are also given freedom to celebrate the eucharist as they think right (10: 7). The Didachist, and probably his source, thought of the eucharistic president as exercising pastoral and priestly functions. In Ignatius the bishop's action when celebrating the eucharist is described as a sacrifice, but the term *hiereús*, normal word for a pagan or Jewish priest, is not found used of a Christian minister in the New Testament writings, other than of Christ. In the first epistle of Peter Christ is also the one shepherd or pastor. The Christian minister, insofar as he exercises either pastoral or priestly functions, acts only as representing Christ, not independently.

When with Tertullian the Church first began to speak in Latin, it was natural to use the word *sacerdos* to refer to the president of the assembly, the bishop. In the *Apostolic Tradition* of Hippolytus (3) priestly language is found in the rite for ordaining a bishop. His people understood him to be their intercessor with God, and soon they would rely on him to be their intercessor with secular authorities who, in turn, would come to expect the bishops to teach morality, loyalty in paying taxes, stability in marriage and family life.

Because the primitive Church was setting itself free from the ordered structures of the Synagogue and from the professional authority of interpreters of the Mosaic Law, and because of the emphasis on 'freedom' in the teaching of the apostle Paul, a tendency was apparent to rely on authorities that did not derive their standing from tradition or from ordinary forms of legitimation. It was simpler to look to personal and special gifts of the Spirit, which at Corinth (in the manner of some highly regarded pagan oracles) took the form of 'speaking with tongues', i.e. unintelligible ecstatic utterance which then needed to be interpreted before it could be a source of edification. Yet at Corinth itself a group invoked Peter, leader among the Twelve, for their direction and guidance, and implied that direct commission from the Lord in the days of his ministry before the Passion was a source of authority superior to immediate inspiration. An inherent tension lay near the historic roots of Christianity between the derivation of supreme authority from the Jesus of history and his sending out of the apostles, and, on the other hand, from the immediacy of the Holy Spirit.

The importance of the Didache, apart from its antiquity and its position as the earliest surviving church order, lies in its witness to a very early attempt at reconciling this tension.

II

MARCION

The apostle Paul insisted on the utter newness of what God had done in Christ (e.g. 2 Cor. 5: 17). A reader of Galatians 4. 24–6 would naturally deduce that the Mosaic law was a bondage into which no Gentile Christian, perhaps not even Jewish Christians, ought to be tied. Freedom from that law was a priceless gift of Christ in response to faith. By faith Gentile believers had deliverance from the 'elements of the world', the planetary powers of fate which also determined when Jewish feasts, such as new moon, were celebrated. If they listened to teachers telling them now to observe circumcision, sabbaths, and Jewish feasts, they would be returning to bondage (Gal. 4: 9). Such utterances could easily produce a radicalized Paulinism which put a negative interpretation on the Old Testament.

A root-and-branch separation of old and new was proclaimed about 140 at Rome by Marcion, a shipmaster from Pontus on the Black Sea coast, who was struck by the partly gnostic ideas of a certain Cerdo. Marcion was disturbed by the problem of evil in a world said to be created by a God wholly good, all-powerful, and possessing foreknowledge, who must have known that human nature would lapse into sin. If this fall could have been simply averted by the intervention of divine grace and that grace was withheld, does not the God who failed to give help bear ultimate responsibility? Marcion further reasoned that an environment containing scorpions and other noxious insects or poisonous plants must reflect some deficiency of goodness in its Maker. And then the sexuality of the animal and human parts of creation seemed particularly repulsive and humiliating.

These shortcomings discerned in nature and in human society appeared to Marcion strikingly similar to the moral imperfections of the God of the Jews who in their scriptures is revealed to be the Creator of this unhappy world. Marcion saw the God of the old covenant as a stern judge severely punishing transgressions of the Mosaic Law even for trivial matters, contrasting with the kindness and mercy of the God revealed in Jesus. Paul had taught that love transcended law, goodness was more than strict justice. Marcion drew a drastic conclusion: the Creator-god who gave the Law is inferior to a higher, supreme God of goodness and love first revealed by and incarnate in Jesus. The Creator was indeed divine, but far from supreme. Gnostic teachers liked to quote Isa. 45: 7 'I am the Lord, there is none beside me: I am the one who creates evil.' They attributed these words to the creator Ialdabaoth who was deficient in competence and good will. Marcion called the merciful kind deity, above and unknown to this Creator, 'the Stranger', and Marcionite believers were to live as aliens in the dark world of law. Granted that the Creator and his people had rational natural virtues, their moral standards were well below those of the 'strangers', the Marcionites, who were strongly ascetic towards the physical world. They were to abhor civic entertainments, the savagery of the amphitheatre, the low eroticism of theatre and music-hall, above all polytheistic cult. Only celibates or eunuchs or dedicated widows could be admitted to Marcionite baptism. Their rejection of secular society and its gods produced martyrs.

Revulsion from the physical world manifested redemption from the realm of the Creator. Marcion could see no good purpose served by the natural world with its mosquitoes and midges and gnats and snake-bites. Moreover, childbirth was painful, pregnancy nauseating, sexual intercourse undignified and revolting; it was inconceivable that Jesus could have been born of Mary. With appeals to Luke 4: 30 and Rom. 8: 3 ('the likeness of sinful flesh'), Marcion declared that the body of Jesus was an optical illusion. Yet his death on the cross 'paid our debt' to the just Creator at the purchase price.

The Stranger 'constrains us to conquer in the region of evil and in the body of sin.'

Important for Marcion was the saying of Jesus that new wine had to be kept in new wineskins (Luke 5: 36). He wholly rejected all claims that the Old Testament was susceptible of Christian interpretation. Prophets such as Isaiah looked forward to a Messiah, but by that they meant a national military leader which Jesus obviously was not. The prophets' concern was for a leader who would unite the dispersed Jews. No prophet of the Creator's tradition foretold a crucified Messiah. The Hebrew word Emmanuel, 'God with us', cannot be a proper title for the Redeemer.

So the values of the Hebrew scriptures were to be stood on their head. The serpent in Eden, Cain, and the people of Sodom were redeemed by the Stranger in Jesus from the Creator's condemnation, whereas for the Creator's heroes like Enoch, Noah, the patriarchs and prophets, the Stranger could do nothing.

In the natural humanity formed by the Creator there can be no divine spark, since Adam was made in his image and likeness and, at the insufflation of Gen. 2: 7, received the Creator's bad breath into his lungs. So the human soul installed by the Creator is no less evil than the body in which it dwells.

Tertullian records that, in Marcion's writings, astrology played a part; but no specimen survives to make a judgement possible. Marcion diverged sharply from ordinary gnosticism by having no mythology about a primaeval cosmic conflict between good and evil angels ending in the incarceration of some element of the supreme Stranger in the Creator's handiwork. In his radicalized Paulinism the entire human race is by nature alien from the commonwealth of God. Marcion's strong doctrine of total depravity was abandoned by his pupil Apelles, who affirmed the soul to be of celestial origin, imprisoned in flesh.

To Marcion's thesis there was a sharp negative reaction in the Church. So Marcion developed his theme of the contradiction between old and new covenants by compiling a book entitled *Antitheses* (a gnostic thesis, 1 Tim. 6: 20). The opening paragraph enunciated the basic exegetical principle of an absolute contrast between law and gospel. Included were instances of inconsistency and infirmity of purpose in a Creator who could forbid images but then order the making of the brazen serpent; could prohibit all work on the sabbath but then order an eight days march round Jericho. He could advise the Hebrews to steal Egyptian gold and silver; as if ignorant he could ask Adam where he was, and had to send to find out what precise state of vice was prevalent at Sodom and Gomorrah. At the making of the golden calf he simply lost his temper and had to be tranquillized by Moses' intercessions. This catalogue of contradictions was perhaps more impressive in the second century than in modern times. Leviticus (15: 19 ff.) forbids touching a woman suffering a flow of menstrual blood, whereas Jesus (Luke 6: 43–8) broke this law by healing a woman in this condition. Jesus loved little children, whereas the Creator-god sent bears to avenge children's mockery of the bald prophet Elisha. And how deeply did Jesus 'hate' the sabbath and break it! He forbade the calling down of fire from heaven to consume opponents, whereas that was precisely what Elijah had done.

Marcion judged it unimaginable that Jesus could really have said that he had come not to destroy but to fulfil the Law. His exegesis of the Old Testament inevitably required a rewriting of substantial parts of the Christian documents which were in process of becoming treated not merely as a record of the apostolic testimony but as a normative guide to the authentic gospel. Many of these texts presupposed continuity with the old covenant and assumed that the coming of Jesus the expected Messiah was a fulfilment of aspirations in the ancient prophets; even the Law was treated already by St Paul as a charter for the universal extension of the gospel in the Gentile world. A few stories current in the gospel tradition could suggest that the Twelve had failed to understand Jesus' intention. The apostle Paul in the letter to the Galatians complained of teachers who wanted to impose Judaistic customs on Gentile believers, and to Marcion it seemed clear that these Judaizers had interpolated the epistles. Accordingly Marcion produced a canon or list of approved texts, consisting of ten Pauline letters in the order: Galatians, 1 and 2 Corinthians, Romans (chs. 1–14 only),

1 and 2 Thessalonians, 'Laodiceans' (i.e. Ephesians), Colossians, Philippians, Philemon. A few manuscripts of the Old Latin version also give Ephesians the title Laodiceans, and there are also manuscripts which likewise attest a text of Romans which had lost the last two chapters, probably by an early accident in transmission. The form of the Pauline corpus which Marcion received did not include Hebrews or the Pastoral epistles to Timothy and Titus. For the Gospel he decided for one rather than four, and this was an expurgated edition of Luke, behind whose pen Marcionites believed to be the mind of Paul himself.

Marcion did not eliminate all references to the Old Testament in early Christian writings, but he removed references to Abraham as Judaizing interpolations in Romans and Galatians, and to Christ's flesh in Colossians and Ephesians. His method was to give Old Testament references a negative significance.

JUSTIN

Marcion's rejection of the unity and coherence of Old and New Testaments entailed abandonment of the contention that ancient prophecies were fulfilled in Christ and his Church. That contention was important in the conversion of Justin. He was born to Gentile parents in Samaritan territory at Nablus (Neapolis), and travelled in search of philosophical education. He claimed to have sat at the feet of a Stoic, a Peripatetic who disappointed him by concern for his fee (this was a cliché about Aristotelian tutors), and a Pythagorean who expected him to have mastered arithmetic, geometry, music, and astronomy so as to grasp immaterial truths. It was a search for truth in the soul, and of the various schools of philosophy the Platonists had most to offer by way of a religious quest. Plato's *Phaedrus* held up the goal of a celestial vision of God. But Justin was persuaded to abandon Platonism by a seashore conversation with an old man who told him about the Hebrew prophets and the fulfilment of their predictions in Jesus' virgin birth, incarnation, passion, descent to Hades, ascension and 'Son of God' title. Since a substantial part of New Testament Christology was formulated in terms derived from the Old Testament, the argument had force. The old man also deployed Aristotle's arguments against Platonism.

Justin remained positive towards Platonism, 'not radically different from Christianity but not quite the same' (*Apol. II* 13). He believed the thesis of earlier Jewish argument that Plato had studied the writings of Moses, especially Genesis 1, in composing his *Timaeus*. Moreover the Platonic theodicy which attributed responsibility for evil to free choices by rational beings Justin welcomed as derived from Moses (*Apol. I* 44). Greek philosophers derived from the prophets their true ideas of the soul's immortality and judgement hereafter, A foreshadowing of the insight that in God there is a threeness is evident in Plato's second letter. In classical philosophical schools there are 'seeds of truth, sent down to humanity' (*Dial.* 2. 1; *Apol. II* 8), but not in the hedonism of Epicurus. Socrates, Heraclitus, and the Stoic Musonius Rufus exiled under Nero were martyrs for truth. Jesus's parable of the sower could be applied to the seeds of philosophical truth scattered along the wayside by providence.

Of the superiority of Christ's ethical teaching Justin was confident, though aware that some could think it impracticable (*Dialogue* 10). Lustful eyes and remarriage after divorce were censored by Jesus. Numerous Christians were living celibate lives throughout their time. Justin never suggests that Christians have a monopoly of virtue. Observant Jews who keep the law of Moses live good lives (*Dial.* 45. 3). They will be saved if they come to acknowledge Jesus to be Messiah before they die (47. 4). Justin several times mentions the pain felt by the prayer inserted late in the first century in the Eighteen Benedictions of the synagogue liturgy: 'For apostates let there be no hope . . . and let the Nazarenes (*notzrim*) and the heretics (*minim*) perish. Let them be wiped out of the book of life . . .'. (text preserved in the Babylonian Talmud, *Berakoth* 29a). This was placing Christians, both Jewish and Gentile, under a curse.

Justin probably had a book of 'Testimonies' or fulfilled prophecies, including texts not found in scripture which he supposed Jews had suppressed, e.g. a Christian interpolation in Psalm 95 'The Lord reigns *from the tree*', which had a long future to the famous hymn 'Vexilla Regis' of Venantius Fortunatus and much later. This and other like insertions are met in both Justin and Irenaeus. Otherwise Justin carefully avoided appealing to texts not admitted by the Synagogue to be canonical, and is a crucial witness to the notion in his time of a canon of the Hebrew scriptures. An important exception for him was Isa. 7: 14, where the Septuagint's 'virgin' translated the Hebrew word for 'young woman'. Justin judged the Septuagint version correct on the ground that the birth is said by the Hebrew prophet to be a miraculous 'sign' which could not be true of a woman not a virgin.

Justin addressed a vindication of Christianity to the emperor Antoninus Pius and the Roman senate and a later short supplement to Antoninus Pius and Marcus Aurelius (*Apol. II* 2, 16). The two Apologies are interconnected, the shorter text containing references back to the longer piece. In addition, a few years later, he composed a *Dialogue* with a Jew named Trypho, a refugee from Bar Cocheba's messianic revolt of 133–5, which severely harassed Christian Jews and resulted in Hadrian's decree excluding all circumcised persons from Jerusalem, replaced by Aelia Capitolina (*Dial.* 16. 17; *Apol. I* 47). The *Dialogue* shares many concerns apparent in the two Apologies, but is more directly concerned with the fulfilment of prophecies. It is a major source on the mid-second century relation between Church and Synagogue, and illustrates the sense in which early Gentile Christianity was stamped by its need to define itself in contrast with the observant synagogue where circumcision, sabbaths, and new moons were necessary. The *Dialogue* attests numerous Jews who recognized Jesus as Messiah and adhered to the observances of the Mosaic Law; to a Gentile believer such as Justin this was acceptable provided they did not insist on observance by Gentiles. Justin portrays in Trypho a benevolent inquirer, sympathetic to much that he says, and delighted by assertions of the verbal inspiration of the Hebrew scriptures which both read in the Greek version of the Septuagint.[1] With Trypho, however, are his friends who are less amenable and at moments treat Justin with mockery. Possibly they represent the standpoint of Gentiles attached to the synagogue, resentful of the Church carrying off proselytes. Justin (122. 2) records that Gentile proselytes attached to the synagogues were far more hostile to the Church than observant Jews.

He strongly disowns heretics such as Valentinus, Basilides, Satornilus, Simon Magus dominant at Samaria, a magician at Antioch named Menander, and especially Marcion (*Apol. I* 16; *Dial.* 35. 6). He is decisively against 'docetism' and gnostic determinism. He puts repeated stress on freedom of choice given by the Creator's endowment to both angels and men, the fall of angels being important to his theodicy as explaining evil. Once in defending King David's fall with Bathsheba as being his only grave lapse, he argues that David's restoration is a refutation of determinism (*Dial.* 141. 3–4). An interpretation of Christ from which he distances himself is that Jesus was a human being of such perfect virtue that at baptism he was adopted as Son of God. He judged that incompatible with the adoration of the infant Christ by the Magi. Trypho could not accept a Messiah as a pre-existent being born of a Virgin. He has no difficulty about messianic hope: 'All Jews expect Messiah, and refer to him the biblical texts cited by Justin' (89). 'But if Messiah is or has been, he is unknown and is himself unaware of his nature until he is awakened by the coming of Elijah' (*Dial.* 8. 3; 110. 2; cf. Matt. 11: 14; 17: 10; Babylonian Talmud Sanhedrin 98ab).

A significant point new in Justin is a repeated suggestion that for correctly interpreting the Old Testament one needs to recognize that sentences have to be ascribed to different speakers, e.g. the Father and the divine Logos (*Apol. I* 36. 2; 53. 3). The theme became important for Tertullian and later writers. The terminology (*prosopon*) influenced elucidations of the triadic doctrine of God (Cf. *Apol. I* 36. 2ff.; *Dial.* 25. 1, 42. 2–3; 88. 8).

A major theme for Justin is the demonstration that the God appearing in the theophanies of the Old Testament, as for example at the Burning Bush to Moses, cannot be the supreme Father of all, who is utterly transcendent, but must be the Son/Logos, who therefore represents divine immanence within the world and is 'a God other in number but not in will', yet as united as sun and sunlight (128).

Philo the Alexandrian Jew had felt no inhibitions when writing of the Word or Logos of God as 'another' or a 'second' God. Texts to that effect would be gratefully cited by Eusebius of Caesarea in his *Preparation of the*

---

[1] Justin used a revised Septuagint for the Twelve (Minor) Prophets, also attested among the Dead Sea Scrolls.

Gospel (7. 15). Justin may not have read Philo directly but very probably had contact with theology in the Greek synagogue.

Justin's Platonist background helped him to show that the 'otherness' of the divine Logos distinct from the Father did not mean a transfer or loss of divinity from the Father. The principle of 'undiminished giving' applied, like a fire lit from a fire in no way reducing the parent blaze (*Dial.* 128. 4, 61. 2). In the *Dialogue* (128) Justin had misgivings about the analogy of sun and sunlight, which in his judgement might not sufficiently stress the otherness of the divine Logos. The argument presupposes that on this subject there was already debate and disagreement.

The short *Second Apology* deploys Justin's positive evaluation of philosophy, partly by pointing to close analogies between Christian beliefs to which pagans objected and familiar positions of Stoics or Platonists. Christians were more homogeneous and united than the philosophical schools. When pagans asked if martyrs were not mere suicides (the emperor Marcus Aurelius was to think them 'theatrical'), Justin could ask if the same was not true of the admired Socrates.

Christian language about the fire of divine wrath was not far from Stoic belief that periodically the cosmos dissolves into fire. Platonists think divine retribution for wickedness is precise and just. Parallels between the Christian story and some ancient myths (e.g. virgin births) he explains as diabolical counterfeits. Pagan cults and myths are all devilish work. Worshippers of Mithras were led by demons to meet in a cave imitating the cave of Bethlehem where Jesus was born (evidently already a pilgrim shrine) and to have a sacred meal of bread and water caricaturing the Christian eucharist. The acts of demons can be discerned in magic, dreams, the Roman prohibition of the Sibyl and of the oracle of Hystaspes. Trypho was unimpressed by the theme of virginal conception for Messiah, and thought Christians ought to be ashamed of a story so close to pagan myths (*Dialogue* 67).

The different philosophical schools have fragmentary aspects of truth, whereas Christ is the divine Logos and mediates the whole truth. Whether in Abraham or in Greek sages, there were 'Christians before Christ'.

Millennium

In discussion with Trypho Justin upholds with determination the notion, not shared by all Christians, that Christ would return to a renewed Jerusalem there to reign with his saints for a thousand years in accordance with the prophecy of John of Patmos. The millenarian expectation picked up older convictions about the centrality of Jerusalem in the messianic age, and the interpretation, found in the book of Jubilees (4: 29–30), that the seven days of creation in Genesis 1 each signify a thousand years, in that with the Lord a day is a thousand years (Ps. 89: 4; 2 Pet. 3: 8). In Luke's gospel, when on his travels Jesus came near Jerusalem, some disciples thought the kingdom of God must be imminent (19: 11). The epistle of 'Barnabas' was sure that the world is to last for 6,000 years since with the Lord a thousand years are one day (15: 8–9).

A belief close to Justin's appears in Irenaeus of Lyon a generation later. For him redemption means the restoration of what was God's will for Adam and Eve before the Fall resulting from their youthful inexperience. Belief in a literal millennium without symbolic interpretation was useful to Justin and Irenaeus by being directly incompatible with gnostic and spiritualizing understandings of language about the end of time. It also had affinity with the motivation of incipient pilgrimage to gospel sites. Millennial expectation and pilgrimage have often been nearly akin in Christian history. According to the calendar calculated by Dionysius Exiguus in the sixth century the great division in the historical process occurred at the time of the incarnation. (Dionysius nowhere explains how he arrived at his date for the incarnation.) This created excitement at the time of the millennium of the incarnation and the passion of Christ, the latter being marked (according to the record of Rodolf Glaber) by a western pilgrimage of huge dimensions to the Holy Land.

Naturally there was an alternative view to the literalism of Justin and Irenaeus, and Justin was well aware that some Christians, not heretics, understood the millennium as symbol. Tertullian in north Africa understood prophecies about a restored Jerusalem to be an allegory of Christ and his Church, yet the incarnate Lord and the Church are historical realities, so that even in this life believers may hope for a new Jerusalem coming from heaven which is a way of talking about the life of the people of God now, not hereafter. Tertullian, much influenced by Justin, understood the millennium, therefore, as a training period making ordinary believers fit for heaven.

In the background of the debate lay argument with learned rabbis who contended that Jesus could not be the expected Messiah because earthly felicity had not arrived. No lions were to be seen lying with lambs and crops were not growing automatically without human agriculture. Above all the Jews' messianic hope was one of national liberation from enemies, though the disastrous consequences of the revolt against Hadrian under Bar Cocheba, who was Messiah to his followers, suggested the contrary.

Justin wrote against a background of persecution of the Christians which he attributed to harassment by the Synagogue, and he himself, a freelance lecturer in Rome, was to die a martyr's death. At the same time martyrs gave thanks to God for their sentence (*Apol. II* 11. 1) to the amazement of pagan listeners. The accusation of 'atheism' meant rejection of polytheism, which was common among philosophers, and the result of persecution was to give the Church the maximum of publicity: 'Persecutions increase the number of Christians' (*Dial.* 110. 4). 'Every day some become disciples' (39. 1). Popular rumours that Christians indulged in cannibalism and sexual orgies after the lights were turned out were believed by some, not by Trypho (10), but were useful (e.g. to Nero) to justify pogroms.

Christian families found that their slaves were tortured until they gave evidence of vicious acts (*Apol. II* 12. 4) . Torture was similarly threatened during persecution at Lyon in 177. The need for such threats is evidence that popular belief in vicious practices was very limited. As governor of Bithynia the younger Pliny was surprised to find that the Christians he subjected to examination and torture did not actually indulge in cannibalism. But Fronto, a pagan contemporary of Justin, is credited (by Minucius Felix, 9. 6) with diffusing the slander. As late as the mid-third century Origen knew virtuous pagans who shunned Christian company. Credibility would have been enhanced by the fact that Jews were commonly accused of ritual murder, a charge which the Jews themselves passed on to smear the Christians according to Origen (*c. Cels.* 6. 27; Josephus, *c. Ap.* ii 89ff.). A macabre scene in a Greek romance, preserved in a papyrus codex of the second century AD at Cologne, describes a comparable ritual.

Both Justin and Trypho concur in the *Dialogue* that the scriptures (i.e. the Old Testament) provide an inspired authority. They differ, however, in the criterion of interpretation. Justin regards rabbinic exegesis as pettifogging, too literalist, anthropomorphic in thinking of God (114. 3), and in effect trivial (112, 115). However, though the principles of exegesis are crucial to the debate between the two positions, Justin cannot achieve consistency himself since he insists that the meaning of the prophets is first made clear by divine grace (92. 1), yet at the same time he wants to say that the scriptures are so clear as to require no commentary (76. 6, 55. 3). Paradoxically 'Jews understand the Hebrew prophets less well than Gentile believers inspired by the Spirit inspiring the prophets' (118. 3, 119. 1). Justin has no New Testament in the sense that Irenaeus a generation later can be said to have one. But once (18. 1) sayings of Jesus are appended as of equal authority to citation from the Hebrew scriptures. He has 'memoirs by the apostles', the Apocalypse of John with belief in the millennium, and probably a book of Testimonies or prophecies fulfilled in the gospel records. The book of Acts was not in his library. The Gospel of John he probably knew, since he writes of the 'Only— begotten Son' (105. 1), the Logos of God.

Justin's best-known text is his description of Christian worship at baptism and the Sunday congregation (*Apol. I* 65–7), designed to demonstrate that these rites are not black magic.

To the assembled people called brethren we bring the believer united to us. We pray for ourselves, for him who has been enlightened, and for all others everywhere that we may learn the truth and be found worthy by good works and keeping the commandments to receive eternal salvation. After prayers we greet each other with a kiss. Then the president of the brethren is given bread and a cup of water and diluted wine, and he takes them and offers praise and glory to the Father of the universe in the name of the Son and of the Holy Spirit and in a long prayer offers thanksgiving (*eucharistia*) to have been counted worthy. His prayer concludes with the people saying Amen, a Hebrew word meaning 'So be it.' After the president has given thanks and all the people have made response, those we call deacons give to each person present a share in the bread and wine and water over which thanksgiving has been said, and they take a share to members not present. This food called 'eucharist' none may share unless a believer in the truth taught by us, who has been washed for the forgiveness of sins and for regeneration, and whose life conforms to what Christ taught. We do not receive these things as common bread or common drink. Just as our Saviour Jesus Christ was made flesh through God's word, and had flesh and blood for our salvation, so we have been taught that the food over which by prayer with a word coming from him, thanksgiving has been said, food which is changed into the constituents of our body, is the flesh and blood of Jesus who was made flesh. . . .

In *Dial.* 117. 4–5 the eucharist is now universal among all races, including nomads, and fulfils Malachi's prophecy (Mal. 1: 11) of sacrifice being offered to God from all peoples, never realized in the Jewish Dispersion.

13

IRENAEUS OF LYON

Diversity was a mark of mid-second century Christianity with different groups adopting different gospels as their supreme authority. Questions were asked such as whether the divinity of Christ was taught in the gospel according to Matthew, and whether it was not simpler and no less religious to hold Jesus to be merely the son of his father Joseph; what measure of authority attached to the letters of Paul, how one could answer Marcion's exclusive acceptance of a text of Luke's gospel from which references to fulfilled Old Testament prophecy had been removed as Judaistic interpolations, or his belief that Paul was the only apostle emancipated from Judaism and deserving recognition.

Born probably about 140, Irenaeus constitutes a major link between the Church of his own time, spread throughout the Roman Empire and beyond, and the heroic age of the past with Bishop Polycarp of Smyrna who could recall St John, who had shown the heretic Marcion the door, and who had visited Bishop Anicetus of Rome to defend the tradition of Asia Minor concerning the celebration of Easter, achieving peace with the recognition of diversity. Like other Greeks from Asia Minor, Irenaeus moved to the Rhône valley. He was probably author of the moving account of the inhuman persecution inflicted by order of Marcus Aurelius on the Christians of Lyon and Vienne in 177, preserved in the *Church History* of Eusebius of Caesarea. Continuing controversy between Rome and Asia Minor about the calculation of Easter Day and the form of the preceding fast drew him in to write a conciliatory letter to Pope Victor inviting him to be tolerant of diversity. That was hard for Victor to do for the reason that at Rome there were migrant Christians from Asia Minor, and it seemed hard to tolerate differences within one city. It seemed an advertisement of disunity. Victor's bid for uniformity was supported by several bishops in the Greek East. The disagreement was the earliest instance of tensions between Greek east and the west, the latter being still Greek-speaking.

Gnosticism

Irenaeus' greatest work was a five-part argument against gnosticism, especially against the followers of Valentinus. In its original form his was the least bizarre form of gnostic theosophy, the form most likely to capture the attention of church members. Valentinus was one of a succession of preachers or teachers who were attracted to the Roman Church, where such persons were held in respect and valued. In the capital there gathered people of different ethnic groups and cultures. Irenaeus once spoke of Rome as a microcosm of the universal Church, and thought that this enabled this Church to provide a norm of Christian truth.

The principal characteristic of gnosticism in its many shapes and forms is a negative evaluation of the material world and therefore of its Creator. Dualistic language about spirit and matter, usually cast in mythological form, is common, and the distinctiveness of different sects often lies in the imaginative myths in which individual teachers expressed their dualism. They speculated about the origins of the cosmos and how the human soul came to be imprisoned in a body of flesh. The theme from St John's gospel that the divine Logos had united human flesh to himself was difficult to grasp for anyone touched by Platonic ideas of the soul's destiny, impossible if one thought the flesh vile. It seemed altogether easier to think of the divine Logos being united to the human soul and not to the body.

Irenaeus refused to see the origin of evil as located in matter. Its root for him lay in a wrong use of free choice, initially by angelic powers corrupting women (Gen. 6: 4). There was therefore an association between the original Fall and the erotic. Irenaeus did not think Adam and Eve experienced sexual desire before the Fall (*Epideixis* 14).

There were to be those who asked if the pure Logos of God could be one even with the soul, considering that the human mind is not characteristically pure in heart. But for most teachers the soul was a divine spark that had a longing to return to its heavenly home, and *gnosis* or knowledge was an explanation of the way in which it had come to be here and what knowledge was needed, e.g. of planetary powers barring the ascent to the divine realm. This conception of powers barring the soul's ascent did not in the least need to be associated with heresy, and it is explicitly found in Justin (*Dial.* 105. 3), Clement of Alexandria and Origen as well as in later writers with no gnostic tinge. But it was a picture of the soul's earthly situation which easily lent itself to resort to magic. Astrologers could sell one an amulet which could coerce the planetary power obstructing ascent to open the great doors and allow one through to the next stage. Experts in the occult could disclose the secret barbaric names which gave power over hostile spirits. The teachers and sects were rivals to each other and not at all on friendly terms.

Valentinus is no simple figure to delineate because he had pupils able to develop the teachings of their master, and because in all probability the citations from his homilies or poems or letters, mainly found in Clement of Alexandria, reached Clement through the medium of his disciples. The three most prominent disciples, themselves independent teachers, were Ptolemy, Heracleon (author of the first commentary on St John's gospel and the object of refutation in the exegesis by Origen), and Theodotos, of whom Clement of Alexandria gives excerpts. He is never actually described as Valentinus' pupil but is clearly a kindred spirit. It is certain that Valentinus was uncomfortable with any idea that the physical body of Christ needed food and drink and had to dispose of body waste. Clement of Alexandria felt the force of his difficulty and answered with the doctrine that Jesus did not actually need to eat or drink but did so to forestall heretics who said that he produced an optical illusion of doing so. Irenaeus first formulated the classic orthodox reply that any part of human nature, body, soul, or spirit, which the Redeemer did not make his own is not saved.

The power and attractiveness of the Valentinian school lay in its presentation of the true meaning of dark biblical symbols. Genesis 1 and the parables of Jesus could be made rich in symbolic significance. If Jesus lived for thirty years before going public, and if the hours worked by the labourers in the vineyard add up to thirty, that number coincides with the days in most months, and signifies the thirty celestial powers or Aeons constituting the Fullness (*pléroma*) of the evolving divine being. Of these thirty aeons the twelfth is obscurely referred to in Luke's statement (8: 41–2) that the young girl raised from the dead was twelve years old. She symbolizes the heavenly Wisdom (Sophia) who suffered emotional distress by falling in love with the supreme Aeon or 'Depth', which was to set her cap above her station and to precipitate the pre-cosmic Fall.

From the distress of Wisdom failing to recognize her ceiling in heaven there have come three natures: (*a*) spirit, (*b*) a psychic stuff, (*c*) matter. Humanity may be divided into (*a*) spiritual people sure of being the Elect predestinate to salvation, who could safely eat meats sacrificed to idols; (*b*) ordinary church members or psychic people who have a chance of a better lot hereafter through ascetic restraint and self-discipline; and (*c*) earthy clods for whom salvation is not an option. The threefold division was using a theme from Plato's *Timaeus*.

One teacher named Mark was the object of special horror in the mind of Irenaeus, not least because he fascinated women, using sorcery with the eucharistic wine, and charging substantial fees for the revelation of mysteries. But not all gnostics were crooks. Valentinus did not look like a heretic.

Gnostics liked to explain the creation as the consequence of emanations from the supreme being. They were a natural overflow of causation percolating down to lower levels of being. Irenaeus opposed this by stressing that the creation had come about by a free and inscrutable decision of the divine will. To ask why such a decision was made or how it can have come about is inquiring into matters God has not thought fit to reveal. At the same time as stressing the impenetrable will of God, Irenaeus could also follow the *Timaeus* of Plato (29 e) in the proposition that the creation of this world is an overflow of God's goodness which is free from all envy (*AH* 3. 41). Moreover just as the created world has come from an inscrutable decision of the divine will, so too the begetting of the divine Son is beyond all human investigation: 'Who can declare his generation?' (Isa. 53: 1). But there is the difference that the material world belongs to the realm of time and temporal successiveness, while the divine Son belongs to the eternal realm transcending time. There were themes here which would become important and influential for Athanasius in the fourth century.

The doctrines and myths associated with Valentinus and his pupils are clear that the central figure in the story of redemption is Jesus. That was not necessarily true of all gnostic myths. The sect which followed Simon Magus of Samaria made Simon the redeemer; the book of Genesis provided the fallen female figure, symbol of a pre-cosmic smudge in the creative process. The serpent in Genesis 3 fascinated speculation, and one sect, the Ophites or snake-worshippers, judged that the creature through which the human race acquired its knowledge of good and evil must be beneficent. Origen (*c. Cels.* 6) preserves substantial pieces of Ophite liturgy, known to the pagan Celsus who rightly saw that it adapted matter from Mithraic rites. Ancient magical papyri and amulets illustrate the cosmic snake with his tail in his mouth signifying eternity. Magicians liked barbarian words and names, and this liking strongly influenced some gnostic mythologies.

At the time when gnostic sects were shaping their mythologies there was no fixed canon of New Testament writings, and gnostic teachers were proud to be able to produce Secret Sayings of Jesus, accounts of what Jesus had said to his disciples between the resurrection and the ascension, or other occult and cabbalistic information. Gospels, Acts, Letters, and Apocalypses widely current were not limited to those which in course of time became the New Testament, and gnostic leaders liked texts which 'the Great Church' was not going to recognize as authoritative and appropriate to be read in the lectionary. Irenaeus affirmed that it is of the nature of things to have four gospels, as there are four principal winds, the cherubim have four faces—a lion for John, calf for Luke, a man for Matthew, and an eagle for Mark (an allocation later altered). There long remained groups and individuals who valued apocryphal or secret texts and who thought it improbable that so profound a mystery would be in publicly accessible books.

Norms of true teaching

Irenaeus contended that if the apostles really had handed on secret traditions, they would have entrusted them to the clergy responsible for the communities of apostolic foundation. Any church founded by an apostle would prove the point, but best of all one can turn to the glorious church at Rome, founded (Irenaeus believed) by Peter and Paul the apostolic martyrs. At Rome the tradition of catechism is conscientious, and with many Christians coming there from other parts of the Roman Empire the community is subject to external control. So it is impossible to suppose that the authentic tradition is not to be found in this church which enjoys pre-eminence by virtue of antiquity. Here one can meet the common faith of all believers, and Irenaeus can cite the succession of bishops through which the tradition is visible.

'Through God alone can God be known', and therefore as revealer of the Father Christ is himself true God. God has become human so that we might become divine, which is the meaning of salvation. 'Christ became what we are that we might become what he is'. Therefore Christ 'recapitulates Adam'. This participation in the divine nature is given through sharing in the eucharistic gifts, the pledge of immortality, as the Word of God comes to the mixed cup and bread to become the body and blood of Christ. 'We there offer God his own', in the spiritual sacrifice of Christians of which the Levitical sacrifices are a prefiguration.

Irenaeus repeatedly emphasizes that the one faith is shared by believers in every part of the known world, and what is universal is apostolic. So the universal Church is the repository of truth. Where the Church is, there is the Spirit, and where the Spirit is there is the Church. Therefore one must not separate from the Church. Would-be reformers want to leave the Church because of moral faults and hypocrites. If they end by splitting the Church, they do more harm than good.

The marks of the Church are the Bible in which Old and New Testaments are a unity and coherent. Marcion was wrong to think them incompatible, but was at least right in thinking that there should be a canon or fixed list of books accepted. The Pauline epistles were vindicated by Luke–Acts, but Irenaeus did not regard the epistle to the Hebrews as Pauline and canonical, though he has allusions taken from it. He has no citation from 2 Peter, 3 John, or James.

Like Justin Irenaeus declares the meaning of the Bible to be clear, so that the heretics get their private meaning by forced exegesis. Yet the Bible has hard sayings, and the necessary rule is to interpret obscure passages by the clear. The exegete needs grace. And beside the written texts of scripture he can rely on tradition in the orthodoxy of apostolic foundations. The sacramental laying on of hands in ordination endows the bishop with grace to hold and teach the truth to his people.

That there are difficulties in the Old Testament is not denied. In the plagues of Egypt why did Egyptians have to suffer massacre? The hardening of Pharaoh's heart? Spoiling the Egyptians of their jewels? The incest of Lot's daughters? In each case Irenaeus is sure of an edifying typological sense. The gnostics and Marcion had a strong argument in the contention that the Christian revelation must presuppose its superiority to what went before. Irenaeus allowed revelation to be gradual and progressive, just as Adam and Eve fell at first because like children they could not always stand upright. Even the Christian revelation is not absolute, for we see through a glass darkly and do not have the full truth until the final fulfilment of God's plan (*AH* 4. 9. 2). The Bible is an obscure collection but as a self-disclosure of the Creator it is not more obscure than the world of nature. (This is the earliest statement of the proposition in Joseph Butler's *Analogy of Religion* that there is no difficulty in revelation not paralleled in nature.) Irenaeus was well educated in philosophy and literature, with citations of Homer and Plato and others. He is well aware that the sources of the Nile remained unknown, and the causes of bird-migration, tides, thunder, and lightning belonged in the realm of mystery.

Although the original Greek of Irenaeus' great work survives only in later citations, and its survival is owed to early Latin and Armenian versions, he was certainly influential during the following two centuries. He provided the classic rebuttal of dualistic mythology, affirming the centrality of the incarnation as medium of redemption, and the goodness of the created order. 'The glory of God is a living human being' (*AH* 4. 20. 7). The authentic Church is that with the ministerial succession from the apostles, though that (he added) does not sanctify proud or avaricious presbyters.

Extant in Armenian is his 'Demonstration of the Apostolic Preaching' (*Epideixis*), the essence of which (much indebted to Justin) is a vindication of the fulfilment of prophecy in the gospel story.

Irenaeus embodies the process towards standardization, towards having a more or less fixed list of writings to be deemed authoritative in debate. The canon of the New Testament is visibly emerging out of the mist. Nevertheless this in no way signified the destruction of alternative or 'apocryphal' Gospels, Acts, Letters, and Apocalypses, which continued to be produced and read. Many of these bore the names of Old as well as of New Testament authors. Some were being produced during the same decades in which books received into the canon were being composed. Some were written after the main shape of the New Testament canon was already formed. Their literary form is different from that of canonical books. They are not distinctive because their title ascribes them to Old or New Testament heroes, for some books admitted to the canon are not by their stated authors. Admission to the canon was inextricably linked with the orthodoxy of the doctrine contained in the text. It was not enough to bear an apostolic title. Apocryphal Gospels wanted to convey traditions about Jesus of an esoteric nature, or sayings of Jesus which the canonical evangelists might not have. Apocryphal Acts could recount the missionary wanderings of apostles in distant lands, such as Thomas in India, and a major theme could be the neces-sity of celibacy for the baptized. Letters could supplement the preserved corpus or adopt the apostolic form to correct the errors of a later time. Apocalypses could describe heaven and hell, the latter in lurid and horren-dous images to which some congregations would object.

Christian apocalypses could recycle older Jewish material. The *Ascension of Isaiah*, probably early in the second century, not only narrates how Manasseh sawed the prophet in half but describes the descent from heaven of the 'Beloved' to set up his kingdom on earth for a thousand years. It offers a sombre picture of the quality of church leaders 'who love office but lack wisdom'. A supplement to biblical material is 'the Penitence of Jannes and Jambres', the magicians who opposed Moses, providing them with a sorceress-mother, a kind of Sycorax, and (in anticipation of the Faust legend) introducing a pact with the devil. Numerous apocryphal texts were enjoyed by gnostic sympathizers. The *Acts of John* describe a 'docetic' crucifixion; that is, while Roman soldiers on Golgotha are under the illusion that they are putting Jesus to death, the real Christ is with John looking down on the scene. These Acts are also famous for the Hymn of Jesus, perhaps to be chanted in a dance (a piece known to Augustine, *ep.* 237). The *Acts of Paul and Thecla* are said by Tertullian to have been written by a presbyter in the province of Asia (i.e. near Ephesus) who resigned office because he advocated the view that women could preach and baptize. The surviving text is fragmentary, dependent on Greek and Coptic papyri. Thecla attracted high veneration, especially at a shrine in her honour at Seleucia in Cilicia (Silifke in southern Turkey). The martyrdom of Paul in Rome after a confrontation with the emperor is the last part. These Acts are cited by orthodox writers as edifying matter.

Such documents have an affinity with Jewish Midrash, embroidering a sacred story either to fill in gaps or to advocate celibacy. An infancy Gospel such as the 'Protevangelium of James' in the second century is at pains to stress Mary's perpetual virginity, and in time other apocryphal texts extolled the glory of the Mother of God in the communion of saints.

Among the most interesting texts is the Clementine romance, written in the style of ancient love stories. This composition of the late second century survives through fourth-century adaptations, one in Greek, one in a Latin translation by Rufinus of Aquileia entitled 'Homilies' and 'Recognitions' respectively, the latter having been revised partly in a more orthodox direc-tion, partly also by a radical Arian, but still retaining much of the original sense. The second-century original disliked the apostle Paul and put great stress on Peter. The Clementine Homilies and Recognitions include an

influential fiction, a letter from Clement to James saying that at Rome
Clement had been formally ordained and commissioned by St Peter himself
entrusting him with the power to bind and loose. In short, the bishops of the
Roman see have derived their Petrine office from Clement by juridical succession. That theme made this document immensely influential with
medieval canonists a millennium later. The author may also have wanted to
affirm Roman primacy over against the successors of James at Jerusalem. The
implication is that the Second Coming has not arrived and the Church has to
come to terms with a continuing existence in history with a reasonably
ordered form of government. The principal purpose, however, of the
Clementine romance was to utilize the novel-form to make Christian
doctrine sweeter to the inquiring reader.

14

THE NEW TESTAMENT TEXT

Marcion had put a critical question about the integrity of transmission of texts which in and soon after his time were in process of being formed into the New Testament. A major objection to his view that these documents had been interpolated in a pro-Judaistic sense consisted in the total lack of manuscript authority for his drastically expurgated form of text. No autograph existed then (as now, of course); but autographs of ancient documents other than letters and documents of daily life preserved on papyrus are extremely rare. About the middle decades of the second century a scribe of Gospels and Acts produced a copy which came to enjoy a famous descendant in the late fourth-century Codex Bezae from Lyon, a bilingual manuscript presented by the Calvinist Beza to Cambridge University to encourage Reformed sympathies. Here there is mild enhancement of words or phrases critical of Judaism. But the principal families of ancient manuscripts, numbering several thousand, offer forms of text where differences are numerous but not often deeply significant theologically. Scribes wanted to harmonize Gospels or to clarify a sentence by paraphrase. Naturally the majority of variants were created by scribes' mistakes. It has never been easy to transcribe a substantial text by hand without a single slip.

The numerous manuscripts can be subjected to ordered classification in families, i.e. groups which share the same variants or other idiosyncrasies. These originally arose from differing local usages—Egyptian churches followed Alexandria, Jerusalem and Palestinian churches followed Caesarea the metropolis, where Origen and later Eusebius and his master Pamphilus were much interested in variant texts. A very early manuscript of the Caesarean family is preserved on papyrus in the Chester Beatty collection, containing the Pauline epistles with Hebrews but without the letters to Timothy and Titus. The handwriting is not later than AD 200. One scrap of St John's Gospel at Manchester (Rylands papyrus 457) is in a hand unlikely to be later than 135. Experts in ancient handwriting can offer decisive judgements about the approximate dating of a text on papyrus or parchment. Naturally a form of text does not enjoy superior authority because it happens to have been preserved on papyrus. It is a rule of good textual criticism of all ancient writings that an early manuscript is not necessarily superior to one written later whose scribe could have been copying a very careful and even older model. In any event, reason is of greater authority than any manuscript in deciding on a variant reading.

In the course of time there was a tendency towards standardization, and this would produce the text commonly labelled *koine* or 'Byzantine', the normal Greek text familiar to medieval writers. The vernacular versions of the sixteenth century depended on this, and sometimes western Protestants mistakenly supposed that by translating the Greek (Byzantine) text they had a Bible far closer than Jerome's so-called Vulgate Latin (i.e. the common Bible of the medieval West) to what the apostles wrote. There was only a limited sense in which this was true, and Jerome used Greek manuscripts much earlier than, and at times superior to, those available to the vernacular translators.

In the second century the Greek original of the New Testament writings was translated into the languages immediately required by the missionaries, especially Syriac and Latin. The old Syriac version began with the four gospels. Justin's pupil Tatian, a native of Mesopotamia, made a gospel harmony in Greek, the 'Diatessaron', a fragment of which was found at Dura-Europos and therefore earlier than 256, and in Syriac translation this became the normal text used in the Syriac-speaking churches at Edessa and the contiguous region. The old Syriac gospels were also known as 'The Gospels of the Separated'. Only two manuscripts survive. Late in the fourth century a revised version of the Syriac New Testament called the Peshitta, i.e. the 'simple' or 'current' text, was produced. The Syrian churches did not admit the Revelation to the canon. The Peshitta included the Old Testament, and probably came from a variety of translators, some perhaps Jewish.

The Old Latin or Vetus Latina was produced in southern Gaul and in north Africa by various translators, and had different forms of text, one of which is well attested in Cyprian's biblical quotations. Differing versions survive in early manuscripts. In some parts of the Old Testament the translators found their task of exceptional difficulty, and their Latinity is idiosyncratic. In the fourth century north Africa had a group which read no book other than the Old Latin Bible, and in consequence had problems in making their intentions clear to shopkeepers in the bazaar because they used biblical idioms. They spoke the equivalent of Quaker English.

The Old Latin translations remained current until Jerome produced a revised version. Even then the Old Latin Bible long continued to be used in places distant from Rome and the main arteries of travel and trade. Although parts of the Bible in an Old Latin version do not survive, the text can often be reconstructed from the quotations in Christian writers. It is currently in process of being edited under the hand of R. Gryson.

15

CELSUS: A PLATONIST ATTACK

The first grave conflict between Church and Roman Empire after Pilate's execution of Jesus was the accidental consequence of Nero needing to blame an unpopular scapegoat for fire at Rome in AD 64. But the Christian refusal to acknowledge the gods by whose favour the empire enjoyed fertile crops and wives and secure frontiers, or to take an oath by the genius of the emperor, provoked distrust and fear. The customs and institutions of society involved participation in idolatrous sacrifices. It was accepted that Jews were exempt from these; that was their ancestral religion and justifiable, even if bizarre. But Christians were being converted from all sorts of ethnic backgrounds. It could help one to lie low if one was vegetarian, as were a few philosophers mainly in the Pythagorean tradition. Little meat was eaten which had not first been offered at some altar. But soldiers could not avoid being present at polytheistic rites, which enhanced Christian reluctance to serve as army officers. A public stand would end in trial and martyrdom.

The apparently suicidal, almost theatrical impression created by martyrs drew much attention to the Church, where the model of the Maccabees' resistance to Antiochus Epiphanes was closely followed, short of military conflict. In Bithynia the governor Pliny was surprised to discover no secret vices practised at nocturnal assemblies, but reported to the emperor Trajan that the refusal to offer sacrifices was an obstinacy worthy of capital punishment. One governor, confronted by a Christian explaining that simply on ground of conscience he could not co-operate, saw further discussion as a waste of time and ordered immediate execution.

In Rome Justin, soon followed by Tertullian in north Africa, recorded that martyrdoms had the effect of providing huge publicity and attracting converts, notably by offering an obvious refutation of popular accusations of nocturnal vice. In Rome a public disputation between Justin and a pagan philosopher Crescens did nothing to diminish the already substantial community in the city even if it led on to Justin's own trial and death.

In the middle years of the second century the Cynic writer Lucian of Samosata (Syria) composed a witty sketch of a confidence trickster and charlatan, Peregrinus Proteus. Having murdered his father, he deceived a Christian community into making him their leader, so that he received adulation and opulent gifts, suffering imprisonment for his 'faith' but thereby enjoying even greater veneration from widows and orphans. Bribed gaolers allowed prominent Christians to spend the night in his company in the prison. He was hailed as a new Socrates, finally dropping any Christian pretence and committing a dramatic suicide by fire in 165. Lucian's Voltairean portrait shows him aware that the Christians have sacred books which are expounded at their assemblies, and that Jesus taught them universal brotherhood and sharing of property.

Roughly contemporary with Irenaeus a Greek observer of the Church named Celsus became alarmed by Christianity's rapid growth. His philosophical sympathies were those of an eclectic Platonist, and he wrote a series of critical studies, substantial fragments from one of which survive in quotations made by Origen in a reply (*contra Celsum*) 75 years later. Celsus' book was entitled *Alethes Logos*, the true doctrine or authentic tradition. His criterion of religious truth was adherence to ancestral customs. He understood the penumbra of gnostic sects to be part of the same phenomenon as the body which he called 'the great Church', and was struck by the ferocity of the disagreements among the different groups. He had first-hand information about Marcion and Ophites. A knowledge of Justin's work is possible.

Celsus understood the supreme god called Zeus to preside over a pantheon of lesser deities who guarded individual tribes or nations. He was offended by Christian scorn for polytheistic cult as worship of evil daemons, by cheap abuse of the legend of Zeus' tomb in Crete, by provocative insults and assaults on cult-statues. It seemed extraordinary, even mad to proclaim that a crucifixion could be a victory over the devil (2. 47, 6. 42), and to have a longing for martyrdom as sharing in that victory (6. 48). To refuse to swear by the Genius (Tyche) of the emperor (8. 62) declared Christian alienation from the cause of the empire. It was extraordinary to suppose the exaltation of Jesus to divine honour was compatible with monotheism and incompatible with honouring the divine emperor. Yet they could dream of a day when the emperor himself would be converted and when their 'law' would be universal (8. 69–72). Irenaeus acknowledged the debt owed by the Christian mission to the peace and civil order of the empire (*AH* 4. 30. 3). Justin saw the cross-symbol in the Roman army standards (*Apol. I* 55 followed by Tertullian and Minucius Felix in Africa).

Celsus' portrait of the Church is of a society far from monochrome, largely artisan and uneducated in the majority, yet also including intelligent people capable of interpreting Genesis allegorically and well read in the dialogues of Plato (1. 27, 7. 35–45). At the same time he writes of good people wanting to stay aloof, repelled by the crowd of simple believers, but evidently attracted by an austere ethic of contempt for wealth, honour, and pride in high culture (3. 73). That the mission of the Church was pulling people in large numbers distressed Celsus much (8. 39, 69). Polemic led him at times to scorn the Church as an insignificant body (3. 10, 73), but had that been true he would hardly have written his book. His final appeal to Christians to accept public office and serve in the army presupposes that among them he knew some of a station in society fit to become magistrates. A few years later in north Africa Tertullian was contending against the view that, if Joseph could hold such office under Pharaoh, the people of God could do so now. Origen's reply shows that debate within the Church concerned the appropriateness of a Christian holding any office of power and authority in society or the Church. He allowed the latter.

Theological disagreements inside the Church caught Celsus' attention, not merely dissension between the great Church and the sects. He knew of some for whom Christ was simply God; or 'Jesus is God' while the Father is 'the great God' (1. 66). He was aware that between Jews and Christians the contentious issue was merely whether in Jesus Messiah had come or not (3. 1, 4. 2), but not perhaps of the degree to which this disagreement was related to the Christian understanding of messiahship as implying divine status. He knew that Jesus was entitled 'saviour' (2. 9, 3. 1), 'child of God' (often) and God's messenger or 'angel', this last being a common second-century title found in the *Shepherd* of Hermas and in Justin and a target in the polemic of the epistle to the Hebrews. He had met Christians who said the Son of God is the 'Logos' (2. 31), and were concerned to say that the title 'Son of God' is being used in a special sense.

Celsus was aware that the differing gospels were like flags for rival groups, and mentions people who altered the text (perhaps a deduction Celsus made from differences of wording or perhaps a reference to Marcion's textual alterations).

The Christology of one group is presented as a doctrine that 'since God is great and hard to perceive, he thrust his own spirit into a human body and sent it down here' (6. 69). A puzzling sentence in 6. 72 mentions 'some who do not grant that God is spirit, but only the Son'.

Celsus was intrigued by the tension in the Church between the differing standpoints of various theologians leading to sharp controversy and by the mutual love (*agápe*) which the Christians also manifested towards one another (1. 1). 'Their agreement is amazing, the more so as it can be shown to rest on no trustworthy foundation.' What in Celsus' diagnosis holds them together is the bond created by being in revolt against their roots in Judaism and indeed Hellenic culture generally, the mutual advantage created by sticking together, and 'the fear of outsiders' (3. 14). Their problems of disunity result from their growth in numbers: 'Since they have expanded to become a multitude, they are divided and rent asunder, and each wants to lead his own party' (3. 10). Now the only thing they still have in common is the name which alone they are ashamed to abandon (3. 12). It was an ancient argument of Epicurean philosophers that the one reason why people co-operate is its necessity for survival.

The affirmation that in the man Jesus, illegitimate son of Mary, a god was present was for Celsus incomprehensible. A divine being would unquestionably have visited retribution on those who tortured and crucified him, would have vanished from the cross (as Apollonius of Tyana did before the emperor Domitian), would above all have appeared after death to Pilate, to the soldiers who crucified him, and to all people everywhere. That at the resurrection he appeared only to one woman and to his own confraternity is unimaginable. After death the wounds he showed were an optical illusion, not real. (In other words, Celsus would have found a docetic Christology credible.) But *a priori* it is inconceivable that a god would have been born in a human body as Jesus was, could have eaten lamb (at the Last Supper), and could have spoken with an ordinary voice. A divine figure would have had an enormously loud speaking voice (2. 61–8, 1. 69–70, 2. 70, 74, 6. 75). The disbelief which met his teaching is evidence that he could not have been divine (1. 70).

Celsus knows that the Christians have sacred writings, but except for Genesis these do not loom large in his attack. He has no interest, for example, in pointing to contradictions or moral difficulties, despite his attention to arguments used by Marcion about the Old Testament. He is ready to concede that Jesus did miracles, but that was by magical means. The prophecies which were claimed to be fulfilled he regards as far too ambiguous, and in any event lacking persuasiveness to Jews. What scares him is the success of the Christian mission undermining an entire cultural tradition. And the quiet mutual toleration of polytheistic cults is being replaced by fierce internal contentions recalling the conflicts of Greek philosophical schools.

16

MONTANISM: PERPETUA

Celsus had met extremely enthusiastic Christians given to delivering excitable prophecies 'at the slightest excuse', proclaiming the imminent end of the world (7. 9). Probably in 156 Bishop Polycarp of Smyrna was martyred. His church wrote a moving account of his end, stressing that he was no voluntary martyr, and contrasting him with a Phrygian named Quintus who provoked the authorities. Perhaps Quintus was a Montanist. In Egypt the Coptic churches would suggest that Polycarp's heroism compensated for St John's dying in his bed.[1]

In Phrygia (Asia Minor) a major movement of ecstatic prophecy began in either 157 or 172. A leading theme was a special revelation by the Holy Spirit to call the Church away from gnostics and others anxious to reinterpret symbolically the literalist eschatology of resurrection of the flesh and a physical millennium, Phrygia was a region where there had been prophetesses and charismatics especially at Hierapolis and Philadelphia, and so the new movement in Phrygian villages could answer critics by invoking the idea of a legitimating succession. The 'New Prophecy' as it was called by its adherents (Montanists or Kataphrygians to opponents) began with a charismatic ecstasy on the part of Montanus, whom Jerome (*ep.* 41. 4) claims to have been a converted priest of Cybele (i.e. accustomed to scenes of religious frenzy) together with two women, Prisca and Maximilla, who abandoned their husbands. Critics of the 'New Prophecy' liked to represent it as having pagan origins as well as working with an irrational notion of inspiration as based on suspension of the rational faculty. The inspired oracles of the trio were peculiar in being direct utterances of the Paraclete using their vocal chords as his own. The content was a proclamation of the imminent end, in view of which special fasts were to be observed. The new Jerusalem was to descend from heaven, not indeed in Palestine as was normal millennial expectation e.g. in Justin or Irenaeus, but (with a touch of regional patriotism) in Phrygia. Missionaries from Phrygia spread the message through the empire, reaching Rome, Lyon, and Carthage among other towns. In that

---

[1] F. W. Weidman, *Polycarp and John* (Notre Dame, 1999).

extension there is a measure of the movement's power and success. An austere puritan ethic was impressive.

The New Prophecy was strictly orthodox, and claimed to be vindicated by numerous martyrdoms, a sign of being the authentic Church. However, the claim was being made that anyone who failed to recognize the movement as an authentic operation of the Spirit of God was on that ground deficient in the presence of the Spirit. The distinction made at Corinth and in Paul's first epistle to the Corinthians between the 'natural' (psychic) and the spiritual (pneumatic) was crucial. Therefore the movement became extremely divisive.

The claim to spiritual validity was a demand for recognition. A decisive question was to be the attitude of the great sees such as Rome. Tertullian at Carthage became a convert to Montanist sympathies, and reports that for a time the bishop of Rome, unnamed, almost decided to acknowledge its authenticity but was argued out of that by urgent representations from Asia Minor. There some bishops were horrified by the divisiveness of the Montanist claim, whereas at the town of Thyatira the entire population, bishop and clergy and laity, became Montanist. Phrygian inscriptions 'Christians to Christians' may well be of Montanist origin, not merely an expression of strong self-consciousness of being a society apart, 'strangers in this world' (John 17. 14), though that defiant feeling in Phrygian churches could have helped to create a seed-bed for the New Prophecy to take root.

Besides regretting the divisive effect of the New Prophecy, critics pointed to the very unusual form of inspired utterance. The prophetic trio did not adopt the pattern of biblical prophets, 'Thus saith the Lord . . .' reporting in the third person. Their oracles were the Paraclete's words, and the three prophets were not at the time in possession of their rational faculties. Bishops who failed to recognize the oracles of the Holy Spirit found themselves cold-shouldered, in effect dismissed as godless and secular. Tertullian wrote a (lost) tract 'On Ecstasy' pinpointing the loss of mental control as the central issue between 'psychics' and 'pneumatics'. At the back of the debate was a much older disagreement, whether inspiration is conditional on a suspension of reason or whether it brings an enhancement of it. It became necessary for bishops to affirm that the word of God in Bible and sacraments entrusted to the apostolic ministry was the locus of divine grace to believers, not emotional excitements.

To assert that in the Montanist oracles the Holy Spirit was giving new revelation was not obviously compatible with the presupposition in the making of the New Testament canon that divine revelation was exhausted in these writings. It is difficult to estimate whether Montanism reinforced an already embryonic notion of a closed canon or whether it was an influential factor in creating it. The former seems more probable.

Did Montanism have to be so divisive? In north Africa at Carthage Tertullian thought it a mighty reforming spirit in the Church, but not a mere rejection of the Church. His writings, however, attest a widening sense of alienation, and a concern to bring reform often causes splits. 'Prophecy' is inherently hard to control and even to define other than in the loose sense of inspired insight into the contemporary scene and the power given to speak to its condition. The New Prophecy's rigorism answered to a mood of the time. A sharply contentious question in the second- and third-century West was whether the power of the keys to bind and loose extended to granting for-giveness to church members who confessed to adultery. Montanists were not the only people who thought not. Tertullian (*De pudicitia*) was appalled when about 220 the bishop of Carthage, probably after consultation with Rome, ruled that a bishop possessed such power in the name of the Church. A hun-dred years earlier the *Shepherd* of Hermas had presented the possibility of absolution and restoration to communion as a single amnesty. That was more than enough for Montanists and other readers of the epistle to the Hebrews.

Perpetua

Montanist 'oracles' were collected, and to that degree had something in common with the oracles given at shrines of Apollo at Didyma or Claros or Hierapolis. Apart from the surviving Montanist oracles, mainly reproduced by Eusebius and Epiphanius but with some in Tertullian, the most remark-able extant Montanist text is the *Martyrdom of Perpetua*, the slave-girl Felicitas and some fellow Christians who about 203 were thrown to wild beasts in an amphitheatre in north Africa. The moving document survives in two Latin lines of transmission and one Greek. The Greek tradition locates the bloody scene at Thuburbo Minus, not far from Carthage; the Latin manuscripts give no location at all. But the presence of the proconsul of Africa Hilarianus sug-gests Carthage.[2] The Montanist author had one priceless document, Perpetua's prison diary recording the visions which she was granted. He presents his story as a refutation of some strict biblicists who wanted to restrict the operation of the Holy Spirit to old texts in scripture. It was to remain a subject of contention for at least two centuries to come whether accounts of martyrdoms qualified beside biblical texts in the lectionary to be read during acts of worship.

Perpetua is expressly described as being a lady of good family. Tertullian's writings make it certain that by the end of the second century the church at

---

[2] Perpetua and Felicitas were buried at Carthage in the Basilica Maiorum (Victor of Vita, *Historia persecutionis Africanae provinciae* 1. 3. 9), which correlates with an inscription in the Mcidfa basilica recording the presence of the martyrs (*ILCV* 2041 = *CIL* VIII., 25038).

Carthage included a number of people with wealth, at least enough to bribe authorities in time of persecution (not an action approved by Montanist rigorists). They were also qualified by their social standing to serve as magistrates, and saw biblical precedent in the life of Joseph in Egypt. Tertullian composed a tract 'On Idolatry' setting out a detailed job description of a Roman magistrate, noting that every one of his public duties entailed compromise with some form of idolatry.

Perpetua and her fellow martyrs were cared for by deacons of the local Church and she had a vision in which she achieved a happy reconciliation between the bishop Optatus and his presbyter Aspasius. Nothing is said in the text identifying possible sources of tension that required healing. However, the passage could be related to the kind of bitter feeling of alienation from the official clergy expressed in Tertullian, *De pudicitia*, contrasting charismatic Montanists with psychic bishops untouched by the Spirit. Such a sense of alienation reappears late in the fourth century among the Messalians of Syria and Asia Minor. But the Montanists are misrepresented if they are interpreted as protesting against order or a pastoral ministry in apostolic continuity or against church finances based on endowments. No doubt it is very possible that Phrygian villagers and peasants did not feel quite integrated in the largely urban structure of a Church with episcopal authority located in the empire's towns. Once they had become a separate body with their own life in the hills of Phrygia, their organization was well developed and efficient. It is unusual for a charismatic body to have chaotic finances. It was true, however, that for Montanists authority depended on the 'vertical' gift of the Paraclete, not upon the horizontal transmission of authority from pastor to pastor in apostolic continuity, mediating a valid sacramental life.

17

TERTULLIAN, MINUCIUS FELIX

On 17 July AD 180 twelve Christians from the north African town of Scillium were sentenced to execution by the proconsul. The record of their cross-examination survives in Latin and Greek. The proconsul expected them to practise secret vices and asked what books they had in their box. 'Books and letters of a just (innocent) man Paul', they replied. After refusing thirty days in which to change their mind, they declined to swear by the emperor's genius and were condemned to be beheaded, to which they answered 'Thanks be to God.' The sentence suggests that they possessed Roman citizenship and therefore were not Punic peasants, though one had a Punic name Nartzalus. If as is probable the Pauline letters in their box were in Latin, that is the earliest evidence for the Old Latin Bible of the second century.

During the last decade of the second century Christianity successfully penetrated the educated classes of Carthage, chief town of Roman Africa and a place of high culture. Among the converts was a brilliant advocate Tertullian, master of eloquent Latin and fluent in Greek as well. Not only familiar with Latin authors, including Juvenal and Tacitus, he had also read Herodotus and Plato in Greek. A fair proportion of the population at the trading port of Carthage spoke Greek, and he published a few of his tracts in that language. Tertullian came into a Church already under sharp persecution, and the polarity in society provoked him to write tracts of superb militancy, especially his *Apologeticus* of AD 197, in which his defence of Christianity is a trenchant attack on the superstitions of polytheism. His practice as an advocate in the courts familiarized him with points of law.

His skills in attacking pagans could be turned against fellow Christians from whom he dissented. He defended a 'natural theology' in the sense that the soul, created by God though now fallen, still has a subconscious memory of God innate within and from this can advance to truths only revealed through scripture. He shared the opinion that the Greek philosophers had derived their correct insights from the Old Testament, which made possible a positive estimate of their value. But within the Church disputed questions rested largely on whether a text in scripture could be seen to settle the point. Some Christians were arguing that since scripture had no express prohibition of attending public shows such as beast fights in the amphitheatre, they were free to go. Artisans working in factories making idols for pagan cult pleaded that no scripture forbade this occupation. Military service was particularly delicate. John Baptist had not required soldiers to abandon the Roman army. People argued that at least a soldier converted could remain in the army as a catechumen, even if he deferred baptism until retirement. Some even contended that a baptized believer was free to join the colours.

One Christian soldier caused a storm of debate by refusing to wear the regulation laurel wreath at a distribution of largesse to his military unit by a visiting grandee. This took him to prison. Other Christians in his unit thought the wreath a matter of moral indifference, so that he had achieved nothing except giving the Christians a bad name. At Carthage many, including clergy, thought the man had been stupid, exhibitionist and provocative. What scripture forbade a laurel crown?

Tertullian (*De corona*) defended the soldier on the ground that scripture is not the sole authority to be invoked. There is also tradition, going back to the apostolic beginnings of the Church. None would question traditions not mentioned in scripture, such as the baptismal renunciation of the devil and his angels, threefold immersion, the baptismal formula now more elaborate than that prescribed by the Lord, the neophyte being given milk and honey symbolic of entry to the promised land, and the customary abstention from a bath for seven days. Similarly universal custom was to receive the eucharist before dawn from the bishop's hands, not at a meal, to remember martyrs on the anniversary of their death, not to kneel between Easter and Pentecost, to make the sign of the cross at grace before meat or when lighting the evening lamp. In short, liturgical usage does not require a biblical text.

If the Bible were reckoned to be the exclusive source of divine truth and there were no clue other than individual judgement to its correct interpretation, then the Church would be defenceless against theosophical exegesis by gnostic sects. To that problem Tertullian addressed a brilliant tract arguing that there is (as Irenaeus had said) a rule of faith inherited from the apostles that there is one God creator of the world by his mediating Word; that this Word manifested in Old Testament theophanies has become incarnate by the Virgin Mary; and that the incarnate Lord taught the new law, was crucified, risen, ascended, is seated at God's right hand, and has sent the Holy Spirit as his deputy; he will return to take the saints to heaven and to send the wicked to hell after resurrection of the flesh. Gnostics claim that their teachings only reinterpret the scriptural story. Tertullian replies that orthodoxy does not appeal to scripture at all but only to the apostolic rule of faith. Heresy is later than orthodoxy and on the test of priority fails. Orthodoxy is attested universally, and is unanimous. An awkward text for unanimity was Galatians 2: 11 ff. on the disagreement between Peter and Paul. That is mitigated by reflecting that it occurred soon after Paul's conversion when he was still a neophyte, and it was on food, not dogma. Christ installed the apostles on his own teaching chair (*De monogamia* 8; *Praescr.* 6). That teaching has been faithfully transmitted by local churches, especially at Rome. The apostolic succession lies in the communities. Gnostics being outside the Church are not entitled to cite or interpret the Bible, the Church's books. Moreover, though there had been some diversity of custom in Africa in regard to the acceptability of baptism given by heretics, Tertullian himself thought it impossible outside the Church, and his view was confirmed by an African council under Agrippinus bishop of Carthage. The decision was to be crucial for Cyprian.

Tertullian received an understanding of the Church where high importance attached to the body of laity. Lay believers are priests. In Tertullian's time there was argument about the standing of the clergy or *ordo* on the one hand and the lay congregation or *plebs* on the other. 'In case of necessity when the clergy are absent you as a lay Christian can offer the eucharistic sacrifices and may baptize' (*Exh. cast.* 7). Earlier, writing on Baptism, Tertullian had warned laity not to usurp clerical functions and on no account to allow a woman to baptize or to offer the eucharist (*Bapt.* 17). The normal giver of baptism is the bishop, the 'high priest'. Presbyters and deacons may do so only with the bishop's leave. Likewise the bishop's responsibility is to reconcile and absolve the penitent. Tertullian was aware that those who compromised their faith in persecution could turn to martyrs for absolution if they were refused by the bishop (*Mart.* 1). Yet the power to bind and loose is vested in the community, not in the bishop apart from the Church. The north African church had not yet finally made up its mind that the administration of baptism and eucharist should rest with ministers authorised to perform those crucial functions.

The Montanist tract 'On Modesty' (*De pudicitia*) vehemently denies the power of the Church to absolve any sinner. The Church may intercede, but not remit. 'The *Shepherd* of Hermas is not now recognized as authoritative, even at Rome' (*De pudic.* 10). The Church's authority to remit sins has been revoked by the Paraclete through the New Prophecy. Inconsistently Tertullian adds that the power to absolve, not entrusted to the apostles' successors, is granted only to spiritual men. The true Church is constituted by the Spirit, not the collective of bishops. This final thrust was to provoke a negative response from Cyprian bishop of Carthage half a century later and an admirer of much in Tertullian.

During the second century it had become established custom in the Greek churches for ascetic women to take or to be invested with a veil. In north Africa veiled virgins were living side by side with Latins who thought the veil a matter of indifference and private choice. But the New Prophecy had ruled that all virgins must be veiled. 'Christ did not say, I am custom, but I am the truth.' Paradoxically Tertullian declares that while the rule of faith is unchangeable, that implies that anything else can be altered, which is what the New Prophecy has done. Revelation is a story of growth and is not static. Revelation is the education of the human race and a process of intellectual advance. Tertullian hovers on the brink of the progressivist ideas of Joachim of Fiore (AD 1200) that the Old Testament is the age of the Father, the New Testament that of the Son, but now has come the age of the Paraclete which can supplement or amend scripture by removing options previously open.

Two writings from Tertullian's pen had marked influence on later western theology, both written when his sympathy for the New Prophecy was explicit, namely *Adversus Praxean* and *De Anima*. Justin had written of the Logos as being 'other' than the Father, and it was a hot question whether or not this was compatible with biblical monotheism or if it weakened Christian criticism of the plurality of polytheism. In Asia Minor some theologians wanted to say that Father and Son are one and the same, different names for one God in different aspects. At Rome factions produced sharp dissension. Tertullian as a Montanist sympathizer wished to speak of the independent being of the Holy Spirit, but without prejudice to the unity of God. The plurality was to be seen in the 'economy', manifest in the missions of the Son and of the Paraclete. But it remains a 'monarchy' just as the rule of the one emperor is not infringed by a royal family or provincial administrators. Praxeas was an opponent of Montanism in Asia Minor who was also opposed to the pluralism of the Logos theology. He came to Rome and convinced the then bishop of his cause, to the distress of Tertullian: 'He put to flight the Paraclete and crucified the Father.' Tertullian affirmed unity of 'substance' in Father and Son, and (following a suggestion already in Justin) introduced the term 'person' to distinguish the divine titles: 'one substance in three persons.' Yet the distinction implies no difference in deity. The Son is God made visible. Father, Son, and Spirit are one entity but not one person (*unum, non unus*), just as the Son is vine, the Father husbandman (John 15: 1), just as Christ, a title meaning anointed, implies one who anoints him (a point already in Irenaeus). Moreover, Christ died, but the transcendent Father is immortal and cannot suffer or die. Admittedly Christ died as man, not as divine. Tertullian's terminology for the Trinity became decisive for the Latin West.

The origin and nature of the soul was of special importance because Tertullian held to the Stoic opinion that everything real is in some sense material, and soul is a kind of invisible thinking gas. Gen. 2: 7 seemed to show that the human soul was a breath from God, and indeed that God himself is a unique kind of not quite immaterial substance—an opinion which drew direct criticism in Augustine's *Literal Commentary on Genesis* (10. 25. 41). Tertullian defended his view of the soul by an argument from heredity: children resemble their parents both physically and mentally, and their

character is determined partly by that fact, partly by their free choices. The
devil seizes every newborn child, so that every soul is in fallen Adam until
converted and baptized in Christ. There is both evil coming from the evil
spirit and evil from the fault in its origin; nevertheless, the image of God is
obscured, not destroyed, and hence even in very good people there is some
evil, even in very bad some touch of goodness. The sacred water of baptism
brings second birth and the soul is captured by the Holy Spirit. The intimate
union of body and soul explains the efficacy of the sacraments, baptismal
water, anointing of chrism or laying on of hands in confirmation, the body
feeding on the body and blood of Christ that the soul may fatten on God
(*De resurr. carnis* 8).

The rigorism of Montanism was only a little exaggeration of a puritanism
characteristic of the main Christian body. In his *Apologeticus* Tertullian could
be censorious of the everyday morality of pagan society, e.g. decisively ruling
against abortion, a condemnation repeated by Minucius Felix and Clement
of Alexandria, as being in principle no different from infant exposure or
murder. The Christians were glad to find support for their view in Plato's
Laws 838 E. Similarly their hatred of pederasty had precedent in Plato, though
the homosexual love of Plato's *Symposium* was not so supportive. Ancient
pagan moralists had much to say about the advantages and disadvantages of
marriage, and anticipated arguments for asceticism which recur in Tertullian
and Clement of Alexandria.

Tertullian's discerning of a link between heredity and the egocentric
selfishness of the human heart bequeathed huge problems to successors.
Brilliant in writing Latin prose, trenchant and at times obscene, he made his
successors anxious at the same time as he fascinated them.

Minucius Felix[1]

Minucius Felix, a north African Christian, who owed much to Tertullian but
wanted something less aggressive, composed a charming Latin defence of his
faith entitled *Octavius*. The scene is a sea-shore dialogue at Ostia between
Octavius and a pagan Caecilius, who is converted by arguments drawn from
Cicero, 'On the Nature of the Gods.' As they walk along the shore, they
watch boys playing ducks and drakes, bouncing flat stones on the water. The
sceptical contentions of Cicero are deployed against pagan cult and divination. Stoic arguments are deployed to defend divine design in the world.
A central thesis is that today the Christians are the philosophers and that

[1] A good annotated translation in the series Ancient Christian Writers is by Graeme Clarke.

the old philosophers support the Christians. The pagan arguments against Christianity, in the mouth of Caecilius, were probably drawn from Fronto, twice mentioned (9. 6, 31. 2). The concluding defence of the Christian doctrine of the Last Things can appeal to the philosophers who also held that virtue is divinely rewarded, and wickedness punished. But Minucius is reticent about the Christian scriptures and sacraments.

18

CLEMENT OF ALEXANDRIA

At the western mouth of the Nile Alexander the Great founded a great Greek city, a citadel of high culture under his successors the Ptolemies until their last representative Cleopatra succumbed to Rome. With its double harbour, this rich mercantile centre was second city of the empire, and the Jewish quarter contained a million Jews. Here the Greek version of the Hebrew scriptures was produced, and early in the first century AD Philo wrote his allegorical commentary and other writings in defence of Jewish monotheism and belief in providence. Alexandrian Jews suffered unpleasantnesses from the empire, but most of Philo's voluminous works survive copied by Christian scribes. The Jews of Alexandria were anxious not to be thought too liberal because many of them were well educated in Greek literature and interpreted Moses philosophically. This did not dispense them from literal observance of the Torah. Philo was hostile to Jews who so asserted freedom. Their synagogue at Jerusalem did not admire the less conservative views of Stephen (Acts 6: 9). The apostle Paul found a mission to Gentiles parallel to his own in the work of Apollos, an Alexandrian Jew familiar with his Bible. At Corinth one group looked more to Apollos than to Peter or Paul.

Second-century Christianity at Alexandria was not all by later standards orthodox. There were teachers such as Basilides who would soon seem to be deviant from the Irenaean rule of truth. The spirit of the Christians was to be open to speculations reaching out beyond simple faith. They wanted to explore a higher knowledge (*gnosis*), and this word came to be associated with a certain scorn towards naïve orthodoxy. Clement candidly described some writings by Basilides and Valentinus as pretentious nonsense (*Strom.* 2. 37. 1). He did not think naïve orthodoxy possible either.

Towards the end of the second century Titus Flavius Clemens settled at Alexandria after travels to sit at the feet of Christian teachers in various places. A well read and thoughtful person, he was strongly influenced by the contemporary (Middle) Platonism which provided his bridge towards Christianity, as had happened with Justin. At Alexandria he encountered a Christian named Pantaenus who had once taught Stoicism. Clement found him excellent, and called him a 'Sicilian bee' (the island was famous for honey). Together they shared a programme of instruction in Christian faith and ethics, at first freelance but in time a more formal catechetical school under the bishop. Clement's writings have references to his role as catechist and also to the pastoral authority of the bishop. *Paid.* 1. 25 is a section on baptism, 50–1 on milk and honey given to neophytes, and 42. 1 praises 'one Father, one Word, one Holy Spirit, and one virgin mother the Church.' More than once there is polemic against sects which celebrate the eucharist in bread and water, not wine (*Paid.* 2. 20. 32; *Strom.* 1. 6. 1). At some time during his two decades at Alexandria, Clement was ordained presbyter, but whether this was by Bishop Demetrius, with whom Origen was soon to encounter difficulties, there is no certainty. Of Clement's career little is known, but his personal ideal is writ large in his writings. It seems unlikely that he stayed on at Alexandria to the end of his life, perhaps because of sporadic persecutions. Martyrdom was an issue for him and for contemporary Christians. He knew of trouble resulting for a believing wife with a wicked husband or a son with an unsympathetic father or a slave with a bad master (*Strom.* 4. 67; on persecuting laws 6. 67; on tortures 2. 125. 2).

He began with a trilogy: Exhortation (*Protreptikós*) inviting pagans to conversion to the gospel; the Tutor (*Paidagogós*) in three books on ethics and etiquette; and Miscellanies or Patchwork (*Stromateis*) in seven books. An eighth book consists of notes from his reading in dialectic. His stated intention was to call the third constituent of the trilogy the Teacher (*Didáskalos*), containing a systematic statement of doctrine. This he never wrote. He decided it would be risky to be entirely clear. The Christian story was a mystery. The *Stromateis* are deliberately elusive, constantly shifting ground and changing the subject, in the manner of contemporary pagan authors such as Aulus Gellius and Aelian or a modern *Reader's Digest*.

Rich converts were troubled by Jesus' saying about the camel having difficulty in passing through a needle's eye; so he wrote an exposition explaining that the ethical crux lay in use, not in possession, which was morally neutral. His prescriptions for use were extremely austere. Other writings include 'Excerpts from the Prophetic Scriptures', excerpts from a mildly heretical gnostic Theodotos, and 'Outlines' (*Hypotyposeis*) briefly commenting on Bible texts in eight books, unhappily extant only in fragmentary quotations and in Cassiodorus' Latin version of the exegesis of 1 Peter, Jude, 1 and 2 John. Eusebius reports that the work also expounded the epistle of Barnabas and the lurid *Apocalypse of Peter* with its descriptions of hell that offended congregations (so says the Muratorian canon, an ancient list of approved texts found by Muratori in the Ambrosian library at Milan). Cassiodorus did not translate these pieces. Photios in the ninth century judged the work to contain dangerous doctrines, which explains its failure to survive (*Bibliotheca* 109).

The *Shepherd* of Hermas and Clement of Rome to Corinth were sacred texts included in his Alexandrian canon. Eusebius had before him tracts on

Easter mentioning Melito and Irenaeus (evidently for their part in the paschal controversy), fasting, slander, an exhortation to newly baptized on endurance, and a book against Judaising Christians. These are lost. So also is a tract on the resurrection (*Paid.* 1. 47. 1; 2. 104. 3).

Clement's library was extensive and he used it freely, so that his pages are often a mosaic of allusions or quotations from Homer, Euripides, Plato, Aristotle, Musonius Rufus, the Bible, from which he especially liked the wisdom literature (Proverbs and Ben Sira had much to commend in good education). His numerous quotations from poets are demonstrably using school anthologies; he often has the same citations in the same order as appear in Athenaeus or the large fifth-century anthology of Stobaeus, which was assembled from a number of anthologies of both prose and poetry.[1] No contemporary pagan reader could have repeated Celsus' accusation that Christians were ignorant or even illiterate. Clement's conversation at a dinner party would have been entirely in the style of the time, indeed probably more sophisticated than that of other guests present. The *Paidagogós* offers advice on behaviour when a guest at dinner. The Christian guest may certainly drink wine, though not too much, and in his heart that glass will remind him of the eucharistic memorial of the Lord's passion. Clement adds in passing that the wine should not be drunk in voracious gulps or spilt down one's front. Wine refreshes the body, but to the spirit it is blood (*Paid.* 1. 15). At dinner guests should not spit or wipe their noses as some do (2. 60). Ethical issues loom large in the *Paidagogós*, especially the therapy of the passions or emotions. There were evidently both men and women receiving Clement's instruction, and he is assertive that men and women are equal in moral and spiritual matters (*Paid.* 1. 10–11; especially *Strom.* 4. 62 echoing Musonius). The identity of the Tutor oscillates between Clement himself and the divine Word. There is much advice about sex, about modest clothing and cosmetics (admissible for Christian wives if their husbands have a wandering eye), and frugal diet. He disliked homosexual practice and abortion.

The *Paidagogós* concludes with a striking anapaestic hymn of praise to the Word of God, instructor of God's children in the Church's way of peace, using Homeric epithets and idioms from classical Greek poetry.

Gnostic teachers closest to orthodoxy as Clement understood it, especially Basilides and Valentinus, were convinced that simple faith was insufficient and that there was a specifically Christian 'knowledge' (*gnosis*). Clement did not accept that there was no such thing as an orthodox gnosis. True gnosis was possible but only on a foundation of faith (*pistis*), and that faith rested on the grace of God, to which free will responded. The gnostic sects held too deterministic a view of salvation, not taking seriously the act of repentance

---

[1] See my article in *RAC* s.v. Florilegium.

indispensable to baptism (*Strom.* 2. 11), losing the Pauline theme of 'working together with God'. The sects also disparaged the order of creation, above all sex and marriage, appealing to 1 Corinthians 7. The third book of the *Stromateis* constructs a middle path between licentious sects such as the followers of Carpocrates whose love feasts ended in the extinction of lights and general wife-swapping promiscuity (*Strom.* 3. 10. 1), and the world-rejecting sects, followers of Marcion or Tatian for whom to be born is to die and is therefore an evil. Both types of sect were giving Christianity a bad name, which Clement resented, notably when the ascetics dissolved marriages (46. 4), invoked the example of Christ in demanding general celibacy (49. 1), and did not see marriage as co-operating with the Creator. 'The marriage of two true lovers of wisdom is a concord bestowed by the divine Word, telling women that beauty lies in character, not appearance and men that they are not to treat their wives as sexual objects' (*Strom.* 2. 143. 1).

Clement's ideal, the true or orthodox gnostic, embodies both biblical and Greek ideals of perfection, like the Stoics' wise man who is, they reckoned, prophet, priest, and king (*Strom.* 2. 19. 4), or the Platonic ideal (*Theaetetus* 176 B) of being 'as like God as possible'. What the Old Testament law was to the Hebrews, philosophy has been to the Greeks, and now the two streams providentially have their confluence in the gospel (*Strom.* 1. 29. 1). Accordingly the believer may adopt a positive estimate of Greek philosophical ethics but setting aside Stoic materialism and Platonic notions of reincarnation. Clement liked Plato's *Gorgias* on the remedial purpose of punishment (*Paid.* 1. 67), and this helped him to see divine punishment for sinners here and hereafter as therapeutic. 'God's anger is full of love' (*Paid.* 1. 74).

Clement devotes a long section to the theme, inherited from Philo and Josephus, that the Greek philosophers and writers plagiarized the Old Testament. He could find in Plato a doctrine of the divine Triad, creation, the cross, the life to come and judgement, the evil world-soul of Plato's *Laws* which is his way of speaking about the devil, the resurrection of the righteous, and Socrates' prophecy that a truly good and just man is so unacceptable to corrupt human society that he is crucified. At the same time Clement disliked Plato's notion that the celestial bodies are homes for divine souls, which explained the strict order of their movement. Clement here foreshadows a major controversy of the sixth century between the pagan Neoplatonist Simplicius, for whom the divinity of the sun, moon, and stars is a basic pagan principle, and the Alexandrian John Philoponos for whom they are merely natural physical objects. After Philo it was easy to find the account of creation in Plato's *Timaeus* dependent on Genesis. But Clement could not accept the eternity of the world. Another sensitive point for him was Plato's idea of the soul falling to be imprisoned in matter. He regarded as gnostic heresy the exegesis of Adam and Eve's 'coats of skins' to mean the bodies acquired at the Fall (*Strom*. 3. 95. 2), a view found also in Philo which implied that in paradise they had no sexual union before they fell, and therefore reflected a negative valuation of the created order (*Strom*. 3. 102).

In the development of the doctrine of the divine Trinity Clement (*Strom*. 5. 103. 1) followed Justin in finding an anticipation of the Christian triad in contemporary Platonist exegesis of Plato's second letter (312 E) (not today regarded as Plato's but not doubted in antiquity): 'All things lie round the king of all and exist for him; beings of the second rank lie round the second king, beings of the third round the third'. Plotinus (5. 1. 8) wrote that the good is 'Father of the creator/cause, the cause itself is intelligence (*nous*) which produces Soul.' Behind this was interpretation of the first two hypotheses of Plato's *Parmenides*: the One cannot be an object of knowledge (142 A), for God is ineffable, neither whole nor parts, has no dimensions or limit, no form, no name (137 CD, 142 A). The first One is above being, the second is intelligible being and the totality of ideas. Within this stream of thought Clement writes that 'the Father transcends the Son' (*Strom*. 7. 2. 3). The merging of the Neoplatonic triad with the Christian concept of God was followed by Origen (*c. Cels*. 6. 18) who was also credited with strongly 'subordinationist' ideas about the Son's relation to the Father.

Clement's answer to the question in Celsus how monotheism can be consistent with the incarnation reads that the divine Logos is the Father's will and energy and minister to the created order. He rejects, as Justin did, the notion that Jesus was so good a man that, like Heracles, he was raised to divine status (*Paid*. 1. 25). Jesus is the embodiment of the ideal of perfection in humanity realizing, as believers cannot do, union with God in this life. For believers the knowledge of God is a growth in maturity of faith, hope, and love. This knowledge is identical with salvation. A true gnostic invited to choose between a dynamic advance in knowing God and a static possession of salvation would choose the former (*Strom*. 4. 136. 5), a saying famously plagiarized by Lessing. The Creator has endowed all rational beings, angelic and human, with freedom, allowing that which derives being from him to turn from him and to be other. Opposition to the determinism of the sects made Clement firmly assertive about free choice.

But the Creator is utterly transcendent, beyond our power to grasp, so that we can comprehend only what he is not, a negative process analogous to thinking of a geometrical point. We have to abstract all corporeal and even incorporeal ideas and images, casting ourselves upon the greatness of Christ for the final ascent (*Strom*. 5. 71). Accordingly Clement was much aware of the symbolic and metaphorical nature of religious language, a characteristic not only of Christians but also of Egyptians, Greeks, and Jews. The principle he found particularly exemplified in allegorical interpretation of biblical texts. In theology truth is wrapped in mist, and the esoteric is to be seen in Pythagorean symbols, in Plato's unwritten doctrines, and also in Aristotle. Celsus had attacked Christian talk of God as anthropomorphic. Clement finds far more anthropomorphism in polytheism with its temples and idols and animal sacrifices, as if a god could be hungry. True prayer is expounded in the seventh book of the *Stromateis*, and is 'conversation with God' for which vocalised words are unnecessary. Any time or place which offers the occasion for thinking of God is thereby made holy (*Strom.* 7. 43).

The seventh book of the *Stromateis* provides a theology of spirituality which anticipates the monastic aspirations of believers two hundred years later. Clement adapted for Christians a Pythagorean concept of spiritual direction. The true gnostic is not egotistically concerned with his own soul. He is to be a mediator of truth and moral leadership to less advanced believers. It is he who fills 'the place left vacant by the apostles' and who can therefore interpret scripture with authority (*Strom.* 7. 52, 77).

Clement could not but be aware that he belonged to a faith which was rapidly spreading (expressly *Strom.* 2. 30. 1), but which was regarded as non-Hellenic and therefore 'barbarian', an outsiders' culture. Critics whom he would like to win over are 'Greeks' (e.g. *Strom.* 1. 163). The plagiarism theme made it much easier for him to surmount this considerable obstacle. He devoted pages to an argument that all important skills accepted by the Greeks have been of barbarian origin. Nevertheless his own high culture is very Greek. His critique of pagan society where people were enslaved to the pursuit of pleasure with mistresses or in many cases young boys, 'more licentious than animals' (*Strom.* 2. 138. 6), is in line with ancient classical satire. What needed changing in polytheistic society was its religion, which was idolatrous superstition. Remove the threat of active persecution and Clement comes before us as a fully paid-up member of the most cultivated class of ancient Alexandria. At the same time he is no less puritan than Tertullian in his assessment of occupations unsuitable or inappropriate for a baptized Christian or even a catechumen. He writes severely of pornographic art and literature, and is sure that beauty is no sufficient defence of artistic work which is morally corrupting. There is a potent self-consciousness of belonging to a community committed to a critical stance in regard to pagan culture and social mores.

19

JULIUS AFRICANUS

A comparable contemporary of Clement was another learned Christian, Sextus Julius Africanus, whose surviving writings show him to have been a rare polymath. He was capable of writing on military matters (of which he had some first-hand knowledge), on history, magic, Christianity, and architecture. He had a strikingly varied career in the army, in medicine, and law. His birthplace seems to have been Hadrian's replacement of Jerusalem, Aelia Capitolina (P.Oxy. III 412). He came to know relatives of Jesus from the Nazareth region, and knew at least some Hebrew. On a visit to Edessa he met King Abgar VIII (177–212) and his son and especially a Christian theologian who also wrote Syriac poetry, Bardaisan or (for Greeks) Bardesanes (below p. 166), whose skill in archery he admired. Bardaisan or an immediate pupil was author of an extant tract 'on the laws of the nations',[1] copied by both Christians and pagans. At Edessa Africanus studied the archives to grasp the history of Edessa's kings. He compiled a pioneer chronicle in five books, providing a synchronous account of biblical or church history together with Greek and Roman history.

His reputation reached the ears of the emperor Severus Alexander to whom he dedicated a kind of encyclopedia, and perhaps he influenced this emperor towards the construction of a private chapel with statues of principal heroes of the various religions of his subjects, including Abraham and Jesus. The emperor invited him to design a library for the Pantheon in Rome. For an otherwise unknown Aristides he composed an extant harmonization of the two gospel genealogies of Jesus, the differences between them being a point of negative criticism against the reliability of the records. (Late in the fourth century their diversity played a crucial role in repelling the adolescent Augustine from his mother's faith.)

In touch with the equally learned Origen, he persuasively argued that the story of Susanna should not be cited as authoritatively showing up Jewish elders in an unhappy light, since the Greek text contained a pun not

---

[1] Edited by H. J. W. Drijvers (Assen, 1965), by F. Nau in *Patrologia Syriaca*, I. 536–611 (1907), discovered by W. Cureton, *Spicilegium Syriacum* (London, 1855). Professor Drijvers followed his edition with a monograph (Assen, 1966).

reproducible in Hebrew, demonstrating that the text was not original and authoritative.

Africanus had the curiosity of a traveller. Visiting Egypt he called on Heraklas, bishop of Alexandria. He obtained a copy of the sacred Book of Cheops, 'a great acquisition'. In old age he lived in Palestine at Emmaus (Nicopolis) and once represented his town on an embassy to Rome, success-fully obtaining its elevation to the rank of *municipium*.

From the varied evidence it is an inevitable conclusion that Julius Africanus was not regarded as an outsider to high culture, but was a distin-guished man of respected and admired learning with access to the imperial court. His faith can hardly have been a secret, yet there is no evidence of anyone harassing him or threatening torture and martyrdom. The fierce persecution under the emperor Decius (251) was not even on the horizon.

20

HIPPOLYTUS AND LITURGY

During the third and fourth centuries the Christian community in Rome gradually became predominantly Latin-speaking, and memories of its Greek beginnings were lost in mist. The last ancient Christian of Rome to write in Greek was Hippolytus. The calendar of Filocalus of the year 354 records under the year 235 that Bishop Pontianus and Presbyter Hippolytus were exiled to Sardinia, no doubt to sweat as labourers in the mines under the usual lethal conditions. Both names occur in the list of martyrs. A number of works by Hippolytus were known to Eusebius, for example *On the Pascha* together with an Easter table on a 16-year cycle starting in AD 222; a *Hexaemeron* expounding the six days of Genesis 1; *Against Marcion*; *On the Song of Songs, On Ezekiel*; and *Against all Heresies*. Extant also is a commentary on Daniel, written to discourage millennial excitements (in Syria a bishop had lately led his flock out into the desert to await the second coming, and had had to be rescued by imperial authority). The work twice alludes to personal envy against the author. His colleagues may have found him difficult. Other works transmitted under his name, probably correctly, are *On the universe* attacking Plato for incompetence, *On Christ and Antichrist, On the Benedictions of Moses*. Fragments survive of a letter on the resurrection theme in Paul's Corinthian letters addressed to the empress Mammaea.

Two works attributed to him by modern scholars have been the subject of controversy, namely his *Elenchos* or 'Refutation of all Heresies', found on Mount Athos and first printed in 1851, and a Church Order which presupposes a situation at Rome early in the third century and was composed by a passionate conservative anxious about recent innovations. In 1551 a statue on a chair was discovered in Rome, on which was a list of titles of Hippolytus' works, including his Easter table (not the *Elenchos*), and recording work on spiritual charisms and the *Apostolic Tradition*. The *Elenchos* is indispensable to students of pre-Socratic Greek philosophy because of the number of quotations of otherwise lost texts; Hippolytus' thesis is that the gnostic heresies have been plagiarized from very uninspired philosophers. The climax of the work turns into a direct and very personal assault on Bishop Callistus of Rome, who had enraged the author by denouncing his Logos theology as ditheism.

The Church Order survives through several dependent texts in various languages, and whatever dispute there may be about authorship (attribution to Hippolytus is uncertain), the probability of an early third-century date at Rome is high. The Church is vulnerable to persecution, and is given a decision on the status of confessors who have been in prison for their faith. The community assembles for worship in a private house. The eucharistic prayer lacks a Sanctus, which was common in the Greek east but not in the west until the fifth century. The bishop is expected to use the prayer as a model, but is not required to know it by heart and is free to make his own text. The shape of the liturgy is defined: thanksgiving, reciting the Institution with Jesus' words, the anamnesis or memorial, invocation of the Holy Spirit upon the Church's offering and the community. There is no commemoration of saints. But at this date liturgy had not yet acquired a fixed form.

The Church Order rules that the slave of a Christian master may be admitted as catechumen with the master's consent. Certain trades and professions are banned, e.g. a pander or harlot, a sculptor who makes idols, an actor, a charioteer, a gladiator or trainer of gladiators or any official concerned in such matters, a pagan priest, a soldier or magistrate who may have to kill (a distinction is made in that a soldier may become a catechumen but a catechumen may not join the army), a magician. The process of instruction lasts three years with exceptions made for individual cases. In the assembly the sexes are segregated and the kiss of peace is to be men with men, women with women.

For baptism candidates undress and women untie their hair (a rule also known to Tertullian) and put off any gold ornaments. They are anointed with consecrated oil by way of exorcism in a renunciation of Satan, his service, and all his works. Naked in the water they profess the faith with answers to interrogations:

Do you believe in God the Father almighty?

Do you believe in Jesus Christ the Son of God, who was born of Holy Spirit and the Virgin Mary, who was crucified in the days of Pontius Pilate, and died, and rose the third day from the dead, and ascended into heaven, and sat down at the right hand of the Father, and will come to judge the living and the dead?

Do you believe in Holy Spirit in Holy Church, and the resurrection of the flesh?

To each question the candidate answers 'I believe', and is immersed in the font; after which a presbyter anoints with oil, an act which the bishop repeats laying his hand on the head with the sign of the cross on the forehead. The newly baptized are then admitted to the assembly for the eucharist, to which they may otherwise not come. The bishop says the prayer of Thanksgiving by which the bread and wine become the 'antitypes' of Christ's body and blood. Entry to the promised land is symbolised by milk and honey. (A prayer is provided for blessing cheese which recalls the African martyr Perpetua's dream-vision of receiving cheese in heaven.) Some water is added to the wine. As the bishop gives a fragment of bread to each communicant he is to say 'The Bread of heaven in Christ Jesus', and the recipient says Amen. Care is emphatically enjoined to ensure that none of the sacred bread and wine falls to the ground. An order to see that no mouse or other animal eats from the bread makes sense if it was customary to take the bread home, reserved to be consumed during the week with private prayer.

The interrogations are the parent of the later so-called Apostles' Creed, the baptismal confession of the western Church.

Family prayers at home are to be at cockcrow, the third, sixth, ninth hours, before retiring to bed, and at midnight, the hour at which every creature is hushed to praise the Lord.

21

ORIGEN

When early in the fourth century Eusebius Bishop of Caesarea came to write his history of the Church, his sixth book offered a triumphant climax in a biography of his intellectual hero Origen.

Eusebius knew Origen's writings intimately, and felt himself to be a pupil, though Origen, born about 184, died in 254 and the two men had never met. However, Origen's library was preserved at Caesarea (Palestine), a church proud to have been the place where St Peter was granted the first conversion of a Gentile, Cornelius (Acts 10). Origen was a prolific producer. Jerome, who in his early years as a biblical exegete, thought Origen 'the greatest teacher of the Church since the apostles', preserves in one letter (33) a long catalogue of Origen's writings, with the cry 'Which of us can read everything he has written?' Origen was helped in producing this overflowing mass of matter by a wealthy patron named Ambrosius who provided shorthand writers to take down what he dictated and to make copies. (Publication in antiquity was by the reading of the text usually by the author to a circle of friends, who would then commission copies to be made at commercial rates. Once an author was known he might send a letter to a distant correspondent suggesting that he should pay for a copy to be made of his latest pieces.)

The central task for his lifework, as Origen himself understood it, was to write biblical commentaries, to interpret the scriptures for his generation in the Church, thereby warding off gnostic exegesis and also rebutting criticism from the pagan intelligentsia. He needed to provide exegesis implicitly refuting Marcion's rejection of the Hebrew scriptures but also disallowing rabbinic literalism. In addition to full-scale commentaries, some of remarkable length so that none survives complete, he was in demand as a preacher. Sermons on the Hexateuch, on the Song of Songs, Isaiah, and Ezekiel were translated into Latin by Rufinus or his one-time friend Jerome. Sermons on St Luke's gospel also survive in Latin. Commentaries on some Pauline epistles, notably Ephesians, survive mainly through the work of Jerome making use of Origen for his own exegesis. The sermons belong to the second half of his life after he had migrated from Alexandria to Palestinian Caesarea, where he received ordination as presbyter, an event highly displeasing to Bishop Demetrius of Alexandria. Throughout the medieval millennium the Latin versions of the sermons found grateful and admiring readers in the West. The Greek East was more reserved. Eusebius had before him a collection of about 100 of Origen's letters; of these only three survive.

Origen was a precise observer of variant readings in manuscripts of scripture. A major undertaking was his 'Hexapla', bringing together in parallel the different Greek versions of the Hebrew Bible, including a transliteration of the Hebrew in Greek. The Hexapla had practical utility in discussions with rabbis. It also facilitated correction of the Septuagint.

Origen knew of heretics who disparaged Moses as a murderer (Exod. 2: 12), but greater injury to Moses' reputation was, in his opinion, caused by those who refused allegory 'who interpret the spiritual law carnally'. 'Simple Christians believe things of God that would be incredible of the most unjust and barbaric men.' He rejects the suggestion that he has a low estimate of the Torah, every word of which he understands to be dictated by the Holy Spirit (*Hom. on Num.* 7. 1–2, 1. 1).

Already by the end of the second century congregations expected their bishop not only to be their spiritual pastor in an office and succession assuring them of apostolic faith and sacraments, but also to fulfil a social role. This social role could include banking their savings, lending money at normal commercial rates (12 per cent a year), and where bishops had the necessary rank in society supporting individuals in trouble with tax-gatherers or magistrates. A bishop would attend an agape or love-feast at which the poor could be well fed and even, with the leave of the wealthy provider, take food away for the morrow.[1] Towards the more secular aspects of being a bishop, Origen had deep reservations. He knew of at least one bishop who went about with an attendant bodyguard (*Comm. on Matt.* 16. 8) as, soon after Origen's time, Bishop Paul of Antioch is recorded to have done. The churches were crowded out (17. 24), but had become too concerned for financial success (16. 22–3). A church had become a piece of property which a bishop might try to bequeath to a relative or at least he would nominate his successor (*Hom. on Num.* 22. 4; *on Lev.* 6. 6). The necessary assent of the laity to an election was no control against abuse (*on Lev.* 6. 3). Celibacy was desirable in a bishop, not required canonically.

Origen expected immensely high standards of personal morality from bishops, presbyters, and deacons, with the consequence that he can be read as that familiar type in church history, an anticlerical high churchman. He can write scathingly of 'bishops of great cities, waited on by ladies of wealth and refinement, who will not converse with ascetic Christians on equal terms.' His exegesis of the woes of Matthew 23 is fierce reading. Demetrius of

---

[1] On generous gifts by ancient hosts see W. J. Slater, 'Handouts at Dinner', *Phoenix*, 54 (2000), 107–22.

Alexandria seemed to him this kind of worldly prelate. Several of the Caesarean sermons directly address catechumens. At the age of about 18 Origen was entrusted by Demetrius with the school for catechumens, a group which he soon divided into two streams, taking the more able himself and delegating the slower minds to an assistant. Simple minds in the Church gave him problems. They were prone to understand everything in scripture as plain prose to be taken literally: 'The stupidity of some Christians is heavier than the sand of the sea' (*Hom. on Gen.* 9. 2). Their idea of God was wholly anthropomorphic, as if he had a physical frame like an old man in the sky. Moreover, the renunciation of evil at their baptism was often not more than half-hearted, so that they continued to consult astrologers and trusted in fortune tellers to interpret their dreams (*Hom. on Josh.* 5. 6, 7. 4). They went to the theatre for erotic dramas (*Hom. on Lev.* 11. 1). It also troubled Origen that a substantial number attended the synagogue on Saturday and the church on Sunday, and observed Jewish feasts and fasts (*Hom. on Lev.* 10. 2). (They may of course have been Jews.) Infidelity to spouses was a source of frequent difficulty (*on Josh.* 5. 6). Origen asked the laity for austerely disciplined personal lives, but qualified his exhortations by saying that abstinence should never be immoderate (*Hom. on Num.* 27. 9; *on Judg.* 5. 6). Renunciation of the world had to be unqualified (*Hom. on Lev.* 11. 1). Too many lapsed after baptism, and among those who continued, good sexual discipline was unusual (*Hom. on Josh.* 4. 2). Yet secularized believers 'bow to the priest and honour God's servants' [i.e. ascetics] (10. 3).[2] It saddened Origen that many spent 'less than two or three hours a day' in prayer and Bible study and worship (*Hom. on Num.* 2. 1).

Cardinal to Origen's exegesis is his resort to allegory. Not that the literal sense is excluded except in rare cases. Normally everything in the Bible has a good literal sense. But it is a fundamental axiom that nothing unworthy of God can be the inner meaning. And if there are difficult or apparently unedifying passages, allegory offers a solution. The size of Noah's ark can be defended literally if one cubes the figures, but its inner meaning is what most matters: 'Outside the Church there is no salvation' (*Hom. on Josh.* 3. 5). The hardening of Pharaoh's heart or the inhumanity shown by Joshua to the Canaanite tribes were weapons in the arsenal of Marcion, but then he rejected allegory and should not have done so. The story of Adam and Eve was clearly symbolic of the fallen human condition. Moreover, the propriety of allegorical exegesis applied not only to the Old Testament but also to the New (*Hom. on Lev.* 7. 5). That allegory was justified seemed demonstrable from the authority of the apostle (Gal. 4: 24). Like Clement, Origen was familiar with Philo's writings.

---

[2] This is the earliest allusion to the custom of giving honour to clergy. Socrates, *HE* 6. 11. 16 noted the custom to stand when a bishop entered the room.

In the commentary on St John he asks the significance of the fact that while the synoptists place the cleansing of the temple at Jesus' final entry to Jerusalem, St John places it early in his ministry and is clearly incorrect at the literal historical level; but as symbol of the Church's need for purification this is profound and right, 'spiritual truth in historical falsehood'. And the entry to Jerusalem refers to the Lord's ascent to the heavenly city, conquering opposing powers and purifying his people.

The Septuagint Bible was the supreme source of God's revelation, and Origen, who had an excellent memory, could recall the text by heart with only few occasional lapses. The preacher begs his congregation to pray that he may be granted a true interpretation, since his task is dangerous. But the congregations included critics with serious doubts about his allegories, which to them seemed almost like divination, subjective guesswork (e.g. *Hom. on Ezek.* 6. 8; *on Jer.* 5. 2; *on Luke* 25). Or perhaps excessive allegory looked indistinguishable from gnostic methods. Origen's commentary on St John's gospel was undertaken to refute an earlier exegesis by the Valentinian Heracleon who found the gospel's highly symbolist writing congenial.

A major answer to Marcion and Valentinus was embodied in his fascinating work 'On First Principles' (*De principiis*), much of which survives only in a Latin paraphrase by Rufinus of Aquileia, explicitly glossing or amending passages where the Greek original seemed too speculative and risky. But there are substantial quotations of the Greek text, especially from the section on the interpretation of the Bible in the *Philokalia* made by Basil and Gregory of Nazianzos in the sixties of the fourth century. This work, however, provoked criticism late in the fourth century from Epiphanius and Jerome, and in the sixth century from the emperor Justinian when it was being invoked to justify speculative theology alarming more conservative minds. From Plotinus onwards the Neoplatonic philosophers disliked Gnosticism with its negative estimate of the material creation. Origen's thought in his *First Principles* is akin to that of Plotinus, but is more tied to the question of the meaning of scripture. The work emphatically begins with a statement of the apostolic tradition of doctrine; that is the criterion. But what is left undefined in the rule of faith is left for investigation and free inquiry; moreover, the theologian may try to discern the reasons underlying doctrines authoritatively affirmed in the apostolic rule. Origen also expressed respect for liturgical tradition as a norm of truth. Prayer is offered to the Father through the Son in the Holy Spirit, and this determines the eucharistic prayer.

Origen's reputation brought invitations to other churches and places. He was invited to meet the emperor's mother Mamaea. A papyrus preserves the record of a visit to Arabia invited to correct the monarchian doctrine of one Heraclides. He visited Rome and met Hippolytus.

About 229 Origen travelled to Athens invited to dispute with a Valentinian heretic named Candidus, who defended a dualism of good and evil by pointing to the orthodox assumption which had no room for the possibility of the devil's salvation. That meant that a keystone of gnostic theology was in principle conceded by the Church. Origen answered him that the devil, a fallen angel and Lucifer, fell by will, not by nature, and remains evil by will. If so, it is not impossible for God's power and goodness to bring even Satan to repent. Candidus published his version of the debate. At Alexandria Bishop Demetrius was perturbed at the thought of the devil being saved. A storm ensued, but Origen was invited to Caesarea in Palestine where to Demetrius' wrath he was ordained presbyter. He astringently commented that just as the archangel Michael, contending with the devil, did not revile him (Jude 9), so he himself would not speak evil of the devil any more than of the bishop of Alexandria. Bishop Demetrius complained that Origen was under his jurisdiction; that he was advancing heretical doctrine; and in any event he was a eunuch and therefore by Leviticus 21: 16–24 (cf. Deut. 23: 1), disqualified from priesthood.

Eusebius reports the story (expressly from oral tradition, not from documents) that Origen in youth had sought to facilitate pastoral work in catechizing women by castrating himself. Epiphanius has a different story, that he maintained his celibacy by drugs. In his commentary on Matt. 19: 11–12 Origen deplores literal understanding of Jesus' words, though aware of some who acted on them as plain prose. The council of Nicaea (325) ruled against ordination after self-castration but allowed it in case of loss by accident or enemy action or other involuntary cause. In later centuries a number of monks, among whom some became bishops, were eunuchs. A collection of gnomic maxims, *The Sentences of Sextus*, in which old Pythagorean sayings appear in a Christian setting, did not hesitate to recommend cutting away sources of temptation. Origen informs us that among Christians these maxims were widely read. Translated from Greek into Latin by Rufinus and anonymously into Syriac, they enjoyed wide reading for centuries in the West and passed into other languages as well. Ambrose of Milan liked to quote from them. One maxim is cited in the Rule of St Benedict.

The principal ground for anxiety about Origen's thinking centred on his use of allegorical method and on the inner meaning which he found in the biblical text. For example, like Clement before him he was sure that divine wrath is no emotional reaction, and that each sinner 'treasures up for himself' pain at the final judgement. Simple believers were mocked for their literal belief in the fires of hell by the pagan Celsus (though Celsus was quick, as a good Platonist, to affirm his belief in judgement hereafter). Origen defends simple believers: they are right about divine punishment, but wrong about the intention which is remedial. Fire purifies. It does not merely destroy.

Origen's ideas of creation also caused misgiving. God, he states, is wholly incorporeal, pure spirit beyond space and time, without needs, and good not in the sense that this happens to be his character, but in the sense that he is the very source of goodness. To be and to be good are in God identical, and creation is an overflow of divine goodness (as Plato said in the *Timaeus*). First created were pure spirits endowed with reason and freedom but bodiless. Origen sharply rejects the notion that matter was a kind of sludge as eternal as God who did the best he could with it. God himself created matter out of nothing with a pedagogic purpose. Accordingly this purpose was highly positive; it was to discipline those rational souls which exercised their freedom of choice by falling away from God, some only a modest distance who might therefore ensoul stars, others a more drastic fall into human bodies or even demonic. This was an idea Origen found in Philo of Alexandria.

It followed that Origen did not have a high estimate of sexuality. For married partners there is no sin in the sexual act, but that is not to say that it is holy (*Hom. on Num.* 6. 3). Restriction to procreation should control the motive (*Hom. on Gen.* 5. 4). Otherwise sexual union ties the partners to the flesh and hinders their rise to the realm of spirit (a judgement shared by Platonists of Origen's time, such as Porphyry). He disowns the view that the erotic impulse is of the devil; it is natural given by the Creator. But like anger it is hard to control by reason or will. The practice of baptizing infants is justified by the suggestion that there is some pollution to be washed away. It cannot be accidental that the only two persons recorded in scripture to have celebrated their birthday are Pharaoh and Herod. (The early Christians used *natalis* of the anniversary of a martyr's death.) Gnostics took the 'coats of skins' assumed by Adam and Eve to symbolise material bodies. Origen was far from sure that this could be correct.

There was a problem about the body assumed by the incarnate Lord. Christ had a human soul and body identical with ours. But Origen agreed with Clement that he did not need to evacuate body-waste. Nor did he experience erotic urges (*Hom. on Lev.* 9. 2; *on Exod.* 4. 8). Though in the flesh he suffered pain, the divine nature within did not suffer; yet in devotion Christians may say with some philosophers 'the impassible suffers' just as the apostle could say that he who was without sin was made sin for us (*Hom. on Lev.* 3. 1).

Christ's soul was the mediator between the divine Logos and the body, and the union of soul and Logos is our example. As the believer advances in faith and love, he or she finds that the Christ who is all things to all is to each according to need. The titles of Christ in the New Testament are rungs on a ladder of mystical ascent until, like Moses, one 'enters the darkness where God is', a knowledge confined to few (*c. Cels.* 6. 17). For God is known not by mere dialectic but by grace and purity of heart (*c. Cels.* 7. 33. 42).

About the year 234 Origen composed for his friend Ambrosius a treatise *On Prayer*. The practice depends on belief in providence, but also in freedom of will. Christian prayer differs from pagan in that it is worship in spirit and in truth, not merely asking for success in this world, for fertility of crops or spouse, success in some mercantile venture, or some worldly concern. Prayer for supernatural benefits brings the mind into acceptance and submission, in tune with the world-soul.

Forgiveness of sins was still a debated issue for Origen. Writing on prayer (18. 10) he attacks 'some who claim higher than priestly rank but have less than priestly knowledge, boasting that they are empowered to grant remission for murder, adultery, and apostasy'. On the other hand, he was sure that no sinner could pass beyond redemption point. He would not censure bishops who, to avert worse occurring, allowed remarriage after divorce in the lifetime of the former partner. Evidently the majority opinion was otherwise.

About 248 at the request of Ambrosius he wrote a long rebuttal of the able anti-Christian book by Celsus written almost seventy years earlier (above p. 110). His refutation preserves a large part of Celsus' work by citing it paragraph by paragraph, and is therefore a major source for the debate between pagan intellectuals and the Church especially for the antithesis between Celsus' insistence that true religion consists in keeping ancient custom and Origen's inference that he must think it right for barbarians to keep ferocious customs, whereas the personal conviction of Christians goes with an exalted and universal ethic. Celsus is among the earliest pagan writers to discern how dangerous to traditional society and culture the Church has become. His contempt is mingled with apprehension. Origen's answer urges that the stories of Jesus' miracles and the astonishing fulfilment of ancient prophecies in the life, death, and rising again of Jesus are vindicated by the equally miraculous expansion of Christianity to pervade the entire Roman empire (e.g. *Hom. on Luke* 7). If the resurrection of Jesus had been fiction on the words of a hysterical woman, the apostles would not have risked their lives for its truth. To convince a person about a historical event unless he was there at the time is difficult. 'To substantiate any story as historical fact even if certainly true and to produce complete confidence in it, is one of the most difficult tasks, in some cases impossible. Everyone is sure there was a Trojan War but the sole evidence is in Homer's poem with many impossible and supernatural stories' (*c. Cels.* 1. 42). And should the story of Jesus' birth be scorned when pilgrims go to the very cave, famous even among people alien to Christianity?

Origen's sermons to Christian congregations are less optimistic about Christian expansion: 'Look at our crowded congregations in the churches; how many are conformed to this world, how few transformed by the renewal of their mind' (*Comm. on Matt.* 13. 24). Devotion was far more serious when persecution was serious. Most of Origen's sermons on the Hexateuch were delivered when there were no martyrs, which he seriously regretted. But by the time he wrote his reply to Celsus, he could sense a rising hostility to the Church, held responsible for the civil wars of the 240s and for natural disasters, sent by the gods in their anger at being neglected and starved of the rich smell of animal sacrifices beloved of inferior deities and daemons.

Celsus did not believe that evil in this world could be diminished: its quantity was fixed. Origen affirmed the freedom of God to purify by the word of prophets, by the law taken spiritually, and above all by the incarnation, which to Celsus seemed to presuppose an unthinkable mutability in God. For a Platonist such as Celsus this body, product of a painful birth and destined to humiliating death, could not be united to God. Paul in Romans 8 implied for Origen that the material creation was felt by souls to tie them down (*De princ.* 1. 7. 5).

Platonists such as Plotinus were unsure whether the descent of souls to inhabit bodies was a result of a mistaken free choice or some natural necessity which had to be tolerated. But they also spoke of the soul's power to ascend, leaving behind the downward pull of matter and bodily desire for pleasure in food or sex. Platonists thought this capacity inherent in the soul. Origen thought only divine grace could make it possible. For late Platonists God or 'the One' makes no move towards the created order, whereas for Origen the Father loves this world he has made and all that is by nature part of it. In Plato the goal of a vision of the Good is attainable in this life, but not in Origen.

The concept of resurrection was important to Christians who understood immortality of an immaterial soul as destined to lose all individuality and therefore all responsibility hereafter. In fact Platonists believed that the soul, freed from this earthly body, still needs a less material 'vehicle', ethereal perhaps, to shine like the stars, which 'rejoice in their celestial bodies'. Origen pondered St Paul's saying that 'flesh and blood cannot inherit the kingdom of God', and understood this to make possible a rapprochement with high-minded Platonists. His language drew fire after his death especially from Methodios bishop of Olympus in Lycia (SW Asia Minor) and from Epiphanios bishop of Salamis (Cyprus, beside Famagusta).

Thoughtful believers in his time confessed great difficulty in comprehending New Testament language about Christ's second coming and the millennium of the Apocalypse with a rebuilt Jerusalem. Origen was outspokenly critical of the literal interpretation of the millennium, advocated by Justin and Irenaeus. The second coming he understood to refer either to the universal extension of the gospel to all parts of the world or, more mystically, to the coming of the divine Logos to the soul especially in illuminating the meaning of scripture.

Before Origen, perhaps nearly contemporary with Celsus, a Platonist philosopher Numenius of Apamea had distinguished levels of divine being. Plotinus, junior contemporary of Origen, spoke of three divine hypostases, the One, Mind (*Nous*), and the World Soul, which are distinct grades in the hierarchy of being. Some similar language would be useful to Origen in explaining the doctrine of the Trinity. The Son is no creature. As philosophers said of the eternity of the cosmos, there was never a time when the Son was not (e.g. *Comm. on Rom.* 1. 5). Yet he is ministerial to the Father, in that sense subordinate, mediating between the Father and the inferior created order. The Son comes into being as a distinct hypostasis by the Father's will. Origen was opposed to the idea that Father and Son are merely names for one and the same divine being. There is indeed one God, but the Father is Father and not Son. Origen explicitly opposed the 'monarchian' answer that Father and Son are different titles for one God. If he then wanted to affirm monotheism, it seemed necessary to say that the Son is divine but not as fully divine as the Father. That proposition would bring a legacy of controversy in the following century.

There remained a problem about the correct understanding of the Holy Spirit. St John's gospel said of the Logos that 'all things were made by him'. Does that include the Spirit? Origen reviewed various possible answers, but suggested that the simplest solution was to say that the Spirit is supreme at the head of the entire created order. That doctrine would be troublesome a century or more later. Basil of Caesarea, aware of many passages in Origen passionately affirming his intention to be orthodox and to believe what the Church believes, was deeply concerned to assert the equality of the Trinity as three *prosopa* or 'persons' (an inadequate translation). He therefore marked Origen down as using orthodox language but not having an orthodox heart. This impugned Origen's integrity; it was already a common view among critics of Origen. Eusebius of Caesarea together with his mentor Pamphilus composed a *Defence of Origen* rebutting this attitude. So it would come about that Origen's intention to provide a coherent biblically based theology to overcome the differences between Christians ended by generating other problems for less philosophical successors.

Origen once complained that he found himself an excessively admired paragon for some, maliciously misrepresented by others. He regretted both attitudes. Despite an undercurrent of mistrust, especially from those less well educated than himself, he was occasionally invited by bishops to assist in correcting the doctrines of their episcopal colleagues. Eusebius records that Beryllus, bishop of Bostra (Syria), came to deny that Christ pre-existed his birth of Mary, and said that his deity was the Father dwelling in him. Numerous bishops in synod debated with him, but they had to call Origen in to discover what he really believed, and Origen's cross-questioning brought him back to orthodoxy. A papyrus find in 1941 has preserved a discussion between Origen and a bishop Heraclides, probably in Arabia, similarly concerned with the unity of God and the incarnation. The immortality of the soul was also a problem debated in Arabian churches where Origen was invited to help. Some held the soul to be blood.

Origen's Christian critics were obviously correct in thinking that his system was incorporating large elements of Plato. Merely to have entitled a work 'On First Principles' was to take a stand in the discussions of contemporary Platonists. At the same time, however, he was rewriting Platonism, and incurred the wrath of the pagan Neoplatonist Porphyry for whom a basic axiom was the incompatibility of pagan culture and Christianity.

Among Origen's letters Eusebius found correspondence with Fabian bishop of Rome and many other bishops on the subject of his orthodoxy (Eus. *HE* 6. 36. 4). The matter was an issue after his exchanges with Demetrius of Alexandria. Eusebius also found correspondence between Origen and the emperor Philip the Arab and his wife Severa when the palace was friendly to the Church. Under the fierce persecution of the Church by Philip's successor Decius (250–1) he was arrested and severely tortured. He died at Tyre about 254. His tomb in Tyre cathedral was there for Crusaders to see in the twelfth century.

In his doctrines of the Trinity and the person of Christ Origen had no authoritative conciliar decrees to which he was expected to conform. Adherence to the apostolic and biblical faith was primary for him. But beyond what was affirmed in the apostolic rule he was free to speculate, and such freedom was going to alarm later generations, though Athanasius was to defend his approach. At the same time his teaching about prayer and the devout soul's call to aspire to union with God, and his powerful exploitation of allegory to solve the problem of interpreting the Old Testament and some of the New, remained enormously influential. His powers as a teacher are directly attested in a panegyric on his method by Gregory, a pupil who became the apostle of Pontus by the Black Sea of whom such wonders were popularly reported that he acquired the sobriquet 'the Wonderworker' (Thaumaturgus).[3]

---

[3] On Gregory of Nyssa's largely fictitious biography of Gregory see Stephen Mitchell, in *Portraits of Spiritual Authority*, ed. J. W. Drijvers and J. W. Watt (Leiden, 1999), 99–138 with rich bibliography.

22

CYPRIAN OF CARTHAGE

For the story of the Church (and of much else) in the middle decades of the third century the principal sources of information are the letters and tracts of Cyprian, bishop of Carthage during the decade 248–58, and the excerpts from the writings and letters of Dionysius of Alexandria mainly preserved in the *Church History* of Eusebius of Caesarea. Unfortunately sources for the secular history of the time are jejune. Cyprian and Dionysius both shed much light on the internal problems of the Church at a period when the crisis of a disintegrating Roman empire provoked passionate popular hostility to the Christians. The empire faced a series of civil wars between legitimate and less legitimate emperors. Goths poured across the lower Danube, Persians under King Shahpuhr I invaded Syria and captured the great Syrian city of Antioch-on-the-Orontes. In Asia Minor there had been earthquakes which people blamed on the Christian neglect of the traditional gods. In addition plague[1] spread from Egypt reducing the population of many cities and weakening the imperial armies. Writing against Celsus about 248 Origen noted rising attacks on Christians as responsible for these disasters (*c. Cels.* 3. 15). In 248 a celebration of Rome's millennium provided a context for a pagan revival. At Alexandria in 249 the mob subjected the Christians to a violent pogrom, a sign of what was to come (Eus. *HE* 6. 41). The dimensions of the Christian presence in third-century north Africa are manifest in the exceptionally large number of bishoprics attested in Cyprian's letters and councils, which record more than 130. Pagans could easily have felt swamped. The notorious Alexandrian mob could be roused to frenzy.

Cyprian had enjoyed a successful career at Carthage as a master of Latin rhetoric. In 246 he was converted from polytheism and idolatry to Christianity. An open letter to a friend and fellow convert Donatus provides some account of the motives underlying his conversion. He described himself as disgusted with the cruelties of contemporary society, the corruption of the judges easily bribed, the savagery of judicial tortures which left innocent people maimed if they did not die on the rack and did not confess

---

[1] In 252 plague struck Carthage and its province; Cyprian described it with echoes of Lucretius (6. 1138 ff.) on the pest at Athens from Thucydides (*De mortalitate* 14; *ad Donatum* 10–11).

to capital crimes which they had not committed merely to stop the fearful pain. He hated the inhumanity of gladiatorial combats in the amphitheatre, the violence and murder on the streets, the sexual promiscuity of the under-class, and in the empire incessant battles. It was a formidable indictment of a society coming apart at the seams. He found his own conscience washed clear in baptism. Before long he was ordained presbyter. The extant panegyric by his friend Pontius (2) noted that he prized celibacy as being of special value before God. At this date there were still married Latin clergy, but already celibacy was regarded as manifesting a higher moral dedication—an axiom for Platonic philosophers as well as for admirers of the apostle Paul (1 Corinthians 7). In a society where the emperor's soldiers were expected to be free of marital ties (forbidden until the early third century, not encouraged thereafter), it would be natural to expect the same of front-line soldiers in the Church. After becoming bishop and primate he expected all clergy to avoid any entanglements in worldly business and to devote themselves exclusively to their spiritual responsibilities (*ep.* 1). A prominent Christian characteristic was to manifest their abhorrence of pagan cult by turning their eyes away from temples and idols (*ep.* 31. 7) and to invoke against evil powers the protection of the sign of the cross (*ep.* 58. 9).

Cyprian was probably of curial class, well to do, and respected in the city. Like other Christians in the vicinity of Carthage (*ep.* 55. 14), he was a landowner with a country estate. Generous with money, he also took it for granted that those dependent on his bounty would take care not to dissent from policies he thought necessary. Two years after his baptism the *plebs* demanded of the provincial bishops his consecration to succeed the dead bishop Donatus. The choice was intransigently opposed then and thereafter by five senior presbyters, a substantial proportion of the older clergy. There was already among the clergy a feeling that those chosen to be bishops should ascend through each different grade of ministry. His consecration was by lay-ing on of hands in traditional form by bishops of his provinces (perhaps including some from Numidia, a province he regarded as part of his primacy, and early in the fourth century Numidian bishops regarded themselves as properly concerned in the choice of a bishop of Carthage). They represented both due succession and the universal episcopate of a universal Church (*epp.* 47. 1; 67. 5).

Cyprian's upper-class and educated background appears in his familiarity with Apuleius and Seneca, and in his use of the then conventional aristocratic manner of addressing important personages as abstractions (e.g. 'your holi-ness' for bishops).

The bishop was financial controller of his community. Presbyters received a monthly dividend of the people's offerings (*ep.* 34. 4). There was no system of tithe (*De unitate* 26).

It was natural for senior clergy to look askance at the promotion of a wealthy novice over their heads. But by the mid-third century the laity were coming to expect their bishop to perform a social role, not only in hospitality (*ep.* 7) but also in advising and defending their secular interests if they were in difficulties with tax authorities or with the law or if they needed a bridging loan for their business. The church chest could be used for redeeming captives taken by barbarian tribes in southern Numidia (*ep.* 62), or to give (frugal) help to converts, such as an actor in a disreputable profession and therefore expected to give up his job (*ep.* 2). Since the ruling of the apostle Paul that Christians should not sue each other in the lawcourts, bishops were expected to provide an arbitration service, which might be a very delicate task. Commonly they heard such cases, flanked by their presbyters, early each Monday morning, which gave the maximum of time to achieve reconciliation of the contending parties before the eucharist on the following Sunday. Cyprian's past social standing and public experience in secular society would have made him an attractive choice to the laity. In any event, a qualified orator could preach well. Pontius' panegyric reports (9) that when plague arrived in Carthage, Cyprian mobilized the laity to render crucial help to the sick, whether Christian or not.[2]

The bishop was the normal minister of baptism, for which the water was consecrated. Renunciation of the devil and all his works was emphatic. Infant baptism was normal, but since Tertullian ('why should the age of innocence hurry to the remission of sins?') a tradition of doubt persisted. Cyprian (*ep.* 64) defended it. People were accustomed to nudity at the baths, and nudity at the actual moment of baptism 'occasioned no blushes'.[3] The sick or dying were baptized by affusion, which some disparaged.

From the start of his episcopate Cyprian made it a point of democratic principle that he would consult his clergy, especially about ordinations on which the laity would also have views. (The stated policy evidently distanced critics who thought him bossy.) To clarify his episcopal function and responsibility he took the lead from the Levitical precepts for priesthood in the Old Testament. Priests and high priests were there by divine authority, and it was no less so for ministers of the new covenant of Christ. His role was to pray for his flock and to preside in the offering of the Church's sacrifice

---

[2] Similar care in Egypt: Eus., *HE* 7. 22. 7, 9. 8. 14.

[3] Ps.-Cyprian, *De singularitate clericorum* p. 189 Hartel (probably a third- or early fourth-century text). In Ambrose's time some covered themselves at the public baths (*De officiis* I. 18. 79); but at the moment of baptism any sexual shame signified sin (*in Ps.* 61. 32). Visiting baths at Thagaste the young Augustine and his father were naked (*Conf.* 2. 3. 6). Martial regarded mixed bathing naked as normal; G. G. Fagan, *Bathing in Public in the Roman World* (Ann Arbor, 1999), 24–9. At Jerusalem baptizands stripped (Cyril of Jerusalem, *Cat. myst.* 2. 2). Loincloths were Arian custom: Barhadbeshabba on Eunomius, PO 23. 281. Augustine observed that to remain covered at the baths was barbarian (*City of God* 14. 17).

to the Father. That required clean hands and a pure heart (*ep.* 66. 9). Moreover as bishop of Carthage he exercised leadership not only in the province of Africa Proconsularis but also in Numidia and Mauretania (*ep.* 48. 3). The empire's provinces had become the normal units of church organization (*ep.* 67. 5). Cyprian's relations with bishops in Mauretania became cooler and more distant during the controversy of 256 about baptism, but Numidia followed his lead at that time.

As in Tertullian's time (*De oratione* 6, 19), the church at Carthage had a daily celebration of the eucharist (*epp.* 39. 4, 57. 3, 58. 1) using a movable wooden altar (*altare* being the Christian word, not the pagan *ara*), and the baptized faithful received the Lord's body in their right hand (*ep.* 58. 9). A church had only one altar, a symbol of unity. 'The Lord's passion is the sacrifice of the Church' (*ep.* 63. 17) and is offered in intercession for the departed. Anniversaries both of dead Christian relatives and of martyrs are commemorated by the eucharist (*epp.* 39, 12. 1). The Lord's command is to be kept exactly. Cyprian warns against communities where the cup contained only water and no wine (*ep.* 63. 9), attested also by Clement of Alexandria. Gnostic sects such as the Manichees regarded wine as diabolical. (In ancient society wine was diluted with much water except among Scythian tribes north of the Black Sea.) The celebrating priest 'does what Christ did', offering his true and complete sacrifice (63. 14). 'Without wine the Lord's blood is not present.' Africa had a noteworthy parallel with the *Apostolic Tradition* of Hippolytus in a eucharistic blessing of oil (*ep.* 70. 2).

The African liturgy included the dialogue 'Su(r)sum corda—Habemus ad dominum.' Prayers were daily at the third, sixth, and ninth hours. It is certain that by the mid-third century in large towns the churches had begun to abandon house-churches for designated buildings, since they were confiscated in time of persecution and restored by the emperor Gallienus (Eus. *HE* 7. 13). This was paralleled outside Africa, e.g. a small converted building with frescoes at Dura in Mesopotamia. Hippolytus (*On Daniel* 1. 20) records attacks on church buildings during worship. At Oxyrhynchus in Egypt at the end of the third century the main church had fine bronze, confiscated during the Great Persecution. At Edessa in Syria the church had a special building as early as 202.

For five years until 249 the empire was ruled by Philip the Arab, who professed sympathy with Christianity. He had not solved political problems. The new emperor Decius reacted vehemently in the opposite direction. He initiated formal anti-Christian action, no doubt in hope of allaying the gods' wrath, perhaps because he shared some of Cyprian's diagnosis of the ills of society and looked to the cult of the old gods to bring reform and to foster loyalty. Persecutors could have high moral ideals, excluding toleration.

The persecution of the emperor Decius[4]

The see of Carthage turned out to be an extremely hot seat. Within two years of Cyprian's consecration Decius startled the Church throughout the empire, which in most places had enjoyed some decades of relative peace (*ep.* 11), by an edict late in 249 instructing provincial governors that everyone in the empire must offer sacrifice to the gods, and everyone was to have a signed and officially countersigned certificate (*libellus*) attesting the act. Forty-four of these certificates have survived in the dry sand of Egypt. To offer incense or to taste of meat sacrificed on an altar of the Roman gods would surely placate the evident anger of heaven. It was universally known that, like the Jews, Christians were unwilling to have anything to do with the old gods which Ps. 95. 5 taught them to consider evil powers and their cult to be sorcery. But the Christians had become numerous and therefore seemed a threat. Although the edict was of universal application, they were the community prominently in the firing line.

The long peace was seen by Cyprian, as much as by Origen, to explain why Christians had become too much at ease in society, less than totally serious in remembering their baptismal renunciation of the world, the flesh, and the devil. Some bishops 'moonlighted' with secular jobs, or abandoned their flocks and wandered, trying to get legacies and engaging in trade (*Laps.* 6). The number of church members who apostatized from Christ by obeying the edict was large, and it was a special shock that many clergy, including a number of bishops, were among the lapsed (*ep.* 10. 4, 11. 1, 14. 1, 40. 1). To disobey entailed loss of property and exile, soon much worse.

Some did as the edict commanded and directly offered sacrifice at smoking altars. But a larger proportion found an easier way, namely that of bribing officials in charge of the operation to provide them with a certificate even though they had not sacrificed. At Alexandria during the great persecution of Diocletian the bishop approved of bribes to evade moral compromise with the worse sin of idolatry. Officials expected a good tip for any service rendered; resort to bribery was regular standard procedure if one was hoping to get anything done, and those who passed money to officers of state who then took no steps to meet their requests felt a powerful sense of grievance. In the context therefore bribes to obtain *libelli* were not obviously corrupt morally to those who obtained them, though they could be denounced by the unsuccessful. Cyprian deeply disapproved of any bribery, above all if used to produce a paper attesting falsely that the possessor had compromised with

---

[4] See H. A. Pohlsander, 'The religious policy of Decius' *ANRW* II 16. 3 (1986), 1826–42. A portrait of Decius apart from religion is by A. R. Birley, 'Decius reconsidered', in E. Fiezouls and H. Jouffroy (eds.), *Les Empereurs illyriens* (Actes du colloque de Strasbourg octobre 1990; Association pour l'étude de la civilisation romaine, 1998), 57–80.

demonic powers. To people who had bought their *libelli* and therefore escaped imprisonment and worse without polluting their own conscience, it seemed harsh and inhuman when austere bishops such as Cyprian excluded them from eucharistic communion and regarded them as having lapsed, with no assurance of readmission until, after persecution had ceased (as past experience showed that it would), bishops could meet in synod and agree on the proper terms for penitence. Those who had bought *libelli* were resentful at being treated like those who had actually offered sacrifice, and at being penalized more severely than adulterers. In the past, apostasy (and that was surely what in public records it was) had been ranked with murder and adultery as sin so mortal and so injurious to the community that, in the exercise of the dominical commission to bind and loose, the Church was not clearly authorized to grant remission. It could be sure only of authority to intercede that, at the Last Judgement, the lapsed might be treated with mercy by the divine Judge of all. In time a deathbed or gravely sick application could be considered. It remained valid if one recovered. Moreover, the reconciliation of a penitent man or woman was an act before the congregation, not a private absolution, and for the eucharist celebrating restoration and Christ's forgiveness the penitent person provided the bread and wine (*ep.* 34. 1; Victor of Vita, *Historia persecutionis* 2. 51). The bishop accepted the offering and placed the elements on the altar.

Nevertheless for these lapsed believers there was a ray of light. Christians who refused either to sacrifice or to buy a certificate had been arrested and confined in extremely unpleasant dungeons. Their sufferings there put them under great strain, and their courage in standing firm conferred the exalted status of 'confessors' and 'witnesses' (that is martyrs), endowed with the Holy Spirit and thereby charismatic authority to hand out tickets of readmission. This claim was bound to raise embarrassing questions for bishops if it sidelined their responsibility and divine commission to be judges (*ep.* 68. 2), and so to be spokesmen for the community in exercising the power of the keys after carefully considering each individual case. Some confessors injured their own dignity by being careless in handing out certificates of readmission, giving blank certificates which the applicant could fill in (*ep.* 15. 4), accepting bribes too. Cyprian was informed that intoxicating liquors were reaching the confessors (possibly as anaesthetic for their pain?) and that there were quarrels among them and in some cases sexual irregularities (*ep.* 13. 4 ff., 14. 3, 20. 2).[5] The situation was difficult for bishops, some of whom found themselves jostled and mobbed by crowds of impatient and irate people armed both with

---

[5] How far the sexual problems went is hard to say with assurance. That men and women were thrown into prison together is clear. But among the Christians in north Africa Cyprian encountered ascetics of both sexes living together in continence, an abstinence which he thought hard to credit, *ep.* 4. Released confessors may have followed this pattern.

certificates for which they had paid to escape compromising their faith and with tickets of readmission from confessors in the gaol (*ep.* 27. 3). Yet it was axiomatic that the glory of martyrs was at death to be granted the Lord's kiss with immediate admission to paradise and to share with Christ in judgement (*epp.* 6, 37. 3, 62. 2, 31. 3, 58. 3; likewise Dionysius of Alexandria in Eus. *HE* 6. 42. 5). For them there would be no waiting state. And if the martyred person happened to be unbaptized catechumen, provided the faith of the Church be held complete, then martyrdom was baptism of blood (*ep.* 73. 22). Cyprian was most anxious to safeguard both the full honour of martyrs and the authority of bishops.

From Africa a number of Christians became refugees, finding a hiding-place in the great city of Rome only a few days' sailing distant. The wealthy church at Rome could secretly feed them. It is noteworthy that persecution brought negligible interruption to travel and the conveyance of letters in the Mediterranean. There may well have been Christian shipowners. The Lord had said: 'If they persecute you in one city, flee to the next.' Cyprian being well known in his city was the object of mob hatred, his name being shouted by crowds at circus or amphitheatre. A formal proscription of him by name was placarded. It seemed clear that if he stayed in the city he would bring serious trouble upon his people, who would prefer him to lie low. He therefore retired to a hiding-place near the city, communicating with his presbyters (whom he expected to stay in Carthage) and continuing to supply money to those in need. Naturally there were those who questioned his flight. The *Quo Vadis* legend of St Peter being sent back into Rome to be crucified like his master (upside down) was not yet current, but the attitude presupposed is found in Tertullian's essay *On Flight in Persecution*. At Rome after the execution of Bishop Fabian in January 250 the Roman church continued for several months without electing a successor, and the clergy wrote not to Cyprian but to his clergy and laity frankly regretting that their bishop had not stayed to face the music. Christ's soldiers were expected to fight the devil on the battlefield rather than to run away, and in martyrdom Christ himself was the victor in his human servant. Cyprian obtained a copy of the Roman letter, felt it to be insulting, and returned it asking if it was authentic. After his martyrdom Pontius' panegyric (7–8) still found it necessary to defend his hero from accusations of cowardice.

The government did not find the initial penalty of imprisonment sufficient to achieve what they wanted, and a second edict arrived requiring severe tortures to be inflicted on prisoners who remained obstinate. Under the savagery suffered a number of confessors finally capitulated (*ep.* 56. 1); they were cruelly flogged, some died in the torture chamber, their limbs torn by the rack, by hooks on a wheel lacerating their flesh, with virtual starvation. It seems that the usual resort to bribery for prison officers was made

ineffective. Cyprian directed his clergy to make note of the dates of martyrdom, evidently with a view to the future church calendar. The Carthage calendar of saints in a recension of about 505 survives, edited by Mabillon (*Vetera
Analecta*, 1682), from a now lost Cluny manuscript. It includes names found
in Cyprian's record of the Decian persecution.

A local church could have no greater glory than to have among its
members some accorded the supreme dignity of martyrdom (*ep.* 10). Their
sufferings united them to their crucified Lord—a theme already found in the
epistle to the Colossians (1: 24) where the apostle, or perhaps a disciple writing in his name, regards his sufferings as making good any deficiency in the
redemptive cross of Christ. The theme also appears in Origen's tract *On
Martyrdom* (50).

The ancient Church understood the whole Church to include the faithful
departed as well as the church militant here on earth, and among the faithful
departed a special place was naturally held by the greatest saints. Just as believers were asked to intercede for each other on earth in accordance with the
apostolic model (Col. 4. 3; Eph. 6. 19), and just as they regarded intercession
as a particular responsibility of a pastoral bishop for his flock, so they could
invoke the prayers of saints and martyrs in the Church triumphant. The
assumption that the intercessions of a potent friend would be effective was a
natural axiom. In Roman imperial society where the client/patron relationship was dominant, and where the weaker members of a group depended on
the rich and powerful if they were in trouble over taxes or with the magistrates or were wanting an attractive post, it was taken for granted that an
intervention by an influential friend was indispensable. Bishops were continually badgered for help of this kind in worldly terms. It was not in principle so very different invoking a martyr's aid. And the ancient Church
fervently held that martyrs were qualified for admission to heaven without
further ado.

The charitable duty to bury martyrs was dangerous to those who collected
corpses for burial (*fossores*), especially because Christians preferred Christian
cemeteries (the Roman letter, *ep.* 8. 3). Carthage also had Christian burial
grounds (*ep.* 67. 6). Such sites were well known (*ep.* 9. 3).

Cyprian's strength lay in his burning conviction that the church in north
Africa was a constituent member of a universal body, visibly continuous in
the episcopate. On several occasions he affirmed the individual responsibility of a bishop to reach his own pastoral decisions, for which he would answer
to God at the Last Judgement: 'A bishop is responsible to God alone'
(e.g. *ep.* 57. 5). Nevertheless consensus among bishops was pastorally important. Collectively bishops were responsible for 'every act of the Church'
(*ep.* 33. 1). They were 'as essential to the Church as the Church to bishops'
(*ep.* 33), and should be regarded as the 'glue' that imparts coherence

(*epp.* 66. 8, 68. 3). It was obviously important that the lapsed when they aspired to be restored must receive equal and just treatment. Bishops needed to reach a common mind. Cyprian issued a programmatic statement 'On the Lapsed' defending the position that those who bought certificates were polluted and needed to make confession before their bishop and the people.

In Cyprian's mind the unity and unicity of the Church are symbolized by St Peter on whom the Lord built his Church (*epp.* 43. 5, 49. 2). Bishops are accordingly the visible earthly organs or instruments by which this Petrine unity is maintained and validated. Therefore a problem arises when there is disagreement, especially when an entire regional synod reaches decisions which are not acclaimed and accepted in other regions.

Novatian and Cornelius

Correspondence between Carthage and Rome initially ensured that Cyprian's policies were not out of line with the austerity of Rome, where the leading presbyter during the vacancy in the see was Novatian, a respected theologian, author of a valued Latin treatise on the Trinity which owed much to Tertullian. However, when the Roman church came to elect a new bishop, the choice of the *plebs* and probably also of the consecrating bishops fell not on Novatian but on another senior presbyter named Cornelius. Cornelius favoured a more relaxed policy towards the lapsed: as persecution died down, it was a duty to restore the fallen so that by participation in the eucharist they might be spiritually strengthened if attacks were to return. Novatian was appalled at this choice of bishop, and refused to acknowledge Cornelius. Three country bishops were brought to Rome to give him consecration as rival bishop of Rome. He was recognized by prominent Roman confessors (*epp.* 43 and 46). Later texts say Novatian was martyred under the emperor Valerian. According to Pacian of Barcelona Cyprian heard this and said 'My opponent has gone before me.' An inscription found in 1933 in Rome on the Via Tiburtina records 'Novatian a most blessed martyr'.

The split at Rome was not at first centred on the terms of restoration for the lapsed. But quickly that painful issue became cardinal to the controversy. The news of the split in Rome soon reached bishops in Carthage where there was also high tension between factions; the group of five dissident presbyters found in the unrest with Cyprian's policy about reconciliation of the lapsed a rod with which to beat him. They were led at Carthage by one of their number (confusingly named Novatus), and their candidate to be rival bishop of Carthage was named Fortunatus. Novatus' honour was diminished when his wife had an abortion, the ancient method used for this being the husband kicking his wife in the stomach, a technique which the mother seldom survived (*ep.* 52. 2); Christians regarded abortion as morally indistinguishable from infant murder. Cyprian and his supporting bishops at Carthage were at first far from clear which of the two rivals in Rome they ought to recognize. The final decision to opt for Cornelius took time and a special mission of inquiry which naturally offended Cornelius.

When Cyprian's support came, it was strong, virtually an echo of an imperial panegyric: Cornelius had been consecrated by rigorously correct procedure without any bribery and (unlike Novatian) when the see was vacant. Cornelius could name his predecessor in the see: Novatian could not. His church was 'man-made'. As Cyprian and Cornelius came to draw together, the anti-Cyprian presbyters at Carthage opted for Novatian, a move which strengthened Cyprian's hand. A shift in the situation occurred when Roman confessors held in high respect, who had supported Novatian, changed sides and joined Cornelius, who did not require of them a penitential reception. Their adhesion was very welcome to him. He was also glad to have support from Cyprian, in whose eyes Novatian had moved entirely outside the Church, so that no one needed now to pay the slightest attention to his words. 'One who has lost charity has lost all' (*ep.* 55. 24). The principle stated in Tertullian's polemic against heretics that once they have left the one Church their opinions are of no relevance or consequence became sharply reformulated by Cyprian. Cyprian used language about Novatian which Cicero had used of Catiline, the arch-conspirator against the Roman republic. As for Cornelius, 'the tyrant Decius would have been more alarmed to hear about a new bishop in Rome than of a rival emperor' (*ep.* 55. 9).

On unity

The dissidents at Carthage provoked Cyprian to write the first Christian treatise on the Church, 'On the Unity of the Catholic Church'. If the universal Church is one, the local community also has to be united. Only so is it the Church which Christ founded. 'He cannot have God for his Father who has not the Church for his mother.' Schisms and heresies are the devil's invention to undermine faith, deceiving believers into supposing that there is some new way forward bringing light into their darkness. Splits result from opposition to the one bishop who is bond of unity in his church. And the community of the episcopate is a united universal body, in which each individual 'holds his part in its totality'. The local church is a microcosm of the universal Church, the very spouse of Christ. She does not sleep around. 'If anyone could escape who was not inside Noah's ark, then there can be salvation outside the one Church.'

The fourth chapter of the tract on Unity has two variant forms of text in the manuscript tradition. In one form (commonly called the 'Received Text') stress is laid on the equal power bestowed by the Lord on all apostles, while the unity of the apostles is signified by the giving of the same power of the keys to only one, namely St Peter. The other form or 'Primacy Text' begins from the Lord's commission to Peter ('Feed my sheep'). 'And though to all the apostles he gives equal power, yet he established a single teaching chair . . . the origin and ground of unity.' So while other apostles were all that Peter was, yet the initial place (*primatus*) was given to Peter to manifest one Church and one teaching chair. It has been plausibly conjectured by Maurice Bévenot that Cyprian was responsible for both forms of text, representing a first edition directed against Carthaginian dissidents, and a second edition in the Primacy Text where the target is Novatian and the trouble in Rome. It is equally possible that the two forms of text originated in the fourth century with the Donatist schism in North Africa, the Donatist ecclesiology being conciliar with strong emphasis on apostolic succession, producing the Received Text, and that of their opponents stressing the value of communion with Rome, producing the Primacy Text.

In the spring of 252 a letter from Cyprian answered a report from Cornelius that a Carthaginian dissident Felicissimus had come to Rome, evidently to appeal for support, and with a crowd of supporters had coerced Bishop Cornelius into receiving his letters, but had not been received to communion. Cyprian replied with an outline of his autobiography in becoming bishop four years previously with a providential survival of the persecution, and recorded outrage that the African faction had had 'the audacity to sail to Rome to Peter's chair, the primordial church and source of unity among bishops'. Disunity was their business (*ep.* 59. 19). Exalted language about the Roman church also occurs in *ep.* 48. 3: 'it is the womb and root of the Catholic Church.'

Pope Stephen

A year later in the time of Decius' successor Gallus, Cornelius was arrested and exiled to Centumcellae (Civitavecchia). He died in exile and was ranked by Cyprian among martyrs. His tomb survives, the earliest papal stone to have its inscription in Latin. He was succeeded at Rome by the shortlived Lucius (253–4) in office less than eight months, and he by Stephen. With Stephen Cyprian found agreement difficult. His enthusiasm for harmony with Rome when he needed support in the problem of reconciling the lapsed was quite gone when he discovered Rome to be recognizing the validity of schismatic or heretical baptisms.

The first tensions seem to have arisen when Bishop Faustinus of Lyon wrote to Carthage to report that Marcianus bishop of Arles was refusing all reconciliation to the lapsed, and Cyprian sent a letter telling Stephen what he ought to be doing about it 'with the full weight of your authority'.

A second source of abrasion came when two Spanish bishops named Basilides and Martialis from Legio-Asturica (León and Astorga) and Emerita (Mérida) had compromised their faith by buying *libelli* in the persecution. On the strict view therefore they could return only as penitent laity, and in both sees bishops had been elected to replace them. Naturally enough the two extruded bishops had their supporters. The two replacements found it difficult to exercise their episcopate, and wrote to Cyprian who upheld their view with a letter regretting 'Stephen's negligence' in allowing Basilides to claim reinstatement with Rome's support. For the Africans it was unthinkable that God could hear the prayers and heed the eucharistic sacrifice of a bishop whose hands were defiled. A report on Bishop Martialis was not only that he ignored the need for penitence but also that he habitually attended a pagan dining-club with obscene entertainments (ancient dinner parties commonly included an act by scantily dressed dancing girls) and had had members of his family interred in a pagan burial-ground.

Stephen affirmed the old Roman tradition that if a person had been baptized in the name of Christ by a dissenting body, he or she should be received into the communion of the one Church not by baptism but by laying-on of hands as a penitent. His predecessor Cornelius had followed Cyprian's sharper doctrine that to recognize the baptism given by a schismatic was a full recognition that the dissenting body was part of the true Church. One could not recognize part of the sacrament. It must be all or nothing. It is impossible to think that an enemy of Christ outside the one Church can cleanse and sanctify (*ep.* 71. 1). He had learnt from Tertullian, whom he counted his 'master', that the Lord said not 'I am custom' but 'I am the truth'. (It could not be denied that Cyprian's position was not the old tradition; cf. *ep.* 73. 23.) Roman criticism of this position appeals to custom rather than reason. Moreover, appeals to Petrine authority have to meet the point that in dispute with Paul (Gal. 2: 11 ff.) Peter claimed no *primatus*, no seniority or right to demand obedience (*ep.* 71. 3). So said Cyprian to a bishop in Mauretania named Quintus. He sent a copy on to Rome with a covering letter of absolute courtesy urging Stephen to agree with the African bishops in council, whose tolerance allowed for disagreeing individuals. The Africans acknowledged that the Roman see had a special position, in that Peter was both the origin of unity and the source of episcopal authority. But it was also axiomatic that the African synod excommunicated no one, and allowed 'some' to adhere to past traditions (*ep.* 72. 3).

A difficult point for Cyprian was that at Rome Novatian did not recognize the baptisms of the rival community, which to critics seemed indistinguishable from Cyprian's position. Between Stephen and Novatian this was a wide difference, with Stephen accepting Novatianist baptism, and Novatian refusing Stephen's (*ep.* 73. 2). Cyprian could answer only with the apparently weak reply that what Novatian might or might not do was irrelevant: he was an outsider. Stronger was an amazement that Rome was seeming to acknowledge Marcion's baptism though the man did not believe the doctrine of the Trinity. A biblical passage against the African synod was Acts 8: 14–17, where Peter and John came to Samaria and hands were laid upon those already baptized to give the Holy Spirit, but the converts were not rebaptized. However, the rock-solid position of Stephen was the appeal to tradition: 'Nihil innovetur nisi quod traditum est.' Those baptized outside the Church should be admitted to the one Church by laying on of hands. The sacrament of baptism must on no account be repeated, for that was a slight to the majesty of Christ's name invoked upon the candidate. The sacred tradition to which Stephen appealed was attributed by him to Peter and Paul (*ep.* 75. 6). Cyprian sought to answer this contention by appealing to scripture, pointedly asking where he could find this tradition attested in Gospels, Epistles, or Acts (*ep.* 74). With the African doctrine of the right of an individual bishop to take a personal position and answer to God at the Judgement, Cyprian strongly resented Stephen's threats of excommunication for the disagreement (*ep.* 74. 8). A bishop's responsibility is not only to teach, but also to be teachable (74. 10). Much pain was caused when Stephen refused to receive episcopal envoys from Carthage and forbade his community to offer the visitors any hospitality whatever (75. 25). That was the way in which Novatian's envoys had been received at Carthage (44. 1).

Stephen was not without some support in Africa, and a manifesto on his side entitled 'On rebaptism' has survived among works ascribed to Cyprian, whom the anonymous author, a bishop, disliked as 'arrogantly correcting other churches'. In his view Stephen was correct that baptism in Jesus' name should not be repeated, and that the gift of the Spirit came with the imposition of the bishop's hands as reconciliation with the Church. Exorcism outside the Church was potent; so why not baptism? The apostles could hardly measure up to the demand for perfect faith in the baptizer; and what of ignorant uneducated clergy who get the baptismal questions wrong? God's power overrules such cases. Some of Cyprian's later letters show that probably because of the tension with Rome Cyprian had to reply to critics in Africa, discontented both with him and with his sacramental theology. In both 255 and 256 he presided over councils at Carthage considering the baptismal controversy. The record of 1 September 256 survives with judgements uttered by the 87 bishops from Proconsularis, Numidia, and Mauretania, each assenting to Cyprian's position. The preface by Cyprian stresses that there is no excommunication of any who may disagree. 'None of us has set himself up as bishop of bishops.' It is remarkable that Cyprian's mind moved far from his earlier view that no serious Christian could suppose heretical or schismatic baptism valid, to allow at least the possibility of individual independence. (This last proposition enabled Augustine to defend Cyprian while judging him wrong on baptism.)

Firmilian

Cyprian appealed to the Greek East, writing to Firmilian bishop of Caesarea, metropolis of Cappadocia, who reinforced the doubts about apostolic traditions at Rome by observing that Roman liturgical practices differed from those of Jerusalem. Yet this diversity was no source of disunity in the catholic Church (75. 6). He regretted that the bishop of Rome wanted his own kind of uniformity, and for authority appealed to the locus of his see as successor of Peter with a resultant debate throughout the (Mediterranean) world. Firmilian also asked what Stephen would make of an ecstatic woman at Caesarea who not only baptized with the right formula but celebrated the eucharist with the usual ritual words: On the Roman view that must be valid. Stephen answered the Greek opposition by excommunicating Firmilian, the bishop of Tarsus, and all bishops in the provinces of Cappadocia, Cilicia, and Galatia. Firmilian was scandalized that Stephen had denounced Cyprian as a false Christ, a false apostle, and a crafty operator (*ep.* 75. 25). Cyprian had himself described supporters of Novatian's baptism as antichrists and traitors, fighting the Church from within (*ep.* 69. 10). Stephen had given such persons a strong lead.

Pope Sixtus

Notwithstanding this tough language, Cyprian did not break communion with Stephen, and probably Stephen's successor Sixtus (or Xystus) would have been able to re-establish harmony. Cyprian's Life by Pontius expressly refers to Sixtus as a 'man of peace', and the news of his martyrdom was for Cyprian a very grave matter (*ep.* 80). Both he and Cyprian suffered execution under Valerian, Sixtus in the Roman catacombs with his deacons. The theological debate so far as the West was concerned could not be resolved for a further half-century, when the consequence of the persecution of Diocletian was a major schism in north Africa. The Donatist faction followed Cyprianic sacramental theology of baptism with the refusal to grant that a lapsed priest could offer the Church's sacrifice with hands polluted by surrendering Bibles to the secular authorities, agents of Antichrist. Any sacrament celebrated by a defiled bishop or presbyter must be deemed invalid. Cyprian would have agreed with that proposition, though he was aware that the Church contained both wheat and tares (*ep.* 54. 3) and that he could claim fidelity to the gospel only for 'most bishops' (*ep.* 63. 1), for on occasions 'unworthy men are appointed' (*ep.* 67. 4). Tares were no sufficient reason for abandoning the Church. He would have had to add that insofar as the Donatists had renounced the universal Church, they had become of no importance. Donatist appeal to Cyprian was not unqualified.

Fresh persecution

In 257 the emperor Valerian (253–60) with his son Gallienus abandoned an initially friendly attitude to the Christians (who may have found themselves included in a general remission of exile), and initiated a persecution in which capital punishment was a penalty to come to Cyprian, and other clergy were sent to work in the mines—a penalty estimated as being virtually death. Prisoners sent to the mines in Numidia had no bed or straw to lie on, no washing facility, little to eat. Their heads were half-shaven like slaves suffering punishment. Their legs were chained to prevent escape. They were flogged with heavy cudgels. Work had to be done in smoky underground tunnels in a fearful stench. Survival was unusual (*epp.* 76 and 77).

Cyprian's social standing in the city ensured that he was treated according to the dignity of his class. At first exiled to Curubis, on the coast 55 miles from Carthage and not unpleasant, he was then allowed to return to his own rural gardens. But a new proconsul arrived. Cyprian was able to learn what the emperor had decided for him through Christians working in the palace at Rome, so that he knew the decree before the proconsul did. His biographer and panegyrist Pontius (a high official at Curubis attested in an inscription, *CIL* viii. 980, may be identical with Cyprian's biographer) joined him in his house arrest, and the Proconsular Acts record the dialogue before the proconsul to whom he was taken on 13 September 258. On 14 September, with a huge crowd watching, Cyprian was formally cross-questioned 'Are you Thascius, also called Cyprian?' 'I am'. 'The emperors have commanded you to perform the ceremonies . . .'. The outcome was known in advance, and the examination ended with the proconsul reading his decision from a tablet: 'Thascius Cyprianus is sentenced to die by the sword'. Bishop Cyprian said: 'Thanks be to God.' Uproar followed among the Christian spectators. Cyprian handed his executioner 25 gold pieces, blindfolded himself, and went to his death. The body was taken for burial close to Carthage. He was the first north African bishop to be executed under the persecution. The anniversary of the martyrdom was to become a major popular festival in Carthage.

The emperor Valerian suffered disastrous defeat fighting the Persians in Syria, and was captured, a dramatic event which the Persian king Shahpuhr celebrated with a triumphant inscription, which has survived.

Cyprian was not given to inquiries into theology proper. He marked no distinction between heresy and schism (*ep.* 69. 1). To be outside the Church was enough to decide the issue. Like the garden of the beloved in the Song of Songs, the Church has high walls, a *hortus conclusus*, in Cyprianic ecclesiology. He well knew the western baptismal creed, but produced nothing resembling the speculations of Clement of Alexandria or Origen. He owed much to Tertullian. Jerome reports that he read some of 'the master', as he called him, every day; and the debt is evident, especially in the tracts, but also in the basic presupposition of his stance in the baptismal debate. He believed in a divine guidance prompting him through his episcopal responsibilities, and reported the gift of dreams and visions (mocked by some, *ep.* 66. 10). At a time of crisis when the church in Carthage suffered massive losses by 'apostasy', both among laity and among clergy, Cyprian had the strength of character to hold the fort. The African churches looked back on him as their hero.

Veneration was not slow in becoming established. At Carthage three different shrines in the city were erected in addition to a small oratory by the harbour. Together with Bishop Cornelius he had later an honoured place in the Roman calendar of Saints and in the Latin canon of the mass. At the same time Stephen's tenacious adherence to Roman tradition concerning schismatic baptism, which Cyprian slightingly regarded as mere 'custom', was to remain in force, and a criterion for the adverse criticism of the Donatist sacramental theology. By recognizing baptism given by ministers not in communion with the one catholic Church and with its bishops embodying visible continuity, Roman tradition implied some provisionality in the temporal element in the sacrament. It made clear that the question to be asked of a sacrament is not about the sanctity or status of the minister but rather whether what God has commanded to be done has been done; the grace bestowed in incorporation into the one Church is his, not the minister's. Medieval schoolmen lucidly defined the difference as that between *ex opere operantis* and *ex opere operato*, with the proviso that there is intention to do what the Church does. Cyprian's absolutist conception of the Church constructed mighty defences against schismatics and heretics with the aid of ideas already in Tertullian's *De praescriptione haereticorum*. Stephen allowed the Church a penumbra extending beyond its apparent frontiers.

In the cleavage between Rome and Carthage in 256 Cyprian was supported by major Greek bishops. The issue has long remained a point of divergence between Latin west and Greek East, acutely felt when rigorist elements in the east have felt hesitant about recognizing western baptism. Stephen provided more potential for a positive approach to separated ecclesial bodies regretful of their exclusion.

23

DIONYSIUS OF ALEXANDRIA

Dionysius, presbyter of Alexandria, succeeded Heraklas as bishop about 247, shortly before the elevation of Cyprian. He was a cultivated man of good education, and in the retrospect of the fourth century was much admired and respected as 'the great'. Within a few months of his consecration his people were the target of mob violence, perhaps especially because the city was beset by plague and civil war, and from early in 250 Decius launched persecution.

At Alexandria bishop Dionysius was target of attacks essentially similar to those suffered by Cyprian. Responsible for a number of people in his house, he decided to take flight when persecution came, was captured after a few days and arrested by soldiers, but then liberated by an onslaught from revellers at a wedding party outraged by their bishop's capture; they forced the guards to run for their lives. Dionysius' letters, cited by Eusebius of Caesarea, record the horrors endured by elderly Christians during the pogrom of 249 and then, in 250 under Decius, the sad lapse of many, and their ferocious treatment by the Alexandrian mob. He found it necessary to defend himself against sharp criticism from another Egyptian bishop Germanos who directly accused him of cowardice: ought he not to have stayed at his post and shared martyrdom with the confessors of his flock?

In his *Preparation of the Gospel* (book 14) Eusebius preserves substantial pieces of Dionysius' treatise 'On Nature', defending design in the cosmos against the random chance of Epicureanism. The context is likely to have been a widespread loss of inward security and confidence in providence resulting from the chaotic state of the Roman empire in the mid-third century. Dionysius was clear that even during terrible times divine care had not ceased to operate.

The political disasters of the age could easily have fostered millennialism. The interpretation of the Apocalypse of John of Patmos was no easy matter, but chapter 21 if taken literally (as had been done by Justin and Irenaeus) offered a strong lead for belief in a thousand-year reign of Christ at a rebuilt Jerusalem. Origen, on the other hand, who deeply influenced Dionysius by his biblical exegesis, had been clear that John was writing symbolically and allegorically.

Before Dionysius' time a bishop Nepos of Arsinoe, south of Memphis, had exercised profound influence in Egypt by his spiritual qualities both in bible studies and in writing hymns. His writings retained enthusiastic admirers, especially a work entitled 'Refutation of the Allegorists' devoted to a vindication of the literalism of Irenaeus in expounding the Revelation of John. Nepos' doctrine seemed dangerous to Dionysius, and he made a pastoral visit to Arsinoe and the surrounding churches to correct what was amiss. He frankly admitted that he found large parts of the Apocalypse incomprehensible; but on faith he accepted that the author was at least one of two Johns whose tombs were held in honour at Ephesus. This was directly contrary to the opinion of an early heretic named Cerinthus who was credited by his admirers with authorship of the Gospel, Epistles, and Revelation of John. (The chances are no doubt that the two tombs at Ephesus were actually rival sites both claiming to have the bones of a single John, reckoned, since the apocryphal Acts of John in the mid-second century, to be the beloved disciple and author of the Johannine Gospel, Epistles, and Apocalypse.) However, the highly eccentric grammar of the writer of the Apocalypse could hardly be the style of the author of the Gospel, and in a percipient critique Dionysius set aside the Apocalypse as inconceivably the work of John the son of Zebedee. He accordingly wrote a book in criticism of Nepos entitled 'Concerning the Promises' (i.e. the last things). He did not question that the John of the Apocalypse was holy and inspired.

Dionysius inherited from his master Origen a sense of the supreme importance of biblical exposition. Considerable fragments of his exegesis of Ecclesiastes (mentioned by but apparently not known to Eusebius) have survived through a catena; that is, through the work of a commentator who summarized a series of exegetes on the text, and included among them several citations from Dionysius.[1]

Dionysius was much perturbed by Novatian's dissent at Rome. He was in favour of mild discipline for the lapsed, and thought Novatian very wrong to start a schism, so easy to begin, so difficult to end.

The baptismal controversy into which Cyprian and Stephen had drawn Greek bishops inevitably involved Dionysius. Like Firmilian of Caesarea, he sympathized with Cyprian and wrote accordingly to Stephen of Rome. A letter he wrote to the Roman confessors who initially supported Novatian (Eus. *HE* 6. 46. 5) would have helped to bring them back to catholic communion.

Despite considerable sufferings he survived the persecution of Valerian. Gallienus' edict of toleration and restoration of churches and cemeteries moved him to the language of panegyric on the emperor. The first bishop named in Gallienus' edict was Dionysius, whom Eusebius took to be the Alexandrian. The Roman Dionysius is at least as probable.

---

[1] *Catena Havniensis in Ecclesiasten*, ed. Antonio Labate (CCSG 24; Turnhout, 1992).

Questions of canon law were brought before him by a bishop in the Libyan Pentapolis (Cyrenaica) named Basilides. He was asked to rule on the hour at which the Holy Week or Paschal fast should end: cockcrow, or before midnight on Holy Saturday. He drily commented that it was easier to fast rigorously for two days than moderately for six. As the precise hour of Christ's rising cannot be determined, Dionysius thought that individual conscience was properly a deciding factor. The same held for other questions put to him, namely, whether menstruating women should abstain from communion (to which he assented—a view on which patristic writers long remained divided); whether married couples should decide for themselves when they ought to abstain from sexual union for the sake of prayer (he thought they should so decide and not be directed); and whether nocturnal emissions had some sinful character (which he thought could only be a matter for the individual conscience). These rulings later became a part of Greek canon law. They are striking for what they did not rule. He did not sympathize with the opinion that bishops should penetrate the marital bedroom and tell married people in detail just what they might or might not do.

With so large a region for his oversight Dionysius realized that to inform every bishop of the correct date of Easter it was necessary for him to send round an encyclical. Festal letters announcing the date, accompanied by homiletic reflections, were accordingly issued by him. He insisted that Easter must not be celebrated before the vernal equinox.

The responsibilities of the bishop of Alexandria for the churches in Libya brought Dionysius into disagreement with bishop Stephen of Rome's successor, who bore the same name as himself, Dionysius. The bishop of Berenice, Ammonios, sent a complaint to Rome about the Alexandrian's language concerning the subordination of the divine Logos/Son to the Father. The complaints were five in number: he separates the Father from the Son; he denies the eternity of the Son, implying that 'there was once a time when he did not exist'; he names the Father without naming the Son and vice versa; he refuses to allow that Christ is of one being (*homoousios*) with God; he speaks of the Son as created by the Father and as having a distinct being (*ousia*), just as a vine differs from a husbandman and a boat from a boatman.

Dionysius of Rome brought the matter before a synod, which endorsed a condemnation of those who were dividing the divine 'monarchy' into three separate hypostases. Insistence on three distinct hypostases was characteristic of Origen, who was opposed to the formulation of the doctrine of the Trinity by which Father, Son, and Spirit are three subjective ways of talking about one God, grammatically adjectival rather than substantival. The opinion opposed by Origen was associated with a presbyter at Rome named Sabellios, and later Greek theologians called it Sabellianism. In the Latin west it was felt to imply that in the life and passion of Jesus the Father himself suffered, and this was objectionable, by Latins soon labelled Patripassianism. A major theme of Christian criticism of pagan theology was the polytheistic belief in gods vulnerable to all too human passions, as the myths illustrated.

Christians such as Justin had identified the deity worshipped by Christians with the impassible transcendent needless One of Platonism. The Platonic tradition was critical of the old myths of Homer whose poetry Plato had wished to exclude from the educational curriculum. Origen judged it vital to maintain biblical monotheism; but that seemed to require a doctrine of Christ which allowed the Father to stand higher in the chain of being than the Son. The divine Logos had therefore to be what Philo of Alexandria had said: a mediator between the transcendent Creator and the creaturely realm, half-way between the two.

Dionysius of Alexandria had behind him the critique of Sabellianism in the commentaries of Origen e.g. on St John's Gospel. He composed *Refutation and Defence* frankly conceding in his usual irenic manner that he had used incautious language. He protested that he made no division or separation between Son and Father, who are one as light derived from light. (Dionysius did not comment on whether the analogy is of sunlight and sun or of one torch lit from another, where the latter is more emphatic about the distinction.) However, at the crucial point Dionysius refused to give ground to his Libyan or Roman critics: 'They may say that to speak of three hypostases implies that they are separated from one another, yet they remain three, whether they like it or not; otherwise they entirely destroy the divine triad.' Father and Son are of one nature but like seed and plant, spring and river. 'I expand the monad into a triad without splitting it up and again unite the triad into the monad without reducing it.'

Most of these citations from the controversy are preserved through Athanasius in the mid-fourth century (*De sententia Dionysii*) when he was attempting to vindicate Dionysius against the Arians' appeal to the authority of his name. Because of this context doubts may be (and have been) raised about the complete reliability of the citations. It favours their authenticity that nothing in the texts is anachronistic in the years 259–60, and the involvement of the bishop of Alexandria in a debate in the Libyan churches is wholly probable. Because of the destiny of the term *homoousios* in the creed of the council of Nicaea in 325, special interest naturally attaches to the complaint that Dionysius denied that this assertion of identity of being could properly denote the relation of Son to the Father. The term was in regular philosophical use at the time, often in the context of discussion about the divine nature of the soul. It would have been a word to occur to anyone involved in this debate, and its presence in the report on Dionysius is no argument for thinking the language has to be post-Nicene Arian fiction.

In view of what was to come, it is highly significant that the western bishop at Rome was primarily concerned to protect the affirmation of monotheism: there is but one God, and no statement about the divine triad can be allowed to prejudice that. The eastern bishop at Alexandria was concerned to protect the threeness of the Christian understanding of God, and felt it to be important to state the plurality first and then to explain that the three are one.

The exchanges between Alexandria and Rome illuminate a broad difference of approach to the Christian doctrine of God as between the Latin west and the Greek east. The contrast is not absolute in antiquity. One can find Greek theologians using language close to that of Dionysius of Rome, Marcellus of Ankyra in the 330s being a striking example. There were Latin theologians who found Dionysius of Alexandria congenial; they, how- ever, were severely criticized for Arianism.

A second respect in which the third-century controversies anticipate what was to come may be seen in the different approaches of east and west towards the baptismal controversy. Writing to Cyprian, Firmilian of Caesarea referred at one point to the attack on the eastern tradition in regard to the celebration of Easter by Victor of Rome in the time of Irenaeus. Firmilian evidently felt that the disagreement about baptism, in which he and Dionysius of Alexandria agreed with Cyprian and the Africans, marked an incipient divergence between east and west. Stephen's insistence that baptism outside the Church should be deemed valid and on no account repeated offered irenic or, as one might say in modern terms, 'ecumenical' possibil- ities that the eastern negative view excluded. Down to the twenty-first century the Orthodox tradition of the Greek and Russian churches has found it easier to agree with Cyprian than with Stephen.

Eusebius of Caesarea records that Dionysius of Alexandria[2] wrote a letter to the Armenian Christians on the subject of repentance. They had a bishop named Meruzanes (*HE* 6. 46). This notice is the earliest evidence of Christianity among the Armenian people, though it is very possible that the 'Armenians' addressed were Greek-speaking inhabitants of the Roman province of Armenia rather than Armenians of the independent kingdom, which became officially Christian with the conversion of the king in the next generation. That conversion, however, is more likely to have occurred if there was a previous movement among his people. By the year 312 the Armenians were devotedly Christian (Eus. 9. 8. 2).

[2] Most of the extant remains of Dionysius are gathered by C. L. Feltoe (Cambridge, 1904), to be supplemented by Armenian matter edited by F. C. Conybeare in *English Historical Review*, 25 (1910), 111–14 (cf. Conybeare in *Journal of Theological Studies*, 15 (1914), 432–42) and by M. van Esbroeck in *Orientalia Christiana Periodica*, 50 (1984), 18–42. Good discussion by W. A. Bienert, *Dionysius von Alexandrien* (Berlin, 1978).

24

PAUL OF SAMOSATA

The Persian capture of the Roman emperor Valerian and his great city of Antioch in 259/60 resulted from the constant weakness of an eastern frontier without natural barriers and in any event ill defined and fluctuating. Roman collapse made possible for a decade in the 260s the emergence of an autonomous kingdom under Queen Zenobia based on the largely Arab city of Palmyra in the Syrian desert. The political independence was contemporaneous with a controversy about the style and teaching of the bishop of Antioch on the Orontes, Paul from Samosata on the Euphrates, whose doctrines of Christ and flamboyance in general delighted some of his people and alarmed others. Paul was sharply critical of the interpretation of scripture generally current in the Greek churches. 'He spoke disparagingly of dead exegetes', said his critics, and the reference is probably to the lately dead Origen, whose commentaries and sermons were still influential. It is a measure of their influence and of the opposition aroused that about AD 300 Eusebius and his master Pamphilus undertook a considerable *Defence of Origen* in six books; the first of the six survives in a Latin version by Rufinus of Aquileia.

Greek culture had come to pervade Syria and most of the Semitic world, but not so much as to suppress the languages, Aramaic, Nabataean, Syriac, Arabic. Most people spoke Greek, which was the medium of cultured communication. Paul may well have had Aramaic as his mother's-knee tongue, but was certainly fluent in Greek. Critical as he evidently was of the way in which Origen and his admirers spoke of the incarnate Lord, there is no sufficient reason to think him a conscious vehicle of nationalist Syrian culture over against a Hellenic Christian society. Greek was the dominant Christian language for worship and theology. In the second century a Greek harmony of the four Gospels made by Justin's pupil Tatian and called 'Diatessaron' became a standard text translated for Syriac-speaking churches. At Edessa in 200 Bardaisan was bilingual in Syriac and Greek. The Palmyra court under Queen Zenobia became host to the excellent scholar Longinus, who tried to persuade the polymath Porphyry to come and join him (*Life of Plotinus* 6). The name Iamblichus, borne by the famous Neoplatonist, is that of a princely Phoenician family fluent in Greek but whose first language was Aramaic (Photius, *Bibliotheca* 94).

From Palmyra Zenobia's kingdom expanded for a short time to fill a vacuum of power northwards and southwards in Asia Minor and in Egypt until her rule was ended in 272 by the emperor Aurelian, 'restitutor orbis' as his coins proclaimed.

Paul of Samosata was appointed bishop of Antioch in 261. The *plebs* admired his flair for making the church noticed in the city, and the Syrian bishops consented to consecrate. But very soon he was causing alarm, which in 264 led to a synod of bishops remonstrating and asking for amendments. Dionysius of Alexandria was invited to the synod and declined on health grounds; he was already sinking to his death, but wrote a letter to the synod on the corrections in theology for which he hoped. Paul assured the synod that he intended improvement. That, however, did not occur and the growing rumbles of misgiving led to a second synod at Antioch in autumn 268 which addressed its formal letter to Bishop Dionysius of Rome (died in December 268) and to Maximus of Alexandria.

Eusebius quotes at some length the part of the synod's encyclical criticizing Paul's worldly life-style, modelling himself on high officers of the empire (*ducenarius* or procurator), having a tribunal and elevated throne (evidently an even higher throne than most bishops already had) and a *secretarium* like a provincial governor. So great was his pressure of business that he dictated letters to secretaries in the streets. On Easter Day his adherents sang hymns in his praise (much as occurred among the schismatic Donatists in fourth-century north Africa). They were invited to contribute on a generous scale to his stipend and expenses. He evoked deep fixations in women, and had relationships with them which shocked the bishops by their openness, though they conceded that sexual contact did not occur. The bishops were outraged by the applause and waving of handkerchiefs, as if in a theatre. More problematic was his criticism of the Origenist notion that Son and Father in the Trinity are distinct hypostases. To the bishops' pain he wished to affirm that they are *homoousios*, identical in being. He disliked the pluralist language of the Apologists from Justin to Origen. The bishops feared his doctrine of Christ was indistinguishable from what could be acceptable at the synagogue.

The synod's method was to send him a letter (in effect an ultimatum) signed by six bishops. The letter's theme was that the pre-existence of the Son of God is proved by the exegesis of the theophanies of the Old Testament on the line worked out by Justin Martyr, namely that since the transcendent Father cannot be the one seen by Moses at the burning bush or by Abraham at the oak of Mamre, the Son must be the God encountered on earth. 'If anyone refuses to confess that the Son of God is God before the foundation of the world, and says that it is preaching two Gods if we say that the Son of God is God, we declare him to be alien to the rule of the Church; and all Catholic

Churches agree with us.' The pre-existent Son took the body from Mary and deified it, they added.

Much as Origen had been called in to help synods with problems of orthodoxy, so in 268 the bishops assembled at Antioch invited the help of Malchion, a presbyter who was also head of a secular school of philosophy in the city. Fragmentary citations from dialogue between Malchion and Paul occur in anthologies of dogmatic excerpts compiled during the Christological controversies of the fifth and sixth centuries. Because of the milieu from which these citations come, there has been inevitably a degree of hesitation about authenticity. Nevertheless, if the citations were created after the time of the council of Chalcedon in 451, the forger was extremely ingenious. It is impossible to avoid subjective judgement but many citations have a ring of genuineness. The one ground for doubt is that for Malchion as mouthpiece of the synod's orthodoxy 'the divine Logos was in Christ what the inner man is in us'. That suggests doctrine associated with the late fourth-century heretic Apollinaris of Laodicea, whose admirers were never short of ingenuity. The possibility cannot be excluded that Apollinarian hands either created or at least shaped some of the matter. Nevertheless there are texts in Origen where 'the inner man' is the Soul (e.g. *c. Cels.* 6. 63). An Apollinarian forger is not needed.[1]

The synod understood Paul to be teaching that Christ was a man assumed into union with God, but by inspiration rather than by incarnation. This way of thinking about the person of the Lord had been current in the second century, since in the *Dialogue with Trypho* Justin opposed it, but during the third century was increasingly being sidelined. So far as the surviving fragments go, his Christology taught that Jesus was indwelt by the divine Logos. The gift of the Holy Spirit he associated only with the apostles at Pentecost; so at least it was reported in the sixth century by Leontius of Byzantium. His name long remained a bogey word to engender alarm among Greek theologians, especially of the tradition of Athanasius and Cyril of Alexandria. In the West similar ideas were not unknown but not prominent until the Adoptianists of Spain in the age of Charlemagne.

The resolution of the synod that Paul be removed from office failed to persuade him to vacate the church building. His supporters at Antioch remained enthusiastic. The fall of Zenobia—and the near-independence of Palmyra—before the forces of the emperor Aurelian altered the political situation. If

---

[1] Marcel Richard, *Opera minora* (Turnhout, 1976–7), ii, no. 25, doubted the authenticity of the fragments. But see argument in favour of authenticity in papers by M. Simonetti, 'Per la rivalutazione di alcune testimonianze su Paolo di Samosata', in *Rivista di storia e letteratura religiosa*, 24 (1988), 177–210; G. C. Stead, 'Marcel Richard on Malchion and Paul of Samosata', in *Logos*; *FS Luise Abramowski* (Berlin, 1993), reprinted in *Doctrine and Philosophy in early Christianity* (Aldershot, 2000), no. 3; U. M. Lang in *JTS*, NS 51 (2000), 54–80.

Paul was receiving any support from Palmyra, that would help to explain how the aggrieved bishops were able successfully to appeal to imperial authority. On being petitioned, Aurelian ruled that 'the church-building should be assigned to those with whom the bishops of the doctrine in Italy and Rome should communicate in writing.' This initial benevolence of Aurelian towards the Christians did not last long; soon it was rumoured that persecution would come again, but Aurelian died after six years and his successors were short-lived until in 284 Diocletian took power.

25

MANI

In the middle years of the third century gnostic dualism found a fresh and vigorous embodiment in Mani (216–76). He was brought up in Mesopotamia among a Jewish Christian baptist sect, followers of Elchasai, but left them at the age of 24 to found his own group. Like other sects since, he intended to supersede all the separate religious societies and to embrace all major religions of the time. He understood himself to be an inspired prophet, identical with the promised Paraclete, and therefore one of the line of prophets not only from the Old Testament to Jesus but also including Buddha and Zoroaster. He declared that his religion was not confined to one region or linguistic area but was to be taken by missionaries to all lands. Previous founders of religions had written next to nothing and failed to ensure a stable coherent future; Mani's writings would rectify that. Well within his lifetime his missionaries established communities in the Nile and Oxus valleys and had soon reached Chinese Turkestan and Spain. For over nine years the young Augustine was an adherent in north Africa, and after his conversion in 386 his anti-Manichee writings offer much information. In the twentieth century major finds of Manichee documents have been made in Egypt (Coptic probably translated from Syriac) and Turkestan. In the Persian empire the mission had success, and from there successfully infiltrated the Roman empire, soon to cause anxiety to the imperial authorities and also to bishops. In Persia Mani himself fell foul of authority and was executed in 276. His followers had an annual spring festival, called the Bema, for a memorial of his death and for confession of sins.

Central to his thinking was the problem of evil, the permanence and ineradicability of which showed that if the supreme God was good, he was not also omnipotent. What his angels could do was to contain evil and prevent a complete takeover. Cosmic conflict between powers of light and darkness, spirit and matter, had resulted in a mixture felt in human nature's awareness of tension between physical appetites and higher aspirations of the soul. Mani divided followers into a celibate Elect and a lower order of Hearers who cooked selected food for the Elect and were allowed sexual relations at safe periods of the monthly cycle. They were discouraged from having children since this incarcerated sparks of divine light in soggy matter. Wine was strictly forbidden as an invention of the devil.

The crucifixion of Jesus and the wretched wanderings of his apostles described in apocryphal Acts were themes of Manichee literature and preaching, only the cross was not a particular instrument of divine redemption so much as a symbol of the horrible human situation in a tormented world. Christian language was used in Manichee hymns, some of which had a chorus-like refrain 'Glory to the soul of Mary'. The missionaries found church members a profitable recruiting ground. Clergy detected Manichee influence when communicants at the eucharist accepted the consecrated bread but not the cup of wine. An attraction also was the splendid calligraphy and fine binding of Manichee liturgical books and the high solemnity of their chants. But for church members much of the drawing power of the Manichee conventicle lay in its gospel of asceticism, closely akin to much in the New Testament and in incipient embryonic monasticism. The Elect ate no meat, drank no wine, never washed at the baths, slept on rough mats, were forbidden to own land or practise agriculture. Because of the part played by an apple in the Fall of Adam, no Elect person could pick an apple or eat one.

Compromise made it possible for the Hearers to do much that was out of bounds to the Elect (though not all Elect kept the rules). The higher aspirations were (it was claimed) in line with Plato. Some Manichees held high office in the State, but that was not very welcome to emperors. About the end of the third century Diocletian issued an edict suppressing them; they were deemed a dangerous infiltration from his enemies in Persia. The earliest anti-Manichee document extant is a pastoral letter by a bishop of Alexandria shortly before AD 300 preserved on a papyrus in Manchester (P. Rylands III 469). The bishop objected to their disapproval of marriage, to their veneration of the sun, sun and moon being staging-posts on the Manichee soul's ascent to heaven, and to the use of menstrual blood in their ceremonies.

There were well-educated Manichees. Teaching in Rome Plotinus (2. 9) had found to his distress that some of his pupils were deeply attracted by gnostic sects. An Egyptian Neoplatonist about AD 300, Alexander of Lycopolis, who wrote a tract against Manichaism, conceded that some among them 'are not ignorant of Greek traditions', and pupils from his lecture-room had become Manichees. A standard claim was that Mani had solved every problem in the interpretation of the Bible. That is, he followed Marcion in the thesis that the New Testament writings had been interpolated in the interest of asserting the continuing validity of the Old Testament for believers in Jesus, which Mani rejected. He entirely set aside any idea that Adam and Eve were both created by God; they were the offspring of princes of darkness, Saklas and Nebroel.

To the orthodox Church the Manichees, like all gnostic sects, seemed a diabolical parody of authentic faith, infiltrating the Church, scorning the

Church's stress on faith and authority. Insidiously the missionaries concealed the Manichee myths about the making of this world and the cosmic wars in heavenly places and began by criticizing embarrassing texts of the Old Testament, moving on from there to the contradictory genealogies of Jesus in Matthew's and Luke's gospels. At a late stage they would raise the problem of evil and the weakness of orthodox approaches to it.[1]

[1] Important texts with bibliography are collected by Alfred Adam, *Texte zum Manichäismus*, 2nd edn. (Berlin, 1969). A bibliography with more recent finds and monographs in *Cambridge Ancient History*, xiii (1997); see especially the monograph by S. Lieu.

26

PLOTINUS, PORPHYRY[1]

In the middle years of the third century a modern version of Platonism was taught by Plotinus, a philosopher born in Egypt in 204–5 who studied in Alexandria under a teacher of whom all too little is certain, Ammonios Sakkas, whose lectures had also been attended by the Christian Origen. Plotinus was fascinated by Ammonios and adhered to his lectures for eleven years. Between Origen and Plotinus parallel interests can be detected. Plotinus moved to Rome to teach, and acquired a considerable following in the Latin West. He had rapport with the writings of Numenius of Apamea (c. 260), who had probably read some tracts by Philo of Alexandria; he understood Moses to be a kindred spirit to Plato. On the other hand, it embarrassed Plotinus when Gnostic sectaries of dualistic and pessimistic opinions about the cosmos attended his lectures. The obscurity of some pieces in Plotinus' tracts, then and later made him a magnet for those inclined towards theosophy. Several streams of thought had a confluence in him.

Plotinus' most notable pupil was Porphyry, a Phoenician from Tyre and a polymath, who edited Plotinus' lectures in six sections, each of which had nine chapters (hence given the title *Enneads*). To accompany his edition Porphyry wrote a biography of his hero, describing the awe in which Plotinus was held by pupils, male and female, notably for his aspiration to ascend to the experience of mystical union with the One. Plotinus achieved this four times in his life, Porphyry only once. Plotinus lived a disciplined ascetic life with the minimum of food and sleep, no meat and no baths. 'He always seemed ashamed of being in the body.' Like the Christian Origen, he did not think one should celebrate the anniversary of one's birth. By introspection Plotinus analysed the process of human thought and decided that this mental process contained the key to reality, rather than the empirical observation of the material world. His philosophy was therefore concerned with things of the spirit, with the great chain of being ascending through the World-Soul, through Mind (*nous*) to the ultimate reality of the One. The lowest level of this chain of being is formless matter which first acquires any

---

[1] Plotinus is edited and translated by A. H. Armstrong (Loeb Classical Library, 7 vols.). Fragments of Porphyry are gathered by A. D. Smith (Teubner).

semblance of goodness as it receives form from Soul. Accordingly evil is a deficiency of goodness and of being; it is non-being. At the same time erroneous choices in the will engender evil, as the human soul (or that of midway daemonic powers) is seduced by material attractions. Following Plato, Plotinus was sure that God is not responsible for the evils in the cosmos. Nevertheless the power of providence overrules evils to transform them into agents of good.

Plotinus used ecstatic, erotic analogies for his mystical ascent to the divine beauty. He was sure that the soul, if purged from all physical images, has the capacity for union with God which is an experience of identity (4. 8. 1). The soul is elevated above the successiveness of temporal events to reach the simultaneity of eternity. But the distractions and multiplicity of events in time (notably the role of words in speech) make the experience rare and short-lived (6. 9. 10).

Late in the second century a collection of pagan oracles was produced under the name 'Chaldaean Oracles'. They became influential among pagan theosophists and were valued by Porphyry, who was especially interested in the oracles of Apollo and Hecate delivered at their shrines. Porphyry disliked animal sacrifices, a leading characteristic of pagan cult, and was a fervent vegetarian. In a treatise about vegetarianism he regretted that animal sacrifices were needed to placate malevolent daemonic spirits who could injure those who neglected to worship them by their offerings. The highest God would not desire them. True worship for Porphyry as for Plotinus is quiet meditation and introspective contemplation. Thereby the soul returns to its ground of being and is to 'enjoy God'. Language of this kind offered a religious version of Platonism which could be adapted to include a more positive estimate of polytheistic cult, and therefore would come to provide an alternative to Christianity for conservative pagans who regarded Christianity as dangerously revolutionary and unauthorized abandonment of ancestral custom.

Some ancient writers affirm that in his youth Porphyry had been attracted to Christianity (below, p. 178). This could be correct. In the second half of his life he wrote pieces remarkably close to Christian spirituality. But he also became a vehement critic of Christian beliefs, and especially of the Bible. The work he wrote against the Christians was naturally not copied by Christian scribes, and its content is largely conjectural. Augustine's *City of God* and *Harmony of the Evangelists* together with Eusebius' *Preparation for the Gospel* are the principal sources for any reconstruction.

Porphyry wrote a short 'Introduction' to philosophy, especially to the logic of Aristotle, entitled *Isagoge*. A masterpiece of clarity, it remained a standard textbook for more than a millennium, and later Neoplatonists wrote explanatory commentaries on it. Theologians such as Cyril of Alexandria early in the fifth century found it indispensable. Augustine of Hippo found much that Porphyry had to say deeply congenial. Pagans, however, anxious to maintain polytheistic cults (e.g. Iamblichus early in the fourth century) were uncomfortable with his writings. Porphyry could easily seem to have surrendered too much to Christian critics. This opinion of him was held by Iamblichus (*c.*300–25) and Proclus of Athens (d. 480), both being fervent believers in theurgy or the high value of traditional ritual forms.

Both Plotinus and Porphyry wrote of the supreme triad of the One, Mind, and Soul as three hypostases. Porphyry once suggested that the three constituted a single *ousia* or being. The Christians had been speaking of God in triadic terms long before they encountered late Platonism's exegesis of obscure texts in Plato; but the Neoplatonic interpretation of Plato's *Parmenides* showed that the best respected school of philosophy had closely comparable ideas, and that disarmed pagan critics who found the Christian language about God as Trinity incomprehensible. Pagans such as Julian the Apostate are found using Neoplatonist triadic language to give rationality to the worship of the sungod as possessing three meanings, namely, a supreme sun of the world of intelligence, a second sun which mediates between intelligible and sensible, and a third sun which is that which gives the earth heat and light. Some Christian influence may reasonably be discerned here.

Solar monotheism in the fifth century pagan Macrobius (*Saturnalia* 1. 17 ff.) proclaimed each god's name to be a title of the Sun-god. With the Christian feast of Christ's nativity popularly established on 25 December, it would be easy for Pope Leo I's congregation at the entrance to St Peter's to turn east and venerate the sun before facing west in Constantine's basilica (PL 54. 218–19). A classic discussion in F. J. Dölger, *Sol Salutis* (2nd edn., Münster, 1925).

27

DIOCLETIAN AND THE GREAT
PERSECUTION; RISE OF CONSTANTINE

Eusebius of Caesarea prefaces his account of Diocletian by describing the Church's prosperity in the decades before the coming of sharp persecution. Even in the time of Origen there were individual governors and highly placed officials who, though not believers, did everything in their power to help the Christians, and Christians believed that there could be mercy hereafter for them (Origen, *In Matt. ser.* 120). Eusebius records that more recently there had been provincial governors who were Christians and had even been allowed by authority not to participate in pagan sacrifices; moreover, bishops had been treated with honour by governors. Since the emperor Gallienus had enacted that Christians could legitimately own and assemble for worship in their church buildings and could have their cemeteries (Eus. *HE* 7. 13), the numbers of Christians had swelled, and larger buildings had to be erected to contain the overflowing congregations. Prosperity and success weakened the morale of believers, and there were some painful contentions between bishops (8. 1. 8). To Eusebius this justified a divine judgement.

Diocletian's reorganization

In November 284 the empire acquired an energetic new emperor, Valerius Diocles who expanded his name to Diocletianus. He eliminated rivals and set about reorganizing the empire better to defend frontiers, improve administration, check inflation by (vainly) controlling prices by edict. His legislation was remarkably successful, much of it surviving to be included in Justinian's Code more than two hundred years later. In 293 to make civil wars less likely many provinces were divided. This increased the cost of bureaucracy and therefore raised taxes, bankrupting farmers, but smaller provinces made it harder for a military commander to revolt. Estate duty on the dead helped funding. High officials were given grand titles with distinctions in the epithets applying to their rank, the grades being distinguished by the number of curtains one passed before being admitted to an audience. (There would be a succession of guarded rooms through which a petitioner would move, a procedure familiar today to those granted a private audience at the Vatican.) Provinces were grouped into twelve 'Dioceses', each administered by a deputy (*vicarius*) for the praetorian prefect. At the top the territory was divided among four, two with the rank of Augustus (himself and a colleague Maximian), two entitled Caesar, the title used since Hadrian's time for the nominated successor to the Augustus, but confusingly used by Germanic tribes for the Augustus (as Jerome records, *in Soph.* 3. 1–7, 41–5; cf. *in Hiez.* 9. 29. 1–2). All four members of the Tetrarchy wore purple, forbidden to everyone else. Diocletian called himself Jovius, Maximian Herculius. To enhance imperial honour ceremony characteristic of the Persian court was enjoined.

   Not that Diocletian was pro-Persia. He was shocked by endogamous brother–sister marriages in Roman Mesopotamia, a Persian custom not unknown in the Nile valley. War on the eastern frontier was a continuing problem, and the infiltration of Mani's missionaries from Mesopotamia, refugees from persecution in Persia, provoked a severe rescript of suppression. Diocletian was conservative, wanting the gods' help to preserve the empire. A new religion was the last thing he needed. The Augustus was an absolute autocrat. Rome with its opulent aristocratic families became largely ornamental in government, though the office of city prefect remained prestigious and senators were natural candidates for the office of provincial governor or even praetorian prefect. (The senate at Rome had lost any power to nominate an emperor since the third century, when this effectively passed into the army's hands.) Diocletian's palace was at Nicomedia in Bithynia, Maximian's at Milan. Sirmium, metropolis of Illyricum, and Trier became residences of the Caesars.

Church expansion

Before the middle years of the third century Origen could observe that church buildings were packed with worshippers. The expansion continued in the later part of the third century, moving beyond the empire with the conversion, led by the king, of the Armenians and at about the same time or soon afterwards the Georgians to the north-east of the Black Sea. The Christian heartlands lay in the Greek east, some towns in Asia Minor being wholly inhabited by believers. Growth in numbers brought problems. Bishoprics attracted ambitious, power-hungry candidates, and among laity there were factions in a war of words. Eusebius regarded the insults and tortures suffered by bishops in Palestine a well-deserved divine judgement for their unlawful ordinations and for continual innovations (*Martyrs of Palestine* 12; *HE* 8. 1. 7).

Porphyry

The success of third-century Christianity produced an embattled defensiveness in those called by the Christians of 300 'pagani', a term meaning either bucolic peasants (towns being more Christianized than rural areas attached to them) or, more probably, 'civilians' not enrolled in Christ's army by baptism. Porphyry produced an intellectual attack on the Christians—regarded by pagans as apostates from the traditional gods and therefore atheists, enthusiasts for Jewish myths but refusing the prescribed Jewish ceremonies, insistent in proclaiming faith in disregard of reasoned argument. Porphyry directed attack on the Bible, on the veracity of the evangelists, on the to him dishonest employment of allegory to rescue the Old Testament, on the book of Daniel, which Porphyry saw to be no prophecy of the age of the captivity in Babylon but to belong to the time of Antiochus Epiphanes in the second century BC. He also observed that bishops owed their election to prominent women (cited by Jerome, *in Esai.* 3. 12, p. 57 Vallarsi). Like Celsus before him, Porphyry rejected the exclusive claim to offer the one path to salvation. He had himself searched for a universally valid way, and failed to find it (Augustine, *City of God* 10. 32), a sentence which gives some colour to the statement in the historian Socrates (3. 23. 38) that at one time Porphyry had been a Christian. He knew his Bible well. Writing on oracles he cited one praising Jesus, a holy man rightly elevated to heaven, while mocking believers who deified him (Eus. *Dem. Evang.* 3. 7; Aug. *City of God* 19. 23). An open letter written to Marcella the wife of his old age, much being a mosaic of Neopythagorean and Epicurean maxims, illustrates how close his moral and spiritual ideals stood to Christianity. Many of the same maxims had been incorporated a century earlier in a Christian collection by an otherwise unknown (or at least uncertainly identifiable) Sextus (p. 139).

   The Christians regarded the pagan gods as evil spirits—paradoxically an opinion for which Porphyry himself provided support exploited by Eusebius of Caesarea (*Praep. Evang.* 4. 23 and 5. 6; also in Porphyry's work on vegetarianism, *De abstinentia* 2. 37–40). It followed that Christian officers in the Roman legions were even more unlikely to think sacrifices helpful in battle, and would make the sign of the cross to avert malevolent powers widely believed to cause catastrophes. Eusebius (*Praep. Evang.* 5. 27) comments that down to his own time oracles had misled rulers into waging damaging wars, and cites Porphyry that inferior daemonic powers delight in erotic pleasures and in battles (5. 5).

Christian intellectuals, Arnobius

Until Diocletian's nineteenth year as emperor Christians were largely unmolested. In Alexandria Christian teachers, Theognostos and Pierius, could continue Origen's themes and command respect among the city's educated society. Unfortunately for the historian, in the period before Constantine's victory of 324 the archaeologist's spade and even the papyrologist's documents and letters are reticent about Christians. In the province of Numidia in north Africa a well-educated critic of Christianity named Arnobius, familiar with the writings of Porphyry, felt led by a dream to convert to the faith he had been criticizing. To persuade the local bishop of Sicca that his change was genuine, he wrote a defence of Christianity in seven books. He had read some Tertullian and Cyprian, but was largely unfamiliar with the Bible. On the other hand he discerned in the Neoplatonism of Porphyry an intended rival to Christianity, offering a philosophic salvation for the soul, attacking the true saviour Christ as 'destroyer of religion and author of impiety' (2. 2), claiming that the immortality of the soul is incompatible with a Christian doctrine of judgement hereafter and that because of the soul's innate divine quality it needs no redeemer. The advent of Diocletian's persecution convinced Arnobius that Rome's domination of the world had become catastrophic for the human race (7. 51) because of the insistence on the old polytheism.

Persecution

The long peace for the Church was suddenly ended. The wars of Diocletian had not all gone smoothly for the legions. Before a campaign sacrifice was offered to win the favour of the gods, and Christian army officers made the sign of the cross, a trophy of victory over the evil demons to which the sacrifices were being offered. Might that cause heaven's displeasure? Might the old gods prefer a religiously united empire from which sceptical dissent was excluded? Moreover, although there were Christians serving in the army, some stricter believers were still refusing to serve, as is shown by the Acts of the conscript and martyr Maximilian in north Africa, executed in 295. At least it seemed right to the Augusti to eliminate Christians from the legions, and in 302 a policy of purging the army was carried through. Lactantius, living in Nicomedia at the time, treats the eastern Caesar Galerius as prime mover in the persecution; it is uncertain that this was actually so. Both Christians and pagans (as the rhetor Libanios, *or.* 19. 45 shows) looked back on Diocletian as the embodiment of irrational ferocity in liquidating anyone who failed to conform.

In February 303 Diocletian acquiesced in the verdict that it was time to act against the Christians. The oracle of Apollo at Didyma by Miletus endorsed the decision. In a dawn raid the church at Nicomedia, visible from the palace, was dismantled and destroyed; Bibles were burnt. Next day an edict was published removing privileges from upper-class Christians including the conventional immunity from torture, which equated Christian loyalty with high treason. At roughly the same time Christians were harassed in Roman Armenia and northern Syria (Eus. *HE* 8. 6. 8), possibly because the conversion of the Armenian king to Christianity and the easy movement of traders across the frontier aroused fear that Christian citizens and soldiers in that region were being influenced to feel more attachment to Armenia than to Rome. The bishop of Nicomedia was executed together with other clergy and lay people. Worse was to come when two fires broke out in the palace for which Christians were thought probably responsible. Diocletian's wrath knew no bounds. At Antioch in Syria the magistrates prided themselves on refined and hitherto unpractised methods of horrendous torture (Eus. *Mart. Pal.* 2). All who refused to offer sacrifice to the gods were to be killed.

In practice the number of martyrs appears not to have been large, at least in the first year, unless one includes 'voluntary' martyrs who had provoked the authorities. More numerous, it seems, were those maimed for life by the rack or scorched on gridirons. In Spain and Italy Maximian enforced the measures; Constantius Chlorus, the Caesar ruling Britain and Gaul, did not do more than demolish some churches. In Africa persecution was sharp, and forty-nine Christians who had gathered to celebrate the eucharist at Abitina were executed at Carthage under the judgement of the proconsul. Ladies of wealth and refinement were not exempted from the death penalty as the laity came to be included in the imperial bloodbath. The churches in Spain were proud to commemorate the courage of Vincent, deacon of Saragossa, whose veneration also entered north African calendars. Both the poet Prudentius and Augustine of Hippo possessed the record of his trial and martyrdom. His bishop Valerius came of a prominent family at Saragossa which supplied a succession of bishops to their city; Valerius was not much affected. Ossius bishop of Corduba is recorded by Athanasios (*Hist. Ar.* 44) to have been a 'confessor'. The Acts of Vincent's martyrdom record that the persecution in Spain was directed by a *praeses* named Datianus; this probably represents good memory at Saragossa. In Egypt Bishop Peter of Alexandria was in time able to issue canons to regulate the treatment of the lapsed. The Alexandrian church could gratefully recall the way in which pagan friends hid Christians from the searching authorities with their instruments of torture at the ready.

Pierios at Alexandria was noted for yielding to the authorities, but was able to migrate to Rome where the great city could hide him. His colleague Phileas was martyred after his declaration that it was for him a matter of conscience.

A papyrus letter illustrates how some Christians lived through the dangerous years. A certain Copres went down to Alexandria to present his suit in a magistrate's court concerning some property. When he arrived, he found to his surprise that the lawcourt now had an altar at which he was expected to offer incense at the start of the case. This as a Christian he did not wish to do, so he arranged to confer the power of attorney on a pagan friend to stand in for him, for whose conscience it would not be a problem. For Copres the persecution appeared as a minor inconvenience to his plans.[1] In Egypt at least two bishops were so loved by their people that they could offer sacrifice without any loss of honour or office.[2]

Diocletian retires. Galerius and Constantius I. Constantine

During 304 the persecution was worse, no doubt because, after visiting Rome late in 303 to celebrate his twentieth anniversary of accession, Diocletian fell ill, and it would have been easy to blame Christian prayers for that. His illness persisted, and he was persuaded by the ambitious Caesar Galerius to retire to his palace at Split. He insisted that Maximian in the West should also relinquish office as Augustus. At Nicomedia on 1 May 305 the two Augusti solemnly handed over supreme power to Galerius and to Constantius Chlorus. The two new Caesars were boorish roughnecks, Severus in the West, Maximin Daia in the East. Maximian's son Maxentius and Constantius' son Constantine were given nothing, but they wanted power too. Constantine, initially kept virtually as a hostage at Galerius' court, escaped to join Constantius in Gaul, then in York, where Constantius died. The legions at once proclaimed the young son successor as Augustus (25 July 306). At Nicomedia Galerius acknowledged Constantine only as Caesar and promoted Severus Augustus over him. But in 307 Severus committed suicide. At Rome Maxentius was similarly acclaimed—but to his father Maximian's displeasure, perhaps because he foresaw that the break-up of the Tetrarchy was leading to the civil wars which Diocletian wished to avert, but also because he had resigned power unwillingly. His daughter Fausta had married Constantine. Her father Maximian invested Constantine with the title Augustus. The young Constantine nursed aspirations to become supreme and sole ruler of the empire. Maximian failed in an attempt to murder Constantine so as to recover power, and committed suicide in 309 or 310.

Council of Elvira

The aftermath of persecution in Spain can be deduced from the Acts of a substantial council of 19 bishops at Elvira (Illiberis) by Granada. The council's date cannot be determined but is likely to have been about 310 rather than 'at

---

[1] P.Oxy. XXXI 2601; for altars being installed in lawcourts, Lactantius, *De mort.* 15. 5.

[2] E. A. E. Reymond and J. W. B. Barns, *Four Martyrdoms from the Pierpont Morgan Coptic Codices* (Oxford, 1973), 147.

the time of the council of Nicaea' as claimed by the Escorial manuscript. Ossius of Corduba was among those present. The 81 canons reflect a situation when Christians were again free for worship in their churches. The council was against pictures on church walls (36), excommunicated those who did not attend worship for three consecutive Sundays (21), while those who did not appear 'per infinita tempora' are ranked as apostates readmissible only after ten years' penance (46). Women are warned not to keep vigils at cemeteries because of the risk of immoral goings-on (35).[3] Bishops, presbyters, and deacons are required to live with their wives without begetting children (33). Among bishops there is one who has 'the first see' (58), presumably the senior by date of consecration, as in north Africa apart from Carthage and the Proconsular province. Some laity are magistrates (56), and a mistress who beats her slave-girl to death is excommunicate for seven years if it was intentional, five years if it was unintentional (5). Several canons show that prominent laymen are combining their faith with pagan priesthoods (2–4), while rich ladies are providing decorative garments and drapes for pagan processions (57). Mixed marriages are a problem because there are more Christian girls than boys (15). It was not easy to avoid all concessions to pagan tradition. Masters of households are asked 'as far as possible' not to allow their slaves to have idols in their houses (41). Christians who provoked authority by smashing idols are not ranked as martyrs (60). Some canons seek to rule against remarriage after divorce (8), gambling (69), clergy who fail to expel their adulterous wives (65), clergy who lend money at interest (20), pantomime actors and jockeys who on conversion continue in their jobs (62). Former prostitutes, however, are to be received without hesitation if they are married (44). Pimps are rejected (12). Clergy may not live with women to whom they are not related (27), and should not neglect their duties because of business interests (19). Stress is laid on keeping the fasts, including Saturday (26) as at Rome, and on the high importance of Pentecost (43), a feast from which some stay away apparently with some separatist intention. It is clear that some church members were drawn to Judaism or to return to paganism (1–4. 50).

---

[3] Jerome had trouble with a deacon at Bethlehem who used to visit the Cave of the Nativity to make assignations with women, and had a substantial record of all too successful seductions (*ep.* 147. 4). At Carthage Bishop Aurelius had to order separate entrances to the church for the sexes, because women were jostled by some of the men. See the recently discovered sermons from Mainz city library found and edited by F. Dolbeau, *Vingt-six sermons* (Paris, 1996), specifically Mainz 5 = Dolbeau 2. Jerome, *ep.* 22. 28 to Eustochium, mentions lonely hearts who wanted to be presbyters or deacons to gain easier access to the opposite sex, and has a portrait of a cleric who spent every day in attendance on women. The records imply such cases were uncommon.

Death of Galerius. Licinius. Daia

Both Constantine and Maxentius established freedom of worship. In the West persecution ended, and Maxentius at Rome found it wise to have friendly relations with the substantial Christian populace. He was, however, an obstacle to Constantine's ambitions, and the picture of Maxentius as a debauchee in the pro-Constantine sources, Eusebius and Lactantius, is hostile. There was little relief for Christians in the East until Galerius died in May 311, having published an edict on 30 April declaring toleration for the Christians, exhorting them to pray for his and the empire's welfare. The edict is preserved by both Lactantius (*De mort.* 33–4) and Eusebius (*HE* 8. 17).

To the vexation of the Caesar Maximin Daia, Galerius had named one of his army commanders, Licinius, Augustus in 308. He also was born a peasant. Daia answered the elevation of Licinius by proclaiming himself Augustus too. Not a man of moderation, less than six months after Galerius' edict Daia resumed the harassment of Christians in the East, and the martyrs included Bishop Peter of Alexandria, the learned scholar Pamphilus at Caesarea (teacher and patron of Eusebius the historian), and another learned man named Lucian at Nicomedia. Many were maimed by torturers. Cities were encouraged to submit petitions that the Christians be suppressed. Daia realized the weakness of old polytheism, and produced a kind of blueprint for the emperor Julian's pagan revival half a century later. He created a highpriest for each city and in each province a central high priest in charge of all religion. (One could ask if Daia the persecutor suggested the authority given to the bishop of a provincial metropolis by the canons of the council of Nicaea in 325.) A duty of each city-priest was to offer daily sacrifices to all gods worshipped there and to prevent the Christians either building churches or holding rival assemblies in public or in private. If they refused to sacrifice to the gods, they must be taken to court. However, even Daia found the policy of suppression impracticable. He changed course, issued an edict of toleration including the right to build churches, but soon afterwards suffered a fatal stroke. His colleagues in the Tetrarchy immediately denounced him as a usurper, so that his pictures and statues were destroyed; and his children, close relatives, and principal officers of state were executed.

It is hardly possible to read the extant records of those martyred in the Great Persecution without horror at the degree of violence let loose upon good people and without sympathy for those maimed by grisly methods of inflicting sustained agonies. It was not necessary for their numbers to be very large for their honour and integrity to be long remembered by the Church. Eusebius recorded the sufferings of his own province, Palestine, with forty-three martyrs (who, however, included no bishops). Some of them were provocative of the authorities. Tertullian had declared that 'Christ is in the martyr' (*De pudic.* 22). The Acts of Saturninus observe the 'stupidity' of a proconsul who failed to realize that in the martyrs he was fighting not men but God. Nevertheless, Cyprian had already found problems with the pride of confessors, who had been in prison and in chains but disregarded the need for any reference to the bishop. They had a kind of martyrdom of desire. There could be debate whether a confessor needed ordination to act as a presbyter (*Apostolic Constitutions* 8. 25. 2). He already possessed the charism.

Schisms

The persecution of Diocletian precipitated two serious and long-lived schisms, the Donatists at Carthage and North Africa and the followers of Melitius bishop of Lycopolis in Egypt. In both cases the argument turned on the question whether, when the state forbade Christian meetings for worship and required the surrender of Bibles and sacred vessels, one could quietly co-operate with the authorities, or if one was obliged in conscience to resist them as agents of Satan. The bishop of Carthage, Mensurius, surrendered medical treatises, accepted by the searchers without scrutiny. But one zealot Numidian bishop who found himself in prison with his young nephews thought it right to kill the boys to prevent them from apostasy. (The story, however, comes from a hostile source.) Mensurius and his archdeacon Caecilian pursued a policy of lying low; the persecution would not last long. Caecilian even picketed the Carthage prison to prevent food being supplied to defiant church members who, in his view, had been needlessly provocative. On Mensurius' death Caecilian was hastily consecrated to succeed him. The bishops of Numidia expected to be well represented at the ordination of a bishop of Carthage; they sympathized with the zealots and believed a rumour that Caecilian's principal consecrator Felix bishop of Apthugni had surrendered the scriptures to the authorities. In short, if so, Caecilian had been made a bishop by polluted hands guilty of apostasy. Caecilian was supported by the bishop of Rome. Since, however, Bishop Marcellinus of Rome had also compromised his faith under the persecution, to the Numidians he represented a polluted Church lacking authority in the matter. It became a zealot presupposition that pollution could be transmitted by the fault in the succession of ordinations. That assumption would be utterly denied by Augustine, for whom even if Caecilian had been ordained by a bishop who surrendered the sacred books, it could in no way compromise his successors or those in communion with that line of bishops.

The Carthaginian group hostile to Caecilian were soon led by Donatus, who was to give his name to the party. The Donatists appealed to Constantine, especially when they were not included in substantial funding from the imperial treasury. The emperor referred the dispute to the bishop of Rome who in turn called a synod to consider the issue. The synod met in Fausta's palace on the Lateran and decided for Caecilian, a factor being his readiness to abandon Cyprianic baptismal theology and accept the old custom defended by Pope Stephen. The Donatists appealed to Constantine against the synod's verdict, and their appeal was sent on to a Gallic synod meeting at Arles on 1 August 314. As the persecution had not affected the Gallic churches, the Africans could not claim that they would be prejudiced. Naturally at Arles the Roman verdict was upheld. The Gallic bishops held the first of western sees in great respect. Eventually Constantine left the Donatists 'to the judgement of God', a decision which a century later Augustine was to describe as most ignominious. The outcome was a schism which left a substantial proportion of the African churches out of communion with those north of the Mediterranean. It was the more formidable because full support was given to the Donatist cause by Numidian bands of peasants armed with clubs. Before the persecution they had perfected an unstoppable charge against the musicians playing at pagan festivals, which brought to some the crown of martyrdom. They were now able to turn their militancy on catholic clergy and their congregations by maiming, blinding, and even murder. The mutual hatred engendered drove at least some recent converts back to the polytheism they had left.

In Egypt Bishop Melitius of Lycopolis was shocked to find that at Alexandria Bishop Peter had gone into hiding, perhaps had left Egypt, and that the presbyters were not providing pastoral care and teaching for the people. He concluded that Peter had ceased to be recognizable as bishop, and established a rival episcopate both at Alexandria and south into the Thebaid where his strength was to lie. At the council of Nicaea (325) a major concern was to achieve reconciliation with the Melitian faction, and to the later chagrin of Athanasius they were offered easy terms.

Rise of Constantine

In the West the rise of Constantine was secured by his famous victory over Maxentius at the battle of the Milvian Bridge or Ponte Molle on 28 October 312, when Maxentius was drowned. The senate honoured Constantine in 315 with a triumphal arch by the Colosseum, the inscription (*ILS* 694) declaring that he had won the battle not only 'by the greatness of his mind' but also 'by the prompting of divinity', the relief portraying Maxentius' forces drowning in the Tiber. The motifs of the representation are solar symbols. Panegyrists acclaimed divine aid, indeed the support of his father Constantius with a heavenly host. Constantine had been inspired to attack defying the omens of the augurs. To Eusebius of Caesarea the victory was prefigured by Moses' victory over Pharaoh's army, drowned in the crossing of the Red Sea. A statue was erected in Rome showing Constantine with a cross in his hand and an inscription to explain that this was the saving sign by which he had delivered the city from the tyrant-usurper. God vindicated his legitimacy. Pagans invoked only inferior deities, Constantine the most high. So declared a pagan panegyrist of 313.

It is hard to know whether the victory at the Milvian Bridge was crucial in deciding his allegiance to the God of the Christians who had signally granted military success against larger forces, or whether there was some Christianity present in his family much earlier and that he was in practice associating himself with the Church as early as his elevation by the troops in 306. What is clear is that from 306 Christians in his realm had liberty. Until reluctantly recognized as a Caesar by Galerius he was actually a usurper without proper title to the authority claimed. In those circumstances it would have seemed desirable at least to have divine sanction, and not merely that of his legions. It is also ambiguous whether or not the 'vision' and the direction to put a Christian symbol on his soldiers' shields were actually connected. The language of Eusebius implies that the vision was granted when he was campaigning against barbarians, presumably in Gaul; and this may be linked with a statement in a panegyric of the year 310 that at Autun Constantine had had a vision of the god Apollo (also the Sun-god). Solar theology could, of course, be merged with the veneration of 'the sun of righteousness'. In Tertullian's time there were pagans who deduced from Christians meeting for worship on Sunday that they worshipped the Sun-god (*Adv. nat.* 1. 13). If from 306 the emperor was leaning towards Christianity, there could well have been some element of syncretism. Most of the capable administrators on whom he had to rely were certainly still pagan. That could have encouraged caution in negatives on polytheism, at least for a considerable time. A ruthless soldier could be capable of political concession.

Lactantius (*De mort.* 44) records that before the battle in 312 Constantine had directed the cross to be depicted on the soldiers' shields in the form of **X** with a vertical line through it rounded at the top, the Chi-Rho symbol of Christ. It was an adaptation of a mark for 'NB' or Nota Bene. The story receives a different and developed treatment in the funerary panegyric by Eusebius of Caesarea of 337 or 338, more than quarter of a century later, namely, that a parhelion, with a cross athwart the midday sun, had the inscription 'By this conquer'. The following night in a dream Christ appeared to Constantine and told him to make the monogram his standard. It was called *labarum*. The shape was capable of being interpreted as the double axe of Zeus, but was certainly taken to be a sign that Christ was giver of military victory, since during Julian's pagan revival it was abolished. Any who might question whether the defeated Maxentius was not just as friendly to the Church as Constantine were answered by Constantine's publication of letters showing a close secret alliance between Maxentius and the avowed persecutor Daia in the East.

At Rome Constantine's identification with the Christians was further publicized later by the gift of his wife Fausta's palace, once home of the Laterani family, to be the house of the bishops of Rome. (Perhaps he hoped it might help with propitiation for his wife's murder?) Soon a basilica was constructed beside it and a baptistery. More difficult to build was a basilica on the slope of the Vatican hill with its focal point above the *memoria* constructed in AD 165 in honour of St Peter. Other churches and shrines were built in Rome by Constantine or his mother Helena or his daughter Constantina. This was the beginning of Christian conquest of urban space in the first city of the empire.

At Aquileia a wealthy Christian Theodorus gave the church an exquisite mosaic floor which survives. The benefaction may have been in celebration of the peace brought to the Church by Constantine.

Constantine's agreement with Licinius (313)

Just as Maxentius had sought alliance with Daia, so also Constantine had protected his flank by an alliance with the Augustus, Licinius. In Milan he joined Licinius there to enter into an alliance by marriage and to draft a protocol of agreement on freedom of worship for all religions, so that 'whatever god may be in heaven, he may be propitious to us and those over whom we rule'. Property confiscated from the Christians was to be returned, private buyers being indemnified by the state treasury. The text surviving is in the form of Licinius' edict to the praetorian prefect of the Diocese Oriens at Antioch.

The consequence of the agreement at Milan was to make possible Constantine's programme, making it clear to the empire that this emperor venerated the God of the Christians and this was going to affect his policies.

Death of Daia

From Milan Licinius moved east and encountered Daia's forces at Adrianople in April 313. Daia was defeated, retreated through Asia Minor, and finally committed suicide by poison at Tarsus. The empire was now divided between Constantine and Licinius. Licinius killed off all close relatives of Galerius, Severus, and Daia to eliminate any rivals. From the start relations with Constantine were tense, and in 316 a war ended in Licinius' surrender of Illyricum to Constantine, a province destined to become a source of pain between East and West, since while largely Latin-speaking, it was close to the eastern centre of imperial power.

Tension between Constantine and Licinius: War

Nevertheless it was a matter of time before Constantine decided that Licinius was superfluous in the government of the empire. Licinius was a pagan monotheist. He was bound to think that synods of bishops, such as those which occurred at Ankyra and at Neocaesarea in Asia Minor (regulating reconciliation for the lapsed), were potential sources of conspiracy in favour of his western rival. By negotiating behind his back with the Christian king of Armenia, Constantine could encircle him. Licinius played into Constantine's hands by forbidding episcopal synods, ordering churches rigorously to segregate the sexes (stories of sexual abuse were circulated, Eus. *HE* 9. 5. 2), and harassing Christians near the Armenian frontier. In this region occurred the famous martyrdom of forty Christian prisoners from various places, exposed to freezing death on a lake near Sebaste. Several bishops were executed too. Here, then, was more persecution, and Constantine could invoke the divine giver of victory in the West to dispose of his enemies in the East. The forces met at Chrysopolis opposite Byzantium at the entrance to the Bosporus in September 324, and Licinius lost. At first detained at Thessalonica, he was soon to lose his head.

Constantinople

It was momentous that Constantine had set eyes on the strategic site of Byzantium and, guided (he said) by a vision from the Lord, decided that with its splendid harbour the Golden Horn, and control of all traffic to or from the Black Sea, that would be the ideal site for a new Rome, an eastern capital rather than Nicomedia used by Diocletian. (Troy had also been considered at the entrance to the Dardanelles.) Byzantium needed strong walls on the landward side (Constantine's were replaced in 413) and, as the population grew, better cisterns and an aqueduct. Huge land-walls made it almost impregnable.

Moreover, while old Rome was dominated by the buildings of pagan classical culture and polytheism, Byzantium offered scope and space for a new and Christian foundation, decorated by the recycling of columns and other building materials from the Greek past. Here Constantine could build a church dedicated to Peace, and nearby to begin a church of Holy Wisdom, which was not completed until 360 under his son Constantius II. But he could also reuse an image of Apollo the sungod for the large statue of himself in the Forum of his new city. The population of the city would not have been overwhelmed by signs of Christianization. That is not to say that the battle of Chrysopolis in 324 did not mark a watershed in minds. After 324 Egyptian papyri become reticent about recording pagan cults and associated themes.

If Constantine had not become a Christian, his transference of the seat of government to Constantinople would still have carried huge consequences for Old Rome. He created a new senate for his new capital, including a number of Christians promoted to this status. There was to be a city prefect, and other officers of state paralleled in Italy. The erection of a parallel church authority in the Greek east imported into the political tension a difference in ecclesiology, with the Latin West thinking of the Church as a sphere or circle with Rome at its centre, the East understanding the Church of the empire as an ellipse with two foci, virtually equal in jurisdictional power, yet granting a genuflexion of supreme honour to the bishop of Old Rome who represented the Latin west. Old Rome would continue to be ceremonially visited, but it was no longer to be the western emperor's residence. That gave a degree of freedom to bishops of Rome, while the proximity of the emperor at Constantinople to the bishop of New Rome could cause awkwardnesses.

Coins of Constantinople minted during the fourth century often portray Old and New Rome sharing a throne of equal authority. See Gudrun Bühl, *Constantinopolis und Roma* (Zürich, 1995).

28

CONSTANTINE: LACTANTIUS, EUSEBIUS OF CAESAREA, ARIUS, AND THE COUNCIL OF NICAEA

Lactantius[1]

Two Christian contemporaries, one Latin, the other Greek, commented on the new situation resulting from the rise to sole power of a Christian emperor, an advent of which second-century Christians had dreamed. Tertullian (*Apol.* 21. 24) was sure emperors would be believers if they were not necessary for unspiritual duties in the secular world. After the establishment of Christianity by Theodosius I, Augustine could declare (*En. in Ps.* 93. 19) 'the emperor has become a Christian, but the devil has not'. Ambrose could write that every secular office is under Satan's power (*in Luc.* 4. 28). That kind of coolness towards a Christian empire was not characteristic of Lactantius or Eusebius, for whom it seemed almost the coming of the millennium, the fulfilment of Hebrew prophecy that God's word would spread throughout the inhabited world. It accompanied the realization that Christian missionaries of spiritual but no great intellectual power had enabled the gospel to take hold of the entire Roman empire with Persia, Armenia, Parthia, Scythia, and even Britain (Eus. *Dem. Evang.* 3. 5, p. 112 D). Celsus had met Christians who looked forward to a Christian empire in which all the diversities of religion and morals would give way to a single law appropriate for the recognition of monotheism. Could empire and church together establish a global ethic? Eusebius (*Dem. Evang.* 8. 3, p. 407 A) hailed Constantine's rise to sole power as happily ending all civil wars.

Diocletian's restructuring and reorganization of the empire reflected a sharp awareness of the huge problems of controlling a Mediterranean society, half of which spoke Greek, the other half Latin, besides tribal tongues which politically did not count. The civil wars among the members of his Tetrarchy will have enhanced this consciousness. Eusebius of Caesarea (*Vita Const.* 2. 19) observed that by his elimination of all rival emperors ('tyrants')

---

[1] See E. D. Digeser, *The Making of a Christian Empire: Lactantius and Rome* (Ithaca, NY, Cornell Univ. Press, 2000).

Constantine had united east and west under a single monarchy. That the impact of the Great Persecution was to sow a seed of separation between Latins and Greeks is not discernible, though the far western provinces suffered much less than those in the east or in Latin north Africa and Italy. The early Syriac martyrology of the year 410 records that in Phrygia the persecution united the Novatianist community with the orthodox churches, and therefore diminished the schismatic urge for ecclesial divorce. It would be more persuasive to say that, by liberating the churches from the threats of hostile government, Constantine set them free to indulge in uninhibited internal conflict without feeling a need to stay together bonded in brotherhood to ensure survival. The Christian writers of the time regarded polemic against polytheism as a primary task. Both in Lactantius and in Eusebius this was a main preoccupation. The relief from state persecution did not end verbal pagan attacks calling for reply (*Dem. Evang.* 2. 3, p. 82 c).

Lactantius from north Africa had a secular career teaching Latin literature and rhetoric after studying under Arnobius, and was invited by Diocletian to teach at Nicomedia. At what precise stage of his career he decided to be a Christian, and whether during the persecution of Diocletian he resigned office at Nicomedia, is unclear. There he found only few pupils keen to learn Latin and in due course used his powers of good Ciceronian prose to write books of Christian exposition and vindication, at first cautiously but in time explicitly. At Nicomedia Lactantius was eyewitness of the initial act of persecution—the demolition of the city church. He wrote on divine creation, on the notion of divine wrath, and drafted an introduction to his Christian faith, dedicated to Constantine. The text transmitted was composed after Lactantius had left Nicomedia, probably in his old age when he was invited to Gaul to teach Constantine's son Crispus. He called his book *Divine Institutes*, a title modelled on lawyers' textbooks. Much of the matter is fairly conventional. He attacks polytheistic superstitions and the mutual contradictions of philosophers. In the fifth book his subject is the justice that goes with faith in God being the Father of all, who desires that we injure no one and keep an open door for the stranger. The fifth book is a passionate engagement with the pagan mind that could think persecution justified. To end persecution, what is needed is education since it is rooted in ignorance.

All the religions and cults of polytheism were regarded by the people as equally true and by philosophers as equally false (2. 3) as Cicero's Academic scepticism illustrated. Only fear and timidity prevented Cicero from recognizing monotheism to be true.

Some ask why, if monotheism is true, so many people have a diversity of cults with different gods. The answer given is that virtue is only discerned when there is evil opposed to it. 'There cannot be good without evil' (6. 15. 7), a sentence which is only one of several dualist formulations. Lactantius dissents from those who say that no one is just, but is sure that on earth justice is incompatible with polytheism which of itself breeds diversity and contradiction. Latent here is the Platonic antithesis of the one (good) and the many (evil). If all worshipped the one God alone, that would end quarrels, wars, conspiracies, robberies, adulteries, harlotry. Sexual union is intended only for procreation. In a society where males restrained their lusts and the rich supported the destitute with alms, there would be no prostitutes. (Lactantius recognized that desperate poverty drove women into brothels.) In short, if everyone observed God's laws in the way we Christians do, there would be no such social evils, and we should then have no need for prisons and capital punishment. Lactantius thought one should never bring a charge where the penalty for the convicted was death.

But the Christians have been subjected to mindless tortures for no other reason than that they are just and good. Why is there such profound hatred? Perhaps people resent anyone witnessing their crimes, and feel put to shame. Why are those who apostatize praised and honoured except to encourage others to yield? Why tear apart the bodies of those whom everyone knows to be innocent? Christians do not attack travellers by land or sea, are not poisoners, do not strangle or expose infants, practise no incest, do not conspire against the empire, do not rob temples, do not hunt for legacies and forge wills. If they are provincial governors or magistrates called to judge, they do not accept bribes to send the innocent to their deaths or to acquit the guilty.

And what ghoulish delight officials have taken in the tortures inflicted, sometimes supposing it might bring them promotion, some being merely cruel by nature! 'In Bithynia I saw the governor (*praeses*) overjoyed as if a barbarian tribe had been conquered because a Christian who held out for two years was at last yielding' (5. 11. 15). The policy was to torture with such care that the victims did not die but were allowed respite to provide the pleasure of inflicting at intervals yet further cruelties, a relentless method likely to cause surrender in the end. Intermittent onslaughts on a victim's genital organs induced fear of agonies to come which could win the psychological battle. Christians were deprived of eyes and limbs or had their noses slit, then after a protest from Constantine to Daia were surreptitiously drowned. A (lost) collection of imperial rescripts directing how Christians should be punished, compiled by the famous lawyer Ulpian, became a handbook of guidelines.

From this summary of Lactantius it is evident that the memory of the persecution was vivid to him and its ending was close in time. His work was a protreptic to conversion addressed to the educated critics in the Latin West, unfamiliar with the high ethic of the community admired by Constantine. He deployed his extensive knowledge of Cicero, Virgil, and Seneca, and supported his faith by citations from Thrice-greatest Hermes (Trismegistus) and the oracles of the Sibyl, authors external to the biblical tradition at least in form. (Sibylline Oracles, which in the second century Celsus censured as interpolated by Christians and in any event were largely of Jewish composition, were positively appreciated by Constantine as also by Lactantius, both of whom were aware of pagan suspicions of authenticity. Origen never cites them or the *Hermetica*.) Constantine himself thought his providential mission to bring Christianity to the empire was prefigured in Virgil's fourth Eclogue.

The exposition of Christian ethics follows in book 6. Primary is 'humanity'; that is, support for the weak, widows and orphans, prisoners, sick, burial of the poor and strangers, self-denial in pleasures, and the right directing of the emotions. Concubinage, sexual comedies on stage, and exciting spectacles under polytheist auspices are wrong. The seventh book expounds the Christian understanding of the end of history. The world is not eternal and will end. In two hundred years' time Christ will return to establish the millennium of God's kingdom, the golden age of which Latin poets have sung; then will come a final struggle to eliminate evil and the redemption of humanity, which is the goal of providence. (Like other forecasters of the end of the world Lactantius did not make the date fall in his lifetime.) The conversion of Constantine and his imperium are decisive steps towards this ultimate objective. And while in the providential plan, the Roman empire is to come to an end, nevertheless it will continue as long as the city of Rome stands (7. 15, 25).

The myth of the phoenix was a regular symbol for the 'regeneration' or a new world after the end of the old. Lactantius wrote a poem about the bird dying to be at once replaced by its offspring.

The fourth book of the *Institutes* has a statement about God as Father and Son (4. 29), who are one spirit and have one mind, one substance, but distinct as the sun and sunlight, or the spring and the flowing stream, or the vocal chords and speech. Jerome's commentary on Galatians observed that on the Holy Spirit Lactantius was modalist, insufficiently distinguishing differences in the Trinity.

Late in the year 314 Lactantius wrote *De mortibus persecutorum*, a special book of great candour and historical value in which he saw providence vindicating the persecuted martyrs by the extremely painful deaths suffered by the emperors responsible, especially Galerius and Daia. This theme of poetic justice also came to expression in Eusebius (*Dem. Evang.* 3. 7, p. 140 D) and in Constantine's letter to the inhabitants of the eastern provinces, cited by Eusebius (*Vita Const.* 2. 24–7), in which the emperor repeatedly declared himself to be the chosen instrument of providence to remove all evils. Lactantius dedicated his book to a heroic confessor Donatus who had undergone torture with nine successive treatments before being left to moulder in prison until released under Galerius' edict of toleration.

Eusebius of Caesarea

Eusebius had contact with the emperor Constantine at various points in his life. A presbyter of Caesarea in Palestine, bishop from about 314 until his death in 339, he had learnt to be a scholar under the guidance of the learned martyr Pamphilus, who familiarized him with the extensive library left at Caesarea by Origen, including both biblical manuscripts and Origen's own works. Copies of manuscripts written by Pamphilus survive. Caesarea, being the metropolis of the province of Palaestina, was bound to be important to an emperor who held the Holy Land in great veneration and after his defeat of Licinius had nursed an ambition to be baptized in the river Jordan. The persecution had destroyed many Bibles. Constantine turned to Eusebius to ask him to arrange for scribes to provide replacements. It is probable that the two great biblical manuscripts of the fourth century, one in the Vatican, the other from Sinai via St Petersburg now in the British Library (acquired by sale from the Soviet Union when Stalin needed foreign exchange) originated in the scriptorium at Caesarea.[2]

In building Aelia Capitolina Hadrian had placed not only a statue of Zeus on the site of the holy sepulchre but also a statue of Aphrodite on Golgotha. Eusebius (*Dem. Evang.* 8. 3, p. 406 D) was saddened to see the stones taken from the ruined Temple reused for pagan temples housing idols and for theatres to entertain the Gentile population; Mount Sion had become a farm.

At Jerusalem Constantine financed the erection of the church of the Anastasis or Resurrection beside Golgotha which, since the replanning of the city, was now well inside the new city wall. Remnants of Constantine's building survive today under the Crusaders' church of the Holy Sepulchre. At Bethlehem over the cave of the Nativity, already being visited by pilgrims in the second and third centuries (in competition with pagan veneration of Adonis installed by Hadrian), he also funded the building of a basilica. In 335 the construction of the church of the Resurrection (for the Crusaders the Holy Sepulchre) was completed in time to be the setting for an episcopal council to celebrate Constantine's thirtieth anniversary of accession. Naturally it became a pilgrims' shrine. There remained voices critical whether of the veneration of the Holy Sepulchre in particular (attested by Jerome, *ep.* 46. 8) or of pilgrimage in general.

Eusebius had visited Jerusalem to work in the library of Bishop Alexander (*HE* 6. 20. 1). He also enjoyed friendship with Bishop Paulinus of Tyre, where it is likely that he would have found other manuscripts. From his travels and manuscript researches he laid the foundation for a pioneer work,

    [2] See T. C. Skeat, 'The Codex Sinaiticus, the Codex Vaticanus, and Constantine', *JTS*, NS 50 (1999), 583–625.

his History of the orthodox Church down to his time, characterized by the invaluable habit of citing substantial extracts from the original documents. Successive revisions took account of events during his lifetime. In his mind the story was in itself a vindication of the divine preservation of the true faith. The continuity of the Church was assured to him by the succession of bishops in the great sees, which he conscientiously listed. The main weight of the history falls on the Greek East. The biography of Origen in book 6 represents a climax. Origen's commentaries and his vindication of Christianity against pagan criticism fascinated Eusebius.

During the persecution of Diocletian he composed a reply to the attack of Hierocles, governor of Bithynia, owing much to Origen's *contra Celsum*. He compiled lists of parallel passages in the gospels, and wrote a special book about contradictions which was known to Jerome. Probably he followed the thesis of Origen that contradictions at the level of historical fact were a providential sign of deeper spiritual truth. His two massive works of Christian defence were the *Preparation for the Gospel*, again with numerous excerpts from authors, many being otherwise lost, and the *Demonstration of the Gospel* restating the argument from the fulfilment of prophecy. Eusebius' method was to leave judgement to his readers. His *Demonstration of the Gospel* does not survive complete.

His memorial panegyric, 'On the Life of Constantine',[3] has been treated with some reserve; it was an ancient commonplace that panegyrists were not writing on oath and offered what their audience wished to hear (Plotinus 5. 5. 13. 14; Augustine, *Conf.* 6. 6. 9). Nevertheless good narrative history can be extracted from Eusebius' work and documents cited are demonstrably genuine. He also had apologetic aims, his Constantine being explicitly Christian and regarding the sun as the visible symbol of the one God whose deputy on earth he was (1). Other works by Eusebius include his *Chronicle* to show the superior antiquity of biblical religion to paganism. It survives through an Armenian translation and a Latin version continued by Jerome to 378. Also extant are an *Onomasticon* on the topography of the Holy Land, commentaries on Psalms and Isaiah, and a work on Easter (fragmentary but informative on his view of the eucharist).

Arius

Eusebius and Pamphilus co-operated in writing a defence of Origen against his critics, with an arsenal of orthodox citations. The first of the six books survives in a Latin version by Rufinus of Aquileia. From Origen and no

---

[3] The *Vita Constantini*, the most important single source for Constantine, has received a masterly translation and commentary by Averil Cameron and Stuart Hall (Oxford, 1999).

doubt from Pamphilus, Eusebius understood the doctrine of Father, Son, and Spirit to exclude what the Greeks called Sabellianism, the Latins Patripassianism (or the notion that God the Father suffered on the cross, being identical with the Son). He was therefore alarmed when Bishop Alexander of Alexandria excommunicated his popular dockland presbyter Arius for opinions which to Eusebius seemed close to Origen's. He took Alexander's action to be that of a pastor unfamiliar with advanced theology and scholarship. His *Demonstration of the Gospel* restates Origenism with a strongly subordinationist Christology. To ensure external support, Alexander of Alexandria kept Bishop Silvester of Rome informed. Arius invoked high-calibre help in the bishop of Nicomedia, another Eusebius, who was not only living next to the emperor's eastern residence but also related to the emperor's family; he had been used by Constantine as envoy to Licinius (the first occasion when a bishop was used by an emperor as ambassador, a role in which neutrality between the parties could be dangerous; Constantine found Eusebius of Nicomedia too neutral). For unclear reasons he was not on good terms with Alexander, possibly because the bishop of the second city of the empire resented the influence of the highly political Eusebius on the emperor.

The west was receiving a strongly anti-Arius picture, and that was passed on to the Spanish bishop Ossius of Corduba who had accompanied Constantine on his move to the East.

Appalled by a report about the dispute, Constantine sent Ossius to Antioch and wrote to Alexandria telling the bishop and his presbyter to stop arguing about trivialities (see the letter in Eusebius, *Vita Const.* 2. 64–72.) At a Council in Antioch early in 325 Eusebius of Caesarea with two other bishops supported Arius and was himself provisionally excommunicated, this decision to be reviewed at a forthcoming synod at Ankyra. To Ossius' ear the issues did not sound trivial. The bishops at Antioch produced an anti-Arian statement of faith, not using the term *homoousios* (identical in being) to the amazement of the scribe of the manuscript. The document is strident that the Son or Logos transcends the created order and is not made out of nothing, so that he is not morally mutable.

Since the apologist Athenagoras in the second century, theologians knew that they should distinguish between the derivation of the Son from the Father and the derivation of the created order. Athenagoras had said 'begotten, not made'. Nevertheless a consensus among pre-Constantinian theologians would have found no difficulty in saying that the Son was begotten in dependence on the Father's will. Arius stressed this dependence on the will of the Father and reiterated the phrase already current in Alexandrian thought in the time of Origen that 'there was when the Son was not'. Arius did not say 'there was a time when he was not'; in fact he said that the Son was begotten 'before all times', 'created by the will of God before times'. That was to say that the 'creation' from God's will was before the world was made when there was no time. However, Arius made no apology for the use of terms implying time such as 'before'.

By contrast Athanasius at Alexandria wanted to avoid the notion of dependence on the Father's will, while granting that the phrase had been used in an acceptable sense by writers with an orthodox intention lacking to Arius (*Or. c. Ar.* 3. 59). He preferred to say that the Son is from the Father's being or nature, from the Father's *ousia*. To avoid the ambiguous implications of saying the Father and Son are one and the same *ousia*, he would write that they are 'like in *ousia*', though this did not escape ambiguity. 'Like' implies a degree of difference.

The issue raised by Arius affected the Christian doctrine of God: no less. At the same time the controversy included large elements of a power struggle between bishops of important sees, so that to the church historian Socrates of Constantinople writing about 444 in conscious succession to Eusebius of Caesarea, all theological disputes were to be treated as a mere figleaf for contentions about power and authority. (A similar opinion of Jerome, before his breach with Rufinus, held that the censure of Origen at Rome was merely envy of his eloquence, not really doctrinal: *ep.* 33).

Like Origen, Arius did not see how an assertion of the divine presence in Christ the redeemer could be made by a monotheist without some qualification, viz. that the Son is subordinate to the Father from whom he derives his divinity. Indeed since he is the mediator, his metaphysical position is best seen as halfway between Creator and creature, at the summit of the created order, yet not in the same category as the creation generally. Arius was convinced from the gospels that the temptations of Jesus were real; that is to say, as a fully human being, he might not have conquered them and was morally mutable, as a fully divine nature cannot be. God is inherently immutable and cannot err without ceasing to be what we mean by the one supreme God. The Lord who 'grew in wisdom', who wept, who did not know the hour of the end, who cried in dereliction on the cross, must belong to a lower order of being than that of the Father of all. Exegetes were agreed that Proverbs 8 was an utterance of the divine Wisdom, that is of Christ; and in the Septuagint version it said 'The Lord created me the beginning of his ways with a view to his works.'

Arius defended his position with biblical texts. His subordinationist doctrine ran head-on into the principle stated by Irenaeus that only God can make God known, only the Creator can also be our redeemer, and one who is himself a part of the world needing salvation cannot by definition save the world. In Athanasius of Alexandria the principles of Irenaeus would be reaffirmed; and any kind of Arian doctrine was treated not as a tolerable mistake but as heresy for which toleration was impossible, since it cut the lifeline of salvation.

Arius had a tradition behind him, as Origen shows. Rufinus of Aquileia's epilogue to his translation of Pamphilus' *Apology for Origen* comments that the entirely orthodox Clement of Alexandria could sometimes speak of the divine Son as 'created' by the Father. But behind Athanasius stood Irenaeus and the theology of Asia Minor in the second century.

The Council of Nicaea

The Council of Antioch in 325 with Ossius presiding referred the dispute to the forthcoming assembly to be held at Ankyra, evidently already summoned. This assembly was primarily intended to celebrate Constantine's victory over Licinius. It had as a principal item on the agenda the question of agreement on the date of Easter. It was transferred to Nicaea by the authority of Constantine himself, on the ground that bishops were coming from the West for whom the city would be more accessible, that Nicaea had a lovely climate, and that (since he had a palace there) he himself would take part in the proceedings. The western presence was small but important. It particularly included two presbyters sent by Silvester bishop of Rome, the bishop of Carthage, and most influential of all Bishop Ossius of Corduba, who, after being sent by the emperor to the Council of Antioch to preside there, had learnt a lot about the theology and politics of the controversy. The emperor was determined to stop any one narrow faction imposing its will. An attraction of the word *homoousios* (probably agreed in advance by anti-Arian leaders because Arius had mocked the word) was its ambiguity: it was not clear whether it meant specific or generic identity, and that enabled bishops of differing standpoints to agree to it. The original list of signatures shows that about 220 bishops attended; Constantine claimed '300 or more'. Thirty years later someone saw that if the total was 318, that would be the sacred number of the servants of Abraham (Gen. 14: 14) and in the Greek letters for 318 TIH the emblem of the cross of Jesus, thereby affirming the unique authority of Nicaea against rivals.

The Council met at Nicaea in Bithynia in May–June 325. Eusebius submitted his baptismal creed of Caesarea and found himself vindicated by the emperor himself, who declared that he agreed with it and advised everyone present to agree also. Eusebius was reinstated in his see. Eustathius of Antioch was appalled by Constantine's inclusiveness and his friends' silence; in his eyes the text produced by 'Eusebius' (probably of Caesarea not Nicomedia—the point is disputed) was blatant heresy (Theodoret, *HE* 1. 8). The creed of Caesarea did not exclude Arius. The irritation of Eustathius at the silence of his friends must mean that he himself voiced dissent from the emperor's vindication and thereby annoyed Constantine, which helps to explain why he did not last long in his see after the council. But to lose the scholarly Eusebius of Ceasarea would not have been compatible with Constantine's endeavours at comprehensiveness. His earlier letter to Bishop Alexander and Arius had expressly stated that he did not expect them to reach precise agreement in detail, but surely they could share the essentials. The remarkable success of that policy and of Constantine's decision to be present can be judged from the fact that when the creed and canons were taken round by a high-ranking civil servant for signature, all the bishops except two from Libya signed, and the two dissenters (who were exiled by the emperor) probably objected less to the creed than to canon 6 subjecting them to the jurisdiction of Alexandria. Eusebius of Nicomedia signed. He and the likeminded bishop of Nicaea offended by admitting Arius to communion after he had refused to sign, but were allowed to recover favour.

The crucial word in the creed was the philosophical term *homoousios*, suggested perhaps because in a rash letter prior to the council Arius had ridiculed his bishop, Alexander, whose view would end in the opinion that the Son was identical in being with the Father (i.e. Sabellianism). The word had not surfaced at the council of Antioch a few months earlier, but had certainly been agreed by a caucus of anti-Arians before the Nicene assembly. Constantine insisted on its insertion into the creed. That was to combine a term congenial to Alexandria and the West with a formula which the Origenist camp could, with only a little difficulty, swallow.

Nevertheless the word *homoousios* aroused remarkably little interest in the subsequent controversy until the fifties, and in the aftermath of the council the anathema attracted more attention. This condemned propositions that the Son once had no existence, was not incapable of moral error, and was of a different *ousia* or hypostasis from the Father. Eusebius of Nicomedia and the bishop of Nicaea, Theognis, expressed reservations about this anathema, and were temporarily exiled by Constantine who would tolerate no dissent. They were reinstated on affirming that with the creed they had no difficulty, and their question was only whether the anathema was a fair representation of Arius.

Eusebius of Caesarea signed the Nicene creed and canons but published an open letter to his church at Caesarea explaining in what sense he understood the term *homoousios* (of one being), which as a scholar he knew to have some orthodox tradition behind it. He had difficulty with the Nicene clause which condemned those who said the Son is 'of a different *ousia* or hypostasis' from the Father, since he wanted to preserve Origen's language that Father and Son are two hypostases; but a subtle replacement of 'or' by 'and' mitigated the problem.

The council of Nicaea was far the largest assembly of bishops hitherto. It initiated a pattern common to most later ecumenical assemblies in that the interpretation of its decisions, especially those intended to make for peace, was divisive at least in the East. The West was initially not much interested in the subtleties but would be sucked in.

Unanimity was axiomatic for a council's authority. Dissenters had to be excluded from the Church. They had no minority rights. Despite the emperor's dominance, the decisions were made by the bishops which Constantine then confirmed and enforced. It long remained the rule that a general council of many provinces had to be called by the emperor. It is remarkable that Ossius of Corduba signed the Acts before the Roman legates.

29

THE SEEDS OF REACTION

The terms of the Nicene creed and appended anathema were not altogether familiar vocabulary to numerous Greek bishops. Alexander of Alexandria (accompanied at Nicaea by his young deacon Athanasius who succeeded as bishop in 328), Eustathius bishop of Antioch, and Marcellus of Ankyra were wholehearted supporters, but were therefore likely to be the target of a back-lash from bishops who (correctly, as must be conceded) did not see in the creed any defence against their bogey, Sabellianism. That last question engendered decades of controversy. Eustathius and Marcellus both regarded the Nicene formula as insufficient to exclude heresy in that the creed could be accepted by men such as Eusebius of Caesarea. Constantine did not remove their difficulties when, in pursuit of his policy of maximal inclusion, Arius himself signed the creed (probably not the anathema) and Athanasius was asked to receive him back to communion—which was out of the ques-tion. In about 334 Arius, living with friends in Libya, submitted an emotional appeal to Constantine for restoration. His old friends, like Eusebius of Nicomedia, had found him an embarrassment and dropped his cause. The emperor answered in a high theatrical style with no encouragement. The Alexandrian presbyter was now hardly even marginal. Nevertheless, Athanasius relates that Arius made his way to Constantinople and, on his way to being readmitted to communion by the then bishop there, died in dis-gusting circumstances in a public lavatory. Gibbon thought the story left the historian a choice between miracle and poison. Athanasius thought it providential.

Eustathius, Athanasius

In the decade following the council the first prominent anti-Arian to fall was Eustathius of Antioch, an overt critic of Origen's exegesis, who gave vent to sharp criticism of the emperor's mother Helena on her pilgrimage to the Holy Land in 326–7, during which it was later said that she recovered the True Cross. His exile left behind a small intransigent congregation firm for the Nicene creed and especially the anathema with its 'one hypostasis'. A proposal that Eusebius be translated to Antioch from Caesarea was vetoed by Constantine. In Egypt the Melitian schismatics were troublesome. In 328 Alexander of Alexandria died and was succeeded, controversially, by the deacon Athanasius, already known for his unbending aversion to Arius and to the Melitian party. Soon the Melitians were accusing him of violence, and the survival of a papyrus find with the letter-file of a Melitian priest proves that there was truth in the charge (H. I. Bell, *Jews and Christians in Egypt* (London, 1924), 53–71 at p. 60.[1] A council at Caesarea in Palestine summoned him, but after many hesitations, having his baggage put on the ship and then taken off again, he refused to attend. The following year his irritated opponents tried again at a synod at Tyre, and this time he had to go and present a vigorous defence, his main argument being that his opponents were sympathizers with Arius and therefore disqualified as heretics from judging. He was declared deposed, not for erroneous doctrine but for acts of violence unfitting in a bishop. He escaped from Tyre and appealed to Constantine at his new capital on the Bosporos. His opponents, however, reported a damaging story from Alexandria, likely to be true, that Athanasius had threatened a dock-strike cutting off the Egyptian supply of grain to Constantinople if the emperor did not support him.[2] Constantine, enraged, exiled him to Trier. There he was well received by the bishop. The emperor had thereby set the controversy on the way to becoming a confrontation between East and West.

Marcellus

There were other Greek bishops who were deposed from their sees on reports that they were opposed to the prominent bishops sympathetic to Arius. The most distinguished of these was Marcellus of Ankyra, an outspoken critic of Origen. He thought it essential to stress the unity of God, affirming that the proceeding of the Holy Spirit from the Father also included the Son, and expounding 1 Cor. 15. 28 to signify this unity by the delivering up of the kingdom to the Father. His opponents would reply with

---

[1] This is explicable after Constantine had invested bishops with the powers of magistrates, which would have entitled Athanasius to secular assistance in restraining or suppressing delinquency. At the council of Constantinople in 536 Syrian monks submitted to the patriarch Menas an accusation partly against Severus of Antioch, who had put Chalcedonians in prison with bonds and beatings (*ACO* III 39–40 = PO 2. 341–2). That some bishops used prisons for delinquent clergy appears in Moschos, *Pratum spirituale* 108 (PG 87. 2969 D).

[2] At Tyre Athanasius sufficiently defeated the opposition to compel them to send six of their number to Alexandria and Mareotis (Lake Mariut) to gather evidence against him. This commission of inquiry obtained the story of the bishop's threat to the corn supply. Two of their number were Valens of Mursa (Osijek) and Ursacius of Singidunum (Belgrade), who became lifelong opponents of Athanasius and convinced many of their fellow bishops in Illyricum of the dangers of the Nicene formula.

Luke 1. 33 ('of his kingdom there shall be no end'). He had a running pamphlet war with Eusebius of Caesarea, and was synodically deposed in 336. He
lived on for long years in the vicinity of his old city, and kept in touch by correspondence with the intransigent little congregation at Antioch loyal to the
memory of Eustathius, who were led by a presbyter, Paulinus. They had the
use of Antioch's 'old church', and in time acquired a mounting but divisive
importance in church politics, recognized by Alexandria and Rome but not
elsewhere.

The canons of Nicaea

The council approved of twenty disciplinary canons. Self-mutilation is to be
a bar to ordination; so too being a neophyte, or to have lapsed in the persecution. Clergy must not have women living with them in ascetic cohabit-
ation. Usury is forbidden to clergy (acting as bankers and money-lenders for
their congregations and especially for the poor, who would find it hard to
repay the interest, normally in antiquity 12 per cent a year). It troubles
the council that in some cities deacons are giving the eucharist, not only the
chalice, to presbyters; their commission includes no authority to offer the
oblation of the body of Christ. Deacons are also forbidden to sit on the bench
with the presbyters. Canons rule on the reception of clergy converting from
Novatianism, whose baptism and orders are valid, and from the followers of
Paul of Samosata, whose baptism and orders are invalid, no doubt because of
his unitarian doctrine of God.

Paul's group included women deacons ('deaconesses' is a variant reading
reflecting post-Nicene usage). Women deacons were potentially controversial; in the 370s Epiphanius of Salamis (Cyprus), always fierce for orthodoxy
and sure that only heretical sects would have women priests, was glad to say
that he had never ordained even a woman deacon (in Jerome, *ep.* 51). The
council ruled that, although hands are laid upon them, this does not constitute ordination with liturgical functions, which probably they had been
exercising previously and, despite the canon, no doubt continued to do in
out-of-the-way-places.

The most important canon is numbered 6. This rules that, despite
Diocletian's dividing of provinces, the ancient customs are to remain in force
whereby the bishop of Alexandria has jurisdiction in Egypt, Libya, and the
Pentapolis (the region of modern Benghazi). This is justified by the extra-
provincial jurisdiction belonging to the bishop of Rome, i.e. the suburbicarian churches of Italy (not the whole of the West), and by the similar but again
undefined authority of the bishop of Antioch. The three cities named are
those which were held to be the three senior cities of the empire. In 451 at the
council of Chalcedon a Roman legate cited this sixth canon with a text

revised in Rome to say 'the Roman church has always had primacy'. In reply Greek bishops produced the original text of 325.

Canon 7 rules that on the basis of old custom the bishop of Aelia (Jerusalem) has appropriate honour, but Caesarea retains the dignity and rights of the metropolis. The canon is evidently the first evidence of the process ending in the erection in 451 of a patriarchate of Jerusalem, which in effect submerged the rights of Caesarea.

Canon 4 legislates for the choice of bishops, which is to be subject to a veto by the bishop of the provincial metropolis and for consecration requires all the bishops of the province if possible, or at least three (not necessarily the metropolitan). The concern was evidently to avert partisan elections. There is no denial of the voice of the laity, which the Council took for granted.

The 20th and last canon forbids kneeling for worship either on the Lord's day or in the period from Easter to Pentecost. Kneeling being a sign of servility is inappropriate at a time of joy at the victory of the risen Lord.

Easter

An original cause for the calling of the council was to discuss the date of Easter (above p. 25). In the second century there had been unresolved disagreement between Rome and Asia Minor, each keeping to its own tradition which in Asia Minor implied adhering to the date of the Jewish Passover. In the west, at Alexandria, and in Syria the celebration of Easter was commemorating the Lord's resurrection, still taking note of the full moon, as with the Passover, but on the Sunday following the full moon after the spring equinox. Even so unison was not easily obtained. In Syria and Cilicia the date of the relevant full moon was still discovered by inquiry of the Jewish synagogue. Rome and Alexandria used different systems of computus to calculate. Alexandria used the old Greek observation by Meton that the relationship between sun and moon is roughly constant every nineteen years. A nineteen-year cycle was worked out. Rome, however, abandoned Hippolytus' cycle and had an 84-year cycle.

In Syria and Cilicia the Jewish Passover was, for many, decisive as the time of the Lord's Passion. The Jews, we are told, mocked the Christians for being unable to determine the time of their principal festival without asking the neighbouring synagogue for the correct date. But this calculation was not unanimous and in consequence there could be two celebrations of Easter at a great city like Antioch with different uses in different congregations. Perhaps they were amicable, but perhaps not entirely brotherly. At least they were agreed in keeping a Sunday for the celebration, but not necessarily the same Sunday.

In the mid-third century Dionysius of Alexandria began the custom of issuing a paschal letter to every bishop in his jurisdiction (i.e. including Libya and Thebais); he stressed that Easter must not fall before the spring equinox. At Alexandria this was reckoned to fall on 21 March. At Rome since the time of Julius Caesar the equinox was customarily reckoned to fall on 25 March; this difference would cause friction. Moreover Alexandria had no objection to Easter falling as late as 25 April. It was long custom in Rome for 21 April to be a secular feast with horse-races celebrating the foundation of the city on this day. Therefore bishops of Rome were unhappy if Easter was as late as 21 April. Only after they had acquired high social standing in the city could they successfully ask for the city's foundation to be celebrated without races. It would have been an embarrassing demand.

Constantine thought it dreadful to depend on the synagogue for discovering the correct date. He demanded and no doubt obtained agreement from the bishops that all churches ought to celebrate the feast on the same Sunday. It is unlikely that during the council more was achieved than a commission to the church of Alexandria to notify a date to the other great sees. Roman inhibitions about 21 April soon made their bishops unwilling to accept this date when that was notified from Alexandria. That at Nicaea a full cycle was worked out is unlikely for the reason that in 342 at Serdica the two synods both thought it necessary to produce an Easter table, which they would not have done if the work had already been decided in 325. The eastern council of Serdica produced a table not only for Easter but also for the Jewish Passover, which the computering experts of Antioch evidently had in front of them (below p. 250).

The title 'ecumenical council'

In the late thirties Eusebius of Caesarea and Athanasius are both found applying to the council of Nicaea the epithet 'ecumenical', that is to say of authority coextensive with the universal Church or at least with the Roman empire. The word *oikoumene* meaning the inhabited world was often used in this age simply to mean the Roman empire from Hadrian's wall to Mesopotamia, from the Danube to the Sahara. Was it the presence of Constantine which gave the council's decisions universal authority, as some Greeks held? or the representation of all, East and West, North and South, in the deliberations? or the assent of Roman legates and the subsequent ratification of the council by Silvester (Pope Damasus' view)?

The actual formula 'ecumenical synod' can be shown to be borrowed from a worldwide association of professional actors and athletes who in the third century succeeded in obtaining tax exemption. The survival of tax exemption certificates on papyrus is decisive.[3] No doubt since the Nicene council asked and obtained from the emperor tax exemption for the churches, one must allow the possibility that in popular usage someone applied the actors' title to the assembly of bishops, and it was then taken up as soon as there began to be debate about the authority of the Nicene council after Constantine's death, especially if (as some held) its worldwide authority depended on his presence and sanction for its decisions.

Eusebius of Caesarea's theology was in conflict with that of bishop Marcellus of Ankyra, whose Trinity was an expansion of the unity of one God, and in the mid-330s Eusebius wrote two books against him. Marcellus felt such antipathy to everything that Eusebius and his friends represented that he refused to come to Jerusalem with them to greet the emperor and to celebrate the dedication of his new church of the Resurrection. Marcellus' endeavour to keep his hands clean was construed as insulting to Constantine, and was a factor in his deposition and exile. In 336 Eusebius was honoured by being invited to deliver an oration in praise of Constantine's thirtieth anniversary of elevation to the purple.

The Christian Constantine of Eusebius

After the emperor died at Pentecost, 22 May 337, Eusebius was responsible for the important Panegyric, 'On the Life of Constantine', in which there is no doubt about the dead emperor's faith. To this end Eusebius recycled much matter already used in his *Church History* and a panegyric of Constantine in 335. Encomia were statements of what the emperor being praised, or his successor(s), wanted to be understood and as a matter of respect accepted. They were a species of propaganda. Interpretation of the religion of Constantine much depends on the evaluation of Eusebius' panegyric, which includes good historical narrative. Naturally one cannot make windows into the soul of a man so long dead, and there is no utility in debate to what precise degree or sense he was a believer. That his self-association with the Church was a public fact is certain, and he understood the main shape of Christian doctrines. Lactantius reports that on his acclamation to be Augustus in 306 he decreed toleration for Christian worship in his part of the empire. He made no secret of his belief that the God of the Christians inspired his victory over Maxentius in 312. His military standard, the *labarum* with the Chi-Rho monogram for Chr(ist), was generally understood to be a Christian statement or Julian would not have abolished it. The pagans thought he had changed everything they held dear. If any Christians felt qualms of uncertainty about his faith, pagans did not.

---

[3] The evidence is collected in my *History and Thought in the early Church* (London, 1981).

Naturally Constantine seemed to pagans to be overthrowing hallowed traditions of the imperial past in law and custom, a verdict which Ammianus cites as the view of the emperor Julian (21. 10. 8). At the same time he was in fact a continuator of Diocletian's reforms and in striking respects resembled his Illyrian predecessor. To build his 'queen city' of New Rome, the city of Constantine at Byzantium, he needed a great deal of money, and the captured estates of Licinius would hardly have sufficed for so huge a project. Taxes were sharply raised. If wealthy people fell foul of the administration, they would find their property confiscated for higher purposes. When the pagan orator Libanius delivered a panegyric (*or.* 59) on Constantine's sons Constantius II and Constans, he heaped praises on Constantius Chlorus for not soaking the rich, with the implication that Constantine had done so to their lasting anger. The probability is that the rich who suffered confiscation of their estates had been supporters of Maxentius, Licinius, or Daia. Senators who had been deprived of property by Maxentius at Rome had their wealth returned to them (Eus. *VC* 1. 41; Nazarius *Panegyric* 4. 31).

Reluctant toleration of the old cults

Constantine's declared policy towards pagan cult was tolerant, but (according to Eusebius) in the sense that he did not hide his conviction that it was wrong and should be discouraged, not forbidden. The tone of his edict on haruspicy (CTh 9. 16. 2) bears out Eusebius' view. His toleration was not indifferentism. Some endowments of old temples were diverted to other uses. The initially sixth-century *Liber Pontificalis* with biographies of bishops of Rome included under Silvester an impressive catalogue of Constantine's endowments of the Roman churches, evidently taken from Roman archives. He enacted by edict that 'the day of the sun' should be a day of rest (CTh. 2. 8. 1 of 321).

To the amazement of high pagan officials Constantine invested bishops with the authority of magistrates, and more, since he ruled that from their decisions there could be no appeal. Bishops were already accustomed to holding a court with their presbyters, at which disputes among members of their congregation could receive arbitration. The apostle Paul (1 Cor. 6: 1–6) forbade Christians to take disputes against other believers before a pagan court. The consequence was to lay a heavy burden on bishops. Naturally unsuccessful parties were left with angry resentment and there could be counter-claims that the other side used bribery. Bribery of secular magistrates was almost universal. Ambrose found the property disputes among members of a family were extremely painful to adjudicate.

The emperor Julian deprived bishops of the powers given by Constantine, but they were restored and the 'episcopalis audientia' was the subject of imperial legislation under Justinian (CJ 1. 4).[4]

Constantine's eldest son by his first wife Minervina was Crispus, proclaimed Caesar in 317. But report of an affair between Crispus and his stepmother Fausta precipitated a storm of anger in Constantine, and the two were murdered early in 326, Fausta in a scalding hot bath. It is possible that Helena's pilgrimage to the Holy Land in that year was in part motivated by a desire to make propitiation for a ghastly tragedy. Pagans put into circulation the story that Constantine had turned to Christianity to seek forgiveness for the murders. No doubt that was in a sense true, but not that he was first moved towards trust in the God of the Christians by this crime.

Pagan reactions

Constantine's pro-Christian policy provoked some hostile reactions. Eusebius (*Vita Const.* 3. 4) reveals that there were some riots and places where the emperor's statues were damaged. There was bound to be anger at the prohibition of pagan sacrifices (CTh 16. 10. 2). In 328 he forbade gladiatorial combats (Eus. *Vita Const.* 4. 25. 1), the bloody cruelty of which provided a magnetic attraction for city mobs. These shows did not stop either for Constantine or, at the end of the century, for Theodosius. An early edict, later repealed (CTh 16. 9. 1; Sirm. 4), forbade any Jew to have a Christian slave. No one was to resort to magic or private haruspicy, public use being allowed (CTh 9. 16. 1–3). Divination was strongly frowned upon since it normally required a sacrifice and some astrology. Even the aggressively pagan Porphyry had to concede that 'daemons are often mistaken in their astrology' (cited by Eusebius, *Praep. Evang.* 6. 5, p. 241 c). Confidence in oracles had suffered grave doubts. Plutarch (*Mor.* 411 E) told a story of a man in the time of the emperor Tiberius sailing across the Adriatic who by the island of Paxi heard a voice declaring 'Great Pan is dead.' A Cynic writer of about AD 200, Oenomaus of Gadara, wrote a sustained invective against belief in oracles and divination. Nevertheless people remained attached to oracles and might continue to guide their life by soothsayers and fortune-tellers even if they did not confidently believe in them. One could not be too careful. The elder Pliny (*NH* 29. 9) remarks on the way in which ancient physicians would not treat a patient without consulting sundry astrological almanacs. Roman aristocrats in the time of Ammianus (28. 4. 24), though 'lacking all belief in gods', did not go out of doors or eat a meal or take a bath if the stars were unfavourable.

From the pagan historian Eunapius, Zosimus (2. 29ff.) preserves a catalogue of adverse comments on Constantine as a disaster for the empire,

---

[4] See Jill Harries, *Law and Empire in Late Antiquity* (Cambridge, 1999), 191–211.

e.g. moving army garrisons away from frontier forts into nearby cities where the soldiers were a pest to the inhabitants and spent their leisure in enervating entertainment. There was therefore no frontier control on barbarian entry. In 332, Constantine recruited Germanic tribesmen to defend the frontier (Themistius 8. 119C; date in Mommsen, *Chronica Minora*, 1. 234). In time some barbarians rose to be generals and powerful in affairs of state. Themistius interpreted Constantine's universalist ideology to entail the conclusion that frontier fighting was a mistake: barbarians should be peacefully settled and educated under the civilizing influence of Roman law and Christianity (Themistius 10; also 13. 166C). It could be a disastrous model for Valens in 376. It was resented by those who wanted barbarians to be merely helots.

Marriage legislation

An intricate problem is the question of Christian influence on Constantine's marriage legislation. He repealed old penalties for celibacy. But in contrast to a number of Christian writers (not unanimous anyway), he allowed divorce on grounds other than a wife's infidelity, even including consent between separating spouses. He did not enact the widely accepted judgement of Christians that wives had as much right as husbands to demand fidelity. Here 'the laws of Caesar and Christ differ' (Jerome, *ep.* 77. 3; Ambrose, *in Luc.* 8. 5; Augustine, *Nupt.* 1. 10). Perhaps he anticipated Augustine's estimate that trivial infidelities are a common male disease (*Adult. coniug.* 1. 6). It was as difficult in the fourth as in later centuries to harmonize high moral aspiration with practical legislation.

Legal marriage was little used by persons of modest means, who preferred to buy a slave-girl as partner and mother for their children (Jerome, *ep.* 69. 5; Justinian, *Novel* 71). The Church asked for a monogamous relation with one sexual partner, not necessarily for a legal marriage recognized by state law, which, for reasons of property inheritance, was required of persons of substance.

Eusebius' oration for celebrating the thirtieth anniversary of Constantine's accession states a political theory for a Christian empire. Constantine's monarchy as supreme ruler is a mirror image of the divine Monarch in heaven; he is earthly representative of God. Such ideas were known in pagan panegyrics. Plutarch (*Mor.* 780EF) wrote of the wise king, model and image of the divine Logos or Reason. Pagans wrote of emperors as a god present among men. Christians could adapt this to declare their emperor ruler by divine grace, by his legislation enacting the divine will. This would entail a link between legitimacy and orthodoxy. In choosing his most senior administrators Constantine often liked to select Christians, even for such offices as consul or prefect of Rome, though he was careful not to alienate powerful pagan aristocrats by leaving them on the sidelines. Remarkably, as early as 317 the consul Gallicanus turns out to have bestowed a substantial benefaction on the church at Ostia (*Liber Pontificalis* 34. 19, p. 184 Duchesne; *ILCV* 2763). He was evidently a Christian or had become one after holding office. If the identification is correct, a policy of favouring Christians for major posts began after the war with Licinius in 316, and may have been partly motivated by a determination to deepen the religious divide between himself and his eastern colleague. This divide was an explicit factor in the subsequent war culminating in Licinius' defeat of 324.

In May 337 Constantine fell ill. He was about 65 years old and realized death was approaching. He moved from Constantinople to Helenopolis, once Drepanum in Bithynia renamed after his mother, then to the palace at Nicomedia, where he received laying-on of hands and became a catechumen. Bishops gathered to be greeted by him as 'brothers' with the memorable remark that he was 'bishop of those outside' (the Church). He now needed purification of his sins by baptism, which he had once hoped to be given in Jordan. Now there was to be no more ambivalence or uncertainty. Baptized by Eusebius of Nicomedia in a church dedicated to the martyrs, he put on a shining white robe, no longer secular purple. Senior army officers came to wish him recovery. About noon on 22 May, the day of Pentecost, he died at a modest country villa near Nicomedia. The body was to be buried with full military honours.

Eusebius of Nicomedia was prominent for his support of Arius before the council of Nicaea; afterwards Arius was grieved to have been abandoned by him. Eusebius of Caesarea called him 'the great Eusebius', and he was certainly a brilliant fixer. Later legend originating in Rome in the mid-fifth century found his name embarrassing for so important a sacramental function, and preferred to give the honour of baptizing the emperor to Pope Silvester. Much later legend in the late eighth century explained that Constantine's reason for making New Rome the centre of his government was so that he could leave Silvester and future bishops of Rome a free hand in coping with the universal jurisdiction, even over eastern patriarchs, that went with their office.

On the highest hill of his city by the Golden Horn he had constructed his mausoleum alongside a five-aisled martyrion of the Twelve Apostles, each being accorded an empty sarcophagus with a thirteenth in the middle of the row intended for his own mortal remains. At first the building's purpose was secret. It was an ambiguous version of the kind of mausoleum that Diocletian made for himself at Split (now the cathedral). Some Roman emperors had been buried in mausolea with statues of the twelve gods of Olympus. Clement of Alexandria (*Protr.* 96. 4) and John Chrysostom (*Hom. in II Cor.* 26. 4) say the

Roman senate held Alexander the Great to be thirteenth god. Probability favours the view that Constantine's mausoleum was ambivalent, with pagans and the army taking its symbolism to be analogous to that of Alexander and with Christians like Eusebius, anxious to claim Constantine for their cause, interpreting its thirteen sarcophagi very differently. By the fifth century Constantine was hailed in hymns as 'the apostles' equal' (*isapóstolos*). About 1320 the church historian Nikephoros Kallistos Xanthopoulos (*HE* 8. 55) says that on the site of Constantine's tomb there had been an altar dedicated to the twelve gods; his source is unknown.

The funeral ceremonies were entirely for the army chiefs with Constantius II, second of the three surviving sons, not for the bishops, who were allowed in only after the state's obsequies were complete. The customary funerary pyre was impossible; but there was a ceremony of *consecratio* signifying the emperor's deification. From late in the third century emperors were made by the army alone, and the army chiefs could assume that the funeral was theirs. No doubt, beside a requiem, bishops gave thanks for this greatest benefactor of the Church. The sharp separation of state funeral from Christian memorial reflected awareness that Constantine identified himself with two distinct entities still unsure of their mutual relation. The Church did not yet think it was bound to the particularity of the empire. A coin was minted showing Constantine ascending to heaven in a chariot drawn by four horses, that is with the ancient symbol of the Sungod (cf. 2 Kings 23: 11).

According to Eusebius of Caesarea Constantine had decreed that imperial power should be inherited by his three sons, Constantine II (illegitimate), Constantius II, and Constans, his sons by Fausta, and by no one else. This was also the choice of the army generals. The reality was less simple. That decision was actually taken during the ensuing summer and given Constantine's posthumous sanction. Just as Diocletian and Licinius had liquidated possible rivals for power, so the senior army officers murdered Constantine's near relatives, his nephew, Hannibalianus and Dalmatius (proclaimed Caesar in 335), his half-brother Julius Constantius, whose young sons by his two wives, Gallus and Julian, were spared because of their tender age. While the three brothers negotiated about dividing the territories, for six months the empire was governed in the name of their dead father. It was significant of the extraordinary authority of this tough soldier that this could be. Long after he was gone people appealed to his authority, and no greater salute could be made to a new emperor than to call him a new Constantine, a formula first used in 364 by Themistius (*or.* 5. 70D) in greeting Jovian as an emperor not born into the Constantinian dynasty. Philostorgius (2. 17) reports that in Constantinople a porphyry column bearing a statue of Constantine with a radiate crown like the sungod was popularly venerated with propitiatory sacrifices and lights and incense.

30

THE CHURCH AT PRAYER

Most of the history of the Church concerns its institutions with its canon law, social and political operations, the degree of subjection to forces such as regional or national patriotism, the struggles to be independent of the secular forces to which the Church is often bound. Yet the point of the Church in its own self-understanding lies in faith in God who became and is present to believers in Christ and through the experience of the Holy Spirit. This is not very visible in the meetings of synods or the decisions of primates, but is pre-eminently the case when Christians in a particular place assemble together to worship, to give thanks for their creation and redemption, to pray for forgiveness, renewal, courage, and humility, but especially to hear the word of God and to celebrate the covenant signs in water, bread, and wine as means of divine grace and as ordered rites which provide both form and vitality to the disorder of human life. Characteristic of Christian worship is a dialogue between God and the people of God. The forms which this takes are called liturgy, which is not so much a precise and prescribed pattern of sentences as a pattern of symbolic words and actions through which the presence of the Lord is realized.

At the same time liturgy is expressive of the Christian story, that is, a narrative commonly formulated in a creed or confession of faith. Therefore liturgy is often intimately associated with belief or doctrine, though not with its more technical formulation. Normally the vocabulary of liturgy is severely limited; certain words and turns of phrase become character-istic vehicles of prayer and aspiration and, because of the spiritual desire which motivates them, tend towards verbal beauty, lost when the meaning is translated into more everyday and less poetic terms. Liturgy is an act of a community. But often human beings do not find it the easiest thing to be trying to pray if too much is going on around them, and they long for silence and solitude. A consequence of this in the past has been the feeling among the clergy that so sacred a text as the central eucharistic prayer of consecration and offering, in Latin the 'canon of the mass', in Greek 'anaphora', should be mumbled, not said aloud, because it has mystery at its heart. Nevertheless it is obvious to any student of ancient eucharistic prayers[1] that they are expressing the longing of the community rather than only that of an individual, and this is particularly the case with the ancient Latin canon of the mass.

The first followers of Jesus, being Jews, were accustomed to meet on the sabbath for worship at temple or synagogue, as their Master had done. But to commemorate the Lord's resurrection in the breaking of bread they also met on the first day of the week, or Sunday. The breaking of bread was from the earliest time a central act of the apostolic community. It was also called the Thanksgiving; in the Didache, Ignatius, and Justin this word is already technical: *eucharistia*. Like almost all the other technical terms of Christian vocabulary, this Greek word passed into Latin transliterated and so into modern European languages. This thanksgiving was an offering of the gifts (1 Clement) or a sacrifice (Ignatius). To be qualified to share in the eucharist it was necessary to have been baptized, requiring a renunciation of evil and an affirmation of faith. The solemnity of baptism was soon marked by stripping at the actual moment of being immersed in the water and immediately on emerging being robed in white and in many places being given to drink milk and honey, symbols of entry to the promised land beyond Jordan. The presiding bishop then anointed and laid hands on each candidate.

Baptism was one of the normal ceremonies of the synagogue at the admission of a proselyte, from which the Christians dropped circumcision. In the reform proclaimed by John the Baptist it signified repentance. So for the believers in Jesus the Messiah, baptism signified forgiveness of all past sins and inward renewal by the coming of the Holy Spirit. The Lord himself identified himself with the penitent in the baptism of John in Jordan. To be baptized in Messiah's name was identical with being baptized in the name of Father, Son, and Holy Spirit (Matt. 28: 19). The trinitarian formula took the form of three questions requiring the answer 'I believe.' 'Do you believe in God the Father? Do you believe in Jesus Christ, Son of God, born of Holy Spirit and the Virgin Mary, who was crucified in the time of Pontius Pilate, died, rose on the third day alive from the dead, and ascended into heaven, and sat at the right hand of the Father, who will come to judge the living and the dead? Do you believe in the Holy Spirit in holy Church and the resurrection of the flesh?' At each answer the candidate was immersed in the font. So says the *Apostolic Tradition* of 'Hippolytus', a Church Order from Rome early in the third century. (That it is the work of Hippolytus or the author of the *Refutation of Heresies* is possible but uncertain.)

It is noteworthy that the earliest baptismal confession is not a simple affirmative creed but an answer to interrogations, as is implicit in 1 Pet. 3: 21.

---

[1] A convenient collection is *Prex Eucharistica*, ed. A. Hänggi and I. Pahl (Spicilegium Friburgense, 12; Fribourg, 1968).

In this, there were no doubt regional variations. A laying-on of the bishop's hands in blessing could be before or after the water-rite, and an anointing symbolizing the Spirit's gift could vary in position. However, the anointing and laying-on of hands were not regarded as merely marginal and decorative ceremonies beside the one essential water-rite. Christians bear the name of Christ, said Theophilus of Antioch in the second century, because they are anointed with the oil of God (*ad Autol.* 1. 12). Cyprian's famous letter to Jubaianus (*ep.* 73. 9) comments on Acts 8: 14–17 that the Samaritans did not need to be baptized again; Peter and John completed what was lacking, namely that by prayer over them and the laying-on of hands they invoked the Holy Spirit which was poured out upon them. 'That also occurs with us: those who are baptized in the Church are brought before the bishop of the church and, by our prayer and imposition of hands, they receive the Spirit and by the Lord's seal are perfected.' Tertullian (*Bapt.* 7. 8) reports: 'As we come out of the water, we are anointed, then hands are imposed'; the purifying water prepares for the Spirit's coming. Heb. 6: 2 shows that this was very early practice and regarded as a foundation rite. Clement of Alexandria (*Paid.* 1. 6) thought the water-rite alone incomplete. For Cyril of Jerusalem the 'seal' was baptism with anointing (*Cat. myst.* 3. 4). Cornelius objected to Novatian that his clinical baptism had not been completed by 'sealing' by the bishop (Eus. *HE* 6. 43). In Ambrose (*Sacr.* 3. 2. 8) the seal of the Spirit followed baptism 'to bring completeness'.

Already in the apostle Paul triadic language shapes his words (1 Cor. 12: 4–6; 2 Cor. 13: 14). Believers offered their prayers to God in the Holy Spirit, not on their own merits, but through the grace of Jesus the Christ the mediator. But in the first generation it is unlikely that there would have been a prescribed form of words for baptism. Of the Greek churches John Chrysostom (*Hom. in Act.* 1. 5) reports that the bishop or presbyter does not say, 'I baptize you in the Holy Spirit', but 'You are to be baptized'. Theodore of Mopsuestia a few years later says that the words make clear that it is Christ who is baptizing. The Coptic church has the more western form, 'I baptize you . . .'. The words used were obviously no less important than the immersion in the water, since the words imparted significance to the act.

At Carthage in Tertullian's time the rite was preceded by fasts and all-night vigils; then exorcism, the water-rite with the triadic interrogation (Tertullian noted that this included belief in the Church), anointing with invocation of the Holy Spirit, the sign of the cross, and laying-on of hands by the bishop. The normal minister of baptism was the bishop, but he could delegate to presbyters and deacons, or in urgent necessity at sickbed even laymen, but not women, despite Thecla (in the Acts of Paul) having given baptism. In the west the bishop came to give the laying-on of hands himself when the water-rite had been ministered by a presbyter or deacon. The regular times for baptisms were Easter and Pentecost, but in emergency it could be at any time. Unlike Jewish lustrations, baptism is unrepeatable; it applies to the believer the once-for-all redemption of Christ.

Tertullian answers questions which were being put: if baptism is necessary, as John 3: 3–5 (and Hermas, *Sim.* 9. 12. 8), why is there no record that the apostles were baptized? The answer (characteristic of Tertullian) could be the splashes in the storm on the lake (affusion) or St Peter's total immersion. How did Christian baptism differ from the water in cults of Mithras and Isis reckoned to be for expiation and regeneration? The answer is that they are correct in using water but have the wrong god, the devil's counterfeit. How can bodily washing cleanse the conscience? The answer is that the candidate and the Church have faith. Latent questions about the relation of baptism to conversion were first debated in depth by St Augustine of Hippo (*De baptismo*). Prayer for the sanctification of the water in the font became fairly common.

Solemnity surrounded the renunciation of the devil and his works and his angels, often in this or a similar triadic form. The essence of the matter was the impossibility of serving God and Mammon. Tertullian (*De anima* 35. 3) was sure that if the baptized person went back on the vow, the devil resumed his rights. At baptism women untied their hair, no doubt with the intention of warding off the devil who might think it a place of beauty in which to hide. Undressing for the act of baptism would prevent the devil from getting into the water too (Clement of Alexandria found this in the gnostic Theodotus: *Exc. Theod.* 83). Stripping at the moment of baptism presupposed that the devil could be in the detail of clothing.

The baptismal renunciation, dramatically reinforced by exorcism, affected people's jobs. Certain kinds of employment were incompatible with Christian ethics. A married man who also had a concubine or mistress or slept with his slave-girls had to change his ways. A priest serving idols could not so continue. (It is instructive that there were applications from people employed in this way.) Actors and actresses, who in antiquity were mostly slaves, or professional gladiators had to find different work, raising inevitable questions about trying to finance emancipation, perhaps with help from the church chest. In general the public entertainments industry was looked on with aversion. Considerable qualms attached to those whose duty, as soldiers or as prison gaolers, involved them in taking human life, and the same held good for provincial governors, whose duties constantly required attendance at idolatrous ceremonies, not to mention ordering torture and execution of criminals. Sufficient evidence of the bribery of judges survives to make it certain that this was a widespread problem, and especially offensive when used to bring about a death sentence. (Capital punishment was not approved by Christians.) The list of those before whom the Church erected barriers is not only a sign of the Christians' determination to be a society of purged saints rather than a school for sinners continuing in unacceptable positions but also a testimony to the wide cross-section of society attracted by the gospel. School teachers who were expected to teach Homer and his gods, and artists whose commissions could also ask them to portray idolatrous or erotic themes (even if allegorical), were regarded with anxiety and unanimity was not easily attained. There were thorny problems in the case of those who were divorced and remarried: does baptismal remission wipe out the past completely? or since marriage is no sin, is it a state that survives the washing of regeneration?

Because baptism marked regeneration and adoption into God's family, the person baptized could fittingly receive a new name. He or she now bore 'the name of the Son of God', and so might bear a name with Christian and scriptural associations.

Candidates for baptism were called 'catechumenoi', people under instruction. Admission began with a ceremony foreshadowing baptism: sign of the cross, prayer invoking divine aid and guardian angel, laying-on of hands and, as an act of exorcism, salt placed upon the tongue. The length of catechumenate varied with individuals, but could last up to three years. Anxiety about the consequences of possible sins after baptism could make a considerable number content to remain catechumens for several years. A variation between east and west becomes visible, in that western catechumens were being reformed morally, and the creed or doctrinal instruction was brought in at a very late stage; in the east instruction took a more theological form with the moral issues being sorted out later, perhaps even after baptism. Wisdom literature of the Old Testament was suitable to give moral education. So too, but very surprisingly, the books of Judith and Tobit were to be read. It became customary for instruction to be given by the bishop in the weeks preceding Easter, baptism being conferred on the evening before 'the day of resurrection'. A catechumen was counted to be Christian, but not a full believer, *fidelis*. At the synaxis or assembly he or she left after the readings and sermon before the eucharist proper. Catechumens were not present at the exchange of the kiss of peace, reserved only for those whose kiss[2] was purified by baptism and who were not in heresy or schism. Schismatics being in protest against the Church were not going to be present anyway. By contrast many heretics wished to be acknowledged as members. Tertullian once sharply observed that heretics seek to subvert the orthodox, not to convert the heathen, and are easy-going in discipline, careless about order, offering

---

[2] In ancient society the kiss was common for greeting distinguished persons, especially emperors, and did not necessarily have the partly erotic association common in the modern west. The *Apostolic Tradition* forbids a kiss of peace between the sexes. There will have been places and cases where this kind of rule was not observed.

communion to anybody and everybody, casual about ordinations, many of their clergy being apostates from the Church (*De praescr.* 41–2).

Baptism's unbreakable character soon gave it the name 'seal' (*sphragis*), a term not only for the seal of a letter or signet ring but also becoming a synonym for a formal contract, or for the tattoo marking a slave or a herd or a soldier. Devout pagans might bear the 'seal' of their god, and carry on travels a wooden image or idol commonly called seal, *sigillum* (Apuleius, *Apol.* 61–4; Tertullian, *orat.* 16). Among Christian texts the most striking example is the inscription written about 182 for his own epitaph by Aberkios bishop of Hieropolis in Phrygia. Much travelled, he had visited the church at Rome 'a queen in golden robe and golden sandals, and there saw a people having a shining seal'. He journeyed through Syria as far as Nisibis in Mesopotamia, crossing the Euphrates and finding Christian brethren everywhere. He followed with a codex of Pauline letters. 'Everywhere faith led the way and everywhere served food, the Fish from the font, vast, pure, which the pure virgin caught and gave to her friends to eat for ever, with good wine giving the cup together with the loaf.'[3] The inscription is a very early instance of the fish symbol for Christ. The Greek word ΙΧΘΥC forms an acrostic for 'Jesus Christ Son of God Saviour', the earliest instance in full being in the *Sibylline Oracles* (8. 217). Catacomb art provides examples of fish as symbols of Christ.

The baptismal seal was for some like an amulet protecting against the planetary powers of fate or other evil forces. Origen cites a gnostic dialogue called 'The Seal' (*c. Cels.* 6. 27). Ignatius wrote to Polycarp 'May your baptism abide as weapons of defence' (*Pol.* 6. 2). Here was the word of God, the sword of the Spirit. Gregory of Nazianzos (*orat.* 40. 17) tells catechumens that once they have received the seal, they will need none of the devil's amulets and magic spells. A sermon by Basil (13. 4) reminds his hearers that the destroying angel at the exodus passed over houses that were sealed. The homiletic language was clearly designed to encourage perseverance to the end of life and, in a stern writer such as Tertullian, becomes the threat that to break the seal of one's baptism is to condemn oneself to the fire (*Bapt.* 8). Experience soon showed that the baptized could lapse into various sins. The *Shepherd* of Hermas mitigated the absoluteness of the epistle to the Hebrews (6. 4–6) offering, by unique revelation, a possibility of penance and restoration for one occasion only. His argument, however, presupposed that some renewed absolution would be needed, and in the third century terms for the restoration of the lapsed in persecution created the earliest attempts at an ordered canon law. A description of Christian penitential discipline in the pagan Celsus (in Origen, *c. Cels.* 6. 15) as 'disgraceful and undignified', with a

---

[3] See J. B. Lightfoot, *The Apostolic Fathers*, ii/i, 496 ff.; H. Leclercq in *DACL* i. 85–7; text and full commentary in F. J. Dölger, *Ichthys*, ii. (Münster, 1922), 457–507.

closely similar account in Tertullian (*Paenit.* 9. 11), shows that public penance was felt to be shameful and disgusting by Christians as well as pagans. As late as Augustine (*sermo* 352) pagans were insulting Christians for the laxity of the system. Pagans declared that Constantine's conversion was motivated because the Church offered cheap grace to remove his guilt over the deaths of Crispus and Fausta. But in fact the ancient system was both embarrassingly public and severe. It was also judgemental rather than therapeutic.

Eucharist

The principal act of the eucharist was sharing in consecrated bread and wine, at first as part of a solemn and sacred memorial meal. 1 Corinthians 11 shows that for some at Corinth the food and drink was primary and the sacred ritual of the act secondary. It was not more than a fellowship meal of a brother-hood of love or agape. (There was tension between the poor who could not afford to bring good food and the rich who brought fine fare. But as wealthy people were converted, the agape became a way of providing the poor with a square meal.) The apostle was disturbed that they were failing to 'discern the body of Christ'. He tells the Corinthians that they can eat and drink at home; but this act of obedience to Jesus' command is a sacred act re-enacting through ritual symbolism the breaking of the Lord's body and the pouring out of his blood for the redemption of humanity. The act is a proclamation of the Lord's death and uses bread and wine which at the Last Supper he had for ever associated with his redemptive self-offering.

The use of bread and wine was part of the Passover ritual. The canonical gospels are not agreed whether the Last Supper was the Passover meal or not. (Probably their differences reflect the traditions of different communities.) Paul earlier told the Corinthians 'Christ our passover is sacrificed for us' (1 Cor. 5: 7), which may imply that Passover fell on the day of crucifixion. Redemption was foreshadowed in the exodus of the children of Israel from the bondage of Egypt (an underlying theme in the epistle to the Hebrews), annually recalled in the Passover by every devout Jew. Early Christian paschal liturgical prayers have direct relation to Passover prayers of the synagogue with verbal echoes.

Fixed forms of prayer were slow to develop. What was expected was a pat-tern of themes, but in expressing these themes the presiding presbyter/bishop was free. Justin says the president offered 'the best of which he is capable'. After that prayer the people answered with the Hebrew word, 'Amen', immediately preceding the distribution and sharing of the bread and wine (water being added to the wine, as was almost universal in antiquity); deacons took the food to the absent. Justin is emphatic that these gifts are not received as ordinary bread and wine. Evidently by the prayer and the sacred ritual of breaking bread and pouring out wine in analogy to the death of Christ they have a unique dignity. There was also an offering of money to help the needy and destitute.

There were local and regional varieties. The eucharistic prayer in the Didache lacks the redemption theme that a reader of 1 Corinthians 11 would expect, which the apostle evidently regarded as central. In the period from the fourth to the sixth century forms of prayer were becoming regular and fixed in east and west, but in different ways. Western liturgy was shorter, while in the east it was altogether more extended.

The eucharistic 'president' (Justin's word) composed his own eucharistic prayer, but there soon came to be a generally used and very ancient dialogue between president and congregation, each praying for the other and the president bidding the people to concentrate for the great prayer to come:

> 'The Lord be with you'
> 'And with your spirit'
> 'Lift up your hearts'
> 'We lift them to the Lord'
> 'Let us give thanks to the Lord . . .'
> 'It is fitting and right.'

From this point the president says the 'Preface', a kind of panegyric of the majesty of God in creation and the glory of nature (Justin, *Apol.* 1. 13; Origen, *c. Cels.* 8. 33),[4] before the actual commemoration invoking the blessing of the Holy Spirit on the congregation and the consecrated gifts and the offering of broken bread and poured out wine. In the *Apostolic Tradition* the commemoration is emphatically Christological, praising the Lord who has conquered the devil and trodden down hell and brought light to the righteous, going on to the words of institution and the 'anamnesis' or memorial of Christ's death and resurrection in which the bread and cup are offered. The prayer concludes with an invocation of the Holy Spirit on the oblation of the holy Church, that all may be united, their faith confirmed in the truth.

Here it is noteworthy that the text has both the institution narrative and an invocation or *epíklesis*. Later the east would stress the latter, the west the former, and much later there could even be argument which of the two constituted the moment of consecration. The bedrock essentials consisted of the prayer, the bread and wine, and the explicit association with the Last Supper and Christ's death and resurrection.

---

[4] How natural it was to employ the language of imperial panegyric can be judged from the occurrence in an ancient Latin panegyric of the formula that expressing gratitude to the emperor would be right at all times and all places but particularly so in the present context; e.g. the beginning of Mamertinus' panegyric on Maximian delivered on 21 Apr. 289 (*Paneg. lat.* 10 (2). 1). See below p. 523.

In Justin the first part of the service consists of readings and prayers. In short, the eucharist had two rather distinct sections, and that remained characteristic for the future. In the west the dismissal of the catechumens after the readings and the homily gave its name to the service as a whole, *missa* or mass. But the word could mean an act of worship where the congregation was sent away with a bishop's blessing.

Tertullian (*De corona* 3) tells us that the communicant received the sacred elements in the hands. For many centuries that was to remain standard practice. Some communicants could take the consecrated bread home, but needed to ensure that a mouse did not eat it. Origen mentions the distress caused to communicants if with bread or cup there was a spill. In antiquity to receive the sacrament in only one kind was not approved. But there were problems with peasants who gulped rather than sipped on being offered the chalice or with very young children.

Ministry

Tertullian (*Exh. cast.* 7. 3) once observed that the Church has marked a distinction between the 'order', i.e. the clergy, and the laity (*plebs*). Christian writers found it natural to regard the appointed church officers with pastoral and priestly responsibilities as people received into an existing collective order. No surviving text from the very early period provides a form of ordination other than possibly 1 Tim. 6: 11–16. But prayer and the laying-on of hands emerged as the basic actions, with the pastoral commission being handed on from pastor to pastor, which required the ordaining bishop to have received this power from his predecessors. A bishop was called to do for his people some of the essential caring once done by the apostles. His responsibility was not only to his own people but to the whole Church and the episcopate collectively. The episcopal order became the most evident and visible element in the continuity of the entire community. Correspondence with other churches was conducted through bishops, and at the ordination of another bishop in the same province all bishops of the province were expected to be present. The council of Nicaea prescribed a minimum of three, but there were unusual instances where only two had to be taken to suffice.

The *Apostolic Tradition*, the fourth-century *Apostolic Constitutions*, and the fourth-century sacramentary of Serapion of Thmuis all provide for the consecration of oil for anointings, including that of the sick (Jas. 5: 13–16). But what liturgy was used for funerals is not attested.

While by the third century there were many places where the eucharist was celebrated everyday, that was not the practice everywhere. The regular daily services were the 'hours'. Paul had exhorted the Thessalonians to 'pray without ceasing', and Clement of Alexandria wrote that this unceasing prayer was characteristic of the entire life of the higher spiritual or 'gnostic' Christian (*Strom.* 7. 40. 3). Origen's careful treatise on prayer (12) suggested that this way of speaking was the only possible way of understanding Paul's command. At least the devout will pray three times a day, like the prophet Daniel. Ps. 53: 17 speaks of prayer each evening and morning. Psalm 118: 62 speaks of prayer at midnight. At Philippi Paul and Silas sang a hymn and prayed in the middle of the night. Origen took all these as models to be followed. A characteristic of the 'hours' was to use the Psalter in sections. The Christian writers of the second century had prepared the ground for a Christological reading of the psalms. This, combined with the emotional range of these ancient poems, made the Psalter, with some exceptions where they are cursing, remarkably suitable for daily use. The Christological interpretation prepared the way for the Trinitarian doxology ('Glory be to the Father . . .') at the end, the form of which became a controversial subject in the middle years of the fourth century; it was still being debated in the 370s in Basil's time.

Tertullian similarly attests regular prayers at the third, sixth, and ninth hours of which the very rough equivalences would be 0900, 1200, and 1500 hours. The early morning and evening prayers were not merely optional extras, but obligations, and in practice these two were those most commonly observed by devout laity. Lastly a prayer and a short hymn were customary at the lighting of the evening lamp. An old extant hymn of the ancient Church praises the cheerful light which God brings—the *Phos Hilaron*,[5] cited as an ancient tradition by Basil the Great of Caesarea (*De Spir. S.* 73) and probably dating from the third century. A third-century papyrus (P.Oxy. XV 1786) preserves an anapaestic hymn with signs (neums) for the music of the chant: 'While we hymn Father, Son, and Holy Spirit, let all creation sing Amen, Amen. Praise, power to the sole giver of all good things. Amen, Amen.'

Church buildings

The first generations of Christians did not have special purpose-built buildings for their worship, but met in private houses with a large room. For them 'the Church' was the community ('God's temple,' 1 Cor. 3: 16; 2 Cor. 6: 17), not a physical structure. God does not live in a house made by human hands (Acts 7: 44–50; 17: 24). The discernment of the Church as God's temple is an act of faith, not of the eyes. But by the first years of the third century they

---

[5] A version of this occurs in modern English hymnbooks, e.g. Hymns Ancient & Modern New Standard edition 8, or New English Hymnal 247, or the American *Hymnbook* 1982, 36. Technical discussion in F. J. Dölger, *Antike und Christentum*, 5 (1936), 11–26.

were beginning to have special houses of prayer, as the Synagogue had. One at Edessa in 202 is expressly attested as destroyed by a flood. After the persecutions by Decius and Valerian the emperor Gallienus restored church buildings which had been confiscated. A 'house of the church' which Paul of Samosata declined to vacate is attested for Antioch in 268. Excavation of the Roman fort at Dura Europos on the Euphrates, destroyed by the Persians in 256, revealed a synagogue finely decorated with biblical figures and nearby a small house-church with a baptistery (likely to be in demand among soldiers in an isolated stronghold whose last hour was imminent). The walls had paintings of the Good Shepherd, Adam and Eve, Christ healing the paralytic and walking on water, the Samaritaness at the well, David and Goliath. There were still house-churches well into the fourth century. At Cirta in north Africa early in the fourth century the substantial but far from enormous congregation was meeting in a private house and had no special place necessitated by the growth of the congregation. But growth in numbers required bigger places of assembly (Eus. *HE* 8: 1). Rome about 350 had over forty basilicas (Optatus 2. 4). At Nicomedia in 303 the imperial palace looked across to the main church building in the city. Constantine funded the replacement of churches destroyed under the persecution. Eusebius' panegyric on the new church building at Tyre (*HE* 10. 4) presents it as modelled on Solomon's temple with the decorations from Isaiah 54. Nevertheless, the reticence of early Christianity means that many buildings used by Christians are not identifiable as such. That changed with Constantine. He told Macarius bishop of Jerusalem that the new church of the Resurrection was to be the noblest basilica yet seen (*Vita* 3. 34).

Today it is no longer necessary to deny the romantic notion that early Christians celebrated their mysteries underground in catacombs. But the popular art on the walls of Roman catacombs heralded an extraordinary efflorescence of brilliant and beautiful Christian art in the age of the Christian empire.

Although it occurred, it was not a Christian characteristic to erect church buildings, like pagan temples, in locations already held in reverence for their numinous associations, e.g. because of a spring. Late in the fourth century when under Theodosius I pagan temples were being closed down, some of these old and beautiful buildings could be adapted for Christian worship. Christians valued places as holy not in themselves but because of what holy people had said or done there. This at least was the verdict of Pope Gregory the Great. Naturally this pre-eminently marked the sites in Jerusalem or Galilee where the gospel had been acted out by Jesus and the apostles. In the second century Melito of Sardis journeyed to Jerusalem sure that the (now Gentile) community there would have preserved the authoritative and authentic canon of the Old Testament. Origen reports on pilgrims to the cave of the Nativity at Bethlehem (*c. Cels.* 1. 51, known to Justin, *Dialogue* 78), and says that he himself had travelled round the Holy Land following the traces of places where Jesus had been (*Comm. in Joh.* 6. 40 (24) 204). In the Jordan valley he had even made a discovery closely analogous to the Dead Sea Scrolls (Eus. *HE* 6. 16. 3).

Because the great majority of Christians at first were Jews, it was utterly natural for Jewish festivals to be selectively continued. Passover merged imperceptibly into Easter, and continued with the name Pascha. Pentecost, fifty days later, was also continued, though now as a feast commemorating the outpouring of the Holy Spirit on the apostolic company. The account of this in Acts 2 is astonishingly close to language used by Philo when he expounded the story of Noah's inebriation (*De ebrietate* 145 ff.). Ascension Day seems not to have been a special day in the calendar before the fourth century. One rather contentious matter was the length of the fast before Easter. At first this was only a few days, and Dionysius of Alexandria would timelessly observe that a short fast was taken far more seriously than a long one. But the fast in the Greek east was soon lengthened to the seven days of Holy Week. When Athanasius was exiled to the west, he made the disconcerting and shaming discovery that churches in the west were keeping a prepaschal fast of forty days, which he immediately sought to establish in his own jurisdiction.

Evidence of special vestments for clergy is first found in fourth-century texts. But the custom whereby the newly baptized wore white (giving English speakers the name Whitsunday for Pentecost) is well attested for the second century. In Latin books the Sunday after Easter is 'Dominica in albis' with the same meaning.

All these matters are the accidental features of liturgy. For the substance it would be hard to come closer than words of Augustine commenting on Psalm 85: 1 that God's supreme gift to human beings is himself through the Son of God and Son of man. 'Addressing God in prayer we do not separate God from his Son. . . . He prays for us as our priest, he prays for us as our head, we pray to him as our God. Let us recognize our words in him and his words in ourselves.'

Christian Art before Constantine

In the pre-Constantinian period Christians had to tread carefully. They had no public status or privileges. The surviving monuments of their art are mainly underground in the catacombs. Nevertheless, we know a little. Clement of Alexandria (*Paid.* 3. 59) gives readers advice on their choice of signet ring—in ancient society an indispensable means of assuring the recipient of a letter that it was authentic. A Christian would avoid representations with idolatrous or too carnal associations. But it would be suitable to have a fisherman with a fish caught on his line, or a portrait of a good shepherd with his lamb on his shoulder, or a dove or a ship or a lyre, like Polycrates of Samos in Herodotus' famous story, or an anchor, like King Seleucus I, but nothing suggesting drink or sex. Such themes as these had the merit that they were ambiguous. They were in no way specifically Christian. Moreover, Neopythagoreans disapproved of signet rings with a seal representing a god (Iamblichus, *V. Pyth.* 35). The shepherd carrying his sheep was a common symbol of *philanthropía* or humanity, hospitality, generosity. The symbolic figures might also be engraved on an amulet hung round the neck. When a memorial monument had been erected to St Peter on the Vatican hill, a roof mosaic was painted close by showing Christ as a sungod driving his chariot across the sky. It again had the merit of being capable of a Christian interpretation but of appearing neutral to a non-Christian observer. Another favoured theme was the figure at prayer with arms raised, the orant, again a neutral symbol of piety towards the divine, but for Christians easily capable of being an allegory of divine blessing.

Philosophers and teachers were represented holding a book-roll, and this could be utilised to signify the teaching Christ with the written word of God in his hand. Naturally portraits of human figures were invaluable. What over-curious pagan investigator could guess that this head was St Peter and that St Paul if he was unaware of the evolving iconographic conventions of the artists? There was not a serious problem in having a portrait of the Virgin Mary, since no one by this age knew what she looked like. In any event a portrait of Christ performing a miracle was not in the least significant for its actual resemblance to his face. One did not need to be able to look at a representation of the twelve apostles and be sure just which was which.

On sarcophagi portrayals of harvest scenes or bunches of grapes were popular themes in pagan culture, but obviously suitable for a Christian funeral. Loaves of bread and grapes also symbolized the eucharist. Elijah's ascent to heaven in a chariot of fire invited exploitation of the chariot theme from contemporary conventions; emperors ascending to heaven in a chariot were part of the stock-in-trade. The mother and child could be acquired from the regular themes on sale at the stonemason's yard or artist's studio. Funerary art portraying the transitoriness of human life could use symbols from plants, and peacocks for immortality.

In the fourth century we hear of contention about the decoration of church walls with frescoes and, since there is an echo of the debate in the canons of the council of Elvira, perhaps about 310, it is certain that some of these pictures antedate Constantine. Celsus knew about Jonah and his gourd and about Daniel and the lions (*c. Cels.* 7. 53), who may have come to his attention because they were favourite subjects for Christian artists. The rich decoration of the Dura synagogue (now in Damascus museum) proves that there was precedent for pictures of biblical scenes in Jewish symbols.[6]

In the second decade of the fourth century Theodorus of Aquileia decorated his church with a magnificent floor mosaic, vividly portraying Jonah being swallowed and then vigorously ejected as indigestible by the sea-monster. The boats portrayed are strikingly similar to those visible today on the Venetian lagoon.

[6] See the classic discussions by E. R. Goodenough, *Jewish Symbols in the Greco-Roman Period*, 13 vols. (New York, 1953–65); C. H. Kraeling, *The Synagogue: The Excavations at Dura-Europos final report VIII*, 1 (Yale, 1956).

31

ATHANASIUS, MARCELLUS, AND THE GATHERING STORM

Fourth-century church history is simultaneously the history of the emperors, Christian with most of the Constantinian dynasty, briefly pagan in Julian; but Julian's disastrous campaign against Persia in 363 was taken to be a sign that his old polytheism offered no security to the cause of Roman power and imperial domination. His failure and death provided a contributory cause of Christian success in the conflict with paganism. In this age it was almost axiomatic that military victory was a providential gift not granted to people whose religious rites or moral conduct failed to propitiate heaven. Prayers win battles, wrote the pagan Libanius (*or.* 20. 48). Yet from 375 onwards the barbarian influx in the west transformed the operations of both state and church. The intermingling of church controversy with imperial politics sometimes solved problems for both church and state, but could also create them. The Christian dissensions of the fourth and fifth centuries are misread if they are naïvely interpreted as mere struggles for power. What most mattered to the contending bishops was the theological teaching of their tradition. At Nicaea in 325 Constantine the Great was determined to achieve harmony and consensus, and largely succeeded. The authority of his great council would have been weakened if rival factions had been allowed to create a split with a substantial minority opposed to the central decisions. Wise bishops also wanted consensus and unity in accord with the tradition of scriptural understanding which they had received. There were enemies to combat: pagan critics who read Celsus and Porphyry, schismatics who, while in essentials orthodox, vehemently dissented (like Donatists on moral grounds) to the point of rigid separation from the main Christian body, and heretics who longed for their version of the faith to be accepted as at least a valid option, best of all as the more authentic form of divine truth. In Christian history, however, the most passionate disputes have been, and were in the fourth century, between those who stood very close to one another. The issues were too often logomachies, a feature already troubling as early as 2 Tim. 2: 16, 23.

Reconciling Melitians and perhaps Arius?

The church in Egypt remained beset by problems even after the decisions at Nicaea that the Melitian schismatics should be reconciled with full recognition of their orders (with the proviso of communion with and obedience to the bishop of Alexandria), a ruling to which Alexander of Alexandria must have assented, but which to his deacon Athanasius was most regrettable. A second issue was the rehabilitation of Arius and his episcopal supporters, Eusebius of Nicomedia and Theognis of Nicaea, suspended for their reservations about the Nicene anathema as a misrepresentation of Arius' position. About the end of 327 or early in 328 Constantine had summoned a synod of leading bishops to implement the reconciliation of the Melitian clergy and congregations, but also to reinstate Arius, who could accept the Nicene creed with the explanations being given by Eusebius of Caesarea and Eusebius of Nicomedia. Receiving Arius (who had been sent to exile in Illyricum) could not be very welcome to Alexander of Alexandria, especially when Arius claimed to say only what he had heard his bishop saying. Perhaps Alexander was already failing in health, for he died on 17 April 328.

Athanasius

The Egyptian clergy assembled to choose his successor had the difficult choice of electing as bishop of Alexandria the Melitian candidate or an alternative deeply unsympathetic to this reunion. A small group, no doubt themselves apprehensive about the reconciliation of dissident Melitians, presented their colleagues with a *fait accompli* by consecrating Athanasius. That ensured that the Melitians would remain a separate body (which was the case for a long time to come) and that, at least as long as Athanasius was bishop, Arius could not be received at Alexandria. He would have to find asylum with his friends in Libya such as Secundus of Ptolemais. Arius made his way to Constantinople where, before his intended rehabilitation by the bishop Alexander, he met his end in a public latrine (above p. 201).

Alexander of Constantinople died early in 335 and was replaced by Paul, of whom in time Athanasius came to approve because they shared common enemies. At the council of Tyre (335) Paul signed the deposition of Athanasius, but changed his mind. Constantius disapproved of Paul, removed him from office and authorized the translation of Eusebius from Nicomedia to the capital.

The canonical legitimacy of Athanasius' consecration in 328 was questioned by his less intransigent colleagues, especially of course by Melitians and by sympathizers with Arius and the tradition which he represented. He was under age. In combating the Melitian separatists Athanasius' clergy used an unfortunate degree of physical violence which was to hand means to opponents with which they could attack him. In the Mareotis immediately south of Alexandria a dissident priest named Ischyras, whose ordination had been at the hand of a dissenting presbyter named Colluthus, was celebrating the liturgy when Athanasius' agent Macarius arrived to smash the chalice and overturn the altar. That did not help Athanasius' cause, though witnesses could be persuaded to testify that at the time in question Ischyras had been lying ill and could not have celebrated. Eusebius of Nicomedia and other bishops of his group who wanted Arius reinstated at Alexandria were easily able to produce witnesses with evidence of inappropriate behaviour. There was no doctrinal charge against Athanasius, but he was able to retort that his accusers were foot-faulted by their adherence to Arian heresy. After the council of Tyre in 335, where Athanasius skilfully defended himself and his opponents made the mistake of accusing him of injury or even murder of a man he could produce alive and well, he made a clandestine escape and appealed to Constantine. But the threat to stop the grain supply from Egypt to Constantinople if Constantine failed to support was disastrous. Unfortunately it was certain that he had a close relationship with the sea-captains at the harbour; he would imply that himself (*ep. Encycl.* 5). The charge was all too plausible.

The fourth century was an age of violence. The discourses and letters of Libanius,[1] pagan sophist of Antioch (314–*c.*393), show that peasants were flogged into forced labour, that soldiers were almost always brutal to civilians and if billeted in towns were dreaded; they organised protection rackets to exploit farmers in the countryside. The authorities maintaining law and order resorted to torture, not only for slaves, who regularly suffered punishment with their body and under cross-examination had to be put to 'the question' but for members of city councils who failed to collect sufficient tax. A hypocritical pride led some provincial governors to claim that they had not executed anyone, when with fire and rack their torturers had either maimed the victims for life or left them half-dead. Libanius thought capital punishment a necessary deterrent but hated bloodshed and corporal scourging.

Athanasius theologian

Athanasius' exile to Trier, however, brought him into good contact not only with a sympathetic bishop of the imperial city but also with the eldest of Constantine's three sons, Constantine II. It may also have provided him with the leisure for the composition of his twin works 'Against the heathen'

[1] A. F. Norman, 'Libanius, the Teacher in an Age of Violence', in G. Fatouros and T. Krischer (eds.), *Libanius* (Wege der Forschung, 621; Darmstadt, 1983), 150–69.

(*contra Gentes*) and 'On the incarnation'. On hearing the news of his father's death one of Constantine II's first acts was to give Athanasius liberty to return to Alexandria at his discretion, declaring probably correctly that this had been his father's intention. Since the empire for some months was governed in the name of the dead emperor the declaration was no doubt necessary.

Athanasius' tract *contra Gentes* shows the extent of his sympathy with the kind of reply to pagan critics that Origen had offered in his *contra Celsum*, which Athanasius probably drew from the *Theophany* and the *Preparation for the Gospel* written by Eusebius of Caesarea. Nevertheless there is no allusion to his exile other than a note that he has no copies of his teachers' books by him, and the Arian controversy is never mentioned. In essentials the work presents Christianity as less materialistic than the crudity and superstition of paganism and therefore able to occupy common ground with Platonic notions of the soul as the higher element in human nature. Soul is immortal but needs gospel purification. The tract will have had more Christian than pagan readers.[2]

The tract on the Incarnation is similarly directed against pagan criticism. A proposition declared to be superfluous, impossible, and unworthy of God is actually both necessary for salvation of our lost race and also in line with the highest affirmations about the Creator. Every Platonist agreed to the overflow of divine goodness as ground of creation; this providence continues in redemption. Adam, rational and immortal before his Fall, fell into precarious impermanence and mortality and the image of God in him was gradually destroyed. God's creative goodness cannot be frustrated, but the penalty for sin, for despising the wonder of divine contemplation, must be paid. Hence human repentance is insufficient, and does not answer the problem of our perishing finitude, sinking into nothingness. The incarnate Lord brought incorruption to human nature by rising from the dead; he met divine justice by death. Only God can redeem. His redemption brings eternal life which is to participate in the divine nature and is communicated by sacramental incorporation in his Church.

Athanasius' theology owed much to Irenaeus, for whom it was axiomatic that God alone can make himself known as an inferior mediator cannot do. Although he had imbibed much from the tradition of Origen, it was offensive to him when Arius wanted to keep monotheism by the thesis that the Son of God is at the summit of the created order, 'a creature though not as one of the creatures'. One who is part of this finite transitory world cannot have the power to bring immortality and incorruption to morally precarious

---

[2] See E. P. Meijering, *Athanasius contra Gentes* (Leiden, 1984); *Athanasius de Incarnatione* (Amsterdam, 1989).

souls. The Logos or Word of God took a human body and made it his own to demonstrate divine glory to fallen, mortal mankind, and to make possible purification, directing the soul to be united with *nous*, mind. Athanasius left it unclear whether or not the Logos assumed a human *nous*. That was a problem for the future.

The tract 'On the incarnation' is not always self-consistent; but it makes clear why Athanasius felt threatened by Arius' ideas. Arius by contrast was pleading for the utter otherness and transcendence of God the creator and for pure monotheism. However, Athanasius did not make the Nicene creed the standard for a polemical campaign until the forties and fifties.

Division of the empire: a dynastic massacre

It is certain that Constantine intended the empire to continue being ruled by members of his dynasty. That meant rule by his three sons: Constantine II the eldest, a bastard, already holding the Rhine frontier from Trier, and the two sons by Fausta, Constantius II in the East, the only son to be present at his father's funeral (but not at his deathbed), and Constans, still hardly sixteen years old but as ambitious as any; together with them there were two nephews, Dalmatius already nominated Caesar, and his brother Hannibalianus. Five was only one more than Diocletian's tetrarchy, and the empire was huge. The three sons thought the two nephews superfluous, likely to be an obstacle to the aspirations of each. Hannibalianus was popular in Roman Armenia. The story was put out that the army would tolerate only the sons, and at Constantinople in the summer of 337 there was a blood-bath of the kind customary in that age, the soldiers eliminating all members of the dynasty who might reasonably bid for power and several high officers of state who had been close to Constantine the Great. Emperors were deposed by no democratic vote, but by assassination. John Chrysostom, commenting on the epistle to the Philippians, observes that the pavements of imperial palaces are always soaked in blood of the emperor's own kindred, and that almost all stage tragedies concern kings (*Hom. in Phil.* 15. 5)). Two young boys, Gallus and Julian, grandsons of Constantius I by two different partners, were too young to seem a threat, were protected by Bishop Eusebius of Nicomedia and Mark, who later became bishop of Arethusa in Syria, and so by Constantius' intervention (Greg. Naz. *or.* 4. 21) were allowed to live. It was taken for granted, by Athanasius (*Hist. Ar.* 69), by the emperor Julian in his letter to the Athenians (270 C), and by the pagan historian Zosimus (2. 40), all being hostile witnesses, that the decision for the killings was taken by Constantius, but it is unlikely that he alone was responsible. At least he had no objection. The three brothers and the army had reason to think the coherence of empire was at stake. Julian believed that Constantius suffered from remorse, and attributed to this guilt his childlessness and lack of success in the Persian wars.[3]

Constantius and the eastern frontier

By mutual agreement Constantine II took Spain, Gaul and Britain, Constans I had Italy, Africa and the (civil) 'diocese' of Macedonia. Constantius II had Asia Minor, Egypt, and the East based on Antioch in Syria. He drew the short straw since, unlike his brothers, whose frontiers were subjected only to ill-organized raids by barbarian tribesmen, he had to face the considerable might of a Persia determined to recover Mesopotamian provinces captured for Rome by Galerius in 298. Julian (18 C) recalls that Constans and Constantine II did nothing to make it easy for Constantius to cope with a Persian war. Constantine the Great had written a letter to the Persian king Shahpuhr II, preserved by Eusebius of Caesarea (*Vita Const.* 4. 8–9), expressing pleasure at some kindness he had showed to his numerous Christian subjects; that he would surely not harass them (an evidently possible threat) he might deduce from the capture of the emperor Valerian in 260, which was manifestly divine punishment for his persecution of believers. Unfortunately the letter evidently implied that Christians in Persia should be considered to be under the protective advocacy of a Roman emperor who shared their faith, and in whose eyes they were almost honorary Romans.[4] In consequence, after Constantine's death the young churches in Persia were subjected to persecution by their government which deemed them to be allies of the Roman emperor, required to pay double taxation to finance the war against Constantius and to suffer death if they could not pay. A passage in the Syriac homilies of Aphrahat (5. 1. 24) about 337 shows that there were indeed pro-Roman Christians in Persia, sure that Jesus was with Constantius. Probably Constantius himself shared this confidence. Persian persecution was, of course, the more likely to make Christians look towards the Christian empire for support.[5]

[3] R. Klein, 'Die Kämpfe um die Nachfolge nach dem Tode Constantins des Großen', *Byz. Forsch.* 6 (1979), 101–50.

[4] An analogy is the claim of imperial Russia to be protector of the Ottoman Sultan's Christian subjects.

[5] See the still classic discussion in J. Labourt, *Le Christianisme dans l'empire perse sous la dynastie sassanide* (Paris, 1904); J. M. Fiey, *Jalons pour une histoire de l'Église en Iraq* (Louvain, 1970) following his *Assyrie chrétienne*, 3 vols. (Beirut, 1965, 1968); W. Hage, 'Die oströmische Staatskirche und die Christenheit des Perserreiches', *Zeitschrift für Kirchengeschichte*, 84 (1973), 174–187; especially S. P. Brock in *JTS*, NS 19 (1968), 300–9, and his illuminating paper 'Christians in the Sasanian Empire: A case of divided loyalties', in *Studies in Church History*, 18 (1982), 1–20 with bibliographical references. On the empire's conflict with Persia see P. A. Barceló, *Roms auswärtige Beziehungen unter der Constantinischen Dynastie (306–63)*, Eichstätter Beiträge, Abteilung Geschichte, 3 (Regensburg, 1981), 73–104.

Ulfilas and Frumentius

Constantius' embassies to Persia were not very successful in fostering sympathy for Christianity. The emperor also looked elsewhere outside the empire for Christian missionary work which could help in spreading Roman authority. A Cappadocian taken prisoner in a Gothic raid and named by Goths 'little wolf', Wulfila or Ulfila(s), came to Constantinople with a Gothic embassy about 336–7 (below p. 364f.). Eusebius of Constantinople was to consecrate him bishop in charge of a mission to the Goths north of the Danube. Hostility to this mission pushed him back into the empire south of the Danube where Gothic residents were numerous. He devised a Gothic alphabet and translated the Bible, omitting the books of Kings as too warlike. His sympathies were not with the Nicene creed. Gothic Christians were long considered 'Arians'. Constantius knew that Athanasius had consecrated a bishop Frumentius for the tribes south of Egypt at Axum. He wrote asking the princes at Axum to send Frumentius to Alexandria so that his too Athanasian theology could be corrected (Athan. *Apol. ad Const.* 31). A similar pattern of missionary concern appeared in Constantius' use of an Indian bishop Theophilos to serve as ambassador to peoples south of the Red Sea and to Arabs to keep them friendly towards the Roman empire.

Athanasius returns from exile at Trier: Constantine II dies

All three sons of Constantine had been brought up as professing Christians. They inherited from their father the conviction that by special providence they had a divine mission. Their father had been convinced that he was destined to establish a universal faith and a global ethic intended to bring a worldwide unity to the human race reaching beyond the frontiers from Hadrian's wall to the Tigris. It was going to affect the Church, however, that each of the three brothers shared their father's belief that the unity of their empire was best achieved by only one emperor; in short, each considered his two fraternal colleagues less than necessary. Constantine II assumed that the adolescent Constans must be under his guidance and authority. This led him to underestimate his youngest brother in a military move to be rid of him, and near Aquileia in 340 he met his death. That gave Constans control of two-thirds of the empire's resources, and high tension in the Church created a fusion of political and ecclesiastical interests which enabled him to put threatening pressure on Constantius in the east for a decade to come.

When Athanasius left Trier, he did not immediately return to Alexandria, where a friend of Arius named Pistos had already been put in as bishop; he travelled to the Danube region to have an interview with Constantius going to a meeting of the three sons of Constantine at Viminacium, in Moesia Superior, near the border (Serbian Kostolac) with Pannonia. The agenda was no doubt to petition for support from the civil authorities at Alexandria. After a considerable tour to enlist support he reentered the city to much enthusiasm from his people on 23 November 337 (so the ancient index to his Festal Letters). He had returned to his see without a synodical decision cancelling the deposition at the council of Tyre. He therefore held a synod of bishops at Alexandria at which the bishops under his jurisdiction declared him innocent, objected to the uncanonical translation of Eusebius from Nicomedia to Constantinople, and attacked Athanasius' accusers as compromised by Arianism and by schismatic Melitian support in Egypt. Their encyclical was a valuable juridical weapon for him. Meanwhile his opponents, whom he calls 'the Eusebians', were writing to the three emperors and to Julius bishop of Rome, reiterating the grounds for the deposition of Athanasius by the council of Tyre, especially his responsibility for violence and even murder. At the time Constantius had war on his hands in Armenia; his two western brothers were unlikely to be sympathetic. The Roman see turned out to be friendly to Athanasius. The influence of Constans is no doubt to be discerned there. Under severe pressure a proposal had come from the Eusebians themselves that Pope Julius should call a revising synod and preside in person. But the story (Ath. *Apol. c. Ar.* 20. 1) may be slanted. In *Hist. Ar.* 9. 1 it appears that the Greek legates initially asked Julius to write a letter of communion to Pistos of Alexandria, thereby implying recognition of the council of Tyre's verdict against Athanasius. They could urge that the Greeks recognized Latin synods, and expected the West to respect eastern councils. Athanasius' friends warned Julius that Pistos was associated with those who disliked the Nicene creed, whom Athanasius would label as 'Arians'. His Egyptian council addressed their plea to all churches, not only to Rome, but naturally they wanted the leading Western see to give support. The legates sent by the Eusebians assumed that if there was to be a council to reopen the issue, that would be held in the east where people were well informed, not in the ignorant west.

The prefect of Egypt forced Athanasius' withdrawal. Pistos was soon replaced by a more effective bishop, though not enjoying good health, named Gregory, whom Constantius, at Antioch during winter 338, supported. After a brief stay in hiding Athanasius wisely withdrew and went to Rome, there to seek reinforcement from Bishop Julius in his 'apostolic see'.

Athanasius and Marcellus in Rome as refugees

It was momentous that after a few months at Rome Athanasius was joined by another exile enjoying Constantine II's amnesty, Marcellus of Ankyra. After

Nicaea Marcellus had had a running pamphlet war with Eusebius of Caesarea and a clever layman Asterios, who had misgivings about the Nicene *homoousios* and preferred to use a formula associated with the martyred scholar, Lucian of Antioch, that 'the Son is an indistinguishable image of the Father'. Marcellus addressed Constantine the Great with a text designed to prove Eusebius of Nicomedia and Eusebius of Caesarea to be heretics. It turned out differently from his hopes. Opposition to Marcellus was theological and strong. The bishops, offended by his refusal to attend at the dedication of the new church of the Resurrection at Jerusalem in 336, rejected his doctrines and at a council in Constantinople declared him out of their communion.

Marcellus liked the formula of Neopythagorean mathematicians that the Monad contains the potential to engender the dyad and the triad, but is primary. To preserve immutability, he said that in the generation of the Son, the Godhead 'expands'. Marcellus, who could be critical of Origen but also may have owed him something, did not feel able to stomach the Origenist formula (*c. Cels.* 8. 12) that Father and Son are separate hypostases. Marcellus was enthusiastic for the Nicene creed and anathema. Differing in names, God is one in *ousia* and hypostasis. To suggest that the unity of the Father and the Son consists in harmony of will seemed refuted by Christ's words in Gethsemane. He understood the unity of God to be clear from 1 Cor. 15. 24–8: at the end Christ delivers up the kingdom to the Father. Critics took this to mean that the Son would eventually be merged into the Father. He was sure that if God is a monad, the Son participates in the proceeding of the Spirit from the Father. Yet if the Father and the Logos are one hypostasis, indistinguishable in being, is Jesus more than a mere man? To critics he seemed to combine Sabellius with Paul of Samosata. They thought that to affirm the incarnate Lord to be God entailed his distinctness from the transcendent Father, and Marcellus seemed to prejudice both propositions.

Eusebius of Caesarea felt impelled to write two works in explicit refutation of Marcellus, with plentiful and carefully selected citations, suggesting that even in the Greek east not everyone (Constantine in particular) was convinced that he was heretical. In fact, language used by Marcellus was remarkably close to that used by or at least familiar to Constantine himself.[6] To Greeks of the Origenist tradition Marcellus was Sabellian; he did not believe Father, Son, and Spirit to be essentially three. Western support

---

[6] See Klaus Seibt, *Die Theologie des Markell von Ankyra* (Berlin, 1994); a differing perspective in Markus Vinzent, *Markell von Ankyra, die Fragmenten, der Brief an Julius von Rom* (Leiden, 1997). Vinzent has also published an annotated German translation of Eusebius' tracts against Marcellus (Fontes Christiani; Freiburg i. B., 1999). M. Tetz, *Athanasiana: zu Leben und Lehre des Athanasius* (Berlin, 1995) 61–105, edits and examines Eugenius' document. Eugenius is probably identical with the deacon Hyginos of the Marcellan text in Epiphanius, *Panarion* 72. 11. 1, 5.

for him inevitably confirmed Greek fears for Latin competence in high theology. Marcellus, however, had his supporters in Greece and Macedonia, and after his condemnation at Constantinople in 336 continued to have a congregation in Galatia into the 370s. In 372 a letter by Basil of Caesarea (69) to persuade Athanasius to pronounce him heretical, as a step towards his goal of detaching Athanasius from Paulinus of Antioch with whom Marcellus was in friendly correspondence, was rebutted by a deacon named Eugenius. He was well aware of conciliatory language used at Athanasius' council of Alexandria in 362, his statement being very orthodox; but he avoided any concession to 'three hypostases' in God.

Probably after the Dedication Council of Antioch in January 341 Marcellus submitted to Julius a careful statement of his orthodoxy strikingly akin to the Roman baptismal confession of faith, also attested in Rufinus' *Exposition of the Creed.* This form of words did not answer any of the questions put by his Greek critics, and stressed that Father, Son, and Spirit are a single hypostasis. Pope Julius was rapidly convinced that grave injustice had been done by Greek synods to his refugees. That was certainly what Constans hoped he would think. The refugees successfully persuaded him to invite Eusebius now of Constantinople and his colleagues to a synod in Rome with authority to revise the unjust synods of the East at Tyre (335) for Athanasius and at Constantinople (336) for Marcellus.

At Rome Athanasius' ascetic life found powerful friends and admirers, including Constantine the Great's sister Eutropia. He was treated with deep respect by Constans, to a degree which gave high plausibility to Constantius' later charge that Athanasius was the cause of Constans' rising hostility to his brother. It is likely enough that Constans was not sorry to be able to use the ecclesiastical stand-off as a ground for political pressure. That Athanasius' sympathetic reception in Rome marked a point of high tension between much of the Greek East outside Egypt and the Latin West is obvious. Pope Julius was easily persuaded to write to the Eusebian group at Antioch; his letter was brought to Antioch early in 340 by a count (symbolic of Constans' support) and by two presbyters, who had to wait until January 341 for an answer.

The Dedication Council of Antioch 341

In January the great new Church at Antioch (mosaics of which, unearthed by the American excavators, can be seen at the museum in Antakya) was to be dedicated. Constantius was present and ninety-seven bishops came. The occasion gave the opportunity for a synodical decision on the representations coming from Rome; the greatest anxiety was caused by the Roman reception of Marcellus. Pope Julius' letter had given far more space to Athanasius than to Marcellus, whose case was theologically intricate and in Greek eyes far harder to defend.

On the Dedication Council of Antioch information would be exiguous had its main creed not become prominent in discussions about 358–62. At that time Hilary of Poitiers and Athanasius record various statements of faith produced at the council. The historians Socrates and Sozomen mainly depend on Athanasius. Athanasius lists four creeds (produced, misleadingly it must be said, to illustrate his tendentious theme that in contrast to the one Nicene formula 'Arians' were almost annually rewriting their faith and were incapable of continuing in one stay). His first is cited from the council's letter to Rome. The second is the crux. Sozomen found a tradition, of which he felt uncertain, that this text was the work of the learned biblical scholar, Lucian of Antioch, who won his martyr's crown under Maximin Daia in 311 (Soz. 4. 22. 22). The Eusebians evidently regarded the text as safeguarding their old rule of faith. They had no intention of suppressing the Nicene creed, which enjoyed the nimbus of Constantine the Great's support. They did not suppose they were offering an Arian confession of faith. They declared the only begotten Son of God to be immutable, the indistinguishable image of the Father's Godhead in hypostasis, will, power, and glory, mediating between God and humanity by the incarnation, the firstborn of all creation. (It was a question whether this last Pauline phrase from Col. 1: 15 referred to the humanity of the incarnate Lord or to the pre-existent divine Son; in the latter case it could be interpreted to justify Arius' thesis that the divine Logos stands at the apex of the created order.) So Father, Son, and Spirit stand in an ordered ranking and are 'three in hypostasis, one in agreement of will', positions highly offensive to Marcellus. Anathema is pronounced on the propositions that time could exist before the Son's eternal generation, that the Son is a creature as one of the creatures. (Arius had said 'a creature but not as one of the creatures'.) In their synodical letter they correctly disowned any suggestion that they were followers of Arius; for bishops could not be followers of a presbyter (Athan. *Syn.* 22–3).

Athanasius did not fail to notice that the anathemas were milder than those of Nicaea, though they cover much of the same ground. One striking feature of the text is the amount of scriptural citation. Besides and probably prior to their main text, the synod received a vindication of his faith from the bishop of Tyana (Cappadocia) named Theophronius, who needed to disown and anathematize Marcellus of Ankyra, whose doctrines were coupled with those of Sabellius and Paul of Samosata.[7] Evidently he was not admitted to sit

---

[7] At this point the text of the manuscript tradition (Athan. *Syn.* 24. 5) has a corruption, brilliantly and simply rectified by M. Tetz (*Athanasiana* 230).

as a member of the synod until he had broken communion with Marcellus, a procedure similar to that followed at Nicaea in the case of Eusebius of Caesarea. A theme, pointed against what Marcellus was being taken to say, insists on the endlessness of Christ's kingdom (from Luke 1: 33). Theophronios included one formula on the incarnation directly echoing the Nicene creed, and was cleverly ambiguous on the question of one hypostasis or three, with the formula that the Logos is 'with the Father in hypostasis' (language which Marcellus himself could have used and which occurs in the statement of 372 by the deacon Eugenius). This personal statement of faith is the only explicit condemnation of Marcellus in the admittedly meagre records of the Dedication Council.

The Greek letter to Rome and Pope Julius' reply

The Eusebians' letter to Pope Julius, brought back by the Roman legates from Antioch, was emphatic about the honour in which they held the Roman church as a 'school of apostles and metropolis of orthodox piety', but expressed deep pain at the insult to the eastern churches in the rejection of their synods. They expressed regret that the bishop of Rome preferred communion with two deposed and censured bishops to that of themselves and the Greek east generally. Decisions of synods were not advisory but final. It seemed forgotten in the west that the gospel had come to Rome from the Greek east. The Greeks had never questioned the western censure of Novatian (whose connection had several groups in Asia Minor). Moreover, it distressed the Greeks to note that Julius' letter had not been sent in the name and with the authority of an episcopal synod, but only under his own title. To this Julius replied that he had written after consulting a synod. To him the flattering language used by the Eusebians about Roman orthodoxy seemed ironical. The drafting hand of Eusebius of Constantinople is no doubt detectable in this. He would have been conscious of being bishop of New Rome, where power now lay. Accordingly, as soon as his legates returned to Rome Julius held a synod of about fifty Italian bishops to agree on policy.

Athanasius (*Apol. c. Ar.* 20–35) cites Julius' reply to the Eusebians' letter, from which the main points of their letter can be deduced. He addressed D(i)anius of Cappadocian Caesarea, Flacillus of Antioch, Narcissus of Neronias (Cilicia), Eusebius of Constantinople, Maris of Chalcedon, Macedonius of Mopsuestia (Cilicia), Theodorus of Heraclea, 'and their friends'. He was offended by the lack of charity and the arrogance of the Greek letter. The Pope claimed that the bishops at Nicaea had enacted that the decisions of one council could be reviewed by another. Apparently canon 5 is here in mind, where a member of the clergy or laity excommunicated by the diocesan bishop may appeal to a council, but the possibility of appeal

against an entire council is not considered. Moreover, when the Eusebians
had earlier written to Julius, their legates had been argued into a corner and
had had to concede that the quarrel could be revised by another council.
They did not envisage judgement being given to a single primate, and that
was an issue in the exchanges. If Julius had begun to regard his own office as
analogous to that of (at least) a provincial governor or praetorian prefect, he
could reasonably have supposed that other bishops were his assessors and
counsellors and that he made the ultimate decision.

The Eusebians had complained that the reception of Athanasius and
Marcellus to communion was a breach of canon law. Julius' rejoinder was
that the consecration at Antioch of Gregory, a Cappadocian, for the see of
Alexandria without the least consultation with local clergy and people was
uncanonical; his arrival at Alexandria with a military escort to coerce the
people into accepting him was deplorable and gave the lie to the Eusebian
claim that at Alexandria all was now peaceful and the churches unanimous.
It was appalling that bishops had suffered exile, with bishops present and not
dissenting at the verdict. Julius had forgotten that precisely this had occurred
at the council of Nicaea to two Libyan friends of Arius.

Marcellus had satisfied the Roman synod of his catholic faith and was
testified to be opposed to Arianism by the Roman legates present at Nicaea.
Epiphanius of Salamis about 375 was puzzled by the ambiguity over
Marcellus' orthodoxy, and cites his confession of faith submitted to Julius.
It is emphatic that in God there is but one hypostasis (*Panar.* 72. 2. 4).
Epiphanius adds that he once asked Athanasius for his opinion of Marcellus'
doctrine. 'He neither defended nor criticized him, but only smiled,
indicating that he was not far from wicked error but could be defended'
(72. 4. 4).

Primate versus council

Pope Julius concluded by claiming that by custom decisions concerning the
Alexandrian church were taken at Rome. Probably he had in mind the correction of Dionysius of Alexandria by his namesake of Rome in the mid-
third century. Julius felt himself to be standing by the tradition inherited from
St Peter, resisting innovations. The church of St Mark had a special filial relationship to the see of St Peter. He had a right to hear any appeal from this
church in particular. Alexandria was a special case. Julius was here reacting to
a Eusebian insinuation that Julius was asserting authority on the ground of
the secular importance of his city in defiance of their principle that all
bishops are canonically equal (Athan. *Apol. c. Ar.* 25). Since the Eusebians were
refusing to come to a large council at Rome, there was no alternative to the
exercise and assertion of primatial dignity. At the same time the disagreement

between Rome and the leading Greek bishops of the time marked the first confrontation between a conciliar ecclesiology in the east and a primatial ecclesiology beginning to become dominant in the west. At the council of Serdica the emperors' concern to prevent a collision between two indeflectible bodies was wrecked on this rock.

32

A FIASCO AT SERDICA

Tension between east and west

Some months after the Dedication Council of Antioch the Eusebians sent a delegation of four bishops to Constans at Trier bringing a statement of faith carefully disowning any touch of Arianism and at the same time insisting, against Marcellus, that Christ's kingdom will have no end (Luke 1. 33). The concluding anathema condemns 'any who say that the Son is out of nothing or of a different hypostasis and not of God, and that there was once a time or an aeon when he was not'. One could not find more careful words to distance the Eusebians from the doctrines associated with Arius, and to rebut the accusations of Julius of Rome. The pro-Athanasian bishop of Trier, Maximin, refused to receive them. The legates were Narcissus of Neronias, Maris of Chalcedon, Theodorus of Heraclea, and Mark of Arethusa (Syria). Unsurprisingly they did not include Rome in their itinerary. The first three names were known for their opposition to Athanasius on the ground of his violence in Egypt. Their creed was labelled by Athanasius the fourth creed of Antioch, which is evidently the title he had received for it. Since the eastern bishops were very conscious of authority lying in synodical decisions, it is probable that this document was considered at the Dedication Council as a text more likely to be amenable to the West while still safeguarding themes dear to the Eusebians. It said nothing about three hypostases, slew Marcellus with an unchallengeable biblical text, and had anathemas reinforcing the disowning of Arian propositions. The document was to become programmatic and much repeated.

Eusebius of Constantinople, master-mind and leader of the group, took no part. Probably late in 341 he died. The portrait of him in Athanasius is deeply unsympathetic; he was certainly a formidable opponent of the bishop of Alexandria. His successive translations from the see of Berytos (Beirut) to Nicomedia and thence to Constantinople seemed ambitious hunger for influence. At Constantinople Bishop Paul, expelled by Constantius, returned from exile in the west, but found himself competing for the see with a friend of Eusebius named Macedonius. After a riot in which the army chief Hermogenes, *magister militum*, lost his life, Macedonius was preferred by the prefect and Paul was exiled to Mesopotamia, then to Syria, finally to Cappadocia, where the prefect had him strangled. At many of the towns to which exiled bishops returned under Constantine II's amnesty there were riots; at Ankyra the advent of Marcellus was the occasion of street-fighting. He could not remain there.

Confrontation at Serdica

The abrasive exchanges of 340–1 threatened to divide the Greek East from the Latin West, but the yawning ravine between the principal parties was politically congenial to the western emperor Constans who wanted a good excuse to bring military pressure on his elder brother Constantius II. On the other hand Constans also wanted a Church united in accordance with his policy and dominated by the West. Since no one could question the propriety of seeking church unity, it was not immediately obvious that for Constans and Rome this meant western supremacy over the East. Constans and Constantius concurred that a full synod had to be held with representatives of both east and west as Pope Julius had originally proposed at Rome. The place chosen was Serdica (in Greek Sardike, in Bulgarian Sredéc, modern Sofia) in Illyricum, chief town of Dacia Mediterranea, but close to the Greek-speaking provinces and largely bilingual.[1] It was intended to be an ecumenical council, a title which about 338 is found used of the council of Nicaea (above p. 205), and the assembly is so described in the next century by the historian Socrates (2. 20. 3).

---

[1] The council is dated in 347 by the historian Socrates, which is certainly wrong. The Index to the Festal Letters of Athanasius has 342–3. A Latin collection of documents made in north Africa in the sixth century by a deacon Theodosius and preserved in a contemporary Verona manuscript (LX, fo. 71[b]) has a corrupt entry that the synod was assembled (*congregata*) at Sardica 'consolatu Constantini et Constantini' which invites easy emendation to 'Constantii III et Constantis II', consuls for the year 342. The choice is therefore between a date in the autumn of 342 or in 343. The argument favouring 342 hangs partly on the degree of urgency which the two emperors will certainly have attached to the critical situation following the exchanges of January 341. They cannot have allowed the grass to grow under their feet with open schism imminent. On the other hand, Socrates (2. 20. 6) may preserve an authentic note in the observation that eighteen months elapsed between the issue of the imperial summons to the synod and its actual meeting. This is compatible with the summons going out in spring 341 and the synod meeting in September/October 342. Although autumn 342 is the date better attested in the ancient sources, the case for 343 is strong and either year is possible. 343 has been preferred by a majority of French scholars, especially Annick Martin (SC edition of the *Historia acephala*) and Charles Pietri (*Roma Christiana* (Rome, 1976), 213), supported by L. W. Barnard (*The Council of Serdica*, Sofia, Synodal Publishing House, 1983—a monograph of particular utility) and T. D. Barnes, *Athanasius and Constantius* (Cambridge, Mass., 1993), 259; 342 by most German historians since E. Schwartz Göttinger Nachrichten 1911, 516 = *Gesammelte Schriften*, iii (Berlin, 1959), 325–6; J. Ulrich, *Die Anfänge der abendländischen Rezeption des Nizänums* (Berlin, 1994), 39–44. So also the major study of Marcellus by K. Seibt (Berlin, 1994). F. Loofs was for 343: *Patristica* (Berlin, 1999), 185. Something hangs on whether the question concerns when the Council began or when it ended.

To facilitate attendance the emperors authorized the bishops to use the government postal service or *cursus publicus*, an authorization commonly given for important persons. This put the service under considerable strain laying the bishops open to secular criticism with which the eastern bishops warmly concurred; they came with the utmost reluctance especially as they sweated up the long hill from Philippopolis (Plovdiv) to Serdica (which cost the lives of some elderly and sick bishops). Serdica was 13 days' travel from Constantinople for an unladen traveller (Priscus frg. 11. 2 p. 146 Blockley). On arrival they found the western bishops there before them with Athanasius, Marcellus, and other deposed Greeks already received to communion, a decision anticipated at Rome by Julius and a synod of more than 50 bishops (Athan. *Apol. c. Ar.* 20). The eastern bishops naturally regarded that as a deliberate and scandalous *fait accompli*, prejudging a central question which the council had been called to determine. Writing to Alexandria, the western bishops at Serdica claim that the decision to admit Athanasius to communion was taken only after the eastern bishops had withdrawn from the council: Ath. *Apol. c. Ar.* 36–7. They and Athanasius himself were sensitive to the accusation, which was almost certainly fair. The emperors' summons had set out the agenda, recorded in the western bishops' letter to Bishop Julius of Rome. First, the council was to decide the question of belief and 'the integrity of the truth' which had been violated; second, the cases of persons who had been unjustly ejected; third, the council was to consider the outrages and intolerable insults to the churches. Constans had evidently had a controlling hand in the wording.[2]

Julius sent two presbyters and a deacon. The western president was Ossius of Corduba; the bishops led by him numbered ninety, of whom perhaps over a half were Greek-speaking. The eastern bishops, led by Stephen of Antioch, numbered about seventy-five, and included two Latin-speaking Pannonian bishops, Valens of Mursa and Ursacius of Singidunum. Ischyras of the Mareotis was with them, and a brave Egyptian bishop Callinicos of Pelusium, likely to have a rough ride if and when Athanasius was reinstated. Athanasius mentions his pro-Melitian sympathies.[3]

The emperors' plan for a council of reconciliation was destroyed from the start by the western *fait accompli* and the eastern refusal to hold communion with Athanasius and Marcellus. The western bishops approved of the confession of faith which Marcellus had submitted to Julius; what sufficed for a Pope was enough (Athan. *Hist. Ar.* 6). The two contingents never formally met, since the eastern bishops retired in some anger to another building in

[2] Hilary of Poitiers, CSEL 65. 128, 4–11; Eng. tr. by L. R. Wickham, *Conflicts of Conscience and Law in the Fourth-Century Church* (Liverpool, 1997), 49.

[3] *Fest. Ep.* 4 for 332; his successor Pancratios was present at Sirmium in 358 for drafting the Dated Creed of which Athanasius disapproved, CSEL 65, 162, 15.

Serdica and then down the hill to Philippolis (but dating their encyclical from Serdica), to reaffirm their creed, the so-called fourth creed of Antioch, originally designed to please the west. They significantly reinforced the anathema, condemning not only Arian notions of a time when the Son did not exist but also belief in three Gods, or that Father, Son and Spirit are one and the same, or that the Son is not begotten, or that the Father's generation of the Son was not an act of will. The force of these anti-western propositions becomes more apparent when the western statement of faith is considered. They drafted an incendiary encyclical letter stating their case in powerful terms, preserved by Hilary (CSEL 65. 48–67). Their creed is in the Verona codex LX, fo. 79ᵃ (ed. *EOMIA* i. 638–40)[4], as well as Hilary, *De synodis* 34. The eastern refusal to meet with the western synod was taken by the latter to betray the weakness of their case, perhaps a bad conscience about their unjust synods.

The eastern synod's complaints

To the eastern synod it seemed monstrous that Protogenes bishop of Serdica[5] was sharing communion with Marcellus whose condemnation he had signed at Constantinople in 336; that the same Protogenes who had denounced Bishop Aetius of Thessalonica for living with concubines was now content that Aetius joined in the western assembly; that good evidence of Athanasius' resorting to coercion by prison and fierce beatings was ignored; that Paul exiled from Constantinople was supported by the western bishops and Athanasius though he had signed against Athanasius at the council of Tyre; that these Westerners, led by Julius, were claiming domination over the Church like a usurping tyrant; that the proceedings abandoned 'the old custom of the Church'. The eastern bishops made a gesture of concession: of the six bishops sent by the council of Tyre to the Mareotis to investigate the charges of violence, five were still living and present (Theognis of Nicaea had died and at Serdica his deacons gave evidence against him to the western assembly (Ath. *Apol. c. Ar.* 43). They offered to send a joint commission with representatives from both councils to check the facts. The offer was declined by the western bishops, who regarded the findings of the original commission as flawed by their having taken evidence from pagans and catechumens (Athan. *Apol. c. Ar.* 37). The impression given was that they feared the outcome of such an investigation. Moreover, the west was committed by Julius

---

[4] On the Verona codex LX see W. Telfer, *Harvard Theological Review*, 36 (1943), 169–246. It is a major source for the story.

[5] Subject of a prosopographical note by Stanislava Stoytcheva in *Byzantinoslavica*, 60 (1999), 308–14.

to the vindication of Athanasius, and without massive loss of face could not accept a proposal implying that his reinstatement was still an open question. Rome had dictated a verdict in advance.

Naturally the eastern synod felt unable to consider any compromise for Marcellus. Before his death (about 338–9) Eusebius of Caesarea had convincingly shown up the dangers of his doctrines, and Eusebius's successor Acacius, present at Serdica, had further written an attack, cited by Epiphanius (*Panar.* 72. 6–10), using the language of Asterios and the Dedication Council of Antioch about the Son as 'indistinguishable image of the Father's will and being and glory', differing only in that he is begotten. The western synod further upset the opposition by producing threatening letters from Constans with the acquiescence of his brother. Constans had threatened his brother with war if he did not make his bishops yield. There was already war on the Mesopotamian front, so that menacing words were not only alarming but in eastern eyes politically irresponsible.

The eastern bishops addressed their furious letter to Gregory of Alexandria, Donatus of Carthage, and to some bishops close to Rome such as Campania, Naples, Rimini, and Salona in Dalmatia. (Were these Italian bishops known to be disputing anything with Julius?). They wanted to build up support for their stand. It is surprising if they aspired to change Julius' mind that they looked towards the schismatic Donatus. Later Augustine could argue against Donatists that they had been in alliance with 'Arians'.

The western synod

For the western synod several texts survive through a variety of transmitters. Hilary of Poitiers (CSEL 65. 103–26) preserves the western synod's encyclical without signatories; also in Athanasius, *Apol. c. Ar.* 42–50 with seventy-eight signatories and in Theodoret, *HE* 2. 8 without signatories but with a crucial doctrinal statement attached of which, with the encyclical, a defective Latin version, probably translated from Greek, is in the Theodosian collection of Verona cod. LX (*EOMIA* i. 645–53). Hilary alone gives the synod's letter to Pope Julius (CSEL 65. 126–39; tr. Wickham 47–50); but the Verona codex (fo. 80[b]) preserves a text of another important letter to Pope Julius (addressed as 'bonitas tua, frater dilectissime'), from Ossius and Protogenes of Serdica; though defective and lacunose, the general sense is not obscure, and clearly refers to the statement of faith preserved in Theodoret and the Verona manuscript, vindicating its authenticity.[6]

---

[6] Ballerini text in PL 56. 840; Turner, *EOMIA* i. 644, edits with an unnecessary transposition. Both editions mark a lacuna. An improved edition is by M. Tetz, *ZNW* 76 (1985), 247–51 with good discussion. Ulrich, *Anfänge*, 103, 159 ff. draws attention to Phoebadius of Agen (Aquitaine), who in 358 wrote against Arians, defending the Nicene creed and a single hypostasis and admiring

The authors are anxious to offer reassurance to Julius that there is no intention to replace the Nicene creed, the sanctity and unique authority of which was evidently affirmed by some bishops in the western synod, perhaps with a fervour which Ossius himself did not quite share. (It is important to recall that this synod did not have a majority of Latin speakers.) Sozomen 3. 12. 5–6 neatly summarizes the purport of the letter. But new questions have been raised about the Son: for example, if truly 'begotten', must he not be posterior to and dependent on the will of the Father, even if time is not involved? To be begotten implies a beginning. It is axiomatic that anything which has a beginning must at some point find an end. The thesis the western synod has to answer is therefore that the differentiation between 'begotten' and 'made' is merely verbal, and to rebut this requires some supplement to or clarification of the Nicene formula on which Rome is determined to stand.[7]

The western synod's theology

The western statement of faith attempts to analyse this problem. The argument needing to be met is that, since time comes into being with the creation of the world, both the generation of the Son and the creation are pre-temporal acts of God, but nevertheless whatever is derived is not on the level of its cause. Valens and Ursacius, the Pannonian bishops, are 'two vipers born from an Arian asp', who make claim to be Christians and yet maintain that the Logos and the Spirit suffered in the crucifixion. Since they are singled out as disciples of Arius, it is probable that they issued some doctrinal document justifying their objectionable association with the eastern bishops: they argued that it is axiomatic that the Father is impassible, Son and Spirit are separate hypostases, passible and so at a lower level. The western bishops disclaim belief that the Father is Son, or the Son Father; the Son is the power of the Father. He is both the Only-begotten as divine and the Firstborn of all creation as man (an echo of Marcellus). 'We do not deny that the Father is greater than the Son (John 14: 28), yet not because the Son is a different hypostasis but because the name of Father is greater than that of Son.' Direct attack rejects the affirmation of the Dedication Council of Antioch that the unity of the three hypostases ('I and my Father are one') lies in agreement of

Ossius for his intransigence for Nicaea at Serdica, though not holding the Nicene formula to be the exclusive necessary criterion of orthodoxy.

[7] The issues are well clarified by S. G. Hall, 'The Creed of Sardica', *Studia Patristica*, 19 (1989), 173–84. See also the important paper by M. Tetz in *ZNW* 76 (1985), 243–69, and the substantial consideration in Ulrich, *Anfänge*, 26–109. It is perhaps food for thought that Basil of Caesarea, who was reluctantly pushed into affirming that a supplement on the Holy Spirit was a necessary addition to the Nicene creed, never appeals to the precedent of the Serdican text. But that can be explained by recalling that western Serdica was for one hypostasis while Basil was for three.

will. To the west that seems blasphemy. So also is the idea that the Holy Spirit in Christ suffered; the mortal man suffered, not God. He rose the third day 'not God in the man but the man in God.'

This statement of faith defends Marcellus. In western eyes the eastern bishops too hastily condemn what he merely suggested as questions for consideration; and he never said that Christ's kingdom will come to an end (a proposition of which readers of Marcellus must feel hesitant). More of a problem lay in Marcellus' thesis that scriptural language about Christ's birth refers not to a pre-existent generation before all ages but to the incarnation of Mary. In eastern eyes that was to deny that the Son is 'begotten' before all ages.

One hypostasis or three?

The western bishops insist, with an unambiguous fortissimo, that Father, Son, and Spirit are a single hypostasis, with the gloss: 'which the heretics themselves call *ousia*'. If this is correctly transmitted, this cannot be the earliest attestation of the use of *ousia* to describe the unity of Godhead side by side with three hypostases for the Trinity. More probably the western bishops are deducing from the treatment of *ousia* and hypostasis as simple synonyms, as in the Nicene anathema, that the 'Arians' would be teaching three *ousiai* or essences. Marcellus had found this language in Narcissos of Neronias (Eus. *c. Marc.* 1. 4. 39). But the clause might be a marginal gloss that has crept into the text at an early stage. In 362 at the council of Alexandria representatives of Paulinos of Antioch, presiding over the ultra-Nicene congregation loyal to the memory of Bishop Eustathius of Antioch, defended their insistence on 'one hypostasis' of both Father and Son by appealing to the council of Serdica. Athanasius denied that the council had ruled to this effect. He may have left Serdica before the western statement of faith was finalized. His assertion is wholly insufficient ground for denying the authenticity of the statement of 342, though that opinion has enjoyed support from eminent scholars such as H. M. Gwatkin, Gustave Bardy, and H. J. Sieben. It is also an unlikely possibility that the statement of faith did not constitute a formal part of the synodical letter. By 362 'one hypostasis' was disastrously embarrassing to Athanasius' ecumenism.

At the council of Serdica in 342 the western synod had to disavow the Sabellianism for which their language provided obvious cover, and which had been a central accusation against Marcellus in the work of Eusebius of Caesarea. The weakest point in their statement is the proposition that Father and Son are distinct insofar as their names differ. That again was Marcellus' terminology. It is impossible to determine the relative contributions of Greek and Latin speakers to the composition of the Serdican manifesto. A principal concern had to be the justification of their vindication of Marcellus whose influence on the text is obvious, and if one recalls the fact that this council was effectively the first occasion on which Latin-speaking bishops in any numbers had been confronted by the problems of Trinitarian theology, perhaps the imprudences should not be too censoriously treated. Their learning curve must have been steep.

Excommunications

The eastern bishops declared in their encyclical that they could no longer hold communion with Pope Julius, Ossius of Corduba, Protogenes of Serdica, Gaudentius of Naissus (Niš) with whom Athanasius had stayed on his circuitous route back to Alexandria in 337, and Maximin of Trier, all of whom had accepted Athanasius and Marcellus to fellowship, thereby grossly insulting eastern councils. Ossius was held in the deepest admiration by the western bishops, and therefore had to be the target of a vehement attack, notably for being a close friend of a Bishop Paulinus; the text says he was a bishop of Dacia, but since his magic books were burnt by a bishop of Mopsuestia, Macedonius, an emendation of Dacia to nearby Adana is tempting though perhaps not necessary. Paulinus is described as now living in open apostasy with a bunch of concubines and harlots, an inappropriate intimate friend for the western president of the synod.

The western council addressed important letters to Julius of Rome and to the eastern emperor Constantius. Pope Julius is assured that his reasons for absenting himself are honourable; evidently some criticism of his non-attendance had been voiced. Greeks could have thought it arrogant. The bishops think it fitting and right that every province can report to the head (*caput*), 'that is to the see of the apostle Peter' (CSEL 65. 127. 4), a sentence which anticipates terms next met in Pope Innocent I (402–17) and foreshadows their canonical proposal for Rome to have a role in appeals against unsatisfactory synodical decisions (below). Special attention is paid to the 'irreligious immature Valens and Ursacius'. Valens of Mursa in particular had caused disorder by attempting to oust Bishop Viator of Aquileia, who was trampled to death by a mob. Aquileia was a far more important city than Mursa, and the mosaic floor of the main church (still extant) was an exquisite masterpiece. The see was desirable and central.

The western council declared excommunicate not only Valens and Ursacius but also Theodore of Heraclea, Narcissus of Neronias, Acacius of Caesarea (Eusebius' successor and admirer), Stephen of Antioch, Menophantos of Ephesus, and George of Laodicea who, it was alleged, was too scared to attend and had long ago been degraded by Alexander of Alexandria with Arius. The replacements of Athanasius and Marcellus, Gregory at Alexandria and Basil at Ankyra, were pronounced not to be valid bishops at all.

Constantius is begged to stop the afflicting of catholic orthodox churches, and to enact that provincial governors should not have any part in cases against clergy. All in his realm will enjoy 'sweet liberty' when governors cease to favour heretics and exiled bishops are reinstated. The letter concludes by listing the Arian heretics excommunicated by the western council. The plea for exempting clergy from courts under the aegis of provincial governors is an early step on the path to the establishment of special ecclesiastical courts to hear such cases.

Western canons

The western synod agreed on a series of canons determined by the historical context of the controversy. These are transmitted in Greek and Latin, and probably the diffusion at Serdica was bilingual. Although the Greek text of the canons can be proved to be translated from a Latin original, nevertheless the Greek text preserves more of the directness of the discussion than the Latin, which has undergone some subsequent revision. The bishops are against translating bishops from see to see, for 'none is known to move from a major city to a minor place, and it is obviously mere avarice and ambition'. Censure is passed on those who accept excommunicate clergy, but those persecuted for their true faith are an exception. Ossius was much against the elevation of baptized laymen to be bishops without manifesting their proved worth by their service as presbyters and deacons. A canon deplores the habit of north African bishops badgering the court with petitions for secular causes.

In view of the eastern breach with Julius and the refusal of the Eusebians to acknowledge his authority as successor of St Peter, an important canon brings the Roman see into the appeals process. Ossius proposed that in the case of one bishop having a grievance against another, his appeal should first go to the bishops of his province. If he then appeals against them, the see of Peter is to determine if the provincial verdict is to be upheld. If not, the Roman bishop is to appoint judges to sit with the bishops in a neighbouring province. (Perhaps if that verdict remains unsatisfactory, the aggrieved bishop can go to Rome and the bishop of Rome can nominate presbyters as legates to join the judges; but that is uncertain.) The canons reflect different stages of discussion at the synod with Ossius and Gaudentius of Naissus making varied suggestions. The canons about the appeal procedure are remarkable both for their introduction of the Roman see in exceptional circumstances and for their maintenance of the provincial council as the normal court to which appellants are to go. Moreover, it is assumed that the bishop of Rome first becomes involved when the appellant goes to him; apparently he is not expected to take the initiative. That is analogous to the procedure in civil cases with a provincial governor. However, Julius had invited Athanasius to come to him (Athan. *Apol. c. Ar.* 29, insists on the point, suggesting that some controversy attached to it). Some of the language in the appeal canons shows that the bishops were influenced, as one would expect, by secular legal procedure, illustrated in CTh 11. 30.

Two canons (19–20 Greek; 23–24 Latin, Turner 530–1) record a schism at Thessalonica. Gaudentius asks Bishop Aetius to recognize the validity of orders bestowed by Musaeus and Eutychianus, but this is inconsistently qualified by Ossius urging that neither of these two can be recognized as bishops and that they may be admitted only to lay communion. The church's problems in the city are not explicitly connected with Protogenes' accusations against Aetius' too colourful private life, of which the Oriental synod's letter made some capital. But it would be easy to suppose that Musaeus and Eutychianus were rivals who had owed their followings to local indignation with Aetius and his too devoted women adherents. It may be instructive that when Aetius speaks in the synod, he makes no reference to the schism, but only to the difficulty that too many presbyters and deacons from other churches migrate to Thessalonica and wish to stay there (canon 13 Latin, 16 Greek, Turner 526). Evidently the popularity of the city gave the bishop financial problems.

In the Roman chancery the canons of Serdica were transcribed in a codex following the canons of Nicaea. Later they were cited by popes as having Nicene authority, which led to embarrassment, especially when popes of the fifth century were insistent that the only canons Rome recognized were those of Nicaea. Innocent I (*ep.* 7. 3) could declare that he absolutely rejected the canons of Serdica. In the ninth century Pope Nicolas I and his legates to Constantinople claimed the Serdican canon on Rome's appellate jurisdiction to be unlimited and to justify a papal initiative in deciding who was legitimate patriarch of New Rome. The Greek version of the Serdican canons first entered eastern canon law in the mid-sixth century with the canonist John Scholasticus. Thereafter they were treated with respect, and enjoyed credit in the canons of the council *in Trullo* of 692. However, they were still regarded as the work of a western council without binding authority for the Greek churches, which were free to cite them when helpful.[8]

Both the rival councils produced Paschal cycles for the dates of Easter. The eastern table for the years 328–58 is preserved by the Verona codex LX, edited by Turner, *EOMIA* i. 641–3. The dates suggest that it had been prepared soon after 325 to implement the negative decision at Nicaea in 325.

---

[8] See Hamilton Hess, *The Canons of the Council of Sardica* (Oxford, 1958); a revised edition is forthcoming. Corrections to the 1958 edition are noted by K. Schaeferdiek in *Zeitschrift für Kirchengeschichte*, 70 (1959), 152–5. The western canons in Greek and Latin in Turner, *EOMIA* i. 489–531; episcopal signatories 546–559. The canons say nothing about Easter.

The cycle also has the dates of the Jewish passover for 26 years to 343. This Jewish material relates to Antioch. It was first edited by E. Schwartz in 1905.[9] The dates given are those for full moons in March or April, not Easter Day which would have fallen on the following Sunday.

The western table covered fifty years (so the Athanasian Festal Index) and was motivated by desire to bind Rome and Alexandria to a common date for Easter; this had not always occurred, but now the two churches had need to agree. In practice they differed about the spring equinox before which Easter was ruled out; at Alexandria this was dated on 21 March, at Rome (ideally) on 25 March. Moreover, at Rome desire was strong to avoid Easter on or later than 21 April which already had a longstanding civic celebration of the city's foundation, the Parilia, unsuitable competitor for people's attention at a time holy for Christians[10] At the time of the council of Serdica Alexandria still had Gregory, a bishop with no desire to compromise with Julius of Rome. In 346 and 349 Athanasius compromised with Rome; he needed unity there.

The council of Serdica was spectacularly unsuccessful in its intended purpose of reconciling the alienated east and west; the western statement of faith was not without problematic influence during the next two decades. Disagreements on the doctrine of the Trinity and on Roman jurisdiction had become dangerously exacerbated. Athanasius had needed a large council of ecumenical standing which could agree on the cancellation of the negative decision at Tyre seven years earlier. The profound split between east and west together with the continued survival of the sick bishop of Alexandria, Gregory, deprived Athanasius of any chance of untroubled return to his see at least for the time being. For the emperor Constans the outcome was not bad since it reinforced his determination to put even stronger pressure on his colleague and brother Constantius, whose submissiveness to western power in both church and state during the next few years became striking.

For the Illyrians Valens and Ursacius the polarization at Serdica had disastrous consequences. At Milan they submitted a disavowal of 'Arian' notions of a time when there was no Son or that he was created out of nothing. Soon (347) they had to sign for Julius an abject apology to the effect that their accusations against Athanasius were false, that they willingly accepted communion with Athanasius in return for Julius' pardon, and that if any eastern bishops, or Athanasius himself, brought a legal action against them, they would not appear in court without Julius' consent. Constantine and his successors enacted severe penalties for defamation (CTh 9. 34; CSEL 65. 143; tr. Wickham 55).

---

[9] *Jüdische und christliche Ostertafeln* (Abhandl. Akad. Göttingen). See Sacha Stern, *Calendar and Community* (Oxford, 2001).

[10] CIL I (ed. 2) p. 314 'Roma cond(ita) coronatis omnibus.' In 444 Prosper's chronicle records that under pope Leo I Rome celebrated its birthday (*natalis*), i.e. on 21 April, without the customary circuses (Mommsen, *Chronica Minora*, i. 479), Easter being on the 23rd.

Scandal at Antioch

After the shock of Serdica there was an ominous quiet while the two sides wondered how peace could be achieved. In 344 Constans sent legates to Constantius at Antioch: Vincent of Capua, Euphratas of Cologne, and, significantly, a very senior army officer, a Christian named Salia (*PLRE* i 796). No doubt Salia was there to make a point about Constans' military readiness. A stupid scandal shamed the church of Antioch. Bishop Stephen had a presbyter who set out to discredit the western bishops by a method then common in local politics, namely he introduced a prostitute into the lodging of Bishop Euphratas. Stephen was held responsible for the outrage and was replaced as bishop by Leontius. The scandal weakened the eastern stand of offended moral rectitude upheld at Serdica (Athanasius, *Hist. Ar.* 20–1; Theodoret, *HE* 2. 7–8; Sozo. 3. 20).

The eastern bishops returning from Serdica had adopted a stern line towards any in Constantius' realm who expressed opposition to their stand. Athanasius (*Hist. Ar.* 18) tells of ten lay workers in an imperial armaments factory at Adrianople who refused to hold communion with them and suffered for their opposition by being beheaded. Other bishops in Thrace also suffered exile and execution on false charges. Two priests and three deacons were exiled from Alexandria to Armenia, and measures were taken to prevent Athanasius reentering his city. Such actions were no way to allay the hostility of Constans towards his brother in the East.

Synod of Milan

In 345 at a synod in Milan legates from the east (Eudoxius of Germanicia (Cilicia), Martyrius, Demophilus of Beroea, Macedonius of Mopsuestia) came with a long exposition of the so-called fourth creed of Antioch and its important anathema intended to reassure the west of eastern orthodoxy while safeguarding their stance against Marcellus and Arius. The lengthy statement denies the attribution to the Greeks of opinions attributed to Arius, who is not named: that the Son is created out of nothing, or is of a different hypostasis from the Father. Nor was there a time before the Son came to be, for he is begotten timelessly, yet not without a beginning from the Father. The Father's higher position is clear from 1 Cor. 11: 3 'The head of Christ is God'. Eastern theology does not believe in three Gods when it affirms three entities (*pragmata*) or three *prosopa*. Marcellus had vehemently rejected this pluralist terminology (Eus. *Eccl. theol.* 2. 19. 15; *c. Marc.* 1. 4. 41). It is important to affirm that as God Christ pre-existed his earthly birth or we end with Paul of Samosata. Christ is 'perfect and true God by nature', not a man promoted to be divine. A frontal attack, therefore, inveighs against

Marcellus of Ankyra and his former deacon Photinus (who had lately become bishop of Sirmium, metropolis of Pannonia, an election probably consequential on the Roman defence of Marcellus and approved by Constans); they deny Christ's pre-existence, his deity, and his endless kingdom. A polemic against terms found in Marcellus (Eus. *Eccl. theol.* 1. 17. 7) attacks the view that the Logos of God is merely the immanent reason or expressed speech of the Father; he is the living divine Logos who exists in himself, i.e. is distinct. To him the Father addressed the words 'Let us make man in our image and likeness'. They believe him to be in every respect like the Father (*kata panta homoion*, a phrase found in Athanasius). Accordingly, they hold no communion with (*a*) those called Patripassians by the west and Sabellians by the east who say that the Trinity are the same and a single entity (*pragma*) and *prosopon*, since they make the impassible Father to become passible by the incarnation; (*b*) those who deny the Son to be begotten by the Father's will, attributing to God involuntary necessity, which is contrary to both natural theology and scripture. The east does not understand 'begotten' to mean the same as 'created'. When they say that the Son exists in himself, as the Father does, they are not separating him from the Father, putting physical distance between their conjunction (*synapheia*, a term used of the Trinity by Eusebius of Caesarea); nor do they believe in two Gods but in one with an exact agreement (probably directed against the western Serdican attack on this theme). At the same time the Son is subordinate to the Father. The statement ends by a disavowal of superfluity or ambition; they have written to clear the minds of those who have suspicions of their language, and to assure all in the west of their scriptural faith. (Ath. *Syn.* 26; Socrates 2. 19; summary in Soz. 3. 11.)

The statement is remarkable for its deliberate, careful avoidance of 'three hypostases'. The authors will have become aware that in Latin this would appear as 'tres substantiae' and seem radically tritheistic. Probability lies with the opinion that this omission was motivated by their express wish to make peace with the west.

A letter from Julius' successor Pope Liberius addressed to Constantius about 353–4 includes the information that at Milan the bishops from the east were directly asked if they would condemn the heretical opinion of Arius, and refused, walking out in anger (*Letter Obsecro*, CSEL 65. 91; tr. Wickham 73). Perhaps there was suspicion that while they had denounced Marcellus, they had said no word aganst Arius. Or had some theologian at Milan objected to their statement's clever defence of the anathema against the opinion that there was a time when the Son was not, justified on the ground that time first came into being with the creation of the world, yet maintaining that the begottenness of the Son presupposes his beginning to be? And their explanation of the unity of Father and Son as 'agreement', as in the second creed of the Dedication Council of Antioch and expressly rejected by western Serdica, is likely to have been given hostile scrutiny. Moreover, the Nicene creed had been given no enthusiastic acclaim, and for Rome and the west this creed had become the crucial litmus paper for the presence of orthodoxy or heresy. To be critical of its openness to Sabellian interpretation, of which Marcellus was a living demonstration, was to be labelled as 'Arian'.

33

RELIGIOUS DIVISION:
A NOTE ON INTOLERANCE

The language of mutual condemnation used by the two rival synods at Serdica was strong. There was no inclination on either side to make concessions or to plead for mutual toleration on some such ground as the transcendent mysteriousness of the matters on which east and west were expressing disagreement. Moreover, the western bishops were in a substantial degree the instruments of Constans' ambitions to be rid of his brother Constantius II and to rule the entire empire in the manner of his father, not merely two-thirds of it. Underlying the dispute was an emperor's aspiration to control the east as he was already master of the west. At the same time there was a looming tension between the Roman claim that the bishop of Rome had a unique authority to decide dogmatic and indeed any church questions without needing to be respectful towards synods of the eastern churches and, on the other hand, the Greek assumption that the Roman see was certainly to be respected but should never overrule the customary procedures and synodical authority of Greek assemblies. Naturally it was non-controversial that in questions of fundamental doctrine the eastern and western churches were and at all times needed to be in complete agreement. There might, of course, be room for discussion on the question of defining 'fundamental'. That issue once surfaces in Origen, but did not become prominent until the Pelagian controversy of the fifth century and then only briefly.

The internal dissensions of the Christians offered strong contrast with the peaceful rapprochement of Church and Empire that the Constantinian dynasty (other than Julian) wanted to encourage. That programme of reconciliation derived impetus and drive from the Christian aspiration to be the one faith of every nation and tribe under heaven. A missionary determination to make proselytes underlay the Church's gospel. Constantine the Great had thought this a profoundly congenial imperial theme, since he could use monotheism to justify his own supreme rule (as in Eusebius' panegyric *On the Life of Constantine*). He liked to be told that he was the representative on earth of the unique supreme Deity. When people commonly called the empire by the name *oikoumene*, the inhabited world, it could seem natural to the emperor, though no longer a god, to believe himself the plenipotentiary of the supreme being. Constantine's relationship with the Persian emperor illustrates the attitude. The penalties for dissent, which have appeared painfully intolerant to post-Enlightenment historians, were imposed as a consequence of this imperial ideology. Bishops had no power to exile anybody; that was a decision which lay with the emperor and, under him, with praetorian prefects.

The political rapprochement was probably facilitated by the intellectual harmonization of Christianity and Platonism that had enjoyed its most powerful statements from Justin, Clement of Alexandria, and Origen, and which was soon to be freshly articulated by Augustine. Platonism, especially in its new Plotinian dress, became the dominant philosophy not only in the Greek world but also in the Latin west. Of course there were reservations insofar as Platonic philosophers used monotheistic terms but did not suppose that this excluded them from offering a cock to Asclepios in gratitude for a cure (as in the probably ironic statement of Socrates at the end of the *Phaedo*) or from taking part in a popular pagan festival because that identified them with the rest of society. Numerous philosophers were sceptical about the value of temple sacrifices and cultic rituals, but did not want to initiate a social revolution by proposing alternatives. Porphyry had a theology with close affinities to the Christian faith that he deplored and to which earlier in life he may have felt strong attraction. In his eyes the animal sacrifices that lay at the heart of most pagan cult could only be welcome to inferior powers. Despite the affinity between Porphyry's religious position and Christianity, he warmly supported the great persecution of 303. The paganism of the old empire was in no sense tolerant. It was not experienced as such.

In the bazaar of cults and creeds in ancient society the Christians stood apart by virtue of their gospel being addressed to anyone and everyone irrespective of their class or ethnic origin or education. They took monotheism, as a Jew like Philo of Alexandria did, as necessarily involving a negative judgement on the veneration of other deities, though Philo explicitly qualified his stand by warning his Jewish readers against insulting heathen gods. We meet comparable cautions in Augustine, who would admonish his people that they could never cure their neighbours of pagan attachments merely by smashing their idols (*sermo* 62. 17); first they must change a mental attitude. To destroy pagan shrines was simply to leave a legacy of sullen hatred and occasional outbreaks of ferocious anti-Christian rioting, the penalty and costs for which fell on the members of the town council who had failed to maintain order. It was to be another matter when near the end of the fourth century the emperor Theodosius I gave authority for the dismantling of pagan temples and the withdrawal of temple endowments, which were to be applied to the building of Christian basilicas. Augustine was well aware that Jews and pagans resented the emperor's edicts, but justified them as being like the severity with benevolent intention shown by a schoolmaster with erring pupils (*sermo* 62. 18). In his time paganism had a greater stronghold in hearts than in temples (*En. in Ps.* 98. 1), though the gods venerated in temples were mocked at the theatres (*c. Faustum* 12. 40).

By the end of the fourth century dismantled pagan temples were being refitted as Christian basilicas. Until Theodosius' legislation against pagan sacrifice, pagan cultic acts continued. In any event it was impracticable to suppress private veneration of household deities or to stop people burning incense before a statue or picture of their patron god or to wean peasants from old agrarian rites. At Carthage the great temple of the goddess Caelestis (a lady with an appetite for human sacrifice) continued to be operational for a time even after Theodosius' ban, but from 408 was used, with minimal alterations to the building, as a church, an adaptation which caused such profound offence and wrath to pagans attached to the old polytheistic cult that after about thirteen years Christians ceased to use the building.

Public pagan worship became a target, especially late in the fourth century, for violent attacks on temples and statues by mobs of excited Christians. In 386 Libanius pleaded for the survival of temples after a riot at Beroea in Syria (Aleppo) in which a cult statue was smashed.

In brief, the interpretation of monotheism that was becoming general under the emperors of the Constantinian dynasty involved a belief that the cultic rites of the old temples were actually a dangerous offence to the one true God, whose Decalogue in Exodus had laid down that there must be no compromise with the gods of the heathen. Therefore there was a moral indignation motivating a degree of intolerance at least towards the central pagan act of offering sacrifices. Among the pagans the consequence was a dangerous hatred and anger. Their tradition had regarded Christianity as 'superstitio', and they could not be delighted to find that Christians were describing their acts of worship by this derogatory term. No doubt there were physically strong Christians who regarded their spiritual duty as properly expressed in destructive assaults on statues of pagan deities, and whose intolerance was little underpinned by reasoned argument which would look like weakness. It would not have appeared proper obedience to conscience to treat pagan cults and symbols as matters of indifference or taste.

The observant Jews of the synagogue experienced a gradual increase in the volume of imperial restrictions on their customs. At Nicaea in 325 Constantine himself had already used immoderate language about the need for the date of Easter to be wholly emancipated from the Jews, who were held (not by all but by enough people) to be responsible for murdering the universal Messiah. There is, however, no evidence that Constantine imposed legal disabilities on his Jewish subjects. The late fourth and early fifth centuries after the legislation of Theodosius I saw the foundation laid for the marginalization of observant Jewish life in the medieval period.

The Jews and the Christians read the same scriptures. Jesus was a Jew as were the apostles and all the first Christian believers. But this did not make for peace and harmony. There were two rival bodies with different interpretative principles for the same body of sacred writings. An unpleasant heightening of tension resulted from the decision of the emperor Julian to annoy the Christians by agreeing to encourage (not it seems to fund from his treasury) the rebuilding of the Temple at Jerusalem. During his brief rule over the entire empire without a partner in authority the Jews were not discouraged from assaults on Christian basilicas, which the churches could not answer safely under this emperor. Human nature being what it is, after Julian's death in Mesopotamia in 363 the mood of toleration was strikingly absent, perhaps as part of the psychological reaction to humiliating defeat for the legions and a deeply discreditable peace surrendering much territory. (Themistius was to tell the next emperor Jovian that it had all been a great victory for the empire, which no one believed.) Yet both Justin and Tertullian had insisted that Jews and Christians were worshipping the same God; they differed in their interpretation of the scriptures. That was no minor matter.

In his reply to the Platonist Celsus, Origen had granted that there could be much sharp disagreement between different Christian groups, but for Origen that was a symptom of the seriousness of the matters at stake in the argument. Moreover, there was no profound and serious subject on which human beings found it easy to be unanimous. Respected philosophers were notorious for their dissensions. For the church historians naturally there could be no regrets about the controversies of the age which provided the meat for their books. Socrates in the middle years of the fifth century put it frankly: 'I should have no story to tell if the Church had remained free of division' (1. 18. 15). He agreed with the opinion of a Paphlagonian bishop that too many bishops wanted their personal and private agenda for the Church's teaching incorporated in the creeds approved by the synods which they attended (2. 40. 21).

For obvious social and political reasons the emperors consistently wanted unity and harmony, and combined a conviction that adherence to orthodoxy was important to avert celestial anger with a policy of strong measures to impose the maximum of coherence and unity in the Church of both east and west. They were in search of a majority view and therefore would send into exile bishops who endangered a more general consensus. To say that Christ closely resembled the Father but personally was not wholly identical with the Father would seem to Constantius II and to Valens a doctrine more likely to command the allegiance of a majority than the narrow terms of tough Nicene advocates like Athanasius, who in any event had still a blighted reputation for being a man of violence.

Bad trouble in the churches produced civic disorders in which people were hurt and buildings torched. The philosopher Themistius delivered a (lost) speech before the emperor Valens in which he advised the emperor not to be astonished by Christian disagreements, and to remember that pagans have 'more than three hundred distinct dogmas', i.e. opinions (Socrates 4. 32. 3). The sentence is perhaps an echo of some philosophical catalogue of opinions resembling a lengthy list which in the *City of God* Augustine was able to quote from Varro. Ancient doxographers were more interested in differences than in points of consensus. Themistius also delivered extant orations before the emperor Jovian and ten years later before his successor Valens, in which he commended toleration on the ground that the human mind had no capacity to penetrate the mystery of the divine realm. He told them that in religion coercion is useless, that they must respect freedom of conscience, and that there are 'many paths to God' (*or.* 5. 69A) who likes diversity. For just as differences in religion are pleasing to God, so also are different Christian sects.[1]

The argument was reminiscent of Symmachus' appeal to Gratian to restore the Altar of Victory in the Senate House (below, p. 366).

Socrates observed that assemblies at which the different parties debated their disagreements did not normally lead to solutions of the cause of schism, and made the divisions yet more contentious than before (5. 10. 10). Worst of all, sects not only disagreed with other groups, but experienced disputes within their own party (5. 10. 19; 5. 22. 31). Nevertheless, with his overt sympathies for the Novatianists Socrates found it heartwarming that, when a respected Novatianist bishop died, 'all groups were represented at his funeral' (7. 46. 1). Socrates was therefore particularly interested in the considerable differences of liturgical custom between the different churches of the Catholic and Orthodox great Church, differences which could happily continue without the least inclination to break off communion. Where he found consensus, he understood that to be a miraculous divine gift (6. 30. 5 and 8). At the same time he thought the emperor Theodosius I right not to be tolerant of the extreme Arian Eunomius (5. 20. 4).

The emperors needed persons of 'quality' to serve in major public offices. Such people had the right background and tradition of public service and therefore knew how to be good administrators of provinces, great cities like Rome and Constantinople, or the powerful offices of praetorian prefecture. And the fact that they owned considerable property made them more

---

[1] L. J. Daly, 'Themistius' Plea for Religious Toleration', *Greek, Roman and Byzantine Studies*, 12 (1971), 65–79.

vulnerable to disciplinary action if they turned out to have been unacceptably corrupt. It followed that the imperial court did not cease to make use of unconverted pagans as governors and prefects until well into the fifth and sixth centuries. By Justinian's time it had become an incentive to accept baptism, or at least to become a catechumen probably only intermittently attending church services, that thereby one ceased to be disqualified for high office.

34

ATHANASIUS' RETURN:
A WIND OF CHANGE

Dropping the cause of Marcellus

At Milan in 345 the eastern legates achieved material progress for their cause in that the western bishops assented to reject the opinions of Photinus of Sirmium. That considerably qualified the western Serdican defence of Marcellus of Ankyra, his former bishop, with which it was obviously incompatible. The legates could hardly feel able to accept the Serdican manifesto in favour of one hypostasis, which, for them, was closely associated with Marcellus' denial of Christ's divine pre-existence. There is no evidence surviving that the legates were asked to accept Athanasius back into their communion. But this was the demand put to Valens and Ursacius, and it is significant that, since there was no specific doctrinal accusation against Athanasius, the two Illyrians could concede this without any dogmatic surrender on their part. They simply apologized for not telling the truth. That was bound to appear more difficult for legates from Antioch; Athanasius had come to embody the role of the great divider of the empire and of the emperors' church, because of his refusal to share communion with those whom he called 'Arians'. He was well aware that they did not profess the doctrines condemned in the Nicene anathema. And before 350 he cannot be seen to be zealous for the Nicene term *homoousios*. Surprisingly he was well content to say 'like in essence' (e.g. *ep. ad episc. Aeg.* 17). His opponents did not attack the council of Nicaea (ibid. 18). Nor did they utter a word in defence of Arius (ibid. 10). But Athanasius characterized them as having no respect for 'the apostolic see of Rome, the metropolis of Romania' (*Hist. Ar.* 35), by which he had been acquitted. They were wrong to make charges against his conduct prior to the question of faith, echoing here the imperial agenda for the council of Serdica, a council which had bishops 'from all parts of the world'; and its western half had declared Athanasius innocent (36). Unfortunately it had also approved of Marcellus; and the installing of his disciple Photinus at the major see of Sirmium, seat of the prefecture of Illyricum, can only have been a source of sharp irritation at Antioch. That was taking the western synod of

Serdica seriously, and giving Constans his head. Photinus was well qualified and educated, fluent in Latin as well as in Greek. Probably like numerous other bishops in this age, he had been trained in rhetoric and law, and for all law schools Latin remained the primary language (much to the regret of the sophist Libanius, who lost pupils in consequence). Socrates (2. 30. 45) knew treatises by Photinus in both languages.

Athanasius given leave to return

Pressure from Constans, who cared generously for the churches (Athan. *Apol. ad Constantium* 7), helped Athanasius to return to Alexandria in 346. The rival bishop Gregory died in 345. Constantius wrote several letters inviting Athanasius to return, promising safe conduct. At first Athanasius was reluctant, fearing a trap. But eventually he decided to accept, and had an interview with Constantius, who assured him that an imperial decision, in the eyes of Syrian bishops, made it superfluous to require a conciliar appeal. In another context Constantius is quoted by Athanasius as saying 'Whatever I will, that is to be deemed a canon' (*Hist. Ar.* 34), which is illuminated by Ammianus' observation (23. 5. 18) that an emperor's privilege is that his will is law.[1] Accordingly, his return to his see would be ecclesiastically legitimate, but with the qualification that if the emperor alone could reinstate him, he could also remove him without a synod. Constantius declared that it had been decided 'by God and myself' (*Apol. c. Ar.* 54–5). In practice that was a pious circumlocution for Constans. Among Athanasius' opponents it would become a weapon that no eastern synod had reversed the verdict of Tyre (336), and once Constantius had become sole emperor he found it prudent to use episcopal synods to condemn Athanasius and not to act solely on imperial authority. Hilary of Poitiers was to write a book 'Against Valens and Ursacius' in which he interpreted Jesus' saying 'Render to Caesar . . .' (Luke 20: 25) to mean that while great reverence was due to emperors, nevertheless bishops must judge of ecclesiastical matters and it was wrong in principle for the emperor to appoint bishops (CSEL 65. 101, also 181 ff.).

Usurpation of Magnentius

The western emperor Constans encouraged high culture, inviting the Christian rhetor Prohaeresius to court (Eunapius, *Vi. Soph.* 10. 7. 492). Libanius (*ep.* 275) recalled his excellent education. Like Libanius, Constans

---

[1] The same axiom occurs in Dio Chrysostom 3. 43; Libanius, *or.* 50. 19, written in 384, maintains that an emperor has no power to do what is not morally right. Julian 49 D holds that while emperors are above the law, it is wise for them to act as if subject to it.

failed to conceal his lack of admiration for various senior army commanders, many of whom were now coming to be Germanic soldiers, and they came to think that they would do better without him. Catamites lost him respect. On 18 January 350 at Autun, army chiefs supported a bid for power by Magnentius, who was acclaimed by the troops as Augustus. Constans fled south towards the Pyrenees, but was overtaken and killed. He was hardly more than 27 years old. He had been a princely benefactor of the Church and a bulwark of papal honour.

Magnus Magnentius was of Germanic birth, and had risen to the rank of count, in command of substantial forces. He received unreserved support from the praetorian prefect in Gaul. In Mesopotamia Constantius' army had suffered a serious check from the Persians in 348 at Singara, though it was claimed as a victory, and probably Magnentius nursed hopes of getting rid of the other brother as well. He needed to move rapidly into Italy and take control of Danube provinces before Constantius could prevent that. He reckoned without the sense of family solidarity in surviving members of Constantine's dynasty (e.g. Julian 42 A). Constans' elder sister Constantina encouraged an army commander Vetranio in Pannonia to rebel and be proclaimed as Augustus. Constantius recognized Vetranio; he could then prevent Magnentius moving into his area. Meanwhile a second bid was made in Rome by Nepotianus, son of Constantius' half-sister Eutropia, acclaimed there as Augustus in June 350. His rule lasted a month before he was killed with his mother and other aristocratic friends, whose confiscated estates helped Magnentius to acquire the sinews of war.

Magnentius endeavoured to persuade Constantius to grant him recognition. He used bishops as ambassadors (Athan. *Apol. ad Const.* 9). He also sent a message to Athanasius at Alexandria hoping to enlist his support. It is also very possible that, after the death of Constans, Athanasius perceived that he might need Magnentius' protection against Constantius, and took the initiative of writing benevolently to the new sovereign of the west. This correspondence did not please Constantius, who regarded it as treasonable. Athanasius had to deny its genuineness. Perhaps the messages were discreetly oral. Whether written or oral, genuine or forged, what mattered in harsh reality was simply that Constantius believed the approach was authentic, and Athanasius' protestations were disbelieved. Initially hesitating whether to accept Magnentius out of fear of defeat, Constantius finally decided that the spirit of his father required war. With a substantial force he moved into the Balkans. Vetranio saw that he should not side with Magnentius after his troops made clear their allegiance to Constantius, and by persuasion he was removed from all office. The mystique attaching to Constantine the Great's progeny was an asset.

Synod at Sirmium (351)

The undermining of Photinus was renewed at Milan in 347 and then in 351 by a synod at Sirmium, where Photinus' heresy—in short the provocative opinions of Marcellus—was anathematized and he was declared deposed. The task of refuting Photinus' heresy was entrusted to Marcellus' replacement at Ankyra, Bishop Basil. Arbitration was entrusted to eight senior officials of the court, including Constantius' principal counsellor Datianus. The disputation is recorded by Epiphanius (*Panarion* 71) from the notes made by seven shorthand-writers producing three copies.

Athanasius preserves the creed (= Antioch IV) and anathemas derived from the long commentary of 344–5. Although Athanasius cites the text as further evidence of the inconstancy of the 'Arians', among whom, in oblique honour to Marcellus, he numbers Basil of Ankyra (*ep. ad episc. Aeg.* 8), the document is actually evidence of the solid consistency of the eastern programme. The synod was at Photinus' request while the emperor Constantius was wintering at Sirmium preparing for further battle with Magnentius. The majority of bishops present were Greeks unsympathetic to Marcellus, and no doubt the civil war made it hazardous for western bishops to travel to Sirmium to speak for Photinus had they wished to do so. Hilary of Poitiers reports that the removal of Photinus, made difficult by an enthusiastic local faction, was seen as a reversal of the Serdican acquittal of Marcellus with knock-on consequences for the Serdican judgement accepting Athanasius, at least in drawing attention to its precariousness (CSEL 65. 146; tr. Wickham 56–7). Photinus was replaced by Germinius from Cyzicus (Dardanelles).

Meanwhile the cause of Constantius was strengthened by representations sent to Germanic tribes inviting them to occupy land west of the Rhine so as to harass Magnentius' army in the rear, a move extremely unpopular with those already occupying the land. Fortunately for Constantius Persian attacks at that time were on no great scale and could be held without a massive defence. His young cousin Constantius Gallus was proclaimed Caesar and sent to Antioch with his wife Constantina, sister of Constantius II. A network of informers kept Constantius in touch with Gallus' activities there. After two disastrous years of corrupt government (his wife's erotic orgies forfeited all respect at Antioch) he was dismissed and executed.

By this time Constantius had disposed of Magnentius, their first confrontation being at Mursa in 351 where the loss of life on both sides was heavy. Magnentius consulted soothsayers. This was a godsend to Athanasius who could assure Constantius that he could not imaginably have supported a pagan usurper (*Apol. ad Const.* 7). Magnentius also allowed pagan nocturnal sacrifices, a permission withdrawn by Constantius in 353 (CTh 16. 10. 5); Magnentius was clearly bidding for support from rich pagan aristocrats much given to mantic arts. He needed money to finance his war; some unco-operative senators were executed (Socrates 2. 32. 4). During the battle of Mursa Constantius was being helped to pray for victory in a nearby church with Bishop Valens of Mursa. Valens and his friend Ursacius were thereafter to become influential with the emperor. So too was Basil of Ancyra. These bishops did not offer identical advice.

The death of Constans led some to warn Athanasius that he could not expect from Constantius the kind of support he had been receiving from the west. Constantius even wrote to reassure him that all would be well. But when the emperor was informed that Magnentius had approached him by letter and correspondence was produced, perhaps from captured papers of Magnentius, which Athanasius boldly rejected as forged, Athanasius was dis-believed. Blacklisted for this negotiation, he was still theologically suspect for his association with Marcellus at Rome and especially at Serdica. On his return to Alexandria he had wisely broken his link with Marcellus, who had become an albatross hanging about his neck. That was an act which ultra-orthodox critics did not admire (CSEL 65. 146–7). It seemed incompatible with the decisions at Serdica. Nevertheless he remained the stalwart defender of the Nicene creed against all who opposed it, lumped together as 'Arians'. To be in communion with him was the mark by which supporters of the Nicene creed were identified since he refused to be in communion with anyone who did not accept it.

Magnentius and Athanasius

Constantius pursued Magnentius into Gaul, where his enemy committed suicide (10 August 353). The poetess Proba, wife of the prefect of Rome Adelphius in office in 351 (*ILCV* 1850), composed a verse panegyric on Magnentius' defeat, probably designed to ensure favour for her husband if his loyalty was in doubt. Later she was to compose a Vergilian cento (extant) on the Creation and the life of Christ. The emperor's anger with Athanasius for having anything to do with Magnentius (which Athanasius passionately denied) now spilled over into sustained hostility. He still held Athanasius responsible for Constans' endeavour to impose western domination upon the Greek east, in which charge there was more than a grain of truth; Ammianus (21. 6. 2) records a secular influence also making for this alienation. Constantius proclaimed nominal amnesty for Magnentius' supporters, but Ammianus (14. 5) tells of the severity of tortures and executions meted out by his prosecutor to any associate or supporter of Magnentius, even when the case was no more than suspicion. In 353 at Arles Constantius celebrated the thirtieth anniversary of his imperial crown. In addition to his purge of trai-tors he held a council of Gallic bishops, fortified by Valens of Mursa and

Ursacius of Singidunum. They yielded to his requirement that they condemn Athanasius. An exception was Bishop Paulinus of Trier, who was therefore declared deposed and exiled and who, with the encouragement of his neighbour the praetorian prefect at Trier, could well have favoured Magnentius. The emperor was determined to destroy Athanasius' support in the Latin west and to use synods to this end. Athanasius (*Hist. Ar.* 52) came to realize that the emperor was cleverly claiming the authority of episcopal councils for achieving what he himself wished.

To be suspected of supporting a 'usurper' was to be in danger of death. Until he received a personal letter of reassurance from the emperor Theodosius I, in 388 Libanius was suspected of supporting the western bidder for power, Magnus Maximus, and expected to lose his life for treason (*or.* 32. 27; *ep.* 840). Maximus, a baptized pro-Nicene Christian, was not likely to be supported by a polytheist, for whom Christianity was a disaster. It was the reverse of Athanasius' exculpation.

Pope Liberius

Pope Julius died on 12 April 352, and the deacon Liberius was consecrated in May to succeed him, an office which took him into deep waters. A letter from the eastern bishops and Egypt had come to Rome full of charges against Athanasius. The change from Julius to Liberius may have led to the assumption or at least the hope that Julius' successor might listen better to Greek complaints. As Rome simultaneously had a letter from eighty Egyptian bishops denying the charges against Athanasius, Pope Liberius did nothing and then found himself accused of suppressing the documents, which in fact he had read both to his church and to an Italian council, then sending a reply to the eastern bishops. It is noteworthy that Liberius stresses his consultation of a synod before answering (Letter *Obsecro*, CSEL 65. 90, tr. Wickham 72). But he had probably taken his time about replying to Antioch. His letter to Antioch explained that he had summoned Athanasius to Rome, but he had refused and on that ground Liberius was no longer in communion with him (*Studens paci*, CSEL 65. 155, tr. Wickham 70). That was a startling departure from Julius' position. Liberius may have thought it the only way to reconcile east and west after the split of 342. Or he may have heard rumour of Athanasius being approached by Magnentius, and felt that a defence of one regarded as a traitor could be imprudent.

George bishop of Alexandria

The eastern synod at Antioch is reported by Sozomen (4. 8) to have been led by old opponents of Athanasius: Narcissus of Neronias, Theodorus of

Heraclea, Eugenius of Nicaea (present at eastern Serdica), Patrophilus of Scythopolis, Menophantus of Ephesus, and thirty others. Their encyclical complained that Athanasius' return to Alexandria had not been authorized by a synod, which implied indirect criticism of Constantius, and also announced that a new bishop had been consecrated for the see named George. George had been a well-to-do Christian in Cappadocia with a private library of remarkable richness, from which the young lad Julian, confined to the estate of Macellum near Caesarea, had been allowed to borrow. All bishops were asked to communicate with George, not with Athanasius. There were nasty rumours that his wealth had been obtained by embezzlement. George found his see exceptionally difficult, and for a time had to leave Alexandria. This could be a consequence of Constantius' cool attitude to the decisions of the synod at Antioch. He called Athanasius to an audience at Milan; but Athanasius was unwilling to go, probably because his opponents in his city were becoming a threat and to leave would be to make space for George. He sent five Egyptian bishops and three presbyters; to Athanasius' deep distress, Constantius was unwilling to receive them (*Historia acephala* 3). The Alexandrian situation could explain why his opponents accused him of celebrating the liturgy in the new church being built by Constantius, the Caesareum, before the building was completed (*Apol. ad Const.* 14, 19). He wanted to prevent others using it. The Index to the Festal Letters says that there was a riot in the city and Constantius' officer of state sent to summon Athanasius retreated without achieving his mission. At court Athanasius' stock was in free fall, and he and others had come to realize it.

Council of Arles

At the council of Arles Pope Liberius had two legates who, to his distress, were content to acquiesce in a condemnation of Athanasius but asked the synod to condemn the heresy of Arius; at first welcomed, the latter proposal did not go through. Valens and Ursacius did not want an intricate theological debate in territory with which Gallic bishops could not be familiar. Hilary of Poitiers expressly says that he had been a bishop for some years and was about to go into exile when he first heard of the Nicene creed (*Syn.* 91).[2] The emperor would not have placed Arius on the council's agenda. He mainly wanted a council to condemn on disciplinary grounds a bishop whom he suspected, perhaps with some reason, to have been all too interested in the success of Magnentius. Any who would not consent would be regarded as touched with treason and be sent into exile.

---

[2] Phoebadius, bishop of Agen (357–92) wrote an anti-Arian tract in 358 defending the Nicene creed interpreted as affirming one hypostasis with western Serdica. His writing was influential. See R. P. Hanson, *The Search for the Christian Doctrine of God* (Edinburgh, 1988), 516–19.

Council of Milan

The elimination of Magnentius, leaving Constantius supreme ruler of the entire empire, sent a clear message to Athanasius' opponents that the threat of western domination in the east, a factor influential in ecclesiastical policy since 340, was now at an end. Constantius was determined to ensure that the decisions at Arles were now extended in the west. At Milan in 355 a majority of a council yielded assent to the emperor's demand for excommunication of Athanasius. A handful of three brave dissenters preferred exile: Dionysius of Milan, Eusebius of Vercelli, and the Sardinian firebrand Lucifer of Cálaris (Cagliari), who eventually ended in upper Egypt. Lucifer wrote a pamphlet sent to Constantius explaining that the emperor was Antichrist, and that in the circumstances he felt sure the emperor would not take offence. He also petitioned the emperor to pardon Athanasius' indiscretion in the affair of Magnentius. Dionysius of Milan was replaced by a Cappadocian named Auxentius who had served Gregory of Alexandria as a presbyter and disliked the Nicene creed.

Constantius moves against Pope Liberius

Liberius wrote the three exiles a letter of encouragement. He vainly asked Constantius for a large revisionary synod at Aquileia. The emperor had decided that this bishop of Rome above all others must be constrained to yield. Both Athanasius and Ammianus interpret the emperor's thinking to be that this see had an aura of authority which would carry many waverers. Liberius had read the past letters in the Roman archives, and was convinced that Athanasius must be right that the faith of Nicaea and Constantine the Great was the real issue at stake. Constantius sent to Rome the eunuch high chamberlain Eusebius with rich presents for the Pope. (It was a common criticism of Constantius that he surrounded himself with eunuchs who were too powerful.) Liberius refused the gifts and was then angered to discover that they had subsequently been accepted in ignorance by clergy at St Peter's. He was aware that the issue had come to be a challenge not only to the council of Serdica but to the authority of Peter's see. He declared that he had done nothing to increase or diminish that authority (Letter *Obsecro*, CSEL 65. 91. 10; tr. Wickham 73).

A painful interview between Liberius and the emperor, reported by Athanasius, Sozomen, and Theodoret, has the feeling of a confessor's trial in the age of persecutions; Athanasius regarded all bishops who suffered by being in communion with him as martyrs and confessors. Theodoret and Sozomen use the same document, presented as a secretary's minute of a dramatic dialogue. It is difficult to think the detail authentic. Theodoret himself thought it the composition of devoted believers. The text portrays Constantius as resenting the damage done to himself by Athanasius' enlisting of Constans in his support—damage, he claimed, worse than the two usurpers Magnentius and Silvanus (executed in 355).

Ammianus (15. 7. 7–10) reports Liberius' firm refusal to condemn Athanasius at Constantius' bidding, on the strong legal ground that it was wrong to condemn someone who had not been in court to defend himself. As Liberius was popular in the city, he was kidnapped by night and exiled to Beroea in Thrace. There Bishop Demophilos, no admirer of the Nicene creed or of Athanasius, could be expected to explain to him the finer points of theology and the delinquencies of the bishop of Alexandria.

Felix replaces Liberius at Rome

As a replacement in the Roman see, archdeacon Felix was consecrated. He had previously shared in an oath of clergy that the see must remain vacant during Liberius' exile; Felix exchanged letters of communion with the eastern bishops at Antioch. Many laity at Rome did not want him. He had at least the good fortune that posterity treated him as the true, lawful, and orthodox bishop of Rome, while Liberius was to be regarded as an intruder. The *Liber Pontificalis* of the sixth century has a muddled and largely fictitious account of the story. Another fictional account of Liberius was produced with other forgeries about 501 during the dissensions in Rome about Pope Symmachus and his rival Laurentius (PL 8. 1388–93).

When after three years of exile Liberius returned to Rome, Felix was expelled from the city, attempted to return, and thereby precipitated severe street-fighting between rival supporters. He had to withdraw but left a divided community.

Hilary of Poitiers

In Gaul in 355 Hilary of Poitiers devoted his considerable ability to studying the theological aspects of the controversy underlying the decisions of Arles and Milan, and disliked what he learnt. He addressed a flattering but firm letter to Constantius protesting in favour of the Nicene formula and against Valens and Ursacius. With a few other Gallic bishops he withdrew communion from Saturninus bishop of Arles as the principal spokesman for the less specific theology supported by Constantius. Unfortunately for him his protest more or less coincided with a Gallic revolt led by a Frankish soldier Silvanus (Ammianus 15. 5), voicing extreme dissatisfaction at the way in which lands in Gaul were ravaged by barbarians from the east, many being encouraged by the policy of Constantius to embarrass Magnentius. The revolt was suppressed with Silvanus' execution. At a synod at Béziers (Baeterrae) in 356 Hilary was accused, falsely he protested, perhaps on suspicion of supporting Silvanus, and was exiled to Phrygia.

Meanwhile Constantius was increasingly suspicious of being surrounded by smiling treachery, and two years later intelligence about pagan high officials consulting oracles to discover who would be the next emperor led to bitterly cruel treason trials at Scythopolis in Palestine (Ammianus 19. 12; several victims were known to Libanius). In the fourth century, people who were hostile to divination other than by dreams could nevertheless fear that an oracle might be correct in its predictions and could be serious. A horoscope composed as a practical joke might contain a forecast that turned out to be true. It should not be ignored.[3] It was an age when a priest could be asked by someone to say a requiem, just as pagans would make an offering at a temple, to bring about the death of a rival or adversary (Petronius, *Sat.* 88; Augustine, *sermo* 90. 3). So Constantius was a man of his time in fearing people consulting soothsayers or oracular predictions with sinister intention. Christian conquest of witchcraft was a gradual process.

Constantius at Rome

The division at Rome during his exile alarmed Liberius, and naturally both he and his Roman followers desired his return for the sake of peace and unity. In April 357 Constantius made a visit to Rome with high solemnity which Ammianus in an ironical and cutting account (16. 10) described as exaggerated pomposity. It was designed to celebrate his triumph over Magnentius, though his opponent's defeated soldiers were legions of the Roman army and he himself had been nowhere near the front line of battle. He was also celebrating the twentieth anniversary of his father's death in 337. Other cities sent representatives and golden crowns. The philosophic orator Themistius (*or.* 3) spoke for New Rome, saluting the emperor in a now less distinguished old Rome which, he felt sure, had given no support to Magnentius. (One may deduce that there were stories to the contrary.) The emperor preserved an impassive countenance and at no point was seen to spit or wipe his nose and mouth. The majesty of old Rome moved him deeply. A month of games and public entertainment passed. He erected in the Circus Maximus the obelisk which today stands by St John Lateran. Strangely the inscription (*ILS* 736), lauding Constantius as 'lord of the world', records that it was originally intended for Constantinople. He addressed the senate, but had the pagan

---

[3] *Anthologia Palatina* 9. 158; Augustine, *Gen. ad litt.* 12. 22. 46 f.; cf. 2. 17. 37. See *RAC*, art. Horoskop. Underlying the belief that even a bogus horoscope could be true was the widespread ancient conviction of a hidden cosmic sympathy.

Altar of Victory removed for the occasion (Ambrose, *ep.* 73 Maurist edn. [M.] 18. 32). This and his generally anti-pagan policy could not have pleased the pagan senatorial aristocrats of the city, and after the visit his relations with some of them were certainly not relaxed. The support of courtiers was obtained by simply conveying to them the emperor's property-rights over temples (Lib. *or.* 30. 38).

Firmicus Maternus

A vehement attack on paganism had been written in Rome about 347 by a converted astrologer, Firmicus Maternus from Sicily. His Latin handbook on astrology called *Mathesis*, composed before conversion, is a major treatise on an intricate subject. His post-conversion treatise 'On the error of profane religions' asks the emperors to be relentless in merciless extirpation of polytheism. (Augustine was to urge that pagans could be converted only by persuasion, not by force.) The work is an important source of information about oriental mystery-cults. It could have influenced Constantius.[4] The author evidently thought that the suppression of pagan cult was what the emperor wanted.

During Constantius' stay in Rome,[5] eminent ladies among Liberius' supporters submitted a petition asking for the exiled bishop's restoration. They were assured that they would have him back 'better than he was before' (*Libellus precum*, Coll. Avell. 1. 3, CSEL 35, 2). The following year saw Liberius back in Rome, but on awkward conditions. He was generally understood to have surrendered Rome's authoritative endorsement of the Nicene creed. If so, this would prove consistent with his controversial policy of full acceptance of western bishops who in 359 at Ariminum were surrendering the Nicene formula for the weaker affirmation of 'likeness' (below p. 284). But return to his church was vital if schism was to be scotched. To the Roman ladies Constantius had suggested that both Felix and Liberius should share in the episcopate at Rome. This provoked a cry 'One God, one Christ, one bishop' (Theodoret, *HE* 2. 17. 6).

---

[4] *Mathesis* ed. W. Kroll and F. Skutsch, 2 vols. (Stuttgart, 1968), Eng. tr. J. R. Bram (Park Ridge, NJ, 1975). *De errore profanarum religionum*, ed. K. Ziegler (Leipzig, 1953) or R. Turcan (Paris, 1982); Eng. tr. C. A. Forbes (New York, 1970).

[5] R. O. Edbrooke, 'The visit of Constantius to Rome', *American Journal of Philology*, 97 (1976), 40–61. An exception among the Roman senators, of whom at this time few were Christians, was Junius Bassus (*PLRE* i 155), prefect of Rome, who was baptized on his deathbed; he died in office in 359, and was commemorated with an exquisite sarcophagus now in the museum at St Peter's. Pictures in W. F. Volbach, *Early Christian Art* (London, 1961) pls. 41–5; E. Malbon, *The Sarcophagus of Junius Bassus* (Princeton, 1991).

'The blasphemy of Sirmium'

After leaving Rome in 357 Constantius had gone towards the Danube where barbarian raids were causing trouble. His tour ended at Sirmium, the metropolis of Illyricum. There a small conference of important bishops met: Valens of Mursa, Ursacius of Singidunum, Germinius of Sirmium, the non-agenarian Ossius of Corduba, Potamius of Lisbon. After a lengthy and careful discussion of the disagreements about faith, they issued a statement of what seemed obvious. Everyone agreed that there is one almighty God and Father, one Son Jesus Christ our saviour begotten before the ages; but no one can or should preach two Gods for the Lord said 'I go to my Father and to your Father, to my God and to your God' (John 20: 17). So there is one God of all (Rom. 3: 29–30). On the other articles of faith there was no disagreement. But no one should use the term *substantia*, which the Greeks call *ousia*; that is to put it bluntly, either *Homoousion* or *Homoiousion* of identical or similar essence. For these terms are absent from scripture; they upset people; they make assertions beyond human knowledge, for scripture says 'Who can declare his generation?' (Isa. 53: 8). It is obvious that only the Father knows how he begat his Son, and only the Son knows how he was begotten by the Father. There is no ambiguity that the Father is greater (John 14: 28) in honour, dignity, splendour, majesty, indeed in the very name 'Father'. No one is ignorant that it is catholic to affirm two 'persons' of Father and Son, the Father greater, the Son subordinate with all that the Father subordinated to him. The Father has no beginning, is invisible, immortal, impassible, whereas the Son is begotten of the Father, God from God, light from light. The Son's generation none can know except his Father. The Son of God, our Lord and God (John 20: 28), took flesh and body, that is man, from the virgin Mary's womb, as the angel foretold. All scriptures and especially the teacher of the Gentiles, the Apostle, teach that he took the man from the Virgin Mary, and that through the man he shared in suffering. That the Trinity is always to be maintained is confirmed by that summary of all the faith in the gospel: 'Go and baptize all nations in the name of the Father and of the Son and of the Holy Spirit.' The number of the Trinity is whole and perfect. The Spirit, the Paraclete, is through the Son (*per filium*). He was sent and came according to the promise to instruct, teach, sanctify the apostles and all believers. (Hilary, *Syn.* 11; Greek in Athanasius, *Syn.* 29, Socrates 2. 30; Sozomen summarizes 4. 6. 9–10).

The statement reads as a list of self-evident scriptural truths, with each proposition buttressed by a biblical text. It is as if Potamius of Lisbon had insisted on some Atlantic fresh air in a stuffy debate. 'Two persons', even the subordination of the Son, had been good Latin theology since Tertullian's *Adversus Praxean*, and necessary for interpreting scripture where there appears to be heavenly dialogue between Father and Son. The statement is striking for not resembling a creed and for having no anathemas disavowing opinions ascribed to Arius or Marcellus. The intention of the statement is to further the cause of peace and unity in the wrangling and quarrelling churches. Like his father Constantine in his letter to Alexander and Arius, Constantius regarded the disputes as a cloudland of words of uncertain meaning. Nevertheless, the stress on the inferiority of the Son to the Father is strong. It was at once taken to be emphasizing how dissimilar the Son is from the Father, in whose transcendence he does not share. That was to pour fuel on the embers of dispute. This was the reverse of Constantius' intention.

The reception of the manifesto of Sirmium

In 357 from somewhere in hiding in Egypt Athanasius wrote for the monks a tempestuous attack on Constantius as Antichrist in person. In this incendiary and impassioned invective he tells how pressure was put on Ossius of Corbuba to agree to the condemnation of Athanasius, and how, when Ossius stood firm against this demand, he was taken to Sirmium and kept there for a year, though a hundred years old, by a new Ahab or Belshazzar, until he shared communion with Valens and Ursacius. He still declined to sign against Athanasius. Athanasius does not mention that on his return to Spain Ossius found bishops refusing to hold communion with him on the ground that he had compromised with heretics. That was also the opinion in Aquitaine.

In north Africa (Hilary, *c. Const.* 26, PL 10. 601 B) and Gaul the Sirmium manifesto was frowned upon. Phoebadius bishop of Agen wrote against it (PL 20. 13–30), full of admiration for all that Ossius had steadfastly believed for his first ninety years, sad at his abandonment of all this in his nineties. Hilary named it the 'blasphemy' of Sirmium (*Syn.* 10). He interpreted the statement to be denying the Son to be God because he cannot be said to possess the honour, dignity, splendour, and majesty of the Father, and to be affirming that the Son was born not of the Father but out of nothing. Hilary's last point makes the statement say something which it does not say. He assumed that any theological statement in which Valens and Ursacius had a hand must mean that the Son is a 'creature', and that between 'begotten' and 'created' there is no real difference. Phoebadius picked on the Sirmium statement's argument that in the humanity taken from Mary the Son of God shared in suffering, this implying that being inferior he cannot share in the Father's impassibility. The crux at Sirmium was the attempt to achieve harmony and consensus by forbidding the current use of unscriptural words, namely *homoousion* and *homoiousion*. The second of these terms was becoming the slogan for a well-organized group of Greek bishops, led by Basil of Ankyra, who regarded 'identical in being' as dangerously open to

Sabellianism but were anxious to affirm that in his very being the Son is like the Father, as it were a perfect image of his will and nature. Eusebius of Caesarea had said much the same.

Athanasius' three orations against the Arians

'Like in essence' was language close to that of Athanasius, who in the fifties wrote three powerful discourses against the Arians. (The fourth discourse, attacking Marcellus without naming him, is not by Athanasius but from the school of Apollinaris.) These were designed to argue that his opponents rejecting both himself and the Nicene creed are Arian heretics even if they disown any following of Arius; that Arianism is Antichrist; that Nicaea had ecumenical authority; that 'light of light' means that the Son is the very image of the Father and *homoousios* (1: 9); that Arianism depends on Constantius' support, not on the mind of the faithful; that the Christian eternal Triad differs from the (Neoplatonic) philosophers' graded triad of descending derivation; and that the Son is 'in all respects like' the Father (1: 21). Language used by Marcellus' critic Asterius (of whom Athanasius had no high opinion) such as 'indistinguishable image' is too orthodox for Arian ears. The root fault in the Arian mind is anthropomorphism; they think of God as if he were human. They protest against unscriptural *homoousios*, but have no hesitation in using the equally unscriptural 'unbegotten' (*agennetos*) for the Father.

The first two orations against the Arians offer a single argument that the scriptural texts to which critics of the Nicene creed triumphantly appeal such as Prov. 8: 22 ('The Lord created me') should be otherwise interpreted. The third oration, probably later than the first two, is a more formidable piece of thinking. Neoplatonic philosophers were intrigued by the problem of identity and difference; to say X and Y are identical implies that they are distinct. So Athanasius explains that the Son's identity with the Father in *ousia* does not mean that there is no difference. The third oration rejects the 'low' Christology that the Logos 'came into a man'. He became man and was both divine and human, so that as man he could hunger, thirst, be weary, suffer, while as God he could raise the dead, restore a blind man's sight, or cure the woman with a haemorrhage, acting however, through the body which the divine Logos had made his own. It was 'God's body' (3: 31). So when the body suffered, the Logos was not external to it and yet remained impassible. Salvation enables the redeemed to share in that impassibility by a therapy doing away with the passions that take humanity away from the right and the good. Salvation is 'deification', *theopoiesis*.

Athanasius' sharpness in the controversy was in part a consequence of his sharing some axioms with those he opposed. So he was sure it was irreligious to debate how God the Father begets a Son: 'It is better to be silent when in perplexity than to allow perplexity to erode belief' (*Or. c. Ar.* 2. 36). But he insisted that 'begotten' is distinct from 'created' or 'made'. Creatures have a beginning, but not the Son of God (2. 57). He took trouble to disavow Sabellian modalism (3. 4, 36). Arians have no sense of the broad intention (*skopós*) of scripture teaching that the Redeemer is both God and man so that Mary is 'mother of God' (*theotókos*). Because his body was God's, when the flesh suffered, the Word was not external to this (3. 31–2). Yet the Word is not injured by the human weaknesses and passions, but destroys them, so that believers also are rendered free of passion and impassible (3. 34). Arians want to argue for the subordination of the Son by saying that he was begotten by the Father's will and not 'by nature', language which could be edifying if used by other than heretics (3. 59). The Son is the image of the Father's *ousia*, not of his will, and *ousia* is prior to will (3. 65). The third of the discourses shows Athanasius grappling with the Christological problems which with Apollinarius were soon to occupy the stage.[6]

Liberius' return from exile

Reports of the painful state of division in the churches of Rome alarmed Liberius in exile, and put pressure upon him. Called to Constantius at Sirmium, he was asked to sign the manifesto of Sirmium of 357, and almost certainly did so since that enabled him to return in triumph (Jerome said 'quasi victor') to his see. Hilary (*c. Constantium* 11) thought the conditions attaching to Liberius' return as shameful to the emperor as to his exile. The signing did not endear him to the intransigent opponents of all compromise with Valens and Ursacius, especially to the admirers of Lucifer of Calaris. Back in Rome there was tension with Felix, but after disorders Liberius won support from the civic authorities under the city prefect and the majority of the *plebs*.

Aetius, Eudoxius, Basil of Ankyra

The Sirmium creed acquired importance as a result of a situation at Antioch in Syria. A gifted Syrian named Aetius argued that the difference between the Son and the Father was more important than any similarity; for him there was no question of identity of nature. Though the Son is a perfect image of the Father, in substance the dissimilarity is crucial. In *ousia* Father and Son

---

[6] Charles Kannengiesser's view that the third discourse against the Arians is not by Athanasius has not convinced other Athanasian experts. See E. P. Meijering, *Athanasius, die dritte Rede gegen die Arianer*, 3 parts (Amsterdam, 1996–8). A new critical edition of the first two discourses appeared in 1998 (Berlin, de Gruyter); general editor Martin Tetz.

were unlike—*anhomoios*. The Son is created as instrument of the Father's will. For Arius, who had told Constantine that he accepted the Nicene creed, Aetius had no respect. His disciple Eunomius from Cappadocia became an even more aggressive advocate of this Dissimilarian or Anhomoean theology.

Leontius of Antioch

Under Bishop Leontius Aetius was made deacon, but Leontius' congregation protested against Aetius' views and he left Antioch. Leontius found himself presiding over a divided church. He tried unsuccessfully to reconcile his majority with the small intransigent separatist group faithful to the memory of Eustathius of Antioch and his stand in 325 for the Nicene creed with its implicit 'one hypostasis' of the Trinity. They met together for common prayers but not for the eucharistic liturgy. In addition, there were two learned presbyters at Antioch, Diodore and Flavian, who held special devotional meetings with a considerable following, and who were not in the least sympathetic to Aetius and Eunomius. Leontius used to point to his white hairs and say 'When this snow melts, there will be much mud.' His prophecy was correct. Late in 357 he died.

Eudoxius

In Syria there was an ambitious pushing Bishop Eudoxius of Germanicia (now Maras) in Commagene who aspired to succeed Leontius. He had been fairly prominent in the Eusebian party at Serdica, and had been one of the legates who took to Milan in 345 the long exposition of the fourth creed of Antioch. He was a very able person, whose ambitions did not make him universally admired. On Leontius' death he took charge of the church at Antioch, initially as acting bishop of the see, and (since he did not need consecration) secured possession to the annoyance of rival aspirants, notably George of Laodicea. He had a way of expressing himself that was tasteless. Probably at the council of Seleucia in 359 Hilary of Poitiers (*c. Constantium* 13) heard him discussing the meaning of 'begotten', saying that while God always was and is, yet he was not a Father before he had a Son, for which he would need a wife with whom he had conversation and conjugal agreement and courting and lastly the natural method of begetting. Presumably Eudoxius was mocking too anthropomorphic and literalist an understanding of the notion of fatherhood, ridiculing homoiousians who were insisting that 'begotten' denotes an intimate relation that 'made' does not. The remarks would make sense if he was arguing that the less literalist the understanding of 'begotten', the less clear becomes the differentiation between 'begotten' and 'created'. He continued by saying 'the more the Son extends himself to know the Father, the more the Father superextends himself to be unknown by the Son'. Hilary and his audience thought it merely shocking; there was a tumult. It was an aggressive means of asserting the Father's utter transcendence and otherness, which was a theme in the teaching of Aetius. He was a man who enjoyed putting the cat among the pigeons.

Eudoxius did not enjoy the confidence of the existing clergy. He brought Aetius back to Antioch to teach but without liturgical duties and ordained Eunomius deacon. He called a synod which expressed enthusiasm for the manifesto of Sirmium, for it sought to rid the west of the contentious terms *homoousios* and *homoiousios* and affirmed the Son's subordination. George of Laodicea in Syria had once been an associate of Arius himself at Alexandria, but he was horrified by Eudoxius' actions, and wrote in consternation to Macedonius of Constantinople, Basil of Ankyra, Cecropios of Nicomedia, and Eugenius of Nicaea begging them to save Antioch and the empire from shipwreck, resulting from Eudoxius' promotion of Aetius' disciples to be clergy.

The homoiousian party, a reaction against Eudoxius

Basil happened to be holding a small synod at Eastertide which addressed a letter to bishops in Phoenicia and other bishops who shared their standpoint, voicing horror at the ideas current not only at Antioch but in Alexandria, Lydia, and the province of Asia. (Philostorgius the Arian historian records support for Aetius and Eunomius in 'Lydia and Ionia', 8. 2). The letter, preserved by Epiphanius (*Panar.* 73. 2–11), was composed by a body self-consciously standing in the tradition of the Dedication Council of 341 and the creed of the eastern council of Serdica accepted by the first council of Sirmium (i.e. 'Antioch IV'). If therefore they were enabling rapprochement with Athanasius and the pro-Nicene party, they could not have known it. Nevertheless, their favourite formula 'like in essence' was obviously one that Athanasius too was using. The bishops at Ankyra appended to their letter nineteen anathemas; Hilary of Poitiers (*Syn.* 12–25) gives them in Latin but in a different order. The polemic is directed against opinions which they associated with Aetius, with any talk of dissimilarity between Father and Son, or merging of begetting and making. They much disliked the proposition that divine activity of Father and Son is identical whereas the 'being' is distinct. They liked the reverent language of church usage that there is an individuality of *prosopa* or 'persons' (Epiph. *Panar.* 73. 11. 5). The hypostasis of Christ is from the Father (73. 11. 6). They end with an anathema on *homoousios*, taken to mean identical and therefore Sabellian. There was also an old fear, found in Eusebius of Caesarea and Arius, that *homoousios* might imply too material and physical a notion of the begetting of the Son of God.

Epiphanius (73. 12–22) gives the text of a wordy memorandum by George of Laodicea or Basil of Ankyra, perhaps both, contrasting the faith of 'us catholics' with the beliefs of Aetius; probably it was submitted to the emperor. Its date is unclear. It is noteworthy for insistence on 'like in every respect' (*homoios kata panta*) and also on the 'hypostases' of Father and Son as a term which eastern theologians use to express the individuality of the 'persons' (*prosopa*). Admittedly some are disturbed by this word (73. 16. 1), but it does not mean three Gods or three first principles. The defence of 'three hypostases', about which after Serdica the eastern divines had been reticent, is significant for what was soon to come. (Greeks at the Council of Florence in 1438–9 also liked this statement.) The memorandum has no mention of *homoiousios*.

Basil of Ankyra's representations to the emperor Constantius at Sirmium conveyed the consternation of the homoiousian group at the favour shown to Eudoxius by Constantius and at the encouragement given to Aetius. Eudoxius was fortified by appeal to the Sirmian statement which forbade the use of *homoousios* or *homoiousios* and therefore opened the gate wide for Aetius to urge that the difference between Father and Son is one of *ousia*, though not of will and activity (*enérgeia*). Constantius was impressed and withdrew all support from Eudoxius, Eunomius, and Aetius, who had to leave Antioch (Soz. 4. 14). To uphold Basil of Ankyra was evidently to set aside the statement from Sirmium of 357. On the other hand the homoiousian party affirming the distinct being of the Son was not afraid of saying that the Son/Logos is subordinate to the Father. In a word, what alarmed Basil and his allies in the statement from Sirmium of 357 was that it made space in the Church for Aetius and Eunomius, even though it did not use their language. Basil and his group anathematized any notion of a dissimilarity of *ousia*.

The homoiousian group objected to baptism in the name of the Unbegotten and the Begotten or of the Creator and the Created. They could justify holding that the Son is 'like' God the Father by saying that this is analogous to the Pauline saying (Rom. 8: 3) that Christ took the 'likeness' of sinful flesh (Epiph. *Panar.* 73, 9: 3–5); in short, he was like God and, by his pure virginal conception, like humanity, yet without being totally one or the other. They could reinforce their rejection of the term *homoousios* by discovering that this description of the bond between Father and Son had been censured by the council of Antioch (268) which condemned Paul of Samosata. Obviously it is the case that if, on a wholly modalist position, Father and Son are only different titles for one God, adjectives not substantives, it is then natural to think of Jesus as an inspired prophet but not a union of humanity with God in metaphysical 'substance'. This discovery caused trouble to both Athanasius and Hilary of Poitiers, who offer different explanations of what might have been intended by the bishops in 268.

Basil of Ankyra's programme attracted support from Cyril bishop of Jerusalem. Unfortunately tension was rising between the sees of Jerusalem and of Caesarea, the provincial capital. That prickliness was of some years' standing. At Nicaea in 325 the seventh canon had ruled that the see of Aelia be held in honour without prejudice to the metropolitical rights of Caesarea. The fourth-century growth of pilgrimage and the fine churches founded by Constantine were making the church of Jerusalem a magnet for substantial numbers with increased resources. 'Zion the mother of all churches' declared the Jerusalem liturgy of St James. It was natural that the bishop of Jerusalem would begin to think of his office in the way that pilgrims in ever larger numbers also thought and felt. In the provincial metropolis at Caesarea on the coast that could not be welcome. It would not be very long before claims were made for the see of Aelia at the expense of both Caesarea and Antioch. Therefore if Cyril of Jerusalem was going to support Basil of Ankyra and the homoiousian group, that would provide sufficient reason for the bishop of Caesarea, Acacius, to side with Eudoxius of Antioch, the see which in any event under canon 6 of Nicaea had rights of jurisdiction over the various provinces in the civil Diocese Oriens.

To Constantius it was a deep disappointment to discover that his ambition for unity and harmony in the churches, which had social and political consequences, was threatened by the tension between Basil's homoiousian party and Eudoxius of Antioch's support for Aetius. Philostorgius (4. 10) records that the two old supporters of Arius, Narcissus of Neronias and Patrophilus of Scythopolis, journeyed to Singidunum to explain to the emperor that Basil of Ankyra was not the kind of theologian who could hope to bring peace to the divided Church. After all he had moved Constantius to veto the appointment of Eudoxius to be bishop of Antioch. The emperor decided that there would have to be an ecumenical synod; to prepare for this a small group of episcopal advisers was formed to prepare a creed intended to be imposed as universally acceptable. That would solve all the emperor's problem. This group met at Sirmium in Constantius' presence and on 22 May 359 approved a statement principally drafted by Bishop Mark of Arethusa. To impart solemnity and the style of an imperial edict the document was prefaced with a consular date as had been the Nicene creed of 325, a matter forgotten by Athanasius when he mocked giving the timeless creed of the catholic Church a date. The Dated Creed pursued the course of trying to say nothing that anyone could possibly disagree with.

35

CONSTANTIUS' DOUBLE COUNCIL OF UNITY

Hilary of Poitiers on Councils

The exchanges of 357–8 inflicted some damage on Constantius' ambitions for peace in the Church, especially by creating distrust of his policies among western bishops. This distrust was mightily fostered by the banished Hilary of Poitiers, whose exile in Phrygia did not prevent him writing letters to Gaul. Late in 358 he wrote for the Gallic bishops a weighty tract 'on the synods or concerning the faith of the Orientals' (*De synodis seu de fide Orientalium*). His principal purpose was not merely to tell the uninformed about eastern creeds but also to urge generous western sympathy for Basil's homoiousian group and to explain to the latter that western theology was not Sabellian. He argued that the term *homoiousios* is far from being incompatible with the Nicene formula. The statement of faith from Sirmium in 357, despite its pointed insistence on scriptural authority for each affirmation including the subordinate status of the Son, Hilary presented in lurid colours as the 'blasphemy' of Sirmium and in some degree caricatured by glosses to the effect that Christ is presented as created out of nothing, which the document never says. Because the extreme Arian party of Aetius and Eunomius regarded the statement as granting them citizenship rights of toleration, it was natural to attribute to the statement a radicalism which was not there.

Hilary readily conceded that the Nicene *homoousios* provided cover for Sabellian modalism and could be understood in a way 'as much wrong as right' (*Syn.* 67). A correct understanding takes Father, Son, and Spirit not to be hierarchically graded but to be equal and therefore one; but not one person with two names, and not one substance which is then split up into two halves. An erroneous view understands the one substance to be a prior substance in which the two persons Father and Son participate. But if *homoousios* is ambiguous, so too is *homoiousios* since likeness normally implies some measure of dissimilarity; a vessel may be plated with gold so as to be very similar (*Syn.* 89). The sacredness of the Nicene *homoousios* is sure from the tradition that 318 bishops, the number of Abraham's servants in Genesis 14, approved it (*Syn.* 86). This number first appears in the mid-fifties replacing an older 'about three hundred' (the actual certain figure being two hundred and twenty). The epistle of 'Barnabas' saw in the numerical value of the Greek letters TIH (= 318) a symbol of the cross of Jesus (above p. 56). He incidentally shows that the abbreviation IH for Jesus (in Greek letters IHCOYC) was very ancient indeed. The number 318 was important for the further reason that Constantius' two synods were going to add up to a much larger assembly, and there could be argument that the greater the number of bishops the more potent the authority. That contention could be trumped if Nicaea had a sacred number attending. This argument becomes explicit in 371 with Pope Damasus and Ambrose.

Marius Victorinus at Rome

In his analysis Hilary was close to Marius Victorinus, a philosophically minded teacher of rhetoric to the sons of rich aristocrats at Rome whose dramatic conversion to Christianity about 354 is vividly described in the *Confessions* of Augustine from the memories of Simplicianus of Milan. Victorinus had come from north Africa, which was a bond with Augustine. His oratorical performances do not survive, but treatises are extant on the liberal arts and logic. He made Latin versions not only of Aristotle's *Categories* but also of selected pieces by Plotinus and Porphyry. Like many Greeks and Latins of the fourth century he was deeply impressed by Neoplatonism. But the springs of his conversion lay in the intellectual content of Christian faith; here was the way to 'the knowledge and the vision of God.' The Platonic ideal of liberating the soul from the illusions and imprisonment of the physical world could be realized through Christian practice. Therefore he told Simplicianus that he had no wish to be a fellow-traveller, but wanted his initiation by baptism to be in the customary public form. That would enforce an absolute break with pagan idols. The timing of his conversion was close to the drama of Liberius' exile and the western realization that in the demand for a condemnation of Athanasius the underlying issue was the truth or falsity of 'Arianism'.

Victorinus composed a defence of the Nicene 'consubstantiality' of Father and Son. He was provoked by an old friend named Candidus who was convinced by the logical contentions of Aetius. These were spreading to the west, perhaps encouraged by Auxentius of Milan, and, because of the stress on the absolute otherness of the supreme being contrasted with the contingency of the realm of creation, could be fused with an agnostic mysticism. Aetius was certainly clever, but he was not irreligious. Candidus took this mysticism so far that he even denied that the supreme being is capable of 'begetting' by act of will, since that must imply change in the Immutable. If one uses the term 'being' or 'substance', that is true only if one means the pure simplicity of being without any further predicate. Victorinus' reply urges that Candidus ought to allow potentiality in the supreme being, and the possibility of an actuality of creation. Why cannot there be movement in the Immutable, a movement which is the Word or Logos derived from the very substance of God?

Victorinus had received a copy, probably through Pope Liberius, of the homoiousian dossier produced by Basil of Ankyra at Sirmium in the summer of 358 and was not impressed either by the negative attitude to the Nicene creed approved by 'more than three hundred bishops' or by the fact that Basil was now condemning bishops Valens and Ursacius with whom he had been in communion for years. Basil seemed responsible for persuading Liberius to betray orthodoxy when he accepted Basil's position. However, Victorinus liked the formula 'one substance, three hypostases' and thought it corresponded to Plotinian language about being, life, and understanding. So his exchange with Candidus led him to write a major work 'Against Arius' which took in the contemporary controversies about *homoousios* and *homoiousios* and also a growing debate about the divine status of the Holy Spirit. He was sure that 'like in essence' presupposed a prior substance in which Father and Son both participate. The contention that *homoousios* is to be rejected because not in scripture forgets that the same is true of 'God of God, light of light'. Moreover compound words with *ousia* occur in Bible and liturgy, as when in the Lord's Prayer we pray for *epiousios* bread (Victorinus regrets the mistranslation 'daily') or in the prayer of oblation in the eucharist 'Save the *periousios* people, zealous of good works' (the citation in *contra Arium* 2. 8. 34 presupposes that in 360 liturgy at Rome was still Greek).[1] The argument would be congenial to Ambrose (*De fide* 3. 15. 127).

The twin councils and the Dated Creed

Constantius' plan for a grand council was going to be costly. To reduce travelling expenses the western bishops were to meet at Ariminum (Rimini) and the Greeks in the east, at first planned for Nicaea, but then Nicomedia. An earthquake destroyed much of Nicomedia (24 August 358), killing among others Bishop Cecropios. Constantius decided to defer the synod until 359 and to relocate the eastern half at Seleucia in Isauria with its large shrine of St Thecla.

The Dated Creed drafted at Sirmium in 358 to be proposed at both synods is preserved in Greek by Athanasius (*Syn.* 8) and Socrates (2. 37). It

---

[1] Victorinus was evidently struck by the unusual *periousios* (= 'special') from Titus 2: 14.

was composed far into the night by Mark of Arethusa at the end of a lengthy debate. Constantius himself presided and those present included not only Valens, Ursacius, Germinius, and Basil of Ankyra but also George of Alexandria and Pancratios of Pelusium. It affirms belief in the one and only true God, almighty Father, creator of all; in one only-begotten Son of God, impassibly begotten of God before all time and before all *ousia*, like his begetter according to the scriptures, whose begetting no one understands except the Father. He was incarnate of the virgin Mary by the Father's decision, was crucified, descended to the underworld so that the gates of Hades trembled (the first occasion when the descent to Hades figures in a creed). He rose from the dead. He sent the Holy Spirit the Paraclete. But the term *ousia*, used by the fathers in their simplicity but unfamiliar to laity, causes scandal because not in scripture, and should be entirely abolished in reference to God. 'We say the Son is like the Father in every respect, as the scriptures say and teach.'

Nothing was said of the Son's subordination to the Father. The prohibition of *ousia* naturally affected both the pro-Nicenes and Basil of Ankyra's homoiousian party. Some of the signatures were qualified. Epiphanius (*Panar.* 73. 21. 5–7) preserves the glosses. Valens' signature reveals that the document was signed in the small hours of the morning early on the day of Pentecost. He agreed the Son is like the Father, did not want to allow 'in every respect' but was required to make the addition by Constantius. Basil of Ankyra signed with a gloss on 'in every respect', meaning 'not only in will but in hypostasis and in existence and in being' (a row of synonyms for the word *ousia* which he was not allowed to use). The argument soon began to surface that no one could want to split the Church for the sake of the unbiblical term *ousia* (Theodoret, *HE* 2. 18. 2).

Constantius also decided that each of the two synods should appoint ten of its members to come to the emperor and to reach agreement in his presence; that would constitute the final decision of the whole Church. Constantius was becoming very aware that achieving harmony and consensus among so many different competing factions would not be easy. He could not safely leave so momentous a matter to the bishops unsupervised, especially when each faction had its own favourite slogans.

The western bishops at Ariminum

The Council of Ariminum began work late in June and early in July 359 with more than four hundred bishops required to attend. (Ancient sources give differing estimates of the number, and some bishops gave their signatures afterwards.) The Aquitanian bishops are proudly described by Sulpicius Severus as financing their own travel costs, but among the British bishops three were too poor to forgo state aid. The praetorian prefect of Italy, Taurus, was ordered to allow no bishop to leave until everyone had signed the Dated Creed. The emperor had addressed a testy letter to the western bishops (CSEL 65. 93; tr. Wickham 80–1), admonishing them to reach agreement on matters of faith, and forbidding them to say anything about the eastern bishops; in other words, there was to be no repetition of the disaster at Serdica, for which, it is implied, the western synod was then responsible. A rift appeared between a group of eighty bishops supportive of the prepared Dated Creed, and the majority (according to Athanasius numbering almost two hundred) who did not wish to abandon the Nicene formula which for them expressed the faith delivered to their predecessors guaranteed by the apostolic succession (*successio apostolorum*: CSEL 65. 95).

In the *Chronicle* of Sulpicius Severus a main spokesman for the Nicene formula was Phoebadius bishop of Agen, leader of a group of twenty. He was opposed by Valens of Mursa deploring language not in scripture. An Umbrian bishop of Calle successfully invited the majority to condemn the Illyrians already under censure (i.e. at Serdica), Ursacius, Valens, Germinius, and Gaius who have often changed their beliefs and replaced the Nicene creed by a heretical text. So a letter explained to Constantius that the Nicene Faith, formulated by holy confessors, also had the aura of having been approved by Constantine of famous memory, who had professed it at his baptism (by Eusebius of Nicomedia—the statement is the first indication of the hagiographical tendency which culminated in the replacing of Eusebius by Pope Silvester). The Illyrians had manifested their inconstancy by offering amendments to the Dated Creed. Any abandonment of Nicaea would cause disorder everywhere and especially at Rome. (The reference is perhaps to Pope Liberius' wobbly adhesion to the Nicene creed; at Ariminum Potamius of Lisbon and Epictetus bishop of Centumcellae said that Liberius merited anathema: CSEL 155. 16, tr. Wickham 71.) To Constantius the western majority wrote to beg leave to go home, especially since many were old and poor. Then with their people they could pray for Constantius' salvation and for the peace of the empire. A long list of signatures was appended to this letter to Constantius (Athan. *Syn.* 10; CSEL 65. 78–85).

A tenth-century manuscript (Paris. lat. 2076, fo. 50ᵛ) preserves a list of anti-Arian anathemas approved at Ariminum, almost certainly belonging to this drama at the first session of the council. (The text, not in Hilary, CSEL 65, is reprinted from Coustant in PL 10. 698–9.) The bishops anathematize those who say the Son of God is out of nothing and not begotten of the Father, true God of true God; who say Father and Son are two Gods or that they are one and the same; or (against Photinus and Marcellus) that the Son of God began from Mary, or that there was a time when he was not, or that he is only human. In particular they reject the proposition that Father, Son, and Spirit are three substances (i.e. three hypostases?), or that the Son was before all ages but not before all time or that created things were made without him or before him. The bishops felt sure that they were condemning all heresies that had ever raised their head against the catholic and apostolic tradition. Already it was becoming a repeated formula that the Nicene creed was a bulwark against every deviation, not only Arianism, and therefore needed and must have no supplement. It participated in the sacredness of holy scripture to which no addition or subtraction was possible.

The two separate parties could not easily meet together, and both sent delegations of ten members to Constantius at Constantinople. Meanwhile, their colleagues were detained in Ariminum. The legates found the emperor planning a campaign against Persia and unwilling to see either of them. He was busy gathering Gothic forces by the Danube, and the legations were told to wait for him at Adrianople (Edirne). Meanwhile back in Ariminum bishops were becoming extremely restive at the long delay, and pleaded by letter for release. Constantius was going to grant nothing of the kind. The two legations were told to move to the little Thracian post station of Nike (formerly called Ustodizo) and to discuss until agreement was reached. Even then there was no promise of release.

Western legates at Nike

Nike was probably the kind of desolate place to which exiles might be banished. It is very unlikely that anything was done to make the two delegations comfortable. When Hilary of Poitiers came to write his work 'Against Valens and Ursacius' he included some scraps of information and a few texts shedding a fitful light on the Nike meeting, but almost all the story is shrouded in obscurity. Afterwards it was not in the orthodox interest to provide a proper record of the proceedings. Restitutus bishop of Carthage led the western bishops to capitulate, acknowledging that the dissension at Ariminum had been the work of the Devil (CSEL 65. 86. 6) and that they had been wrong to excommunicate the Illyrians. Significantly he came from a region little involved in the Greek debate, probably finding much of the debate almost incomprehensible, and convinced by experience with African Donatists that no technical disagreement in theology could be worse than the rancour of schism.

The final agreed statement of faith modified the Dated Creed of Sirmium, avoiding 'like in all respects' and content to say 'like according to the scriptures'—in short, the form of words for which Valens had unsuccessfully striven at Sirmium. The statement prohibited the proposition that Father, Son, and Spirit are a single hypostasis (Theodoret, *HE* 2. 21. 7). The ghost of Western Serdica was laid. Except for unimportant concessions in wording, the western delegates suffered an unmitigated defeat, which the pro-Nicene sources strenuously seek to whitewash, blaming the emperor's improper pressure or bitterly cold weather or the bishops' age, weak health, and travel exhaustion or youthful lack of experience compared with those clever old Illyrians who deceived them with diabolically ingenious ambiguity. It seemed unthinkable that the simple-hearted Nicene west could so have betrayed the truth and led the world, in Jerome's famous phrase, to 'groan at finding itself Arian'.

Winter was approaching, when the Balkans can be remarkably cold. The legates from Nike returned to Ariminum, where the bishops composed a letter to Constantius, preserved by Hilary (CSEL 65. 87–8) who was sure it was the work of the non-Nicene leaders. The letter declares that, in consensus with the easterners, they are agreed to avoid the unscriptural terms *ousia* or *homoousios*, words unknown to God's Church and creating scandal. Their colleagues accustomed to use such terms have accepted defeat. So now the bishops, 'we who are in complete agreement with the Orientals', ask leave to return home so that they no longer have to be detained with people infected by perverse doctrine. At the emperor's command they have renounced the unworthy term *ousia*. So please would the emperor tell the prefect Taurus to let them go. A letter has gone to the eastern bishops to inform them of the western council's decision.

This text shows that the legates from Nike did not succeed in winning over all the pro-Nicene party at Ariminum. Yet they write to the emperor in the name of the council as a whole. The emperor's letter to Taurus told the prefect that the bishops could not go home until they had all signed the Nike text. This forced the Nicene bishops' hand, except for twenty led by Phoebadius of Agen and Servatius bishop of Tongres (Sulpicius Severus, *Chronicle* 2. 431–4, probably dependent on lost parts of Hilary's account of the council, but with a touch of Gallic regional patriotism). Phoebadius was convinced that Valens believed the Son of God to be created on a par with the rest of the created order. Under the presidency of a senior African Bishop Muzonius a confrontation followed, which ended in Phoebadius yielding.

'Not a creature as one of the created order'?

According to Jerome's 'Altercation between Luciferian and Orthodox', expressly dependent on the conciliar Acts but perhaps influenced by his reading of Hilary's work against Valens and Ursacius, which he knew (*Vir. inl.* 100), Valens was asked directly if he believed the Son of God to be a creature, and exculpated himself with six anathemas. Valens insisted that the Son was begotten before all ages, is like the Father in accord with the scriptures, is not a creature as other creatures, is not made out of nothing, and there was no time before he came to be. This was received with acclamation. Subtle minds would soon ask if 'not a creature as other creatures' really meant that the Son of God is indeed a creature but in a different category from the rest of the created order. At the time the ambiguity was not detected. When the western legates from Ariminum came to Constantinople and met their eastern opposite numbers, they quoted Valens' anathema; delegates of the eastern synod of Seleucia saw the point, at least according to Hilary (CSEL 6. 176. 5 ff.; *co. Aux.* 6; Ambrose, *De fide* 3. 16. 130). It is difficult to be certain here whether Hilary's comments are his own or if he had an authentic report of a dialogue at Constantinople. In any event he was misrepresenting Valens and his friends in accusing them of regarding the Son as being on the same level as the rest of creation in the hierarchy of being. The form of the Acts of Ariminum that passed into general circulation was determined by the party led by Valens. Marius Victorinus, *De homousio recipiendo*, attacked Valens' party for thinking the Son could be called a creature, but had to admit that they did not actually say 'created out of nothing'. He was aware that Valens and his friends dissociated themselves from the radical Aetius.

The agreement at Ariminum was bound to be represented as compromise and therefore to be an objectionable fudge. The timeless principle common to such dialogues operated, that any proposition acceptable to the opposing group must for that reason alone be inadequate. Jerome was no admirer of the outcome, and even less was Hilary of Poitiers. But they were willing to find excuses for what had happened. An absolute rejection of communion with any bishop who had assented to or excused the agreement at Ariminum was led by Lucifer of Calaris in Sardinia, at the time still an exile in Egypt, and in Spain by Gregory bishop of Elvira: assent had been an act of sheer cowardice before the pressure of an emperor who was a forerunner of Antichrist. A central question would be the policy of Pope Liberius. Wisely he could not agree to the virtual demotion of almost all the western episcopate, and found reasons for thinking that apologetic signatories should be pardoned and remain in office. Lucifer excommunicated him. But that is to anticipate moves after Constantius' death on 3 November 361.

Constantius' driving motive was to avert the split between east and west that had occurred at Serdica. Schism had very adverse political consequences for the empire. Evidence put before him by the influential Valens or by Basil of Ankyra easily convinced him that the Nicene term *homoousios* engendered many disputes and in the Greek east had provoked too much misgiving because of its capacity for embracing Sabellianism, of which the still living Marcellus was the embodiment. His difficulty was to persuade the Latin west, and especially the see of Rome with its close links to Athanasius of Alexandria and its already innate feeling both that St Peter's see must be an ultimate judge of truth in God's Church and that all authority and coherence foundered if the creed accepted by Popes Silvester in 325 and Julius in 340 was jettisoned. At Nike and Ariminum Constantius was granted success, but at a price.

Hilary's anger. Tax concessions?

The outcome at Ariminum vastly angered Hilary of Poitiers, who in 360 wrote a tract 'Against Constantius'. He accused the emperor of persecution as wicked as that of Nero or Decius, and worse because it was veiled in deceitfulness. It was diabolical not to employ torture, which would have given the dissenting faithful the honour of confessor status. In particular he had bought the assent of many bishops by dangling before the churches tax concessions and, like Judas to Christ, greeting bishops with a kiss, bowing his head to receive their benediction (*c. Const.* 10, PL 10. 587). An edict in the Theodosian Code dated 30 June 360 (16. 2. 15) notes a discussion at the council of Ariminum about the privileges of churches and clergy. In 355 Constantius had already granted bishops exemption from having to appear before secular courts; they could be judged only by other bishops (CTh 16. 2. 12; Ambrose, *ep.* 75 = M 21. 2). The edict of 360 grants severely limited exemption from taxes and from obligations to undertake public services, but mainly to impoverished gravediggers, not to clergy who own large estates. It is instructive that there were bishops in this last category. For an emperor in need of funds to finance his intended expedition against Persia, tax exemptions could not be very welcome. Success would need more than the bishops' prayers, important as those would be.

The council of Seleucia (359)

Accounts of the council of Seleucia mainly depend on Sozomen's history (4. 22–3) which drew on a detailed narrative by a strongly partisan homoiousian, Sabinos of Heraclea. Sabinos had little compunction about misrepresenting parties other than his own, but was clear on the main outline of events. The bishops at Ariminum were persuaded to assent by the consideration that agreement with the Greek east was necessary and an expression of the authority of a united Church. At Seleucia in Isauria about a hundred and fifty or sixty bishops gathered late in September 359. It was a significantly smaller attendance than that at Ariminum. Constantius appointed two counts, Lauricius and Leonas, to preside as his representatives. The emperor's letter to the synod was imprecise about the agenda. The first session saw dissension about the question whether the synod should first consider the question of faith or if it should begin by considering accusations against Cyril of Jerusalem and Eustathius of Sebaste in Roman Armenia, who was advocating a radical asceticism that was the subject of much dispute.

Cyril, bishop since 348, was deposed by Acacius of Caesarea in 358 on the ground that to raise funds for the starving during famine he had sold to a dancer a golden decorated robe given to the Jerusalem church by Constantine (so Theodoret, *HE* 2. 27). An alternative version in Sozomen (4. 25) is that a layman who had presented a fine robe was shocked to see it being worn by an actress at a local music-hall (which might raise the question how he had come to see this worldly spectacle). Eustathius had an early association with non-Nicene circles, but became accepted in Asia Minor, and then fell under discipline because of his rigorous asceticism, negative to married believers. His was not a standpoint to which Basil of Ankyra was unsympathetic; Basil was author of an extant treatise on celibacy and its medical consequences, preserved under the name of Basil of Caesarea. Basil of Ankyra had been a physician before ordination.

Absentees at this opening session included Basil of Ankyra, Patrophilus of Scythopolis, and Macedonius of Constantinople (a bishop of the capital of whom the historian Socrates had the lowest opinion). Unkind opinion suspected them of staying away for fear of facing unspecified charges. The theological issue was voted for by the majority as the first question to be debated.

The Council divides: Acacius of Caesarea

That brought with it the problem that immediately the diverse parties closed ranks against each other. Acacius of Caesarea, Eudoxius of Antioch, George of Alexandria, Uranius of Tyre, and thirty-two others were for the Dated Creed. George of Laodicea and Eleusius of Cyzicus were homoiousians, preferring the creed of the Dedication council of Antioch, which rejected Marcellus' Sabellianism as the Nicene creed did not; they had a substantial majority, and, no doubt foolishly, held a separate defiant meeting to endorse the Antioch creed. Acacius of Caesarea and his friends drew up an independent statement, extant in Epiphanius' *Panarion* (73. 25–6), which they put before the count Leonas. Tumult greeted the reading of this document which noted that the emperor had forbidden unscriptural words in any creed, and went on to argue that the synod was invalidated by the presence in the homoiousian group of deposed bishops (Cyril of Jerusalem and Eustathius of Sebaste being instances) and others illicitly ordained; moreover in the first session some bishops had been insulted and others prevented from speaking. Acacius answered accusations of being a turncoat by saying that he did not reject the creed of Antioch (to which he had once subscribed), but the unscriptural *homoousios* or *homoiousios* must now be abandoned in view of the fact that the terms were divisive, and some wanted to stress the dissimilarity between Father and Son, an opinion which Acacius and his group wished to anathematize and which the creed of 341 might conceivably be held to allow. (Sabinos here claims misleadingly that Acacius wanted a formula that did not exclude Aetius. Acacius was soon to preside at a council in Constantinople in 360 which condemned Aetius and his Libyan supporters: Theodoret, *HE* 2. 28). For Aetius' school the similarity of Father and Son resided in will, not in *ousia*. But Col. 1: 15 'image of the invisible God' vindicated 'like'. Acacius' document ended with an edifyingly simple creed, a sound baptismal confession excellent for catechumens, without the least relevance to the controversial issues but declared to be in line with the Dated Creed of Sirmium. Forty-three signatures are recorded by Epiphanius (incomplete in the manuscript tradition, which has only thirty-seven names). The named sees show that Acacius had a strong following in Palestine, Syria, and Libya and, beside George of Alexandria, even a handful from Egypt (Pelusium and Thmuis). Any pro-Nicene bishops from Egypt were wholly without influence.

Acacius withdrew from attending the synod, saying that the emperor had ordered him to be present only if unanimity was achieved. Count Leonas supported Acacius' stand. The homoiousian majority declared excommunicate and deposed George of Alexandria, Acacius, Eudoxius of Antioch, and others (Soz. 4. 22. 25). A presbyter of Antioch, Annianos, consecrated to succeed Eudoxius, then found himself arrested, handed over to the two counts and their soldiers, and later sent into exile. The counts knew that the emperor was opposed to allowing the homoiousian majority to dominate and to exclude, an intolerance which would be no road to the common faith which he desired. At the same time he was no supporter of Aetius and Eunomius, whose language he found disturbing.

By the first day of October the factions in the synod could no longer meet together. It was already all too clear that the count Leonas was not giving any support to the homoiousian majority which was now being led by Eleusius of Cyzicus and Silvanus of Tarsus, zealots for the creed of Antioch 341; they could not be persuaded by Basil of Ankyra to agree to the Dated Creed's modest claim that the Son is 'like the Father according to the scriptures'. For the homoiousians the silences of the Dated Creed were unacceptable. Yet that formula was something almost nobody could reject; hence its attraction for the emperor. It excluded virtually no one, not even Aetius and Eunomius, since the assertion of likeness implies some degree of dissimilarity. Even the assertion of identity becomes interesting if and when there is a significant difference between the beings or objects compared. Epiphanius regarded the differences between the non-Nicene groups as hardly more than hairline cracks. That was fair enough so far as theology was concerned. But the divisions were exacerbated by personal animosities, at least between Acacius of Caesarea and his suffragan Cyril of Jerusalem.

Legates and emperor at Constantinople

The synod faced the imperial requirement of ten legates to confer with him and with the legates from Ariminum. The two legations met with the emperor at Constantinople. There too came Hilary of Poitiers from his nearby exile in Phrygia (Sulpicius Severus, *Chronicle* 2. 45). The emperor appointed the city prefect Honoratus to take charge of the proceedings. The emperor was unimpressed by an interview with Aetius, and wished Eudoxius of Antioch to condemn him. A question arose whether he should be condemned by name or whether the anathema should state the doctrine to which objection was being taken. The homoiousian group feared that they might get only the former from the slippery Eudoxius, and wrote a letter to the western legates from Nike to warn them of a clever plot on this point. They added that they were keeping the western churches informed of everything that was going on. The homoiousian group, led by Silvanus of Tarsus, was aspiring to propose alliance with Rome and the Latin west, perhaps inspired in that direction by Hilary of Poitiers.

Constantius and Hilary want a simple scriptural creed

Acacius and his friends had their own delegation at the court. Although they represented a minority at Seleucia, in Acacius the group had a leader of high ability endowed with determination and persuasiveness. They told the homoiousians that the statement accepted by the western legates at Nike should now be approved. Constantius himself asked all the bishops to agree on the Nike formula which declared the Son to be like the Father, reassuring the homoiousians by observing that though the terms with *ousia* were not used, they were not actually condemned. What he wanted was an agreed statement of faith and he believed the best route to that end was to stick strictly to scripture as all-sufficient or to simple words such as 'like' which expressed the biblical intention and avoided divisive technicalities. Paradoxically that was almost identical with the advice given to the emperor by Hilary of Poitiers (*ad Const.*, CSEL 65. 197–205; tr. Wickham 104–9). Hilary deplored the ceaseless production of competing creeds and mutual anathemas, and declared deep admiration for the emperor's longing for a simple scriptural statement, a baptismal confession which showed true religion to be in the heart, not a written text with signatures and a philosophical debate. Nevertheless, there have been few heretics who have not claimed the authority of scripture. Peace for the church of both east and west would bring honour to Constantius' reign. (Hilary was not so pleased with the simple text that emerged.) In his hope of an audience with the emperor Hilary was frustrated.

After a session through the night of 31 December 359 the emperor finally persuaded the homoiousian legates from Seleucia to accept the Nike text, the formula already approved by the council of Ariminum. Hilary of Poitiers was deeply saddened that the legates from Ariminum had silently acquiesced in communion with Valens and Ursacius, and indeed from the first moment of their arrival in Constantinople had ignored the representations and warnings of the homoiousians and had without hesitation or delay shared the eucharist with the Illyrian heretics on the ground that being westerners, they were 'their own people.' It was shaming that the legates had allowed Valens to cite proof-texts from Latin fathers, 'from your own library', to convince them of the correctness of the Nike formula (CSEL 65. 175–7; tr. Wickham 90–2). The argument presupposed western pride in Western theology.

On 1 January the emperor could celebrate the New Year and his entering upon the office of consul for the tenth time.

Eudoxius' council of Constantinople 360. Homoiousian defeat.

The homoiousian bishops could only retire to lick their considerable wounds. They had been betrayed by the Latin west. Acacius and his friends remained in the capital and gathered a council of seventy-two bishops, including Ulfilas of the Goths. (Was the number present chosen to give the assembly the same sacredness as the Septuagint?) The Great Church of Sophia at New Rome, begun under Constantine, was completed and in February 360 was dedicated. The *Paschal Chronicle* of the sixth century preserves the names of fifty bishops present ('with others' *PG* 92. 735–7). This council reaffirmed the formula of Ariminum, forbade any use of either *ousia* or *hypostasis* in reference to God, and degraded Aetius from the office of deacon. It went on to declare deposed the leading homoiousian bishops, not for their doctrine, but as disturbers of the peace: Bishop Macedonius of Constantinople (who had a turbulent record in the city and caused offence by moving Constantine's body from the church of the Apostles to that of St Acacius to facilitate some reordering of the Apostles' basilica), Cyril of Jerusalem, Silvanus of Tarsus, Eleusius of Cyzicus, and especially Basil of Ankyra who, intoxicated by favour shown to him by Constantius a year earlier, had acted in a violent and arrogant way violating the canons. He had used his influence with the civil authorities to have clergy from Antioch and points east, from Cilicia, Galatia, and Asia, to be arrested by provincial governors. Without trial many of them had been fettered and had had to bribe the soldiers to escape dreadful maltreatment, this being a customary necessity for those in custody. (Libanius observes that prisoners had to bribe their gaolers to escape fearful naked floggings: *orat.* 33. 30; 45. 10.)

To replace Macedonius, Eudoxius was translated from Antioch. At Constantinople he reached the summit of his ambitions, and held the see for a decade. Constantius gave the new basilica at Constantinople munificent benefactions. The building did not have an untroubled history, and ultimately was destroyed in the Nika riot in January 532, thereby making room for Justinian's masterpiece that still stands today.

The extant creed of Eudoxius proclaimed the secondariness of the Son to the Father whom he worships, whereas the Father worships no higher being. As the 'only begotten' the Son is superior to the rest of creation of which, as firstborn of creation, he is supreme. He was made flesh but not man, since he did not assume a human soul. He was not two natures since he was not completely man. God replaced the soul in the flesh. The whole is one nature and was passible only by 'economy' (or condescension). If either soul or body suffered, he could not save the world. It is therefore impossible to say that one who is passible and mortal can be of the same *ousia* (*homoousios*) with God who is superior to such things, transcending suffering and death.

Eudoxius saw to it that the sees compulsorily vacated were now filled by friends of his party. Eunomius himself replaced Eleusius at Cyzicus, which did not please Acacius (Philostorgios 6. 4). Eudoxius advised Eunomius to exercise careful reserve in expressing his real views. It was a grievance for Aetius that though he was exiled, he was only saying openly what others were secretly thinking (Epiphanius, *Panar.* 76. 3. 10). Other bishops unconvinced of the case against Aetius were temporarily suspended and allowed six months in which to see the light (Theodoret, *HE* 2. 28. 3–6 lists them).

Eunomius could not be discreet for long. He was delated to Eudoxius, then to Constantius, who demanded his removal from office. Eunomius retired much aggrieved that Eudoxius had failed to support him, and set up his own sect with bishops and clergy ordained by him to serve the congregations of his connection. He composed an *Apologia* submitted to Constantius; Basil of Cappadocia wrote a refutation of it, to which in 378 Eunomius wrote a rejoinder. A more powerful attack on Eunomius was composed by Gregory of Nyssa.[2]

Meletius of Antioch

For the vacant see of Antioch contenders were numerous. Eudoxius thought well of Meletius from Armenia, bishop of Sebaste in that province, known to be an eloquent preacher as well as a man of virtuous life. Meletius had been consecrated to the see of Sebaste after Eustathius had been deposed in or

---

[2] See the edition of Eunomius by R. P. Vaggione (Oxford, 1987) and his monograph (Oxford, 2001). Gregory of Nyssa's work was edited by Werner Jaeger (1921, 2nd edn. Leiden, 1960).

about 358; but such was the popularity of Eustathius with the congregation that Meletius, who was by nature gentle and unaggressive, found the task impossible and withdrew. So he was a bishop at a loose end, living nearby at Beroea (Aleppo) and available. At Seleucia he had assented to Acacius' non-controversial creed. There was nothing in his past record to alert Acacius and Eudoxius to any risks. Meletius was duly translated to the difficult see of Antioch, where there was a history of division, especially because of the small intransigent continuing congregation loyal to the Nicene creed and to the memory of Eustathius of Antioch, deposed not long after the council of Nicaea to die in Thrace. This congregation had as their pastor a presbyter named Paulinus, whose strength lay in the support received and communion enjoyed from both Alexandria and Rome. Meletius was installed in office by Acacius and his friends, all 'Arians' in the judgement of Paulinus.

Sozomen (4. 28) records that at Meletius' first discourse all parties, including Jews and pagans, crowded in to hear him. He began by ethical teaching, but soon he passed to theology. At Antioch Constantius was wintering and preparing for a campaign against Persia. He decided to hold a sermon festival in which successive discourses by different preachers were to expound the controversial text, Prov. 8: 22 (LXX) 'The Lord created me the beginning of his ways with a view to his works.' He heard George of Laodicea, then Acacius of Caesarea, thirdly Meletius, whose exposition of the Trinity as unity alarmed disciples of Eudoxius. Perhaps he was going to defend the distrusted creed of Nicaea. The text of this discourse is preserved by Epiphanius, *Panar.* 73. 29–33:

Meletius began with a plea for unity in the church, and went on to affirm the Son of God to be God of God, 'one of the One, begotten of the Begetter and worthy Son of him who is without beginning, interpreter of him who is beyond interpretation.' He is not merely an utterance of the Father but is an independent hypostasis, 'like' the Father as accurately revealing his character. But some take Prov. 8: 22 to deny that Christ is God. In scripture there is no contradiction, though it may appear so to those not sound in faith or weak in intelligence. No analogy from this world suffices to show the nature of the Only-begotten, and scripture uses many terms and titles. The Son is like the Father, for he is the 'image'; but not a soulless image of an ensouled being, nor only a piece of activity or energy. Physical birth is no sufficient analogy. Scripture uses both 'begotten' and 'created'. His nature (*physis*) is beyond our grasp, and quarrels about the transcendent mystery make us fall into blasphemy. We should base our words on faith, not our faith on words.

Critical ears noted that Meletius had not expressly said the Son is a created being, and had made no reference to the question whether the suffering Christ could be one with the impassible Father; there were phrases which could be taken to be critical of Eudoxius. His language was so carefully chosen that he was hard to fault on doctrinal grounds. However, he reinstated clergy ejected by Eudoxius, and this gave ground for anger. So the decision was made to remove him from office, to exile him to his native Armenia, and to replace him by an old colleague of Arius at Alexandria named Euzoius. However, like Paulinus, Meletius had his loyal admirers at Antioch, who preferred to continue as a separate congregation apart from Euzoius and to worship in the open air without a building. He was supported by two learned presbyters, Diodore and Flavian. Paulinus' congregation had at least a roof over their heads within the city. They were intransigent for the Nicene formula, but as Meletius moved nearer to this position, Paulinus became defensive.

The closer Meletius moved towards approving of the Nicene *homoousios*, the more painful became the division between him and Paulinus. This was especially true after the death of Constantius in November 361 and Julian's amnesty which released the fiery exiled bishop Lucifer from Sardinia. A zealot for the true Nicene faith, he went to Antioch and with two other bishops consecrated Paulinus. It was harder to reconcile rival bishops than rival creeds.

The schism at Antioch became a cardinal issue during the next decades and even beyond.

36

JULIAN AND THE CHURCH[1]

Julian Caesar

After Constantius had finished his dealings with the west in 357, he moved to Constantinople and sent his young cousin Julian with the rank of Caesar to check possible usurpers and barbarian attacks in Gaul. In 355 both Cologne and Trier were badly damaged. A senior army officer was deputed to keep an eye on the Caesar, and to see that he made no foolish military decisions. In the event the officer led an unwise campaign across the Rhine and was crushed, thereby leaving Julian a free hand. At Strasbourg in 357 Julian led his troops to success, enjoyed adulation from the legions, and himself composed a panegyric on his famous victory.

It was a remarkable achievement for a young man in his mid-twenties whose upbringing and education had been withdrawn and bookish. After Eusebius, successively of Nicomedia and Constantinople, had died in the winter of 341/2, Julian and his elder brother Gallus had been confined to an imperial palace and estate at Macellum, near Caesarea in Cappadocia. He was to be there for six years during which he served as a Reader in the church at Caesarea and with his brother funded the building of a martyr's shrine for St Mamas, a popular hero for the church at Caesarea (Basil, *hom.* 23; Greg. Naz. *or.* 44, 12). He knew his Bible well, better than his guardians, it was said (Eunapius, *V. Soph.* 473). He studied classical Greek literature and the liberal arts under a congenial tutor named Mardonios. He was able to borrow books from the opulent library of George, who in 357 was to be pressed into becoming Athanasius' rival as bishop of Alexandria, where he was singularly unloved by the city populace, both Christian and pagan. The news of Constantius' death in November 361 provoked the mob to lynch George; Julian immediately wrote disapproving of the murder but demanding George's library for himself, to which end torture should be used if necessary. In 347 Gallus was moved to Constantius' court, while Julian studied further first at Constantinople, then at Nicomedia. At that time the distinguished pagan rhetor Libanius was teaching in Nicomedia; Julian was not allowed to

[1] See the article with full bibliography by A. Lippold in *RAC* xix (1999), 442–88.

hear him, but had clandestine contact. In 362, when Julian was at Antioch, they became friends and allies.

Gallus was promoted to the rank of Caesar in 351. He was to be an imperial presence at Antioch in Syria while Constantius was coping with Magnentius' usurpation in the west. His behaviour at Antioch was deplorable; Constantius summoned him and without trial had him executed. Julian had written his brother a sympathetic letter which came to be compromising and a source of anxiety (Libanius, *or.* 12. 35; 18. 25). The execution of his brother without trial was hurtful.

Conversion to polytheism

The young prince's situation was not conducive to open manifestation of convictions. Probably he was confused anyway. Ammianus (22. 5. 1) was sure that from boyhood the gods held him; 'in adolescence he burned with longing to participate in their cult.'

Julian and Gallus used to exchange argument for and against the gods (Greg. Naz. *or.* 4. 30). In a letter (*ep.* 82 Wright) Gallus regretted Julian's too evident sympathy for the old religion.[2] Julian's letter of 361/2 to Alexandria (*ep.* 111 Bidez, 47 Wright) says he ceased to be Christian aged 20; but the change was not publicly known until Constantius' death made it safe. Outwardly he conformed to Constantius' expectations for ten years during which pagan cult was outlawed, and high offices of state were not for avowed pagans. Perhaps for a time Julian's ideas were syncretistic. As late as January 360 he was attending church for the Epiphany.

In 351 Julian had the chance to travel about to Pergamum, then to Ephesus where he was wholly fascinated by a theosophist and wonderworker named Maximus, who combined Neoplatonic doctrines with wonderful occult rites and solemn purifications. He discovered a coterie of Neoplatonic teachers of high culture, deeply admiring the writings of Iamblichus, and in some cases following Iamblichus in the practice of theurgy or the employment of pagan rituals to assist the soul towards purification. A letter from Julian to the philosopher Priscus of Athens asks for a copy of Iamblichus' commentary on the Chaldaean Oracles (*ep.* 12 Bidez = 2 Wright), a late second-century work concerned about the right formulae for compelling the gods to do things.[3] Priscus remained a favourite, went with him to Persia, and was with him when he died.

---

[2] Bidez and Cumont, p. 287, needlessly doubt the letter's authenticity; cf. W. den Boer, *Vig. Chr.* 16 (1962), 179–86.

[3] A good recent discussion of the Oracles by P. Athanassiadi, *Pagan Monotheism in Late Antiquity* (Oxford, 1999), 49–83. Extant biographies of this coterie were written by the pagan historian Eunapius (346–*c*.414); who also wrote a largely lost 'Universal History' bitterly polemical against

Maximus of Ephesus could perform strange wonders, burning incense and reciting a spell which made a torch in the hand of an image of Hecate burst into flame (Eunapius, *V. Soph.* 7. 2. 475), an act which may well have been inspired by an oracle of Hecate quoted by Porphyry in his book on Oracles (cited by Eus. Caes., *Praep. Evang.* 5, 15, 202 D). One of Libanius' letters (606) congratulates Maximus for purging Julian of superstition (*or.* 13. 12). Julian admiringly mentions the writings of Iamblichus, notorious for their rebarbative style. What came to Julian from this source was more theosophy than the art of reasoning. He would have found congenial Iamblichus' book 'On the Mysteries' with its doctrine that a philosopher achieves union with the gods not by cool thinking but through cultic action or theurgy invested with divine power.

The Sun-god

Solar monotheism or henotheism (one god with subordinates) was potent in the third century. Aurelian's victory over Palmyra gave credit to the Sun-god and his temple at Emesa (Homs) in Syria. For astrologers the sun was the most powerful planet. Coins of Constantine the Great and his arch by the Colosseum show symbols of the sun. At Constantinople the statue on his porphyry column wore a radiant crown like Apollo. Devout folk put candles and flowers at the base (Philostorgius 2. 17). Christians venerated Christ 'the sun of righteousness'. A Christian mosaic in the necropolis under St Peter's, probably about 320, portrays Christ as the sun in a chariot crossing the sky. Chariot and horses were an ancient solar symbol (2 Kgs. 23: 11). Popular piety celebrated both Christ and the sun on 25 December, a feast which became popular in the west by about 300 and entered the Roman church's official calendar by 330.[4]

For Neoplatonic philosophers or astrologers no power in this cosmos was superior to the sun, king of planets and all below, believed to have a special relationship with emperors and kings. As Julian looked back on his conversion to polytheism, he felt that under the direction of Zeus, the Sun-god King Helios had healed him of a deep malady (his normal term for Christianity but perhaps it simply means that he fell ill). In his study of rhetoric he owed a debt to Hermes god of eloquence and intellectual life (229–30). 'The greatest gift of Zeus and Helios is Asclepius who has often cured my ailments' (*c. Galilaeos* 235 C). 'His oracles are everywhere.'

Christianity and panegyrical about the 'divine' Julian. See R. J. Penella, *Greek Philosophers and Sophists in the Fourth Century A.D.* (Leeds, 1990).

[4] See F. Cumont, 'La théologie solaire du paganisme romain, *Mémoires de l'Académie des Inscriptions et Belles-Lettres,* 112. 1 (1923), 448–79; G. H. Halsberghe, *The Cult of Sol Invictus* (Leiden, 1972); F. J. Dölger, *Die Sonne der Gerechtigkeit und der Schwarze* (Münster, 1924).

Julian composed a prose-poem in honour of King Helios, in which he recounts how in his youth sunlight so greatly fascinated him as to become a numinous experience. 'By this ethereal light from childhood, my mind was in a state of ecstasy' (130 C). He felt that this had helped to overcome the horror over the massacre of his father and close relatives. He did not recall that his life had been saved by a Christian named Mark, who became bishop of Arethusa in Syria. Despite his dislike of Constantius, he confessed his gratitude at having been born into a dynasty destined to rule 'the inhabited world' (*Helios* 131 B), a sentence implying a rejoinder to charges of illegitimate usurpation. But this was the work of the Sun-god intending him to be his special servant (131 D), language strongly reminiscent of Constantine the Great's almost messianic self-consciousness. Helios delivered him from darkness and opinions about the divine which he was happy to have shed (131 A). His vocation was to undo Constantine's handiwork. He would not have been delighted if the orator Themistius (*or.* 5. 70 D) had greeted him in the way he welcomed Jovian, as a new Constantine. The city he always called New Rome.

In 351 at the age of twenty Julian inwardly abandoned his belief in Christianity and adhered to the gods who had made the Roman empire, above all the Greek culture and religion of the pagan Neoplatonists. Julian knew Latin but Greek was the language he admired. Libanius (*or.* 12. 33), who was not interested in theurgy, hoped that Julian had been converted to the cult of the old gods by the study of philosophy. Julian was aware that he was not actually much of a philosopher (216 A). Influenced by the Platonic *Alcibiades I*, which Neoplatonists regarded as the ideal introduction to the subject, he understood philosophy as a process of self-knowledge: 'Recognize that you are divine, concentrate on pure thinking, and utterly despise the body' (226 C–D). As an adolescent he adopted an extremely frugal life style. At Antioch in 362 his lack of interest in food, wine, and sex provoked mockery.

Julian's writings show him to have absorbed the style and precepts of the 'sophists' with whom he studied. He shared their values. Only a small circle realized that this was now his position, and he wisely kept his own counsel, conforming to Christian expectations at a time when Constantius' harassment of paganism was increasing. His military success in Gaul contrasted with Constantius' lack of success against Persia, and envy entered the emperor's distrustful mind. The Persian war needed more troops and in 360 Constantius demanded the transfer of substantial units from Julian's command. Any soldier on the Rhine frontier who had fought in the summer heat of Mesopotamia in June would have been reluctant. Libanius describes Constantius' weak military ability in *or.* 18. 91. The orders were sent to Paris, Julian's headquarters, but bypassing Julian and going to his subordinates.

Mutiny followed. The army proclaimed Julian to be Augustus. That required a delicate negotiation on Julian's part, asking Constantius for recognition of parity. Constantius did not wish to share equal supremacy in the empire, and refused the request. If Julian was to achieve supreme power, it had to be by military force, which could not be unsuccessful if he was to stay alive. Other usurpers had met with death. He had only a small army, but that had the advantage of making rapid movement possible.

In 355 Julian had married Constantius' sister Helena. In Gaul she suffered a miscarriage (Ammianus 16. 10. 19 says the midwife killed the infant as part of a malicious plot to ensure Julian had no offspring to succeed him). A devout Christian, she worshipped with him at the celebration of the feast of Epiphany on 6 January 360. She supported Julian when he was acclaimed by the army in Paris. But her health was failing and not long after his elevation by the troops she died, to be buried in Rome beside her less edifying sister Constantina, who had been married to Gallus and had died in 354. Constantina founded the church of St Agnes without the Walls at Rome.

Civil war averted when Constantius dies

In the coming civil war with Constantius Julian was going to need all the help available. Being unsure of the loyalty of the army he offered secret sacrifices to the fierce Cappadocian goddess of war Bellona or Ma, and then addressed the troops asking for their fidelity (Ammianus 21. 5). A vehement affirmative met his words, but the praetorian prefect Nebridius dissented and had to be protected by Julian from a lynching; he retired peacefully to his villa in Tuscany (*PLRE* i. 619). Julian advanced into Pannonia, sending part of his small force into Italy to create the impression that he commanded numerous units, while he himself advanced to Sirmium to take control of Illyricum. From there he made a lightning move to the narrow pass of Succi in the mountains between Illyricum and Thrace, on the eastern side a precipitous defile.

Meanwhile a propaganda war denigrating Constantius was launched. From Gallic successes Julian claimed to be able to release documents showing that the unchecked infiltration of Germanic tribesmen into Gaul, to the vexation of the inhabitants, had been encouraged by Constantius himself when he wanted to harass Magnentius. A dangerous and costly siege of well-defended Aquileia, loyal to Constantius, was ended when news came that on 3 November 361 the formidable emperor, who was widely expected to overcome in the imminent conflict, had died of fever at Mopsucrene in Cilicia. The story was put about that on his deathbed he named Julian as his successor, which was no doubt designed to answer some tough questioning of Julian's legitimacy. Julian had found it necessary to address numerous cities offering a justification of his rebellion. The letter to the Athenians survives among his writings. The Roman senate had been unenthusiastic: was he not biting the hand that had fed him? Constantius received a funeral at Constantinople with the customary imperial honours, the body being conveyed by Jovian, a member of the imperial guard, *protector domesticus*. Julian attended the ceremony. Constantius' third wife Faustina, whom he had very recently married, was soon to bear a daughter Constantia who grew up to be wife to the emperor Gratian.

Estimates of Constantius differed then and later. The historian Aurelius Victor regarded him as a good, fair-minded man whose advisers and subordinates were disastrous. He surrounded himself with flattering yes-men. Venal eunuchs, with whom the court seemed to be filled, were the object of cordial dislike. Ammianus thought him judicious and conscientious in promoting military commanders, and in his private personal life a model of chastity; but his suspicious nature led him to appoint merciless judges cruel to those on trial for harbouring treasonable aspirations, in contrast to his ambition to be both just and merciful. His feared prosecutor Paul the Chain too often sentenced defendants to flogging with a scourge lethally weighted with pieces of lead (e.g. Libanius, *or.* 14, 15). Ammianus (21. 16. 12) agreed with 'right-minded people' who would have thought it better for his reputation to renounce power and abdicate than to use such methods of deterrence. At the same time he conceded that the list of rebels to be suppressed was long. 'The simplicities of the Christian religion he bedevilled with old wives' fancies, making it so complicated and contentious that the public transport system was ruined by crowds of bishops attending synods as they call them' (21. 16. 18).

Julian's estimate of Constantius was naturally low, and the unpopularity of Constantius' taxes and the harshness of his subordinate governors gave material help to the new regime. To win popular support Julian issued an edict fixing maximum prices, which was not popular with food-producing landowners, especially when in Syria the needs of the army and poor distribution created a serious food shortage. His way of encouraging loyalty was to grant reduction of or exemption from taxes. When, however, he was preparing for his campaign against Persia, there was a sharp rise in taxes, and people with resources were not convinced of the necessity for so large an operation (Ammianus 2. 4. 23). Julian brooded on and could not forgive the dynastic massacre of 337 in which he had lost his father and his eldest brother, a tragedy for which Constantius disowned responsibility (Greg. Naz. *or.* 4, 22).

From Athanasius, Lucifer of Calaris, and Hilary of Poitiers we hear a harmoniously orchestrated chorus of vehement denunciation of Constantius. They knew a forerunner of Antichrist when they saw one. But from Gregory of Nazianzos kinder words come; Gregory realized that the emperor was determined to achieve unity of creed, marked by simplicity rather than complexity. A disputatious Church seemed to be disintegrating into competing factions with rival slogans excommunicating and persecuting each other in ways prejudicial both to public order and to the credibility of the Christian mission. Gregory did not think Constantius' ideal ignoble (*or.* 4. 37). Naturally he thought the sincerely Christian Constantius, even if poorly advised, a far better monarch than Julian the apostate. For Gregory Christian faith secured the greatness of the empire (*or.* 4. 74). He understood that as Constantius body was being conveyed to Constantinople, a choir of angels was heard singing (*or.* 5. 16).

The restoration of polytheism as religion of the empire

An edict of Constantius in 341 shows that he regarded the essential act of pagan worship to be sacrifice (an opinion which Julian, unlike Porphyry, shared); that was what the 'Vicar' (i.e. deputy prefect) of Italy was instructed to stop (CTh 16. 10. 1). This was soon followed by enactments protecting temples associated with public entertainments, which were necessary to keep the populace quiet (CTh 16. 10. 4. 6). At Antioch the festival of Apollo at nearby Daphne was notoriously not a moral occasion. Gallus Caesar devised a means of purging Daphne by installing there the relics of St Babylas, martyred bishop under the persecution of Decius in 251. Antioch retained a substantial minority attached to pagan cult, but a majority were at least conforming Christians who, on occasion, were seen at church services. John Chrysostom would record that the people of Antioch were excessively attached to theatres and dancing, a weakness already noted in the second century by Lucian of Samosata (*De saltatione* 76). On 22 October 362 the temple of Apollo was destroyed by fire, and the commission to investigate it could not find the culprit. The excitable and impulsive Julian was sure it must have been a Christian (*Misopogon* 346 B), and ordered the great Church of the city to be closed.

Soon after his arrival in Constantinople Julian ordered a trial of Constantius' principal officers of state; many were executed. It is not clear that religion was a factor at this point. Among those who died was the military commander in Egypt, Artemius. He was treated as a saint and martyr by non-Nicene Christians; it is possible that he was a friend not only to Constantius and his anti-pagan programme but also of Bishop George when he needed protection against the angry mob. Artemius' name occurs in P.Oxy. VIII 1103.[5]

---

[5] See J. Dummer, 'Fl. Artemius Dux Aegypti', *Archiv für Papyrusforschung*, 21 (1971), 121–44.

At first Julian wanted religious toleration. His declared ambition was to restore justice on earth. But the bribery and corruption endemic under Constantius was in no degree lessened under Julian, and Ammianus observed that justice was precisely what it was hard to get under this emperor. Too many verdicts seemed arbitrary (22. 9. 12), a judgement with which Gregory of Nazianzos concurred (*or.* 5. 20). An amnesty was granted to exiled bishops, an act which intentionally produced shaming troubles in the cities where an alternative bishop had been installed. Athanasius returned to Alexandria, and was unmolested until he was discovered to have baptized important ladies of the city, which seemed to Julian sufficient reason to require his departure. In 362 he was able to preside over a small but crucially important synod at Alexandria, especially concerned about the situation of competing ortho- doxies at Antioch.

Julian's restoration of polytheistic worship demanded the rebuilding of shrines. All Christians who had participated in dismantling temples and shrines were required to pay for restoration. A layman who had used building materials from a temple for his own house had to surrender them (Libanius, *ep.* 636). At Cyzicus Bishop Eleusius was given two months in which to rein- state a Novatianist church destroyed under his predecessor (Socrates 3. 11. 3). The use of state tax revenue to bolster church welfare was cancelled (Sozomen 5. 5. 2). The military standard of Constantine the Great, the *labarum*, was abolished because its shape, the Chi-Rho (**XP**), was understood to be a monogram of Christ (Greg. Naz. *or.* 4. 66). At Paneas (Caesarea Philippi) a statue of a woman erected to symbolize Hadrian's visit to the province in 129 had been reinterpreted as the woman with a menstrual haem- orrhage healed by Jesus; so Julian had it replaced by a statue of himself which was, to Christian satisfaction, then struck by lightning (Sozomen 5. 21).

Christian reaction to Julian was unfriendly. In the army a few soldiers pre- ferred martyrdom to participation in pagan rites (Theodoret, *HE* 3. 15). John Chrysostom commemorated two martyred soldiers, Juventinus and Maximin (PG 50. 571). Libanius knew of some military units being bribed to offer sacrifice (*or.* 18. 168). Zealots smashed newly restored altars (Julian, *Misopogon* 361 B). In Phrygia new images of gods were destroyed (Socrates 3. 15). At Antioch Bishop Euzoius was commanded to remove the bones of St Babylas from Daphne (*Misopogon* 361 BC; Libanius, *or.* 60. 5; Ammianus 22. 12. 8). Perhaps their presence in the immediate vicinity explained why the oracle of Apollo was silent. The congregation turned the occasion into a massive demonstration with a defiant procession carrying the sacred relics, singing and chanting Psalm 96 to denounce the demonic gods of the heathen. Nisibis had many Christians and the reinstated temples remained ostentatiously empty (Soz. 5. 3. 5), though Ephrem (*Carmina Nisibena* 9) tells of some sun-worshippers and idolaters. In Caesarea in Cappadocia the temple of Fortune (Tyche), the presiding genius of the city, was destroyed by hotheads who suffered for their act (Greg. Naz. *or.* 4. 92–3: 'not unjustly').

Julian's harassment of the Church began mildly but became severe (Greg. Naz. *or.* 4. 92). Christians were not promoted in the army, and were not appointed provincial governors or magistrates, on the ground that they disapproved of capital punishment and torture. There was no change in the system whereby governorships were for sale (Libanius, *or.* 2. 42). Julian was ready to order execution of soldiers who retreated before enemy forces, which embarrassed Libanius. On 17 June 362 an edict laid down the requirement that teachers of classical literature should be in sympathy with the religion of the texts (CTh 13. 3. 5). In effect this excluded Christians from the teaching profession. Thereafter Julian's attempts at toleration ceased, and his hatred of Christianity was given full rein. The sophist, and master orator Prohaeresius resigned his position at Athens, his sympathies being Christian.[6] So also did Marius Victorinus in Rome. The standpoint that culture and religion are indissoluble was not alien to Christian thinking. Nevertheless, it meant that children of zealous Christian families could not go to school. Other than monasteries there were no church schools in this age. Libanius (*or.* 18. 158) judged Julian's edict a praiseworthy deed, as Ammianus did not (22. 10. 7; 25. 4. 20). To Gregory of Nazianzos (*or.* 4. 5–6) it was a barbaric act. The edict gave occasion for the Apollinarioi, father and son of the same name, at Laodicea in Syria to compose versions of biblical books in the forms of Greek epic or tragedy or, for the gospels, Platonic dialogue (Socrates 3. 16. 2–5). A learned writer might suggest that Julian's reason for forbidding Christians to teach Homer and classical Greek literature was to prevent people discovering how ridiculous the myths of the gods were (Socrates 3. 16. 19).

Libanius warmly supported Julian's religious policy. At the same time he maintained amicable relations with Christians of the educated class. Being in need of pupils for financial reasons, he could hardly afford to alienate Christian parents who might send him their sons; he could not make his school an embattled pagan citadel. A count of his known pupils suggests that almost 20 per cent were Christians. The upper classes were tenacious of the old gods. It is striking that in his 'Beard-hater', *Misopogon*, Julian set out to win the hearts of the proletariat. He may have learnt from the Church that the common people were of the first importance, and for bishops a major power-base. In the time of Augustine in north Africa great landowners were particularly difficult to convert to Christianity, saying they wanted to 'associate with Pythagoras and Plato rather than with their domestic servants', whose obedience they ensured by severe floggings; they would be

---

[6] This is mistakenly doubted by R. Goulet in *Antiquité tardive*, 8 (2000), 209–22.

embarrassed to be handing out alms to tenants whom previously they had
been rapaciously oppressing.

Another intellectual who provided important support to Julian was
Sallustius, who had served in Gaul as praetorian prefect 361–3. He wisely
warned Julian against invading Persia; at least he ought to be sure that the
gods were propitious, a matter of which Sallustius felt very uncertain
(Ammianus 23. 5. 4). Probably he was the author of a pagan catechism, 'On
the gods and the cosmos'.[7]

Against the Galileans[8]

Naturally the Christians were hurt and offended by the emperor's abandonment of his childhood faith, and puzzled by the reasons for the decision.
There were critics for whom his accession remained illegitimate, and the two
causes could coalesce. We have documents in which Julian defends legitimacy, but no text directly explaining his change of religious allegiance unless
it be his treatise against the Galileans.

Gregory of Nazianzos reports that an edict directed everyone to call
Christians by the name 'Galileans', which could have been suggested to him
by reading Epictetus (4. 7. 6). The title would convey their insignificance as
'little people' and their lack of any kind of universality such as the empire
possessed. During the winter months of 362/3, while preparing for his coming campaign against Persia, Julian wrote 'Against the Galileans' in three (?)
books, justifying his apostasy. (The title 'Apostate' is met in Malalas in the
sixth century.) This work does not survive intact, though it was known in
medieval Byzantium. Substantial quotations, however, occur in the refutations written in the early fifth century by Theodore of Mopsuestia and especially Cyril of Alexandria, a well-educated man of wide knowledge.
Alexandria remained a pagan citadel, where Julian's work was valued. The
historian Eunapius wrote a panegyric on him. At what stage Cyril wrote is
unclear, except that he sent a copy to John bishop of Antioch (429–41), probably in 433 (Theodoret, *ep.* 83). A few pieces have survived elsewhere.[9]

---

[7] Edited by A. D. Nock (Cambridge, 1926), less well by G. de Rochefort (Paris, 1960), setting
out a positive programme of pagan theology, owing much to Iamblichus.

[8] Sarcasm entered into Julian's anti-Christian arsenal. When the church at Edessa was deprived
of its treasures and endowments to finance the Persian war, Julian mockingly offered the consolation that the Christians could now practise apostolic poverty and get to heaven (*ep.* 115 Bidez,
40 Wright).

[9] A collection of the fragments was published by K. J. Neumann (Leipzig, 1880), and this is
reproduced in the third volume of the edition of Julian in the Loeb Classical Library by Professor
W. C. Wright of Bryn Mawr. These editions are now superseded by E. Masaracchia's (Rome,
1990), to which additional pieces from catenae (i.e. commentaries on scripture with summaries of
a succession of commentators in the margins) are edited from Theodore of Mopsuestia by Augusto

'Jesus lived only 300 years ago'

For ancient society the oldest known seers and peoples possessed insights not granted to later people. Julian liked to contrast the antiquity of polytheism with the modernity of Christianity. Jesus was embarrassingly recent. Polytheism allowed for a supreme deity, Zeus being the correct name which one must get right (236 D). For some pagan monotheists the highest is name-less; under him are lower deities and daemons. It is axiomatic that the supreme power works through provincial governors or satraps. So each nation and tribe has its own god, and this explains the diversities of national character. Hence Celts and Germans are fierce fighters (116 A; *Misopogon* 359 B). Greeks and Romans are humane and alert to political problems. Egyptians are intelligent and skilled craftsmen. Syrians are not warlike but hot-tempered, vain but quick to learn. Western nations have no aptitude for philosophy or geometry, but the Roman world delights in oratory and debate. Persians, Parthians, and all barbarians in east and south are content to live under despotism (138 B). Such differences reflect the character of the god responsible for each. Admittedly climate is also a factor explaining differ-ences, but is taken into account by the gods in charge. If Jewish–Christian monotheism were true, every race would be the same.

For defenders of Christian belief in the Bible, the argument from the fulfilment of ancient prophecy, both in the life of Jesus and in the coming of the universal Church, enjoyed some potency. Origen (*contra Celsum*) allowed that in its popular form it was not cogent, and attached greater force to the astonishing expansion of the Church. Julian astringently rejects the argument from prophecy. True, some prophets of the Old Testament had looked for-ward to the coming of a son of David, a national liberator from foreign occu-pation; but that is very different from finding fulfilment of such predictions in a crucified Jesus. Moreover, the Christians attach high value to the Hebrew scriptures as divinely inspired, but then abandon observance of the laws given through Moses. Moses legislated for the sacrificing of animals in

Guido (see Further Reading, IV). A valuable commentary on Gregory of Nazianzos' first oration (*or.* 4) against Julian has come from Alois Kurmann (Basel, 1988). Gregory's brother was court physician and he had good access to facts, which he presented as if he were prosecuting counsel, treating Julian's successes in government as baits for his diabolical traps. However, the fifth-century church historians Socrates and after him Sozomen got more from the Julianic orations of Libanius, well discussed by H. U. Wiemer, *Libanios und Julian* (Munich, 1995), and Reinhold Scholl, *Historische Beiträge zu den Julianischen Reden des Libanios* (Stuttgart, 1994).

The reference system for *c. Galilaeos* to the pagination of Cyril in Aubert's edition (= PG) differs from Julian's other works (Spanheim). On a planned new edition of Cyril see G. Huber-Rebenich and M. Chronz in J. van Oort and D. Wyrwa (eds.), *Heiden und Christen im 5. Jahrhundert* (Leuven, 1998). A good discussion of the philosophical arguments used by Julian in this work by C. Riedweg in T. Fuhrer and M. Ehler (eds.), *Zur Rezeption der hellenistischen Philosophie in der Spätantike* (Stuttgart, (1999), 55–81.

worship; he was right, for sacrifices are the essential rituals which unite us with the gods. The Christians sacrifice no animals; they say that (in the eucharist) they have a new kind of sacrifice (305 F), but no one would think that their worship contained a sacrifice of any sort. And why have they abandoned circumcision, claiming that circumcised hearts fulfil the lawgiver's intention? Why no passover, no unleavened bread? They reply by citing that dishonest and inconsistent charlatan Paul, and say Christ is their passover. They simply adjust divine laws given to Moses to suit 'shopkeepers, taxmen, dancers, and pimps' (238 E). So Julian dismisses Christianity as mere human folly (*ep.* 83 = 37), which is evident in the extreme austerities of monks or in the ceaseless invocation of Mary under the title of the 'mother of God' (*theotókos*, 262 D). The 'suicidal mortifications' of Christian ascetics are provoked by evil daemons (*ep.* 89b, 288 AB).

The derivation of Christianity from Judaism is a further argument against it. Though Julian respected the antiquity of Judaism, he was unambiguously hostile. Both Jews and Christians hold the same books to be authoritative, but the only thing they have in common is rejection of the Hellenic gods. It was a big mistake of Hebrew prophets to disparage idols and sacrifices. And there is problematic implausibility about the notion that books written in Hebrew, a language not understood even by all Jews, can have been intended by the universal Father of all to be his revealed teaching for the entire human race. Hebrew prophecy is now no less silent than the oracles of the Greeks and Egyptians (198 C). But we have been granted by Zeus fellowship with the gods through theurgy. Admittedly divine inspiration comes rarely and to very few (198 B). (For Julian divination was important evidence of the truth of his religion.) Moreover, the penalties under the law of Moses are harsh, whereas our penal code is 'gentle and humane' (201 E). This last argument is reminiscent of the 'Comparison between the law of Moses and that of the Romans', the *Collatio* familiar to Roman lawyers, composed probably soon after Julian's time, where the argument is that the superiority of Moses is discerned in the greater seriousness and graver penalties which he attached to transgressions.

Julian attacks Judaism and the Hebrew scriptures with the kind of anti-Semitic zest last found in Apion of Alexandria, to whom Josephus replied. He thinks the most brutal Greek and Roman military commanders were not as brutal as Moses (184 B). The God of the Decalogue is confessedly a jealous god, and jealousy is no admirable state of mind. Adam and Eve were forbidden to eat so as to acquire knowledge of good and evil, which had to be learnt from the serpent, a major benefactor of the human race (75 A). The God of the old scriptures becomes angry, swears oaths, changes his mind, as no thoughtful Greek would think possible (160 D). The philosophers tell us to imitate the gods as far as possible, and that this imitation consists in the contemplation of things which have being, which means an unmoved passionlessness or *apatheia* (171 D). As for culture, Julian asks what science or philosophy owes its origin to a Hebrew thinker. Arithmetic, geometry, music, astronomy and medicine have all been Hellenic discoveries (178 B). Eusebius of Caesarea wickedly tried to make out that the ancient Hebrews wrote hexameter epics (*Praep. Evang.* 11. 5. 5), and claimed that they knew about logic (222 A). Surely Isocrates was wiser than Solomon.

The New Testament writings are as unimpressive. Matthew and Luke do not agree on the genealogy of Jesus (253 E). That Jesus was divine is stated nowhere in Matthew, Mark, or Luke, but only in John (213 AB, 327 A). Perhaps John had heard that the tombs of Peter and Paul were secretly being venerated (327 B). Some believe Jesus Christ to be quite other than the Logos proclaimed by John (333 B); Julian knew about Photinus of Sirmium, and wrote a letter (46 B) inviting Aetius to court. Julian is horrified by the cult of the martyrs, for corpses are a source of defilement (335 C). It is instructive to compare his view with Augustine's apprehensiveness (*Sermo* 361. 6 cf. 273) that the veneration of martyrs may take forms hard to distinguish from pagan *parentalia*.

His objection to the 'deification' of Jesus needs to be balanced against the fact that in his own lifetime altars were set up in his honour, and after his death he was invoked by pagans for intercession (Libanius, *or.* 18. 304; 24. 7).

For Julian any providential intervention to rescue corrupt humanity is impossible. The divine realm is immutable, as one can deduce from the unchanging position of the stars, moving in a circle round the Creator and impelled on their way by the World Soul. We know God by nature in the conscience (52 B). Like John Chrysostom, Julian's belief in God rests on the moral law within and the starry heavens above. Julian readily grants that Hellenic myths about the gods contain absurdities and impossibilities, but not more so than Hebrew myths. Julian had probably read Origen's *contra Celsum*, and, though like Iamblichus he disliked his works, Porphyry. He was sure that in ancient myth absurdities are a sign of profound truths discoverable by allegory, without which the myths would be blasphemous (93 E). Otherwise one faces the questions, In what language did the serpent address Eve? Or where did Cain find a wife? (75 A). How inferior the Mosaic cosmogony is to the *Timaeus* of Plato can be seen in the fact that Moses records only the creation of physical matter and, unlike Plato, has nothing to say about incorporeal beings or angels (49 E). If, as some claim, Solomon was expert in theurgy (and he enjoyed a high reputation among magicians as magical papyri show), he owed that to his numerous foreign wives and concubines and their gods. At least the Christians venerate the inferior powers whom we call daemons (221–2). In Julian's copy of St Luke's gospel the angel of the agony at Gethsemane was absent. One may wonder here whether he was discussing the contested place of angels in Christian theology, or variant forms of text (evident in Nestle–Aland's New Testament).

Julian was appalled by the mob violence which led some Christians to attack temples or polytheistic ceremonies. Perhaps he had reports of the Donatist militants (*agonistici*, by Catholics called circumcellions) of north Africa who, shouting 'Laudes Deo' and armed with clubs called Israels, specialized in an unstoppable charge destroying bands playing music at pagan festivals (Augustine, *ep.* 185. 12). He noted that similar violence might be deployed against heretics, whose theology he likewise held in contempt (206 A). All this was as bad as the bitterness of the Jews (205 E). *Ep.* 114 = 41 to Bostra, where Bishop Titus had written proudly of his successful pleas for peace and order, lists Samosata, Cyzicus, Paphlagonia, Bithynia, and Galatia as places where inter-sectarian violence had cost lives. Julian was offended that a bishop could claim responsibility for avoiding disputes. Both Athanasius (*Hist. Ar.* 64) and Ammianus (22. 5. 4) thought Christians fighting each other more dangerous than wild beasts. Like Julian, Ammianus thought the disputes comparable to the contentions of Jews with one another.

The restoration of pagan cult was popular in some places. At Emesa (Homs) in Syria there was an anti-Christian riot. At Arethusa the aged bishop Mark fled, but returned when he discovered how dreadfully his congregation was suffering. Sozomen (5. 10. 13) reports that Mark's courage and pastoral devotion as he endured cruel indignities was much admired by the pagan prefect who thought Julian was making himself ridiculous. The city mob coated his body with honey and exposed him to wasps and bees. Gregory of Nazianzos thought his tortures gross when one recalled what he had done in 337 to save Julian's life (*or.* 4. 91). Libanius (*ep.* 819) wrote of the profound admiration in which Mark's fortitude was held. In ordering the expulsion of Athanasius from Alexandria, Julian wrote that he would be ashamed if any Galilean were to be found in the city (*ep.* 111 = 47). His religious policy had been vindicated by the exceptionally high rise of the annual Nile flood on which the economy of the country depended (*ep.* 108 = 45). (This argument would be used by Christians after the attack on the temple of Serapis in 391.)

In Cappadocia Julian despaired of finding a single pagan (*ep.* 44 = 35). Even where there were pagans to be found, he deplored their apathy, in strong contrast with the passionate zeal of religious Jews (*ep.* 89 = 20 Bidez). Syria was more open to his views. At Batnae he was pleased to find polytheistic cult maintained, and was embarrassed only that the vast clouds of incense greeting his presence suggested that the ritual was being overdone and seemed unprofessional (*ep.* 98 = 58 to Libanius).

The Temple at Jerusalem

Because it would vex the Galileans, Julian planned the rebuilding of the Jewish Temple at Jerusalem, so that once again sacrifices could be offered. This hugely costly project, for which wealthy Jews contributed funds, was intended to leave for posterity a lasting memorial of his reign (Ammianus 23. 1. 2). It would also refute prophecies to which Christians appealed. Julian was anxious to make amends for some adverse treatment of rioting Jews in Syria under his brother Gallus. However, earthquake (19 May 363) and a resulting fire brought the work to a stop and seemed an ominous manifestation of celestial disapproval.[10]

Christian influence on Julian's revival

Julian's programme for a restored cult of the old gods was considerably indebted to the Church. He saw how important bishops were in giving coherence to the churches, and nominated high priests in different regions with responsibility for appointing local pagan priests. He wanted priests to provide a welfare agency for the destitute exactly as the churches had long done. Moreover, the personal life of priests was to be a moral model for worshippers, with no visits to taverns. In Lydia, he appointed the sophist Chrysanthius, beloved teacher of Eunapius, to be high priest for the region. Chrysanthius moved slowly. He may have had little confidence that Julian's revival would last. He rebuilt no temples as other high priests did, and was in no way harsh to the Christians. In consequence the restoration programme in Lydia passed almost unremarked, and after Julian was dead the transition back to an easy-going tolerance was effortless. Chrysanthius was a fervent worshipper of the gods (Eunapius, *V. Soph.* 501). But he wanted quiet coexistence between cults. Zeal embarrassed him.

A comparable figure on the Christian side was the bishop of Troy, Pegasius (*ep.* 79 = 19). When Bishop Pegasius was called upon to give the future emperor a conducted tour of the city and its old temples, Julian was clear that he held the right views of the gods. Altars were still in use, and a statue of the hero Hector had been anointed, defended by Pegasius on the ground that he was a kind of classical martyr and should be honoured. Pegasius gratified Julian by not making the sign of the cross or hissing as many Christians did on coming near a pagan temple. This practice is attested in Tertullian (*Idol.* 11)

[10] Excavations at Scythopolis (Bet Shean) illustrate damage resulting from this tremor; see Y. Tsafrir and G. Foerster in *Dumbarton Oaks Papers*, 51 (1997), 85–146. An inscription from Ma'ayan Barukh, Israel, praises Julian, 'templorum restaurator': A. Kofsky and G. G. Stroumsa, *Sharing the Sacred* (Jerusalem, 1998), 8.

and Theodoret (*Hist. rel.* 3). Later Julian discovered that secretly Pegasius used to pray to the Sun-god Helius.

The bishop was far from being the only Christian of the age to think Christianity and sun worship reconcilable. In the mid-fifth century Pope Leo I found that members of his congregation on coming to worship at St Peter's, where the church is 'orientated' so that the altar is at the west end, used to venerate the rising sun in the east before entering the basilica. At Alexandria we hear of Christians venerating the sunrise with the prayer 'Have mercy upon us' (Ps. Eus., PG 86. 1. 453 CD). Epictetus (2. 7. 13) shows that 'Kyrie eleison' was a common form of prayer for non-Christians. It could be (but did not have to be) associated with a prayer to the Sun-god. In the New Testament *Kyrie eleison* is found at Matt. 15: 22 and 17: 15; cf. 20: 30–1, and similar formulas are frequent in the Psalms. A threefold Kyrie eleison was part of the liturgy at Constantinople in the time of John Chrysostom (*Hom. in Matt.* 71. 4).

Ammianus Marcellinus himself includes in his intelligent and indispensable history many remarks sympathetic both to the kind of Neoplatonism represented by Porphyry and to Christianity, at least in the style represented by humble country bishops. While he admired Julian for personal heroism and other qualities, he certainly thought that the pagan revival was marked by excesses such as huge sacrifices and far too much divination. A sacrifice for an emperor customarily required white cattle. After some of Julian's hecatombs it was feared the supply was running out. The meat and drink handed out to soldiers on such occasions stupefied them so that they had to be carried to their quarters in a debauched state. These cultic acts were costly. Moreover, since the emperor highly valued divination, all manner of people set up shop as fortune-tellers and professed skill in mantic arts (Ammianus 22. 12. 6–7). Ammianus was clear that Julian was taking religion to the point of superstition (25. 4. 27), foolishly dreaming of trumpets and battles (22. 12. 2), and excessive in his trust in omens. Though Ammianus himself was a believer in the value of omens, and in the inflexible power of fate, he disliked zeal. 'Julian would have conquered Persia if heaven had not decided otherwise' (25. 4. 26). 'No human power or merit has ever prevented what the decree of destiny has ordained' (23. 5. 5). In Ammianus there seems to be a stance somewhere between paganism and Christianity, tolerant of both provided there was no excess or violence in either cause.[11]

---

[11] I have not been able to follow Professor T. D. Barnes in the judgement that Ammianus was a Christian: see his *Ammianus Marcellinus and the Representation of Historical Reality* (Ithaca, NY, 1998). I do not think he was more than a fellow traveller, at most a 'flying buttress' on one or two days in the week. For the pagan side of him see J. F. Matthews, *The Roman Empire of Ammianus* (London, 1989), 424–51.

The Persian campaign

There were attractions about following Alexander the Great, even if not as far as India and Afghanistan. After Constantius' defeats at Persian hands, Julian wanted to show how war should be waged; so he would be awarded the epithet Parthicus, and he would vindicate the old gods as givers of victory.

Before the war Julian was given much advice against it by critics whom he ignored, and on all sides the omens discovered by the augurers and soothsayers were uniformly unfavourable. He realized the importance of rapid military movements and also of security regarding his plans. Rumour said that before setting out he had entrusted a purple robe to his kinsman Procopius, and it would be a question whether or not he was designating his successor in the event of death. He set out from Antioch, a city which had greeted him with mockery and insult, on 5 March 363 and moved towards Mesopotamia. At the fortress of Callinicus near the Euphrates he celebrated the ritual of the Mother of the Gods on her day, 27 March. This fierce Anatolian goddess was important to him since he had once visited her great temple at Pessinos, and had written a philosophical exposition of her lurid myth. His army was strengthened by Arab auxiliaries.

A body of soothsayers and a group of Platonic philosophers accompanied the emperor, and the two groups disagreed. When the enemy was engaged, Julian was foolhardy in risking his life, and could ascribe his amazing survival to the gracious protection of the gods. In that respect at least he believed in the possibility of providential interventions. He reached the Tigris,[12] but the courageous Persians vigorously defended Ctesiphon. Rashly Julian ordered that the boats in which his army crossed the river should be burnt, presumably intending to give resolution to the soldiers if there was no possible retreat. During a battle in a moment of excitement he forgot his breastplate, and a spear thrown by an unidentified soldier lodged in his liver. Carried to camp, his blood ebbed away. The accounts of his dying are modelled on Socrates in Plato's *Phaedo* (Libanius, *or.* 18. 272); probably that was in his mind as he made a last speech to his friends. In Ammianus' report he explicitly refused to name a successor. On being told that the place was called 'Phrygia,' he lost hope of recovery, saying he had been told that that was where he was fated to die. During the night he died. Ephrem the Syrian has an eyewitness account of the body being carried into Nisibis. He was buried at Tarsus. The army acclaimed Jovian of the imperial bodyguard to be successor.

Different accounts of Julian's end rapidly came into circulation. Ammianus knew an unverified statement that the fatal spear was of a Roman

---

[12] Julian may have supposed that the fast-flowing Tigris would be like the more leisurely Euphrates.

type. If so, then it was thrown, whether deliberately or carelessly, by one of his own soldiers, either Roman or Arab auxiliary. His Arab auxiliaries had become highly dissatified with what was being done for them (Ammianus 25. 6. 10). Libanius shifted, first saying a Persian did it (*or.* 27. 32), then suggesting (24. 6) an Arab—'but only the gods know' (*ep.* 1187); next that it was a Christian victory (*or.* 17. 7). When the news reached Jerome, then a schoolboy in the west, a pagan friend jested to him that no one could now complain of delay in the execution of divine revenge (*Commentary on Habakkuk* 2. 3, p. 660 Vallarsi). Christians danced in the streets making no secret of their jubilation (Libanius, *ep.* 1220), so that in time Libanius became convinced that the spear was deliberately thrown by a Christian hand (*or.* 24. 6ff.). In his dying speech Julian said he was glad not to be dying by treason. Libanius came to think otherwise: 'Julian died by treason or he would have conquered Persia' (*or.* 30. 40). Soon there were Christians declaring that, if the weapon was indeed thrown by a Christian, that was a righteous and fully justified act of tyrannicide. Sozomen (6. 2) believed that he had been justly struck by divine wrath, and that the act answered many Christian prayers.

Of his last words various reports were put about. Philostorgius (7. 15) writing about 425, had the story that he threw blood from his wound up at the Sun(god) with the words 'Be satisfied'. In the ritual of the Sun-god an offering of blood was normal, since Libanius once comments on the to him remarkable fact that the Manichees venerated the sun without offering blood (*ep.* 1253). Philostorgius' story was also known to Sozomen (6. 2. 10–12) but in the form that he threw his blood at a vision of Christ. Theodoret (3. 25. 7), nearly twenty-five years later than Philostorgius, is the earliest writer to claim that he died with the words 'Galilean, you have conquered'. In June 363 that was already much about what most pagans and Christians supposed to be the case.

By 380 solemn oaths were being sworn at Julian's tomb[13] in Tarsus as a test for perjury (Libanius, *or.* 18. 307). That a particular sacred figure had special power even *post-mortem* to reveal liars and perjurers is paralleled in Gregory the Great and in Augustine, *ep.* 78. 3, who knew of such cases at Milan, and sent two suspects to Nola in Italy to swear before St Felix's shrine. Julian's portrait was erected in temples and prayers addressed to him were being answered, which demonstrated that he had ascended to heaven (Liban. *or.* 15, 36). In the tradition of old Roman religion, the emperor had been granted apotheosis. Libanius' Julianic orations did for Julian what the memorial panegyric of Eusebius of Caesarea had done for Constantine. He left a lasting portrait of his hero which was largely exploited by the Christian

[13] One Christian story of Julian's tomb was that an earthquake ejected his corpse, a manifestation of his fate in hell (Gregory of Nazianzos, *or.* 21. 33).

historians Socrates and Sozomen. At the end Libanius was demanding from Theodosius I vengeance for the murder.

Julian's defeat and death damaged but did not extinguish pagan hopes that public sacrifices to the gods might be restored for the safety of the empire. In 365/6 Julian's relative Procopius, last survivor of the Constantinian dynasty, led a rebellion against the emperor Valens, and was supported by both Gothic forces and pagans. He lasted only a few months. In 370–1 a conspiracy aimed at getting rid of Valens, under whose reign pagans were much harassed, so as to install a pagan emperor Theodore. The plotters were severely dealt with. Eugenius' rising against Theodosius I in 393 similarly enjoyed major pagan support.

Nevertheless Julian's letters and orations survived, partly because they were good models of rhetoric. Even his attack on the Galileans continued to be read. There would long be those who looked with admiration to anti-Christian Neoplatonists such as Proclus in the fifth century or Damascius and Simplicius in the sixth. At the same time, however, there were well-educated and philosophically minded Christian writers of no less ability, notably John Philoponus of Alexandria anticipating some of the discoveries of Galileo and engaging in controversy against Simplicius' view that the heavenly bodies are divine and not merely physical matter. Paradoxically the writings of Proclus, who loathed Christianity, became a major source of inspiration for the unknown and hugely influential Christian author writing under the name of St Paul's convert Dionysius the Areopagite and, much later, for Thomas Aquinas. Dionysius' indebtedness to Proclus was seen by the English Platonist Thomas Taylor in the 1830s.

The tenacity of both peasants and opulent landowners towards the old rituals long created problems for bishops. Had not the well-tried rites propitiated the gods to ensure plentiful crops and victorious legions? The Church had particular difficulty in persuading farmers that the gospel was better for their crops and beasts, especially if they heard someone reading St Paul's considered doubts whether God cared for oxen. There were also parents who brought their sick children to the priest in hope that baptism would include a cure. Augustine's beliefs both that infant disease must be a symptom of original sin and that baptism remitted original sin could have combined to assist such hopes. Disappointed parents might then resort to a clandestine pagan priest and his sacrifices to a god (Augustine, *ep.* 98. 1). Use of amulets and horoscopes was widespread within the churches of the late fourth century.

37

DAMASUS, SIRICIUS, PAPAL AUTHORITY, SYNESIUS OF CYRENE

Election of bishops by the laity

In Cyprian's time at Carthage the laity in north African cities had a substantial voice in the election of a bishop. In the fourth century there appears a tendency for the vocabulary to be assimilated to that of electing a magistrate, which was also a privilege or right of the *plebs* or *populus*. They exercised a 'suffrage', choosing a candidate who had offered to stand and who conducted a campaign for success, perhaps against competition from a rival. The result easily produced faction such as Ambrose coped with at Vercelli, where he had to admonish the people that as consecrator he had the ultimate responsibility. The bishops of the province, especially the metropolitan, had the delicate task of mediating between the parties, and tactfully indicating which candidate they would be willing to consecrate. Decisions were formally recorded in 'ecclesiastical acts' with the acclamations and record of the numbers. Unanimity was always reckoned a sign of a divinely authorized choice; it was not always easily achieved, though at Milan Ambrose received it and the laity could put pressure on their chosen candidate, e.g. by blocking any attempt to leave the town. In 371 the pressure from the laity was enough to force the consecration of Martin of Tours on unwilling bishops who thought him unsuitable (and in the outcome were proved wrong). Martin himself believed he had suffered a loss of charism when the hands of the bishops, in his eyes a worldly lot, were laid upon his head. In 426 Augustine of Hippo wrote (*ep.* 213. 1): 'I know that at the death of bishops the peace of the churches is often disturbed by rivalries and ambitions.' The laity were increasingly coming to expect their bishop to have the social influence to protect them when they were in trouble with taxmen or magistrates or when they needed a favourable reference for a job, and this capacity counted more than holiness. The office of a bishop was inevitably politicized.

Faction at Rome in 366[1]

During Pope Liberius' exile the churches in Rome became sharply divided. Despite the oath of the clergy that they would recognize no successor while Liberius was alive, Bishop Felix, named by Constantius to implement his policies, succeeded in winning over many including the deacon Damasus. When Liberius returned Damasus switched his allegiance. Felix's attempt to return to office failed. Liberius died on 24 September 366. The orthodox of Constantinople early in the sixth century did not count either Liberius or Felix as authentic bishops of Rome (Marcellinus comes, ann. 382).

The animosity of the split at once became acute. Priests with three of the seven deacons of Rome met in the basilica of Julius in Trastevere, and elected deacon Ursinus to succeed. Paul bishop of Tibur (Tivoli) forthwith consecrated. A larger body met at the church of St Laurence (S. Lorenzo in Lucina) and elected deacon Damasus, who at once took possession of the Lateran. On Sunday, 1 October he was consecrated by the bishop of Ostia, who by custom consecrated bishops for the Roman see. Damasus had a few friends among the powerful and rich as Ursinus did not; he won the support of the city prefect who expelled Ursinus. However, Ursinus' supporters occupied the basilica of Liberius. Damasus decided to end this occupation by force, using circus gangs and gravediggers armed with clubs. This resulted in a three-day fight ending with 137 corpses (the figure given by Ammianus). Ursinus claimed to be successor to Liberius, while Damasus he thought merely successor to Felix, the bishop intruded by Constantius in the 'Arian' interest.

Roman deacons

It is worthy of note that both the two rival candidates were deacons, not presbyters. It was common in the ancient history of the Roman see for the people to look for a new bishop among the seven deacons of the city. The contemporary pen of Ambrosiaster (*Qu.* 101) records the startling degree of clout possessed by the Roman deacons, which often led them to treat the city presbyters with less than the respect due to them, seeing that presbyters could preside at the eucharist as deacons could not, and in that liturgical action were 'vicars of Christ' (on 1 Tim. 5: 19). For 'wherever a presbyter celebrates the mysteries, there is the Church' (on 1 Cor. 16: 19). Jerome (*ep.* 146 to Evangelus) reveals that at Rome a presbyter was ordained only on a deacon's

---

[1] Major documents survive through the Avellana collection in a manuscript now in the Vatican (Vat. lat. 3787, s. xi), edited by O. Guenther, CSEL 35 (1895).

recommendation, a custom of which he disapproved; it led deacons to take too much upon themselves, even in the absence of a bishop to take a seat among the presbyters, and to give a blessing. The stipend of Roman deacons was well above that of presbyters. 'Ambrosiaster' (on 1 Cor. 12: 29) noted that Rome had seven deacons, for each individual church two presbyters, but only one bishop over all (on 1 Tim. 3: 12). He also commented that deacons wore a dalmatic like bishops (*Qu.* 46: 8), and did not preach (on Gal. 4: 11). Perhaps Roman deacons felt that in the Christian city where they served, they held a position analogous to senators. In the sixth century in Gregory the Great's correspondence the epithet 'cardinalis' is found applied to Roman presbyters; it was in time extended to deacons and then to bishops attached to the Lateran.[2]

On 15 September of the following year Ursinus returned undeterred to the city (Avell. 6) and to the basilica of Liberius. He did not last long. On 16 November a new city prefect Praetextatus expelled Ursinus again, while his partisans moved to the Via Nomentana to occupy St Agnes. The prefect then prohibited all dissident assemblies within twenty miles of the city. Ursinus' supporters had been holding stational prayers at martyrs' shrines without any clergy until Damasus's supporters disrupted these meetings (Avell. 1. 12). The emperor Valentinian I disliked taking sides in ecclesiastical disputes. In 370 he relaxed sanctions against Ursinus as long as he kept out of Rome (Avell. 11–12). Ursinus then made his way to Milan, where he came to ally himself with Ambrose's opponents. Eventually the emperor Gratian exiled him to Cologne (Avell. 13). In Rome this rival faction to Damasus slowly petered out; Jerome (*ep.* 1. 15) records that his friend Evagrius of Antioch, where there was schism but mutual toleration without violence, showed Damasus not only how to overcome his opponents but also how to reconcile them. Probably this was in 382 when Evagrius came to Rome. But the road to peace was bumpy.

Pope Damasus accused of homicide

In 370 an accusation of responsibility for homicide against Damasus was entered by a converted Jew named Isaac. (Since the writings of Ambrosiaster (below p. 379) show extensive knowledge of synagogue practice, and since he once remarks that the ideal exegete of scripture is a converted Jew (on 1 Tim. 4: 6), it is possible that Isaac was his real name. He explicitly says that he writes when Damasus is 'rector' of the Church: on 1 Tim. 3: 14; 'rector' was Damasus' own term for his office—it occurs for bishops in some of his

---

[2] C. G. Fürst, *Cardinalis* (Munich, 1967).

verse inscriptions.) Rigorist adherents of Lucifer of Calaris, numerous in Sardinia, were outraged by Damasus' lifestyle. People were rudely calling him 'the ladies' ear-tickler' (Avell. 1), which at least suggests that his sermons were popular. His generous hospitality led the pagan aristocrat Praetextatus, who held priesthoods in several cults (his epitaph in *ILS* 1259 = *CIL* VI, 1779), to tease him by saying 'Make me bishop of Rome and I will become a Christian'—cited by Jerome (*adv. Joh. Hieros.* 8), who was sure that Praetextatus was 'now in Tartarus' (*ep.* 23. 2). Evidently the bishop of Rome's office now possessed high social standing, which for Praetextatus was of crucial importance for priesthoods. The resources of the Roman church were building up, but were not comparable with the vast opulence of men like Praetextatus, to whom the papacy would have seemed merely one more distinguished office to add to his long list. Damasus' relations with the rich Roman senators may not have been easy. When the pagan senators urged Gratian to allow the reinstatement of the Altar of Victory, the Pope turned for help to Ambrose, sending him the text of a counterpetition by Christian senators (Ambr. *ep.* 72 = M17. 10).

City morals

The period of Damasus' pontificate was far from easy in Roman society. There was a series of crises over food. In the affair of the Altar of Victory (below p. 366) Symmachus could point to famine in Africa, Rome's main supplier of grain. Revolts in Africa by Firmus (372–5) and then after Damasus' time by Gildo the Mauretanian in 398 caused serious interruptions in the food supply. Such dramas easily led to mob rioting. The populace could also become excited on religious issues; a Luciferian presbyter died as a result of a riot (Avell. 2. 82).

The maintaining of ethical probity in Roman society in this age was not easy. Ammianus (28. 4) paints a sordid picture both of the upper classes and of the plebeians in the city. Some of this portrait is vindicated by Ambrosiaster, who commented that whereas in old Roman society, women did not drink alcohol (an abstinence also attested in other texts), under present custom they had ceased to drink anything else (on Col. 3: 11; *Qu.* 115. 26). Jerome portrays Rome as a society sodden with corruption and mendacity (*ep.* 127. 3). The Briton Pelagius was shocked by the lack of passionate seriousness on such matters.

Roman synod, 378

The course of Damasus' trial on the charge of homicide is hard to reconstruct; we know the outcome in the petition from a Roman synod to Gratian in 378 (*Et hoc gloriae*, PL 13. 575, a document drafted by Ambrose, CSEL 82/3. 191) and Gratian's reply (Avell. 13). The synod took note of his acquittal. The letter also contained an allusion (578 A 11) to tortures which had been used in the cross-examination of innocent Roman clergy, an action which Rufinus (*HE* 11. 10) attributed to a ferocious prefect, Maximin. The synod of 378 asked the emperor to rule that a criminal charge against the bishop of Rome should come not before the city prefect but before either a council of bishops or the emperor; the petition also pleaded that the Roman bishop have authority over other bishops and be enabled to compel them to appear before the Pope if in Italy, or before their provincial metropolitan if outside Italy. If the accused bishops were metropolitans themselves, then their judge should be either the bishop of Rome or bishops nominated by him. Any appeal should be heard either by the bishop of Rome or by a synod of at least fifteen neighbouring bishops. This second plea was occasioned by the support given to Ursinus by 'bad bishops'. The synod was perturbed that the bishops of Parma and Puteoli had been declared deposed and then sat tight ignoring the decisions against them. The synod also wanted Restitutus of Carthage, who had sent an 'insolent' refusal, to answer some unspecified charge, probably his responsibility for the creed of Nike/Ariminum (above, p. 284). (One of Athanasius' last writings was an open letter 'to the Africans' that Nicaea had far greater claims on their allegiance than Ariminum, with a long catalogue of provincial synods enforcing this position. The see of Carthage was wobbly on this.) The underlying and primary question for the synod was the jurisdiction of the 'apostolic see' (the first occurrence of this phrase for the Roman see). In Damasus' time it was axiomatic at Rome that all authority in the Church stems from St Peter, and therefore from episcopal succession since the apostle (Ambrosiaster, *Qu.* 110. 7). For the request that a criminal charge against the bishop of Rome come before the emperor the synod cited an otherwise unattested acquittal of Silvester by Constantine.

Gratian was kinder to the second request than to the first. He ruled that accusations against the pope from malicious or immoral people should be excluded, but otherwise ignored the plea regarding criminal charges against a pope. He agreed that metropolitans should appear before the Pope, who should provide a court of appeal for bishops against their metropolitans. What canons or rules were thus to be enforced Gratian assumed to be evident. The canons of Nicaea were prominent in Damasus' decretals, though the sixth canon as approved in 325 did not help claims for Roman jurisdiction on any universal scale. If it was to do that, it would need some emendation, which in due course the Roman chancery provided by giving the Latin version the opening sentence: 'The Roman church has always held the primacy...' (*EOMIA* i. 121b; PL 56. 819A). At Chalcedon in 451 the Roman legates cited the canon in this form. It caused difficulty to the Greeks.

Roman liturgy: from Greek to Latin

Marius Victorinus (*adversus Arium* 2. 8. 34–5) and Ambrosiaster (on 1 Cor. 14. 14 and 19) show that until Damasus' time the liturgy of the Roman church was still in Greek, though Latin-speakers did not understand it, and indeed preferred the creed to be in incomprehensible Greek. At Rome it long continued to be customary for the Gospel and some lections to be read in Greek. The bilingual Codex Bezae at Cambridge of the fourth century, with the Gospels and Acts, was written for a church normally using Latin but needing a Greek text for the Gospels and Acts for at least certain occasions. Ambrosiaster (on 1 Tim. 2. 3–4) also echoes the general intercessory prayer in the eucharist—for kings, for the subjection of barbarians, for peace, and for all in trouble and necessity. Damasus appears to have been responsible for making Latin the standard liturgy; it was the vernacular of the majority of his congregation.

Dissidents suppressed

Damasus sought above all to impose order on a fractious body. There were Manichees in the city, so the emperor was asked to deal with them, which he did (CTh 16. 5. 3, March 372). A small congregation of Donatists under their bishop Claudianus, probably consisting of expatriate Africans, was likewise made unwelcome. In 383–4 two priests belonging to Lucifer of Calaris' group submitted a lengthy catalogue of Damasus' shortcomings (*Libellus Precum*, Avell. 2), mainly in his suppression of dissident houses of worship by violent means.

Auxentius of Milan. Nicene authority

No doubt the Nicene faction at Milan alerted him to the problem of Auxentius' strict adherence to the Likeness creed of Ariminum. In 371 Damasus presided over a synod, which asked (in vain) that Valentinian I remove Auxentius from office. Damasus asserted the universal authority of the Nicene formula, which derived this special authority from its ratification by Pope Silvester. It seems to have been his custom to invite Italian bishops to an annual gathering on the anniversary of his consecration; Augustine attests such a custom for an individual bishop who would give a substantial meal for the poor on his anniversary, called his *natalis* or birthday (S. Frangipane 2. 4 p. 193 Morin). In Damasus' claim that the authority of Nicaea depended on Roman ratification, it is likely that he meant to assert less a right to speak on behalf of the entire Latin west, thereby giving the council the assent of west as well as east, than a right to be the one ecclesial organ with unique power to confer this status on Constantine's or any other council. But there was a touch of ambiguity at this point. There is no evidence that Damasus influenced the choice and approval of Ambrose at Milan. It is improbable, since he was wholly opposed to making bishops of people in public service who had had responsibility for capital punishment and torture. Damasus' council made the earliest statement that different theologies confuse laity, that all bishops must agree on the Nicene formula that Father, Son, and Holy Spirit are one *ousia* and *figura*, that where disagreements appear, the judgement of the Roman bishop is prior to all others, and that none dissenting is in communion with Rome the touchstone of authenticity.

Priestly celibacy[3]

Damasus expected his clergy to be celibate; then they could offer the daily eucharistic sacrifice in ritual purity. He did not approve of the ordination of laity coming from other churches to Rome, and commended this rule to the churches in Gaul, who were also warned against clergy whose career had been in the army or civil service. He wanted the clergy to be marked out as separate from the laity, but distinguished more by moral probity than by their brains or social class.

New churches and martyria

The juxtaposition of pagan temples and Christian shrines was not at first very close. In time as Christian influence in Rome steadily increased new shrines for martyrs could be sited close to old pagan sites. At Rome, unlike the Greek east, a long time passed before disused pagan temples such as the Pantheon were recycled for Christian use. In 354 in Liberius' time the calligrapher Philocalus produced for an otherwise unknown Christian Valentinus a finely illustrated calendar of festivals for the city. It had lists of city prefects and consuls and then side by side, not fused, pagan feasts and days when the configuration of the planets would be dangerous, the dates of Christian festivals including 25 December, an Easter table from 312 to 411, and a list of Roman bishops enlarged from an earlier document of 235 revised in 336. A further section had emperors to the death of Licinius in 324 and a list of the Regions of the city as in the year 334; it also included the chronicle of world history by Hippolytus in which biblical chronology is inserted into Greek and Roman dates. The Christian feasts are noted in a setting which reflects the calendar of old Rome. It suggests a programme for the sanctification of both places and times in the life of the city.

---

[3] Philo regarded celibacy as a hallmark of true priesthood: *V. Mosis* 2. 68–9.

In Rome Damasus fostered a major programme of building shrines and churches in honour of Rome's martyrs. He recruited the services of the calligrapher Philocalus to incise the martyr's shrines in exquisite lettering with verses which he himself composed. Most of these texts survive in later copies, but about five in their original Philocalian form. One (57 in Ihm, and in Ferrua, Vatican City, 1942) records archives of the Roman church, which Damasus housed and brought into order. This made a valuable arsenal for him and his successors in providing precedents for the affirmation of papal jurisdiction. The inscriptions not only honour the martyrs; they include some which emphasize peace and unity in the Roman church, themes dear to Damasus' heart. By the font at St Peter's the words were 'one chair of Peter, one true baptismal washing' (Ihm 5, Ferrua 4: *Una Petri sedes, unum uerumque lauacrum*). The churches in Rome had a past of separate, probably financially independent congregations. It seems to have been in Damasus' time that wealthy aristocrats were persuaded to fund church buildings, and these came to be called 'title-churches' associated with particular benefactors. Archaeologists have not been able to find evidence of continuity going back to the second- or third-century house-churches, though that is not impossible.

Legacy hunters

In 370 Valentinian I enacted a painful decree addressed to Damasus forbidding clergy to hunt for legacies among opulent ladies (CTh 16. 2. 20). That was the kind of charge Ursinus and his party were glad to bring against Damasus. Jerome concedes that there had been instances to justify the edict.

Damasus and the East

Damasus' condemnation of Apollinaris' doctrines enhanced his reputation in the Greek churches, not so his rigid adherence to Paulinus of Antioch. In this support for Paulinus Basil of Caesarea judged him to be arrogant and uncomprehending (an opinion which was mutual). His support for the Cynic philosopher Maximus to be bishop of Constantinople did not last long, probably on advice from Thessalonica. He was represented neither at the council of Constantinople in May 381 nor at the council of Aquileia controlled by Ambrose in September of that year. The former council he deeply disliked and resented because of its canonical elevation of Constantinople on the ground of being New Rome, a title for the city in normal use well before Damasus' time, as well as because of its decision to refuse recognition to Paulinus of Antioch. In 382 he held a council at Rome, attended by, among others, Jerome, Paulinus of Antioch, and Epiphanius of Salamis. This issued a trumpet blast against the pretensions of Constantinople insisting that the only sees with multi-provincial jurisdiction were Rome, Alexandria, and Antioch—the three sees mentioned in the sixth canon of Nicaea at which time the city founded by Constantine did not exist in the form it had acquired by 381; all three were 'Petrine'. Moreover, the honour of the Roman see depended on no synodical decisions but on Jesus' words 'Thou art Peter . . .' and on Peter's martyrdom at Rome with Paul on one and the same day ('not on different days as heresies say'). Perhaps the tradition that both were martyred on the same day was associated with the shrine to both apostles together on the Via Appia, while the separate sites on the Vatican hill and on the Via Ostiense were linked to separate dates (above p. 48). There was also a current compromise which declared that the martyrdom of the two apostles occurred on the same date (29 June) but a year apart, a view which involved no liturgical complications. This last view is exemplified in Prudentius, *Peristephanon* 12. 5, and the Verona or 'Leonine' Sacramentary.

Jerome's Vulgate

After the council of Rome in 382 Jerome stayed on in the capital as Damasus' secretary until the Pope's death in December 384, and the Pope encouraged him to produce a revised version of the Latin Bible, free of the numerous infelicities and specimens of 'translationese' which marred the Old Latin Bible, especially in the Old Testament. Very gradually Jerome's version succeeded in supplanting the Old Latin until his translation became the standard version in the west, named by the Council of Trent the common version or Vulgata. He had studied Greek and some Hebrew and had Origen's Hexapla to help him with versions of the Greek Old Testament other than the Septuagint. But for the future it was central that his version of the Old Testament books treated the Hebrew text as possessing an authority which the Septuagint did not have. He was also responsible for giving the misleading title Apocrypha to the overplus of the Septuagint canon over against the Hebrew. These books he judged to be good guides in ethical matters, but were not to be appealed to for settling dogmatic disagreements. Their authority was not recognized by rabbis. It was easy to say this as there was next to nothing of dogmatic importance that these books helped to resolve. In the long term the sponsoring of the Vulgate Bible was Damasus' act with the greatest consequences of benefit to the churches.

Memorials of Peter and Paul

Damasus liked tidying things up, and it is reasonably likely that he was responsible for reconciling the cult at the Via Appia with the two independent sites (above p. 48). That on 29 June the Roman churches celebrated Peter and Paul probably with a procession round the ancient sites is very likely. Pope Silvester could not attend the council of Arles on 1 August 314 because of his obligations to be in his city for the festival. A procession from St Peter's to St Paul's and then on to the double shrine on the Via Appia in a hot June would have been remarkably exhausting, and already in Prudentius' time the inclusion of the Via Appia was dropped. Jerome (*adv. Vigilantium* 8) says that the bishop of Rome celebrates mass over the relics of Peter and Paul; this text could tell either way. The Gelasian sacramentary (2. 30–2) has three celebrations, one at St Peter's, one for both apostles together, and one for St Paul; that suggests that at least a presbyter was on duty at the Via Appia. One of Paulinus of Nola's annual visits to Rome was for the celebration on 29 June. By the eighth century the Gregorian Sacramentary shows that the visit to St Paul's was deferred until 30 June. A contemporary observer regretted that the feast of St Paul was attended by more visitors and pilgrims from outside Rome than from those who lived in the city (PL 56. 1139B). It is possible that Damasus sought a justification for dropping the Via Appia from the procession.

In or about 165 the Roman community had erected a memorial monument to St Peter in a necropolis on the Vatican hill outside the old city. A monument to St Paul was also erected on the road to Ostia, and these two monuments were explicitly mentioned with some pride by an anti-Montanist Roman writer Gaius early in the third century cited by Eusebius (*HE* 2. 25. 7). The calendar of Philocalus of 354 has an entry for 29 June which has provoked much discussion: 'III Kal. Petri in Catacumbas et Pauli Ostense Tusco et Basso consulibus' (= 258). The omission of a reference to the memorial monument on the Vatican hill is problematic; perhaps the text has a lacuna. Or perhaps this form of text dates from the time of the Laurentian schism (499–502) when St Peter's was in the possession of Laurentius' successful rival Symmachus, while Laurentius had St Paul's and the Lateran was under the bishop of Altinum. Laurentius' calendar for 29 June would certainly have omitted the Vatican. The site called Catacumbas was some hollow ground near the third milestone on the Via Appia. There by the year 258 there was a shrine to both Peter and Paul, and the graffiti inscribed on the walls (below the church of San Sebastiano) make it certain that devout Christians believed the remains of both Peter and Paul to lie there together; e.g. 'Petre et Paule in mente nos habeatis' or 'Paule et Petre petite pro Victore'. The worshippers also celebrated funerary meals, called Refreshment or *refrigerium*, so that one graffito has 'ad Paulum et Petrum refrigeravi'.

The historical problem is therefore that by the third milestone of the Via Appia we have a third century shrine for both apostles, while late in the second century there were two separate shrines, for Peter in the Vatican necropolis, for Paul on the road to Ostia, evidently on the site of the existing church of St Paul without the Walls. There are two hypotheses to account for these facts. The first is the speculation, first proposed by John Pearson in 1682 but attested in no ancient text, that perhaps during persecution the relics were moved for safety from the Vatican and the Via Ostiense to the Via Appia, and then returned in the time of Constantine. This guess has real attractions. An epigram by Pope Damasus, however, may imply belief that both apostles had originally been buried together on the Via Appia but were subsequently translated to the Vatican and the Via Ostiense; in other words, if there was a translation, it was in the reverse direction to that of Pearson's conjecture. The second hypothesis is that we are dealing with rival sites, and that the worshippers at the Via Appia were perhaps in origin a dissident group, of which Rome never lacked a supply. At Ephesus Eusebius records that there were two tombs dedicated to the apostle John, one of which he thought could be of a different John. It is no doubt likely that they were rival sites, one in the city near the harbour, the other on the hill at Selçuk where now stands Justinian's basilica of the apostle John.

The epigram by Pope Damasus makes it certain that in the fourth century in his time it was believed that the shrine on the Via Appia had at one time in the past possessed the remains of both apostles (Damasus, *epigr.* 26 Ihm, 20 Ferrua). The text may be rendered:

Whoever you may be that seek the relics (*nomina*) of Peter and Paul should know that the saints dwelt here once. The East sent the disciples; that we readily admit. But on account of the merit of their blood (they have followed Christ through the stars and attained to the ethereal bosom and the realms of the holy ones) Rome has gained a superior right to claim them as her citizens. Damasus would thus tell of your praises as new stars.

The image of stars to describe the apostles may imply that Damasus was already thinking of Peter and Paul as replacing Romulus and Remus as founders of a now Christian Rome, a theme expressly formulated by Pope Leo the Great sixty years later. The argument that although Peter and Paul came from the Orient, they are now appropriated by Rome, is a Christianization of an old thesis that each tribe has its own local gods and rites, but the Romans worship all the gods of conquered nations and therefore through their patronage have acquired a world empire. (So explicitly the pagan Caecilius in the *Octavius* of Minucius Felix 6.)[4]

---

[4] Damasus' understanding that both apostles had once been on the Via Appia is repeated in Gregory the Great's letter of 594 to the Byzantine empress Constantina (*Reg.* 4. 30); it also appears in the *Martyrium Petri et Pauli* of pseudo-Marcellus 66 (in Lipsius–Bonnet, *Acta Apost. Apocr.* 1, 174–5), in a Salzburg itinerary of the seventh century (de Rossi, *Roma sotteranea*, 1864, i. 139), and in the sixth-century Life of Pope Cornelius in the *Liber Pontificalis* (i. 150 Duchesne).

The language of the epigram reflects some degree of tension with the eastern churches and might therefore date from 382 when Damasus was visibly cross with the Greek council of the previous year.

The great church of St Paul's without the Walls was constructed in Damasus' time. He evidently did not think that the authority of Rome's bishop depended on succession exclusively to St Peter.

Siricius

When Damasus died late in 384, his erudite but contentious secretary and sermon-writer Jerome aspired to the succession. 'Almost everyone agreed I was worthy of high-priesthood. Damasus spoke no words but mine' (*ep.* 45. 3). He failed to gain enough support. Malicious gossip reported unkindly of the spiritual direction of devout aristocratic ladies by 'a sorcerer and seducer'. Jerome resentfully observed that congregations prefer unscholarly bishops (*in Eccles.* 9. 11, p. 465 Vallarsi). The election went in favour of Siricius, who was to hold the see for thirteen years until 399. After the weakness of Liberius and the embarrassing conflicts of Damasus with Ursinus, the community in Rome needed consolidation and peace to provide leadership for the west more generally.

Siricius responded to the requests for guidance from other western metropolitans. In the archives he found that Liberius had sent out encyclicals addressed to several western provinces, not merely to bishops in the 'suburbicarian' region of Italy. He describes these encyclicals as 'generalia decreta', rulings of universal application concerning the way in which heretics should be reconciled to the Church. It was important that the procedures in one province should not differ from those in another. Converts from Novatian's society should be accepted by laying-on of hands and invocation of the Spirit.

Decretal to Himerius of Tarraco

On 2 February 385 Siricius celebrated his elevation with a council of bishops, which supported him in a directive answering an enquiry from Himerius bishop of Tarraco (Tarragona) in Spain. The Pope saw a lot needing rectification. Baptisms were to be only at Pentecost and Easter unless for a sick baby or for those facing shipwreck, enemy attack, siege, or grave illness. They should not be at Christmas or Epiphany. Apostates could be reconciled with viaticum on their deathbed. It was wrong for baptized persons then to accept office in government service involving prosecutions or presiding at public spectacles. The demand for celibacy was an unbreakable rule without exceptions; bishops and deacons who had children by wives or even concubines, and ascetics of opposite sex who had offspring, needed discipline.[5] No women were to reside in clergy houses, with the exceptions allowed under the fourth canon of Nicaea. None should invoke the Old Testament as justifying marriage for priests now. The penalty was to be 'deposed by the apostolic see'. Siricius optimistically ruled that no bishop should be ignorant of 'Roman decretals and canons'. A surprising rule legislated about the age of ordination: deacon if over 30, presbyter over 35, bishop over 40. Monks of the right age should be welcomed to ordination. To be a lay penitent was a bar to ordination.

This last ruling created a problem. Guided by Augustine, the African churches wanted to offer reconciliation to schismatic Donatist bishops. But a schismatic was reconciled by laying-on of hands just as a penitent was. If Siricius meant that no reconciled schismatic in major orders could be received in his clerical rank, that was awkward for Augustinian ecumenism. A council at Carthage in 397 asked Siricius and Ambrose's successor Simplicianus of Milan please to reconsider this.

Reform of ordinations: celibacy

On 6 January 386 Siricius presided over another council 'gathered by the relics of the apostle Peter from whom apostolate and episcopate originated'. The bishops agreed that in the western churches much needed to be put right, and Siricius felt it to be his responsibility to issue an edict, correcting bishops who presumed to 'follow what their people want and do not fear God's judgement.' He therefore issued a general letter, written 'in fear of hell' if he neglected his duty. It is noteworthy that Siricius felt it necessary thus to justify his decision to write, no doubt foreseeing reaction from bishops of independent spirit. He was perturbed by the unsuitable bishops sometimes elected. 'None may dare to ordain a bishop without consulting the apostolic see', and no single bishop may consecrate a bishop contrary to the fourth canon of Nicaea (a ruling that touched Evagrius' consecration by Paulinus of Antioch acting alone). Other rulings repeated the prohibition of admitting to the clergy baptized persons who had then accepted posts in the public service, the demand for priestly celibacy necessary because of the duty to celebrate the sacrifice daily or in emergencies, and the principle that a cleric ejected at one church may not be reinstated at another. Siricius concluded with a request that there be no dissent, and a warning that disagreement

---

[5] In ancient pagan society it was an axiom that before offering a sacrifice a priest must not have sexual intercourse (Porphyry, *De abstinentia* 2. 50). Soldiers before battle had the same expectation, e.g. 1 Sam. 21: 5.

entailed forfeiting communion with Rome. There is 'one faith, one tradition'. A reminder was needed of the theme to Himerius in Spain: ordination
is no earthly commission; priesthood is heavenly.

Jovinian, Bonosus, Helvidius

Reaction against clerical celibacy as a general requirement was not slow in
coming, and arrived from an unexpected quarter, namely a monk. Jovinian
arrived in Rome from north Italy and proclaimed the equal value before God
of marriage and virginity, the ethical indifference of either fasting or eating
with thanksgiving, and the equality of all the baptized who keep their vows.
He expressed serious doubts about ascribing to the Blessed Virgin Mary a
perpetual virginity; later she could have had other children by Joseph. Similar
opinions were voiced by Helvidius, a layman at Rome, against whom Jerome
wrote a sharp tract. In 390 Ambrose condemned Jovinian's doctrines, and
Siricius concurred. Eight years later Jovinian was exiled to an island off the
Dalmatian coast where he died. In 393 Jerome composed against him one of
his most controversial writings, indebted to Seneca, but to high Roman
society utterly offensive (cf. below pp. 443–44).

 The denial of a need to proclaim Mary to be perpetual virgin was also
heard from the bishop of Naissus Bonosus, whose opinions disturbed the
bishop of Thessalonica. He too encountered condemnation from Ambrose
and Siricius.

One faith, one tradition, one discipline for all

A letter to the bishops of Gaul (sometimes ascribed to Damasus) similarly
addressed problems of diversity as a threat to unity which consists in the tradition of the fathers. 'Many bishops depart from tradition, preferring the
honour of men to the glory of God.' Gallic bishops are now asking for an
authoritative statement from the apostolic see. Catholic bishops should have
a single confession and apostolic discipline, so that there is 'one faith, one
tradition, one discipline for all churches.' (*ep.* 10. 9. PL 13. 1188 A). This discipline requires clerical celibacy, since by priestly hands 'the grace of
baptism is given and the body of Christ made.' A priest who begets children
cares more for the secular world than for God. How can he with integrity
counsel a widow or consecrated virgin (10. 5)? Siricius gives rules on prohibited degrees for marriage: no marrying of an uncle's wife or a niece.
Bishops are not to be chosen from the laity, only from clergy (15). Bishops
should not leave one church for another, for that is like leaving a spouse (16).
They are not to ordain in another's territory, which is 'contrary to the ruling
(*moderatio*) of the apostolic see'. As earlier, Siricius stressed that ordination is

'not something secular, not a worldly promotion' (18). Laity excommunicated by their bishop may not be ordained elsewhere; names of bishops who
do this are to be delated to Rome 'so that we may know who to avoid' (19).

Collegiality and Primacy

Damasus and Siricius both wrote their authoritative letters after holding
synods. It is significant that the letters sent out are all in the name of the see
of Rome,[6] not of the synods, which are thereby implied to be valued counsellors giving the bishop of Rome collective advice and by their assent also
enhancing the honour of the Roman see. This was not unprecedented. In
340 Julius had upset the Greek bishops at Antioch by writing in his own name
only, though he defended that by saying that he had consulted all Italian
bishops (Athanasius, *Apol. c. Ar.* 26). Yet it was not a manner of proceeding
that would be easily understood in the synodically minded East. And Siricius'
repeated insistence on celibacy for presbyters and deacons was constructing a
dividing wall against Greek practice. The eastern churches were beyond the
horizon of his vision. It was enough for him to be bringing ordered discipline to the Latin west which in his time had little of it. Greek experience
of western church policy in 381 and 382 and Basil's prickly correspondence
with Damasus could well have discouraged Greek bishops from looking
Romewards for help with their problems.

No evidence survives of Siricius continuing Damasus' building programme, or of his responsibility for a riot destroying a Jewish synagogue in
Rome, which provoked Magnus Maximus to order rebuilding at some cost
to his popularity (Ambrose, *ep. extra coll.* 1a = M40. 23). The Avellana collection (40) preserves a letter from Magnus Maximus to Siricius about his
suppression of Priscillianists. The Pope sought to avoid being involved in the
dispute between Jerome and Rufinus about Origenism, which was splitting
the aristocrats of Rome into factions but probably hardly excited the main
body of the *plebs*. In this detachment he was more successful than his short-
lived successor Anastasius I. We do not hear of him being prominent, as
Ambrose was, at the time of the uprising led by Eugenius against Theodosius.
His central achievement was to consolidate papal authority in the west and
thereby to lay a foundation for stronger measures by Innocent I.

---

[6] *Papa*, in Greek *pappas*, in the fourth century expresses respectful affection, in the fifth and sixth
centuries gradually becoming the title of an office for bishops of Rome or Alexandria. Originally
African bishops gave the title to the bishop of Carthage. In 400 a council at Toledo used *papa* for
Rome. But bishops in Gaul are found being so addressed until Carolingian times. The title was
important for Symmachus at Rome in 500 during the Laurentian schism. See J. Moorhead in *Journal
of Eccles. History* 36 (1985), 337–50, below, p. 607.

Anastasius, Innocent I

Anastasius succeeded Siricius in November 399. The quarrel between Jerome and his old friend Rufinus about the orthodoxy of Origen led him to censure Origen's doctrines, which pleased Jerome, but to refuse any disciplinary action against Rufinus for translating him. He died in December 402, succeeded a few days later by Innocent I (402–17), who may have been Anastasius' son and was in political terms a major figure for the development of the idea of a universal papal jurisdiction responsible for east as well as west.

Synesius of Cyrene[7]

Parallel to the movement of senators towards the Church there was a comparable shift among highly educated Greek intellectuals. Among the latter the most striking is Synesius. He was born at Cyrene in 370 and studied philosophy with Hypatia at Alexandria. His social standing in Cyrenaica led to him being sent to court to negotiate tax relief on behalf of his province (c.399–402). He also took a lead in mobilizing resistance to raiding nomadic tribes (ep. 32–3). A few years later, perhaps 410 certainly by 412, he accepted an invitation to become metropolitan bishop of Ptolemais and was consecrated by Theophilus of Alexandria. He was a Neoplatonist, and had to reinterpret Christian themes such as resurrection. As a bishop he asserted a right to retain his wife. Theophilus had blessed their wedding. His writings are an unusual mixture. They include a portrait of his ideal prince, delivered as an oration before the emperor Arcadius, an allegorical piece written with an eye to the Goths' bid for power in Constantinople, a covering letter for a gift of an astrolabe, a work on dreams, a defence of the unity of the old Greek rivals philosophy and rhetoric, presented as an echo of Dio Chrysostom of Prusa three centuries earlier. A hundred and fifty-six of his letters survive attesting both his philosophic humanism and his adherence, with qualifications, to Christianity which to him represented a path of ascent for the soul to God and so a way of bringing Neoplatonic ideals into practice for the many. In addition nine hymns are preserved, deeply Neoplatonic in content, in which the Trinity is interpreted in a Plotinian framework.

---

[7] Synesius' works are best edited by A. Garzya (Turin, 1989), the letters also (Rome, 1979), and by N. Terzaghi, opuscula (Rome, 1944), the hymns, ed. J. Gruber and H. Strohm (Heidelberg, 1991), monograph by J. Bregman (Berkeley, 1982). See too W. Liebeschuetz, *Barbarians and Bishops* (Oxford, 1990); Alan Cameron and J. Long, *Barbarians and Politics* (Berkeley, 1993); H. I. Marrou, 'Synesius and Alexandrian Neoplatonism,' in A. Momigliano (ed.), *The Conflict between Paganism and Christianity* (Oxford, 1963), 126–50; W. Theiler, *Forschungen zum Neuplatonismus* (Berlin, 1966), 151–301; S. Vollenweider, *Neuplatonische und christliche Theologie bei Synesius* (Göttingen, 1985).

Synesius had an affinity with Themistius, a philosophic mind at the court, who pleaded before the emperor Valens for a policy of religious toleration on the ground of theology's essential mysteriousness. Synesius liked to stress the esoteric inwardness of true religion. His experience of the practical demands put upon a bishop led at the end of his life to a degree of sad disillusion with his earlier aspirations. Moreover, he had lost his children and too many close friends.

38

BASIL OF CAESAREA (CAPPADOCIA)

Education. Monasticism

The emperor Valens, guided by Eudoxius, was opposed by a struggle to establish bishops supporting the Nicene creed and to marginalize those dissenting. In Asia Minor central to this endeavour became Basil, bishop of Caesarea, metropolis of Cappadocia from autumn 370. He was born into an aristocratic landowning family with close attachment to the Church at Neocaesarea in Pontus, where his father was a successful advocate and the family included more than one bishop. At Neocaesarea the church proudly remembered the evangelization of Pontus by Origen's pupil Gregory the Wonderworker (Thaumaturgos), and treasured his creed and liturgy with such precision that their style of worship had come to seem very old-fashioned a century later (Basil, *De Spir. S.* 74). When Basil's monks chanted the psalms antiphonally, people at Neocaesarea were censorious of the innovation, which seemed a defiance of authority (*ep.* 207). Basil had a high-class education at Athens and heard Libanius lecturing at Constantinople. Letters exchanged between Basil and Libanius were known to Severus of Antioch about AD 500 (PO II i. 13); the authenticity of at least some among those transmitted has been reasonably doubted. His sister Macrina, whom he never mentions, was given a biography by his younger brother Gregory of Nyssa, which fused Neoplatonic aspirations with Christian holiness and portrayed her as an ideal saint. Basil had a past closely associated with the monastic (and homoiousian) movement in Asia Minor, where a leading figure was Eustathius bishop of Sebaste, in whose company in 356 he went on a tour of monasteries in Mesopotamia, Palestine, and Egypt.

Baptized by Bishop Dianios of Caesarea (prominent at the eastern synod of Serdica and no friend to the Nicene creed) for whom he had deep reverence, in the 360s he was ordained presbyter and began to compose rules for monasteries, dominated by texts from scripture. He retreated to family property with lovely scenery at Annisi not far from Caesarea, and there with his friend Gregory of Nazianzos compiled the extant *Philokalia*, gathering Origen's principal discussions of biblical interpretation; this could answer some of the objections to scripture in Porphyry and Julian and at the same time ward off criticism of Origen. Like Eustathius, deposed from Sebaste in 359–60, he wanted to link ascetics with the life of the churches and vice versa, mainly in towns. It was a principle for him that monks should live a common life in community, serving those beyond the walls as well as one another. He also composed forms of liturgy and preached numerous surviving sermons. Eleven homilies on the six days of creation were vastly admired in his time and later; when they were preached cannot be determined, but they were exploited by Ambrose in his discourses on the same subject. Basil may have sent him a copy. They were early translated into Latin by one Eustathius. One theme in the homilies is a disavowal of treating all Genesis as allegory. These homilies constitute a dialogue with philosophical writing on the world of nature. Caesarea had important pagan temples of Zeus, Apollo, and the city's Genius or Tyche. The city population included many pagans. When Bishop Dianios died in 363, Basil was not chosen to succeed, and the election went to an ex-civil servant named Eusebius who understood little about the pastoral office and therefore relied much on Basil. Their relations were not always easy.

Homoiousians. Against Eunomius

During the 360s in the East the homoiousian party attempted to reassemble a coherent and influential body after their virtual destruction by Eudoxius in 360, and by not declaring themselves on the deity of the Holy Spirit gained the support of Pope Liberius. Only the influence of the West was able to provide the East with support which could establish an orthodoxy that might persuade the emperor Valens to be tolerant and perhaps even supportive. After attending the council at Constantinople in 360, Basil saw the threat from radical Arianism. At this stage he had turned for theological guidance to Apollinaris at Laodicea, whose exposition of the Nicene *homoousios* was influential. Later when Apollinaris' name became widely associated with error in Christology, Basil would need to disown the relationship. His past association with the homoiousian group also needed to be consigned to wise oblivion. He wrote a treatise against Eunomius, candidly attacking Eudoxius' 'seizure' of the see of Constantinople and his past support for Eunomius. Appeal to 'The Father is greater than I' was answered from Phil. 2: (equality with God); so one may say either *homoousios* ('identical') or *homoios kat'ousian* ('like in essence'). Basil was seeking to bring together a pro-Nicene group with the battered homoiousian party cruelly excluded at Seleucia 359 and Constantinople 360, probably a party politically damaged by Athanasius' olive branch discharged as if by a catapult. Basil understood the Nicene *homoousios* to be generic: all human beings share the same *ousia*, so also Father, Son, and Holy Spirit have a common *ousia*, while their individuality is expressed as hypostases. The third book, much briefer than the first two, begins to develop an argument about the Holy Spirit, named with Father and Son in the baptismal triadic formula; but it is embryonic in comparison with his later work on this subject.

High culture in decline at Caesarea

The provocation given by Julian's decree forbidding teachers to be un-believers in the gods may have given Basil the impetus to write a short piece to guide the young about the right way to read classical literature. The surviving texts reveal relatively little of Basil's dialogue with pagan intellectuals. One letter (20) to a sophist Leontius (perhaps identical with a sophist from Armenia often mentioned in Libanius' correspondence, whose rhetoric brought him high office under Julian; but probably only a local teacher at Caesarea) ironically apologizes for his own association with the common herd, and then sends him a copy of his work against Eunomius to show him what an educated Christian who has studied Plotinus can do. Gregory of Nazianzos records that throughout his life Basil retained a modest library (*or.* 43, 49, PG 36. 559 c). The peasants surrounding Basil were probably demotic in their Greek and spoke the old Cappadocian dialect (*De Spir. S.* 29. 74 implies that Basil could speak it; another reference in Greg. Nyss. *c. Eunom.* 12, PG 45. 1045 D). *Ep.* 74 laments the decline of all high culture at Caesarea, its closed gymnasia, no street-lighting now, only the barbarous voices of Scythians and Massagetae, no market for produce. Nevertheless Caesarea had fitting accommodation for an emperor.

Basil as bishop with the emperor Valens

During the 360s Basil established a monastery at Caesarea. In 370 at the next vacancy his political skills were deployed in canvassing for his election to be bishop; they did not forsake him thereafter. Other bishops in Cappadocia thought he had used unscrupulous methods in getting himself elected. But Basil had his theological agenda, welcome to Athanasius of Alexandria. His action was not self-seeking. The emperor Valens, advised by Eudoxius at Constantinople, after his death (370) by Euzoius at Antioch, was unsympathetic to the Nicene creed. Its advocates were too intolerant of other views. When he visited Caesarea in the winter of 372 or 373 a pro-Nicene group hoped for a grand confrontation between Basil and the emperor, but Basil did not oblige. Valens had been baptized by Eudoxius probably in 364 when he was seriously ill. At the 'table' or 'altar' (*ep.* 251. 3) he himself presented the bread for consecration. He was given communion without any question, and the emperor was impressed by Basil's qualities. He even entrusted him with a commission to provide bishops for the province of Armenia, where chaos reigned. The commission made insoluble difficulties for Basil, though he was honoured and delighted to be asked. Probably Valens was anxious to recruit him in support of his ecclesiastical policies. Later Basil found himself under bitter attack at the court, and feared for his life. A military commander, Victor, spoke for him (*epp.* 120, 129, 152, 153, 156, 213). Travel, usually by mule, was necessary, but to the cold hills of Armenia unpleasant and, when his health became poor which was not infrequent, hazardous or impossible. A visit to some hot springs failed to cure his ailments. Army deserters in Cappadocia as elsewhere in the empire usually became brigands infesting the highways (268).

Eustathius of Sebaste; Aerius

Eustathius of Sebaste had advocated serious forms of asceticism, and at a council at Gangra in Paphlagonia (of uncertain date, perhaps as early as 343, but Socrates dates it after 360, and Professor T. D. Barnes has suggested 355) there were condemnations of ascetics who rejected marriage or refused to accept the eucharist from a married priest or regarded vegetarianism as obligatory or told slaves that they need not obey their masters. Basil's ascetic writings show the influence of Eustathius, notably in founding a hospice.

Eustathius placed in charge of his hospice an ascetic named Aerius with whom he did not get on. Aerius led a schism teaching that presbyters and bishops are of the same order with identical power so that both may ordain, that it is Judaistic to celebrate the Easter Pasch, that prayers for the faithful departed at the eucharist do no good, and that prescribed times for fasting are needless. He had a mixed following of men and women who fasted on Sundays and ate well on Wednesdays and Fridays. Aerius was 'still alive and still Arian' when Epiphanius wrote his *Panarion* (375). Basil wholly ignored Aerius. Eustathius' and Basil's most striking characteristics were to treat ascetic communities as preferable to hermitages and to be expected to provide a mission to the entire Church, not an exodus from it. The communities needed rules, grounded on holy scripture, and Basil set out to provide these.

Canon law

The gathering of rules for the churches was hardly less important; three of his letters to Amphilochios of Iconium give his collections (188, 199, 217), which became part of Greek canon law. That is a testimony to the authority later enjoyed by Basil, since the canonical letters (especially *ep.* 188. 23) give the impression of being largely his personal rulings, valid in his own jurisdiction, rather than assembled from the rule-books of churches known to him. A letter to the country bishops (*chorepiscopi*) under his jurisdiction rebukes them for departures from canon law, especially in ordaining men for payment, without scrutiny, and without consulting Basil. (Consent of the diocesan bishop was made a requirement by a canon of Antioch about 328.) They had been allowing existing clergy to propose relatives and friends to be subdeacons, an order popular among people avoiding military service (*ep.* 54). When the deputy prefect of Pontus, Demosthenes (who had once been snubbed by Basil), removed Gregory of Nyssa from his office, Basil complained that depositions required a synod of the provincial bishops so that the act by merely secular authority was not legal (225). When his ally Bishop Eusebius of Samosata complained that he was allowing too many episcopal elections to go to the anti-Nicene party, Basil replied that he did what was possible, but canon law gave the metropolitan no autocratic powers (141). *Ep.* 105 addresses sisters who were deaconesses, daughters of a friendly count Terentius near Samosata on the northern Euphrates. The canonical letters include invalidation of oaths in an improper cause, e.g. to injure someone, or to refuse ordination (188. 10); this last may have been necessary to prevent ascetics claiming exemption from orders on this ground.[1] *Ep.* 199. 29 forbids any oath to wreak vengeance. Influence from the synagogue is seen in Christians taking vows to abstain from swine's flesh (*ep.* 199. 28).

Rules for monks and nuns

Monks needed a spiritual director. On arrival novices learnt silence; they could take vows, which should be made in the presence of the clergy to impart special solemnity and public character to the decision. Renunciation is of family, social class, property, friendships. The promise must be to keep celibacy. Fasting is not to be excessive, like the Manichees, and there can be no Manichee restriction on what one may eat; but the food is to be inexpensive and only enough for need, not for pleasure and never eaten to satiety. For drink water suffices. Guests should share in the frugality. Clothing is never to be luxurious or ostentatious, but enough to keep warm; and there is no call for a change of clothing at night. Monks dress like mourners. No loud laughter is allowed,[2] but one may smile. The daily liturgy consists of seven offices and the eucharist, the latter beginning with the liturgy of the word for catechumens, followed by 'the prayer of the faithful' (217. 57). Only in grave emergency may the eucharist be celebrated in a private house. Basil did not

---

[1] Cassian, *Coll.* 17 justifies breaking a solemn vow if by keeping it one abandons a higher spiritual goal. His critic Prosper dissented, *c. Coll.* 5. 2.

[2] Plato thought laughter unseemly.

want private masses, but welcomed customary private reservation by which the host was taken home (*ep.* 93). Consecration is by invocation of the Holy Spirit (*De Spir. S.* 66). Vigils are kept before Easter (*hom.* 14, PG 31. 445) and the festivals of martyrs (PG 29, 484). There is to be no reading, private or communal, of non-canonical books. Hymns and spiritual songs are sung at the offices and during the day at manual work. When young boys are admitted there is need to be on guard against homosexual attachments. Monks must know that to leave a monastery after making vows is to be excluded for ever. There is no way back. Monasteries may have attached a school for children of lay families.

Gradually the number of nuns increased. At the same time there were dramas with lapsed virgins. The model figure was St Thecla, companion of St Paul in the Apocryphal *Acts of Paul*, with a popular shrine at Seleucia in Isauria. Parents might bring girls under the age of sixteen to become nuns, not because they had a true calling to the unmarried life, but to solve domestic financial problems; they should not be accepted unless over sixteen (*ep.* 188. 18). The same problem would be met by Augustine (e.g. *Op. Monach.* 25). One letter (169, probably by Gregory of Nazianzos) tells of Glycerius, a deacon of mean quality, who gave himself the insignia of a patriarch and headed a community of virgins stolen from the normal convents. It is remarkable that the insignia of a patriarch could be identifiable, since at this date the title was hardly as yet in general use. The letter shows how natural it was when it came to be used for bishops with supra-provincial authority a few decades later.

Basil's summary of the Christian ideal borrows Plato's phrase from the *Theaetetus*: it is 'likeness to God as far as possible' (*Homily on the Creation of Man* 1. 17). That is to say, the imitation of Christ, denying ourselves, taking up the cross and being indifferent to danger. The 'retirement' pursued by a monk has to be retirement from his own will (*Reg. fus. tr.* 6. 344–5). Love to God is not taught by human teachers, but is implanted by grace, giving the power to fulfil divine commands so that it becomes as natural as loving one's family or beauty. The desire for goodness is instinctive (*Reg. fus. tr.* 2. 336 B ff.).

Basil not only built a monastic hospice near the city which could provide support for the destitute, but used to kiss the lepers (Greg. Naz. *or.* 43. 63, PG 36. 579). He was a regular visitor (*ep.* 150. 3). As bishop he lived as one of the poor (*ep.* 35; 135 end), sleeping on the ground. Since he wanted all Christians to live ascetic lives, he had deep misgivings about opulence.

Lay reaction to Basil's monks was unfriendly. Pagans gossiped that celibacy was merely a trick to inspire trust, and that the house was a cloak for vice (*ep.* 119). Neocaesarea in Pontus was probably not the only place where Basil's monks were criticized (*ep.* 207). The Caesarean house actually rebelled against him at one stage before he became their bishop (*ep.* 48); Athanasius wrote to rebuke them (Ath. *ep.* 63). Some of his monks had formerly been with Eustathius of Sebaste and could become critical if Basil's theology deviated from that of their former spiritual director. Basil's old friendship with Eustathius made him suspect in the eyes of Eustathius' critics, especially Theodotus of Nicopolis. As Meletius had replaced Eustathius at Sebaste, Basil's friendship with Meletius made Eustathius end amicable relations.

The Holy Spirit

Against those who doubted Eustathius' orthodoxy, Basil assured himself and others that his friend was wholly orthodox (*ep.* 98 and 99) but in consequence found himself disinvited to a council in Armenia. Eustathius caused difficulty: he did not want to state a doctrine of the Holy Spirit which went further than scripture and the laconic clause in the Nicene creed of 325 'And (I believe) in the Holy Spirit.' 'I prefer not to call the Holy Spirit God, but I would not dare call the Spirit a creature' (Socrates 2. 45. 6). Asia Minor still had many bishops who were more than hesitant about affirming the equality of the Spirit with the Father and the Son in the Holy Trinity. Basil himself spoke and wrote with caution on this subject; moreover the question of the Spirit was associated with problems of the homoiousian group which had reservations about the Son's equality with the Father. He thought the condemnation of *homoousios* in the case of Paul of Samosata was a substantial difficulty favouring the homoiousian party, which presupposed tolerance on his part towards those who had qualms about the Nicene term (*ep.* 52). But by 375 the pressure for a bold statement built up, especially on the equality of the Holy Spirit. He had to complain to Bishop Athanasius of Ankyra that he called Basil a heretic without so much as writing a letter (*ep.* 25), and to the church of Neocaesarea in Pontus that their bishop Atarbios 'hated' him and answered no letters (207). Basil may have been sending Neocaesarea too much unwelcome advice.

In the third century Origen declared the Spirit to sanctify the souls of believers, to have inspired the prophets, and to be associated with Father and Son. Yet in his work 'On first Principles' and especially in his *Commentary on St John* 1. 2, at the text 'All things were made by him', he raised the question whether the Spirit belongs to the created order, at least in being derived through the Son and therefore at a lower order of being. Athanasius' letters to Serapion address the position of a group which grants that the Son is no creature but believes the Spirit ranks with the created angels. Athanasius answers that the Trinity is all of similar nature and indivisible. The Spirit sanctifies, given by the Son who proceeds from the Father, and to sanctify is not within the capacity of the created order. The Spirit deifies redeemed humanity, and cannot be alien to the Father's deity.

Athanasius' statement was taken further by the Alexandrian exegete (and admirer of Origen), Didymus the Blind, who wrote both on the Holy Spirit, extant in Jerome's Latin version, and on the Trinity, extant in Greek. Jerome had attended his lectures: though the Spirit is not begotten but proceeds from the Father, all the divine characteristics are there, creating, forgiving, inspiring, touching human lives in word and sacrament. The Spirit's operation is so united with the Father and the Son as to be evidently one *ousia* or nature, though also distinct in operation. The being of the Spirit is derived from the Father and the Son, 'and the Spirit has no hypostasis [*substantia* in Jerome] other than that given by the Son'.

In 374–5 in Cyprus Epiphanius produced his 'Anchor' (*Ancoratus*) and an enormous *Panarion* or 'Medicine Chest for the cure of all heresies'. He strongly affirmed that the Father is God, the Son God, the Holy Spirit God, and that is to say *homoousios*. The Spirit proceeds from the Father, receives from the Son, and is the bond binding the Trinity, 'derived from both'. The Spirit has subsistence (*hypostasis*) from the Father through the Son (*Panar.* 73. 16. 2).

These authors were opposing the party called by others Pneumatomachoi (fighters against the Spirit) or Semi-Arians. Their most notable leaders were Macedonius bishop of Constantinople and his protegé Marathonius bishop of Nicomedia, so that they were also called Macedonians or Marathonians. Marathonius enjoyed a better reputation than Macedonius (of whom the historian Socrates had sombre accounts); previously in high office and therefore rich, he founded monasteries and hospices for the poor. Basil found Eustathius of Sebaste keeping company with people who did not feel the Bible gave authority to affirm the Spirit to be God. This led to a breach between old friends. Basil needed to put a distance between himself and the old homoiousian group.

Against this background it is intelligible that there was sharp polarity between those who denied that the Holy Spirit may be called 'God', and the opposing view that Athanasius, Didymus, and Epiphanius were right. Basil upset some of the latter party by fearing to call the Spirit God lest he be suspected of tritheism. His reticence, motivated also by averting anger from Valens' advisers, aroused distrust and open criticism.

In the autumn of 375 Basil issued a substantial treatise 'On the Holy Spirit' which is constructed round the prepositions used in the *Gloria*. Should one say 'with (*meta*) . . . with' (*syn*) or 'through (*dia*) . . . in' (*en*)? Basil's critics disliked the first pair of prepositions and accepted the second. He accepted both; they had precedent and tradition. The essence is that the opponents deny the ranking of the Spirit with the Father and the Son, and think the Spirit belongs to the created order. This is the unpardonable sin. Appeals to tradition leave the opposition unmoved; they want the Bible and the Bible only. But in revelation there is progressive education, as from Old Testament to New. Immemorial tradition has three immersions at baptism, the sign of the cross, turning east for prayer, chrism, renunciation of the devil and his angels, standing on Sundays, and, particularly relevant, the liturgical doxology. (The treatise is authority for the ancient evening hymn, *Phos hilaron*, 'Hail gladdening light' in Keble's translation.) Not everything is in scripture; Genesis has no record of the creation of the angels; that they are created is non-controversial. To affirm three hypostases does not imply more than one God. Just as the emperor and the emperor's image are not really a duality, so 'the honour of the image passes to the archetype' (a sentence with a major future in the iconoclastic controversy of the eighth and ninth centuries), and the Spirit completes the Trinity. Sanctification comes from the Father through the Son to the Spirit (*De Spir. S.* 18. 47).

The treatment of scripture plus tradition was cited by the medieval canonist Ivo of Chartres (PL 161. 223), and so became influential in the idea of two parallel sources for revelation.

Basil reinforced his argument from tradition by a momentous move, namely a florilegium or anthology of excerpts from respected Christian writers of the past. Adherence to the Nicene creed expresses the continuity of tradition. Moreover at Caesarea pro-Nicenes believed that their bishop, Hermogenes, had been responsible for drafting the Nicene creed. But its third article, so reticent about the Holy Spirit, must now be enlarged to exclude those who say the Spirit belongs to the created order. The Spirit inspired the biblical writers ('the prophets'), is the source of life and holiness, is neither unbegotten nor begotten but 'proceeds from the Father', is joined with Father and Son in the doxology or *Gloria*, and in the formula of baptism (*ep.* 125). Gregory of Nazianzos (*or.* 43. 69) was anxious that Basil's treatise might be taken as a complete and adequate statement of the full truth about the Holy Spirit. He himself wanted to say more.

Episcopal colleagues

The bishops of Asia Minor were in more or less constant disagreement with one another on theology, and Basil comments that each bishop seemed to suspect all his colleagues of heresy (*ep.* 191). It was like a night-battle in which no one knew who was a friend and who an enemy (*ep.* 69; *de Spir. S.* 30. 76). The parties were like circus factions (*ep.* 212). All this seemed profoundly inappropriate in a community formed by divine love. As sees fell vacant, Basil exerted pressure by letter or otherwise to get a Nicene successor. He was only sometimes successful. At Nicopolis (*ep.* 230) he explained to the magistrates of the city, who thought the election of a new bishop was for themselves to decide, that this was a matter for the clergy, and that the laity's role was to ratify (by acclamation?) what had been already determined. He found it hard to discover candidates with the capability for episcopal office; 'mediocrity brings Christianity into discredit' (*ep.* 190. 1). Basil judged it better to have few clergy of high quality than many of low capacity. *Ep.* 115 mentions an emancipated slave becoming a bishop; in such cases quality could be very variable. Regional pride emerged when a fellow Cappadocian Ascholius became bishop of Thessalonica (165), a crucial city on the route from Constantinople to the Adriatic and Italy. Ascholius was shown to be sound by his enthusiasm for Athanasius (154). Basil found his own clergy at Caesarea a poor lot (198). A number of letters mention married bishops and clergy. When his brother Gregory had been expelled from Nyssa by secular power, he noted that the usurper succeeding him named George lived with a 'concubine' (perhaps an ascetic relationship, as was often the case), and this seemed typical of the low standard prevalent (239. 1). A presbyter Paregorius aged 70 continued to live with a woman, perhaps his wife (?), but without conjugal relations; Basil thought the faithful were offended by her house-keeping and wrote threatening excommunication (*Ep. can.* 55. 88).

Basil's episcopal court at Caesarea had to deal with minor delinquents. *Ep.* 286 relates how at a large gathering the clothes of some poor people were stolen. The thieves were arrested by church officers. Unless the count wished to deal with this case, Basil would have them up before his court, and they would be corrected, no doubt by a minor flogging. 'What civil penalties do not achieve, the fearful judgements of the Lord' may do. Basil found himself attacked from all sides, by radical Arians as if he were Sabellian, but by ultra-Nicenes because of his support for three hypostases. Bishops hoping to please the emperor Valens, based at Antioch, were over-anxious to be approved by bishop Euzoios (*ep.* 226), evidently exceptionally influential at court because of his proximity. The Nicene cause at Alexandria suffered after Athanasius' death in 373, and its adherents were fiercely persecuted (139). Athanasius' successor Peter took refuge in Rome. (Basil found Peter unsympathetic: *ep.* 266). In Syria there was similar trouble (183). There Basil had a strong ally in Eusebius bishop of Samosata, who is recorded by Severus of Antioch (*Select Letters* 1. 1, ed. Brooks) to have travelled about disguised as a soldier, carrying out ordinations during the time of Arian domination. He suffered exile but returned after Valens' death.

Ambrose recorded apropos of the council of Ariminum in 359 that the laity preserved the true faith better than the bishops. Basil made a similar observation. The ecclesiastical party in the saddle was discovering that the laity actually disliked 'Arianism', and bishops were claiming to be almost in favour of Nicene faith (240). Even Demophilus at Constantinople, who in 381 preferred to resign the see rather than sign the Nicene creed, was reported to Basil as at least affecting to be orthodox (48). One bishop at Aegae thought that all the theological reasons given for suspending communion were secondary and ultimately indifferent (250). Basil himself more than once says that talk about God is beyond the capacity of the human mind, and that in any event words are inadequate to express what mind thinks (*Homily* 15, PG 31. 464). Frequently he repeats how desirable it is to stick to the words of scripture, and regrets that philosophical terms like *homoousios*, which express the sense of scripture but are not scriptural, have to be used. It was sad that private quarrels were dressed up as theological disagreements (*ep.* 92).

Apollinaris and Vitalis

As an aspiring divine Basil had once corresponded with Apollinaris about God, not Christology, and respected him. Controversy with Apollinaris concerning Christology was unwelcome to him. He thought the entire subject so beset with obscurity that further definition should be avoided. He told Epiphanius in Cyprus that he was opposed to any Christological addition to the Nicene formula (*ep.* 258, cf. 260). If he was going to denounce Apollinaris, then it would be more for his 'Judaistic' millenarianism than for his Christology where his mistake was to have disturbed people (*ep.* 263). Basil also wholly opposed Apollinaris' decision to ordain bishops who were planted in other churches with divisive effect; moreover they had neither clergy nor laity (265). The reference is evidently to the situation at Antioch for which Apollinaris had ordained his own bishop Vitalis (a convert from following Meletius). Perhaps he infiltrated similar supporters elsewhere. He was himself in this position at Laodicea. In opposing Apollinaris' thesis that the divine Logos replaced the human mind in Christ, Basil was content to state the Irenaean principle that what is not assumed is not saved (*ep.* 261). This he called 'brotherly disagreement' at first; but in time Apollinaris ceased to be 'one of us'.

Cappadocia divided

In 371 the emperor gave authority for the province of Cappadocia to be divided into two. This was highly unwelcome to the citizens of Caesarea, which, as a metropolis, was thereby vastly reduced in standing. Cappadocia II had a new metropolis at Tyana to the south-west. There Bishop Anthimos, with whom Basil had no cause for theological disagreement (*ep.* 210), competed with Basil for control of the pilgrim offerings at the shrine of St Orestes in the foothills of the Taurus mountains. Gregory of Nazianzos' panegyric on Basil says that there were rough exchanges at the site (*orat.* 43. 58, on Orestes, see *Acta Sanctorum* Nov. IV. 391). Basil's campaign against the division of the province earned him the hostility of the praetorian prefect and the high chamberlain (*ep.* 79).

The splitting of the province affected Basil's plan to fill as many sees as possible with sound Nicene bishops. He put his younger brother Gregory into Nyssa and sent his friend Gregory of Nazianzos to a miserable posting station named Sasima at a dusty road-junction, both in the new province. Gregory never visited Sasima (to Basil's annoyance, Greg. Naz. *ep.* 49), and evidently thought Basil's policy mistaken. Ecclesiastical jurisdiction for Basil would cease to correspond with the boundaries of the civil provinces. Although Valens may have thought it an additional argument for division that it reduced Basil's sphere of influence, his motive was almost certainly secular, to separate the imperial lands round Caesarea, which became the only city of Cappadocia I, from the more urbanized western region.[3]

Finding good bishops; Armenia

Finding suitable candidates for bishoprics was far from easy. They needed to be of good education, and the economic level of many clergy and laity was low. Basil founded a number of hospices for the poor, for which he was usually able to gain tax exemption (142; 150; 176). His sermons voiced the cause of the very poor; he invited the wealthy to bequeath a third of their estate not only for charity but for the sake of their own soul (*Hom.* 7. 7; 8. 8; *ep.* 32; Greg. Naz. *or.* 43. 20). When charged with finding bishops for the troubled province of Roman Armenia, he faced the difficulty that a good bishop must know the language of the people (*ep.* 99), and this required considerable consultation. The election of a bishop needed a choice by the bishops of the province, and the magistrates representing the laity were expected to assent to that choice (*ep.* 230). A bishop was to care for all, not merely for those of his own party or faction, not only for believers but for all Cappadocians (*ep.* 337). In this role of spiritual father to everyone in his territory Basil was continually badgered to write supporting letters to obtain relief from taxes or from curial duties on town councils (*ep.* 84). (A social problem of the time was the extreme reluctance of the curial class to serve on town councils, since they had to raise taxes and maintain order, and could be flogged severely if they failed in such duties.) Basil's episcopal duties could include gathering a levy to pay for army equipment (*ep.* 88), trying to negotiate tax relief for clergy (*ep.* 104) or monks (*epp.* 284–5) and for iron workers in the Taurus mountains (*ep.* 110). Arbitrations fell to him (*epp.* 72–3, 307). To litigate in court was expensive and, even if one recovered costs, one was out of pocket, so that it was better to go to arbitration (*ep.* 307). Silvanus of Troas in the 350s is the first bishop known to have employed a legally qualified lay adviser for

---

[3] A. H. M. Jones, *The Cities of the Eastern Roman Provinces*, 2nd edn. (Oxford, 1971), 184 ff. Theodosius I reunited the provinces in 379, but in 382 the division became fixed.

the bishop's court or *audientia episcopalis* (Socr. *HE* 7. 37. 17). By a transparent convention those for whom Basil writes supporting references are fictionally 'close relatives.' *Ep.* 317 observes that his letters to officials pleading for special consideration are unanswered. A fair proportion of letters from Basil and Gregory of Nazianzos were, like those of Libanius, written on behalf of someone if not to gain financial relief for clergy or monks. Often these letters were composed in the then fashionable rhetoric, with treacly flattery and wrapped in obscurity.

Some moral problems

Slavery was problematic. 'None is slave by nature; but it happens to prisoners of war and provides for the poor' (*De Spir. S.* 51). Their labour being reluctant, slaves had to be chastised (*epp.* 72–3). Another problem was abortion, which was not morally distinct from homicide (*epp.* 188. 2. 217. 52). Unwanted infants were often exposed (*ep.* 199. 13). Military service was compatible with a Christian life (*ep.* 106); but while killing in war was not murder, it needed three years' purification (*ep.* 118. 13).

Liturgical life

The sacredness of the episcopal or presbyteral office is strongly stressed: with priestly functions (*ep.* 247) they minister the liturgy of the altar (*epp.* 54. 222), 'entrusted with Christ's body and blood' (*ep.* 53). Basil's personal rule was to celebrate the liturgy on Wednesday, Friday, Saturday, and Sunday (*ep.* 93). So clergy are prominent at the memorials of martyrs to which bishops from beyond the boundaries of Cappadocia were invited; e.g. for St Eupsychios, who was executed under Julian, remembered on 5 September, or St Eutyches, taken prisoner by Gothic raiders among whom he became an evangelist before being put to death (*ep.* 164 on the translation of the relics). Pontus celebrated with pride the Forty Martyrs of Sebaste, but they were also commemorated at Caesarea (*Hom.* 19). The florilegium in *De Spiritu Sancto* cites a hymn of the martyr Athenogenes (*De Spir. S.* 74). The high feasts are Easter, after a forty-day Lenten fast, Pentecost, and the Nativity (unclear if this was 25 December or 6 January).

Sects

Asia Minor had its share of dissenters: Encratites who did not recognize married people as Christian; wearers of sackcloth; Renouncers (Apotactitae) who rejected marriage and private property; Novatianists (the validity of whose baptism was judged differently in different regions); Marcionites and

Montanists whose baptism was certainly invalid. *Ep.* 188. 1 says that two former Encratites have been accepted to be bishops. Epiphanius in Cyprus wrote to ask for information about Persian Magi or Magusians; *ep.* 258 explains that in Cappadocia such immigrants are numerous, that they will not kill animals and get someone else to do that for them; their marriages are unlawful, they believe in fire as divine, they claim to be descended from 'Zarnonas' (evidently Zervan).

The emperor Valens was aware that after Julian's proposal to rebuild the temple at Jerusalem, the Jews had become unpopular. Jerome (*adv. Jovinianum* 2. 7) records a strange edict issued by Valens to prohibit the eating of veal. Since observant Jews did not eat pork, they liked veal (cf. Luke 15: 23). The lack of cattle or belief that cows were sacred animals meant that beef was not to be had in Egypt and Palestine. The edict was probably an anti-Judaic pinprick.

Festivals and relics of martyrs

Basil felt it to be tragic that 'Arians' persecuted other Christians, but several times insisted that victims of such harassment should be included in the calendar of martyrs (*ep.* 243). He disapproved of martyrs' feasts being occasions for bazaars (*Reg. fus. tr.* 40). Basil puts this precept into his Longer Rule for monks, but he cannot have been successful in trying to stop a universal custom. He did not want the commemoration of a martyr secularized. But traders were not going to miss so large a gathering. Relics of martyrs were good for sending to the barbarians in the Danube region (*ep.* 155). Among the Goths Christians were suffering persecution; *ep.* 165 thanks Ascholius of Thessalonica for the gift of relics of a martyr who lately suffered death at Gothic hands (perhaps St Sabas?). *Ep.* 197 replies to a request from Ambrose of Milan for the relics of Dionysius of Milan; Basil stridently insists on their authenticity.

He was sure that the individual Christian needs the community of other believers (*Reg. fus. tr.* 7). He was no less sure that particular churches need the universal Church. The wreckage of past conflicts needed to be cleared away if this 'brotherhood' or 'fellowship of the Spirit' imparting unity in diversity (*in Ps.* 44. 9, PG 29. 408 c), was to be realized. His ideal for the Church is found in the Song of Songs.

Searching for unity at Antioch

Basil's supreme quest for church unity with the Nicene creed as its banner of truth was shipwrecked on the schism at Antioch with the two Nicene groups under Paulinus and Meletius unable to worship together. He was clear that only Meletius could command the confidence of the Greek bishops, and that Paulinus' association with Marcellus of Ankyra, who died about 374 in old age, was disastrous. Letters to Athanasius flattered the Alexandrian bishop's incomparable virtue and honour, but failed to move him to abandon support for Paulinus. After some initial friendly exchanges Basil began to raise the question of Antioch and sent to Alexandria Meletius' deacon Dorotheos, asking Athanasius to speed him on his journey to Rome, if possible with someone familiar with the Roman situation (*ep.* 69). In an oblique sentence Paulinus is the target when Basil observes that Marcellus of Ankyra, once received to communion by the west, had never been disowned, and (despite Athanasius' support for his friends) that is now necessary. Noteworthy is a remark that travel to and from Rome should be by sea to avoid interference by hostile bands (*ep.* 68). By 376 the Gothic invasion of the Balkans propelled by the Huns made the Via Egnatia unsafe.

The western reaction was to send Sabinus, Ambrose's deacon at Milan. Basil's answers by his hand were letters to the Illyrians (91) and to Gaul and Italy, actually to Pope Damasus (90), telling him that he and the bishops concerned profess the Nicene faith and agree with all that Damasus has done under canon law. The outcome was painful. Damasus abrasively returned Basil's letter to him as unacceptable and, by the hand of Paulinus' presbyter at Antioch Evagrius, sent a list of propositions to which Basil's signature was demanded (138). This list is likely to have included recognition of Paulinus. The deacon Dorotheus called on Evagrius and invited him to be present when Dorotheus was assisting at the eucharist; Evagrius refused, and Basil wrote to Evagrius to express his regrets and to tell him that he was no longer intending to send a representative to Rome (*ep.* 156).

Meanwhile Basil was under mounting pressure from Eustathius of Sebaste's friends, from Pneumatomachoi, and from supporters of the 'likeness' formula, who were lobbying the court to have Basil exiled. He had enough highly placed friends at court to avert this end to all his endeavours, but could not stop Anthimos of Tyana, metropolitan of Cappadocia II, from ordaining a bishop for Armenia, in his sphere of responsibility. Basil came near to despair. If the Nicene cause in Asia Minor was to be rescued, help was needed from the west.

A renewed attempt was made to persuade Pope Damasus to change his mind. Meletius (Basil, *ep.* 92) wrote to Rome, sad that private and personal quarrels were disguised as disagreement in faith. Basil felt that Damasus became more arrogant and scornful the more courteous the letters to him were (*ep.* 239). There was additional difficulty in that after Athanasius' death in 373, his successor Peter could not safely live at Alexandria, under Arian control again, and was in Rome, no friend to the recognition of Meletius, whose envoy Dorotheus became angry with him. It was time to discard the velvet glove and to be frank. Rome was in effect lifting no finger to help the pro-Nicene bishops in Asia Minor who were being harassed and persecuted. That was not good Roman tradition. A heartening letter came from Epiphanius of Salamis supporting 'three hypostases'. His *Panarion* (73. 16) explained his view. Finally Basil sent a tough letter (*ep.* 263) ironically thanking the western bishops, i.e. Damasus and perhaps Ambrose, for negligible sympathy, and reporting that the churches of Asia Minor were beset by Arian wolves in sheep's clothing, by Eustathius of Sebaste's heresy in Armenia Minor, by Apollinaris' millenarianism and Christology, and last but far from least, by Paulinus of Antioch, whose consecration by Lucifer of Calaris had not been recognized as canonical, and whose theology was hopelessly tainted by association with Marcellus of Ankyra's Sabellianism. The letter was stern stuff. But he was asking Rome to condemn individuals unheard.

The Tome of Damasus of 377 conceded a condemnation in abstract terms of Sabellianism, Photinus, Eunomius, any who preach two Sons or who hold that the divine Logos replaced the rational soul in Christ (Apollinaris not named) and of those who say the Holy Spirit is created. Censure is also pronounced on clergy who move from one church to another, a sentence which reads as an attack on Meletius. The document was much less than Basil had wanted.[4]

Basil died probably in 378; Gregory of Nazianzos says he held the see for eight years. Already in his lifetime he would be awarded the rare title, 'the Great', by his admirers. Gregory of Nazianzos (*or.* 43. 77) remarked that people modelled their gait and their speech, thoughtful, hesitant, and melancholic, on his.

The total failure of Basil's endeavours to restore pro-Nicene consensus and authority in Asia Minor sprang from the unsolved issue at Antioch. Had he lived to see the council of Constantinople under Theodosius in 381, Basil would have been glad that in doctrinal terms the view he advocated had broadly won the day. The article concerning the Holy Spirit exactly reflected his position; and the creed included no complicated matter on the issue of Christology, which Basil foresaw to be a question of unending intricacy (*ep.* 260). But the bishops knew enough of the unhappy way in which Rome had treated him and Meletius to be very unco-operative to the plea made by Gregory of Nazianzos after Meletius' death that Paulinus should be recognized to gratify the west. Gregory thought it a price worth paying to have west and east in harmony, but did not command support. Greek voices disputed Roman assumptions of jurisdiction, saying that the east was where the Lord was born.[5] At least Meletius ended canonized in the Roman

---

[4] *EOMIA* i. 283–96. Two texts are here united.

[5] Gregory Nazianzen's verse autobiography, 1690ff., ed. C. White (Cambridge, 1996), 134; PG 37. 1147.

Martyrology, though never at any time in his life in communion with the see of Rome.

The golden age of Constantine's favour to the Church had long passed. The Arian controversy had split east and west apart; to Rome it bequeathed an ineffaceable impression that the Greek east had too many heretics to be trusted so that even bishops persecuted by Arians could be called Arians by uninformed people at Rome (Basil, *epp.* 242. 266). The Greek orthodox had a deep impression of Rome's incomprehension and perhaps even the beginnings of a feeling that there were separate traditions of ecclesiology. Constantius and Valens saw the Nicene creed, affirmed by most of the Latin west, as divisive and therefore productive of disorder. Basil saw that the reconciliation of east and west could be attained only on the basis of the Nicene formula, and in all essentials of faith there was no dissension between him and Ambrose or Damasus. Ascetic communities could be instruments of general reform in the Church, and would attract less attention from the imperial government than urban churches and their bishops. Laity and monks could carry a torch that among some of the bishops flickered uncertainly. He did not live to witness success in church politics. But he could see that his programme was in line with what many of the laity hoped and prayed for. No one contributed more to the making of the Constantinopolitan creed long shared by east and west. The healing of the schism at Antioch did not come for many further decades, but its importance steadily receded. What Basil pleaded for eventually came about. In his lifetime there can only have seemed ground for despair.[6]

[6] Basil's works (not all authentic) are in PG 29–32. There are separate editions of his book On the Holy Spirit by C. F. H. Johnston (Oxford, 1892) and B. Pruche (Paris, 1968). Letters: text and translation by R. J. Deferrari (Loeb Classical Library, 1926–34); text and French translation by Y. Courtonne (Paris, *Belles Lettres* 1957–66); German translation with good notes by W. D. Hauschild (Stuttgart, 1973–93). *Hexaemeron*: text and French translation by S. Giet (Paris, 1968); a distinguished annotated edition by E. A. de Mendieta and S. K. Rudberg (GCS 1997). *On Greek literature*, text and notes by N. G. Wilson (London, 1975). Ascetical works, English translation by W. K. L. Clarke (London, 1925). The series Sources Chrétiennes also includes editions and French translations of *Contra Eunomium*, on Baptism, and on the Creation of Man.

Major secondary works are by W. K. L. Clarke, P. J. Fedwick, B. Gain, J. Gribomont, F. Loofs, Philip Rousseau, and R. Teja (see Further Reading, IV). On the churches in Asia Minor, see S. Mitchell, *Anatolia*, II (Oxford, 1994). On Basil's doctrine of God the old study of Karl Holl, *Amphilochius von Ikonium* (Leipzig, 1904) remains valuable.

39

AMBROSE[1]

In Ambrose of Milan the Latin west acquired a major figure, a Roman aristocrat deeply attached to tradition, not disposed to think the Greek east a superior guide to right faith. Yet he derived his grasp of the Christian faith from Origen's sermons and other Greek Christians. He once remarked how superior Origen was on the Old Testament compared with his work on the New (*ep.* 65 = M75, 1). He admired Basil's *Hexaemeron*. In polemic against Arianism he exploited Didymus the Blind and Athanasius. His high posthumous reputation in the east was admittedly assisted by pseudonymous texts created in anti-monophysite interest (cited in Theodoret, PG 83. 181 f. pp. 161–5 Ettlinger). The fact that a Chalcedonian supporter had the idea of inventing texts to be ascribed to Ambrose shows that for Greeks his name stood high. The Latin west owed much to him both in the general establishment of orthodoxy as defined by the Nicene creed and in the conversion of society from polytheism. He saw the Church steadily increasing in numbers (*Exameron* 3. 1. 4) while pagan priests were daily diminishing (*in Ps.* 36. 28). For his biography his own writings and especially the letters are a mine of information. The *Life* composed by Paulinus deacon of Milan at the suggestion of Augustine in 422 is mainly concerned to stress the miraculous in the expulsion of demons, healings, and even resuscitation of the dead. As *City of God* 22. 8 shows, Augustine was at this stage of his life interested in answering a pagan objection. Miracles still happen now and could therefore happen in the time of Jesus.

Towards Christian capture of society

With Julian's death the external underpinning of pagan cult by public authority collapsed. But that did not mean the conversion of hearts and minds to the Christian gospel. The last quarter of the fourth century saw a strenuous effort by the churches to evangelize, using a gradual method of persuasion for the educated and asking landowners to erect churches on their

---

[1] Ambrose's letters are cited from the CSEL edition by O. Faller and M. Zelzer but with the addition of the Maurist numbering (M).

property and to bring their labourers, often under some coercion, to worship there. There was tough resistance to the abandonment of venerable peasant superstitions, and there were some bishops who thought it best to compromise. In Spain at Ávila in the 370s Priscillian admitted to allowing sorcery and magic, e.g. anointing sacred stones with oil to ensure good crops (Priscillian, *Tract* 1, p. 23. 22 ff. ed. Schepss). But in the sixth century Martin of Braga tried to wean the rustics from their ancient rites (*De correctione rusticorum*).

There were also merely nominal adherents coming to church services because it might help them to some higher post, or to gain the hand in marriage of a Christian girl (Ambr. *in Ps.* 118. 20. 48–9). The earliest surviving catechetical lectures, by Cyril of Jerusalem, begin by observing that the young men attending have come to see their girls but now they are going to listen to the bishop. Before Ambrose's time Zeno of Verona writes of nominal Christians who in a still predominantly pagan milieu secretly preserved shrines of the old gods on their land (Zeno 1. 25. 10).

Refugees

Germanic tribal incursions in and after the 370s removed from imperial control substantial tracts of territory south of the Danube, and in northern Italy the flood of impoverished and homeless refugees created many social problems which impacted on the churches, whose care for the poor and destitute was well understood. Even in the Po valley rich families were hiding their gold and silver in the ground (Zeno of Verona 1. 14). The billeting of soldiers in towns, always dreaded by the inhabitants, led to frictions which bishops were expected to sort out. In 408 a decree of the emperor Honorius placed formal responsibility for refugees in the hands of bishops (CTh 5. 7. 3). This extended the principle inherent in a decision by Constantine the Great to give bishops the powers of magistrates, and to make astonished secular authority implement the bishop's verdicts (Const. Sirmond. 1). Since there were occasional cases where hesitation about a bishop's decision was referred to the emperor, Ambrose preferred to act as arbitrator in cases where both parties agreed to abide by his verdict (*ep.* 24 = M82. 3). It irritated him to judge disputes 'about money, estates, and beasts'. Holy men could discern guilt and innocence as others could not (an ancient axiom, e.g. in Porphyry's *Life of Plotinus* 11 and his *Life of Pythagoras* 13. 54, and a charism spectacularly claimed by the Roman synod of 378 defending Pope Damasus). The original donors could be offended when bishops sold church plate and furnishings to redeem prisoners captured by the barbarians (Ambr. *off.* 2. 136). On the eastern front with Persia, Acacius bishop of Amida (Dyarbakir) caused a sensation by selling church treasures to pay for the release of Persian prisoners captured by the Romans (Socrates 7. 21). The axiom that charitable aid to the poor must not discriminate in favour of Christians was formulated by Atticus of Constantinople (Socr. 7. 25). Ambrose would be clear about the correctness of the judgement that humanity had first claim (*off*. 2. 142–3). In a law of 529 Justinian prohibited sales of church plate for any other purpose than ransoming prisoners of war (CJ 1. 2. 21).

Capital punishment. Almsgiving

In defiance of the emperors' laws (but obeying Prov. 24: 11) Ambrose defended the right of Christians to try to rescue condemned criminals being carried off to execution, provided it could be done without an affray (*off*. 2. 21. 102). Symmachus when prefect of Rome once complained that people under arrest were kidnapped on their way to court (*Relatio* 28. 2); so this kind of interference with law and order was common. Asylum and kidnapping of criminals naturally gave plausibility to the charge that the Church was overthrowing justice and legality. Edicts in 392 and 398 tried to stop it (CTh 9. 40. 15–16). After all, Christians did not disagree that penalties should be incurred by those who did wrong. Ambrose disapproved of capital punishment (which pagan governors hated also), though not accepting the Novatianist excommunication of Christian governors imposing this sentence (*ep.* 50 = M25). He was critical of the rule that in capital cases judges had no discretion about sentence (*in Ps.* 37. 51).

An acute problem for the poor (not the destitute) was debt. A good custom at Milan was to release debtors from prison in Holy Week (*ep.* 76 = M20. 6). Ambrose would have much to say about almsgiving. 'Honour the poor as images of Christ' (*in Ps.* 118. 10. 26). They were the basis of his power in the city.

From provincial governor to bishop

Aurelius Ambrosius (full name, *ILCV* 1800) unexpectedly became bishop of Milan in succession to Auxentius in 374. The son of a praetorian prefect in Gaul who died about 340 (perhaps at the time of Constantine II's death), he had been educated in Rome, learning Greek as well as Latin literature, and had a career as a civil servant at Sirmium, metropolis of Pannonia II, then as governor (*consularis*) of Liguria. Bishop Auxentius, a Greek from Alexandria who had perhaps trained in law and if so knew some Latin (more than Athanasius thought, *Hist. Ar.* 75), had enjoyed long tenure, strongly supporting the creed of Ariminum that the Son is 'like' the Father. Thanks to Valentinian I's policy of detached toleration he had retained his position after Hilary of Poitiers in 364 had unsuccessfully attacked him and even after Gallic synods in Julian's time declared him unacceptable and Athanasius had badgered Pope Damasus into a synodal demand for his removal. Probably a few years later Evagrius of Antioch is said by Jerome (*ep.* 1. 15) to have 'almost buried Auxentius before death'; perhaps he persuaded Valentinian to take Nicene opposition seriously and to restrict Auxentius' action against it. At least Valentinian ordered a legal inquiry by a quaestor and a magister, Hilary being supported by about ten bishops. Auxentius argued that Hilary had been condemned by Saturninus of Arles and was disqualified, but conceded that Christ is 'of one divinity and substance' with the Father. The lay investigators held this to be a matter of faith and outside their remit. But he would not disavow the council of Ariminum, and his biblicist profession of faith (contained in some, not all manuscripts of Hilary's *contra Auxentium*) utterly denies any knowledge of or link with Arius, such as an Alexandrian ordained by bishop Gregory might be expected to have. Hilary was required to stay out of Milan.[2]

On the death of Auxentius, whose supporters had evidently done little to ensure a likeminded successor, there was disorder among the *plebs*, as was not infrequently the case in an age when the lay congregation played a part in the choice of their bishop and candidates hired claques to shout for them. Auxentius had faced a pro-Nicene group at Milan who refused to accept any sacraments from him (Hilary, *c. Aux.* 13, PL 10. 617B), a group which was encouraged from outside first by Hilary of Poitiers, then by Filaster bishop of Brixia (Brescia), who organized a riot. At the election the pro-Nicene party had their candidate, probably Filaster; those who wanted to continue Auxentius' rock-solid adherence to the ambiguous 'like' formula of Ariminum had theirs. Eight years earlier the election of two rival bishops at Rome, Damasus and Ursinus, had resulted in a ferocious riot costing 137 lives among Ursinus' supporters (above p. 315). It would be bad for both church and state if that occurred at Milan.

Ambrose as governor was brought down to quell the civil disorder (it is unlikely but not wholly impossible that he was directly offering himself for election), and found himself shouted for to be bishop. Perhaps each of the contending parties regarded their impartial governor as so ignorant of theology that each hoped to win him for their cause. During his time as civil servant at Sirmium he had no confrontation with Bishop Germinius, who held no brief for the Nicene creed. There would be advantage for everyone in having a bishop who had influence with taxmen or magistrates or experience at getting dependents good posts. Ambrose knew his way along the corridors of power. Rufinus (*HE* 11. 11) says that Ambrose alone could unite the parties.

---

[2] Auxentius' creed is critically edited by M. Durst in *Jahrbuch für Antike und Christentum*, 41 (1998), 118–68.

That the Milan *plebs* petitioned the emperor for his appointment is certain from his own statement (*ep.* 75 = M21. 7). Probably there were critical voices who shared the view of Pope Damasus and his successor Siricius that former officers of state should not be made bishops. Ambrose himself disarmed critics by declarations of his utter unworthiness to be bishop (*Paenit.* 2. 8. 73). His previous career had been in 'the vanities of this world' (2. 72).

The story in Paulinus' *Life* (not known to Rufinus of Aquileia and treated with hesitation by Paulinus) said that the suggestion first came from a small child. As the voice of children enjoyed oracular status in antiquity, this may well be true. The story does not assume that the child knew what it was saying. On the other hand, a divine oracle may also have been a later hagiographical fiction to justify the exceptional and uncanonical procedure. The proposal was welcomed by Petronius Probus, praetorian prefect of Illyricum, Italy, and Africa; Probus was Christian (buried at St Peter's, 390, in a mausoleum behind the apse, *ILCV* 63). It was then agreed by the emperor Valentinian I, who may have thought that Ambrose could bring peace to Milan and that his lay background could promote the emperor's well-known neutrality in church controversies (Ammian. 30. 9. 5). A bishopric was not what Ambrose himself could have wished, but he came of a Christian family and accepted the duty. 'The call to the *sacerdotium* cannot be refused' (*off.* 1. 1. 2). Moreover, his education in Rome no doubt instilled in him a sense of loyalty to the Roman see; but in his youth that meant the flexible position of Liberius. Augustine (*Conf.* 8. 3) reports that Ambrose was baptized by Simplicianus, a priest who had been at Rome and could have met the young Ambrose there. Which side Simplicianus was on during the dissensions under Auxentius we do not know, but a presbyter from Rome (if already ordained there) would be more likely to be of the Nicene party. It is therefore possible that his migration to Milan was by Ambrose's invitation. Auxentius would hardly have asked him, but he played a prominent role in the conversion of Marius Victorinus, favourite tutor for Roman aristocrats, and had high intellectual qualifications sympathetic to Christian Platonism.

Gradual establishment of Nicene orthodoxy

We do not know which bishops consecrated Ambrose to the episcopate. Ambrose devoted himself to his pastoral office. Close friendship with senators was ended (*Exameron* 3. 7. 30), but friends in high places leaked intelligence to him. He adopted Damasus' policy of regarding the Nicene creed as a criterion of catholic communion. That would become easier after the death of Valentinian I in 375. Nevertheless an early indication of his inclination was his informing Basil of Caesarea (*ep.* 197) in Cappadocia of his election; to Basil's reply a disputed, possibly inauthentic addition (above p. 344) suggests that he asked for help in recovering the bones of Dionysius, bishop of Milan, exiled in 355 by Constantius for his intransigence for Nicaea and Athanasius. His early work *On Paradise* warns against letting a heathen convert, on becoming a catechumen, learn his doctrine from 'Photinus or Arius or Sabellius', all of whom appealed to scripture (12. 58). That he wrote *On Paradise* soon after becoming bishop is expressly said (*ep.* 34 = M45). However, it is necessary to bear in mind that though the pro-Nicene party accused advocates of Ariminum like Auxentius of being 'Arian', the latter did not accept any link to Arius and disowned the title. The emperor Gratian, aged 15, 'Augustus' since 367 but taking over from his father Valentinian I after his death in November 375, was at first cautious and only hesitantly sympathetic to Ambrose. The more open became Ambrose's hostility to Ariminum and the 'likeness' formula, the sharper became the antagonism in Milan from those who preferred the more broad church term, supported at the palace by Valentinian I's widow, Justina (at one time married to Magnentius). Her aversion to the Nicene party first became explicit after Valentinian's death. Soon Milan had a rival bishop who came from the Danube delta or the province of Scythia Minor, 'a Scythian', who adopted the name of Auxentius in admiration for Ambrose's predecessor and lived in the city providing a focus of dissidence for Ambrose's opponents. Crucial for Ambrose was not only support from Damasus in Rome but also the approval of his election by Valentinian I and Probus. With imperial support he was impregnable. After November 375 it was not always self-evident that Gratian, influenced by Justina, would provide that.

Ambrose set out to convince Gratian by writing 'on Faith', the first two books in 378, the last three in 381 replying to an attack on books 1–2 by Palladius bishop of Ratiaria. The sacredness of Nicaea's bishops was proved for him by the scriptural number 318 (TIH in Greek, and so the cross of Jesus); and the provinces where opponents flourished were those over-whelmed by barbarian Goths, the Gog of prophecy (*De fide* 2. 16. 137–40).

Rome the touchstone

A sermon on Psalm 40. 30 cites the Petrine text from Matthew 16 and adds 'Where Peter is, there is the Church'. Similarly *in Ps.* 43. The bishop of Rome is source of the 'iura communionis' (*ep. extra coll.* 5 = M11. 4). Membership of the catholic Church is defined as communion with the Roman see (*Satyrus* 1. 47). So the Novatianists, by not accepting communion with Rome, have lost the inheritance of Peter (*Paenit.* 1. 33). At the same time Ambrose did not think local customs of the church in Rome ought to be observed by other churches with their own independent tradition. When Monnica came to join her son Augustine in Milan, she followed African and

Roman custom in bringing food and wine to martyrs' shrines, and was shocked to be told by the guardians that Ambrose had forbidden this (Aug. *Conf.* 6. 2; Ambr. *Hel.* 17. 62 and *in Luc.* 7. 245). Augustine commented that she accepted the ruling because she admired Ambrose, but would have found the prohibition hurtful from someone else. When she was asking if she should keep the Roman custom of fasting on Saturdays, Ambrose told Monnica to fall in with local church custom, meaning that as she was not in Rome now, she should not be doing that in Milan (Aug. *ep.* 36. 32; 54. 3). The maxim echoes the Delphic oracle's reply to one who asked how to please the various gods, in Xenophon (*Memorabilia* 4. 3. 16), and known by Augustine as a Socratic saying (*De consensu evangelistarum* 1. 18. 26 and *S. Dolbeau* 23 = *S* 374, 10, p. 545. 205). Ambrose evidently did not share the view that this fast was ordered by St Peter himself. By contrast, Ambrose was confident that the baptismal creed used at both Milan and Rome was the apostles' creation and Rome had faithfully preserved it (*ep. extra coll.* 8 = M42. 15). This creed did not take sides between Nicaea and Ariminum, but to catechumens Ambrose could gloss it in a Nicene sense. No doubt Auxentius before him had done that in his sense.

When in 378 a council in Rome directed a plea to Gratian and Valentinian II on behalf of the embattled Pope Damasus, Ambrose drafted the letter for the council (*ep. extra coll.* 7, CSEL 82/3. 191); above p. 318.

The majority of Christians and clergy in Milan had had seventeen years of Auxentius, and were not conditioned to think well of either Damasus or the Nicene council. Ambrose was an unbaptized layman rapidly promoted to be bishop, directly contrary to a canon of the western council of Serdica. It is possible but far from certain that after baptism he passed through the orders of deacon and presbyter during eight days before being consecrated bishop. The ambiguity of the text in Paulinus' biography suggests that he did not. There would be those who disliked such disregard of the Serdican canon and questioned Ambrose's legitimacy. But a consensus of bishops recognized validity. The approval of the election by the emperor and the praetorian prefect will have helped to that end. Moreover, he recognized Damasus as 'elected by God's judgement' (*ep.* 72 = M17. 10), not his rival Ursinus, who rashly came to Milan to join Ambrose's opponents.

Martyrs

Ambrose opened tombs to encourage the veneration of martyrs, valuing annual festivals and writing hymns in their honour, e.g. for Agnes, Nazarius, Laurence, Victor, Nabor and Felix. He took special pleasure in Sebastian, a native of Milan (*in Ps.* 118. 20. 44) and in the discovery of bones believed to be of two gremial martyrs of Milan, Gervasius and Protasius. They seemed a vindication against his opponents and a source for civic pride ('my body-guards', *ep.* 77 = M22. 9). 'Arians' accused him of fraud but the relics brought healings. He buried his brother Satyrus, saved in shipwreck by invoking St Laurence, beside the martyr Victor (*ILCV* 2165), and believed in the advantage hereafter of being buried 'ad sanctos' (*Satyrus* 1. 18), an opinion with which Augustine was to disagree. He was sure the intercession of martyrs would help at the Last Judgement (*Vid.* 9. 55).

He supplied relics to other churches, to nearby Brescia and to distant Rouen, where bishop Victricius, a friend of Paulinus of Nola, celebrated his return from trying to reconcile factions among bishops in Britain with a solemn arrival of relics enabling him to build a new church round them. In the relics the saints were present in his city, almost a divine presence, and Victricius replied to objectors who asked what bits of bone could do by a logical ploy about the whole present in the parts. In Ambrose's oration on the death of Theodosius I in 395, he mentioned that Constantine's mother Helena had used a nail from the cross of Jesus for the bridle of her horse and had put another nail in her crown; but there were people who thought this bizarre, '*insolentia*' (*Ob. Theod.* 47–8; Jerome was one, *in Zach.* 3. 14. 20, p. 935). Milan celebrated the feast of SS. Peter and Paul (*in Ps.* 118. 4. 10), no doubt on 29 June. At Turin Bishop Maximus at this time complained that his people neglected the feast on 29 June (*hom.* 3. 2).

Gentle persuasion

Auxentius and his clergy had refused to recognize the validity of baptism conferred by Nicene clergy. Ambrose declared that he would accept Auxentius' clergy on condition that they did not refuse to receive the sacraments from him. Evidently most were moderates. That decision must have baffled the pro-Nicene party if they were hoping for an uncompromising confrontation. Paulinus' biography (34. 2) records one critic. To a bishop Constantius, Ambrose advised a gentle line with suspected 'Arians' but disowned actual compromise (*ep.* 36 = M2). But almost all Milan clergy submitted.

A related problem, however, would be presented by bishops in Illyricum and along the Danube to Moesia (modern Bulgaria) whose allegiance was shaped in favour of the creed of Ariminum. Admittedly Germinius of Sirmium, the metropolitan of Illyricum, had moved away from the Likeness formula of Valens of Mursa and had come to associate himself with 'like in essence' or *homoiousios*. He was still reserved towards 'identity of essence'. Theodoret (*HE* 4. 9) records that in Illyricum a synod (surprisingly) supported *homoousion*, and Valentinian deplored a suggestion that this doctrine was being accepted merely as the emperor's will.

Ambrose was meeting a phalanx of bishops both in northern Italy and in Illyricum who regarded his Nicene inclinations with foreboding. It would become important for him to fill as many sees as possible with bishops who shared his view that only the Nicene creed could be the universal faith of East and West, 'fides ecclesiae' (*Exameron* 3. 1. 4). This was high on his agenda, and there was fury when he went outside his own province to consecrate a sound bishop Anemius for Sirmium, metropolis of Illyricum and therefore influential in the choice of bishops. The opposition could not block it.[3]

Jerome's estimate of Ambrose

Jerome had little respect for Ambrose's exegetical writings, which he correctly regarded as plagiarized from Philo, Origen, Basil, and Didymus the Blind. He failed to spot the copying of Origen and Eusebius of Caesarea (*Quaest. Evang.*) in the uneven commentary on Luke. He did not notice how much Ambrose could recycle matter from Plotinus and Porphyry, especially when, as the sermons expressly note, his congregation at Milan included pagans (e.g. *in Ps.* 36. 61). Augustine cites a lost commentary on Isaiah (*de grat. et pecc. orig.* 1. 54). Jerome reserved for Ambrose's efforts at exegesis some of the more scathing phrases taken from his little book of insults. His exegesis of Habakkuk (PL 25. 1298 B) hits at Ambrose on the prophet's 'scarabaeus in ligno' (Christ a worm on the cross). Ambrose, for whom it was a repeated principle not to answer an insult, never retorted. (*Ep.* 75 = M20. 28 has a robust reply to a threat from the eunuch chamberlain Calligonus.) He could have replied that Jerome's scorn had not prevented him from borrowing language and ideas from Ambrose's writings (e.g. his consolation on his brother's death, *De excessu fratris* I).[4] Nevertheless, in his *Chronicle* Jerome was not in doubt that the ideological conquest of northern Italy for the Nicene faith was Ambrose's great achievement which he admired. It called for aggressive methods and senatorial clout.

A Christian ethic

In ethics Ambrose especially admired the *Sentences* of Sextus, popular in Greek. (Soon Rufinus would translate the maxims into Latin.) His treatise *On Duties*, addressed to clergy, assumes the gospel to complete and sometimes rectify Cicero's book under the same title, a debt expressly acknowledged. Just as

---

[3] Did the bishop of Sirmium have powers? It is unclear that in North Italy this degree of organization was in force. See Mark Humphries, *Communities of the Blessed; Social Environment and Religious Change in northern Italy* (Oxford, 1999).

[4] Jerome's notorious *ep.* 22 used matter from Ambrose, *De virginibus*; N. Adkin in *Symbolae Osloenses*, 68 (1993), 137 ff.

Cicero had plagiarized the Hellenistic philosopher Panaitius of Rhodes, so Ambrose restates Cicero's treatise *on Duties* which was a current educational handbook directed to the public service. In the bishop's responsibilities, service of the community was carried out by his clergy. On such familiar themes as the four cardinal virtues of justice, courage, prudence, and self-control, no major amendment of Cicero was required. Just as Cicero illustrated them from old heroic precedents, so Ambrose provides biblical examples. Only for Ambrose 'justice' requires putting God and the community before any private interests, which stands in contrast to Cicero's concern for private property. Moreover for Ambrose faith (*fides*) in a Christian sense is not merely keeping contracts but a trust and commitment to God which is the foundation making 'justice' possible (*De off.* 1. 142). Ambrose's treatise could be naturally read as a reassurance to educated Romans that to become a Christian meant no huge break with the ethical principles articulated by Cicero, but it also presupposed that corrections and modifications were necessary in a society acknowledging a Christian way.

Ambrose had difficulty in persuading owners of slave-girls that they ought not to sleep with them, and had to use the argument that sexual indulgence ended in disgraceful servitude to the girl, who lost respect both for her lord (*ep.* 7 = M37. 10–11; *Abrah.* 2. 16 and 65), and for his wife if the slave was more successful in producing children (cf. Gen. 21: 10). The copulation of male with male is forbidden (*Noe* 21. 26).

The discussion of virtue is both Ciceronian and Christian with justice becoming indistinguishable from altruism, benevolence, and an expression of love. His debt to Cicero may well have been influential on Augustine, for whom Cicero's philosophical tracts were central. Like Augustine, Ambrose adventurously conceded that in highly exceptional circumstances adultery was not damnable (*Apol. David altera* 50), but stressed chastity as a basic principle (3. 6). A model for his people was the phoenix, reproducing itself every 500 years at the price of its life (*in Ps.* 118. 19. 13). His homilies on Tobit took matter on usury from Basil. In north Italy there were serious social consequences when poor people took out loans which then could not be repaid, so that a man might have to sell his son into slavery or a widow lose all her furniture or even her house (Maximus of Turin, *hom.* 18). Ambrose remarks that during the menstrual period women should not participate in eucharistic communion (*Apol. David* 56)—an opinion with which Augustine would disagree since for him no natural function could be a source of defilement.

Ascetic discipline. Jovinian. Bonosus

Virginity enhanced standing and authority. Pagans could point to the Vestal Virgins, but as they were not lifelong virgins this failed to impress. In an age when adolescent girls were virtually put up for auction in a marriage market, there were attractions in taking the veil (*Virg.* 1. 56). One girl fled from her mother's pressures and found asylum at a church altar 'where the sacrifice is offered' (1. 63). Virgins could be tempted by pride; Augustine (*de sancta virginitate*) much stresses humility. In 377 Ambrose wrote with Virgilian allusions and examples on the virgin ideal in St Agnes, St Thecla, and his own sister Marcellina, dedicated by Pope Liberius (in whose mouth Ambrose puts some clearly Nicene sentiments). He owed much to Athanasius.

Ambrose as bishop had the advantage of being unmarried. Celibacy was not a canonical requirement, but it was deemed desirable in a bishop. The ascetic movement was producing monks severely critical of married secular clergy living in the Babylon of the urban environment, attending dinner parties at which conversation could be risqué and where half-clad dancing flute-girls were an expected entertainment (*ep.* 4 = M27. 13), participating in contentions about the dangerous subject of biblical exegesis. As Augustine was astonished to discover, in the suburbs of Milan Ambrose had a monastic house. His enemies maligned his chastity and at one stage even tried to kill him (*in Ps.* 61. 21).[5]

Controversy came when the ex-monk Jovinian urged that married Christians were not spiritually or morally inferior to professed celibates, and accused Ambrose of holding a Manichee attitude to sexuality. Ambrose reacted when two monks left their monastery and told the church at Vercelli that celibacy was not superior, sexuality being God's good gift to be enjoyed (*ep. extra coll.* 14 = M63. 7–14). Ambrose wanted to encourage young women to belong to religious communities. Constantinople in John Chrysostom's time had 3000 virgins and widows (*Hom. in Matt.* 66. 3). It was grievous to find that Milan produced fewer novices than Bologna, Florence, or even refugees from Gildo's revolt in Mauretania (*Virg.* 1. 57–60). The supreme model for them was the Blessed Perpetual Virgin, mother of God (*Exameron* 5. 20. 65; *Virg.* 2. 3). Only one must remember that 'Mary was God's temple, not God of the temple'; that is, she is to be held in high honour but not worshipped as divine (*De Spir. S.* 3. 80). That the warning was needed is instructive. He defended Mary's perpetual virginity against Bonosus bishop of Naissus, who thought that she had other children after Jesus. Ambrose shared the fear (also found in Epiphanius of Salamis, *Panar.* 78. 10) that there might be thought some impropriety in the Blessed Virgin going off to share a house with St John (*in Luc.* 10. 134; was this text being used to justify the disputed ascetic practice of both sexes living together in continence? North Italy had examples: Maximus of Turin, *Hom.* 88. 6.

[5] An edition of Ambrose *On Virginity* and *on Widows* with learned notes has come from D. Ramos-Lissón (Madrid, 1999).

Or to justify divorce? Siricius, *ep.* 9). The wealthy aristocrat from Bordeaux, Paulinus, who became bishop of Nola and with his wife gave away most of his substance, was criticized by many, but defended by Ambrose for 'wise folly' (*ep.* 27 = M58; *in Ps.* 118. 22. 11). Paulinus (*ep.* 3. 4) had visited Milan when Alypius was there, as described in Augustine's *Confessions* 6.

Class divisions

Ambrose the senator identified himself with the common people now that he was their bishop. Echoing Alexander the Great on his wealth being his friends, and perhaps the reply of St Lawrence when the prefect of Rome demanded surrender of the Church's wealth, he claimed the poor of Milan as his strength and treasure (*ep.* 76 = M20, 8: 'all I have belongs to the poor'). When high officials expected him to stop the *plebs* from rioting, he replied that calming them was in God's power. Private property he thought unjustifiable, but tolerable if used for communal benefit (*off.* 1. 28. 132). He was aware that as a bishop he was no longer regarded by old senatorial friends as one of their society. But they knew that he retained influence. When in 376 Rome was short of food and foreigners were expelled by Symmachus, his voice was critical of the decision and was glad this had not been done at Milan (*off.* 3. 7. 45–52). At the same time, however, he did not think it good for bishops recruited from plebeian stock to be the object of snide class mockery from persons higher in the social scale. One letter (*ep.* 6 = M38) expresses the hope that, whatever their origins, bishops should maintain the honour and standing of their office by not behaving in a vulgar way (*ep.* 6 = M28. 2). Their walk in the streets should never be pompous or arrogant (*off.* 1. 71), never hurried (74). They should learn to avoid a rustic accent (104). A bishop of Pettau (Poetovio), whose constituency was transformed by the arrival of numerous Goths, shocked Ambrose by adopting Gothic styles in wearing a necklace and bracelets (*Gesta Aquil.* 2). A bishop should be seen to belong to the church of the Roman empire. God's priests, he wrote (*Exh. virg.* 3. 82), have a calling higher than prefects and consuls. He expected clergy, especially bishops, to be celibate; married men could be made bishops but should not have conjugal relations with their wives. He once comments (*off.* 1. 44. 218) that it is rare for sons of clergy to seek ordination. The expectation of celibacy he saw as a cause for this reluctance.

Ambrose judged it an extravagant waste of money to provide popular entertainment at the circus, theatre, or amphitheatre with gladiatorial shows and fights with wild animals (*off.* 2. 21. 109). In any event 'beast-fights are cruel to the animals' (*in Ps.* 118. 8. 42), an observation unique in antiquity.

Barbarians within the empire

To Ambrose barbarians were dangerous enemies of the empire (*ep.* 76 = M20), not to be relied on to defend the frontier (*De fide* 2. 140). The correct course for the state is to buy them off (*Tobias* 15. 51), a policy which got Stilicho into trouble with rich aristocrats required to find the cash. Let them keep their own customs (*ep.* 15 = M69. 6). Boethius in the sixth century had to work with Goths at Theoderic's court, but was distressed by Gothic liking for hairgrease, *Lederhosen*, and ghastly music. There was a problem for Ambrose in that the army of defence largely consisted of barbarians, especially Goths, among whom a proportion were Christians of 'Arian' allegiance.

Liturgy and hymns[6]

Another act by Ambrose to identify with the values of the *plebs* was his popularization of the congregational hymn. Hymns involved both sexes, both the *plebs* and the grandees. Singing a hymn helped to impart a sense of unity to a congregation. Even the emperor could and did join in (*in Ps.* 1. 9). At Easter special efforts were made by a choir (*in Ps.* 47. 1). The hymns he himself wrote combined religious and poetic feeling and were chanted responsorially (*in Ps.* 45. 15). Faith is incomplete without baptism and eucharist (*ep.* 1 = M7. 20). At baptism Psalm 40 (41) was chanted (*in Ps.* 40. 37), and at the vigil before Easter Day a large crowd would be initiated; in April 387 this included Augustine. The rite included the sign of the cross on the forehead (*ep.* 20 = M77).

While baptism is complete cleansing, candidates must understand the meaning of the two necessary sacraments, and therefore a newly baptized person 'does not offer the sacrifice until the eighth day' (*in Ps.* 118, prologue). The catechetical lectures 'on the Sacraments' and 'On the Mysteries' are shot through with awe at the word of Christ in the institution of the 'daily sacrifice' bringing divine 'transfiguration' of ordinary leavened bread and

---

[6] Shortly after Ambrose's time the church in Spain produced a notable poet, Prudentius, who wrote lyric verses in Latin on Christian themes with Greek titles: the Daily Round (*Cathemerinon*), Martyrs' crowns (*Peristephanon*), the Trinity and the deity of Christ (*Apotheosis*), the soul's struggles against temptations (*Psychomachia*), a sustained restatement of Ambrose's reply to Symmachus' defence of the Altar of Victory, and some brief verses to accompany pictorial biblical scenes. Prudentius illuminates the contemporary conflict between Christianity and paganism, especially by the paradoxical thesis of the *Peristephanon* that the martyrs condemned to death by the authority of Rome are the city's and the empire's supreme pride and glory. The repulsiveness of pagan cult is exemplified by a macabre and vivid description of a taurobolium, in which the initiate stood underneath as the blood of a newly killed bull poured over him. It was an initiation that only the opulent were likely to afford.

wine to be in faith Christ's body and blood. Consecration 'changes nature' (*Myst.* 50). 'Daily feed on Jesus' (*in Ps.* 43. 37). At the beginning of the liturgy, which was celebrated before dawn, the celebrant kisses the altar (first attested in *ep.* 76 = M20. 26). Ambrose provides the earliest attestation of 'missa' for the mass (*ep. extra coll.* 15 = M42. 5). In his time the creed, the Lord's Prayer, and the eucharistic prayer of consecration were first known to candidates for baptism by oral instruction, and were not written down. But the six lectures 'On the sacraments' preserved by a shorthand writer (with a biblical text identical with that of Ambrose and to be confidently accepted as authentic) go so far as to preserve the core of the eucharistic canon, concluding with the Lord's Prayer and a doxology.[7]

He had problems with his congregation, who could be turbulent (*Virg.* 3. 3. 11; *off.* 1. 10. 35). The liturgy of medieval Milan included a demand for quiet: 'silentium habete' (Beroldus recording Milan usages in the twelfth century).[8] Church attendance was not good; some preferred rural walks (*in Ps.* 118. 16. 45). While people loved singing psalms and hymns, during the readings they chatted (*in Ps.* 1. 9. 4). Once he needed to admonish communicants that a gulp does not bring more grace than a sip from the chalice (*ep.* 1 = M7. 8). He wanted his flock to realize that the entire body of believers has a priesthood (*in Luc.* 5. 33; 8. 52; *Sacr.* 4. 3; *Myst.* 30). Augustine would be grateful for his statements about the transmission of sinfulness from Adam (e.g. *in Ps.* 118. 11. 25; *Myst.* 2). Some came to church but lived unregenerate lives with sex, drink, and contentiousness (*in Ps.* 118. 14. 12). Sadly there were apostates even under Christian emperors (*ep.* 72 = M17. 4). Evil powers are not prominent in Ambrose's thinking; but it is worth noting that he provides a very early witness to the belief that Satan has horns (*in Ps.* 43. 18).[9]

The conquest of urban space was achieved by building Christian shrines, usually installing the relics of a martyr beneath the altar (Revelation 6. 9). He sent relics to Florence for a new church (*Exh. Virg.* 1. 1. 9).

Literary culture. Sermons

Ambrose had been well educated, and besides an evident debt to Plotinus and Porphyry his writings have quotations and reminiscences of Sallust, Cicero, Virgil, Quintilian, less often of Terence, Lucan, Ovid, and Horace. He knew Pliny's *Natural History*. Augustine mistakenly supposed Ambrose to think

[7] Liturgical material in Ambrose is well gathered by J. Schmitz, *Gottesdienst im altchristlichen Mailand* (Theophaneia, 25; Cologne, 1975).

[8] Ed. M. Magistretti (Milan, 1894), 51. 62–3, or in L. A. Muratori, *Antiquitates italicae medii aevi* (Milan, 1738–42), iv. 833–940.

[9] M. P. McHugh, 'Satan and St Ambrose', *Classical Folia*, 26–1 (1972), 94–106 collects texts. The existence of evil powers was evident to the pagan Porphyry from the disgusting nature of animal sacrifices with which they needed to be placated.

Plato met[10] Jeremiah (*Doctr. Chr.* 1. 28. 43), later correcting himself (*City of God* 8. 11; *Retr.* 2. 4). Ambrose accepted the view that Plato in Egypt had studied Moses and the prophets (*in Ps.* 118. 18. 4; *Noe* 8. 24) enabling him to make a positive evaluation. He could quote Homer (*Noe* 2. 3; 16. 56). Greek theology from Philo, Origen, Didymus, Athanasius, and Basil was freely recycled. Jerome translated Didymus on the Holy Spirit so as to show up the plagiarism.

The educated people at Milan were impressed by the oratorical skill of Ambrose's sermons. The new professor of Latin literature and rhetoric, Augustine from Africa, initially came to the cathedral in admiration for his power with words, and only gradually came to realize how good the content was. The first chapter of Augustine's *Confessions* proclaims the importance of the Milan sermons in moving him towards conversion. In north Africa he would never have heard anything like them. Educated people had difficulties with the Latinity of the Old Latin Bible. He needed to explain to his people that the Latin was a translation from Greek, and was often not as clear (e.g. *in Ps.* 36. 4). Ambrose wanted his people to realize that scripture was the divinely inspired book (*in Ps.* 1. 4; 47. 12) on which they ought to meditate every day (*in Ps.* 118. 20. 9). 'I do not ask Christ for rational argument; if I am convinced by reason, I am denying faith' (*Satyrus* 2. 89).

Jews in Italy

The cities of northern Italy had a strong Jewish population. An author not long after the time of Ambrose, Maximus of Turin (63. 3), noted how very influential Jews were 'in palaces and with provincial governors'. An edict of 418 (CTh 16. 8. 14) encouraged Jews to practise as advocates in lawcourts; probably this was not new. Ambrose (*Ob. Val.* 30–1) contrasts Christian poverty with Jewish opulence. He was aware that at synagogues Bible study was serious; some rabbis knew the Torah by heart (*in Ps.* 118. 13. 26). 'While you, a Christian, sleep on, Jews are studying the Bible night and day' (*in Ps.* 118. 19. 31). Especially under Julian there had been sharp tensions between church and synagogue; a number of Christian basilicas were torched (*ep.* 74 = M40. 25), and Jews were blamed; whether rightly or not cannot be decided. Some Christians were keeping Jewish festivals (*in Ps.* 118. 2. 18). Sharply anti-Judaic matter occurs in *ep.* 74 = M40. The anonymous Roman author known as Ambrosiaster (because his commentary on the Pauline epistles was transmitted under Ambrose's name) writing in the 370s was probably of Jewish birth, and certainly wrote many times of synagogue practice with

[10] Dr Holford-Strevens suggests misinterpretation of Greek *enétuchen* as 'encountered' instead of 'read.'

deep respect. He may be in mind in *ep. extra coll.* 1 = M41. 10, of a Jew with deep admiration for Christian teaching.

Functions of bishops

At ordinations Christ presides (*extra coll.* 14 = M63. 3). The grace given never fails (ibid. 52). Priesthood is shared by bishops and presbyters. Bishops perform apostolic functions in absolution (*Paenit.* 1. 8. 34ff.), especially on Maundy Thursday (*in Ps.* 118. 10. 17); but they are not on a par with those directly chosen by Christ (*off.* 1. 1. 3). In matters of basic doctrine they cannot be judged by laity (*ep.* 75 = M31. 4). Some dishonour the office by using it for gain (*in Ps.* 1. 23. 2). Episcopal insignia include a ring (*Joseph* 7. 40).

For bishops Bible study was a fundamental need (*in Ps.* 118. 10. 39). Not submitting to scripture was a cause of heresy (*De fide* 4. 1. 1). 'In the prophetic scriptures there is much obscurity' (*in Ps.* 118. 8. 48). Some Italian bishops and clergy used to get help from Ambrose with problems of biblical interpretation. With his knowledge of the Greek text, he was qualified to assist. Throughout he wrote with 'sober intoxication' (a phrase borrowed from Philo) that the exposition of scripture is to proclaim redemption in Christ bringing forgiveness of sins and eternal life. The objection to the subordinate Arian Christ is his insufficiency to redeem. Like others of his time, Ambrose was moved by Paul's epistles, though he found them obscure, and a sombre diagnosis of the human condition. Yet King David offered a model of penitence for adultery and no sinner should despair (*in Ps.* 118. 20. 29). Ambrose once mentions philosophical critics who thought absolution merely encouraged sinning (*in Ps.* 118. 18. 3). He himself feared facile indulgence creating more delinquency (*in Ps.* 118. 8. 26).

Influence on Augustine

In view of Augustine's enthusiasm for his sermons, one might expect the personal contact between the two men to have been frequent and fruitful. This was not so. At one time in his distress and puzzlement Augustine found his way to Ambrose, but found him reading silently and did not dare to interrupt his intense concentration. Nevertheless, the reader of Ambrose's sermons on the Psalms or his commentary on the six days of creation or on the story of Isaac (in which Porphyry is an evident influence) cannot escape being aware that many themes particularly characteristic of Augustine are there. The interpretation of 'the letter kills, the spirit gives life' of Old Testament allegory liberated Augustine (*ep.* 64 = M74. 4), who only discovered years later that the text meant something else (*De spiritu et littera*). Ambrose insisted that before God only grace, not human merit, can avail for salvation (*in Ps.* 118. 20. 42).

The essence of religion is not in ceremonies but is inward in the soul (ibid. 8. 39), a 'fire in the heart' (13. 2), 'ordinata caritas' (*in Luc.* 5. 73). All descendants of Adam and Eve are bound by the succession of social cupidity (*ep.* 63 = M73. 8). Yet the fall was a happy event ('felix') giving occasion for redemption (*in Ps.* 39. 20; *in Ps.* 118. 16. 40). This theme became familiar through the Easter 'Exultet' hymn. Baptism derives its validity not from the quality of the bishop conferring it but only from God's gift (*De Spir. S.* 1. 18; *Myst.* 27), a theme of the first importance in Augustine's argument against Donatism. As in the *Confessions* (8. 7), Ambrose observed that something we possess is not much valued if it is easily and cheaply acquired (*Exameron* 3. 2). For Ambrose the Church is the 'City of God' (*in Ps.* 118. 15. 35). Neoplatonic elements in his language occur and, like Augustine, he quoted from Plotinus 'Flee not by ship, chariot or horse . . .' (*Isaac* 8. 78). *Isaac* 7. 28–8, 38 uses much from Plotinus 1. 4. Matter from Plotinus 1. 6 appears in *ep.* 11 = M29. Platonizing influence cannot be detected in his language about God as Trinity, nor in his Christology. But he is emphatic on the unity of God: Father, Son, and Spirit are one God (*De Spir. S.* 1. 13. 132ff.). The nearest theology comes to Platonism is to say (3. 93) that God cannot be a plurality because there are no numbers in God. He is 'the One to whom all things return' (*ep.* 1 = M7). Divine giving leaves God undiminished (*De Spir. S.* 1. 11. 118ff.). Plato was the prince of ancient philosophers (*in Ps.* 35. 1). Towards the logic of Aristotle Ambrose was more reserved: 'God has not been pleased to save his people by dialectic' (*De fide* 1. 5. 42). Profane logic was a tool of radical Arians. A reference to a devout mother pouring out tears in prayers for her son (*in Ps.* 118. 20. 8) might be about Monnica. A striking passage (*in Ps.* 118. 22. 32) 'I sought you, but I could not find you unless you willed to be found' could come from Augustine's *Confessions*. So too *in Ps.* 118. 8. 39 (and 20. 46) 'the conflict is within you yourself'; or the citation of Romans 13. 13–14, at *in Ps.* 118. 14. 12, close to the garden scene of *Conf.* 8. 12. 29. However, in the Pelagian controversy Augustine first invokes Ambrose's authority for orthodoxy, not earlier.

Bishop Ulfilas

A Cappadocian family captured as prisoners in a Gothic raid of the mid-third century had a fourth-century descendant brought up as a Goth with the name Wulfilas or Ulfilas (p. 232). As a young boy he was sent to Constantinople as a hostage at a time when the prevailing Christianity of the capital was inclined to the non-Nicene position. He became a reader in the Church and in time Eusebius of Nicomedia, translated to Constantinople, consecrated him to go as a missionary bishop in Gothia. His mission was remarkably successful, but provoked hostility from Gothic leaders. He therefore took his converts back into the empire to settle in Moesia south of the Danube. He created an alphabet partly Greek, partly runic, and translated the Bible. He disliked the Nicene faith (above p. 232). For Ambrose's critic Palladius of Ratiaria, Ulfilas was a great witness to truth.

To the disaster at Adrianople

The Goths north of the Danube suffered a grave defeat from the migrating Huns which led them to ask the emperor Valens for leave to settle in the empire south of the Danube. Valens and his advisers agreed, but in the short time available could not provide food or shelter for a very large tribal migration of barbarians, inevitably resented by the Roman citizens already working the lands being occupied. Conflicts erupted, and by 378 the abrasions had become serious war. Roman infantry could not cope with massed Gothic cavalry.

The annihilation of the imperial army and the death of the eastern emperor Valens at the battle of Adrianople, 9 August 378, delivered a massive shock (below p. 423). It seemed to prefigure the end of the known world of civilization. Now the barbarian Goths were or seemed to be in control. Their lack of organization was not immediately realized. Before Valens set out for the battle, the monk Isaac at Constantinople had promised victory if he would restore Nicene orthodoxy; Valens ordered him chained in prison (Sozomen 6. 40). Refugees poured into north Italy, and Ambrose sold valuable church plate to ransom prisoners. From Spain Gratian summoned Theodosius to restore order not only in the army but in the administration which, by Ammianus' account, Valens had left in near chaos. He also represented a Nicene faith and a sea change in ecclesiastical policy for the east. In January 379 he was proclaimed Augustus. He saw the impossibility of pushing the Goths back north of the Danube; they had to be settled within the empire and turned into federate allies, without whose aid the difficult frontier could not be defended.

From 378–9 Ambrose began to be able to recruit the emperor Gratian to support Nicene bishops. Ambrose did not fail to point to the prevalence of non-Nicene views in regions under barbarian attack while Nicene Italy remained secure. Valens' death at Adrianople could be catalyst for a change in religious policy. In the imperial consistory Ambrose had opponents, notably Macedonius, Master of the Offices, who used to shut the door against him, an act which after Gratian's death cost him asylum at the church (*Vita* 37). Perhaps remembering Valentinian I's neutrality Gratian felt hesitant about supporting Ambrose and excluding the rival Christian group regarded by Ambrose, not by themselves, as Arian heretics. At least both parties wanted the emperor to be unfriendly to pagan cults.

The Altar of Victory

The rich aristocrats in Italy, especially at Rome, were tenacious in quiet adherence to the old gods. Possessors of huge estates in many parts of the empire, they also owned most of Rome itself. They no doubt hoped that Christian senators could also be quiet in their religious allegiance. Class and high culture were social bonds. A Christian senator Pisidius Romulus may have been disconcerted when, in answer to a query, Ambrose (*ep.* 48 = M66) assured him that Moses acted correctly in arranging a massacre of 3000 idolaters who had worshipped Aaron's golden calf (Exod. 32: 28). In 382 there was a showdown when Gratian directed that the Altar of Victory be removed from the Roman senate-house and renounced the office of Pontifex Maximus.

Q. Aurelius Symmachus, prefect of Rome in 384 and famous for eloquence, pleaded for restoration and mutual toleration: 'It is impossible by only one road to attain to so great a mystery.' This argument from the mystery of God to toleration was anticipated by Porphyry, who believed there must be a universal way of salvation but that it seemed undiscoverable (*City of God* 10. 32). Themistius in the east agreed. In 357 for Constantius' visit to Rome the Altar had been removed, but was replaced. Like Montaigne, Symmachus argued that where so much is uncertain tradition has binding force since reason fumbles in the dark. And emperors are 'priests of justice' preserving for each his due (*suum cuique*, the jurist Ulpian had said). Justice is independent of the predilections of the ruler. Roman religion is governed by Rome's laws. The Altar of Victory is needed to be confident against barbarians; the insulted gods have lately shown anger by a famine (in Africa, granary for Rome, in 383) when the funding of temples was diverted from cult to meet the high price of grain to feed the city. The state survives when law and old custom are preserved, and suspension of the old laws will unnerve people making a will. Symmachus granted that the emperor had authority to alter laws and could issue edicts superior to any existing code. But in religious matters a wise emperor would make no changes.

Symmachus was asking for toleration. Two centuries earlier Tertullian had eloquently stated the case for toleration (*Apol.* 24. 5), though he was sure that the old gods were false, immoral, and offensive to the true deity (*Spect.* 2. 9). The martyr spirit was not conducive to thinking the gods were all right for those who liked that sort of thing. Moreover, the Christians were commissioned with an apostolic vocation to convert the world, similar to the zealous proselytizing by Jewish missionaries on which Matt. 23: 15 has an adverse comment. Yet the Christians were in no doubt that they and observant or liberal Jews worshipped the same God who, in the Christian understanding, had indeed given the Mosaic Law or Torah and the prophets who foretold

Messiah's coming. Tensions could be sharp because they were so close to one another. But with a Christian emperor to support them the churches were not using Tertullian's language, and still felt threatened by powerful pagan landowners and senators or indeed by the devotion and obedience to Moses characteristic of strict Jews.

Ambrose's relation to Symmachus was that of the courtesy due to a member of the same senatorial class and probably a relative. Symmachus was no aggressive militant for polytheism and represented quietly tenacious conservatism. His values were culture and class. He had no determination to harass Christians in Rome (*Relatio* 21). Ambrose may once have thought in much the same tolerant way, but now as bishop he represented the kind of zeal and conviction which Symmachus did not want to possess.

Ambrose's reply tells Gratian that he injures no one by putting the supreme God first. Christianity brought progress, making ancient customs obsolete. A Christian emperor will give a verdict corresponding to the Church's moral code rather than to outworn laws of the old order. Unimpressive is Symmachus' highly aristocratic assumption that in time of famine the income of impotent gods and their temples has prior claim over provision for the hungry poor, who are the Church's great resource. Military victory comes from the brave legions, not from the old religion, the valueless nature of which was proved by Julian's disastrous campaign in Mesopotamia, when he was told by soothsayers to burn his ships and thereby lost all chance of retreat. In any event the majority of senators have now become Christians and are offended by the pagan Altar's presence. The mysteriousness of religion is for believers answered by faith in God's self-disclosure. Christians are therefore certain where Symmachus can offer only guesses in the dark. Ambrose strikingly refuses to meet Symmachus on his chosen ground of legality. In another context he too could argue that the emperor ought to be the first to keep his own laws, yet that his law was surely not above God's law (*ep.* 75 = M21. 9–10).

East and west agree on Nicene faith

In 381 Gratian was disposed to foster a general swing towards the Nicene faith. He called an ecumenical council of east and west to meet at Aquileia; attendance was voluntary and eastern bishops had already attended Theodosius' council at Constantinople in May. Most stayed away. This enabled Ambrose to play the dominant role of a prosecuting counsel against bishops from the lower Danube region who wanted to stand by the formula of Ariminum and who wholly and reasonably disowned any debt to Arius. There was probably some tension between Gratian and Theodosius, both being rivals for guiding the churches in the direction now being favoured.

Magnus Maximus

In spring 383 Gratian, who had vexed senior army officers, was murdered and replaced in the west by Magnus Maximus, commander in Britain, a relative of Theodosius. His inauguration as Augustus coincided with his baptism and resolute declaration for Nicene faith. Maximus' power was a threat to the boy Valentinian II and his mother Justina at Milan. Symmachus composed a panegyric in Maximus' honour which soon embarrassed him after Theodosius had destroyed Maximus (388). The emotional support felt for Gratian by Christians in the west meant that Maximus found it hard to win their hearts. Ambrose saw the treachery of Gratian's murder as making him a Christ figure and Maximus a Judas (*in Ps.* 61. 17–26). The palace would have been glad to hear this.

Justina demands an 'Arian' basilica

Pope Damasus died on 11 December 384. His successor Siricius (*ep.* 5), aware of contentions among Italian bishops, called a council of eighty bishops at Rome on 6 January 386. He pleaded for unanimity, contentiously insisting (against Jovinian) on priestly celibacy and that no new bishop be ordained without the knowledge of 'the apostolic see'. Dissenting bishops were held excommunicate. Surprisingly this council did not refer to problems in north Italy, where Ambrose had plenty. Justina and Valentinian II were a growing problem for him, and he could refer to her as 'that woman' (*ep.* 76 = M20. 12). In January an edict (CTh 16. 1. 4) granted toleration for adherents of the creed of Ariminum. The rival bishop, taking the name Auxentius, demanded and was given a basilica for his flock. Ambrose's people opposed this with a sit-in and hymn-singing at the building, surrounded by armed soldiers, who, however, did not attack.

Ambrose declared excommunicate any officer party to the confiscation. Merchants supporting him were imprisoned. Underlying Ambrose's confidence was the threat of intervention in Italy in the Nicene interest by Magnus Maximus. It was proposed that Ambrose and Auxentius should each nominate assessors to advise the high consistory before whom they were to state their case, after which the emperor would give the verdict. To Valentinian II Ambrose quoted a rescript of his father Valentinian I that in matters of faith or a case involving clergy, the judge should not be someone unequal in standing or in law (*ep.* 75 = M21. 2). That was in line with his policy that bishops should judge bishops, a principle going back to Constantine the Great when anxious to avoid an imperial decision about Donatists. 'Scripture and tradition show that bishops judge Christian emperors, and emperors do not judge bishops.' 'The emperor is a son of the Church . . .

within not above the Church.' From his reading of Philo Ambrose would have learnt that a high priest has authority superior to a king's (*Leg. ad Gaium* 178). Arians wished to assert that the emperor is supreme legislator over the Church. In fact people were saying 'emperors would more wish to be a bishop than bishops would want to be emperor' (*ep. extra coll.* 24 = M63. 28). Jerome (*ep.* 60, 14 to Heliodorus) has comparable reflections. It was prejudicial to justice that a prior edict threatened the death penalty for any resistance to Valentinian II's verdict.

Ambrose interpreted Valentinian I as exempting him as a bishop from appearing before a lay court in a matter of faith, even if the court was the emperor's consistory. It was comparable to the civil service in which different departments were answerable to their own special courts of inquiry. He refused to dispute with Auxentius in a civil trial of which the unbaptized emperor would decide the issue. Moreover, Valentinian I's rescript enabled him to regard the request for a basilica for those refusing communion with him as being a question of faith, *causa fidei*. He did not believe there could be as many churches as there are schisms. Auxentius' demand for a basilica presupposed that he was enjoying sufficient following in Milan, which could only be strengthened if a basilica were transferred to him, thereby entrenching schism. Ambrose appealed to his support among the city *plebs*, and wholly refused to acknowledge the standing of Auxentius as a bishop in the universal Church in which alone there could be authentic priesthood.

In retrospect Ambrose knew he had been close to martyrdom (*ep.* 23 = M36). The doctrine that in matters of faith the emperor yields to the bishop was only a step short of saying that a Christian emperor is subject to the discipline of the Church and that his legislation ought to protect Christian truth and practice. Constantius had already granted that clergy should have their own courts. The alternative society was not simply a heavenly Jerusalem; something of the City of God was present now.

The Schism at Antioch troubles the west

To the emperor Gratian's irritation his council at Aquileia in September 381 had been anticipated by Theodosius' great council at Constantinople in May which not only destroyed Arian dominance in the east but asserted the claim of New Rome to be the second see after old Rome and also reached decisions about the vacancy at Constantinople and the rejection of Paulinus of Antioch unwelcome to Rome and Milan. Gratian's council at Aquileia sent Theodosius a letter, drafted by Ambrose (*ep.* 6 = M12), explaining that both parties at Antioch had written to the west asking for communion; that the Goths' invasion of the Balkans had prevented western legates being sent to investigate; and that now a council should be held at Alexandria to sort out the confusion and restore concord among orthodox catholics. Since Paulinus of Antioch's presbyter Evagrius was present at Aquileia and since the Nicene bishops of Alexandria were in communion with Paulinus, the proposal was not wholly neutral. It came to nothing; but Ambrose was still concerned about Antioch at the synod of Capua in 392. Western anger at the canons of the council of Constantinople of May 381 received expression from a council at Rome in 382 when Constantinople's claim to be the second see after old Rome was answered by Damasus with the proclamation that Rome had the episcopate founded by St Peter and that Alexandria and Antioch stood second and third.

Priscillian of Ávila

In the eighties Ambrose was troubled by the Spanish quarrel about Priscillian bishop of Ávila. Ambrose's aversion to capital punishment was directly expressed when Priscillian, accused of Manichaeism and sorcery, appealed from a synod of Bordeaux to Magnus Maximus at Trier in or about 385. Maximus may have thought that his own position would gain further support from bishops if he accepted the view of Spanish and Gallic bishops and was hostile to this unusual ascetic. It is certain that Priscillian favoured the study of dualistic apocryphal texts, some of Manichee provenance, and asserted the equality of women with men before God and in the Church. He had retreats in country villas where men and women studied together. It was believed that his followers had special private prayer meetings where men and women prayed together naked by way of manifesting their ascetic conquest of desire. If this happened once with three or four, that would be enough for a general charge to become current. Maximus condemned Priscillian and his follow-ers to execution. Sadly the bishop of Corduba, Hyginus, who had first sounded the alarm about Priscillian but then showed kindness to him, was among those exiled; when Ambrose asked the guards to treat the old man less roughly, he was brushed aside (*ep.* 30 = M24. 12). What outraged Ambrose was that accusations entailing a capital penalty were brought before a secular ruler by bishops. He refused to hold communion with bloody bishops and those who were a party to the executions. They could not offer the eucharist with blood on their hands.

Tension between Maximus and Justina

Maximus' rise to power in 383 involved Ambrose in delicate negotiations between Milan and Trier. Maximus had been acclaimed Augustus by army officers angry with Gratian for favouring Germanic soldiery, and a senior army officer (Maximus himself disowned responsibility) was responsible for

Gratian's murder. Maximus sent envoys to Theodosius asking for full recognition and to Justina demanding that the young Valentinian II come to Trier for 'protection'. Justina sent Ambrose to Trier to tell Maximus that the boy emperor was harmless and in wintry weather could not travel. Ambrose implied that Valentinian could come in the spring, and thereby dissuaded Maximus from invading Italy at once. Maximus came to feel, with some reason, that Ambrose had deceived him, and that Valentinian was the mere tool of his Frankish army commander Bauto (*PLRE* i. 159), who had incited barbarian attacks on Maximus to hinder designs on Italy. When Bauto was inaugurated as consul on 1 January 385, Augustine delivered the panegyric (*c. litt. Petil.* 3. 30).

Justina's fostering of the anti-Nicene and pro-Ariminum group at Milan ran political risks since it could provide the pro-Nicene Maximus with ground for interfering. However, she may have calculated that the Goths ravaging Pannonia 'beyond hope of any recovery' (Ambrosiaster, *Qu.* 115. 39) were unstoppable and would soon be at the gates of Milan. They had just destroyed Mursa, which Maximus and Ambrose could independently interpret as a judgement on Bishop Valens' long domination. (Valens died during the seventies.) Justina may well have thought it in the empire's interest to support the version of Christianity which all-conquering Goths would find congenial. Maximus warned Valentinian II directly that conflict with the Church would put him dangerously out of step with all provinces except Arian Illyricum (Avellana 39, CSEL 35. 88). In 387 Ambrose was sent on a second mission to Trier. His report to Valentinian II was designed to avert suspicion that secretly he was supporting Maximus. The letter (*ep.* 30 = M24) describes abrasive exchanges before Maximus' consistory, and how he had refused communion with bishops (including Trier) with hands polluted from the execution of Priscillian, heretic though he was. Maximus was offended by Ambrose's reaction to his execution of Priscillian and his friends. So at least Ambrose reported at Milan.

Theodosius' war against Maximus

Slowly Theodosius decided not to share the empire with Maximus, who bribed barbarians settled in Thrace to give him support. The decision to go to war on both land and sea (Theodosius' coins show him in a ship, and passenger voyages between Ostia and Carthage ceased, affecting the return of Augustine and Monnica to north Africa) entailed a levy to meet the costs. In 388 Theodosius' largely barbarian army moved westwards. Near Aquileia Maximus was defeated and executed. All his edicts were annulled (CTh 15. 14. 7). At Antioch in Syria the city mob was incensed by the rise in taxes. Statues of the emperor and his family were stoned by rioters. Libanius and, to greater effect, Bishop Flavian pleaded for mercy to the terrified population contemplating the impending punishments from a hot-tempered Theodosius. The final outcome was tough but less frightful than they feared. Antioch escaped without a massacre (below, p. 479).

The synagogue at Callinicus

Ambrose's relations with Theodosius were uneasy; perhaps like Valentinian II, Theodosius too suspected him of having been too cosy with Maximus. At the fortress of Callinicus on the Euphrates (today al-Raqqa) Christians had torched the town synagogue, and Theodosius ordered the bishop, who had incited them, to rebuild it at his and his church's expense (*ep.* 74 = M40, *ep. extra coll.* 1a). He also deprived the bishop of exemption from municipal office. In Ambrose's mind this was allowing the synagogue to gloat over the church's humiliation. He told Theodosius that, in the view of many, Maximus' fall had been a consequence of celestial anger at his order that a torched synagogue in Rome must be restored. In Julian's time churches in Alexandria and Syria torched by Jews had been content to receive no compensation. Moreover, Theodosius had lately been merciful to Antioch for insulting his statues; could he not now forgive Callinicus? Indeed Ambrose himself claimed personal responsibility for the Callinicus affair, a claim presupposing not so much his own invincibility as his willingness to raise funds to pay the bill.

About the same time in a Syrian village monks processing to a shrine of the Maccabaean martyrs had been disrupted by some Valentinian gnostics. The monks retorted by torching the gnostic conventicle. Ambrose could not think so trivial a matter worthy of imperial action. Reluctantly Theodosius yielded, but monks were beginning to be disorderly; for a time Ambrose did not enjoy favour. This emperor could not administer his empire without good lawyers, and they could hardly have failed to suggest that the interests of the Church on Ambrose's stand seemed incompatible with fair dealing and justice. In 393 Theodosius, no friend to pagan temples, formally legislated against the destruction of synagogues (CTh 16. 8. 9 to the *comes Orientis*).

Massacre at Thessalonica

Early in 390 the military commander in Illyricum, a German general named Butherich (Soz. 7. 25. 3), stationed there probably to deal with barbarians in Thrace bribed by Magnus Maximus, was lynched by a mob at Thessalonica. Theodosius gave the Goths leave to take revenge. The populace assembled at the circus were indiscriminately massacred. Discreetly but unambiguously Ambrose wrote a remonstrance. He had previously begged the court to sanction no atrocity. Evidently some friend had leaked the decision to him.

(Theodosius could be dangerously irate when confidences were leaked; a *consularis* named Hesychius, *PLRE* i. 429, was executed for improperly obtaining imperial papers dealing with the Jewish patriarch: Jerome, *ep.* 57. 3.) The consistory had obviously discussed the case, which shows that the massacre was not the result of the emperor's blind rage. Sozomen (7. 25. 4) says that the angry emperor's decision was to execute a stated number by way of exemplary punishment. Perhaps the outraged Gothic soldiers thought this too little. Too late Theodosius enacted an edict reaffirming the principle that sentences of capital punishment should not be carried out for thirty days (CTh 9. 40. 13; Rufinus, *HE* 11. 18). News of the massacre came to Milan when a synod was sitting with a delegation of Gallic bishops, probably there to seek accord about the aftermath of the Priscillianist affair which had led many to refuse communion with Felix bishop of Trier. Ambrose could tell the emperor that the synod felt the emperor to need penitence and reconciliation to God, which would restore his honour generally. Public opinion was horrified by 7,000 deaths. Royal penitence had biblical precedent in King David's restoration after his sin against Uriah the Hittite. Ambrose was sure that the story of Bathsheba must be largely allegorical, since no modest lady could imaginably strip to wash in full view of the royal palace (*Apol. David altera* 40; cf. *Apol. David* 20–3). But David's penitence was a model for Theodosius now. The emperor repented, Ambrose absolved and readmitted him to eucharistic communion.

The suppression of polytheistic cult

Theodosius resided at Milan until spring 391, and in that year began serious anti-pagan legislation. Pagan rites at Rome and in Egypt were formally forbidden (CTh 16. 10. 10–11; 16. 7. 5). Bishop Theophilus of Alexandria was delighted to dismantle the great temple of Serapis. The Palatine Anthology preserves epigrams by an Alexandrian schoolmaster Palladas, whose hatred for Theophilus was cordial. Under the prefect Cynegius in 384, at the time of Magnus Maximus' programme for intolerant orthodoxy, Egyptian temples were closed and sacrifices forbidden. Temporary suppression was now succeeded by formal prohibition, which in Syria Cynegius implemented with fervour, even destroying a temple in the largely pagan city of Apamea. His violence in a tour of destruction evoked Libanius' discourse (*or.* 30) pleading for beautiful temples; he never sent the text to the emperor. Already in Augustine's time (*Sermo* 163. 2) a few African temples were converted as churches.[11] Greater instances occurred at Caesarea in Palestine, at

---

[11] The conversion of temples into churches was discussed by F. W. Deichmann in two papers in his *Gesammelte Studien* (1982).

Aphrodisias in Caria (SW Asia Minor), eventually even the Parthenon at Athens; not so much in the west. Most pagan buildings were allowed to collapse. In Rome a Christian aristocrat restored a statue of Minerva about 500 (*ILS* 3132).

Valentinian II's murder: Arbogast and Eugenius

After the elimination of Maximus in 388, Theodosius sent Valentinian II, now 20 years old, to Gaul with the support of a Frankish military general, Arbogast, who was pagan. Emperor and general did not see eye to eye, especially when Arbogast was lobbied by pagan aristocrats to get polytheistic cult restored in the west (*ep. extra coll.* 10 = M57. 5). Valentinian refused. Estrangement became extreme after he attempted to sack Arbogast. At Vienne Arbogast cut Valentinian down. (Socrates 5. 25. 4 says he had the emperor strangled by court eunuchs.) Arbogast had an alternative, more pliable emperor named Eugenius, a master in rhetoric (Zosimus 4. 53–4), a Christian but no zealot for his faith. All actual power remained with Arbogast and with a pagan aristocrat, Virius Nicomachus Flavianus (*PLRE* i. 347), a correspondent of Q. Aurelius Symmachus. He had been *vicarius* in Africa where he was described by Augustine as favouring the Donatists (*ep.* 87. 8); he was praetorian prefect of Illyricum and Italy until Theodosius heard of Valentinian's murder, and was reappointed when Eugenius entered Italy. Nicomachus threatened to stable horses in Ambrose's church (Paulinus, *Vita* 31), his clergy would be recruited as fighting men. He made a Latin version of Philostratus' life of Apollonius of Tyana (Sidonius Apollinaris, *ep.* 8. 3. 1), perhaps as a rival to Jesus. Two inscriptions (ILS 2947–8) record his rehabilitation by relatives in 431, partly on the ground that in 390 he had dedicated to Theodosius 'Annals', whether of the emperor's reign or of a much earlier period of imperial history. Nothing of this book survives unless it be identified with the *Historia Augusta*, composed in the 390s by an anonymous pagan senator. A work for Theodosius is unlikely to have been explicitly anti-Christian. An idealization of Rome's past is probable.[12]

Valentinian's body was sent to Milan. Ambrose stressed with vehemence that, unlike the past, he and Valentinian had become close. He had lately asked Ambrose to come and baptize him. He did not ask local Gallic bishops, which may suggest that he had not made friends in that quarter. But Ambrose never achieved this baptism. The implicit protest looks like an answer to

---

[12] T. Grünewald in *Historia*, 41 (1992), 462–87. It is unclear whether he was the target of a poem 'against the pagans' which may have been directed against Praetextatus, complaining that he used his gold to bribe people into abandoning Christianity. The *Augustan History*, edited and translated in the Loeb Classical Library, has attracted a large literature in part speculative and indecisive. That it was composed late in the fourth century seems certain, also that some is fiction.

gossip that in church interests Ambrose was somehow implicated in the conspiracy to get rid of Valentinian. Arbogast was known to have 'dined often'
with him (Paulinus, *Vita* 30. 1). He now wrote to Theodosius offering the
reuse of a porphyry marble sarcophagus, once occupied by Diocletian's colleague Maximian (*ep.* 25 = M53. 4). The corpse remained unburied for many
weeks, awaiting Theodosius' decision (a hesitation no doubt caused by coolness towards Ambrose if, when Eugenius was master of Italy, he had acknowledged him as Augustus). Ambrose delivered the panegyric at the funeral,
with pointedly numerous biblical references to make the occasion unambiguously Christian, subtly reinforced by a quotation from *Aeneid* 6. 882–6
with Anchises' admission that the customary flowers strewn on a grave could
do nothing for the departed. In any event in heaven his soul had been
welcomed by his half-brother Gratian, similarly murdered.

Valentinian II's sister was Theodosius' wife Galla, who was thrown into
deep distress by her brother's murder. That may be the explanation of delay
about the funeral. But a messenger from Milan to Constantinople could be
expected to need at least five weeks for a summer journey one way. Galla died
in childbirth in 394. Her daughter was the redoubtable Galla Placidia, who
was to enjoy an astonishing career. After appropriate mourning Theodosius
took his army rapidly west to confront Eugenius. Eugenius had been sending
impressive embassies to Constantinople, with Gallic bishops briefed to say
that Arbogast had had no hand in the murder. Eugenius in Italy sought to
enlist Ambrose's support but received no reply to several letters. Ambrose
soon decided to vanish from Milan and not to meet Eugenius. Eugenius
obtained the support of eminent pagans by giving to them personally the
value of endowments lately confiscated from temples, to which they were
then free to return the money. This action convinced Ambrose that he had
been right to keep out of the way (*ep. extra coll.* 10 = M57), but he did not
refuse to recognize Eugenius' title as Augustus. Theodosius' answer to
Eugenius' claims was to name as Augustus both his sons, Arcadius and
Honorius. That was to make civil war certain.

Battle at the Cold River (5 September 394)

Theodosius consulted the Egyptian hermit John of Lycopolis while making
careful military preparations. John foretold success. The emperor also prayed
for success with processions to martyrs' shrines at Constantinople (Rufinus,
HE 11. 33). Eugenius and Arbogast were confronted at the river Frigidus
(today Vipacco) on 5 September not far from Aquileia. Theodosius' standard
was the cross; Eugenius used a picture of Hercules (Theodoret, *HE* 5. 24. 4),
symbolic of the clash between Christian and pagan. At a critical moment in
the battle when Eugenius' forces had the upper hand, Theodosius resorted to

prayer. A freak storm, understood as miraculous (*in Ps.* 36. 25), assisted in the defeat of Eugenius, who was captured and executed. Arbogast fled and fell on his sword. Nicomachus Flavianus, prefect of Rome, also committed suicide; the pagan restoration he had sought to lead had failed. Ambrose (*ep. extra coll.* 3 = M62) was asked to intercede with Theodosius for supporters of Eugenius seeking asylum in churches.

Theodosius' forces at the battle included both Romans and Goths; the Goths suffered particularly severe casualties. Soon resentment would emerge among Gothic military commanders who felt that they had not been adequately rewarded. They wanted land and food, which the emperors were reluctant to provide.

Theodosius had not been serene about Ambrose leaving Milan, as if he were waiting to see who would win the coming battle. Such an ambivalent attitude may have been general, since Theophilus of Alexandria sent his presbyter Isidore with two alternative letters, one congratulating Eugenius, the other Theodosius (Socrates 6. 2. 6). Unfortunately for him both came into the hands of Eutropius the high Chamberlain at Constantinople. In a letter Ambrose had fully recognized Eugenius as emperor. However Theodosius was satisfied by Ambrose's self-justification. The emperor asked for a mass of thanksgiving to be celebrated, which Ambrose was glad to do, laying the emperor's letter of request on the altar (*ep. extra coll.* 2 = M61. 5).[13] Ambrose had a sense of theatre.

Theodosius visited Rome and, to the distress of pagan senators, directed that all public funds be withheld from pagan cult and temples (Zos. 4. 59). The cult of the old gods was now associated with disloyalty. In the minds of pagans the noble temples were the very heart of Rome and its empire, and public funding was of the essence of success. At least public games, without the customary sacrifices, were to continue as entertainment for the populace, for whom they were of huge importance. Moreover they enhanced the public standing not only of emperors but also of opulent senators who paid for them, often being forced to sell land to meet the high cost (Augustine, *Conf.* I. 10. 16; *En. in Ps.* 80. 7; 147. 7; 149. 10). At least that brought the land back into circulation. There was no prestige in soup-kitchens for the destitute, as Augustine critically commented (*En. in Ps.* 118. 12. 2). One of the ways in which pagan senators could subtly discomfort bishops was by giving public shows at the same time as church services which then had slim congregations (Leo M. *sermo* 84. 1, ed. Chavasse, CCSL 138 A).

---

[13] Another instance of a bishop placing a letter with good news on the altar during the eucharist is found in Severus of Antioch, *Select Letters* 3. 2, tr. E. W. Brooks, 4 vols. (London, 1902–4), ii, 233–4.

Theodosius I's death

At Milan on 16 January 395 Theodosius was to celebrate victory by chariot races. Too unwell to preside, he delegated that duty to Honorius. On the following night he died. Forty days later (a customary interval for a requiem), on 25 February, on the eve of the corpse's transport to Constantinople, Ambrose delivered a funerary oration before Honorius and army chiefs. Psalm 114 was chanted (the earliest evidence for its funerary use). He stressed army loyalty to Honorius in a way that suggests the existence of doubts. For the emperor Honorius his father's devotion is the model. Now in *lux perpetua* he had been received into the company of heaven with Gratian and Constantine; and there too would be Helena, Constantine's mother, who found the true cross on her pilgrimage to the Holy Land with two nails of the crucifixion. The emphasis is on the providential protection of the Roman state under the Christian emperors since Constantine.

In the *City of God* (5. 26) Augustine looked back on Theodosius as a truly devout man for whom it was 'more important to be a member of the Church than to be lord of the world', and who mobilized government coercion to suppress public heathen cults. It should be added that by edict he punished over-excited Christians who took the anti-pagan policy to allow attacks on synagogues (CTh 16. 8. 9). He forbade theatres and circus games to be available on Sunday, or on Epiphany, Easter, and Pentecost (CTh 15. 5. 5).

The pagan historian Zosimos, following Eunapius, says (4. 59. 1) that Theodosius made the Vandal general Stilicho guardian of Honorius. That is also implied in Ambrose's memorial obituary for the dead emperor (*obit. theod.* 5). After Theodosius I's death Stilicho was virtually ruler of the empire, commanding the armies of both west and east. He was a Christian (Augustine, *ep.* 97). His tomb is in the church of Sant'Ambrogio, Milan.

Ambrose's death

On 4 April 397, on the day before Easter Day, Ambrose died. He was buried beside the bones of Gervasius and Protasius and was succeeded by Simplicianus. Among Ambrose's last letters is his longest, addressed to the church at Vercelli, where the people were split in their choice of a bishop to succeed the ascetic Eusebius. One party wanted a married man with substantial means, which would reinforce the church chest. Ambrose thought the model to follow was their ascetic Eusebius, who had combined the public duties of a bishop with the monastic life. For a bishop must live his life in the public eye 'in quodam theatro'. He has to be sociable, to fit in easily, and to represent moral discipline. He has to be set apart from the laity and their concerns. He may be called upon to oppose an emperor's commands and by his faith to triumph over soldiers sent by imperial authority. He must be a Bible student and teacher of the gospel, hospitable, compassionate to those in prison, consoling the bereaved. The job description here, like other statements of a personal ideal, is no bad self-portrait (*ep. extra coll.* 14 = M63). Jerome (*adv. Jovinianum* 1. 34) once comments that when choosing a new bishop, individuals look for somebody resembling themselves. But 'many are selected to keep out another who is disliked'.

The mosaic portrait of Ambrose clothed as an aristocrat in the apse of the church of Sant'Ambrogio at Milan was made soon after his death, and may well preserve an authentic likeness.

40

AMBROSIASTER

Contemporary with Pope Damasus (366–84) a theologian of remarkably independent mind was writing in Rome, with a commentary on the Pauline epistles (without Hebrews, which he did not think Pauline) and a book discussing 'Questions' on the interpretation of the Bible ascribed to Augustine. The commentary survived under Ambrose's name,[1] so that he is usually called Ambrosiaster, the name given to him by Erasmus. The anonymous author knew much about synagogue usage, and once allows himself to say that the ideal expositor of scripture is a converted Jew. He may have been referring to himself. Like Justin he was clear that Jews and Christians worship the same God (on 2 Tim. 1: 3). The ministerial structure of the Church interested him. Damasus he describes as the 'rector' of God's house the Church (on 1 Tim. 3: 15). The commentary on 1 Timothy observes that the orders in the contemporary Church do not correspond to those in the epistle. 'Timothy, whom Paul had made a presbyter, he calls a bishop because the first presbyters were called bishops. . . . That is why in Egypt presbyters minister confirmation if the bishop is absent. Because later presbyters were discovered to be unsuited for the highest position, a change was made in consideration of the future, so that not age in years but merit should be the qualification for a bishop.' Bishop and presbyter have the same ordination, both being *sacerdotes*; but while every bishop is a presbyter, not every presbyter is a bishop. Now each city has only one bishop (on 1 Cor. 12: 29). But a presbyter is *sacerdos* no less than he. The author would like to change the custom of reserving that title to bishops.

The seven deacons of Rome cause him anxiety because of their arrogance, the close association with their bishop making them feel superior to the presbyters of the city. In fact their remuneration is greater. It was customary for presbyters to be seated in church, and for deacons to stand. At least at Rome deacons do not presume to sit. They are not commissioned to celebrate the eucharist. They are assistants to the priest. Roman clergy often spare them the indignity of actually pouring water on the priest's hands at the ablutions

---

[1] In 405 Augustine quotes the commentary under Ambrose's name (Aug. *ep.* 82. 24). Later (*ep.* 180. 5) he cites it again with no mention of Ambrose.

(*Qu.* 101. 3). Because they are the bishop's staff, controlling access and the papers put before him, deacons easily get above themselves in the city.

After ordination to diaconate, priesthood, or episcopate, abstinence from conjugal intercourse is to be observed (on 1 Tim. 3: 12). The reason for this is the daily celebration of the eucharist, the apostle having taught that abstinence is necessary for prayer (*Qu.* 127. 35). The celebrant is acting in place of Christ when he prays for the people, or offers or baptizes (on 1 Tim. 4: 13–14). The deacon too administers holy things, by custom ministering the chalice, so that no less is expected there. Once he writes emphatically that 'among the eleven apostles there was no woman'. He deduced from 1 Cor. 11: 5 that woman is not made in God's image. Once (on 1 Tim. 3: 11) there is polemic against a Montanist claim that women deacons should be ordained.

He confirms that in his time the liturgy of the Roman church is still using Greek (on 1 Cor. 14: 14) even though the Latin-speakers do not understand it (cf. p. 281 above). Surprisingly the Latins prefer the creed to be in Greek (14: 19). Perhaps at Rome they did not care to understand what was affirmed. A few allusions to liturgical forms occur, but not direct citations. 'Reserve should be used in uttering the mysteries of our religion' (on 1 Thess. 2: 17).

Of the indifferent quality of clergy available in his time he is candid (on 1 Tim. 5: 22). He is aware that many clergy are depressed by poverty and do not have sufficient to command respect in their congregations (on 1 Tim. 5: 17). But widespread damage is caused by avaricious clergy who use high office to amass riches (1 Tim. 6: 10). Poor ascetics going barefoot live better lives than the well off (on 1 Cor. 12: 23). His portrait of the populace of Rome is almost as negative as that in the pagan historian Ammianus: they are excessively given to wine and women. And the women have taken to drink (*Qu.* 115, 26; on Col. 3: 11). Several passages deplore widespread resort to astrologers even by Christians. The drunken feast on 1 January is not to be celebrated by believers (on Gal. 4: 10).

He stresses the equality of all the baptized (on 1 Cor. 12: 12–3). One should not think of the Church as being the clergy. The emperor's army has officers, tribunes, counts, etc., but the ordinary infantry soldiers are much more necessary than the officers. An army consisting entirely of generals would be useless (on 1 Cor. 12: 22).

Alarming news of Damasus commissioning Jerome to make a new Latin version of the Bible has evidently reached him, since (on Rom. 5: 14) he regrets that some are wanting to dictate from Greek manuscripts, whereas the Old Latin versions were made from early and uncorrupted Greek manuscripts, and have support in Tertullian, Cyprian, and Victorinus of Pettau (Poetovio). In Oea (Tripoli) in north Africa in Augustine's time a reading of Jerome's new version caused a near-riot. Jerome's revision was not regarded with enthusiasm in the west.

Intricacies of theological controversy are not great subjects of interest in either Commentary or Questions. He has met some who valued controversy and thought it useful. But it did not seem right for a people professing one faith (on 2 Tim. 2: 15–16). The Manichees were present in Rome to a degree that caused misgiving, and a number of passages refer to them. He knew Diocletian's edict condemning them.

41

DONATISM

A disputed moral compromise

Some of the sharpest divisions in the Church have centred upon moral issues. In north Africa the party led by Donatus of Black Huts (Casae Nigrae), later dissenting bishop of Carthage, a well-educated man according to Augustine (*Tr. in Joh.* 6. 20), originated in protest against compromise with Diocletian's government ordering the surrender of Bibles and sacred vessels and forbidding Christian assemblies for worship. Remarkably the issue was not treated as crucial and dramatic in other western provinces. But in north Africa bishops who handed over these things, simply wanting a quiet life and rightly confident that the crisis would not last, were in both senses 'traditores', handers-over and traitors. Such action seemed like apostasy, disqualifying a compromised bishop from further priestly functions. If so, the consecrating hands of this ordaining bishop transmitted pollution, not Christ's apostolic pastoral commission. Disqualification followed not merely from proven evidence of having surrendered sacred objects but from suspicion that this might perhaps have occurred. Whether he could be readmitted as a penitent layman would be for the members of the pure Church to decide. It followed in Donatist ecclesiology that all sacraments of this compromising Church were rendered invalid. The harassment the separatists suffered from the government convinced them that they were the authentic persecuted body of Christ. A painful question, on which initially the Donatists were divided, was whether baptism, given to members of the Catholic community before the split, was invalidated and needed to be repeated. Donatists also demanded that any Catholic marrying a Donatist must become a member of their community. Augustine was sad how many Catholic clergy shrugged their shoulders and tolerated this (*Sermo* 46. 15).

Valid baptism

Donatist ecclesiology presupposed that baptism had to be given by a good priest or bishop to be valid. Its power to confer grace varied according to the quality of the minister. They appealed to Cyprian of Carthage for this position. Echoing Cyprian himself, Augustine was sure that 'there were many things the learned Cyprian could teach; but there were also things that the teachable Cyprian could learn', among which he counted the theology of baptism where the question to be asked was whether what God has commanded has been done as scripture lays down. The gift does not depend on the holiness of the human giver who is merely instrumental and ministerial.

Caecilian's ordination

When Mensurius bishop of Carthage died (*c.*308), he was succeeded by his deacon Caecilian, who had been deeply unsympathetic to provocative defiance of the government's edicts. Rumour said that his principal consecrator, Bishop Felix of Abthugni, had surrendered the scriptures, though this was never proved by witnesses. A formal inquiry acquitted Felix. Donatists felt sure he must have transmitted to Caecilian a fatal contagion inherited by all in communion with Caecilian or ordained by him or receiving the sacraments at his or their hand. Therefore fifty or eighty years later, the clergy of the *ecclesia catholica*, all those in the communion of which Caecilian was a member even if they came from Mesopotamia, were not true priests at all but a diabolical counterfeit. The water poured over them in baptism could confer only defilement.

Africa God's own country

The separatists were unmoved by the consideration that they were out of communion with the churches north of the Mediterranean and those in the east, with both Rome and Jerusalem. The truth of God could rest with few or even a single person, for particularity was of the essence of the incarnation. And had not Noah's Ark contained no more than eight people? In the Song of Songs the bride (the Church) says to the divine bridegroom 'Thou dost rest in the south.' They found in Isa. 14: 13 that the devil is in the north. A Latin version of Habakkuk 3: 3 said that 'God will come from Africa' (Aug. *S.* 46: 38). (An appeal to Simon of Cyrene would have cut more ice had there been any Donatists in that Libyan city.) So Donatists located the true Church in their own society in north Africa, and saw the rest of the Christian world as in apostasy by association. Augustine replied 'The whole world judges that without the least anxiety' (*contra ep. Parm.* 3. 24: 'securus iudicat orbis terrarum'). The Lord's parable of the wheat and the tares, both to be left untouched until the final harvest of the last judgement, was incompatible with intolerant puritanism. God's Church is universal, not local, and the sacraments are his, not the minister's. Sacraments correctly given have validity outside the Church, but become authentic means of grace on joining the unique universal body.

Toleration by the government. Macarius' suppression

From the imperial government the Donatists experienced alternating periods of harassment and toleration. After conciliar verdicts against them, Constantine had enacted a severe edict (Augustine, *ep.* 105. 9), but the coercion was unsuccessful and soon abandoned. The Donatists grew in strength, and especially in Numidia, least Romanized of the African provinces, the Donatists had a big majority. In the other provinces their numbers were far from negligible, Families were divided. Augustine himself had a Donatist cousin. In Constans' reign in the 340s severe repression took place under two special commissioners, Paul and Macarius, initially sent to bring relief exclusively to Catholic poor, which to Donatists was bound to look like bribery (Optatus 3. 3).[1] They reacted violently. In protest zealous Numidian Donatists threw themselves over cliffs, and the community proudly commemorated annually their deaths, for which Catholics were blamed. Under Decius and Diocletian the north African churches had endured fierce tortures but survived; so the Donatists would do the same. Nevertheless their memory of the 'Macarian times' remained a smouldering source of anger. Catholics represented an imperial Church, 'the communion of the emperor', a compromising establishment bribed by a secular government with financial subsidies. As bishop of Carthage Donatus believed himself to be first bishop in Africa and to stand higher than any emperor, claims which the Catholic Optatus of Mileu (3. 3) thought arrogant.

Attacks on pagan shrines

In the third century well before the time of Diocletian militant and muscular Christians began to form bands to assault pagan shrines and disrupt festivals. Early in the fourth century one Numidian bishop, Purpurius of Liniata, raided a temple of Serapis and removed casks of vinegar, probably intended for ceremonial ablutions of the statue to remove the deposit left by candles. He was notorious for his strong-arm ways of resistance. There had long been and there long remained a small but hard core of militant believers whose métier was violence against pagan shrines and Jewish synagogues. An edict as late as 8 June 423 (CTh 16. 10, 24 = CJ 1. 11. 6) lays down that Christians may not injure or harass law-abiding Jews or pagans.

---

[1] Dr M. J. Edwards has published an annotated translation of Optatus (Translated Texts for Historians, Liverpool, 1999).

A law of April 423 (CTh 16. 8. 26 = CJ 1. 9. 16) forbids rash Christians either to seize or to burn synagogues.

Circumcellions

Militant bands of African Punic peasants with wooden clubs (metal later) and a terrifying war-cry 'Deo laudes' specialized in unstoppable charges on the bands of musicians, *symphoniaci*, at pagan festivals, smashing their instruments. Young pagans with swords made martyrs of some. Among Donatists they were known as the Militants, *Agonistici*. The Catholics called them 'Circumcelliones', probably because most of them were seasonal agricultural labourers who, when unemployed, wandered round 'cellae', perhaps martyrs' shrines. They were also called Cutzupitae (the Semitic root *qtp* means 'harvest'). Persecution under Paul and Macarius poured fuel on their zeal, except that now they turned their attacks on Catholic churches and clergy, who might be maimed for life, blinded, in rare cases killed, their basilicas being dismantled. Those who failed to support the men of violence had their kneecaps pulverized (Optatus 2: 25). When Donatists took over or recovered a basilica that had been in Catholic hands, they first disinfected it with salt water from the pollution of Catholic liturgy. Consecrated oil, bread, and wine were thrown away as profane. Some of them believed that at a Catholic mass an unmentionable enormity was committed (Aug. *ep.* 93. 17). Wooden altars were broken up and the white cloth customary for the Church's sacrifice to God was discarded. In towns such as Hippo (modern Annaba) the massive Donatist majority could forbid the bakers to sell any bread to Catholic customers (Aug. *c. litt. Petil.* 2. 184). Catholics were excluded from burial in Christian cemeteries where Donatists were in control. Augustine described the situation as civil war.

In upper Numidia in the fourth century disruptive bands were led by Axido and Fasir, who called themselves 'commanders of the saints'; they specialized in intimidation of (not only pagan) landlords who were pushed out of their gigs and forced to run before their own serfs. Law-abiding farmers then had the further embarrassment that the government sent military units to suppress these levellers with their demand for social justice, and the soldiers caused as much trouble as those they were sent to stop (Augustine, *En. in Ps.* 136. 3). The Donatist bishops, not the Catholic, had asked the Count for military intervention to suppress them (Optatus 3. 4). In Numidia the peasants spoke Punic, the old Phoenician language. The Latin of government administration and of much commerce was unfamiliar to them. Augustine's mother Monnica had a Berber name and spoke Latin with a demotic accent and syntax (*De ordine* 2. 45). Augustine reckoned that in Numidia only 10 per cent were Catholics, the rest Donatists (*En. in Ps.* 149. 3).

Augustine describes the Circumcellions as including both sexes, but all celibate, dedicated to evangelical homelessness like Jesus who had nowhere to lay his head. When Augustine began to create monasteries in north Africa, Donatists were critical of the economic security which this meant for the residents, who had at least shelter and a bed with simple food such as Donatist militants did not. On the occasion of a commemoration for one of their martyrs, underfed Donatists celebrated with gusto and consumed quantities of food and liquor. A Catholic celebration in Africa was not notably more sober.

Tertullian (*Apol.* 44; *Scap.* 2) disapproved of Christians who assaulted pagan idols. The same view appeared in Origen (*c. Cels.* 8. 38) who held such action both contrary to scripture and counterproductive in effect. Bishop George of Alexandria enjoyed the support of the military commander Artemius in destroying pagan shrines in Egypt; under Julian he was lynched and Artemius executed. The Catholics in Africa had some horrific experiences when they became the target of Circumcellion assaults. The Donatist bishops wholly disowned the violence, but their country clergy were often a party to the attacks.

Neutral emperors

The death of Constantius and the accession of Julian were causes of rejoicing for Donatists since, although Julian's paganism was now overt, his African policy was to be neutral between Donatist and Catholic. Some high officials had Donatist sympathies. People who had been impelled by the harassment to become nominal Catholics returned to the Donatist fold in large numbers both in town and country. After all there was no difference in essential beliefs; Catholics and Donatists even had the same psalms appointed for certain feasts and the same lectionary. Their bishops were in unquestionable apostolic succession; their leader in the 380s, Parmenian of Carthage, liked to trumpet an exclusive mediatorial role of bishops between God and the laity (language which Augustine thought 'the voice of Antichrist': *c. ep. Parm.* 2. 8. 15).

Catholic opposition mobilized by Augustine

Under Valentinian's express policy of keeping ecclesiastical disputes at arm's length, Donatist and Catholic settled down to living side by side in mutual communal distrust and in a hatred kept alive by Circumcellion attacks. Augustine was sharp against any uncharitable words about Donatists. The polemic against Parmenian, Donatist bishop of Carthage, by Optatus of Mileu about 370 was a substantial statement of ecclesiology. Once Augustine had become bishop at Hippo in 395–6, it seemed to him intolerable that intimidated Catholics were acquiescing in the deadlock. The outrages of

Circumcellions were sufficient ground to petition the government for restraining action. But the legislation of the emperors was not so clear as to make it impossible for Donatist bishops to defend their own position.

Edicts condemned heretics by name. But were Donatists heretics? Augustine oscillated between argument that he was dealing with a schism and the legally much more formidable contention that Donatism had become heresy by repetition of baptism and its rejection of the universal Church, and therefore liable to prosecution under the law. It was easier to recognize the baptism of schismatics than that of heretics. In conciliatory approaches, following Optatus, he shocked less ecumenically minded colleagues by always referring to Donatists as 'brethren' (*fratres*), contrasting with Donatist description of ex-Donatist Catholics as 'pagans' (Optatus 3. 11). To grumblers he gave the razor-sharp answer that Lot had spoken of the inhabitants of Sodom as brothers (Gen. 19: 7). Augustine would never call an ex-Catholic becoming Donatist an 'apostate'. Some converted 'for the sake of worldly advantage' (Aug. *Bapt.* 5. 5). He knew many Donatists who were well educated and brilliant in oratory (*Tr. in Joh.* 13: 15). Petilian, Donatist bishop of Cirta, had been Catholic and an eloquent advocate in lawcourts, but he was coerced by Donatists into becoming their bishop. In favour of the argument that they had fallen into heresy there was the consideration that then under imperial edicts they lost their basilicas and suffered civil penalties, which provided a deterrent.

With converts there was the usual danger that some wanted to change allegiance because they were under discipline, perhaps excommunication, in their original group. Augustine refused to admit excommunicate Donatists. He absolutely opposed the reordination of ex-Donatist clergy. That recognition surprised some of his fellow bishops.

Donatist weaknesses

The people of north Africa honoured the emperor but had an instinctive sense of independence from Rome and the empire. Donatus himself was heard to ask 'What has the emperor to do with the Church?' Donatists weakened their awkward relation with the government by supporting a succession of usurpers asserting their independence of the empire. Gildo, the most threatening of these, received energetic backing from Optatus, Donatist bishop of Thamugadi (Timgad), a brigand who was able to mobilize violent Circumcellion bands. Gildo's fall was disastrous for this Optatus, tarred with high treason.

The thoughtful statement of the Catholic standpoint composed about 370 by Optatus, bishop of Mileu in Numidia, presented a conciliatory argument, directed to his own people, that Donatism was a schism rather than a heresy, with a sustained critique directed against Parmenian, Donatist bishop of Carthage. To his demerit Parmenian was not a native African (2. 7, 3. 3). Optatus' work in seven books survives in a second edition (*c.*390). The catholicity of the Catholic community in north Africa is established for him by communion with Peter's chair at Rome. It seemed absurd for the Donatists to claim that an expatriate Donatist in Rome, bishop to a little congregation of other expatriates, stood in the true succession from the apostle. 'Peter's see is ours' (2. 9). In divine providence there is an intimate link between the Church and the Roman empire, authority to which the Church is subordinate; hence the duty of prayer for the emperor (3. 3). Divine care for this empire is evident from the presence within its frontiers of Christian priests and ascetics, not found among barbarian peoples. He ends with an appeal to the Donatists to return to this communion. Optatus had correctly seen that the central questions were 'where is the one true Church?' and the unrepeatability of baptism.

Another factor that weakened Donatism was that this body separating from the Catholic community had its own internal splits. In 391 the great Donatist leader Parmenian died; he was succeeded by Primianus in a hotly contested election, since he was thought to be a laxist by a Donatist deacon of Carthage named Maximian. Maximian rapidly acquired a strong following among bishops in the neighbouring province south-east of Carthage, Byzacena, as well as in the African provinces other than Numidia, and on 24 June 393 the Maximianist party in synod at Cebarsussi in Byzacena declared Primianus deposed. Twelve bishops (the customary number in Roman Africa) consecrated Maximian in his place. Their party denied validity to Primianist baptism. They issued an encyclical (*tractatoria*) to all Donatist churches in Africa; through state archives this document came into Augustine's hands. He cites parts of the text in *En. in Ps.* 36. 2. 18–23 of the autumn of 403, showing that some bishops signed for absent colleagues. Naturally Augustine's only interest in the story was insofar as it provided him with a potent rod to beat the main Donatist positions.

Primianus' supporters declared Maximian's group 'lost' to salvation, and with official support in law took possession of Maximianist basilicas (Aug. *c. litt. Petil.* 2. 102). Court decisions favoured Primianus. Intimidation organized by Optatus of Thamugadi diminished support for Primianus' opponents. A vast assembly of 310 bishops supporting Primianus met on 24 April 394 in southern Numidia at Bagai,[2] a Donatist stronghold, partly to celebrate the anniversary of Optatus' consecration as bishop (his *natalicium*, on which custom expected a bishop to provide a large dinner for the poor of his diocese), and partly to declare the Maximianist party utterly condemned.

---

[2] Bagai exists today on maps of Algeria.

The Primianists were thereby enabled to persuade the civil authorities that they were the orthodox (within the law) while the Maximianists were heretics who should be deprived of their churches. In time, however, they reconciled returning Maximianists, who were to be accepted virtually without censure including even the full reinstatement of two bishops who had ordained Maximian. This procedure was very different from Donatist treatment of Caecilian and offered Catholic polemic an argument to exploit. Donatist apologists had been accusing the Catholics of appealing to the secular government for support. Now they had been doing precisely that themselves. They had been claiming that they were proved to be the authentic Church by being persecuted by a government in league with the Catholics. Now they themselves had been fiercely persecuting Maximianists. They were recognizing Maximianist baptism; then why not Catholic baptism also? Donatism was wholly inconsistent. Furthermore, the Maximianist council of Cebarsussi had unpleasant things to report of Primianus, ill-becoming a leader of a body claiming to be the one holy Church of the pure. A few names of former Maximianist bishops reconciled to communion with Primianus turn up in the record of the Carthage Conference of 4. 11.[3]

Tyconius

Significant of weakening in the Donatist camp was also the emergence among them of a lay theologian named Tyconius who had earned censure from Bishop Parmenian for his insistence that the true Church of holy scripture must be worldwide and cannot be merely African. Augustine admired this thesis, and had a catalogue of biblical texts to enforce the point, composed perhaps to counter Parmenians collection of scriptural exhortations to separate from all pollution. Tyconius also observed that during the first forty years of the split, before the 'times of Macarius', Catholic converts could be welcomed by a Donatist bishop without rebaptism. Tyconius regretted the Donatist assumption that what was 'holy' was a matter for themselves to define. He boldly expressed the conviction that the Donatist justification for their separation was insufficient and unconvincing. Tyconius especially impressed Augustine by his (extant) book of 'Rules' for interpreting scripture,[4] the influence of which is writ large in Augustine's own exegesis, providing at least a few universal rules or general principles to diminish subjectivity in the interpreter. He also wrote a commentary on the Apocalypse of John (lost but partly recoverable from later users).

---

[3] On the names at Cebarsussi see a valuable examination by C. Weidmann in SB Vienna, 655 (1988).

[4] Critical edition by F. C. Burkitt (Cambridge, 1894); translated by William S. Babcock (Atlanta, Ga., 1989).

Augustine's anti-Donatist writings helped to give the Catholic bishops a greater confidence in facing their at times violent rivals. His aim was to achieve reconciliation, and to that end proposed with negligible success public disputations and conferences where both sides could state their case. Donatist bishops felt incapable of meeting so clever and gifted an adversary in debate. Their social custom was to have nothing to do with the polluted Catholics and their pretended bishops.

Coercion?

As other African Catholic bishops contemplated the problem, some among them began to think that pressure from the imperial government could be the only route to a solution. About 405 the Catholic bishop in Bagai in the far south of Numidia obtained a court ruling for the recovery of his basilica. The following Sunday he was celebrating the liturgy when a substantial band of Donatist hitmen invaded. They smashed the wooden altar over his head, wounded him in the groin with a machete, and then dragged his body out of town to be dumped on a dung-heap at the foot of a water tower there to die. At dusk a peasant and his wife, going home by ox-cart, came by the water tower; the man needed to relieve himself there, his wife modestly remaining in the cart. He returned with the half-dead body of the bishop: if they could nurse him back to health, the Catholic community would surely give them gold. The story illustrates the relative indifference of Numidian peasants to the religious issues in the schism. The bishop, restored to health, travelled to Ravenna and stripped to show the emperor Honorius his terrible wounds and scars. Honorius was outraged and ordered his officers of state to see that this kind of thing was suppressed. It was a turning-point in moving the emperor to action.

Augustine was in two minds about coercion. In the twelfth century the canonist Gratian could compile two collections of his sayings, one for toleration, the other for coercion (the latter being instrumental for the much later Inquisition). Against coercion there were many considerations: it would produce hypocritical conversions, and an increase in Circumcellion atrocities. Moreover, the repression under Macarius about 347 had merely made Donatists intransigent in the extreme. Nevertheless Augustine's misgivings were set aside by his fellow bishops. In favour of coercion, provided it was not too drastic, there was practical success in converting some Donatists. If their conversion was not wholly sincere, in time they would come to appreciate the truth of the authentic universal Church. Owners of property had to convert to be able legally to bequeath anything to their children. In time Augustine acquired a majority following at Hippo.

The two parties meet at Carthage, 411

In May 411 at Carthage a large conference or confrontation was arranged by the government to meet under the presiding hand of a commissioner, a tribune Marcellinus, who was Catholic and was to give the final verdict. He was a friend of Augustine. The Catholic bishops numbered 286, the Donatist 285, Augustine being chief spokesman for the Catholic side, Petilian for the Donatists. In obedience to the biblical prohibition on sitting down with the ungodly, the Donatists refused to sit, with the result that in the summer heat everyone had to stand throughout the proceedings. At the end the Donatists were confident that they had won every argument, everything except the inevitable verdict in favour of the Catholic claim to be the true Church. The Donatists had stated their case and in law had failed. Thereby the government was justified in applying coercion. Augustine made a striking move, offering the Donatists that if they would share eucharistic communion, the Catholics would invite their opposite numbers to share with them in pastoral care. His own supporters were deeply apprehensive that the Donatists might accept the invitation; but there was no chance of that.

The outcome of the Conference, of which the record taken down by shorthand writers survives,[5] was a substantial move by Donatist laity towards the Catholic body, and Augustine was surprised to find what good people many of them were. (Donatist bishops were more intransigent, but it was hard for them to act in a way that in effect conceded that the entire protest for a century past had been a huge error.) Augustine's famous saying 'Love and do as you like' (*in ep. Joh.* 7. 8) was in context a justification of discipline subject to the proviso that it must not exceed what a loving parent might hand out to an erring child. This for Donatist peasants might mean whipping, and not all recipients of the treatment experienced it as loving. The strength of Donatism always remained in the rural world, especially in Numidia's small villages and adjacent estates.

The record of the Conference has illuminating matter on legal procedure which was carefully followed. At the time of the Conference there were refugees from Alaric's Goths in Carthage, one of whom was a distinguished ascetic and spiritual director named Pelagius, described by Augustine as a native of Britain. Pelagius and Augustine saw one another but exchanged no words; Augustine had much on his plate at this time.

The Church

The controversy with the Donatists revolves round the idea of the Church. For Augustine this is in its essence a united body, a universal and visible society

---

[5] A distinguished edition by Serge Lancel in SC (4 vols.).

or fellowship of baptized believers, and not only an earthly society. The Church on earth is one with the angels and saints. African basilicas had murals portraying martyrs (*S.* 316. 5), especially Peter and Paul, and Christians invoked their aid. This visible society is Christ's body, so that Christ with his Church is 'the whole Christ' (*totus Christus*). The Holy Spirit is the soul of the Church (*S.* 267. 4). All who have the Spirit love the Church (*Tr. in Joh.* 32. 8). 'Outside the Church anything is possible except salvation' (*Sermo ad Caesariensem plebem* 6). Yet 'something catholic can exist outside the Catholic Church' (*Bapt.* 7. 77). Donatist ecclesiology excludes the bad and wicked from the Church. Tyconius spoke more wisely when he said that the Church has a right and a left side, a mixture of true Christians and people who are only nominal (*Cons. Evang.* 1. 49). The latter are within the Church until the Last Judgement. Like Noah's ark, the Church has clean and unclean beasts (*En. in Ps.* 8. 13). 'God's house' may contain some chaff.

The whole Church is priestly. While it is customary to call bishops and presbyters 'priests' (*sacerdotes*) or pastors, that is not more than ministerial, since Christ alone is the true priest and shepherd of souls. 'To you I am a shepherd, but to the Chief Shepherd I am a sheep like you' (Aug. *En. in Ps.* 126. 3). People talk of going to church, meaning the building; but the Church is actually the believing body of the baptized. Controversy within the Christian society is unavoidable, but should never lose charity (*En. in Ps.* 33. 2. 19).

A plenary council of bishops is the supreme authority for deciding debated questions. Peter's see at Rome has a leading part to play. The 'rock' on which Christ has built his Church was Peter's confession of faith. 'We Christians believe not in Peter but in him in whom Peter believed', and Peter is symbol of the one Church's universality and unity. When African bishops in synod reached a conclusion, they liked to follow Cyprian's example and check that they were not out of line with Rome. A strong consciousness of different customs between the Greek and Latin churches occasionally surfaces in Augustine's writings. He thought it unimaginable that an eastern council would write to the see of Carthage without simultaneously informing the Roman see (*Cresc.* 3. 38). Unity of east and west was a basic presupposition. The authority of this universal Church had convinced Augustine of the truth of the gospel. It was the ground for his trust in the Bible as conveying to him the word of God.

Of the Church as ideal Augustine uses lyrical and exalted terms. Of the empirical actuality his portrait is often dark. Few African cities had no clergy who had not had to be removed from office for delinquency. Episcopal duties to give hospitality had made a number into alcoholics. At elections faction was common. It did not help that in Africa most bishops were chosen 'by the violence of the laity'. Bishops were expected to be celibate, but clergy accepted this custom unwillingly (Aug. *Adult. coniug.* 2. 22). Some bishops were excellent pastors, but others were there for the temporal honours (*ep.* 208. 2) or in one case to transfer a large private debt to the church chest (*ep.* 96). In one case (*epp.* 209; 20*[6]) Augustine suffered agonies of anxiety about a mistake he had himself made. An ex-Donatist community at Fussala within the jurisdiction of Hippo needed a Punic-speaking bishop. Punic-speaking Catholics were evidently a rarity. Augustine nominated a young man from his monastery to be ordained by the metropolitan of Numidia, and he turned out to be catastrophic, hated with good reason by his flock. The man appealed to the Roman see against his suspension; Augustine had to tell the Pope that he would have to resign Hippo if the decision favoured the appellant. This was not the only case of delinquency in the numerous African episcopate. Some of Augustine's toughest letters were addressed to bishops failing in a conscientious pastorate. The need for total dedication imposed high demands. Augustine was convinced that 'only a preacher on fire can kindle his hearers' (*En. in Ps.* 103. 2. 4). Anyone who looks for good people in the Church is sure to find them (*En. in Ps.* 47. 9).

---

[6] The asterisk refers to the letters of Augustine discovered and first edited in CSEL 88 (1981) by J. Divjak, discussed in my paper in *JTS* NS 34 (1983) 425–51, reprinted in the Variorum volume, *Heresy and Orthodoxy in the Early Church* (1991).

42

MONKS: THE ASCETIC LIFE

A call to discipleship which expects renunciation of even natural goods for the sake of the gospel is a constituent element in the earliest strands of Christian teaching. It is prominent in Jesus' teaching in Luke's gospel, e.g. 14: 26, where the proclamation of the gospel is prior to family ties, or 9: 60, where it takes precedence over the burial of one's father.[1] Martha's activity is necessary but in priority yields to Mary's contemplative dedication (10: 41–2). At Corinth a group of converts were sure that baptism requires a renunciation of marriage. Ancient pre-Christian texts can say that one who has received the love of a god will forgo the love of a mortal, and that physical love distracts the soul in rising to higher things. Paul needed to tell the Corinthians that celibacy is a gift not given to all, and that marriage is no sin, even if celibacy allows for a greater degree of dedication to the Lord (1 Corinthians 7).

The vindication of Christian ethic

Presenting a case to impress hostile pagan readers in the second century, Justin was proud of Christians who had renounced marriage (*Apol.* 1. 15. 6). Origen (*c. Cels.* 7. 48) answered Celsus' scorn for Christians by pointing to believers who, 'like perfect priests', have turned away from sexual experience, and do not need, like the Athenian hierophant (cf. Julian, *or.* 5. 173), hemlock to ensure their chastity; and their motive is not honour or reward but purity of heart. Ascetics were an apologist's asset. Philo of Alexandria had thought similarly when in his treatise 'On the contemplative life' he described the Jewish communities called Therapeutae in Egypt.

Galen

In the second century there was no more intelligent person than the medical writer Galen. In one place he writes of the Christians with critical respect,

---

[1] This saying (Luke 9. 60) has a rabbinic parallel in the Babylonian Talmud, *Berakoth* 19b; cf. *Shabb.* 139ab.

but particularly admires their men and women devoted to the celibate life who also show self-control in food and drink.[2]

Epictetus

A similar attitude appears in his contemporary the Stoic Epictetus for whom it seemed admirable that the 'Galileans' were not afraid of tyrants (4. 7. 6). The renunciation of worldly values was not unheard of in the pre-Christian classical world. In the *Republic* (559) Plato advises that the appetite for food and drink and sexual acts needs to be restricted to what is necessary for survival. It alarmed him that young people were easily seduced by voices telling them that licence is asserting liberty and that moderation is fit only for the stupid and uneducated (560 D). The portrait of Socrates in Xenophon's *Memorabilia* (1. 3) is of an ascetic with a frugal lifestyle, enjoying his food by being hungry, always the best sauce, but only taking what was sufficient, drinking only when thirsty, and rigorously avoiding sexual indulgence, which he saw to entrap people. To pupils, unlike contemporary sophists, he never charged a fee (1. 2. 60). He supported the cult of the divine according to his means (1. 3. 3).

With the ethical ideal of happiness, it became crucial for all ancient moralists to offer counsel for the therapy of emotions. Human beings find themselves in distress in consequence of making decisions based not on reason but on emotion or passion. Therapy to reduce the pain requires self-discipline and a training of the habits which determine character. To yield to a temptation once makes it harder to resist on the next occasion. One quickly falls into a mire of frustration when a strong desire has to remain unfulfilled or when, because of a faulty judgement, a situation has come about which is deplorable. Accordingly ancient moralists advise, as a first necessity in character training, a restraint in the indulgence of bodily appetites, e.g. for delicate food, much wine, or pursuit of sexual pleasures, all of which need to be treated with reserve. Such self-discipline loses its character-building quality if it is ostentatious and advertised to attract admiration. This summarizes the Stoic programme of Epictetus, whose ethical discourses were recorded by an admiring hearer Arrian, to whom we also owe a history of Alexander the Great. Unfortunately only half of Arrian's transcript has been preserved in the manuscript tradition.

Epictetus calls his recipe for therapy *askesis*, like the training of an athlete or a soldier. One of his favourite warnings is the saying of Socrates that 'the

---

[2] R. Walzer, *Galen on Jews and Christians* (London, 1949), 15. On the transmission of this through ninth-century Arab sources see S. Gero in *Orientalia Christiana Periodica*, 56 (1990), 371–411. Galen thought sexual activity good for health in melancholic or manic dispositions, but required strict restraint; sex may drive such people to mad lengths, but (he feared) no sex may drive them madder.

unexamined life is not worth living' (1. 26. 18; 3. 12. 15). Self-scrutiny will reveal that ambitions for honour, fame, and wealth are no road to happiness. Everyone is in search of happiness, yet constantly people are looking in the wrong place (3. 22. 26) as one can judge from the evident unhappiness of the very rich or the holders of high office (3. 22. 27). People nurse illusions that somehow they can escape death; but all that is born must die. If you drown when the ship goes down, that is no ground for accusing God (2. 5. 12). We are transient beings.

Cynic philosophers like Diogenes had manifested a high degree of job satisfaction, living a quietist life (4. 3), serene in having no house, no slave, no city, sleeping on the ground, no privacy and therefore without temptation to do what others do in dark places behind closed doors (3. 22. 45 ff.). Socrates seldom went to the bath (4. 11. 19). (To many ancient people frequent visits to the bath-house were luxurious self-indulgence. In the fifth century a bishop was criticized; why do you take two baths a day? He replied, Because of you I have no time for a third: Socrates 6. 22. 4). Epictetus did not think the path he was commending would be easy. To attempt so difficult an undertaking without the help of God would be to incur disaster and divine anger (3. 22. 2). Epictetus' prayer was 'Lord have mercy', *Kyrie eleison* (2. 7. 12).[3]

Before the third century soldiers in the Roman army were required to be unmarried, and after that marriage remained unusual. Like a soldier or an athlete, said Epictetus, one needs to practise self-discipline to concentrate on living with the minimum of distraction and with as much freedom as possible from social obligations. This raises the question whether one should marry and beget children. The serenity and detachment of a Diogenes requires the conclusion that, though legitimate, it is better not to marry. Some of Epictetus' terms at this point (3. 22. 67 ff.) are strikingly similar to the language used by Paul in 1 Corinthians 7, for whom marriage is no sin but celibacy is better for those so called.

To follow this Stoic way incurred a steep ascent. Epictetus was well aware that among many who called themselves Stoics only few lived their lives in full accord with his ascetic recommendations. Most of them acted as if they were Epicureans, deciding what was right or wrong in accordance with the pleasure or the pain resulting. 'If you have a Stoic, show me' (1. 19. 20). Admittedly he knew that Epicurus the hedonist was strongly averse to all sexual acts (3. 7. 19). (He had no objection to letting the mind linger with pleasure at the thought: Augustine *c. Jul.* 5. 29.) Adultery destroys trust and fidelity, and therefore destroys your humanity (2. 4). But Epicurus' argument

---

[3] This is not the only evidence that *Kyrie eleison* was used by non-Christians, but as we have no pre-Christian evidence of it, influence from the Church, though not probable, is possible.

against it is selfish hedonism (3. 24. 38), indifferent to the community. Zeus has made the nature of the human being such that he cannot achieve his own goods unless he contributes to the common interest (1. 19. 13).

The portrait of Plotinus in Porphyry's biography is of an ascetic saint, perhaps consciously akin to a Christian ideal.

Iamblichus on the Pythagorean Life

About the time of Constantine the Great the Syrian prince Iamblichus was teaching Neoplatonic philosophy at Apamea. He had studied Plotinus and Porphyry and dissented from Porphyry's cool attitude towards polytheistic cult and sacrifices. Iamblichus was much interested in a phrase used by Plato (*Republic* 600 B) about 'the Pythagorean life'. He, like Porphyry before him, saw in the life of Pythagoras a moral ideal of living which they both wanted to commend. So Iamblichus wrote a tract describing the life of his hero,[4] portraying the way of living as withdrawn, elitist, and ascetic. It is worth summarizing: Pagan ascetic training is designed to purify mind and soul together and to check self-indulgence or greed. This entails abstinence from meat, wine; little sleep; contempt for fame, wealth, honour, etc. Hidden within the body there are 'opposing powers'. Only necessary food should be eaten. Beds should never be luxurious. Sexual activity for boys should be after the age of 20 and then very seldom. Sex is for procreation. In the Pythagorean community the novice must keep silence for five years to learn self-control, and bring his property into a common chest. There are chastisements for failures. The cult of the gods is central to this way of life: 'Follow God.' Old ancestral customs must be carefully observed and kept. When attending sacrifices and visiting holy places one must go barefoot. Beside the community there are Pythagorean hermits in desert places. The community had special songs designed to allay depression or anger. But Pythagoras' teaching was esoteric, using obscure symbolic speech.

Ancient Greeks and Romans did not experience sexual encounters as a major source of happiness and ecstasy. That sexuality was important was known to others beside the poet Ovid. But moralists tended to regard sexual activity as animal, necessary for the survival of the family and therefore of the city or tribe, providing heirs for the inheriting of property, but also a disturbing and potentially antisocial thing. It too easily passed out of control, and could easily be more a source of pain than of delight. No moralists appear more reserved than the arch-hedonists, the followers of Epicurus, as one sees in Lucretius' vivid and essentially negative portrait. Epicurus thought sex a

---

[4] The text edited by L. Deubner, revised by U. Klein, is in the Teubner series. Translation by Gillian Clark (Liverpool, 1989); or by John Dillon and J. Hershbell (Atlanta, Ga., 1991).

likely way in which his pupils would get hurt. Cicero's dialogue *Hortensius*, which had a catalytic effect on the young Augustine aged 18, had a solemn warning against indulgence in food, drink, and sex as likely to have a stultifying effect on the mind.

Christian asceticism. Syrian monks

Asceticism has a less prominent place in Christianity than in other world religions. Nevertheless from the New Testament there was a strong stream of asceticism within the early Church. St Luke's gospel in particular can be seen to emphasize the disciple's need for renunciation of natural delights. But in Matt. 19. 11–12 there is the strongest statement of the choice for the celibate ideal. Second-century Christians in Syria took ascetic practice to a refined degree. 'Sons of the Covenant' were celibate. In the fifth century Theodoret of Cyrrhos wrote his *Religious History* with biographies of Syrian holy men, hermits regarding the body as an enemy to the soul, most of them wearing heavy iron belts to punish it. In his youth Theodoret had been taken to visit many by his devout mother. One of them named Symeon found his spiritual life disturbed by crowds coming to consult him, so he mounted a column, at first 3 metres high, then 6, then 11, finally 18 (or more than 60 feet) above ground, topped by a platform with provision at one end for natural functions. He was exposed to heat by day, frost by night. Some thought him crazy, but vast numbers came, grandees as well as peasants, and eventually four (extant) basilicas were built to provide for pilgrims, all focused on his column. He died in 459. Though Syrian ascetics were influential, in time 'the paradise of the fathers' would be Egypt.

Antony

In the first half of the third century Origen knew of Christian ascetics who felt it necessary to leave the hubbub and bustle of cities and escape to the silence of the desert. For Egyptians that was no great physical distance and the climate by day was warm. Origen was not himself persuaded of the merits of the desert as a solution to personal aspirations, on the good ground that people take with them their greatest problem, namely themselves. The spiritual enemy is within. About 271 a young man aged 18 named Antony felt called to the ascetic life, moved by the gospel exhortations 'Sell what you have.' and 'Be not anxious about tomorrow'. Initially he submitted to the direction of an old man living in a small village (so he was far from being a pioneer), but gradually he moved further away from human habitation to a derelict fort, then to a hermitage in a cave near the Red Sea. There he attracted would-be disciples anxious to learn how to combat the demons of temptation. To preserve serenity for prayer he had to remove himself three days' journey to 'an inward (remote) mountain'. Excessive mortifications injurious to health were not his style, but he expected himself and any monk to know by heart substantial parts of the Bible, certainly the psalter, and by basket-making to earn enough to give to destitute beggars. Antony's advice on temptations was that everyone should keep a written record of actions each day, the deterrent to repeating a sin being the shame at the reflection that someone else could know. This simple Copt, idealized for a Greek readership at Alexandria, became the theme of Athanasius' *Life of Antony*, a work having affinities with Iamblichus and with Porphyry's *Life of Plotinus*. It was twice translated into Latin in Athanasius' lifetime and then into other languages, Syriac, Coptic, Armenian, Old Slavonic.

Athanasius' Life of Antony

The Antony of Athanasius' *Life* is a biblically formed holy man, uneducated in Greek literature but held in respect by inquiring pagans. His frugal life is a struggle with the demonic world of sexual fantasies, nightmarish terrors, suggestions that all his self-renunciation is pointless. Desert travel brought alarming threats of death by dehydration, and attacks from hyenas were averted only by Antony's holiness; but the mockery of demonic laughter (possibly articulated by hyenas) was his greatest peril. By listening to readings in church services the demons learnt to quote scripture, might appear in monastic garb, could make plausible forecasts of coming events, and joined in wild dances. Antony became noted for his power to discern demonic disguises, assisted by a vile stench which betrayed their evil identity. They could be put to flight by the sign of the cross so notoriously mocked by pagans, to whom the entire notion of atonement by the cross of Christ defied rationality.

At death the soul's ascent would be harassed by accusing demons with dogs, but the Mother of God and the saints give support. Athanasius' portrait repeatedly emphasizes Antony's respect for town clergy (an unusual feature among ascetics), and in particular his refusal to hold communion with Melitian schismatics or Arian heretics. Early in 356 at a time of high crisis for Athanasius' career he came to Alexandria in extreme old age (Jerome says he died aged 105) to affirm his support for the bishop and the orthodoxy that he represented. In consequence high officers of Constantius' civil and military administration in Egypt harassed the monks among whom Athanasius found refuge. One of the demons' fiercest weapons was military attack. Antony correctly predicted the early death of the *dux* Valacius, notorious for ferocious floggings of male and female supporters of Athanasius. His reputation for faith-healing caused him to be invited to urban churches. He declined, saying that a monk out of his cell was a fish out of water.

Both Gregory of Nazianzos (*orat.* 21. 5) and Jerome (*Vir. inl.* 87–8) are sure the *Life of Antony* was by Athanasius. He may have used matter prepared by Serapion of Thmuis; the preface acknowledges much help from an intimate disciple of Antony. Numerous attempts to deny Athanasius' responsibility for Antony's *Life* depend mainly on the claim in the preface that Athanasius had met Antony more than once, which is possible but unlikely.[5] They may have seen each other a few times before Antony's intervention at Alexandria which occurred after Athanasius had fled from his city. One has to allow for Athanasius' strong political interest in presenting the holy hermit as on his side in the passionate controversy of the 350s. He would have thought exaggeration pardonable in his desperate circumstances. He never wrote a line as a neutral detached historian. The two accounts of the death of the *dux* Valacius (*PLRE* i, 929) in *His. Ari.* 14 and *VAnt.* 86 are not so divergent as to be a problem. Moreover, the text attributes to Antony statements of Athanasius' doctrine of redemption by the incarnate Lord through his Church in terms closely paralleled in his work on the incarnation. His Antony never toyed with Platonic or gnostic ideas of the soul falling into the material body. Ancient tradition has transmitted seven letters ascribed to Antony extant in Latin, Georgian, and Syriac with some Coptic fragments. A Greek version which survived until the fifteenth century was known to Jerome. The letters include some obscurely expressed themes of an Origenist stamp but also have language echoing Athanasius' work on the Incarnation. Ascetic circles were not at first as precise in formulation as Athanasius might have wished.

The *Life of Antony* tells as much about Athanasius and his understanding of the Church as about Antony. The biography presupposes that the ascetic movement stemming from Egypt was already spreading to the West. Fifteen years after its composition one of the Latin versions was being studied in Trier, as described in Augustine's *Confessions*. Though composed at a low moment for the church in Egypt, the *Life* is serenely confident that the crisis is transitory. The Egyptian churches looked back with pride on their survival of the persecutions of Daia and on their martyred hero, Bishop Peter of Alexandria. Antony himself acquired sufficient fame to receive letters from Constantine the Great and from his sons Constans and Constantius. So the *Life* was more than a local record of God at work in the Nile valley and the adjacent desert; it was a message for the whole Church in the

---

[5] A negative view put forward by R. Draguet is modified by T. D. Barnes, 'Angel of Light or Mystic Initiative', *JTS* 37 (1986), 353–68, supported by L. W. Barnard, 'Did Athanasius know Antony?', *Ancient Society*, 24 (1993), 139–49. See also A. Louth in *JTS*, NS 39 (1988), 505–9; for Serapion as ghost-writer, M. Tetz, *ZNW* 73 (1982), 1–30. The case for Athanasian authorship is well stated in the critical edition by G. J. M. Bartelink, (*SC* 400; Paris, 1994).

empire and beyond. Above all it meant that a hero of sanctity supported Athanasius and his cause.[6]

Implicitly the *Life* asserted (no doubt one should say, desired) an integration of urban churches with the hermits and recently formed ascetic communities. From them Athanasius would find it possible to recruit suitable bishops, one such being named, Serapion of Thmuis. Even so monks could remain a source of awkward critical dissent, as Theophilus of Alexandria found in the controversy about Origen's spirituality.

Athanasius' *Life* became a text of high authority among the monks of the Pachomian connection, but surprisingly the *Life* is silent about Pachomius and his monastic communities, possibly because they were determined to have no link with town churches and their clergy. In 346 Pachomius had had trouble with a synod of bishops, distrustful of his visionary experiences.

Pachomius

A papyrus dated 324 is the earliest witness to the actual word monk, *monachós*, a loner. The hermit was, however, not to be the most usual form of ascetic. Experience showed that the beginner needed to learn the ascetic way in community.

In Constantine the Great's time this was clear to a Copt named Pachom, or in Greek Pachomius, an ex-soldier converted from paganism by the moving charity of a Christian community, bestowed without any limitation of their alms to fellow-believers. The Nile valley was at that time facing huge unemployment with many farms and villages altogether abandoned partly because of high taxes. Pachomius was easily able to recruit large numbers of monks to come and live a common life together under a religious discipline and obedience to himself as superior. Their separation from the secular world was made visible by a substantial wall. The wall resembled the boundary normally surrounding ancient temples in the Nile valley. In this case it provided necessary control of the discipline of the monastic society and underlined their seclusion from relatives and visitors. The wall may also have protected the monks from raiding tribesmen capturing them for sale in city slave-markets, a fate to which monasteries long remained vulnerable. (Later there would be instances when rich benefactors could populate a derelict monastery by buying slaves in the local market.) If a monk was seriously delinquent, he might be chastised, perhaps severely. But he would prefer that to the worst of all penalties, which was to be expelled from the community. To be a dedicated professed monk living within the wall was to have a chance of salvation.

---

[6] See David Brakke, *Athanasius and the Politics of Asceticism* (Oxford, 1995).

Pachomius' original monastery not far from Dendera and the loop of the Nile was soon to be one of nine associated houses, some with substantial numbers. The ancient sources offer widely differing totals: Sozomen has 500, Jerome 50,000, the first certainly too few, the second too many. With their large labour force they brought a lot of land under cultivation, and in time there emerged a painful issue which caused division and feeling, namely whether the primary calling of the monks was to grow and sell food and to make a good profit or whether their first duty was to God and the daily round of worship in the monastery chapel. The question of ownership of property by monks was a neuralgic issue. Renunciation of property was possible only to those who owned some, not to the very poor. Moreover, monks needed perhaps a field or some comparable resource to grow their food. The 'Apophthegms of the Fathers' tend to recount the heroic, which was probably not the normal. Hermits might be supported by lay people, their spiritual disciples, which could solve the difficulty of paying for even a very modest diet and for sufficient clothing to cover their bodies. The desert was bitterly cold at night, scorching by day. Not every monk was in the community because he had a deep vocation to the religious life.

A later report of a monk in Palestine records that he went to his superior with the declaration that he was profoundly bored in the monastery and was determined to return to the world. The superior replied: 'My son, it is evident that you think of neither heaven nor hell; for if your mind were on those matters, you would never be bored' (Moschus, *Pratum* 142).

In the early Greek Life of Pachomius, written about 390–400, a hero figure was that of Theodore, to whom the founder was severely repressive but who eventually became the superior of all the houses and insisted that the religious task was prior to agricultural economics. He would not have failed to recognize that a peasant was financially much more secure inside the monastery wall than hoping for employment outside. Moreover in his old age when he would be too infirm to work, his needs would be cared for by the younger monks. The monastic society had two nunneries, but there was virtually no contact between the sexes. Many monks and nuns enjoyed a long life without emotional disturbance.

In the fifth century the Pachomian monasteries acquired a formidable leader Shenoute; austere and authoritarian, he made discipline tougher (more vehement beatings for lapses) but was admired for generous hospitality and for his onslaughts on pagan temples.

Once monks were gathered in communities living a common life and were in most cases living some distance from noisy towns full of worldly and carnal temptations, they became a principal agent for the evangelization of the countryside. Inscriptions show that in Syria monasteries were usually close to villages in the countryside, and became a major social factor. At the same time olive plantations were providing economic development in which the monasteries are likely to have been involved. In north Africa or Italy where bishoprics were numerous and attached to small and minor places it was different.

Augustine as ascetic

The *Life of Antony* played a part in the converging pressures underlying the conversion of Augustine at Milan in the summer of 386. He was amazed to discover that Ambrose had a monastery on the edge of the city. His conversion in the Milan garden was a decision for the celibate life. On returning to north Africa after burying his mother at Ostia, he gathered friends to form an ascetic community at his home in Thagaste in Numidia (Souk-Ahras, Algeria). This was an intellectual society daily chanting the psalms but also reading Cicero and probably some Plotinus in Victorinus' Latin version. In 391 he visited the harbour town of Hippo, his purpose being to establish a monastery there, and was coerced by the congregation into accepting ordination to be their presbyter under the Greek-speaking bishop Valerius. He wept, for he wanted and felt called to the ascetic life of withdrawal. But, like Ambrose, he did not think the call to the *sacerdotium* could be declined. As presbyter and then as bishop, his lifestyle was monastic, and he was allowed by bishop Valerius to found a male monastery beside the church building. Soon there was also a nunnery, over which his widowed sister presided.

His monastic rule is among his most remarkable works. Yet his letters and sermons also record how many problems the ascetics could create. Some of the monks and nuns came to join the communities when they were young, their parents were poor, and the monastery provided a simple means of keeping the struggling offspring fed, clothed, and sheltered. In consequence many of these children felt no vocation for the religious life. No doubt they could make themselves useful by accepting the weekly roster of duties in the sacristy or kitchen or refectory and perhaps also in working nearby land. There were embarrassing cases of sisters taking to the bottle in their boredom.

Monks and Cynic philosophers

Monasteries, in short, could answer to needs other than the single-minded quest for purity of heart to be made fit for the kingdom of heaven. They could provide for a social need of 'internal emigration': to help people disillusioned with society at home in town or village, or who wanted to escape paying taxes. There remained people who in a pagan milieu would have become Cynic philosophers of the type praised by Epictetus (though not admired by the emperor Julian), living rough, homeless, shocking their neighbours by defecating or masturbating in the streets. Augustine once tells us that in his time they no longer copulated in public (*City of God* 14. 20). But provided their behaviour was not indecent, the way of life of a Cynic was compatible with Christian profession (19. 19). In the 370s at Constantinople the Cynic Maximus, also called Hero, made an unsuccessful bid to become bishop of Constantinople; the emperor Theodosius vetoed this.

Seniority in monasteries

In Pachomius' houses order and obedience were strictly enforced. The rule made previous secular rank a matter of indifference: seniority within the wall was reckoned solely from the date of making the monastic profession and undertaking the all-important vow of unquestioning obedience. Moreover, Pachomius would not admit any clergy, for fear that they would begin telling the lay monks what they might or might not do, and assume a superiority that would be hard to live with. Upper-class recruits no longer wore the upper-class clothes or other insignia (girdle or shoes especially) which in cities marked them out. Naturally the majority of his monks were illiterate, but some could read books.

Monks militant

Christian conviction held that the gods worshipped by pagans were malevolent spirits, and in time a cohort of Coptic monks would become a formidable force for dismantling a shrine. They could also be valuable for constituting a Christian fortress in a predominantly pagan milieu. At one such pagan stronghold in Panopolis (Akhmim) the local bishop invited the monks to found a house by the city to strengthen his hand. High culture, if pagan, was scorned. Cultured Christians at Constantinople were outraged when the respected Alexandrian Neoplatonist philosopher and mathematician Hypatia was lynched by a frenzied gang of monks. In 391 militants could be useful when the government's programme of closing down pagan temples and forbidding pagan sacrifices led to the dismantling of the great temple of Serapis at Alexandria. The building, founded by the Ptolemies, was eventually converted into a church.

Palestine: the Lavra, hermits

Monastic houses were founded in Palestine, especially on the edge of the Sinai desert and in the Judaean desert between Jerusalem and Jericho where water was and is scarce and in summer the temperature can be high. A halfway-house between the cells of isolated hermits and the common life of a coenobium was the Lavra, in which a group of semi-eremitical cells were reasonably close together so that at weekends the monks could share common liturgy. Hermits isolated from any form of human society could become unaware of the calendar and might well need a miracle to inform them that Easter Day had arrived. The great majority of hermits attracted disciples who would bring them simple food for the few meals in the week which they allowed themselves.

Hermits in desert caves were vulnerable to attack by hungry hyenas. But ancients believed that innocent and good people were respected by wild beasts (above p. 70). Tradition said of the holy *abba* Gerasimos that he extracted a thorn from a lion's paw and found the animal devoted to him, like a spaniel, wherever he went. On the holy man's death the lion also died of a broken heart. The story is evidently a folklorish adaptation of 'Androclus and the Lion', found in the *Attic Nights* of Aulus Gellius (5. 14), taken from 'The Wonders of Egypt' by Apion of Alexandria. A second-century addition at the end of Mark's gospel predicts that believers will be able to handle poisonous snakes or drink poison without ill effects. Miracles and especially the demonic world are prominent in some of the evidence.

Evagrius of Pontus

A more intellectual and meditative ideal was pursued by monks whose devotion was inspired by the tradition of Origen and his subsequent admirers. Among them the most prominent were from Asia Minor, Evagrius of Pontus, and the great Cappadocians Basil of Caesarea, Gregory of Nyssa his brother, and his one-time student friend Gregory of Nazianzos. Evagrius was brought to Constantinople by Gregory of Nazianzos, but a love-affair forced him to depart to Jerusalem and on to the Egyptian desert until his death in 399. He combined writings on the conquest of the passions with esoteric speculative theology which later caused alarm and led to censure in Justinian's time in the mid-sixth century. His strength was his system, bringing order to the struggle against evil spirits hiding within the soul, demanding silence and aspiring to passionlessness (*apátheia*). Purity of heart is needed for prayer undistracted by images or secular thoughts. Following Origen he listed eight principal or root sins, corresponding to the Canaanite tribes expelled from the promised land; he observed that they can conflict with each another; one may be roused from sloth (*akedía*, in Latin *accidie*) by pride, or delivered from pride by humiliating lust. His list was later shortened by Gregory the Great from eight to seven which made the correspondence with seven Canaanite tribes more persuasive. Evagrius was convinced that pictorial images of God in human form are a deceit and illusion. This provoked the hostility of Coptic monks to the intellectualism of Origenists.

Barsanuphios

Monastic communities in both east and west had only occasional trouble
with chastity and poverty but fairly frequent difficulties in the rule of obedience to the abbot or higumen. Disobedience produced factions in a community. Early in the sixth century a holy hermit near Gaza named
Barsanuphios appointed his devoted pupil Seridos to be abbot of a monastery
in which the old man lived a secluded life, not seen or heard by the community in his private cell. Questions raised were referred to him by the abbot.
But one day there was a rebellion against the abbot, who was accused of
inventing the holy hermit. All the brothers were assembled in the refectory,
and Barsanuphios himself appeared, silently washed the feet of each of the
monks, and retired to his cell never to be seen again.

Again common to east and west was the cutting-off of contact with members of a monk's family or close friends. A blood brother or sister could not
visit. Nor could a monk or nun attend a family funeral. This was a defiance
of natural humanity that provoked severe temptation.

Critics of the monks

Among Roman aristocrats we find occasional critics. Rutilius Namatianus,
prefect of Rome in 414, described in verse a move back to his native Gaul.
Passing the monastic island of Capraria he commented adversely on monks
there; they rejected a life-style that he held dear. The Greek orator Libanius
hated the vandalizing of beautiful pagan temples by bands of monks in Syria.
There could be problems for government if large numbers of people forsook
civic responsibilities and retired to monasteries. They ceased to pay taxes or
to serve in the army or civil service. But in the fourth and early fifth centuries
those who had most difficulty with monasteries were the bishops, whose
urban location and inevitably public role took them far from the quietist
ideals of Cassian or Benedict.

Martin of Tours

The ascetic life was taken up in Gaul by an ex-soldier Martin, whose Life was
written by Sulpicius Severus of Aquitaine, a wealthy widower who himself
took Martin as his model of renunciation. He wanted the west to know that
wonders at least as great as those told of Egyptian hermits could be found in
Gaul. Martin was notable for his outspokenness and directness of manner; if
he was invited to a meal with a powerful luminary, he was abrasively candid.
Sulpicius also wrote a *Chronicle* with an account of Priscillian. He was addressing people who feared ascetic demands as being touched by Manicheism.

John Cassian

Cassian formulated his ascetic ideals by composing reports of *Conferences* (in Latin *Collationes*) held by Egyptian ascetics. Benedict directed that at meals the *Collationes* were read. That gave the Italian language its everyday word for lunch or breakfast, and English the term 'collation' for a light meal. He came from the Dobrudja, the Danube delta, a bilingual region. Before 392 he had come to a monastery at Bethlehem with a friend Germanus, but was impressed by a refugee superior of an Egyptian house, Pinuphios, who found his responsibilities distracting his efforts to pray. Cassian and Germanus decided to go to Egypt, and were allowed to leave after swearing that they would return. But the asceticism of monks in Egypt was better than that at Bethlehem, and they remained in the desert until the Origenist controversy led John Cassian to migrate to Constantinople to be with John Chrysostom. After John Chrysostom's fall in 404, he took a letter to Pope Innocent I and in Rome was ordained priest. His vocation was to take the monastic ideal to Marseille where he founded monasteries for men (St Victor) and women (St Salvator).

At Marseille Cassian wrote his *Institutes*, describing (not necessarily prescribing) the forms of common life current in Egypt and Palestine. The work was an answer to a request for guidance from Bishop Castor of Apt, north of Marseille, who was thinking of founding a monastery. Readers could there learn what to wear, how to chant the psalms, what 'hours' of prayer were to be observed. Books 5–12 set out the Evagrian list of temptations: gluttony, lust, covetousness, anger, dejection or melancholy, accidie (boredom with prayer), vainglory, pride. After Castor's death Cassian wrote the 24 'Conferences' (*Collationes*) with Egyptian hermits whom he had visited.[7] They were dedicated to Leontius of Fréjus and Helladius of Arles. He possessed an early form of the *Apophthegms of the Fathers*, the main collections of which date from the sixth century but include much earlier matter, so that no source brings the reader so close to the spirit of the Desert Fathers. The Apophthegms survive in two forms, one classified by subject, the other divided alphabetically according to the name of the speaker. They were preserved not only in Greek, but in an early Latin version, Syriac, Armenian, Ethiopic. The apophthegms were given in answer to spiritual inquirers. At the same time, though Cassian likes to say that he contributes no ideas of his own but follows 'the fathers', the Conferences can be seen to contain themes dear to his heart, and *Coll.* 13 notoriously attributes to Chaeremon penetrating criticism of the extreme doctrine of grace associated with

---

[7] Ed. M. Petschenig (CSEL 13, 17; Vienna, 1886–8); tr. E. C. S. Gibson (Oxford, 1894), good but incomplete; Boniface Ramsey (Ancient Christian Writers, 57; New York, 1997); nos. 1, 9–11, 15, 18–19 also tr. Owen Chadwick, *Western Asceticism* (Library of Christian Classics, 12; London, 1958).

Augustine and becoming contentious in southern Gaul by 426–7 (cf. below p. 472). Elsewhere there are echoes of Basil's monastic rule and of Jerome's 22nd letter on virginity (*Coll.* 19. 1), besides pieces from Evagrius and Palladius' *Lausiac History*. He had also read the 'History of Monks' translated by Rufinus into Latin. Though Cassian wrote in good Latin, he was early taken to heart by Greek ascetics, and excerpts from him were translated into Greek. Paradoxically Cassian was to be more trusted as a spiritual guide in the Greek Christian world than in the Latin, principally because of his critique of Augustine's absolutist doctrine of predestination.

For reasons of climate the ascetic life of Egypt could not be reasonably practised in Gaul, and Cassian wisely modified the austerity of the desert. In any event he commends moderation. He was obviously uncomfortable with the kind of picture of St Martin of Tours portrayed by Sulpicius Severus where miracle was prominent. Sulpicius wanted to claim that Gaul's ascetics were as impressive as Egypt's.

Cassian insists on the primacy of the community with its centre in the eucharist. Monks who realize their sinfulness should not absent themselves from this sacrament of divine forgiveness. They are not to follow the practice of some who receive the sacrament only once a year (*Coll.* 24. 21), a custom also known to Ambrose (*Sacr.* 5. 25). The Conferences discuss practices where there was diversity of custom in different places, such as fasting in Lent (21). *Coll.* 18 commends hermits as ideal and, as a lower and necessary stage of training for beginners, houses of common life, but warns sharply against indisciplined 'Sarabaites', vagrants who recognize no authority and have no rule. Cassian's description (18. 7) suggests that Sarabaites were actually a survival of the old Christian ascetics living together in twos and threes in houses still with an attachment to town or village churches, but without rule or particular habit and free to move about without being the wandering hippies or *gyrovagi* negatively described by Benedict. The name 'Sarabaites' could be akin to that of wandering Manichee ascetics, homeless followers of homeless Jesus, called in the Manichee Psalm-book 'Sarakoton'.

Origen taught that penitence was a permanent state of mind for the serious aspirant in the spiritual life. He and Clement before him also knew that resistance to temptation can be strengthened by a spiritual director, to whom confession of faults may be made. Cassian did not expect the monk receiving the confession to be a priest. A monk seeking assurance of forgiveness should ask for the intercession of the saints and for the 'grace of satisfaction' by mortifications and fasts. But on no account should the memory of past sins remain to haunt his mind (*Coll.* 20. 8), except to the degree that one who has fallen into sexual sin will take care to avoid getting into an intimate relation with someone of the opposite sex, and one who has eaten or drunk unwisely will take pains to restrain appetite.

Benedict of Nursia

A biography of Benedict's life and wonders was written by Gregory the Great in the second of the four books of his *Dialogues*. Born in the 480s at Nursia he studied in Rome but soon abandoned education to become a hermit near Subiaco. His ascetic way of life led to an invitation to preside over a nearby monastery, but he preferred to return to Subiaco in search of solitude. Aspiring pupils followed him. Local clergy were not pleased by his presence; it was often the case that priests in secular settings in parishes felt uncomfortable in the presence of monks, whose lifestyle seemed critical of theirs. Benedict moved to the summit of Montecassino, where he destroyed pagan shrines and built Christian oratories. There he died about 547.

At Cassino he wrote the justly famous Rule, a text which underwent more than one recension from well-educated revisers ill at ease with his colloquial Latin. Early manuscripts survive at Oxford (Bodleian, Hatton 48) and at St Gallen, both about 700.

The Rule was designed to order the life of an ascetic Christian Community, called to obey the authoritative guidance of an Abbot prescribing rules for the liturgical offices (there was no daily mass), for kitchen, refectory, and dormitory. Punishments were laid down for delinquencies. Errors in reading by young boys had the penalty of a beating. He describes his Rule as designed for a school of the Lord's service, 'a little rule for beginners'. One of Benedict's sources was a much more severe text, the 'Rule of the Master'. Benedict admired and commended the *Conferences* of John Cassian, valued for their restraint and moderation. Characteristic is Benedict's sumptuary law allowing wine, but not to excess. The moderation of the Rule helps to explain its extraordinary success in future centuries.

Syrian ascetics

Perhaps influenced by Tatian in the second century, for whom Paul in 1 Corinthians 7 accepted marriage as non-sinful yet not recommended, and whose gospel Harmony (*Diatessaron*) was a standard text, Syrian churches regarded a celibate ideal as appropriate for all the baptized. They were 'sons of the covenant' engaged in a holy war. Like soldiers in the Roman army, they were without spouses. Early Syrian churches bear the marks of being a close offspring of Jewish synagogues, and the status of married members was controversial between church and synagogue, especially with the Christian homilist Aphrahat (*Dem.* 18. PO 1. 841. 6–9), writing probably in Adiabene, a province that was at times under Roman, at other times under Persian control.

In Mesopotamia about 306 Ephrem was born to a Christian mother married to a pagan priest. He was to become the principal Christian writer and poet in Syriac; besides the hymns that he himself composed, much else was added to the corpus of his works by pupils and admirers, so that it is not always easy to be sure in every case where authenticity lies. He was a native of Nisibis, but in 363, when it was surrendered to the Persians, he migrated to Edessa for the last ten years of his life. (The emperor Julian's courtship of the Jews on the eve of his Persian campaign could not have endeared them to the population of Nisibis.) Both Aphrahat and Ephrem concede that the marriage of the two sexes is a good gift of God, but they do not write about it with enthusiasm, since it is not the highest gift. Monastic communities are not apparent in Syria and Mesopotamia before the middle decades of the fourth century. When they appear they seem more closely bound up with nearby village society than was common in Egypt or Gaul.

The mortifications of some Syrian ascetics went to extreme lengths. Some fed on grass and berries; it was normal to practise self-discipline by wearing a heavy metal belt or worse. In the next century there was Simeon who prayed and meditated on top of a column, and thereby set a fashion for other stylites. Soon after AD 600 the monk John Moschos from Cilicia gathered macabre stories of dramatic austerity especially in Syria.[8]

---

[8] An important study is Robert Murray, *Symbols of Church and Kingdom; A Study in Early Syriac Tradition* (Cambridge, 1975) with full bibliography.

43

MESSALIANS: THE MACARIAN
HOMILIES

The ascetic writings of Basil of Caesarea speak of monks who held that because prayer without ceasing is commanded (1 Thess. 5: 17), the canonical 'hours' can be neglected (*Reg. fus. tr.* 37. 383 B). Some monks stayed away from sermons for reasons of devotion and piety (*Mor.* 70. 33 PG 31. 842 D). There were communities of 'Sleepless' monks which sought to implement the Pauline command by having relays to provide a continual life of prayer twenty-four hours a day; they began in Syria but had an important house on the Asiatic shore of the Bosporos, from where in the sixth century they defended the Chalcedonian cause.

Related groups of ascetic texts coming from Edessa about 370 have survived under the name of Makarios, the Greek manuscripts being of the eleventh century and later. The majority of manuscripts preserve a collection of fifty homilies (H), to which in 1918 seven additional homilies (KlB) were added.[1] During more recent times two further large collections have been edited, and it is clear that these different groups overlap with one another. The texts were evidently edited in the tenth or early eleventh century by an enthusiastic reader. The central theme is the soul's ascent to spiritual perfection in God. Sharp language is used to arouse the soul to a realization of war with Satan whose main agencies are the soul's hidden passions. At Adam's fall sin entered the innermost chambers of the soul (H 43. 1). Overthrown by his pride, Adam became lost in thick fog or smoke (8. 5, 43. 7). Humanity is like a wretch in a prison cell without door or window (KlB, p. 146, 11). Many Christians think the devil is expelled at baptism; but actually he continues lodged in the soul. 'Few and rare are those who are aware that the destroyer of souls is with them' (H 51. 2). This does not mean that humanity is

---

[1] The 50 homilies (H) are edited by H. Dörries, E. Klostermann, and M. Kroeger (Berlin, 1964); English translation by A. J. Mason (London, 1921, repr. 1974) and also by G. Maloney (Denville, NJ 1978). E. Klostermann and H. Berthold, *Neue Homilien des Makarius/Symeon* i (TU 72; Berlin, 1961) here abbreviated as KlB; texts re-edited by V. Desprez in SC 275 (Paris, 1980). H. Berthold, *Makarios/Symeon: Reden und Briefe: Die Sammlung I des Vaticanus Graecus 694* (B), 2 vols. (Berlin, 1973). Texts extant in Syriac and Arabic have been edited by W. Strothmann (Wiesbaden, 1981).

incapable of any good act, as Manichees think (H 46. 3); we are sick, not dead (KlB, p. 144). To despair of salvation is itself sinful (H 4. 21 ff.). At death Satan's customs officers will be claiming their own (43. 9). The devils are our passions and vice versa (5. 3), and Hades is symbolic language for an evil mind (11. 11).

An authentic disciple should be a homeless wanderer (KlB, p. 26. 29). Only a poor church can minister to destitute people, and it is the devil's sophistry which makes people say they need money to give alms (H 5. 6). A holy person receives a stamp or 'character' in the soul (H 15. 35). But mystical union is transitory, an intermittent moment of incomparable delight (B 63), a sober intoxication like the apostolic Pentecost. Makarios insists repeatedly on the 'sweetness', the full conviction and inner feeling. Bridal imagery is used, but with the qualification that it should not be understood too literally (B 63). Grace does not abolish nature; uneducated people remain so even if granted amazing charisms.

Some imagine they can conquer evil by effort of will. The problem is treachery within from passions; to recognize the need for Christ's help is essential (H 26. 17). Those baptized in water have to seek the baptism of the Spirit and of fire (H 27. 17). Charisms include a power of discrimination 6. 3–4), a gift of veridical visions of objective realities in the spiritual realm, powers of healing, profound insights. But those entrusted with charisms have to beware of human admiration leading to pride. 'I have seen a man who had all the charisms and yet fell', flattered by the world (27. 14). The Devil has had six thousand years of experience to plan subtle attacks (H 26. 9). One can never be assured of final perseverance (15. 26), just as a merchant cannot be confident until his ships are in harbour (43. 4).

The homilies lay continual stress on the inwardness of true religion. Organized religion is threatened by formalism and merely physical rules. It is true that God's Spirit is present in baptism and at the holy sacrifice at the Lord's Table. And bishops who speak in agreement with the apostles are building on a true foundation. But there are false teachers, modern whited sepulchres with only outward show (B 34 and 40), eartickling orators, dry disputers about words (KlB, p. 113. 5). Pray for the divine fire. The divine Spirit is not found in Plato, Aristotle, and Isocrates (H 42. 1). There are occasional echoes of Neoplatonic aspiration, but it is never determinative.

Two writers, Timothy of Constantinople in the sixth century and John of Damascus in the eighth, give overlapping but independent catalogues of doctrines held by heretics called Messalians. The quotations were evidently drawn from formal acts of synodical censure. Almost without exception the propositions consist of verbatim citations from the Macarian homilies. The question therefore presses, whether the homilies were composed by a moderate sympathizer with the enthusiastic evangelical sect.

Messalians is a label attached to the last group of eighty heresies in the Medicine Chest or *Panarion* of Epiphanius of Salamis in the 370s. The title transliterates the Syriac for 'people of prayer'. The sect makes up the number corresponding to that of Solomon's concubines in the Song of Songs, and is described as anarchic and undisciplined. Theodoret of Cyrrhos also gives a hostile report and tells how bishop Flavian of Antioch tricked a leader in the sect named Adelphios into telling him of the doctrines and aspirations (*HE* 4. 11). Photius in the ninth century (*Bibliotheca* 52) summarizes a canonical codex containing records of action against Messalians, notably at a synod in Side on the south coast of Pamphylia at which Amphilochios of Iconium presided. The date was probably in or shortly before 400. The date of Amphilochios' death is unknown. Synodical action also occurred at Constantinople in 426 at the time of Sisinnios' consecration when Cyril of Alexandria surprisingly wanted no harsh severity (*ep.* 82). To the wrath of the Syrian bishops, Cyril received to communion at Ephesus twelve Pamphilian bishops infected by Messalianism (Theodoret, *ep.* 170; John of Antioch in *ACO* I i/7. 117–18). But under pressure from not only John of Antioch but also Valerian of Iconium and Amphilochios of Side, the council of Ephesus in 431 confirmed the decisions of 426. The enthusiasm of Messalians had spread through much of southern Asia Minor. It continued underground until the sixth century. In medieval Byzantium Messalian was a common term of abuse for any group or doctrine that was not under episcopal control.

The Messalians won individual sympathizers in a few bishops, despite their tendency to disparage the sacramental and ordered life of the Church. Of their sympathizers the most notable was Gregory of Nyssa. A sermon he preached probably at Constantinople at the time of the council of 381 speaks in glowing terms of ascetics coming from the east whose simple faith and devotion are exemplary. The author of the Macarian homilies had written a 'Great Letter' rebutting the charge of being anti-sacramental.[2] Gregory made his own adaptation of this text, reshaping the argument in places.

The Macarian homilies influenced fifth-century writers, especially Mark the Hermit and Diadochos of Photike. Both had their distinct reservations with the homilies; neither acknowledged the least indebtedness and in one passage Diadochos launched a direct attack (*Centuries* 76–89). Diadochos also disliked the idea that the soul must go in fear until death. But he restates many themes characteristic of the Macarian texts such as inward fire in the soul (*cent.* 59. 67), the soul's full assurance and feelings in enjoyment of divine sweetness. The charisms of the Spirit intoxicate with love (8). Mark the Hermit concentrated on baptism as the foundation without which no good

---

[2] Ed. R. Staats (Abhandlungen der Akademie der Wissenschaften zu Göttingen, 1984).

works have value before God; the sacrament confers inalienable grace (PG 65. 1028 B). Prayer should be unceasing to enable the soul to combat the passions (1081 B). A major writer strongly in favour of the Macarian Homilies was to be Gregory Palamas, by whose recommendation they became and remain standard devotional reading in Orthodox monasteries.[3]

---

[3] See further Columba Stewart, '*Working the Earth of the Heart*': *The Messalian Controversy in History, Texts and Language to* AD *431* (Oxford, 1991) with bibliography; K. Fitschen, *Messalianismus und Antimessalianismus* (Göttingen, 1998).

44

SCHISM AT ANTIOCH: THE COUNCIL
OF CONSTANTINOPLE (381)

Paulinus of Antioch and the Eustathian group

The split in the church at Antioch went back to the time of the council of
Nicaea, soon after which, perhaps as early as 327, Bishop Eustathius of
Antioch was deposed for conduct unbecoming and for discourtesy to the
emperor's mother Helena on pilgrimage to the holy places. A congregation
loyal to his memory met separately in 'the old church' in the city, while the
main body worshipped elsewhere, after 341 in the fine building begun under
Constantine and dedicated in that year. They were led by a presbyter named
Paulinus. When Leontius was bishop in the fifties, the separate congregations
were able to meet together for devotions other than the eucharistic liturgy,
but did not share communion.

Paulinus' congregation, however, was recognized as the true church of
Antioch by Athanasius of Alexandria and by Rome. This western and
Alexandrian recognition became a difficulty after 360 when Meletius
became bishop. Being rejected by Eudoxius and his friends, he soon supported the Nicene creed; there were then two Nicene congregations in the
same city. They were theologically divided, however, by the fact that, like
Basil of Caesarea and his Cappadocian friends, Meletius with his homoian
background was sympathetic to saying that the Trinity is 'three hypostases',
which asserted the independence of Father, Son, and Spirit and which had
formed part of the central eastern bishops' programme since 341. In strict
accord with the Nicene anathema, Paulinus insisted (like Marcellus of
Ankyra, with whom he had compromising correspondence) on only one
hypostasis. He thought Meletius a hypocrite, since he pretended to profess
Nicene faith when expressly glossing the creed to say that the Son is 'like' the
Father: 'the kingdom of God is like a grain of mustard seed, but not much.'
Moreover, when Athanasius visited Antioch (probably on return from Jovian
at Hierapolis in 363), Meletius did not share communion with him (Basil,
ep. 89; 258), a decision fateful for the future. Politically communion with
Athanasius in 363 could have been highly disadvantageous. Perhaps Meletius

rebuffed an approach from Athanasius because Paulinus was already recognized at Alexandria as bishop, perhaps because he was not invited by Athanasius to his synod in 362. When Jerome was an ascetic near Antioch, he found it bewildering that the term hypostasis was a point of clear-cut division and that his preference, with Damasus, for one hypostasis led to accusations of Sabellian heresy (*ep.* 15).

Athanasius' Council of Alexandria

In 362 Athanasius' little synod at Alexandria sought a way to reconciliation, declaring that both one hypostasis and three hypostases were being held with orthodox intention by the divided factions. (Athanasius' conviction that correct doctrine was more a matter of intention than of verbal formula was not easily grasped, especially when the formulas were mutually incompatible.) However, the firebrand Lucifer of Calaris in Sardinia, released from exile in Egypt by Julian's amnesty, had ignored the disagreement of Eusebius of Vercelli, who had shared exile with him (Rufinus, *HE* 10. 31), had hurried to Antioch and with two other bishops had consecrated Paulinus bishop. That made reconciliation much more difficult. Paulinus was represented at the Alexandrian synod by two deacons, which suggests that his ordination as bishop was already known to the synod before it disbanded. The deacons surprisingly committed Paulinus to assent to the synod's conciliatory programme. In practice, however, it was otherwise.

Nevertheless, the council of Alexandria dispatched a Tome, or short summary of essential doctrines, to the church at Antioch. It was drafted by Athanasius, Eusebius of Vercelli, and Asterios of Petra after the other bishops had already gone home. A primary problem for the council was to propose procedure for the reconciliation of bishops who had not hitherto accepted the Nicene creed, but who had been scared by Eudoxius and the counterproductive effect of his synod at Constantinople. They now saw that the assertion of 'identity of being' expressed their faith as the anaemic 'likeness' formula did not adequately do. The council's policy was to demand no more of those seeking rapprochement than anathema on Arianism, profession of the Nicene creed, and a supplementary denial that the Holy Spirit belongs to the created order. On these conditions, a preference for affirming the divine Triad to be 'three hypostases' would be acceptable. The supplement on the Holy Spirit confronted one wing of homoiousian bishops, such as Eustathius of Sebaste, who stood firm on the Nicene formula in which the third article simply said 'and in the Holy Spirit' without further addition. The synod's generous policy was unlikely to please Lucifer of Calaris, who judged all bishops who had failed to uphold the Nicene creed under Constantius to be capable of reinstatement to communion only as penitent laity. He included Pope Liberius.

One or three hypostases?

Eusebius of Vercelli was at the council as a liberated exile, and was evidently responsible for querying the statement that 'three hypostases' could be maintained with orthodox intention. To anyone from the Latin West the formula sounded like three Gods. He recalled that the western council of Serdica had affirmed one hypostasis. He was met by Athanasius denying that that council made a formal statement to this effect. At Serdica, Athanasius recalled, some bishops had wished for a supplement to the Nicene creed and had even drafted such a document, but the argument had prevailed that it was vital to treat the Nicene creed as all-sufficient. Otherwise it could justify adversaries in their attempt to supplant it. It had become evident that the rambling doctrinal statement of the western council of Serdica was a potential block to Athanasius' hopes of a united front among pro-Nicene groups. If 'three hypostases' simply meant that the Triad was not merely in name but corresponded to existence and truth, then the Tome was sure it was unobjectionable. Eusebius of Vercelli glossed his signature by saying that, since it was important to affirm the Nicene creed to be sufficient without further supplementation, he agreed that the document of Serdica should now be regarded as a less than formal conciliar act. Its status was a retrospective judgement; previously he had thought otherwise.

The Tome took it for granted that the authentic Nicene group at Antioch was that led by Paulinus. In effect Athanasius was asking Paulinus to welcome the congregation of Meletius to his liturgy, and (yet more difficult no doubt) asking the Meletian congregation to accept Paulinus as their pastor? The familiar pattern appeared that those closest to one another found it hardest to unite. In its immediate purpose the Tome suffered the fate of other carefully drafted statements of agreement. Gregory of Nazianzos regarded the Tome as Athanasius' greatest single achievement.

Apollinaris of Laodicea

At Alexandria in 362 there were present some monks sent as his representatives by Apollinaris, bishop of a dissident Nicene congregation at Laodicea in Syria (Latakia), where the main congregation now had Bishop Pelagius, an ally of Meletius who in 381 was among those named by Theodosius as offering a touchstone of Nicene orthodoxy (Soz. 7. 9. 6). Although strongly anti-Arian, Apollinaris was associated with a thesis also held by Eudoxius of Constantinople, that in Christ the human mind was replaced by the divine Logos or Reason. He did not think Christ could have had a mind 'full of filthy thoughts'; there was no such thing as a human mind (*nous*) of such purity as to be one with the divine Word. Apollinaris was insistent that redemption depends on the Word 'made flesh'; that in the eucharist believers receive 'the body and blood of Christ' with no mention of soul or mind; that this doctrine of salvation determines Christology. He expounded 1 Cor. 15: 47, 'the second man is from heaven', to mean that Christ had deified human flesh before the incarnation. In opposition to the Origenist tradition he believed in a literal earthly millennium. He had no sympathy for an opposing view advanced by the presbyter Diodore of Antioch, soon to be bishop of Tarsus, and probably present at the Alexandrian council, that redemption depends on the perfect obedience and self-offering of the humanity of Christ. Apollinaris understood Diodore to be teaching that Jesus was an inspired man rather than God incarnate, and therefore to be making the Virgin Birth an unnecessary miracle. Apollinaris' Christology had a head-on collision with the basic principle, evident in the epistle to the Hebrews, that Jesus was one with all the human race and was not ashamed to call all believers his brothers and sisters. On the other hand, he expressed exceptionally clearly the beliefs of the devout that in Jesus God himself was present to redeem, and therefore that in him the human nature was utterly united, not merely juxtaposed or even bonded, with the very nature of the divine. He was more than an inspired man.

The Alexandrian Tome sent to the church of Antioch laid down as agreed by all that, while there was no question of Jesus being merely an inspired man like one of the prophets, he must have had a soul since otherwise salvation would be only of the human body. The axiom from Irenaeus was limpidly stated by Origen: 'what was not assumed is not saved'. This was the first serious surfacing of the Christological controversy which, as Basil foresaw, was to occupy the centre of the stage for several centuries to come.

On the opposite side, Paulinus at Antioch, represented at Alexandria by two deacons, received the Tome and signed it with a surprising gloss: he accepted the statement concerning the equal orthodoxy of both three hypostases and one, disowned 'the heresy of Sabellius and Photinus' (i.e. the opinion attributed to Marcellus who is not mentioned by name), and anathematized all who rejected the Nicene creed. He thought it impossible to suppose that the Saviour's body was lacking in *psyche* or *nous*.

At Antioch in the early seventies Apollinaris had his own separate group of followers, and consecrated a bishop Vitalis to care for them. This corresponded to his own position at Laodicea as pastor planted for a small dissenting congregation. That was bound to cause pain to Paulinus, who alerted Pope Damasus to the need for Roman censure of Apollinaris. Damasus demanded and received Vitalis' confession of faith and at first accepted it, but then decided that he had been misled (Greg. Naz. *ep.* 102). In the 370s, therefore, Antioch had four rival bishops for the different groups, Euzoius holding the great church founded by Constantine, Paulinus in the 'old church',

Meletius' congregation worshipping in the open air, and Vitalis' small group perhaps in a private house. Probably there was also yet another group following the theology of Eunomius.

Instruments of law and order at Antioch

About this time probably from the chancery of Bishop Euzoius of Antioch, wanting to establish order amid near-chaos, came three texts unsurprisingly concerned with episcopal authority, namely, the longer recension of the letters of Ignatius of Antioch, a major handbook of Church Order called the *Apostolic Constitutions* in which pride of place was given to the Apostolic Canons, and a codification of Greek canon law which put together in sequence the canons of several Greek councils and gave them a consecutive numbering by which they were subsequently cited. A synod called by Meletius met in 363, asserting Nicene faith.

The emperor Jovian 363–4

The death of Julian on the night of 26/27 June 363 left his army surrounded and leaderless. Senior army officers met urgently to choose a new emperor. A pagan prefect and old friend of Julian declined the honour, and the choice fell on the commander of the imperial guard, Flavius Jovianus. Jovian was born near Singidunum in Pannonia. With considerable difficulty he got his hungry and thirsty men and animals west across the Tigris. News of Julian's death reached the Persian king who wisely proposed peace on terms favourable to his empire. Jovian, desperate to give his army food and drink, agreed to terms which included the surrender of two strong fortresses, Singara and Nisibis. Ephrem's *Carmina Nisibena* had celebrated the city's divine protection and survival of successive Persian sieges, trouble which he was inclined to ascribe to continuing pagan cults and poor church attendance on Ascension Day. Though writing when Jovian was emperor, he did not yet know of the city's surrender (21. 13, ed. E. Beck, Louvain, 1961). The humiliating terms were mitigated only by an agreement that the Roman inhabitants could leave in peace. From Nisibis the angry, betrayed people would move to a shanty town outside Amida (Dıyarbakir in Turkey) on the northern Tigris. Ephrem went to Edessa. At Antioch in Syria the peace was regarded with a sense of shame. Propaganda announced it as a mighty victory for the Roman empire. Few believed that.

On Jovian's return towards the Euphrates, at Edessa he found himself surrounded by bishops of various parties competing for his support. They included Athanasius of Alexandria and Apollinaris of Laodicea. Athanasius assured Jovian that all orthodox Christians held the Nicene creed; since accepting that creed was his definition of orthodoxy, there was a tautology. Jovian was a soldier, a very untheological Christian who simply thought that the factions must reach agreement, if only for the sake of public order. At Antioch he disappointed zealous Christians, perhaps Bishop Euzoius, by decreeing toleration. He moved on to Ankyra and on 1 January 364 heard Themistius' oratory saluting him as the new consul and new Constantine and congratulating him both on his recent 'victory' and on his religious toleration. This last theme was dear to Themistius, who was convinced that certainty in religious thought was unattainable by finite human minds. On 17 February at Dadastana in Bithynia, Jovian was found dead in his bed after having drunk unwisely the previous evening. His body was buried in Constantinople.

Valentinian I and Valens

On 26 February he was succeeded by another Pannonian soldier, Valentinian, chosen by the army leaders. A Christian of sorts, he was superstitious and would not accept the nomination until a day of ill omen (the intercalary day in leap year) had passed. The ancient statue of an emperor with sword raised, standing in the main street of Barletta in Apulia, is often thought to represent him. (There are other candidates.) He proceeded through Nicaea and Nicomedia to Constantinople where, in the western suburb of Hebdomon, he was formally acclaimed by a military parade. He brought with him his brother Valens, to be acclaimed as Augustus for the east while Valentinian himself went west to the Rhine frontier.

Valentinian announced his policy in church matters, that he would not intervene or take any part in ecclesiastical disputes. Valens began by an encouraging attitude to the Nicene party, but his wife influenced him in favour of Eudoxius, bishop of Constantinople and therefore adjacent to the imperial palace. The two brothers announced a policy of freedom in worship, including divination provided noxious practices were avoided (CTh 9. 16. 9).

'Like in essence' again

The homoiousian group revived under this toleration and commissioned one of their number, Bishop Hypatian of Heraclea (Perinthus), to ask Valentinian on his journey to the west for leave to hold a council. He answered that bishops could meet at their discretion without his permission. The group met at Lampsacus on the Hellespont (Soz. 6. 7 from Sabinus) for a long conference lasting two months. They decided to reject the decisions of Eudoxius' council of Constantinople (360) and the west's creed of Ariminum and Nike. But they insisted on 'like in being' (*homoiousios*) as the only safeguard for the plurality of hypostases in God. The too nearly Sabellian Nicene creed could not serve them. True faith lay in the creed of the Dedication council of Antioch (341). All bishops deposed by the Dissimilarian party (protected if not advocated by Eudoxius) must be reinstated, but were not to be exempt from facing charges, on the two understandings that the judges would be orthodox bishops and that, if the charges failed, the accusers must be liable to the penalty attaching to the crime being alleged (a common principle in Roman law). However, when they presented their findings to Valens, they discovered him already influenced against them by Eudoxius, with whom they refused to share communion. In anger Valens sent them all into exile. He then moved to Antioch, and exiled Meletius, who could return to Antioch in 366 but was again exiled in 371 until after Valens' death in 378. Valens so admired the quiet inoffensive life of Paulinus that he left him undisturbed. Paulinus had some wealthy ladies supporting his little congregation. Otherwise all not in communion with Euzoius were harassed. Valens evidently felt that in cities with more than one claimant to be bishop, he could not be assured of order unless he supported only one of the rival bishops, being the one recognized to be officially in possession of the majority and the greatest church. For his brother in the west the situation was different and such intervention was not necessary.

Disappointed homoiousians appealed to Pope Liberius and, by necessarily declaring assent to the Nicene creed which at Lampsacus they had not favoured, achieved acceptance and letters of communion. They were not asked to clarify their position in regard to the deity of the Holy Spirit. Thus fortified they held a synod at Tyana in Cappadocia and then attempted to hold a vastly larger assembly at Tarsus. On Eudoxius' advice Valens prohibited this meeting. But they were already in trouble from division in their own ranks; thirty-four of the bishops from the province of Asia met in Caria (SW Asia Minor) to state the unacceptability of the Nicene *homoousios* and to insist on the 'Lucianic' creed of Antioch in 341, in defence of which their predecessors had endured much.

The Holy Spirit

A further subject of disagreement among the homoiousian party was the equality of the Holy Spirit in the Godhead. The denial of this was associated with Macedonius, bishop of Constantinople through the forties and fifties under Constantius. Deposed by Eudoxius' council at Constantinople (360), he died soon thereafter, but his name continued to be attached to this position. Those holding it were labelled 'Pneumatomachoi' or fighters against the Spirit, sometimes 'Semi-Arians'. At least the Nicene creed presented no difficulty for them because of the extreme reticence of its third article. The geographical strength of this group lay in the Hellespont, while their opponents within their own homoiousian party were mainly in Asia Minor. The religious power of the party lay not merely in their trinitarian theology but also in their general sympathy for the monastic movement, especially in Asia Minor.

The people of Constantinople had not much loved Bishop Macedonius, though he retained a group of admirers in the city. In the thirties and forties his rival had been one Paul, who was exiled and was strangled about 350 at Cucusus. In 381 the emperor Theodosius I decided to facilitate the obliteration of Macedonius from the city's memory and to bring Paul's bones back to the capital to be enshrined in a church built by Macedonius but now dedicated to Paul. The people soon supposed the dedication was to the apostle.[1]

Growing conflict between pro-Nicenes and Valens' bishops

Valens decided that Athanasius must be turned out of Alexandria, but the people of the city staged demonstrations in support of their bishop. To avoid rioting he secretly left the city and hid. The threat of major civil disturbance, perhaps also a desire not to vex Valentinian, led Valens to accept the advice that the city would be quieter if Athanasius were allowed to return. Exiled homoiousian bishops did not fare equally well. When Eudoxius died in April 370, an attempt by a small pro-Nicene group of clergy and laity in the capital to get their own candidate elected was crushed. Eudoxius was replaced by translating a bishop of similar opinions, Demophilos, from Beroea in Thrace to succeed him. The bishop of the old metropolis of Heraclea successfully claimed the right to consecrate and install, a custom destined to survive. (For the medieval canonist Balsamon on the 12th canon of Chalcedon, the custom was less than a right.) At the installation there were hostile catcalls. The admirers of Aetius and Eunomius thought Demophilos a loquacious muddler (Philostorgios 9. 14). Respect for him was shaken when a body of eighty presbyters regretting his appointment, who appealed to Valens against their treatment and had much angered him by what they unwisely said, were put into a small ship that was set on fire a little way out to sea. All perished. After Athanasius' death (373) Valens supported his 'Arian' rival Lucius. Any refusing communion with him were sent to the mines in Pontus and Armenia (Cassian, *coll.* 18. 7). Both Valens and Valentinian I were feared for the ferocity of their penalties. (Valentinian kept two man-eating she-bears called Gold-dust and Innocence to whom those angering him were thrown:

---

[1] The ingenious paper by W. Telfer, 'Paul of Constantinople', *Harvard Theological Review*, 43 (1950), 31–92 has not been upheld. See G. Dagron, *Naissance d'une capitale* (Paris, 1974), 431 f.

Ammianus 29. 3. 9.) Of Demophilos' episcopate from 370 to 380 relatively little is known. For the story of the churches in Asia Minor the principal sources are the writings of the Cappadocian fathers, Basil bishop of Caesarea from 370, his younger brother Gregory bishop of Nyssa, and his friends Amphilochios of Iconium and Gregory of Nazianzos, who, under pressure from Basil, was made bishop of a wretched dusty road junction named Sasima (above p. 342), and for a short time became bishop of Constantinople in 381.

Goths in Thrace: the battle of Adrianople (378)

In the 370s the emperor Valens was faced with huge problems in defending the frontiers. The Persian army was active in attacking Armenia and Mesopotamia, while the Goths on the Danube were increasingly restless. The Goths' desire to settle within the boundaries of the empire was given force in 375 by the arrival in their rear of Huns from the steppes of central Asia, a hugely potent horde on horseback. In August 378 at the great battle of Adrianople the Roman legions were utterly defeated by the Goths and Valens was among the dead (above p. 365). The catastrophe seemed enormous to contemporary observers, and it was to be the apocalyptic climax of Ammianus' history. Libanius saw the battle as celestial revenge for the death of Julian in 363. A military author, Vegetius, was moved to compose in Latin a programme for the reform and better training of the army, sadly weakened by the reluctance of old Roman families to want a career for their sons as soldiers. With Valens dead, Theodosius was brought from the west to take charge. He was pro-Nicene, and his advent was to make the Nicene *homoousios* the required standard of orthodox faith in the Greek churches.

Gregory of Nazianzos

Basil's friend Gregory was a gifted orator who, like Basil, had sat at the feet of Libanius and other sophists of distinction. Son of the bishop of Nazianzos in Cappadocia, his father having been converted by his wife from a sect which worshipped 'the most high God',[2] Gregory composed orations of florid eloquence and wrote letters with rich references to Greek myths and literature. He also liked writing didactic verses with serious subjects. Classical learning could be used for higher ends in the fear of God and should not be distrusted, for these works with beautiful language and profound thought are part of God's good creation. He was strongly drawn to the ascetic life, in which Neoplatonic aspirations could merge with Christian ideals.

---

[2] See Stephen Mitchell in P. Athanassiadi (ed.), *Pagan Monotheism* (Oxford, 1999), 81–148.

He was ordained presbyter but the duties were alarming, and he fled north to Pontus in retreat (*or.* 2 justifies his escape). He later returned to give his father a helping hand. There was schism in the church at Nazianzos which he tried to settle (*or.* 6). He composed two well-informed discourses attacking the anti-Christian acts and words of the emperor Julian (*or.* 4–5). In 372 on the division of the province of Cappadocia Basil pressed him to be bishop of Sasima in the separated part of the old province, where also Nazianzos lay. To the end of Gregory's life Basil's action rankled. He never admitted going to Sasima and fled to the hills. After his father's death he refused election to the see of Nazianzos and for some years withdrew to Seleucia (Silifke) to live beside the shrine of St Thecla. Gregory was one of those who like to be offered positions but withdraw in face of the practical obligations.

Basil was aware that at Constantinople there was a small group whose faith was Nicene. With Peter of Alexandria he encouraged Gregory to go to the capital to give them episcopal care. Gregory converted a private house into a little chapel called Anastasia, and there several of his most important discourses were delivered, including five famous orations on fundamental theology. Against Eunomius he argued, like Basil, for the unknowable mystery of God in contrast to the radical Arian view that if we are to understand what is being said, everyday speech should and can be used. Reverence excludes logic-chopping. Talk of the Trinity is ascending into a darkness like Moses on Sinai. Without prayer a theologian learns nothing. Orthodoxy is a middle path between Sabellios and Arius, affirming one *ousia* and three hypostases or prosopa. A battleground was the doctrine of the Holy Spirit. Revelation that the divine Triad is an equality has been gradual, requiring time to reach the right conclusion, the Son begotten, the Spirit proceeding from the Father. What 'proceeding' means and how it differs from 'begotten' the human mind cannot know, but the words are given by scripture.

Sound on the Nicene creed and the deity of the Spirit, Apollinaris was harder to defend after Pope Damasus' censure in 377, canon 1 of Constantinople, 381, and the edict CTh 16. 5. 12 of December 383. (No mention in 16. 5. 11 of July 383.) Vitalis, Apollinarian bishop at Antioch, had put his creed before Gregory, who found no fault in it.[3] After the council of Constantinople (381) attitudes changed. Gregory told Vitalis that his friends were unacceptable (*ep.* 75). Although Gregory briefly assumed care for Nazianzos when his father died, canonically he was not bishop of the see, and sympathizers with Apollinaris wanted to install their candidate. Gregory sent two treatises to fortify a presbyter Cledonios (*epp.* 101, 102): 'whatever of human nature Christ did not assume is not saved' (101. 21). Because sin's root

---

[3] It is cited by Cyril of Alexandria, *ACO* I i/5. 67–8 = H. Lietzmann, *Apollinaris* (Tübingen, 1904), 273.

is in the mind, Christ must have a mind to provide redemption for it. Gregory's Christ is one prosopon by a fusion of two natures so as to be one out of two (*or.* 37. 2). *Ep.* 101 insists that Mary's title mother of God (*theotókos*) is necessary. *Ep.* 202 asks Nektarios to stir the emperor against Apollinarians. At Chalcedon in 451 he was given the title Theologian (see R. Schieffer's index, *ACO* IV iii/2. 211).

Gregory of Nyssa. Amphilochios of Iconium

After Basil's death probably in 378, his defence of the Nicene faith, dissociation from Apollinaris, and fostering of the ascetic life were carried on by his clever younger brother also named Gregory, who, although married in his youth, and sure that to celebrate the liturgical sacrifice sexual abstinence must be necessary (*De virginitate* 3 and 27), had reinforced Basil's position by accepting consecration for the see of Nyssa in 371/2. Bishops hostile to the more illiberal Nicene group held synod to depose him and he was exiled. But after Valens' death Gregory could return and compose treatises on Basil's themes, e.g. on celibacy and defending 'one *ousia*, three hypostases' against charges of tritheism. He also preached eloquent homilies on caring for the poor and for lepers, and attacking usury and the entire institution of slavery as inhuman. Among his ablest and longest works is a rebuttal of Eunomius' assertion of the adequacy of everyday human language for talk about God. About 386 he composed a substantial answer to the contentions of Apollinaris. His training in rhetoric helped him to rebut paganism with an attack on fatalism and astrology and two expositions of the creation (*Hexameron* and *On the Creation of Man*). His exegeses show influence from his reading of Origen; e.g. on the titles of Psalms, on the Song of Songs, and a Life of Moses, all of which turn on the theme of the soul's mystical ascent to God, who is infinite and so an unending mystery. Of his letters *ep.* 2 expresses considerable misgivings about the growth of pilgrimages to Jerusalem. His sympathy for asceticism helped him to be remarkably conciliatory to Messalian language about the inward life of prayer.

Amphilochius, cousin of Gregory of Nazianzos and a pupil of Libanius in rhetorical training for his career as an advocate in Constantinople, likewise supported Basil who in 373 consecrated him as bishop of Iconium, metropolis of Lycaonia. His wife had died, leaving him three children. Libanius wrote to express pleasure that as bishop he would have opportunity to deploy his rhetorical skill (*ep.* 1543). As widower Amphilochius was himself ascetic, but shared Basil's judgement that radical, church-rejecting forms of ascetic life must be unacceptable. Compared with Gregory of Nyssa, he was therefore much less sympathetic to the Messalians' non sacramental evangelicalism, and in 383 was at a synod of Side on the coast of Pamphylia to present a common front against them. Some iambic verses addressed to a friend Seleucus were preserved by Gregory of Nazianzos, and include a remarkable catalogue of the biblical canon, recording disagreements on the number of accepted epistles of John and the rejection of the Apocalypse by 'most churches'; he defended the Pauline authorship of the epistle to the Hebrews (PG 37. 1594–8).

The schism at Antioch at the council of Constantinople, May 381

At Thessalonica in 379, where he fell ill and received baptism, Theodosius announced his programme for the Church, which required communion with Damasus of Rome and Peter of Alexandria.[4] That implied recognition of Paulinus. On moving to Constantinople with closer knowledge of the Greek churches, the emperor soon changed his tune and invited Meletius to preside over his council in the capital in May 381. The existing bishop of Constantinople, Eudoxius' successor Demophilos, was a supporter of the Likeness formula of Ariminum and Seleucia. Given by Theodosius the option of accepting the Nicene creed or retiring, he preferred to go. This ruled him out. It was believed that a special revelation had come to the emperor in a vision directing him to look to Meletius, who was known to long for restored communion with Rome. In 379 Meletius had presided over a council of 153 supporters at Antioch, a sacred number from John 21: 11, (PL 13. 353–4), declaring approval of every utterance of Pope Damasus of which he could get a copy (no doubt through Dorotheus' visits to the west), probably also producing the creed which at least from the year 451 onwards was held to be that of the council of Constantinople (381) and may in fact have been welcomed there. Meletius, however, died during Theodosius' council. So the council needed to find new bishops for Constantinople and, if Paulinus was not recognized, for Antioch.

Distrust of Gregory of Nazianzos; Maximus the Cynic

Problems bristled at this point. The see of Alexandria and Egyptian bishops had been distrustful of Gregory of Nazianzos when he was ministering eloquently to the little Nicene congregation in Constantinople, and had privately consecrated a rival, a Cynic philosopher, author of an anti-Arian tract, named Maximus. Gregory had initially found Maximus an ally at Constantinople, and wrote a panegyric on his virtues, but he became

---

[4] The edict was addressed to 'every one' (*cunctos populos*), but in practice only church people were involved. When the edict came to be included in Justinian's Code in the sixth century, it was then assumed to be for all citizens and subjects of the emperor. A universal faith required the acquiescence of all.

disillusioned. The little Nicene group was divided, and Gregory's command of their loyalty was weakened when he discovered some financial malad-ministration. Maximus' bid to oust Gregory was wholly unacceptable to the emperor Theodosius, and, though persistently backed by Ambrose of Milan, he was soon dropped by Pope Damasus, probably on the advice of the bishop of Thessalonica. However, there was a difficulty in Gregory's judgement about the schism at Antioch. He deeply admired Meletius, but also held his rival Paulinus in great respect, and was aware that Alexandria and Rome were solid for recognizing Paulinus. It could not have escaped notice in 381 that the bishop of Alexandria, Peter's successor Timothy, did not come to Theodosius' great council, nor had the Roman see sent any legates, and that this absence was obviously connected with Alexandrian and Roman non-recognition of Meletius, whom the emperor had invited to preside. The Maximus affair spelt tension between Gregory and the see of Alexandria, but Gregory wanted to avert estrangement between Old and New Rome. He called Rome and Constantinople the two supreme lights, outshining in the east the sun, in the west the evening star (*De vita sua* 565). His verse autobiog-raphy, addressed to the nobility of new Rome (ibid. 11), wanted them to respect old Rome.

The synod, having initially recognized Gregory of Nazianzos as bishop of Constantinople, painfully decided on his rejection, on the ground that a translation from another see (the dismal Cappadocian posting station Sasima which he had never visited) would be uncanonical, but mainly because after Meletius' death he wanted the unwilling council to recognize Paulinus of Antioch. A senator Nektarios, who had served as praetor of the city and had the merit of no past association with any one faction, was baptized and put into the see of Constantinople. It is possible that the creed he professed at his baptism was that which Meletius had approved at his council of Antioch in 379. That creed, associated at Chalcedon in 451 with the council at Constantinople, was later to be treated as if it had Nicene status, despite its different wording, especially on the Holy Spirit. Nektarios had to confront a hostile group attached to his non-Nicene predecessor Demophilos. His house was torched. He survived quietly on his episcopal throne for sixteen years, during which he relaxed the procedure for ministering reconciliation to penitents and won support by generous hospitality. He apparently ignored Ambrose's hasty and strongly hostile reaction to his election.

Gregory's failure to persuade the council to make peace with the west by recognizing Paulinus at Antioch reflected a fairly general feeling of alienation in the Greek east that Rome and the west had not much helped in the elimination of 'Arianism'. Roman support for Marcellus, now being dis-owned by Pope Damasus, was not easily forgiven or forgotten. There was no willingness to please the west by unity at so high a price as an acceptance of

Paulinus. For Antioch the council therefore chose and consecrated Flavian, a presbyter of Antioch held in deep respect.

Canons of Constantinople

The council of Constantinople approved disciplinary canons not all of which were calculated to tranquillize western observers. Canon 1 rules that the 'faith and canons' of the 318 fathers of Nicaea remain authoritative, and imposes a special anathema on 'Eunomians, or Anomoeans, Arians or Eudoxians, and Semi-Arians or Pneumatomachoi', Sabellians, and Marcellians (variant reading: Marcionites), Photinians and Apollinarians. The named heresies appear to have been taken from the _Panarion_ by Epiphanius of 375.

The creed later associated with the council of Constantinople has modifications of the Nicene creed of 325; it includes the crucial term _homoousios_ (so that much later it could be described as 'Nicene') but has some changes which show assimilation to the Roman baptismal creed. In line with the position adopted by Basil of Caesarea (Cappadocia), it much expands the third article on the Holy Spirit to rebut (though not expressly) those who denied the deity of the divine triad; for the Spirit 'proceeds from the Father', has inspired scripture, and is joined with Father and Son both in the baptismal act and in the liturgical doxology.

Canon 2 directs that bishops have to observe proper limits to their jurisdiction and are not to make rulings beyond the boundaries of their province or civil 'diocese'; churches among the barbarians are ruled according to precedent (which is not further explained).

Canon 3 affirms that 'the bishop of Constantinople has the privileges of honour after the bishop of Rome because it is new Rome'. This was to offend Pope Damasus greatly. It was also most unwelcome at Alexandria and Antioch. The implication was the inevitable erection of the see of Constantinople into an administrative centre to which one turned for decisions. The canon spoke of honour when the reality was virtual jurisdiction. This can be illustrated by three letters in the correspondence of Gregory of Nazianzos (_epp._ 183–5). In 383 he asked Nektarios of Constantinople to intervene when a Cappadocian bishop, Bosporios of Colonia, was being troubled by civil bureaucrats; evidently the metropolitan of the province lacked the clout of supra-provincial authority which the bishop of New Rome would possess with the imperial government.

Canon 4 rules invalid the ordination by Egyptian bishops of Maximus the Cynic philosopher. Canon 5 approves of 'the Tome of the Westerners' and 'those at Antioch who confess one deity of Father, Son, and Holy Spirit'. The western Tome is probably Damasus' Tome of 377, which had an evident bearing on the position at Antioch; probably it was one of the Roman documents welcomed by Meletius and his council at Antioch in 379. A lengthy Canon 6 deals with unreasonable accusations against bishops, requiring scrutiny of the accusers, but providing that any plaintiff with a personal grievance has a right to be heard, as long as he or she is not a heretic or schismatic or excommunicate.

The western reaction

Both Nektarios and Flavian were unacceptable to Rome and initially also to Alexandria. Ambrose of Milan thought the Roman see insulted, and told Theodosius that the canonical decisions of the council severed communion between east and west. More than forty years later Pope Boniface (*ep.* 15. 6) discovered in the papal archives that a delegation of bishops and high officials was sent by Theodosius asking Damasus to recognize Nektarios, who needed strength for the struggle against Arians. Pope Damasus held a council at Rome in 382 which Paulinus and Jerome attended. This council systematically opposed the disciplinary canons of Constantinople, and asserted the superior authority of the sees of Rome where Peter and Paul were martyred, Alexandria, and Antioch. As long as Paulinus was alive, there was no prospect of Rome or Alexandria acknowledging Flavian. A sermon by Nestorius on the incarnation, preserved in Latin by Marius Mercator,[5] records that Theophilus of Alexandria's letters to Flavian were 'tyrannical'. Latin writers could not bring themelves to mention the Council of Constantinople. As Jerome had received ordination to the priesthood from Paulinus, he could not be expected to enthuse about the proceedings. In 381–2 an unbaptized Augustine would have had no interest in such a meeting of Greek bishops, and there is no reason to think that then or later he knew anything at all about its creed or other decisions. Even Rufinus (*HE* 11. 20–1) records nothing of any conciliar meeting, only the ordination of Nektarios.

Evagrius of Antioch

Gregory of Nazianzos hoped that when Paulinus died, the schism would die of inanition. But in 384 on his deathbed Paulinus consecrated his able presbyter Evagrius to be bishop. Bilingual in Latin and Greek, owner of property at Maronia east of Antioch, and at one time a provincial governor (*PLRE* i. 285–6), Evagrius had travelled to Italy in 362 with Eusebius of Vercelli on his return from exile after the synod of Alexandria, probably trying to persuade him that Lucifer's consecration of Paulinus was correct. He translated

---

[5] *ACO* I. v. 39–45, F. Loofs, *Nestoriana* (Halle, 1905), 300.

Athanasius' *Life of Antony* into Latin. He had acted for Damasus when Basil of Caesarea was vainly trying to persuade the Pope to recognize Meletius and to withdraw from communion with Paulinus, who in Basil's eyes was compromised by his association with Marcellus and insistence on one hypostasis, not three. On his visit to Caesarea Evagrius had laid before Basil a theological document demanding Basil's signature; this Basil felt he could not give and was offended by the request (*ep.* 156). A colleague of the distrusted Paulinus could not be congenial to him. In 381 as 'presbyter and deputy' (for Paulinus) Evagrius turns up in the record of Gratian's council at Aquileia, dominated by Ambrose.

Evagrius had consented when Paulinus acted alone in his consecration. That was in conflict with the canon of Nicaea requiring a minimum of three bishops of a province for a valid consecration. That fatally weakened his position, Theodosius deplored it. Theophilus of Alexandria and his Egyptian synod felt unable to recognize him, and there was much hesitation in Damasus and Ambrose (*ep.* 70 = M56). A proposal was made, probably from Italy, that both Flavian and Evagrius should submit their cases to a council which would arbitrate. In fact two councils considered the issue, one at Capua which was less than decisive, and then, on the decision of Pope Siricius, another at Caesarea in Palestine. The synod of Capua had proposed that Theophilus of Alexandria should adjudicate. He preferred to refer the intricate issue to a Greek synod. Flavian, willing to discuss anything other than the legitimacy of his position, refused the summons to both councils, and won over Theodosius to support him. At Antioch he treated Evagrius and his congregation as wilful schismatics to whom no recognition whatever should be given; in this rigorist policy he was eloquently supported by his presbyter John, whose brilliant sermons were later to win for him the epithet 'Golden Mouth' or Chrysostom (*Homily on Ephesians* 11, PG 62. 85 ff.). John delivered a panegyric on Eustathius of Antioch ending by claiming that his authentic successor was Meletius (PG 49. 597–606). He warned Flavian's people that they must be very reserved towards heretics and ice-cold towards orthodox schismatics whose essential orthodoxy made their dissent much worse. In any event their ordinations were null and void. It was offensive that any delinquent disciplined by Flavian could simply migrate to the other community. Women were distressingly prominent in maintaining the split.

On 25 December 386 John (Chrysostom) preached to explain and defend the very recent introduction of this feast at Antioch: 'we have received this from the Romans' (PG 39. 352–3). The congregation of Paulinus had close links to Rome and probably had the feast in their calendar already. Flavian's people needed to celebrate it whether in rivalry or to facilitate reconciliation.

To many critics at Antioch the hard line maintained by John against Evagrius seemed too tough, deficient in charity. They felt that if both groups were affirming Nicene orthodoxy, as was the case, it was unimportant which group commanded adherence. However, the very devout, not those coming to church once a year, were those most passionately determined to maintain division.

Bishop Flavian adopted a gentler tone. He deplored those in his own flock all too ready to pronounce anathema on the separated body (PG 48. 943–52; *Clavis* 3430). Only charity could overcome the mutual rancour. Those who cursed Paulinus and Apollinaris must remember that both were now dead and should be left to God for judgement.

About 394 Evagrius died. Already Theophilus of Alexandria had decided to recognize Flavian as lawful bishop, and the two of them co-operated in affectionate terms at a council in 394 to deal with a problem at Bostra in Syria. Flavian wisely accepted the clergy of Evagrius' congregation. The names of Paulinus and Evagrius were commemorated among the saints of Antioch in Flavian's liturgy, though they had never been in communion with him. The memory of Meletius himself, though at no time in his life in communion with the see of Rome (to his regret), was to be honoured by inclusion in the Roman Martyrology. He was buried beside St Babylas, martyr bishop of Antioch whose relics had interfered with Julian's cult of Apollo at Daphne.

Unhappily this was not the end of Antioch's trouble. In 397–8 the great preacher John Chrysostom was taken from Antioch to be bishop at Constantinople. Flavian of Antioch died in 404, saddened by lack of success in reconciling a small intransigent core, fiercely loyal to the memory of Eustathius, Paulinus, and Evagrius. In the same year Theophilus of Alexandria succeeded in unseating the uncompromising John Chrysostom from Constantinople; the emperor exiled John, and Theophilus' nominee Arsacius was intruded into the see. He had to cope with a substantial body of bishops, clergy, and laity tenaciously attached to John, labelled Johnites. Schism at Constantinople was at least as intransigent as the smaller split at Antioch. Theophilus sought to justify his action by issuing a bitterly hostile portrait of John (lost; Facundus 6. 5. 15 ff. quotes from this). A small split at Antioch was now joined by a much greater schism at Constantinople. At Antioch Flavian was succeeded by Porphyry (404–12) who distressed John's numerous admirers at Antioch by recognizing Arsacius and supporting Theophilus' negative view of John. Johnites were persecuted in Constantinople and Antioch. Numerous refugees fled to Rome and were received by Pope Innocent I (402–17), whose relations with the three patriarchates of Constantinople, Alexandria, and Antioch became icy. Innocent demanded a rehearing of John's case at a new synod and then, after John's

death in exile in 408, the insertion of his name in the diptychs commemorating saints with whom the church was in communion.[6] Communion with
Rome and the west could be restored only after the great eastern sees had
admitted John to the diptychs. Diptychs became an instrument of ecclesiastical polemic, but could also be a positive means to the reconciliation of
memories, inserting the heroes of a smaller ecclesial group into the calendar
of the mainstream body.

When Porphyry of Antioch died, he was succeeded by Alexander who set
out to reconcile both the Johnites and the old Nicene congregation left by
Evagrius. He perceived that if he pleased Innocent by adding John's name to
the diptychs at Antioch, the Pope could be persuaded to withdraw the comfort of Rome's longstanding support from the old Nicene Eustathians who
now lacked a bishop. At a tiny price he could solve a huge problem. In
solemn procession Alexander went to the old church and gathered as many
members of the little dissenting congregation as were willing to follow him,
chanting hymns as they all went to the great church of the city. Even
Alexander, however, could not win all of them. A small embattled continuing group survived until 482 when the then bishop of Antioch Kalendion
brought the bones of Eustathius from Thrace to be enshrined at Antioch.

Alexander sent legates led by John Cassian to report success to Innocent.
Johnite refugees in Italy were fully recognized by the Pope and the clergy
included in the Roman's church's payroll. A passionate surviving account of
the Johnite perspective on the story was written by Palladius of Helenopolis
in Bithynia, also author of the famous history of Egyptian holy men, notably
the circle of Evagrius of Pontus, dedicated to the high chamberlain Lausos
(*Lausiac History*). The final step for the Johnites came when Cyril of
Alexandria, who in 412 succeeded his uncle Theophilus at a contested election (when Cyril was supported by the governor of Egypt), realized that he
too could need Roman support. Reluctantly he came to admit John
Chrysostom's name to the diptychs at Alexandria. It had become evident that
John's posthumous fame as a holy man was irresistible. A saint could be more
potent after death than during his lifetime.[7]

---

[6] See Robert E. Taft, *The Diptychs* (Orientalia Christiana Analecta, 238; Rome, 1991). Diptychs
are folding tablets of ivory originally used by late Roman senators as invitation cards to celebrate
special occasions or inaugural games. About AD 400 they began to be used in churches, inscribed
with the names of departed saints and living bishops with whom the church was in communion.
The names were read by the deacon in the liturgy. When great sees experienced high tension in
disputes, inclusion or exclusion became highly sensitive.

[7] The Antioch schism is subject of a justly famous monograph by F. Cavallera, *Le Schisme
d'Antioche* (Paris, 1905).

45

JEROME AND RUFINUS: CONTROVERSY ABOUT ORIGEN

Jerome (Hieronymus) from Dalmatia and Rufinus of Aquileia, born at nearby Concordia, were old friends who shared the aspiration to make good Greek theology accessible to an ignorant Latin world. To help western Christians acquire a sense of their tradition, Jerome composed, after the manner of Suetonius, the *Lives of Illustrious men* (392/3) with brief biographies of Christian writers, and translated the *Chronicle* of Eusebius, continued down to 378. Jerome briefly sat at the feet of Didymus the Blind at Alexandria (*ep.* 50. 1; *in Osee*, prol.), a disciple of Origen's way of writing biblical commentaries whose own expositions have been partly recovered in consequence of a papyrus find near Cairo in 1941, thereby showing how much Jerome owed to him. At Antioch he studied exegesis under Apollinaris (*ep.* 84. 3). In 379 he had been at Constantinople listening to Gregory of Nazianzos (*ep.* 52. 8; *in Esai.* 3. 6. 1), and Gregory is a probable voice to have directed him towards Origen's expositions of scripture. He met Gregory of Nyssa, who read him his refutation of Eunomius, and also Amphilochius of Iconium. Like other Latin contemporaries, he could not bring himself to mention the council of Constantinople of 381. Augustine wrote to remonstrate against his use of Origen, Didymus, and Apollinaris, whose reputation for orthodoxy was uncertain (*ep.* 116. 23). Jerome was not much disposed to pay serious attention to criticism from the younger African, 'the new wealth of Africa', especially when Augustine criticized his (Origenist) commentary on Galatians 2, where he saw the dissension between Peter and Paul as edifying playacting.

Origen's biblical exegesis

Jerome found excellent matter in Origen's exegesis of scripture and in his impassioned sermons, and decided to make some Latin translations. They would be valuable guides for western exegetes. 'The interpretation of scripture is the one art where all claim to be masters', he wrote ironically (*ep.* 53. 7). Origen could teach the point that biblical commentaries are not for entertainment, but to disclose spiritual meaning (*in Osee*, PL 25. 839A). *Ep.* 33 provides an invaluable list of Origen's numerous writings. Jerome had access to Origen' *Hexapla*. He claimed that Origen was 'the greatest teacher of the Church since the apostles'. He also wrote commentaries under his own name on e.g. the epistles to the Galatians and Ephesians, in which the exegesis provided by Origen was exploited to an extent which makes it possible to reconstruct much of Origen's lost work. Rufinus also made Latin versions of Origen's sermons on the Old Testament, which characteristically interpret the Old Testament as an allegory of New Testament truths and treat contradictions or moral difficulties as symbolic of deeper insights.

Critic of Ambrose

Jerome made a Latin translation of Didymus' treatise on the Holy Spirit, motivated, however, by a desire to show up the plagiarisms in Ambrose's treatise on this theme. Dislike for Ambrose's commentary on Luke's Gospel led Jerome to translate Origen's homilies on Luke. Jerome was an academic of a familiar type, armed with powerful erudition, who wrote noble letters to younger people and scornful references to contemporaries who looked like rivals. He shared the Greek criticism of Ambrose's ordination. He was disgusted that 'a catechumen today becomes a bishop tomorrow; yesterday at the amphitheatre, today in the church; in the evening at the circus, in the morning at the altar; a little time ago patron of actors, now dedicator of virgins' (*ep.* 69. 9).

Ascetic women

Aquileia had a community of monks supported by the bishop. Both Rufinus and Jerome were drawn into the ascetic movement with its military ideals of fasting, vigils, hardship, and sexual abstinence. They had the support of rich Roman widows from families of the highest distinction determined to pursue the ascetic way. Some of Jerome's most remarkable letters were written to Marcella, a cousin of his friend Pammachius, at Rome; *ep.* 127 is a memoir of her. Melania the elder lost her husband when only 22 years old, and sailed to Egypt where she assisted orthodox monks harassed by the Arian bishop Lucius after Athanasius' death (373). Probably at Alexandria she met Rufinus, and became 'his companion on the spiritual path' (the phrase of Paulinus of Nola, *ep.* 28. 5).

Melania's sights were on Jerusalem, to which she moved perhaps about 375. She founded a monastery on the mount of Olives to house fifty virgins and to provide hospitality for pilgrims in a religious house. Rufinus joined the community. He translated a 'History of the Monks' (*Historia*

Monachorum) extant in both Greek and his Latin, describing an Egyptian pilgrimage by seven monks from the house on the mount of Olives to visit holy men in the desert. It is less valuable than the *Lausiac History* by Palladius (one of the circle round Evagrius of Pontus), which is less dominated by the miraculous. Both documents have a complex transmission, and underwent anti-Origenist revisions; Rufinus himself modified the text he translated, which was close to that used by the historian Sozomen. He adapted Basil's monastic Rules, thereby much influencing western readers. For his part Jerome encountered Pachomian monks at Alexandria and made a Latin version of their Rule.

Jerome's Lives of Paul, Hilarion, Malchos

The success and influence of Athanasius' Life of Antony may have spurred Jerome to compose brief essays in hagiography: a Life of Paul the first hermit written when Jerome was an ascetic in the Syrian desert in 374–5; later a Life of Hilarion near Gaza, who moved to Cyprus, popularly admired for his healings, for curing a woman's infertility, for enabling a chariot-race at Gaza to be won by horses owned by a Christian in competition with steeds owned by a devotee of the god Marnas, thereby paving the way for the overthrow of the pagan cult in an anti-Christian city. Like the temple of Serapis at Alexandria, the temple of Marnas was soon converted into a church (Jerome, *ep.* 107. 2; *in Esai.* 7. 17. 1, p. 279). A third Life was that of Malchos living on Evagrius' estate Maronia, east of Antioch. Jerome's hagiography encountered sceptics who thought his lives of holy men fictitious 'logrolling'; it is likely that they contain legendary elements given to him by folk tradition, but not that he invented these. The topography of the three Lives is impeccable.

Paula and Eustochium

Jerome at Rome had become spiritual director to a group of aristocratic ladies. In his ascetic aspirations he was especially supported by the widow Paula, mother of the young Eustochium for whom at Rome he wrote a notorious letter (22) on virginity, causing such scandal and pagan mockery as to ensure that the author could not achieve his ambition to become bishop of Rome. Her elder sister Blesilla died of excessive mortifications for which Jerome was widely blamed. Paula 'knew the Bible by heart' and could chant the Psalter in Hebrew without a Latin accent (*ep.* 108. 27; he once remarks that 'Jews laugh at our pronunciation of Hebrew gutturals', *in Titum* 2, PL 26. 621 B). She constructed a large monastery at Bethlehem, to which a school was soon attached where Jerome could teach Latin grammar and literature. He took lessons in Hebrew from a Bethlehem Jew named Baranina who came by night (*ep.* 84. 3). For a few years relations with Rufinus remained good; Jerome paid Rufinus' monks for making copies of texts, especially of Cicero's philosophical Dialogues for which Jerome paid particularly generously, 'more than for biblical texts.' In the light of Jerome's famous dream brilliantly recounted in the letter (22) to Eustochium, in which in his cell in the Syrian desert haunted by erotic temptations, he was accused before the divine Judgement Seat of being a Ciceronian rather than a Christian and promised to change his ways, Rufinus could not resist mentioning his inconsistency after their relationship was soured. Jerome's promise was not kept.

Copying manuscripts

It is noteworthy that Jerome turned to Rufinus' monastery for scribes capable of copying the texts which he needed. For ascetics the transcription of manuscripts was thought an appropriate manual labour. Monks copied texts partly for sale, but in the main for their own libraries. Naturally not all the monks were themselves necessarily students of what they were copying, and the original author had no control over the accuracy or the final destination of the copies. An unkind reference by Jerome in the later controversy with Rufinus shows that Rufinus travelled with a substantial library (*Apol. c. Ruf.* 3. 29; cf. *ep.* 5. 2). Jerome did much the same. Both men surrounded themselves with an admiring school of disciples who helped to diffuse their works and indeed other patristic texts as well. In an age when the barbarians were invading the empire, they played a notable role for the west in preserving monuments of Christian culture.

Origen and allegory

Origen was the master exegete, for whom the many books read in the lectionaries of the churches constituted a single divine Author's book. Moreover, he urged, the sense of the Scriptures is often obscure to ordinary readers who fail to discern that beyond the literal or surface sense there must be a hidden spiritual meaning, clues to which are found when the surface text seems impossible or absurd or unworthy of God. Normally the literal meaning is right and good, and he thought it rare for this to be impossible. But it is not the most important meaning. Origen believed that the Pauline threefold division of spirit, soul, and body, also applied to Scripture. Beginners understand the surface meaning, but beyond that lies a moral sense and higher still a spiritual or mystical sense. The person of Christ offers a close analogy. The visible humanity of Jesus answers to the literal sense; but for those with ears to hear, the divine presence within him is to be discerned by the exegete given to prayer and enlightened by the divine Word himself.

'On First Principles'

With some exceptions, among whom was Eustathius bishop of Antioch, Origen's allegories were not thought problematic. But the system of theology which he founded upon his exegesis worried some especially alarmed by his anti-gnostic work 'On First Principles'. This masterly work was primarily directed against Gnostic determinism and was an able vindication of providence. The two foci of his thinking were the goodness of God and the indestructible free will of the rational creature, axioms from which he reasonably deduced that no rational being created by God can sink to be totally depraved and that divine love will never fail to redeem even the fallen angel Lucifer. (To make Satan irredeemable is to concede victory to gnostic dualism.) If this seems impossible, that only indicates that it may take a very long time, but God is content to educate slowly. Nevertheless, because free will is indefectible and lasts for ever, Origen speculated that the fall might occur all over again. Augustine sharply expressed all this as a doctrine in which long periods of real misery alternate with illusory bliss (*City of God* 12. 20).

Athanasius was aware, and did not object (*Decr.* 27), that Origen allowed room for speculative flights in his theology which were experimental, leaving the intelligent reader to make up his own mind on the issues presented. In the third century the Church had not defined such matters. The preface to the work 'On First Principles' catalogues articles of the apostolic Rule of Faith which are taken as given; but the apostles did not explain their reasons for holding these truths, so that there is plenty of room for the theologian to set about serious inquiries. By the last quarter of the fourth century this licence for speculation in fundamental theology had come to look dangerous and less than orthodox.

The last things: Origen on resurrection

Christian language about the last things puzzled educated believers. The resurrection of the body was difficult for a Platonist, though he would grant that the soul needs a material vehicle hereafter. Origen's interpretation was not literalist, and this alarmed simple believers and those responsible for teaching them their catechism. He was sure that flesh and blood could not inherit the kingdom of God. And would the wicked dead be provided with teeth to gnash with? At the end of the third century Origen's account of the resurrection and his belief in the pre-existence of souls were attacked by Methodius bishop of Olympus in south-west Asia Minor. This was restated by Epiphanius of Salamis in 375. By 303 the body of criticism of Origen was sufficiently weighty for Pamphilus and Eusebius of Caesarea to compile an *Apology for Origen* addressed to the confessors in the mines in Palestine,

vindicating him against charges of heresy. Of the six books only the first survives in a Latin translation by Rufinus. But the major onslaught on Origen
came from Epiphanius in Cyprus, a bishop who had been born in Palestine
and had close attachments there; he found his way to the Latin monasteries.
In Cyprus Salamis was a Marcionite stronghold (John Chrysostom, *ep.* 221);
he was sensitive on heresy.

Epiphanius critic of Origen

Origen was unhesitant in affirming the divinity of Jesus the Christ. At the
same time he safeguarded monotheism by allowing that the divine Logos is
mediator between the Father and this lower world, and, while God, is not the
very source of deity. Such language seemed to Epiphanius to make him the
father of Arianism.

Epiphanius visited the Holy Land where he had himself founded a
monastic house, and influenced Jerome in his monastery at Bethlehem.
Jerome is likely to have discovered at Alexandria that the Pachomian monks,
whose Rule he translated into Latin, regarded Origen with some horror. In
382 both Epiphanius and Jerome had been present at Damasus' council of
Rome. In 393 a self-appointed heresy-hunter named Aterbios, probably
briefed by Epiphanius, arrived in Jerusalem to detect Origenist enormities
and to ask monks to condemn such doctrines. Jerome obliged. Rufinus on
the mount of Olives replied reasonably enough that he would answer questions from the diocesan bishop John of Jerusalem, but not from Aterbios.

A suspicion of Origenism in Bishop John was the next stage. He was on
very good terms with Rufinus and Melania. Bishops of Jerusalem were in
communion with Flavian of Antioch, not with Jerome's friend Evagrius,
whose episcopal standing, after his uncanonical ordination, was coming
under embarrassed criticism in both Rome and Alexandria. Jerome could
insinuate that Bishop John had an unresolved Arian past. John's relations with
Jerome were already less than cordial, especially after Epiphanius uncanonically, without the consent of Bishop John, ordained Jerome's adolescent
brother Paulinianus to be priest to the community; this was desired because
of Jerome's refusal to exercise his presbyterate (his mortifications were to
atone for sexual indiscretions in his youth, memories of which still troubled
him); but Epiphanius' act was declared invalid by Bishop John, so that
Paulinianus had to retire to Cyprus. The acid pen of the monk of Bethlehem
was all too ready to be critical of Greek liturgical custom where it differed
from Latin usage, e.g. in celebrating Jesus' Nativity on 6 January. To Bishop
John's charge that the monks of Bethlehem were schismatic, they replied that
his jurisdiction was invalidated by Origenist heresy. They sent their catechumens to be baptized by the anti-Origenist bishop of Diospolis (Lydda), with

whom Jerome was in communion. Apart from Origenism, Jerome was also known to think that the mortifications of the well-heeled monastery on the mount of Olives were insufficiently austere. The parting of friends began to look possible. Nevertheless, Theophilus of Alexandria was able to bring reconciliation and when in the spring of 397 Rufinus left Palestine for Italy, Jerome accompanied him to the ship.

Rufinus the Syrian

A Syrian presbyter also named Rufinus entered the Bethlehem monastery and as a zealous anti-Origenist was soon sent by Jerome to Rome and Milan (*ep.* 81. 2). The inclusion of Milan suggests that support from the bishop and Honorius' court was hoped for; John of Jerusalem was asking the emperor Arcadius at Constantinople for state action against the Bethlehem house (Jerome, *ep.* 82. 10). This was decreed but never implemented. Rufinus the Syrian was the author of an extant book *On the Faith*, sharply critical of Origen but also containing ideas congenial to the British monk Pelagius and his ally Caelestius.

The translation of Origen 'On First Principles'

The breach between Bethlehem and the Mount of Olives was soon to become actual. Rufinus on landing in Italy met a philosopher named Macarius asking questions about Origen's view of providence and determinism; he was composing a book against astrology (Rufinus, *apol.* 1. 11). For Macarius Rufinus translated the first of the six books of Pamphilus' apology for Origen and wrote a warning treatise on the falsification of Origen's works by heretics. Such falsifications he could detect wherever Origen expressed opinions deviating from those accepted by orthodoxy. Rufinus could quote three instances: a letter from Origen complaining of a falsification, an experience of Hilary of Poitiers, who found that his book *De synodis* had been altered by his opponents, and a manuscript of Cyprian at Constantinople in which work by a very different author (Novatian) had been inserted, he thought, by followers of Macedonius. In Rome about 398 Rufinus was urged by Macarius and others to translate Origen 'On First Principles'. Imprudently he yielded. A storm ensued.

Rufinus' preface to his translation of this work refers to the Latin hunger for Origen resulting from Jerome's translation of Origen on the Song of Songs. Since Jerome had now abandoned translations in favour of books in his own name and therefore must be supposed to have abandoned his intention of translating *De principiis*, Rufinus could inherit the mantle and had now yielded to the pressure of Macarius and many others. Jerome is claimed as his model in changing the sense wherever it would be offensive to Latin readers. With total candour Rufinus explains that wherever the text is contrary to Origen's orthodox opinions in his other writings, he has either omitted it as an interpolation or altered it to conform to his doctrine elsewhere.

Rufinus' preface aimed at warding off attacks from a group in Rome known to be hostile to Origen. A Bethlehem monk, Eusebius of Cremona, took a copy of his unfinished draft (Rufinus was characteristically careless in allowing copies of his versions to be made before they were in final form) and passed it to an old friend and correspondent of Jerome, Pammachius, formerly proconsul in Africa, son-in-law of Paula, a fellow pupil with Jerome of the grammarian Donatus. Pammachius and his friend Oceanus were alarmed that the translation was presenting to the Romans an impression of Origen as orthodox when he was not, and by invoking Jerome as model the preface implicated Jerome as responsible for diffusing heresy. A letter to Bethlehem rapidly alerted Jerome to a dangerous work being put about as enjoying his approval. Jerome sent in reply an exact translation of Origen's work, which so alarmed Pammachius that, after allowing a copy to be made, he hid it away. It has not survived, while Rufinus' version has.

Rufinus had had no reason to suppose that Jerome had modified his favourable opinion of Origen. That modification resulted from the influence of Epiphanius and the consternation of his Roman friends, who campaigned against Origenism in Italy. Nevertheless when consulted by Paulinus of Nola needing an explanation of God's hardening of Pharaoh's heart, Jerome himself recommended that he read the excellent work of Origen 'On First Principles' (*ep.* 85. 3). Rufinus defended Origen's exploratory theology in matters where the Church had expressed no verdict, and urged the utility of the work in answer to philosophical cavils. Moreover, the council of Nicaea had uttered no word of censure (though 'identity of being' was not the terminology of Origen, who vehemently opposed Sabellian modalism). The polemical exchanges between Rufinus and Jerome make painful reading, and Jerome injected venom into his satirical portrait of his opponent.[1] He had no support from Pope Siricius, but was able to win sympathy from his successor Anastasius and felt sure that his successor Innocent would hold the same view (*ep.* 130. 16). Augustine was horrified by the breach between the two old friends and the manner of their quarrelling. His remonstrance (*ep.* 73. 6) was ineffective. Jerome (*ep.* 115. 3) was pained that Augustine had not supported his side against Rufinus and had been neutral.

---

[1] Jerome's *Apology against Rufinus* has been edited by Pierre Lardet both in CCSL 79 (Turnhout, 1982) and in SC 303 (Paris, 1983), with a detailed commentary in *Vigiliae Christianae*, Suppl. 15 (Leiden, 1993).

Anthropomorphite monks in Egypt

Controversy in Palestine was exacerbated by trouble in Egypt. In the Egyptian desert some monks, notably Evagrius of Pontus, profoundly admired Origen's teaching on prayer. In particular they held that physical images of God as a benevolent old man in the sky have to be utterly set aside. Images of God in human shape must be absolutely negated. This proposition alarmed other monks, who felt that the Origenists were 'taking away their God', who certainly became flesh in the incarnation. Theophilus bishop of Alexandria initially defended the Origenists and denounced Epiphanius, but then found that he had a huge protest on his hands and changed sides. In 399 or 400 he held a synod at Alexandria condemning Origen for suggesting the pre-existence of souls and the final restoration or *apokatastasis*.[2] He gave important support to Jerome. Four Origenist monks, known as the Long or Tall Brothers, found that Egypt was no place for contemplation, and began to look to Constantinople for help. There since 397 was a new bishop John, chosen because of his fine sermons as presbyter at Antioch on the Orontes, and sympathetic to admirers of Origen. From the seventh century he would be called 'Golden Mouth', Chrysostom.

Rufinus' retreat to Aquileia

Jerome's Roman friends ensured that Rufinus could not long stay in Rome, though he there made versions of the pseudo-Clementine Recognitions, and, more important, of the letter of Clement to James of Jerusalem (destined to be influential in medieval canon law because of its account of Peter appointing Clement as his successor as bishop of Rome, but problematic because it called James 'bishop of bishops'). Fortified with a commendation from Pope Siricius, he retreated to Aquileia where he continued translating Origen's sermons, now on Psalms 36–8 (37–9) concerned with penitence, and issued a version of nine sermons by Gregory of Nazianzos (gratefully exploited by Augustine in debate with Julian of Eclanum and later by Pope Leo I). Two manuscripts of the translation of Gregory of Nazianzos (Bodl. Laud. misc. 276, s. xi and Arras 621, s. x) carry a note that at Rome an ancestor of these copies was collated to the end of *orat.* 7 with the copy left by Melania the younger, granddaughter of the elder. She was a keen collector of Greek and Latin Christian texts, and daily practised calligraphy (*Vita Melaniae* 23, 26).

For the aristocratic Apronianus and his wife Avita, who had decided to live together in continence, Rufinus translated 451 ascetic maxims entitled 'The

---

[2] Synodal fragments, ed. J. Declerck, *Byzantion*, 54 (1984), 495–507.

Sentences of Sextus' (or Xystus). Rufinus noted a tradition that these, compiled partly from Neopythagorean sources, were by the martyred Pope
Xystus II. Jerome was to be scathing about the ascription of non-Christian
ethical maxims to a bishop of Rome. They were widely read by Christians in
the first half of the third century, and were admiringly quoted a few times by
Ambrose, who used the Greek original. Rufinus' Latin version was very
popular as a medieval handbook of moral education, extant in many manuscripts. In the fifth century it is twice cited by Caesarius of Arles (*S.* 1. 7;
5. 2), in the sixth in St Benedict's Rule (7 and 9). Jerome shared the admiration for the maxims, but was sure they must be by a Pythagorean, 'a rank
pagan' not a Christian at all (*in Hiez.* 6. 18; *ep.* 132. 3. *in Jerem.* 4. 22).

Bishop Chromatius of Aquileia persuaded Rufinus to translate Eusebius'
Ecclesiastical History; he merged books 9–10, omitting most of 10, and added
not only details in the life of Origen but also two valuable books of his own
to bring the story down to Theodosius I.[3] He was able to use a history by
Gelasius bishop of Caesarea (Palestine), some fragments of which survive.[4]

At Aquileia Rufinus translated a work which he supposed to be the work
of Origen, attacking erroneous doctrines in Bardaisan, Marcion, and the followers of Valentine: *De recta in Deum fide* ascribed to Adamantius. The
unknown author used Methodius' attack on Origen's spiritualizing doctrine
of resurrection. Rufinus' preface deplored writers who plunder Origen and
then accuse him of heresy.

Defending his own orthodoxy, soon after 402 Rufinus' wrote a commentary on the Apostles' Creed, the baptismal creed of Rome 'where no heresy
has originated'; he carefully affirmed the resurrection of the body. His exposition owed a debt to Cyril of Jerusalem's *Catecheses*. Remarkably, since he was
writing before Augustine's *De Trinitate* was current, he was sure that the Holy
Spirit proceeds from both the Father and the Son (36). About 406 he made
an abbreviating paraphrase of Origen's enormous commentary on the epistle to the Romans, not all of which was available to him, so that he filled gaps
by inserting summaries of what he found elsewhere in Origen's writings. His
epilogue pointedly observed that it was against his conscience to publish this
adaptation of Origen as if it were his own work, contrasting that with 'secular authors' (an evident code for Jerome) who put out under their own name
works they have translated from the Greek. The adaptation of Origen on
Romans was primarily intended to deprive heretics of texts used to deny free
will. The theme was to be congenial to Pelagius, who could use Rufinus'

---

[3] See J. E. L. Oulton, 'Rufinus' Translation of the Church History of Eusebius', *JTS* 30 (1929),
150–74.
[4] See F. Winkelmann, *Byzantinoslavica,* 34 (1973), 103–98, and his paper in *Byz. Forschungen,* 1
(1966), 346–85.

work in his own commentary on the Pauline epistles. The Origenist controversy was to lead into the Pelagian controversy.

Jerome's gift for sharp language and the element of rancour introduced by
the breach in a former friendship made the controversy often merely personal abuse. But there were issues in which Rufinus was echoing criticism
widespread in the west. It was uncomfortable that Jerome was critical of the
Septuagint and regarded the Hebrew text as primary and superior. In reply to
Rufinus Jerome had to explain his methods of translation and his intentions
in writing commentaries. With an excellent knowledge of both pagan and
Christian literature Jerome lay open to puritan critics who thought Rufinus
had a good point in observing that he had remained a very Ciceronian
Christian.

Rufinus moves to Sicily

Rufinus was in Aquileia when the city was captured by Alaric and his Goths
(November 401). Alaric did not stay (he was to return later), but before 407
Rufinus decided to move south through Rome and perhaps to a monastery
at Pinetum near Terracina on his way to Sicily. There, with friends for company, he translated Origen on Numbers and in 410 watched from Messina as
Alaric set fire to Rhegium (Reggio) across the straits. In 411 he suddenly
died. One manuscript of Origen's Commentary on Romans (Copenhagen,
Gl. kgl. S. 1338, 4°, written at St Amand early in the ninth century) records
that it copied an uncorrected unfinalized copy found among his papers by his
followers after his sudden death. Several manuscripts of his translation of
Origen's Homilies on Numbers record that they were written at Syracuse. In
all probability this was a monastic society to which Rufinus and his fellow
refugees moved, and which saw to the perpetuation of their master's works.
Writing a preface to his commentary on Ezekiel Jerome was delighted to
report that the 'scorpion' Rufinus was dead; the hydra had ceased to hiss. In
the last decade of Jerome's life, he continued to mock Rufinus 'the grunter'
(Grunnius). The controversy rumbled on; he was finding that Rufinus'
memory was treasured by friends who had not ceased to express their
reservations about himself.

Jerome's polemics

Jerome was a master of polemic. Marcella at Rome feared that he was continually beginning new quarrels (*ep.* 27. 2). Western critics of ideas and practices dear to the ascetic movement drew his fire. Against Helvidius he
defended the perpetual virginity of Mary; against Jovinian the moral superiority of celibacy to marriage (a work owing much to Seneca); against

Vigilantius (a priest from the north side of the Pyrenees, once a monk at Bethlehem) the devotional value of the veneration of relics. Vigilantius deplored candles in broad daylight, dubious miracles of healing, vows of continence that might well not be kept, and adolescents cuddling in the dark at martyr's shrines. Jerome was hurt that Vigilantius also opposed sending money to the monastic hospices in the Holy Land when the poor of Gaul were starving. His tract against the schismatic followers of Lucifer of Calaris, besides being a crucial source for the history of the Council of Ariminum (359), is merciful by comparison. Towards Pelagius, however, he reserved some of his fiercest language. The polemic against Jovinian was read as so negative to femininity that Augustine wrote a book 'On the Good of Marriage', where the ostensible target of criticism is Jovinian but the actual unnamed target Jerome. Jovinian was formally censured by councils and the Roman see, so that his influence was modest. Nevertheless Jovinian correctly perceived that Jerome's ascetic principles stated in his letter 22 to Eustochium assumed that sexual intercourse between Adam and Eve occurred only after the Fall, not in paradise, and was therefore inherently flawed by sin. This exegesis was attacked by Ambrosiaster at Rome (*Quaest* 127) and disowned by Augustine (e.g. *City of God* 14. 23) though much earlier he wrote as if he were sympathetic to Jerome's view (e.g. *de Genesi contra Manichaeos*, and the correction in *Retractationes* I. 13. 8).[5]

The Latin Bible

Jerome may not come too well out of the Origenist controversy. But there is much to his credit in the fascinating biblical commentaries and letters rich in historical information. The letter of consolation to Heliodorus bishop of Altinum on the death of his nephew Nepotian (*ep.* 60) is a noble document. Above all he made most of the revised translation of the Latin Bible, much later to be called the Vulgata, widely current in the western churches. (For Jerome 'vulgata editio' meant the Septuagint: *ep.* 57. 7.) The Old Latin version of the second century was produced by a variety of missionaries, and there were not only passages of translationese in the Old Testament (above p. 322) but also considerable variants between different manuscripts. An educated reader could not help being repelled by the barbarisms. Damasus in 382 asked Jerome to embark on revision, and in 384 Jerome produced a new version of the four Gospels. His first task with the Old Testament was to retranslate the Psalms, a work which he had earlier undertaken on the basis of the Septuagint column in Origen's *Hexapla*. From 392 he realized that he needed

---

[5] On Ambrosiaster see D. G. Hunter in *Harvard Theological Review*, 82 (1989), 283–99; on Jovinian his paper in *Theological Studies*, 48 (1987), 45–64.

to set aside the Septuagint, and to translate directly from the Hebrew original, noting that the New Testament writers often used the Hebrew. He did not share the view, held by Augustine, that the Septuagint translation was inspired. He observed that in his homilies to the people Origen cited the Septuagint, whereas in the commentaries addressed to the learned he cited the Hebrew. Jerome's Hebrew Psalter was not particularly welcomed, and it was his first translation which was copied and became standard for Latin liturgical use. Jerome used good Greek manuscripts for his translation of the Gospels, and the Vulgate, though not all of it necessarily comes from his work, is a major witness to Greek manuscript readings of his time of high value.

Resort to the Hebrew original was not popular. In north Africa the reading from Jerome's version of the book of Jonah caused a near riot at Oea (Tripoli). The people resented the abandonment of the old language with which they were familiar, and which had evidently acquired numinous associations. Acceptance of the Vulgate as an authorized version came only slowly. Readings from the Old Latin manuscripts found their way into manuscripts of Jerome's Vulgate, so that the Oxford edition of the Vulgate New Testament (edited by Wordsworth, White, Sparks, and Adams) is an indispensable source for the Old Latin as well as for Jerome's revision.

Jerome was not a thinker or in the stricter sense a theologian. He applied his secular education to the philological interpretation of scripture, and affirmed such an education to be an indispensable equipment (*ep.* 130. 17). But he was the most learned scholar of his time, and his revised Latin Bible eventually, not at once, earned him the lasting admiration and gratitude of the western churches. He died on 30 September 420, buried at Bethlehem in a grotto below the Church of the Nativity close to Paula and Eustochium.

46

PELAGIUS, CAELESTIUS, AND THE ROMAN
SEE IN GAUL AND NORTH AFRICA

Morality and faith in God

In Christian history there is discernible a distinction between two classes of believers. For one the essential substance of the true worship of God resides in authentic moral life in imitation of Christ and in obedience to the values and precepts of the New Testament and the prophets of the Old. 'This is love, that we follow God's commandments' (2 John 6). For the other class this same moral life is an external fruit rooted in a prior internal dedication of heart and soul in a penitent response of faith, often involving deep emotion, continually committing the individual believer to the gospel of divine forgiveness and regeneration of which baptism is the sacrament of acceptance and the community eucharist the repeated renewal. In the New Testament the two patterns are obviously represented by the epistle of James and Paul's epistle to the Romans. At the end of the fourth century they are embodied in Pelagius and Augustine. The two standpoints are not unrelated to Christology. In the former pattern Christ is above all the supreme example by the perfection of his inspired humanity in obedience to his divine vocation, which is redemptive. In the latter pattern Christ is St John's divine Word made flesh, whose incarnate life imparts atoning power to the self-sacrifice of his life upon the cross; and it is the presence of the divine in him which makes his person and work redemptive, conqueror of both death and sin, of both human transitoriness and proud resistance to the good.

Underlying the issues being debated lies the question, What makes a Christian? If the answer is the believer's moral achievements grounded in the decisions of his or her determined will, assisted by divine grace to keep the Lord's commandments, these achievements may appear as ground for meriting further grace and the reward of salvation. That seems to conflict with the penitent believer's need for mercy and forgiveness. If, on the other hand, the assistance of divine grace is an initiating and persisting, perhaps all-embracing factor in producing the will to do what is good and right, then any merit is itself a divine gift. There is then a question about the freedom or independence of the human will and, within that, a problem about asserting the power to make an independent moral decision when, for a variety of possible reasons such as the storms of passion, the actual capacity to perform what the will wishes to do is weak or lacking or otherwise insufficient. Therapy of the emotions comes by grace.

The questions at issue in the Pelagian controversy are perennial in Christian history and are of considerable profundity. At the same time they were no reflection of the political and economic troubles of the empire's citizens in that age, from which the theological and anthropological problems of the main protagonists were quite remote. Suggestions that the Pelagian group (they were never a coherent party with common aims in church politics) had social or political objectives have been unconvincing. The controversy was largely western, although Pelagius and his supporters received at first a measure of support in the Greek east, where Augustine's way of talking about vitiated nature and corroded free will was not customary.

Pelagius in Rome

Pelagius is the earliest surviving British writer. His writings found sympathetic readers for a long time in both England and Ireland. A lay ascetic, he came to Rome probably in the 380s and, without any demand for extreme acts of self-denial, was shocked by the undisciplined and unregenerate style of life being lived by nominal but in many cases baptized Christians. (His portrait resembles the negative pictures of Roman society in Ammianus Marcellinus, Jerome, or the critic on whom Augustine commented, *ep.* 36. 3–4.) Among them many preferred to remain catechumens, i.e. counted as Christians but not baptized and so not 'faithful' (*fideles*). They left church services after the readings and sermon, not qualified for the eucharist. One well-to-do aristocrat with a baptized wife once answered Augustine's plea that he should be baptized by saying that he had not as yet the will to do that and (following Augustine's doctrine that the will to do right is God's gift) was awaiting this gift (*ep.* 2*). Some, like their pagan friends, had mistresses as well as wives and took it for granted that they had the right to sleep with their slave-girls, even if that incurred the probable outcome of the slave's scorn for an infertile wife. Augustine (*En. in Ps.* 80. 20–1) sadly records how many felt confident in the illusion that, in accord with 1 Cor. 3: 15, their adultery, perjury, even compromises with pagan cult, would all be happily purged 'as if by fire' hereafter. Augustine granted that minor or 'venial' sins would be purged by the fire of divine love at the Last Judgement, or perhaps earlier during the waiting state between death and Judgement, but St John's serious 'sins unto death' injuring the community, still unrepented at life's end and unabsolved, could hardly be in this category. Moreover we are no judges of what is venial and what is not (*City of God* 21: 27).

At Rome Pelagius became well liked among the great Christian houses, especially the powerful Anicii, and enjoyed good relations with a presbyter Sixtus who became pope, 432–40. He was in rapport with Paulinus of Nola. In 417 Augustine and his colleague Alypius bishop of Thagaste had to write to Paulinus to warn him against Pelagius (Aug. *ep.* 186). A large burly figure ('weighed down with Scottish porridge', wrote Jerome), in Rome perhaps about 405 he wrote a commentary on the letters of the apostle Paul.[1] He had not been happy with his reading of a short book which Augustine addressed to Ambrose's successor at Milan (influential in his own conversion), the *Questions to Simplician*, nor with everything in the *Confessions*, e.g. the affirmation that in rewarding human merit, God crowns his own gifts (*Conf.* 9. 13. 24; 10. 39. 64), though the anti-Manichee polemic in the *Confessions* and especially the essay *On Free Will* would have been welcome to him. Writing as a presbyter at Hippo about 394, Augustine had expounded the epistle to the Romans to mean that divine election must be grounded on human deserts and that faith is a decision of the free will. But to Simplician, he had shifted: grace is prior to merit, unredeemed humanity is a 'mass of sin', and the punishment of the first sin in Adam is transmitted to the entire race. Hence the universality both of death and of desire for what is evil.

In his *Questions to Simplician* Augustine expounded Rom. 9: 17–18 on the hardening of Pharaoh's heart in a way that provoked Pelagius to write a tract with an alternative exegesis, that God treated Pharaoh as he deserved.

Pelagius regarded human sins as a disastrous following of Adam's example, not as something hereditary. He agreed with Augustine that sin is determined by habit which can be hard to break. But Pelagius felt certain that it must be possible to break a bad habit. Accordingly he wrote a book entitled 'On Nature', some fragments of which survive in the answer which Augustine wrote to it ('On nature and grace'). Pelagius begins from the proposition that in humanity there exists the possibility of free choice, and therefore by the constitution of human nature sin is not inevitable. If it were so, one could not censure a fault. People try to excuse their faults by the argument that it is only human to fail. They blame nature, not themselves. Pelagius does not claim that actual examples of sinless human beings can be seen to exist; all that he affirms is the possibility. Texts such as Matt. 11: 30 and 1 John 5: 3 justify the assertion that keeping the commandments is not very difficult. He grants that habit is the root of the matter; sin so weakens the will that the sinner commits more sins. But to say that our nature is responsible for sin is to accuse the Creator. Pelagius vigorously denies that he has nothing to say about the grace of God helping us not to sin. The endowment of free will is itself a gift of the

---

[1] The Commentary on the epistle to the Romans is translated with notes by Theodore de Bruyn (Oxford, 1993).

Creator. We have the possibility by nature not to fall into sin; yet the power to avoid sin requires divine grace, and it must be allowed that nature is vitiated by custom, example, and environment until baptism brings a mysterious uncaused gift of forgiveness and renewal.

Letters to Demetrias

Among the noble refugees who fled from Alaric's Goths to north Africa was the great lady Anicia Faltonia Proba, widow of Petronius Probus (consul 371). She brought her granddaughter Demetrias, who decided to take a vow of virginity when about to marry aged fourteen (a common age for marriage in Roman society, though often a fright for the girl: *City of God* 6: 9). In 413 Proba elicited letters of counsel for her niece from both Jerome (*ep.* 130) and Pelagius (PL 30. 15–45; 33. 1099). Pelagius' ardent letter, asserting the possibility of perfection since God would not have imposed impossible commands, alarmed Augustine, who therefore wrote some rather different unsolicited advice (*epp.* 150, 188). Demetrias' distinguished family was not impressed by the implication that their young nun, of whom they had reason to be proud, might be touched by heresy.

Rufinus the Syrian

At Rome Pelagius had sympathizers, among whom was Rufinus the Syrian (not Rufinus of Aquileia). This Rufinus had been in Jerome's monastery at Bethlehem, and therefore was much exercised about the speculations of Origen. He was author of an extant book *De fide* preserved in a sixth-century manuscript at St Petersburg.[2] To this work Augustine wrote an answer 'On the deserts of sinners and the forgiveness of sins and on the baptism of infants' (*de peccatorum meritis*). Rufinus the Syrian attacked the traducianist notion that there is inherited sinfulness incurring guilt and was horrified by the idea that 'Christ could destine unbaptized children to everlasting fire'. His principal target was Origen, in whom he could see no good whatever. The doctrine of the soul's pre-existence he rejected as heresy. The correct view he believed to be that each human soul is created by God as the embryo is conceived. He wrote at Rome in the time of Pope Anastasius, and later was treated (e.g by Marius Mercator in 429: *ACO* I v. 5. 38) as if he were the founder of Pelagianism. That he was not. But some of his opinions, not all, were in line with Pelagius' concerns. If he knew Augustine's book addressed to Simplician of Milan, which is very possible, he could not have felt in the least comfortable with it. He was certain that infants need baptism to be admitted to the

---

[2] Ed. M. W. Miller (Ann Arbor, 1967); also PL 48. 451–88.

kingdom of heaven, but also that, in the special case of infants, baptism meant not the remission of sins but regeneration and adoption. Rufinus understood the death resulting from the Fall to be the spiritual death of the soul; the death of the body he regarded as a natural biological event.

Is infant baptism for the remission of sins?

Augustine insisted that for infants baptism must mean remission of sin. In his *Confessions* he had described the egotism of helpless infants in their demand for attention. Baptism brings remission of both actual and original sin. Therefore there is 'condemnation but of the mildest kind' for unbaptized infants, even if their parents could not get them to a priest before death intervened. The root of sin is therefore sexual reproduction which in marriage is 'good use of an evil impulse' and is nevertheless an animal act of the 'old Adam'. (Augustine's low view of sex goes with a high view of marriage as the seed of society.) That infants are in this state is shown by their helplessness and ignorance to which the infant Christ must be an exception. None except Christ is without sin (later there would be an open question about Mary whom Pelagius affirmed to be sinless, but who was not in Augustine's view free of original sin because she died, *En. in Ps.* 34. 3). Yet sinlessness is possible by grace which gives not only free choice as a neutral capacity between good and evil but also the actual desire to do what is good and right because it makes this pleasurable. Augustine did not always achieve consistency in his language, since he could write of free will as a neutral possibility. He was confident that before the Fall Adam and Eve were immortal, and that physical death is universal in consequence of sin. It distressed him that so good and holy a man as Pelagius was reported to be could make a mistake in interpreting Romans 5. Augustine was unaware that the Latin translation of Rom. 5: 2 (*in quo*, taken to say that in Adam all died) was inaccurate.

On the spirit and the letter

This was soon followed by a more important tract 'On the spirit and the letter'. The moral law kills if the Spirit is absent. There is a psychological paradox, namely that what is forbidden becomes for that reason alone more desirable and pleasurable. Grace is necessary to overcome this morbidity. To do what is good and right we need not only the capacity of choice and wise authoritative teaching but also an inner psychological delight in the good which is the very nature of God. Hence Paul's saying that 'the love of God is shed abroad in our hearts by the Holy Spirit given to us'. Without that love and the delight in righteousness, our efforts must fail for lack of the emotional feelings required (*Sp. litt.* 5). The tract vigorously denies that

Augustine abolishes freedom of the will. Plotinus (6. 8. 7. 1) had taught him that freedom is the consequent, not the prior condition of virtuous action, and to attain the good is to maximize choices. Nevertheless though justification is antecedent to doing good works, it is false to suppose that our human will plays no part in our justification. The will co-operates with God's doing. It is wrong to take Paul to mean that Judaism is a religion of works, whereas Christianity is of faith. The law is right and good. But it establishes human frailty and need of grace, which sets the will free to do good. The tract *On the spirit and the letter* broke new ground. It was highly influential later, e.g. on Adam of St Victor's hymns in the twelfth century or on Martin Luther in the famous 1545 preface to his Latin works.

Caelestius

Beside Rufinus the Syrian Pelagius had a more vocal sympathizer named Caelestius, a member of an aristocratic family who had trained as an advocate. Augustine found him 'more outspoken' than Pelagius, and at Carthage his arguments made an impression. But in 412 before a council of bishops he was suddenly accused of heresy by Paulinus deacon of Milan and future biographer of Ambrose, who had come to consult Augustine. He accused Caelestius on seven charges of teaching (1) that Adam was mortal by creation and would have died even if he had not fallen; (2) Adam's sin injured himself, not his entire posterity; (3) newborn infants are as innocent as Adam before the Fall; (4) even unbaptized infants receive eternal life; (5) just as all humanity will not rise again because of Christ's resurrection, so Adam's Fall did not bring death upon the entire race; (6) keeping either the Law or the Gospel can qualify for heaven; (7) before Christ there were some without sin. Caelestius affirmed that infants ought to be baptized and need redemption since from birth they are capable of sin. They are baptized in view of what is the probable future. Caelestius was declared excommunicate by the bishops. He decided not to appeal to the see of Rome and sailed to Ephesus. He was later to return to Rome in 418 when Pope Zosimus was giving a sympathetic ear to Pelagius and his friends. The main source for Caelestius was to be a Latin layman, Marius Mercator, who about 429 at a monastery in Thrace compiled a Memorandum (*commonitorium*) on Pelagianism and Nestorianism (PL 48; *ACO* I v. 5–70). Both in Sicily and in north Africa the questions caused a continuing buzz of debate.

Pelagius and Orosius in the Holy Land

From north Africa Pelagius had travelled to the Holy Land, and as late as 413 Augustine wrote him a courteous letter. A friendly personal reference also came in 415 in Augustine's work 'On nature and grace' (71), where Augustine appealed to the authority of Ambrose for a defence of his position. About this time he persuaded Paulinus, deacon of Milan, to write a Life of Ambrose. Pelagius had also appealed to Ambrose but with less reason. Early in 415 a presbyter from Spain named Orosius, a refugee from the invading barbarians, arrived at Hippo to consult Augustine about Priscillianist and Origenist views. On Origen Augustine thought that he should go and see Jerome, and entrusted him with letters (*epp.* 166–7) telling Jerome about the Pelagian controversy. These moved the old monk of Bethlehem to write his *Dialogue against the Pelagians*, some said in rivalry. In Jerusalem Orosius met both Pelagius and Bishop John who had heard of the western controversy and asked for information. Communication through an incompetent interpreter did not facilitate comprehension. Bishop John understood Orosius to hold that even with divine help human beings could not live without sin. Orosius had to write an Apology in his defence. He had abruptly told Bishop John that the Pelagian controversy was above the heads of him and his bishops, and should be referred to Pope Innocent. Orosius returned to the west with newly discovered relics of St Stephen, enshrined in north Africa and Menorca to be a focus for healings.

Synod of Diospolis

The next western visitors to Jerusalem were not more successful. Two Gallic bishops, Heros of Arles and Lazarus of Aix, had owed their position to a shortlived usurper from Britain named Constantine (407–11) and had unwisely supported him when a force from Honorius brought his life to an end. They had been violently deposed. They sought refuge in the Holy Land where the Pelagian question was a lively subject of discussion. They studied the subject and drew up a formal accusation of heresy submitted to the metropolitan of Palestine, Eulogius of Caesarea. He called a synod at Diospolis (Lydda) in mid-December 415. Neither of Pelagius' accusers appeared. Pelagius had little trouble in answering a list of ten charges, and dismissed a question about the possibility of a sinless life by saying the propositions were foolish rather than heretical. He denied ever having said that anyone had lived wholly without sin, disowned any responsibility for Caelestius' statements, and assured the council that divine grace was a necessary help to human moral effort. Indeed he anathematized anything and everything alien to the catholic Church. He was accordingly recognized as being in catholic communion. Among Pelagius' sympathizers in Italy it was rumoured that he had condemned his own teaching but, even if he had done so, his followers would still stand firm (Aug. *ep.* 186. 29).

Pelagius exulted in the synod's acquittal, and composed four books

On Free Will of which Augustine has preserved a few citations. For Augustine the central question was whether the gift of divine grace is the power which inspires the will to cooperate or whether it is a reward for the merit of an initial unprompted resolution. Pelagius used language perhaps suggesting the latter. Augustine concluded that at Diospolis Pelagius had been disingenuous, using ambivalent language.

Two African synods. Pope Innocent I

In 416 two African synods met at Mileu and Carthage, denounced Pelagius, and asked Pope Innocent to confirm their condemnation especially of two propositions: that prayer for God's help against sin is needless, and that baptismal grace is not required for infants to attain eternal life. Answers from Rome came in February 417. Innocent expressed pleasure that the council of Carthage had recognized their need to refer to the apostolic see of St Peter from whom the entire authority of the episcopate was derived. The propositions must be condemned unless repudiated. He observed that Augustine's account of grace corresponded to that of one whose conversion was like that described in his *Confessions* (Aug. *ep.* 181. 7). To the council of Mileu Innocent sent a similar reply, glad that they showed awareness of his practice in sending rescripts from the apostolic fount to petitioners in all provinces, since all arguments about the faith should be referred exclusively to St Peter. Pelagius and Caelestius should be restored to communion if they repudiated the two propositions. Since the propositions entirely misrepresented them, they would find that simple to do. In a sermon Augustine rejoiced: two African councils had upheld his view, and now the Roman see had sent 'rescripts'. 'Innocent had no alternative' (*c. Jul.* 1. 4. 13). In juridical terms 'the case is concluded' (*causa finita est*), language which he had also used after the verdict against the Donatists at the Carthage conference of 411. He knew, however, that Pelagianism was far from dead.

Pope Zosimus

On 12 March 417 Innocent died. He was succeeded by Zosimus, said to be a Greek by the sixth-century *Liber Pontificalis*. He admired what Innocent had affirmed regarding Roman authority. Some of his problems turned out to be caused by the failure of this message to be fully taken on board by bishops in all provinces. He shared the experience of his predecessor Innocent in dealing with John Chrysostom that the louder he proclaimed his Petrine authority, the less notice was taken of what he was saying. The character which he brought to the Pelagian affair was given a preview in his dealings with southern Gaul.

Zosimus and Patroclus of Arles

In Gaul the enhancement of the city of Arles by becoming the seat of the Gallic prefecture made the bishop aspire to greater authority. Ausonius thought Arles a city second only to Trier. Archaeological finds have underlined the importance of the church there. Patroclus was bishop of Arles from 412 to his assassination in 426. He had been present in Rome at Zosimus' consecration, perhaps influential at the election, and they were intimate friends. Both owed their positions to the favour of the army commander Constantius (*PLRE* ii. 321–4),[3] who had restored Honorius' writ in Arles by eliminating the usurper Constantine. Constantius had roughly deposed bishop Heros of Arles, who offended by attempting to save Constantine's life. He not only defeated Goths but married Galla Placidia, putting himself on the path to imperial power. As Heros was an admirer of Augustine, it was likely that Patroclus would not be, and therefore that his view might influence Zosimus. In a Gaul that had lately been politically independent of Honorius, it would have appeared to Zosimus that papal authority there needed an active representative to be both symbol and instrument of Rome's ecclesiastical power. With Constantius' support that would be facilitated.

However, Patroclus' ambitions alarmed episcopal neighbours. The bishop of Narbonne soon applied successfully to Innocent to confirm that as metropolitan of the province he had responsibility for ordaining bishops there. Perhaps Patroclus' presence in Rome at the very time of Innocent's death was an endeavour to alter that confirmation. Arles had become politically important. But Marseille was the bridgehead from which the Christian mission had spread and which was felt to be the mother church. On 22 March 417 Zosimus began his tenure of office by an immediate letter to the bishops of Gaul and the Seven Provinces (i.e. Viennensis, Aquitania I and II, Novempopulana, Narbonensis I and II, and Alpes Maritimae), informing them of a decision by the Apostolic See that any bishop or cleric in any grade travelling to Rome or anywhere else outside his province must have a letter of recommendation (technically called *formata*) from Patroclus bishop of Arles; this decision had been necessary because of many pretenders who received a veneration that was unwarranted. Further, 'we have given order' that the metropolitan bishop of Arles is to ordain bishops in the provinces of Vienne and Narbonne I and II, which Zosimus claimed to be in accord with old tradition. Anyone otherwise consecrated to be bishop will find himself unrecognized. One ground for giving this privilege to Arles Zosimus stated to be the splendid personal qualities of Patroclus, a formula which may have

---

[3] See also W. Lütkenhaus, *Constantius III: Studien zu seiner Tätigkeit und Stellung im Westreich 411–421* (Diss. Bonn., 1998).

been intended to placate opposition by the (false) implication that it was not necessarily a permanent arrangement. An imperial edict was obtained from Honorius that the bishops of the named provinces should hold an annual synod at Arles (Zosimus, *ep.* 13, ed. Coustant).

This was a snub to Marseille, whose jurisdiction had been reaffirmed at a council in Turin perhaps in 398. Zosimus laid down that all bishops were to be content with the customary parishes; the bishop of Arles as successor of St Trophimus (legendary disciple of St Peter who sent him to evangelize Gaul: *PL* 54. 880 B) is justified in claiming two places very close to Marseille, Citharista (Ceyreste) and Gargarius (Saint-Jean-de-Garguier). Both happened to lie in the civil region once administered from Arles, Marseille being originally confined to a small area. But in 417 Marseille had a much-respected bishop Proculus who naturally assumed that these nearby parishes should continue to be his responsibility, as they later became. He ignored Zosimus' command and answered the pretensions of Arles by consecrating bishops for the two places in dispute. Another letter from Zosimus to a Bishop Remigius (see unnamed) supported Remigius in claiming parishes cared for by Proculus.[4] Proculus wholly disregarded Zosimus' orders.

Zosimus met strong opposition. The bishops of Vienne and Narbonne protested that their metropolitan rights were wrongly challenged. Proculus of Marseille continued with ordinations as before, and naturally was represented by Patroclus as grossly insulting the Apostolic See. Zosimus declared him deposed, wrote to the clergy and people of Marseille, and instructed Patroclus to ordain a replacement. If he attempted to do so, which is uncertain, we may be sure there would have been a local riot.

The bishop of Narbonne, Hilary, also stood up for his traditional rights. He claimed the support not only of the Nicene canon entrusting the ordination of provincial bishops to metropolitans, but also of a letter from Innocent I. On 26 September 417 Zosimus accused Hilary of dishonesty in persuading Innocent to confirm rights which were surely not traditional. He insisted on absolute obedience, and told Hilary that no bishop ordained by him would be recognized by Rome. When in 421, after Zosimus' death, Patroclus ordained a bishop in Narbonensis, the clergy and people sent a protest to the then Pope Boniface I, who rebuked Patroclus and reasserted the system of the fourth Nicene canon (*ep.* 12, PL 20. 772–4).[5] Boniface's successor Celestine adopted the same line in 428, and this decision was followed by Leo about 441, who fought a verbal battle with the then bishop of Arles, another Hilary.

---

[4] Text in Duchesne, *Fastes épiscopaux de l'ancienne Gaule*, 2nd edn. (Paris, 1907), i. 101–2 or *PLS* i. 797; not in PL 20 or Coustant.

[5] Pope Boniface also received a protest from the clergy and people of Valence in the province of Vienne that their bishop Maximus was an ex-Manichee (Priscillianist?) unworthy of the office. So Patroclus may also have consecrated him.

Zosimus and north Africa

The autocratic insensitivity shown by Zosimus in dealing with southern Gaul reappeared in his correspondence with north Africa on the subject of Pelagius and Caelestius. The African bishops had gladly hailed Innocent I's confirmation of their synodical decisions. That was their understanding of Petrine authority. But they would have less exalted opinions of papal decisions when Zosimus spectacularly failed to concur with their judgement.

Caelestius had been accepted and ordained priest in the east, but when he tried to settle at Constantinople Bishop Atticus would not have him, perhaps lest the continuing stand-off with Rome over John Chrysostom, which he wanted to end, were to be exacerbated. The accession of Pope Zosimos led Caelestius to return to Rome and to submit a statement of his faith, declaring himself ready both to accept Innocent's judgement and to submit without reserve to any correction now required of him by the successor of St Peter. He granted that infants need to be baptized for the remission of sins according to the rule of the universal Church and the gospel (John 3: 5), but opposed the transmission of sin by heredity. Zosimus was impressed by his confession of faith and by his docile submissiveness to Roman authority. Pelagius also submitted a protestation to Zosimus that he had been much misrepresented. He assented to Innocent's two stipulations. Only he would not concede that human sin is wholly unavoidable, a symptom of corrupt nature. He was able to append a commendation from Praylios, John's successor as bishop of Jerusalem. After a hearing of Caelestius in the church of St Clement Zosimus was supported by his Roman clergy (he did not act alone in this case) in a ruling that Pelagius and Caelestius were within the bounds of orthodoxy, and in September 417 he wrote to all African bishops implying that they had been hasty in their condemnation.

The Africans thought that if anyone was being hasty it was the Pope. They replied in January 418 that they adhered to the decision of Innocent. In short they were going to ignore Zosimus and his virtual acquittal of Augustine's critics. In March an alarmed Zosimus assured them that he had always intended to consult them and as yet had made no final verdict. He thought the Africans had dealt with a delicate problem too fast, and that a considered reflection by the whole Church was appropriate. It seemed self-evident that whether or not faith was always a divine initiative, there was a human decision to be made. The impatient Africans, for whom the issue was not an open question or a matter of opinion on which disagreement should be tolerated, decided to mobilize the court at Ravenna. There Alypius bishop of Thagaste, a trained lawyer who knew his way round the corridors of power, won support—by vast bribery, it was said; and since little was achieved at the imperial court without large backhanders to high officers of state, the story is probably in principle correct. On 30 April Honorius issued from Ravenna a rescript ordering the expulsion of Pelagius and Caelestius from Rome and all followers to be exiled also. On 1 May the African bishops in synod formally insisted that biological death is a consequence of the Fall, that unbaptized babies cannot be saved, and that grace is more than help to make obedience easier.

Zosimus' Tractoria

Zosimus could not defy the emperor. He yielded to the Africans and issued a statement entitled 'Tractoria', an authoritative Encyclical (PL 20. 693–5) of which surprisingly little survives through a tiny handful of quotations in Augustine, in Prosper of Aquitaine (who frankly thought it a necessary act to rectify an 'error by the sacrosanct see of blessed Peter', PL 51. 228 A), and in Pope Celestine I (422–32). Its effect is described in Marius Mercator (*ACO* I v. 68). So little of this major letter survives that perhaps it contained sarcasms uncomfortable for the Africans and could only be cited selectively. It is hard to suppose the Pope failed to reconcile his past and present verdicts. In this document Zosimus explicitly and pointedly appropriated as his own judgement several canons of the African synod of May 418. It was addressed to all bishops (Aug. *ep.* 190). Bishops at least in Italy were required by the emperor to sign their assent, which entailed deposition and exile for a bishop such as Julian of Eclanum who strongly sympathized with Pelagius. Most of Julian's allies in the fight yielded. Praylios of Jerusalem was impelled by Theodotus bishop of Antioch, a see now in restored communion with Rome, to withdraw his support for Pelagius, who was forbidden to visit the holy places but not otherwise disciplined (*ACO* I v. 69. 3–5). Cyril of Alexandria, however, who had not yet made any move to restore John Chrysostom's name to the diptychs, caused some upset in Italy by long delay in taking action (Avell. 49). He may already have been receiving representations from Carthage about canons invoked by Zosimus which lacked Nicene authority. Yet among Greek divines none would have a closer affinity with Augustine.

Zosimus' *Tractoria* was surrendering much of his own discretion in face of the powerful and dominant Africans. But it was dangerous for a bishop of Rome to find himself widely accused of comforting heretics and to be risking the good will of Ravenna. Not unnaturally Zosimus was bound to feel no little resentment and to ask himself how he could impose his authority on the too independent African bishops who had been dictating to him with such lack of docility.

Late during the summer of 418 a Bishop Numunianus in the African province of Byzacena got into financial difficulty with tax authorities. The provincial bishops held a synod to which the lay tax officers were admitted.

The bishop in trouble wrote to Zosimus, who on 16 November addressed a sharply worded rebuke to the provincial bishops who had defied canon law by admitting laity to sit with them in judgement. The Pope was not impressed by African indifference to proper procedure.

Apiarius: a presbyter's appeal to Rome

Probably a little earlier a stormier row broke out over a presbyter named Apiarius of the diocese of Sicca Veneria in Proconsular Africa. His bishop Urbanus had excommunicated him for misdemeanours (glossed over in the jejune records but probably sexual). Bishop Urbanus had been a monk at Hippo and was intimate with Augustine. Apiarius thought himself unfairly treated, and appealed to Pope Zosimus stating his case. Zosimus decided that his case was good, and that Bishop Urbanus must correct his mistake under pain of excommunication. A delegation from Italy led by Faustinus bishop of Potentina in Picenum would go to Africa fortified by a *commonitorium* in which, among other things, a presbyter's appeal to the Roman see was justified by mentioning canons on Rome's appellate jurisdiction. The African bishops in short would have to acknowledge the right of appeal to Rome, even by a presbyter over the head of his bishop. Apparently it did not emerge until after Zosimus' death (26 December 418) that the unlucky Pope had in mind the canons of Western Serdica which he (and no doubt his chancery) supposed to have not Serdican but Nicene authority because they were transcribed without break after those of Nicaea in the Roman archives.

In Rome itself Pope Zosimus had contemporary critics, notably a group of rebellious presbyters. He complained that 'contrary to the canons' they had submitted a complaint against him to the court at Ravenna, of which he had been informed by a report from a presbyter Archidamus residing there. He wrote to his clergy at Ravenna to warn them that the rebels were excommunicate and under anathema by the holy and apostolic Church (*ep.* 14, 3 October 418). The substance of the grievance is not specified.

Sympathy for Zosimus can be based on a letter to Honorius from the city prefect Symmachus (29 December 418, Avell. 14), recording that his death had long been preceded by bouts of grave illness and that rumours of his dying had been frequent before the final demise. He succumbed to the temptation to use plausible appellants to Rome as levers for asserting the authority of his see in a time when that was indeed respected but not understood to be absolute.

Since Damasus there was a growing conviction in successive popes that they were called to be managers governing the entire Church with a centralized control over different departments, with local bishops acting as provincial governors did for the emperor, implementing his edicts in their separate regions. The conciliar African and Gallic bishops (and those in northern Italy) valued the Petrine primacy but understood its function to be that of seeing that rules made by church councils, in short canon law, were observed and enforced by pastors responsible for their own way of conducting the common enterprise.

Papal schism. Popes Boniface and Celestine

Zosimus' death was followed by schism at Rome and delays. The archdeacon Eulalius was ordained in the Lateran basilica by a doddery old bishop of Ostia, who by long custom was principal consecrator for bishops of Rome. A rival consecration chose the senior presbyter Boniface, who had represented Innocent I at Constantinople, in the basilica of Marcellus, moving from there to St Peter's. At first the city prefect supported Eulalius. At Epiphany Eulalius celebrated in St Peter's, Boniface at St Paul's. On Honorius' instruction Boniface was expelled, his supporters sending a protest to Ravenna. After a hopeless meeting at Ravenna, Honorius called a council at Spoleto with Gallic and African bishops to decide what should be done. On 15 March Honorius banned both Eulalius and Boniface from Rome. Meanwhile about seventy Roman presbyters supported Boniface, who also received strong backing from Galla Placidia (Avell. 25, 27–8), while the deacons and a handful of presbyters supported Eulalius, and the bishop of Spoleto took care of the Easter baptisms at Rome. There were riots as Eulalius destroyed his own cause by defying Honorius and the bishop of Spoleto, occupying the Lateran palace with the acquiescence of the city prefect and claiming himself to preside at Easter. The prefect blamed Boniface for the disorders. But the irate and offended Honorius decided for Boniface (Avell. 31. 2; 33. 3). Almost all documents of the schism are in the Avellana collection (CSEL 35).

Surprisingly there is no evidence that argument for or against Pelagius was an issue in the split, but Boniface's handling of the Pelagians was less abrasive than some of the Africans might have liked. He was Pope for the years 418–22 and was then succeeded by Celestine. Both were as zealous for papal authority as Zosimus had been. Boniface expressly affirmed that the judgement of the Apostolic See was not open to debate (*ep.* 15. 5). Boniface took it for granted that a council of bishops in southern Gaul would have Patroclus of Arles as presiding bishop. Boniface sought to use Rufus bishop of Thessalonica as his deputy to resist the infiltration of the jurisdiction of Constantinople into Illyricum, insisting (without naming Constantinople) that by canon law the second and third sees after Rome were Alexandria and Antioch (*ep.* 15. 5), as Damasus had said. Boniface prompted Honorius to check encouragement given to the see of Constantinople by Theodosius II (CTh 16. 2. 45 of July 421 on Illyricum where 'Constantinople has the privileges of old Rome'). Rome had the principal bishop (*principium sacerdo-tum*: *ep.* 10). He was alarmed to hear of some eastern bishops indifferent to communion with blessed Peter, delighted when on another occasion he received a delegation of eastern bishops grieving at the breach and asking for 'peace' (*ep.* 14. 2; 15. 6). He found in the archives that Theodosius I had sent an embassy of court officials and bishops asking Damasus or Siricius to send a letter of communion to Nektarios of Constantinople to strengthen him in his contested position againt Arians (*ep.* 15. 6). That was a recognition of Roman authority over the see of Constantinople.

Serdican canons cited as Nicene

The case of Apiarius dragged on from Zosimus to Boniface and then Celestine. A synod at Carthage on 1 May 418 had modified the procedure for appeals, allowing not only bishops but inferior clergy to complain to an African council or their provincial primate, but anyone appealing abroad across the sea would be held excommunicate. The last clause suggests that Apiarius' appeal to Rome was already an issue but that the bishops were con-ceding that their appeals legislation in canon law needed the amendment agreed. The canons cited by Zosimus as Nicene were not in the African archives under that title. At a great council at Carthage on 25 May 419 African copies of the Nicene acts were produced, and in the presence of Faustinus' delegation from Italy the bishops affirmed their unreserved assent to the Nicene decisions. Alypius of Thagaste remarked that the Greek copies of the Nicene acts did not contain these things. The new Pope Boniface should be invited to check his records, and letters should be sent to Constantinople, which would have the authoritative original text, Antioch, and Alexandria asking for their copies. The debate produced a careful record of the corpus of African canons and of the negotiation with the papacy.[6]

The Roman chancery may have been unimpressed by the scepticism of Carthage and the support from the Greek churches. It was an ingrained preju-dice at Rome that Greeks were expert at falsifying records. This opinion was expressed later in lapidary terms by Pope Gregory the Great, who was sure that the Greeks had falsified the Acts of the council of Chalcedon: 'The Roman codices are more reliable than the Greek; we have no falsifications' (*Reg.* 6. 14). The minor Roman modification of the sixth Nicene canon shows that this last clause was an exaggeration. That the episode of 419 did not affect scribes in the Roman chancery could be deduced from a group of early manuscripts from the sixth century to the ninth (listed by Turner,

---

[6] Ed. C. Munier (CCSL 149; Turnhout, 1974); also *EOMIA* i. 561–624.

EOMIA i. 443) where the Nicene and Serdican canons in Latin are run together without any break.

The council of Carthage wrote to Boniface 'appointed bishop by God' to say that after some disagreement consensus had been reached; that Apiarius, who had brought scandal not only on Sicca Veneria but on the whole church of Africa, apologized for his faults and was readmitted to communion; that Urbanus his bishop had corrected whatever was felt to be amiss; that for the future Apiarius be moved to another church at his own request. Pending the arrival of Greek copies the African council accepted the two canons of Serdica on the assumption that these stood in the authentic record of the acts of Nicaea. However, the bishops felt confident that under Boniface they would not be treated with insolence or be asked to endure the unendurable. Although they had consulted many codices, they had not found the canons cited by Zosimus in them, either in Latin or in Greek. Since the Greeks would have the original text, Boniface is asked to write himself to the bishops of Antioch, Alexandria, and Constantinople. Until the answer comes, the Africans will loyally observe the canons cited in the *commonitorium* of Faustinus. Greater courtesy, when the Africans obviously thought the canons not Nicene, can hardly be imagined. The council called itself 'humilitas nostra'.

The Africans were in any event aware that, under the canons cited, Apiarius would have no right to appeal to Rome. They did not conceal their irritation that Zosimus had not himself kept to the letter of the canons he was citing. They also found the legate Faustinus unbearably high-handed and haughty, but abstained from expressing their anger on this point. On 6 November they sent Boniface the Nicene acts from Constantinople and Alexandria.

A later council wrote to Boniface's successor Pope Celestine saying that Apiarius had again suffered excommunication in his new post at Thabraca, had appealed to Rome once again, and had been reinstated. Faustinus was once more sent to Africa to see that the Pope's wishes were implemented. After insulting the council in the interest of papal authority which he embodied, he discovered that Apiarius' delinquencies and 'filthy passions' were of such offensiveness as to make reinstatement absurd and impossible. The African bishops concluded by begging the Pope not to be too ready to listen to malcontents from Africa and to adhere to the canons of Nicaea (by which bishops were forbidden to admit inferior clergy and laity excommunicated by other bishops). It had caused astonishment that both Boniface and Celestine had upheld the decision of Zosimus in face of appalled consternation in the African churches which the Popes were so obviously anxious to control. The Africans were particularly surprised that anyone should think the authority of 'one individual whoever he may be' superior to that of a large episcopal council. They did not recognize the papal custom of sending a curial legate from the Pope's side (*a latere*) with power to order everyone about, and concluded a vehement letter with an irate hope that they would never again have to endure Faustinus.

The African assumption was that the bishop of Rome had authority to enforce conciliar canons. They also took it for granted that the canons he would enforce were, please, to be as authentic as Rome thought they were. The African Catholics were profoundly conscious, in face of the Donatists, of the importance to them of communion with Rome and the churches north of the Mediterranean. They had deep respect for St Peter's see, and felt distress when, apparently in the interest of asserting Roman autocracy, serious mistakes were made. Their thinking about the nature of the Church was conciliar, and this would appear again in the following century when the African bishop Facundus of Hermiane protested against Pope Vigilius' condemnation of the 'Three Chapters' in defiance of the general mind of Latin bishops and to the prejudice of the authority of the council of Chalcedon. At a time when the Roman empire in the west was threatened with serious disintegration it may well have been apparent to the bishops of Rome that only they had the tradition of authority to provide order necessary in church and society.

During these minor conflicts which, however, raised large questions of principle, the Pelagian controversy had taken a fresh turn. Augustine's doctrine of grace was meeting thoughtful and intelligent criticism, the effect of which was to drive him to extremes.

Imperial changes

On 27 August, 423 Honorius died. At Constantinople his sister Galla Placidia, with her children by Constantius Honoria and Valentinian, decided that her hour had come; she would claim the western empire for her little son Valentinian aged four. That would reassert the Theodosian dynasty. A senior civil servant named John had assumed the purple at Rome on 20 November and had army support. Galla Placidia was able to ensure that he received no recognition in the east, and he upset the churches by suspending privileges of the clergy such as exemption from prosecution in secular courts (like civil servants). He also appeared sympathetic to those who sympathized with the Pelagian cause (Const. Sirmond. 6). Aspar, an army general, was sent with a force to eliminate him at Ravenna in 425.

Galla Placidia talked Theodosius II out of attempting to be the one emperor of both east and west, and took possession of the palace at Ravenna. Her son was declared Valentinian III. One of the first acts was to restore ecclesiastical courts for cases involving clergy and to direct the praetorian prefect at Arles to support Patroclus of Arles in harassing Gallic supporters of Pelagius and Celestius. One prominent sympathizer with moderate Pelagianism was Sulpicius Severus of Aquitaine, popular biographer of St Martin of Tours. The same law (July 425) decreed banishment from all cities for Manichees and astrologers, and deprived Jews and pagans of the right to sue in court or to be employed in the imperial service.

47

JULIAN OF ECLANUM: AUGUSTINE'S CRITICS IN GAUL AND NORTH AFRICA

Bishop Julian of Eclanum[1], a little town between Naples and Benevento, now Mirabella, was the son of Memorius, a south Italian bishop of good education. A correspondent of Augustine, Memorius once obtained from a reluctant Augustine (*ep.* 101. 4) the sixth and last book of his treatise *On Music* (of which the first five books are mainly about metre) for his son Julian to study. Such a textbook in the liberal arts seemed to its author trivial. Probably Julian was sent to learn the liberal arts at Rome and if so would have been studying there when Pelagius was acquiring a following in the city. Julian married the daughter of the bishop of Beneventum and Paulinus of Nola wrote a wedding poem for the occasion, which was something of a pastoral idyll. The marriage was clearly a success; but either before long he was widowed or the couple decided to live ascetic lives in separation. His wife disappears from the story. Augustine soon spoke of Julian as vowed to celibacy. He may have accompanied Pelagius to Africa. He was consecrated bishop of Eclanum by either Innocent I about 416 or (perhaps more probable) Zosimus in the following year. His first contribution to the debate about the doctrine of grace was in two (lost) letters to Pope Zosimus.

The Pope's encyclical *Tractoria* had delighted devoted Augustinians. Prosper of Aquitaine looked back on it as Zosimus' 'decapitation of the impious with St Peter's sword' (PL 51. 271 A). Conversely it caused Julian acute pain. In north Italy there were sympathizers with his cause. He and eighteen other Italian bishops felt unable to sign the *Tractoria* when it was circulated for assent; he wrote to Zosimus to explain his position and later to Pope Boniface. He addressed to a fellow bishop Turbantius a work of which Augustine preserves numerous citations. He made no secret of his dislike of Augustine's opinions on marriage and sexual reproduction, thereby leading Augustine in 419–21 to write two books 'On Marriage and Concupiscence', with a positive valuation (unlike Jerome's tract against Jovinian).

---

[1] See *RAC* Lieferung 149/150 (1999) art. Julianus IV by M. Lamberigts, and his papers on Pelagius in *Revue d'histoire ecclésiastique* 95/3 (2000) 97–111 and on Julian of Eclanum in *Augustinianum*, 42 (1992) 311–30.

The work was dedicated to an influential soldier, Count Valerius at the court in Ravenna (PLRE ii. 1143–4). Valerius had already been lobbied by Julian. The dedication shows Augustine aware that to defend himself in controversy he still needed friends in high places. Valerius was a zealous member of the Church; Augustine flatteringly called him a model of conjugal chastity and addressed him formally and conventionally as 'your sublimity' (*ep.* 200), but had not actually met him as Julian had. It is instructive that a married layman was being appealed to by both sides. The two main disputants, however, were not sexually inexperienced. Moreover both accepted celibacy as appropriate for bishops and clergy.

The expulsion of the Pelagians led to a demand for a general council of east and west. Augustine sharply rejected the notion, correctly observing that very few questions of essential doctrine have needed to come to a general council for determination (*c. du. epp. Pelag.* 4. 34).

After Julian's militant rejection of Zosimus' *Tractoria* led to his deposition and exile from Italy, he was not thereby silenced. His fellow bishops submitted. Julian was made of sterner stuff. He candidly declared that the Roman clergy had been inconsistent, had compromised the truth, and had sanctioned a crypto-Manichaeism surviving in Augustine as a hangover from his early years in that sect. Wanderings eventually took him to the east where, for a time, he was hospitably received by Theodore bishop of Mopsuestia in Cilicia. His reception in the east was made impermanent by the distribution there of Zosimus' *Tractoria*. Atticus of Constantinople was not going to allow the Pelagian problem, which few in the east understood, to sour already prickly relations with the west. Julian was confident that eastern theologians represented a more sympathetic tradition than those in the west, from whom, to vindicate his orthodoxy, Augustine had numerous quotations defending original sin, including Ambrose and the learned Jerome scorned by Julian as a mere presbyter. In Julian's view Latin theologians were less well educated and understood little or nothing of logic, a subject he had specially studied himself in Aristotle's *Categories* (*c. Jul.* 2. 37). Logic was a discipline in which Augustine was far from ignorant. But Julian desired an estimate of humanity more appreciative of humane values and of the goodness of the Creator.

In opposing Augustine Julian confessed to feeling like David encountering Goliath (Aug. *c. Jul.* 3. 4). He was angered by the way in which allies of Pelagius had been treated by Zosimus, and suggested that the papal schism of 419 was a divine judgement for the injustice and tergiversation (6. 38). After Pelagius and Celestius had yielded to authority Julian felt himself to be called to stand alone in defence of the truth of reason and the goodness of God (2. 36). He and his allies were a minority; but then so were the orthodox bishops at the council of Ariminum in 359 (*Op. impf.* 1. 75). Augustine's doctrines seemed to Julian like yet another Punic war against Italian life and culture. He felt sure that Augustine's black doctrine of human nature was not the native air of the Italian churches where a number of the bishops were now well educated men of good family who valued a humanist country-house culture, and therefore was unimpressed when Augustine appealed to church tradition and to the convictions of the majority of believers. Julian was appealing to reason and the logic of Aristotle. What reason rejects, authority cannot be invoked to defend (Aug. *Op. impf.* 1. 3 ff.; 2. 6).

Augustine's language disturbed Julian deeply. The theme of the overwhelming power of predestined grace left no real room for human free will; in spite of his disavowals Augustine seemed a determinist. Addressing Simplician of Milan in 397 Augustine grasped the nettle and affirmed that divine predestination is based on no prior conditions such as foreseen merits, as he had once thought himself, and must mean that souls not predestinate are reprobate. Their damnation is what all deserve, but God saves a substantial minority of humanity by an act of pure grace, and the justice of his decision cannot be put in question. The notion of original sin as a 'contagion' transmitted from Adam through the reproductive process necessarily meant that the soul is physically derived from the parental sperm, a doctrine not recognized as orthodox and akin to Manichaeism. To prove this affinity Julian cited a letter from Mani to a lady Menoch. Augustine did not know it and doubted authenticity. The letter teaches that sexual desire is the root of all evil.[2]

Julian was sure that the sexual impulse was implanted by the Creator, and cannot be evil in itself; without it the human race would have died out. Jesus himself possessed male genital organs perfectly controlled (*Op. impf.* 4. 54). Julian could quote Cicero (*De natura deorum* 2. 136–7) on the beauty of the human body. What the Creator had made beautiful and a source of delight could not be reckoned a devilish snare. He was appalled by Augustine's declaration that the sexual drive is evil, corrupt in its very nature, though free of sin within marriage in which context it is 'forgiven' (*Nupt.* 1. 16). Augustine was applying to sexual desire the doctrine found in Plotinus' discussion of the problem of evil, namely that God can make use of evil things for good ends. Julian forced Augustine to concede the more nuanced proposition that sexual desire is not sin, though the act is sinful when contrary to God's law. Nevertheless, Augustine had taken from Porphyry the theme that the inability of the human will to control genital excitement, whether to arouse or to quench, was a kind of punishment (e.g. *c. Jul.* 5. 19; *ep.* 184. 3; *Nupt.* 2. 18). Augustine was particularly emphatic about the common phenomenon of impotence as a demonstration of the flawed nature of the will. Before the Fall Adam could control the urge by reason and will, an opinion mocked by Julian (*c. Jul.* 5. 29). Since the Fall the act has become one of which we feel

---

[2] M. Stein, *Manichaica Latina*, i. (Opladen, 1998).

shame; and we think loins should be covered (*Grat. Chr.* 2. 41). Taboo words are part of the evidence of corruption and distortion, when all the same phenomena can be described by medical writers in strictly clinical terms. If usage were to make words now taboo acceptable in polite society, the consequence would only be the invention of a new 'rude' vocabulary. What is being expressed is an attitude of mind.

Outside the context of the debate about original sin, Augustine's letters, sermons, and other writings rarely discuss problems of sexuality, an exception being the fourteenth book of the *City of God*.

The Neoplatonic tradition was in general negative towards sexuality. In Marinus' *Life of Proclus* it is stated more than once (17 and 20) that he thought it good to be celibate. Proclus was sure that disordered matter pulls the soul down (*in Tim.* iii. 325 Diehl); therefore the body and its appetites are at the root of evil. Similarly Ammianus (25. 4. 2) thought it a notable virtue in the emperor Julian that after his wife died he had no sex life. Platonism was a factor in the making of Augustine's mind. But more important than all was the influence of Cicero's *Hortensius*, deploring lack of sexual restraint and recommending frugal austerity as the way of happiness.

In agreement with Plato and the Stoic moralists, Augustine's ideal marriage was one in which libido was given rein exclusively for procreation, though he allowed it to be a venial fault if married couples had conjugal relations without such intention e.g. because they loved and delighted in one another, or if, as Epicurus recommended (cited *c. Jul.* 5. 29), celibates lingered with pleasure on thoughts of sexual experience which they were not going to have (*c. Jul.* 2. 33). During Lent as a time of prayer all sexual relations should be avoided (*Sermo* 205. 2; 210. 9). A perfect Christian marriage would have as little sex in it as that of Mary and Joseph (*c. Faustum* 23. 8; *Sermo dom. in monte* 1. 39 and 42). That would anticipate the condition of the redeemed in heaven. A really good Christian man loves God's creature in his wife, but should hate her femininity (ibid. 41).

Julian took Augustine to imply that Adam's Fall had had wider and more momentous consequences than the redemptive work of Christ (*Op. impf.* 2. 97); it involved the entire race, whereas in Augustine's theology Christ died only for the elect. Augustine's language about humanity as a 'mass of perdition' (*massa perditionis*) must mean a denial of any individual responsibility, which contradicts Ezekiel 18 (*Op. impf.* 3. 38 ff.). He thought it irresponsible Manichaeism to divide humanity into two blocks, the saved and the lost, by a decree prior to and irrespective of the moral quality of their lives. This doctrine was inducing moral despair (*c. Jul.* 3. 65). How much more wisely Augustine had written on Free Will in his earlier days. He now appeared to deny the goodness of the creation.

The evident weakness of Julian's position was that he did not reckon with the emotional constraints that press upon human beings in their social environment and from within their personalities. Augustine's notions of original sin being hereditary sounded offensive to him; but he would have been wise to say much more than he did about the effect of heredity on character and decision-making. Augustine was surely correct in refusing to accept Caelestius' proposition that between right and wrong the scales are evenly weighted in all situations. What choices human beings are capable of making depends on their character. Julian would have said that their character is determined by the free choices they have made and are making.

Augustine took Gen. 3: 16 clearly to mean that pain is a consequence of the Fall (e.g. *Grat. Chr.* 2. 40). To Julian that seemed utterly wrong. Pain was natural to the human condition as to animals. And how could a God of pure goodness allow, not to say decree, innocent infants, who have done no wrong, to be eternally damned because their parents could not get them to a priest in time to be baptized? Augustine, on the other hand, believed that serious diseases of mind or body with which some infants are born proved that this was a punishment for the contagion of sinfulness inherited from their parents (*c. Jul.* 3. 9–12). And if at baptism infants are exorcized and exsufflated to drive out the Devil, must not that liturgical custom demonstrate that they have inherited a vitiated flawed nature? The cries of infants at baptism show that the expulsion of Satan is painful and unwelcome. Original sin or the presence of a radical evil in the heart is not merely an empirically observable fact about human nature; for Augustine it is also necessary for his theodicy to reconcile the justice of God with the problem of pain and the storms of irrational passion.

In the *Confessions* Augustine's brilliant description of infant behaviour (no doubt modelled on that of his natural son) did not portray it as free of envy and egotism. Babies would often attempt to injure their mother or their nurses if only they had the power. He was wholly unsympathetic to the opinion held by some that before puberty children cannot sin 'as if sins were only acts done through the sexual organs' (*Gen. ad litt.* 10. 13. 23).

Augustine vigorously denied that he had no room for free will in his system. What was lost at the Fall of Adam was the power to do what is good and right. Humanity fully retained the power of free choice to opt for what is evil (*c. Jul.* 1. 5). Augustine would say repeatedly that the only thing of our own which we contribute to our salvation is the sin from which we need to be redeemed (*Tr. in ev. Joh.* 5. 1; 49. 8 and elsewhere). Controversy turned on the interpretation of St Paul in Romans 7, describing the will to do good vitiated by lack of power: was he being autobiographical? That is, was he describing a person under law or a person under grace? Augustine insisted that Paul described the inner conflict of a person under law.

A quality of relentlessness entered the dispute between Augustine and

Julian. Each was confident of the complete consistency and coherence of his position in reason and did not listen to what the other was saying. The protagonists misrepresented each other in matters of detail and neither fully comprehended the other's position. As the controversy developed, the language became sharp and at times (especially on Julian's side) distasteful. Augustine issued a series of replies to Julian, and the last of these remained incomplete in six long books at the time of Augustine's death on 28 August 430. Much of this work was written during long hours of labour into the small hours of the morning (*ep.* 224) as he was writing by day his 'Reappraisals' (*Retractationes*) in which he reviewed his numerous writings and made corrections. Both were works with a substantial element of self-justification. Since the argument proceeds by citations from Julian's work for his friend Florus, to which Augustine then replies, the incomplete work against Julian is of special value for reconstructing the views of Augustine's most notable adversary. He can be heard speaking for himself, admittedly in considerable anger and frustration.

Against Julian's charge of believing in 'traducianism', i.e. the physical transmission of the soul from the parental seed, Augustine never found a satisfactory answer. He accused Julian of merely creating a screen of dust (*c. Jul.* 3. 26), taking refuge in a question of deep obscurity (5. 17). Whether the soul preexists the body, or is transmitted with the parental seed, or is created *ad hunc* or *ad hanc* by God at the moment of conception, Augustine did not wish to speculate.

Julian was well educated and widely read in Cicero and the Latin classics. Augustine in reply went back to the *Hortensius* of Cicero, the philosophical dialogue which profoundly influenced him at the age of eighteen (*Conf.* 1. 4. 7). His polemic against Julian was decorated by quotations from Horace and Cicero, evidently because Julian had written in a similar vein. The style presupposed that both authors expected to be read by readers belonging to the same well-educated section of society. One issue between them was destined to have a long life in subsequent Christian history. Like liberation theologians of the twentieth century, Julian believed that altruism was not wholly impossible, and that human beings would behave much better if they accepted the proposition and authentic hope that the ideal is practicable. Pelagians generally assumed that the Church here and now could be without spot or blemish. Augustine believed human nature to be so flawed by egotism, sexuality being the most striking demonstration, that altruism could not be achieved in this life in the world as it is, and that the faults in the empirical Church would never be purged away before the Last Judgement. That difference is relevant to the question whether Pelagius and his friends had social aims and nursed aspirations to remedy the miserable poverty of great numbers in their time (above p. 447). At least they worked with an estimate of human nature which could have made such a programme imaginable. This is not to say that Augustine did not care deeply about the relief of the destitute as a Christian duty.[3]

Julian lived on until about 455. Augustine died on 28 August 430 during the Vandal siege of his city Hippo.

Julian was not the only writer to feel sharp misgivings about Augustine's uninhibited move towards ever more extreme positions. At Hadrumetum (Sousse) south-east of Carthage a monastery was disturbed by Augustine's pronouncement that 'in crowning human merits God is rewarding his own gifts'. The ascetic life asked for effort to a strenuous degree. To attribute every good and right action, every holy thought, exclusively to divine grace and to deny that the human will has a responsibility to want it and may even be the initiator of the process seemed dispiriting. In 426 two monks went to visit Augustine to ask for explanations. He thereupon wrote 'On Grace and Free Will', asserting both uncaused unmerited grace and the necessity of free will as long as its exercise is not thought to initiate or even to continue the life in grace. In other words, the human will had nothing positive to contribute. Moreover, the crucial quality of perseverance is wholly a divine gift. The question was then asked whether this implied that rebuking people for faults is superfluous. To this Augustine wrote 'On Rebuke and Grace' (*De correptione et gratia*) asserting grace to be for those predestinated by God before creation. Did not this mean that missionary evangelism became preaching not for a decision but to awake an awareness of being elect in the predestinated persons present?

Further problems were inherent in the very notion of a predestinate number of believers fixed by divine decision before all ages. How could this be reconciled with the scriptural saying that God wills all to be saved? Augustine's solution was to take the text in 1 Tim. 2: 4 to mean that representatives of every race, age, and class would be saved (*De correptione* 44 and elsewhere). A second question was whether, if predestination is true, it can be preached. The answer (*De dono perseverantiae* 57 ff.) is that it has to be explained very tactfully. A congregation should not be told 'Some of you are decreed to be rejected'. The third person should be used, not the second. Then there was a further question. Augustine held that true happiness excludes any anxiety or fear that it will not last. Yet no one can be sure of being one of God's elect, and those who are sure that they are so are peculiarly liable to pride and presumption (*De correptione* 40).

---

[3] Julian's works with the fragments of his *Ad Turbantium* are edited in CCSL 88. The first six books of his *Ad Florum* survive virtually intact in Augustine's *Opus Imperfectum contra Julianum*, of which an edition is in progress in CSEL 85 by M. Zelzer. See also Peter Brown, *The Body and Society* (New York, 1988); J. Lössl, *Intellectus Gratiae* (Leiden, 1997).

For Augustine the grace of God was not merely help to making good free choices and to carry them out so much as an irresistible power. If at any point in the process the human will is 'on its own', he thought something was certain to go wrong. God predestinates by his absolute fiat; otherwise his will would be frustrated, which is unthinkable. Plotinus did not believe that chance ever operates in the realm of the supreme One (6. 8. 7. 32). Augustine did not believe that anything happens by chance. If an infant of Christian parents dies before clergy can come and baptize it, that is not chance but inscrutable providence (*De dono perseverantiae* 31). The usage of words such as 'perhaps' or 'with luck' does not affect this point. Augustine's two books 'On the gift of perseverance' and 'On the predestination of the saints', written in 427 for the monks of southern Gaul, did nothing to allay anxiety.

At the monastery of St Victor at Marseille founded by John Cassian Augustine was understood to be leaving no real room for free choice, to be at heart a determinist and, with the notion of two bodies of predestined souls, one of grace the other of perdition, to be indistinguishable from a Manichee.

A slightly older monastery was located on the island of Lérins off Cannes, then under the direction of an austere noble, Honoratus. There lived a learned ascetic named Vincent, to whom the extreme predestinarianism to which Augustine had moved was out of line with tradition. In 434, after Augustine's death, Vincent composed a 'commonitorium' with a careful discussion of the development of doctrine, controlled from innovation by retaining internal consistency and coherence with the authoritative past in scripture and the great exegetes. Vincent's analogy is biological growth in human beings or in plants, or the logical elucidation of what was already true but obscure. In short, development is not the adding of new doctrines unheard of previously. Authority cannot be exclusively in scripture because heretics appeal to it; therefore the authentic sense of scripture is received by the Church and interpreted in the tradition of the community. This continuity of belief and practice is assured by being ancient, universal, and a matter of consensus among the faithful. By 'universal' Vincent was content to mean 'held by the great majority'. Consensus can be expressed by a general council or otherwise by the agreed interpretation by the majority of the great Christian writers who have died in communion with the one Church. Hence Vincent's famous criterion or canon of orthodoxy: 'Quod ubique, quod semper, quod ab omnibus'— what is held everywhere, always, by all. The formula was directed against Augustine's extreme predestinarianism and sidelining of free will.

Vincent was seriously disturbed by Augustine's explanation that only a minority of the human race are believers for the reason that the majority are destined to eternal damnation (e.g. *c. Cresconium* 4. 53. 63; *ep.* 93. 30), on the ground that those who are not saved by the special intervention of grace cannot be saved at all. Moreover, if our nature has become so sodden with sinfulness that we can do no other, does not that reflect on our Creator? Can it be correct to say that perseverance is God's gift in such a sense that it hangs wholly on predestination, not at any point on human resolve?

Controversy in southern Gaul moved Celestine, Pope 422–32, to write in defence of Augustine's reputation, 'a man never out of communion with the Apostolic See'. Under his name there is transmitted a document, perhaps Roman but Prosper of Aquitaine is also a probable author, occasioned by some who, while rejecting Pelagius and Caelestius, suggest that attacks upon their heresy have been overstated; they declare themselves wholly obedient to all that has been defined by papal authority. The document accordingly gathers doctrinal decisions of popes since Innocent I, and is unambiguously Augustinian in its general position. But at the end the text disclaims debate about particularly profound questions, no doubt meaning predestination and perseverance, on which no censure is called for.[4]

A few years before Augustine's death, John Cassian's thirteenth *Conference* ('Chaeremon') described the ascetic path of the Desert Fathers which promised the gift of grace to all who aspired for it. Cassian did not think Adam's Fall had rendered humanity wholly incapable of doing the right and the good, only that the tension between flesh and spirit made this much more difficult. One should not despair of the will's power which is integral to the life of prayer that is in turn dependence upon God.

This *Conference* much offended Prosper of Aquitaine, who correctly saw Cassian as endeavouring to qualify Augustine's doctrine of grace so as to make it less absolute (PL 51. 213–76). Prosper was at this time so zealous an Augustinian that he wrote a guide to his master's thought in verse. He later served Pope Leo I, and modified his early zeal at least to the extent of holding that when scripture declares that God wills all to be saved (1 Tim. 2: 4), the text means what it says.

A monk at Lérins named Faustus came from Britain, and became abbot of the monastery (433 until about 460), then becoming bishop of Reii (Riez) and influential throughout Gaul. After falling into disfavour with the Visigothic king Euric, perhaps for an attack on Arianism, he suffered exile in 477–86 and died about 495. He defended John Cassian's standpoint against the ultra-Augustinians of Gaul, holding that the initial move of the heart and final perseverance are free human decisions, but at the same time wrote against Pelagius. His position did not delight north Africans, then suffering under Vandal harassment, and Fulgentius of Ruspe, exiled to Sardinia, wrote a lost work against him. Caesarius bishop of Arles (470–542), arranged for Faustus to be condemned at a synod at Orange (529) [below p. 652].

---

[4] *Clavis* 527 under Prosper; best edited by the Ballerini, *S. Leonis opera* (Venice, 1756) 251–7. In Migne PL 45. 1756 and elsewhere.

48

AUGUSTINE[1]

Born on 13 November 354, the son of a small-time farmer at Thagaste (Souk-Ahras in north-east Algeria) and a Christian mother Monnica, Augustine's training was as a teacher of the liberal arts, notably Latin literature ('grammar'), rhetoric or the art of persuasive public speaking, and logic. He was also informed about arithmetic, geometry, musical theory (though he never wrote a book on pitch), astronomy and medicine. Love of Cicero's prose and Vergil's poetry permanently marked his style. He also much admired the sombre writings of Sallust and knew well the comedies of Terence. Occasional allusive quotations from Juvenal and Seneca show him at home there. Aged 18, he read Cicero's defence of philosophy, the (lost) dialogue *Hortensius*, offering a guide to life and happiness. Briefly he picked up parts of the Bible, but was repelled by the banausic style of the Old Latin version, by the patriarchs' polygamy, and by the two divergent genealogies of Jesus. In any event he was attracted by the Manichee theosophy and explanation of the problem of evil, namely that while God is good, he is not all-powerful. For a decade he associated with a Manichee ascetic community, which did not discourage him from acquiring a concubine of low class sharing bed and board with her in much contentment. By her he had an unintended son Adeodatus who was educated as an orthodox Catholic; a boy of high intelligence, he died at the age of 16. In his memory Augustine wrote on non-verbal communication, often discussed with his son; gestures and tone of voice are more revealing than words, which in any event are incapable of expressing the deepest things. Texts show that in this age it was normal for young men to take a concubine until such time as they were earning their living and could acquire a regular wife.

In adult life he earned his bread by teaching, but riotous students at Carthage made him aspire to a similar post in Rome. There, however, he found the students evading payment of their fees. With the support of the powerful pagan prefect Aurelius Symmachus he was able to get a teaching post at Milan, residence of the western emperor Valentinian II as also of

[1] On Augustine I have written at greater length in the Oxford series Past Masters (1980), reissued 2001.

Bishop Ambrose, who personally welcomed him to the city and was held in deep respect by his widowed mother Monnica, who followed her son to Italy. At Milan he met a Neoplatonic circle, and was convinced by Plotinus' account of providence and the problem of evil, especially his thesis that God can transform evil to good ends. He was attracted by hearing Ambrose preach sermons fusing high oratory with Christianized Neoplatonic themes, and especially deploying Philonic allegory to interpret the Old Testament in a way 'worthy of God'. Ambition made him aspire to become governor of some minor province (the kind of post to which well-educated literary men were often appointed), but for that end he needed money to grease the palms of the high court officials or at least to express gratitude to them afterwards. So he needed a wife with resources. Monnica found for him a suitable girl, though too young for wedding, and Augustine's concubine had to be sent back to Carthage, the breach being a source of deep pain for both partners. But she would hardly have been suitable for a provincial governor, which in any event he could not become without money. Public offices were for sale.

Conversion

Augustine's sex drive was strong, but left him feeling incomplete. In Ambrose he encountered a man obviously happy, yet unmarried. Ambrose's sermons taught him that the catholic faith of the universal Church was other than he had supposed. The level of preaching in north Africa had been inferior. Without having close personal contact with Ambrose he was inexorably drawn to conversion, spurred on by the tedium of calling on powerful senators in hope of gaining their support for his ambition, and made the decision under extreme stress in a friend's garden at Milan in July or August 386. The scene is brilliantly and poetically described (with sophisticated literary allusions) in the eighth book of his later *Confessions*. Conversion for him meant a celibate life, though at the time he had no intention of offering for the priesthood. Neoplatonist ideals combined with the apostle Paul convinced him that he must forgo his plans for a secular career and for the marriage that was to make that financially possible. Monnica, although she had been looking forward to grandchildren, was glad at his change of heart. On Easter Eve 387 he was baptized by Ambrose, and accepted the forgiveness of his past sins. The archaeologists' spade has excavated the font below the Duomo at Milan. Some decades later he retained a vivid memory of Ambrose's catechetical discourses (*Fid. et Op.* 9).

Return to north Africa was delayed by the civil war between Theodosius and Magnus Maximus which closed down the ferries, and during the wait at Ostia Monnica died. The description of her dying and requiem is a high emotional climax of the *Confessions*. Her tomb was accidentally discovered in

1945 when some boys were digging a hole for their basketball post. An admirer of Augustine's *Confessions* had erected a memorial inscription there. In 388 Augustine was back in Thagaste with a society of friends sharing his family house and studying the Bible and Neoplatonic themes. In Rome Augustine had read Jerome's 22nd letter to Eustochium, describing the monasteries of Egypt, and was moved to write a book (*De moribus*) to argue that the catholic Church was a better home for the ascetic life than Manichee communities. He wanted to found monastic houses attached to north African churches.

On a visit to the harbour town of Hippo in 391 with this end in view, he attended the Sunday morning service. The bishop, Valerius, a native Greek-speaker who owned estate in southern Italy, espied him in the congregation and preached a sermon telling his congregation that here was an ideal man to become presbyter in Hippo; he was already noted for Latin eloquence. At Hippo people were not readers of books, as they were at Carthage (so expressly *ep.* 118. 9), and if they knew the story of Dido and Aeneas that was from the local music-hall, not from Vergil. Augustine found himself mobbed by the *plebs*, and forced to accept ordination at Valerius' hands. In Africa this was a common procedure which admittedly led to some unsuitable ordinations, for Augustine himself once records that north Africa had few churches where clergy had not been removed from office (*c. litt. Petil.* 3. 32. 36; cf. *ep.* 208. 2 on some bishops whose motive was only the secular honour). 'The Church is often deceived in those from whom much is hoped' (*ep.* 93. 34).

Five years later Valerius felt his end coming and persuaded the elderly primate of Numidia to come to Hippo to consecrate Augustine as coadjutor bishop with right of succession. Though the council of Nicaea disapproved of having two bishops in one city (a rule of which Augustine and probably all bishops in Numidia knew nothing), it was not without precedent (Eus. *HE* 7. 32. 21). For personal reasons the proposal caused a storm. There were those who remembered his past, his sex life and theosophy in particular, and suspected his monastic enthusiasm of being a concealed infiltration of Manichee practices. Adherents of Mani had houses with similar lifestyle. At Rome Augustine had met a wealthy Manichee who tried unsuccessfully to form an ascetic house (*c. Faustum* 5. 5). The primate received letters attacking the unsuitable plan and wrote to Valerius a letter damaging to Augustine which came into Donatist hands and was exploited. To a married woman he had given some blessed bread, which critics asserted to be a love-charm intended to further an inappropriate affair. (Clergy could be asked for such assistance.) The consecration, however, went ahead. 'No one has the right to refuse ordination' (*Qu. Hept.* 4. 54). One of Augustine's motives in writing his partly autobiographical *Confessions* was to vindicate himself, not only before Christian critics but also in answer to educated pagans who could not forgive him for abandoning his distinguished literary career. The *Confessions* is a book with close affinities to anti-Manichee tracts written in the same period. He needed to answer suggestions that he was a crypto-Manichee.

A stimulus for writing the *Confessions* came from an accidental correspondence between his pupil Alypius, lately made bishop of Thagaste, and the *grand seigneur* from Bordeaux, Paulinus.[2] A pupil of Ausonius and a poet, Paulinus had been governor of Campania and owned estates there and elsewhere. Ordained at Barcelona, he decided to retire to Nola in Campania with his wife and to build a shrine in honour of St Felix for whose assistance he felt gratitude. He replied to Alypius suggesting an exchange of letters on the way in which each had been led to adopt the ascetic life of a bishop. Alypius shared this letter with Augustine; he had sent Paulinus some of Augustine's anti-Manichee writings, asking for a copy of Eusebius' *Chronicle* in exchange. The sixth book of the *Confessions* includes a brief biography of Alypius. Paulinus and Augustine exchanged a number of letters, and at Paulinus' inquiry Augustine wrote 'on proper care for the dead', discouraging Paulinus from thinking that burial in proximity to a saint's tomb must necessarily be advantageous hereafter.[3]

The selection of autobiographical matter in the first nine books was designed to show the course of his life which had led him to be bishop at Hippo. A striking theme is the providential overruling of events, at the time apparently purely secular, that eventually led him to Milan and Ambrose. Nevertheless the work is only in outward form an autobiography; the last four books discuss memory, time, creation, and the allegorical meaning of Genesis 1, where the creation story is interpreted of the Church and its providential functions on behalf of humanity. The autobiographical chapters illustrate the wandering homelessness of the human soul alienated from God and in quest of peace and inward repose (a notable Plotinian theme). Time as a succession of mainly meaningless events is what the eternal God of love wants to rescue us from. Plotinus had seen time as in itself beyond our understanding, but intelligible if contrasted with eternity and if seen as given meaning by the goal to which history moves. God is found in the deepest level of the soul, in the subconscious where the soul longs for completeness. 'You have made us for yourself and our heart is restless until it rests in you.' 'At long last I came to love you, beauty so old and yet so new . . . You were within me, and I had been seeking you in the external world' (*Conf.* 1. 1; 10. 38).

A leading theme is the dependence of humanity on divine grace for a good moral life. We have no merits which are not God's gifts (*Conf.* 9. 34; 10. 64). God has commanded continence and if that is attained, it is by his gift.

[2] Dennis E. Trout, *Paulinus of Nola* (Berkeley, 1999).
[3] On burial beside a saint, see Ambrose, *De excessu fratris* i. 18; Yvette Duval, *Auprès des saints corps et âme; l'inhumation ad sanctos* (Paris, 1988) especially discussing Augustine, *De cura pro mortuis gerenda*.

The language of the *Confessions* is sophisticated, and an undercurrent in the work is a demonstration that he a Christian can write creatively and beautifully and with the adornment of allusions to Vergil or Terence that contemporary pagans of high education liked. The same undercurrent is beneath the surface in his major work on Christian culture, *De doctrina Christiana*, in which he defines a Christian curriculum based on scripture.

At first Valerius had allowed Augustine as presbyter time to study the Bible and to acquire a better knowledge of Christian doctrine. Scripture had played no part whatever in his education. What he knew by heart consisted of pagan classics. His eloquence made him much in demand for addressing episcopal synods. He influenced Aurelius, primate of Carthage, to mobilize synodical action against the schismatic Donatists, and was to play a central role in rebutting the Stoic ideas of Pelagius about the capacity of the human will to do what is right and good. Augustine understood the human mind to have amazing powers and at the end of the *City of God* gives a vast list of artistic and technological achievements. Yet he saw humanity as flawed by egocentricity, expert in knowledge (*scientia*) but sadly deficient in wisdom (*sapientia*), prone to mendacity.

'No one who has not been a bishop would believe what we are expected to do', he once lamented. The administrative and financial cares; the frequent need to arbitrate between disputing members of his flock; problems when an illtreated slave sought asylum at the altar and the owner was a powerful landowner sure of support from the magistrates; anxiety when a man owing large sums in tax succeeded in getting himself elected a bishop so that the debt could be transferred to the church chest ('I have never before known a bishopric used as a tax-fiddle'); bishops whose hospitality duties made them alcoholics; illusory expectations among his people that he would have influence with governors or their deputies to intercede on their behalf, whether for a job, or because they were involved in litigation; their anger if he refused a benefaction because of the strings attached (e.g. obligation to replace a ship in the event of shipwreck); endless matrimonial cases on which distressed partners, especially wives ('infidelity is a male disease'), came to consult him; a tenant farmer who sold his wife to a slavetrader and replied to Augustine's protests that he preferred the money; the low level of ethical commitment among many of his people ('drunk in church and especially at martyrs' shrines'); 'the church almost swamped by a multitude of adherents whose morals are at variance with the way of the saints'; some who consulted their astrologer to discover when it would be a good day to become a Christian; the catalogue of a bishop's 'rucksack' (*sarcina*) is unending. Hardest of all was to be vulnerable to alternating flattery and vituperation.

Alaric's brief sack of Rome in August 410 made many ask how the eternal city could be allowed by providence to succumb to the barbarians, how the patron saints Peter and Paul could fail to defend a city claimed as their own, and how an empire whose emperor worshipped the true and supreme God could suffer such humiliation. The temple of Romulus now had far fewer devotees than Constantine's church housing the shrine of St Peter (Aug. *En. in Ps.* 44. 23). Augustine had been meditating long on the problem of divine providence in human history, and his reading of Lactantius' *Divine Institutes* had already influenced an early tract 'On true religion' in ways which were to be developed. The *City of God* opposes the symbols Jerusalem and Babylon as contrasting ethical ideals, Babylon representing fallen humanity, 'the city of the devil', Jerusalem being the people of God in the Old and the New Testaments and in the Church. Having a Christian emperor had not made the empire Christian. It might have political virtues, but the lust for dominion had not died away. In any event Augustine thought that smaller units would be easier to administer with justice. Half a century after his time the western empire was in process of being replaced by independent barbarian kingdoms.

A major work designed to rebut pagan critics was on the doctrine of the one God as Trinity. The work took many years to write, and when finished left Augustine deeply dissatisfied. The Neoplatonic idea of the soul helped him to affirm unity and trinity to be present in human psychology. The term 'substance' and above all 'persons' can only be inadequate, used because the alternative is silence. The inspired prologue to St John's Gospel shows that the Word of God is second in the Trinity. Threeness is to be found in the inner relation of love in the being of God. Argument with Neoplatonist themes pervades his *Literal Commentary on Genesis*, the literalness being the actuality of divine creation, and his cautious work *On the Soul*. Although his idea of the transmission of Adam's sin by heredity obviously implied that the soul is transmitted through the parental seed and egg, he was never willing to affirm this, mainly because it easily sounded Manichee.

Theosophical Manichees, schismatic Donatists, and Pelagians shocked by his sombre estimate of human moral capacities occupied much of his energies, but not all. The heart of his religion is in the sermons, especially those on St John's Gospel and Epistles and on the Psalms.

Augustine died on 28 August 430 during the Vandal siege of Hippo. His last recorded words were a quotation from Plotinus. His last lengthy book was a Reappraisal of his writings (*Retractationes*), in about half the books correcting faults, and in the other half defending his works against criticisms. He once commented that only fools never express regret for their mistakes.

49

JOHN CHRYSOSTOM

Vandalized statues at Antioch

At Antioch in Syria a presbyter of bishop Flavian named John had acquired a considerable reputation, mainly for his strongly ethical and candid discourses. In 387 there was a crisis at Antioch, when Theodosius I needed to raise money by a high tax to pay for his campaign against Magnus Maximus;[1] in a riot statues of Theodosius and his first wife Flaccilla were overturned. This was an insult to imperial authority, as such legally counted as 'sacrilege' (e.g. Augustine, *S. Dolbeau* 6, p. 463; *En. in Ps.* 66. 4). For this a price would be paid by the city councillors held responsible for a failure to keep order. The pagan orator Libanius wrote letters interceding for mercy. The city of Syrian Seleucia, port of Antioch, interceded, though in a way that much offended the Antiochenes proud of their superiority (Chrys. *Hom. in Col.* 7. 3, PG 62. 548). Commissioned by the city council (*Hom. in Stat.* 21. 1), the old bishop Flavian went to Constantinople in person to beg for pardon for his city, and seems to have been more effective than the pagan representations. While Flavian was absent, presbyter John preached a series of sermons, in broad terms rebuking the people of the city for their moral laxities, especially their love of swearing, which in his view was responsible for the disaster. Educated pagans were present. Temporarily Antioch lost its title of metropolis. The hippodrome and city baths were closed, so that people took to the river Orontes as a substitute. Among the magnates, but not the poor and destitute sleeping rough, there were some exemplary executions, tortures, and confiscations, for failing to enforce order (as usual in edicts in the Theodosian Code). But the final upshot was less dreadful than had been feared. And John's homilies made him famous.

Antioch's Jewish community

John had also given expression to Christian feelings of anger that, through a collection made by their patriarch, the numerous and wealthy Jews of

---

[1] Jerome on Isaiah (16. 58, p. 690 Vallarsi) notes that a prime cause for riots in cities was high interest rates, driving many into hopeless debt.

Antioch and elsewhere had co-operated with Julian the apostate in the aborted plan to rebuild the Temple at Jerusalem, where Julian's foundations were still visible (*Quod Christus sit deus* 16. 9–10, PG 48). He was upset to find how many Christians worshipping with the church on Sunday had been at the synagogue on the previous day and were keeping Jewish festivals. His anti-Judaic homilies at Antioch (not much at Constantinople), passionate and scurrilous, make painful reading.[2] On the other hand, like Ambrose (p. 361 above), he rebuked Christians for their indolence in prayer and Bible study and worship in comparison with the stricter devotion of Jews (*Hom. in Ps.* 121 (122), PG 55. 347). The attraction of worship in the Greek synagogues of Antioch may be measured from the fact that the anonymous author of the *Apostolic Constitutions*, probably written at Antioch *c.*375–85, included in his liturgical matter a lightly Christianized version of synagogue prayers.[3]

Education and training

John had high ideals for himself and everyone else. The son of a high-ranking civil servant who died when John was young, he had received an excellent education, studying under Libanius. He agreed with Libanius in observing that the study of rhetoric and Latin was the route to success in the civil service (*Oppugn. vitae monasticae* 3. 5, PG 47. 559). But he took up the ascetic life. His mortifications injured his health. Meletius baptized him and later ordained him deacon at Antioch. He described his ideals for a bishop in a remarkable book *On the Priesthood*, partly designed to justify his reluctance to be ordained by portraying the vocation as too exalted for his character.

Antioch's population he records as 200,000 (*Hom. in Ignat.* 4, PG 50. 537f.); racially it was mixed, with many whose first language was Syriac, not Greek (*Hom. in Gen.* 2. 3, PG 53). The city was prosperous, the third or even the second city (in a tie with Alexandria) of the empire. The Christians were proud that they had first acquired this title at Antioch (Acts 11. 26) and that those who first took the gospel to Rome and the west came from Syria (*Hom. in Rom.* 2. 2). The great city of Rome retained its old aura, but its greatest glory was to possess the relics of Peter and Paul the apostolic martyrs, who came from Syria. The body of Paul so defended Rome as to make it impregnable (*Hom. in Rom.* 32. 4–5, PG 60. 678–9). At Rome people so believed until Alaric arrived.

---

[2] PG 48. 843–942; R. L. Wilken, *John Chrysostom and the Jews* (Berkeley, 1983).
[3] Set out in English translation by E. R. Goodenough, *By Light Light* (New Haven, 1935), 306–58 on the basis of work by Wilhelm Bousset.

Conversion and baptism

John had a strong missionary vocation: ascetics were called to convert pagans, including barbarians beyond the frontier. He observed that convincing people of the truth of the faith was more difficult than giving baptism, important as the latter was. As the sacrament of the remission of sins, baptism offered cleansing for everyone, even for harlots, idolaters, practising homosexuals, thieves, drunkards (*Catech.* 1. 15 Wenger, SC 50). Baptism was preceded by catechetical instruction, and immediately by renunciation of evil and an 'agreement' with Christ. The priest anoints the candidate, like an athlete, but in the name of Father, Son, and Holy Spirit with the sign of the cross. At nightfall all clothing is set aside, and the entire body receives anointing, after which the candidate descends into the water. The priest uses the candidate's name and, as he or she is three times plunged into the water, says 'He or she is baptized in the name of Father, Son, and Holy Spirit.' He does not say, 'I baptize you' because the baptizer is Christ. The form of words suggests John was aware that the Latin usage was different. The candidate ascends out of the font, receives a kiss and then the eucharist (*Catech.* 1. 21–7 Wenger). For seven days after baptism a white robe is worn (3. 18). After baptism, remission of sins is only by tears of penitence, confession, almsgiving, prayer, and pious practice. John had deep reservations towards the traditional practice of public confession before the bishop and congregation. What the Church brings is therapy for sick souls, not judicial punishment, and that is to be given in confidence. ('The errors of fellow Christians not to be made public': PG 51. 353–64.)

In the churches numbers were steadily increasing, while polytheism was suffering inward collapse and the old pagan festivals had fewer supporters (*Babylas* 14 and 43, ed. Schatkin—a work with polemic against Julian). But the number of Christians whose moral life needed reform was large, and John's sermons made this objective a main target. The congregation vigorously applauded his oratory, but were reluctant to change their ways. He warned that the bright lights of the city could be deceptive; the lives of admired actresses and actors were notoriously miserable (*ad Theodorum* 1. 19).

Correct doctrine

Although moral questions dominate his discourses, it was not that orthodoxy was of no interest. One should believe with the Church (*Hom. in Gen.* 8. 12). Some sermons vigorously rejected radical Arians; processions against them were encouraged. He was familiar with the terminology of current Trinitarian and Christological discussions. His sermons attacked Marcellus of Ankyra and his followers (e.g. *Hom. in Joh.* 7. 2). He affirmed 'three hypostases' and was strongly opposed to the schismatic community of Paulinus. He rejected Apollinaris' Christology (*Hom. in Phil.* 7); 'one must neither confuse nor separate the natures in the one Christ'. This 'union' is also a 'joining together' (*synapheia: Hom. in Joh.* 11. 2). But 'orthodoxy without a good life is useless' (*Hom. in Gen.* 13. 16).

Posts for sale

Reform was needed not only among the laity. Church offices were for sale, like those of the state (CTh 2. 29. 2 of 394 takes this for granted, imposing penalties on those who failed to reward influential benefactors arranging their promotion as contracted). Those influential in managing an appointment expected to be rewarded afterwards. Officials who, when asked for help, held out their hand for a bribe were not only petty and local. Corruption pervaded the entire system. An exposition of Psalm 148 (PG 55. 491) warns against the deduction that the institutions of government are inherently evil.

The quality of clergy and laity

A full scrutiny of those being baptized or receiving Easter communion would disclose the common practice of divination, use of charms and omens, fornicators, adulterers, drunkards, and office-holders set only on gain and profit from getting promotions for people by receiving bribes (*Hom. in Eph.* 6. 4, PG 62. 48). John was firm that the ambition of some women to serve as priests or bishops had to be resisted as contrary to 'divine law' (*Sacerd.* 2. 2. 2; 3. 9). They were and could be deacons. He was anxious about the power well-to-do women exercised in the election of bishops (*Sacerd.* 3. 9). It was customary for virgins not to attend funerals (3. 17). Experience showed that holy ascetics did not always make good bishops (3. 15). Bishops wore dark clothes (1. 4. 7). John thought it important that bishops were elected by the clergy in the presence of the laity, whose participation in the consecration of a bishop 'by acclamations which only the baptized know' was crucial (in 2 *Cor.* 18. 2–3).

Liturgy

John stressed the heavenly commission of bishops and priests, but at the same time valued the participation of the laity in major decisions. In the New Testament there was less difference between priest and layman than under the old covenant where only the priest partook of the sacrifice. The congregation participates in the eucharistic offering, as is 'meet and right'

(*Hom. in 11 Cor.* 18. 3, PG 61. 527). The church's sacrifice in the eucharist is none other than that of Calvary being ritually reenacted (*Hom. in Heb.* 17). Consecration is by Christ's words, which change the gifts on the altar by the coming of the Spirit. Just as the emperor's throne was behind curtains (PG 49. 241), so also the altar was behind curtains, lifted aside at the climax of the liturgy (*Hom. in Eph.* 3. 5, PG 62. 29). In the churches of Syria the sanctuary was at the east end of the basilica, but in the centre of the nave was a platform called *bema*, shaped like a horseshoe, the round end towards the west end. It had seats for clergy and an altar with cross and gospel-book, and in the centre a chair for the bishop. Psalm-chanting (without instruments) gave the soul wings (*in Ps.* 134, PG 55. 388). Incense was used (*Hom. in Matt.* 88. 4), the eucharist three or four times weekly (*adv. Jud.* 2. 4); where it was celebrated daily, worshippers were few (*in Eph.* 3. 4). Holy relics are commended for devotional value (*Babylas* 2. 81). Much of the Liturgy under John's name goes back to him.

Bishop and emperor

The bishop is representative or ambassador of Christ, standing in succession from the Lord, and ambassadors are honoured even among barbarians (*Hom. in Col.* 3. 5). His role stands in strong contrast to that of the emperor, whose tenure of office is always precarious, some having been slain by their own bodyguard (*Hom. in Stat.* 18. 5). The list of disasters to emperors of the fourth century is long (*Hom. in Phil.* 15. 5). Emperors rule by force, bishops only seek to persuade. John was aware that on occasion bishops had served as ambassadors for their city or for the emperor (*Sacerd.* 6. 4). But priests had an office higher than that of emperors (*Sacerd.* 5. 1; *Hom. in Stat.* 3. 6). The power of the keys was more than symbolic or declaratory; it was instrumental (*Sacerd.* 3. 5–6). A bishop was expected to be celibate and, if married, not to cohabit with his wife (*in 1 Thess.* 10. 1).

Rich, poor, slaves

John wanted a classless society; at least in worship there were no distinctions. The emperor and his officers wore no insignia in church (*Hom. ad Gothos* 3, PG 63. 475). John asserted a common humanity shared by all alike. He could not disagree with sharp criticism of clergy richly dressed in silk, riding a horse (in antiquity a sign of not being poor), accompanied by attendant slaves to clear a way in the crowd, and constructing a second fine house (*Hom. in Phil.* 9. 4). The church chest of Antioch maintained 3,000 widows and prisoners (*Hom. in Matt.* 66. 3). Slavery was a problem, since free wage labourers were worse off (*Hom. in Matt.* 5. 6; *in 1 Cor.* 20. 5; *in Heb.* 11. 3), so that one was better fed, clothed, and housed as a domestic slave. (Libanius once comments that free manual workers have to labour night and day simply to avert starvation: *Orat.* 25. 37.) But the flogging of slaves was deplorable, above all when irritated wives had slave-girls stripped and then whipped by their husbands (*Hom. in Eph.* 15. 3, PG 62. 109–10). Later it would become a formal accusation against John that he disciplined a presbyter who had beaten his slave. At least caring masters saw that after being whipped slaves had medical help for their weals (*Hom. in Gen.* 9. 11). Slavery originated in lust for domination (*in Eph.* 22. 2; *Lazaro conc.* 6. 7, PG 48, 1037). Unlike Libanius John was wholly opposed to corporal punishment for schoolchildren ('On vainglory and the right way for parents to bring up children' 31, ed. Malingrey, SC 188 (1972); *Clavis* 4455). Very poor parents could be reduced to selling their children to slavetraders. Roman law provided that they could contract to recover their freedom and citizenship after twenty-five years (Augustine, *ep.* 10*; cf. CTh 3. 3. 1). A recurrent theme in John's sermons is the dignity of manual labour, not to be despised by educated intellectuals (*Hom in 1 Cor.* 5. 6). He deplored wealthy people possessing Christian books but valuing them only for their fine binding and calligraphy (*Hom. in Joh.* 32. 3, PG 59).

Alms

John was particularly concerned for the beggars thronging the porches of churches and baths (*in 1 Thess.* 11. 4), and was incessant in exhorting his hearers to give alms, thereby to be sure of escaping the fires of hell which would find out the stingy (*in 1 Cor.* 21. 7; cf. Tobit 12: 9). In the diversity of punishments hereafter, the avaricious would particularly suffer. A disciple of John named Martyrius wrote a biography of him recording that his decision to build a leper hospice on land outside the city reduced property values, vexing wealthy landowners in that vicinity (F. van Ommeslaeghe, in *Analecta Bollandiana*, 97 (1979), 151). He understood Christian aid to be for everyone including pagans and Jews (*Hom. in Heb.* 10. 4). Like Basil of Caesarea, he supported a hospital (Palladius, *Dialogue* 5).

So persistent were his pleas for generosity to the destitute that such discourses came to be resented by the wealthy, whose ostentatious style of life he frequently lambasted. The rich owned numerous houses decorated with marble and mosaic, and had hundreds of slaves in their retinue. Some defended this by citing Abraham's 318 servants (*in Ps.* 48, PG 55. 507). Unlike Ambrose, who won the support of merchants in Milan (above p. 368), John succeeded in losing the friendship of powerful rich people. They should give alms for the destitute and forgo silver chamber-pots—a theme incurring mockery (*Hom. in Col.* 7. 5, PG 62. 350); John insisted that private property was a consequence of the Fall (*Hom. in Joh.* 74. 3). So also was sexual intercourse (*Hom. in Gen.* 16. 4). By contrast *Hom. in Col.* 12. 5 (PG 62. 388) is warm and positive about physical conjugal relations. He told men that they no less than their wives had a duty to be faithful and chaste (*Hom. in Matt.* 7. 7, PG 57. 81–2), and that it was false to say 'fornication is my private affair' (*Hom. in 1 Thess.* 4. 4, PG 62. 420). To people who thought outspoken sermons on sex in poor taste and too candid, he replied with good reason that he was less frank than the prophet Ezekiel (*in 1 Thess.* 5. 3, PG 62. 427). He opposed abortion (*in Rom.* 24. 4). Christian marriage he thought the sweetest experience on earth (*Hom. in Matt.* 37. 7, PG 57. 428). To second marriage he was reserved (*Virg.* 37, ed. Musurillo, SC 125), but not wholly negative (*Eutrop.* 2. 15).

Social customs

There were other aspects of the customary 'culture' which came under his lash: sexy dancing and songs at wedding receptions after a bridal procession through the agora by torchlight with abuse customarily hurled at the bride-groom while pipes played (*Hom. in 1 Cor.* 12. 5–6, PG 61. 103). Too much alcohol was drunk at wedding parties, the celebration of which lasted a week (cf. Gen. 29. 27), and also by soldiers, for whom hard drinking was a matter of honour (12. 4, PG 61. 102). At funerals professional female mourners were hired to sing dirges; John did not think well of this, nor of an old custom whereby a child's name was decided by the last of a row of candles to burn out (12. 18). 'Not one of you can repeat a psalm but you can readily sing an improper song' (*Hom. in Matt.* 2. 5–6). Drink and dances at the New Year were also deplored (PG 48. 953–62). It was still common for people to wash on returning from a visit to a tomb (*Hom. in Matt.* 37. 6), and to wear white when children died (31. 5).

Another target for his criticisms was the hostility of many at Antioch towards the monks living in their caves in the nearby Mount Silpios. Some opponents went so far as to inflict physical assaults on monks when they came into the city, and would then boast about it (*Oppugn. mon.* 1. 2, PG 47. 322). Possibly these assaults occurred during the troubles about the statues, when the monks were fervent in supplications for mercy to the delinquent, and may have annoyed the authorities. John wanted the laity in the city to pursue holiness as zealously as the monks. Feminine arts, clothes, and cosmetics were also a threat to the higher life of the soul. Church services were so crowded that the people had to be warned against pickpockets (PG 48. 735), and sternly rebuked for jostling and shoving at the distribution in the eucharistic liturgy (PG 49. 360–1). His sermons were applauded. He was aware that applause for polished oratory did not mean that the hearts and wills of his hearers had been touched. During the readings from scripture, there was gossip and inattention (*Hom. in 2 Thess.* 3; *in Ps.* 43, PG 55. 172). It upset John that many stayed until the sermon was over, but did not remain for the liturgy, some receiving communion only once a year. That was presumably at Easter or Christmas (*Hom. in 1 Tim.* 5; *in Heb.* 17. 7). But he was sad that on Easter Day there were horse-races and plays at the theatre (*Catecheses*, 6. 1 Wenger). No doubt his influence lay behind a law of August 399 prohibiting shows on Sundays (CTh 2. 8. 23). But public amusements were to continue (16. 10. 17). He did not approve when at Constantinople the emperor attended the races (*Hom. in Gen.* 5. 17); the great ladies in their low-cut provocative fashions were 'a parade of whores' (6. 6). Such language may have been fair comment but was hardly calculated to win friends at court, where it would seem vulgar abuse. He made it easy for ladies close to the empress Eudoxia to suggest that he had her in view. A sermon on Psalm 48 (PG 55. 507) criticized women in the gallery of Sancta Sophia bedecked in jewellery—'a theatrical display'. Defying 1 Tim. 2: 9 hindered pagan conversions.

Ascetic cohabitation

At both Antioch and Constantinople John deplored the practice of clergy having a woman (ascetic) housekeeper living with them. There was no sexual relation, but it did not look well to outsiders. He was anxious when deaconesses, who could not dress in the fashionable style, nevertheless contrived to make even rough cloth very feminine (*Ep.* 1 to Olympias, PG 51. 566).

Oaths. Amulets

In a lawcourt and elsewhere solemn oaths were taken on a gospel book (*Hom. in Stat.* 15. 14). But all too commonly judges took bribes. Miniature gospel-books were used as amulets (ibid. 19. 14; *in Matt.* 72. 2). Some had amulets of Alexander the Great (PG 49. 223). Amulets were in use when a child was sick (*Hom. in Col.* 8. 5), or a fragment of the true cross encased in gold might be worn round the neck (*Quod Christus sit deus* 10. 4). On arriving at the entrance to a church simple people would kiss the lintel columns (*in 2 Cor.* 34. 2).[4]

John gave thought to Christian education of children. He asked parents to give them Christian names like Peter, Paul, etc. Near the end of his time at Antioch he wrote a homily 'on vainglory and how parents should bring up children'[5].

---

[4] See an important discussion by F. J. Dölger, *Antike und Christentum*, ii. 156–8. The practice is recorded in north Africa in an embarrassed sermon of Augustine discovered by F. Dolbeau, *Vingt-six sermons*, 374, l. 233.

[5] Translated with notes by M. L. W. Laistner, *Christianity and Pagan Culture in the Later Roman empire* (Ithaca, NY, 1951, 1967).

Bishop of New Rome

On 26 September 397 the easygoing, hospitable bishop of Constantinople, Nektarios, died. There were factions for rival candidates to succeed. Theophilus of Alexandria hoped to get his presbyter Isidore appointed. Alexandria resented the rapidly growing authority and power of the see of Constantinople, and Theophilus may have imagined that if he could get his own man into the post, he would keep New Rome subordinate. The court under the emperor Arcadius, aged 20, his Frankish wife Eudoxia, daughter of the great general Bauto, and the eunuch Eutropius, wanted a good preacher. Eutropius could arrange that.

Late in October 397 John was commanded by the Count of Oriens at Antioch to go at once to the martyrs' shrine outside the gate on the road north to Tarsus and on to Constantinople. He was in effect being kidnapped lest the people of the city should hear of the plan for Nektarios' successor and make it impossible for him to leave. He evidently had a powerful and massive following. John was conducted to the capital. The court wished the installation of the new bishop on 26 February 398 to be a solemnity worthy of the dignity of New Rome, and among the many important bishops invited for the enthronement was Theophilus of Alexandria. He was wholly opposed to John's appointment. The court wanted him to play a leading role, and found him extremely reluctant. But the powerful eunuch Eutropius (*PLRE* ii. 440) possessed compromising letters, evidently those with which Theophilus had treasonably corresponded with Eugenius, and told Theophilus that they would be published if he did not consent. Blackmail persuaded the bishop of Alexandria. The opportunity would come for Theophilus' revenge.

A saint hard to live with

A large quantity of John's sermons and other writings survives, and they remain edifying and powerful, leaving no question about the judgement of posterity that he was a great saint of the time. At Constantinople, however, he succeeded in making enemies who regarded him as a considerable nuisance to them and their customary ways. There is no necessary incompatibility in the two assessments. Saints are not always easy neighbours. No doubt it is less common to find saints who can be a nuisance than to find nuisances who are not saints. On taking office as bishop and moving into the *episkopeion*, which Nektarios had rebuilt after it was torched by the anti-Nicene faction in the city, John understood his duty to be that of a reformer called to clean the place up. In a sermon soon after arriving he observed that 'people praise a bishop's predecessor when they mean to disparage the present incumbent' (*Hom. in Act.* 3. 4). Several of his clergy he found to be involved in scandals of one kind or another, and simply removed them from office. He did not like clergy in the city keeping the offerings of the faithful for themselves and for maintaining their parish church, and sought to centralize financial control. Nektarios had kept a generous table for guests. John had a weak stomach after his ascetic mortifications; he ate alone and deplored invitations to dinner parties (e.g. *in Ps.* 141. 8, PG 55. 439). This immediately diminished his influence on behalf of church members needing his patronage. It was also badly received by bishops visiting him. Acacius of Beroea (Aleppo) took offence that when he went to see John, a decent lodging was not offered (Palladius, *Dialogue* 6).

Tension with local monks

Constantinople had a number of monasteries, for which the acknowledged leader was named Isaac. John thought the monasteries should look to the bishop, not to Isaac, for authoritative guidance and rulings. Tension grew on this issue, remarkable when one recalls John's strong defence of the monastic movement. One of his sermons on Matthew (8. 5, PG 58. 88) commends the reading of Athanasius' *Life of Antony*. Orthodox dissenters such as the adherents of Novatian, and old believers called Quartodecimans who celebrated Easter on the date of the Jewish Passover, were harassed, and the distress this caused is reflected in the unsympathetic portrait of John in book 6 of Socrates' history, which portrays him as unbendingly rigid and uncompromising—'like a man with no knees'.

Stilicho

When Theodosius I moved west in May 394, he left his son Arcadius under the care of the praetorian prefect Rufinus. Rufinus was soon challenged by the mighty soldier Stilicho of Vandal origin (Orosius 7. 38) in the west, claiming to be regent for both sons, Honorius and Arcadius (Ambrose, *obit. Theodos.* 5; Claudian, *c. Rufinum* 2. 155; Zos. 5. 4. 3). Thereby Stilicho (*PLRE* i. 853) could hope to take all Illyricum, an important source of army recruits, from the east (Zos. 5. 26. 2). Honorius had married his daughter Maria and on her death in 407 her sister Thermantia, so Stilicho could not have been closer to the centre of power in the west. He was zealous for Christianity and against pagan cult (Augustine, *ep.* 97). His ambition to control both east and west may be reflected in the contemporary list of officers of state, *Notitia Dignitatum*, where east and west are separately listed. In 408 after Arcadius' death he was suspected of wanting to install his son as emperor at Constantinople, and accusations of treason led to his execution and so the removal of the one man able to keep Alaric out of Italy.

The prefect Rufinus, Gainas, Eutropius

Relations between east and west at this time were distinctly cool. A measure of the tension can be seen in the fact that at one stage Stilicho fortified western ports to repel all trade with the eastern empire, a decision cancelled after his death in 408 (CTh 7. 16. 1). When Arcadius elevated his eunuch Eutropius to be consul (399), a reward for military success against Huns in Anatolia, Honorius and the west were disgusted and refused to recognize him (Claudian, *in Eutrop*. 1. 319). Claudian's verse invectives against Rufinus and Eutropius marshal a broad attack on the government at Constantinople, reflecting Latin dislike of New Rome. The prefect Rufinus got Arcadius to order Stilicho to withdraw from opposing Alaric in Greece and to release his eastern forces needed to repel Huns from North Syria and Visigoths from Thrace and southern Greece. But Rufinus was unpopular for selling honours, confiscating rich estates, and enjoying torturing people (so at least Claudian, for whom Stilicho was a flawless hero). The furious Stilicho arranged for Rufinus to be brutally murdered by the troops of the eastern military commander Gainas, a Goth who had started in the army as a common soldier and, after a distinguished role at the battle of the Frigidus, received rapid promotion. He was an Arian. In intriguing to eliminate Rufinus, Eutropius co-operated. The prefect's head was triumphantly carried into Constantinople on the point of a spear (Jerome, *ep*. 60. 16; Claudian, *in Rufin*. 2. 335). However, Gainas' ambitions got rid not only of Rufinus but also in autumn 399 of Eutropius, who at Gainas' demand was dismissed by Arcadius and charged with high treason. The contemporary writings of Synesius of Cyrene show that high officials at the eastern capital had come to think overwhelming German influence in the army command was a public danger and should be diminished.

Available choices before the youthful Arcadius and his advisers were thorny. Though Gainas' aspirations were no more than to have power equal to that of Stilicho in the west, that ambition seemed insupportable. On the other hand, the emperor needed an effective army which only Gainas and his Goths could provide. With Rufinus dead and Eutropius cashiered, it was no easy matter to confront Gainas.

Though Eutropius had a big hand in John's appointment as bishop, in power he had vexed him by removing a right of asylum in churches. Now, in his fallen state, he sought asylum himself in Sancta Sophia. John preached a sermon intended to plead for his life, but understood by critics to be kicking Eutropius when he was down. Granting asylum to Eutropius was sharply criticized as implying that John thought the charge of treason false (PG 52. 393–4). No doubt adverse words about Eutropius were necessary to protect John from accusations of being a party to his treason, which Eutropius may have been suggesting. 'A man on a charge attempts not to prove his innocence but to disclose accomplices in his crimes . . . Let no one take offence, I mention no one by name' (*Hom. in Eph.* 6).

Gainas decided that he must control the city of Constantinople and billet his Goths there. He extracted from Arcadius the taking of three hostages from among officials obstructing his ambitions, one of whom, Count John, was on close terms with the handsome empress Eudoxia, reputedly her lover; some said the father of the future Theodosius II. Arcadius and Eudoxia saw in Bishop John the one man who might be a persuasive envoy to soften Gainas and prevent the hostages being killed. The fourth century had had several instances of bishops serving as ambassadors on delicate matters of state. In the negotiation John seems to have told Gainas where to find Count John, which was to lead to lasting accusations of betrayal. Whatever Bishop John may have done (perhaps refusing to allow asylum?), that was unlikely to endear him to Eudoxia. Had John failed both the empire and his church? Some critics thought so. Gossip may have damaged John when Eutropius was taken and executed, with his name deleted from the list of consuls.

In Constantinople Gainas asked Bishop John for a church to be used by his Arian Goths, and was absolutely refused. However, under pressure from the city prefect he may have later relented since Synesius thought that allowing Goths to have their own church services was a move which (by chance) led to them leaving. The billeting of the Goths in the city was hated by the people, and when in July 400 seven hundred of the troops found themselves under attack from a furious mob and sought asylum in a church, they were gruesomely incinerated with the building. The court found in a pagan Goth named Fravitta a commander willing to attack and defeat Gainas, who retreated into Thrace and there was killed by a Hun commander. His head was sent to the emperor.

A column to commemorate Gainas' defeat was erected in the Forum of Arcadius with a statue of this emperor on top. It survived until the eighteenth century.[6]

Bishop John's principal enemies turned out to be clergy, but he also succeeded in losing the support of the palace. In 401 a woman complained that Eudoxia had taken over her property. Did John mention Naboth's vineyard (1 Kings 21) and Jezebel? It was reported that a sermon by John offended the empress (Palladius, *Dialogue* 8 end). Probably he used the fateful words.

---

[6] Gainas' story is in Socrates (6. 6) and Synesius (*De providentia*), who was in Constantinople at the time negotiating tax reduction for his city Ptolemais in Cyrenaica. Critical studies in T. S. Burns, *Barbarians within the Gates of Rome* (Bloomington, Ind., 1994); J. H. G. W. Liebeschuetz, *Barbarians and Bishops: Army Church and State in the age of Arcadius and Chrysostom* (Oxford, 1990); Alan Cameron and Jacqueline Long, *Barbarians and Politics at the Court of Arcadius* (Berkeley, 1993). A clear summary of complex intrigue in Warren Treadgold, *History of the Byzantine State and Society* (Stanford, 1997, 78 ff.).

Origenism

The arrival in Constantinople of ascetic admirers of Origen expelled from Egypt by Theophilus was bound to be awkward for John. His sympathies like theirs were against anthropomorphic language about God. Evagrius of Pontus was aware that an anthropomorphic deity (an old man in the sky on a throne) is creaturely, finite and limited, and cannot satisfy the needs of true religion. John's commentary on Psalm 43, PG 55. 172, is explicit:

The soul grows up with the body and never sees anything bodiless; it longs for the things of the senses. It needs to be led by the hand from visible to mental entities. That is why when the prophets spoke about God, they needed to speak of human limbs, not to give that undefiled nature the shapes of bodily parts, but to educate the soul brought up among things of sense to advance from human imagery to truths transcending humanity. While the activity of God is a concept of the mind, the psalmist offers a material image lest the people of that time should fail to believe.

A similar polemic occurs in the commentary on Psalm 7 (PG 55. 97–8): language about God having bow and arrows is used because of the stupidity of thick hearers, and must be interpreted in a way worthy of God. The author of these words was bound to be sympathetic to the Origenist Tall Brothers from Egypt, Bishop Dioscoros of Hermopolis Parva (Damanhur), Ammonius, Eusebius, and Euthymius. Their stormy exodus had been accompanied by numerous other monks. They went by Jerusalem to Scythopolis, but Theophilus' pursuit took them to Constantinople. They were accompanied by the former confidant of Theophilus, Isidore, who had objected to a shady financial deal by Theophilus and found himself called to answer to a synod on a charge of sodomy many decades previously. There was therefore an inescapable problem for John in events which must end in him arbitrating for or against the bishop of Alexandria, who not unnaturally considered his own see, not New Rome, to be the second see of the empire's church and himself the bishop entitled to sit in judgement on the bishop of an upstart city which sought to enhance its standing by gathering relics of holy people from elsewhere.

Trouble at Ephesus; simony

Already in Nektarios' time the see of New Rome had been called upon to preside over inquiries into disputes well outside not only the diocese but the province. On 30 September 394 Nektarios presided at a synod of 37 bishops, including Alexandria and Antioch, to adjudicate between two rival bishops of Bostra in Arabia. In April 400 John was presiding over a synod of bishops coming from the province of Asia for which Ephesus was metropolis;

unexpectedly the bishop of Ephesus, named Antoninus, was attacked by one of his suffragans, Eusebius of Valentinopolis, a tribal village community in the hills at the source of the river Kaystros, elevated to city status by Valens. Eusebius refused to be silenced, and excitedly interrupted the synod's liturgical celebration by brandishing his list of seven accusations. He claimed that Antoninus had melted down church plate and used the proceeds of sale for his son; he had taken marbles from the baptistery and used them for his private bath; in his dining room he had erected columns belonging to the church (admittedly they had been lying about for some years); he had not got rid of a slave who was a murderer; he sold lands given to the church by the emperor Julian's mother, Basilina, and pocketed the cash; after separating from his wife, he rejoined her to beget children; he regularly charged a fee for ordaining bishops proportionate to their diocesan revenues.

Antoninus and bishops alleged to have paid him fees denied the allegations and, as Eusebius could not prove his case, deadlock was reached. John thereupon announced that three bishops would investigate. One of the three bishops was Palladius of Helenopolis, to whom we owe a strongly partisan narrative of John's career and tragedy.[7] One, a friend of Antoninus, excused himself. The third was Syncletus of Trajanopolis, another tribal community in the hills inland. The inquiry was held at Hypaipa and, since no witnesses arrived, achieved nothing. Antoninus died and the next problem was dissension at Ephesus about a successor. John was invited to sort things out. After baptizing Eudoxia's infant the future Theodosius II on 6 January 402 (Soz. 8. 18. 5 cites Eudoxia describing John as 'baptizer of her children'), he embarked on a winter sea-journey, leaving the administration of the capital's churches to his abrasive archdeacon Sarapion, who had a genius for giving offence. Episcopal duties he entrusted to Severian, bishop of Gabala, a small but beautiful town on the coast of Syria (Jeble, south of Latakia), who, despite his Syrian accent, had won popularity by his homilies and appreciated the financial rewards of good preaching in the capital. Severian was especially favoured by the empress Eudoxia.

At Ephesus John summoned a large synod, seventy bishops from Asia, Lydia, and Caria, with some from Phrygia as well. A choice between rival candidates proved difficult. John arranged for his own deacon, Herakleides, to be elected and consecrated, having presumably brought him from Constantinople. He was a disciple of Evagrius of Pontus and therefore a devoted Origenist; before long that was to cause trouble. At the time the laity of Ephesus were much dissatisfied and rioted (Socrates 6. 11. 11).

The old complaint that Antoninus had charged ordination fees was not yet dead. Six bishops were proved by good witnesses to have paid up, and they

---

[7] Edited and annotated by A. M. Malingrey and P. Leclerq (SC 341–2; Paris, 1988).

eventually admitted their guilt, pleading in extenuation that their motive for becoming bishops had been to gain exemption from the heavy duties of town councillors. At a time when this was a frequent form of tax avoidance which the government was trying to stop (CTh 9. 45. 3 of July 398), it did not seem dreadful. They asked to have their money back if they could not continue as bishops; they could need it for curial responsibilities. John agreed: they could only have lay communion, but Antoninus' heirs should repay them, and John would petition the emperor to allow them exemption from curial duties.

It was soon claimed that 'on a single day' John had deposed not merely six but thirteen bishops for simony; it is likely enough that seven from provinces other than Asia were also removed from office. All were replaced. John further arranged for the shutting of churches belonging to Novatianists, Quartodecimans, and other dissenters. Novatianists at Constantinople enjoyed respect; Socrates' history, sympathetic to Novatianists, presents John's actions as high-handed.

On the way home John passed through Nicomedia and removed from office the local bishop Gerontius, who had once been a deacon in Milan but was sacked by Ambrose and went east to find alternative church employment. The laity of Nicomedia liked Gerontius, were angry at what had been done, and were not placated by the replacement, once Eudoxia's tutor, installed over their heads by John. Riots followed. Naturally the deposed bishops and their supporters claimed that John's actions were an innovation, ignoring traditional customs and local rights (Soz. 8. 6. 9). It was obviously a true claim. But John must have had support from the emperor in his reforming zeal and his assumption that the bishop of New Rome had wider responsibilities and power beyond his own diocese or province. Soon after Easter 402 he was back in Constantinople.[8]

Severian of Gabala

While John was away, Severian of Gabala had not been loyal to him. Indeed he had been ambitious enough to be denigrating John and charming the court ladies by his relaxed and easy-going style. Paradoxically a number of Severian's sermons have survived under John's name. John had many critics who were glad to use Severian as a focus for their discontents. He and the archdeacon Sarapion were in no kind of rapport. It was customary to rise in the presence of a bishop (Socrates 6. 11. 6). A day came when Sarapion failed to rise, probably because he had not noticed Severian come by, and Severian

---

[8] The sermon preached on his return is printed by A. Wenger in *Revue des études byzantines*, 19 (1961), 110–23. The chronology of his movements is examined by Cameron and Long (n. 6), 405–8.

exploded with anger. On learning of this fracas, John asked Severian to return to little Gabala, and according to reports put robust members of his staff called 'deans' to expedite his departure. Eudoxia begged for his retention.

Olympias

John lost influential friends by persuading wealthy widows to give more support to churches and monasteries than to their dependent families. The widow Olympias had a close friendship with him, which could be compared to that between Bishop Francis de Sales and St Jane Frances de Chantal early in the seventeenth century, intimate and affectionate but with distance kept. There were sly accusations that he received women alone, but the relationship of admiration between Olympias and John was careful and controlled. Among these ladies some had connections with the Latin west.

The synod of the Oak

In late summer 402 Arcadius granted leave for a synod to investigate the charges against Theophilus of Alexandria. John was reluctant to preside, but gathered forty bishops, including seven metropolitans. His enemies at Constantinople meanwhile manufactured evidence against him, presenting selected perhaps doctored homilies as mockery of Eudoxia and the court. Theophilus did not arrive until 403, according to Palladius (8) 'laden with bribes like a beetle laden with dung'. He avoided contact with John, and rapidly gathered round him those alienated by John's reforms or those removed from office. Fortified by their complaints, he assembled his own synod on the other side of the Bosporos in a place called 'the Oak' at Rufinianae, an estate formerly owned by the murdered prefect Rufinus who had founded there a martyrion for the apostles Peter and Paul and a monastery with Egyptian monks. A summary of the synod of the Oak was preserved in the ninth century by Photius (*Bibliotheca* 59). Of the thirty-six episcopal signatories, twenty-nine were Egyptian. The synod was dominated by enemies: Theophilus, Acacius, Antiochus of Ptolemais, Severian of Gabala, and Cyrinos of Chalcedon, who was from Egypt.

Theophilus saw that there could be a case against John if he were shown to have received Origenists to communion. He therefore invited the respected heresy-hunter Epiphanius of Salamis to come from Cyprus. On arrival Epiphanius manifested his extreme distrust of John's orthodoxy by ordaining a deacon in defiance of canon law (much as he had done at Bethlehem, p. 438). Nevertheless John warmly invited him to reside at the bishop's house, an invitation which he curtly rejected. He would not share communion with John until he had expelled the refugee Origenists from the capital and had signed a condemnation of Origen (Socrates 6. 14). He assembled the bishops then in Constantinople and similarly invited them to sign a censure of Origen and his works; some did but the majority refused, led by Theotimus of Tomi (Constanţa in Romania). Stories circulated about Epiphanius and what had been discussed when he met Eudoxia. Sozomen reports that the Tall Brothers met Epiphanius, extracted an admission that he had never read any of their writings, and flatteringly declared that they unreservedly admired his works. Epiphanius left Constantinople in disillusion, perhaps even with some glimmering of realization that he had been a pawn in Theophilus' hand. He died on his return voyage to Salamis.

Theophilus had travelled from Alexandria by land, sending his suffragans by sea, and passing through Asia Minor he had discovered the apprehensions shared by metropolitans in Asia Minor as they contemplated the authoritarian ways of the bishop of Constantinople. Probably there was already fear that John's successors, if not himself, would be charging ordination fees. Naturally enough bishops deposed by John were among the angrier malcontents. Theophilus landed at the port where Egyptian grain ships discharged their cargoes, and so was acclaimed by the Alexandrian sailors. Hospitality offered by John was abrasively declined, and Theophilus wholly refused to share in prayer or communion with him. Ominously he accepted hospitality from Eudoxia herself, an act which must presuppose either that Eudoxia was already irritated with John or less probably that she dreamt of reconciling the two protagonists. The palace was an impressive address from which to be recruiting support.

Arcadius' synod to examine charges against Theophilus was transformed at the Oak into a trial of John, the defendant being absent. John's absence defied an instruction from Arcadius and no doubt cost him the support of the court. Pointedly the presidency of the synod was given to the bishop of Herakleia, the old metropolis to which Byzantium had once been suffragan. At the Oak Makarios bishop of Magnesia accused the Origenist Herakleides of Ephesus, installed by John after simony had been discovered.

Against John no one specifically mentioned Origenism; there were complaints which Socrates (6. 15. 13) thought absurd. He had sold marbles from Gregory of Nazianzus' little church of St Anastasia. He had treated his clergy as a corrupt lot, spoken contemptuously of Epiphanius, treated Severian abrasively, nominated one Antony to be a bishop despite his robbery of tombs, betrayed Count John to Gainas, conducted ordinations of deacons and presbyters outside the eucharistic liturgy,[9] failed to attend the funerals of

---

[9] The same charge was brought against Bishop Domnus of Antioch at the Council of Ephesus, in 449. Probably this was not liturgical custom of Antioch.

those who, on his verdict, had gone to prison and died there, refused to speak to Acacius of Beroea, handed over two presbyters to Eutropius for punishment, had a bath heated only for himself. Eating alone, 'he feasted like a Cyclops'. He gave money to bishops ordained by him so that he could maintain power. Palladius bishop of Helenopolis (and admirer of Evagrius of Pontus) was also a target for attack. The monk Isaac presented a separate list of complaints, including one that he offered easy and repeated absolution to baptized sinners. By quoting a sermon against radical Arians, Isaac was able to attribute to John the opinion he was engaged in refuting. He disapproved of John's ordaining to be bishops slaves who had not been emancipated and did not belong to him.

The case of the sale of marbles from St Anastasia was presented by the archpriest (*protopresbýteros*) Arsacius, who succeeded John in the see, and by the priest Atticus who was to be Arsacius' successor.

Although summoned four times, John refused to appear before a synod of his avowed enemies. He could therefore be declared deposed for contumacy. In his pulpit John declared 'again Herodias dances and seeks John's head'. The weak Arcadius ratified the verdict and a military escort conducted John by sea to Prainetos in Bithynia, a port on the south side of the gulf of Astakos not far from Nicaea. The people of Constantinople were outraged and let their feelings be known. However, the following day Eudoxia recalled him, sending her chamberlain Brison, because in the imperial bedroom there had been a 'catastrophe' (*thrausis*), a still-birth. Eudoxia no doubt took this as a sign of divine anger; John's supporters did so. With Brison she sent a note that she had no responsibility for the wicked conspiracy. No doubt John could have had reason to suspect this. When eventually found, John declared that until the decision of the Oak was formally cancelled, he could not resume office. Brison was not the last imperial messenger to bring persuasion to bear until finally John yielded. Without entering the city he returned to a villa near the capital. The longer he stayed away, the hotter was the anger of the populace against the palace. A synod could soon annul the decision against him. Meanwhile Theophilus rapidly withdrew to Alexandria.

Eudoxia's statue

John's opponents were not pleased at his recall. The great church of Sancta Sophia was occupied by furious monks opposing John, disrupting the regular services and demanding that worshippers denounce him. Soldiers were called in to turn them out and the violence left several monks dead. Under pressure John came in to preach to his supporters (PG 52. 440), welcomed by an enthusiastic crowd of many thousands. The opposition could use the weapon that there had been no annulment of the verdict against him except by the empress which for the Church did not count. They cited a canon of a council of Antioch (ascribed to the council of 341, but actually a dozen or so years earlier) forbidding appeals to the secular power; this invited the rejoinder that this was an 'Arian' synod. A better chance came in November 403 when the city prefect honoured Eudoxia with a marble statue placed close to the great church. The silver base with a dedicatory inscription survives (*ILS* 822), now in the garden beside Sancta Sophia; it shows that the gift was as much to honour the city prefect as the empress. Hubbub at the dedication disturbed worshippers inside the church, and John unwisely gave vent to irritation.

The erection of such an honorific statue to an emperor's consort was politically significant. Statues of Eudoxia were also sent to the provinces, to the distress of Honorius (Avell. 38). John was taken to be joining with the critics of a cause dear to Arcadius and the city prefect. The anger of the palace confined John to his house.

John's expulsion, exile, and death

At Easter 404 the customary baptism was in the hands of John's clergy. Four hundred soldiers, untrained recruits, were told to break up the proceedings. Half-naked women fled the bloody scene; the sacrament was defiled. John had lost support at the palace, and soon after Pentecost a deputation of bishops who had led the synod of the Oaks demanded John's permanent removal. In June Eudoxia endorsed the decision to exile him. (Her death in October seemed to John's supporters a divine judgement.) John appealed to Pope Innocent I and to the bishops of Milan and Aquileia, bade his supporters to be peaceful and loyal to his successor, and then crossed the Bosporus. The furious Johnites rioted, and the church of Sancta Sophia suffered severe damage from fire.

Arsacius was named John's successor, and Johnites refusing communion with him were harassed, Olympias being heavily fined and exiled. Arsacius lasted only a few months, and was succeeded by Atticus, who was no more acceptable to the Johnites. Hostile monks endangered John's life as he was being conducted by guards across Asia Minor to the desolate town of Cucusus in Armenia Secunda. After a year he was moved to Arabissos in Cappadocia, but that was too easily reached by old friends from Antioch (Palladius, *Dialogue* 11). Meanwhile Innocent of Rome was putting strong pressure on the court and the patriarch to a degree and in a manner of assertive authority that were much resented, producing the decision that John had to be eliminated. In 407 he was moved to a military fort on the Black Sea coast; but the long journey on foot in the summer heat killed him as without doubt it was intended to do. He died on the road near Comana in Pontus on 14 September 407.[10]

From the seventh century John was named 'Golden Mouth', and preachers used anthologies of his sermons.[11]

---

[10] A funerary oration, delivered not in Constantinople but not far away, was delivered by a devoted Johnite, a deacon Cosmas, which survives (Paris. gr. 1519, s. xi–xii). Its important content is clarified by T. D. Barnes, *Studia Patristica*, 37 (Leuven, 2001), 328–45.

[11] The best study of John in English is J. N. D. Kelly, *Golden Mouth* (London, 1995). A full bibliography is appended to the fine article in *Reallexikon für Antike und Christentum* by R. Brändle (1997). Palladius' *Dialogue on the Life of Chrysostom* is critically edited by A. Malingrey (SC 341–2, Paris, 1988). In the same series she has edited several works by John. But for most of his writings one must use Montfaucon, reprinted by Migne's PG. A catalogue of works and editions is best found in Geerard's *Clavis Patrum Graecorum*, ii (Turnhout, 1974) and *Supplementum* (1998). The English translation (London, 1959–60) of C. Baur's *Johannes Chrysostomos und seine Zeit* (Munich, 1930), has to be used with caution; so too E. A. Clark, Jerome, *Chrysostom and friends* (Lewiston, NY, 1979). G. Dagron's studies of Constantinople in John's age are important, as are the studies of Antioch by J. H. G. W. Liebeschuetz, G. Downey, and A. J. Festugière.

50

INNOCENT I AND
JOHN CHRYSOSTOM'S HONOUR:
ALARIC AND THE FALL OF ROME

Without excommunicating Theophilus, Innocent opposes him

Theophilus tersely and belatedly notified Pope Innocent I of the decision taken by the synod at the Oak deposing John. John's appeal was taken to the west by four bishops; already John had a representative at Rome supportive of his cause. The harassment of Johnites at Constantinople soon led to a flood of refugees travelling to Italy, among whom Palladius of Helenopolis (author of the *Lausiac History* and chronicler of John's troubles) was one. Theophilus realized that Innocent was listening to adverse reports on his goings-on, and accordingly sent a longer statement with a copy of the synodical acts of the Oak; these thereby became available to Palladius for his account of the tragedy. In reply to John's appeal to the canon of Constantinople (381) forbidding bishops to interfere outside their own diocese, Theophilus cited a canon of Antioch to persuade Innocent to excommunicate John, and was to receive the sharp reply that the Roman see recognized no canons other than those of Nicaea. (No doubt he thought the canons of Serdica had Nicene authority; in fact Innocent rejects any authority in canons labelled Serdican, *ep.* 7.3). Theophilus also composed a defence of his conduct, clearly convinced that in judging John he had been upholding the right and the good and that John would go to hell. Jerome put it into Latin for him (*epp.* 113–14). A Latin citation survives in Facundus in the sixth century. In Egypt Isidore of Pelusium estimated Theophilus as a worshipper of gold, whose faults were seen in the tragedy of John (*ep.* 1. 152, PG 78. 285 A).

The persecution of the Johnites abated after a damaging storm with hail, thunder, and earthquake at Constantinople, taken by the populace to indicate celestial disapproval of the harassment (*Chronicon Paschale*. a. 408).

In a letter now lost Innocent wrote to Theophilus expressing dissatisfaction about the treatment of John, and repeated this in a second letter inviting Theophilus to a 'canonical' synod held under the Nicene canons which alone Rome accepted. He had evidently been told that Theophilus' faction had been appealing to an Arian canon. He wrote to the clergy and laity at Constantinople deploring their acceptance of a bishop replacing John, and declared that the matter should be reconsidered at an ecumenical synod; that implied that Innocent was not regarding the matter as one to be decided by his own Petrine jurisdiction. The fact that John's appeal had been not only to Rome but also to Milan and Aquileia shows that John himself understood the west's authority to be diffused and not concentrated in one influential bishop.

Greek resentment at the west's stand

In 404 the western emperor Honorius was moved to write to his brother the eastern emperor Arcadius asking for agreement that a synod be held at Thessalonica, which Theophilus should be compelled to attend. If that synod upheld John's excommunication, that would be accepted; if not, the bishops censuring him faced excommunication. The western synod laid down that the proposed council at Thessalonica would cross-question John on the basis that he appeared fully reinstated in office prior to any decision. (This model was to reappear in the ninth century at the retrial of the patriarch Ignatius.) In other words, the synod of the Oak was considered null and void, which was hard for Constantinople and the court to take. Honorius' envoys were disgracefully treated, imprisoned in Thrace, not allowed to deliver their letter, and only in 406 allowed to go home to Italy. At Constantinople the western legates were regarded as a gross interference in eastern affairs. The Greek prefect Anthemius was much opposed to allowing Stilicho and his friends to take over Illyricum. Meanwhile in his third year of exile, John wrote a wretched letter to Innocent telling of his trials—hunger, disease, isolation, and daily murders by Isaurian thugs in the vicinity. Bandits controlled all roads, but he was sending this sad letter by a presbyter and a deacon, hoping they would get through. In practice Innocent's representations to Arcadius and to Theophilus were ineffective; all he could do was to write to John recommending patience, a virtue he had to practise himself. Nevertheless the Pope had taken a stand on the issue of imperial intervention in an ecclesiastical matter, and that was a powerful position. Moreover, he had the support of influential Roman aristocrats.

Thessalonica as a location for the desired ecumenical synod was a prudent choice. It implied western authority in Illyricum. Innocent's first extant letter had been to Anysius bishop of Thessalonica, renewing the appointment of papal vicar in Illyricum, an office already held under Damasus, Siricius, and Anastasius. He was assured that Anysius would support whatever judgement Rome reached. Innocent was aware of conflict between Honorius and

Arcadius concerning the control of Illyricum (*ep.* 8), a disagreement casting a long shadow forward to later centuries. Innocent's letters show particular concern for orthodoxy and good order in the churches of Illyricum and Macedonia. The see of Rome, wrote Innocent (*ep.* 17. 1), is 'caput ecclesiarum', the head of the churches; it embodies the tradition of the apostles (17. 9, 25). Apostolate and episcopate take their origin from St Peter (*ep.* 2. 2). Nevertheless in relation to the east, only synodical procedure would be effective. The synod he gathered had to be entirely western but was strong. Moreover, politically Honorius and Stilicho were blaming the inertia of Constantinople for a Gothic rampage in the Balkans.

Innocent versus three eastern patriarchs

Innocent's representations being ignored, he assumed a breach of communion with John's second successor Atticus,[1] with Porphyry successor of Flavian at Antioch, and with Theophilus of Alexandria, but apparently without giving formal notice. It was public that he was in communion with the bishops supporting John. The bishop of Jerusalem upheld John. But three of the four eastern 'patriarchs', as they would soon come to be called, stood together in opposition to Innocent, and continued to do so after Arcadius died on 1 May 408. His consort Eudoxia had predeceased him on 6 October 404. Arcadius was succeeded by the young Theodosius II, seven years of age, destined to rule until 450, when he fell off his horse and died. Actual power was exercised with high ability by the praetorian prefect Anthemius, whose career had included a succession of major offices. Anthemius was responsible for rebuilding the great walls of Constantinople (ILS 5339). He was certainly a Christian. Among the letters congratulating him on his appointment as prefect was one from John Chrysostom in exile (*ep.* 147).

There was one predictable source of weakness in an otherwise unanimous western stance, namely the Catholics of north Africa. The bishops decided to write to Pope Innocent urging that the churches of Rome and Alexandria should be at peace (Register of the church of Carthage 101, CCSL 149, p. 217 Munier). They wanted compromise and an end to the damaging quarrel. It was a plea comparable to that proposed from Carthage in 359 at the time of the synod of Nike. Rome surely disliked it; wicked injustice needed rectification.

---

[1] Atticus was reputed to be a dull preacher, and not much of his work survives. Professor F. J. Thomson has lately found one sermon in Slavonic: *Analecta Bollandiana*, 113 (2000), 5–36.

Rome at peace with Antioch

After a decade, and then only slowly Innocent began to win. The death of Porphyry of Antioch brought to that see Alexander, who saw a chance to break the lifeline of the little Eustathian congregation dependent on the now fading recognition given by successive bishops of Rome. If Innocent would withdraw support from the Eustathians, who since Evagrius' death had no bishop, Alexander would include the name of John Chrysostom in the dip-tychs commemorating the saints with whom his church was in communion. The deal succeeded. Alexander told Atticus he was coerced by his laity into a decision unwelcome at Constantinople and Alexandria.

Innocent told Alexander of Antioch that the two Petrine sees should give a lead to the other sees. Acacius of Beroea, who had been bitter against John, saw which way the wind was beginning to blow, and wrote to Innocent asking for a letter of communion. Innocent reasonably assumed Beroea to be within the jurisdiction of Antioch, and therefore replied that this was indeed in order provided that Bishop Alexander was satisfied with Acacius' sincerity.

Jurisdiction of Antioch

Alexander of Antioch was acutely conscious of the jurisdiction of his see in relation to other provinces in the civil Diocese, and wanted the support of Rome for his conviction that he had to have a controlling say over the choice and ordination of new bishops. No one was contesting his right to ordain metropolitans; he wanted the right to veto the metropolitans' choice of unsuitable suffragans favoured by local interests. Innocent answered his every wish saying that, in the entire civil Diocese Oriens, no bishop should be con-secrated without leave from the bishop of Antioch, who embodied the authority of St Peter and whose extra-provincial jurisdiction was acknow-ledged in the sixth canon of Nicaea. For Innocent episcopal jurisdiction had nothing to do with the secular dignity of the city. That was something on which bishops of Rome could be expected to feel strongly. He advised that if the see in question was near Antioch, the bishop of Antioch should conse-crate; if it was distant, he should delegate authority to the metropolitan in writing.

Innocent's directions no doubt reflected the situation for the Roman see in Italy. They did not necessarily correspond to the actualities of Syrian cus-tom, where metropolitans decided on ordinations of bishops in their province as directed by the sixth Nicene canon, and the see of Antioch might be referred to only in case of serious trouble. Evidence, however, supports the view that Innocent had some influence. At the second session of the council of Ephesus in 449, preserved in a Syriac manuscript in the British Library,[2] Photius bishop of Tyre, appointed to be metropolitan in September 448, records that Domnos of Antioch had written to him directing him to ordain a bishop to replace a Nestorian in the see of Byblos.

Alexander also asked Pope Innocent if, when a province was divided into two by the imperial government, a new metropolitan bishopric had to be created. This was no theoretical question but involved matters of principle as well as actual practice. Innocent was against any such notion: like Basil of Caesarea when Cappadocia was divided, he wanted church structures to be wholly independent of the state, a view also found in Gregory of Nazianzos (*ep.* 185). With few exceptions this was far from being the case. Not long before the time of Alexander's correspondence with Innocent, the provinces of both Syria and Palestine had been divided, as is evident from the *Notitia Dignitatum* or official list of civil and military offices of about 408 with some subsequent updating. In March 409 Palestine already consisted of three administrative units (CTh 7. 4. 30). In the *Notitia Dignitatum* Syria stands beside Syria Salutaris, as it does not in earlier lists. Probably therefore the bishops of new metropoleis (in Syria II, Apamea; in Palestine II, Scythopolis) were asserting rights that Antioch was being reluctant to recognize.

From Hadrian onwards the title 'metropolis' could be awarded by the emperor as an honour without implications that such a city would be the residence of the provincial governor. This was certainly the situation in the sixth century in Justinian's time (Procopius, *Aedif.* 5. 4. 17–18, and instances in Malalas).[3] But the Nicene canons assume only one in each province; probably that was normal in the east in 325.

Tension between Tyre and Berytos

At the council of Chalcedon in 451 (19th session) there was tense consideration of a dispute in Phoenicia where the bishops of Tyre and Berytos (Beirut) presided over cities both with the title 'metropolis', Theodosius II having awarded this title to Berytos. At Ephesus in 449 Photius of Tyre did not come well out of an investigation of Ibas of Edessa, whereas Eustathius of Berytos had supported Dioscorus of Alexandria and was therefore favoured. Anatolius of Constantinople and his resident synod had given the bishop of Berytos a consequential right to ordain bishops in six nearby towns, hitherto under the old metropolis of Tyre. This decision was put to Maximus of

---

[2] Ed. J. Flemming, pp. 76–7; see below, Ch. 53 n. 3.

[3] See R. Haensch, *Capita Provinciarum, Statthaltersitze und Provinzialverwaltung in der römischen Kaiserzeit* (Mainz, 1997), 24–5. That the governor of Syria Phoinike resided in Tyre is assumed by Socrates *HE* 1. 19.

Antioch, at the time in Constantinople though not in the synod; on seeing Anatolius' signature, he signed also. Photius was threatened with deposition if he did not acquiesce but he refused. Notice of excommunication was sent to him by the synod; he had not been heard in his defence.

The honour of Berytos could have secular grounds. It was known for luxury silks (Procopius, *Anekdota* 25. 14). The city's law school was famous with a long history and was more than a private institution. The mid-fourth-century *Expositio totius mundi et gentium* (25, ed. J. Rougé SC 124. 1966) and texts of Libanius (*or.* 2. 44, 48. 11, 62. 21–3) tell of its glories as the source of good Roman law, sending out learned men to be assessors to provincial governors, and as a repository for texts of imperial constitutions. The Theodosian Code was compiled, 429–38, by high officials in Constantinople. In part perhaps this imperial honour for Berytos reflected the emperor's pleasure at the contribution of lawyers trained there towards the making of the great law code of 438, even though some were not more than research assistants helping in the mammoth task of unearthing texts of past constitutions. Antiochos Chuzon, however, almost certainly a former student at Berytos, an ex-quaestor (i.e. minister of justice) then praetorian prefect in the East and consul, 'sublime in all respects', holds the first place among those thanked by Theodosius when the Code was finally promulgated (NTh 1. 7). He might well have been an effective petitioner on Berytos' behalf. (His career in *PLRE* ii, 103–4. He was dead by November 444: NTh 26.)

The decisions about Tyre and Berytos were determined by the side each was on in the dramas of the council of Ephesus in 449. At that council Ibas of Edessa was condemned, though previously acquitted by Photius of Tyre and Eustathius of Berytos, appointed by the emperor to hear complaints of Edessene presbyters. At Ephesus in August 449 Photius had to support Dioscorus of Alexandria in the condemnation of Ibas. The emperor Marcian ordered Photius' reinstatement. Did removing excommunication cancel the split into two provinces? After the split, Photius ordained two bishops for the cities now under Berytos; Eustathius demoted them to be presbyters. At Chalcedon Photius condemned Dioscorus, and signed for bishops in the northern part of the province. Luckily for him Eustathius of Berytos was under a cloud for active support to Dioscorus at Ephesus, and the council of Chalcedon restored the *status quo ante*.

At Chalcedon there was debate whether this conciliar decision was determined by canon law or by the emperor's constitution. Canon law prevailed. Bishop Photius of Tyre was upheld by the council in objecting to Bishop Eustathius of Berytos' claiming ordination rights over six sees in his province, one of which was Byblos (*ACO* II i. 465. 5). This decision was enforced by canon 12. But Berytos retained the title of honorary metropolis. That was not the council's business.

Eustathius of Berytos disowned responsibility for obtaining the imperial constitution on the status of his city proud of its law school (*Act. Chalc.* 19. 23). The petition to the emperor had not come from him. No one thought this a problem to be settled merely by the bishop of Antioch.

Nicomedia and Nicaea

There were precedents for honorific titles of metropolis. In Bithynia Nicomedia, the actual metropolis with the seat of administration, had long had competition from Nicaea (Dio Chrysostom 38) where the title was an honour without practical consequences in provincial government. Bishops of Nicaea were not slow to ask for rights and to claim precedents. The fourteenth session at Chalcedon in October 451 decided in favour of Nicomedia's exclusive rights for ordinations.

Domnos of Antioch

Domnos of Antioch risked Alexandrian anger by asserting that Peter's see must be superior to Mark's. There could also be difficulty with Juvenal, an ambitious bishop of Jerusalem wanting to extend his jurisdiction at Antioch's expense. Domnos translated to Arka in Phoenicia I a bishop that Juvenal of Jerusalem had expected to appoint to a Palestinian see (Syriac Acts of Ephesus 449, p. 127 ed. Flemming). When bishops of the province of Phoenicia Libanensis had ordained one Peter to be bishop of Emesa, Domnos had over-ruled their decision and, merely by placing the gospels on his candidate's head without assembling the provincial bishops, had ordained Uranios instead (ibid., p. 125). He was a friend of Theodoret and therefore more congenial to Domnos, whose close affinity with Theodoret in theology led him to pro-vide a special lodging for him at Antioch to encourage frequent visits. This affair at Emesa was resented. Nevertheless these episodes suggest that Innocent's letter to Alexander had a marked effect on the powers asserted by the see of Antioch. The story helps to explain why at Ephesus in 449 Dioscorus of Alexandria was determined to overthrow Domnos. During the painful internal Syrian disputes whether John of Antioch's compromise with Cyril of Alexandria in 433 could honestly be accepted as other than a fudge, John much offended metropolitans who dissented from him by consecrating bishops in their jurisdiction.

Cyprus

A special problem for Alexander and successive bishops of Antioch was the status of the church in Cyprus, whose bishops regarded their island as autocephalous on the ground of their foundation by St Barnabas. Innocent (*ep.* 24) held this claim to autocephaly to be excluded by the sixth canon of Nicaea. In practice the future favoured the claims of Cypriot bishops to be independent of Antioch, and Innocent's ruling was ignored. At the council of Ephesus in 431, where Bishop John of Antioch was in a weak position, the Cypriot bishops successfully pleaded that they had always chosen and consecrated their own bishops without interference from Antioch. Autocephaly did not imply a breach of communion or a different code of canon law.

Reluctance to canonize John Chrysostom

The lead given by Alexander of Antioch in inserting the name of John Chrysostom in the diptychs of his liturgy was not at once followed by Atticus of Constantinople. A letter from Innocent to a Bishop Maximian in Macedonia discloses that Atticus had sent a deputation of clergy to Rome asking for restored communion, but would not agree to the condition imposed by Innocent, namely that John's name be included in the diptychs (Theodoret, *HE* 5. 34. 12). Another extant letter from Innocent (*ep.* 23, PL 20. 546), preserved by the sixth-century canonist Dionysius Exiguus, asks a presbyter named Boniface to inform Atticus' supporters that to be out of communion with the Roman see is to forsake the unity of the one Church.

Atticus finally yielded if only to reconcile the Johnites, and wrote to Cyril, Theophilus' successor at Alexandria, to inform him (reported in Nikephoros Kallistos, *HE* 14. 26): if the body of the Arian Eudoxius could lie under the altar at the Church of the Apostles in Constantinople, surely one could remember the dead John without unbearable insult to the memory of 'your father Theophilus, the equal of the apostles'. Cyril was Theophilus' nephew, and was so reluctant to jettison Theophilus' hostile stance that his initial reaction in reply to Atticus was to describe John as a Judas Iscariot. We owe to Nestorius the clear information that even Cyril ultimately and most unwillingly agreed to honour John's memory. Perhaps that was after Nestorius' elevation in 428 when Alexandria needed Roman support in the long rivalry with Constantinople.[4]

Constantinople's jurisdiction undiminished

Under Atticus there was no diminution of the jurisdiction of New Rome. Insofar as John's opponents at the synod of the Oak aspired to stop the

---

[4] Nestorius cited by Severus of Antioch, *Contra impium grammaticum* 3. 39. ed. Lebon (CSCO). The Atticus/Cyril correspondence is edited by E. Schwartz, *Codex Vaticanus graecus 1431*, Abh. Bay. Akad. 32/6 (Munich, 1927) pp. 23–8 with discussion 94–6; PG 77. 347–59.

exercise of wide jurisdiction by the bishops of Constantinople, they had failed. Socrates (7. 36) records that Atticus consecrated a bishop Silvanus to the metropolitan see of Thrace, Philippopolis, an act which Innocent might have regarded as intruding into Roman jurisdiction exercised through the vicariate of Thessalonica. Silvanus found the climate too cold and retreated to live in Constantinople, whence Atticus soon despatched him to the see of Troas where he became notable for launching a large ship obstinately adhering to the 'shores' (or launching woodwork) and for referring litigants in his court to a lay judge, never to clergy. Socrates (7. 25) also tells of Atticus consecrating for the see of Nicaea in Bithynia. His successor Sisinnius got rid of an inconvenient rival for his own see, Proclus, by nominating him for Cyzicus, where, however, the people would not accept the decision, claiming perhaps correctly that the emperor's ruling that the bishop of Constantinople had a right of nomination applied only to Atticus, not to successors. Sisinnius did not dispute their view.

By the time of Atticus' death (10 October 425) communion between Rome and Constantinople had been restored, and John's name had been included in the diptychs of New Rome. Atticus had greatly pleased the Roman see by his cold treatment of Caelestius the zealous Pelagian.

The dignity of Constantinople asserted in the too explicit canon of the council of 381 had offended Pope Damasus, and Rome did not then recognize the council which was claimed to be 'ecumenical'. It is remarkable that Innocent's stand against the proceedings of Theophilus had the effect of imparting a nimbus of sanctity to the memory of John, and thereby enhancing the honour of the see of New Rome. Admittedly, there were anxious doubters long after this time who felt unsure about John. Writing before 634 John Moschos (*Pratum* 128) implies that John's death in exile still embarrassed his admiring defenders: a sixth-century abbess needed a vision to reassure her that he was indeed to be reckoned among the authentic patriarchs. But the sermons were taken as models, and anthologies were made, which ill-equipped preachers were encouraged to use.

Pope Innocent and Priscillian of Ávila

Innocent's correspondence ranged more widely than the affair of John Chrysostom. The controversy concerning Priscillian bishop of Ávila moved into prominence the question of 'apocrypha' written in the name of apostolic authors. Priscillian's view was in fact not much different from that of Augustine of Hippo that one could profitably read non-canonical texts such as the Acts of John or legends in which Mary's father was named Joachim, provided that one did not derive doctrine from them. But for Priscillian the acceptability of apocrypha was a positive principle, qualifying and correcting the stuffy narrowness of orthodoxy. The Priscillianist controversy was not confined to Spain; it also involved churches in Aquitaine. Innocent found it necessary to write to Bishop Exuperius of Toulouse warning against the reading of dangerous apocryphal books, favoured by 'Manichees', and providing him with a list of the books in the biblical canon (*ep.* 6. 13).

Innocent and Roman liturgy

One of Innocent's more interesting letters discloses his confidence that Roman liturgical usage has been derived from St Peter and ought to be followed everywhere. He wrote (*ep.* 25) to Bishop Decentius of Eugubium (Gubbio) in central Italy on the limit of the suburbicarian region and open to the influence of Milan. A papal concern was that various sacramental acts should be performed by the bishop. Presbyters could anoint the sick as Jas. 5. 24 prescribed, but that did not mean that a bishop had not consecrated the oil, as was apparently not required at Milan. It was pre-eminently for him to perform this sacramental act. Again, he ruled that exorcism should be under the authority of the bishop, not independent. 'Presbyters are priests of the second rank.' The laying-on of hands in confirmation should also be for the bishop and is joined with the sign of the cross with the oil; through the bishop the Holy Spirit is bestowed, as in Acts 8. 17. It was a good custom at Rome to have no celebration of the eucharist on Good Friday; 'we fast because of the Lord's Passion.'

The insistence on the bishop's right and duty to reserve to his office certain sacramental functions was no doubt motivated in part by a desire to keep unity within the city of Rome, where the separate churches of the large city could easily become centrifugal—a factor that would have been influential in the civil war between Damasus and Ursinus and was to be troublesome in the future in the schisms between Eulalius and Boniface in 419 and worst of all in 498 between Symmachus and Laurentius. Innocent attests the custom of the 'fermentum', distributing blessed bread from the bishop to the various congregations and their presbyters.

Resistance to Milan's customs

Innocent was peremptory in insisting that a fast be observed on Saturday in agreement with Roman custom, not kept at Milan. He did not approve of the Milanese usage placing the kiss of peace before the central action of the eucharist rather than before communion (a custom long to continue to the present day). Nor did he welcome Milan's custom of naming donors before the prayer of consecration rather than in the middle of it (i.e. at the prayer *Hanc igitur* of the Latin canon, which in the Verona Sacramentary, 1138, ed.

Mohlberg, petitions that this offering offered for the soul of a dead relative may be mercifully accepted by the Lord; in the Gelasian text the prayer is more general that this offering by the faithful may be accepted).

The conviction that Roman usages should be the norm for western churches generally emerged in an earlier letter from Innocent to Victricius of Rouen (*ep.* 2 of 404). All 'major matters of dispute' (*causae maiores*) should be referred to the Apostolic See after the provincial bishops have discussed the issues (2. 6). He affirmed to the Africans that the Roman see was the origin and basis of all episcopal authority (*ep.* 29. 1). Innocent's strongest affirmations of Roman authority are in letters to western metropolitans. Nevertheless, at Constantinople the historian Socrates (7. 11. 4) did not conceal his regret that the bishops of both Rome and Alexandria had 'extended their priestly authority to become domination.'

Pelagianism

The Pelagian controversy in north Africa was not something from which the Roman see could hope to escape, and the determination of Augustine of Hippo to bring the matter to an issue involved Innocent being asked to give support for African decisions, an action of which Augustine remarks that he 'had no alternative' but to confirm (*c. Jul.* 1. 4. 13). Jerome in Bethlehem received support from Innocent when his monastery had been attacked by unfriendly people and Pelagius, then in the Holy Land, was somehow thought to be associated with the outrage, probably without foundation. Innocent complained to John bishop of Jerusalem (he could not know that he had lately died).

Alaric

During Innocent's time the empire was in political trouble. Tension between Constantinople and Ravenna (where the western emperor resided from 402) had been acute since Stilicho's ambition to be effective ruler of both west and east and, because of the alienating disagreement about John Chrysostom's sanctity, was not resolved before Honorius' death (27 August 423). This created a power vacuum. The pagan Goth Radagaisus invaded Italy with a vast army checked only at Florence when Stilicho brought in Huns and rival Goths to combat his threat. A triumphal arch in Rome confidently commemorated the emperors' 'extinction of the Goths for all time' (*ILS* 798). But the Gothic soldier Alaric, who had ravaged Greece and Illyricum, soon followed. The execution of Stilicho and the murder of his friends at Ravenna created a huge opportunity for Alaric in the west. His negotiations with Honorius at Ravenna proved frustrating; he took his formidable force in 408 and then again in 409 to the walls of Rome, retreating only after having been presented with a huge tribute of gold, silver, pepper, and precious silk garments. Honorius and his anti-Gothic advisers had no army capable of confronting him. It was easy to put the blame for the predicament on Stilicho's failure to eliminate Alaric, who, he had hoped, might become a notable ally to the empire. In Rome the defenceless starving populace resorted to the churches and temples; Pope Innocent consented to offer no objection if pagan cult was offered as long as it was private, not public (Zos. 5. 41) . Pagan senators insisted that the ceremonies must be public to be effective, but whether they had the courage to perform them is not clear.

Alaric's ambition was to be in effect supreme commander of the imperial army in the west, and Honorius, correctly judging that he would always tend to act independently, not necessarily in the empire's interests, did not feel able to trust him with such responsibility. Nor would he grant land and food. Pope Innocent was one of the counsellors who made his way to Ravenna to be consulted by the emperor (*ep.* 16; Oros. 7. 39; Zos. 5. 45. 5). At Ravenna as much as at Constantinople high-ranking officials were opposed to complete barbarian control of their defensive forces. In 397 an edict (CTh 14. 10. 2) was posted in Rome forbidding the wearing of barbarian dress such as trousers in the city; it was an evident sign of what was felt to be socially unacceptable. Stupidly, Stilicho's death was marked by Roman troops massacring the wives and children of barbarian soldiers serving in auxiliary units. More than 30,000 Gothic soldiers therefore left to reinforce Alaric, now convinced that Romans could not be trusted (Zos. 5. 37. 5). The Roman problem was that they lacked any satisfactory alternative defensive force. Advice from the military writers Vegetius or an Anonymous, *De rebus bellicis* (ed. E. A. Thompson) of the age of Valentinian had not been heeded.

Barbarians invade Gaul

The invasion of Italy necessitated moving troops from the Rhine frontier and Britain with the transfer of the Gallic prefecture from Trier to Arles at much the same time as the emperor's move from Milan to Ravenna. In consequence the bishop of Arles became more important, and soon the Popes would want to make Arles the seat of a papal vicariate comparable to that at Thessalonica. The absence of defending forces along the Rhine opened the road for the west German tribes to sweep across into Gaul. Control in Britain, precarious since a dangerous barbarian uprising in 367 and native Celtic hostility to Christianity, dwindled before the immigration of raiding Angles and Saxons. On 31 December 406 the Rhine froze, and huge numbers of Asding and Siling Vandals, Suevi, and (non-Germanic) Alans crossed the river in an unstoppable incursion as far as the Pyrenees. Soon they passed through into Spain. Towns as far south as Toulouse, where Bishop Exuperius was regarded as a hero in encouraging defence, suffered siege. The power of the Roman empire in Gaul, Britain, and Spain was receiving a body blow with lasting consequences.

Alaric's sack of Rome

Failure in Alaric's pressure to extract concessions from Honorius led him in fury to Rome for the third time, and on 24 August 410 he gained entry: the Porta Salaria was opened for him by Proba, a high-ranking Christian lady, appalled by the cannibalism, starvation, and misery in the city into which no food was being admitted (Procopius, *Wars* 3. 2. 27). Famine was made worse by hoarding on the part of distributors (Zos. 6. 11). An accusation of treachery was soon made. For three days the city was plundered. Churches were ransacked for treasure. Though not orthodox, Alaric was a Christian and respected asylum at the altars of the large basilicas of Peter and Paul. There was some loss of life and much damage to property. Leading senators were murdered (Soc. 7. 10. 4). Gothic soldiers raped women, including some nuns (Augustine, *City of God* 1. 16). 40,000 slaves and numerous barbarians living in the city left Rome to join Alaric's force (Zos. 5. 40. 3; Soz. 9. 6. 3).

Galla Placidia: Alaric's death

On 27 August Alaric withdrew with plunder and prisoners, one of whom was Honorius' half-sister Galla Placidia who, to the distress of anti-Gothic people in the east, became consort of his brother-in-law and more moderate successor Athaulf. She was to have an astonishing and strange career.[5] Alaric's seizure of her suggests that he had aspirations to be western emperor in all but name, a position closely parallel to that of Stilicho. At Rome he appointed the prefect Attalus to be western emperor in place of Honorius, who was able to reply by appointing a rival Gothic commander to defeat Alaric before Ravenna. Attalus did not last long. For the western empire the general chaos was not mitigated by successive usurpers in Gaul and Britain and the lack of determination at Ravenna. Alaric left Rome to move south to Calabria but a storm in the Straits of Messina wrecked his ships. The pagan historian Olympiodoros records that this check to Alaric was believed to be caused by a sacred statue, later demolished, which averted Etna's lava and barbarians from the Straits (fr. 16 Blockley = Photius, *Bibl.* 80). His ambition to reach Africa, a rich source of food, perhaps also of land, was frustrated. He retired

---

[5] S. I. Oost, *Galla Placidia Augusta* (Chicago, 1968).

northwards, and before the year was out this brilliant leader of a huge tribal migration was dead.

Alaric's brother-in-law Athaulf led for five years. He is reported by Orosius from Spain and north Africa (7. 43. 4–5) to have begun in office by being cool towards the traditions of Rome. At Bethlehem Orosius, visiting Jerome's monastery, heard a distinguished soldier from Narbonne telling Jerome that he had been intimate with Athaulf, who had initially wanted to replace the Roman empire by a Gothic empire: Gothia instead of Romania. But experience as the Goths' ruler and discussion with Galla Placidia had convinced him that his barbarous Goths were incapable of observing laws indispensable to any state. It was therefore better to use Gothic power to uphold and restore the Roman empire with the Goths in charge militarily. However, his policies of peace with the empire were not congenial to some of his followers, and they murdered him at Barcelona. A Gothic bishop in his entourage vainly attempted to save his children from sharing the same end (Olympiodorus, *fr.* 26 = Photius, *Bibl.* 80). A similar fate befell his successor Sigeric for similar reasons. The next Gothic king Wallia served the Roman interest and simultaneously satisfied the warlike instincts of his soldiers by warring against Alans, Vandals, and Suevi in Spain. He returned Galla Placidia to Honorius. Meanwhile Honorius' general Constantius III eliminated a western usurper at Arles, drove many Goths into Spain, and re-established some degree of imperial control in at least southern Gaul (411), qualified by the Goths' retention of a settlement in the Garonne valley.

Orosius (7. 40. 1), who had some apologetic interest in minimizing the momentousness of the fall of the Eternal City, had met Romans who survived the siege of Rome and thought it, in retrospect, something of a non-event without enormous lasting consequences for the city other than a few remains of burnt-out buildings. Moreover, the population of the city, once the food supply from Africa had been restored, was larger afterwards than it had been before. Honorius announced and presumably funded a transfer of population from elsewhere to fill the city again (Philostorgios 12. 5). No doubt the city and its churches were accustomed to having numerous migrants temporarily resident. An edict of 419 (CTh 14. 4. 10) specifies the distribution of 4000 pounds of meat each day to cope with the increased numbers.

The fall of 410 was, however, symbolic of a decline in morale of which discerning people had already become conscious. The pagan historian Zosimos could not bring himself to mention the disaster. Emotionally, if not politically, especially to people distant from Italy, the fall of the Eternal City seemed to contemporaries an unimaginable catastrophe heralding the world's end. Jerome at Bethlehem was thrown into deep dejection and sadness by the news, especially that Marcella, Pammachius, and other old friends were dead.

'In one city the whole world has perished.' (Prologue to commentary on Ezekiel, III, pp. 79–80, Vallarsi.) Jerome was among those who agreed with the rich aristocrats that the person to blame was Stilicho who, despite the many years in which he had dominated western Europe, had left the heart of the empire defenceless against bellicose barbarians on or within the frontier and, by his treacherous policy of giving the barbarians money raised by taxing the aristocrats to buy them off, merely enabled them to arm themselves to attack the empire (*ep.* 123. 16).

'Christian times'

For both pagans and Christians there were grand and agonizing questions about divine providence and the fearful evils of the city's fall. Pagans were sure that the disaster was the result of the gods' anger at the imperial ban on the traditional sacrifices which lay at the heart of polytheistic cult. To Christians who claimed that 'Christian times' must be good times for society, pagans replied that Christian times spelt nothing but catastrophe for the Roman empire. For believers it was axiomatic that the city's protection had passed from the old gods to the glorious martyrs, Peter, Paul, Laurence, and others, whose noble shrines had been expensively erected by aristocratic converts. Peter and Paul had replaced those unsatisfactory characters Romulus and Remus. People were asking how such potent patrons could have failed to defend what had become in their minds a now holy city, sanctified by the tombs of apostolic martyrs and the constant intercessions of the faithful. In the minds of many 'converts', Christ and his saints were fulfilling the roles once ascribed to Jupiter (Zeus) and subordinate deities and heroes. It was natural religion, the criterion of which lay in physical preservation and the secular success of the tribe and the family.

Ausonius[6]

It had not become difficult to find nominal Christians, as Ambrose complained. In his time Ausonius in Bordeaux (who educated the young Gratian and died in 394) wrote poetry in which Christian themes mingle with pagan rhetorical conventions, and there is no discernible element of ethical commitment. He was proud that, thanks to his imperial pupil who nominated him first to be quaestor, then praetorian prefect, and finally consul for 379, he ruled the empire (*ep.* 22). A combination of finer poetry with a more strenuous faith was manifested south of the Pyrenees by Prudentius (above p. 360), commemorating the martyrs, embattled against pagan cult, and

---

[6] See H. Sivan, *Ausonius of Bordeaux* (London, 1998).

composing memorable hymns for the Hours of prayer during the day. He especially celebrated in verse the Roman senate's decision to expel Jupiter and to honour the Christian God (*contra Symmachum* 1). Theodosius' legislation had made pagan sacrifice a capital offence.

The City of God[7]

Under the impact of Goths in Italy rich Romans poured into north Africa, and some travelled as far as the Holy Land perhaps to intercede for homes and relations as much as for personal safety. The city's fall provided the occasion for Augustine in north Africa to begin on a huge work which he had already been planning, contrasting pagan society or 'Babylon' with the City of God or heavenly Jerusalem. With his well-read mind, he had no difficulty in demonstrating that, in the idealized times of the Roman Republic, there had been numerous disasters against which the cult of the old gods had provided no defence. In Sallust's telling phrase, which Augustine much admired, it had been a society of 'private affluence and public squalor', flawed by a lust for domination over other peoples. His sermons on Rome and its empire offended some among his hearers unimpressed by the remark that he was quoting Sallust (*City of God* 3. 17; *S.* 105. 12 preached at Carthage about 410–11). Augustine did not hesitate to affirm that in the purposes of God the Roman empire had a providential role (*Conf.* 13. 34. 49). He was generally more positive than negative towards Rome and the empire. But the gospel of Christ was addressed to all races, not only to the Romans (*ep.* 199. 47). The Church embraced barbarians as well as Jews, Greeks, and Romans (*En. in Ps.* 64. 5). The empire could be the agent through which under God's mysterious hand the barbarian peoples could become Christians. Admittedly conversion to the gospel was much commoner among barbarians settled within the empire than those beyond the frontier (*ep.* 199. 46). He dissented from Ambrose's view that Gog and Magog, bringers of doom in biblical prophecy, prefigure the Goths and Massagetae (*City of God* 20. 11 on Ezekiel 38 and Revelation 20.8) and represent an assault on the city of God itself.

[7] See G. J. P. O'Daly, *Augustine's City of God, A Reader's Guide* (Oxford, 1999).

51

THE CHRISTOLOGICAL DEBATE, I:
TO THE FIRST COUNCIL OF
EPHESUS (431)

Beginnings

The gospel traditions in the New Testament portray Jesus as teacher, prophet, Messiah, Son of God, Son of man, and therefore one who has come to bring to fulfilment God's plan for his people both by his actions and by his words. 'No man spoke as this man', said his audience. He shocked people by forgiving sins. He faced a rising tide of hostility from conservative experts on the Law of Moses which showed how things would end, but in Mark 10: 45 foretold that he would be giving his life as a ransom for many. The authority with which he taught was derived from certainty that he was speaking for God his Father. In the synoptic gospels he is not described as God nor did he call himself God. But a very short time elapsed before the disciples felt sure that in him God had visited his people. The apostle Paul wrote to the Corinthians that in him God was reconciling the world to himself (2 Cor. 5: 19). In Philippians 2 terms applied to Jesus are taken from Isaiah's language about Yahweh. In St John's prologue he is the divine Word (Logos) who was made flesh and brought 'grace and truth' in contrast with Moses who brought the law. To see Jesus is to see the Father. The first chapter of the epistle to the Hebrews has polemic against the evaluation of Jesus as a ministering angel.

The synoptic gospels present a man, though one through whom miracles may be wrought. In Luke the child grew in wisdom. In Mark he is ignorant when the end will come, and on the cross experienced a sense of dereliction, which his dying would certainly have meant to his then disillusioned disciples. Even in St John's gospel 'Jesus wept'. Any Gentile educated in the liberal arts and in the commonplaces of eclectic Stoic and Platonic philosophy would be aware that ascribing to a divine figure the capacity to be ignorant or to suffer was stretching accepted ideas to breaking point, unless one could use the analogy of heroes like Dionysus or Heracles who heroically suffered and struggled to the benefit of the human race and were rewarded with divine honour. Such language in the evangelists and St Paul (Phil. 2) was to bequeath problems of interpretation.

A change in God?

The pagan critic Celsus objected to the concept of incarnation as implying change in the immutable supreme Being. Origen, like Clement before him, understood the incarnation as a very special instance of divine providence. If providence could care for this inferior world of matter and humanity, which would be generally conceded by thinkers other than the relatively few followers of Aristotle or Epicurus, there was no reason why this had to exclude so startling an event as the Word being made flesh. Or was there not still a difficulty in that the supreme Being could not be involved in matter, least of all in the pain and mess of human birth? (Celsus regarded the virginal conception by Mary as a cover-story for illegitimacy; cf. John 8: 41.) How could the Immutable suffer change or the Impassible take flesh?

Origen on Christ's human soul

In his treatise 'On first principles' Origen offered the solution that the pre-existent soul of Christ, which had never fallen like other souls, was so perfectly holy as to be the mediator between the divine and the physical body. The notion that the cosmos consists of three elements, matter, soul, and mind (*nous*) was helped along by Plato's *Timaeus*. That Christ had a human soul was to Origen a necessary deduction from the argument already deployed by Irenaeus against gnostics who wanted to deny the reality of Christ's flesh, namely that if any part of the composite human being was not assumed in the incarnation, then that part is not being saved. Origen uses precisely this proposition to affirm that Christ possessed a soul in solidarity with all souls. But by being united to the divine Logos this soul adhered to the divine love indefectibly and inseparably.

   To illustrate this union Origen used a simile which Stoic philosophers had used to illustrate the union of soul and body, saying that the union was like that of white-hot iron in the fire which acquires the properties of fire. In *contra Celsum* 3. 41 Christ's mortal body and human soul received the highest elevation not merely by communion with the Logos but by actual union and intermingling, so that they were rendered divine. Such language suggests that Origen was solving the Christological problem by absorbing the humanity of Christ wholly into the divine Logos. In fact he says no more than that the properties of the one nature are shared by the other (later called *communicatio idiomatum*). He is against dividing Christ; 'we speak of him no longer as of two entities but as of one' (*In Ev. Joh.* 1. 28 (30)). But the manner of the union is a question 'for private investigation by believers' (*c. Cels.* 1. 66).

The terms for discussing the union of divine and human were derived from philosophical debates about the union of soul and body. A question common to both debates was whether the soul feels the sufferings endured by the body. Those who upheld that the soul is immortal and impassible ascribed all suffering to the body. Others said that humanity is constituted out of both, and that joy and fear are experienced by the whole person, soul and body in common.[1]

The soulless Christ of Arius

At the time of the Council of Nicaea Eustathius of Antioch was a sharp critic of Origen for his excessive allegorism, writing a critique of Origen's exposition of Saul's visit to the sorceress of Endor who brought Samuel's soul back from the dead. But he was not in disagreement with Origen on the moral quality of Jesus' humanity in union with the divine Logos. Arius' thesis that the Logos is inferior to the Father because of the human limitations of the incarnate Lord presupposed that the Logos in effect replaced the human soul, which therefore had no function. Although Eustathius noticed this point, some time passed before the question became prominent in the debate, and Augustine confessed to surprise at this silence (*Haer.* 49). Gregory of Nyssa criticized Eunomius for denying Christ had a soul. John 1: 14 declared that the Word was made flesh, and this text was taken to support Arius' and Eunomius' thesis. The implication for the Arians was evidently that the Logos and the flesh of Christ constituted a single nature.

Marcellus and Athanasius

Marcellus of Ankyra was explicit that in Christ 'the man was united to the Word' (fr. 42 Klostermann). His disciple Photinus of Sirmium took this to mean that the moral excellence of Jesus was the ground on which the Logos was united to him; naturally to his critics, such as Hilary of Poitiers (*De Trin.* 10. 3), this meant that Jesus was so good a man as to merit adoption by God. By contrast the writings of Athanasius in effect ascribe no significant role to the human soul of Christ; he does not deny that Christ had a soul, but for him this is not really salvific. Two eventually rival views were emerging: the first, that the Logos was united to flesh and constituted a

---

[1] See Pseudo-Plutarch, *De libidine et aegritudine*, ed G. N. Bernadakis in the old Teubner edn. of Plutarch's *Moralia*, vii. 1 ff.; re-edited by F. H. Sandbach in the new Teubner edn., vi/3. 51–9, and also in his Loeb edn., xv. 38–59.

single nature; the second that the Logos was united to (or 'took' or 'assumed') a man, endowed with a soul as well as a body. A problem for the first view lay in the suffering of Christ. The 'one nature' answer allowed for the divine nature to suffer in the crucifixion. Neoplatonists could offer help. Plotinus could say that in the union of body and soul, the higher soul cannot share the sufferings of the body, but can be said to have 'impassible sufferings' (3. 6. 1. 34). The aggressively paradoxical expression was to be useful in the fifth century for Cyril of Alexandria in answering the complaint that in his Christology the impassible Logos suffered. A problem for the second view was to avoid the suggestion that the elevation of Jesus to divine honour was based on the perfection of his human character and obedience to the Father's will.

Apollinaris on Christ's soul

Among the paradoxes of debate in the fourth century one of the most striking is that the most eminent and intelligent of theologians to deny to Christ a human soul, Apollinaris of Laodicea,[2] was deeply opposed to Arianism and wholly committed to the cause of Athanasius and the Nicene creed. He thought it simply impossible psychologically for two centres of will and action to be a unity. He said that the human soul is open to temptations, 'filthy thoughts', unimaginable for the redeeming Word of God. Under pressure Apollinaris grants that in his humanity Christ is 'of one being (*homoousios*) with us'; nevertheless he can also affirm that Christ was not a man, but like a man. He has the name 'human', but not the full reality. Here the text of Rom. 8: 3 ('in the likeness of sinful flesh') was influential. Apollinaris opposed Diodore, presbyter of Antioch, later bishop of Tarsus, who sought to rebut the emperor Julian's anti-Christian arguments by distinguishing the divine Logos from the human Jesus in such a way as to give an uresolved duality. Apollinaris thought this was making the virginal conception of Jesus a superfluous miracle.

At the little council of Alexandria in 362, where Apollinaris was represented, among other aims Athanasius needed to find a compromise between two orthodox parties at Antioch—an Apollinarian group and the adherents of Paulinus who would certainly have followed Eustathius. Athanasius was opposed to the proposition that Christ was 'soulless'; the Greek word *apsychos* carries the sense of lifeless. There was a touch of ingenious ambiguity whether the source of life was the human soul or the indwelling Logos.

---

[2] The works of Apollinaris survive in large part through quotations by his critics, collected by H. Lietzmann (1904), well discussed by C. E. Raven, *Apollinarianism* (Cambridge, 1923), E. Mühlenberg, *Apollinaris von Laodicea* (Göttingen, 1969). See also R. A. Norris, *Manhood and Christ* (Oxford, 1963).

But Athanasius decided the issue by adding that Christ's possession of a soul meant that our human soul could be saved. In his third oration against the Arians Athanasius had sought to undermine Arian appeals to the human weaknesses of Christ by arguing that his ignorance was merely that of human nature, not the Logos; his moments of emotional stress were similarly a condescension to our frailty which the Logos purges. A critical question attached to the Descent to Hades (1 Pet. 3: 19). In a famous letter to Epictetus bishop of Corinth Athanasius explained that Christ's body ate and drank and was tired and crucified; yet within was the impassible Logos. The Logos was separated from the body when the body was buried in the tomb. This refuted an opinion reported by Epictetus that the Word was changed into the physical body and deified it, implying that Mary had played no real part in the human formation of Christ. In the struggle against Arianism Athanasius naturally wanted to put the strongest emphasis on the full deity of Christ, but not in such a sense that the reality of his humanity became lost.

Apollinaris was explicit in affirming that the unity of Christ must be asserted by the formula 'one nature (*mia physis*) of the incarnate divine Logos'. This was a requirement of worship. 'Just as body and soul constitute a single man, so also Christ was made in the likeness of men.' For this unity or 'synthesis' he had three technical terms: *ousia, physis, hypostasis*—especially the last of these. His writings enjoyed wide diffusion (Basil, *ep.* 263. 4).

Basil's warning

Basil of Caesarea, who before he was a bishop had had some profitable correspondence with Apollinaris in the early 360s, deeply regretted the Christological debate. He could foresee that in so intricate and delicate a matter there was going to be no quick conclusion, and that on the issue good believers were going to be divided and the simple bewildered to the injury of the Church (*ep.* 258 to Epiphanius, who was involved in the dissensions at Antioch). He did not want an anti-Apollinarian addition to the Nicene creed. In writing to the west he penned an attack on Apollinarianism (*ep.* 263). Paulinus of Antioch had already alerted Pope Damasus to the strange doctrine of the Apollinarian group in his congregation. The Roman condemnation of Apollinarianism was influential at Antioch. Basil's attack, in which he had the unqualified sympathy of his friend Gregory of Nazianzos and of his brother Gregory of Nyssa, may have been motivated by a desire to disavow any association with Apollinaris, since critics trying to dig up dirt against him had discovered his early correspondence with a man now tarred with the brush of heresy. Damasus and Paulinus' group at Antioch were not as quickly convinced as Athanasius of the reliability of Basil as theologian and ecclesiastical politician.

Gregory of Nyssa and Gregory of Nazianzos

Gregory of Nyssa loomed large in controversial writing against Apollinaris, and decisively opted for affirming a duality in Christ. The Logos assumed humanity, he would write; the *ousia* of the Logos is distinct from the humanity, which at the Resurrection was deified by union with the Logos. He did not feel comfortable with Apollinarian language about a single hypostasis as a term for expressing the unity of Christ. Gregory of Nazianzos had trouble at Nazianzos with advocates of Apollinarian theses, and wrote two important letters in criticism (101; 102). He reassured a group which looked to Apollinaris by affirming his attachment to the popular devotional title 'mother of God' (*theotókos*) to which Apollinarians appealed. He liked Origen's language that through the medium of the human soul God was mixed with the flesh; the analogy of union between soul and body was useful. It was a conjoining in *ousia*. Gregory of Nazianzos appears less emphatic about the duality than Gregory of Nyssa. He had more pro-Apollinarian sympathizers breathing down his neck.

Didymos the Blind

The neuralgic problem became that of technical terms. In a context very different from Apollinaris, Didymos the Blind at Alexandria could distinguish the one hypostasis that is Christ from the many aspects and titles of the redeemer as expounded by Origen's commentary on St John. Once in a polemic against Eunomius transmitted under Basil's name, Didymus insists that the distinction of divine and human natures in Christ is made only in detached thought, not in worship (Ps.-Basil, *contra Eunomium* 4, PG 29. 704 C). He also insisted that in the union the divine remains divine and the human human (*De trinitate* 2. 7, PG 39. 589 A).

Theodore of Mopsuestia

A strenuous opponent of Apollinarianism was Theodore, from 392 bishop of Mopsuestia, a pagan town near Adana in Cilicia, a friend of John Chrysostom. By his numerous biblical commentaries, for the churches of Syria he was so great an exegete as to be simply entitled 'the Interpreter'. He was born at Antioch about 350 and became a pupil of the rhetor Libanius. It is out of focus to label Theodore as no more than a follower of Eusebius of Emesa and of Diodore who became bishop of Tarsus, though at Antioch with John Chrysostom he had joined Diodore's group of ascetics; some anticipations of Theodore were ascribed to Diodore, who shared his dislike of Apollinaris' ideas, and also preferred historical to allegorical exegesis of scripture. Theodore's commentary on Galatians 4 carried an attack on Origen and allegorists. Diodore did not teach Theodore his stress on Christ's human soul. Like Gregory of Nyssa, Theodore insisted that the divine Word took or assumed a man or human nature.

The western censure of Apollinaris in 377 enhanced the respect for a Christology of 'two natures'. For Theodore this implied a high estimate of human nature, an implication which initially led him to treat Pelagius with a sympathy later abandoned. Originally, he thought, God had created this world to be a bond of visible and invisible in a great chain of being from angels down to inanimate matter. The linchpin of the created order was humanity of this earth, yet linked to the spiritual world by the possession of a rational soul. This bond between heaven and earth, however, suffered disruption at the fall of Adam. By death body and soul were separated, matter and spirit divorced. The spiritual powers pleaded successfully for the restoration of humanity, and this was achieved by the incarnation and atonement, in which the divine Word or Son assumed from Mary a complete human nature, not merely a body. It is in the will of the soul that sin originates, not in the flesh. The Lord assumed and made this soul immutable by union with himself, inaugurating a new humanity. The moral achievements of Christ in his humanity enable us to be saved by giving redemptive value to his sacrifice. The indwelling divine Logos was not vulnerable to suffering and death. At Heb. 2. 9 Theodore's text had the ancient reading, known to Origen, Jerome, and Ambrose, that Christ tasted death 'without God' rather than 'by the grace of God'. 'If Christ conquered sin only by his deity, there is no advantage to us.' By eliminating a human soul from Christ, Apollinaris betrayed the truth to Eunomius and radical Arians. Moreover, he could not explain the fear in the garden of Gethsemane, Jesus' prayer with strong crying and tears, the drops of blood, the angel to strengthen him. When Christ said to Peter, 'Get thee behind me, Satan', the temptation was not play-acting. He needed empowerment by the Holy Spirit to set aside the temptations in the wilderness.

In view of later criticism of Theodore it is noteworthy that his book 'On the incarnation' (lost)[3] suffered corruption and alteration. His complaint to this effect was known to Facundus (10. 1. 5) and through him to the Roman deacon Pelagius (p. 4. 19 Devreesse), both being dependent on Theodoret's defence of Theodore.

Theodore's critique developed into more than a censure of Apollinaris. He was in practice dissenting from the Alexandrian understanding of salvation as set out by Athanasius and then by Cyril, bishop of Alexandria 412–44. In Theodore's view the alternative Christology which he was opposing 'humiliated the Word', subjecting the Word to human limitation and suffering.

---

[3] A copy found in 1914 was destroyed in war before being copied.

Theodore experimented in trying to state a doctrine of the incarnation which escaped objection. Two main ways of thinking are reviewed: some were saying that the manner of the divine indwelling in Christ is one of 'being' (*ousia*); but that would mean that the Logos does not exist outside the incarnate Lord, which is to circumscribe the infinite. Others were saying that the indwelling is one of activity (*energeia*), a view to which the same objection holds. It is wiser to affirm that the union is one of moral will determined by God's gracious love (*eudokía*: Col. 1: 19). This concept allows a particular presence of God in Christ without excluding immanence in the rest of creation. By the grace of God, the Son assumed a man to become a single person (*prosopon*). The union is the ground of Christ's special achievement.

To speak of a union must imply two entities being bonded. Theodore would say 'two natures' which remain distinguishable even in the union so that they may be described as two hypostases forming a single prosopon.[4]

Salvation is mediated through baptism and eucharist. In the eucharistic liturgy the Son's eternal and heavenly sacrifice to the Father is ritually re-enacted, so that the liturgy on earth is an image and symbol of the action in heaven. Theodore expounds this from the epistle to the Hebrews. Bread and wine are transformed by the invocation of the Spirit so that they are no mere figure but the very body and blood of the Lord. This is an awesome mystery to be approached in dread and fear as worshippers bow before their king.

Theodore's rite is one of ritual splendour and it is here, rather than in his rather prosaic and literalist biblical comentaries, that he can be felt to touch the subject with awe. His language of a holy and awful sacrifice is anticipated in Cyril of Jerusalem (*cat. myst.* 5. 9) and in the *Apostolic Constitutions* (Syria, *c.*370–80); it is not found in the Cappadocians or in an ancient collection of prayers by (or ascribed to) Athanasius' colleague Bishop Serapion of Thmuis. It brought a pastoral difficulty: bishops wanted to inculcate in their *plebs* the greatest possible reverence for the Lord's presence in the liturgy of the faithful. This was only to adhere to the teaching of the apostle in 1 Cor. 11: 27–30. But then communicants were afraid to receive (a problem not only for Theodore but also for Cyril of Alexandria).[5]

---

[4] Dogmatic pieces of Theodore are conveniently printed in H. B. Swete's edition of his *Commentary on the Minor Epistles of St Paul*, ii (Cambridge, 1882) appendix A. His important *Catechetical lectures* were edited and translated by their finder, A. Mingana, Cambridge, 1932), reedited by R. Tonneau (Vatican City, 1949). Among many monographs there are good studies in English by R. A. Greer (London, 1961), R. A. Norris (Oxford, 1963).

[5] In the west exhortations to serious reverence were sometimes attached to controversy about daily celebration of the eucharist, which since at least Cyprian's time was customary in Latin-speaking churches, while remaining unusual in the east (Augustine, *Sermo dom. in monte* 23. 26). Some thought believers came without due preparation (Augustine, *Ep.* 54. 4; *En. in Ps.* 49. 23). But daily attendance was obligatory for clergy in Spain (Council of Toledo 400, canon 4). One consequence of stressing

Latin Christology

Western theologians such as Ambrose were content to affirm that Christ was perfect and complete in his humanity, fully sharing in our infirmities and emotions (*in Ps.* 61. 4–5), but thanks to his virgin birth free of any taint of sin. Augustine says the same and rechoes Tertullian's language that Christ is 'one person both God and man' (e.g. *En. in Ps.* 88. ii. 3; *sermo* 130. 3, two *substantiae* but one person; *sermo* 186. 1, the same is both God and man, without confusion of natures but in unity of person). 'It is hard to grasp how the human soul and the Word of God can be united' (*c. Faustum* 22. 40), but a possible way of finding an analogy is through the union of the human soul and body where the soul 'knows itself to be immaterial' and undergoes no change by union, just as light can pass through air and remain light (*ep.* 137. 11–12 borrowing analogies from Porphyry, who wrote an extant treatise on 'how the embryo is ensouled'). In *City of God* 10. 29 the incarnation is presented as the supreme instance of Grace. But the language of incarnation rather than inspiration is used to differentiate Christ from prophets and saints (*de agone Christiano* 22). It is the greatest act of humility, and therefore objectionable to proud pagans such as Porphyry (*City of God* 10. 29) who characteristically praise Christ for his wisdom and say that Christians claim more for him than he really was (*De consensu evang.* 1. 7. 11). Pagans have to attribute his miracles to magic (1. 9. 14).

This unity of person means that in Christ two wills were united into one (*En. in Ps.* 93. 29). Therefore the assumption of human nature excluded the possibility of sin by free choice of will (*De correptione et gratia* 1. 30). To Augustine it was more important to deny that the incarnation implied change in God than that there was change in the human nature assumed. The humanity of Christ is the step on the ladder by which the believer ascends to perceive that he is also God (*S.* 141. 4). 'Do not think it unorthodox to say that as man Christ was predestinated' (*Tr. in Joh.* 105. 8).

By a fusion of theology with devotion it had become usual to affirm that he who was born of Mary and died on the cross was God, and that the miracles were done by the human Jesus; there was a sharing of properties (*City of God* 17. 18) between the two natures in the one person, known since Bonaventura as *Communicatio idiomatum.* This was a way of affirming the unity

the awesome sacredness and importance of the rite was that women communicants dressed themselves elaborately with fine jewellery asking for admiration (Augustine, *sermo* 22. 23, 25).

The stress on the kingship of Christ was concomitant with an elaboration of ceremonial and sometimes of liturgical vocabulary which owed something to the imperial court. One fourth-century panegyrist is found initiating his approach to the sovereign with the words that it would be proper for his audience to be praising the emperor 'at all times and in all places', but particularly at the current moment (*Paneg. Lat.* 2 (12).1; 7 (6).1; 10 (2).1). The language is reminiscent of a eucharistic Preface.

of Christ. In Augustine's time this strong language was sharply criticized by a Gallic monk, Leporius, as being 'unworthy of God'. In 418 in Africa he signed a document of correction drafted by Augustine (*ep.* 219): the Word became flesh 'personaliter', not 'naturaliter' with the Father and the Spirit (CCSL 64. 115). In the sermons on St John's gospel Augustine wrote that 'Mary is mother of Christ's humanity, not of his divinity; in the birth the Creator of Mary became known in his power, and in his death Mary's child hung on the cross' (*Tr. in Joh.* 119. 1).

Mediated through Pope Leo I, this western Christological language was sure to surprise and even shock inheritors of the Alexandrian tradition of Athanasius and Cyril.

Greek terminology

In the Greek churches the question of terminology became more and more prominent. Neoplatonic logicians were already discussing how a union of disparate elements should properly be described. Union needed to be distinguished from mixture, which sounded like a compound or confusion. One Greek word, *synapheia*, meaning conjunction or joining together, was useful. In his commentary on Plato's *Timaeus* (ii. 102, ed. Diehl), Proclus of Athens puts first the highest possible degree of union, that of mind with mind. On a second level is the union of mind (*nous*) with soul (*psyche*) for which the term *synapheia* is appropriate. In the case of material bodies a sharing or participation (*methexis*) is the fitting term. The discussion emerges from the problem of identity and difference in which Neoplatonic logicians were especially interested.[6]

It was agreed that the term union or *hénosis* needed some qualifying adjective to indicate the quality of the bond. In the controversy about Apollinaris, a writer in the name of Athanasius was content to write of a 'natural union', a union of *physis* or a single nature, but not of a union defined as constituting one hypostasis, a term which Apollinaris had used in this context (Ps.-Athan. *c. Apollin.* 1. 12).

Alexandrian Christology: Cyril of Alexandria[7]

In 377, when Apollinaris was condemned for heresy by Bishop Damasus of Rome, Peter of Alexandria was present and consenting to the act. Similarly Bishop Theophilus (in Jerome, *ep.* 98) stood more firmly against Apollinarian theses than rumour reported to Gregory of Nyssa, who wrote a warning to

---

[6] W. Beierwaltes, *Identität und Differenz* (Frankfurt, 1979).
[7] A recent introduction to Cyril with bibliography is by Norman Russell (London, 2000).

him.[8] But with Theophilus' successor and nephew Cyril, bishop 412–44, the Christological issue became central. Cyril had accompanied his uncle to the synod of the Oak which condemned John Chrysostom, and wholly shared Theophilus' opinion that the power of bishops of Constantinople needed to be checked. Until he came to need Rome's support in controversy with Nestorios, he did not welcome Pope Innocent I's request that John's name be included in the diptychs.

Cyril was an intelligent and well-read theologian, who could apply to difficult problems of theology logical terms and distinctions which he had learnt from studying Porphyry and other Neoplatonic writers. He also knew some Latin. Cyril competed for the see with the archdeacon Timothy, but in the turbulent contest received crucial support from Abundantios, count of Egypt and commander of the army (Socrates 7. 6. 3 Armenian version; Greek MSS say he supported Timothy). However, Cyril was not given to toleration of pagans, heretics, and Jews, and in 415 the prefect Orestes, a Christian baptized in Constantinople, had confrontations with his strong-arm methods. Isidore of Pelusium, who did not admire either Theophilus or Cyril, curtly described him as 'his uncle's nephew'. The historian Socrates also did not admire Cyril, who began his episcopate by closing Novatianist churches and confiscating all their moveable property. Socrates goes on to record high tension between Cyril and Orestes; the prefect resented the bishop's intrusions into secular affairs. This was exacerbated when the large Jewish populace of the city attacked the Christians by night and killed many. Cyril's response was to mobilise an expulsion of Jews from Alexandria and to take possession of their synagogues. Orestes was irate that the city should lose a substantial proportion of its population, many of whom were cultivated persons of substance.

Monks from the Nitrian desert heard of the riot, and saw that Cyril needed a private army which they could provide. Some five hundred of them left their monasteries, confronted Orestes, who was met by a shower of stones, one hitting him on the head. The monk who threw the bloody stone was arrested and died under torture, after which Cyril (in Socrates' view unwisely) could declare him a martyr.

The murder of Hypatia[9]

Neoplatonic philosophy flourished at Alexandria under Hypatia, daughter of Theon the mathematician. Among her pupils was Synesius of Cyrene, who under Theophilus became bishop of Ptolemais in Libya. The prefect Orestes had a good relation with her, but she was suspected of prejudicing

[8] Ed. F. Müller (Leiden, 1958); also PG 45. 1269–77.
[9] See Maria Dzielska, *Hypatia of Alexandria*, tr. F. Lyra (Cambridge, Mass., 1995).

Orestes against Cyril. Moreover she represented a philosophy that for many pagans offered an alternative to Christianity. But Alexandria was notorious in antiquity for mob violence. In March 415 a gang of Christian bigots lay in wait for her, dragged her off to the church named Caesareum, stripped her, and then murdered her with bricks. Christian opinion at Constantinople and elsewhere was highly critical of Cyril and his church for this outrage. Cyril does not appear to bear responsibility for the act other than by having given a general encouragement of hostile attitudes towards active paganism.

Anti-pagan moves at Alexandria

Cyril had the intellectual equipment to engage educated pagans in dialogue. His refutation, only in part extant, of the emperor Julian's book 'Against the Galileans' was evidently evoked by the use that Alexandrian pagans were making of Julian's arguments. Cyril was strong enough to suppress a cult of Isis at nearby Menuthis, replacing the goddess by the Christian saints Cyrus and John, whose relics were transferred from the church of St Mark at Alexandria and became famous for healings.[10] The suppression of pagan rites was not entirely successful; cult at the site continued into the sixth century (Zacharias, *Life of Severus of Antioch*, PO 2. 17ff.) Cyrus gave his name to the place as Aboukir (Abba Kyros), the site of Nelson's battle of the Nile.

Perhaps as a defensive militia as well as a useful instrument of aggression Cyril mobilized hospital aides (*parabolani*) normally serving the sick in hospices founded by the church. In 416–18 imperial edicts (CTh 16. 2. 42–3) limited their numbers to a maximum of 600, and directed that they should be under the command of the bishop of Alexandria, but were not to interfere in secular business.

Cyril on St John's Gospel

Cyril was concerned about his duty to repress heresies. He meditated deeply on the Christology presupposed by the Gospel of St John, and felt its incompatibility with the language used by Theodore of Mopsuestia. His commentary has much criticism of Sabellians and Arians, who were evidently far from extinct in the provinces under his jurisdiction. Though written in undistinguished prose, in content his exegesis of the gospel, almost all extant, must rank among the greater achievements in ancient biblical exposition. He also wrote studies in allegorical interpretation of Old Testament passages, especially the Pentateuch, and commentaries on Isaiah and the Minor Prophets.

---

[10] Cyril, PG 77. 1100–5; Sophronius of Jerusalem, *Miracles of Cyrus and John*, PG 87/3. 3113. On an unprinted Life of Cyrus and John by Sophronius see T. Nissen, *Anal. Boll.* 57 (1939), 65–71.

Arian objections to the Nicene doctrine of the Trinity were answered at length, and these occupied space in the commentary on St John restating Athanasius' arguments. Homilies on St Luke survive in Syriac. While the exegesis of Johannine theology is hostile to the 'two-natures' Christology of Theodore, the commentary mentions no names as targets for criticism. Cyril's commentary on the epistle to the Hebrews with its theme of Christ the pioneer made perfect through suffering was more uncomfortable and attracted sharp criticism in Syria.

Influences on Cyril from Alexandrian tradition

Influential on Cyril's Christology were writings of Apollinaris of Laodicea circulating under the name of Athanasius, and he liked the terms of one polemical piece from this arsenal in which 'Athanasius' declared the one Son not to be two natures, one worshipped the other not worshipped, but 'one nature of the divine Word incarnate, worshipped with his flesh in a single worship'; moreover, not two Sons, one Son of God, the other son of Mary becoming Son of God by grace, adopted as we are.[11]

Nevertheless Cyril was careful never to concede that Christ lacked a human mind and soul. Otherwise his thinking was closely akin to that of Apollinaris, facilitated by the fact that the ideas came to him under the cover of Athanasius' name and authority. Of Athanasius' authentic writings he especially exploited the third discourse against the Arians and the letter to Epictetus of Corinth which he took to be a criterion of orthodoxy. The letter to Epictetus, however, was known to him in a recension improved by Apollinarian editors.

Nestorius bishop of Constantinople (428–31)

Educated at Antioch on the Orontes, Nestorius became a priest and learnt his theology at the feet of Theodore of Mopsuestia (d. 427). His sermons were much admired; the question could be asked if he was even more eloquent than John Chrysostom. After the patriarch Atticus of Constantinople died (8 October 425), the succession was competed for between Atticus' former secretary Proclus and a learned but confused historian Philip of Side in Pamphylia. The laity, however, preferred a less eloquent and less learned parish priest named Sisinnius, admired for his holy simplicity. Proclus was sent to be metropolitan of Cyzicus on the south coast of the sea of Marmara, armed with an imperial edict giving patriarch Atticus the right to be consulted.

---

[11] Cited in his address to the emperor's sisters, Arcadia and Marina, ladies devoted to the religious life: *ACO* I i/v. 65; PG 76. 1212; ed. P. E. Pusey, 161–2.

The people of Cyzicus successfully argued that the emperor's ruling named Atticus but no successor; Proclus returned to the capital and on Sisinnius' death late in 427 again competed with Philip of Side. Theodosius II and his court advisers decided to bring in an outsider. Nestorius, presbyter of Antioch, was proposed and installed in April. He was entering shark-infested waters.

Nestorius against heresies

Nestorius, like Cyril of Alexandria who sent him a friendly note on receiving the notification of his consecration, felt it his primary task to suppress heresy. His programmatic enthronement sermon before the emperor on 10 April 428 promised Theodosius II that if he were supported in getting rid of heretics, he could promise the emperor heaven and the legions victory over the Persians, a matter crucial at Antioch always close to the battle (Socrates, *HE* 7. 29. 5). He started five days later by dismantling a little chapel used by surviving Arians; the Arians in anger set the building ablaze, which then spread through the entire quarter of the city. Nestorius was popularly held responsible. Moves against the city's Novatianists were checked by the emperor. But in Asia Minor he harassed groups of Quartodecimans who still observed their Easter on the same day as the synagogue passover; consequent riots in Miletus and Sardis cost many lives. Adherents of the doctrines of Bishop Macedonius, who denied the equality of the Holy Spirit in the Godhead, were fiercely treated both in Constantinople and in the Hellespont where they were numerous.

Theotókos: *mother of God*

Nestorius failed to endear himself to clergy and monks at the capital by bringing his own team from Antioch, one being a presbyter Anastasius (later bishop of Tenedos) who particularly shared his antipathy to Apollinarianism. For Apollinaris' devotion the Blessed Virgin Mary was important. In reply to Diodore of Tarsus he had insisted on the wonder of Christ's virginal conception, and stressed the long traditional title *theotókos*, mother of God, attested from the mid-third century. Nestorius and his presbyter regarded this title as dangerously deifying Mary, whose essential vocation in salvation was to be human and, by her obedience to a divine call, to contribute the humanity to her Son, thereby making redemption possible. *Theotókos* could imply that for salvation the humanity of Christ was insignificant. It was acceptable if *anthropotókos* was added, mother of man. But to deny the legitimacy of the devotional title caused huge offence, and led to widespread misrepresentation, led by an able and zealous advocate named Eusebius (later bishop of

Dorylaeum in Phrygia), that Nestorius was denying Christ to be more than a mere man. The detached historian Socrates studied his utterances and was clear that this charge was unjust; but the title was used by Origen and Eusebius of Caesarea, so that Nestorius' ignorance of great Christians of the past was responsible for his indiscretion. An anathema had been pronounced by Gregory of Nazianzos on any who rejected *theotókos* (*ep.* 101). Nevertheless there were orthodox ears who heard 'mother of God' as redolent of paganism (Isidore of Pelusium sought to reassure them, *ep.* 1. 201, PG 78. 312 B). Nestorius' coldness to the title sprang from his aversion to devout folk treating the Virgin as a goddess (*ACO* I i/6. 31. 33).

Rivalry between Alexandria and Constantinople

The enthronement at New Rome of a bishop consciously averse to language and understandings of salvation which were native to the tradition of Alexandria was to inject a heady mixture into the already existing rivalry between these two great sees.

In 429 four Alexandrians disciplined by Cyril escaped to Constantinople to appeal to the emperor, who naturally asked Nestorius to hold an inquiry. Cyril had representatives (apocrisiaries or nuncios) at the court to watch his interests. When Nestorius asked them for details of the appellants' case, he was forcefully advised to dismiss them out of hand and to listen to no charges against their 'Papa'. Nestorios protested that he could not be a respecter of persons. The apocrisiaries made a full report to Cyril, who prepared for a coming war. His defence would be to attack Nestorius' orthodoxy, thereby undermining his authority to judge. His apocrisiaries saw to it that the dispute about *theotókos* was not allowed to die down, and that Cyril was sent copies of Nestorius' sermons, from which he could glean inflammatory matter. This was Nestorius' own reading of the record in his partly autobiographical *Book of Heraclides* extant in Syriac.[12]

Cyril was aware that at Constantinople many of the monks were alarmed by their new patriarch. There was already a tradition of distrust between the monasteries and the patriarchate, which had operated in John Chrysostom's time. Important supporters of Cyril's cause in the capital were an archimandrite Dalmatius and a respected monk named Eutyches (*ACO* I iv. 223. 23–5); the last-named was to become a major player on the stage in 448–9.

Cyril's first move was to publish an encyclical nominally addressed to the monks of his jurisdiction but circulated at Constantinople, in which he vigorously defended the title 'mother of God' and wrote of the monks' distress

---

[12] Preserved by the harassed Nestorian community in south-east Turkey until 1917, but four copies were made before the manuscript was lost and the text printed (1910) and translated.

at what they heard about Nestorius. The priest Anastasius was sent to Cyril's apocrisiaries to assure them that Nestorius in no way dissented from Cyril's letter to the monks. Cyril's reaction was irate rejection. He accused Nestorius of putting up the four Alexandrian malcontents, 'the refuse of the city', to slander their bishop, and refused to discuss further with him until he repented of his heresy (Cyril, *ep.* 10; *ACO* I i/1. 110ff.). Nestorius made a fateful error: he asked the emperor, not renowned for being tough, to call a synod to examine the accusations against Cyril. And if true doctrine was an issue, Nestorius was confident that he was orthodox and Cyril a heretic.

At the palace the emperor's wife Eudocia liked Nestorius whereas his sister Pulcheria was offended by him. Theodosius had to live with two quarrelling ladies. (See Theodosius' complaint to Cyril, *ACO* I i/1. 73. 22–5.) Pulcheria avowed support for Cyril, though after the council of Ephesus her activity on his behalf came to seem weak and insufficient (*ACO* I iv. 223. 15).

Cyril's doctrinal manifesto to Nestorius

Cyril needed some damaging matter from Nestorius' pen, and suggested that Nestorius and he might exchange letters. Unwisely Nestorius accepted. Cyril's letter to him began with a contemptuous reference to three of the malcontents (fraudster, matricide, thief—the fourth he was turning to favour him) but devoted the rest to a long dogmatic statement and a demand for assent. Cyril emphatically asserted that the divine Word united to himself flesh with a rational soul, and this union was 'hypostatic', not a mere union of will or a relation of good pleasure, nor by assuming a *prosopon*; 'not that the difference of the natures is abolished by the union'. This language was unconcealed polemic against the 'Antiochene' Christology of Theodore of Mopsuestia. Care is taken to deny that the divine nature suffered; but the body which he made his own property suffered. There is no worshipping of the Word in distinction from the man; the Christ we worship is a single person. Only a hypostatic union averts two Sons. On that ground we may make bold to call the Virgin *theotókos*. The letter is known as his Second Letter to Nestorius. Its wording was intended to be provocative. Meanwhile Cyril was able to enlist support at Rome from Pope Celestine, assisted by Nestorius' naïve imprudence in receiving refugee Pelagians and asking the Pope what was wrong with them.

The Council of Ephesus (431)

On 19 November 430 the emperor summoned a council under imperial authority to meet in Ephesus at Pentecost, 7 June 431. The agenda was formulated so that the doctrinal question alone was to be discussed. No accusations of crime or bribery were to be brought before the synod or a law-court; they were to be referred to the emperor and his consistory. Nestorius' sermon on 6 December 430 complained that he was being attacked with 'golden arrows', in other words by generous bribes with which Cyril's agents were capturing influential officers of state (*ACO* I v. 43. 17). The coming struggle was one which Cyril could not afford to lose. To maintain order in Ephesus Candidian, *comes domesticorum*, commander of the imperial body-guard and a major military figure, was commissioned. His endeavours to see that proceedings were correct brought complaints that he was biased in favour of Nestorius, especially when he tried vainly to stop Cyril holding a synod before John of Antioch and his suffragans had arrived. They were delayed by torrential rain and floods.

The metropolitan bishop of Ephesus, Memnon, was not likely to be friendly to the see of Constantinople or to have forgotten John Chrysostom's intrusions into metropolitan rights in Asia Minor. He could easily mobilise his people to hostile demonstrations against the bishop of Constantinople.

Nestorius obtained leave to be accompanied by a friend, Count Irenaeus, subject to the condition that he took no part in the debates or in Candidian's responsibilities. His friendship with Nestorius was to be fatal to his future; for a time exiled to Petra, he wrote a history of the controversy entitled 'Tragedy', of which a few fragments survive in Latin translation (*ACO* I iv. x–xv), but emerged in 445 as bishop of Tyre for three years before being again exiled. He was twice married, which made him vulnerable to criticism from those who disliked his theology.

Cyril's Twelve Anathemas

For Cyril there was perhaps a danger that Nestorius might find a way round the propositions in his Second Letter. Nestorius had written to Pope Celestine conceding the legitimacy of the *theotókos* title. He was advised so to do by John of Antioch (*ACO* I i/7. 93). Cyril had to present Nestorius with propositions that he could not imaginably accept without vast loss of face at Antioch. He also felt much emboldened by support from Pope Celestine and his Roman synod, demanding that Nestorius correct his heresy within ten days of receiving the papal letter. Cyril accordingly sent a Third Letter, endorsed by his Egyptian synod, formally declaring his opponent excom-municate; to this he attached twelve 'Chapters', propositions to be rejected under anathema (*ACO* I i/1. 33–42; Cyril, *ep.* 17, PG 77. 105). They were strong meat. They moved Theodoret bishop of Cyrrhos in Syria to a seriously considered refutation.

In the course of his book Theodoret objected to Cyril's belief, expressed in his ninth anathema (and elsewhere, e.g. *In Ev. Joh.* 2, p. 126, PG 74. 443 B), that the Holy Spirit proceeded from both the Father and the Son when Jesus (John 15: 26) said the Spirit proceeds from the Father. The bold theme was anticipated in Epiphanius (*Panar.* 62. 4). Cyril never acknowledged the creed which at Chalcedon was associated with the council of Constantinople in 381. Remarkably, during the long medieval debate between east and west from the mid-seventh century concerning the legitimacy of the *Filioque* in the creed, Theodoret's observations were not noticed until the twelfth century.[13]

Cyril regarded the Nicene faith with awe as the one inspired conciliar statement of necessary belief to which no addition should be made. (This may have originated as an Alexandrian formula designed to censure everything associated with the hated council of Constantinople in 381.) The creed was widely used both at baptisms and at the ordination of bishops (e.g. *ACO* I i/2. 16. 8). But he refused to allow Nestorius to vindicate his orthodoxy by assent to the Nicene creed. One must also follow the fathers as authentic interpreters (Athanasius being evidently in mind with the Apollinarian texts being attributed to him). That meant affirming the hypostatic union of Logos with the flesh, and that Christ was not a man indwelt by God; not a 'conjoining' (*synápheia*) of two distinct beings. *Synápheia* was for Cyril appropriately used of the bond between the divine Logos and the believer. The impassible Logos made the flesh his property and therein suffered. So in eucharistic unbloody worship we receive the body and blood of our Saviour, not as ordinary flesh, not as that of a human being joined to the Logos by divine indwelling, but as lifegiving because the personal property of the Logos. Christ was 'out of two different entities', united like soul and body, one hypostasis of the incarnate Word. We should not say that he 'offered himself on behalf of both himself and us' (evidently a quotation from one of Nestorius' sermons), nor that he was inspired by the Holy Spirit. Accordingly, we must affirm Mary to be *theotókos*; we must not divide the sayings of Christ between his divine and human natures for the Son is one in his nature (*physis*). We must affirm that the Word of God suffered in the flesh and was crucified in the flesh. To speak of God suffering horrified Syrians.

Cyril's Third Letter and the attached anathemas embody a passionate statement of the devotional belief of the ascetics that Christ is God and Man, but that the humanity is absorbed within the divinity. He can redeem because he is God not merely an inspired man. The passion upon the cross derives redemptive value from being the suffering of God himself. Whereas for

---

[13] See André de Halleux in *RHE* 74 (1979), 597–625 reprinted in *Patrologie et Œcuménisme* (Leuven, 1990), 367–95. At the council of Florence in 1439 Theodoret's claim that Cyril yielded to his criticisms (*ep.* 171) was used by Mark Eugenikos to neutralize citations from Cyril by John de Montenero OP (*Acta Latina* 202–22).

Theodore of Mopsuestia the stress in eucharistic theology lies on the self-offering of perfect obedience by the mediator and redeemer, in Cyril it lies on the presence of Christ so that the liturgy is a reenactment of Bethlehem and the coming of Emmanuel, of 'God with us'. Cyril's problem lay in the intimate affinity between his language and that of Apollinarius. Nestorius' friends were bound to think Cyril crypto-Apollinarian, perhaps not crypto.

The emperor had called the synod for 7 June. On 22 June John of Antioch with his suffragans had not arrived, and because of bad travelling conditions in appalling weather wrote courteously to Cyril to explain a late arrival; some of their party had died *en route*. A delay in starting out had been caused by riots at Antioch caused by famine. Cyril sent a message to John that he would wait (*ACO* I i/5. 125. 6). In defiance of Candidian, who was insulted and roughly treated, Cyril, urged on by Memnon of Ephesus and claiming to have delegated authority from Rome, insisted on holding in St Mary's church a synod of a body of bishops, who besides fifty Egyptians, forty of Memnon's province of Asia, and twelve from Pamphylia (tainted with Messalianism in Antiochene eyes) were mainly supporters from Palestine and Asia Minor. Candidian was forced to read the imperial letter (*sacra*) giving authority to the synod to meet (for which by custom all stood). The gospel book was placed on the throne, symbol of Christ's presence. Nestorius was three times summoned. Since for his protection his house was surrounded by soldiers, he could not physically come without Candidian's consent; he agreed to come when all bishops had arrived. Cyril's second letter to Nestorius was approved by 124 bishops, each assenting individually, as the true meaning of (i.e. 'no addition to') the Nicene creed.

Cyril's third letter was later read and Cyril was ready with an explanation of each proposition (*ACO* I i/5. 15–25) which Nestorius thought more heretical than the text being explained. The text passed by without receiving either criticism or formal approval (*ACO* I i/2. 36). Cyril would later claim that the great council had approved his Twelve Anathemas so that he could not withdraw them (*ACO* I. vi. 222. 18–19). John of Antioch understood that 'several bishops' with Cyril had signed them (*ACO* I i/3. 40. 10 = Theodoret, *ep.* 170). At least it is clear that Cyril's synod did not reject them. In 532 there was dispute whether Cyril's Twelve Anathemas, inserted in the Acts of Ephesus, enjoyed a stamp of approval at Chalcedon (Innocentius of Maronea, *ACO* IV. ii. 173. 20).

Bishop Theodotus of Ankyra witnessed to hearing Nestorius say 'a baby two or three months old cannot be called God'. A selection of texts was then read either supporting Cyril including Apollinarian forgeries, or citing from Nestorius. One hundred and ninety-seven bishops declared Nestorius deposed on the basis of 'the canons and the letter of Cyril' (evidently the second to Nestorius is here meant, p. 530). Finally an apology for absence was received from the bishop of Carthage, whose provinces were being ravaged by Vandals.

Four bishops who supported Nestorius were declared deposed: Helladius of Tarsus, Eutherius of Tyana, Himerius of Nicomedia, and Dorotheus of Marcianopolis in Thrace.

Juvenal of Jerusalem was prominent on Cyril's side. He was already nursing ambitions (Cyril being unsympathetic) to create a patriarchate at the expense of Antioch, and at one point declared that the bishop of Antioch ought to acknowledge the superiority of Rome and Jerusalem (*ACO* I i/3. 18. 30). Cyril's synod ended in the evening and, as he and his supporters walked back to their lodgings, numerous citizens of Ephesus conducted them enthusiastically with torches. Ephesus resented the jurisdiction of Constantinople's patriarch.

Sixty-eight bishops, twenty being metropolitans, who had already arrived in Ephesus, signed a protest to Cyril, since his partial and partisan synod could be reckoned invalid (*ACO* I iv. 27–8). It certainly could not be counted 'ecumenical' as Candidian pointed out. An imperial decree on 29 June confirmed the right of the protesters (I i/3. 9). The emperor did not want schism. John of Antioch and his party arrived two or three days after Cyril's meeting. In contrast with Cyril's body, John obeyed the emperor's instruction and brought only two or three bishops from each province. On 26 June forty-three bishops (the Latin version says fifty-four) met in a rival synod which heard Candidian again read the imperial *sacra*, complained bitterly that Memnon of Ephesus had excluded them by force from all churches and shrines including that of St John, declared Cyril and Memnon deposed and excommunicated all participants in Cyril's particular synod (*ACO* I i/5. 119–24).

John's synod produced a conciliar doctrinal statement (*ACO* I i/7. 69–70) which offered a basis for future reconciliation and was mainly drafted by Theodoret bishop of the Syrian town of Cyrrhus, the most notable of Syrian theologians: it affirmed Christ to be perfect God and perfect man, of one being with the Father in his divinity, and of one being with us in his humanity, a union from two natures, and accordingly affirming *theotókos*. (This last concession caused pain to some Syrian bishops, especially Alexander of Hierapolis: *ACO* I i/3. 45. 25; I iv. 130.) The Syrians' synod asked for the withdrawal of Cyril's Twelve Anathemas, and no demand for subscription to more than the all-sufficient Nicene creed.

Roman legates (two bishops and a presbyter) arrived early in July after a rough voyage and Cyril recruited their support; on 16–17 July Cyril's synod and the legates declared John of Antioch deposed, Cyril and Memnon insisting that on 22 June they had acted canonically and were now supported by more than 200 bishops, where John's riffraff numbered only thirty or thirty-seven and had ignored canonical procedure (*ACO* I i/3. 15–16). Moreover, the bishop of Antioch had 'no sufficient authority to sit in judgement on the bishop of a greater see' (Alexandria). On 22 July this synod decreed that no faith other than the Nicene creed should be composed or proposed for assent (*ACO* I i/7. 105. 20).

The court's decision

In the long run the adherence of Roman authority to Cyril's partisan council was to give the condemnation of Nestorius a general authority. It later came to be believed that the council had specially sanctioned the title *theotókos*, a subject on which strangely Cyril's council in actuality gave no definition other than that implied by welcoming Cyril's second letter to Nestorios. The immediate question was what decision would be made by the weak emperor and especially by his court advisers, who were a corrupt lot, their support being for sale. Cyril knew how to buy them. At the court every man was for himself.

Count Candidian had been instructed to prevent anyone from leaving Ephesus or sending communications to the court. In practice such tight security was impossible, and for the monks in Constantinople a pro-Cyril report about the course of events reached the capital hidden in a reed carried by a poor beggar (*ACO* I i/2. 65. 23). Demonstrations and chanting on the streets were designed to influence the court. The holy archimandrite Dalmatius, who had not emerged from his cell for forty-eight years and was consulted by the emperor when earthquakes occurred, led the people.

The Egyptian delegation to the court arrived three days before Count Irenaeus representing the Antiochene cause. The top people at court considered numerous possible courses of action. Bankrupting the Alexandrian church chest to the consequent poverty of the clergy (*ACO* I iv. 223. 32), the Egyptian Pharaoh, as the Syrians called Cyril, used vast bribes (the list of recipients and douceurs survives: *ACO* I iv. 224) to win over the powerful courtiers, especially the eunuch high chamberlain Scholasticius, upset that at Ephesus the title *theotókos* had not been formally promulgated but influential with a *praepositus* known to be highly critical of the Church. Both were on good terms with the Antiochenes (*ACO* I i/5. 133). The emperor was known to be attached to the title.

The outcome was acceptance by the emperor of the deposition of Nestorius, Cyril, and Memnon as an act by a united council, all other acts being rejected. Theodosius was not inclined to recognize any schism. The august Count of the imperial treasury John (*comes sacrarum largitionum*) was sent to Ephesus to sort things out, which meant putting the three bishops under house arrest and military guard if only to avert riots. His request to Cyril and to John of Antioch to produce statements of belief was scorned by

Cyril as an insult. An unsigned poster followed by an announcement in the church of St John demanding that Memnon of Ephesus be replaced was badly received by his people (*ACO* I i/3 47. 1 ff.). While at Ephesus, Count John was promoted to be Master of the Offices (*PLRE* ii. 596). He was among those bribed by Cyril's agents, was won over (*ACO* I i/3. 51. 1 ff.), and was later sacked in disgrace (*ACO* I iv. 113. 23). He instructed the two parties to send delegates to court at Chalcedon across the water from the palace, and allowed Nestorius to appeal to Theodosius to allow him to retire without censure to his monastery by Antioch; the appeal was granted. Food and transport were provided for him (*ACO* I i/7. 71). He was taken to be resigning his see, though that was not what he himself thought.

Cyril escapes. Nestorius' successor consecrated. Schism

Initially John of Antioch's delegation had success. The bishops were given leave to return home; but both parties stayed put, Cyril's demanding the release from prison of Cyril and Memnon. The living conditions of the bishops remaining in Ephesus in the summer heat were bad enough to cost some lives (*ACO* I iii. 178). By a modest bribe to his guard, rewarding him by promise of promotion among the Alexandrian clergy, Cyril escaped; he was not able to enter Constantinople but could arrange that on 25 October Juvenal and seven bishops consecrated a successor to Nestorius named Maximian, a personage of little consequence who was to last three years and was found by Cyril ineffective in supporting his cause (*ACO* I iv. 223. 1). Cyril returned to Alexandria in triumph on 31 October (*ACO* I iii. 179. 11). Memnon likewise returned to Ephesus. But it had been a humiliation for Cyril that the emperor had refused to concede any censure of John of Antioch's group, 'with whom no opponent had debated' (*ACO* I i/7. 142. 28–9). Meanwhile John of Antioch in synod again declared Cyril excommunicate. The feared schism had arrived.

The Cyrilline council of Ephesus pleased Pope Celestine by a censure of Pelagians, some of whom had taken refuge in the east.

Cyprus autocephalous. Messalians

The bishops of Cyprus had long aspired to be independent of the patriarch of Antioch. With the stand-off between Alexandria and Antioch they were in a strong position to win Alexandrian support for their cause. They grounded their plea on their foundation by St Barnabas. Their alienation from Antioch had been enhanced by some forcible coercion lately inflicted in the time of Patriarch Theodotus (424–28). Early in 431 the metropolitan bishop of Constantia (by Famagusta) had died. The military commander at Antioch

Dionysius wrote to the Cypriot bishops forbidding them to consecrate a successor before the council of Ephesus had considered their claims. In the outcome, on 31 August 431 the synod agreed that there was no ancient custom by which the patriarch of Antioch consecrated the metropolitan, and that it was for the assembled bishops of the island to act (*ACO* I i/7. 118–22).[14]

Another problem that came before the council was that of the Messalians (above Ch. 43), the men of prayer who disregarded canonical order and had their *Asketikon*, a collection of homilies on the spiritual life akin to the Macarian Homilies composed probably at Edessa about 370 (above, chapter 43). At the request of Valerian of Iconium and Amphilochius of Side the synod agreed that the 'enthusiasts' should be condemned (*ACO* I i/7. 117–18).

---

[14] A fresh angle appears in C. Petrinus, 'L'église de Chypre entre Constantinopel et Antioche', *Byz. Forsch.*, 15 (1999), 131–42.

52

THE CHRISTOLOGICAL DEBATE, II:
FROM REUNION (433) TO
A BREAKDOWN OF UNITY (449)

Negotiation for peace after the council of Ephesus (431)

The emperor with his elder sister Pulcheria, whose dislike of Nestorius was unmitigated, was much distressed and displeased by the quarrel. He wrote to John of Antioch instructing him that he and Cyril must set aside antipathy and get together. Schism could spell disaster for the empire. A tribune and notary named Aristolaus was entrusted with the delicate negotiation. He travelled to Antioch, then to Alexandria, and lastly back to Antioch. The terms demanded by the emperor were clear. John must agree to the deposition of Nestorius to enable Cyril to grant agreement (*ACO* I i/4. 1 ff.). A comparable letter was sent to Cyril. Meanwhile Theodosius begged Symeon Stylites, the holy man on his column not far from Beroea, to pray for unity. Symeon later approved of the Chalcedonian Definition, and although some Monophysites claimed him for their party, Severus of Antioch (*Select Letters*, 5. 11, p. 333, tr. Brooks) acknowledged that it was not so. Two Syrian bishops were ordered to be involved in the conversation, namely Paul of Emesa (Homs) in the province of Phoenicia and Acacius of Beroea. Acacius had the authority of great age and in his history of the monks of Syria (2. 16; 21. 10) Theodoret wrote of him in panegyrical terms; moreover at Alexandria he was held in respect for his role supporting Theophilus in the condemnation of John Chrysostom. But he disliked Cyril's Twelve Anathemas and thought Cyril's attack on Nestorius to be driven by non-theological motives (*ACO* I i/7. 141). He was also outraged by hard evidence of Cyril's bribery (*ACO* I iv. 85). His confession of faith (ibid. 243–5), stressing the distinction of the two natures, would not have pleased Cyril.

At an early stage in the negotiations, John of Antioch heard an alarming report that an anathema was to be imposed on all who spoke of 'two natures'. He feared that the emperor might support this. Yet even Cyril had never explicitly said such a thing (ibid. 91). The rumour reflected the view of Cyril's more extreme supporters such as Acacius of Melitene.

The Syrians ask Cyril to withdraw his Twelve Anathemas

The chronology of the peace negotiations is obscure, but the essence is not doubtful. At first the Syrians conferred with Acacius of Beroea and decided that they must press Cyril to withdraw his letters and 'tomes' and ask for assent to no more than the Nicene creed. Theodoret of Cyrrhus wrote a sustained indictment of the Twelve Anathemas (*ACO* I i/6. 107 ff.). Cyril's reply was sharp: all he had written against Nestorius was in accord with Nicaea; the Syrians must condemn Nestorius and recognize Maximian as his successor, and if they condemn Nestorius they cannot consistently ask him to withdraw writings attacking his heresy. The Syrian bishops bitterly complained of Apollinarian language in Cyril, and John of Antioch wrote an uncomfortable letter to say so, but added that the Syrians were ready to 'anathematize' Nestorius (a term not used at Ephesus). For that anathema John himself used the ingenious formula that he condemned 'whatever Nestorius said contrary to apostolic doctrine' (*ACO* I iv. 173. 3). It soon offended Cyril that Syrian bishops were claiming that Nestorius was condemned only for his criticism of *theotókos* (*ACO* I iv. 25). Cyril had zealot supporters who wanted the Antiochenes to admit 'one nature' and thought the modest terms of peace inadequate.

Cyril accepts an Antiochene formulary

Accordingly, John of Antioch sent to Cyril as a basis for reunion the formulary of faith which his Syrian synod had approved at Ephesus, fortified by an additional sentence insisting (against Cyril's fourth Anathema) on dividing the sayings and actions of Christ between his divine and human natures. Cyril replied approving the document as true. In return John of Antioch would accept Maximian as valid and canonical bishop of Constantinople and sign the condemnation of Nestorius. Paul of Emesa took John's agreement to Alexandria and on 25 December 432 preached a Christmas sermon at Alexandria which went as far to meet Cyril as an Antiochene theologian could possibly go, especially emphasizing *theotókos* with anathema on its rejection and thereby evoking acclamations of pleasure from the congregation (*ACO* I i/3. 11–12). On 1 January 433 Paul preached a second sermon, again receiving acclamations for his fidelity to the tradition of Athanasius, Theophilus, and Cyril.

Cyril disavows Apollinarianism

The outcome was evident: Cyril sent an enthusiastic letter to John of Antioch to say that Paul of Emesa had shown the split to be unnecessary, and that the title 'mother of God' added nothing to the Nicene faith; he then incorporated in his letter the Formulary of Reunion being the text sent by John of Antioch. The letter disavows any Apollinarian ideas, e.g. that Christ's body came from heaven. Christ is perfect in Godhead and perfect in humanity; Christ is not two but one, one even though a difference of natures is acknowledged. Slander has ascribed to Cyril belief in a confusion or mixing of the two natures. But that 'Christ suffered in the flesh' is certain from 1 Pet. 4: 1. In everything Cyril strictly follows Athanasius. Many authoritative citations could have been added. The Nicene creed was inspired by the Holy Spirit who proceeds from the Father but is not alien from the Son in respect of his essence. Finally 'since we have learnt that Athanasius' letter to Epictetus has been corrupted by some', Cyril sends a transcript checked from old copies in the Alexandrian archives. From Cyril's later letter to Succensus of Diocaesarea it emerges that Cyril thought the corruption to Athanasius' text had been by Nestorians and that Paul of Emesa's copy was incorrect (*ACO* I i/6. 156. 19 ff.). In actuality Cyril was using an Apollinarian recension. It was an element in the agreement that both parties affirmed the sufficiency of the Nicene creed but accepted Athanasius' letter to Epictetus of Corinth as its valid interpretation.

The peace process said nothing about the reinstatement of the four supporters of Nestorius who were also declared deposed at Ephesus, and when Paul of Emesa put in a plea on their behalf Cyril initially dug his heels in. He was already agreeing to much, and was unwilling to consider a new requirement not previously mentioned. The point was important if he was to be able to carry his most fervent supporters, already anxious about a compromise (*ACO* I i/4. 32. 18). Nevertheless in correspondence with Pope Sixtus III he did not disagree with Sixtus that all bishops who assented to the Cyrilline synod of Ephesus should be pardoned, with the single exception of Nestorius (*ACO* I i/7. 143–5; PL 50. 583 and 587).

'One from two natures'?

The Formulary of Reunion affirmed Christ to be one with God in his divine nature, one with us in humanity, yet one from two natures. To many of Cyril's more zealous supporters Cyril's assent to this Antiochene document was incomprehensible. His apocrisiaries at the court needed a letter to explain how Cyril had come to agree (*ACO* I i/7. 154). To them Cyril had implicitly condemned his own teaching (*ACO* I iv. 129. 22). Even one of the presbyters of Antioch, Eusebius, who dissented from his bishop and was later to become prominent in the controversy about Theodore of Mopsuestia, wrote to Cyril in distress that he could have put his name to a fudge. To the pained Acacius bishop of Melitene (Roman Armenia) Cyril protested that all the surrender was on the side of the Syrians, that he accepted two natures in detached mental contemplation, but 'after the union, the division into two is removed' and the incarnate Lord is one nature, *mia physis*. Cyril was vexed that John of Antioch had been writing to the effect that Cyril had conceded two distinct natures, allocating some sayings to one, other sayings to the other. It was also vexatious that some were producing a letter from a Roman presbyter Philip, saying that Celestine's successor Xystus III was annoyed by the condemnation of Nestorius, whereas the truth was rather that Xystus (or Sixtus, Pope 432–40) had confirmed the decision of his synod at Ephesus.

Similarly to Dynatos bishop of Nicopolis in Old Epirus Cyril penned a letter of explanation, assuring him that there was no question of rehabilitating Dorotheos of Marcianopolis and others who had supported Nestorius. Later Cyril was more relaxed. In 436 the emperor rewarded Cyrus bishop of Aphrodisias with tax exemption for his anti-Nestorian labours (CTh 11. 1. 37).

Cyril reassures zealous supporters: Diodore and Theodore

A major statement of Cyril's position was given in two letters to an Isaurian bishop, Succensus of Diocaesarea (Cyril, *epp.* 45–6; *ACO* I i/6. 151–62), who was especially anxious about 'two natures or one?' Cyril's answer to his questions begins by an attack on Diodore of Tarsus, who (he says) had once disbelieved in the equality of the Holy Spirit with the Father and the Son, and then having abandoned that heresy fell into another by asserting that the son born of Mary is one person and the eternal Logos is another. The true doctrine is 'one nature of the Logos incarnate', as the fathers said (actually Apollinaris under the name of Athanasius). Succensus wrote that after the resurrection Christ's body was changed into a divine nature. Cyril corrects him: it is true that after the resurrection his body became free of all human weaknesses, lifegiving, no longer corruptible.

With the hostile reference to Diodore, Cyril gradually supported a sustained argument against Diodore and Theodore of Mopsuestia which might vex Syrian theologians but could do much to tranquillize his critics. Antiochenes coerced into rejecting Nestorius unwisely began to trumpet the orthodoxy of Diodore and Theodore, which led Cyril to warn the emperor that Theodore was the father of Nestorianism (*ACO* I iv. 211). A defence of Diodore and Theodore was written by Theodoret, remnants of the work being preserved by the sixth-century African Facundus. The remains of Cyril's work against them were acutely assembled by Marcel Richard (*Opera Minora*, ii (Turnhout, 1977), no. 51).

A second letter to Succensus affirms that Christ is 'one nature'. Succensus asked how 'one nature' is compatible with the language of the Formulary of

Reunion, perfect God and perfect man. Cyril's reply grants that the two natures are distinct but only to the contemplating mind, not to the worshipper.

Cyril distrusted by his own sympathizers

The Formulary of Reunion was in practice being differently interpreted at Alexandria and Antioch. Cyril reasonably protested that he could not anathematize his own writings, and sought to reassure supporters who felt that he had betrayed their cause and convictions, emphasizing his belief in 'one nature of the incarnate Logos', not two. At Chalcedon in 451 Eustathius bishop of Berytos observed that this substantially modified the language in his letter to John of Antioch (*ACO* II i. 112. 10 ff.). Nevertheless under pressure Cyril pleaded that anything in his Twelve Anathemas which might seem reprehensible (i.e. implicitly admitting that he might have gone too far) was occasioned by zeal for Christ (*ACO* I iv. 222. 24). The distrust felt by some who had gone all the way with him at Ephesus was palpable, especially when a rumour, in which there was more than a grain of truth, went round that the Antiochenes were refusing to concede any criticism of Nestorius' doctrines (this not being a constituent clause of the peace treaty). That Cyril had agreed remains astonishing, and one might wonder if he had simply run out of money for further bribery to keep the court in firm support. But the Carthaginian Liberatus in the mid-sixth century says that Cyril and John both yielded under threat of exile (*ACO* II v. 106. 14), which is inherently probable.

Deep division in Syria and the East

Meanwhile John of Antioch had to be dragged into signing a condemnation of Nestorius and recognition of Maximian under strong pressure from the tribune Aristolaus, who threatened to tell the emperor that the bishop of Antioch was to blame for the schism if he failed to sign. John's reluctance was determined not only by personal belief that Nestorius was orthodox even if imprudent but also by his acute difficulties with the great mass of bishops in the region of his jurisdiction, a number of whom were militant in hostility to Cyril's Apollinarian language and were outraged by the treatment of Nestorius. In Syria the most important figures were Theodoret of Cyrrhus, Alexander of Hierapolis (east of Antioch near the Euphrates), and Andrew of Samosata. Alexander was regarded by many as making a heroic stand against a shoddy political compromise, and John found several suffragans refusing communion with him. Andrew of Samosata described a nightmare in which he found himself being blessed by Apollinaris (*ACO* I iv. 100). The bishop of Mopsuestia, who venerated the teaching of his predecessor Theodore (ibid. 168. 23), was ejected from his see by military force and exiled to Melitene in Armenia. Theodoret saw that survival entailed yielding, but Alexander of Hierapolis remained intransigent. The news that Theodoret would yield probably provided occasion for Cyril to send him a copy of his refutation of the emperor Julian (Theodoret, *ep.* 83), a notably friendly act.

Sisyphus and the experience of ecumenism

On 23 April 433 Cyril preached at Alexandria declaring peace with Antioch achieved on the basis of Nestorius' removal. It had been a struggle for both protagonists to reach a compromise. In time its precariousness would become all too evident. Firmus bishop of Cappadocian Caesarea (whose letters, rich in literary clichés and social history, show almost no interest in theology but who supported Cyril) commented that trying to reach agreement between Christians in combat was like the Homeric misery of Sisyphus in Hades (*Odyssey* 11. 593), for ever pushing his boulder up a steep hill and almost at the top losing control of it every time (*ep.* 38, PG 77. 1508; SC 350). In 432 a synod of pro-Nestorian bishops at Tarsus vainly tried to depose him. But one letter (41) asks the Nestorian bishop of Tarsus to excommunicate a nun who seduced a man and went off with his wife's property. After the peace of 433 Firmus was to be a merciless harasser of bishops in Cilicia II whose conscience would not allow them to accept it (*ACO* I iv. 141. 6–7 'implacabile proelium'). Among Firmus' letters one (5) is from a rural bishop (*chorepiskopos*) Alypius who sought reconciliation with Firmus after the tensions. It is noteworthy that at sixth-century Tarsus Nestorius was still being commemorated in the calendar of martyrs. Severus of Antioch (*Select Letters*, i. 24, p. 84, tr. Brooks) remonstrated with the then bishop.

The Cilician dissenters long refused communion with bishops who acquiesced in the peace agreement. Their neighbour Eutherius metropolitan of Tyana supported them and opposed Firmus.

Theodoret

Theodoret's long-delayed yielding to the agreement was based on his judgement that when Cyril had signed the Formulary of Reunion, then, whether or not he admitted it, he had in effect surrendered the hard-line doctrines of his Twelve Anathemas. Theodoret had acute difficulty with the demand for condemnation of Nestorius if that implied censure of a theology which he affirmed to be wholly orthodox. Perhaps it could suffice if the Antiochenes were to anathematize those who speak of two sons or say that Christ is a mere man. However, the only possible way forward was compromise.

During the negotiations at court immediately after the council of Ephesus Theodoret had discovered Nestorius to be cordially hated at the imperial court; both Theodosius and the consistory reacted with a reflex knee-jerk abhorrence when his name was mentioned (*ACO* I i/7. 80. 7ff.). The 'hatred' for Nestorius at the capital is also twice mentioned in Ibas of Edessa's letter to the Persian Mari (*ACO* II i. 301–3). The hostility of Pulcheria was well known enough to be an acclamation (ibid. 69. 32). Theodoret, who had friends in the consistory, could not have failed to realize that any attempt to reinstate Nestorius at Constantinople was out of the question. Nestorius had made himself extremely unpopular and had almost no supporters among his own clergy and the monks. Moreover Pope Celestine, writing to the emperor about estates bequeathed to the church in north Africa by Proba, where the income was being diverted to secular purposes by the person in charge of the property, took the occasion to ask for 'the rapacious wolf' Nestorius to be exiled (*ACO* I ii. 88–90). The pope recognized Maximian as Nestorius' successor, warning him against the Pelagian errors of Caelestius (ibid. 90–1). Maximian staged a procession with crosses and torches in the Forum of Constantine at which the people were told that peace had been settled and he was now recognized as valid bishop (*ACO* I iv. 144).

Alexander of Hierapolis

Alexander of Hierapolis became leader of a substantial group of Syrian and Cilician bishops who thought the proposed deal faced them with a kiss of peace for blatant heresy; they preferred death. He and others who looked to his leadership regarded John of Antioch and Theodoret as 'chameleons', traitors to orthodoxy by favouring peace. He harboured pride that at Ephesus he had not been party to the drafting of the doctrinal statement, now the Formulary of Reunion, in which the admission of *theotókos* was for him a fatal step down a slippery path (*ACO* I iv. 130–1). That title he deemed to be the keystone of Cyril's heresy (ibid. 134. 2). When Nestorius' friend Count Irenaeus came to write his history of the controversy, he judged the peace treaty to be utterly unscrupulous (ibid. 114–15). Eutherius of Tyana and Helladius of Tarsus appealed to Pope Xystus (ibid. 145–8). But pressure from the imperial government was hard to resist. In Isauria Bishop Archelaus was fined the substantial sum of 8,000 solidi by the 'Augustalis' (adjutant to the prefect) at Seleucia, and John of Antioch had to ask his suffragans to make contributions (ibid. 113. 29). As Seleucia in Isauria had the pilgrim shrine of St Thecla, perhaps the church there had good resources. The condemnation of Nestorius was a requirement imposed by the emperor himself, and refusal incurred state penalties. For Alexander of Hierapolis there was a painful issue in the fact that Nestorius had not been censured for corruption of life but for alleged heresy, and Alexander was sure that he was orthodox and the leader condemning him Apollinarian. He felt especially hurt when Andrew of Samosata joined Theodoret in accepting the peace.

Alexander was distressed that the sharp division of opinion among the eastern bishops gravely weakened their position, which would have been much stronger if they had faced the emperor united. On the other side, John of Antioch considered the unity of the churches more important than refinements of doctrine. Pagans and Jews were openly laughing at the excommunications; at Laodicea (Syria) in the theatre some Jews had lately lynched the archdeacon (ibid. 210. 21).

The monasteries could also be divided. Alexander was astonished to learn that in Alexandria there were holy monks who cursed Cyril and wished to find refuge in Syria (ibid. 186–7). Meanwhile, in Syria some monks thought Cyril right. Theodoret's *Religious History*, with short biographies of holy men in Syria, especially Symeon the Stylite, was probably written both to vindicate his own solidarity with the monks and to affirm that these holy ascetics were no less to be venerated than the Egyptian monks on whose support Cyril relied.

Imperial pressure for union

John of Antioch's apocrisiary at Constantinople succeeded in obtaining an imperial letter compelling the dissenters to hold communion with John of Antioch or leave their churches. It was never published. The praetorian prefect of the East, Taurus, told the emperor that his *sacra* would produce 'further riots in cities', and that Cilicia and Thrace were almost the only provinces which loyally paid taxes (*ACO* I iv. 155). This was a fiscal argument such as had persuaded Arcadius to resist a request from the Christians of Gaza to give authority for the demolition of the great pagan temple of Marnas (Syriac for 'Our Lord').[1] Some Cilician bishops were in any event only lukewarm for the Nestorian cause (ibid. 277). Nevertheless the emperor's command was conveyed orally to Alexander of Hierapolis. He and his allies remained defiant and in provincial synod made formal protest (ibid. 154. 32).

The dissension in the *Dioicesis* Oriens was further embittered when John of Antioch ordained two bishops in the province of Euphratesia, ignoring the rights of Alexander the metropolitan; he installed at Doliche an unsuitable replacement for a bishop who had signed no letter of resignation (*ACO* I iv. 160–1). Moreover, Resapha near Callinicus (Raqqa) with its shrine of St Sergius had lately been elevated into a city by Theodosius because of the place's importance as a military base for defence on the Euphrates frontier.

---

[1] Mark the Deacon, *Life of Porphyry of Gaza*, 41.

There John ordained a bishop, probably Marianus, who turns up as 'bishop of Rosapha' in the record of a council of Antioch in 445 (*ACO* II i. 428. 28; *Act. Chalc.* 15. 15); at Chalcedon Alexander's successor Stephen of Hierapolis signed for the see. On a big pilgrim church at the shrine of St Sergius, the ruins of which survive, Bishop Alexander had spent the large sum of 300 pounds of gold, and he felt wounded by this intrusion, which conflicted with the canons of Nicaea (but not with Pope Innocent I's advice to Alexander of Antioch).

Rabbula and Ibas of Edessa

An additional difficulty was the enthusiastic support given to Cyril by Rabbula metropolitan of Edessa (412–35), allied with whom was the bishop of Perra, Gemellinus. Rabbula, a rich pagan landowner of Chalcis, was converted by his mother. At the council of Ephesus he had been with John of Antioch but changed sides. He supported Cyril with the fanaticism of a convert. Rabbula had the advantage of understanding both Greek and Syriac; the revised Syriac Bible, the Peshitta, slightly antedated his time. He warned Cyril that the Christology of Theodore of Mopsuestia was being advocated now that Nestorius was under a cloud (*ACO* I iv. 212). Rabbula's Christology was opposed at Edessa by Ibas, who in 435 succeeded him as bishop. In 433 Ibas wrote a famous letter to Mari of Nisibis, a Persian monk, perhaps a refugee from persecution living in the Roman empire, rejecting Cyril as Apollinarian and sending Mari the Formulary of Reunion. Rabbula he described as 'tyrant of our city'. Edessa had schools for Syriac-, Armenian-, and Persian-speakers, and had links with churches in Persia. Christian Armenians in the Persian empire after their land was divided in 387 naturally looked to Edessa for fellowship. As the school soon became a hotbed of Nestorians, in time harassment forced it to move to Nisibis in Persian territory.

   Approved at Chalcedon, Ibas' letter to Mari was to become a major object of delighted hate to critics of the Chalcedonian Definition, and therefore an issue in the sixth-century controversy concerning the 'Three Chapters' (Theodore of Mopsuestia, Theodoret, and Ibas' letter). In that controversy the approval given to Ibas' letter at Chalcedon required the fiction that the fourth general council had approved a different document from the letter to Mari which was not the authentic work of Ibas. At the council of Ephesus in August 449 Ibas was condemned, and needed rehabilitation at Chalcedon.[2]

----

[2] On the identity of Mari see a different view in M. van Esbroeck, *JTS*, NS 38 (1987), 129–35.

At Edessa Ibas' too overt sympathy, though he accepted the deposition of Nestorius, divided his clergy and the monks. He obtained military aid to suppress his opponents, but they submitted a complaint to the court that he not only was Nestorian but had misappropriated money from the sale of sacred vessels, sold to ransom captives, for his own use. The emperor remitted his case to the bishops of Tyre and Berytus. Proceedings at Berytus were attended by a large crowd of supporters and opponents, intimidating the judges who for their personal safety reached no verdict. A riot ensued.

Proclus of Constantinople

On 12 April 434 Maximian bishop of Constantinople died. Rioters demanded the reinstatement of Nestorius with a threat to burn down the great Church. Even before Maximian was buried, the emperor, who was accustomed to issuing orders appointing new bishops for Constantine's city and elsewhere,[3] decided in favour of Proclus, disappointed in three previous elections but resident in the capital and valued for fine eloquence and orthodoxy. Proclus sympathized with the local clergy and monks who had been deeply offended by Nestorius. He echoed some of the Christological language of Cyril, who was delighted by his installation. Devotion to the Blessed Virgin Mary was prominent in his preaching. John of Antioch also expressed pleasure at his elevation (*ACO* I iv. p. 154). Proclus was far from benevolent to the pro-Nestorians in the capital (ibid. 179. 23). His installation was wholly unwelcome to the Syrians refusing communion with compromising John of Antioch (ibid. 173–4; 179. 24).

The failed coup to reinstate Nestorius as bishop had its depressing effect. In the province of Cilicia II the bishops yielded to holding communion with John, and Theodoret himself decided to do the same on being assured by John that he would not demand a signature in writing to the deposition of Nestorius. He judged that refusal would entail consequences much worse. He faced a threat that his church's well-known shrine of SS. Sergius and Bacchus would be reduced to ashes (ibid. 160. 28). Isauria and Cilicia I quickly followed suit in surrender. At Mopsuestia the intransigent bishop, ejected by force, fostered civil disorders until exiled to Melitene in Armenia, where rough treatment killed him.

The same harsh treatment was accorded to Alexander of Hierapolis. The

---

[3] Firmus of Caesarea (Cappadocia) in the 430s attests the imperial custom of sending a *congé d'élire* in gold ink for an episcopal appointment (*ep.* 30); cf. R.Cormack, *Writing in Gold* (London, 1985). The patriarch Anatolius could explain to Pope Leo (*ep.* 53) that by custom the clergy of Constantinople submitted a list of possibles; the emperor would then give the clergy permission to elect 'their choice' (in practice probably his). In 520 Epiphanius patriarch of Constantinople notified Pope Hormisdas of his accession 'by the choice of the emperor Justin and his empress' (Avellana 195).

imperial order for his expulsion came in April 435; he retired quietly but his people in tears shouted abusive acclamations against those deemed responsible for his ejection, probably including the emperor himself. Shockingly, he was exiled to labour in a mine in Egypt, probably surviving only a few days in the appalling conditions; he was not heard of again (*ACO* I iv. 203. 28). On 8 August 435 an edict imposed penalties on a long list of heretical sects, concluding with Nestorians who are to be called 'Simonians' (followers of Simon Magus); Nestorius' writings were to be burned (CTh 16. 5. 66). Cyril argued that the emperor's classification of Nestorius as a Simonian implied the condemnation of his doctrine, not merely of the man himself or his criticism of *theotókos* (*ACO* I iv. 206, cf. 230), but the imperial tribune Aristolaus had no instruction other than to demand the deposition of Nestorius. Even Cyril realized that it would be a mistake to ask too much if he was to retain support at court. In 437 John of Antioch presided over a large synod which condemned Nestorius but insisted that the one all-sufficient faith was the Nicene creed (implying reserve towards Cyril's Twelve Anathemas). Nestorius himself was exiled to Petra, later to the great Oasis in Egypt.

Proclus' Tome to the Armenians[4]

Armenia, long disputed between the Roman and Persian empires, was split in 387. Armenian Christians in Persia naturally looked to Edessa, metropolis of the province of Osrhoene, for guidance. From Edessa Rabbula's sharply negative estimate of Theodore of Mopsuestia soon penetrated Persian Armenia beyond the frontier of the Roman empire. Two Armenian presbyters named Leontius and Abel stirred their bishops to write to Proclus asking for his advice and authoritative help. The bishops were hesitant, aware that Cilician bishops were more favourable to Diodore and Theodore than Rabbula of Edessa or Acacius of Melitene in Roman Armenia. To meet the Armenians' question Proclus composed a long statement called his Tome; he sent a copy to Cyril of Alexandria.

Proclus' Tome of 435 is a diffuse and in some respects amateurish document. But at the time it was important and at Chalcedon in 451 received the synod's approval. It begins with non-controversial questions about ethics, listing the four cardinal virtues followed by the three theological virtues of faith, hope, and love. Then follows a doctrinal statement of the Christian

---

[4] PG 65. 836–74; critical edition by Schwartz, *ACO* IV ii. 186–95 (taking account of two Syriac versions) followed by the Latin version of Dionysius Exiguus. A French translation of the early Armenian version in M. Tallon, *Livre des Lettres* (Beirut, 1955).

On the tangled history see Schwartz, *Konzilstudien* (Strassburg, 1914), and M. Richard's paper 'Proclus de Constantinople et le théopaschisme' reprinted in his *Opera Minora*, ii (Turnhout, 1977), no. 52.

story of an impassible incarnation which implies no addition to the divine Triad. Christian faith requires not only good works but also right belief. This entails an affirmation of free will, the Fall of Adam and Eve, and the incarnation. Some of Cyril's language in his synodical letter to Nestorius is borrowed, but Proclus can be independent, explaining (perhaps more pretentiously than logically) that just as a Monad cannot be divided without becoming a Dyad, so the one being resulting from the union cannot be split into two. The Logos became flesh, i.e. perfect man. There are not two sons. The Alone begat the Only-begotten. So the generation of the divine Son did not require two partners. Christ is not distinct from the divine Logos, which would make him a mere man. One should not be scandalized by the human weaknesses in the gospels. 'I am astonished at the folly of those who follow new paths of deceit; for I acknowledge and am taught that there is one Son; I confess the hypostasis of the incarnate divine Logos.' That the Logos remains impassible is indisputable. 'One of the Trinity was enfleshed'; but that does not mean that the Son/Logos suffered; he overcame the disruptive force of passion in the incarnation.

Proclus' lapidary phrase 'one of the Trinity' points to the conclusion that 'one of the Trinity suffered' was already a liturgical acclamation in use by some monks at Constantinople.[5] At Chalcedon in 451 a monk Dorotheus affirms 'We confess that he who suffered is one of the Trinity' (*ACO* II i. 316).

At one point Proclus has a modified echo of the Formulary of Reunion of 433, namely in the affirmation that Christ is of one *ousia* with the Father in his divinity, and of the same race (*homophylos*) with the Virgin in his flesh: 'It would not be much of a miracle if the Virgin's child were not God; many women have given birth to righteous men.'

Surprisingly and no doubt significantly there is not a word naming either Nestorius or Theodore, merely a mention of a 'new blasphemy' unspecified. But excerpts from Theodore, sent by the Armenians, were appended without naming the author or explicit request for censure. The Tome seemed hopelessly inadequate to a deacon and archimandrite at Constantinople named Basil, who took a copy of it with the Armenian correspondence to Cyril at Alexandria and on returning home composed indignant pamphlets against Theodore (Innocentius of Maronia, *ACO* IV ii. 68). Basil was soon joined by the dissident presbyter of Antioch Maximus. The excerpts from Theodore sent to Proclus from Armenia were imprudently translated into Syriac and Armenian and widely circulated by their admirer Ibas of Edessa,

---

[5] Ephrem, Patriarch of Antioch (527–45; *PLRE* ii. 394–5) after high secular office as Count of the East, a native Syriac-speaker who wrote defences of Chalcedon in Greek, correctly observed that the Monophysite interpolation *crucified for us* in the Trisagion was orthodox at Antioch, where it referred to Christ, not at Constantinople, where it was understood of the Trinity and therefore theopaschite (Photius, cod. 228).

an act which aroused alarm not only among clergy but among highly placed laymen (Proclus to John of Antioch, PG 65. 875 A from the Acts of the council of 553, *ACO* IV ii. 240–3); by Maximus' hand Proclus now sent these excerpts without naming the author for the consideration of John of Antioch, who was invited to be critical of them (Facundus 8. 2).

Enthusiasm for the problem now being raised was almost non-existent with Proclus, John of Antioch, and even Cyril of Alexandria who cannot have been pleased by a threat to the peace achieved in 433, which he interpreted to allow him to speak of 'one nature of the incarnate Word'. All three patriarchs were under different pressures. John of Antioch summoned a substantial synod of seventy-five or eighty bishops, which wrote to Proclus on the happy unity between Antioch and Constantinople manifested by a unanimous approval of the Tome to the Armenians; but the synod warned Proclus to ignore nomadic monks all too ready to delate bishops to the authorities at the capital. The synod wrote to Theodosius II reminding him of the favour shown to Theodore by his grandfather Theodosius I and of the close friendship between Theodore and John Chrysostom, whose relics had lately been enshrined at Constantinople. For teachers in the Church to be a target for vituperation was normal.

The synod's letter to Cyril, who was in Jerusalem, survives complete in a Latin version found in the Arsenal library (cod. 341 s. xiii), Paris, edited by Schwartz (*Konzilstudien*, 62–6 = *ACO* I v. 310–14). In the sixth century the Roman deacon Pelagius (later Pope Pelagius I) writing in Defence of the Three Chapters (ed. Devreesse, Vatican City, 1932) also gave a summary. John writes of Theodore's noble battles against Arians and Eunomians; of the similar doctrines found in Athanasius, Basil, both Gregories, Amphilochius, Theophilus, and indeed in the Tome of Proclus himself; moreover in Eustathius of Antioch, Alexander of Alexandria, Meletius, Flavian, and many western writers 'better known to you.' The contention is about words. None of us can escape saying something that upsets someone. Sayings of Theodore that seem harsh were written in controversy with heretics, and similarly words of Cyril himself in combat with Nestorius had been mitigated by their author to meet difficulties among the Syrian bishops. The critics had taken pieces entirely out of context. In this battle in the dark Cyril is asked to write to Proclus advising him to discourage this storm against the Syrian bishops. While two different natures in Christ are affirmed and indeed conceded by Cyril himself, that is no prejudice to the absoluteness of the union. The Nicene creed should have no additions or subtractions. The synod accepts Proclus' Tome. To condemn Theodore would strengthen the Nestorians. Further, to judge a dead man is to usurp the rights of the divine Judge. (This was a question that much exercised the Council of 553.)

Proclus was naïve to suppose that the excerpts in which he had suppressed Theodore's name would not be immediately identified. He expressed some vexation when the matter was public, and deplored the suggestion that one could condemn a dead man. But he wanted John of Antioch to return the copy of his Tome with the excerpts attached so that the censure of the latter would be beyond doubt. However, the question of Theodore was now a very public issue. Cyril was irritated by John of Antioch's claim that one could find opinions like Theodore's in Athanasius, in his revered uncle Theophilus, or in Alexander at the time of Arius. He wrote to John that none should preach the impious doctrines of Theodore (*ep.* 70, PG 77. 341 AB). This was not the answer John would like to have received. But popular enthusiasm for Theodore at Antioch was uncontrollable. Cyril addressed urgent letters to the emperor and the princesses suggesting an edict against Theodore, and circulated his book against Diodore and Theodore. Proclus can only have been much displeased. Cyril's shifting stance, however, was to be that while Theodore was a heretic, he was dead and should not now be under anathema; economy should be exercised in the interest of peace. Zealots among his supporters were not pleased by such words. But for the last six years of his life until his death in 444 Cyril's relationship with Antioch was free of acrimony.

Cyril's relationship with Proclus was uneventful, perhaps mainly because the latter's ambitions for his jurisdiction were directed towards Illyricum.

Preparation for controversy about the 'Three Chapters'

Rabbula died on 8 August 435, to be succeeded by his active opponent Ibas. Diodore was long dead, and Theodore died in 427. Moreover, neither of them had played any part in tension between Alexandria and Constantinople, so that it was hard to persuade either Proclus or Cyril to be deeply excited about them. Nevertheless, in the long run the attack on Theodore left a lasting mark, and a determination one day to obtain his condemnation was embedded in the more extreme supporters of Cyril's Christology. In the next century under Justinian they succeeded. The sixth-century controversy about the orthodoxy of Theodore, the letter of Ibas to Mari, and Theodoret had all its foundations laid in 438.

Dioscorus and Eutyches

John of Antioch died in 442 and was succeeded by his weak nephew Domnos. In 444 Cyril was succeeded as bishop of Alexandria by his tough deacon Dioscorus, who strongly sympathized with the zealot supporters of Cyril's Twelve Anathemas and regretted Cyril's assent to the compromise

Formulary of Reunion with Antioch in 433. He also represented the clergy of Alexandria resentful of the ways in which Cyril had disbursed the resources of his Church, whether to bribe court officials or to look after his relatives (*ACO* II i. 218. 2 ff.). But he warmly concurred with Cyril's determination to weaken and if possible humiliate the see of Constantinople, and was to succeed in overthrowing Proclus' successor Flavian, patriarch from 446, at a second Council of Ephesus in 449. He could use the Christological debate as a stalking horse. (His reaction to Flavian's installation was curmudgeonly, so perhaps he had a rival candidate: *ACO* II ii. 77. 25). He was also angered by Domnus of Antioch's claim that his Petrine see was superior to St Mark's, and at Ephesus in 449 eliminated him also.

In this project he was assisted by the archimandrite of a monastery of Job at Hebdomon on the west side of Constantinople named Eutyches, godfather and close friend of the immensely powerful eunuch and *spathários* (emperor's sword-bearer) named Chrysaphius, also called Ztummas (*PLRE* ii. 295–7). Eutyches had had friendly correspondence with Cyril of Alexandria, who had sent him records of the decisions at Ephesus in 431. Like the archimandrite Dalmatius, he was among the monks of Constantinople who sustained deep reservations about successive patriarchs. Chrysaphius kept the emperor entertained so that he would not interfere in the control of government. His power approximated to absolutism. To Eutyches he was a potent ally.

Cyrus of Panopolis

How dangerous it was to cross Chrysaphius' path is clear from the career of the city prefect and perhaps still pagan poet Cyrus from Panopolis in Egypt, in 439 praetorian prefect and friend of Eudocia the empress, consul in 441. He became too popular in Constantinople and was sacked. Since 438 public office was barred to pagans, heretics, Jews, and Samaritans (NTh 3). In 443 Cyrus submitted to be baptized and was sent by Chrysaphius to be bishop of Cotyaeum in Phrygia, where the populace had lynched the four previous incumbents (*Life of Daniel the Stylite*, 31). By the brevity of his sermons he won the hearts of the people, and after the deaths of Theodosius and Chrysaphius (450) could return to lay life in the capital, composing verses for the nearby pillar of Daniel the Stylite his spiritual director (located at the site of the Turkish castle Rumeli Hisar on the Bosporus), and famously generous to the poor.

Cyrus had a friend in the emperor's wife Eudocia. They shared pagan classical culture. His fall may be connected with hers. Eudocia had been on pilgrimage to Jerusalem in 438, but on return was accused perhaps falsely of an affair with Paulinus, former Master of the Offices. He was executed. From

443 to her death in 460 she lived in Jerusalem. She composed a Homeric cento with a Christian theme.

Eusebius of Dorylaeum and the archimandrite Eutyches

In 428–9 the affair of Nestorius had become a major issue in part from a denunciation of the patriarch by a professional advocate named Eusebius. This Eusebius had meanwhile become bishop of Dorylaeum (Phrygia). He was a fanatic for precise orthodoxy. Visiting Constantinople he came into conversation with Eutyches, and was perturbed to hear him challenge the orthodoxy of the Formulary of Reunion of 433. The Christology of Eutyches seemed extreme not for the doctrine that in Christ incarnate there was after the union but one nature, not two, but rather for his denial that in his human body the Lord was of one substance with us. This was a crucial clause in the Formulary of Reunion. Eusebius of Dorylaeum denounced him before the patriarch Flavian, and on 8 and 12 November 448 the case came before the 'resident synod' (*synodos endemousa*) made up of thirty-six bishops who happened to be in Constantinople on their own business and could be gathered by the patriarch for a hearing. It was risky to arraign an intimate friend of Chrysaphius, who was in any event on bad terms with Flavian. After Flavian's installation Flavian had a poor start with the emperor. Theodosius needed money to cope with Attila's Huns, and Flavian refused help from patriarchal funds (Nestorius, *Heraclides* 298 Nau; Theophanes AM 5940). A variant of this story (in Evagrius, *HE* 1. 10) told that Chrysaphius indicated to Flavian that some sign of gratitude would be appropriate for his consecration. When Flavian sent blessed bread, the eunuch returned it saying that gold would be preferred.

At a preliminary discussion the resident synod, whose proceedings were formally minuted as at a meeting in 'Constantinople Rome', listened with approval to Cyril's second letter to Nestorius and then to the Reunion letter to John of Antioch (not the Twelve Anathemas). Bishops repeated their belief in the Nicene creed 'dictated by the Holy Spirit' (*ACO* II i. 121. 19). They then decided to send for Eutyches, who heard the charges, refused to abandon a vow he had made never to leave his monastery, and affirmed that Eusebius of Dorylaeum had long been his enemy, motivated by malice. He affirmed the Nicene creed and especially the scriptures, which provocatively he thought more solid ground than the fathers. The incarnate Lord had only one nature. It was slander to accuse him of saying the Logos brought his body from heaven. The proposition that Christ was constituted of two natures hypostatically united he could not find in the fathers or, better, in the scriptures. He granted that the Virgin Mary's son was perfect God and perfect man, but not that his body was of the same nature as ours (*ACO* II i. 124).

Eutyches' attachment to this latter point no doubt originated in his eucharistic faith. At holy communion he received 'the body of God',[6] and that could not be merely a human body of the same nature as ours. Born of Mary, crucified for us, it was united to and transformed by the divine Logos. (This is not far from the ruling of Trent (XIII 3) that under the form of bread is the true body of our Lord together with his soul and divinity.) By the same reasoning, to stress two distinct natures must seem to make everything about the human body and soul of Christ less than divinely lifegiving. In Cyril's Christology, the eucharist was central. Cyril too did not want 'two natures after the incarnation'. A eucharist was not commemorating a dead hero. It was unjust that Eutyches was to be labelled a heretic by both Chalcedonians and Monophysites. But his denial that the body of Christ was of one substance with ours was open to caricature. Philoxenos (Xenaia), bishop of Mabbug (Hierapolis), 485–519, no admirer of Chalcedon's two natures, judged Eutyches' language gnostic.[7]

Flavian persisted; Eutyches was like a wasp in his nose. Three formal summonses were sent. When Eutyches finally arrived, he was escorted by a body of soldiers, monks, and members of the praetorian prefect's guard, who would leave him in Flavian's care only if assured that he would be at liberty to leave after the investigation. With him there came also a silentiary from the emperor with a request: that at the trial of Eutyches an eminent patrician named Florentius, formerly praetorian prefect and consul, moreover an orthodox Christian, should attend by delegation from the emperor apparently to see that justice was done. It was not clear how neutral he was, but at the conclusion his interventions towards the end of the trial made explicit Eutyches' divergence from the Formulary of Reunion and therefore seemed designed to make condemnation by Flavian's synod certain. In reply to Flavian Eutyches answered: 'Until today I have refused to say that our divine Saviour's body is of one substance with ours, but that of the Virgin Mary is so; since you say this, I will say it; but it is not the language found in the Bible or the Fathers.' The implication in this humility to patriarchal authority was evident that he himself did not believe it and thought Flavian a heretic. Florentius warned him: 'You will be deposed if you do not say "Two natures after the union."' Back came the cutting answer: 'Read Athanasius and you will learn that he says nothing of the kind.' The verdict deprived Eutyches of priesthood and of being higumen of his monastery. It had fifty-three signatures of bishops and other archimandrites.

---

[6] John Rufus, PO 8. 147, says that Monophysite celebrants distributing at the eucharist preferred to say 'the body of God the Word' rather than 'the body of Christ'.

[7] A. de Halleux, *Philoxène de Mabbog* (Louvain, 1963), 364.

Eutyches challenged the accuracy of the minutes of his trial. His appeal to Rome, Alexandria, Jerusalem and Thessalonica was missing. The nitpicking inquiry, ordered by the emperor on 8 April 449 not long after he had also summoned an ecumenical council to meet at Ephesus to consider the Christological debate, began on 13 April and was regulated by senior judicial officers. The cross-examination of the notaries who took the minutes disclosed that they were not impeccable, and the mighty Florentius himself was a witness to this effect. In a situation highly dangerous for the notaries themselves, one of the four accused a colleague of falsification. Disastrous for Flavian was testimony of the silentiary from the emperor that Flavian had told him the presence of Florentius was unnecessary, since the condemnation of Eutyches was already determined in advance. Therefore there was an accusation against Flavian of being guilty of fraud and of grossly incorrect procedure. Bishops who had supported him scuttled for cover and where possible sought to disown their indiscretions during the trial.

Eutyches held to the Christological formula 'one nature after the union'. He believed that only heretics could admit two natures after the union. In dealing with the human body of Christ one was speaking of 'the body of God'. That was a deduction drawn from Cyril's eucharistic doctrine of divine presence in the host. There could be no question of an independent humanity of the body and soul of Christ not transformed into a divine nature. Therefore the double *homoousios* of the Formulary of Reunion of 433 was abhorrent to him.

In December 448 the emperor asked Flavian for a written statement of his faith. His answer (*ACO* II i. 35) affirms the scriptures and the councils of Nicaea and Ephesus (431). These authorities are understood to teach that Christ is perfect God and perfect man with rational soul and body, of one substance with the Father in his divinity and of one substance with his mother in his humanity. Christ is constituted 'from two natures . . . in one hypostasis and one prosopon . . . one nature of the divine Logos incarnate, one out of both.' This last clause echoed Cyril using pseudo-Athanasius. Flavian anathematizes those who say two Sons or two hypostases or two *prosopa*, and especially Nestorius. He was clearly anxious to reduce the gulf between himself and the ultra-Cyrilline position. Some of the terms anticipated the council of Chalcedon.

Another momentous anticipation of the language of Chalcedon at the trial of Eutyches came from Basil of Seleucia, whose irenic formula was a gloss on Cyril of Alexandria to the effect that Christ is 'acknowledged (*gnorizomenos*) in two natures' (*ACO* II i. 117. 22), perfect God and perfect man.

It is hard to read the proceedings, preserved in the first session of the Acts of Chalcedon, without drawing the tempting conclusion that Flavian fell into an ingenious trap designed and laid by Eutyches' godson the mighty eunuch Chrysaphius. Eutyches had made himself objectionable to the patriarch; Flavian replied by using Eusebius of Dorylaeum as a professional accuser; by condemning Eutyches Flavian acted as Chrysaphius must have hoped, and thereafter his doom was fairly simple to arrange. By the time he arrived at Ephesus on 1 August 449, he cannot have failed to realize that his situation was desperate.

53

THE CHRISTOLOGICAL DEBATE, III:
FROM THE SECOND COUNCIL OF
EPHESUS (449) TO CHALCEDON (451)

Dioscorus of Alexandria was deeply convinced that in his Twelve Anathemas his predecessor Cyril, despite later shilly-shallying, had seen the truth about the person of Christ and expressed it in ways that no good Christian could criticize. Cyril's concessions to Antioch were a mistake which now needed rectification. Through the Constantinopolitan archimandrite Eutyches, this view found a sympathetic ear in the hugely powerful eunuch chamberlain Chrysaphios, and therefore with Theodosius II.

Theodoret confined to Cyrrhos

The direction of imperial policy was revealed in 448 when an order confined Theodoret to his diocese. As he had expended much money on fine public buildings and bridges in his city, making it attractive to pilgrims visiting the local shrine of the saints Cosmas and Damian, he was naturally upset. The order made ruffians at Cyrrhos unwilling to obey their bishop (*ep.* 79). Theodoret was prominent for his forthright criticism of Cyril's Twelve Anathemas as well as for his friendship with Nestorius, and the drama of Eutyches' confrontation with Flavian moved him to compose a general critique of Alexandrian Christology in the form of three dialogues entitled *Eranistes*. This title meant a person piecing together a garment from discarded rags, i.e. abandoned heresies. Each dialogue was fortified by a florilegium of weighty citations from orthodox authors.[1]

An element in Theodoret's argument, noteworthy because found congenial by Pope Gelasius (492–6) in his treatise 'On the two natures' (14, p. 541 Thiel), reasoned from the analogy of the eucharistic presence. The heretic Eranistes argues that just as the epiklesis by the priest changes the antitypes or symbols of the Lord's body and blood, so the Lord's body was transformed

---

[1] Critical edition by G. H. Ettlinger (Oxford, 1975).

into divine substance. The orthodox replies that even after consecration the symbols are not deprived of their nature, but 'are venerated as being what in faith they are now believed to be'. Theodoret further argues that if the Lord's humanity is not of one substance with that of the Virgin Mary (as Eutyches had claimed), then the redeemer's mother is superfluous.

Theodoret also wrote, probably about 448, a history of the Church, particularly valuable for Antiochene records, from the Arian controversy to the death in 427 of Theodore of Mopsuestia (ed. G. C. Hansen, Berlin, 1998). It is not accidental that his story stops before the Nestorian controversy broke out. The story has an underlying theme, that emperors who support heresy have met with failure and misfortune. Athanasius of Alexandria ranks as a hero. Theodoret was evidently aware of the emperor's fear of the consequences of allowing heresy. The Vandals had conquered north Africa, and the Huns were ravaging the Balkans. So the government had enough problems on its hands to arouse apprehension of celestial displeasure. Theodoret repeatedly affirmed that the security of the empire depended on right belief in the one Church.

Confinement to Cyrrhos did not stop Theodoret writing letters. In December 448 he wrote to Flavian of Constantinople congratulating him on his censure of Eutyches (*ep.* 11). He was also the Syrian bishop most congenial to Patriarch Domnos of Antioch, who provided a special lodging for him on his visits. He was in sophisticated correspondence with high officers of state in letters adorned with allusions to Homer and Greek literature. His 230 letters are a major source of information. At the same time his *Religious History* manifests deep sympathy for the ascetics, especially Symeon on his column near Beroea. His own schooling had been at an Antioch monastery. Probably because of his being temporarily under a cloud, scribes circulated two of his works under the names of Justin Martyr and Cyril of Alexandria. Though he had no very philosophical mind, he composed a treatise on 'Healing sicknesses of paganism' and also a book on Providence. Following Theodore of Mopsuestia, he wrote commentaries on biblical books, mainly from the Old Testament. The weight attaching to his name made him a bogy to Dioscorus.[2]

Second Council of Ephesus 449

At the end of March 449 Theodosius issued a summons to an ecumenical council at Ephesus on 1 August. The only matter on the agenda was the Christological disagreement between Flavian and Eutyches. Theodoret was

[2] Editions of the *Religious History, Letters, Healing Sicknesses of Paganism, Commentary on Isaiah,* in SC; otherwise PG 80–4.

debarred from attending. But a Syrian archimandrite Barsumas of strongly Alexandrian sympathy was specifically invited on the emperor's authority, this being to silence critics who regarded bishops as the only proper members of synods. The secretary of the imperial consistory wrote to Dioscorus investing him with full authority over the synod in nominal consultation with Juvenal of Jerusalem and Thalassius. Thalassius was a former praetorian prefect who had been ordained by Proclus to be bishop of Caesarea in Cappadocia, a city where he had grown up and of which he had been a bene-factor when a lay official (Firmus, *ep.* 17). Before the synod met, Dioscorus restored Eutyches to communion.

Pope Leo I's Tome to Flavian

Theodosius sent an invitation to Pope Leo who had already received from Flavian full details of his encounter with Eutyches and also Eutyches' appeal. The emperor's message was received in less than five weeks, which was rapid transit. It stressed desire for Leo's Petrine authority in support of the emperor's policy. Leo interpreted this as a request to endorse the decision to call the council. Initially impressed by Eutyches' appeal, Leo changed his mind on reading Flavian's record of the proceedings. In Leo's ears, 'two natures before the union, one after it' was nonsense. But the Christ in two natures is a single *persona.* An axiom in discussions of the union of body and soul held that each constituent performed its individual functions. So Leo could say that in the one Christ 'each nature performs what is proper to it with the co-operation of the other, the divine Word performing divine acts, flesh the bodily actions.' This sentences would cause a furore among eastern bishops wanting a 'one nature' formula.

From his secretary Prosper of Aquitaine, who drew on Augustine (whose texts he knew intimately) and Gaudentius of Brescia, the Pope commis-sioned a simple western statement affirming Christ to be both God and man, and therefore able to be mediator. This was the teaching of the Apostles' Creed, i.e. the old Roman baptismal creed which western Christians for many centuries assumed to be universally known. (In 1439 they had a shock at the Council of Florence.) On 13 June 449 he sent this to Flavian as a Tome (*ep.* 28) to be put before the coming synod for its docile assent to Petrine authority. Indeed Leo (*ep.* 36) regarded this council as superfluous; all it had to do was to assent to St Peter's successor and his Tome.

The authority of St Peter's see

For Leo the claims for his see were important. His city had lost political power, and in his time was subjected to appalling raids on its treasures by

Vandals and threats from Attila's Huns. He could console his sad people by telling them that the greatest apostles, Peter and Paul, remained guardians of the city possessing their bones, replacing Romulus and Remus 'Thanks to Peter's see, you have become head of the world; you reign over a vaster empire by virtue of divine religion than by terrestrial supremacy' (*sermo* 82). This church taught by Peter and Paul is grounded upon the rock, is so protected from error as to be renowned for orthodoxy, is predestined by God for leadership in the universal Church, and has a presiding bishop with jurisdiction not only over his own community but over every church (*plenitudo potestatis*). The Tome sent to Flavian of New Rome manifested this teaching authority even over the churches of the east, and Leo could strengthen its authority in Greek eyes by demanding its reception by Gallic bishops who also needed to be taught to bow to his teaching authority. (Leo had had some trouble with independence in Hilary of Arles.) In a letter, after the council of Chalcedon had acknowledged its teaching to be in line with the apostles, Leo could claim that the Tome was the greatest event since the incarnation (*ep.* 120. 2, PL 54. 1049A to Theodoret). He was the unworthy but juridical inheritor of all Peter's powers. Recognized in the west, this was now to be allowed in the east as well.

Leo's Tome not read at Ephesus

For the council announced by the emperor as 'ecumenical', Leo sent four legates, one of whom, Renatus priest of St Clement, died on the journey at Delos (Avell. 99. 6). The others were Julian bishop of Puteoli (Pozzuoli), Hilarus a Roman deacon, and Dulcitius a notary. They were hospitably received by Flavian at Ephesus. None of them understood Greek, but when needed one of the Lydian bishops acted as interpreter. On a sudden summons by Dioscorus of Alexandria, the synod began work at Ephesus at dawn on 8 August. The Roman legates were seated in an exalted position beside Dioscorus who was virtually the emperor's plenipotentiary. When they asked for Leo's Tome to be read, Dioscorus courteously agreed but of course letters from the emperor must take precedence. Despite further later attempts to have the Tome read, the proceedings were so managed that this did not occur. Had it been read in Greek translation, Leo's aversion to Eutyches' language could not have been concealed. This fact was obviously known to Flavian and his friends, who were not few but were intimidated into silence or actually debarred from speaking on the ground that their verdict about Eutyches was under judgement. Flavian and Eusebius of Dorylaeum were there as defendants. When a copy of the Tome eventually reached Nestorius, he was delighted by this vindication of his position (*Heraclides* 298, 302–3 Nau).

Flavian deposed

The proceedings before Flavian against Eutyches at the capital were patiently read, and then the scrutiny of the minutes. There was enough to put Flavian on the back foot in self-defence, especially the admission that he had a verdict prepared before hearing the case. The minutes of 448 included Flavian's confession of faith, very close to a statement already submitted to Theodosius at the emperor's request. In the main these texts reproduced the Formulary of Reunion from Cyril's letter to John of Antioch, but for the emperor Flavian had added 'one nature of the divine Word incarnate' (*ACO* II i. 35). He had obviously become aware of Theodosius' sympathy for Eutyches. Nestorius reports that Flavian offered his resignation (*Heraclides* 300 Nau). The patriarch was no enemy of Cyril's Monophysite terminology and did not suspect this famous formula of originating with Apollinarius. But critics of Eutyches were not allowed to speak at Ephesus. No defence of their position was allowed. Abruptly Flavian's demand that Eutyches accept the double *homoousios* of the Formulary of Reunion was taken by Dioscorus to justify the charge that Flavian and Eusebius of Dorylaeum had added to the sacrosanct creed of Nicaea in defiance of the ruling at the first council of Ephesus in July 431. That was ground for a summary sentence of deposition. Flavian cried 'I appeal.' The Roman deacon Hilarus protested in Latin: 'Contradicitur.'

Violence in St Mary's church: Flavian's appeal to Rome

The submission of many bishops was ensured by Dioscorus' strong-arm methods. A hundred and forty signatures to the condemnation survive in the sixth-century Latin version of the Acts of Chalcedon (*ACO* II iii. 252–8), a few of the bishops being illiterate. Dioscorus explained that any dissenters faced deposition and prison, and then, to enforce his point, allowed into the assembly the military officers with soldiers, their swords drawn, and a large mob of monks, physically coercing reluctant bishops to sign—in many cases to sign blank papers. Refusing to sign would insult the emperor. The only notaries allowed to keep a record were those of Dioscorus, ensuring that there could be no dispute about the record (a method employed in the papal consistory in the sixteenth century: *Concil. Trident.* VI, 1, p. 686).

Eutyches was declared orthodox. That verdict, when Cyril's Twelve Anathemas and his eucharistic doctrine were adopted as criterion (e.g. *in Ev. Joh.* 10. 1; 11. 11, PG 74. 341. 560) was justifiable—much more so than later estimates of Eutyches were to allow. Unjustifiable was Flavian's treatment. His attempt to find asylum at the altar was blocked by soldiers. Under guard he found a corner of the church to compose an impassioned appeal asking Leo to call for a synod of both east and west to re-examine the matter (*ACO* II ii. 77–9). The paper was entrusted to the Roman legates in hope that they could get it away from Ephesus (which would be difficult) and carry it home to Italy. Eusebius of Dorylaeum also submitted an appeal, transmitted by a presbyter and a deacon (ibid. 79–81).

Flavian was condemned to exile, possibly by a prepared imperial decision but more probably after proper reference to Constantinople. Nestorius (*Heraclides*, 316 Nau) records that in name the edict sent him back to his original home, whereas the intended destination was the grave, since that would facilitate the appointment of a successor. Writing to the emperor's sister Pulcheria on 1 October, Leo had had no news of his death.

Whatever the date of his removal from prison at Ephesus, he was taken away by rough soldiers. The accounts of the manner and time of his end vary. He was old but, like John Chrysostom, was hurried along. Exiled persons were commonly beaten to keep them moving (e.g. *ACO* II i. 482. 17). Nestorius (*Heraclides* 316 Nau) understood that four days of the journey finished him. This coheres with a story which reached Pope Gelasius in the 490s (Avell. 99. 9, CSEL 35. 443) that on reaching the town of Hypaipa, about 60 km to the north-east on the road to Sardis, he died of exhaustion. To his friends it was martyrdom.

Vacancy at Constantinople

Flavian's death would have seemed a help to Dioscorus' cause; in the long term it was a disaster. Immediately it ensured that devoted supporters at Constantinople could not refuse a successor on the ground that their bishop was still alive. But for the longer view Dioscorus made an immense misjudgement. He was able to get the emperor and Chrysaphius to agree to the succession of his apocrisiary or nuncio in the capital, named Anatolius. Probably Dioscorus himself was among the consecrators (Theodore the Reader in the sixth century, ed. Hansen, p. 99, may imply this.) But since the emperor was sure in due course to wish that Anatolius would receive recognition by Rome, participation by Dioscorus in his sacring would not have been given publicity, least of all in letters to Leo. Perhaps because of the delicacy of any negotiation with Pope Leo, the consecration may well have been delayed until April 450. However, Dioscorus' intention was clear at the time. He wanted a puppet patriarch to ensure Alexandrian domination over New Rome. The outcome was the opposite of that intended. Moreover, Dioscorus' resort to physical violence brought discredit on him and on Eutyches' case.

A second session at Ephesus, 449

On 22 August the synod was reassembled, no one having been allowed to leave the city. The record of the second session survives in Syriac in the British Library Ms. Add. 14530.[3]

The Roman legates declined to attend on the ground that in the emperor's letter to Leo the question about Eutyches was the sole item on the agenda, and that had been decided albeit without the legates' assent. Hilarus the deacon was threatened with 'terrors' by Dioscorus if he refused to yield (so in his letter to Pulcheria in Leo, *ep.* 46). He found his way to the shrine of St John the Evangelist on the hill 2 km distant from the church of the synod, where the visitor now sees the ruins of Justinian's great basilica. There he prayed for escape. St John interceded for him, and he found a way across trackless country (*per incognita et invia loca*) no doubt to another, less guarded port such as Miletus. Of the three surviving legates he alone returned to Rome (Leo, *ep.* 45. 1). He lived to succeed Leo in 461. In the Lateran baptistery stands to this day the moving inscription in which he recorded his gratitude to St John: 'Liberatori suo beato Iohanni Evangelistae Hilarus Episcopus Famulus Christi' (*ILCV* 980).

Ibas of Edessa

On 27 June 449 the emperor had sent a further missive instructing the synod to cope with the matter of Ibas of Edessa who should be replaced. Ibas had Nestorian sympathies. The bishops of Tyre and Berytos, entrusted with a prior investigation which had reached no satisfactory verdict, were to report. Domnos of Antioch, whose predecessor John had ordained Ibas bishop, excused himself on ground of illness, but assented to any anti-Nestorian measures the synod might decide. Critics of Ibas from Edessa, who included the ascetic 'Sons of the Covenant', submitted a complaint that Ibas was bringing discredit on the metropolis of Osrhoene, proud to have the bones of St Thomas, for which a silver reliquary had been presented in 442 by the military commander on the eastern frontier (*Chronicon Edessenum* s.a. 753). Although at Berytos Ibas had disowned heretical homilies being attributed to him, he was now being accused again of selling sacred vessels to collect money to ransom captives (from Arabs or Persians or both) but then using some of the cash for his relatives. Ibas was neither the first nor the last ecclesiastic expected to provide for impecunious dependants. Because of the shortfall in

---

[3] English transl. by S. G. F. Perry (Oxford, 1867, fuller, Dartford, 1881); German by J. G. E. Hoffmann (1873) reissued with Syriac text by J. Flemming in Abhandlungen of the Göttingen Academy, 1917; French version by J. P. P. Martin (Amiens, 1874) with corrections to Hoffmann.

ransom money, captive monks had been forced to venerate idols worshiped by barbarian Arabs, while nuns were made to work as prostitutes. Ibas, the critics demanded, should be exiled with his archdeacon, his inspector of hospices, and numerous subdeacons. Domnos had weakly procrastinated over a decision, and the complainants had had to take their case to Flavian and his resident synod, evidently without result. So Ibas' letter to Mari the Persian lay before the synod at Ephesus, with a claim that he had diffused unorthodox texts (i.e. of Theodore of Mopsuestia) among the Persian churches. This produced shouts that Ibas and Nestorius should be together burnt alive at Antioch. (This did not occur. But it is an alarmingly early suggestion of a possibility, not in law, but from a lynch-mob.)

Other casualties: cheese magic

The synod condemned not only Ibas but also his nephew Daniel, who shortened proceedings by resigning his little bishopric at Carrhae not far from Edessa. He lived with a woman, which in ascetic Syria was offensive to his people. Nestorius' friend Irenaeus, ordained by Domnos to be bishop of Tyre about 445 despite having been twice married, had been exiled early in 448. The synod at Ephesus declared him deprived of priesthood without more ado or any debate. It was an open and shut case. A friend of Irenaeus, the bishop of Byblos was another to bite the dust.

Sophronius, bishop of Tella and cousin of Ibas, was deposed on charges both of Nestorian sympathies and of addiction to magic, astrology and pagan methods of divination. He had been requiring people suspected of stealing that they should take oaths not only by the Gospel but also by eating bread and cheese and other more dramatic techniques involving the appearing of a spirit: A censer was placed under a table on which was placed a phial containing oil and water with a naked small boy beside it. Then a spell was recited at the bishop's prompting. It was supposed that a thief would be unable to eat the food after spells were pronounced. For the magical properties of this food there are several ancient allusions, and among sorcerers bread and cheese were a known way of uncovering a thief.[4] The magician bishop's astrological handbooks had been copied for him by a subdeacon and two deaconesses and, alarmingly, studied by the local town physician. Ancient and medieval medical prescriptions were much determined by astrology.

---

[4] For priests given to sorcery see John Moschos, *Pratum Spirituale* 145, or a reference in the letter of the oriental synod of Serdica in 342. For cheese magic there is a well-known reference in Augustine, *City of God* 18. 18. Much ancient magic was for unmasking thieves.

Theodoret and Domnos of Antioch

Theodoret of Cyrrhus was next to fall for the same reason as Flavian, that the Formulary of 433 'added to the Nicene creed'; he had also written a defence of Diodore and Flavian from which damaging excerpts were cited. Like Flavian he despatched an appeal to Leo: fulsome in praise of Rome, mistress of a great empire which has given the name 'Roman' to all its subjects, but especially famed for having the tombs of Peter and Paul, though they came from the east. Probably through Domnos a copy of Leo's Tome had reached Theodoret, 35 days' travel from Ephesus in his confinement at Cyrrhus; for Leo he felt full of admiration. Dioscorus had declared him deposed, the decision being taken in his absence with no examination of his doctrine. There was no complaint about his lifestyle. From the offerings of the faithful he had acquired no personal property and built no tomb for himself (evidently what less ascetic bishops did). When his parents died, he had distributed everything to the poor. His diocese had 800 churches, and he had reclaimed for the Church numerous heretics—a thousand Marcionites, and many Arians and Eunomians. Leo was impressed and in due course would declare Theodoret orthodox and reinstated.

After Theodoret, 'condemned without trial as no bandit would be', the synod declared deposed patriarch Domnos of Antioch, who at the first session is reported by Nestorius (*Heraclides* 303–4 Nau) to have protested against Dioscorus but, according to the Greek minutes of the Alexandrian notaries, did not utter a squeak in Flavian's support. Charges against Domnos were his friendship with Theodoret, his ordination of Irenaeus of Tyre, and his claim that the Petrine see of Antioch was superior to that of Peter's disciple Mark at Alexandria. If someone were to cite the canon of Constantinople (381) to assert that the bishop of Alexandria had no jurisdiction outside Egypt, Dioscorus recognized no authority in decisions of that council. Moreover, at Antioch some were claiming that Nestorius was deposed for contumacy, not for heresy. The Church must be guided by 'the two councils', i.e. Nicaea and Ephesus 431, with Cyril's Twelve Anathemas accepted as correct interpretation. Domnos had to admit that, were he publicly to assent to the Anathemas, he would face a massive riot. That sealed his doom. He was deposed. In the sixth century Cyril of Scythopolis says that Domnos retired to the monastery of St Euthymios in Palestine (*Vita Euthymii* 20). Anatolius consecrated Maximus at Constantinople to replace him. Leo, (*epp.* 104 and 106 of May 452; *ACO* II iv. 57. 7) judged it unprecedented for the bishop of Antioch to be made at Constantinople but acquiesced for the sake of peace. Maximus' retention of his see may have been dependent on his surrender of three Palestinian provinces to Jerusalem; if so, the secret negotiation is not openly recorded. This Maximus is in all probability the

Antiochene presbyter whose zeal for Cyril of the Anathemas had distressed patriarch John in the 430s (above pp. 503, 549).

Theodosius ratified the depositions enacted at Ephesus in an edict issued by Chrysaphius, ending with an order that Theodoret's writings should be burnt (*ACO* II iii. 347–8). This edict was repealed by Marcian on 6 July 452.

Politically Dioscorus had grossly overreached himself. Under the new régime after Theodosius' death in July 450, Anatolius was potent for the supremacy of Constantinople in the east. Meanwhile in the west Alexandria faced an insulted and enraged bishop of Rome. Leo was given an eyewitness account of the first session at Ephesus by the deacon Hilarus. Of the other two legates nothing further is heard, which raises the possibility that under violent beatings they succumbed to Dioscorus and judged that Rome might be too hot to hold them if they returned. Leo described the proceedings at Ephesus as a 'bandits' den' ('latrocinium', *ep.* 95. 2). Eusebius of Dorylaeum also made his way to Rome, having been replaced in his Phrygian see (Leo, *ep.* 79. 3).

Leo's protest

In October 449 Leo began a campaign of letters to the emperor, demanding that everything be open for reconsideration at a new synod held in Italy with eastern bishops invited. Apart from the Roman legates western representation at Ephesus had been negligible; it was an instinctive assumption in east Roman emperors that the Roman see could speak for the entire Latin west. Leo understood himself to be St Peter's mouthpiece, a chosen instrument for correcting Greek errors. On 13 October Leo wrote to Theodosius to convey the judgement of a synod, probably held on his anniversary (29 September), solemnly warning the emperor not to find himself burdened with responsibility for Dioscorus' sins and alerting him to Flavian's appeal to Rome. The canonical authority of the Roman bishop to judge this was in the canons of Nicaea—actually western Serdica. Leo also wrote to the emperor's sister Pulcheria affirming that Flavian remained in full communion with Rome. On 13 October Leo assumed that though in custody he was alive, which could be correct. Leo was also able to find Galla Placidia venerating St Peter, and persuaded her and other grandees to add their remonstrance.

Theodosius unmoved

It was not easy for Theodosius to put policies for the Church into reverse. In a battery of letters to the west he declared himself content with the decisions at Ephesus; he had ordered the expulsion of those condemned, notably Flavian 'the chief cause of contention', and peace reigned (Leo, *epp.* 62–3). Nothing could be further from the imperial mind than a breach with the pope whom he addressed as 'patriarch', equipollent with the bishops of Constantinople, Alexandria, and Antioch. An undated letter to Licinia Eudoxia, wife of the western emperor Valentinian III (*ep.* 64), contains the first news that Flavian had now died and was beyond reinstatement.

An earthquake: Trisagion

On 26 January 450 a major earthquake damaged Constantinople, especially weakening the towers in the defensive walls (Nestorius, *Heraclides* 318; *Chronicon Paschale*) which may have encouraged second thoughts. Moreover, Huns in the Balkans were threatening. Nestorius says that the earthquake inspired the Trisagion (evidently for wider use at Constantinople) 'Holy God, holy mighty, holy immortal, have mercy on us.' The prayer appears in the Acts of Chalcedon (*ACO* II i. 195). At Ephesus in 431 there is a reference to some trying to alter it (*ACO* I i/7. 72. 37).

Anatolius' orthodoxy

The reaction from Rome to the proceedings of 449 cannot have been welcome to the emperor. Schism on this scale was harmful to the empire. Both Theodosius and Pulcheria would have wanted Anatolius to receive recognition in Rome, and the emperor could not afford to alienate a western figure of large influence at a time when Constantinople itself was under threat of Hun attack. Anatolius and his consecrators both wrote to Rome to notify Leo of his elevation, which may have been as late as April–June 450, but nothing was said of his beliefs. How soon after his consecration Anatolius opened negotiation with Rome is obscure. With reason Leo suspected that Anatolius had been consecrated 'by the wrong people'. He sent legates to demand that the new bishop manifest his orthodoxy by assent to Cyril's second letter to Nestorius and also to his own Tome. If Anatolius was glad to give assent to the Tome, that could be either because Theodosius II told him to do so or because the emperor was dead and his sister was in charge.

Theodosius' death

On 28 July 450 Theodosius II, thrown by his horse, died of injuries. Barbarian invasions had not made his reign simple; but he continued his grandfather's policy of using Arian Germanic soldiers for the army. Orthodoxy was intensely important to him, and heretics and Jews were subjected to some restrictive edicts. Montanists and Eunomians were forbidden right of assembly, provoking fierce resistance (CTh 16. 5. 57–8). Synesius *ep.* 128 is to an Egyptian bishop who had to leave his see because of Arian opposition. The Jewish patriarchate was abolished, and Jews were forbidden to own slaves who were Christians at the time of purchase. Though new synagogues were forbidden, existing buildings were to be protected against vandals (16. 8. 21). Theodosius shared the general Christian aversion to capital punishment and to bloody shows in the amphitheatre. His clemency was thought remarkable by Socrates (7. 22). Chrysaphius relieved him of much administration, so that he often signed papers unread (so Theodore the Reader, p. 99–100 Hansen). Rationalist historians (Seeck, Bury) have scorned him; but at the time, except for his domination by Chrysaphius, people thought reasonably well of him, even if he could not be 'the Great' as his grandfather was already commonly entitled.

Pulcheria and Marcian

Control of the eastern empire now fell to his determined sister Pulcheria aged 54, hitherto living a life of ascetic devotion. She was fluent in Latin as well as Greek. Before her brother's death was widely known, one of her first acts of government was to order the execution of Chrysaphius, who had kept her out of all power. Another major decision was that the empire needed a soldier-emperor. She remained a nun but took as her consort a Thracian with military experience named Marcian who, it was said, had been suggested by the dying Theodosius. He had held large responsibilities under the general Aspar, an Alan and Arian. On 25 August 450 Marcian was proclaimed and invested by Pulcheria herself, signifying that the Theodosian dynasty was not defunct. The patriarch Anatolius was present with the senate at this ceremony, and is said by some later sources to have crowned him. The western emperor Valentinian III was offended that he had not been consulted as was customary, but eventually in March 452 granted recognition. Initially Marcian's elevation would have suggested to Italy that the eastern half of the empire was too independent. Gold coins were issued with Marcian and Pulcheria together, and a reassuring claim to be bringing victory over the barbarian menace. Attila had given notice of an intention to capture Constantinople and had extracted a huge annual tribute of gold from Theodosius, glad to buy him off. Marcian discontinued this payment and preferred to fight Attila. Among his first acts was an attempt to abolish the system whereby all public offices were for sale (Theodore the Reader, p. 100 Hansen). He was a Christian.

Pulcheria's wind of change

While Marcian's task was primarily to cope with the Huns, who had already sacked Naissus, Philippopolis, and Constantia, Pulcheria implemented a radical change of policy in the Church. Politically it was vital to re-establish good relations with Rome and Ravenna, so Theodosius' pro-Monophysite moves had to be quickly jettisoned. Exiles were recalled. Flavian's body was returned to the capital to be buried in the Church of the Apostles with his predecessors; Anatolius inscribed his name in the diptychs. Eutyches was placed in custody, not in his monastery from which a master of intrigue could operate. In due course he would be exiled to Doliche in Euphratesia, where he would be surrounded by Christians more sympathetic to Nestorius than to him. Bishops who at Ephesus had yielded to give their signatures now fell over one another in protest that they had been coerced by Dioscorus. Maximus of Antioch required all Syrian bishops to sign Leo's Tome. A number of ill content persons in Egypt who had suffered under Dioscorus contributed valuable stories against him, one being that when the imperial insignia of Marcian had arrived at Alexandria, the tyrannical bishop so resented anyone other than himself controlling Egypt that he ignored the ceremony of homage in which the bishop was expected to participate (*ACO* II i. 220. 8 ff.).

Council at Constantinople, October 450

A Syriac manuscript in the Borgia collection at the Vatican shows that on 21 October 450 patriarch Anatolius presided over a synod in the baptistery of the Great Church at Constantinople. Pope Leo sent two legates to attend: Abundius of Como and Aetherius of Capua with two presbyters from Naples and Milan. Greek bishops present were selected from those who had not assented at Ephesus in 449. A deacon of Constantinople interpreted Latin interlocutions. The legates brought a copy of Leo's Tome, now fortified with a florilegium of proof-texts shrewdly including a few from Cyril's *Scholia* on the Incarnation (composed by Cyril when he needed to mitigate his Twelve Anathemas and had sent them to Rome), and a declaration that all bishops who had not signed Flavian's deposition and who now signed the Tome were thereby in communion with St Peter's see. It was also decided that bishops who had agreed to the deposition of Flavian and the orthodoxy of Eutyches might continue undisturbed pending a decision at a forthcoming council which would adjudicate on terms for readmission of the lapsed.[5]

---

[5] Acts edited from Borgia syr. 82 by P. Mouterde, *Mélanges de l'université S. Joseph Beyrouth*, 15. 2 (1930). See also Pulcheria to Leo (*ACO* II i. 8) dated 22 November, and Leo to Anatolius, *ep.* 90.

At court a decision was made to hold a council to clear up the mess, and this should not be in Italy, as Leo asked, but at Nicaea. The Greek churches could not comprehend Leo's contention that, since his legates were empowered to absolve penitent supporters of Dioscorus and to punish the impenitent, no council was now necessary. Moreover, since Leo thought his Tome settled all the theological questions, he saw no place for debate which could imply that the definition of orthodoxy was still in dispute. In April 451 Leo directed Anatolius not to commemorate Dioscorus, Juvenal of Jerusalem, and Eustathius of Berytos in intercessions (*ep.* 80. 3). The deacon Hilarus had evidently reported that Juvenal and Eustathius had been prominent supporters of Alexandria at Ephesus. Dioscorus cannot have remained ignorant that Leo regarded him as excommunicate in advance of the coming council.

Pope Leo excommunicated by Dioscorus

An angry and decisive reaction came with Dioscorus' decision to declare Leo excommunicate, presumably because of the latent Nestorianism detectable in the Tome and for his rejection of the 'ecumenical council' at Ephesus in 449. This was done as the bishops assembled at Nicaea before being transferred to Chalcedon, and may have been a factor contributing to the court's decision to take total control, which the move to Chalcedon meant. A letter from Pulcheria to the *consularis* of Bithynia (*ACO* II i. 29) tells of serious rioting at Nicaea preventing an imperial visit to the council: the governor is to expel monks, laity, and clergy with no business to be there or he will face the consequences.

Dioscorus was not going to go down without a manifesto of blazing anger. He had utter contempt for colleagues scuttling for shelter or for the treachery, as it would have seemed to him, of his own creatures Anatolius and Maximus of Antioch, who had been content to sign Leo's Tome as the palace wished. He would not have begun to understand Leo's view that to be out of communion with Peter's successor was to put oneself and one's people outside the Church. Nor would he have understood the judgement of the court that the empire's unity, facing the huge threat of Attila, and indeed the visible catholicity of the Church, demanded a different stance from that of 449. If Leo excommunicated him, he would retort in kind.

The Council of Chalcedon begins

In practice Nicaea became an impracticable location because Marcian wished to attend the principal session himself; he therefore wrote from campaigning in Thrace directing the bishops to move to Chalcedon immediately across the water from the palace. There the synod could meet in the lovely church of St Euphemia the martyr in a beautiful setting lyrically described by the historian Evagrius (2. 3). The shrine was associated with marvels and a famous odour of sanctity. The martyr herself had authorized the patriarch to come to her silver shrine and recover miraculous blood. There was space for an assembly of over 500 bishops. Apart from two African refugees from Vandal harassment, the only western representatives were the Roman legates. These were Paschasinus bishop of Lilybaeum (Marsala) in Sicily, bishop Lucentius of Ascoli in Picenum, and a Roman presbyter Boniface. In addition responsibility was entrusted by Leo to Julian bishop of Kos, born and brought up in Rome, fully bilingual, and able to help with interpretation.[6]

Lay presidents

No bishop was to preside at most of the sessions. That task was entrusted by Marcian and Pulcheria to a high-powered lay body, an array of nineteen leading officials or former officials of the empire. All were to be in charge of the first session, later sessions having only a handful of them. The second council of Ephesus in 449 had shown that when bishops were in unfettered control, faction created trouble.

The holy gospels were enthroned in the centre. The supporters of Dioscorus sat on one side, the supporters of Leo on the other. The Roman legates held first place among the bishops, and in contrast to the procedure at Ephesus called attention to their decision to put Anatolius of Constantinople second. 'That is because you know the canons', observed bishop Diogenes of Cyzicus, who throughout the proceedings played the part of an upholder of the canon of Constantinople in 381 about the privileges of the see after Old Rome. The alternative, however, would have been Dioscorus, the 'usurper of Flavian's primacy' (*ACO* II i. 78. 3; iii. 304. 29). From the start the jurisdiction of his see was in Anatolius' mind as a goal to be reached at the council. Leo had forewarned his legates on this matter; but they could not begin their task by angering the Greek bishops. Leo needed Anatolius at least as much as Anatolius needed him. Proceedings began on 8 October 451 with the legate Lucentius demanding that Dioscorus be not allowed to sit as bishop, and declaring that he himself would withdraw if Dioscorus were admitted. 'He called a council without leave of the Apostolic See, for which there was no precedent and ought never to occur.' Dioscorus reasonably retorted that

[6] In the list of those present Julian appears after metropolitans of Nicomedia, Nicaea, and Chalcedon; in two Mss his see is put in Bithynia, which would require Kos to be emended to Kios, a trading port on the sea of Marmara (Propontis). This emendation was supported by W. M. Ramsay, *Historical Geography of Asia Minor* (London, 1890), 428, and by A. Wille, *Bischof Julian von Kios* (Diss., Würzburg, 1909).

the recent council of Ephesus had been called by the emperor. The imperial officials immediately asked if the legates were judges or accusers; they could not be both, a point the foot-faulted legates were not quick to appreciate. The dialogue resulted in Dioscorus being specially treated in the position of a defendant as if to stand trial, but he was not stopped from speaking in synod. Eusebius of Dorylaeum appeared in his customary role as prosecutor but also at liberty to speak.

It was correct that ancient ecumenical councils were summoned by emperors, not popes; but in the case of Nicaea and the first council of Ephesus there was Roman assent and representation. An ecumenical council lacked general authority without Rome and the other principal sees. At Constantinople in 381 there were no Roman legates, though the bishop of Thessalonica came late, and Pope Damasus was ignored when the canonical decisions were made, all of which offended him.

Dioscorus' supporters

At Chalcedon Dioscorus asked for issues of faith to be first item on the agenda (*ACO* II i. 67. 30). He evidently thought his case strongest on the doctrinal platform. He foresaw that the opposition would concentrate on non-theological factors where he had offered fortune hostages. Even from Egyptian suffragans he did not enjoy unanimous loyalty, four being openly critical of his methods. But he was far from lacking support, especially at first from bishops of Palestine and Illyricum (they later abandoned him); and he resolutely stood his ground, becoming steadily more isolated as the Council proceeded. His supporters were pained by the early entry of Theodoret, who had friends among the lay commissioners and was admitted as an accuser after hostile shouting, but not until a later session allowed to sit as a full member of the synod.

Eutyches and Flavian reconsidered

The lengthy record of Ephesus in 449 was read and also that of Flavian's synod at Constantinople earlier that year ending in censure of Eutyches. The presiding officials asked what the assembly thought of Flavian's claim to be in line with Cyril of Alexandria. Paschasinus of Lilybaeum thought this correct. Juvenal of Jerusalem agreed and having said so crossed the floor of the church taking the Palestinians with him. The Illyrian bishops followed this lead and also moved across. Atticus metropolitan of Nicopolis in Old Epirus, had a not unfounded anxiety about disharmony between Leo and Cyril's Twelve Anathemas; rather than join his suffragans he withdrew with a severe illness (*ACO* II i. 116–17; 278–9). Two days later he was back in his seat. Probably someone had reassured him. The need for reconciliation of Leo with Cyril was an issue foreseen by Theodoret (*ACO* II i. 278. 30).

Near the end of a long day a bishop of Chersonese declared his support for Flavian's 'from (*ek*) two natures'. Dioscorus imprudently intervened at once, saying 'I accept from two; I do not accept two. . . . It is for me a matter of conscience. . . . There are not two natures after the union' (*ACO* II i. 120–1). At Constantinople in 448 Eutyches had rejected the preposition *ek* (II i. 136. 13). The issue of the theology of prepositions was going to loom large. Later supporters of the Chalcedonian Definition were going to accept both prepositions, *ek* and *en*. Dioscorus misjudged the feelings. Already anything acceptable to him was going to be insufficient for opponents, especially the Roman legates. The exchange about the right preposition was to be fateful.

The first session ended with a surprise from the presiding officials, no doubt following an instruction from Pulcheria, namely that the synod ought to depose six leaders of the council of Ephesus in 449, not only Dioscorus but also five others: Juvenal, Thalassius of Caesarea, Eusebius of Ankyra, Basil of Seleucia (Isauria), and Eustathius of Berytos (*ACO* II i. 288). All were held responsible for the miscarriage of justice at Ephesus. Other bishops would think that a long list. To persuade the Roman legates to co-operate, it could be necessary to sacrifice Dioscorus, even though that was certain to bequeath lasting alienation and fury in Egypt. If the story was true that Dioscorus had declined to pay homage on the news of Marcian's accession, the court may well have felt that he must be a special target. But the other five were not in the same degree a party to the offensive actions at Ephesus. They could have yielded to Alexandria under no less intimidation than others. It may be that Marcian and Pulcheria included the other five with the motive of avoiding a politically dangerous isolation of the pope of Alexandria. Guilt could seem less if distributed and not concentrated on one, especially if the other five could present a persuasive defence.

A new confession of faith?

On 10 October the six bishops named were absent. The presiding officials demanded that each bishop should submit a written statement of belief, in the knowledge that the emperor accepted the Nicene creed, the creed of the 150 fathers associated with Constantinople 381, and the traditional interpretation by eminent fathers. One bishop explained that this tradition was embodied in Athanasius, Cyril, Celestine, Hilary, Basil, Gregory (Nazianzen) to which list Leo was to be added. Nothing was said of Cyril's Twelve Anathemas.

The prospect of yet another definition of faith was looming, and was most unwelcome (*ACO* II i. 274). The bishops were aware that pagans laughed at the Church for a continual succession of synods creating new creeds (Evagrius 1. 10). Following Athanasius and Cyril they wanted to adhere to the Nicene creed and no more. That raised a question whether the creed being associated with the 150 fathers of Constantinople was accepted as being consonant with the Nicene formula. Latent was the impassioned antipathy of the Alexandrians to anything said to emanate from Constantinople in 381. On the other hand, since Pulcheria and Marcian wanted a fresh statement of faith, it could overcome the objection to any addition to the Nicene creed if at Chalcedon the council accepted the creed of 381 as a legitimate and necessary supplement. One supplement would jus-tify a second.

The assembled bishops saw amber light. There was noisy opposition to any proposal for a new confession of faith. But the lay presidents were clearly voicing the mind of Marcian and Pulcheria. The metropolitan of Nicomedia read the Nicene creed with its anathema dated 19 June 325, which was acclaimed by the bishops as the faith in which they were baptized and which was affirmed by Cyril and Leo. At the demand of the lay presidents the archdeacon of Constantinople then read the creed of the 150 fathers (of 381), 'concordant with the great synod of Nicaea', and bishops acclaimed this as orthodox. The same archdeacon also read Cyril's second letter to Nestorius and the letter to John of Antioch with the Reunion Formulary. These were similarly acclaimed as the faith of Cyril, Leo, and Anatolius. A Greek version of Leo's Tome was then read by no less a personage than the secretary of the imperial consistory, whose authority would be hard to challenge. An attached florilegium was omitted. Acclamations at this point included 'Peter spoke through Leo', and 'Why was this not read at Ephesus? Dioscorus hid it' (*ACO* II i. 277).

Nevertheless, during the reading of Leo's Tome, specific criticisms from Illyrian and Palestinian bishops were answered by the archdeacon with pre-pared citations from Cyril, implying the assertion of agreement between Cyril and Leo (ibid. 278). The Illyrian bishop Atticus metropolitan of Nicopolis asked for Cyril's Twelve Anathemas to be read, but he was ignored. The lay presidents instructed Anatolius to select a committee and to return in five days with a statement of faith. The session ended with rival shouts, Syrians asking for Dioscorus' exile, the Illyrians and their friends for mercy all round, since 'we have all sinned'.

Action against Dioscorus

On 13 October the official commissioners absented themselves, and left the presidency to the legate Paschasinus. The synod's task was to put Dioscorus in the dock. Three times messengers were sent to call him, but he declined to attend unless the official lay commissioners were present. It also disturbed him that the other five bishops in the commissioners' black list were not being called. The absence of the lay presidents evidently meant that on behalf of the court they disowned responsibility for the impending action against the bishop of Alexandria. By imperial command the proceedings were under canon law. The emperor's representatives were not to be seen to be in charge. The synod had to treat the case as one of contumacy. The Roman legates had accusations ready: Dioscorus had uncanonically admitted Eutyches to communion before the council of Ephesus declared him acquitted in 449; he had not allowed Leo's Tome to be read. Above all, he had excommunicated the archbishop of Rome.

The Roman charges included no point of theological doctrine. No word indicated that the Ephesian council of 449 was null and void. But the impression given by the reading of the proceedings at Ephesus in 449 was inevitably that the man who supported Eutyches and condemned Flavian was in agreement with Eutyches. Dioscorus affirmed that there is 'one nature in Christ after the union'. But Dioscorus did not at all share Eutyches' view that the body of Christ was not of one substance with ours and with his mother's, and after Chalcedon from exile in Gangra Dioscorus could write a letter to one Secundinus eloquently stating his position (Ps.-Zach., *Chronicle* 3. 1, Eng. tr. p. 45). He distanced himself from Eutyches, and this became the normal pattern for those whom the pro-Chalcedonians called Monophysites and who called themselves Orthodox.

Scurrilous evidence was produced from Egyptians who had been offended by Dioscorus, notably Cyril's relatives and dependants. A presbyter whom Dioscorus had removed from office had gone to Constantinople to appeal for help to Chrysaphius and Nomos, former Master of the Offices and consul. He borrowed huge sums to bribe the influential Nomos, who was understood to be willing to get support from the chamberlain, but failed to gain for him an interview with Chrysaphios. In consequence he was living in reduced circumstances with only two slaves. One witness reported popular gossip of Dioscorus' liaison with a courtesan Pansophia, nicknamed Oreine, Mountain Girl, a story to which there is probably a reference in the *Palatine Anthology* 16. 19: 'As he comes in, the bishop says Peace (Eirene) to everyone. How can this be for everyone when he has her to himself in his inner room?'[7] Naturally a bishop could not grant a private audience to a lady of such repute without gossip becoming imaginative and malicious. One story alleged that she shared his bath.

---

[7] See B. Baldwin, *Vig. Christ.*, 35 (1981), 377–8. The Latin version translates her name as Montana (*ACO* II ii. 107. 13). It was pronounced *Orini* (II iii. 290. 20). Hence the epigram's Irini.

The emperor personally authorized the trial of Dioscorus who remained intransigent, 'unable to add to what he had already said'. In the synod individuals added the further charge that he had been responsible for the murder of Patriarch Flavian, condemned merely on his own authority without due canonical procedure. Paschasinus of Lilybaeum finally summed up the adverse case and concluded: 'Leo archbishop of the elder and great Rome acting through us and the present synod with the thrice blessed apostle Peter, the rock and foundation of the catholic Church and the orthodox faith, has stripped him of his episcopate and deprived him of all priestly dignity.' It is noteworthy that the authority for the condemnation is that of the Roman see with which the synod is asked to show a nod of support, a distinction that pleased Leo (*ep.* 103 to bishops in Gaul). Anatolius of 'Constantinople New Rome' declared concurrence. 250 bishops added their signature, concluding with a Persian bishop who signed in Persian. Those signing after the session included Juvenal of Jerusalem, Thalassius of Caesarea, Eustathius of Berytos, Eusebius of Ankyra, and (perhaps) Basil of Seleucia. At the session on 17 October there were cries asking pardon for 'the five'. A formal notice of the deposition was addressed to the clergy of Alexandria, together with a warning that rumours of Dioscorus' early reinstatement were false.

Dioscorus' suffragans. The Council has a jolt

Thirteen Egyptian bishops submitted a petition to the emperor stating their faith to be read to the synod. The thirteen formally acknowledged their signatures to this document in accord with correct procedure in a court of law. The secretary of the imperial consistory read the paper to the synod, in which the claim was that Alexandria had been orthodox from the time of St Mark and the martyred Bishop Peter and from Athanasius, Theophilus, and Cyril. They now confess the Nicene creed and believe with Athanasius and Cyril, anathematizing Arius, Eunomius, Mani, Nestorius and those who say the Lord's body is from heaven and not from Mary (i.e. extreme Apollinarians).

The petition is met with cries: 'Why did they not anathematize Eutyches? They do not mention Leo's Tome. Eutyches is the reason for this synod.' The Egyptians answer through their leader Hierakis that 'as for Leo's Tome, we in all things adhere to the judgement of our archbishop. The sixth canon of Nicaea placed all the Egyptian (civil) Diocese under Alexandria (a claim to which Eusebius of Dorylaeum surprisingly objects).' Faced with barracking the Egyptians cry: 'Anathema to Eutyches and those who believe him', but refuse to put this in writing by signature without the judgement of their archbishop, the implication being that they must wait to know who Dioscorus' successor is to be. Moreover, they are only a small number from Egypt which has many bishops. To submit to the synod would be to lose their lives in riots at home. 'Archbishop Anatolius knows Egyptian custom and will understand. We must wait until a new archbishop of Alexandria is ordained.' The presiding commissioners declared that the request should be humanely granted. Paschasinus made it a condition that the Egyptian bishops did not leave Chalcedon until the matter was resolved.

Monks for and against Eutyches

The next problem before the synod concerned the ultra-Cyrilline monks led by the Syrian Barsumas, whose spirit pervaded some of the monasteries of Constantinople sympathetic to Eutyches. Monks were troubled by the treatment of the Egyptian bishops. A *libellus* was submitted claiming that the emperor responsible for calling the synod at Chalcedon had assured the monks that the Nicene creed was a sufficient norm of orthodoxy and no addition should be made. It followed that the deposition of Dioscorus was not reasonable, and would be a cause of schism since one could not remain in communion with bishops who set the Nicene creed aside. It is accepted that the Ephesian decree deposing Nestorius was only confirming the Nicene faith.

The *libellus* was answered by the archdeacon of Constantinople reading the fifth canon of Antioch (ascribed to the Dedication Council of 341 but actually earlier, 328–30). This canon ruled that monks must obey their bishop and that if they cause disorder then the secular arm is to be invoked.

Enthusiastic acclamations from bishops then met a protest from an archimandrite Carosus (of Constantinople), saying that Theotimus bishop of Tomi who baptized him with the Nicene confession told him never to consider any other creed.[8] Carosus was similarly supported by archimandrite Dorotheus, and by Barsumas speaking in Syriac but with his private interpreter. The archdeacon's answer is that Cyril and Celestine and now Leo have interpreted the creed by letters but not setting forth a creed or a 'dogma'. The question put is whether the monks anathematize both Nestorius and Eutyches. Carosus is content to say Anathema on Nestorius, as he has done many times. On Eutyches, however, he wishes not to judge and can only say that if Eutyches' belief differs from the catholic Church, let him be anathema.

Eighteen presbyter-archimandrites then submit their petition attacking Eutyches as a corrupting influence and a heretic. The monk Dorotheus protests that Eutyches himself should be examined on his affirmation that

---

[8] In 457 Theotimus wrote to the emperor Leo that he accepted the ruling of Ephesus that Nicaea was all-sufficient; he did not recognize the anti-Chalcedonian Timothy Ailourus (the Weasel) whose ordination by two excommunicated bishops was uncanonical. Theotimus said nothing (if the text is correct) of the creed of Constantinople and the Chalcedonian Definition (*ACO* II v. 31).

there are two natures before union, one afterwards. The official commissioners wisely prefer to receive comment on Eutyches' denial that the body of Christ was of one substance with ours. Dorotheus sidesteps the question; he affirms the creed of his baptism: the incarnate and crucified Christ is 'one of the Trinity'. He will not sign acceptance of Leo's letter, whatever the synod may hold its own authority to be. The Nicene creed and the decision of Ephesus (431) are all he will accept. The commissioners' offer of two or three days for reflection is abrasively rejected by Carosus as an invitation to compromise his conscience. So the session ends with the promise of a draft statement.

The Chalcedonian Definition

At the fifth session on 22 October the council moved to consider the new definition of faith which, to the bishops' unconcealed distress, was required by the emperor and Pulcheria. The draft, produced by a committee chaired by Patriarch Anatolius, had been informally considered by numerous bishops on the previous day and then met with approval. However, now it immediately met with criticism from a Cilician Bishop John of Germanikeia, spokesman for the Syrian sympathizers with Nestorius and friend of Theodoret; he thought the term *theotókos* insufficiently precise to be used. There was an unopposed proposal from a deacon of the Great Church at Constantinople that the draft be not entered in the minutes. The draft pleased all except the Roman legates and those from the east in the (civil) Diocese of Oriens under Antioch who were suspected of Nestorianism. The legates were not sure it agreed with Leo's Tome. Since the draft was not recorded in the Acta, its detail can only be conjectural; but it is at least certain that it affirmed Mary to be *theotókos*, declared Christ to be 'from (*ek*) two natures', and approved Leo's Tome (*ACO* II i. 320. 15 and 21). Whether or not it included the creeds of Nicaea or Constantinople is wholly uncertain and perhaps unlikely.

The official commissioners proposed a new committee, six from Oriens, three from Asiana, three from Pontus, three from Illyricum, three from Thrace, meeting with Anatolius and the Roman legates in the oratory of St Euphemia. The commissioners observed that Dioscorus claimed to depose Flavian for saying two natures; 'the draft has from (*ek*) two natures'. Anatolius intervened with the significant words 'Dioscorus was not deposed for heresy, but because he excommunicated the Lord Leo and refused three summons to attend' (*ACO* II i. 320. 17). The commissioners insisted that the content of Leo's Tome be included in the Definition. This immediately renewed cries hostile to any new confession of faith, certainly to one which dropped *theotókos*. Eusebius of Dorylaeum was among the many who felt that if a new text was to be proposed, that considered on the previous day sufficed. (Monophysites thought it miraculous that he of all people could support a text which Dioscorus could sign: Ps.-Zach. 3. 1). That should be signed upon the gospels. 'It was enough that the draft confirmed the letter to Flavian. Leo said the same as Cyril; Celestine and Xystus confirmed what Cyril said.'

It was a more hazardous matter to put into the new definition material drawn from the Tome with its emphasis on two natures after the union. That alteration might make Leo's agreement with Cyril less clear. These cries being reported to the emperor, a peremptory statement came from court that if the revised draft produced by Anatolius' committee in the oratory of St Euphemia was not to be accepted, the synod would be transferred to the west. The politically crucial plan for harmony between east and west would then be destroyed. The Roman legates would be leaving. They had already said that if the text did not agree with Leo's Tome, they would ask for their passports (*rescripta*). The reluctant council was being forced not only to surrender to the court in admitting a new unwanted definition, but also to accept a form of it imposed by Rome's legates which far-sighted Greek bishops discerned to be a source of unending trouble to come.

Bishops from Illyricum (earlier supporters of Dioscorus) cried that opponents of the draft were Nestorians: 'Let them leave for Rome', where the critics sarcastically thought Nestorians would feel at home. The commissioners then disclosed the difficulty: the draft said 'from (*ek*) two natures', words which Dioscorus had unwisely declared acceptable to himself and had also been used by Flavian. But 'Leo's Tome rules that in Christ there are two natures united without confusion, without change, without separation. This authoritative decision must be put in the definition' (*ACO* II i. 321. 18). Remarkably, the words quoted by the commissioners as if from Leo do not occur in the Tome. The adverbs, however, had been expressed more than once by Basil of Seleucia (ibid. 143. 25; cf. 298. 39). The Acts record the names of the oratory committee; they do not include Basil of Seleucia but an Isaurian suffragan. Basil had supported Dioscorus at Ephesus, and his one-time admirers could not forgive his 'apostasy' (John Rufus in PO 8. 54 ff.). The committee had Basil's colleagues, Juvenal of Jerusalem, Thalassius of Caesarea, and Eusebius of Ankyra. In due course the oratory committee produced its momentous text.

The text of the Definition

After a preface on the Lord's desire for peace in his Church, the Nicene creed (N) is correctly cited; the original text is certain from Eusebius of Cacsarca's letter to his church in 325. This is followed by that associated, perhaps rightly, with the council of Constantinople (C) in 381, included as confirmation of Nicaea but also as dealing in its third article with more recent heresies. The presence of C justified the council in providing a new statement of faith adding to N; no doubt it served to impart a nimbus of authority to the see of Constantinople as being where C was drafted. During the first session there had already been a sharp exchange about the authority of the council of Constantinople and the legitimacy of its addition to the Nicene faith; in 381 they included a clause alleged to be repugnant to Apollinarians, 'from the Holy Spirit and the virgin Mary' (*ACO* II i. 91. 21 ff.).

In the manuscript tradition two forms of text occur; in the best line of tradition N and C are given in their pure form, already identified in the third session of the council; but in a Latin summary of the climax of the synod, probably compiled after Leo's time, the two creeds are fused with one another, evidently to exemplify how unanimous they are (*ACO* II ii. 104).

The creeds are followed by a substantial piece about heretics who deny *theotókos*, or who merge and mix divine and human in Christ with their doctrine of 'one nature', involving the divine nature in suffering; about those who combat the deity of the Holy Spirit, condemned by C; about Cyril of Alexandria's 'synodical letters' to Nestorius and to the Antiochenes (i.e. the second letter to Nestorius and that to John of Antioch); about Leo's Tome opposing Eutyches, upholding St Peter's confession of faith; finally about those who teach two Sons. The piece concludes with anathema on Eutyches' proposition that there are two natures before the union and one after it.

The council therefore follows the fathers' tradition teaching (as in the Formulary of Reunion of 433, rejected by Eutyches) that the one Christ is perfect God and perfect man with rational soul and body, of one substance with the Father in his deity, of one substance with us in his humanity, in everything like us except sin. In the last days he was born of Mary *theotókos* 'known (or acknowledged) in two natures without confusion, without change, without separation, without sharp distinction' (the crucial verb and adverbs from Basil of Seleucia, one of whose suffragans was a member of the drafting committee). There follows an acutely chosen quotation of a concessive clause from the second letter of Cyril to Nestorius: 'the difference of natures not being abolished by the union'. The next clauses translate from Leo's Tome: 'salva proprietate utriusque naturae et in unam coeunte personam . . .'. Each nature preserves its individuality running together to constitute one *prosopon* and one hypostasis. Here 'one prosopon and one hypostasis' cites Flavian's confession of faith, a tribute to a patriarch now being honoured as a martyr whose relics were enshrined by Anatolius in the Church of the Apostles where dead patriarchs were buried. Anathema is pronounced on any who teach a different faith.

As is evident, the Definition is a mosaic deliberately drawn from different sources: from the originally Antiochene Reunion formula of 433 composed by Theodoret and John of Antioch and accepted by Cyril; from Basil of Seleucia's happy but ambiguous turn of phrase, 'known in two natures', easily reconcilable with Cyril; from a concessive clause in Cyril; from a central clause in Leo's Tome (which is in effect the most Antiochene moment in the text); and from Flavian, a new martyr and saint bringing fresh glory to Constantinople, though for that reason, as well as for his adherence to the formulary of Reunion, unacceptable to supporters of Dioscorus. Yet 'one hypostasis' was a technical term congenial to minds wanting to affirm one nature rather than two. Taken as a whole, the definition was more at home at Antioch than at Alexandria, though it had bits of Cyril.

It was not a text free of all ambiguity. Few great dogmatic statements in Church history can be so described. The Definition did not succeed in clarifying the thorny problem of affirming the unity of Christ and simultaneously conceding that his miracles were divine acts and his sufferings human. It was and is unclear whether hypostasis carries the sense of 'person' or the sense of 'nature'. Although there is an evident degree of homogeneity to the thinking that has made the Definition, the principal compiler or compilers achieved some of the desired ends by juxtapositions. Is the one hypostasis that of the divine Logos? Different interpreters took the text in divergent ways. Because of its mosaic character, the Definition had something for almost everyone other than Eutyches and ultra-Cyrillians. The generous allowances made for Antiochene concerns could make one wonder if, behind the scenes, Theodoret had been consulted. He was one of the best theological minds available. The council's allocution to Marcian has so many echoes of his *Eranistes* as to give plausibility to the conjecture of Eduard Schwartz (*ACO* II i/3. xiii ff.) that he was the author.

A substantial majority of the bishops at Chalcedon felt a large debt to Cyril of Alexandria, and many among them would have wished the Definition to pick up more of his anti-Antiochene themes. The title *theotókos* was affirmed, but might not seem enough. The chorus of noisy protests greeting Theodoret's appearances is solid evidence of the pro-Cyril attitudes and feeling present in the assembly. The Definition could not easily be shown to include propositions that Cyril would have rejected, but it contained nothing that an admirer and friend of Nestorius such as Theodoret would find objectionable. Above all, it affirmed the full humanity of Christ, which was crucial for the future.

The Definition or Cyril?

There was to be long controversy whether or not the Definition was in line with Cyril of Alexandria and his fondness for the absent formula 'one nature of the divine Logos incarnate'. The Greek bishops assumed not that Cyril was orthodox because in agreement with Leo, but rather that Leo's Tome was accepted for its agreement with the revered Cyril. About thirty years after the council a considerable florilegium was compiled to prove the agreement of Cyril and the Definition; the anti-Chalcedonian Severus, patriarch of Antioch 512–19, wrote an extant refutation of this called 'Lover of truth', *Philalethes* (ed. R. Hespel, Leuven, 1955). Noteworthy in the Definition is the presence of a single citation from Cyril of Alexandria which is a concession to the Antiochene tradition. Otherwise Cyril is represented by the Formulary of Reunion in his letter to John of Antioch and by Flavian's 'one hypostasis'. Of his Anathemas or letters to Succensos and Acacius there is no trace. Basil of Seleucia's 'acknowledged' or 'known in two natures' is equivalent to Cyril's concession that the twoness of the natures is a matter for the detached reflective mind, not for the worshipping soul.

Controversy after the council particularly concentrated on the technical vocabulary, *physis* (nature), *prosopon*, and hypostasis. This terminology was at home in Neoplatonic logic. In the contemporary pagan Proclus of Athens comparable terms appear. In his commentary on Plato's *Parmenides* 129 A, the same negative adverbs occur which enter the Chalcedonian Definition. But the Definition is misjudged if the presence of the term hypostasis or *physis* is taken to mean that the dominant framework is drawn from Platonic logic. That situation came about in the sixth century when rival logicians of high ability went to work on the text. The bishops at Chalcedon were concerned to affirm a doctrine of redemption, for which the Redeemer is fully divine and fully human. Those were the two poles represented by Cyril and Theodoret. In 433 those two theologians briefly if reluctantly recognized the validity of the other, and at Chalcedon that was reaffirmed.

Formal approval by the emperor and Pulcheria

At the sixth session on 15 October, the emperor Marcian himself came to the council supported by a particularly large body of eminent lay officials. Despite the perhaps deliberate silence of the Greek Acts, old Latin tradition shows that Pulcheria was also present (Avellana 99, CSEL 35. 444. 7; *ACO* II ii. 97. 17). The emperor was hailed as 'New Constantine', Pulcheria as 'New Helena', in an avalanche of formal acclamations. Proceedings were first in Latin, then in Greek. Four hundred and fifty-two bishops signed the Definition of faith, some as proxies for others or by their deacons or other helpers. Towards the end of the list metropolitans signed on behalf of numerous absent suffragans.

It would be naïve to suppose that every signature was given in full conviction and a clear conscience. Amphilochius of Side needed to be cuffed on the

head by the archdeacon of Constantinople to be persuaded to sign; his dislike
of the Definition emerged again later. Eustathius of Berytos added in shorthand symbols 'I have signed this under pressure, not being in agreement'
(Ps.-Zach. 3. 1, Eng. tr. p. 47). After the council he was a persistent figure
among critics of the Definition.

The canons

Marcian conferred on Chalcedon the honorary title of metropolis without
prejudice to the customary rights of Nicomedia. Twenty-seven canons were
enacted. There is no record of discussion about them, but the imperial consistory had a hand in some of them. The emperor wanted order in the
churches and an end to bishops squabbling and declaring schisms. Canons of
previous councils were reaffirmed: Nicaea, Constantinople, Ephesus, with
local eastern councils of Ankyra, Neocaesarea, Antioch (attributed to 341),
Gangra, Laodicea. No Latin council was put in the list. The canons' main
concern was the good order and discipline of clergy and monks. They are
forbidden to take secular employment, to farm estates or to trade for gain.
Only in certain circumstances may they be guardians for minors. Clergy must
not migrate from church to church. No ordination is allowed without title,
i.e. a specific appointment to a town, village, martyrium, or monastery.
Clergy going to law against other clergy must not go to secular courts but
only to their own bishop or an arbitrator appointed by him. Cases of contested jurisdiction, where a provincial synod or even the bishop of the capital of the civil diocese cannot resolve the issue, are to be referred to the see
of Constantinople 'the imperial city' (canons 9 and 17). Church provinces are
not to be split. Women deacons, whose age must be 40 or more, receive
imposition of hands, and may not make a bequest to a cleric or a pauper; they
must remain unmarried, as are dedicated virgins or monks. A special problem is located in wandering undisciplined clergy and monks causing disturb-
ances in Constantinople. The *defensor* (*ékdikos*) of the church is empowered
to expel them by force. All bishops must have stewards, finance officers to
manage ecclesiastical revenues. A hagiographical Life of Markianus, steward
in the time of Anatolius' successor Gennadius, records that he allowed minor
churches in the city to retain the offerings of their congregations; evidently
he exercised power.

Particular petitions brought to the council

On 26 October by Marcian's direction, as a reward for changing sides, Juvenal
of Jerusalem was granted the three provinces of Palestine for his patriarchate,
while Antioch retained the two Phoenicias and Arabia. After more painful

friction Theodoret was admitted on his anathema of Nestorius and of any-one who says Mary is not *theotókos* or affirms two Sons. The Roman legate Paschasinus observed that long ago Leo had accepted Theodoret (Leo, *ep.* 120); the decision was already made. The Cilician John of Germanikeia was required to anathematize Nestorius, and Amphilochius of Side had to condemn Eutyches.

Ibas again

The case of Ibas of Edessa was to prove more complicated. The passionate interest in him during the controversy over the Three Chapters in the next century had a disturbing effect on the transmission of the debate in 451. He had petitioned the emperor to ask the council to consider his case. This entailed the reading of the proceedings at Tyre (25 February 449) at which the judges Photius of Tyre and Eustathius of Berytos noted that in Edessa he had already anathematized Nestorius and affirmed the Formulary of Reunion; he accepted the decision of the council of Ephesus in 431 con-cerning the faith of Nicaea. On this he was acquitted of charges. As for finan-cial maladministration, Ibas assured them that he would in future follow the example of Antioch and use stewards chosen from his clergy. Although Photius and Eustathius supposed that they had settled the disputes at Edessa, the plaintiffs had renewed their grievances before Flavian at Constantinople and before Domnos of Antioch. The accusations were little different from those heard at the second session of Ephesus in 449, the most serious being embezzlement on behalf of a nephew's woman partner and Nestorian sympathies. Ibas was understood to have declared that he could not hold communion with Cyril of Alexandria unless Cyril condemned his Twelve Anathemas. Ibas countered by saying that after Cyril had put a gloss on his anathemas, he had written letters of communion to Ibas. The princi-pal document, however, is the text of Ibas' letter to Mari the Persian (of Nisibis) summarizing the controversy between Cyril and Nestorius and concluding on the Formulary of Reunion. On this basis the Roman legates declined to have the record of Ephesus 449 read (that assembly having been annulled by Leo) and declared Ibas orthodox. The council therefore accepted Ibas and his letter. In the controversy about the Three Chapters in the next century it became necessary to acquiesce in a fiction that a letter described as by Ibas to Mari was not that actually approved but a different and innocuous document. Thereby it became possible to condemn the letter to Mari as Nestorian without prejudice to the orthodoxy of Chalcedon. Maximus of Antioch was asked to decide about shifting Ibas' replacement Nonnos at Edessa. Juvenal of Jerusalem welcomed Ibas as 'a repentant heretic'.

New Rome's jurisdiction

At the end of October the council turned to a sensitive question—the jurisdiction of the bishop of New Rome. The Roman legates and imperial commissioners stayed away, the legates saying that from Leo they had no instructions on this subject (*ACO* II i. 447. 19). The proceedings were not secret but canonical (ibid. 447. 24). Following a wish expressed by the emperor, the Greek bishops with Anatolius presiding approved a restatement of the canon of Constantinople in 381 that its dignity rested on being New Rome 'on an equality with Old Rome', but adding that the bishop of Constantinople should be responsible for the ordination of the metropolitans only of the civil dioceses of Pontus, Asia, and Thrace, and of all bishops working among the barbarians. Otherwise each metropolitan should ordain the bishops of his province as laid down in the canons. The proposal marked no innovation in the regions named. It gave recognition to existing custom, admittedly resented by some metropolitans.

Pope Leo had given his legates a written instruction, read by the presbyter Boniface: 'Do not allow the constitution promulgated by the holy fathers to be violated by any rash move, preserving in every way the dignity of our person which you represent; and if perhaps any, relying on the splendour of their cities, attempt any usurpation, repel this with the determination which this merits' (*ACO* II iii. 548. 13). Did Leo have reason to fear a rival claim to jurisdictional primacy from Constantinople? Or were his apprehensions looking more in the direction of Dioscorus of Alexandria?

The imperial commissioners wanted to know if bishops agreeing to the proposed restatement of the canon of 381 had been under any pressure: had it been a free vote? The overwhelming answer was that it was so. The bishop of Phrygian Laodicea replied that 'the glory of the see of Constantinople is the glory of our city' (*ACO* II i. 456. 9). The archbishop of Ankyra was anxious that in time the patriarchs of Constantinople might expect ordination fees; while the intentions of Anatolius were clear, 'no one is immortal' (ibid. 457. 25).[9] It had long been customary for the bishop of Constantinople to ordain metropolitans in the three civil dioceses named, 'not to enhance the powers of the see of Constantinople but because often when bishops die tumults have arisen' (*ACO* II i. 477. 8ff.; Latin, II iii. 356. 30ff.). An answer given by Eusebius of Dorylaeum was significant: when he had been a refugee at Rome shortly before Easter 451, envoys arrived from Constantinople; Eusebius had quoted to Leo the canon of 381 on the dignity of New Rome

---

[9] In 544 Justinian, Novel. 123. 3 and 16 enacted that the customary fees for consecrations, namely 20 lbs of gold for patriarchs, 100 solidi for metropolitans, otherwise graded according to the income of the see, should not be exceeded; and the fees go to lawyers, not to the consecrating bishop.

and Leo accepted it (*ACO* II i. 456. 28–30). Evidently six months before Chalcedon the clergy sent by Anatolius were raising the question with Leo, and they would have returned to report that there was no cloud on the horizon. Leo's letter to Pulcheria of 20 July 451 (*ep*. 95. 2) laid emphasis on the disorder at Ephesus in 449 where some were 'robbed of their privilege of honour'. He was referring to the record of Ephesus which showed that Flavian had been demoted to fifth place. In short, Leo himself was implicitly acknowledging the third canon of 381. At the time he needed good relations with Constantinople to achieve what he desired.

Roman appeal to the sixth canon of Nicaea

At the first session at Chalcedon, almost ingratiatingly, the Roman legates had themselves drawn attention to the placing of Anatolius in the second place after the legates of Pope Leo (so consistently throughout the council), and had been congratulated for their knowledge of the canons (*ACO* II i. 78. 1–4). If the legates were to achieve the deposition of Dioscorus, they would need a lot of Greek support. At points during the conciliar discussions the privilege of the bishop of Constantinople to ordain metropolitans in the nearby provinces was mentioned, as in the fourteenth session on the metropolitan rights of Nicomedia versus Nicaea (ibid. 418), but provoked no grunt of intervention from the Roman legates. Nor did they query the procedure when a dispute between two rival bishops of Ephesus was decided by patriarch Anatolius (ibid. 410–11). However, when the Greek bishops approved the vote (it was not called a canon at the time) on Anatolius' jurisdiction, the legate Lucensius objected that the see of Rome was being insulted: 'sedes apostolica nobis praesentibus humiliari non debet' (*ACO* II iii. 552. 30). His question was how the canon on the dignity of Constantinople could be reconciled with the sixth canon of Nicaea, which named Rome, Alexandria, and Antioch as the three sees with supra-provincial authority beyond that of a metropolis. Since in 325 the city of 'Constantinople New Rome' (as it is consistently described in the Greek Acts of Chalcedon) had not yet been formally inaugurated, naturally it could not be mentioned.

Since Damasus and his council at Rome in 382, the claims to authority of the Roman see had been based on St Peter, and this Petrinity was shared by Alexandria through St Mark and by Antioch. This doctrine was restated by Innocent I, for whom Peter and therefore all his Roman successors were the source of authority and authentic ecclesiality for all bishops throughout the entire Church. In the 420s and 430s there had been tension between Rome and Constantinople concerning jurisdiction in Illyricum. Anatolius particularly enraged Leo by asking the churches of Illyricum to recognize the jurisdiction of his see (Leo, *ep*. 117. 5, 21 March 453, written after a report from

Thessalonica). Moreover, when Anatolius had consecrated Maximus for the see of Antioch in succession to Domnos, Leo came to see this action as personal ambition for his office, an act in which Leo had reluctantly acquiesced for the sake of harmony (which in the run-up to Chalcedon he needed).

Anatolius had been taken aback by the protest of the Roman legates. They had expressly said that the subject was one on which Pope Leo had given them no instructions. Yet after the decision to confirm the canon of 381 had been made and confirmed by signatures, they had 'disparaged the see of Constantinople-Rome and insulted Anatolius personally', even though all had received the approval of the imperial commissioners. Anatolius wrote a sad letter to Leo asking him to 'let everyone know that your true mind is unchanged' (*ACO* II i. 248–50). Leo's reply (*ep.* 106) did not pour oil on the troubled waters.

After the council of Chalcedon disbanded, during three years of subtly acrimonious correspondence with both Anatolius and Marcian, Leo was so vexed by the conciliar vote confirming the canon of Constantinople (381) that he astonishingly withheld his ratification of the council's doctrine, and thereby greatly comforted the numerous extreme advocates of Cyril's Twelve Anathemas for whom the council's 'two natures' Definition was tantamount to treachery. Leo observed that the canons of Constantinople (381) were not in the canon-collection acknowledged at Rome, and he believed that the text had never been transmitted to Rome at the time. Constantinople was a great and imperial city, but it was not an apostolic foundation; 'secular matters are one thing, divine another' (*ep.* 104. 3 to Marcian, 22 May, 452). Leo's polemic was turning the issue into an expression of rivalry between east and west, and heralded the fierce exchanges half a century later in the time of the Acacian schism. That the council of Chalcedon intended hostility towards old Rome is improbable. Admittedly, the Roman legates could feel embarrassed by the assertion of 'equality' between the Old and New Romes.

Troubles at Alexandria: Proterius and Timothy the Weasel

The Chalcedonian vote on the privileges of Constantinople was also offensive to the churches of Egypt, not only to Rome. At Alexandria, by long tradition proud to be second city of the empire, it became an additional reason for strong reservations about the Christology of the synod as well as its idea of the structure of the Church. Dioscorus' successor and former presbyter Proterius had been given a formidable task. His conversion to support Chalcedon did not endear him to some of his people, and his resort to coercion made the situation worse. He used the resources of his church chest to grease the palms of powerful people in the city and infuriated those whose anti-Chalcedonian prejudices rendered them in his view disqualified for alms. As long as Dioscorus was alive in exile at Gangra Proterius was confronted by a strong faction urging the absurdity of a synod which anathematized Nestorius and then, through Leo's Tome, canonized doctrine hard to distinguish from Nestorius' stance. (This ironic estimate of Chalcedon's achievement was probably shared by Nestorius himself if still living.) On Dioscorus' death (4 September 454) Marcian sent a silentiary named John, who had been present at Chalcedon, to explain the Chalcedonian decisions to the Alexandrians and to persuade them to receive Proterius (Ps.-Zach. 3. 11; Leo, *ep.* 141). John was so impressed by the massive opposition to Proterius that he returned to court to present the case against him.

In 455 Leo wanted Easter to fall on 17 April when the Alexandrian date was 24 April. The emperor Marcian, appealed to, thought the Alexandrians correct. Proterius persuaded Leo to have the celebration on 24 April.[10]

Timothy the Weasel (Ailouros)

Marcian died on 27 January 457, to be buried with Pulcheria in the church of the Apostles. The news led Egyptian monks to persuade the presbyter Timothy Ailouros or the Weasel (so called on account of his emaciated countenance) to be consecrated bishop for the 'believing' community opposed to Proterius. This Timothy had been ordained by Dioscorus and had a close ally in a deacon named Peter Mongos ('Stammerer') who was later to be patriarch (for a few weeks in 477, then 482–9) and objectionable to the west. By the Nicene canon a minimum of three bishops were required. Two Egyptian bishops, excommunicated probably by Proterius, were the best Timothy could find. (A story concerned about the uncanonical ordination says that the two were assisted by the anti-Chalcedonian bishop of Gaza, Peter the Iberian, who happened to be in the city.) The issues were admirably suited to the notorious Alexandrian mob which, in a society where they had no democratic vote, customarily expressed feelings through a centuries-old tradition of urban riots. The military commander Dionysius arrested Timothy and lives were lost in the affray at the hands of the troops (*caetrati*). The conflict ended on Maundy Thursday, 28 March 457, when a soldier murdered Proterius, who had sought asylum in the baptistery of the main church. His corpse was triumphantly incinerated by the mob in the hippodrome. His episcopal chair was burnt as polluted. His relatives were persecuted and deprived of his family estate. Timothy the Weasel was left in control. Egyptian bishops accepting Chalcedon were expelled. Timothy wrote a

---

[10] See B. Blackburn and L. Holford-Strevens, *The Oxford Companion to the Year* (Oxford, 1999), 793.

measured letter to the emperor Leo, Marcian's successor and Augustus from 457 to 474, explaining that Pope Leo's Tome was Nestorian in separating the 'natures'.

Monophysite aversion to Chalcedon and Leo was not allayed by the tenacity with which some churches in Cilicia and some monasteries persisted in commemorating Nestorius in the diptychs. Close to Constantinople itself there was a monastery of Sleepless monks (Akoimetai) who firmly supported Chalcedon but also venerated Nestorius in their calendar as a martyred saint (Ps.-Zach. 7. 7). Early in the sixth century Severus of Antioch discovered this canonizing of Nestorius at Tarsus authorized by the Bishop (Severus, *Select Letters*, ed. Brooks, 1. 24).

The emperor Leo was, like Marcian, a protégé of Aspar and a soldier from Thrace without comprehension of theological questions. Pope Leo sent him a revised version of his Tome to Flavian, strengthened by a substantial florilegium of proof-texts. Riots in Alexandria became the new emperor's headache. Timothy the Weasel's delegation to the capital insisted that the Church of Alexandria could not accept the council of Chalcedon and demanded a new council to declare Chalcedon null and void. His moderation, which irritated Ultras, led him to recognize all Proterius' ordinations as valid (a decision defended by Severus of Antioch) and, after initially negative noises (*ACO* II v. 22), to approve the creed of 381.

Persuaded by Aspar, the emperor Leo exiled Timothy the Weasel. In his place the see was filled by another Timothy called Salofakiolos ('Wobblecap'), who realized that the Monophysites at Alexandria were strong and could not reasonably be subjected to coercion. To placate them he even put Dioscorus' name into the diptychs, and told Anatolius' successor at Constantinople, Gennadius, that he could not accept the decision of Chalcedon regarding the jurisdiction of New Rome (Ps.-Zach. 4. 10–11).

At Rome the news of Proterius' sordid death had serious effects on trade between Rome and Alexandria, and an Alexandrian delegation visited Rome to reassure their trading partners that the death of Proterius was no regrettable event and no ground for a trade war (Leo, *Sermo* 96). The sack of Rome by Geiseric's Vandals (June 455), vividly described by Procopius, led Alexandrian Monophysites to interpret the disaster as a divine judgement on Chalcedon (Timothy Ailouros, ed. Nau, PO 13. 216).

Troubles in Palestine

At Jerusalem also the news of Chalcedon's Christology sparked a major riot of monks, led by an excitable Alexandrian named Theodosius whom Dioscorus had had occasion to treat as a delinquent (Evagrius 2. 5). Juvenal temporarily lost his see to this man, who soon fled to the monks on Mount

Sinai. Juvenal's tenure was already precarious in that Maximus of Antioch was seeking Leo's support for annulling Chalcedon's act rewarding Juvenal for changing sides by depriving the Antioch patriarchate of three provinces (Leo, *ep.* 119). Maximus of Antioch was not in a strong position since his predecessor Domnos was still alive, though at Chalcedon there was an informal agreement to pay a lump sum pension to Domnos of 250 solidi from the chest of Antioch (*ACO* II ii. 113. 18). Juvenal recovered his see late in 453 and naturally, when the alternative was the anti-Chalcedonian Theodosius, Leo was bound to support him. The see of Palestinian Caesarea inevitably lost metropolitan rights of ordination. In 457 the bishop of Caesarea was signing second after Juvenal of Jerusalem (*ACO* II v. 9. 27).

In Palestine the anti-Chalcedonian cause had a zealous champion in a Georgian prince Peter, who had been brought up at the court of Theodosius II, where he had been sent as a hostage. At court in charge of the emperor's horses, he resigned to follow the ascetic life in Palestine. The brief tenure of Archbishop Theodosius at Jerusalem was enough to consecrate Peter to be bishop of Gaza, a predominantly pagan city but with a largely Christian population in its port Maiouma. The *Life of Peter the Iberian* (ed. R. Raabe, Leipzig, 1895) contains illuminating information about the intransigent opponents of the council's Definition.

The emperor Leo's *Encyclia*

For more than a century to come, the canonical legitimacy of Chalcedon was a bone of contention in the east, an issue contributing to alienation between the Greek east and the Latin west, but more to division among the Greek churches. The critical question was how the Definition could be reconciled with the more vehement anti-Nestorian writings of Cyril of Alexandria. In the autumn of 457 the emperor Leo received rival petitions, one from fourteen Egyptian bishops, refugees in Constantinople, favouring Chalcedon and denouncing Timothy the Weasel's uncanonical ordination, the other from the rival party at Alexandria declaring their absolute rejection of the councils of Constantinople (381) and of Chalcedon. They accepted both synods of Ephesus. The refugee bishops complained that Timothy was allowing alms only to his own criminal supporters, and depriving the poor. Moreover he anathematized Leo of Rome, Anatolius of Constantinople, Basil of Antioch, and the entire council of Chalcedon. Naturally a sharp question was whether his rejection of the council of 381 implied acceptance of Apollinarian heresy.

The emperor Leo decided against holding another council, but asked all metropolitans, Symeon Stylites, and some others to write with their opinion. Forty-eight answers out of an original fifty survive in a Latin version (*ACO* II v). Since the emperor required replies almost by return, several answers appear rushed but broadly agree that although the Chalcedonian Definition had nothing like the status of the Nicene creed, it was a useful barrier against heretics. Apart from the collected replies it is recorded by Ps.-Zacharias and Evagrius (2. 10) that Amphilochios of Side, who at Chalcedon had been required to anathematize Eutyches, answered with a rejection both of the Chalcedonian Definition and of Timothy's ordination. None of the metropolitans' answers embodied serious reflection on the Christological question. A few registered enthusiasm for Cyril: Isauria, Pamphylia, Cappadocia, Armenia, and Cyzicus. The metropolitan of Melitene in Armenia II expressed gratitude for not being summoned to another council: 'We are in a remote corner of the world and live with Armenians, faithful indeed, but not speaking good Greek (or Latin); and because of the mixed population with barbarians from across the Euphrates, we cannot deliver long sermons. We uphold the Nicene creed but avoid difficult questions beyond human grasp. Clever theologians soon become heretics.' At Melitene the church venerated the memory of Cyril's friend Acacius, no advocate of 'two natures' (*ACO* II v. 71–5). Aversion to a new synod was general: 'many bishops have to sell church plate to pay travel costs' (84–6).

In 459/60 the emperor Leo, persuaded by Aspar, exiled Timothy the Weasel first to Gangra in Paphlagonia, then to the Crimea. In 475 Timothy was briefly recalled to Alexandria by a pro-Monophysite but short-lived emperor Basiliskos; patriarch Acacius of Constantinople refused communion with him. Critics had tarred him with the brush of Eutyches, which he strenuously disowned; moreover, he embodied a breach with Rome and the west which the emperor's consistory could not welcome. Timothy's writings, which survive in Syriac and Armenian, include a sustained invective in three books against Leo's Tome and the Chalcedonian Definition, arguing their incompatibility with the authentic Cyril. He died in 477.[11]

The Alexandrian church long remained a divided body, each party being convinced that the other was an invention of Antichrist. A minority were loyal to the decisions of Chalcedon, but faced a substantial majority venerating the memory of Dioscorus and alienated from the emperor and patriarch at Constantinople. That set Egypt on the way to being lost to the east Roman empire under the Islamic invasion and the Arab capture of Alexandria in 641.

---

[11] R. Y. Ebied and L. R. Wickham have published letters of Timothy Ailouros, *JTS*, NS 21 (1970), 321–69, vehement against Eutychianism, and part of his work against the Chalcedonian Definition in a *Festschrift for Albert van Roey, After Chalcedon* (Leuven, 1985), 115–66. His main weapon was the florilegium of excerpts either from Nestorius or from Cyril.

54

THE AFTERMATH OF THE COUNCIL OF CHALCEDON: ZENO'S HENOTIKON

The last decades of the fifth century were disturbed for the Roman empire in both east and west. In the west a succession of shortlived emperors, few of whom were recognized in the east, ended with all control passing into barbarian hands, first under Odoacer, then under his conqueror the Ostrogoth Theoderic. Theoderic's rule at Ravenna admirably restored order in Italy, but his independence of east Rome and positive determination to keep the Latin and Greek churches apart was resented by old Roman families and in 525 brought death to Boethius, his father-in-law Symmachus, and Pope John I. In the east the emperor Leo had trouble with Goths after he had murdered Aspar the senatorial leader and also his sons, which may presuppose that Aspar meditated making himself or a son emperor. Some anti-Arian legislation followed. Under Leo, Isokasios, philosopher and quaestor, was accused of paganism; after examination by the praetorian prefect he was forced to submit to baptism. Leo also legislated that Sunday be a day of rest undisturbed by music.

The emperor Zeno the Isaurian[1]

Leo was succeeded in 474 by a shortlived son and then by his personal favourite Zeno, an otherwise unpopular Isaurian. Zeno's power was precarious under attack from three quarters, namely Goths, a briefly successful usurper Basiliskos brother of his mother-in-law, and a fellow Isaurian named Illus, who was backing an alternative monarch.

Before becoming emperor Zeno had visited Antioch as a military commander and there discovered something of the ecclesiastical controversy. A former presbyter of Chalcedon, Peter the Fuller, came to Antioch and acquired a following of anti-Chalcedonian supporters, zealous for affirming in liturgy their faith in 'God crucified' (language painful to the ears of the emperor Marcian). Peter was the first to insert the (hitherto baptismal) creed in the eucharist (Theodorus the Reader, p. 118 Hansen). The old bishop of

---

[1] See the article on Zeno in Pauly–Wissowa by A. Lippold.

Antioch, Martyrius, found the chaos hard to bear, and resigned the see. A small synod at nearby Seleucia chose Peter the Fuller to succeed, and he enjoyed Zeno's support. But at Constantinople Peter's doings provoked anger with Patriarch Gennadios and the emperor Leo. Peter was summoned to Constantinople and interned in the monastery of the Sleepless monks on the Asiatic shore of the Bosporos, a house dedicated to continuous prayer in relays and militant in defence of the council of Chalcedon.

Basiliskos' usurpation (475); pro-Monophysite policy withdrawn

Nevertheless support for negative opinions of the Chalcedonian Definition was sufficiently evident for Basiliskos, during his eighteen months as usurping emperor, to recall Timothy the Weasel from exile and to issue an Encyclical affirming the Nicene and Constantinopolitan creeds, confirming both councils of Ephesus but condemning the Chalcedonian Definition and the Tome of Leo. Bishops were asked to sign this and did so. At a synod in Ephesus, led by Timothy the Weasel, a bid was made to cancel Chalcedon's decision about the privileges of Constantinople, thereby restoring the bishop of Ephesus' metropolitan rights, and to reaffirm the validity of the council of Ephesus of 449. Naturally Basiliskos' pro-Alexandrian policy was not acceptable to the patriarch of Constantinople, Acacius, a Chalcedonian who succeeded Gennadius about 471. A measure of Acacius' intransigence can be deduced from the fact that he succeeded in persuading Daniel, a Stylite saint on his column on the European shore of the Bosporos and Chalcedonian believer, to accept ordination and to come into the city to be received at the great church by Acacius. The patriarch also alerted the then Pope Simplicius (468–83) to the threats to Leo's Tome coming from Alexandria. The outcome was Basiliskos' withdrawal of his Encyclical and the restoration of patriarchal ordination rights to the see of New Rome. Zeno was menacing him with military force, and Basiliskos fell in August 476.

The Henotikon

Zeno saw that the passionate divisions arising from decisions at Chalcedon in 451 were politically dangerous. The air was thick with the language of conflict and of choice between exclusive alternatives. He wanted this replaced by inclusion, reconciliation, even ambiguity as long as it enabled bishops and their congregations to live together peaceably. Proterios' murder in an anti-Chalcedonian riot at Alexandria warned what could happen to patriarchs. The patriarch of Constantinople Acacius, who was on good terms with Pope Simplicius, had an acute intelligence and drafted for Zeno to enact by edict an instrument of union popularly entitled *Henotikon*, addressed in July 482 to the churches threatened by schism in the jurisdiction of the bishop of Alexandria. It was a law of the empire issued by authority which popes and bishops who disliked it would think secular. It reflected Zeno's awareness that discord in the Church had large political consequences which were an emperor's proper concern. New Rome depended for food on Egyptian corn.

Evagrius[2] (3. 14) cites the text: The emperor begins from the empire's need for unity on the sole basis of the Nicene creed, confirmed by the council of Constantinople in 381. Enemies will be defeated, the weather will be kind, and the food supply will not fail (which had occurred in Leo's time taken by Monophysites to mark heaven's displeasure at his Chalcedonian policy) if and when Christ, born of the ever virgin mother of God, accepts our worship. Petitions (of Monophysite provenance) have been coming to court from archimandrites and anchorites asking for unity to be restored, for the sacraments to be assured to people who at present die deprived, and for bloody murders (occasioned mainly by urban riots) to cease. The Nicene faith used at all baptisms was followed by the council of Ephesus which condemned Nestorius, who with Eutyches is anathematized. We accept Cyril's Twelve Anathemas. So (echoing the Reunion of 433) we affirm Christ to be of one substance with the Father in his Deity, one with us in his humanity, made flesh of the Holy Spirit and of Mary ever virgin mother of God, one not two. Both the miracles and the sufferings are those of one (person). (This last sentence dilutes a proposition in Leo's Tome.) We do not accept those who teach division or mixture. He who took flesh was one of the Trinity. This is no new creed. We anathematize all who think or who have thought other-wise 'whether at Chalcedon or at any other synod'. Controversial terms like 'nature' or 'hypostasis' are wholly absent.[3]

Monophysite hostility to the Henotikon

Though unenthusiastic about aspects of Chalcedon, in comparison with Basiliskos' Encyclical the Henotikon offered less to hard-line Monophysite opinion. The *Plerophoriai* of John Rufus (PO 8. 1), who succeeded Peter the Iberian as bishop of Maiouma by Gaza, have stories of miraculous dreams and prophecies condemning Leo's Tome and Chalcedon with visions of the

---

[2] Evagrius wrote late in the sixth century and was a Neo-Chalcedonian convinced that on essentials the parties were agreed (1. 11, 2. 5). See Michael Whitby's well-annotated translation: (Translated Texts for Historians, 33, Liverpool University Press, 2000).

[3] The critical text of the Henotikon is in E. Schwartz, *Codex Vaticanus gr. 1431*, 52–6 (Abh. der Bay. Akad. 32/6, 1927), editing both the Greek original and Liberatus' Latin version. Other texts are edited by Schwartz, *Publizistische Sammlungen zum acacianischen Schisma* (ibid., NF 10, 1934). For an English account of the controversy see W. H. C. Frend, *The Rise of the Monophysite Movement* (Cambridge, 1972).

emperor Marcian in hell. Favourable references to Basiliskos' Encyclical are frequent, but the Henotikon is unmentionable.

The Henotikon sought to state what pro- and anti-Chalcedonians were agreed upon as a highest common factor. It was notable for an ambiguous reference to Chalcedon, or at least to what some said there, and for the thunderous silence about the Tome of Leo or indeed about the crucial dispute whether one must speak of one nature or of two and with what preposition, in or of. For Zeno and perhaps for the patriarch of Constantinople, it had become important and immediate to reduce the Alexandrian aversion to Chalcedon, which was gradually spreading influentially through some Syrian monasteries. Theodoret had died in 466 but at Cyrrhos about 520, perhaps in delight at Justin's restoration of Chalcedonian faith, his icon was defiantly hailed at a celebration of Diodore, Theodore, and (so critics claimed) Nestorius (*ACO* IV i/199. 22 ff.). In 482 peace in Egypt was more urgent than serene relations with Rome and a now largely barbarian west. After all, a cool supporter of the Chalcedonian Definition could conscientiously sign the Henotikon as a return to the pre-Chalcedonian position of Cyril. The Definition was not mentioned.

Timothy Salofakiolos (Wobblecap) against Peter Mongus (Stammerer)

In 477 Timothy the Weasel died peacefully in Alexandria; a decision to exile him again, already taken at court, arrived just after his death. News of his impending demise may have reached the capital, since control by the government ensured that a Monophysite successor, Peter Mongos, could be consecrated only in secret at midnight and then by a solitary bishop (Theodore of Antinoe) before Timothy Salofakiolos returned from his refuge making baskets in the Pachomian monastery at Canopus. The dead hand of Timothy the Weasel was laid on Peter Mongos' head—by old Alexandrian custom, otherwise attested, and older than the Nicene canon requiring three bishops for a canonical consecration (Liberatus 20, *ACO* II v. 135. 2).

The return to the city by Salofakiolos precipitated fresh rioting. But he had government support. He notified Rome of his return, apologizing that earlier he had commemorated Dioscoros in the diptychs, and affirmed his assent to the Chalcedonian Definition. It would help, he suggested, if Pope Simplicius could persuade the emperor to exile Peter Mongos as far as possible from Egypt, which the Pope attempted for him (so Gelasius, *tract.* 1. 8, p. 516 Thiel); but Mongos, in hiding no doubt among the monks, could not be found. The mildness and moderation of Salofakiolos towards the opposition seems only to have confirmed their suspicions of him. Timothy the Weasel had initially refused to recognize Chalcedonian orders as valid, but relaxed his rigour. Zealot Monophysites would not receive communion at Chalcedonian hands and on journeys carried the host in a pyx (e.g. Moschos, *Pratum* 79; John Rufus, *Pleroph.* 38).

Under the impact of the moderate Henotikon ultra anti-Chalcedonians were becoming determined to resist compromise and to act independently of their opponents. They were not yet a coherent organized body; that did not come until the time of the emperor Justinian. But they had success from time to time in getting supporters of their cause into important and influential positions in the Church; if only they could win an emperor, they might conquer the empire at least in the east and even in the long run bring the west to heel by a discreet use of gold for a Roman see harassed and impoverished by barbarian invasions of Italy. In the mid-sixth century Pope Vigilius turned out to be a vulnerable target to this end. The death of Justinian's Monophysite wife Theodora (548), however, shattered hopes. Egypt and Syria became marked by a different culture. Lasting aversion to 'in two natures' survives in Copts, Ethiopians, Armenians, and the Syrian Orthodox (often called Jacobites).

John Talaia of Alexandria

The Monophysites had many setbacks, as when Acacius of New Rome at the emperor's command consecrated an avowed Chalcedonian Calandion to be patriarch of Antioch (479–84), his predecessor Stephen having been murdered at the altar by a Monophysite fanatic (Avell. 66). His successor Calandion accepted the Henotikon, but was attacked by Philoxenos of Hierapolis and for political reasons fell (Evagrius 3. 16; Ps.-Zach. 7. 10). At Alexandria Salofakiolos was succeeded by his presbyter and steward John Talaia (482) who was Chalcedonian but for reasons of political intrigue unwelcome to the emperor Zeno, who had made him swear that he had no ambition to be bishop. Zeno ordered Talaia's expulsion; he fled to Rome. Zeno shocked Pope Simplicius by approving for Alexandria Peter Mongos (482–9) on condition that he accepted both the Henotikon and all adherents of the Proterian party also willing to accept it. After hesitation Peter Mongos accepted the Henotikon, qualifying this by a statement that, by affirming Cyril's Twelve Anathemas and the body of Christ to be of one substance with our body (i.e. disowning Eutyches), the Henotikon was in line with Dioscoros and Timothy the Great (the Weasel) and so by implication annulled the doctrine of Chalcedon and the Tome of Leo even though it contained no express anathema of them (Ps.-Zach. 5. 7). The absence of any such anathema naturally made the Henotikon suspect to Mongos' more fervent followers at Alexandria, who, with deep reluctance, accepted moderate Proterians or adherents of Salofakiolos. But Mongos saw that the Henotikon was the best he could hope for, and labelled Ultras rejecting it and seceding from his communion as 'separatists' (*aposchistai*) or 'headless' (*akephaloi*) since they had no patriarch. They included two Egyptian bishops, but that was a tiny number.

That the Henotikon annulled Leo's Tome and the Chalcedonian Definition was obviously untrue, neither being mentioned, but this inter-pretation became standard among the anti-Chalcedonians not separatist extremists. Monophysite confidence in Peter Mongos was eroded especially among the monks who constituted the shock troops of the cause (Severus of Antioch, *Select Letters*, 4. 2). Peter had to make his anathema on Chalcedon explicit. Many monks judged it a bar to recognizing him that he was in full communion with Acacius of New Rome and Calandion of Antioch, who offered no such anathema and had no objection to the Chalcedonian Definition. For zealots Mongos was a two-timer. A letter from Mongos to Acacius cited by Evagrius (3. 17) proves how right they were. When he found his support in Egypt ebbing away, he was looking to Constantinople to bol-ster his authority, mendaciously denying that he could ever have pronounced anathema on Chalcedon.

Greek supporters of Chalcedon could accept the Henotikon. But the appeal to Rome by John Talaia made bishops of Rome hostile. This was made complicated by the fact that Pope Simplicius had withdrawn his confirmation of Talaia's appointment (Avell. 68). That could seem a weak surrender of papal authority.

Pope Felix: legation to Constantinople

After long illness Simplicius died on 10 March 483, and his successor Felix was in office three days later, probably supported by the powerful praetorian prefect Basil (*PLRE* ii. 217), who acted as deputy for Odoacer at the papal election (*MGH AA* xii. 445). Felix came of an aristocratic Roman family; Pope Gregory the Great counted him among his ancestors (*Dial.* 4. 17). One of Felix's first acts was to notify the emperor Zeno of his elevation. At this stage no copy of the Henotikon had officially been sent to Rome, but prob-ably through Talaia its text was known. Felix decided to send his letter con-taining an unmarked quotation from the Henotikon by the hand of two bishops, Vitalis and Misenus, later followed by the Defensor of the Roman church, as legates to Constantinople. Their brief was to protest against recog-nition of Peter Mongos once suspect to Acacius himself, and to insist on the authority of Chalcedon as upheld by the emperor Leo, 'the royal Via Media between Eutyches and Nestorios'. The legation was disastrous for the Pope. On arrival at Abydos, the customs-post on the Dardanelles, they were confined in custody and their letters confiscated. They were then conducted to Constantinople and most hospitably received. Misenus and Vitalis and then the Defensor were persuaded by Acacius' charm and political skill, and decided that the patriarch had a good case. They were present when Acacius celebrated the liturgy and for the first time openly and in no whisper named Peter Mongos in the diptychs (Evagrius 3. 20). To the horror of Sleepless monks who despatched a report to Pope Felix, the legates entered no protest. On their return they were excommunicated by a Roman synod unimpressed by their defence that they had done what seemed to them for the good of the Church.

Felix's relations with Acacius were not smoothed when the patriarch of New Rome claimed to share headship of the entire Church with 'the care of all the churches' (Felix, *ep.* 2. 8, p. 237 Thiel; cf. Gelasius, *ep.* 1. 40, p. 310). It was becoming an axiom that in canon law 'Rome' included both Old and New Rome. Spurred on by an impatient letter from the abbot of the Sleepless monks, Felix formally summoned Acacius to come to Rome and 'before St Peter' to answer charges brought by John Talaia. But for the emperor Zeno John Talaia was *persona non grata*, whereas with his signature to the Henotikon Peter Mongos could be entirely acceptable at Alexandria. Calandion of Antioch likewise wrote to Rome calling Peter Mongos an 'adulterer' (as an intruder in another's see) and candidly calling Cyril of Alexandria a fool. Calandion did not last at Antioch, being implicated in a conspiracy to get rid of Zeno. Peter the Fuller returned to the see, and accepted the Henotikon. Honeyed, almost treacly words were exchanged, and communion between Constantinople, Antioch, and Alexandria was restored on the basis of Zeno's Edict. Felix was ignored.

A question of primatial jurisdiction

Felix and successive bishops of Rome were offended. How could the patriarch of New Rome enter into communion with a known adversary of the Chalcedonian Definition, and fail to consult the Roman see? He was assuming that the east fell entirely within his jurisdiction, not Rome's. But Mongos was uncanonically ordained by a single bishop, and in distorting Roman eyes was an adherent of Eutyches' heresy. The precise and justified disavowal of Eutyches that Peter Mongos offered would have seemed over-subtle at Rome, where any doubter of Leo's Tome and of Chalcedon was assumed to be an adherent of Eutyches, just as defenders of Chalcedon and Leo were assumed by Monophysites to be Nestorians, Chalcedon's condemnation of Nestorius being deemed disingenuous. That seemed clear from the respect shown to the works of Theodore of Mopsuestia, Theodoret, and Ibas of Edessa. Rumour said that Theodoret had bribed Pope Leo (Ps.-Zach. 3. 1, 7. 8). Support for Mongos by the emperor Zeno evoked a Roman declaration that in matters ecclesiastical emperors should bow to Christ's priests (Felix, *ep.* 9, p. 250 Thiel). Like Innocent I in the Chrysostom affair, Felix felt that he had a duty to excommunicate not only Acacius but also the patriarchs of Alexandria and Antioch, in short the entire eastern Church.

This declaration was confirmed by a Roman synod in October 485 attended by forty-three bishops asserting the right of St Peter's successor who is 'head of all' to judge of the matter, a power, it is claimed, confirmed to the Roman church by the 318 fathers of Nicaea on the ground of Matt. 16: 18 'Thou art Peter . . .' and by Christ's grace guarded by succession to our own time (Coll. Avell. 70. 9, CSEL 35. 159). This claim is evidently an appeal to the revised Roman version of the sixth canon of Nicaea that 'The Roman see has always had the primacy', and perhaps the Serdican appeal canon counted as if Nicene. The formula is a momentous assertion of Roman superiority to the eastern patriarchates and of the subordinate authority of even an ecumenical council such as Nicaea. In 487 a similar synod warned the monasteries in and near Constantinople to be on their guard against their patriarch.

On 26 November 489 Patriarch Acacius died. He had been a skilful operator in his influence over both emperor and bishops and in the skill with which he had won the papal legates. Schism with Rome had resulted, nevertheless, and this was particularly associated with his name as the 'Acacian schism'.

Patriarch Fravitta

He was briefly succeeded by Fravitta, of Gothic ancestry, who had been a presbyter at Sykai on the Bosporos (Malalas 405 Bonn) at the church of St Thecla, an important saint for the Isaurian emperor in view of her great shrine at Seleucia. His synodical letter to Alexandria condemned Nestorios and Eutyches but said nothing of Chalcedon or of Leo's Tome. His epistle to Rome was the soul of courtesy and anxiety to be in agreement with the Roman see in doctrine, on which basis 'separated fragments might be joined again'. Pope Felix reacted in a friendly manner, but for restored communion there was a non-negotiable condition, namely that the names of Acacius and Peter Mongos be excluded from the diptychs. That exclusion could cause considerable upset in Constantinople where Acacius' memory was held by many in much respect. Emperors had reason to fear possible cause for urban riots. Moreover Acacius might have been too liberal towards Peter Mongos but was himself Chalcedonian. The Pope could hardly have been kept in the dark that a synodical letter from Fravitta had gone to Peter Mongos, whose answer insisted on the upholding of the Henotikon. Mongos realized how helpful its ambiguities were. Could there be two parallel and incompatible integrities agreed on pre-Chalcedonian faith?

Patriarch Euphemius

Patriarch Fravitta died (spring 490), replaced by a strong Chalcedonian from Syria named Euphemius, in Monophysite eyes 'tainted with Nestorian heresy' (Ps.-Zach. 6. 4). Euphemius could not delete Acacius' name from the diptychs without facing a storm. The Blues and Greens of the circus would unleash riots. He begged the Roman bishop to show 'condescension'. Pope Felix was glad to know the new patriarch's strict adherence to the Chalcedonian Definition, but that in itself was not enough to heal the wounds inflicted on Roman authority by Acacius, whose omission from the diptychs remained an indispensable condition of reunion. It is painful to observe that even when the bishops of Rome and Constantinople were in total harmony about Chalcedon's doctrine, the issue of Roman authority persisted in keeping them apart. It was never going to be enough to agree with Rome in dogma if that was not accompanied by total submission to Roman jurisdiction. Politically, because Odoacer and then Theoderic the Ostrogoth ruled over Italy, the bishop of Rome was encouraged to be free of obligations to please the emperor in east Rome. In a letter to Zeno of direct candour Felix told Zeno he must choose between the communion of the apostle Peter and the communion of Peter Mongos (*ep.* 8. 2, p. 248 Thiel). The former would be more likely to get the emperor to heaven.

The emperor Anastasius

On 9 April 491 Zeno died. His widow Ariadne had influence enough to achieve the rapid election of Anastasius, aged sixty, 'decurion of the silentiaries', a native of Dyrrhachium on the Adriatic (now Albanian) coast. His coronation was on 11 April, Maundy Thursday; Ariadne was to be his consort. A record of the accession ceremony was preserved by Constantine Porphyrogenitus (*De Caeremoniis* 1. 92). It was the end of Isaurian power in Constantinople fostered by Zeno. Anastasius turned out to be a very able ruler of the east Roman empire for two and a half decades, bequeathing to his successors Justin and Justinian a well-filled treasury and well-fortified defences (Procopius, *Anekdota* 19. 4 ff.) especially on the troubled frontier with Persia, where, after a difficult war, he rapidly built a major fortress at Dara as an alternative and threat to the now Persian stronghold of Nisibis. The walls of Constantinople were also restored with a new defensive wall from forty miles west of Constantinople to the Black Sea. Like Marcian he tried to end the purchase of official positions, and also granted immensely welcome tax relief.

To the emperor Anastasius religion was a serious matter in his personal life, and at an earlier stage of his career he had been mentioned as possible bishop for the bankrupt see of Syrian Antioch where disastrously bishops had been borrowing to pay interest on prior loans. The churches of east Rome needed to be prevented from squabbling and rioting, and the only reasonable platform on which this could be achieved was the Henotikon of his predecessor Zeno. That this edict vexed Rome by its silence about Leo's Tome and the Chalcedonian Definition and infuriated numerous Monophysites in Egypt by its lack of a formal anathema on those two statements could be awkward; but the Henotikon looked a very plausible Via Media, the more so perhaps because of the intolerant extremes which it irritated. If some recalcitrant bishop had to be exiled, Anastasius would personally direct that there should be no bloodshed, and that if bloodshed was a possible outcome of exiling somebody, then the decree should be annulled (Evagrius 3. 34).

The pro-Chalcedonian patriarch Euphemius of Constantinople refused to crown Anastasius unless he swore in writing that there would be no innovation in the Church and the faith would be pure. That may have meant that Anastasius affirmed the Chalcedonian Definition, but it made no difference to his tolerant policy towards the Henotikon.

Pope Gelasius I (492–6)

Pope Felix died on 1 March 492. He was succeeded by Gelasius, one of the Roman deacons (a customary pattern of promotion) who had already been responsible for drafting letters for Felix. In his four years as Pope, Gelasius injected the strongest and toughest language into the controversy with Constantinople. In the next generation Dionysius Exiguus the canonist looked back on him as his ideal. In the ninth century Pope Nicolas I borrowed freely from Gelasius' letters in his denunciations of patriarch Photius; the chancery archive of Gelasius' correspondence was his arsenal. A master of precise statement and vigorous contender for the supremacy of his office, Gelasius had plenty of problems in the west. In Rome itself he protested, probably without much effect, when Roman aristocratic families maintained the ancient celebration of Lupercalia in which young men roamed the city stripping and whipping women reputed to be of easy virtue, a tradition claimed to be 'neither pagan nor Christian'. In north Africa orthodox Christians suffered persecution from Arian Vandals. In the Balkans and in northern Italy Pelagianism was not yet defunct. In southern Italy with an acute shortage of priests he tried to suppress women priests celebrating mass, and to stop presbyters of the Greek rite from giving chrism after baptism, a matter which a century later exercised Gregory the Great (*Registrum* 4. 9, 26). He judged it hazardous to ordain sufferers from epilepsy, taken to be demon-possession (pp. 373, 487 Thiel). There was embarrassing trouble in Calabria at Squillace where two successive bishops had been lynched by the mob. He directed that the offerings of the faithful be divided into four portions, for the bishop (to provide hospitality), for his clergy, for the poor and homeless, and for the fabric of the church building. He upheld the right for clergy to stand trial in ecclesiastical, not in secular courts. Many of his rulings on matters of church law survive through their use by Gratian, Anselm of Lucca, and other medieval canonists. In the sixth-century *Liber Pontificalis*, Gelasius is said to have contributed to liturgy. The so-called 'Gelasian Sacramentary' of the eighth century is not attributed to Pope Gelasius in any manuscript. That is not to say that no material in the famous manuscript given to the Vatican by Queen Christina of Sweden (Reginensis lat. 316) may bear his mark. There is probably more of him in the Verona (Leonine) Sacramentary.[4]

Gelasius and the east

The sour relations with Constantinople occupied much of his attention.

Gelasius was put under pressure by Anastasius' demand that the Roman senate support their emperor and persuade the Pope to yield. Happily for Gelasius, King Theoderic had no especial interest in smoothing relations between the Latin and Greek churches. He wanted interventions from the highest level at Constantinople as little as did the bishop of Rome. It cannot have helped Gelasius to acquire confidence in the emperor when in 494 the Chalcedonian patriarch Euphemius fell by an accusation that he had given encouragement to a movement of sedition. One of his presbyters Macedonius was nominated to succeed, but on two incompatible conditions: that he signed the Henotikon and reconciled the Sleepless monks. He signed and so could not reconcile.

In addition to such irritants for Gelasius, there was renewed trouble about ecclesiastical jurisdiction in Illyricum. The bishop of Thessalonica was papal vicar for Illyricum, but he was uncomfortably close to Constantinople which governed this region by secular administrators. He needed the support of papal authority to have any clout with the other bishops of the civil Diocese. Gelasius warned the bishops of eastern Illyricum (Dardania) to be on their guard against the admission of Acacius and Peter Mongos to the diptychs, especially when that was being conceded by Chalcedonians. It was absurd to prefer communion with condemned heretics to communion with St Peter (*ep.* 3 to Euphemius, who had been telling Gelasius that Acacius was orthodox and not remotely akin to Eutyches).

---

[4] See Antoine Chavasse, *Le Sacramentaire gélasien* (Paris, 1957). On Gelasius' role in the controversy with Constantinople see W. Ullmann, *Gelasius I. (492–96): Das Papsttum an der Wenden der Spätantike zum Mittelalter* (Stuttgart, 1981).

In the matter of the diptychs, Gelasius' critics thought he was making a mountain out of a molehill of mere names, especially when the most eminent was dead. His claim to lay down the law for the Greek churches was felt to be 'proud and arrogant' (*ep.* 12. 12). His obstinate refusal to negotiate and compromise when the interest of the empire was at stake was 'diminishing the dignity of his see'. They said that his personal excommunication of Acacius did not conform to the rules of canon law, to which he replied claiming that the (Serdican, for him Nicene) canon made Rome court of appeal for the entire Church. In any event he was confident that, in the words of his predecessor Felix, which he himself had probably proposed (*ep.* 7, p. 247 Thiel), the excommunication of the patriarch was an act of no pope or synod but of God himself. It was irreversible. He repeated the argument from Petrinity in Rome, Alexandria, and Antioch, respectively first, second, and third sees of the Church in the empire, appealing to the silence of the sixth Nicene canon as excluding Constantinople. Similarly he scorned the see of Constantinople as merely a suffragan of the old metropolis of Heraclea. He expressed himself with anger when he found the bishops of the Diocese Oriens complaining that he had not informed their patriarch of his attacks on the patriarchate of New Rome, and threatened excommunication if they did not change their tune. In fact he regarded the Greek churches generally as sodden with heresies (*ep.* 7. 2), whereas the Roman see under St Peter's care stood beyond criticism. To Gelasius any synod was advisory and consultative. If condemnation of Athanasius or John Chrysostom by an oriental synod was invalid without papal ratification, it followed that the bishop of Rome needed no synod to ratify his verdicts of censure (*ep.* 1, p. 288 Thiel in Felix's name).

The excommunicate legate Vitalis died, but Misenus was granted rehabilitation in advanced years. The relaxation was one of Gelasius' only modifications of steely rigorism, evidently in response to social pressure for mercy to a dying man.

Emperor and Pope, power and authority

Gelasius' relation with the emperor Anastasius, whose piety he handsomely acknowledged (*ep.* 12. 4), was abrasive. He told Anastasius in set terms that this world is governed by two things, the sacred authority of bishops, and royal power ('auctoritas sacrata pontificum et regalis potestas', *ep.* 12. 2). This meant more than mere division of labour. Authority was a moral question, whereas power meant raw coercion whether right or wrong (*ep.* 12. 2, p. 351 Thiel). In ecclesiastical or divine matters an emperor bows his head to bishops, who provide the means of his salvation. Bishops acknowledge that rule over the empire is entrusted to the emperor by divine appointment, and obey him in legislation affecting public discipline. Gelasius begs the emperor not to be offended when love for him encourages hope that his reign will be perpetual, so that after reigning on earth he will reign with Christ.

The argument that removing Acacius' name from the diptychs would cause a riot left Gelasius unimpressed. Macedonius in the fourth century and Nestorius recently were removed from office though the *plebs* of Constantinople wanted to keep them. A tumult caused by circus factions had lately been suppressed (*ep.* 12. 10). So why not heresy?

Gelasius' tracts

Six tracts survive from Gelasius' pen. The first, a factual history of the Eutychianists or an account of the affair of Acacius, was probably composed for Felix his predecessor (Avell. 99). It was exploited by Liberatus of Carthage half a century later (*ACO* II v. 119–30). The second similarly concerned Peter Mongos and Acacius, designed to defend the Roman position held in view of his responsibility to answer before Christ's judgement seat. The third 'on two natures against Eutyches and Nestorius' (pp. 530–57 Thiel; PL Suppl. iii. 763–87) answers the opinion that Gelasius has caused the breach. More importantly, he allows either 'from' (of) or 'in' two natures (p. 537. 3 Thiel). Several times the preposition 'from' without using 'in' is employed. He also criticizes the illusion that the favoured Monophysite formula 'one incarnate nature' is incompatible with 'two natures' (a momentous reinterpretation of Chalcedon). One cannot remove 'nature' from 'substance' without abolishing the substance (p. 539). In the eucharist 'the substance or nature of bread and wine does not cease to exist' (p. 541). The third tract concludes with a substantial florilegium mainly drawing on Theodoret's *Eranistes*. The fourth tract seems to be a collection of excerpts from a document, possibly drafted for Pope Felix, on the binding force of an anathema. Like Leo, Gelasius affirms that papal ratification of the Chalcedonian Definition is not weakened by disapproving the council's other decisions. A 'permanent' anathema on Acacius could have been lifted if he had repented. No authority attaches to the emperor in ecclesiastical matters. Priest-kings such as Melchizedek in the Old Testament have been imitated by the Devil in the claim of pagan emperors to be *Pontifex Maximus*.

Pope Anastasius (496–8)

Gelasius died on 21 November 496. The senators and many of the parish clergy in Rome wanted a successor rather more amenable to good relations with Constantinople, where their emperor resided. Their preferred candidate, Pope Anastasius, wanted a policy of pragmatic compromise, and sent bishops Cresconius of Todi and Germanus of Pesaro to the Emperor

Anastasius (not to the patriarch) with a letter announcing his election (*ep.* 1, p. 615 Thiel). Theoderic appointed the patrician Festus to lead the delegation which travelled east in 497. The new Pope proposed that while Acacius' name be no longer in the diptychs, there should be no formal condemnation since it was inappropriate to pass judgement on the dead. In other words, the anathema on Acacius by Felix in 484 was to be put aside. It was non-controversial that the Church should not be divided about the name of a man already dead some years. Yet surely the emperor as God's vicar on earth had it in his power by edict to bring the church of Alexandria back to the path of catholic truth as taught by tradition. Acacius' baptisms and ordinations are held valid, the contrary impression having been given by Pope Felix; his recognition of Peter Mongos injured none but himself.

Alexandrian apocrisiaries participated in the conversations on this programmatic statement, and their letter addressed to the western party survives in a translation by Dionysius Exiguus preserved in the Avellana collection (102, CSEL 35. 468; pp. 628 ff. Thiel). The Alexandrians wholly disavowed any affinity with Eutyches, but suggested that the Greek version of Leo's Tome was misleadingly translated by Nestorians such as Theodoret. 'The bishop of Rome supposing us to be against the faith handed down from the apostles suspended himself from our communion.' An Alexandrian delegation to Rome had been maligned by John Talaia, and rebuffed without even a greeting so that it returned home. A little time back Photinus, deacon of Thessalonica, had been sent by his bishop to Pope Anastasius and, being bilingual, had been able to say that while the Latin text of Leo's Tome was in line with the Nicene creed, the Greek version contained errors. He had reported this to the Alexandrian apocrisiaries. The official faith of the church of Alexandria was accordingly presented as the Henotikon, which was paraphrased with a diplomatic rewriting of the clause about possible conciliar mistakes, Chalcedon not being named and with no mention of Zeno or Acacius. Like Rome, Alexandria condemned Nestorius and Eutyches.

The Roman delegation promised to report all this to Pope Anastasius but added, to the amazement of the apocrisiaries, that since the Alexandrian patriarchs Dioscorus, Timothy the Weasel, and Peter Mongos had been opposed to the creed paraphrased, they must be omitted from the diptychs. For the emperor it would be a major success if the bishop of Rome accepted the Henotikon, interpreted as a gloss on the Chalcedonian Definition but not as a rejection. The surviving record of these astonishing exchanges is a report addressed to the Pope by the Alexandrian apocrisiaries. From another source (Anon. Valesianus) we learn that the patrician Festus had successfully submitted to the emperor a request by Theoderic for leave to wear kingly insignia. This success was an important political backdrop to the softening of ecclesiastical negotiations. But in the version of the *Liber Pontificalis* favourable to Anastasius' successor Symmachus, Anastasius' sudden death in November 498 is seen as a striking instance of providential intervention to preserve the see of Peter from heresy.

The Laurentian schism at Rome

Festus' proposal to ask Pope Anastasius to approve the Henotikon in the embalmed form presented by the Alexandrian apocrisiaries came to nothing. He returned to Rome to find Anastasius dying or dead (19 November 498). The ensuing election produced two rival bishops, Symmachus, a deacon of Sardinian origin, and a senior presbyter named Laurentius, much favoured by many senators and many parish clergy in Rome. The two represented oppos-ite policies towards Constantinople. The double election produced tumults, but the outcome was victory for Symmachus who by borrowing substantial sums, later embarrassingly hard to repay, won support from Theoderic's offi-cials at Ravenna. By selling church land for largess he gained most of the Roman *plebs*. For a time Symmachus had possession of St Peter's, Laurentius had St Paul's without the Walls. During the stand-off Theoderic appointed a Visitor, Peter bishop of Altinum (now under the Venetian lagoon), who celebrated Easter at the Lateran basilica.

There were nasty rumours about Symmachus' too amicable continuing relationships with courtesans, old flames of his pagan youth. Theoderic insisted that this be cleared up by a synod. Italian bishops were unaccustomed to the calling of synods by a secular prince. They liked Symmachus' defence that without papal consent and ratification no synod had juridical validity, and that under canon law the legitimate holder of the first see could not be judged anyway. On 23 October 502 an ill-attended synod declared Symmachus canonically immune from being judged by inferior bishops. The synod noted that he now enjoyed the favour of 'almost all the *plebs*' (prob-ably some exaggeration), and asked Theoderic to allow Symmachus to draw the temporalities of the see.[5] Symmachus enjoyed important support from Ennodius, then at Milan, but soon to be bishop of Pavia 513–21, author of 197 extant letters and sundry tracts and poems, both prose and verse being in a sophisticated rococo style. Ennodius particularly supported the more

---

[5] The text of the synods concerned with Symmachus is edited by Theodor Mommsen with his edition of Cassiodorus' *Variae* (*MGH AA* XII (1894 = 1981). A fragment with some of the Laurentian side of the story is printed in Duchesne, *Liber Pontificalis* I 43–6. On Ennodius see S. A. H. Kennell, *Magnus Felix Ennodius: A Gentleman of the Church* (Ann Arbor, 2000). Symmachus was from Sardinia. In November 1998 a congress was held at Oristano assembling papers about him: *Il papato di San Simmaco* (Cagliari, 2000). The Laurentian schism is well treated by John Moorhead, *Theoderic in Italy* (Oxford, 1993) and by Patrick Amory, *People and Identity in Ostrogothic Italy 489–554* (Cambridge, 1997).

papalist ideology of Symmachus in preference to the conciliar language of his opponents.

Perhaps because of the coolness between Rome and Alexandria Symmachus ignored the Alexandrian computation for Easter in 501, preferring 25 March rather than the Alexandrian date of 22 April observed in northern Italy and by Gothic communities.

The outcome of the synod's quasi-acquittal, which left the moral question wide open, was chaotic rioting with a certain amount of bloodshed. Symmachus' supporters forged documents attributed to the time of Xystus III, said to be maliciously accused of adultery, but exempt from trial because of the traditional supremacy of St Peter's successor over all synods. Theoderic had left it to the bishops to solve the problem, but in the outcome they left it to him since the synod decided that the question lay beyond its competence. That was what the forgeries made clear. Riots in Rome did not quickly come to an end, but ultimately Theoderic recognized Symmachus; his rival Laurentius retired to a country estate where he died. Meanwhile the bishops of Rome and Constantinople remained out of communion, and Theoderic was going to do nothing to bring them together. No power was going to shift the emperor Anastasius from his support for the Henotikon. But this did not mean that in the Greek east all was peace and quiet.

The Roman claim to a supreme teaching authority elicited a request from an unnamed Greek bishop, probably a prominent metropolitan (Thessalonica being very possible), who asked Pope Symmachus for a more constructive policy to the Greek churches. The Pope should surely use his authority to loose as well as to bind. The patriarch Acacius had made a mistake and in consequence Rome had cut off communion with all the Greek churches, including bishops who affirm Chalcedonian Christology and Leo's Tome, on the ground that they accept bishops who had signed the Henotikon. But when accepting the Henotikon is made a condition of keeping one's see, refusal means abandoning the flock to the wolves. Rejection of the Henotikon is treated as a manifestation of Nestorian sympathies, and rejecting bishops are compelled to abdicate. Could not the Pope use his authority to indicate a middle path between Nestorius and Eutyches? Some voices in the east deny that logically there can be any such middle path; they think that 'two natures' Christology cannot show the unity of Christ, and 'one nature' Christology loses the Lord's humanity. The middle path ends in a row of negations. We must affirm Christ to be both in and of two natures (both prepositions already used by Gelasius).[6]

---

[6] The letter, printed by Thiel as Symmachus, *ep.* 12, survives through an awkward sixth-century Latin version printed in T. Herold's *Orthodoxographia* (Basel, 1555), 906–9. The dilemma that only Nestorius and Eutyches had coherent solutions was put to Severus of Antioch by his correspondent Sergius; see I. R. Torrance, *Christology after Chalcedon, Severus of Antioch and Sergius the Monophysite* (Norwich, 1988).

Boethius' tract 'Against Eutyches and Nestorius' records a meeting in Rome of clergy and senators at which a letter was read from a Greek bishop affirming in and of two natures. Boethius was appalled at the incoherence and arrogance of participants in the discussion.

Dionysius the Areopagite

Under the name of Paul's convert at Athens (Acts 17) an unknown Greek author round about AD 500 composed a body of writings partly intended to make a home within the Church for mystical Neoplatonic language used by Proclus, leader of the Platonic school at Athens who died in 485. The texts naturally have important matter on God and Christ, and the Christological passages were capable of being interpreted either by Chalcedonians or by their critics. Probably therefore the works were composed under the emperor Anastasius and reflect the reserve of the Henotikon of Zeno. Soon competing groups would be quoting from the Areopagite in support of their party, and the earliest references to his work occur in Severus, Monophysite patriarch of Antioch 512–18. Soon too there were doubters of the authenticity of these texts, who argued that these writings were never mentioned by Origen or by Eusebius of Caesarea, or that they presupposed ceremonies and church customs first established long after the first century. The Areopagite was a help to ecumenists aspiring to reconcile Monophysite and Chalcedonian.

Severus of Antioch[7]

The emperor Anastasius did not discourage the Egyptian decision to accept the Henotikon. But this acceptance was given provided its silence could be interpreted as a rejection of the Christology of Chalcedon (about which it said nothing specifically negative), and this gave heart to anti-Chalcedonians not only in Egypt and Syria but also in Constantinople itself. There by reaction they provoked pro-Chalcedonian monks such as the Sleepless (Akoimetai) to very public opposition. In Constantinople Monophysite sympathizers were being strengthened by the advent of the most competent theologian of the age, Severus of Antioch who much impressed the emperor by his qualities as theologian and preacher. He came from a Christian family in Pisidia, studied law at Berytus, and there came under the influence of a zealous ascetic, Evagrius of Samosata. This decided him in favour of being a monk rather than an advocate. He was soon devoting himself to the study of canon law and the writings of Cyril of Alexandria, every sentence of whom he believed to be binding on the Church.

[7] The classic monograph is by J. Lebon, *Le Monophysisme séverien* (Louvain, 1909).

Nephalius, a neo-Chalcedonian

The Egyptian churches produced a controversialist named Nephalius, who at first vexed Peter Mongos by his ultra-Monophysite stand, highly critical of the Henotikon, but then switched allegiance to support Chalcedonian themes. He became a cleric at Jerusalem, persuading the bishop Elias, who was notoriously weak and indecisive, to allow him to harass Palestinian Monophysites, especially at their citadel of Maiuma by Gaza. Nephalius' thought can be reconstructed only from the reply to him by Severus, extant in Syriac. He deployed Aristotelian logic in defence of the 'two natures' formula, and urged recognition not only of the Chalcedonian definition but also of Cyril's Twelve Anathemas; like Pope Gelasius, he affirmed of and in two natures, and also asked his allies to affirm the liturgical formula, hated by Nestorians, 'one of the Trinity suffered in the flesh', chanted as an addition to the Trisagion. The enlarged Trisagion, supported in the capital by Scythian monks who were Chalcedonian, was ordered by the emperor Anastasius in November 512, but a bloody riot ensued, and the order had to be cancelled. To Sleepless monks theopaschite language was objectionable. Soon it would become evident that bishops of Rome disliked it also. Nephalius was far from being the only person to switch his allegiance from one extreme to the other in the controversy. There was traffic in both directions.

In Syria Philoxenus bishop of Hierapolis was fervent in his aversion to Chalcedon. He attacked Patriarch Flavian of Antioch for tolerating such belief. The resulting disorder led to the deposition of Flavian and his replacement by Severus, nominated by the emperor Anastasius on condition, which he did not fulfil, that he did not attack Chalcedon. Meanwhile the emperor's relations with Pope Symmachus were passing from bad to worse. Anastasius declined to recognize Symmachus as validly elected, and, probably correctly, thought him responsible for a rebuff received from Roman senators, who could not afford to anger Theoderic by favouring east Rome, as the life and death of Boethius would demonstrate in 525.

Pope Hormisdas (514–23)

On 19 July 514 Symmachus died and was succeeded by his deacon Hormisdas—his name indicates Persian ancestry. His eastern policy meant no change, but he sent two legations vainly trying to persuade Anastasius to abandon the ambiguous Henotikon. Negotiations ended in deadlock with Hormisdas insisting that the emperor's duty was to submit to the superior authority of the bishop of Rome, and with the emperor's last letter to Hormisdas complaining 'I can tolerate being insulted but not being ordered about' (Avell. 138 = Hormisdas, *ep.* 38, p. 814 Thiel). Anastasius correctly foresaw that the imposing of Rome's conditions on the Greek churches would produce urban riots and loss of life, as indeed turned out to be the case, and would do nothing to reconcile Egypt.

Justin, emperor 518–27

The emperor Anastasius died aged 88 on 9 July 518, and was succeeded by Justin, a Balkan soldier born of a peasant family, who had risen to high office checking rebellion by a Gothic soldier Vitalian in Thrace. Vitalian had gained support against Anastasius by declaring his allegiance to Chalcedonian faith, which went with his cordial dislike of Severus of Antioch. (Bishop Flavian, whom Severus had ousted at Antioch, was his godson.) Justin won support by bribery and, though elderly and white-haired, was invested as Augustus on 10 July 518. *The Book of Ceremonies* (1. 93) describes the procedure. His nephew Justinian in practice administered his empire, and was declared co-emperor on April 527. Justin died four months later. He and Justinian saw before long that political control of the west could be recovered from the barbarian kings and princes more easily by restoring unity between the bishops of Old and New Rome. That might not be sufficient, but it was not less than necessary. The new church policy cost non-Chalcedonian officials their positions at court, and one or two of them even lost their lives. Justin realized that the Greek bishops must submit to any demand that the bishop of Rome might make. They were going to comply, but at a cost.

The formula of Hormisdas

In 515 Pope Hormisdas had sent to Constantinople a formula to be signed as a condition of restored communion. This famous text was astonishingly silent about the Christological issue and said not a word about nature or person or hypostasis. It censured Nestorius, Eutyches, Dioscorus, Timothy the Weasel, Peter Mongos, Peter Fuller of Antioch, but especially the Chalcedonian Acacius who had insulted the papacy by communion with heretics without consulting Rome. All those names were to be deleted from diptychs. So too were the names of Acacius's successors at Constantinople, even if they happened to be firm for Chalcedon and Leo. Assent was required to 'all Pope Leo's letters about the Christian faith'. In conclusion, signatories were requesting communion with St Peter's see 'where the catholic religion always remains intact'. (Avellana 116). John bishop of Constantinople in 519 accepted this formula, prefaced, however, by insisting on the authority of the council of Constantinople in 381 as confirming the Nicene faith and by declaring assent to all Leo's letters concerning the correct faith. (One notes the subtle wording; for the Greek mind it is implied that Leo's Tome had authority because he proclaimed what is true, but it was not true merely because he proclaimed it.) John gave his signature with the express assent of Justin (Avellana 159). Hormisdas hailed Justin as 'the dissipator of schism and pride' (*ep.* 140. 2).

The ending of the Acacian schism reduced Italian independence of east Rome. But Italy remained territory governed by the Arian Ostrogoth Theoderic, and relations with Constantinople were uneasy. In 522 the east Roman emperor Justin nominated as the two consuls for the year the two young sons of Boethius whose delight and pride in the honour was enormous. In September of that year Boethius was named Master of the Offices at Ravenna. It could not be without risk to him, however, that it signified favour to him at Constantinople. The ending of schism between Rome and Constantinople was important to him, and his writings on theology (*Opuscula Sacra*) decisively support a neo-Chalcedonian approach to Christology; that is, a reconciliation of Cyril with the Chalcedonian Definition by accepting 'out of two natures' provided 'in two natures' is also affirmed. His attempt to eliminate bribery and corruption won him many enemies among those whom he called 'court dogs', mainly Roman aristocrats like himself. Dangerous gossip speculated who might be successor to the septuagenarian Theoderic. Hostile plots produced Boethius' imprisonment at Pavia (Ticinum) where he wrote his masterpiece 'The Consolation of Philosophy' with an impassioned discussion of the logical problems for belief in providence and freedom in face of evil. At the end he was clubbed to death.

A possible occasion for the judicial murder may well have been reaction to the decision by Justin to close down Arian churches in the east, provoking Theoderic's wrath. Theoderic sent Pope John I to Constantinople with senior senators to express his anger. Unfortunately for the Pope's standing at Ravenna, John was received with immense acclamation, celebrating a Latin mass at Easter 'with full voice' (contrasting perhaps with the incipient custom of silent recitation of the canon), and even crowning Justin. The western embassy won a concession which excepted Goths from Justin's anti-heretical edict (CJ 1. 5. 12. 17). But on returning to Ravenna they met extreme displeasure from king Theoderic, were imprisoned, and there Pope John died. This and Boethius' death were tyrannical acts very damaging to the reputation and honour of Theoderic's rule. As part of the subsequent mending of fences between Ravenna and Constantinople, the noble mosaic portraits of Justinian and Theodora at San Vitale in Ravenna stand as a monument.

55

JUSTINIAN, ORIGEN, AND THE 'THREE CHAPTERS'

Theodora

In 527 the emperor Justin died and was succeeded by his nephew Justinian, aged 45, also a native of Illyricum but unlike Justin well educated (*PLRE* ii. 648). During his illiterate uncle's reign he already in effect governed the empire, and was joint emperor from 1 April 527 until Justin's death on 1 August. In 523 he had married Theodora, like himself of modest social origins, who in a colourful and turbulent past had been mistress to a governor of Libya and then, after being discarded, earned a precarious living as a low music-hall artiste. The historian Procopius nursed cordial hatred for both her and her imperial husband and on death his 'Secret History' (*Anekdota*) was found among his papers making a ferocious attack, a high proportion of which appears factually true.[1] At one point in her miserable past life at Alexandria she had turned for help to a Monophysite priest, and in consequence her sympathies were marked by strong reserve towards the Chalcedonian 'two natures'. To her resolute courage during the seditious Nika riot in January 532, a revolt which destroyed much of the city including St Sophia, Justinian owed his survival. He wanted to flee and was stopped by her adapting Isocrates (*Archidamus* 45), that 'this purple robe will make a fine winding-sheet for my burial.' She was a compound of catgut and steel. The riot by destroying the old church of Holy Wisdom, enabled the building of the extant engineering and architectural masterpiece dedicated in 537. The dome partly fell after an earthquake in 558. Rededication was in 562. Theodora's monogram is on half the columns, Justinian's on the other half. She was reckoned to share fully in the imperial office, at least as potent as Justinian (Procopius, *Anekdota* 17. 27 and 30. 24. At audiences her feet were kissed (15. 15). Her monogram was also on state seals.

[1] Averil Cameron, *Procopius and the Sixth Century* (London, 1985). See also *Antiquité tardive*, 8 (2000), *passim*, for his panegyric on Justinian's buildings.

Justinian supreme governor of the whole Church[2]

Theology was a subject in which Justinian was expert, but he was also able to put his jurists led by Tribonian to produce a *Digest* of great lawyers of the past like Ulpian, and also a revised code of currently valid edicts and his own new laws or Novels. A proportion of these laws concerned the Church which he ruled. In addition he expended large sums on fine buildings, many of which were churches, of which the most famous are two still standing in Constantinople dedicated to Holy Wisdom and to the Syrian saints Sergius and Bacchus. The latter building served as a home for Monophysites for whom Theodora provided a sanctuary of refuge. At Constantinople he also rebuilt the church of the apostles for which he asked Rome to supply relics of St Laurence (Avell. 218). This, a model for St Mark's Venice, lasted till 1453. Several of his new churches were dedicated to the Mother of God.

For Justinian it was self-evident that the primatial authority of Old Rome, 'caput orbis terrarum', was fully shared with New Rome (CJ I. 17. 1. 10), but that the highest dogmatic authority in the Church was in practice as well as in theory the consensus of the five patriarchs, among whom Old Rome was acknowledged leader (Novel 123. 3; 131. 2). The emperor did not understand the Roman see as possessing jurisdiction over the eastern patriarchs.

Monks dispute about Origen

'Any difference between priesthood and empire is small' (Novel 7. 2. 1), and responsibility for protecting orthodoxy lay with the emperor (Novel 6, preface). When the monks of Palestine became passionately divided about the more mystical teachings of Evagrius of Pontos, Didymus the Blind, and Origen,[3] it was Justinian's duty to issue in 543/4 a decree of condemnation which cited excerpts from or ascribed to Origen. He then successfully invited the five patriarchs to assent (*ACO* III 189–214). Pope Vigilius signed (*ACO* IV i. 114. 11). Legislation combining secular and ecclesiastical matters laid the foundation for the later 'Nomocanon' in which imperial laws and conciliar canons would be fused.

---

[2] See K. L. Noethlichs in *RAC* s.v. Iustinianus (1999) and K. H. Uthemann, 'Kaiser Iustinian als Kirchenpolitiker und Theologe,' *Augustinianum,* 39 (1999), 5–83.

[3] See A. Guillaumont, *Les Kephalaia Gnostica d'Évagre le Pontique et l'histoire de l'origénisme chez les Grecs et les Syriens* (Paris, 1962). Offence was caused by speculation, attributed to Origen, that resurrection bodies will be spherical, that being the perfect shape in Plato's *Timaeus.*

Rescuing the west from barbarian control

Besides theology, law, and buildings Justinian dreamt of restoring the empire, and the historian Procopius brilliantly recorded his wars of reconquest against the Persians, against Vandals in north Africa,[4] against Goths in Italy (this being particularly destructive and long drawn out), and against Visigoths in Spain, where the success of Roman arms was limited. These barbarians were Arians. He probably planned war against the Franks in Gaul, but their leader Clovis had recently been converted to catholic orthodoxy and brought his Franks with him in a tribal conversion. Fighting them would therefore have seemed inappropriate. He seems to have foreseen trouble from the Arabs on the eastern frontier, and built some strong points to withstand minor raids. Their insufficiency was to become clear not long after his time.

Rescuing the east from anti-Chalcedonian Christology

A restored and unified empire was to be complemented by a splendidly united Church. Both heresy and paganism were to be excluded. An astonishing law (Novel 146) rules that in synagogues (evidently using Greek for worship) Jews must use the Septuagint or the painfully literal version of Aquila so that prophecies may convert them. Small sects could be given severe treatment, but the Monophysites were strong in Egypt, Syria, and Asia Minor. Moreover, his wife's heart was with them, and he did not believe they were really heretical. His method of conciliation was to concede to the Monophysites everything they asked for, but they must allow the legitimacy of the preposition in the Chalcedonian 'in two natures'. Severus the extruded bishop of Antioch who, with numerous anti-Chalcedonians loyal to him in Syria and beyond the Euphrates, had lost his see on the death of Anastasius and the lapse of the Henotikon in 518, was invited to the capital, but remained in hiding in Egypt.

The debate of 532

In 532 a debate was held in Justinian's presence between five Chalcedonian bishops and five (perhaps more) anti-Chalcedonians, contemporary accounts of which survive both in Syriac from a Monophysite standpoint, and in a Latin version from the Chalcedonian side, the latter probably less trustworthy

---

[4] After the recovery of Carthage new baths were named after Theodora: Procopius *Aedif.* 6. 5. 8–10.

on detail. Among the Chalcedonians were Leontius of Jerusalem and Anthimus of Trebizond, later to be patriarch of Constantinople, inwardly sympathetic to the Monophysites. The leading Chalcedonian was Hypatius of Ephesus. The Monophysite bishops had left their sees after 518 when they had been required to sign the Roman libelli from Pope Hormisdas demanding condemnation of Peter the Fuller of Antioch, Acacius of Constantinople, and Peter of Alexandria (probably Mongos), i.e. supporters of the Henotikon. In 532 Severus of Antioch had been invited, but his whereabouts remained unknown. Among the Monophysites was Sergios of Cyrrhos, surprisingly an admirer of his predecessor Theodoret. The Chalcedonians asked how one could defend Dioscorus when at Ephesus in 449 he had received Eutyches to communion as orthodox. Objection was also raised to Monophysite appeals to an inauthentic 'Dionysius the Areopagite' and to their use of Apollinarian forgeries. Next day the Monophysites countered by asking how one could defend the decision at Chalcedon to accept Theodoret and Ibas of Edessa, sharp critics of Cyril's Twelve Anathemas. They could accept Chalcedonian ordinations as valid if they held communion with the orthodox (i.e. Severan Monophysites or 'Syrian Orthodox'). The Chalcedonians offered no defence of Theodoret and Ibas, and faced citations from Cyril of Alexandria affirming one nature.

Justinian came to their rescue, in conciliatory manner affirming the anti-Chalcedonians to be orthodox in intention but with scruples about details and about names in diptychs. The record shows Justinian conceding virtually everything including censure of Diodore, Theodore, Theodoret of Cyrrhos, Ibas, affirming Cyril's Twelve Anathemas, even allowing 'one nature of God the Word incarnate' provided the Monophysites did not anathematize two natures after the union or the Tome of Leo. As Chalcedon condemned Eutyches, it deserved their approval. They need not accept the Chalcedonian Definition, but could agree to its censure of Eutyches and Nestorius. (Severus of Antioch, cited in Ps.-Zach. 9. 20, regarded this as unscrupulous.) However, 'the *libelli* of the *Rhomaioi* should not be suspended.' In other words, as a condition of reinstatement they must assent to the censure of the Henotikon and its supporters, on which Rome was intransigent.

This last proposition would in practice make it impossible for the Monophysite bishops to return to their sees. Justinian's intention was to make it clear that if the Monophysites refused reunion, that would not be on any theological ground and their obstinacy would get the blame.[5] His ingenious

---

[5] The letter of the Balkan bishop Innocentius of Maroneia to Thomas priest of Thessalonica describes the Chalcedonian side (*ACO* IV ii. 169–84); the Monophysite or Syrian Orthodox side in Harvard MS. syr. 22, found and published by S. P. Brock, *Orientalia Christiana Periodica*, 47 (1981), 87–121. It was probably written by the monk John of Aphthonia who accompanied the

compromise adumbrated the issue of the Three Chapters. Justinian realized that the Monophysite participants in the colloquy were not important enough, and in any event the outcome had not been positive; the rival accounts answered to the need of the parties to justify their unyielding stance. He needed to capture the mind of Severus, soon afterwards persuaded to come to Constantinople, where Severus won the mind of the patriarch Anthimus.

Patriarch Anthimus

After the debates of 532 Theodora was able to use a vacancy in the patriarchate of Constantinople to have installed Anthimus bishop of Trebizond (Trapezous). A respected ascetic, he had participated in discussions of 532 as one on the Chalcedonian side, but was inwardly persuaded by Severus' moderate brand of Monophysite doctrine. There was no wide gulf between Severus and neo-Chalcedonians insisting on the concord between Chalcedon and Cyril, i.e. that Chalcedon be interpreted by Cyril, not vice versa. Admittedly it was no simple task to prove Cyril an unqualified Chalcedonian or Chalcedon fully Cyrilline. Confidentially Patriarch Anthimus held communion with Severus and Theodosius, Monophysite patriarch of Alexandria (resident in Constantinople), on the ground of the first three councils and the Henotikon. Naturally this crucial fact leaked. Alarm bells were rung by Ephraim of Antioch, a former Count of Oriens and a well-equipped Chalcedonian, writing not only to Justinian but also to Pope Agapetus. Agapetus travelled to Constantinople, deposed Anthimus (given shelter by Theodora, who was already housing 500 monks), and consecrated Menas, who had been responsible for a hospital in the capital. To Agapetus it was a source of glowing triumph that the bishop of Rome had consecrated for the see of New Rome. Perhaps he hoped it would be a precedent for the future. Justinian undertook to maintain Chalcedonian faith. Agapetus fell ill and died (22 April 536). Justinian saw to it that his funeral was of immense solemnity. His body was buried at St Peter's, Rome. In 536 a council in Constantinople condemned Severus and fellow Monophysites; Justinian enforced the decision (Novel 168). A similar exile was imposed on the militant Syriac-speaking Monophysite, Philoxenus of Mabbug (Hierapolis),

---

bishops; he wrote a Life of Severus extant in a Syriac version (PO 2. 2. 1907). An important summary of the colloquy in PO 13 (1919), 192–6. A Monophysite position paper in Ps.-Zach. 9. 15: they stood by Nicaea, Constantinople 381, and Ephesus 431, rejecting Eutyches, but also the innovations of Leo and Chalcedon. See W. H. C. Frend, *The Rise of the Monophysite Movement*, 362–6; discussion by J. Speigl, *Annuarium Historiae Conciliorum*, 16 (1984), 264–85. J. W. Watt, 'A portrait of John of Aphthonia', *Portraits of Spiritual Authority* (Leiden, 1999), 155–70.

important for his labours on the Syriac version of the Bible and for his exegetical writings.[6] Another, quieter critic of Chalcedonian language was Jacob of Serug (Batnae near Edessa), who observed that definitions are divisive.[7]

Three Chapters

To Monophysites the (to them) blatant Nestorianism of Chalcedon was unmasked by the liking which some partisans had for Theodore of Mopsuestia, Theodoret of Cyrrhus, and Ibas of Edessa or at least for the letter critical of Cyril, attributed to Ibas addressed to the Persian Mari of Nisibis, approved at Chalcedon. The scheming bishop Theodore Askidas of Caesarea in Cappadocia (who lived in Constantinople) admired Origen and, because Theodore of Mopsuestia had written against Origen's allegorism, saw possibilities in suggesting to Justinian that he should allay the controversy about Origen by concentrating on these patrons of Nestorius (Liberatus 24, *ACO* II v. 140, writing at Carthage about 565). Ingeniously, one could condemn the person as well as the doctrine of Theodore as Chalcedon said nothing about him, but only the doctrine of Theodoret and Ibas' letter.

A terrible plague which swept through much of the empire from 542 and which Justinian was lucky to survive could easily be interpreted as a judgement on Christian division. Justinian became convinced that reconciliation between Chalcedonians and Monophysites might be possible if he issued an edict condemning these three names; this was issued about 544, and he then planned to have it confirmed by a substantial synod of bishops in 553 at Constantinople. It was necessary to this end to deny that the letter of Ibas approved at Chalcedon was the anti-Cyrillian piece in the Acts of that council, which must therefore be a forgery in Ibas' name infiltrated into the conciliar acts by Nestorian sympathizers. This fiction would leave the great council of 451 untarnished.[8]

John Philoponus

At predominantly Monophysite Alexandria a very able teacher of Neoplatonic exegesis of Aristotle was John Philoponus. He was unimpressed

---

[6] A. de Halleux, *Philoxène de Mabbog* (Louvain, 1963).

[7] See T. Jansma, 'Encore le Crédo de Jacques de Saroug', *Orient syrien*, 10 (1965), 75–88, 193–236, 311–70, 475–510.

[8] Edict condemning the Three Chapters: PG 86. 1041–95 has suffered abbreviation; full critical edition by E. Schwartz. *Drei dogmatische Schriften Iustinians*, Abh. der Bay. Akad., NF 18, Munich, 1939; repr. Milan 1973; English version by K. P. Wesche, *On the Person of Christ: The Theology of Emperor Justinian* (New York, 1991). Since the colloquy of 532 Justinian was now aware of Apollinarian forgeries.

by appeals to the ecumenical authority of Chalcedon, Rome, and the emperor Marcian; Leo's Tome undermined any special teaching authority in St. Peter's successor. The ecumenicity and imperial ratification of the second council of Ephesus in 449 had not counted for much in Leo's or Pulcheria's eyes. Philoponus presented a logical critique in a work entitled *Arbiter*, extant complete in Syriac (ed. A. Šanda, Beirut, 1930); substantial fragments of the original Greek survive. It is a remarkably irenic work, even allowing 'in two natures' provided one adds that the union produces 'one composite nature'. Such concession attracted sharp criticism from his own party, and he had to write two works in defence. Neo-Chalcedonians could be content to say that Christ of two natures is composite, but 'one composite nature' seemed too much for them to grant. Philoponus wrote to Justinian expounding his position, and he can be seen to have affected Justinian's language from 551 onwards and even the wording of canons approved at the council in 553.

Pope Vigilius[9]

If Justinian's substantial synod was to rank as 'ecumenical', the emperor would need the presence and support of the bishop of Rome, Vigilius (pope 537–55) son of a praetorian prefect of Italy and brother of a prefect of Rome. Made deacon by the Goth Boniface II (the first German pope, 530–2), Vigilius had served Pope Agapetus (535–6) as apocrisiary at Constantinople, and came to know the empress Theodora. She saw in him a possible agent for her Monophysite objectives if her influence could somehow install him at the Roman see. She provided him with 700 gold pieces to encourage his support. He returned to Rome probably with Agapetus' body during the Gothic war. There by bribery in June 536 the Gothic king Theodahad had fixed the election of Hormisdas' son Silverius to be Pope, but Theodahad was soon replaced by another Goth, Vitiges, and Justinian's general Belisarius was able to capture Rome (December 536). By March, however, Vitiges returned to lay siege. Some prayers preserved in the Verona ('Leonine') Sacramentary probably belong to the time of this siege.

Belisarius' wife was a friend of Theodora, and it soon became clear that Silverius could not remain in his post unless he was willing to play Theodora's game. In any event he appeared in league with the Goths to whom he owed his election. In December 537, deposed by Belisarius for treachery (Procopius, *Bell.* 5. 25. 13) and starved by Vigilius (so the *Liber Pontificalis*) he died. Procopius (*Anecdota* 1. 14 and 27) agrees that Silverius was murdered. While Silverius was still alive, Vigilius was already in office as Pope since the

⁹ See A. Lippold, art. Vigilius, in PWK Suppl. XIV (1974); E. Schwartz, *Gesammelte Schriften*, iv, reprints his paper of 1940 (his last) on Justinian; a list of Vigilius' pieces in conciliar Acts by R. Schieffer in *ACO* IV iii/1 488–90.

end of March 537, a situation raising awkward questions about validity. Theodora's arm had been long. He was to hold the papacy for eighteen years. The Gothic war did not make the city agreeable to live in. Perhaps it was so briefly in 544 when the poet Arator recited to him his versification of the Acts of the Apostles in the church of St Peter 'in Vincoli'. In any event most of the surviving evidence for his pontificate is either his correspondence with Caesarius of Arles, through whom papal authority in Gaul was maintained, or his dealings with the policies of Justinian at Constantinople. Despite service as apocrisiary he knew no Greek (Avell. 83, CSEL 35. 297. 2–4). A letter to Profuturus of Braga is important for liturgical evidence about the canon of the Latin mass at this date. Famine at Rome made the city population critical of Vigilius to the point of bombarding him with stones. (It is instructive that the *plebs* regarded him as in part responsible for ensuring the food supply.) Could he not sail to Sicily and arrange for better food supplies from papal estates? Vigilius himself thought Sicily would be a more congenial place to be.

In November 545 while Goths generalled by Totila were besieging Rome, imperial soldiers, perhaps stage-managed by Belisarius to forestall a Gothic capture of the pope with the city, interrupted a festival service on 22 November at St Cecilia's church (Trastevere) to inform Pope Vigilius that the emperor commanded his presence in Constantinople without delay. A ship took him to Sicily where he stayed some months seeing to the sending of food to Rome. He was probably glad to be for a time in neither Old nor New Rome. While in Sicily he began to receive alarming information from the bishop of Milan about Justinian's intentions to arrange a conciliar condemnation of the 'Three Chapters', Theodore, Theodoret, and Ibas.

Vigilius' Judicatum (548) condemns the Three Chapters

To bishops in northern Italy, Illyricum, and Africa the emperor's plan was a subtle indirect attack on Chalcedon and Pope Leo, 'selling the pass to the Monophysites'. On his slow journey east Vigilius informed patriarch Menas that he was against the proposal. He finally arrived in Constantinople in January 547 to be welcomed by the emperor. Months were spent studying writings of Theodore of Mopsuestia done into Latin for his benefit, and in Holy Week 548 he issued a verdict or 'Judicatum' extant only in fragments[10] in which he condemned Theodore's writings, the letter of Ibas, and the writings of Theodoret against the Twelve Anathemas of Cyril, while also affirming Chalcedon. This was addressed to patriarch Menas. Copies were widely circulated by Vigilius' nephew and deacon Rusticus, who actually

---

[10] *ACO* IV i. 11 f. and Avell. 83. 299–302, CSEL 35. 316–17.

regarded the condemnation as a mistake and seems to have circulated copies to arouse opposition (*ACO* IV i. 188–9). Vigilius felt betrayed by him. He had not been instructed to send the text to north Italy, north Africa, and southern Gaul. From Arles came tough questions: had not the Pope sacrificed Leo's Tome?

The Judicatum withdrawn, then maintained in private on oath

Episcopal synods in the west were seriously alarmed. Bishops in Illyricum and north Africa expressed disapprobation, and those in north Africa went so far as to declare Vigilius excommunicate. He seemed to be undermining the council of Chalcedon, which had accepted two of the three now named 'heretics'. A bishop of Rome denounced by many western provinces was no use to Justinian. The pope decided that he had made a mistake and pleaded that the verdict had been extracted under coercion. He had not been clear about the emperor's intentions; surely the mistake had been Justinian's. Behind the scenes, however, on 15 August 550 he took a secret and solemn oath to the emperor that he would sustain his condemnation of the Three Chapters, on condition that the oath was kept secret and the privileges of his see were preserved. This clandestine oath was formally witnessed by Theodore Askidas of Caesarea and Cethegus a patrician and senator (*ACO* IV/1. 198–9).

Justinian's Edict on the true faith (551)

Vigilius' attempts to avert Justinian's wrath could no longer rely on Theodora who died of cancer in June 548. In any event she would have been vexed by a failure to damn the Three Chapters. Justinian would not allow him to leave Constantinople. Vigilius urged that the question be referred to a council, but painfully few bishops came from the west to attend. In 551 Justinian impatiently issued a new edict condemning the Three Chapters, a small part of his argument being perhaps an implicit reply to Philoponus since there are echoes of his philosophical terms. The edict keeps the Chalcedonian distinction of the two natures of God and man but approves of Cyril's Apollinarian formula 'one nature of God the Word incarnate'. The analogy of human body and soul was no argument for Monophysite Christology. Thirteen anathemas condemn Theodore, Theodoret, and Ibas' alleged letter. The contention that heretics who died in the peace of the Church cannot be posthumously censured, a consideration which weighed with Cyril of Alexandria, is refuted from precedents.[11] Vigilius could be reminded that he had agreed to the condemnation of the long-dead Origen.

---

[11] Text in PG 86. 993–1035; critical edition by E. Schwartz, English version by K. P. Wesche (see n. 8). This major text, though included in the *Chronicon Paschale*, is omitted on ground of

The text was posted at St Sophia and elsewhere. Vigilius was angered by a breach in an agreement made with Justinian that, until the western opponents had stated their objections, there should be no formal condemnation of the Three Chapters, and in synod used anti-imperial language to a degree which led him and his western allies to seek asylum at a church altar. He excommunicated Theodore Askidas and Patriarch Menas on 14 August 551 but without publishing this fact. Askidas and Menas were able to restore communion with Vigilius by assuring him that they had issued no condemnation of the Three Chapters. But the emperor ordered his arrest, and he was rescued from the soldiers by a mob (evidently no admirers of their emperor). Eminent senators were sent to assure him that if he returned to his lodging, he would be unmolested. In practice it was house arrest, and before Christmas 551 he escaped by night across the water to find asylum at Chalcedon in St Euphemia's shrine. No one would interfere with him in so venerated a place. And it would be cold.

The emperor was sensitive to the criticism that his decision to condemn the Three Chapters was motivated by a political need to keep the loyalty of Egypt and Syria in his endeavour to maintain the unity of the empire. He strenuously denied this: his only motive was to uphold the true faith. Naturally he realized that a condemnation should please the Monophysites, whom he evidently respected. The hinterland of the province of Asia was still largely pagan. Justinian could commission and finance a Monophysite monk, John, to use Ephesus as a base for evangelism. John claimed to have built 98 churches, 12 monasteries, and converted 80,000. In 550 to harass Montanists he burnt the relics of Montanus, Maximilla, and Priscilla (F. Nau, *Revue de l'Orient chrétien*, 2 (1897), 489). After Theodora's death Monophysite refugees housed by her in the palace of Hormisdas (now Küçükayasofya) were often visited by Justinian asking for their blessing (so John of Ephesus, *Lives of the Eastern Saints*, PO 17. 680). John wrote a church history, the extant part of which is a major source for Justinian's last decade.[12]

Council of Constantinople, May 553

Justinian realized that he needed to conciliate rather than to bully or torture. In time Vigilius could return to his lodging. The emperor remained determined on the plan for a great council. He would not listen to a request by Vigilius that simultaneously he hold a council in Italy to consider the Three Chapters. But he granted that the Pope could name a few western bishops to

length in the valuable English translation by Michael and Mary Whitby (Translated Texts for Historians, Liverpool, 1989). A second edition (forthcoming) will include it.

[12] J. van Ginkel, *John of Ephesus, A Monophysite Historian* (Diss., Groningen, 1995).

attend in Constantinople. At the four earlier ecumenical councils there were present 'only two or three' bishops from the west. Request for delay did not come well from a bishop of Rome who had already been in Constantinople for several years. In preparation Vigilius was formally asked for a statement on the Three Chapters. That took him time, and the council meanwhile opened on 5 May at St Sophia in the secretarium of the patriarchate with 152 bishops.

Vigilius and his western supporters did not attend (Avell. 83. 308 ff.). His reason given was that the Greek bishops outnumbered the Latin (a plea which was weak in face of the overwhelming Greek majorities at the four ecumenical councils). He amazed the Greeks by proposing that the question of the Three Chapters be referred to a body of eight, viz. himself with three western bishops, balanced by three Greek patriarchs and one bishop. It was explained to him that each Greek patriarch would expect to be supported by as many as the Latins supporting Vigilius. To the Greek council Vigilius' absence seemed arrogance. He assumed that the council was advisory, an expression of popular opinion, and that it was for him then to judge of the consensus of east and west. If he would not attend, neither would his Latin colleagues: 'Papa non praesente non venio', they said (*ACO* IV i. 29. 33). For the Greeks, if the Latins stayed away, that could not invalidate proceedings. Moreover, Vigilius' absence was understood to mean that, whether from personal conviction or because of strong pressure from the Latins, he was against any censure of the Three Chapters.

Patriarch Menas having died (24 August 552), the council was under the presidency of his successor Eutychius. The first session heard Justinian's letter specifically citing Vigilius' 'Judicatum' of 548 and other papal disparagements of the Three Chapters quoted from his letters notably to Justinian and to Theodora. The emperor defensively emphasized that at Nicaea Constantine had been present; at Constantinople in 381 Theodosius was there; Theodosius II directed the council of Ephesus in 431 by appointing judges; and Marcian attended at Chalcedon. Evidently he was meeting criticism of the too active participation by the lay theologian in the palace. Pope Agapetus had bluntly expressed reservations on this subject (Avell. 82. 3, CSEL 35. 229. 21 'non quia laicis auctoritatem praedicationis admittimus').

Vigilius behaved as if he had juridical authority over all the eastern patriarchs as well as over the emperor. Justinian was clear that the five patriarchs were equal in canonical authority and that Rome was no more than *primus inter pares*, as it were a dean among colleagues. Moreover, the bishop of Rome had become a disputant in the case, and disputants could not simultaneously be judges. At Chalcedon that point had been made to the Roman legates by the presiding lay grandees and was not disputed.

Vigilius' first Constitutum

On 14 May 553 Vigilius sent in his first 'Constitutum' addressed to Justinian (Avell. 83). He was offended that his request for a synod in Italy and Sicily had been rejected. He reiterated his absolute allegiance to the 'four councils', i.e. including Chalcedon in his canon (a matter on which of course the emperor, who had lately directed that the ecumenical councils be included in diptychs, wholly agreed). He then devoted many pages to quoting damaging passages from Theodore of Mopsuestia. Despite their admitted shortcomings, it was wrong in principle to excommunicate those who died in the peace of the Church; in the Acts of Chalcedon there stood no allusion to Theodore. Therefore 'we do not dare to condemn or to allow that he be condemned by anyone else' (CSEL 35. 292. 24) . Theodoret is briefly treated, Ibas at great length. The document ends with a substantial quotation from the 'Judicatum' of 548 anathematizing any questioning of the four councils because they were confirmed by the apostolic see, evidently carrying the implication that Justinian's synod would also need Vigilius' ratification if it were to be generally accepted. Appended are seventeen episcopal signatures with three Roman deacons, one being Pelagius, hitherto a loyal supporter of his bishop and the author of an eloquent extant defence of the Three Chapters, but in time to become hesitant and to change his mind. As a deacon, in collaboration with another deacon John, he made an extant Latin translation of the *Apophthegms* of the desert Fathers (edited by H. Rosweyde, Antwerp, 1612).

Vigilius dropped from the diptychs; the Three Chapters condemned

Vigilius' absence from the council was thought by the Greek bishops to be incompatible with his claim to act as the senior bishop in the universal Church. At a seventh session on 14 July 553 the emperor's letter was read directing that Vigilius' name be deleted from the diptychs. Communion with the apostolic see was unaffected if the transitory incumbent was excluded (a text which became important for seventeenth-century Gallicans). No formal condemnation was enacted thereby.

At its eighth and final session the council approved fourteen technical theological canons, defending Chalcedon's 'two natures' and disavowing in canon 5 a doctrine ascribed to Chalcedonian divines by John Philoponus, namely that the one hypostasis in Christ can be interpreted to cover a plurality of hypostases. The fourth canon affirms 'union by synthesis' (Greek: *ACO* IV i. 240–5; Latin 215–20), terms congenial to Severus of Antioch and to Philoponus. A formal synodical verdict condemned the Three Chapters. At the same time some terminology of the canons went far to offer appeasement to the Monophysites. John Philoponus was decisive that such language was irreconcilable with that used at Chalcedon.

The Latin transmission of the Fifth Council's Acts

When one considers the aura of sanctity attached by the Orthodox churches of the east to the Seven Ecumenical Councils, it seems at first sight paradoxical that the record of the Fifth Council survives in the very early Latin translation with only a few bits and pieces in Greek. The reason for this refusal of Greek scribes to copy the Acts may be at least partly explained by a letter of Vigilius quoted at the seventh session, in which he affirmed that in Christ there is not only one *subsistentia* and persona but also 'one operation', or in Greek 'one *enérgeia*' (*ACO* IV i. 188. 14). At the Sixth Council at Constantinople in 680 this hazardous doctrine, exploited by the advocates of 'one activity, one will', was disowned by the Roman legates. The Council of 680, being opposed to 'one *enérgeia*', wanted to believe that the record had been tampered with. But authenticity is more probable.

Vigilius' second Constitutum (554) capitulates

On 8 December 553 Vigilius, still in Constantinople, addressed a letter to patriarch Eutychius, regretting that he had made a mistake; but even the brilliant Augustine had written *Retractationes* when he changed his mind. Reflection had convinced the Pope that the Three Chapters were rightly condemned, that Cyril's Twelve Anathemas were correct, and that therefore anything written by Vigilius himself or by others in defence of the Three Chapters was hereby annulled (*ACO* IV i. 245–7). On 23 February 554 Vigilius issued his second 'Constitutum' reiterating the ratification of the Council implied by his letter to Eutychius of December (*ACO* IV ii. 138–68) which was freely quoted. That meant that at long last he could be free to return to Rome. He stayed on at Constantinople until 13 August, perhaps delaying to gain information about the degree of fury in the west. He died on the journey at Syracuse on 7 June 555, evidently after a long stay in Sicily. The probability is high that reports from Rome and the mainland were to the effect that his reception there would be hot. Perhaps in anticipation of trouble, Justinian (Novel app. 7. 1) when issuing a pragmatic sanction for the restoration of public order in Italy after Totila's Goths had been defeated, gave prominence at the beginning of this long document to the fact that it had been issued on the petition of Vigilius. The document was dated 13 August 554; perhaps Vigilius took it with him on taking leave before embarkation.

Pope Pelagius I

After a lengthy interregnum Justinian decided that the deacon Pelagius, who had written in defence of the Three Chapters, could also change his mind if offered the see of Rome. By long tradition bishops of Rome were consecrated by the bishop of Ostia, but in this case finding three bishops willing to consecrate him turned out to be difficult. Eventually it was done by two. The imperial nomination of the bishop of Rome established a precedent for future elections. Pelagius faced defiant schisms in north Italy and in north Africa, but told the Roman clergy and people that he had done Vigilius no injury. By abstaining from giving any reasons and relying wholly on the authority of his see, Pelagius maintained the correctness of the Fifth Council, which had in no way diminished the standing of the council of Chalcedon. Pope Gregory the Great and later canonists wrote of the first four ecumenical councils as possessing a greater aura of authority than the subsequent assemblies. Already in Justinian's time people spoke of a canon of four councils parallel to four gospels.

Any estimate of Vigilius is problematic. He does not figure in the story as an impressive character, and he was not a theologian capable of coping with Christological intricacies. He owed promotion to Theodora, and one would wish that he had not accepted her gold. Yet with a Gothic war in Italy and a society of intense intrigue at Constantinople, his task was extremely difficult. Sympathy can at least go to the length of being sorry for him in the situations confronting him, representing a Latin west in high tension with the eastern emperor and the Greek churches. He was in dangerous waters.

The failure of appeasement

The ecumenism of Justinian was not blighted by nationalism or by non-theological factors, but by the inherent intransigence of the parties he sought to reconcile. Those who felt that they had learnt from Cyril of Alexandria to affirm 'one nature in the incarnate Lord' were convinced that Chalcedon's 'two natures' must be condemned. They could accept the Henotikon only by insisting that it be interpreted as saying what it did not say, namely that Chalcedon and Leo be anathematized.

Justinian's reassertion and defence of the 'two natures' doctrine of Chalcedon, admittedly with what was bound to seem dilution, did nothing much for the communities loyal to the memory of Theodore, now mainly flourishing in the Persian empire east of the Euphrates, and carrying the gospel across central Asia to China where 'Nestorian' monuments have been found.[13]

---

[13] The school at Edessa, closed by Zeno in 489, refounded at Persian Nisibis, had a great theologian Babai. Nestorian monks are attested in sixth-century north Africa (S. P. Brock in *Anal. Boll.* 91

His endeavours to placate the Monophysites had the reverse affect to that intended. In his brief years as patriarch of Antioch Severus had taken pains to see to the ordination of soundly anti-Chalcedonian bishops. His endeavours had been systematically destroyed under Justin and Justinian. Deposed bishops had Chalcedonian successors. The Monophysites had come to feel that they had an identity which, either by force or by blandishments, this emperor was threatening.

The Jacobite succession

In 542 Theodosius the Monophysite patriarch of Alexandria moved from Constantinople to Derkos, a fort some 50 km distant in Thrace. He secretly ordained Jacob Burdʿ ana[14] (Baradai) to the see of Edessa and Theodore for Arabia. This was of momentous consequence for the survival of the succession among the Monophysite communities. Otherwise candidates for ordination had to go to Alexandria where they found asylum, though there was always a Chalcedonian patriarch controlling the main sacred sites, such as the shrine of SS. Cyrus and John at Aboukir, famous for curing the ophthalmia common in a dry dusty climate (effective, it was claimed, only for Chalcedonians). Jacob in disguise travelled round Syria and Asia Minor secretly ordaining presbyters for dissenting Monophysite groups. They operated mainly from monasteries. He performed his task with such profusion that the ex-patriarch Anthimus had to ask him to exercise discrimination: too many who could not read or write would be an embarrassment (*PO* 18. 516–17). In time he began also to ordain bishops. Thereby he ensured that the Syrian Orthodox Church and its allies among the Armenians, Copts, and Ethiopians had and still have a due succession of episcopal ministry.[15]

One of the anti-Chalcedonian bishops removed from office by Justin in 518–19 was Julian of Halicarnassus, who like Severus of Antioch found refuge in Egypt.[16] To exclude all duality from the person of Christ, he held that from conception, not only from resurrection, Christ's body shared in 'incorruption' and was without moral taint. He did not share sin and the sting of

(1973), 317). Nestorius had some following among Palestinian monks (Cyril of Scythopolis, *Vita Sabae* 38). In the time of Pope Donus (676–8) Syrian Nestorian monks were discovered in Rome (*Liber Pontificalis* i. 348 Duchesne; *Anal. Boll.* 91 (1973), 318). Severus of Antioch tried to stop the commemoration of Nestorius at Tarsus in Cilicia. In 561–2 Justinian held a discussion between Chalcedonian divines and Paul bishop of Nisibis (*Dumbarton Oaks Papers*, 23/4 (1969–70), 41–66.

[14] Dr Holford-Strevens has acutely suggested that *Burdʿ ana* meaning horse-cloth was Jacob's disguise.

[15] E. Honigmann, *Évêques et évêchés monophysites d'Asie antérieure au VIᵉ siècle* (Louvain, 1951), 157 ff.

[16] R. Draguet, *Julien de Halicarnasse et sa controverse avec Sevère d'Antioche* (Louvain, 1924); also in *Dictionnaire de théologie catholique*, viii. 1931–40.

death. His doctrine, in some respects close to Augustine, was easy for Chalcedonian critics to misrepresent as Eutychian or even Docetist. Severus of Antioch composed tracts against Julian whose book was polemical against Chalcedonian Christology.

One eminent Chalcedonian was impressed by the argument, the emperor Justinian.

Shortly before his death in 565 Justinian issued a last theological edict. For the text there are only indirect reports, but the essential point was a simple declaration that even before Resurrection the body of Christ was free of all corruption, and that he ate food before his Passion in the same way as after it (Evagrius 4. 39–41; a probable fragment in *Doctrina Patrum*, ed. Diekamp, 134). This was to look like an approximation to Christology professed by Julian of Halicarnassus, with a pre-history in Clement of Alexandria's insistence that Christ ate and drank not because he needed to do so but to forestall heretics who said that it was an optical illusion. In the sixth century the doctrine took the form of teaching that the human suffering or experience of Christ was indeed real, but only because the indwelling Logos miraculously allowed it. Justinian's edict was not necessarily out of line with Cyril of Alexandria but it caused distress. The question at issue between Julian and Severus had become a matter of contention among the Monophysites at Alexandria which had resulted in a split. A minority group looked to the moderate bishop Theodosios who was a friend of Severus of Antioch, while a majority followed Gaianus, to whom the physical body of the Lord shared in the incorruptibility of the divine from the moment of conception, not merely from resurrection. Theodosios found that he had to live in Constantinople. His moderate position was one with which orthodox Chalcedonians found it easy to hold conversation. The Alexandrian split, not the only division within the fissiparous Monophysite community, continued well into the seventh century.

Justinian died aged about 83 on 14 November 565, to be succeeded by his nephew Justin II. His Fifth Council at Constantinople in 553 was conceded e.g. by Gregory the Great but without discussing the Three Chapters which were treated in silence. In medieval times the fact that Theodoret criticized Cyril of Alexandria for language associating the Son of God with the Father in the 'procession' of the Holy Spirit and that he was censured by an ecumenical council, became an argument for defending the *Filioque* against Greek critics of this doctrine.

56

THE ANCIENT ORIENTAL CHURCHES

For the apostles Peter and especially Paul Rome was the capital of the Gentile world, and therefore became a focus of Gentile Christianity. The identification of interest between Church and Empire left the legacy that Christianity is commonly thought of as a European religion, even in an age when the majority of believers are not Europeans, and the conversion of Constantine the Great and of his successors other than Julian reinforced a conviction already widely held among the Christians of the Mediterranean world.

But the missionary spirit of the ancient churches looked beyond the frontier. To this day there are substantial Christian bodies with ancient roots in countries where Christianity is not necessarily the predominant allegiance of most of the inhabitants. The Armenians, centred on their much contested native land, were soon rooted in the Holy Land with an ecclesial body at Jerusalem, and the natural abilities of the race carried them to form a colony in Constantinople. The Armenians acquired an extensive dispersion. Unlike the Greek churches of Orthodox tradition they used unleavened bread for the Eucharist, a fact which caused some sharp differentiation in medieval times. They dissented from the Christological Definition of the Council of Chalcedon to which it is unclear whether they were actually invited. In any event Persian hostilities at the time were giving them grave matters to think about. The libraries of the Armenian Church have preserved ancient Christian documents otherwise lost, notably an early version of Irenaeus and the attack on the council of Chalcedon by Timothy the Weasel (Ailouros). The detachment of the Armenians from doctrine and customs normative in the Greek Orthodox communities no doubt assisted the survival of their churches under Persian pressure.

In Persia most of the Christians were expatriates from the Roman Empire, which did not help to assimilate them with the indigenous people. The Persian churches had their focus not at Antioch in Syria but at Seleucia-Ctesiphon (Koke); this structure of authority was in fact set up at the suggestion of the patriarchate of Antioch which sent a deputy, bishop Marutha of Maipherqat, to urge this ordered organization on them at their synod in 410. Fourteen years later their synod formally declared independence of the west. It was also important that they and the Romans (i.e. of New Rome)

celebrated Easter on the same date and that they accepted the Nicene creed
and canons. They suffered insofar as, during the continuous wars between
the Roman Empire and the Persians, they were suspected, with some reason,
of supporting Rome. State persecution led many to seek refuge west of the
Euphrates. The frontier fortress of Nisibis, surrendered to the Persians after
the humiliating débâcle of Julian's campaign in 363, retained its role as a
bridge between Christians on either side with a school partly devoted to
Syrian, partly to Persian Christianity. Theodore of Mopsuestia 'the
Interpreter' long remained the authoritative teacher for its Syriac-speaking
Christians. Nisibis was not to be the home of supporters of Cyril of
Alexandria in the Christological debate.

Syria was the citadel of numerous bishops who venerated Theodore and
therefore his disciple Nestorius, promoted from Antioch to the great see of
Constantinople but with unhappy results. Harassment drove many Christians
who thought Nestorius had been unjustly censured at Ephesus (431) and
Chalcedon (451) to migrate into Persia. It was an easy frontier to cross with
constant trade when war ceased and impossible to guard even during war.
Unfortunately the divisiveness of the Christological controversy made the
churches within the Roman Empire dismiss them as heretics, a split which
had huge effects on the church at Edessa with its two incompatible bishops
Rabbula and his successor Ibas. Similar incompatibility occurred at the metropolitan see of Hierapolis (Mabbog), where Bishop Alexander had opposed
Cyril of Alexandria to the point of being exiled to the mines whereas Bishop
Philoxenos (Xenaia) was a fervent upholder of Cyril's Twelve Anathemas.
The Nestorian Church carried its mission across central Asia to China. Until
1917, when their sympathy for the Russians at war with Turkey brought
upon them a terrible massacre, the Nestorian community survived in south-
eastern Turkey in the vicinity of Hakkari, and Anglican and American
Presbyterian missionaries were able to assist them from a base on the Iranian
side of the frontier (later moving a few thousand survivors to San Francisco).
There in about 1895 it was discovered that this community had preserved
Nestorius' autobiography in Syriac, the *Book of Heraclides*. Before the original was lost in the massacre of 1917 four copies had been made, one of
which, now lost, was used by Bedjan for his printed edition of the Syriac text
(1910). One copy is in Cambridge University Library.[1]

The Syrian Orthodox Church has retained sympathy for Cyril in his least
Chalcedonian moments. In Syria and Jerusalem there are active congregations and, while for everyday use their language today is Arabic, they have

---

[1] Bedjan's text was translated into French by F. Nau (1910). The English version by G. R. Driver
(1925) is unsatisfactory, but the English version by Dom R. H. Connolly of extracts included by
J. F. Bethune-Baker, *Nestorius and his Teaching* (Cambridge, 1908), is reliable.

kept a knowledge of Aramaic. The Arabs first had knowledge of Greek philosophy and science through versions made by Syrians.

The Iberian Church in Georgia, north-east of the Black Sea, had close contacts both with Constantinople and with Armenia, and was conscious of intimate links with Jerusalem. An account of the evangelization of Georgia in the mid-fourth century is given first by Rufinus (*HE* 10. 11) probably dependent on a partially lost history by Gelasius of Caesarea; it was achieved by a woman prisoner, later called St Nino, who converted the queen by wonderful healing.[2] All Greek accounts of the mission depend on Rufinus or Gelasius. However, through Georgian documents we know the calendar and lectionary of the community in Jerusalem in the fifth century. By 400 monasteries were founded there, and Georgian records have been preserved by their monastery on Mount Athos, Iviron or 'Of the Iberians', Iberia being the ancient Greek name for Georgia, Kartli the Georgian name. In the fifth century the prince Peter 'the Iberian' was a prominent monk and critic of the Chalcedonian 'two natures'. Nevertheless in the long run the churches of Georgia did not associate themselves with the anti-Chalcedonians and dissociated from the Armenians probably from 519. In 601 Pope Gregory the Great was in correspondence with the Iberian catholicos and his bishops about the reception of former Nestorians to communion (*Registrum* 11. 52).[3]

Rufinus (11. 6) drawing on Gelasius of Caesarea also records the origins of the church among the Arabs. Late in the fourth century the Arab queen Mavia or Mawiya was leading attacks on the borders of the Roman provinces of Palestine and Arabia. The chronicler Theodoros the Reader (p. 69 Hansen) reports that she had been a woman prisoner from the Roman Empire. Rufinus says nothing of the kind, and it seems unlikely to be true. But that Arab tribes at this time could be led by a woman is otherwise attested (*Expositio totius mundi* 20, SC 124. 154–5) . For Romans any leader of a barbarian tribe would be accorded the title king or queen. Characteristic for the age is the indissoluble link between religion and politics. She agreed to peace on condition a holy monk named Moses was ordained bishop for her Arabs. He would not have been the first bishop for the Arabs, if the record in the manuscript tradition of Socrates (3. 15. 18) with a bishop 'Theotimus of the Arabs' present at a council of 363 under Meletius of Antioch is correct. (G. C. Hansen emends the reading to 'of Arados'.) The implication was evident that she either already was or had decided to be a Christian and that if her Arabs were to be Christians, that could imply an intimate association with the Roman Empire, but that within this association she wanted her Arab

---

[2] The story is examined by F. Thelamon, *Païens et chrétiens au IVᵉ siècle* (Paris, 1981), 85–122.
[3] For the history of the churches of Georgia with rich bibliography see M. van Esbroeck in the Paris journal *Bedi Kartlisa*, 40 (1982), 186–99; G. Garitte in *Dictionnaire de Spiritualité*, vi (1967), 133–56.

Christians to have an organization independent of the empire's structures. She did not think the conversion of her tribe entailed Romanization. Moses' ordination was a matter of some drama. He was taken to Alexandria (not Antioch, where the emperor Valens was resident) to be made bishop. But the then bishop was the Arian Lucius; on the ground that Lucius was responsible for persecutions (in Valens' time), Moses refused to be defiled by his hands, and insisted on being consecrated by pro-Nicene bishops whom Lucius had caused to be exiled or sent to mines. Strangely there is no evidence of Arabic versions of the Bible prior to the Koran and the immense expansion of Islam diffusing Arabic as a widely spoken tongue.[4]

It was natural for the Copts of the Nile valley to adhere to the teachings of Cyril and the anti-Chalcedonian stand of Dioscoros and Timothy the Weasel. There continued to be a Chalcedonian patriarch of Alexandria, but his flock was a minority of the population. Sophronius (*On the Miracles of Cyrus and John* 12, PG 87. 3461) describes Alexandrian Chalcedonians celebrating the Christmas liturgy in the church of St Theonas while a larger Monophysite crowd led by a hundred clergy of the Gaianite faction waited in the square outside, only entering the church after the modest number of Chalcedonians had finished. Then all together they were able to venerate a holy icon of the Mother of God, *Theotókos*. A factor which was to give impetus to the veneration of icons was ecumenism in association with the honour of the Mother of God; both sides of the divide were equally able to honour the Blessed Virgin and the saints in this way. Something of the same non-theological ecumenism evidently played a part in the ceremony at Jerusalem of the holy fire on Easter Eve or Holy Saturday, when the Greek and Armenian patriarchs co-operated (as continues today). At Menuthis near Alexandria, in order to neutralize a pagan shrine, Cyril had installed relics of the saints Cyrus and John, and pilgrims going to their shrine received healing. However, the shrine was in Chalcedonian hands, and the clergy in charge would admit only those who professed the conciliar faith. A deacon from upper Egypt came to the shrine, and candidly switched allegiance to Chalcedon for as long as he was at Menuthis or Abbakyros (Aboukir) as the holy place was already called. On returning home gratefully cured he would be expected to succeed his father as bishop and to resume his stand as a loyal Monophysite. In the seventh century the Alexandrian patriarch John the Almsgiver found that his most effective means of recruitment to the Chalcedonian cause was to disburse wealth from the church chest (*Mirac.* 37). Patriarch Sophronius of Jerusalem observed that 'Egyptians are not a race to change their mind' (PG 87. 3573 B).

---

[4] See Irfan Shahîd, *Byzantium and the Arabs in the Fourth Century* (Dumbarton Oaks, Washington DC, 1984) with a sequel (1989) on the fifth century; G. Graf, *Geschichte der christlichen arabischen Literatur*, I (Studi e Testi 118; Rome, 1944). C. D. G. Müller, *Kirche und Mission unter der Arabern in Vorislamíschei Zeit* (Tübingen, 1967).

The Ethiopian Church had close links to Egypt and followed the Monophysite majority there, but the worship was able to include beautiful slow dances, unique in ancient Christian history and still in use today. Ethiopic is a Semitic tongue, and the people of the country had links to the Israelites (cf. the story in Acts of the Ethiopian eunuch, and in the Old Testament the Queen of Sheba's visit to King Solomon). In antiquity 'Ethiopian' was a generic name for black people to the south of Egypt. Under the name Kush the land south of Assuan is mentioned in the Old Testament. Rufinus received information about the Ethiopian church from a presbyter Aedesios of Tyre, who had gone to Ethiopia with Frumentius (above p. 232). Among Roman merchants trading with Ethiopia there were Christians, and through them groups of Christians began to form congregations and to construct church buildings. Athanasius himself consecrated Frumentius to be bishop of Axum (*Apol. ad Const.* 31). The Coptic and Ethiopian churches have preserved important Christian documents of late antiquity such as the liturgy associated with the *Apostolic Tradition* ascribed to Hippolytus.[5] The Ethiopic holy books included texts such as the book of Enoch, Baruch, Jubilees, the *Shepherd* of Hermas, the first epistle of Clement, and the *Apostolic Constitutions*.

---

[5] Dr Holford-Strevens points out that Otto Neugebauer (SB Vienna 347, 1979) has been able to use Ethiopic MSS to reconstruct the Alexandrian computus in its pure un-westernized form: *Oxford Companion to the Year*, 803–5.

57

THE CHURCH AND THE BARBARIAN
INVASIONS IN THE WEST: SALVIAN,
SIDONIUS, CAESARIUS

Rural Gaul was evangelized by Martin of Tours,[1] founder of monasteries at Ligugé and Marmoutier, made famous by Sulpicius Severus' story, mocked by Jerome, of cutting his cloak to give half to a beggar. The Rhine frontier was fortified; but pagan Germans overwhelmed it.

Hilary of Arles

While the eastern churches were engaged in a divisive controversy concerning Christology, the west had different problems. Pope Leo sought and obtained support in Gaul for his Tome and had earlier persuaded John Cassian to write against Nestorius, of whom Cassian knew next to nothing; but, with rare exceptions such as Gennadius of Marseille fluent in Greek who about 470 wrote (lost) works against Nestorius and Eutyches, the Gallic churches were far more disturbed by the consequences of barbarian movements into their territory. Leo also had difficulties when in 445 Hilary, an aristocrat trained in the ascetic life at the idiorrhythmic monastery founded by a noble named Honoratus on the island of Lérins (near Cannes) and an energetic bishop of Arles active in building churches in his city, replaced a bishop of the metropolitan see of Besançon (Vesontio), Chelidonius. He was accused of having married a widow and of having, as a provincial governor (*praeses*) before ordination, imposed capital punishment. Germanus of Auxerre, whose career from governor to bishop had run closely parallel to that of Chelidonius, was a party to Hilary's action. The deposed bishop had evidently said or done something to give serious offence to Hilary and his network of aristocratic bishops. By custom the bishop of Arles had the right to gather bishops in synod (explicit in canon 18 of a collection ascribed to the second council of Arles, perhaps in or soon after 443; Germanus died

---

[1] See Clare Stancliffe, *St Martin and his Hagiographer* (Oxford, 1983).

probably in 446). Hilary had a council to provide consensus for the deposition, and force was used to eject the deposed bishop, who appealed to Leo. Hilary owed his see and continued support to a military commander (*magister militum*) named Cassius who may have provided the coercion.

Hilary had to go to Rome to defend his actions and even disputed the right of the Roman see to intervene and overrule when a Gallic council had made a decision. Hilary left Rome *incognito* without waiting for Leo's reaction. Leo's fiery anger produced furious correspondence. Leo demanded Chelidonius' reinstatement with a synod in 445 (PL 54. 628–36) humiliatingly reinforced by an edict of Valentinian III (Nov. Val. 17. 101, PL 54. 636–40).[2] There was already tension between the sees of Arles and Vienne, and Leo transferred to Vienne the metropolitan authority that Hilary had exercised from Arles. Hilary had supporters and after his death in May 449 Leo decided to divide metropolitan authority between the two sees, different cities being assigned to each.

Between Arles and Vienne tension remained. Avitus of Vienne, bishop from 490, failed to win Rome's support for his see. He converted the Burgundian king's son.

Pope Leo I and Priscillianism in Spain

Pope Leo had other more local problems, such as the custom of his congregation at St Peter's to turn east to venerate the sun before entering the basilica where the apse was (and is) at the west end. An inquisition also uncovered a nest of Manichees, detected by their acceptance of the consecrated bread but refusal of the chalice. Manichee infiltration was also a factor among the Priscillianists of north-west Spain. A private letter from Turibius bishop of Asturica (Astorga) alerted Leo to their hold on the churches of Galicia and to the mutual toleration between the Priscillianist bishops and the others. They were receiving communion together without any friction. Moreover, at Priscillian's tomb in Galicia (possibly at Compostela?) healing miracles were occurring. Barbarian domination of the land made synods impossible. Turibius sent Leo a list of sixteen heretical propositions, one of which taught that 'the scriptures are accepted under the names of the patriarchs, symbolizing the twelve virtues which cause a reformation in the inner man.' This idea turns up in a Chinese Manichee text of about AD 900.[3]

[2] M. Heinzelmann in J. F. Drinkwater and Hugh Elton, *Fifth-Century Gaul: a Crisis of Identity?* (Cambridge, 1992), 239–51.

[3] H. Chadwick, *Priscillian of Ávila* (Oxford, 1976, repr. 1999), 214.

Pelagianism in Britain. Patrick in Ireland

The Pelagian cause had not died in the British Isles. Pope Celestine, alerted by a deacon Palladius, commissioned bishop Germanus of Auxerre, former advocate and governor or military commander, to correct the error. Later he paid a second visit. Celestine also sent Palladius as bishop to Ireland. A mission to Ireland was soon to be in process.

A British (not of course English) Christian named Patrick (Patricius) also called by the native name Sucat, sixteen-year old son of a Romano-British landowner and decurion who had taken deacon's orders, had been captured by raiders and carried off to Ireland; but he escaped and returned to Britain from where, about 432, he went back to Ireland as bishop to evangelize the north and west of the island, with Armagh as his see, at that time inhabited by Scots, with Picts in the south. Two documents survive from Patrick's pen, composed in an uneducated Latin. A letter to the soldiers of a Welsh prince Coroticus, who had killed some of his lately baptized Irish converts and had sold others into slavery, shows that just as Patrick himself had been taken by raiders from Ireland, so too raiders from Britain were responsible for murderous reprisals. In old age Patrick wrote a *Confessio*, partly a profession of orthodox faith, partly a self-vindication against critics probably in Gaul, of his admittedly deficient education, and against some of his own converts accusing him of simony. He admitted the sins of his youth, but affirmed that his achievement in Ireland was the work of divine grace.

Churches in Germany

Although the Christian mission aspired to penetrate beyond the Rhine into Germany, before the mission of Boniface the Church was not successfully established in Germany except in Cologne, Mainz, and Trier, which lay within the empire.[4] Ammianus records that Germans attacked Mainz on a Christian feast (27. 10. 1–2). Cologne and later Trier (c.475) were to pass into the power of the Franks. Salvian of Marseille (*ep.* 1) knew a noble lady at Trier reduced to serving barbarian wives as a charlady. Trier was long the residence of the prefect and headquarters for the defence of the Rhine frontier. In 355 it needed a larger church (Athanasius, *Apol. ad Constantium* 15). Valentinian I resided there. After Athanasius' exile there it had a monastery (Aug. *Conf.* 8. 6. 15) and it was reckoned the richest and principal city in Gaul. But these three cities were the target of barbarian attacks, and early in the fifth century the prefecture was moved south to Arles. On 31 December 406 the Rhine

---

[4] In the fifth century a Roman bath at Boppard on the Rhine was adapted to become a church. See E. Dassmann, *Die Anfänge der Kirche in Deutschland* (Stuttgart, 1993).

froze, and the crossing of the river was relatively easy for Vandals, Alans, and Sueves in large and uncontrollable numbers (above p. 510). Stilicho already had his hands full coping with Alaric and troops had been moved from Gaul into Italy, as no doubt barbarian intelligence had discovered. Moreover, Stilicho was at the time more concerned with his personal ambitions to dominate the east as well as the west. It was part of the indictment against him that while the western empire was being dismembered by barbarians, he served only his own interests.

Visigoths and Vandals

Co-ordination among the tribes was probably small.[5] Nevertheless Gaul was ravaged, and towns were ablaze. Bishop Exuperius of Toulouse was notable for the encouragement he gave to the defenders of his city, which was larger than others. Of the invaders the Vandals were the most numerous with two main groups, Asdings and Silings, who had come to the west from eastern Europe. They had become Arian Christians like the Visigoths. In 409 some of them crossed the Pyrenees into Spain, partly to escape the counterattack of the great general Constantius and the unwelcome attentions of Visigoths, but also to find pasture and land. They had no doubt slaughtered many beasts on the north side of the mountains. Spain already had Sueves and Visigoths, and the Iberian peninsula had to be divided among them. In 429 the Vandals were invited by a foolish Roman general Boniface to assist him in establishing his own rule in north Africa. The outcome was a Vandal conquest and the establishment of a kingdom at Carthage in 439, from which they could harass shipping and trade in the Mediterranean like the Barbary raiders of medieval times. They were Arians and under Vandal rule Catholics were sharply persecuted, a story eloquently told by Victor of Vita in Byzacena about 488. It fell to Justinian's general Belisarius to end the Vandal pirate kingdom, and to Procopius his *consiliarius* to tell the story.[6]

The Burgundians successfully attacked both sides of the Rhine and Rhône valleys, and the Alemanni were also far from inactive mainly in sharp brief raids on old Roman forts. The Burgundian centre became Worms. They put great pressure on Lyon (Lugdunum).

---

[5] The orgy of murder and burning in Gothic attacks in Thrace (378) is vividly described by Ammianus 31. 6. In Gaul the invaders were probably substantial guerrilla bands rather than a well-organized invasion.

[6] Christian Courtois, *Les Vandales et l'Afrique* (Paris, 1955 = Aalen, 1964). Victor's text: CSEL 7, English transl. by John Moorhead (Liverpool, 1992). Procopius is in the Loeb Classical Library. H. Wolfram, *The Roman Empire and its Germanic Peoples* (Berkeley, 1997), 159–82.

The Visigothic kingdom in Aquitaine[7]

The barbarians wanted land, and the Roman authorities were forced to yield on this. The Visigoths were granted the fertile land of Aquitania II, i.e. from the Loire south to the Garonne and further south to Toulouse, which became the centre of Visigothic power, under King Theoderic I from 451, then his son Thorismund, murdered by his brother Theoderic II in 453. At first the administrators of the empire remained in office for non-military matters, and the great landowners retained possession of a third of their property. To refuse to share one's estate with a 'guest' was to risk the loss of nearly everything, as was the experience of Paulinus of Pella, grandson of the poet Ausonius. At the age of 83 he wrote an extant thanksgiving for his survival, wishing that he could have persuaded his wife to leave Aquitaine and blaming her for the damage that his property suffered on no less than four occasions. She was determined to see the Visigoths off her estate. A poem by Rutilius Namatianus, master of the offices 412 and then prefect of Rome 414 (*PLRE* ii. 770), describes his journey from Rome to Gaul in 417, necessitated by the damage to his property. He did not value monks in black on Capraria island who did not share his 'country-house culture'. He was also no admirer of Stilicho's role in making the chaos possible.

That the number of landowners who were forced out and left was large seems evident. Sidonius (*ep.* 6. 10) writes on behalf of one refugee. Provided that Gallo-Roman landowners conceded to the immigrants, they did not fare too badly, and there was more continuity than could initially have been expected. But although some Romans were able to serve in the Visigoth army, much of the military power was barbarian, and the Visigoths from Toulouse soon nursed ambitions to conquer Arles as well, if only to scare the Gallo-Romans into greater concessions of land. At first they were *foederati* or allies of the empire, recognizing the emperor's supremacy in name while pursuing their own interests. The survival of a peace treaty with the emperor depended on the Goths getting their way, and there were some sharp encounters. But the Visigothic king Theoderic II (king 453–66) supported the emperor Avitus (briefly Augustus 455–6, ousted by Majorian). Relations were more strained between the empire and Theoderic's successor Euric (king 466–84).

Successive emperors in Italy were almost impotent to deal with the barbarians in Gaul and Spain. The weak Honorius died in 423, succeeded by a short-lived John, not recognized in the east, and a longer-lived child, Valentinian III, aged four at accession, effectively governed for twelve years by

---

[7] On the political situation see J. F. Drinkwater and H. Elton, *Fifth-Century Gaul: a crisis of identity?* (Cambridge, 1992), especially the paper by P. Heather.

his mother Galla Placidia. His father, the able general Constantius, died of illness in 421.

Aetius and Boniface

With the barbarian invasions the real power in the empire was increasingly exercised by army leaders. The empire still had an able military commander named Aetius, who came from the lower Danube. For three years in youth (405–8) he had been hostage with Alaric the Visigoth, and later with the Huns, with whom he established good relations. In Gaul he repulsed a Visigoth attack on Arles, but he had a potent rival in Boniface, the man responsible for checking the barbarians in Africa but fatally inviting help from the Vandals in Spain. Boniface lost his life in battle against Aetius near Rimini. Civil war at such a time was a luxury the empire could not afford. Aetius in Gaul continued successful in checking the Visigoths. From Britain a futile plea for his help in 446 is reported by Gildas. An invasion of Gaul by Attila in 451 led him to ask the Visigoths to help in resisting the Huns, and they agreed. Aetius stopped Attila from occupying Orléans, thanks to the prayers of Anianus (St Aignan), bishop of the city, it was said (Sidonius, *ep.* 8. 15. 1). The prefect Ferreolus' diplomacy kept the Visigoths out of Arles in the following year. The emperor Valentinian III personally murdered Aetius in Rome in September 454, but was himself murdered the following year by two of Aetius' bodyguards.

Ricimer, Odoacer, Theoderic in Italy

Thereafter barbarian army commanders, Ricimer and then Odoacer, effectively made the western empire's decisions. In 476 the last of a series of nonentity emperors, Romulus Augustulus, was sent into pleasant retirement by Odoacer, who acknowledged the nominal sovereignty of the Roman emperor in Constantinople but in practice acted independently. He in turn was removed by Theoderic the Ostrogoth, whose verbal recognition of the eastern emperor as his lord made him suspicious of Roman senators in Italy who would have preferred to be ruled by a Catholic, not an Arian, and by a king less independent of the Roman imperial ideal. That was to lead to the death of Boethius in 525. Theoderic was nevertheless a great governor of Italy and guardian of Gothic interests. When he visited St Peter's, Rome, he reverenced the apostolic shrine 'like a Catholic' (Anon. Valesianus, a Ravenna chronicle). But during the Roman schism between the rival popes Symmachus and Laurentius he was detached and cool.[8]

---

[8] H. Chadwick, *Boethius, the Consolations of Music, Logic, Philosophy and Theology* (Oxford, 1981, repr. 1998).

Church reaction to the collapse of the western empire

The weakness of both Honorius and Arcadius and the alienation between eastern and western governments associated with Rufinus and Stilicho and with the irate Roman reaction to the treatment of John Chrysostom were evident contributory factors facilitating collapse. Stilicho was able to check a frightening invasion of Italy by the Goth Radagaisus in 405. But the unstoppable loss of control in Gaul in and after 407 and Alaric's invasion of Italy with the sack of Rome in 410 made Christians ask if the end of the world was at hand. In the *City of God* (21. 24. 4) Augustine observed that a 'city' is overthrown by moral collapse though its walls may remain standing. But the barbarian invasions deprived the empire of much revenue in taxes on land, and therefore of the ability to finance the legions, the cost of one soldier being reckoned as one gold solidus. In Africa the Vandals were to capture the richest of all parts of the empire, the principal source of olive oil and grain for the northern side of the Mediterranean. Financial advisers were telling people to move their investments from west to east (Aug. *S.* 38. 9).

Augustine on the disintegration of the western empire

Augustine annoyed some of his hearers by his sombre language about the moral quality of Rome and the empire, not allayed when he replied that he was quoting Sallust (*City of God* 3. 17. 1). But Christians must acknowledge that Christ's gospel is for all races, not a promise simply for the Romans (*ep.* 199. 47), and in Africa at least they can be grateful: 'none of us is at present a prisoner of barbarian invaders' (*En. in Ps.* 8. 4). Ambition to dominate is not good, and small kingdoms would give better societies (*City of God* 4. 15). The Roman Empire is now deservedly tasting the medicine it has administered to others (*En. in Ps.* 93. 1). Augustine did not think a restoration impossible; there had been bad times in the past and recovery was achieved (*City of God* 4. 7).

Salvian of Marseille[9]

An almost uniquely gloomy view was proclaimed by Salvian, presbyter of Marseille from about 440 (died *c.*480). How much he really knew about the barbarians is unclear. He saw the barbarian victories as providential reward for their moral qualities at least in comparison with a Roman society corrupt

[9] J. Badewien, *Geschichtstheologie und Sozialkritik im Werk Salvians von Marseille* (Göttingen, 1980); I. Opelt, 'Briefe des Salvian von Marseille: zwischen Christen und Barbaren', *Romanobarbarica* 4 (1979, 161–82; R. W. Mathisen, *Studies in the History, Literature and Society of Late Antiquity* (Amsterdam, 1991).

from the top downwards. Perhaps he had read Tacitus. 'The Roman empire is dying, strangled by taxes' (*De Gubernatione Dei* 4. 6). Educated people in Spain and Gaul flee to the barbarians (5. 5). The rich evade paying the crushingly heavy charges, so that the poor have to pay more (a complaint vindicated as no exaggeration by a law of the emperor Majorian, Novel 2. 4 [March 458],[10] which said exactly that and, since this emperor resided mainly in Gaul endeavouring to enlist loyalty there, reflected the real situation). A rise in tax levels was no doubt necessitated by the loss of much territory to the barbarians. 'The Roman fisc has collapsed' (6. 8). 'Once the barbarians paid tribute to the empire; now it is the other way round' (6. 18). Nobles are dishonest thieves; high officials embezzle state property (4. 4; 7. 21). A man who seized another's property outrageously justified himself by saying that he had bound himself to do so by an oath (4. 74–5). *Curiales* (members of town councils responsible for tax-gathering) are mere instruments of injustice (3. 10; 5. 5). Runaway slaves are fiercely flogged; but the reason for their flight is fear of being brutally beaten by stewards and other slaves, so that some flee to their masters for mercy. But some masters see no crime in killing a slave, no doubt by beating as recorded in e.g. Libanius, *or.* 46. 8, Synesius, *ep.* 72, or canon 5 of the council of Elvira, above p. 182 (Salvian 4. 5; Cod. Just. 9. 14. 1). Orphans and widows are oppressed (7. 16). The trade of Gallic cities is in the hands of Syrian merchants (4. 14; the same was true in Spain, attested in Jerome's commentary on Ezekiel). The sexual shenanigans of the rich and powerful are disgraceful. Nobles treat wives and slave-girls alike as mere sexual objects for their gratification (4. 5; 7. 3). Slaves despise such vicious masters (3. 9). The cities of Aquitaine are notorious for sexual scandals (7. 3), much like Carthage, which, until the Vandals cleaned it up, seethed with vice both heterosexual and homosexual (7. 16–18. 22), a picture akin to that in Augustine's *Confessions* 3. At Trier, which Salvian knew well, top people were given to inebriation and adultery (6. 13) and some nobles were feasting when barbarians broke into the town. After the place was destroyed, the powerful men of the city asked the emperor to fund public games (6. 14). But such unethical entertainments (beast-fights kill people) were no longer possible in Trier four times destroyed, or in Cologne occupied by the enemy (Franks), or in Mainz, wholly destroyed.

A disastrous social consequence of the corruption in society had been the concentration of land in the hands of big landowners and the reduction of *coloni* to be serfs; they had been forced to sell their smallholding to a rich neighbour or at least to become dependent on him for protection.

Tragically Salvian's Church is not untouched by comparable scandals.

---

[10] Text in T. Mommsen and P. M. Meyer, *Theodosiani Libri* . . . ii (Berlin, 1905; repr. Dublin and Zürich, 1971), 159.

Some clergy lapse into fornication (cf. canon 18 of the council of Elvira on adulterous bishops and clergy). The congregation in church is small if a high festival happens to coincide with shows in circus or amphitheatre (6. 7; a complaint also voiced by Augustine in Africa). Religious activities are a subject of mockery to Romans who proudly boast of being 'faithful' (i.e. baptized) and Catholics, not heretics like the Arian barbarians (7. 11). Worldly Africans especially mock monks, whistling at them, and bullying them (8. 4). Salvian had once been a monk at Lérins and upheld an ascetic morality. In contrast with the Cappadocian fathers who advised Christians to bequeath a third of their estate to the Church, or Augustine who advised leaving to the Church the proportion that would go to an additional child, Salvian held that relatively little wealth should pass by inheritance to children, the Church being the sole agency of welfare to the innumerable destitute and homeless.[11]

In a few places Salvian praises the high morality of barbarians, e.g. Goths 'hate fornication' (7. 6). That they are heretics is caused by the faults of Romans; Arianism was created within the empire and was not their own idea (5. 3). Heresy and barbarism are not coterminous. They accuse Romans of heresy because their version of the Bible has interpolations and mistranslations (5. 2). But rhetoric apart, not all barbarians are in reality so superior; Saxons are savage, Franks traitors, Gepids merciless, Huns lecherous, Alemanni drunkards, Alans rapacious (4. 14). Arian Goths and Vandals, however, live lives worthy of catholic faith (5. 3). Salvian bitterly regretted the decline of old Rome's high moral standards and the dependence of the empire's survival on, of all people, the Huns. He wanted citizens of the empire to recover the austere virtues of Rome's early history, and implied that the Church was the providential agent with the capacity to make this possible.

Britannia

Salvian's portrait of corrupt government in Roman Gaul may explain why in the first decade of the fifth century there were three successive usurpers in Britain, rising up against the Roman officials. One of them reached Arles before being crushed. The Roman imperial presence in Britain may have been rendered impossible as much by local social protest against abuses and high taxes as by the destruction caused by the infiltration of Anglo-Saxon invading parties, who, at least at first, are unlikely to have been very numerous or formidable.[12]

---

[11] Augustine (*sermo* 355) judged it wrong to bequeath everything to the Church in disregard of family needs.

[12] Argument in part to this effect is in Michael E. Jones, *The End of Roman Britain* (Ithaca, NY, 1996). However, the burials of treasure in East Anglia, e.g. Hoxne or Water Newton, certainly point to the conclusion that the threat came to the east coast of Britannia.

Apollinaris Sidonius[13]

As barbarian power in Gaul increased, there were fewer top jobs for the rich Roman nobles. Redundancy threatened. A bishopric, therefore, was an attraction, and some Gallo-Roman aristocrats found this a useful position from which to preserve old cultured Roman values. Of these the most prolific writer was Sidonius Apollinaris (*PLRE* ii. 115), a Gallo-Roman aristocrat, son of a praetorian prefect in Gaul (*ep.* 6. 5), son-in-law of the emperor Avitus, concerning whom his letters show cautious reservations. In 468 he rose to be prefect of Rome (a reward for a panegyric on the emperor Anthemius nominated by Constantinople which stressed the restored unity of east and west in the empire). He was bishop of Clermont (Augustonemetum) for ten years or more from 470. At Rome he contracted a fever but had been cured after praying at the 'limina apostolorum' (*ep.* 1. 5).[14] He was a man glad to be able to rely on apostolic prayers of devout Christians holier than himself.

He was as clear as Salvian that the Roman Empire had suffered an unmitigated and irremediable catastrophe. The world was now in its dotage (8. 6. 3). The important town of Burdigala (Bordeaux), controlled by Visigoths, had now a mixed population of Saxons, Heruls, Burgundians, Ostrogoths, and Scythians (8. 9). But what great ideals the empire had! Surely it would not die and yield to uneducated barbarians who could only be despised. The tall Burgundians were 'uncouth in body and mind' (5. 5. 3). Barbarians were malodorous, had bad breath, used 'rancid butter' for hairgrease (*carmen* 12. 7), wore clothing of skins and spoke an alien language. Admittedly barbarian nobles were trying to learn good Latin (*ep.* 3. 3–4). Sidonius could congratulate a Frankish governor of Trier, Arbogast, descended from the military commander defeated by Theodosius I, on the excellence of his Latin (4. 17). But Visigothic kings needed an interpreter to negotiate with an imperial ambassador (Ennodius of Pavia, *Vita Epiphanii* 90).[15]

If the old position of Gallo-Roman aristocrats could not long be maintained, at least a bishopric could give some modest degree of independence

---

[13] Text and translation in the Loeb Classical Library by W. B. Anderson and W. H. Semple. Studies: C. E. Stevens (Oxford, 1933); J. Harries, *Sidonius Apollinaris and the Fall of Rome* (Oxford, 1994); K. F. Stroheker, *Germanentum und Spätantike* (Zürich, 1965); R. P. C. Hanson, 'The Church in Fifth-century Gaul: Evidence from Sidonius Apollinaris', *Journal of Ecclesiastical History*, 21 (1970), 1–10; R. W. Mathisen, *Roman Aristocrats in barbarian Gaul* (Austin, Texas, 1993). Full bibliography in Alberto Ferreiro, *The Visigoths in Gaul and Spain AD 418–711* (Leiden, 1988), though he is there confused with Apollinaris of Laodicea.

[14] This classic Latin phrase becomes common in this period, especially for St Peter's basilica in Rome; the visit to the 'threshold' is possibly derived from the ancient custom of venerating holy entrances.

[15] Edited with translation and notes by Genevieve M. Cook (Washington, DC, 1942).

over against barbarian overlords, and Sidonius' letters and poems show him determined to preserve the tradition of high culture in Latin literature. He would write letters and, before he became bishop, poems with literary allusions that his equally well-educated correspondents would recognize. The technique was a quiet assertion of a network of friends and relatives sharing in the preservation of a Latin civilization now awash in a Sargasso sea of barbarism. Naturally this had the consequence that the Gallic churches were profoundly controlled by and allied with the old highly literate aristocracy.[16] To belong to the upper class could apparently extenuate misdemeanours, such as seducing slave-girls, which in some inferior person would incur ecclesiastical discipline. But the people wanted bishops who had the know-how to represent them before powerful kings and emperors, to gain remission of harsh taxation, to intercede for them if they were under accusation, to address authority with the fearless devastating candour of a St Martin of Tours at Valentinian's or Magnus Maximus' table.

Sidonius accepted the bishopric of Clermont from two motives, namely to preserve a small corner of high Roman culture and Christian values, and secondly to attempt (unsuccessfully) to prevent the Visigoths established at Toulouse from taking over the Auvergne. That was to identify the bishop of Clermont as a leader in a community which did not want to be dominated by barbarians, and it was in the upper-class tradition of public service. The king of the Visigoths Euric (466–84), brother of his predecessor Theoderic II whom he murdered, determined to capture the Auvergne in 475 and in the next year took Arles and Marseille, conquered Spain, and attacked the Burgundians in the Rhone valley. He attributed his military successes to his Arian faith; Bishop Sidonius feared his attack on the remaining pockets of Roman power less than his hatred of Catholic church life, faith, and influence (Sid. *ep.* 7. 6. 4 and 6). Euric forbade eight Catholic sees to be filled when bishops died, and that was to give advantage to the Arians. Sidonius himself and two other bishops suffered exile for about a year. The Roman emperor Julius Nepos commissioned four Gallic bishops (Arles, Riez, Marseille, and Aix) to be his ambassadors to negotiate a treaty of appeasement which, to Sidonius' anger, abandoned the Auvergne to Visigothic control but at least obtained leave for vacant sees to be filled and for exiled bishops to be restored to their people. Sidonius' antipathy to the Goths after Euric's tearing up of the treaty with the empire indicates modification of an earlier opinion; before becoming a bishop he had been dangerously sympathetic to a praetorian prefect of Gaul named Arvandus who favoured division of Gaul

---

[16] Jerome on the prophet Micah (1. 2. 9–10, p. 457 Vallarsi) deplored co-operation between bishops and magistrates in suppressing the poor; a bishop's prime duty was to protect the poor against the powerful.

between different barbarian tribes and (probably) merely nominal recognition of Roman imperial sovereignty; for Arvandus this caused accusations of treason brought to trial at Rome in 469, the death penalty being commuted to exile (*ep.* 1. 7. 3).

The barbarian occupation made difficulties for bishops needing to communicate with one another. Sidonius had to warn bishop Faustus of Reii (Riez) that in consequence of Euric's aggression a courier carrying a letter would encounter guards on the roads questioning him about his business; if nervous when being examined, couriers 'are thought to be carrying messages not committed to writing and suffer maltreatment' (*ep.* 9. 3). Barbarian rivalries added to the problems. Bishop Aprunculus of Langres was suspected by the Burgundian king Gundobad (*c.*474–516) of treasonable friendliness to the Franks in the north; he took refuge with Sidonius at Clermont and was to succeed him as bishop there.

Despite the harassment of Arian barbarian control, Sidonius is witness to the building of some new churches, especially a new building at Lyon for which Sidonius composed a memorial inscription and Faustus of Riez preached the inaugural sermon (Sid. *ep.* 2. 102–3; 9. 3. 5). It was an achievement since the people of Lyon were deeply divided among themselves, and were under Burgundian attack (3. 8). The cause of division is not recorded, but a very possible disagreement could have been whether necessity forced a coming to terms with the barbarians or whether they should be resisted to the death. The former alternative was bound to win in the end.

At Lyon psalms were chanted antiphonally. Sidonius' recording of this fact implies that it was not so everywhere. Bishop Perpetuus of Tours, author of a description of miracles at St Martin's tomb versified by Paulinus of Périgueux (CSEL 16. 1), rebuilt St Martin's church (4. 18), perhaps inadequately since Gregory of Tours repeated the operation (*HF* 2. 40; 4. 20; 10. 31). Unlike Gregory of Tours, Sidonius shows no interest in relics. Visigothic occupation did not facilitate the repair of dilapidated churches (7. 6. 8). But churches retained land bequeathed to them since Sidonius could request a loan of church land to a deacon refugee from the Visigoths (6. 10. 1–2). Sidonius was conscious of the responsibility and dignity of the episcopal office as high priest, *summus sacerdos*, and many letters to other bishops salute them as 'domine papa'. Married himself (as also other Gallic bishops), he expected lay married couples to abstain from sexual intercourse after having one or two children (9. 6. 4); and bishops were expected not to have sexual intercourse with their wives (council of Elvira, canon 33). Intermarriage with barbarians was self-evidently not encouraged; imperial law against it went back to CTh 3. 14. 1 of 373. There are several references to monks, and a flattering letter to bishop Principius of Soissons praises his ascetic life attested by a former abbot of Lérins now a bishop (8. 14). The monasteries at

Lérins and Marseille supplied many of his colleagues. Curiously he has no mention of the bishop of Rome. Following the example of Mamertus of Vienne, he introduced Rogation processions (5. 14).

Not all Gallic bishops entirely approved of Sidonius. A wistful letter to Remigius of Reims expresses a hope that his work will not be shunned (9. 7. 3); perhaps Remigius disapproved of the choice of a former imperial official of eminence to occupy a bishopric. It would not have been welcome to Pope Siricius a few generations earlier.

A vacancy occurred in the metropolitan see of Bourges in Aquitania I. Rival candidates were numerous and, at a date when Clermont was the only city in Aquitaine still Roman and as yet unoccupied by Goths (7. 5. 3), Sidonius was invited by the laity to come and make a choice for them. This delegation of the power of decision was unwelcome to presbyters who sat in a corner exchanging resentful whispers. There was the possibility of choosing a monk; but the laity would think him better fitted to be their intercessor at the Last Judgement than their earthly defender in immediate situations here and now, and neither clergy nor laity would be enthusiastic about strict monastic discipline. Another possibility was to promote one of the presbyters; but then clergy not selected would be tempted to envy, and would expect him to pick the senior man, whatever shortcomings he might have. One of the candidates had queered his chances by offering bribes. There was the possibility of rewarding supporters by the sale of church land after election and consecration (a method employed at Rome in 498–9 by Symmachus in rivalry to Laurentius). Candidates who had been twice married could be excluded on the ground of 1 Tim. 3: 2. Finally Sidonius picked on Simplicius, a layman whose forebears included prefects as well as bishops; he was a native of the city and had served its interests on embassies to the emperor and to Visigothic kings. He had also suffered imprisonment in Gothic gaol (7. 9. 20).[17] For Sidonius Simplicius had the merit of being of the requisite class. 'He had the energy of a young man and the good judgement of an old one.' For the consecration Sidonius was assisted, after overcoming some reluctance, by Agroecius of Sens. It was customary and not obviously incompatible with Gallic canon law for a consecration to be performed by only two bishops provided that the proposal had written support from a metropolitan.[18]

The barbarian invasion certainly caused considerable suffering for the population, and the Church became the principal organ of relief. One of Sidonius' poems (16. 116–26) lists the charitable actions of Bishop Faustus of

---

[17] At Lyon the ascetic bishop Eucherius was so intransigent in loyalty to the empire that he was executed (Gregory of Tours, *HF* 2. 20).

[18] Canon 5 of the second council of Arles (443?).

Riez, seeing to the supply of food to the starving, to wretched prisoners wasting away with their legs in chains, and to the burial of the poor.

Sidonius was orthodox but no theologian. When a priest and monk named Riochatus passed through Clermont carrying sermons by Faustus of Riez to his fellow Britons, Sidonius hastily dictated copies to scribes, and then wrote to Faustus with a friendly appreciation of his prose style, not of the content which could have been above his head (*ep.* 9. 9). After becoming bishop he seldom wrote poetry, but once sent an otherwise unknown bishop Megethius copies of some eucharistic prayers which he had composed (7. 3. 1). However, he had two congenial friends who were in intellectual controversy with one another, bishop Faustus himself and Claudianus Mamertus, a presbyter at Vienne where his brother was bishop.

Faustus of Riez in controversy with Claudianus Mamertus

Faustus was born in Britannia, but in adolescence became a monk at Lérins and was abbot there from 433 until about 452 when he became bishop of Riez.[19] He was much opposed to Pelagius but also to Augustine's doctrine of predestination as leaving no room for free will,[20] and was very reserved towards the degree to which, at least in some passages, Augustine accepted Platonic notions of the immateriality of the human soul. Faustus (*ep.* 3, CSEL 21) thought the soul a constitutive element in the body and as such to be physical. If it was granted as it was by Augustine that the soul is created, Faustus thought it easy to think that at every human conception, the Creator provides a soul so that body and soul are created together.

Sidonius was not much of a theologian but he was made anxious by an anonymous tract arguing for the corporeality of the soul transmitted through the parental seed. He asked Claudianus Mamertus to write a reply. The author under fire turned out to be Faustus of Riez, and there was some resulting cooling of relations between Faustus and Sidonius. Augustine had recognized that 'traducianism' most easily explained the hereditary transmission of the innate propensity to evil from the Fall of Adam and Eve and the consequent necessity of baptism for infants (*De Genesi ad litteram* 10. 11. 19). But it sounded dangerously Manichee (cf. above p. 469). The alternatives were either a Platonic idea of the soul's natural immortality or creationism, i.e. that as human bodies are conceived, the Creator creates a soul *ad hunc* or *ad hanc*. Augustine had rejected 'creationism' in a letter (166) to Jerome. It seemed to involve the Creator in endless fuss and in providing souls for

---

[19] A. L. F. Rivet, *Gallia Narbonensis* (London, 1988), 243–6.

[20] In 470 a synod at Arles was moved by Faustus to condemn his presbyter Lucidus, who had ignored an admonition to beware of a high doctrine of predestination.

pregnancies by adultery or fornication. He maintained that the cause of concupiscence was not in the body alone, nor in the soul alone, but in both
together (*Gen. ad litt.* 10. 12. 20). He wanted to differentiate a Christian view
of the soul from that of Plato and Porphyry, whose book 'on the soul's return
(to God)' influenced both him and Claudianus Mamertus, by insisting that
the soul is created out of nothing; hence its moral precariousness and vulner-
ability to temptation through attachment to the body.

In 419 Augustine was criticized by Vincentius Victor, a convert to catholic
unity from a Donatist sect in Mauretania, for his indecision and uncertainty
on the issue whether traducianism or creationism is correct (above p. 469f.).
The critic agreed with Augustine that on the creationist hypothesis the transmission of original sin is hard to understand, but then regarded that as dis-
proving the idea of hereditary sinfulness. Augustine's long reply, *De anima et
eius origine*, insists that indecision in face of a mystery is not dithering but
correct and that while there is much in the natural order that we can grasp,
we find ourselves incomprehensible; but in any event it should be regarded
as certain that the soul is spirit and not body. If, as Victor held, the soul is a
physical entity, the question must arise whether male and female souls differ.
Victor upheld the sexlessness of the human soul. Augustine could not know
that male and female brains are not identical.

Behind Faustus' idea of the soul as a physical entity lay Tertullian
(*de Anima*), Hilary of Poitiers, and John Cassian who held that only God is
wholly incorporeal, and everything created is in some degree corporeal.

Claudianus Mamertus admired Porphyry's book 'On the soul's return',
which he could have read either in Greek or more probably in a Latin translation by Marius Victorinus. While he had evidently read Augustine on the
Trinity, he had direct access to a Latin version of Porphyry and quoted, with
an enthusiasm that the mature Augustine could not share, Porphyry's dictum
that 'Everything bodily is to be shunned' (*omne corpus fugiendum*).[21]

Ruricius of Limoges

Another friend and correspondent of Sidonius was Ruricius, who became
bishop of Limoges after Euric relaxed his insistence on keeping this see
vacant. Like Sidonius he was a blue-blooded aristocrat, related indeed to the
potent aristocratic family of Anicii. During most of his tenure of the see his
city was under Visigothic control. It is remarkable that of the numerous
letters by him that are extant, none refers to the Visigoths. One (*ep.* 2. 45)
refers to probably Frankish raids causing distress about 494–8. He also

---

[21] On Claudianus see P. Courcelle, *Les Lettres grecques en Occident* = *Late Latin Writers and their
Greek Sources* (Harvard, 1969); and a fine monograph by E. L. Fortin (Paris, 1959).

corresponded with Faustus of Riez who found refuge with him when exiled under Euric. His grandson after him was a later bishop of Limoges. He died about 507.[22]

Caesarius of Arles[23]

Born in 469–70 the son of upper-class parents at Chalon-sur-Saône or Cabillonum, Caesarius aged seventeen aspired to serve the Church. Aged twenty he moved to the monastery at Lérins, but ascetic practice injured his health and the abbot sent him to Arles to recover under the aegis of another aristocratic and ascetic bishop Aeonius. There he had fruitful encounters with a local teacher of rhetoric, Julianus Pomerius, whose book 'On the contemplative Life' survives intact. It may have been written to ward off criticism that any study of rhetoric was worldly. He thought bishops should have a way of life more ascetic than aristocratic. Similar reformist ideas were expressed at this time by an unknown priest of Arles who compiled the extant *Statuta ecclesiae antiqua* (ed. C. Munier, Paris, 1960; also CCSL 148). Aeonius ordained Caesarius deacon, then presbyter and in 499 abbot of the monastery at Arles. In 502 the dying Aeonius obtained King Alaric II's consent for the nomination of Caesarius to succeed him. Trouble in southern Gaul led to Caesarius being briefly exiled to Bordeaux, but he returned to Arles to lead bishops of southern Gaul in council at Agde in 506.

Numerous sermons survive under Caesarius' name, and it is clear that he recycled several by Augustine, Faustus of Riez, and others, often with personal modifications for his hearers at Arles. He exhorted his fellow-bishops that they should heed the lections at their ordination (Ezek. 3. 17 to be watchmen to Israel, and John 21 'feed my lambs'). They were not to be primarily stewards of their vineyards or farmers of their own estates. He deplored sermons in high language which few understood. (One thinks here of the elaborate Latin of Sidonius or Avitus of Vienne or the ultimate in rococo prose by Ennodius of Pavia.) The language of every preacher should be ordinary. Christ chose fishermen to be his apostles (*Sermo* 20, echoing a common observation in Augustine). If some bishops have no gift for preaching, then let them follow the eastern custom of reading a good sermon by a master such as Hilary, Ambrose, or Augustine. Any presbyter, however uneducated, knows how to tell people not to tell lies or swear oaths, not to be proud or drunk, and at a dinner party not to have immoral songs and dances. Women needed to be warned that abortion was morally indistinguishable

---

[22] R. W. Mathisen's annotated translation of *Ruricius and Friends* in Translated Texts for Historians (Liverpool, 1999).

[23] W. Klingshirn (Cambridge, 1994) with bibliography. On Arles in the empire see A. L. F. Rivet, *Gallia Narbonensis* (n. 19).

from murder. Sexual intercourse should be avoided before receiving communion. Let there be no drunkenness on saints' festivals, no shameful songs or dancing after church services (*Sermo* 13. 4). (Augustine had similar problems in north Africa.) All Christians should know by heart the creed and the Lord's Prayer. The preacher should not be afraid of talking frankly about heaven and hell. Severe and threatening discourses can be a duty.

The people were deplorably reluctant to stay in church for the entire celebration of the eucharist, and many would leave after the lections and sermon (*sermo* 74), a phenomenon appearing in later church history, even in the twenty-first century in parts of South America. Women were too inclined to gossip with their friends during services (78). Rogation processions no doubt encouraged a feeling of togetherness in the congregation (*Sermones* 207–9). If anyone was in difficulty, one could rely on the intercession of the saints (20. 4).

Caesarius judged inappropriate 'in Christian times' that young men were commonly living with concubines until such time as they acquired a wife 'with more money than they had themselves'. The numbers involved were so large, the practice so universal, that the clergy could not reasonably impose ecclesiastical suspension or any discipline. Everyone took it for granted that this was customary and socially acceptable behaviour. But men want their bride to be a virgin and should themselves be virgins when they come to marriage. Men ought to be as faithful to their wives as they expect their wife to be to them (*Sermo* 43).

Old pagan customs were persistent especially among rural peasants who probably came to church as well. In fertility rites on 1 January some put on animal head-dress especially as stags for the Celtic god Cernunnos, and soldiers dressed as prostitutes (*Sermo* 13. 5; 192).[24] In honour of Jupiter some did not weave on Thursdays but, perhaps defying the bishop, did so on Sundays (13. 5). People consulted fortune-tellers and diviners and went to sorcerers to obtain spells (*Sermo.* 54). They relied on amulets obtained from clergy (*Sermones* 50. 1, 204. 3). There were foolish people who thought that during a lunar eclipse reciting magic formulas helped the moon to recover, blowing trumpets and shaking bells, presumably to scare away evil spirits (*Sermo* 52. 3). In Spain church bells were hung to repel demonic powers. Caesarius wanted his people to destroy pagan shrines (*Sermo* 53); so there were evidently plenty of semi-pagans still surviving and practising their rituals in sixth-century Gaul. Christianization had some way to go.

Barbarian attacks made life precarious, and many estates in the region of Arles suffered (*Sermo* 6. 6). The biography of Caesarius composed by various friends among his fellow bishops records that when in 508–10 Arles was put

---

[24] R. Arbesmann discusses these rites in *Traditio*, 35 (1979), 89–119; Klingshirn 217.

under siege by Burgundians and Franks, he was regarded by defending Goths as having excessive sympathy for the enemy and was delated to King Alaric by one of his own notaries named Licinianus with 'a savage accusation'. He went to Bordeaux and cleared himself. No doubt Caesarius judged that it must be in the overriding interest of the Church to survive even if that involved apparent treachery to the current transitory government. He sold church silver to have resources for the redemption of prisoners, including many nobles (*Life* of Caesarius 2. 80). Arles passed under the Ostrogothic rule of Theoderic at Ravenna from 510. But when summoned he impressed Theoderic. Going on to Rome he also won the support of Pope Symmachus.

Pope Symmachus reinstated the papal vicariate of Arles, conferring on Caesarius the privilege of wearing the pallium 'in all the Gallic regions'. (It was no longer correct to speak of 'provinces'.) He replied to an inquiry from Caesarius that by canon law there must be no alienation of church property unless for special needs to fund clergy, monks, or pilgrims, and then only for a time, not permanently. Simony for ordinations must stop, and it should be a difficult path for a layman to be ordained. Rapists of virgins or widows were to be excommunicated, and no leave given for widows and virgins wanting to marry and abandon their vows. Bribery of 'powerful persons' must be unsuccessful in candidates for the episcopate; for a consecration it was indispensable to have the declaration of a deputy for the metropolitan (*visitator*) that the choice was unanimously supported by the clergy and the citizens (Symmachus, *ep.* 15, p. 723 Thiel = *MGH Epp.* iii 37, dated 6 November 523).

Two months later Pope Symmachus learnt that the assertion of privilege for the church of Arles, which he supposed to have antiquity and the 'authority of the fathers' in support, was meeting opposition. Critics said it was a presumptuous innovation. The bishop of Aix in particular was unwilling to bow the knee to the metropolitan of Arles and in principle refused to obey his summons to a synod or an ordination. In January 514 Symmachus sent a second letter to Caesarius, threatening 'ecclesiastical discipline which we do not wish to impose' on the bishop of Aix should this continue. This was a decree by the primatial apostolic see, the entire episcopate being derived from St Peter, and was in accord with precedents supported by 'pragmatic' constitutions—probably referring to Valentinian III's edict of 445 (Symmachus, *ep.* 16, p. 728 Thiel = *MGH Epp.* iii 41, dated 11 January 514).[25]

---

[25] 'Pragmatic sanctions' were issued by emperors from the fifth century onwards. See PWK, Suppl. XIV (1974), 460–6 s.v. pragmatica sanctio.

Caesarius and Rome

The transfer of the region of Arles to Theoderic at Ravenna facilitated Caesarius' task. Moreover, a highly sympathetic prefect was appointed named Liberius, who had a distinguished career of public service in Italy and Egypt as well as in Gaul.

Between Provence and the papacy Caesarius ensured good and warm relations, even if that sense of ultramontane benevolence was not easily shared by the bishop of Aix and the province of Narbonensis. Bishops of Rome were expected by Caesarius and most of his episcopal colleagues to be reliable guardians of true belief, empowered by Peter to give a determinative judgement in cases of dispute. Since the Roman church possessed estates in Provence from which it derived support, apparent in the letters of Pope Pelagius I, Arles was far from unimportant in maintaining the papal curia. There were admittedly difficulties about transferring money from Gaul to Italy because the weight of coins minted in Gaul differed from that used in Italy. (This difficulty was also to cause complex arrangements for Gregory the Great in his plans for the Anglo-Saxon mission: below, p. 662.)

Pope Symmachus (*ep.* 16, p. 728 Thiel; *MGH Epp.* iii 41) entrusted to Caesarius a responsibility for correcting theological errors 'not only in Gaul but also in Spain.' All bishops from these regions travelling to Rome were to have a commendatory letter from the bishop of Arles.

In practice most of the councils over which Caesarius presided reflected his concern for discipline more than for correct doctrine and show him expecting from bishops and clergy the kind of ascetic and self-restrained lifestyle which the sermons held before his laity. Caesarius also aimed to achieve liturgical uniformity taking Roman usage as a model; so the Gallic churches were to fast on Saturdays.

At Arles Caesarius had founded a monastery. Fearful of what his successors might do about its resources, he successfully obtained from Pope Hormisdas (514–23) a confirmation that bishops of Arles were not to interfere in the monastery's affairs. Hormisdas was not a pope to be shy of a measure which expressed the universal authority of his see. It is the earliest instance of papal authority isolating a monastery from diocesan interference. A trickier matter was obtaining papal support for a grant which Caesarius had made for a women's monastery, the funding being obtained by sale of church land—an alienation such as Pope Symmachus had hoped to discourage. Hormisdas assured him that his action was eminently pleasing but should on no account occur again.

The council of Orange 529

From 511 onwards some Gallic councils were being called under the authority of the Frankish king Clovis. His recent tribal conversion had been to
catholic unity, not to Arianism with the Visigoths. The first of these assemblies at Orléans not far north of the frontier with Visigothic Aquitaine did not
involve Caesarius. One council among several over which Caesarius presided
but under the aegis of Theoderic rather than Clovis stood apart by being
concerned with doctrine rather than discipline; this was the council at
Orange (*Arausica civitas*) in the province of Arles held in July 529 on the occasion of the dedication of a basilica constructed at the cost of the praetorian
prefect Liberius.[26] Both Liberius and his sick wife had been healed by the
touch and prayers of Caesarius. The *Life* of Caesarius which records this had
a special interest in encouraging pilgrimage by narratives of miraculous
healings, but the substance of this story is probably correct. There was a
special bond therefore.

Caesarius' contacts with Rome may have alerted him to a current of opinion in the circle of Pope Hormisdas that Provence had a bishop of contested
opinions named Faustus of Riez. In 520 an African bishop named Possessor,
then resident at Constantinople, had written to Hormisdas (Coll. Avellana
230) partly about the Scythian monks' programme of ecumenism between
Chalcedonian and Monophysite but mainly about Faustus as an author insufficiently respectful of the authority of the fathers, especially Augustine, concerning the doctrine of grace and free will. To African admirers of Augustine
this was painful. Hormisdas' reply to Possessor (Avellana 231; *ACO* IV ii. 44–6;
Thiel p. 926) enclosed a copy of the 'Gelasian Decree' or fifth-century index
of prohibited books inserting Faustus' name as a dangerous author. If
Hormisdas was disturbed to think that writings of a bishop of a see close to
Arles were still widely respected, he is likely to have admonished Caesarius
to take action. That would explain the unusual agenda of the synod at
Orange.

The *Life* of Caesarius (1. 60) records that Bishop Julian of Vienne was raising questions about Caesarius' orthodoxy in the matter of grace, and held a
council at Valence which Caesarius declined to attend, probably in 528. At
Orange Caesarius presided himself; Julian of Vienne's signature comes
second.[27]

At the assembly of fourteen bishops in Orange, which had been taken into
Ostrogothic rule by Theoderic in 523, Liberius was present representing

---

[26] James J. O'Donnell, 'Liberius the Patrician', *Traditio*, 37 (1981), 31–72.
[27] The Acts of the council are edited by C. de Clercq (CCSL 148A. 53–76; more accurately in
SC 353 (Paris, 1989) by J. Gaudemet and B. Basdevant.

royal authority, and his signature of assent together with that of seven other 'magnificent' bureaucrats follows that of the bishops. The synod's duty was to correct the errors made in simplicity by the venerated Faustus of Riez (whose name was not mentioned but whose writings were widely and persistently admired) regarding the Augustinian doctrine of grace and predestination. Prosper's critique of John Cassian provided important matter. Nothing new was put forward. The main object was to crush the reservations of the churches in Provence which a century earlier had caused tension between Augustine's followers and the main Gallic theologians. In the eyes of John Cassian of Marseille and Vincent of Lérins Augustine was a great theologian who in a few important matters had been a dangerous innovator in conflict with the canon of orthodoxy, viz. that it is what all Christians have believed everywhere in all ages. No doubt on his visit to Rome Caesarius had acquired a copy of an approved list of propositions. The outcome of the council of Orange was a reaffirmation of Augustinian ideas about grace but explicitly disowning double predestination, i.e. to both heaven and hell. One must affirm the need for grace because of the weakening of the human will resulting from Adam's Fall, but also the positive and necessary part played by free choice in accepting salvation. 'All the baptized with Christ's help and co-operation can and have a duty to fulfil what things belong to the soul's salvation if they are willing to work at it.' Caesarius did not want anyone to suppose that with grace no effort or act of will was required.

Caesarius sent a copy of the decisions to Rome for Pope Felix IV to confirm, but he had lately died, succeeded by Boniface II who wrote a substantial letter of ratification.[28] To this Caesarius attached a prefatory note that anyone dissenting from the council's canons must realize himself to be contradicting the apostolic see and the universal Church throughout the world. A further addition was a florilegium of texts designed to show that Augustine's doctrine was held in deep respect by Ambrose and Jerome, therefore no innovation.

One other major dogmatic statement probably came from Arles during the time of Caesarius, namely the *Quicunque Vult* or so-called Athanasian

[28] The year 530 was marked by a papal schism at Rome. The dying Felix IV nominated as his successor a Goth who had risen to be archdeacon. To seal the appointment Felix invested him with the pallium, on the understanding that in the event of his recovery from sickness it would be returned. The Gothic archdeacon was wholly Romanized, and naturally he was firmly supported by the Gothic government at Ravenna. That, however, meant coldness to peace moves with Constantinople and the Greek churches. Felix's action was canonically questionable; Pope Hilarus in the 460s had forbidden Spanish bishops to name their successors. An opposition party formed, including a large majority of the Roman clergy, and they elevated a deacon from Alexandria named Dioscorus whose policy was to favour harmony with the east. Dioscorus was consecrated in the Lateran basilica, while his rival Boniface II had to make do in the less important basilica of Julius. Unfortunately for the opposition Dioscorus died less than a month later. Boniface II has the distinction of being the first German pope.

Creed. One form of the text appears among Caesarius' sermons (*S.* 3). Many pieces composed by others were reused by Caesarius so that this fact does not necessarily point to him as the probable author, but he may well have sponsored its production; in any event early sixth-century Arles is the milieu from which the document comes.[29]

Caesarius was bishop of Arles for forty years, during which time he saw the territory governed successively by Visigoths, Ostrogoths, and finally Franks. He lived to see the domination of Gaul by the Franks and the arrival of the Merovingian rulers. His death in 542 was profoundly mourned not only by his own flock but also by Jews and others. He had become the authority holding the Gallic churches together during a time of threatened disintegration. The western empire might be dismembered but not the Church. Christians could perhaps recall that once they had been proud to be a counterculture and barbarian, and that the apostle (Romans 1) regarded all ethnic and cultural differences as irrelevant in the Church.

The struggle on the Danube frontier

In the Danube region of Noricum (now roughly Austria) the situation was more difficult than in Gaul both for upholders of the empire and for the churches. A vivid picture is to be seen in the *Life of Severinus* by Eugippius, abbot of a monastery near Naples and a devoted admirer of Augustine, of whose writings he compiled an invaluable anthology. He described how the frontier was long defended by soldiers in many towns, paid for by the imperial treasury 'as long as the empire lasted' in the west. But the garrisons and indeed the frontier defences had disappeared. At Passau a military unit had held out but needed to send a detachment of men to Italy to bring their pay; the entire detachment was wiped out by barbarians. By second sight St Severinus knew what must have happened. The bodies of the dead men were found being carried down the river by the current. Severinus moved about from town to town, some deserted, many seriously damaged. When asked to mediate with the barbarian Rugians to allow the people to trade, he expressed doubt whether there would be any merchant alive to buy their produce. Once he was invited to meet a man on the other side of the Danube who presented him with relics of John the Baptist. At many of the places which he visited, barbarian raiders had killed Christians, in one place crucifying a presbyter. One of Severinus' main themes of intercession was that churches might be spared massacre or captivity. The sombre hagiographer vividly illustrates the horror which, in the Danube territory at least, was experienced by the people.

---

[29] See J. N. D. Kelly, *The Athanasian Creed* (London, 1964).

A factor which saved southern Gaul from this degree of awfulness was the desire of at least Visigoths and then Franks to have a positive association with the empire, as was illustrated when Alaric II produced a law-code that substantially restated the Theodosian Code of 438, and therefore preserved much of the text in the first five books that would otherwise have been lost. When the imperial army already consisted largely of Gothic soldiers, the forces had become barbarian up to the highest level of authority. So many barbarians were already living within the frontiers of the empire that any strong awareness of difference of race was beginning to fade. A Gallic inscription (*ILCV* 1516) records two barbarians whose racial origin was among the stains washed away by baptism. The latent presupposition was that to be baptized was to be fully Roman as well as Christian.

It was important that although the barbarians had their own separate Arian churches and bishops, they were Christians and, as Salvian observed, lived moral lives. (Augustine made a similar discovery about Donatists.) The conversion of the Franks to catholic faith and their military superiority to Burgundians and Visigoths would create the possibility of Francia, and so of France.

In Spain the Visigoths remained bellicose, and astonishingly the Mozarabic liturgical books include a form of service in Toledo cathedral 'when the king of the Visigoths goes forth to war'.[30] The Visigoths in Spain did not make life comfortable for Jewish communities, and this was not alleviated when, led by King Reccared in a council at Toledo in 589, Arianism was abjured and an Augustinian orthodoxy accepted. Under Reccared's father Leovigild the Visigothic kingdom was enlarged by incorporating the Basques and the north-west territory of Gallaecia occupied by Suevi who had converted to catholic orthodoxy in 448, then back to Arianism, but finally ending in catholic faith. A degree of unity in the Visigothic kingdom was thereby achieved. The Visigothic kings effectively controlled a succession of episcopal councils at Toledo. Relations with the papacy were marginal, but Gregory the Great possessed a major ally in Leander bishop of Seville. The Spanish churches remained concerned to teach the errors of Arianism but also of the Jewish synagogue. Isidore of Seville looked back with regret on a harassment of Jews conducted with 'more zeal than knowledge'. It was evidently a reflection of the quest for unity in the Iberian peninsula.

The Spains

In Spain the situation for both Church and State during the fifth century was close to chaos. The south in Baetica was more Romanized than the north,

---

[30] M. Férotin, *Liber Ordinum* (Paris, 1904), 149.

and disparities between the regions were considerable. A central administration had become impossible. From 490 the Visigoths began to settle in considerable numbers, and were not in the business of sharing power with old Roman landowners. After the conversion of king Reccared and the council at Toledo (589) condemning Arianism, relations were easier. At Toledo a series of episcopal councils was held. In 531 Montanus bishop of Toledo had held a small council at which a bid was made to erect the see of Toledo to metropolitan status in the province with authority to summon synods. This synod also prayed for 'divine clemency for our glorious King Amalaric' with the hope that he would allow the council's canons to be in force. The Visigothic king was understood to have a sacred character; after all he in practice nominated new bishops. The Visigothic crown was and remained central in the life of the Church.

As always, the canons of the Visigothic church councils vividly portray what the bishops thought it their duty to discourage or suppress. They wanted to stop people at baptisms throwing coins into the font; secular girls' choirs singing in church services; concubinage; clergy who took to the bottle or who had adulterous relationships; fees charged for ordinations; clergy with hunting dogs and hawks; marriages during Lent and of any girls against their parents' will; corpses at funerals being given the eucharistic host (once a common north African custom) or kissed (usual in the Orthodox east to this day); the ordination of manumitted slaves; people not staying to the end of mass; failure to consume the consecrated remains at the end of mass. They welcomed incense to mark the liturgical Gospel and the offertory. It seemed important to them to make it clear that women deacons were not ordained. They state the principle that no diocese should have a bishop thrust upon it against the will of the people (*nullus invitis detur episcopus*); in a world where Visigothic kings were nominating, this must have been hard to achieve.

In 418 when Orosius deposited in Menorca relics of St Stephen the first martyr (which he was supposed to deliver to Braga), Bishop Severus reported the conversion of 540 Jews. Severus' encyclical betrays feelings of considerable tension between Christian and Jewish communities at that time. See Scott Bradbury's edition (Oxford, 1996). Contact between the Church in Spain and the rest of Christendom seems to have been limited. At a council of Seville in 619, however, a Syrian bishop turned up who endeavoured to persuade the bishops of the grave error of the definition of Chalcedon. He was himself converted to western orthodoxy by the council (canon 12). The Spanish churches had some internal controversy about the use of the *Gloria Patri* at the end of every psalm, and some were critical of the *Gloria in excelsis* on the ground that after the biblical text it continued with non-scriptural words (*C Toledo* IV. 633, canon 13). This dispute may have anticipated a problem which surfaced in ninth-century exchanges between Pope Leo III and the Franks at Aachen, namely that there was objection to the words 'You alone are holy' *Tu solus sanctus*, addressed to Christ in the *Gloria in excelsis*. A particular concern of the fourth council of Toledo was to achieve liturgical uniformity. It was a mark of the intimate link between Church and Crown that the Visigothic kings were appointing bishops even to serve on commissions investigating high treason; the council agreed that bishops could serve but could only give a verdict of pardon, never of capital punishment (canon 31). The main problem of dissidence centred upon the Jewish communities who could not easily be integrated into so tightly knit a state (canons 57–66). In east Rome the legislation of Justinian about Jews marked a deterioration. Under the barbarians other than the Visigoths in Spain it was not so bad, and in Theoderic's Italy their position received good protection.[31]

The authority of the see of Rome appears rather distant. But Pope Gregory the Great had caused some impact when he dedicated his homilies on the book of Job to Leander bishop of Seville; they had met in Constantinople when Gregory was 'deacon apocrisiary' to the emperor and the patriarch about 580. Leander played a leading role in the conversion of Reccared from Arianism to Catholicism. The council of Toledo marking the conversion not only affirmed the creed of the council of Constantinople in 381 (of which assembly Gregory the Great was to have negative views) but also included the Augustinian *Filioque* as part of proper catechetical doctrine. In the western churches of the sixth-century the truth of this doctrine was taken for granted as a necessary safeguard against Arianism. The council ordered that the Constantinopolitan creed, probably with *Filioque* (but that is not stated), was to be recited by the congregation at the end of the canon of the mass before the Lord's Prayer (canon 2).

About 600 Leander was to be succeeded in the see of Seville by his younger brother Isidore, who dedicated to Leander his book modelled on Jerome with brief biographies 'of Illustrious Men', and became hugely important for medieval education by his '*Etymologiae*' or *Origines* in twenty books, explaining liberal arts and much else besides—zoology, medicine, medicine, law, and statecraft (edited by W. M. Lindsay, Oxford Classical Texts, 1911, repr. 1985). A number of other writings illustrated the extraordinary range of information possessed by this polymath. His book *De officiis* is a mine of material on clergy and on the liturgy of the sacraments (CCSL 113, learnedly edited by C. Lawson). Isidore thought the etymology or origin of a word could explain its essential meaning. The Spanish churches before the arrival of the Arab invaders in 711 were well educated by Isidore's labours.

---

[31] H. C. Brennecke, 'Imitatio-reparatio-continuatio: die Judengesetzgebung im Ostgotenreich Theoderichs des Großen als reparatio imperii', *Zeitschrift für Antikes Christentum*, 4 (2000), 133–48.

58

POPE GREGORY THE GREAT (590–604)

Gregory was son of a Roman senator and when still in his thirties rose to be praetor and could well have gone to the top as a praetorian prefect. His grandfather had become Felix III, pope 483–92 in the early years of the long Acacian Schism with Constantinople. Three of his father's sisters had become nuns, one of the three abandoning the religious life, marrying the steward of her property and failing to find happiness (*Hom. Evang.* 38. 15; *Dial.* 4. 17). He aspired to be a monk and founded his own monastery of St Andrew in Rome. Self-discipline and humility were basic virtues in the ascetic life. It is not clear that his monastery used the Rule drafted by Benedict of Nursia as a 'little rule for beginners', considerably mitigating an earlier and more strenuous 'Rule of the Master'; but when Cassino was destroyed in 585 and the monks took refuge in Rome, Gregory had informants to brief him for a biography of Benedict which was to be the second of the four books of his *Dialogues*.

Pope Pelagius II ordained him to be deacon and sent him to Constantinople as apocrisiary; it was normal for apocrisiaries to the court and the patriarch to be in deacon's orders, and they were officially accredited to convey documents from emperor to pope and vice versa. Gregory held this post for six years, 579–85. During this time he appears not to have learnt Greek, so he probably had a local translator.[1] At this time it would be easier to find a civil servant in Constantinople with a legal training and therefore some grasp of Latin (John Lydus could be an example) than to find a Latin-speaker in Italy capable of fluency in Greek. His residence in Constantinople brought him into contact with influential people, and among those he met there was Leander bishop of Seville for whom he wrote his commentary on Job, carefully expounding the text as one in which 'lambs could paddle and elephants swim'. Gregory's preaching was profoundly biblical, allowing for both a literal or moral sense and for an allegorical inner meaning.

---

[1] *Reg.* 11. 29 ('Graecae linguae nescius') and 11. 55 ('nos nec graece novimus') seem fatal to the contention of Joan M. Petersen (*Studies in Church History*, 12 (1976), 121–34) that Gregory knew Greek.

Bishop of Rome 590

He returned to his monastery in Rome. In 589 a flood brought disease and Gregory organized litanies and processional prayers for the ending of the plague. In 590 Pope Pelagius II died. Gregory found himself nominated by the east Roman emperor Maurice for consecration. In Gregory's view this was 'asking an ape to act like a lion'; rough would be the storm in which he felt that he had been put in charge of a leaky ship (*Reg.* 1. 4 to John bishop of Constantinople). Moreover it meant that 'under the colour of the episcopate he had been brought back to the secular world' (1. 5 to the emperor's sister Theoctista). At east Rome matters were to become even more tempestuous in 602, when the emperor Maurice was murdered by Phocas, who usurped the imperial title. Gregory wrote a formally correct letter of salutation to the new emperor, to which Phocas answered with a decree on papal authority. A surviving column in Phocas' honour was erected in the old Roman Forum.

In the west the Frankish kingdoms established in Gaul had been catholic since the conversion of Clovis in the 490s. In 587 the Visigoths in Spain had been brought to abandon Arianism by king Reccared. The greatest problem was the Lombards' threat to churches in Italy. Gregory might and did strive to convert them but their determination was conquest. Surprisingly Gregory's task was alleviated by the fact that some wives of Lombard military commanders (dukes) were catholic in faith. In Rome itself since Theoderic's rule there had been an Arian basilica. Gregory reconsecrated it with relics of SS. Stephen and Agatha (*Dial.* 3. 30).

Justinian's Gothic wars were past and had left much in ruins, but from 568 the Lombards had arrived in the north and were soon to move southwards. Italy was under the sovereignty of the emperor at Constantinople who governed through a viceroy or exarch at Ravenna, and it was his duty to marshal defence against Lombard attack and infiltration. For the Church memories of the Ostrogothic domination of Italy had left a bitter taste, principally because of Theoderic's reaction to Boethius by which the philosopher-logician was bludgeoned to death in custody at Pavia and his father-in-law Symmachus with his close friend Pope John I lost their lives. Gregory would recall a holy hermit on the Lipari islands who had a vision of Theoderic's death by being plunged into an erupting volcano (*Dial.* 4. 33). Gregory thought that a just end. In general Gregory's estimate of Goths, many of whom had remained in the countryside as labourers (*Dial.* 2. 6), was not laudatory but not hostile; he found them excessively bibulous (*Dial.* 1. 9. 14).

The Roman clergy were not comfortable with so ascetic a bishop. Gregory found it necessary to sack his archdeacon and to install one more amenable to his ways named Honoratus, later to be sent to Constantinople as apocrisiary. After Gregory's time, the local clergy reasserted their role

(*Liber Pontificalis*). He was no builder of new churches in his city, but a conscientious restorer of old church buildings. The ancient buildings of imperial Rome were crumbling away (*Dial.* 2. 15. 3). Opulent aristocrats occupied their leisure in producing calligraphic editions of classical Latin authors such as Livy or Vergil.

In 592 Lombards from Spoleto under King Agilulf arrived before the walls of Rome and in the following year returned to besiege it. References to the resulting hardships for the people occur in his Forty *Gospel Homilies* preached in various Roman churches, especially on martyrs' festivals. At martyrs' shrines prayers for healing are being answered, perjurers harassed by evil powers, and the demon-possessed liberated (*Hom. Evang.* 32). Help comes from the angels of whom, as taught by Dionysius the Areopagite, there are nine ranks (*Hom. Evang.* 34, restated from *Moralia in Hiob* 32. 23. 48). People losing their earthly home should contemplate their heavenly destiny. Under siege the people fill the churches (*Hom.* 17) but how few have real faith; some are Christians merely because everyone else is (*Hom.* 32).[2] Some come to pray for their enemy's death (27). Yet the bishop's problems are not much with the laity. 'God suffers great harm from none more than priests.' Almost no worldly act is not done by clergy living evil lives, avaricious, mocking at chastity (17). Bishops have to ask themselves how at the Last Judgement they will answer when asked how many they have converted or turned away from a sinful life or brought to renounce avarice or pride. We bishops have become secular. All that we are ambitious for is human praise. And many are charging fees for ordinations which canon law forbids (17, 39).

His *Homilies on Ezekiel* were also preached during this siege. He saw people coming into the city with their hands cut off, and news came of some being captured and others killed (*Hom. in Hiez.* 2. 10. 14). Gregory raised 500 pounds of gold to persuade Agilulf to go away; though successful in outcome, to the emperor this was the action of a fool; it would only encourage hunger for more gold. Gregory expostulated that the Roman garrison had been withdrawn by the exarch to defend Perugia, and that he had had to witness undefended Romans being bound with ropes and led off into captivity (*Reg.* 5. 36). The exarch was not interested in the fate of Rome. Bishops had inherited secular functions, acting as magistrates, arbitrators in disputes, providers of food in times of barbarian attack or famine. He could have echoed Augustine's timeless comment that 'no one who has not been a bishop can imagine what people expect us to do' (above p. 477), or his

---

[2] This sentence illustrates how different Gregory's society was from that of Augustine 200 years earlier. The next sentence however is exactly paralleled in Augustine, *Sermo* 90. 9 (do not come to a eucharist to pray for your enemy's death). That was pagan: e.g. Petronius, *Sat.* 88 (offering in temple to cause death).

outraged reminiscence 'I have been consulted on how to obtain someone else's villa' (*Sermo* 137. 14).

Gregory owed much to his reading of Augustine who had taught that the Church's present enemies may become her future members (*City of God* 1. 35). He instinctively saw that his primary duty was to convert the Lombards and thereby to transform them into men of peace. The exarch and the military commanders could not be expected to share that view. It was not that Gregory did nothing for the defence of the city. He found that respons-ibility was left to him to ensure that there were guards on the walls to protect the citizens against sudden surprise attacks (*Hom. in Hiez.* 1. 14. 16). Defence was not easy if the remaining garrison within the walls was in revolt (*Reg.* 1. 3 of September 590).

As bishop of Rome Gregory was expected to act as the city's protector, whether by invoking SS. Peter, Paul, and Laurence, or by direct action. The defence of the city against Lombard attacks brought him into close touch with the Roman military commander (2. 4, 27). On the future of Ravenna, he negotiated with the Lombard king (v. 36). His public and Roman role found lapidary expression in his epitaph now in the crypt of St Peter's, the author of which described him as 'God's consul' (text in *MGH Epp.* ii. 470).

Gregory's irritation with authority at Constantinople may have been sharpened by the old feeling of distrust between Old and New Rome, vastly exacerbated during the Acacian schism. Nearly two centuries earlier as is clear in Augustine people thought of the empire as a duality with two churches, eastern and western, which tried to speak as if they were one but were visibly not so. The emperor Theodosius II and his lawyers had drafted the Theodosian Code with the intention that it be accepted as valid for both halves of one empire. That presupposes that there was a sense of needing to bridge a widening crack affecting both Church and State. Once the western provinces had been dismembered to become barbarian kingdoms mutually watchful against each other, and once there was no one western king (*rex*) who could become an effective centre of government for the old empire, there was in the Latin west only one locus of real authority. That now resided in the bishop of Rome.

Head of an investment corporation

A solid proportion of Gregory's large extant correspondence, almost 850 letters in all, is concerned with the administering of properties outside Italy vested in the Roman church by gift or legacy. Each estate was cared for by ecclesiastical 'rectors'. So large had been the benefactions of the faithful that the bishop of Rome's most time-consuming duty was to be executive president of a large investment corporation, used partly to maintain the basilicas of the city but also to provide aid for the numerous poor and destitute. He did not deploy his resources for magnificent new buildings or for the spectacular adornment of Rome's city churches. Money was often needed to ransom captives held by the invaders. The medieval canonist Deusdedit preserves a fragment of a letter from Pope Gelasius to Agilulf (on ground of chronology not the same as the Lombard king attacking Rome in Gregory's time), from which it is clear that a century earlier the papacy possessed estates in Dalmatia (fr. 2, p. 484 Thiel). The deacon Peter, who had once been Defensor of the church at Ravenna, and to whom Gregory dedicated his *Dialogues*, was entrusted with substantial estates in Sicily, later in Sardinia. In Gaul the land, mainly in the region of Arles, was administered by a priest Candidus (*Reg.* 6. 10). In 556 Pope Pelagius II had been writing to Sapaudius bishop of Arles begging him to release the income from the papal estate on the ground of desperate poverty in Italy (*MGH Epp.* iii. 72, no. 49); the request had to be repeated a few months later (*MGH* p. 76). It is instructive that even in chaotic times the revenues from distant estates could somehow be transmitted to Rome without loss. In Gaul there was a special problem: the coinage had lately become of a weight lighter by an eighth than that in Italy, and therefore was not accepted by bankers in Rome (*Reg.* 6. 10; 3. 33 'Gallicanos solidos'; Majorian, Novel 7. 14, p. 171 Mommsen, on the *solidus gallicus* 'cuius aurum minore aestimatione taxatur'). Moreover, many countries had no banks at all (*Hom. Evang.* 10).

Gregory believed that at the Day of Judgement when the angelic accountants would inspect his books he would be answerable for his stewardship. In consequence no detail was too small for his attention (*Reg.* 2. 38). Like Augustine he was unsympathetic to benefactors who, in faith that their piety would be rewarded in the world to come, starved their relatives of help in their will. When wealthy people built a church on their land, it was crucial that the benefactor's endowment was sufficient to pay for both priest and overheads. Another danger was that a monastery would be founded and sufficiently endowed, but then the local bishop would assert his right to control the monastery and might judge that he could use its endowment on other favoured projects. Therefore it was prudent to lay down that a monastery be exempt from diocesan control. When a religious lady wanted to found a monastery in Corsica, Gregory judged it wise to provide not only that there be sufficient endowment but also that the proposed site be replaced by one on the coast fortified against raiders (*Reg.* 1. 50).

Vicariates

The old vicariates of Thessalonica and Arles were much diminished in importance. In Gaul the bishop of Arles was not someone ordinarily consulted by Frankish kings who were more likely to turn to Lyon or Autun. Moreover, at Arles there happened to be a bishop (Virgilius, 588–610) in whom Gregory had less than complete confidence, though there was no polemic or quarrel and Gregory invested him with the pallium and appointed him as his vicar or deputy. But the Arles vicariate had become nominal, and lasted only a few decades after Gregory's death.[3]

The situation in Gaul was one of power conflicts among the kings and nobles, and in the churches no one could hope to become bishop without laying down a substantial sum in gratitude to the lay prince who made it possible (*Reg.* 5. 58). In consequence the clergy lost public respect. Prominent laymen were elevated to become bishops *per saltum*,[4] but in both word and behaviour remained unpriestly and unedifying (5. 60). That was particularly true of successive bishops of Arles in the late fifth century. Gregory became hard to persuade that the necessary reforms in the Gallic churches could ever be led by his Vicar in Arles. His only hope lay in mobilizing members of the royal families, and a chance came when Queen Brunhilde requested a pallium for her bishop Syagrius of Autun, a bishop who was no metropolitan, his metropolitan being at Lyon. Gregory could therefore use Syagrius to implement the necessary reforms, and simultaneously could rely on support from the queen whom he gratified.

Canon law

Gregory was much aware of the decretals of his predecessors, from the times of Damasus and Siricius. He extended the rule made by Leo that subdeacons should be as celibate as bishops, presbyters, and deacons. He sought to introduce this rule in Sicily where many laity and some clergy were Greeks who would not expect celibacy to be required of any clergy not bishops. Other letters concern divorce, consanguinity and prohibited degrees for marriage, Sunday observance. About episcopal elections he insisted on being 'consulted'. The theory remained that bishops nominated by local people by inspired acclamation were then consecrated by the metropolitan with other provincial bishops. But episcopal elections had become so frequently a matter of faction and strife that in the event of a vacancy Gregory would try to get an appropriate person appointed. When a see fell vacant, he would appoint a neighbouring bishop to take charge of the diocese. In 593 he even directed that in north Italy under the aegis of Milan Rome should still retain a power of veto (*Reg.* 3. 30–1).

---

[3] G. Langgärtner, *Die Gallienpolitik der Päpste* (Bonn, 1964).
[4] That is, without first being deacon and/or presbyter.

Natalis of Salona

A series of remarkable letters deals with problems at Salona in Dalmatia (a few km from Split). There Bishop Natalis was a *bon vivant* who liked a good table richly furnished with guests and high standards of hospitality. He justified this by citing the hospitality of Abraham to guests who turned out to be angels and by declaring himself glad to share in the accusation levelled at the Lord himself of being a gluttonous man and a winebibber. His purposes were charitable and his entertainments were reconciling many heretics to the Church. To the monk now in the papal office such worldliness was shocking. Apparently the archdeacon Honoratus of Salona was a critic of Natalis, and the bishop got rid of him by promoting him. Gregory demanded his restoration (*Reg.* 2. 20; 11. 50). A year later Natalis died and Gregory wrote to the subdeacon in charge of papal estates in Dalmatia; he was to see that the Salona election was properly conducted (5. 10). The local city clergy were anxious to please Gregory and chose Honoratus. But the Dalmatian bishops regarded him as unsuitable, and instead consecrated a certain Maximus, first having secured support for him from the emperor at Constantinople who no doubt was glad to have Dalmatia regarded as under his jurisdiction in such a matter. For the same reason the consecration of Maximus was unwelcome at Rome. Gregory demanded that the Dalmatian bishops suspend communion with their new bishop of Salona. Only one bishop could be found to submit to this amazing demand. Maximus himself obtained a letter from the emperor to Gregory regretting that the consecration had gone ahead without his good will. The emperor did not apologize; he was sorry that Gregory felt the way he did. After three or four years of wretched controversy, Gregory gave way under pressure from the exarch at Ravenna. After examination by an ecclesiastical court at Ravenna, all complaints against Maximus were withdrawn, and Gregory invested him with the pallium. At least Gregory had won his main point that in future a major episcopal election in Dalmatia needed Roman ratification if fuss was to be avoided.

Unity and authority

Gregory was confident that the Roman empire would be protected by God if it protected the Church and orthodoxy and suppressed paganism and heresy. In return for the support of the Church, including church property, the intercessions of God's priests would assure security and victory for the empire. Divine favour surely requires unity in the universal Church, so that in harmony all bishops can offer a single propitiatory sacrifice to the Lord; the sacrifice of the altar pleads for forgiveness since Christ suffers for us afresh in his mystery and (in ritual) we are renewing his passion (*Hom. Evang.* 37). The departed long for requiems (*Dial.* 4. 57. 7). In the one Church Gregory did not ask for precise liturgical uniformity; unity was for him compatible with diversity of custom, much as Augustine (*En. in Ps.* 44. 14) wrote of 'many languages, one faith'. Disunity occasioned mockery from pagans (Aug. *util. ieiun.* 8. 16). The demand for unity could be uncomfortable for those who naturally fell outside the tradition that Gregory represented. Gregory did not understand authority to be coercive. In his *Moralia in Hiob* (8. 3) he wrote that the Church is humble and does not command when it gives correct instruction to erring sinners; assent is won by reason. If she says something that cannot be comprehended by reason, she reasonably points out that human reasoning cannot be looked for in hidden mysterious truths.

On Jews, moreover, there must be no coercion. Jewish business men complained of the zeal of the bishop of Marseille who used to catch them at the harbour on a trading journey and drag them by force to the baptismal font (*Reg.* 1. 45). Gregory wrote a stern rebuke to the bishop.[5] Such mistaken measures would be ineffective unless accompanied by teaching. Similarly the bishop of Terracina was admonished to use gentleness with Jews and no rough methods (1. 34). Moreover at Terracina the Jewish synagogue occupied its site with Gregory's explicit permission. They were to be treated with reason, not force, and if the sound of their worship was disturbingly audible in the church, the bishop of Terracina ought to find them an alternative place. By law Jews might not have Christian slaves, who could acquire their freedom by running away, though then there would still be difficulties for them in finding a job and food, so that they could be better off where they were (2. 6). And while no physical coercion should ever be used to gain conversions, there was no objection to modest financial inducements (2. 38).

Paganism was another matter; cult was prohibited by law and could properly be suppressed by force. The old pagan practices of the rural peasantry had to be stopped, and rustics could be beaten into church with blows. Blows seem to have been the accompaniment of almost everything for poor manual labourers in the fields. Flogging remained the severest penalty imposed by church courts, but Gregory was alarmed when it was not administered with care and discretion. *Dial.* 4. 37 reports on a sadist who administered whippings with cruel blows.

There were difficulties for Gregory in the asylum granted by bishops to runaway slaves. In Sicily landowners complained that slaves who ran for protection, probably hoping for manumission by the church, then declared themselves to have become the church's property, and at least one bishop was

---

[5] In the ninth century an imperial policy of forced baptism for Jews was vigorously denounced by the Sicilian bishop Gregory Asbestas, consecrator of patriarch Photius. His treatise is edited in *Travaux et mémoires* 11 (1991), 313–57 by G. Dagron.

refusing to return them to the lawful owners. Gregory ruled that after their grievance had been examined, runaways should be restored (*Reg.* 1. 39a, a document surviving through the Spanish canon collections: 3: 1).

Pagans, heretics, and orthodox Christians in this age assumed that the security of the empire against the barbarians, or good crops in the fields, required right belief. At the root of Gregory's moments of intolerance lay the assumption that too many practising pagans or heretics could provoke celestial wrath and explain famine or drought or other disasters. That pagans and heretics were associated with disloyalty to the empire is evident from the oath required of bishops returning to communion with Rome: 'By the four gospels held in my hand and by the health (*salutem*) and genius of the emperors' (*Reg.* 12. 7).

Popular piety: relics

Evidence of providential protection was visible in miraculous happenings which might be almost everyday occurrences in Gregory's circle. In 593–4 at the request of his deacon Peter he compiled his *Dialogues* with accounts of wonders performed by Italian holy men and women, avowedly motivated by local patriotism and a desire to prove to the world that Italy did not fall behind Egypt's Desert Fathers and Mothers. He devoted the second book to a Life of Benedict and his thaumaturgic powers. The atmosphere of the *Dialogues* is closely akin to the *Spiritual Meadow* of John Moschos. Many of Gregory's anecdotes are repeated from his forty *Gospel Homilies*.

When Gregory wished to send a notable present to some important personage, he liked to send 'Keys of St Peter', the metal of which included shavings from the very chains that had once bound the apostle. King Reccared of Spain received such a present together with a cross incorporating wood from the True Cross and some hairs of St John the Baptist (*Reg.* 9. 228). Gregory was the grateful recipient of relics from the East such as oil from the cross or the tunic worn by St John (3. 3). On the other hand the empress Constantina, wife of the emperor Maurice, peremptorily ordered him to send to Constantinople 'the head of St Paul or some other part of his body' to be enshrined in a church which she was building within the palace precinct. She may have recalled how two hundred years earlier the prefect Rufinus obtained from Rome relics of SS. Peter and Paul for his church at Chalcedon.[6] Gregory absolutely refused to obey her wish, and explained his refusal by relating horrific stories of the gruesome and sudden deaths which in the past had been visited on unfortunate folk who had dared to dig in the vicinity of the graves of St Paul and St Laurence. Moreover, it was contrary to

---

[6] Callinicus, *Vita Hypatii* 8. 6, SC 177, p. 98; Soz. 8. 17.

western custom to move bones of saints in the deplorable manner customary among the Greeks. Roman practice was to put a cloth in a box close to the sacred body, such cloths in time acquiring the miracle-working powers of the relics themselves. If the empress should doubt this, let her ponder a story of Pope Leo the Great. Greeks had expressed scepticism of the wonderworking efficacy of such cloths. Leo refuted their doubts by cutting one such cloth with scissors, whereupon blood had flowed. Nevertheless, Gregory wished well to Constantina and hoped to send filings from St Peter's chains. Success in this project could not be taken for granted since, for unworthy applicants, the holy chains have been known to withstand filing (4. 30).

Pilgrimage was encouraged by Gregory, whether to the holy places at Jerusalem (within a generation to pass under Arab control) or to Mount Sinai or to the apostolic shrines in Rome, especially on the annual festival of 29 June (e.g. *Hom. Evang.* 37 on Cassius bishop of Narni; on Jerusalem pilgrimage abandoned, then pursued to Sinai by the patrician lady Rusticiana, *Reg.* 2. 27, 4. 44). Rome in his time had a calendar of saints' days[7] but no collection of 'legends' to be read on these days such as Eusebius of Caesarea gathered for the emperor Constantine. He had only a small number in one codex. The Roman calendar recorded name, place, and date and nothing further (*Reg.* 8. 28 to Eulogius of Alexandria). Gregory also tells us that a festival of the Blessed Virgin Mary was being observed in Sicily in the month of August (*Reg.* 1. 54). This is the earliest western reference to a feast of the Dormition, celebrated in the east on 15 August and formally recognized for the Greek churches by the emperor Maurice (Nikephoros Kallistos, *HE* 17. 28, PG 147. 292A).

Portrayals of Christ, the Virgin, angels, and saints had become common in the west. At Marseille the bishop was iconoclast in reaction to adoration being offered by simple people to images. The bishop felt it to be his duty to destroy pictures that led to such devotional practice. However, members of his flock were outraged by his puritanism. Gregory wrote a stern censure: he was right to tell people not to worship the images, but wrong to destroy them (*Reg.* 9. 195, 208; 11. 10). A majority were illiterate, and icons were the poor man's Bible.

To the barbarian Christians the right policy was one of accommodation and conciliation. There was an educational task for the Church, and abrupt methods could only alienate them. One of Gregory's strengths, and part of his legacy to medieval Catholicism in the west, lay in his combination of ascetic devotion to the supernatural with acceptance of natural aspirations,

---

[7] Saints explicitly named by Gregory are: Agnes, Andrew, Clement, Felicity, Felix, Juvenal, Laurence, Marcellinus and Peter, Menas, Nereus and Achilleus, Pancratius, Philip and James, Processus and Martinianus, Sebastian, Silvester, Stephen, besides St John Lateran; many appear in connection with sermons preached on their feast day in churches dedicated to them.

hopes, and fears of ordinary uncultured unheroic men and women with needs which they looked to the Church to meet. In his mind there was no such thing as an inferior 'popular religion' distinct from that of the well-educated. All religion was popular. Educated senators wanted relics and icons as much as peasants.

Gregory and east Rome

Gregory inherited the Roman tradition of firm adherence to Chalcedon and the two-natures Christology. In line with the neo-Chalcedonian language favoured by Justinian, he affirmed both *of* and *in* two natures (*Hom. Evang.* 38). The four councils of Nicaea, Constantinople, Ephesus I, and Chalcedon are a canon as sacred as the four Gospels, though as an afterthought one must add the fifth council condemning the Three Chapters (*Reg.* 1. 12, 3. 10, 4. 4). Gregory evidently inherited from Vigilius and Pelagius I the judgement that the condemnation of the Three Chapters could not be taken as a rejection of Chalcedon if the authority of that council was simultaneously being reaffirmed. He accepted the fifth council's censure of Origen (*Moralia in Hiob* 3. 35), though without alluding to the council as authority. On the other hand in accord with Roman tradition since Damasus, he could not accept the canons of Constantinople (381) (7. 34). He reaffirmed Damasus' insistence against Constantinople of the superiority of the three Petrine sees, Rome, Alexandria, and Antioch (*Reg.* 5. 42; 6. 58; 7. 40). The theme that episcopal jurisdiction is derived from St Peter's successor in Rome is expressed through the conferring of the pallium which the recipient is to wear when celebrating mass (iii. 56–7; cf. 5. 11, 15; both London and York were to receive one: 11. 39).

When Gregory had been Roman apocrisiary at Constantinople he had been critical of the then patriarch Eutychius who had written a book teaching that the resurrection body will be impalpable and subtler than wind or air. In the middle of the sixth century the Alexandrian anti-Chalcedonian divine, John Philoponos, urged that the resurrection body is created out of nothing and will be a suitable medium for the soul hereafter, discontinuous with the physical body in this life (Chabot, *Documenta ad hist. monoph. pertinentia*, p. 230). Gregory did not know about Philoponos, but he was alarmed by the patriarch, whose exegesis of 1 Corinthians 15 seemed to him too spiritualizing. The dispute came before the emperor Tiberius Constantine at a private hearing, and this emperor decreed the burning of Eutychius' book, a signal victory for the Roman nuncio.[8]

---

[8] The controversy is delicately mentioned in Eustratius' Life of Eutychius (PG 86. 2376), and described more independently by the Monophysite historian John of Ephesus (*HE* 2. 36, pp. 101–2, ed. Brooks).

Both in this controversy and in the fourth book of the *Dialogues* Gregory's doctrine of the Last Things is physically realist. His sermons on Job (6. 48) restate the doctrine of Tertullian (*De spectaculis*) that an ingredient in the felicity of the righteous in heaven will be to contemplate the damned receiving their just reward in hell. He adds, with an echo of ancient Stoicism, that compassion is an infirmity from which the saints in heaven will be free. This stoicizing doctrine is also found in the Gospel *Homilies* (40). The fourth book of the *Dialogues*, in which he explores stories of the soul's experiences in the waiting state between death and judgement, was to provide later theologians with proof-texts for 'purifying fire' for venial faults (*Dial.* 4. 41. 3).

Strained relations with Constantinople

Gregory inherited the old pre-Christian suspicions that Latins felt towards intelligent Greeks, who seemed 'too clever to be honest' (5. 14). Moreover, his predecessor Pelagius II had complained when the contemporary patriarch John IV the Faster, 582–95, allowed correspondents to apply to him the title 'ecumenical patriarch', which to Latin ears sounded like 'universal patriarch'. The title had already a long history. At the Robber Council of Ephesus in 449 Dioscorus of Alexandria was acclaimed by one enthusiastic supporter as 'universal archbishop' (*ACO* II iii. 187. 12). Perhaps this was customary for Constantinople in the time of Patriarch Acacius, seeing that Pope Felix asked him how he could assert himself to be leader of the entire Church (*ep.* 2. 8, pp. 237–8 Thiel). The title was certainly used in a letter of 20 July 518 addressed to Patriarch John II of Constantinople by his synod (Mansi viii. 1038. 1042. 1058–9). Thereafter several sixth-century texts have it. Likewise letters from the court at Constantinople to Rome address the Pope as 'universal archbishop' (Avellana 163, 165).

Gregory's letter of complaint to John the Faster has the earliest known allusion to the claim that the church in Constantinople had been founded by Andrew brother of Simon Peter (4. 44). For Gregory the appropriate self-designation probably seemed that borrowed from Augustine, who applied it to his mother Monnica and also to himself (*Conf.* 9. 9. 22; *ep.* 217 title), 'servant of the servants of God.' In *Reg.* 5. 37 Gregory writes 'I am the servant of all priests insofar as their lives are priestly.'[9]

On three occasions documents incorporated with the Acts of Chalcedon refer to Leo as 'ecumenical archbishop and patriarch of great Rome' (*ACO* II i. 211, 31; 213. 11; 216. 17). In 517 it had been used of Pope Hormisdas (Mansi, viii. 425) and of Pope Agapetus in 535 (Mansi, viii. 895). The title patriarch was not a problem. In Gregory's age this title could be applied to the

---

[9] Pope Agatho in 680 can use the title as normal (*ACO* II ii. 123. 12).

metropolitan bishops of Tyre (Mansi, viii. 1083, 1090), Phrygian Hierapolis (CIG xx. 8769) or Thessalonica (Theophanes, AM 6008). Patriarchs of Constantinople are found using the term 'ecumenical patriarch' for Jerusalem (Mansi, viii. 1066–7), so that they evidently did not think of themselves as asserting their own particular prerogatives. The epithet implied for the Greeks a dignity of imperial range extending beyond their own region, but not universal jurisdiction over both east and west, as Gregory was understanding it. The sensitivity was long-lasting. When Pope Gregory VII in the eleventh century drew up his famous 'Dictatus papae', he included 'That only the Roman pontiff is entitled universal' (*Reg.* 2. 55a, i. 202, ed. Caspar).[10]

In Gregory's time western Christians, especially at Rome, had prejudices unfavourable to eastern Christians. A Sicilian visitor to Rome noted as borrowings from the east the Alleluia sung outside Eastertide, letting subdeacons process to the altar without linen tunics, using the Greek Kyrie Eleison, and placing the Lord's Prayer at the end of the canon. The visitor may have been asking how Gregory could be less than polite to the patriarch of Constantinople when he had borrowed so much from him for Roman liturgy. Gregory had to write to bishop John of Syracuse (9. 26) to rebut these charges.

North Africa

Justinian's reconquest of north Africa from the Vandals was long past in Gregory's time. The region was administered by an imperial exarch at Carthage. Gregory found the north African churches too independent-minded, and took this independence to be a revival of Donatism. Professor Robert Markus has given good reasons for thinking Gregory misinformed, namely that his letters show no awareness of two rival churches embattled against one another as was the situation in the time of Augustine of Hippo, from whose writings Gregory had learned virtually all that he knew about this region. We hear of no town with two competing bishops. All that can be safely asserted is that here and there remnants of the Donatist legacy were discernible in a few rural areas especially, as one would expect, in Numidia. One thing disturbed him, namely the old practice in Numidia whereby the primate among the provincial bishops was decided not by merit but by seniority in date of consecration; it obviously tended to make the metropolitan elderly, in some cases too much so to discharge his duties correctly. Gregory otherwise confirmed an assurance by his predecessor Pelagius II that the north Africans should maintain their traditional customs (*Reg.* 1. 72 and 75). A minor fuss was caused by an appeal to Rome by a Numidian bishop Paul

[10] Illuminated by H. E. J. Cowdrey, *Pope Gregory VII* (Oxford, 1998), 502–7.

who had been excommunicated by the Numidian bishops for making a nuisance of himself, and who claimed perhaps misleadingly to Gregory that he
had been roughly treated by Donatists. It seems evident that Donatist sur-
vivals and Vandal persecutions had left the African churches ill at ease with
each other, and there were stories of rebaptisms that should not have been
allowed. Gregory exhorted the African bishops to have unity among themselves as a basic priority.

The conversion of the Angli

Gregory's letters are the fundamental source for hard information about the
mission to the Anglo-Saxons in Kent led by the Roman monk Augustine.
Augustine arrived in the spring of 597 at Thanet with a party of forty. In
Frankish Gaul he had been helped along the way, though at first the terrifying accounts he had had of the ferocity of the Angli drove him back to Rome
in fear. The Franks were no friends to the Saxons, and had used Britannia as
a useful source for capturing slaves to sell on the mainland. Gregory's first
awareness of the existence of Angli could have come from an Italian slave-
market. Tension between the Franks and the Saxons or Britons explained
why, as Gregory sadly noted, the Franks had not been disposed to carry out
evangelistic missions on the north side of the Channel. However, now King
Ethelberht of Kent had a Frankish wife Berhta who was a Christian and at
Canterbury the capital of the little kingdom had her own Frankish bishop to
provide pastoral care for her and her circle. In northern Gaul from bishops in
the region called Germania by Gregory Augustine received consecration as
bishop so that he arrived in Kent already having episcopal authority.

Augustine's procession into Canterbury was impressive, with vestments, a
silver cross, and an icon of Jesus painted on wood. It is as good as certain
that he also brought books such as biblical manuscripts, no doubt including
the Italian gospel-book now in the library of Corpus Christi College,
Cambridge (MS 286; Lowe, CLA ii. 126). King Alfred records that Augustine
brought a copy of Gregory's book on *Pastoral Care*, written to guide bishops
in an ascetic way of life in their onerous office. Gregory's intention was that
Augustine should found a primatial see at the principal city of Londinium,
already a major trading centre, but it was still in pagan hands and Canterbury
was to remain the first see. Gregory also wanted a primatial see at the Roman
city of York, Eboracum. That took more time to arrange.

A hundred and thirty-five years after Augustine's mission the learned
Christian historian Bede of Jarrow looked back with idealizing eyes on
Gregory's achievement. Shortly before Bede the first known biography of
Gregory by a monk of Whitby recorded Northumbrian legends of the Pope
seeing handsome English boys for sale in the slave-market, and, on being told

they were *Angli*, replied *Angeli*. Gregory knew that his mission was not the first implantation of Christianity in Britannia. In 595 in his sermons on the book of Job he had spoken of Alleluia now being heard in the *lingua Britanniae* (*Moralia* 27. 11. 21). In the same year a letter from Gregory to his agent or 'rector' in Gaul directs him to buy Anglian boys in the market and to put them into monasteries to be taught and baptized. The project was to be funded by income from the papal estates in Gaul which it was hard to transmit to Italy (above, p. 662).

Augustine's mission was burdened by Gregory's additional concern for the state of the churches in Frankish Gaul. He was specifically asked to make contact with the bishop of Arles and to see what could be done to end the virtually universal simony being practised. Bishops who had had to reward lay supporters in achieving their diocese naturally assumed that they could reasonably charge fees to candidates for ordination so that they could recoup their outlay. In practice Augustine found better support at Autun partly because of Queen Brunhilde and her bishop Syagrius.

Augustine the monk had not come to a land with no Christians, bishops or churches. But the British Christians, whose tribes had rashly invited the Saxons and Angles to assist them in fending off the Picts north of Hadrian's wall, found their foreign warriors no good friends. They had been driven west into the mountains of Wales, and the Germanic Saxons gave them their name 'Welsh', meaning 'foreign'. Celtic Christianity especially in Ireland was based on monasteries. The land had few towns anyway and an episcopal system based on urban settlements was inappropriate. The British Christians resented the Germanic invaders, and were not impressed when Augustine explained that by the direction of the bishop of Rome he was to be primate with authority over all bishops in the land. Furthermore, they calculated differently the annual memorial of the resurrection at Easter, the name given by Saxons to their spring festival and their goddess Eastre, and they used a different shape of tonsure for priests and monks.

The conversion of the king of Kent was tribal. In 601 Gregory learnt that the conversion had produced ten thousand for baptism, comparable to the baptism of three thousand Franks which accompanied the baptism of Clovis (Gregory of Tours, *HF* 2. 31). A letter from Gregory assured the convert king that the clergy's intercessions would keep heaven propitious. They would also teach the dangers of worshipping trees and stones.

A substantial letter to Augustine (11. 56a), until recently much disputed, answered a series of questions he had put to Gregory, at least some of which may have been put to Augustine by British clergy. During his travels through Frankish Gaul Augustine noticed that the liturgy differed from that at Rome, and at Canterbury the queen's Frankish chaplain/bishop certainly used a Gallican rite. Augustine asked Gregory if he was to use the Roman or

Gallican order. Gregory, who like Augustine of Hippo did not ask for liturgical uniformity, encouraged him to be flexible. A second question concerned episcopal consecrations. At Rome three or four bishops were normally required. But Augustine was a missionary bishop who found the existing British bishops uncooperative. Gregory told him to consecrate alone until he had two others to assist. Augustine also asked for guidance over church finance. His monks had each received the same modest pocket-money, living a common life. But a diocesan bishop normally allocated a quarter of the offerings of the faithful to episcopal needs, including hospitality and transmitting letters, a quarter for other clergy, a quarter for the poor, and a quarter for buildings (cf. p. 602).

Augustine's graver questions concerned marriage. Germanic tribal custom allowed marriages between first cousins or between stepson and stepmother. The gospel could cease to be good news if converts had to be told that their marriages were outside the permitted degrees and that from the day of their baptism they had to be excommunicate. To this painful issue Gregory sent a reply anything but hard-line, and he horrified the Roman curia and St Boniface evangelizing Germany in the next century. Boniface felt sure the good pope Gregory could not have yielded on such an issue; archivists assured him that no such letter was in Gregory's Register so that it could not be authentic.

Other questions concerned ritual purity after childbirth, monthly periods, and conjugal union. Augustine of Canterbury was asked if a pregnant woman could be baptized, and for how long she should stay away from communion after delivery. Some of these questions are strikingly paralleled in the Irish Penitentials, of which Ludwig Bieler produced a fine edition (Dublin, 1963). This enhances the probability that such questions were being put by British Christians. Gregory's answers do not uphold legalistic purity. He says Levitical precepts are to be interpreted spiritually.

Gregory at first directed King Ethelberht to destroy old pagan shrines. He came to see this as too drastic. The right course was to Christianize them.

Gregory a European?

In 731 Bede looked back on Gregory's mission to the Angli and, from the instruction that Augustine as bishop of Canterbury (if not London) was to be primate for the entire region he saw the Church as the one linchpin capable of holding together the quarrelling tribes now occupying the half of Britannia south of Hadrian's wall, which they were busy transforming into England. The question arises how far he may have anticipated the thinking of Charlemagne with a concept of Europe as more than a spatial region but also a state of mind pervaded by Christian values and with a common market.[11] Eighty years after Gregory's time Pope Agatho opposed the Monothelete Christology favoured at Constantinople by invoking the support of bishops throughout the western half of Europe, putting special emphasis on the then archbishop of Canterbury, the Greek monk Theodore of Tarsus, 'a philosophic mind living on the edge of the world' (*ACO* II ii. 133. 18).

Gregory's aura of authority steadily grew after his death in 604. Later Roman chant was attributed to him in Carolingian times when the Frankish churches needed a high authority to vindicate the abandonment of the old Gallican style in favour of the Roman. And a collection of liturgical prayers, including some which he may well have composed, passed under the name of the Gregorian Sacramentary. Though his Anglo-Saxon mission enjoyed only brief success and the conversion of the English owed more to the Irish monks at Lindisfarne or Iona, Northumbrian memory looked to him as linking the English churches to a more universal entity. The careful preservation of his letters, his Pastoral Care, his homilies on the Gospels, on Job, and on Ezekiel reflects the sense of awe that readers felt in the presence of this great and devoted Christian. Apart from his skirmish with the see of Constantinople about the title 'ecumenical patriarch', he was not much concerned about the dignity and power of his office. Living in a time of social catastrophe, he saw that if people did not set high value on material goods and property, they could survive and better times would come. Above all, the ascetic attitude to excess and luxury was one which in any circumstances all believers were invited to share.[12]

---

[11] Charlemagne did not include England in his common currency.

[12] Gregory's letters are edited by P. Ewald and L. Hartmann in *MGH Epp.* 1–2, reprint 1957. A better edition of fewer letters, i.e. excluding those thought not to be transmitted in his Register, is by D. Norberg, Corpus Christianorum 140. 140A. (References here are to the *MGH* edition.) *Dialogues*: ed. A. de Vogüé, SC 251, 260, 263.　　　*Homilies on the Gospels*: Maurist edition reprinted in PL 76. 1075–1312. Dom David Hurst's English translation (Cistercian Publications, Kalamazoo, 1990) numbers the homilies differently.　　　*Moralia in Iob* in CC 143 A and B, translated in the Oxford Library of the Fathers.　　　*Homiliae in Hiezechielem*: CC 142; also in SC 327, 360 with translation by C. Morel.　　　*Regula pastoralis*, ed. F. Rommel, SC 381–2. On the Song of Songs and 1 Kings: CCSL 144, SC 324, 351.

59

WORSHIP AFTER CONSTANTINE

Like the various types of biblical text, ancient liturgies differed according to the region where they were in use. Naturally they influenced one another. The liturgy of Jerusalem or Rome or Constantinople or Alexandria would impress visitors from other churches, who would then introduce at home a form of prayer akin to or identical with what they had witnessed on their pilgrimage. The church at Jerusalem seems to have exercised particularly potent influence, as one can see in the pilgrim diary of the lady Egeria from the Atlantic coast of Spain or Gaul, who recorded in colloquial Latin a succession of visits in about 384, including Euphemia's shrine at Chalcedon, Thecla's at Seleucia (Isauria), Ephesus for St John, and above all the ceremonies at Jerusalem. Pope Innocent I had to invoke Petrine authority to dissuade churches in central and southern (suburbicarian) Italy, such as Gubbio, from following the use of Milan. The kiss of peace was normally a prelude to the offertory, but at Rome Innocent had it before the actual communion, the text of Matt. 5: 24 being influential. Augustine warned against the introduction of too many ceremonies, and especially the borrowing of customs seen abroad (*ep.* 54. 3). He thought it caused confusion to the faithful. At Carthage he had to defend a psalm chanted either at the offering of bread and wine by the people or during the distribution, which encountered wrath from a conservative and influential layman (*Retr.* 2. 11). The diversity and the mutual influence can be illustrated from the fact that the Sanctus, which by the age of Constantine had a secure place in the eucharistic prayer in Syria and Palestine, was used in few western churches before 400. It was to become universal in the west until Calvinist worship in the sixteenth century.

Despite regional variety, it is surprising to discover how much the different forms of worship had in common. Psalms and readings were very ancient, but all churches seem to have continued with them and each region developed its own lectionary of scripture lessons, in many places (not all) allowing also the reading of Acts of Martyrs on the appropriate anniversaries. There was a general sensitivity and aversion to the reading of apocryphal texts in the lectionary, though the evidence shows that these were widely known and therefore read in private or in small groups, as with the followers of Priscillian of Ávila who was an enthusiast for non-canonical books; for him they represented a protest against the narrow view that all God's revelation was confined to the canonical books. Augustine had to combat the opinion that the Acts of Perpetua prove baptism to be unnecessary for salvation (*De anima et eius origine* 1. 12). Although apocrypha had no authority, Augustine could allow that they contained much truth (*City of God* 15. 23. 4). He accepted from the Acts of John that John was celibate and that there were bizarre movements of earth at his tomb (*Tr. in Joh.* 124). 'That Joachim was the name of Mary's father is contained in an apocryphon; therefore one is not required to believe it' (*c. Faustum* 23. 9; cf. 11. 5). 'The canon's limits are determined by the use of the majority of churches, especially those worthy of an apostle or recipients of an apostolic epistle' (*De doctrina Christiana* 2. 8. 12).

Church decoration

Until late in the third century and even well into the fourth in some places, Christians assembled for worship together in house-churches, as in the earliest surviving example excavated at Dura-Europos, a substantial military fort on the Euphrates to provide defence against Persian attacks (above, p. 222). The house-church had frescoes e.g. of Jesus healing the paralytic man, the Good Shepherd (caring for goats rather than sheep), and the Lord walking on water. One room was arranged as a baptistery much used during the Persian siege. The fort fell to the Persians about 256. The church was not far from an opulent and richly decorated synagogue with paintings of Old Testament figures. These pictures show that the prohibition of Exod. 20: 4 was not interpreted at Dura to forbid such portraits.

If among the synagogues of the dispersion there was division of opinion, that soon passed to the Christians. Decoration of churches began in converted houses, but became common when late in the third century special buildings were erected for congregations. Canon 36 of the Spanish council of Elvira early in the fourth century disapproved of mural paintings. When Eusebius of Caesarea was asked to provide a picture of Jesus for the imperial lady Constantia, who evidently thought Palestine was the right provenance for an authentic likeness, he replied that such pictures were not compatible with Christian custom. A similarly negative opinion was expressed by Epiphanius of Salamis. The expression of disapprobation shows that in many places a puritanical principle rejecting icons was not being accepted. The Roman catacombs already had pictures of biblical figures, and with the coming of Constantine sarcophagi came to be decorated with Christian themes. In north Africa in Augustine's day it was common to have pictures of Christ either alone or at the Father's right hand, Peter, and Paul; not uncommon to have pictures of Mary, of Abraham's sacrifice of Isaac, and of Adam and Eve with genitals covered. It troubled Augustine that superstitious Christians could take the veneration of martyrs to the point of using icons virtually for worship (*De moribus* 1. 34. 74). At Nola Paulinus had pictures in his churches. The mosaic floor of the church at Aquileia early in the fourth century retained portrayals of Jonah's encounter with a sea-monster.

Baptism

Although the ceremonies of baptism were held to be a private and secret mystery of initiation, all pagans knew (and mocked) that baptism in water in God's name was what makes Christians (Aug. *De unico baptismo* 1. 2; *En. in Ps.* 80. 11). It was preceded by exorcism and the renunciation of the devil and 'all his works and pomps', followed by anointing or chrism with laying-on of hands by the bishop. For an infant child the three interrogations about faith in Father, Son, and Holy Spirit were answered by parents and sponsors. Baptism was the act of Christ, not of the minister; lay baptism was justified in case of urgent necessity. Augustine was confident that if at critical times the actual rite was not possible, true conversion of the heart sufficed for salvation (*Bapt.* 4. 22. 29). Baptism was an indispensable qualification for admission to the 'sacrament of the altar', and it was unrepeatable, like ordination. The sign of the cross was normal. Augustine judged that a dying catechumen should be baptized even if consciousness had been lost; a dying person should be allowed the benefit of the doubt (*Adult. coniug.* 1. 33).

Eucharist

A common feature of eucharistic liturgies in both east and west remained the ancient dialogue between presiding bishop and people: 'The Lord be with you—And with your spirit'. 'Lift up your hearts or "Hearts up"; in north Africa "Heart up", *sursum cor*—we lift them to the Lord'. 'Let us give thanks to the Lord.—It is right and fitting'. Then followed a panegyric on the glory of God in creation and redemption, a prayer that in his mercy God will accept 'this sacrifice offered through Jesus Christ', and a naming of those who had made special offerings which at least in some places might consist of more than bread and wine. By old custom the wine was mixed with a little water. At some point saints and martyrs were mentioned, and there was a com-memoration of the faithful departed.

At Milan Ambrose attests a prayer, perhaps an invocation of the Holy Spirit, asking God that the offering be 'approved, spiritual pleasing, the figure of the body and blood of our Lord Jesus Christ' (*De sacramentis* 4. 21). The narrative of the Institution is sealed by the people saying Amen (4. 25), and followed by the recalling (*anámnesis*) of the passion, resurrection, and ascension of the Lord. The oblation is in the form of prayer: 'We offer you this unbloody sacrifice, this spiritual sacrifice, holy bread and cup of eternal life; and we beseech you to take up this offering by the hands of your angels (or angel) to your heavenly altar, as you accepted the gift of your righteous servant Abel, the sacrifice of our father Abraham, and the offering which the high priest Melchisedek made to you' (4. 27). The doxological ending of the prayer could praise 'God by whom and through whom and in whom all things are made' (Rom. 11: 33; Aug. *S. Dolbeau* 26 = Mainz 62, l. 1431). In north Africa the great prayer or 'canon' was audible. Augustine never mentions a Sanctus, but the prayer included the church universal.

Augustine attests a solemn breaking of the bread (*ep.* 149. 16). The great prayer ended with the congregation joining in the Lord's Prayer, preceded by the formula 'we make bold to say . . .' ('*audemus dicere*': Aug. *sermo* 110. 5; Jerome, *Adv. Pelag.* 3. 15). The bishop presiding says 'Peace be with you'. At the distribution the people receive 'with hands joined together' and say Amen to the words 'The body of Christ' or 'the blood of Christ'. The cup was distributed by a deacon, as in Cyprian's time (*Laps.* 25). Psalm 34 ('Taste and see how good the Lord is') could be sung during the communion.

The kiss of peace, at the offertory in Milan (as today), was immediately before communion in the Rome of Innocent I (*ep.* 25. 8) and in Africa (Aug. *S. Denis* 6. 3; *c. litt. Petil.* 2. 53). Whether before receiving communion or at the end the celebrant dismissed the people with a blessing from the altar (Aug. *En. in Ps.* 117. 22). Augustine's normal word for the eucharist is 'dominicum', but the dismissal gave the service the ordinary name 'missa' or mass, which could also be used by soldiers for a major military parade. In Africa 'missa' was a vulgarism treated as neuter plural.

The celebrant faced the people, moving from the apse to the altar in the nave. A number of African and Spanish churches had an apse at each end, probably with a shrine to a martyr in one.[1]

North African texts show that the liberty of the celebrant to improvise was becoming restrained. The Donatist Petilian once scathingly declared that catholic clergy were simply (schismatic) laity who happened to know the liturgy by heart (Aug. *c. litt. Petil.* 2. 68). Canon 203 of the council of Carthage in 407 limited freedom of improvisation.

Funerals

For burials, Augustine was aware that each nation had its own customs (*Tr. in Joh.* 120. 4), and knew that in his time in Egypt embalming was practised (*sermo* 361. 12). Christians celebrated the eucharist as a plea for divine mercy; in Africa burial preceded the requiem, not in Italy (*Conf.* 9. 12. 32). The usual

---

[1] N. Duval, *Les Églises africaines á deux absides* (Paris, 1973), ii. 303.

form was to have prayers and readings with psalms chanted during the procession to the graveside where the eucharist was celebrated in petition for mercy. The funeral of a suicide was wholly silent.

Ordination

Ordination of a bishop was by laying-on of hands and prayer by the primate of the province (cf. Jerome, *in Esai.* 16. 695 Vallarsi). There was no anointing until considerably later. The *plebs* had a role in approving by acclamation. In Rome ordinations were always on a Sunday (Avellana 24, *CSEL* 35. 59).

Marriage

Marriages were not solemnized 'in face of the Church' in antiquity but gradually this came about. Ignatius of Antioch, writing to Polycarp, expressed a hope that Christian couples would come to him for a blessing. Late in the fourth century Bishop Timothy of Alexandria warned against clergy blessing a marriage if the union was illegal. The eucharistic liturgy was celebrated in the house of the marrying couple. Synesius of Cyrene received his wife at the hand of Theophilus of Alexandria.

In Roman law marriage was constituted by the consent of the two parties, and this remained a principle in Christian times. But the blessing of the couple and the priest's participation in the wedding party were gradually to enlarge the part played by the Church. In Cappadocia Gregory of Nazianzos (*ep.* 231) expected a priest to say psalms and prayers for the couple, but the priest would also place a crown on their heads and join their hands, customs already known in Africa to Tertullian, who thought the crown pagan. John Chrysostom once presupposes that the priest's blessing occurred on the day before the civil ceremony (PG 51. 211). This would take place in the private house of the bride, not in a church building. It was well to keep the priest out of the wedding party with its risqué ditties. But Jesus at the marriage at Cana provided a precedent for bridegrooms to invite the priest. A priest would come to bless only the first marriage, not the second (or more). Ambrosiaster writing at Rome in the time of Pope Damasus also says that only a first marriage can be blessed by the Church (*in 1 Cor.* 7: 49; *in 1 Tim.* 3: 12 and 5: 3).

Egypt

The church in Alexandria was proud to claim the tomb of Mark the evangelist, disciple of St Peter. So Church and city both enjoyed second place after the imperial capital at Rome. The liturgy of St Mark was the title given to the use. Surprisingly the surviving witnesses for the ancient period tell us much less than western texts. It seems certain that the Alexandrian eucharistic prayer opened with the familiar and very ancient 'Lift up your hearts . . . It is worthy and right . . .' A fourth-century papyrus at Strasbourg has a distinctive preface with themes of offering and prayer for the living and departed members of the Church. Unusually an invocation of the Holy Spirit comes before the recalling of the Lord's words of institution. A papyrus of the late sixth century (from Deir Balyzeh) asks God to send his Spirit to make the bread and wine Christ's body and blood and, partly echoing the Didache, to gather his Church as the bread scattered on the mountains was made one body and as the wine of David's holy vine and the water of the Lamb were mingled to become a single mystery.

Sarapion

A sacramentary with peculiarities of its own, found in a manuscript of the eleventh century in the great Lavra (cod. 149) on Mount Athos by A. Dmitrievski (1894) re-edited by G. Wobbermin (TU 17; Leipzig, 1899), provides a collection of prayers, to two of which is attached the name of 'Bishop Sarapion of Thmuis' in the Nile Delta, friend of Athanasius and Antony, author of an extant work against the Manichees. The prayers cover the eucharistic liturgy, baptism and confirmation, ordination, anointing of the sick, burial of the dead, and are those needed by the celebrant. Nothing is said of any duties of the deacon.[2]

Sarapion's rite of baptism has the customary elements of renunciation, exorcism with an anointing, a naming of each catechumen with threefold immersion and sign of the cross, chrism, and laying-on of hands.

The eucharistic prayer or anaphora is preserved from the words 'It is meet and right . . .' as far as the Sanctus, 'heaven and earth are full of your glory', and then an offering of the bloodless oblation, the bread as a likeness of the holy body of the Lord. A shortened institution narrative is followed by prayer that by this sacrifice God may be reconciled to us; 'and as this bread was scattered on the mountains and gathered to be one, so also gather your holy Church out of every nation . . . and make one catholic Church.' The cup follows, again with citation of the Lord's institution. The Holy Spirit is invoked that the bread may become the Word's body and the cup blood of the truth. An invocation of the Spirit is attested for Alexandria by a letter of Peter II cited by Theodoret, *HE* 4. 22. 7. Intercession for the living and departed and for those who have brought offerings leads to the distribution, preceded

---

[2] Sarapion's Greek text is edited by F. E. Brightman in *JTS* 1 (1899), 88–113 and 247–77; translated by John Wordsworth (London, 1923). The sacramentary has been much debated; its idiosyncrasies strongly suggest a fourth-century origin.

(as in Augustine) by a blessing of the people. There is no mention of the Lord's Prayer as concluding the anaphora, nor of 'Holy things for holy people', but one cannot assume that these were not used.

Sarapion's church had 'interpreters', an office otherwise attested in Palladius' *Lausiac History* 43. Egeria records that at Jerusalem the bishop preached in Greek but had beside him a presbyter to translate into Aramaic, and that there were also translators for Latin pilgrims (73–4). For Epiphanius of Salamis (*De fide* 21. 11) 'interpreters' of lections or homilies were an order of ministry without ordination. Coptic speakers in Egypt, like Aramaic speakers in Syria and Palestine, and the numerous pilgrims, made the office necessary.

Syria and Cilicia

Fairly full liturgical texts survive for Syria and Cilicia. A verbose version in *Apostolic Constitutions* 8, the catechetical lectures given by Cyril of Jerusalem, reused by his successor John (to whom part of the manuscript tradition also ascribes them), in the middle years of the fourth century, and the catechetical lectures of Theodore of Mopsuestia (extant through a Syriac manuscript at Selly Oak, Birmingham), all provide light on the themes and wording.

Cyril of Jerusalem knew that his mixed audience included young men whose motive for attendance included a desire to catch the eye of a lady, and vice versa. He bade both sexes to listen with most serious attention, and to regard their instruction in the sacraments as an arcane mystery. He did not ask the sexes to be segregated, but stressed their distinctive roles, women being especially valued for their singing (*Procatech.* 14–15). At the baptistery the candidates began by facing west, raising a hand and renouncing Satan with all his works and pomp. For baptism candidates stripped, received anointing, approached the font to answer three interrogations on belief in Father, Son, and Holy Spirit. At the eucharist 'in the figure of the bread is given Christ's body, in the figure of the wine his blood', and by reception 'Christ is in us'. The deacon provides the celebrant with water to wash his hands to symbolize inner cleansing of his conscience. Then comes the kiss of peace, a sign of community of soul and oblivion of all wrongs. The priest begins the dialogue 'Lift up your hearts . . .' The preface praises the Creator of heaven and earth, and with angels, archangels, and all the company of heaven the congregation cries 'Holy, holy, holy, Lord God of Sabaoth.' 'We call on God to send his Holy Spirit on the gifts spread before him, that he may make the bread the body of Christ and the wine the blood of Christ.' Consecration is followed by prayer for the peace of both Church and world, for emperors, the army, the sick, and asks that the sacrifice may be propitiatory for the faithful departed. Cyril knew many who asked what good intercession does for the departed, a prayer the utility of which was doubted by Aerius (above p. 334), an Arian in fourth-century Asia Minor (Epiphanius, *Panar.* 75. 2), and by Vigilantius in Gaul; Augustine received the custom as ancient and universal in all churches on the ground that the faithful departed remain members of the one Church in the Lord of both living and dead. The Lord's Prayer follows. The priest says 'Holy things for holy people', to which the people reply 'One is holy, one is the Lord Jesus Christ'. A chanter sings Psalm 34 ('O taste and see the Lord is good'). Cyril tells the people to make a cup by putting their right hand on their left for reception, and to say Amen as the priest says 'The body of Christ . . .' Cyril does not record use of Jesus' words of institution as necessary to consecration, for which the crux is the invocation of the Spirit.

For Antioch the richest source of information is scattered in the voluminous extant writings and sermons of John Chrysostom, who never wrote a connected exposition of the Syrian liturgy but has numerous allusions from which a virtually complete picture can be reconstructed.

In John's time at Antioch the people washed their hands before entering the building, and would commonly kiss the stones of the porch (a custom also attested by Augustine in north Africa). In the nave the sexes were segregated. Like Cyril of Jerusalem, John critically observes that young men often came to church to make eyes at girls. Church buildings already had finely cut capitals, mosaic floors, and frescoes on the walls. The bishop sat in the middle in the apse, but after the dismissal of catechumens he came to the stone altar ('table' is John's word) in the middle of the nave to celebrate the 'liturgy of the faithful'. The altar was covered in a white cloth and had a cross upon it. Sacred vessels were of gold. To counter the odours of an unwashed congregation, incense could be used. At Antioch the eucharist was usually celebrated on Friday, Saturday and Sunday, and on martyrs' festivals. John preached critically of Christians who received communion only at Easter.

In the Greek east it was not customary for a celebration to be provided every day; at Alexandria and in Palestine it was only on Sundays. John's word for a eucharistic assembly is *sýnaxis*.

The eucharist at Antioch began with the congregation presenting their gifts at the altar; deacons place bread and wine on the altar, which curtains veil from the people. Then the usual opening dialogue or a variant of it. Theodore and Theodoret used 'The grace of our Lord Jesus Christ and the love of God the Father and the fellowship of the Holy Spirit be with you'; but (Theodoret records) 'some bishops say, "The grace of our Lord be with you".' 'Lift up your mind and hearts . . .' follows. Then an *anámnesis* of God's many gifts, and intercessory prayer for the world (or the Roman empire, *oikouméne*), the living and departed, and future believers. Thanksgiving for creation and redemption introduces the Sanctus sung by the whole congregation, the narrative of the Institution, an Invocation of the Spirit (the two together constituting the decisive consecration). The curtains were then lifted. The great prayer or anaphora ended with a doxology. The priest declares 'Holy things for holy people.' Distribution follows. Finally the deacon says 'Go in peace.'

John's discourses at Constantinople show only minor differences. The anaphora ended with the Lord's Prayer, not attested for Antioch but usual at Jerusalem. In the capital the eucharist was celebrated twice weekly.

Naturally the liturgical texts contain no sort of theory about the change in the offered and consecrated elements or species. They all presuppose and indeed emphasize the change, especially Cyril of Jerusalem. John Chrysostom lays repeated stress on the awesomeness of the rite, and mentions the hushed silence of the congregation at the Invocation of the Spirit.[3]

It is noteworthy that the liturgical texts do not have echoes of contemporary controversies in the churches. They tell us what sublime simplicities mattered to ordinary Christians in everyday congregations, whether in great cities like Antioch and Constantinople, or in small and predominantly rural towns and villages such as those cared for by Theodore and Theodoret in Cilicia and Syria.

---

[3] The material from John Chrysostom is gathered by F. E. Brightman, *Liturgies Eastern and Western*, i (Oxford, 1896, reprinted) and, with a few corrections to Brightman and good commentary, by Frans van de Paverd, *Zur Geschichte der Meßliturgie in Antiocheia und Konstantinopel gegen Ende des vierten Jahrhunderts* (Rome, 1970).

60

PILGRIMS

On their travels ancient pilgrims were affirming detachment from home and its economic problems. 'Here we have no continuing city'. The saints 'acknowledged that they were strangers and exiles on the earth' (Heb. 13: 14, 11: 13). Pilgrimage is not, of course, a specially Christian activity, and is common to most of the higher religions in the world. Relics and pilgrimages have a role in entirely secular and non-religious travels.

Before Constantine the Great Christian pilgrimage was rare and individual; groups would have attracted a lot of dangerous attention. Before Hadrian banned Jews from Jerusalem in 135, it would have been inevitable for Gentile Christians to think of the holy city as under rabbinic masters, though there had long been a community of believing Jewish Christians there. This community retained an aura of authority. This was not lost after the Bar-Cocheba war and the expulsion of Jews from the city under Hadrian. About 170 Melito of Sardis turned to the church in Jerusalem to learn the precise canon of the Old Testament (Eusebius, *HE* 4. 26. 14). That was 'where the gospel history had been acted out'. The usages of the church there had authority for others. In the mid-third century Origen at Caesarea travelled round Palestine specifically to visit places where Jesus and his disciples and also the prophets had once been (*Comm. on John* 6. 40). He identified mount Tabor as the scene of the Transfiguration (*in Ps.* 88. 13, PG 12. 1548). A Cappadocian bishop Alexander was invited to move to Jerusalem, where he was already well known, and received a vision directing him to accept and evidently justifying him in so doing. During the baptismal controversy between Rome and Carthage, Firmilian of Caesarea wrote to Cyprian to the effect that the Roman church's liturgical tradition was inferior in authority to that of Jerusalem. That was the place to find authenticity. These visits were apparently not motivated by the desire to be nearer God at a sacred site, but they were close to the pilgrimage theme.

Constantine's aspiration, hindered by the Arian controversy, was to receive baptism in the river Jordan. The Holy Land was to be for him a focus of church unity, and numerous Greek bishops attended the synod of 335 at Jerusalem when the dedication of the church of the Anastasis or Resurrection (predecessor of the crusaders' Holy Sepulchre) coincided with the celebration of his thirtieth anniversary as Augustus. His mother Helena in 326 had gone to the Holy Land perhaps to propitiate heaven for the killing of the emperor's wife and son, Fausta and Crispus. Half a century later Ambrose reports that she was guided to discover the true Cross. The church at Jerusalem had a deep sense of Zion being 'the mother of all churches', which found explicit expression in the Liturgy of St James and in the catechetical lectures of Cyril of Jerusalem in the middle of the fourth century.

The ancient Church did not think particular places (or stones, springs, or trees) numinous in separation from the holy men and women who had said or done things there or whose bones were there located.[1] Bishops of Caesarea, the provincial metropolis, like Eusebius were naturally reserved towards the sanctity of Jerusalem, a suffragan see but with a far grander aura which was already engendering rivalry as early as the council of Nicaea. Relics were not inherently necessary for a site to attract devout visitors. Because the Old Testament was part of the Christian Bible, people visited Jacob's well, the rock at Sinai on which Moses smashed the tables with the Ten Commandments, the site of the burning bush. Demand was soon met by supply. A pilgrim from Bordeaux in 333 was shown where Solomon wrote the book of Wisdom, gruesome traces of Zechariah's murder before the altar, the pinnacle of the temple from which the Lord was tempted to throw himself down (despite Roman sieges, much of Herod's temple remained in ruined condition), and, perhaps most inventively, the very stone which the builders rejected. Already in the third century they could show the actual throne where St James had preached (it could easily have been authentic).

In Jerome's time (*ep.* 103. 13) healings occurred at the rock of Golgotha and in Sebaste at the tomb of John the Baptist; and his letter (108. 8–14) on the death of Paula catalogues the holy sites of Palestine which she visited with a climax at Golgotha and the church of the Resurrection. He had travelled with her and her group. She was shown the column to which the Lord was bound for scourging, still bloodstained. At Bethlehem Paula visited the cave and the inn of the Nativity, and then at Hebron the tombs of Abraham, Isaac, and Jacob with a fourth said by the Jews to be Adam or Caleb. The Hebron site came to be amicably shared by both Christians and Jews—and Arabs prizing Abraham's tomb. Other sites visited were a cross on the mount of Olives to mark the Lord's Ascension, Lazarus' tomb and the house of Mary and Martha, Jericho (where remnants of Rahab's house were shown), Zacchaeus' tree, the stone where Jacob dreamt, Jacob's well, Samaria, Nazareth, and finally Egypt for the monks of the Nitrian desert where 'in

---

[1] See S. G. MacCormack, 'Loca Sancta, the organisation of sacred topography in late antiquity', in R. Ousterhout (ed.), *The Blessings of Pilgrimage* (Chicago, 1990), 7–40; P. W. L. Walker, *Holy City, Holy Places?* (Oxford, 1990), shows that Eusebius had no idea of places being holy. Gregory the Great would say that places were made holy by holy people, not in themselves.

each holy man she saw Christ himself'. To help pilgrims Jerome made a Latin translation of Eusebius' *Onomasticon*, identifying the sites of biblical towns and adding notes on churches at sacred sites.

Probably in the 380s a rich lady from northern Spain named Egeria kept a diary of a pilgrimage to Sinai and the Holy Land. Her colloquial Latin, different from Cicero's, has made the document central for Latinists.[2]

Her baggage had a Bible (in manuscript a weighty and costly item), and she recorded how at every site she gave time to pray. Her record was made for 'sisters' at home. A pilgrim journey could be dangerous, but Egeria, being a lady of social consequence, received a military escort for the hazardous parts. She knew little or no Greek but relied on interpreters (she called them *grecolatini*) especially for the liturgy at Jerusalem and Bethlehem, which was also translated into Aramaic. Evidently western pilgrims in her time were numerous. They brought money to the places visited, and the church of Jerusalem's resources became a target for envious sniping. She records vast crowds in September attending the dedication (*encaenia*)[3] of the church of the Resurrection by Golgotha and the Tomb. About fifty bishops would be present, and for eight days there was a cycle of liturgical celebrations at various holy sites. At Epiphany on 6 January Christ's birth was celebrated at Bethlehem, ending in a huge procession back to Jerusalem. On Palm Sunday the bishop rode into Jerusalem on a donkey. On Good Friday the True Cross or some part of the wood was visible to the people for veneration; it was guarded but unsuccessfully, and pilgrims made off with chips to be treasured as talismans. At Pentecost people went to the church on Mount Zion and processed to the mount of Olives to commemorate the Ascension where Christ's parting footprints were preserved. Egeria used the word 'missa' to describe any act of worship at which the bishop dismissed the people with a blessing, not necessarily a eucharist. The rituals were centred round a reenactment of events of Christ's life and therefore included biblical lections. Egeria was surprised by the custom of preaching on the themes of these readings.

In the west the shrines of Peter and Paul in Rome were magnets for pilgrims, who flocked to the city for the feast on 29 June. Paulinus of Nola travelled to Rome for 29 June every year. They would also visit the catacombs and Damasus' memorials for Rome's martyrs and in time made records of inscriptions to be seen. When the emperor Honorius visited Rome, Augustine was glad to record that instead of visiting Hadrian's mausoleum (the Castel Sant'Angelo), the emperor venerated 'Peter the fisherman' at his basilica on the Vatican hill.

[2] See a magistral philological commentary by Einar Löfstedt (Uppsala, 1912; repr. Oxford, 1936; Darmstadt, 1967), exclusively examining the language, not the liturgy.

[3] Enkainia, Greek equivalent of Jewish Hanukkah.

Pilgrimage soon attracted critics. Gregory of Nyssa (*ep.* 2) held it to be entirely optional, not a Christian duty, and its value depended wholly on the devout state of mind of the pilgrim. Ascending the mount of Olives does nothing for someone filled with pride and lust and envy. 'The Holy Spirit is not nearer to you in the Holy Land than anywhere else.' For women there were practical cautions. The inns at which they would stay on the way would not be morally salubrious. It would long be a problem that thieves might rob them of money, and then penniless virgins might have to survive as barmaids, in which occupation they could not long hope to remain virgins. Even Jerome, drawn to live as a monk in Bethlehem ('I am none the better for living here'), advised Paulinus of Nola not to suppose that a visit to Jerusalem, full of noisy crowds, harlots, actors, and vulgar comedians, would enlarge his faith (*ep.* 58. 4).

There could, of course, be pilgrimage without such hazards. Gregory of Nyssa himself visited the shrine of St Theodore at Euchaita (Avkhat) on the border between Cappadocia and Pontus. Paulinus the multi-millionaire from Barcelona and Bordeaux settled at Nola in Campania specifically to live and die beside the shrine of saint Felix. Would it be good at the final resurrection to have been buried close to the shrine of a holy man or woman? Paulinus of Nola believed it would be, but he put the question to Augustine of Hippo. The answer may not have delighted him: To be buried near saints, he was told, is a 'solace to the survivors, no help to the dead'. One may commend the faithful departed to saints, but that can be done wherever they are buried. What helps is not the place but the prayer. The eucharistic sacrifice is an act of intercession which includes departed believers, and the liturgy has a memento of the dead. So in the account of Monnica's burial in *Conf.* 9. 35–7 Augustine affirms that in the requiem beside her grave 'we plead Christ's passion for her that the Devil do not hinder her ascent.' The faithful departed and the Church on earth are one fellowship in Christ, so that mutual prayer is appropriate. There is no custom, however, of praying for martyrs who are already with Christ in bliss.

Senior bishops often feared popular pilgrimage. It was hard to control and to keep it edifying, but the urge was too deeply ingrained in human nature for any hope of suppressing it. In any event the offerings of the faithful at the shrine could often be important to the financial resources of the local church. In sixth-century Spain we hear of a developer who constructed a shrine in partnership with the bishop on the understanding that the proceeds would be divided between them fifty–fifty; a council at Braga strongly disapproved (C. Bracara II canon 6). More edifyingly, the aspiration to become a homeless traveller in imitation of the Son of Man who had nowhere to lay his head was a potent factor leading Irish monks in the sixth and seventh centuries to move to the continent and, like Aidan at Lindisfarne, to become evangelists of major importance for the countries where they went.

61

PENANCE

From the beginning there has been a stream of Christian moral thinking which has expected Christians not to sin and has believed in their capacity and potentiality to avoid it altogether. It is problematic to demand of human beings a personal standard of morality which is in practice unattained. The difficulty was already felt by the great Stoic moralists, Seneca and Epictetus. Perhaps any moral code worthy of commanding the allegiance of serious minds is one beset by the hardness of the ideal's practicability. But it is easy to think of a minimum standard as being commanded, and of higher ideals as being a counsel of perfection, by which impracticability for all but rare individuals is normally meant. The ascetic movement of the fourth century was a quest for perfection. Jesus' words in the Sermon on the Mount (Matt. 5: 48) 'Be perfect as your Father in heaven is perfect' prescribed some such ideal. His words to the rich young ruler (Matt. 19: 21, not in Mark's telling of the same story) 'If you aspire to be perfect, sell what you have and give to the poor' have obviously had huge influence in bequeathing the distinction between precept and counsel.

The absoluteness of the vows undertaken at baptism commits the believer to follow Christ in keeping to the path of a good moral life. But the frailty of human nature constantly leads to failures, and the question arose very early in the development of the Church: what ought to be done to restore the penitent and to exclude the impenitent and mocking apostate as long as their mind does not seriously change?

Jesus was understood to have entrusted the forgiving of believers' sins to the Church (Matt. 18: 15–17); in the last resort, one unwilling to heed the community's admonition is to be treated as an outsider and a heathen. The community is given power to 'bind and loose', and this is expressly said in the sense that decisions on earth have consequences in heaven. In John 20: 21–3 this power and duty are entrusted to the apostles. In Matt. 16: 19 the power of the keys is entrusted to Peter. In the first century it was a general axiom that reconciliation with the Church is the path to reconciliation with God and vice versa. At Rome late in the fourth century Ambrosiaster (*Quaestiones*, 102, CSEL 50) took it for granted that if a sin has not been absolved on earth, it remains on the debit side in heaven. In the third century the Roman presbyter Novatian separated from Bishop Cornelius on this issue.

In the Corinthian community Paul had difficulties with a man who had been in love to the point of incest with his stepmother. He is excluded from communion ('delivered up to Satan'), but with the hope of impressing on him the gravity of his offence and inducing deep penitence. So 'his spirit may be saved in the day of the Lord' (1 Cor. 5: 3–5). The community's judgement is pronounced 'in the name of Jesus'. 2 Corinthians 2 discloses that Paul's apostolic authority had been insultingly challenged by an unnamed member of the local church. Although this had not been initially regarded by the Corinthian Christians as requiring action to disown the man and his deeply offensive language, they had come to see such action to be needed. Paul asks them to restore the man in love, now that he is full of regret. Moreover, the apostle himself 'in the person of Christ' now declares the man pardoned. For his calling is to be Christ's ambassador (2 Cor. 5: 20), empowered to speak in his name.

The epistle to the Hebrews

The anonymous but weighty letter to which was given the title 'to the Hebrews' (6: 4–6 and 10: 29) points to the psychological impossibility of repentance and restoration in anyone who, having once been baptized and believing, should then discard the faith and treat it as a subject for open mockery, 'trampling under foot the Son of God and insulting the Spirit of grace'. These texts are closely akin to solemn warnings in the tradition of Jesus' sayings about the consequence of sin against the Holy Spirit for which pardon is impossible (Matt. 12: 32). The problems of apostasy hit the churches at a very early stage of their history. 2 Pet. 2: 22 quotes the proverbial saying. 'The dog returns to his own vomit.' The evidence of 1 Corinthians makes it certain that Paul's message of freedom from the law produced some antinomian sexual licence. Nevertheless, it is also clear that the apostle expected baptized believers to manifest a huge change in their moral life (1 Cor. 6: 11).

Mortal and venial

Since 'in many matters we all offend' (Jas. 3: 2), it can only be self-delusion to suppose that one can be free of sin (1 John 1: 8). But the light of the gospel can show up the dark recesses of the mind and heart by arousing contrite awareness of fault which is also a condition of forgiveness. However, there are degrees of sins, some being 'unto death', others less grave (1 John 5: 16). Later theology interpreted these words to distinguish mortal and venial sins, mortal being adultery, murder and apostasy (or idolatry), so classified in that they injure not only the individual in his or her private character but also the religious community by virtue of their very public nature. However, there would be a difficulty in attaining confident certainty on the question which sins fell into which category.

Hermas

The evidence of the *Shepherd* of Hermas early in the second century has received contradictory interpretations. The possibility of remission for sin after baptism is central to the work. The work can be read as a subtle challenge to an evidently prevalent belief that baptism not only brings total remission of previous sins but endows the believer with the indwelling Holy Spirit who renders the soul lastingly sinless, white, and pure. The title may imply that pastoral concern for the Lord's sheep asks for modification of church discipline.

The author of the *Shepherd* presents his work as if it were naïve autobiography, but in actuality the work bears the marks of literary artifice. Hence the bizarre opening of the work in which Hermas is struck by the physical beauty of a naked woman bathing in the Tiber, no doubt intended to take note of the difficulty of achieving entire freedom from desire merely as a consequence of an accidental and almost commonplace occurrence. In *Mand.* 4. 3. 1–6 there is direct polemic against the rigorist judgement that after baptism there is no further opportunity for repentance and remission. Hermas claims that by a prophetic revelation he is authorized to announce one further chance; for 'the Lord knows the human heart and the devil's wiles'. What remains out of the question for him is the wholly laxist view that repeated sins can have repeated absolutions. Nevertheless once the absolute and final character of the remission in baptism is denied, it would be hard to see where and why a line should be drawn, unless it be a consequence of the coming of the End. Hermas implies that the penitent person has to remain classified as a penitent, not necessarily restored to eucharistic communion, but begging the congregation to intercede for him so that at the Last Judgement he may find mercy.

Tertullian at the stage when his sympathies were with the Montanists deeply objected to the accepting of the *Shepherd* as an authoritative book to be read in the lectionary, an opinion which he himself had once hesitantly shared (*De orat.* 16. 3). He dismissed the *Shepherd* as 'pastor of adulterers' (*De pudicitia* 20). The Muratorian Canon (above p. 80) famously contains polemic against the authority of Hermas.

In his tract 'on penitence' Tertullian describes the startling degree of open self-abasement made before the Church in the hope of gaining the sympathy and compassion of the congregation. A 'public' rebuke before the entire congregation had been specially commended by 1 Tim 5: 20 as inducing fear in others. The penitent, dressed in rough sackcloth and rags and humbly kneeling in prayer and humility, underwent self-prostration before the presbyters and 'confessors' (heroes under persecution) and asked the congregation to intercede for mercy. This act is described by the transliterated Greek term 'exomologesis'. Tertullian's tract shows that penitents found the process extremely painful to undergo. It was of course deeply shaming to be admitting to adultery or idolatry before all the congregation. The judicial verdict of the congregation would be pronounced by the bishop, and was more judgemental than therapeutic. But to refuse to submit to this discipline would have been to incur the greater penalty of excommunication. Tertullian came to consider that while God might forgive adultery, murder, and idolatry, it lay beyond the Church's authority in such cases to offer reconciliation (*De pudicitia* 3 and 21). It shocked him when a bishop, probably of Carthage not Rome, granted that murder and apostasy could not be forgiven, but allowed reconciliation to adulterers (*De pudicitia* 5). Origen, on the other hand, was outraged by bishops who 'have assumed powers beyond priestly authority, and claim to forgive idolatry, fornication, and adultery' (*De orat.* 28. 10). Cyprian (*ep.* 55. 21) regretted that in Africa there had been some bishops refusing reconciliation to adulterers. At least it had not been an occasion for schism.

The astonishing success of the Christian mission much enhanced the difficulty not only of rigorism but also of the 'public' character of the penitent's plea for mercy and intercession. Pagans criticized the system with the argument that absolution encouraged licence; and it is certain that absolved penitents often reverted to their old sins, after which obtaining absolution could be much harder, normally refused outright (Augustine, *ep.* 153. 7). Adultery was the most frequent problem (Augustine, *ep.* 22. 2–3 and many texts). On Ash Wednesday there would be a very long line ('ordo longissimus', *sermo* 232) of applicants for admission to the status of penitents, hoping for reconciliation on Maundy Thursday as at Rome in the time of Innocent I.

Gradually there was a convergence of two movements, first to treat the penitential process as therapeutic rather than judgemental, and secondly to allow the penitent to make confession in private to bishop or priest. Augustine stated the principle that those whose sins were public deserved public admonition, but private sins could be corrected privately (*Sermo* 82. 10). Matt. 18: 15 laid down 'if your brother sins against you, go and tell him his fault between you and him alone.' Nevertheless there is no clear evidence in Augustine for private confession and priestly absolution. Once he brought before the congregation at Hippo a Christian who had been a practising astrologer, and asked his people to pray for him as well as to see that he behaved properly in future (*En. in Ps.* 61: 23). There was a need for the congregation's knowledge and support to guard against future lapses. The earliest declaration that absolution necessarily requires formal action by the Church is found in Pope Leo the Great (*ep.* 18. 3), but he simultaneously grants that penitence of the heart expressed in penitential actions is indispensable.

Excommunication was rare. If as in fourth-century north Africa there was schism, to impose excommunication or even austere discipline on a penitent was always to risk that the penitent would migrate to the schismatic body. Donatist bishops were louder than Catholics in asserting the possession by their bishops of the power of the keys (Aug. *sermo* 99. 8–9 insists that only God forgives, and would insist that to join a schismatic body was self-excommunication with binding effect in heaven: *Bapt.* 3. 18. 23). Moreover, to make a criminal's delinquency public could incur great dangers. The person concerned might be resentful and take revenge upon the local church. A bishop could not make public that he had privately heard a confession from a murderer without exposing the guilty person to due process of law, and a bishop should not be responsible for action ending in a magistrate's verdict of capital punishment, a penalty of which in any event Augustine disapproved.

The underlying question was whether the Church was to be a society of saints or a school for sinners. If at first the former view prevailed, the latter view gradually became dominant. But that severe disciplining of delinquents should be moderated to achieve therapy rather than condemnation already had its seeds in the Pauline epistles. In Clement of Alexandria the intention of discipline imposed on penitents must be directed towards healing their wound. That was in line with the principle that divine punishments are always remedial, which Origen, more puritanical than Clement, also conceded. Hereafter a baptism of fire will purge the Christian soul, but it may be well if the soul experiences austere discipline in this life. The persecutions raised the acute question of the terms for restoration of the penitent lapsed. It was not disputed in Cyprian's time that the penitent lapsed could be readmitted; his problem was to achieve uniformity and fairness of treatment, which could be done only by concentrating authority in this matter in the hands of the bishop. It is here that one can discern the origin of canon law. Much of the evidence of a penitential system in the fourth and fifth centuries is found in the canons of church councils, then in papal descretals. In three letters (188, 199, 217) Basil of Caesarea gathered canons with many rulings on penances for sins varied according to their gravity. In Asia Minor, not apparently elsewhere, the distinction in the degrees of austerity demanded of penitents led to a grading or categorizing of different classes of penitent under discipline. At the eucharist some were dismissed with the catechumens while others were allowed to remain for the central act of offering but excluded from reception of communion, probably until their deathbed.

A single act of confession and restoration was parallel to the unrepeatability of baptism. Just as baptism was often deferred to near the end of life, so also that became a common pattern with penance. Ambrose advised that it should be put off until the age when the sexual drive cooled (*Paen.* 2. 11. 107). Because the discipline required sexual abstinence, sixth-century councils in Gaul could rule that married persons must have their partner's consent before undertaking penance. It was wholly impracticable to impose penance on a soldier or a married civil servant, also reckoned to be *in militia*. But already in the time of Pope Siricius, Bishop Himerius of Tarragona was asking if this had to be so. And was it the case that a person under penitential discipline who failed to keep the rules had to be excluded as permanently and irretrievably lapsed? (Siricius, *ep.* 1. 5). Almost contemporary with this, John Chrysostom offered hostages to his critics by advocating repeated absolutions of serious sinners ('even a thousand times' (Socrates, *HE* 6. 21. 4). In 589 the third council of Toledo censured the 'execrable presumption' that 'priests in certain Spanish churches' ignore the canon and reconcile people however often they sin.

Origen had bequeathed to the monks the need for a spiritual director. Evagrios in the east and John Cassian in the west passed on this ideal. A monk had a spiritual 'father' to whom he laid bare his evil thoughts, and this director was often not a priest. Devout laity appropriated this method, and would consult their bishop or priest or director about faults of which they were conscious, asking him for prayer. This practice marked a step on the path towards private confession, which might be either to a priest or, in venial cases, to a lay person.

The Celtic and Anglo-Saxon churches produced Penitentials prescribing the discipline appropriate to various listed offences, especially fasting for varied lengths of time and almsgiving. The handing over of money facilitated the practice of commuting a penance for payment. This steadily increased despite being deplored by the synod of Clofesho in 747, canon 26.[1]

---

[1] Haddan and Stubbs, *Councils*, iii. 371–2, briefly discussed by C. Cubitt, *Anglo-Saxon Church Councils* (London, 1995), 101.

FURTHER READING

A proper book list for so long a period of history as that sketched in this volume could easily be much longer than the volume itself. A recent catalogue for Athanasius alone by C. Butterweck (Opladen, 1995) runs to a few hundred pages. Origen and Augustine have specialized bibliographies. For Tertullian and Cyprian (1975–94) see R. Braun (1999). The list here given is therefore a selection, which, for reasons of space, cannot include many items which would be desirable. The publisher Ashgate (Aldershot) publishes many volumes of collected studies with papers from Festschriften and periodicals. A bibliography of New Testament problems would be enormous, and that part of the story is therefore omitted here, since any good Introduction to the New Testament (e.g. that by Raymond E. Brown, New York, 1997) provides book lists.

I. Sources

The nineteenth-century French editor J. P. Migne printed 221 volumes of Latin texts as late as Pope Innocent III, Greek writers to 1439 in 162 volumes. A. Hamman produced 5 supplementary volumes (Paris, 1958–74). The volumes from Migne do not fully answer to expectations of modern critical scholarship, but are often the only edition easily available. Collections of Latin texts edited critically are the Corpus Scriptorum Ecclesiasticorum Latinorum, CSEL (Vienna, 1866ff., still in progress), and Corpus Christianorum, Series Latina (CCSL published by Brepols, in Turnhout), also in progress but for the first six centuries not far from completion. The Corpus Christianorum series graeca (CCSG) does not yet include early texts of the first five or six centuries, but includes writings important in the Christological controversy.

Critical texts of early Greek Christians are in the series under the Berlin Academy, *Die griechischen christlichen Schriftsteller der ersten drei Jahrhunderte* (1899ff.), especially Hermas, Clement of Alexandria, Origen, and the historians, Eusebius of Caesarea, Socrates, Sozomen, and Theodoret, and Karl Holl's three-volume edition of Epiphanius. Evagrius' history is edited by J. Bidez and Parmentier (London, 1899. reprinted).

Athanasius is in process of being edited, also under the Berlin Academy, but in a separate series. For the second century apologists the old edition by E. J. Goodspeed (1914), who did not include Theophilus of Antioch, is in process of being replaced piecemeal. The older edition by J. C. T. Otto remains useful. Justin (and pseudo-Justin) is edited by M. Marcovich in Patristische Texte und Arbeiten; the Apologies by C. Munier in Paradosis, a series from Fribourg, Switzerland. For Irenaeus, five volumes in Sources Chrétiennes. Tertullian, Cyprian, and Novatian, are in Corpus Christianorum, the edition of Cyprian's letters being recent (1997) and replacing the old CSEL edition by Hartel (1866). For commentary on Cyprian's letters, the annotated translation by Graeme Clarke in Ancient Christian Writers (4 vols.) is expert.

Oriental texts: Patrologia Orientalis (Paris 1907ff.) and Corpus Scriptorum Christianorum Orientalium (CSCO) 1903 ff., now published by Peeters at Leuven. Both series provide texts and translations into modern European tongues or into Latin. For Aphrahat see *Patrologia Syriaca*, I (1894–1907). The only complete edition of Ephrem the Syrian including spuria, though unsatisfactory, is by J. S. Assemani in 6 folio vols. (1732–46). CSCO includes some of his works. C. W. Mitchell edited his *Prose Refutations of Mani, Marcion, and Bardaisan* (1912–21). The letters of Severus of Antioch were edited and translated by E. W. Brooks, partly in PO, partly separately. Other works by Severus in CSCO, esp. edited by J. Lebon and R. Hespel; Severus' biography is in PO 2. Major Armenian texts are translated by Robert Thomson. CSCO includes some Coptic texts but they are more widely scattered.

For numerous texts the French series Sources Chrétiennes (Paris, Cerf) gives both a critical text and French version with good introductions and notes; there are now over 400 volumes. The Collection Budé includes Ammianus Marcellinus, Libanius, and Zosimus. Much of Augustine is in the Bibliothèque Augustinienne with French translation and good notes. Some authors are in Oxford Early Christian Texts with English version and notes.

Some basic texts are edited in the Monumenta Germaniae Historica (MGH), especially Auctores Antiquissimi (AA) and Epistolae I–III. A few individual early Christians have editions in the Teubner series of classical authors e.g. the epitome of Lactantius, Nemesius of Emesa, Theodoret. Likewise the Loeb Classical Library has the Apostolic Fathers, selected items of Clement of Alexandria, Tertullian, Minucius Felix, the Church History of Eusebius, Jerome (letters), Augustine (letters, Confessions, and City of God), Ausonius, Ammianus and the Anonymus Valesianus, Libanius, Prudentius, Sidonius Apollinaris, Boethius, Procopius, Bede. Didascalia Apostolorum: ed. R. H. Connolly (Oxford, 1929) with English version.

The imperial laws of the *Codex Theodosianus* (CTh) were edited by Theodor Mommsen, 3 vols. (Berlin, 1905) . The English translation by C. Pharr (Princeton, 1952) has to be used with caution, but is useful. For Justinian see Codex Juris Civilis, ed. P. Krüger (Berlin, 1915). There is no satisfactory English translation of his Code or (more important) his new edicts (Novels), many of which bear on ecclesiastical history. The Digest is translated ed. A. G. Watson (Princeton) with Latin text, paperback.

English translations exist for many texts from the ancient Church, especially the Oxford Library of the Fathers in 48 vols., 1835–85, beginning with E. B. Pusey's good translation of Augustine's Confessions and including Augustine on the Psalms, John Chrysostom's homilies on the New Testament, and Gregory the Great's Moralia; the Ante-Nicene Christian Library in 28 vols. (1886–1900), later reprinted in Grand Rapids, Mich., by Eerdmans. Variable in quality (but the volumes of Athanasius and Gregory of Nyssa are remarkable) are the Nicene and Post-Nicene Fathers in 14 vols., vol. 14 with conciliar canons (Oxford and New York, 1887–93); a second series 1890–1900 for select writings of Augustine. Ancient Christian

696 *Further Reading*

Writers (Westminster, Md., 1946 ff. still in progress); Fathers of the Church (Catholic University of America, Washington DC, 1947 ff. still in progress and now extensive). W. Bright's commentary on the canons of the first four general councils (Oxford, 1892) has good matter.

Papal letters: Letters to Xystus III were learnedly edited by P. Coustant (Paris, 1721, repr. 1967); his edition is reproduced in various volumes of Migne's PL. Leo I's letters were edited by the brothers Ballerini, repr. in PL 54; from Hilarus to Hormisdas (461–523) by A. Thiel (1867, reprinted), but several were included in the Avellana collection (CSEL 35, 1897). Numerous papal letters of the fifth and sixth centuries, especially Leo and Vigilius, are in Eduard Schwartz's Acta Conciliorum Oecumenicorum (1914 ff.) and his Göttingen and Munich Academy monographs with masterly discussions both there and in his Latin prefaces to fascicles of ACO. On the history of the papacy, indispensable is Erich Caspar's incomplete but brilliant *Geschichte des Papsttums*, 2 vols. (Tübingen, 1933). Walter Ullmann wrote an admirable biography of Pope Gelasius I (1981); see too C. Pietri, *Roma Christiana*, 2 vols. (French School at Rome, 1976). The *Liber Pontificalis* was edited by L. Duchesne with supplement by C. Vogel, 3 vols. (Paris, 1955); Duchesne's commentary is valuable. An English translation with good notes by Raymond Davies in the Liverpool series 'Translated Texts for Historians' in 3 vols. Theodor Mommsen also produced (in MGH) a clear edition of this text without commentary and excluding the medieval biographies.

Canon Law: C. H. Turner *Ecclesiae Occidentalis Monumenta Iura Antiquissima* (Oxford, 1899–1939), remains basic for the early Latin west. See too H. T. Bruns, *Canones apostolorum et conciliorum*, 2 vols. (Berlin, 1839); Spanish councils edited by J. Vives, *Concilios Visigóticos* (Barcelona and Madrid, 1963).

Papyri: J. van Haelst, *Catalogue des papyrus littéraires juifs et chrétiens* (Paris, 1976); Kurt Treu, 'Christliche Papyri 1940–67', *Archiv für Papyrusforschung*, 19 (1969), 169–206 and reports in subsequent issues down to 1991; Kurt Aland, *Repertorium der griechischen christlichen Papyri*, i (1976), ii (1995) ed. H. U. Rosenbaum (excludes texts written on parchment); Berliner Klassikertexte VI (1910) ed. S. Schmidt and W. Schubart; art. Papyrus in DACL 13, 1 (1937); G. H. R. Horsley, *New Documents illustrating early Christianity*, ii, iii, and v (1982–9), North Ryde, Australia; R. A. Pack, *The Greek and Latin Literary Texts from Greco-Roman Egypt*, 2nd edn. (Ann Arbor, 1965); Stanley E. Porter, 'The Greek Apocryphal Gospels Papyri', in *Akten des 21. Internationalen Papyrologenkongresses*, 1995 = *Archiv f. Papyrusforschung*, Beiheft 3 (1997), 795–803; C. Wessely, 'Les plus anciens monuments du Christianisme écrits sur papyrus', in *Patrologia Orientalis* 4 (1907), 95–310; 183 (1924), 344–510; José O'Callaghan, *Cartas cristianas griegas del siglo V* (Barcelona, 1963), M. Naldini, *Il cristianesimo in Egitto* (Florence, 1968). *Zeitschrift für Papyrologie und Epigraphik* often carries reports on new finds.

Inscriptions: E. Diehl, *Inscriptiones Latinae Christianae Veteres* (Berlin, 1925–31) with Supplements (1967) by J. Moreau and H. I. Marrou and then Ferrua (1989) (*ILCV*). H. Dessau, *Inscriptiones Latinae Selectae* (*ILS*), reprinted 1974. J. Vives (ed.), *Inscripciones cristianas de la España romana y visigoda*, 2nd edn. (Barcelona, 1969). Annual reports of new finds are in *L'Année épigraphique*.

II. Bibliographies

Annual bibliographies appear in *Bibliographica patristica* (Berlin, 1959 ff.), *Revue d'Histoire ecclésiastique* (Louvain-la-Neuve), and *L'Année philologique*.

Good reference bibliographies are B. Altaner, *Patrologie* (Freiburg, Herder, 8th edn. 1978) English translation of sixth edn. 1960. Larger is J. Quasten's *Patrology*, 3 vols. (Utrecht 1950–60), supplemented by three further volumes edited by A. Di Berardino, 1978, 1996, and 2001 (Marietti, Genoa) reaching to the eighth century.

The standard catalogues of documents and editions are the *Clavis Patrum Latinorum*, ed. Dekkers (new edn. 1999), and the *Clavis Patrum Graecorum*, ed. M. Geerard (5 vols. and supplement), both published by Brepols of Turnhout in Belgium. See also H. J. Frede, *Kirchenschriftsteller*, 4th edn. (Freiburg, B., 1995), with supplement by R. Gryson (1999).

III. Reference books

Various encyclopaedias cover much of the subject. e.g. *Dictionary of Christian Biography*, 4 vols. (London, 1877–87), where contributors include J. B. Lightfoot, B. F. Westcott, H. B. Swete *et al.*; the 50 vols. of Pauly-Wissowa, *Realenzyklopädie der classischen Altertumswissenshaft*, with 15 supplementary volumes (few fail to contain valuable information about early Christians or others who affected them); *Dictionnaire de Théologie catholique* 15 vols. (Paris, 1903–50). *Dictionnaire d'Archéologie chrétienne et de liturgie*, 15 vols. in 30 parts (Paris, 1924–53); *Dictionnaire de Spiritualité ascétique et mystique* 17 vols. (Paris, 1937–95). *Encyclopedia of the Early Church*, ed. A. Di Berardino, with bibliographies by W. H. C. Frend, 2 vols. (Cambridge, 1992), translated from Italian. *The Oxford Dictionary of Byzantium*, 3 vols. (New York, 1991), contains brief articles on Greek theologians and councils of the fifth century. Exceptional is *Reallexikon für Antike und Christentum* (Stuttgart, Anton Hiersemann), which since 1940 has covered subjects and persons from A to J with substantial matter on the continuity and discontinuity between pre-Christian and Christian society in antiquity; this work continues the questions put by F. J. Dölger, *Antike und Christentum*, 6 vols. (1919–40, reprinted 1975) (a mine of antiquarian information) and his large monograph on the fish-symbol, *Ichthys*, 5 vols. (Münster, 1922–40). The Harvard *Dictionary of Late Antiquity: A Guide to the Post-Classical World* (1999), does not exclude Christians, as is largely the case with the *Prosopography of the Later Roman Empire*, 3 vols. in 4 (Cambridge, 1971–92). See too E. Ferguson (ed.) *Encyclopedia of Early Christianity*, 2nd edn. (New York, 1997). A. Mandouze edited a Prosopography of the African Churches (Paris, 1982). There is a recent Prosopography of the Italian churches (1999).

Augustinus-Lexikon (Basel, 1986 ff.) is to cover every aspect of Augustine. *Augustine through the Ages*, ed. A. D. Fitzgerald (Grand Rapids, Mich., 1999), also has articles of high quality and good bibliographies.

The *Oxford Dictionary of the Christian Church* (3rd edn. by E. A. Livingstone, 1997) contains many articles on persons and subjects in the ancient Christian period, with valuable bibliographies. A broad survey of Latin Christian writers is by P. de

Labriolle, *History of Latin Christian Literature* (London, 1924), translated by Herbert Wilson from French (Paris, 1920, revised 1947).

Edward Gibbon's *Decline and Fall of the Roman Empire* (ed. J. B. Bury in 7 vols., London, 1896–1900) depended on the distinguished Le Nain de Tillemont, *Mémoires pour servir à l'histoire ecclésiastique des six premiers siècles*, 16 vols. (Paris, 1693–1712), which remain essential on many details. Tillemont's *Histoire des Empereurs* (6 vols.) also has valuable matter. In England his contemporary William Cave (1637–1713) did useful spadework on texts and authors. Joseph Bingham's *Antiquities of the Christian Church* (London, 1708–22; repr. Oxford, 1875), is invaluable on all but theological ideas; J. Gaudemet, *L'Église dans l'empire romain* (Paris, 1958), on institutions.

On the background history of the Roman empire, the *Cambridge Ancient History*, vol. XI, XII and especially XIII, has good bibliographies. Among expert authors to consult see A. Harnack, J. B. Bury, Otto Seeck, Ernest Stein, Fergus Millar, Ramsay Macmullen, Timothy Barnes, Robert Markus, Peter Brown, W. H. C. Frend, A. Demandt, A. Dihle, Victor Saxer, C. Markschies. On the earlier period Robert M. Grant. Relevant articles are gathered in *Aufstieg und Niedergang der römischen Welt (ANRW) II* 23.

IV. Other works

ALÈS, A. D', *La Théologie de Tertullien* (Paris, 1905).
—— *La Théologie de S. Cyprien* (Paris, 1922).
ALFARIC, P., *L'Évolution intellectuelle de S. Augustin*, i [all published] (Paris, 1918).
ALLBERRY, C. R. A., *A Manichaean Psalm-Book* (Stuttgart, 1938).
AMAND, D., *L'Ascèse monastique de S. Basile* (Maredsous, 1949).
ARMSTRONG, A. H. (ed.), *The Cambridge History of Later Greek and Early Medieval Philosophy* (Cambridge, 1967).
ATHANASSIADI, P., *Julian: An Intellectual Biography* (London, 1992).
—— (ed.), *Pagan Monotheism in Late Antiquity* (Oxford, 1999).
ATIYA, A. S., *A History of Eastern Christianity* (London, 1968).
AUBINEAU, M., *Hésychius de Jérusalem*, 2 vols. (Paris, 1976–80).
AUDET, J. P., *La Didaché* (Paris, 1958).
BADEWIEN, J., *Geschichtstheologie und Sozialkritik im Werk Salvians von Marseille* (Göttingen, 1980).
BAGNALL, ROGER, *Egypt in Late Antiquity* (Princeton, 1993).
—— CAMERON, ALAN, SCHWARTZ, S. R., and WORP, K. A. (eds.), *Consuls of the Later Roman Empire* (Atlanta, Ga., 1987).
BANNIARD, M., *Genèse culturelle de l'Europe, V^e–VIIe siècle* (Paris, 1989).
—— *Viva voce: communication écrite et communication orale du VIe au IXe siècle en Occident latin* (Paris, 1992).
BARDY, G., *Paul de Samosate*, 2nd edn. (Paris, 1929).
—— *Recherches sur Lucien d'Antioche et son école* (Paris, 1936).
BARNARD, L. W., *Athenagoras* (Paris, 1972).
—— *The Council of Serdica* (Sofia, 1983).

BARNARD, L. W., *Studies in Church History and Patristics* (Thessaloniki, 1978).

BARNES, T. D., 'The Editions of Eusebius' Ecclesiastical History', *Greek, Roman and Byzantine Studies*, 21 (1980), 191–201.

—— *Constantine and Eusebius* (Cambridge, Mass., 1981).

—— *The New Empire of Diocletian and Constantine* (Cambridge, Mass., 1982).

—— *Tertullian*, 2nd edn. (Oxford, 1985).

—— *Athanasius and Constantius* (Cambridge, Mass., 1993).

BAUER, W., *Rechtgläubigkeit und Ketzerei im ältesten Christentum*, 2nd edn. (Tübingen, 1964) = *Orthodoxy and Heresy in Earliest Christianity* (London, 1972).

BAUMSTARK, A., *Liturgie comparée*, 3rd edn. (Chevetogne, 1953) = *Comparative Literature*, tr. F. L. Cross (London, 1958).

BAYNES, N. H., *Constantine the Great and the Christian Church* (London, 1932; 2nd edn. 1972).

—— *Byzantine Studies and Other Essays* (London, 1955).

BECK, H. G., *Kirche und theologische Literatur im byzantinischen Reich* (Munich, 1969).

BELL, H. I., *Jews and Christians in Egypt* (London, 1924).

—— 'Evidences of Christianity in Egypt during the Roman Period', *Harvard Theological Review*, 37 (1944), 185–208.

—— *Cults and Creeds in Graeco-Roman Egypt* (Liverpool, 1953).

BERKHOF, H., *Die Theologie des Eusebius von Caesarea* (Amsterdam, 1939).

BERTHIER, A., *Les Vestiges du christianisme antique dans la Numidie centrale* (Algiers, 1942).

BIDEZ, J., *Vie de l'empereur Julien* (Paris, 1930; 2nd edn. 1965).

BIENERT, W. A., *Dionysius von Alexandrien* (Berlin, 1978).

BINNS, J., *Ascetics and Ambassadors for Christ* (Oxford, 1994).

BINNS, J. W. (ed.), *Latin Literature of the Fourth Century* (London, 1974).

BIONDI, D., *Il diritto romano cristiano*, 3 vols. (Milan, 1952–4).

BONNER, G., *St Augustine of Hippo: Life and Controversies*, 2nd edn. (Norwich, 1986).

—— *God's Decree and Man's Destiny* (London, 1987).

BOUSSET, W., *Apophthegmata* (Tübingen, 1923).

BOWDER, D., *The Age of Constantine and Julian* (London, 1978).

BOWERSOCK, G. W., *Julian the Apostate* (London, 1978).

—— *Hellenism in Late Antiquity* (Ann Arbor, 1990).

—— *Martyrdom and Rome* (Cambridge, 1995).

BRADBURY, SCOTT, *Severus of Minorca: Letter on the Conversion of the Jews* (Oxford, 1996).

BRAKKE, D., *Athanasius and the Politics of Asceticism* (Oxford, 1995).

BRAUN, R., *Deus Christianorum* (Paris, 1962).

BREGMAN, J., *Synesius of Cyrene* (Berkeley, 1982).

BRENNECKE, H. C., *Hilarius von Poitiers und die Bischofsopposition gegen Konstantius II.* (Berlin, 1984).

—— *Studien zur Geschichte der Homöer* (Tübingen, 1988).

BROWN, P. R. L., *Augustine of Hippo* (London, 1967; 2nd edn. Berkeley, 2000).

—— *Religion and Society in the Age of Saint Augustine* (London, 1972).

—— *The Making of Late Antiquity* (Cambridge, Mass., 1978).

BROWN, P. R. L., *The Cult of the Saints* (London, 1981).
—— *Society and the Holy in Late Antiquity* (London, 1982).
—— *The Body and Society* (New York, 1988).
—— *Power and Persuasion in Late Antiquity* (Madison, Wis., 1992).
—— *Authority and the Sacred* (Cambridge, 1995).
—— *The Rise of Western Christendom* (Oxford, 1996).
BROWNING, R., *The Emperor Julian* (London, 1975).
BURKITT, F. C., *The Religion of the Manichees* (Cambridge, 1925).
BURTON-CHRISTIE, D., *The Word in the Desert* (Oxford, 1992).
BUTLER, E. C., *The Lausiac History of Palladius*, 2 vols. (Cambridge, 1898–1904).
BUYTAERT, E. M., *L'Héritage littéraire d'Eusèbe d'Émèse* (Louvain, 1949).
CAMERON, ALAN, *Claudian* (Oxford, 1970).
—— and LONG, J., *Barbarians and Politics at the Court of Arcadius* (Berkeley, 1993).
CAMERON, AVERIL, *Agathias* (Oxford, 1970).
—— *Procopius and the Sixth Century* (London, 1985).
—— with HALL, S. G. (tr., comm.), *Eusebius: Life of Constantine* (Oxford, 1999).
CAMPENHAUSEN, H. VON, *Ambrosius von Mailand als Kirchenpolitiker* (Berlin, 1929).
—— *Die asketische Heimatlosigkeit im altkirchlichen und frühmittelalterlichen Mönchtum* (Tübingen, 1930); repr. in id., *Tradition und Leben* (Tübingen, 1960), 290–17 = *Tradition and Life in the Church*, tr. A. V. Littledale (London, 1968), 290–317.
—— *Kirchliches Amt und geistliche Vollmacht in den ersten drei Jahrhunderten* (Tübingen, 1953) = *Ecclesiastical Authority and Spiritual Power in the Church of the First Three Centuries*, tr. J. A. Baker (London, 1969; repr. 1997).
—— *Die Entstehung der christlichen Bibel* (Tübingen, 1968) = *The Formation of the Christian Bible*, tr. J. A. Baker (London, 1972).
—— *Die Idee des Martyriums in der alten Kirche*, 2nd edn. (Göttingen, 1964).
CAVADINI, J. C. (ed.), *Gregory the Great* (Notre Dame, Ind., 1995).
CAVALCANTI, E., *Studi eunomiani* (Rome, 1976).
CAVALLERA, F., *Le Schisme d'Antioche* (Paris, 1905).
—— *Saint Jérôme: sa vie et son œuvre*, 2 vols. (Louvain, 1922).
CHADWICK, HENRY, 'Enkrateia', *Reallexikon für Antike und Christentum*, v (1962), 343–65.
—— *Early Christianity and the Classical Tradition* (Oxford, 1966).
—— 'Florilegium', tr. K. Engemann, *Reallexikon für Antike und Christentum*, vii (1969), 1131–59.
—— *Priscillian of Avila* (Oxford, 1976; repr. 1999).
—— 'Gewissen', tr. Heinzgerd Brakmann, *Reallexikon für Antike und Christentum*, x (1978), 1025–1107.
—— *Boethius* (Oxford, 1981; repr. 1999).
—— *History and Thought of the Early Church* (London, 1982).
—— *Augustine* (Oxford, 1986; repr. 2001).
—— *Saint Augustine: Confessions* (Oxford, 1991).
—— *Heresy and Orthodoxy in the Early Church* (Aldershot, 1991).
—— 'Humanität', tr. Georg Schöllgen, *Reallexikon für Antike und Christentum*, xvi (1994), 663–711.

CHADWICK, HENRY, *Antike Schriftauslegung* (Berlin, 1998).
CHADWICK, OWEN, *John Cassian*, 2nd edn. (Cambridge, 1968).
CHAPMAN, J., *Studies on the Early Papacy* (London, 1928).
CHESNUT, G., *The First Church Historians* (Paris, 1977).
CHESNUT, R. C., *Three Monophysite Christologies* (Oxford, 1976).
CHITTY, D. J., *The Desert a City* (Oxford, 1966).
CLARK, E. A., *Ascetic Piety and Women's Faith* (Lampeter, 1986).
—— *The Origenist Controversy: The Cultural Construction of an Early Christian Debate* (Princeton, 1992).
—— *The Life of Melania the Younger* (New York, 1984).
CLARK, GILLIAN, *Augustine: The Confessions* (Cambridge, 1993).
CLARKE, W. K. L., *St. Basil the Great: A Study in Monasticism* (Cambridge, 1913).
—— (tr.) *The Lausiac History of Palladius* (London, 1918).
COCHRANE, C. N., *Christianity and Classical Culture* (Oxford, 1940).
COLEMAN NORTON, P. R., *Roman State and Christian Church*, 3 vols. (London, 1966).
COLLINS, R. J. H., *Early Medieval Spain* (London, 1983).
COURCELLE, P., *Les Lettres grecques en Occident de Macrobe à Cassiodore* (Paris, 1948) = *Late Latin Writers and their Greek Sources*, tr. H. Wedeck (Cambridge, Mass., 1969).
—— *Les Confessions de S. Augustin dans la tradition littéraire* (Paris, 1965).
—— *Recherches sur les Confessions de S. Augustin*, 2nd edn. (Paris, 1968).
COURTOIS, C., *Les Vandales et l'Afrique* (Paris, 1955; repr. Aalen, 1964).
CRACCO RUGGINI, L., *Il paganesimo romano tra religione e politica, 283–394 d.C.* (Memoria della Academia de Lincei, ser. VIII, 23/1; Rome, 1979).
CREED, J. L., *Lactantius: De mortibus persecutorum* (Oxford, 1984).
CROKE, B., and EMMETT, A., *History and Historians in Late Antiquity* (Sydney, 1983).
CROUZEL, H., *Origène* (Paris, 1984) = *Origen*, tr. A. S. Worrall (Edinburgh, 1989).
DAGENS, C., *S. Grégoire le Grand: culture et experience chrétiennes* (Paris, 1977).
DAGRON, G., *Vie et miracles de S. Thècle* (Brussels, 1978).
DAL COVOLO, E. (ed.), *Storia della teologia*, i (Rome, 1995).
DANIÉLOU, J., *Platonisme et théologie mystique*, 2nd edn. (Paris, 1953).
DASSMANN, E., *Die Frömmigkeit des Kirchenvaters Ambrosius von Mailand* (Münster, 1965).
DAUBE, D., *The New Testament and Rabbinic Judaism* (London, 1956).
DEANE, H. A., *The Political and Social Ideas of St Augustine* (New York, 1963).
DECRET, F., *Aspects du manichéisme dans l'Afrique romaine* (Paris, 1974).
—— *Mani et la tradition manichéenne* (Paris, 1974).
DEICHMANN, F. W., *Ravenna: Hauptstadt des spätantiken Abendlandes* (Stuttgart, 1958–89).
—— *Einführung in die christliche Archäologie* (Darmstadt, 1983).
—— *Rom, Ravenna, Konstantinopel und Naher Osten: Gesammelte Studien zur spätantiken Architektur, Kunst und Geschichte* (Stuttgart, 1982).
DELEHAYE, H., *Les Légendes grecques des saints militaires* (Paris, 1909).
—— *Les Passions des martyrs et les genres littéraires* (Brussels, 1921; 2nd edn. 1966).
—— *Les Saints stylites* (Brussels, 1923).
—— *Les Origines du culte des martyrs* (Brussels, 1933).

DELEHAYE, H., *Les Légendes hagiographiques*, 4th edn. (Brussels, 1955) = *The Legends of the Saints*, tr. Donald Attwater (London, 1962).

DEVREESSE, H., *Essai sur Théodore de Mopsueste* (Studi e Testi, 141; Vatican City, 1940).

DI BERARDINO, A., and STUDER, B. (eds.), *Storia della teologia*, i (Casale Monferrato, 1993).

DIESNER, H. J., *Isidor von Sevilla und seine Zeit* (Stuttgart, 1973).

DIGESER, E. D., *The Making of a Christian Empire: Lactantius and Rome* (Ithaca, NY, 2000).

DOIGNON, J., *Hilaire de Poitiers* (Paris, 1971).

DOLBEAU, F., *Augustin: Vingt-six sermons au peuple d'Afrique* (Paris, 1996).

DÖLGER, F. J., *Ichthys*, 5 vols. (Münster, 1922–40).

—— *Sol Salutis* (Münster, 1925).

—— *Antike und Christentum*, 6 vols. (Münster, 1929–40; repr. 1975).

DÖRRIES, H., *Symeon von Mesopotamien* (Texte und Untersuchungen, 55/1; Leipzig, 1941).

—— *De Spiritu Sancto* (Göttingen, 1956).

—— *Wort und Stunde*, i (Göttingen, 1966).

—— *Die Theologie des Makarios/Symeon* (Göttingen, 1978).

DOWNEY, G. A., *A History of Antioch in Syria from Seleucus to the Arab Conquest* (Princeton, 1961).

DRAGUET, R., *Julien d'Halicarnasse* (Louvain, 1924).

DRAKE, H. A., *Constantine and the Bishops* (Baltimore, Md., 2000).

DREUILLE, C. DE, *L'Église et la mission au VIe siècle* (Paris, 2000).

DRIJVERS, H. J. W., *Bardaisan of Edessa* (Assen, 1966).

DRINKWATER, J. F., and ELTON, H. (eds.), *Fifth-Century Gaul: A Crisis of Identity?* (Cambridge, 1992).

DUCHESNE, L., *Liber Pontificalis*, 2 vols. (Paris, 1886–92); reissued with suppl. vol. by C. Vogel (Paris, 1955).

—— *Fastes épiscopaux de l'ancienne Gaule*, 3 vols. (Paris, 1894–1915).

—— *Histoire ancienne de l'Église*, 3 vols. (Paris, 1906–10) = *Early History of the Christian Church* (London, 1909–24).

—— *L'Église au VIe siècle* (Paris, 1926).

DUDDEN, F. HOMES, *Gregory the Great*, 2 vols. (London, 1905).

—— *The Life and Times of St. Ambrose*, 2 vols. (Oxford, 1935).

DULAEY, M., *Le Rêve dans la vie et la pensée de saint Augustin* (Paris, 1973).

DUVAL, NOËL, *Les Églises africaines à deux absides*, 2 vols. (Paris, 1973).

DUVAL, YVES-MARIE (ed.), *Ambroise de Milan: XVIe centenaire de son élection épiscopale* (Paris, 1974).

DUVAL, YVETTE, *Loca Sanctorum Africae*, 2 vols. (Paris, 1982).

—— *Auprès des saints, corps et âme: l'inhumation ad sanctos* (Paris, 1988).

—— *Chrétiens d'Afrique à l'aube de la paix constantinienne* (Paris, 2000).

DZIELSKA, MARIA, *Hypatia z Aleksandrii* (Kraków, 1993) = *Hypatia of Alexandria*, tr. F. Lyra (Revealing Antiquity, 8; Cambridge, Mass., 1995).

EBIED, R. Y., and WICKHAM, L. R., 'A Collection of Unpublished Syriac Letters of Timothy Aelurus', *JTS*, NS 21 (1970), 321–69.

EBIED, R. Y., and WICKHAM, L. R., 'Timothy Aelurus against the Synod of Chalcedon', in C. Lapa, J. A. Munitiz, and L. Van Rompay (eds.), *After Chalcedon: Studies in Theology and Church History Offered to Professor Albert Van Roey for his Seventieth Birthday* (Leuven, 1985), 115–66.

ELM, S., *Virgins of God* (Oxford, 1994).

ENSSLIN, W., *Theoderich der Große* (Munich, 1946).

—— *Die Religionspolitik des Kaisers Theodosius des Großen* (Abhandlungen der Bayerischen Akademie der Wissenschaften, 1953/2; Munich, 1953).

EVANS, D., *Leontius of Byzantium* (Dumbarton Oaks Studies, 13; Washington, DC, 1970).

EVANS, R. F., *Pelagius: Inquiries and Reappraisals* (London, 1968).

—— *One and Holy: The Church in Latin Patristic Thought* (London, 1972).

EYNDE, D. VAN DEN, *Les Normes de l'enseignement chrétien dans la littérature patristique des trois premiers siècles* (Gembloux, 1933).

FABRE, P., *Saint Paulin de Nole et l'amitié chrétienne* (BEFAR 167; Paris, 1949).

FAVALE, A., *Teofilo d'Alessandria* (Turin, 1958).

FEDER, A. L., *Studien zu Hilarius von Poitiers* (SB Vienna, 162/4, 166/5, 169/5; 1910–12).

FEDWICK, P., *The Church and the Charisma of Leadership in Basil of Caesarea* (Toronto, 1979).

—— (ed.), *Basil of Caesarea*, 2 vols. (Toronto, 1981).

FERRUA, A., *Epigrammata Damasiana* (Rome, 1942).

—— *The Unknown Catacomb*, tr. I. Inglis (London, 1991).

FESTUGIÈRE, A. J., *Antioche païenne et chrétienne* (BEFAR 194; Paris, 1959).

—— *Les Moines d'Orient*, 4 vols. (Paris, 1961–5).

FICKER, G., *Amphilochiana* (Lepizig, 1906).

FIEDROWICZ, M., *Das Kirchenverständnis Gregors des Großen* (Rome, 1995).

FIEY, J. M., *Jalons pour une histoire de l'Église en Iraq* (Louvain, 1970).

—— *Nisibe, métropole syriaque orientale* (Louvain, 1977).

FITSCHEN, K., *Messalianismus und Antimessalianismus* (Göttingen, 1998).

FONTAINE, J., 'Isidore de Séville', *Dictionnaire de spiritualité*, vii (Paris, 1961), 2104–16.

—— *Études sur la poésie latine d'Ausone à Prudence* (Paris, 1980).

—— *Naissance de la poésie dans l'Occident chrétien: esquisse d'une histoire de la poésie latine chrétienne du IIIe au VIe siècle* (Paris, 1981).

—— *Isidore et la culture classique* (2nd edn., Paris, 1983).

—— (ed.), *Sulpice Sévère: vie de S. Martin*, 3 vols. (Paris, 1967–9).

—— GILLET, E., and PELLESTRANDI, S. (eds.), *Grégoire le Grand* (Paris, 1986).

FORTIN, E. L., *Christianisme et culture philosophique au Ve siècle: la querelle de l'âme humaine en Occident* (Paris, 1959).

FOWDEN, G., *Empire to Commonwealth* (Princeton, 1993).

FREND, W. H. C., *The Donatist Church* (Oxford, 1951).

—— *The Rise of the Monophysite Movement* (Cambridge, 1972).

—— *Town and Country in the Early Christian Centuries* (London, 1980).

—— *The Rise of Christianity* (London, 1984).

GAIN, B., *L'Église de Cappadoce au IVᵉ siècle d'après la correspondance de Basile de Césarée* (Rome, 1985).

GARDNER, I., *The Manichaean Kephalaia* (Leiden, 1995).

GARNSEY, P., *Ideas of Slavery from Aristotle to Augustine* (Cambridge, 1996).

GARNSEY, P. and HUMFRESS, C., *The Evolution of the Late Antique World* (Cambridge, 2001).

GAUDEMET, J., *L'Église dans l'empire romain* (Paris, 1958).

GEFFCKEN, J., *Der Ausgang des griechisch-römischen Heidentums* (Heidelberg, 1920) = *The Last Days of Greco-Roman Paganism*, tr. S. MacCormack (Amsterdam, 1978).

GEYER, P. (ed.), *Itinera Hieroslymitana saeculi V–VIII* (CSEL 39; Vienna, 1898).

GIBSON, M. (ed.), *Boethius: His Life, Thought, and Influence* (Oxford, 1981).

GILSON, E., *Introduction à l'étude de saint Augustin*, 3rd edn. (Paris, 1949) = *The Christian Philosophy of Saint Augustine*, tr. L. E. M. Lynch (London, 1961).

GIRARDET, K. M., *Kaisergericht und Bischofsgericht* (Bonn, 1975).

GOEHRING, J., *The Letter of Ammon and Pachomian Monasticism* (Berlin, 1986).

GOODMAN, M., *Mission and Conversion* (Oxford, 1994).

GOULD, G., *The Desert Fathers on Monastic Community* (Oxford, 1993).

GRANT, R. M., *Augustus to Constantine: The Thrust of the Christian Movement into the Roman World* (London, 1971).

—— *Greek Apologists of the Second Century* (Philadelphia, 1988).

GRASMÜCK, E. L., *Coercitio: Staat und Kirche im Donatistenstreit* (Bonn, 1984).

GRAY, P. T. R., *The Defense of Chalcedon in the East* (Leiden, 1979).

Gregorio Magno e il suo tempo, 2 vols. (Rome, 1991).

GREENSLADE, S. L., *Church and State from Constantine to Theodosius* (London, 1954).

—— *Schism in the Early Church*, 2nd edn. (London, 1964).

GRIBOMONT, J., *Saint Basile, évangile et église: mélanges*, 2 vols. (Beyrolles-en-Mauges: Abbaye de Bellefontaine, 1984).

GRILLMEIER, A., *Jesus der Christus im Glauben der Kirchen* (Freiburg i. B., 1979–90).

GRYSON, R., 'Les elections épiscopales en Orient au IVᵉ siècle', *Revue d'histoire ecclésiastique*, 74 (1979), 301–45.

—— 'Les elections épiscopales en Occident au IVᵉ siècle', *Revue d'histoire ecclésiastique*, 75 (1980), 257–83.

—— *Scolies ariennes sur le concile d'Aquilée* (SC 267; Paris, 1980).

GUIDA, AUGUSTO, *Replica a Giuliano Imperatore* (Florence, 1994).

—— 'La prima replica cristiana al *Contro i Galilei* di Giuliano: Teodoro di Mopsuestia', in F. E. Consolino (ed.), *Pagani e cristiani da Giuliano l'Apostata al sacco di Roma* (Soveria Mannelli, 1995), 15–33.

GUILLAUMONT, A., *Les Kephalaia Gnostica d'Évagre le Pontique et l'histoire de l'origénisme chez les Grecs et les Syriens* (Paris, 1962).

—— *Aux origines du monachisme chrétien* (Beyrolles-en-Mauges: Abbaye de Bellefontaine, 1979).

GÜLZOW, H., *Cyprian und Novatian* (Tübingen, 1975).

GUMMERUS, J., *Die homöusianische Partei bis zum Tode des Konstantius* (Leipzig, 1900).

HADDAN, A. W., and STUBBS, W., *Councils and Ecclesiastical Documents Relating to Great Britain and Ireland*, 3 vols. (Oxford, 1869–78).

HADOT, P., *Porphyre et Victorinus*, 2 vols. (Paris, 1968).

—— *Marius Victorinus* (Paris, 1971).

HAEHLING, H. VON, *Die Religionszugehörigkeit der hohen Amtsträger des römischen Reiches seit Constantin I.* (Bonn, 1978).

HAGENDAHL, H., *Augustine and the Latin Classics* (Göteborg, 1967).

HAMMOND BAMMEL, C. P., *Origeniana et Rufiniana* (Freiburg i. B., 1996).

HANSON, R. P. C., *The Search for the Christian Doctrine of God* (Edinburgh, 1988).

HARDY, E. R., *Christian Egypt* (New York, 1952).

HARNACK, A., *Dogmengeschichte*, 4th edn., 3 vols. (Tübingen, 1905) = *History of Dogma*, tr. N. Buchanan *et al.*, 7 vols. (London, 1894–9).

—— *Militia Christi* (Tübingen, 1905; repr. Darmstadt, 1963).

—— *Der kirchengeschichtliche Ertrag der exegetischen Arbeiten des Origenes* (Leipzig, 1919).

—— *Die Mission und Ausbreitung des Christentums*, 4th edn., 2 vols. (Leipzig, 1924).

—— *Markion* (Leipzig, 1924).

HEATHER, P., *Goths and Romans* (Oxford, 1991).

HENGEL, M., *Kleine Schriften*, 2 vols. (Tübingen, 1996).

—— and LÖHR, H., *Schriftauslegung im antiken Judentum und im Urchristentum* (Tübingen, 1994).

HESS, H., *The Canons of the Council of Sardica* (Oxford, 1958).

HEUSSI, K., *Der Ursprung des Mönchtums* (Tübingen, 1936).

HILLGARTH, J., *Christianity and Paganism 350–370* (Philadelphia, 1986).

HINCHLIFF, P., *Cyprian of Carthage* (London, 1974).

HOLL, K., *Enthusiasmus und Bußgewalt beim griechischen Mönchtum* (Leipzig, 1898; repr. Hildesheim, 1969).

—— *Amphilochius von Ikonium in seinem Verhältnis zu den großen Kappadoziern* (Leipzig, 1908).

—— *Gesammelte Aufsätze*, ii–iii (Tübingen, 1928).

HOLUM, K., *Theodosian Empresses* (Berkeley, 1983).

HONIGMANN, E., *Évêques et évêchés monophysites d'Asie antérieure au VIe siècle* (Louvain, 1951).

HONORÉ, T., *Law in the Crisis of Empire 379–455* (Oxford, 1998).

HORBURY, W., *Jews and Christians in Contact and Controversy* (Edinburgh, 1998).

HUNT, E. D., *Holy Land Pilgrimage in the Later Roman Empire* (Oxford, 1982).

IHM, M., *Damasi Epigrammata* (Leipzig, 1895).

JAEGER, W., *Early Christianity and Greek Paideia* (Cambridge, Mass., 1962).

JAMES, E. (ed.), *Visigothic Spain: New Approaches* (Oxford, 1980).

JEREMIAS, G., *Die Holztür der Basilica S. Sabina in Rom* (Tübingen, 1980).

JONAS, H., *The Gnostic Religion* (Boston, 1963).

JONES, A. H. M., *Constantine and the Conversion of Europe* (London, 1948).

—— *The Later Roman Empire*, 3 vols. (Oxford, 1964).

JUNGMANN, J. A., *Missarum Sollemnia: eine genetische Erklärung der römischen Messe*, 4th edn., 2 vols. (Vienna, 1958) = *The Mass of the Roman Rite*, tr. Francis A. Brummer, 2 vols. (New York, 1951).

JÜRGENS, H., *Pompa diaboli* (Stuttgart, 1972).

KANIUTH, A., *Die Beisetzung Konstantins des Großen* (Breslau, 1941).

KATZ, S., 'Pope Gregory the Great and the Jews', *Jewish Quarterly Review*, 12 (1933), 113–26.

KELLY, J. N. D., *Early Christian Creeds* (London, 1950).

—— *Early Christian Doctrines* (London, 1958).

—— *The Athanasian Creed* (London, 1964).

—— *Jerome: His Life, Writings, and Controversies* (London, 1975).

—— *Golden Mouth: The Story of John Chrysostom—Ascetic, Preacher, Bishop* (London, 1995).

KING, N. Q., *The Emperor Theodosius and the Establishment of Christianity* (London, 1961).

KINZIG, W., *In Search of Asterius* (Göttingen, 1990).

—— *Novitas Christiana: die Idee des Fortschritts in der alten Kirche bis Eusebius* (Göttingen, 1994).

KIRK, K. E., *The Vision of God* (London, 1931).

KLAUSER, T., *Die römische Petrustradition im Lichte der neuen Ausgrabungen unter der Peterskirche* (Cologne, 1956).

—— *Gesammelte Arbeiten zur Liturgiegeschichte* (Münster, 1974).

KLAUSNER, J., *Yeshu ha-Notsri* (Tel Aviv, 1945) = *Jesus of Nazareth*, tr. H. Danby (London, 1979).

KLEIN, R., *Kaiser Constantius II. und die christliche Kirche* (Darmstadt, 1978).

KLINGSHIRN, W. E., *Caesarius of Arles* (Cambridge, 1994).

KOCH, H., *Cyprianische Untersuchungen* (Bonn, 1926).

—— *Cathedra Petri* (ZNW Beiheft 11; Giessen, 1930).

KOFSKY, A., and STROUSMA, G. G., *Sharing the Sacred: Religious Contacts and Conflicts in the Holy Land* (Jerusalem, 1998).

KOPECEK, T. A., *A History of Neo-Arianism* (Philadelphia, 1979).

KOTILA, H., *Memoria Mortuorum: Commemoration of the Departed in Augustine* (Rome, 1992).

KÖTTING, B., *Peregrinatio Religiosa* (Münster, 1950).

KRAUTHEIMER, R., *Corpus Basilicarum Christianarum Romae* (Vatican City, 1937–77).

LA BONNARDIÈRE, A.-M. (ed.), *Saint Augustin et la Bible* (Paris, 1986).

LABOURT, J., *Le Christianisme dans l'empire perse sous la dynastie sassanide* (Paris, 1904).

LABRIOLLE, P. DE, *La Réaction païenne* (Paris, 1934).

LACROIX, B., *Orose et ses idées* (Paris, 1965).

LADNER, G., *The Idea of Reform* (Harvard, 1959).

LAISTNER, M. L. W., *Christianity and Pagan Culture in the Later Roman Empire* (Ithaca, NY, 1951).

LAMIRANDE, E., *Paulin de Milan et la Vita Ambrosii* (Paris, 1983).

LAMPE, P., *Die stadtrömischen Christen in den ersten beiden Jahrhunderten* (Tübingen, 1989).

LANCEL, SERGE, *Actes de la conférence de Carthage en 411*, 4 vols. (SC 194, 195, 224, 373; Paris, 1972–91).

—— *Saint Augustin* (Paris, 1999).

LANE FOX, R., *Pagans and Christians* (Harmondsworth, 1986).

LAWLOR, H. J., *Eusebiana* (Oxford, 1912).

LAYTON, B., *The Gnostic Scriptures* (London, 1987).

—— (ed.), *The Rediscovery of Gnosticism*, 2 vols. (Leiden, 1980–1).

LAZZATI, G. (ed.), *Ambrosius Episcopus: atti del Congresso internazionale di studi ambrosiani nel XVI centenario della elezione di sant'Ambrogio alla cattedra episcopale, 2–7 dicembre, 1974*, 2 vols. (Milan, 1976).

LEONARDI, CLAUDIO, 'Alle origini della cristianità medievale: Giovanni Cassiano e Salviano di Marsiglia', *Studi medievali*, 18 (1977), 491–608.

LEPELLEY, C., *Les Cités de l'Afrique romaine*, 2 vols. (Paris, 1981).

LEPPIN, H., *Von Constantin dem Großen an Theodosius II.* (Göttingen, 1996).

LIÉBART, J., *La Doctrine christologique de S. Cyrille d'Alexandrie avant la querelle nestorienne* (Lille, 1951).

LIEBESCHUETZ, J. H. W. F., *Antioch* (Oxford, 1972).

—— *Barbarians and Bishops* (Oxford, 1990).

—— *The Decline and Fall of the Roman City* (Oxford, 2001).

LIETZMANN, H., *Apollinaris von Laodicea und seine Schule* (Tübingen, 1904).

—— *Petrus und Paulus in Rom*, 2nd edn. (Berlin, 1927).

—— *Geschichte der alten Kirche*, 4 vols. (Berlin, 1933–44) [English translation to be used with caution].

—— *Kleine Schriften*, 3 vols. (TU 62, 67, 74; Berlin, 1958–62).

LIEU, S. N. C., *The Emperor Julian: Panegyric and Polemics*, 2nd edn. (Liverpool, 1989).

—— *Manichaeism*, 2nd edn. (Tübingen, 1992).

—— *Manichaeism in Mesopotamia and the Roman East* (Leiden, 1994).

LIGHTFOOT, J. B., *The Apostolic Fathers*, 5 vols. (London, 1889).

LIM, RICHARD, *Public Disputation, Power, and Social Order in Late Antiquity* (Berkeley, 1995).

LIPPOLD, A., *Theodosius der Große und seine Zeit* (Munich, 1980).

—— 'Theodosius II.', *PWK* Suppl. XIII. 961–1044.

—— 'Vigilius', *PWK* Suppl. XIV. 864–85.

—— 'Zenon', *PWK*, NS XA. 149–213.

LIZZI, R., *Vescovi e strutture ecclesiastiche nella città tardoantica* (Como, 1980).

—— 'Ambrose's Contemporaries and the Christianisation of northern Italy', *Journal of Roman Studies*, 80 (1990), 156–73.

LLEWELLYN, P., 'The Roman Church in the Seventh Century', *Journal of Ecclesiastical History*, 25 (1974), 262–80.

LOOFS, F., *Eustathios von Sebaste und die Chronologie der Basilius-Briefe* (Halle, 1898).

—— 'Pelagius und der pelagianische Streit', *Realenzyklopädie für protestantische Theologie und Kirche*, XV (1904), 747–74.

—— *Nestorius and his Place in the History of Christian Doctrine* (Cambridge, 1914).

—— *Paulus von Samosata* (Leipzig, 1924).

—— *Patristica*, ed. H. C. Brennecke and J. Ulrich (Berlin, 1999).

LORENZ, R., *Arius Iudaizans?* (Göttingen, 1980).

—— *Der zehnte Osterbrief des Athanasius von Alexandrien* (Berlin, 1986).

LUBAC, H. DE, *Histoire et esprit* (Paris, 1950).

McLYNN, N. B., *Ambrose of Milan: Church and Court in a Christian Capital* (Berkeley, 1994).

MacCORMACK, S. G., *Art and Ceremony in Late Antiquity* (Berkeley, 1981).

MADEC, G., *Ambroise et la philosophie* (Paris, 1974).

—— *La Patrie et la voie* (Paris, 1989).

MAIER, J. L., *Le Dossier du donatisme* (TU 134–5; Berlin, 1987–9).

MALBON, E. S., *The Iconography of the Sarcophagus of Junius Bassus* (Princeton, 1990).

MANGO, C., and SCOTT, R., with GREATREX, G., *The Chronicle of Theophanes Confessor* (Oxford, 1997).

MARAVAL, P., *Lieux saints et pèlerinages d'Orient* (Paris, 1985).

—— *Le Christianisme de Constantin à la conquête arabe* (Paris, 1997).

MARKSCHIES, CHRISTOPH, *Ambrosius von Mailand und die Trinitätstheologie* (Tübingen, 1995).

—— 'Was ist lateinischer Neunizänismus?', *Zeitschrift für antikes Christentum*, 1 (1997), 264–98.

—— 'Innerer Mensch', *Reallexikon für Antike und Christentum*, xviii (1998), 266–311.

—— *Zwischen den Welten wandern* (Frankfurt am Main, 1997) = *Between Two Worlds: Structures of Earliest Christianity*, tr. J. Bowden (London, 1999).

—— *Alta Trinitas Beata: Gesammelte Studien zur Trinitätstheologie des antiken Christentums* (Tübingen, 2001).

MARKUS, R. A., *From Augustine to Gregory the Great* (London, 1983).

—— *The End of Ancient Christianity* (Cambridge, 1990).

—— *Sacred and Secular* (London, 1996).

—— *Gregory the Great and his World* (Cambridge, 1997).

MARROU, H. I., *S. Augustin et la fin de la culture antique* (Paris, 1938); reissued with 'Retractatio' (Paris, 1949).

—— *Patristique et humanisme* (Paris, 1976).

—— *Christiana Tempora* (Rome, 1978).

MARTIN, ANNICK, *Athanase d'Alexandrie et l'Église d'Égypte au IVe siècle* (BEFAR 216; Paris, 1996).

MATHEWS, T. F., *The Clash of the Gods* (Princeton, 1993).

MATHISEN, R. W., *Ecclesiastical Factionalism and Religious Controversy in Fifth-Century Gaul* (Washington, D.C., 1989).

MATTHEWS, JOHN, *Western Aristocracies and the Imperial Court* (Oxford, 1975).

MAY, G., *Schöpfung aus dem Nichts* (Berlin, 1978) = *Creatio ex nihilo*, tr. A. S. Worrall (Edinburgh, 1994).

MAYR-HARTING, HENRY, *The Coming of Christianity in Anglo-Saxon England* (London, 1972).

MAZZARINO, S., *Stilicone* (Rome, 1942).

—— *La fine del mondo antico* (Milan, 1959) = *The End of the Ancient World*, tr. George Holmes (London, 1966).

MEER, F. G. L. VAN DER, *Augustinus de zielzorger* (Utrecht, 1947) = *Augustine the Bishop*, tr. B. Battershaw and G. R. Lamb (London, 1961).

MEIJERING, E. P., *Orthodoxy and Platonism in Athanasius* (Leiden, 1968).

—— *Athanasius: De incarnatione* (Amsterdam, 1989).

MERKELBACH, R., *Mani und sein Religionssystem* (Opladen, 1986).

MESLIN, M., *Les Ariens d'Occident* (Paris, 1967).

METZGER, B. M., *The Early Versions of the New Testament* (Oxford, 1977).

MEYVAERT, P., *Benedict, Gregory, Bede and Others* (London, 1977).

MILBURN, R. L. P., *Early Christian Art and Architecture* (Aldershot, 1988).

MINNS, D., *Irenaeus* (Washington, DC, 1994).

MITCHELL, S., *Anatolia*, ii (Oxford, 1993).

MOINGT, J., *Théologie trinitaire de Tertullien*, 4 vols. (Paris, 1966–9).

MOMIGLIANO, A. (ed.), *The Conflict between Paganism and Christianity in the Fourth Century* (Oxford, 1963).

MONCEAUX, P., *Histoire littéraire de l'Afrique chrétienne*, 7 vols. (Paris, 1901–23).

MOORHEAD, J., *Theodoric in Italy* (Oxford, 1993).

—— *Justinian* (London, 1994).

—— *Ambrose* (London, 1999).

MORINO, C., *Chiesa e Stato nella dottrina di S. Ambrogio* (Rome, 1963) = *Church and State in the Teaching of St. Ambrose* (Washington, DC, 1969).

MÜHLENBERG, E., *Apollinaris von Laodicea* (Göttingen, 1969).

MUNIER, C., *L'Église dans l'empire romain* (Paris, 1979).

MURPHY, F. X., *Rufinus of Aquileia (345–411): His Life and Works* (Washington, DC, 1945).

—— *A Monument to St Jerome* (New York, 1952).

MURRAY, C. M., *Rebirth and Afterlife: A Study of the Transmutation of Some Pagan Imagery in Early Christian Funerary Art* (Oxford, 1981).

MURRAY, R. M., *Symbols of Church and Kingdom* (Cambridge, 1971).

NAUTIN, P., review of Meslin (1967): *Revue d'histoire des religions*, 177 (1970), 115–53.

NIEDERWIMMER, K., *Die Didache*, 2nd edn. (Göttingen, 1993) = *The Didache*, tr. Linda M. Maloney (Minneapolis, 1998).

NOCK, A. D., *Conversion* (Oxford, 1933).

—— *Essays on Religion and the Ancient World*, ed. Zeph Stewart, 2 vols. (Oxford, 1972).

O'DONNELL, J. J., *Cassiodorus* (Berkeley, 1979).

—— 'The Demise of Paganism', *Traditio*, 35 (1979), 45–88.

—— 'Liberius the Patrician', *Traditio*, 37 (1981), 31–72.

—— *Augustine: Confessions*, 3 vols. (Oxford, 1992).

OOST, S. I., *Galla Placidia Augusta* (Chicago, 1968).

PABST, A., *Divisio Regni* (Bonn, 1986).

PAGET, J. CARLETON, *The Epistle of Barnabas* (Tübingen, 1998).

PALANQUE, J. R., *Saint Ambroise et l'empire romain* (Paris, 1933).

PALMER, A. M., *Prudentius on the Martyrs* (Oxford, 1989).

PAREDI, A., *Ambrogio e la sua età* (Milan, 1960) = *Saint Ambrose: His Life and Times* (Notre Dame, 1964).

PASTORINO, A., *Stilicone* (Turin, 1974).

PAVERD, F. VAN DE, *St John Chrysostom: Homilies on the Statues* (Rome, 1991).

—— *Zur Geschichte der Meßliturgie in Antiocheia und Konstantinopel gegen Ende des vierten Jahrhunderts: Analyse der Quellen bei Johannes Chrysostomos* (Orientalia Christiana Analecta, 187; Rome, 1970).

PELIKAN, J., *The Emergence of the Christian Tradition*, i (Chicago, 1971).

—— *Christianity and Classical Culture* (New Haven, 1993).

PERLER, O., *Les Voyages de S. Augustin* (Paris, 1969).

—— *Sapientia et Caritas* (Fribourg, 1990).

PETERSON, E., *Der Monotheismus als politisches Problem: Ein Beitrag zur Geschichte der politischen Theologie im Imperium romanum* (Leipzig, 1935), repr. in *Theologische Traktate* (Munich, 1951).

—— *Frühkirche, Judentum und Gnosis* (Freiburg i. B., 1959).

PIETRI, C., *Roma Christiana*, 2 vols. (Rome, 1976).

—— *Christiana Respublica*, 3 vols. (Rome, 1997).

PIETRI, L., *La Ville de Tours du IVe au VIe siècle* (Rome, 1983).

PLINVAL, G. DE, *Pélage: ses écrits, sa vie et sa réforme* (Lausanne, 1943).

PONTAL, O., *Histoire des conciles mérovingiens* (Paris, 1989).

POSCHMANN, BERNHARD, *Die abendländische Kirchenbuße im Ausgang des christlichen Altertums* (Munich, 1928).

—— *Paenitentia Secunda* (Bonn, 1940).

—— *Buße und Letzte Ölung* (Freiburg i. B., 1950) = *Penance and Anointing the Sick*, tr. F. Courtney (London, 1964).

PRESTIGE, G. L., *St. Basil the Great and Apollinaris of Laodicea* (London, 1956).

PRIGENT, P., *L'Épître de Barnabe* (Paris, 1961).

—— *Justin et l'Ancien Testament* (Paris, 1964).

—— *Le Judaïsme et l'image* (Tübingen, 1990).

PRINZ, F., *Frühes Mönchtum im Frankenreich* (Munich, 1965).

PUECH, H. C., *Le Manichéisme* (Paris, 1949).

—— *En quête de la Gnose*, 2 vols. (Paris, 1978).

QUASTEN, J., *Musik und Gesang in den Kulten der heidnischen Antike und christlichen Frühzeit* (Münster, 1973) = *Music and Worship in Pagan and Christian Antiquity*, tr. Boniface Ramsey (Washington, DC, 1983).

RAHNER, KARL, *Penance in the Early Church*, tr. (from *Schriften zur Theologie* XI) by Lionel Swain (Theological Investigations, 15; London, 1983).

RANKIN, D., *Tertullian and the Church* (Cambridge, 1995).

RAVEN, C. E., *Apollinarianism* (Cambridge, 1924).

REBENICH, S., *Hieronymus und sein Kreis* (Stuttgart, 1992).

REES, B. S., *Pelagius* (Woodbridge, 1988).

RICHARD, M., *Opera Minora*, 3 vols. (Turnhout, 1976).

RIEDMATTEN, H. DE, *Paul de Samosate* (Fribourg, 1952).

RIST, J. M., 'Hypatia', *Phoenix*, 19 (1965), 214–25.

—— *Augustine, or Ancient Thought Baptized* (Cambridge, 1984).

RITTER, A. M., *Das Konzil von Konstantinopel und sein Symbol* (Göttingen, 1965).

—— *Charisma im Verständnis des Joannes Chrysostomus und seiner Zeit* (Göttingen, 1972).

ROBERTS, C. H., *Manuscript, Society, and Belief in Early Christian Egypt* (London, 1979).

ROBINSON, J. M. (ed.), *The Nag Hammadi Library in English*, 3rd edn. (Leiden, 1988).

ROOS, B. A., *Synesius of Cyrene* (Lund, 1991).

Roques, D., *Synésios de Cyrène et la Cyrénaïque du Bas-Empire* (Paris, 1987).

Rousseau, P., *Ascetics, Authority, and the Church in the Age of Jerome and Cassian* (Oxford, 1978).

—— *Pachomius* (Los Angeles, 1985).

—— *Basil of Caesarea* (Berkeley, 1994).

Rudolph, K., *Die Gnosis: Wesen und Geschichte einer spätantiker Religion* (Leipzig, 1977) = *Gnosis: The Nature and History of an Ancient Religion*, tr. R. McL. Wilson (Edinburgh, 1983).

Russell, N., *Cyril of Alexandria* (London, 2000).

Ste. Croix, G. E. M. de, 'Why were the Early Christians Persecuted?', *Past & Present*, 26 (November 1963), 6–38; repr. in M. I. Finley (ed.), *Studies in Ancient Society* (London, 1974), 210–49.

—— 'Why were the Early Christians Persecuted? A Rejoinder', *Past & Present*, 27 (April 1964), 23–33; repr. in M. I. Finley (ed.), *Studies in Ancient Society* (London, 1974), 256–62.

Sanders, E. P., *Jesus and Judaism* (London, 1985).

—— *Jewish Law from Jesus to the Mishnah* (London, 1990).

—— *The Historical Figure of Jesus* (London, 1993).

Savon, H., *Ambroise de Milan* (Paris, 1997).

Saxer, V., *Morts, martyrs, reliques en Afrique chrétienne* (Paris, 1980).

Schäferdiek, K., *Die Kirche in den Reichen der Westgoten und Suewen bis zur Errichtung der westgotischen katholischen Staatskirche* (Berlin, 1967).

—— 'Zeit und Umstände des westgotischen Übergangs zum Christentum', *Historia*, 28 (1979), 90–7.

Schatkin, M. A., *John Chrysostom as Apologist* (Analekta Vlatadon, 50: Thessaloniki, 1987).

Schneemelcher, W., *Reden und Aufsätze* (Tübingen, 1991).

—— (ed.), *Neutestamentliche Apokryphen*, 5th edn., 2 vols. (Tübingen, 1989).

Schöllgen, G., *Ecclesia Sordida* (JbAC Suppl. 12; Münster, 1984).

Schürer, E., *History of the Jewish People in the Age of Jesus Christ*, tr. and rev. G. Vermes and F. G. B. Millar, 4 vols. (Edinburgh, 1973–87).

Schwartz, E., *Konzilstudien* (Strassburg, 1914).

—— *Gesammelte Schriften*, iii–v (Berlin, 1959).

Seeck, O., *Regesten der Kaiser und Päpste für die Jahre 311 bis 476 n. Chr.* (Stuttgart, 1919; repr. Frankfurt am Main, 1964).

—— *Geschichte des Untergangs der antiken Welt*, 6 vols. (Stuttgart, 1920).

Seibt, K., *Die Theologie des Markell von Ankyra* (Berlin, 1990).

Selb, W., 'Episcopalis audientia von der Zeit Konstantins bis zur Nov. XXXV Valentinians III.', *Zeitschrift für Rechtsgeschichte*, kanon. Abt., 84 (1967), 167–217.

Sellers, R. V., *Two Ancient Christologies* (London, 1940).

—— *The Council of Chalcedon* (London, 1953).

Setton, K. M., *Christian Attitude towards the Emperor in the Fourth Century* (New York, 1941).

Shahîd, I., *Byzantium and the Arabs in the Fourth Century* (Dumbarton Oaks, 1984).

—— *Byzantium and the Arabs in the Fifth Century* (Dumbarton Oaks, 1989).

SIEBEN, H. J., *Die Konzilsidee der alten Kirche* (Paderborn, 1979).

SIEVERS, G., *Leben des Libanius* (Berlin, 1867).

SIMON, M., *Verus Israel* (Paris, 1948); reissued with 'Post-Scriptum' (1964); tr. H. McKeating (Oxford, 1986).

SIMONETTI, M., *Studi sull'arianesimo* (Rome, 1965).

—— *La crisi ariana nel IV secolo* (Rome, 1975).

—— *Ortodossia ed eresia tra I e II secolo* (Soveria Mannelli, 1994).

SMULDERS, P., *La Doctrine trinitaire de S. Hilaire de Poitiers* (Rome, 1944).

SOLIGNAC, A., 'Pèlerinages', *Dictionnaire de spiritualité*, xii (Paris, 1984), 888–940.

SORABJI, R., *Emotion and Peace of Mind* (Oxford, 2000).

SPANNEUT, M., *Recherches sur les écrits d'Eustathe d'Antioche* (Lille, 1948).

SPARKS, H. F. D., *The Apocryphal Old Testament* (Oxford, 1984).

STAATS, R., *Makarios-Symeon, Epistola Magna* (Göttingen, 1984).

STEAD, G. C., *Divine Substance* (Oxford, 1977).

—— *Substance and Illusion in the Christian Fathers* (Aldershot, 1985).

—— *Doctrine and Philosophy in Early Christianity* (Aldershot, 2000).

STEIDLE, W. (ed.), *Antonius Magnus Eremita* (Studia Anselmiana, 38; Rome, 1956).

—— 'Die Leichenrede des Ambrosius für Kaiser Theodosius und die Helenalegende', *Vigiliae Christianae*, 32 (1978), 94–112.

STEIN, E., *Histoire du Bas-Empire*, ed. J. R. Palanque, 2 vols. (1959, 1949).

STEWART, COLUMBA, *'Working the Earth of the Heart': The Messalian Controversy in History, Texts, and Language to AD 431* (Oxford, 1991).

—— *Cassian the Monk* (Oxford, 1998).

STRAUB, J., *Regeneratio Imperii*, 2 vols. (Darmstadt, 1972).

STRAW, C., *Gregory the Great: Perfection in Imperfection* (Berkeley, 1988).

TANNER, N. P., *The Councils of the Church* (New York, 2001).

TEJA, A., *Organización económica y social de Capadocia en el siglo IV según los padres capadocios* (Salamanca, 1984).

TELFER, W., *The Forgiveness of Sins* (London, 1959).

TENGSTRÖM, E., *Donatisten und Katholiken* (Göteborg, 1964).

TETZ, M., *Athanasiana* (Berlin, 1995).

THEISSEN, G., *A Theory of Primitive Christian Religion* (London, 1999).

THELAMON, F., *Païens et chrétiens au IVᵉ siècle* (Paris, 1981).

Théologie de la vie monastique: études sur la tradition patristique (Théologie, 49; Paris, 1961).

THOMAS, C., *Christianity in Roman Britain* (London, 1981).

TURNER, V., and TURNER, E., *Image and Pilgrimage in Christian Culture* (Oxford, 1978).

ULRICH, J., *Die Anfänge der abendländischen Rezeption des Nizänums* (Berlin, 1994).

URBACH, E. E., *The Sages*, 2 vols. (Jerusalem, 1975; Cambridge, Mass., 1977).

URBAINCZYK, T., *Socrates of Constantinople* (Ann Arbor, 1997).

VAGGIONE, R. P., *Eunomius: The Extant Works* (Oxford, 1987).

VALLI, F., *Gioviniano* (Urbino, 1953).

VAN DAM, R., *Leadership and Community in Late Antique Gaul* (Berkeley, 1985).

—— *Saints and their Miracles in Late Antique Gaul* (Princeton, 1993).

VEILLEUX, ARMAND, *Pachomian Koinonia*, 3 vols. (Kalamazoo, 1980–2).

VINZENT, M., *Markell von Ankyra: Fragmente* (Leiden, 1997).

VOGT, H. J., *Coetus Sanctorum: Der Kirchenbegriff des Novatian* (Bonn, 1969).

VOGÜÉ, ADALBERT DE, *Histoire littéraire du mouvement monastique dans l'Antiquité*, 5 vols. (Paris, 1991–8).

VOLBACH, W. F., *Early Christian Art* (London, 1962).

WALLACE-HADRILL, D. S., *Eusebius of Caesarea* (London, 1960).

WALLACE-HADRILL, J. M., *The Frankish Church* (Oxford, 1983).

WALLRAFF, M., *Der Kirchenhistoriker Sokrates* (Göttingen, 1997).

WARD-PERKINS, B., *From Classical Antiquity to the Middle Ages: Urban Public Buildings in Northern and Central Italy AD 300–800* (Oxford, 1984).

WASZINK, J. H., *Tertullian: De Anima* (Amsterdam, 1947).

—— with WINDEN, J. C. M., *Tertullianus: De Idololatria* (Leiden, 1987).

WATKINS, O. D., *A History of Penance*, 2 vols. (London, 1920; repr. New York, 1960).

WEISMANN, W., *Kirche und Schauspiele* (Würzburg, 1972).

WERMELINGER, O., *Rom und Pelagius* (Stuttgart, 1975).

WES, M. A., *Das Ende des Kaisertums im Westen des römischen Reichs* (The Hague, 1967).

WICKHAM, L. R., *Cyril of Alexandria: Select Letters* (Oxford, 1983).

—— *Conflicts of Conscience and Law in the Fourth-Century Church* (Liverpool, 1997).

WIDENGREN, G., *Mani und der Manichäismus* (Stuttgart, 1961).

WILKEN, R. L., *John Chrysostom and the Jews* (Berkeley, 1983).

—— *The Land Called Holy* (New Haven, 1992).

WILKINSON, JOHN, *Jerusalem Pilgrims before the Crusade* (Warminster, 1977).

WILLIAMS, D. H., *Ambrose of Milan and the End of the Arian–Nicene Conflicts* (Oxford, 1995).

WILLIAMS, R. D., *Arius: Heresy and Tradition* (London, 1987).

WIPSZYCKA, E., *Storia della Chiesa nella tarda antichità*, tr. (from Polish) V. Verdiani (Turin, 2000).

WOLFSON, H. A., *Philo*, 2 vols. (Cambridge, Mass., 1947).

WOOD, IAN, *The Merovingian Kingdoms 450–751* (London, 1994).

WYTZES, J., *Der letzte Kampf des Heidentums in Rom* (Leiden, 1977).

YARNOLD, E. J., *The Awe-Inspiring Rites of Initiation* (Slough, 1972).

YOUNG, F., *From Nicaea to Chalcedon* (London, 1983).

ZIEGLER, J., *Zur religiösen Haltung der Gegenkaiser im 4. Jh. n. Chr.* (Hellmünz, 1970).

ZUMKELLER, A., *Das Mönchtum des heiligen Augustinus* (Würzburg, 1950) = *Augustine's Ideal of the Religious Life* (New York, 1986).

DATES OF ROMAN EMPERORS

Tiberius 14–37
Caligula 37–41
Claudius 41–54
Nero 54–68
Four Emp. 68–9
Vespasian 69–79
Titus 79–81
Domitian 81–96
Nerva 96–8
Trajan 98–117
Hadrian 117–138
Antoninus Pius 138–61
Marcus Aurelius 161–80
Commodus 180–92
Septimius Severus 193–211
Caracalla 211–17
Macrinus 217–18
Elagabalus 218–22
Alexander Severus 222–35
Maximin 235–8
Gordian 238–44
Philip the Arab 244–9
Decius 249–51
Gallus 252–3
Valerian 253–60
Gallienus 260–8
Claudius II 268–70 (Gothicus)
Aurelian 270–5
Probus 276–82
Carus 282–3
Carinus 283–4
Diocletian 284–305
　　Tetrarchy 293: Diocletian,
　　　　Maximian, Constantius
　　　　Chlorus, Galerius
From 305: Constantius Chlorus

(died 306), Galerius, Severus,
Maximin Daia. Constantine (died
337) acclaimed after Constantius:
Maxentius' coup at Rome.
Severus died 307. Licinius
Augustus. Maximian died 310.
Galerius died 311. Maxentius
crushed by Constantine 312.
Constantine and Licinius agreed on
toleration at Milan 313. Licinius
defeated by Constantine 324.

Constantine sole emperor 324–37
　His three surviving sons:
　Constantine II 337–40 in west;
　　　Constantius II in east; Constans
　　　Italy and Africa. Constans
　　　defeated and killed
　　　Constantine II 340, but
　　　was ousted and killed by
　　　Magnentius 350. Magnentius
　　　falls to Constantius (battle of
　　　Mursa 351) and takes his life
　　　353. Gallus Caesar killed 354.
　　　Julian to Gaul 355–58.
　　　Constantius II died
　　　3 November 361.
Julian sole emperor 361–3
Jovian 363–4
Valentinian I 364–75 (west); Valens
　　364–78 (east); Gratian
　　co-emperor in west 367;
　　murdered 383
Theodosius I 379–95
Magnus Maximus' revolt 383–8,
　　defeated near Aquileia.

Eugenius' revolt 394, defeated on Frigidus

Arcadius (east) 395–408, succeeded by Theodosius II (408–50)

Honorius (west) 395–423, briefly succeeded by John, then by Valentinian III 425–55, son of Galla Placidia.

Pulcheria and Marcian 450; Pulcheria died 453, Marcian 457, succeeded in east by Leo 457–74.

Avitus (west) 455–6

Majorian 457–61 (west)

Fainéant emperors to Romulus Augustulus 476 and Nepos 480 (under Ricimer, Odoacer, then Theoderic 493–526)

Leo II 474 (east)

Zeno the Isaurian 474–91 (Basiliscus 475–6)

Anastasius 491–518

Justin 519–27

Justinian 527–65

Justin II 565–78

Tiberius II 578–82

Maurice 582–602

Phocas 602–10

LIST OF BISHOPS OF ROME, ALEXANDRIA, ANTIOCH, CONSTANTINOPLE, AND JERUSALEM

Rome

The principal lists for second-century Rome are derived from Irenaeus, Hesippus, Hippolytus' chronicle, the Calendar of 354, and various later indexes. The sixth-century *Liber Pontificalis* gives each a brief biography, but is not reliable for the early period, during which all precise dates are conjectural.

Peter and Paul, apostles
Linus
Anencletus
Clement
Euaristus
Alexander
Xystus I
Telesphorus
Hyginus
Pius
Anicetus *c.*156
Soter
Eleutherus
Victor I *c.*190
Zephyrinus
Callistus *c.*220
Urbanus
Pontianus 235
Antherus 236
Fabian 236–50
Cornelius 253
Lucius 254
Xystus II 256–7
Stephen 257
Dionysius 258–68
Felix I 268–73
Eutychianus 273–83

Gaius 283–96
Marcellus 296–304
Marcellinus 308–9
Miltiades 309–14
Silvester 314–35
Marcus 336
Julius 337–52
Liberius 352–66
   (rival Felix II 355–8)
Damasus 366–84
   (rival Ursinus)
Siricius 384–99
Anastasius 399–401
Innocent I 401–17
Zosimus 417–18
Boniface I 418–22
   (rival Eulalius)
Celestine 422–32
Xystus III 432–9
Leo I 440–61
Hilarus 461–8
Simplicius 468–83
Felix III 483–92
Gelasius I 492–6
Anastasius 496–8
Symmachus 498–514
   (rival Laurentius)

Hormisdas 514–23
John 523–6
Felix IV 526–30
Boniface II 530–2
    (rival, briefly, Dioscorus 530)
John II 533–5
Agapetus 535–6
Silverius 536–7
Vigilius 537–55
Pelagius I 556–61
John III 561–74
Pelagius II 579–90
Gregory I 590–604
Sabinianus 604–6
Boniface III 607

Alexandria

Demetrius c.189–233
Heraklas 233–47
Dionysius 247–64
Theonas 282
Peter c.300–12
Achillas 312
Alexander 312–28
Athanasius 328–73
    Arians: Pistos 336
        Gregory 341–4
        George 357–61
        Lucius 365; 373–80
Timothy I 375–8
Theophilus 384–412
Cyril 412–44
Dioscorus* 444–51 (died in exile 454)
Proterius 451–7
Timothy Ailouros (Weasel)* 457–60;
    475–7
Timothy Salofakiolos 460–75; 477–82
Peter Mongos* 477; 481–9
John Talaia, June–Dec. 482
Athanasius II Keletes* 489–96
John I* 496–505
John II* 505–16
Dioscorus II 516–17
Timothy III* 517–35

Theodosius* 535–66
    (rival: Gaianus* 535)

Chalcedonian (Melkite) patriarchs of Alexandria

Paul 537–40
Zoilus 540–51
Apollinarius 551–5
John II 570–80
Eulogius 581–608
Theodore 608–09
John the Almsgiver 610–19

Antioch

Until Constantine, the main sources are
    Eusebius' *Church History* and his
    Chronicle
(Peter)
Evodius
Ignatius
Hero
Cornelius
Eros
Theophilus (author of *ad Autolycum*)
Maximin
Serapion (*HE* 5. 19, 6. 12)
Asclepiades (*HE* 6. 11. 4)
Philetus (*HE* 6. 21. 2)
Zebennus (*HE* 6. 23. 3)
Babylas (*HE* 6. 29. 4)
Fabius (Chron. a.251)
Demetrianus (*HE* 6. 46. 4)
Paul of Samosata (*HE* 7. 26–8)
Domnus I (Chron.)
Timaeus (Chron.)
Cyril (*HE* 7. 32. 2)
Tyrannus (Chron.; Theodoret,
    HE 1. 3) 304–14
Vitalis (Theodoret: 'he built the church
    in the old town') 314–20
Philogonius 320–4 (Jerome, Chron.;
    Joh. Chrysostom preached on his
    day)
Eustathius 324–7/8

* Monophysite

Paulinus 330, former bp of Tyre
(Eus. contra Marcellum 4)
Eulalius (Theodoret, *HE* 1. 22)
Eusebius declined translation from
Caesarea; Euphronius 332–3
Flacillus 333–42
Stephen 342–4 (deposed)
Leontius 344–57 (died 357)
Eudoxius 357–60
Anianus, soon ejected
Meletius 360, translated from
Melitene, Armenia; soon ejected
(died 381)
Euzoius 361–76
(rival: Paulinus consecrated by
Lucifer of Calaris for the
Eustathian community 362
(died *c*.382))
Vitalis consecrated by Apollinaris of
Laodicea for his disciples
Flavian 381–404
Evagrius uncanonically conse-
crated by Paulinus on his
deathbed
Porphyry 404–13
Alexander 413–21
Theodotus 421–6
John 428–41
Domnus II 441–9 (deposed at Ephesus
449; nephew of John)
Maximus 449–55
Basil 456–8
Acacius 458–9
Martyrius 459–70
(rival: Peter the Fuller (Theodore
the Reader, p. 111 ff.,
117–8 Hansen) (died 491))
Julian 471–5
John II Codonatus 476–7
Stephen II 477–9
Calandion 479–86
Peter the Fuller returns 485–9
Palladius 490–8
Flavian II 498–512
Severus 512–18 (died 538)

Paul II 519–21
Euphrasius 521–6
Ephrem 527–45

Constantinople

Metrophanes 306–14 (bishop of
Byzantium)
Alexander 314–36/7
Paul 337–9
Eusebius (formerly of Berytus, then
Nicomedia)
Paul again 341–2
(rival Macedonius 342–60)
Eudoxius 360–70, translated from
Antioch
Demophilus 370–80, translated from
Beroea; deposed by Theodosius
Gregory (of Nazianzos) 380–1
(rival: Maximus the Cynic)
Nectarius 381–97
John I (Chrysostom) 398–404 (died in
exile)
Arsacius 404–5
Atticus 406–25
Sisinnius 426–7
Nestorius 428–31 (died in exile about
450–1)
Maximian 431–4
Proclus 434–46
Flavian 446–9 (deposed at Ephesus 449
(died 449–50))
Anatolius 449–58
Gennadius I 458–71
Acacius 472–89
Fravittas 489–90
Euphemius 490–6 (exiled)
Macedonius II 496/511 (exiled)
Timothy 511–18
John II 518–20
Epiphanius 520–35
Anthimus 535–6 (deposed)
Menas 536–52
Eutychius 552–69; 577–82
John III Scholasticus 565–77 (canonist)

John IV the Faster 582–95
Cyriacus 595–606
Thomas 607–10

Jerusalem

Hymenaeus 260–98
Zabdas 298–300
Hermas 300–14
Macarius 314–33
Maximus 333–48
Cyril 348–87 (including exiles)
John 387–417
Praylius 417–22
Juvenal 422–58 (first Patriarch)
    (rival in protest against Chalcedon:
      Theodosius★ 451–7)

Anastasius I 458–78
Martyrius 478–86
Salustius 486–94
Elias I 494–516
John III 516–24
Peter 524–52
Macarius 552
Eutychius 552–64
Macarius 564–74
John IV 574–94
Amos 594–601
Hesychius 601–9
Zacharias 609–31
Modestus 632–3
Sophronius 634–8

After the Arab capture of Jerusalem, a vacancy for 50 years

INDEX